JEFFERSON DAVIS

JEFFERSON DAVIS

Perry Scott King

CHELSEA HOUSE PUBLISHERS
NEW YORK
PHILADELPHIA

Chelsea House Publishers
EDITOR-IN-CHIEF: Nancy Toff
EXECUTIVE EDITOR: Remmel T. Nunn
MANAGING EDITOR: Karyn Gullen Browne
COPY CHIEF: Juliann Barbato
PICTURE EDITOR: Adrian G. Allen
ART DIRECTOR: Maria Epes
MANUFACTURING MANAGER: Gerald Levine

World Leaders—Past & Present
SENIOR EDITOR: John W. Selfridge

Staff for JEFFERSON DAVIS
ASSOCIATE EDITOR: Terrance Dolan
COPY EDITOR: Michael Goodman
DEPUTY COPY CHIEF: Mark Rifkin
EDITORIAL ASSISTANT: Nate Eaton
PICTURE RESEARCHER: Lisa Kirchner
ASSISTANT ART DIRECTOR: Loraine Machlin
DESIGNER: David Murray
ASSISTANT DESIGNER: James Baker
PRODUCTION MANAGER: Joseph Romano
PRODUCTION COORDINATOR: Marie Claire Cebrián
COVER ILLUSTRATION: Paul Chadwick (from a photo by Mathew Brady)

First Printing

1 3 5 7 9 8 6 4 2

Library of Congress Cataloging-in-Publication Data

King, Perry Scott.
    Jefferson Davis/Perry Scott King.
    p.   cm.—(World leaders past & present)
    Includes bibliographical references.
    Summary: A biography of the man who was the president of the
Confederate States of America during the Civil War.
    ISBN 1-55546-806-3
         0-7910-0693-X (pbk.)
    1. Davis, Jefferson, 1808–1889—Juvenile literature.
2. Statesmen—United States—Biography—Juvenile literature.
3. Confederate States of America—Presidents—Biography—Juvenile
literature. 4. Confederate States of America—History—Juvenile
literature. [1. Davis, Jefferson, 1808–1889. 2. Confederate States of
America—Presidents.] I. Title. II. Series.
E467.1.D26K56   1990
973.7'13'092—dc20   89–38911
[B]   CIP
[92]   AC

Contents

WORLD LEADERS   PAST & PRESENT

John Adams
John Quincy Adams
Konrad Adenauer
Alexander the Great
Salvador Allende
Marc Antony
Corazon Aquino
Yasir Arafat
King Arthur
Hafez al-Assad
Kemal Atatürk
Attila
Clement Attlee
Augustus Caesar
Menachem Begin
David Ben-Gurion
Otto von Bismarck
Léon Blum
Simon Bolívar
Cesare Borgia
Willy Brandt
Leonid Brezhnev
Julius Caesar
John Calvin
Jimmy Carter
Fidel Castro
Catherine the Great
Charlemagne
Chiang Kai-Shek
Winston Churchill
Georges Clemenceau
Cleopatra
Constantine the Great
Hernán Cortés
Oliver Cromwell
Georges-Jacques
   Danton
Jefferson Davis
Moshe Dayan
Charles de Gaulle
Eamon De Valera
Eugene Debs
Deng Xiaoping
Benjamin Disraeli
Alexander Dubček
François & Jean-Claude
   Duvalier
Dwight Eisenhower
Eleanor of Aquitaine
Elizabeth i
Faisal
Ferdinand & Isabella
Francisco Franco
Benjamin Franklin

Frederick the Great
Indira Gandhi
Mohandas Gandhi
Giuseppe Garibaldi
Amin & Bashir Gemayel
Genghis Khan
William Gladstone
Mikhail Gorbachev
Ulysses S. Grant
Ernesto "Che" Guevara
Tenzin Gyatso
Alexander Hamilton
Dag Hammarskjöld
Henry viii
Henry of Navarre
Paul von Hindenburg
Hirohito
Adolf Hitler
Ho Chi Minh
King Hussein
Ivan the Terrible
Andrew Jackson
James i
Wojciech Jaruzelski
Thomas Jefferson
Joan of Arc
Pope John xxiii
Pope John Paul ii
Lyndon Johnson
Benito Juárez
John Kennedy
Robert Kennedy
Jomo Kenyatta
Ayatollah Khomeini
Nikita Khrushchev
Kim Il Sung
Martin Luther King, Jr.
Henry Kissinger
Kublai Khan
Lafayette
Robert E. Lee
Vladimir Lenin
Abraham Lincoln
David Lloyd George
Louis xiv
Martin Luther
Judas Maccabeus
James Madison
Nelson & Winnie
   Mandela
Mao Zedong
Ferdinand Marcos
George Marshall

Mary, Queen of Scots
Tomáš Masaryk
Golda Meir
Klemens von Metternich
James Monroe
Hosni Mubarak
Robert Mugabe
Benito Mussolini
Napoléon Bonaparte
Gamal Abdel Nasser
Jawaharlal Nehru
Nero
Nicholas ii
Richard Nixon
Kwame Nkrumah
Daniel Ortega
Mohammed Reza Pahlavi
Thomas Paine
Charles Stewart
   Parnell
Pericles
Juan Perón
Peter the Great
Pol Pot
Muammar el-Qaddafi
Ronald Reagan
Cardinal Richelieu
Maximilien Robespierre
Eleanor Roosevelt
Franklin Roosevelt
Theodore Roosevelt
Anwar Sadat
Haile Selassie
Prince Sihanouk
Jan Smuts
Joseph Stalin
Sukarno
Sun Yat-sen
Tamerlane
Mother Teresa
Margaret Thatcher
Josip Broz Tito
Toussaint L'Ouverture
Leon Trotsky
Pierre Trudeau
Harry Truman
Queen Victoria
Lech Walesa
George Washington
Chaim Weizmann
Woodrow Wilson
Xerxes
Emiliano Zapata
Zhou Enlai

CHELSEA HOUSE PUBLISHERS

ON LEADERSHIP

Arthur M. Schlesinger, jr.

LEADERSHIP, it may be said, is really what makes the world go round. Love no doubt smooths the passage; but love is a private transaction between consenting adults. Leadership is a public transaction with history. The idea of leadership affirms the capacity of individuals to move, inspire, and mobilize masses of people so that they act together in pursuit of an end. Sometimes leadership serves good purposes, sometimes bad; but whether the end is benign or evil, great leaders are those men and women who leave their personal stamp on history.

Now, the very concept of leadership implies the proposition that individuals can make a difference. This proposition has never been universally accepted. From classical times to the present day, eminent thinkers have regarded individuals as no more than the agents and pawns of larger forces, whether the gods and goddesses of the ancient world or, in the modern era, race, class, nation, the dialectic, the will of the people, the spirit of the times, history itself. Against such forces, the individual dwindles into insignificance.

So contends the thesis of historical determinism. Tolstoy's great novel *War and Peace* offers a famous statement of the case. Why, Tolstoy asked, did millions of men in the Napoleonic Wars, denying their human feelings and their common sense, move back and forth across Europe slaughtering their fellows? "The war," Tolstoy answered, "was bound to happen simply because it was bound to happen." All prior history predetermined it. As for leaders, they, Tolstoy said, "are but the labels that serve to give a name to an end and, like labels, they have the least possible connection with the event." The greater the leader, "the more conspicuous the inevitability and the predestination of every act he commits." The leader, said Tolstoy, is "the slave of history."

Determinism takes many forms. Marxism is the determinism of class. Nazism the determinism of race. But the idea of men and women as the slaves of history runs athwart the deepest human instincts. Rigid determinism abolishes the idea of human freedom—

the assumption of free choice that underlies every move we make, every word we speak, every thought we think. It abolishes the idea of human responsibility, since it is manifestly unfair to reward or punish people for actions that are by definition beyond their control. No one can live consistently by any deterministic creed. The Marxist states prove this themselves by their extreme susceptibility to the cult of leadership.

More than that, history refutes the idea that individuals make no difference. In December 1931 a British politician crossing Park Avenue in New York City between 76th and 77th Streets around 10:30 P.M. looked in the wrong direction and was knocked down by an automobile—a moment, he later recalled, of a man aghast, a world aglare: "I do not understand why I was not broken like an eggshell or squashed like a gooseberry." Fourteen months later an American politician, sitting in an open car in Miami, Florida, was fired on by an assassin; the man beside him was hit. Those who believe that individuals make no difference to history might well ponder whether the next two decades would have been the same had Mario Constasino's car killed Winston Churchill in 1931 and Giuseppe Zangara's bullet killed Franklin Roosevelt in 1933. Suppose, in addition, that Adolf Hitler had been killed in the street fighting during the Munich *Putsch* of 1923 and that Lenin had died of typhus during World War I. What would the 20th century be like now?

For better or for worse, individuals do make a difference. "The notion that a people can run itself and its affairs anonymously," wrote the philosopher William James, "is now well known to be the silliest of absurdities. Mankind does nothing save through initiatives on the part of inventors, great or small, and imitation by the rest of us—these are the sole factors in human progress. Individuals of genius show the way, and set the patterns, which common people then adopt and follow."

Leadership, James suggests, means leadership in thought as well as in action. In the long run, leaders in thought may well make the greater difference to the world. But, as Woodrow Wilson once said, "Those only are leaders of men, in the general eye, who lead in action. . . . It is at their hands that new thought gets its translation into the crude language of deeds." Leaders in thought often invent in solitude and obscurity, leaving to later generations the tasks of imitation. Leaders in action—the leaders portrayed in this series—have to be effective in their own time.

And they cannot be effective by themselves. They must act in response to the rhythms of their age. Their genius must be adapted, in a phrase of William James's, "to the receptivities of the moment." Leaders are useless without followers. "There goes the mob," said the French politician hearing a clamor in the streets. "I am their leader. I must follow them." Great leaders turn the inchoate emotions of the mob to purposes of their own. They seize on the opportunities of their time, the hopes, fears, frustrations, crises, potentialities. They succeed when events have prepared the way for them, when the community is awaiting to be aroused, when they can provide the clarifying and organizing ideas. Leadership ignites the circuit between the individual and the mass and thereby alters history.

It may alter history for better or for worse. Leaders have been responsible for the most extravagant follies and most monstrous crimes that have beset suffering humanity. They have also been vital in such gains as humanity has made in individual freedom, religious and racial tolerance, social justice, and respect for human rights.

There is no sure way to tell in advance who is going to lead for good and who for evil. But a glance at the gallery of men and women in *World Leaders—Past and Present* suggests some useful tests.

One test is this: Do leaders lead by force or by persuasion? By command or by consent? Through most of history leadership was exercised by the divine right of authority. The duty of followers was to defer and to obey. "Theirs not to reason why / Theirs but to do and die." On occasion, as with the so-called enlightened despots of the 18th century in Europe, absolutist leadership was animated by humane purposes. More often, absolutism nourished the passion for domination, land, gold, and conquest and resulted in tyranny.

The great revolution of modern times has been the revolution of equality. The idea that all people should be equal in their legal condition has undermined the old structure of authority, hierarchy, and deference. The revolution of equality has had two contrary effects on the nature of leadership. For equality, as Alexis de Tocqueville pointed out in his great study *Democracy in America*, might mean equality in servitude as well as equality in freedom.

"I know of only two methods of establishing equality in the political world," Tocqueville wrote. "Rights must be given to every citizen, or none at all to anyone . . . save one, who is the master of all." There was no middle ground "between the sovereignty of all and the absolute power of one man." In his astonishing prediction of 20th-century totalitarian dictatorship, Tocqueville explained how the revolution of equality could lead to the *"Führerprinzip"* and more terrible absolutism than the world had ever known.

But when rights are given to every citizen and the sovereignty of all is established, the problem of leadership takes a new form, becomes more exacting than ever before. It is easy to issue commands and enforce them by the rope and the stake, the concentration camp and the *gulag.* It is much harder to use argument and achievement to overcome opposition and win consent. The Founding Fathers of the United States understood the difficulty. They believed that history had given them the opportunity to decide, as Alexander Hamilton wrote in the first Federalist Paper, whether men are indeed capable of basing government on "reflection and choice, or whether they are forever destined to depend . . . on accident and force."

Government by reflection and choice called for a new style of leadership and a new quality of followership. It required leaders to be responsive to popular concerns, and it required followers to be active and informed participants in the process. Democracy does not eliminate emotion from politics; sometimes it fosters demagoguery; but it is confident that, as the greatest of democratic leaders put it, you cannot fool all of the people all of the time. It measures leadership by results and retires those who overreach or falter or fail.

It is true that in the long run despots are measured by results too. But they can postpone the day of judgment, sometimes indefinitely, and in the meantime they can do infinite harm. It is also true that democracy is no guarantee of virtue and intelligence in government, for the voice of the people is not necessarily the voice of God. But democracy, by assuring the right of opposition, offers built-in resistance to the evils inherent in absolutism. As the theologian Reinhold Niebuhr summed it up, "Man's capacity for justice makes democracy possible, but man's inclination to injustice makes democracy necessary."

A second test for leadership is the end for which power is sought. When leaders have as their goal the supremacy of a master race or the promotion of totalitarian revolution or the acquisition and exploitation of colonies or the protection of greed and privilege or the preservation of personal power, it is likely that their leadership will do little to advance the cause of humanity. When their goal is the abolition of slavery, the liberation of women, the enlargement of opportunity for the poor and powerless, the extension of equal rights to racial minorities, the defense of the freedoms of expression and opposition, it is likely that their leadership will increase the sum of human liberty and welfare.

Leaders have done great harm to the world. They have also conferred great benefits. You will find both sorts in this series. Even "good" leaders must be regarded with a certain wariness. Leaders are not demigods; they put on their trousers one leg after another just like ordinary mortals. No leader is infallible, and every leader needs to be reminded of this at regular intervals. Irreverence irritates leaders but is their salvation. Unquestioning submission corrupts leaders and demeans followers. Making a cult of a leader is always a mistake. Fortunately hero worship generates its own antidote. "Every hero," said Emerson, "becomes a bore at last."

The signal benefit the great leaders confer is to embolden the rest of us to live according to our own best selves, to be active, insistent, and resolute in affirming our own sense of things. For great leaders attest to the reality of human freedom against the supposed inevitabilities of history. And they attest to the wisdom and power that may lie within the most unlikely of us, which is why Abraham Lincoln remains the supreme example of great leadership. A great leader, said Emerson, exhibits new possibilities to all humanity. "We feed on genius. . . . Great men exist that there may be greater men."

Great leaders, in short, justify themselves by emancipating and empowering their followers. So humanity struggles to master its destiny, remembering with Alexis de Tocqueville: "It is true that around every man a fatal circle is traced beyond which he cannot pass; but within the wide verge of that circle he is powerful and free; as it is with man, so with communities."

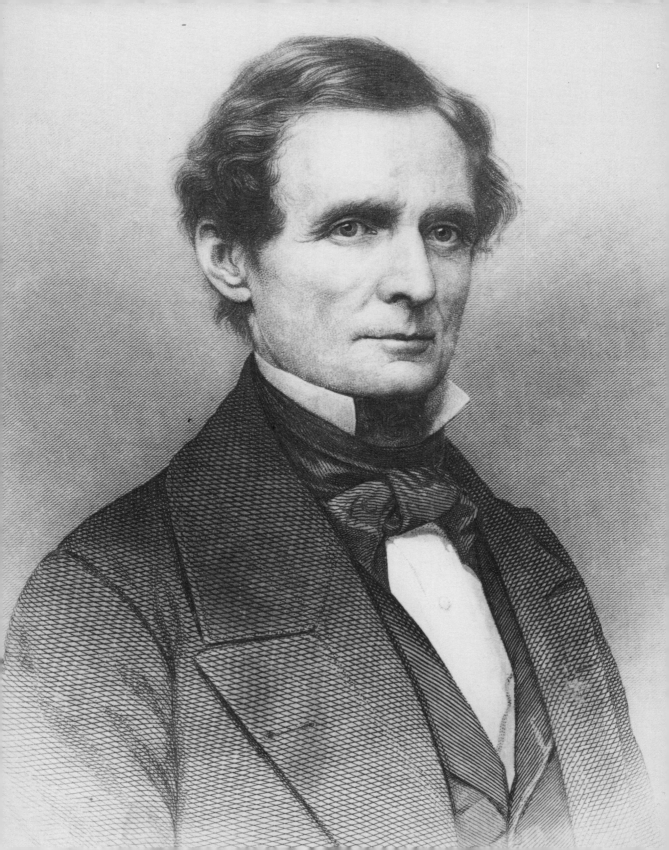

1

The Man and the Hour

The last glimmer of dusk was fading from the southern Mississippi sky on February 10, 1861, when a rider turned his galloping horse off the road to Natchez and clattered up the drive to Brierfield manor. Passing a group of exhausted slaves returning from their day's labors in the cotton fields beside the Mississippi River, the rider reined in his horse at the entrance to the main house, dismounted, and ran inside with a message from the Vicksburg telegraph office.

Brierfield's owner, former U.S. secretary of war and senator Jefferson Davis, was helping his wife, Varina, trim back some tangled stalks in the estate's rose garden when he heard the sound of the horse in the drive. He continued pruning until his steward appeared with the messenger. The telegram was from Montgomery, Alabama, and it stated that the delegates to the newly formed provisional government of the Confederate States of America had unanimously voted to offer him the presidency. Davis retired to his study to write a reply for the waiting messenger.

> *Our present political position . . . illustrates the American idea that governments rest on the consent of the governed, and that it is the right of the people to alter or abolish them at will whenever they become destructive of the ends for which they were established.*
> —JEFFERSON DAVIS
> from his inaugural address to the provisional government of the Confederacy, February 18, 1861

West Point cadet, plantation owner, hero of the Mexican War, U.S. senator and secretary of war, Jefferson Davis of Mississippi was the first — and only — president of the Confederate States of America.

On February 10, 1861, the calm at Brierfield, Jefferson Davis's plantation on the banks of the Mississippi, was broken by the arrival of a messenger, who presented Davis with a telegram informing him that he had been selected as the president of the newborn Confederacy.

As Davis sat down at his desk, he wondered if he was equal to the task presented to him in this time of national crisis. Three months earlier, Abraham Lincoln, the candidate of the antislavery Republican party, had won the U.S. presidential election, and the country that Davis had served as soldier, senator, and secretary of war had split apart under the weight of irreconcilable differences between the antislavery North and the slaveholding South.

At the age of 52, the tall senator with the striking, gray-streaked hair and sightless left eye was the most well known and respected political figure in the South. Ironically, Davis did not feel that he was a particularly able politician. Like most Southern men of that era and his social position, Davis was deeply conscious of his honor and dignity and disliked having to haggle for votes in Congress. He much preferred leading troops into battle, and he had hoped that he would be offered the command of the South's armies in the expected conflict with the North.

Despite his belief that his true talents lay in the science of war rather than politics, Davis knew that he had to accept the position of president of the Confederacy. In this hour of danger, the fledgling government at Montgomery needed the force of his character and strong reputation to weld together the loosely connected Confederate states. Beyond his sense of duty to the South and his home state, however, the proud and imperious Mississippian felt the irresistible pull of history and destiny. He wrote a letter of acceptance, emerged from his study, gave the messenger the letter, and dispatched him. Then he announced to his wife that he was the new president of the Confederate States of America. Varina immediately ordered the servants to pack her husband's bags and began making preparations to follow him to Montgomery.

According to Varina Howell Davis, the first lady of the Confederacy, her husband informed her that he had been chosen as president of the rebel Southern states in a way that "a man might speak of a sentence of death."

Abraham Lincoln of Illinois was elected 16th president of the United States on November 6, 1860. Lincoln was to become the principal adversary of Davis in the calamitous years that followed the secession of the South from the Union.

The next morning, Davis bid a reluctant farewell to his family and slaves and commenced his journey to Montgomery, the capital of the new Confederacy. By the time he reached the train station at Vicksburg, the news of his selection as president had reached the public, and huge throngs had gathered to cheer for "gallant Jeff Davis and the Confederacy." Smiling, he listened as brash young men shouted about what they would do to any Yankee who dared set foot on Southern soil. The buoyant spirit of the people helped to uplift his own mood and steel him for the job that lay ahead.

During the six-day ride east to Montgomery over the maddeningly uncoordinated Southern train lines, Davis was met by enthusiastic crowds at Jackson and other cities in Mississippi and Alabama. Enjoying the festivity of the impromptu gatherings, he roused the people's pride with eloquent speeches about the "nobility" of the Southern way of life, and he warned the North not to use armed force against the South to try to restore the Union. To those who were frightened by the enormity of the step the Confederate states had taken in seceding from the United States, he offered reassurances that the South was well prepared to fight a war to preserve its independence.

In reality, Davis knew that the South's situation was not as bright as he indicated in these speeches. As his train rattled through the Mississippi countryside, he saw stark evidence of the dangers that awaited the South if, as he said to a friend, the Confederacy was forced to fight a "long and bloody" war. The slow, roundabout train ride reminded him of how inferior the South's crude transportation system was to the North's advanced rail and canal networks. And the sight of slaves working in cotton fields beside the train tracks underscored other problems: the Southern economy's dependence on one crop, "King Cotton," and a labor force of questionable loyalty.

Chief among the Confederacy's strengths, on the other hand, was the superb fighting ability of Southern officers and common soldiers, who would also have the advantage of defending their home territory. But despite boasts by Southerners that "any Mississippi farm boy could lick seven Yankees," Davis knew that a formidable struggle loomed ahead. Not only did the South have a nonslave population that was scarcely one-third of the North's; it also lacked the North's heavy industry, financial resources, and naval power.

As the Southern states prepared for war, Davis worried about the large population of black slaves. He believed that they might revolt once the war began or abandon the cotton fields and go north, leaving the agricultural economy of the South in a shambles.

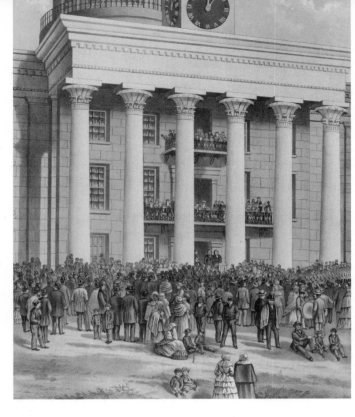

On February 18, 1861, on the steps of the Alabama state capitol at Montgomery, Davis was inaugurated. Describing the scene in a letter to his wife, he wrote, "The audience was large and brilliant. Upon my weary heart was showered smiles, plaudits, and flowers; but, beyond them, I saw troubles and thorns innumerable."

Other questions weighed heavily on Davis's mind. Of the Union's 15 slave states, only 7 — South Carolina, Mississippi, Florida, Alabama, Georgia, Louisiana, and Texas, in that order — had seceded so far. What about Virginia, the most populous of the Southern states? What about North Carolina, Maryland, Arkansas, and Tennessee? What about Missouri, Kentucky, and Delaware? Would their sympathies for the Southern cause finally win out over their loyalty to the Union and bring them into the Confederacy's fold? Without these states, the South would not have the factories and produce that would be needed to support an extended war effort.

The task of securing independence for the South was enormous, but by the time Davis reached Montgomery, he had cast aside whatever doubts he had harbored about the splitting of the Union. He was sure of the righteousness of the Confederacy's cause. For too long, he believed, the South had been the despised and mistreated sister of the North. The South had lain virtually helpless as Northern businessmen gained a stranglehold over its economy, as Northern abolitionists attempted to instigate bloody slave rebellions, and as Northern congressmen conspired to block the spread of slavery into the West. Now the South had risen up and seized control of its own destiny; no longer would it be subjected to the North's bullying and arrogance.

Davis's arrival in Montgomery was greeted by jubilant fanfare. Bands played "Dixie," the newly adopted Confederate anthem, while Davis basked in the applause and accolades, gratified by the size of the crowds in Alabama's stately capital, which had been transformed into a center of activity during the two weeks it had served as the Confederate convention center. Among those who had gathered to greet the president-elect were Georgia congressman Alexander H. Stephens, who had been elected vice-president, and Georgia senator Robert Toombs, whom Davis planned to name secretary of state. William L. Yancey, the fiery leader of the Southern secessionist movement, made a speech that paid tribute to Davis's past services to the South and concluded with the statement "The man and the hour have met."

The next morning, on February 18, Davis was installed as president in the capitol building in Montgomery. In his inaugural address, he praised the constitution drawn up by the provisional congress, a document closely modeled on the U.S. Constitution, except for provisions added to protect slavery and limit federal jurisdiction over the states. To the crowd gathered in the capitol's courtyard, he proclaimed that the popular will of the people of the South had brought about the creation of a new government "in a manner unprecedented in the history of nations." He denied Northern allegations that the South was engaged in an act of illegal rebellion, and he quoted sections of the Declaration of Independence to prove that Americans had the right to "alter or abolish" their own government when it betrayed their trust. If the North refused to recognize the Confederacy's independence, he stated, "it will remain for us with firm resolve to appeal to arms and invoke the blessing of Providence on a just cause."

> *Even if slavery be the product of rapine and violence; even if it be the hideous wrong the Abolitionists declare it to be, still the South is wedded to it in eternal union.*
> —LAWRENCE M. KEITT
> South Carolina
> congressman

2

A Southern Gentleman

Jefferson Finis Davis was born near Fairview, Kentucky, on June 3, 1808, the 10th child of Samuel and Jane Davis. His first name was a tribute to the country's southern-born third president, Thomas Jefferson, whom his parents revered. His unusual middle name, the Latin word for "final," was a product of his father's wry sense of humor; Samuel was certain that his 45-year-old wife would bear no more children. The prediction proved correct, but the name would hover as a dark omen over the career of the first and last president of the doomed Confederate States of America.

The nation into which Jefferson Davis was born was a young, rapidly growing one, pushing inexorably westward as it attempted to stretch its dominion to the Pacific Ocean. A quarter century after the end of the American War of Independence, the United States included 17 states and more than a dozen large western territories, many of which, such as Mississippi and Indiana, would soon be admitted to the Union as states. The country's growth was fueled by an inexhaustible supply of immigrants from Europe, some of whom took jobs in the budding textile industries of northeastern cities; others moved westward to settle on land recently seized from Indian tribes.

Can it be required of a Gentleman, is it part of the character of a soldier, to humble himself beneath the haughty tone, or quail before the angry eye of any man?
—JEFFERSON DAVIS
at his court-martial, 1835

As a youth, Jefferson Davis was spoiled, headstrong, and arrogant. He had no interest in school or in work on his father's farm. But West Point, a stint in the army, and the untimely death of his first wife would curb his willful inclinations.

The cabin in Fairview, Kentucky, where Davis was born in June 1808. Abraham Lincoln was born less than a year later and but 100 miles away.

The national hunger for land and economic wealth — America's Manifest Destiny — was part of the country's desire to establish itself on an equal footing with Great Britain and the other European powers. By the beginning of the 1800s, however, the country's expansion westward had begun to generate the divisive issue that would eventually pit Americans in the North against their southern brethren: Should slavery be allowed in the new western territories, as southerners wished, or should it be prohibited in them, as northern abolitionists advocated? (The Constitution encouraged the abolition of the overseas slave trade, which was accomplished in 1808, making it illegal to bring new slaves into the country. But the Constitution said nothing about all the slaves that were already held captive within the Union.)

Slavery had existed in North America for almost two centuries at the time of Jefferson Davis's birth. Assailed by its opponents as brutal and dehumanizing and stridently defended by its champions as a proper, even noble institution, slavery aroused explosive passions. More than 1 million black people were held in bondage in the United States, the vast majority in the South, whose agricultural economy and large plantation system made it dependent on slave labor.

By 1808, all of the northern states — Rhode Island, Vermont, Pennsylvania, Massachusetts, New Hampshire, Connecticut, New York, and New Jersey, in that order — had passed laws that either abolished slavery or instituted a gradual emancipation process that ensured slaves their eventual freedom. The southern economy, however, had become increasingly dependent on slavery because of the international market's growing demands for cotton, a crop that was especially well suited to production by slave labor.

One of the men eventually to take advantage of the cotton boom was Samuel Davis, Jefferson's father. A Georgian of Welsh ancestry, the elder Davis had fought for the patriotic cause during the American Revolution. After war's end, he married a South Carolinian named Jane Cook and settled on a farm near Augusta, Georgia, where the first six of Jefferson's brothers and sisters were born. In 1793, the family moved to Kentucky, settling down to raise tobacco on a farm in Christian County, in the southwestern part of the state. There, in a modest log cabin, Jefferson was born in June 1808, about 100 miles from the Kentucky cabin where Abraham Lincoln was born 8 months later.

A settlers' wagon train is attacked by Indians in a scene that became increasingly familiar in 19th-century America, as pioneers pushed westward and the Indians were driven from their homeland.

Captive African men, women, and children are unloaded from a slave ship in Charleston, South Carolina, where they will be sold by auction to southern farmers and plantation owners.

Jefferson had no memories of his birthplace, for when he was two years old, his father again got the itch to pull up stakes. The Davises traveled first to the Louisiana bayou country, but unhappy with the malarial delta's swampy soil and swarms of mosquitoes, they moved to southwestern Mississippi and settled on a farm near the town of Woodville. With the assistance of his sons and his half-dozen slaves, Samuel Davis cleared a plot of land near the Mississippi River and established a cotton plantation, which he named Rosemont.

As the youngest member of the family, Jefferson enjoyed close, loving attention from his older siblings. His sisters Anna and Lucinda pampered and spoiled him during his early years, and he was the favorite of his oldest brother, Joseph, a lawyer who owned a large plantation near Natchez, Mississippi. Samuel Davis also treated Jefferson with special regard, for he wanted his youngest son to be thoroughly educated in the courtly ways of a southern gentleman.

The cultural traditions of the southern planter-class gentry were expressed in a code of conduct that emphasized honor, courtesy, and hospitality; it was designed to foster a style of graceful living. The members of the southern aristocracy saw themselves as the spiritual descendants of medieval knights and noblemen, and above all they prized personal honor, chivalry, and courage. The black man, they believed, was an inferior species, and the right to own blacks, they felt, was theirs by birth. Highly sensitive to real or imagined insults, southern gentlemen were known for their impulsiveness, their quick tempers, and their penchant for fighting duels.

Newly entered into the ranks of the southern gentry, Samuel Davis was determined that his youngest son receive the best education possible. On the far western frontier by the Mississippi River, however, there were few schools of any merit. Therefore, in 1816, Jefferson's father decided to send him to the College of St. Thomas Aquinas, a Catholic school in central Kentucky that taught both younger and older students. The decision was bitterly opposed

For southerners such as Samuel Davis, cotton represented potential success and possibly great wealth. Although his father never quite achieved the prosperity depicted here, Jefferson Davis would eventually own a comparable plantation on the banks of the Mississippi.

by Jane Davis, who was upset that her son was being sent to a school hundreds of miles from the Davis home. She was also uneasy about a young boy from a Baptist family being exposed to Roman Catholic teachings. But Samuel Davis had his way, and 8-year-old Jefferson joined a friend of his brother Joseph's, Major Thomas Hinds, and his family on an overland journey through the wilds of Mississippi, Tennessee, and Kentucky.

The arduous trek to the school gave young Jefferson his first real taste of the wilderness, and the journey was crowned by a visit to Nashville, Tennessee, and the home of General Andrew Jackson. The hero of the American victory over the British at the Battle of New Orleans during the War of 1812, Jackson left a deep impression on Jefferson. The boy admired the gruff charm and noble bearing of the man who would be elected president of the United States 12 years later.

Davis's interest in the military was sparked at the age of eight, when his father took him to meet General Andrew Jackson, a heroic figure who would later become the seventh president of the United States.

Jefferson spent two years at St. Thomas Aquinas, showing himself to be a fair student and an accomplished mischief maker. In 1818, he returned home by steamboat, traveling much of the distance unaccompanied by a guardian. For the next five years, Jefferson attended local schools. A handsome, willful boy who much preferred horseback riding to schoolwork, he was never a particularly attentive student, and he frequently rebelled against classroom discipline. Once, after he refused to go to school, his father warned him that he would either have to take his books and return to class or work in the cotton fields. It took just two days of picking cotton alongside his father's slaves to convince Jefferson that school was the lesser of the two evils.

While Jefferson was laboring over his schoolwork, his nation's leaders were trying to arrange a compromise that would satisfy the demands of both southern slaveholders and antislavery northern Free-Soilers concerning the lands west of the Mississippi River. This huge territory, bought from France by Thomas Jefferson as part of the Louisiana Purchase, included Missouri, which in 1819 requested to be admitted to the Union with laws that protected slavery. After a heated debate, Congress passed the Missouri Compromise, which admitted Missouri to the nation as a slave state but set a line even with the state's southern boundary as the limit for slavery in the rest of the western territories.

When Jefferson was 15, he again returned to Kentucky, this time to attend Louisville's Transylvania University. One of the most highly regarded schools in the South during the early 1800s, Transylvania was attended by the sons of some of the South's most aristocratic families, and Jefferson met many young men who would eventually become the leaders of the South and West. The curriculum included the study of Latin, Greek, and other languages, and Jefferson proved to be a fair linguist. While at Transylvania, he also developed a talent for debating, and he began to think about pursuing a law career, which would allow him to put such a skill to good use.

> *We have the wolf by the ears, and we can neither hold him nor safely let him go. Justice is in one scale, and self-preservation in the other.*
> —THOMAS JEFFERSON
> on maintaining slavery in a democratic nation

François de Barbé-Marbois (left) of France and Robert R. Livingston (center) and James Monroe (right) of the United States sign the Louisiana Purchase. Much of the territory included in the purchase, which was made in 1803, was at the center of the later debate over the status of slavery in the American West.

Before Jefferson's first year at Transylvania was completed, he was shattered by grim news from home. His father had incurred sudden severe debts and had been forced to sell Rosemont. Shortly after this catastrophe, Samuel Davis contracted malaria and died. Jefferson was despondent over his loss, but far from home, he could only turn for comfort to one of the last letters he received from his father, which counseled him to "use every possible means to acquire useful knowledge as knowledge is power."

With Samuel Davis gone, Joseph Davis stepped in to take over the role of supporting and advising Jefferson. The young man was relieved to hear that his wealthy brother had bought Rosemont to save it for the family, but he was less pleased to learn that his father and Joseph had arranged for him to go to the U.S. Military Academy at West Point, New York. Jefferson Davis had set his sights on becoming a lawyer and was not particularly interested in the military. Joseph, however, persuaded him to spend at least one year at West Point before settling on a law career.

The choice of West Point was a natural one for a distinguished southern family. In part because of the constant danger of slave uprisings, the South had developed a strong martial tradition that fostered — or so it was hoped — a fighting spirit that combined the courage of legendary pioneer Daniel Boone, the bold generalship of Andrew Jackson, and the shooting eye of frontiersman and Indian fighter Davy Crockett. Southerners were proud of their military prowess, and they composed a majority of the cadets at West Point.

In September 1824, the 16-year-old Davis entered West Point. Founded 22 years earlier, the military institute on the Hudson River molded officers for the U.S. Army. From the ranks of its cadets came the men who would become generals in the country's future wars. Among Davis's fellow cadets at West Point were Confederate general Robert E. Lee and many others who would play commanding roles — for both the North and the South — four decades later in the Civil War.

President James Monroe (right) gratefully clasps the hand of Speaker of the House Henry Clay in a political cartoon depicting the adoption of the Missouri Compromise in 1820. Although the compromise temporarily preserved the Union, it did so — as the cartoon shows — at the expense of the black race.

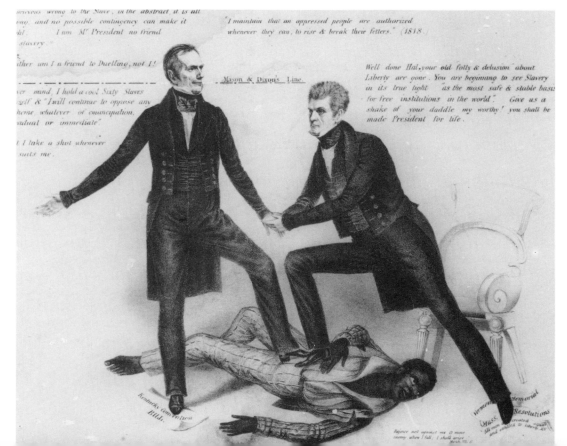

The United States Military Academy at West Point, New York, which Davis entered at the age of 16. Although he spent much of his time at the academy breaking the rules and getting into trouble, he managed to graduate in 1828 with the rank of second lieutenant.

Davis's four years at West Point were not particularly distinguished. Younger than most of the students in his class and no longer bound by his father's stern guiding influence, he took delight in joining other high-spirited cadets in rebelling against the academy's rigorous code of behavior. He was disciplined for slovenly dress and appearance, for disobeying instructions during drills, for firing his rifle out of the window of his room, for spitting in public, and for numerous other infractions. On one occasion he fell into a ravine while escaping from disciplinary officers and was seriously injured. Thoroughly unrepentant, he broke the academy's prohibition against drinking and was twice on the verge of expulsion.

But Davis learned more than just the art of disorderly conduct at West Point. Less than thrilled about the idea of following a military career when he entered the academy, he gradually developed a deep interest in military science. He also forged strong bonds with some of his fellow cadets and developed many friendships that would last a lifetime. Two typically southern traits emerged in Davis during his West Point years: a deep loyalty to his friends and an icy and often unforgiving manner toward those he assumed to be his enemies.

By the time Davis reached his final year at West Point, he had resigned himself to the life of an army officer for at least a few years. When he graduated in June 1828, he was ranked 23rd in a class of 32. After graduation, he returned home for the first time in more than five years. He then took up his commission of second lieutenant and was stationed at an army base near St. Louis, Missouri. Apparently, he still entertained some thoughts of eventually becoming a lawyer, for he began reading law books in his free time. He also spent a great deal of time attending balls and other social events. The dashing young officer made a favorable impression on the young ladies of St. Louis, one of whom described him as "witty, sportful, and captivating."

In the spring of 1829, Davis was reassigned to Fort Winnebago, an army outpost on the Wisconsin River in the Michigan Territory. This region, which eventually became present-day Wisconsin and Michigan, was rapidly being settled by immigrants from the East who were seeking to push the resident Indian tribes off their lands. In this northern territory, Davis got a true taste of the general boredom and loneliness that accompany a soldier's life in peacetime. Instead of leading assaults on enemy fortifications or other such gallant work, he found himself saddled with the job of supervising the building of an army barracks and a sawmill. He was assisted by his slave, Jim Pemberton. Pemberton nursed his master back to health after Davis caught pneumonia during the brutal winter of 1830–31. Although Davis eventually regained his strength, he suffered permanent damage to his health.

After his arduous winter at Fort Winnebago, Davis was transferred to Fort Crawford, another military outpost in the western part of the Michigan Territory, near the Mississippi River. But soon he was sent to Galena, Illinois, to help keep peace between local Indian tribes and the white settlers who were flooding into the area to mine its vast lead deposits. Davis had little sympathy for the tribes' claims to their native lands and viewed Indians as uncivilized and hostile savages who had to be kept under control while the United States expanded westward.

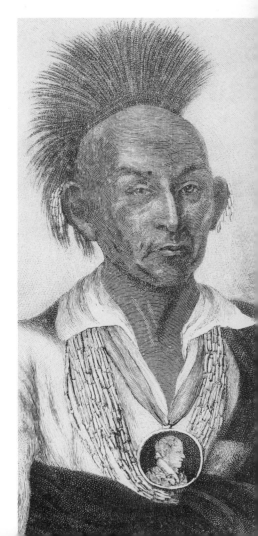

Chief Black Hawk, leader of the Sac and Fox tribes in the Black Hawk War, an Indian uprising in the Michigan Territory. Black Hawk and a war party of 1,000 braves were crushed by U.S. troops at Bad Axe River in 1832. Davis escorted the defeated chief to prison in St. Louis.

Sarah Knox Taylor, daughter of future U.S. president Zachary Taylor, married Davis in June 1835. The marriage was ill fated, however; Sarah contracted malaria on the honeymoon and died on September 15.

Davis remained in Illinois until the spring of 1832, when he asked for a furlough so that he could visit his family. While he was in Mississippi, the tensions between the Indians and settlers in the Michigan Territory erupted into the Black Hawk War, named after the chief who led the Indian resistance. The war was brief, ending after a confederation of Indian tribes was routed by American troops at the Battle of Bad Axe in August 1832. Davis missed the fighting, but he returned in time to be given the assignment of guarding the captured Chief Black Hawk when he was moved from Fort Crawford to St. Louis.

In 1833, Davis was stationed at Fort Gibson in the Arkansas Territory. Still a second lieutenant, he had become frustrated that he had not yet been promoted after five years in the army. Always stubborn and quick-tempered, he let his personal disappointments spur him into insubordination toward his commanding officers, most of whom he despised. In May 1834, he finally was promoted to first lieutenant of cavalry, but his conduct toward his superiors did not change. Ten months later, he was court-martialed for being disrespectful to his commander, Major R. B. Mason. Taking his defense into his own hands, however, Davis argued successfully that his gentleman's pride had been provoked by Mason's own arrogance.

Davis had found other pleasures besides baiting his superiors. His personal charm, which had gained him many friends among his fellow officers, had also succeeded in capturing the affections of Sarah Knox Taylor. The daughter of Colonel Zachary Taylor, Davis's commander at Fort Winnebago and future president of the United States, Sarah had disobeyed her father's rule against writing to the reckless young officer with the small inheritance. For 3 years, Jefferson and Sarah exchanged love letters, and in June 1835, the 21-year-old Sarah agreed to Davis's marriage proposal. Davis immediately resigned his commission and traveled to be with his fiancée. They were married in Louisville, Kentucky, on June 17, despite the objections of Sarah's parents, who refused to attend the wedding.

Tragedy struck the young couple within three months of their wedding. After first visiting Jefferson's brother Joseph at his home in Natchez, the newlyweds continued their honeymoon trip by traveling to the home of Jefferson's sister Anna in Louisiana. Malaria season was at its height at the time, and both Jefferson and Sarah caught the disease. Sarah died on September 15, 1835, and Jefferson was confined to his bed for several weeks.

Heartbroken by the death of his young wife, Davis returned to his brother Joseph's plantation to mourn and recover from his own near-fatal bout with malaria. Feeling that a winter of recuperation in balmy Cuba would improve his health, he sailed to the island at the end of 1835. Although generally bored during his stay there, he used the time to observe the situation in the politically troubled Spanish colony.

When Davis returned to the United States, he spent a few weeks in Washington attending congressional sessions. The main topic of interest in the capital was the revolt of American settlers in the Mexican province of Texas against the government in Mexico City. After suffering hard-fought defeats at the Alamo mission and Goliad in March 1836, the Texans routed the army of General Antonio López de Santa Anna at the Battle of San Jacinto in April. The founding of the Republic of Texas shortly afterward sparked a national debate over the wisdom of admitting the huge young republic to the United States. Southerners, including Davis, overwhelmingly supported admitting Texas, but many northerners were leery about allowing such a large slave territory to join the Union.

From Washington, Davis returned to Mississippi, where he intended to take up his brother Joseph's offer of 800 acres on the Mississippi River. There, on an estate he christened Brierfield for the profusion of briers that covered the land, the young widower began his life as a gentleman landowner. For the next seven years, the strenuous effort of carving a prosperous cotton plantation out of his wild woodland estate would provide him with the activity he needed to help heal the pain in his heart.

The Alamo mission in San Antonio, Texas, where 182 Texans, under the command of Colonel W. B. Travis, fought to the last man against several thousand Mexican soldiers, March 6, 1836. The Mexican-American conflict would reignite in 1846, providing Davis with a chance to experience war firsthand.

3

The Hero of Buena Vista

At Brierfield, Davis became absorbed in the task of building and managing his plantation. With the help of 10 slaves, he cleared the land, raised a small, comfortable house, planted groves of oak and fig trees, and put in his first crop of cotton on the fertile black soil of the riverside estate. The "Father of Waters," as the Mississippi is known, would prove to be both friend and enemy; Brierfield would be heavily damaged in years when the river swept over the levees containing it and flooded the cotton fields.

For the first time in his life, Davis was responsible for a large group of slaves. Like most southerners, he had no qualms about slavery and believed that well-armed county militias were necessary to maintain order among the slaves and to hunt for runaways. Several rebellions, including the bloody revolt of Nat Turner and his disciples in Virginia in 1831, had demonstrated all too clearly to southerners that slavery was a dangerous institution for both master and slave. Although he was a firm defender of slavery and white supremacy, Davis disagreed with those slaveholders who believed that slaves were animals that had to be whipped to make them work.

> *Our doors are unlocked at night. . . . We live among [the slaves] with no more fear of them than of our cows and oxen. We lie down to sleep trusting to them for our defence.*
> —JEFFERSON DAVIS

Following the death of his wife, Davis went into seclusion at Brierfield. While he grieved, the issues of slavery and American expansion heated up once again. After seven years of isolation, Davis grew restless, and soon he succumbed to the call of politics and war.

Brierfield, the product of years of toil. With the help of a handful of slaves, Davis succeeded in transforming 800 acres of rough scrubland into a beautiful and productive cotton plantation.

Davis had a much closer relationship with his slaves than many masters. He allowed the field hands to help themselves to the corn supply and borrow guns to go hunting. He never resorted to using the lash on disobedient slaves, provided decent health care for sick slaves, and even allowed juries of Brierfield's slaves to sit in judgment on their fellows for petty infractions.

The lenient master of Brierfield was hardly typical of most slaveholders, whose more savage ways were described on the pages of northern antislavery journals, such as William Lloyd Garrison's *The Liberator*. During the 1830s, many journals such as Garrison's were published by organizations that wanted the United States to abolish slavery. Intent on exposing an evil institution for what it was, the abolitionists focused on the most brutal aspects of slavery. Their lectures and writings described how slaves were sometimes maimed or murdered by their masters for small offenses, how slave families were ruthlessly torn apart in public auctions, how slave masters and overseers often raped their female slaves, and how underfed and underclothed slaves were worked to death in the sweltering cotton fields of the South. Slavery brutalized both master and slave, the abolitionists warned, and it was a stain on the national conscience in an era when most countries had long since banned the ugly institution.

Southern spokesmen hotly defended slavery as an institution that provided great wealth for the United States and allowed black slaves to benefit from their masters' "racially superior" Christian civilization. Claiming that most masters were "paternalistic" toward their slaves, the South's defenders denied that atrocities were commonplace. They insisted that slaves in the South were better treated than free blacks in the North, most of whom lived in poverty and neglect as despised second-class citizens. The proslavery advocates claimed that the abolitionists, whom they called "Yankee fanatics," were trying to establish economic, political, and cultural domination over the South by destroying the institution upon which the southern way of life so heavily depended.

But it was not just the issue of slavery that was dividing the North and South. Crucial economic problems were causing friction as well. One point of dispute was the tariff, or tax, levied on imported products to protect the North's growing manufacturing industries from being undercut by foreign competitors. High tariffs drove up the prices of

Nat Turner, the leader of a slave insurrection in southeastern Virginia, is brought to bay, October 30, 1831. Turner and his band put 55 whites to death during their spree, fueling southern fears of a massive slave uprising.

THE LIBERATOR.

VOL. I.] WILLIAM LLOYD GARRISON AND ISAAC KNAPP, PUBLISHERS. [NO. 33

BOSTON, MASSACHUSETTS.] OUR COUNTRY IS THE WORLD—OUR COUNTRYMEN ARE MANKIND. [SATURDAY, AUGUST 13, 1831.]

The front page of William Lloyd Garrison's *The Liberator*, the foremost abolitionist journal of the 1830s. Such publications enraged southerners, who believed they were the work of "Yankee fanatics" intent on ruining the South.

goods, especially manufactured products, which benefited the industrialized North but hurt the agricultural South. The South's resentment of high import duties was voiced most effectively by John Calhoun, an eloquent senator from South Carolina who led an unsuccessful effort to have the tariff nullified in the early 1830s. Calhoun's threat to take South Carolina out of the Union unless the tariff was repealed led to a dangerous battle of wills with President Andrew Jackson; the conflict was resolved when Henry Clay, the persuasive Kentucky senator known as the Great Pacificator, arranged the passage of a lower, compromise tariff in Congress — but not before the inflammatory word *secession* had become common on Capitol Hill and in the nation's newspapers and households.

The master of Brierfield was following these developments closely. Davis supplemented his daily diet of newspapers by reading extensively in history, political science, constitutional law, economics, and military theory. His schooling in Latin, Greek, Spanish, and French allowed him to read from many different sources. Among his other chief pleasures was his stable of fine horses, which he kept for riding and hunting. His activities were somewhat limited by occasional spells of ill health, including relapses of malarial fever, but after 7 years of isolation as a grieving widower and with his plantation well established, the 34-year-old Davis began looking for something else to occupy his energies. He found that outlet in politics.

American politics in the mid-1800s, especially in the South, were a tempestuous affair, and bitter arguments in the legislative chambers sometimes resulted in an invitation to continue the debate with pistols at 20 paces. Political campaigns between the two main national parties, the Democrats and the newly formed Whigs, were characterized by language considered unfit for the ears of women and children. It was not the opportunity for dueling or election-platform fisticuffs that drew Davis to politics, however. No longer the rebellious young officer who thumbed his nose at his commanders, it was a quieter, more thoughtful and mature Davis who was now seeking an arena in which to acquire the knowledge — and the power — his father had written of shortly before his death.

Instead of joining the Whigs, the party favored by most of the southern aristocracy, Davis decided to follow family tradition and join the Democrats, the party of Thomas Jefferson and Andrew Jackson and the one preferred by smaller planters. It was a difficult choice for Davis. The Democrats had a stronger popular appeal and a broader national following than their rivals, but the Whigs dominated politics in Warren County, Davis's voting district.

A slave wedding on the Davis plantation. Davis belonged to the more benign category of southern slaveholders, who did not beat or mistreat the blacks they owned and allowed them a certain degree of "freedom" within the limits of the plantation.

Senator Henry Clay of Kentucky was known as the Great Pacificator because of his ability to defuse some of the potentially explosive conflicts that arose between the North and South in the years leading up to the Civil War.

Once Davis made his decision, however, his rise in politics was rapid. His command of state and national political issues and his talent for public speaking so impressed the local Democratic leaders that they assigned him a large role in debates with Whig candidates for state office.

In 1843, Davis made his first run for public office, campaigning for a seat in the Mississippi legislature. (It was this body rather than the general public that elected the state's representatives to the Senate.) Davis lost the election to his Whig opponent, but his spirited campaign addresses brought him to the attention of the state's Democratic power brokers. Selected as a delegate to the Mississippi Democratic Convention, he spoke out for the rights of southern states with such eloquence that he was chosen as one of the state's presidential electors for James Knox Polk's candidacy in 1844 against the Whig Henry Clay.

Given the task of marshaling support for Polk in Mississippi, Davis undertook an extensive lecture tour throughout the state. Mixing insightful comments on burning political issues with barbed descriptions of Whig politicians — he referred to them as "galvanized frogs" and "dung beetles," among other things — Davis succeeded in portraying himself as a strong spokesman for the South, a supporter of an aggressive national foreign policy, and a combative and dangerous opponent on the debating platform. He was especially vocal in his support for the annexation of Texas, a move that would almost certainly trigger a war with Mexico. He also advocated the end of tariffs, the establishment of free trade policies, and the annexation of the entire Oregon Territory, a huge section of land in the West stretching from Alaska to the present southern boundary of Oregon.

Davis's tour on behalf of Polk helped to introduce him to voters throughout Mississippi, but it also endangered his none too robust health, and he was forced to take breaks to recover from periods of illness and exhaustion. Something more than political campaigning occupied his thoughts, however: In early 1844, he became engaged to 17-year-old

Varina Howell of Natchez, Mississippi. Haunted by the memory of his first wife, Davis had been cool to all efforts by his brother Joseph to match him with eligible young ladies. But after meeting Varina at Joseph's Christmas celebration in 1843, he quickly became enthralled by the tall, attractive young woman who displayed such an extensive knowledge of both literature and politics. Davis also discovered, to his delight, that Varina was a fine horsewoman.

After an engagement of more than a year, Davis and Varina were married at the bride's family home on February 26, 1845. This time, there were no protestations from the bride's family; Jefferson Davis was now a distinguished citizen of Mississippi. After a honeymoon trip to New Orleans, the couple returned to Brierfield to begin a period of more than four decades of deep marital devotion. Although never happy with the demands that public office imposed on Davis, Varina used her abilities as a wife, mother, manager of the Davis estate, counselor, and hostess to help advance her husband's political career and nurse his fragile health.

Manifest Destiny in action: settlers pushing inexorably westward. While Davis was campaigning for a seat in the Mississippi legislature in 1843, he established himself as a strong proponent of American expansionism. In 1845, during his first term in Congress, he would lead the movement for the annexation of the Oregon Territory.

In 1843, at his brother Joseph's Christmas party, Davis, then 36, met 17-year-old Varina Howell. Despite the difference in age, Davis successfully courted Varina, and they were married in February 1845.

By late 1845, James Polk had been elected president, and Davis's political star was on the rise. Happily married and thoroughly enjoying life with his new bride at Brierfield, he decided to run for the House of Representatives. Again he made a speaking tour through Mississippi, and his straight, handsome bearing and superb oratory won over the voters. In November, he was elected to his first term in Congress.

Reluctant to leave Brierfield but excited at the prospect of joining Washington's political and social circles, the Davises departed for their new home late in November 1845. Arriving at the capital three weeks later, Davis immediately became busy organizing support for the annexation of the Oregon

Territory and for other measures he considered of vital importance. He opposed a bill that called for setting aside federal money for the improvement of the nation's waterways, because as a believer in a strict Jeffersonian interpretation of the Constitution, he felt that the states were responsible for improving transportation. He also attacked the Native American party, a xenophobic political faction that wanted to restrict the voting rights of foreign-born Americans, especially the Irish. Davis stated that the antiforeign platform of the Native American party violated the spirit of American democracy; paradoxically, however, he believed that slavery did not.

In March 1846, three months after Davis began his congressional term, public attention was shifted to the Southwest. One year earlier, Congress had approved the Republic of Texas's request to enter the Union, an act that led to the severing of relations with Mexico. The Mexican government had never fully recognized the independence of Texas, and it also disputed the Texans' claim to the Rio Grande as their southern boundary. In the spring of 1846, tensions between the United States and Mexico reached the breaking point after the American army occupied positions along the Rio Grande. Citing a small border incident as a pretext, President Polk asked Congress for a declaration of war against Mexico on May 11. Davis joined with the vast majority of his colleagues in the call to arms.

As usual in time of war, the president asked the states to organize regiments of volunteers to supplement the small U.S. Army. War preparation began in earnest, and Davis found himself hungering to be in uniform again. Determined not to miss the chance for military glory, he resigned his seat in Congress and assumed the position of colonel and commanding officer of the First Mississippi Rifles infantry regiment. Varina was aghast, but Davis could not be swayed from his decision. After joining his regiment in New Orleans and outfitting his men — at his own expense — with the best rifles available, he sailed for Texas to join the army of his former father-in-law, General Zachary Taylor.

During the conflict with Mexico that broke out in May 1846, Davis and his rifle regiment served heroically under the command of General Zachary ("Old Rough and Ready") Taylor — Davis's former father-in-law.

Once enemies but now close friends, Davis and Taylor were to play prominent roles in the American victory over the weak and outdated armies of its neighbor. Known affectionately as Old Rough and Ready to his troops, the stolid, unkempt Taylor showed a genius for using difficult terrain to his advantage. Davis joined him after Taylor had already won two battles over the Mexicans on Texas soil. The general's next assignment was to win control of northern Mexico, and in September, Taylor's army marched into Mexico and besieged the fortress town of Monterrey. Despite a heroic defense by the Mexicans, Monterrey fell to the Americans after a week-long assault. Davis's troops were the first to scale Monterrey's walls and race to the town's central citadel.

But Taylor's victories only seemed to saddle him with more difficulties. Fearing that Old Rough and Ready's extreme popularity with the American public would make him an invincible opponent in the next presidential election, President Polk stripped Taylor of many of his troops, which supposedly were needed for General Winfield Scott's campaign against Mexico City. Hearing about Taylor's predicament, Mexican general Santa Anna marched

A victorious General Winfield Scott leads American troops into Mexico City, September 14, 1847. After the defeat of Mexico, Davis hoped that the United States would annex the entire country. President Polk settled for California and New Mexico.

against the Americans with a large army. Outnumbered by more than four to one, Taylor's troops encountered Santa Anna's forces at the mountain pass of Buena Vista on February 22, 1847. After heavy fighting, during which Davis was shot in the foot, the Mexicans drove through Taylor's front lines and seemed on the verge of victory. At that point, Taylor ordered Davis's men to attempt a desperate assault on the charging enemy. Rushing his riflemen forward and arranging them in an unorthodox wedge formation, Davis shattered the Mexican advance and shifted the advantage to the Americans. By day's end, Taylor had won a stunning victory over Santa Anna. Davis's actions during the battle won him the title of "the hero of Buena Vista." Sent home with his regiment soon afterward, he was toasted as the pride of Mississippi.

Davis was at home, recovering from his wound, when he learned of General Scott's capture of Mexico City in September 1847. An ardent expansionist, Davis wanted the United States to annex the whole of Mexico, or at the very least the territory between Texas and the Pacific Ocean. Early in 1848, the helpless Mexican government agreed to American demands and gave up California and its other northern territories. Coupled with a recent treaty with Great Britain that gave the United States control of Oregon, Washington, and Idaho, the new territories increased the nation's size by more than one-half.

The Mexican War expanded America's territory, but it also added new fuel to the slavery controversy. If the political balance between the northern free states and the southern slave states was to be maintained, slavery would have to be allowed to expand westward into the new territories. To Davis, this policy seemed only natural, but the leaders of the antislavery forces wanted slavery contained within its already established boundaries. The struggle over this issue would give the military hero from Mississippi and his fellow southerners the chance to show that they were ready to stand up to the North for their rights — including the "right" to own slaves and to export slavery to the new territories.

I began to know the bitterness of being a politician's wife, and that it meant long absences, pecuniary depletion from ruinous absenteeism, illness from exposure, misconceptions, defamation of character; everything that darkens the sunlight and contracts the happy sphere of home.
—VARINA HOWELL DAVIS
reflecting on her husband's election to Congress

4

Conflict and Compromise

In December 1847, after a one-and-a-half year absence from Congress, Jefferson Davis returned to Washington to assume a place in the Senate as the unanimous choice of the Mississippi legislature for the state's vacant seat. Now a national hero, Davis was greeted by his colleagues as he hobbled on crutches — he was still suffering from the wounds he received at Buena Vista — into the Senate chambers to begin his first term.

By the time Davis took his seat in the Senate, the thin wall of restraint that had thus far kept the North and South from each other's throat was crumbling fast. The first large cracks in the wall had appeared with the passage of the Wilmot Proviso (named for Pennsylvania representative David Wilmot) by the House of Representatives in February 1847. Designed by northern congressmen to curb the expansion of slavery, the measure prohibited

I make no terms. I accept no compromises.
—JEFFERSON DAVIS

In late 1847, after the successful conclusion of the Mexican War, Davis returned to the Senate as a hero. But the feeling of national unity that followed the war quickly faded in the face of the growing conflict between the North and South, and Davis's loyalty to the Union began to fade as well.

slavery in any territories captured from Mexico. The southern states, whose volunteers had played a large part in the victory over Mexico, were incensed by the Wilmot Proviso, and Virginia led them in condemning the measure. To Davis, the Wilmot Proviso was the clearest sign yet of a movement by northern antislavery extremists to isolate and dominate the South.

Following on the heels of the Wilmot Proviso controversy, the discovery of gold in California in 1848 was the catalyst for a momentous national debate over the future of slavery in the American republic. When news of the discovery spread, thousands of Americans and foreigners joined the rush to the gold fields. By 1850, California's population had ballooned to five times its pre-gold-rush size, and its legislature requested that Congress recognize the territory as a state.

Boomtowns sprouted like wild mushrooms during the gold rush of 1849. While fortune hunters flooded westward, a fierce debate raged in Congress over the future of slavery in California.

California's request for statehood sparked one of the most angry and divisive debates that has ever rung through the halls of Congress. At stake was the balance of power in Congress; the admission of another free state would upset the equal division of seats in the Senate and give the North the upper hand in both houses. Already rent by disputes between proslavery southern Democrats and members of the newly formed antislavery Free-Soil party, Congress now faced an issue that threatened to split the nation in half.

Proslavery and antislavery forces spewed out torrents of invective against each other. Tempers flared in both houses; fistfights broke out, and threats were made. Southern politicians again began to invoke the grim specter of secession. Militant abolitionists accused the South of trying to reintroduce slavery into the North and of scheming to extend its slave empire into the West and Latin America. Radical proslavery fire-eaters retaliated with a fierce defense of the South's right to expand anywhere it pleased. Certain that antislavery groups were conspiring to ruin the South, the fire-eaters urged the southern states to secede from the United States and form their own nation.

California gold miners — including newly arrived Asian immigrants — call a momentary halt to their labors and pose for a photograph with prospecting tools in hand.

In this time of extreme passions, Davis stepped forward to take up the standard for the southern states and lead a campaign that he hoped would guarantee the integrity of the South's place within the Union. Davis took a more moderate position than the fire-eaters, but in his speeches in the Senate he was no less firm in his assertions that the South must be allowed its fair share of the West. He now saw himself as the champion of southern expansionism and the much-maligned institution of slavery, and he was hoping to increase the South's political power in Congress and his own political power in the South. Most significantly, Davis had come to believe that a state had the constitutional right to secede from the United States.

Davis's belief that the South had the right to secede rested on one basic principle: The United States was founded on a compact that promised that the federal government would not interfere with the vital institutions of the individual states. In the opinion of Davis and other southerners, that compact was being violated by the North's insistence on prohibiting the spread of slavery. Slaves were property, Davis pointed out, using the arrogant and immoral logic of the southern slaveholder, and any attempt to interfere with the southerners' constitutional rights to do what they wanted with their property — which included the right to transport the property to another state or territory — was illegal and would oblige the South to secede from the Union.

As the national debate over the future of the western territories raged during 1849 and 1850, a growing southern states' rights movement, supported by Davis, called for secession if the South's demands were ignored in Congress. The secessionist appeals aroused deep concern in President Zachary Taylor — who had succeeded Polk in 1849 — and many congressional moderates. Hoping to arrange an agreement that would defuse the crisis, Henry Clay proposed a group of resolutions in the Senate that he hoped would satisfy the demands of the majority of northerners and southerners. Known collectively as the Compromise of 1850, the resolutions called

Nothing can be more unfounded and false than the prevalent opinion that all men are born free and equal . . . it rests upon the assumption of a fact which is contrary to universal observation.
—JOHN CALHOUN
U.S. senator, South
Carolina

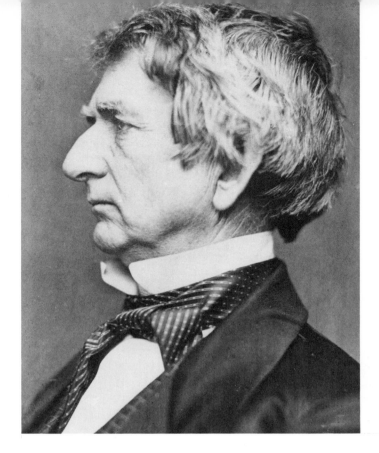

In 1850, Senator William H. Seward of New York led Northern opposition to Henry Clay's proposals concerning the issue of slavery in California. Seward and the other antislavery radicals in Congress believed that Clay's resolutions were weak and immoral.

for the admittance of California to the Union as a free state; the rest of the territories captured from Mexico would decide for themselves whether they wanted slavery or not. To appease the South, the compromise advocated the use of stronger measures to assist in the capture of fugitive slaves at large in free states. The resolutions also called for the abolition of the slave trade — but not slavery — in Washington, D.C., where it was still legal.

Clay's proposal succeeded in dividing public opinion in both the North and South. In the North, New York senator William H. Seward led the antislavery groups' denunciation of the bill as immoral; Massachusetts senator Daniel Webster and Illinois senator Stephen A. Douglas hailed it as a means of preserving the Union. In the South, Clay and other moderates pressed southerners to accept the compromise; the aged but intractable John Calhoun called the bill an insult to the South and organized a campaign to block its passage in Congress.

Davis agreed with Calhoun that the compromise bill was totally inadequate in protecting the rights of the South. He doubted that the northern states would enforce the stricter fugitive-slave law, and he saw no guarantees that the rights of slaveholders would be protected in the western territories. He joined his colleague from South Carolina in leading the fight to defeat Clay's bill in the Senate.

Throughout February and March of 1850, some of the greatest orators in American history rose to defend or attack the compromise bill in the Senate chambers. Clay, Webster, and Douglas made eloquent and impassioned appeals for national unity. Calhoun, barely able to speak and dependent on a colleague to read his address, demanded that the South be given equal footing within the Union. Davis's speech echoed Calhoun's address, calling for constitutional guarantees that neither slavery nor its expansion into federal territories would be challenged.

The campaign by Calhoun and Davis to defeat the compromise bill was unsuccessful. The passage of a revised compromise bill in the summer of 1850 momentarily stemmed the growth of the southern states' rights movement. Not yet ready to engage in a major sectional confrontation, most southerners were content to avert secession and accept a compromise with the North. Davis was slow to realize how quickly the temper of the South had cooled, but the results of a meeting of delegates from southern states at a Nashville convention in June 1850 gave him a clear signal that sectionalist fervor had subsided and unionist sentiments were on the rise. The convention's delegates rejected secessionist proposals and called for moderation and national unity.

Having suffered defeat in the compromise bill struggle, Davis soon found that even his hold over public opinion in his own state was in jeopardy. John A. Quitman, the Democratic candidate for governor of Mississippi, withdrew from the race one month before the election in the fall of 1851. The party leaders asked Davis to assume the candidacy, and he resigned his Senate seat and returned home.

The great evil of Northern free society is that it is burdened with a servile class of mechanics and laborers, unfit for self-government, yet clothed with the attributes and powers of citizens.

—South Carolina newspaper, 1856

Davis's Whig opponent was his former colleague in the Senate, Henry S. Foote, a blustering little politician who had strongly supported Clay's compromise bill. The election turned out to be a referendum on Foote's unionist sympathies and Davis's states' rights views. In his campaign speeches, Davis denied that he was an ardent secessionist, but he urged Mississippi and the rest of the southern states to work together to develop their industries and political organization so that they could lessen their dependence on the North.

In November 1851, Davis lost the election to Foote by a narrow margin. Bitter about the defeat, Davis returned to Brierfield and petulantly vowed to stay out of politics until the people of Mississippi came to their senses and asked him to represent them again. Varina, however, saw the defeat as a blessing

Combative Senator John Calhoun of South Carolina offered a virulent resistance in Congress to Henry Clay's proposals regarding slavery in California and New Mexico; despite Calhoun's efforts, Clay's resolutions were passed in amended form in the summer of 1850.

in disguise; it gave her husband a vacation from the rigors of politics and let him relax on his plantation, which badly needed his attention.

Davis's respite from politics lasted for more than a year, during which he enjoyed the opportunity to cultivate Brierfield's acres, finish construction of a large mansion to replace the old cottage, and participate in Natchez society. In the summer of 1852, after seven years of marriage, he and Varina had their first child. Named Samuel after his paternal grandfather, he would be followed by 3 brothers and 2 sisters, of whom only the girls, Margaret and Varina Anne, would live past the age of 21. The other Davis sons included Jefferson, Jr., Joseph, and William.

Davis was overjoyed to be a father at last, but as usual, politics came first in his life. Deeply immersed in campaigning for Franklin Pierce, the Democratic candidate for president in 1852, he was in the midst of a lecture tour through the North when Samuel was born. His work for his party's ticket paid off when the victorious Pierce offered him the position of secretary of war. A northern "doughface" politician — one who sympathized with the South — the new president was much to Davis's liking. Davis would have preferred to be representing the South in the Senate, but after some hesitation he accepted the cabinet post.

Davis's term in Pierce's cabinet marked his rise to the highest ranks of power in Washington. What should have been a period of general happiness for him and Varina was shattered, however, by the sudden death of their son Samuel in 1854. The loss was partly offset by the birth of their daughter Margaret the following year, but Davis was inconsolable for months after his son's death.

Despite the tragedy that haunted Davis's personal life, the War Department was well managed during his term at its helm. His forthright dealings with congressmen and military contractors enhanced his reputation of being a man of strict honesty and incorruptibility, traits that were in short supply in the capital. He kept up an exhausting pace while striving to improve and expand the country's armed forces, sometimes working nearly the whole day through when he had one of his frequent bouts of insomnia.

As secretary of war, Davis introduced a number of innovations to the nation's military, including the formation of an army medical corps. One of the original members of the board of regents of the Smithsonian Institution when it was founded in 1846, he was keenly interested in new technological advances in weapons and fortifications. He instituted a system of mobile cavalry units and strategically placed forts to drive Indian tribes from their lands in the West. One of his most unusual actions as secretary of war was the acquisition of camels from North Africa to serve as military supply animals in the arid Southwest.

Besides managing the War Department, Davis took on extra responsibilities, including supervising the construction of the dome and new wings of the Capitol building. His most significant work, however, was his direction of efforts to map a route for a transcontinental railroad. In 1854, he dispatched four exploration teams to survey different western regions and determine their suitability as rail routes. Always looking out for the interests of the South, he favored a route that would pass through Texas and New Mexico.

Davis's close relationship with Pierce allowed him to have a commanding voice in administration decisions. In fact, many in the capital viewed the pliable president as Davis's puppet. Davis used his influence to steer the president toward policies and ventures that would expand the southern slave empire. One such project was an ill-conceived attempt to force Spain to sell Cuba to the United States. Davis hoped to transplant slavery to the island and make it a part of the South. He also supported the unsuccessful attempt by the American adventurer and proslavery advocate William Walker to found a dictatorship in Nicaragua in 1855.

While Davis was working to improve the U.S. armed forces and bending the president's ear, the country's sectional quarrel was heating up again. The new focus of contention was the Kansas and

A motley artillery brigade of Free-Soilers stands ready to defend the abolitionist stronghold of Lawrence, Kansas, against an advancing army of proslavery Missourians in November 1855. The bitter struggle for control of Kansas offered Americans a prophetic glimpse of the terrible conflict that loomed on the horizon.

Nebraska territories, which had been designated nonslave areas according to the Missouri Compromise of 1820. Southerners wanted the areas opened up for slavery, however, and in the early 1850s, slaveholders started to settle there. Antislavery groups saw the violation of the Missouri Compromise as proof that the South was conspiring to spread slavery into the territories.

In 1854, Senator Stephen Douglas had proposed a plan that he hoped would end the dispute over the Kansas and Nebraska territories. Douglas's proposal, which he called the Popular Sovereignty Doctrine, called for the inhabitants of the two territories to decide for themselves whether they wanted to allow slavery. After yet another ferocious congressional debate, Douglas's "squatter's rights" bill was passed as the Kansas-Nebraska Act. Almost immediately, groups of gun-toting proslavery and antislavery settlers flooded into Kansas and engaged in a battle for political power. Ambushes, kidnappings, massacres, and other incidents of terrorism by bands from both sides earned the territory the nickname "Bleeding Kansas."

While the preliminary actions of an American civil war were erupting in Kansas, enraged antislavery

groups were forming the Republican party, whose purpose it would be to halt the further expansion of slavery. Aided by a new wave of popular support for the abolitionist movement aroused by atrocities in Kansas and the publication of Harriet Beecher Stowe's antislavery novel *Uncle Tom's Cabin*, the Republicans quickly won over a large percentage of the North's voters and emerged as the main rival of the Democrats. The Republican leaders, an incisive group of men that included William Seward of New York, Charles Sumner of Massachusetts, and Abraham Lincoln of Illinois, called for an end to any further compromises with southern slaveholders.

Davis watched in consternation as the battle lines between the North and South were drawn. In 1848, he had ended a speech about the need for allowing slavery into the Oregon Territory with the words "If the folly and fanaticism and pride and hate and corruption of the day are to destroy the peace and prosperity of the Union, let the sections part like the patriarchs of old and let peace and good-will subsist among their descendants. . . . Let the flag of our Union be folded up . . . untorn by the unholy struggle of civil war." But the unholy struggle, as Davis could plainly see, was approaching fast.

5

A Nation Divides

Davis's term as secretary of war ended in the spring of 1857; he wished good luck to the administration of new president James Buchanan and returned to Mississippi. His respite from the capital's business was only temporary, however; he was to return to Washington at the end of the year to resume his old seat in the Senate.

Davis's reelection to the Senate in the fall of 1856 had been engineered for him by his friends in the Mississippi legislature; he made no attempt to campaign for the seat. He may have felt that his position as the South's most well known and powerful advocate in Washington assured him a victory in the election in his home state. But the narrow margin of his victory in the 1856 election convinced him that he needed to get back in touch with the people of Mississippi.

There is really no Union now between the North and the South. . . . No two nations upon earth entertain feelings of more bitter rancor toward each other.
—BENJAMIN WADE
U.S. senator, Ohio

By 1857, the rigors of public office during a time of national upheaval had taken its toll on Jefferson Davis, who for health reasons spent the summer of 1858 under the care of his wife at an oceanside resort. But he returned to Washington in time to assume his place in the vanguard of the secessionist movement.

Democrat James Buchanan, known — somewhat derisively — as "Old Public Functionary," was elected president in 1856. Although he was a seasoned politician, Buchanan proved unequal to the task of extinguishing the sectional fires that were burning out of control in the United States.

During the nine months before Davis took his place in the Senate again, he worked to rebuild his base of power in Mississippi. He made the rounds at large social gatherings and listened to farmers, lawyers, and doctors give their opinions on the same issues that he and other congressmen tangled over in Washington. Having often felt that he was cut off from popular sentiment while in Washington, he found it extremely valuable to hear his fellow Mississippians talk about such topics as southern expansion and Yankee treachery.

Davis was searching for the answer to an increasingly urgent question: Would southerners support an effort to secede from the United States if the South felt that slavery was threatened? To answer this question, he needed to know the feelings not of congressmen or plantation owners but rather those of the common farmer — the backbone of the South. The majority of southerners did not own a single slave, and Davis was uncertain whether they were prepared to defend slavery to the death. Still another question for Davis was whether Virginia and the other six states of the Upper South — Maryland, Delaware, North Carolina, Kentucky, Tennessee, and Missouri — would support the more militant stance of the states of the Lower South — South Carolina, Mississippi, Georgia, Florida, Alabama, Louisiana, and Texas.

While probing the feelings of his constituents, Davis refined his southern-rights rhetoric with speeches in which he expressed a firm, unflinching defense of slavery. Arrogantly, he stated that the South had nothing to apologize for; it was the North that was antagonizing the South. He acknowledged that the South's dependence on cotton and slavery was a wasteful economic system that depleted the land, but he also said that the answer to the problem was simply for the South to acquire more territory.

A runaway slave is recaptured and punished. Southern slaveholders frequently pursued escaped slaves into the free states of the North, a practice that enraged abolitionists.

And he took up the issue of legalizing the African slave trade, which had resumed again in the slave-hungry Deep South despite a national ban dating back to 1808. Davis took a typical states' rights view on the issue, arguing that each state should decide for itself whether it would import more African slaves. He did not, however, take into consideration the feelings of the Africans themselves.

A fateful turn in national affairs occurred in March 1857, when the Supreme Court announced a decision in the case of a slave named Dred Scott, who was suing for freedom after the death of the man who had owned him. Writing that blacks "had no rights which the white man was bound to respect," Chief Justice Roger B. Taney declared that Congress could not place any limits on slavery. The Missouri Compromise and the Compromise of 1850 were wiped away as unconstitutional, and the western territories were opened to the expansion of slavery.

Dred Scott, the slave of a Missouri army surgeon who brought Scott with him when he moved to Illinois, sued for his own freedom on grounds of established residence in a free state. In March 1857, the Supreme Court ruled against Scott — a decisive setback for the abolitionist cause.

In his ruling on the Dred Scott case, Chief Justice Roger B. Taney, a native southerner, declared that blacks had no constitutional rights because they were "regarded as beings of an inferior order."

To Davis, the Supreme Court's decision confirmed what he had been saying all along — that slaves were property. Now the South was free to press ahead with efforts to expand its boundaries into the American West, Cuba, even Central America. Taney's ruling gave Davis just the ammunition he needed to mount a congressional offensive for southern expansion, but even as Davis traveled to Washington in December 1857, moral outrage in the North was reaching new heights, and northerners were closing ranks behind the banner of the Republican party. When he returned to the Senate, Davis listened to Republicans such as William Seward and Benjamin F. Wade damn slavery as an immoral system and was incensed. What was most galling to him was that many antislavery advocates had begun to insist that there was a higher law than the Constitution that could be appealed to — God's law. Like most defenders of slavery, Davis was sensitive to any attacks on slavery that invoked the Almighty, and he irrationally called for the tarring and feathering of anyone who argued for their own version of divine will over constitutional law.

Runaway slaves take shelter in the Louisiana swamps. Many escaped slaves rode the Underground Railroad — a network of safe houses organized by abolitionists — to freedom in the North.

As the ineffectual President Buchanan struggled halfheartedly to hold together a nation that was twisting apart, the atmosphere in the Senate grew increasingly bitter. Arguments sometimes became violent, and in one notorious incident, a South Carolina congressman beat Charles Sumner with a heavy cane, incapacitating the Republican senator for three years. In the midst of this anarchy, Davis pressed ahead with his crusade to acquire more territory for slaveholders. Aided by a powerful coalition of southern congressmen, he drew up plans for achieving the South's own manifest destiny based on the unrestricted growth of slavery. But Davis was striving to realize his dream of a southern slave empire at a time when increasing numbers of his countrymen were seeking new ways to eradicate the evil institution. He failed to understand that international opinion had turned against slavery forever and that the United States would be the butt of worldwide condemnation as long as it was the only one of the major nations that still accepted the barbarous practice. All of Davis's eloquence about constitutional guarantees and states' rights could not muffle the crack of the slave driver's bullwhip.

The Supreme Court's nullification of the congressional limits on slavery boosted the influence of extremist factions in both the North and South. Waving the banner of southern solidarity, southern fire-eaters called for planters and businessmen to end their association with northern merchants and take a direct role in selling their cotton abroad. The southern radicals also demanded that the South's aristocratic families stop patronizing northern colleges and resorts and devote their time and money to building up the South's institutions. Meanwhile, northern abolitionists pressed for an immediate end to slavery and called on northern merchants to loosen their bonds to King Cotton. The radicals' appeals for sectional economic independence went unheeded, however, because the business ties connecting the North and South were far too tangled to unravel at this late juncture.

The strain of upholding the southern cause in the Senate was beginning to take a toll on Davis. A chronic ailment had robbed him of his sight in one eye, and by the winter of 1857–58, he was so ema-

Senator Charles Sumner of Massachusetts, an ardent abolitionist and the founder of the Free-Soil party, was assaulted in the Senate on May 22, 1856, by Congressman Preston Brooks of South Carolina. Brooks beat Sumner violently over the head with a heavy cane. He was fined $300 for his behavior.

ciated from various illnesses that his doctor ordered him to take a break from his public duties. In July 1858, he finally gave in and took his family to a beachside resort — in the North — for an extended stay.

When Davis returned to Washington in late 1858, he resumed his battle for southern expansion and began drawing up plans for a campaign to annex Cuba. He fought bitterly with Republican leaders, especially over the situation in Kansas, which had turned in favor of the antislavery Free Soil groups. He was also at odds with Stephen Douglas, one of the Democrats' most prominent spokesmen, over the Illinois senator's refusal to support the absolute rights of slaveholders in the West. Davis's conflict with Douglas was indicative of the growing rift between southern and northern factions within the Democratic party.

Americans remained deeply divided over what steps should be taken to resolve the sectional differences. But in October 1859, the abolitionist agitator John Brown took matters into his own hands by launching a raid on the federal arsenal at Harpers Ferry, Virginia. Brown's plan of inciting a massive slave rebellion failed, and he was captured and executed after being convicted of treason. His raid shattered the country's tenuous peace, however, fueling southern distrust of the North while also providing a martyr figure for the abolitionists to rally around.

In the wake of the Brown raid, Davis decided that Congress must make a sweeping gesture to guarantee the South's liberties. Backed by a coalition of southern senators, he forced his fellow Democrats to fall into line behind a series of resolutions he drew up to assure greater protection for the rights of slaveholders. The passage of the Davis Resolutions in May 1860 partially redressed the grievances of the South, but it also led to a wider rift between northern Democrats and their southern colleagues. Meanwhile, southern fire-eaters were enjoying great success in persuading the citizens of the South that further association with the "Yankee rascals" be terminated.

I believe every man in both houses is armed with a revolver—some with two—and a bowie knife.
—JAMES HAMMOND
senator from South Carolina, speaking of the tense atmosphere in Congress in 1860

Watching from Washington, Davis found it difficult to gauge the emotions of the southern populace. But as the time for choosing candidates for the 1860 presidential election neared, he found himself being drawn into a closer alliance with the southern radicals. In April 1860, Democratic delegates gathered in Charleston, South Carolina, to select a candidate for president. Davis had widespread support throughout the South and even among some northern delegates, but he knew he was too controversial a choice and made no effort to seek the nomination. The only one who seemed able to win broad support was Stephen Douglas, but Davis and the southern radicals did not trust him and they engineered his defeat. Rent from within, the convention broke up, and the Democratic party divided into two camps. Douglas was the choice of the northern camp, the National Democrats, and John C. Breckinridge was supported by the southern camp, the State Rights Democrats. A few weeks later, Abraham Lincoln secured the nomination of the Republican party on a platform that promised to curb the spread of slavery.

Learning of Preston Brooks's attack on Charles Sumner, abolitionist zealot John Brown of Kansas and four of his sons kidnapped and murdered — with broadswords — five proslavery settlers. Three years later, Brown led a failed attempt to incite a massive slave uprising in Virginia. He was executed in 1859.

The willful Davis, blinded by his dislike of Douglas, realized too late that he must attempt to reunite his fractured party. He tried in vain to bring the Democrats together behind another moderate doughface candidate, but as the election neared, Davis could see that Lincoln was unbeatable.

In November, the fears of Davis and the South were realized. Crippled by the Democrats' split, Douglas and Breckinridge trailed far behind Lincoln, who swept almost all of the northern states' electoral votes. United behind a strong surge in antislavery sentiment, the North used its overwhelming advantage in population to swamp the South at the polls.

An uneasy period of waiting set in after Lincoln's election as the southern states debated whether to seek a compromise with the future administration or secede from the Union. In spite of Lincoln's assurances that he had no intention of trying to abolish slavery, the South could not be mollified. As usual, traditionally militant South Carolina took the lead in promoting secession. On December 20, 1860, the state legislature unanimously agreed that "the union now subsisting between South Carolina and the other states, under the name of the 'United States of America,' is hereby dissolved." With South Carolina's departure, other states of the Lower South found it impossible to resist the swelling tide of popular support for secession. Mississippi seceded on January 9, 1861, and Florida, Alabama, Georgia, Louisiana, and Texas soon followed. Virgina and the Upper South hesitated, hoping that a compromise could be arranged.

Davis remained in the Senate until he learned that Mississippi had seceded. On January 21, he gave a farewell address to the Senate. Looking haggard and gray from sickness and the rigors of public office, Davis declared to the assembled senators that Mississippi and the other seceding states were taking the only path left to them by northern provocations. Every state had the right to secede, he claimed: "There was a time when none denied it." He departed after conveying his hopes that the divorce of the North and South could be accomplished in a peaceful and friendly manner.

You dare not make war on cotton. No power on earth dares make war on it. 'Cotton is King.'

—JAMES HAMMOND
U.S. senator, South
Carolina

MERCURY

EXTRA:

Passed unanimously at 1.15 o'clock, P. M. December 20th, 1860.

AN ORDINANCE

To dissolve the Union between the State of South Carolina and other States united with her under the compact entitled " The Constitution of the United States of America."

We, the People of the State of South Carolina, in Convention assembled, do declare and ordain, and it is hereby declared and ordained,

That the Ordinance adopted by us in Convention, on the twenty-third day of May, in the year of our Lord one thousand seven hundred and eighty-eight, whereby the Constitution of the United States of America was ratified, and also, all Acts and parts of Acts of the General Assembly of this State, ratifying amendments of the said Constitution, are hereby repealed; and that the union now subsisting between South Carolina and other States, under the name of "The United States of America," is hereby dissolved.

THE

UNION

IS

DISSOLVED!

The Charleston *Mercury* proclaims the fateful news, January 20, 1860.

As Davis reentered his home state, delegates from the legislatures of the seceding states were already meeting in Montgomery, Alabama. On February 8, 1861, the delegates issued a constitution for the new Confederate States of America that ensured strong protections for slavery and safeguarded the independence of each state. Davis was selected to be president; the delegates agreed that only he had the necessary prestige and experience for the Confederacy's highest office.

6

Victory and Defeat

As Davis stood on the steps of the Capitol in Montgomery on February 18, 1861, and delivered his inaugural address, he faced a people who were filled with high spirits and naive bravado. Davis played to the emotions of the crowd, praising the traditions that united the South and recalling the "spirit of '76" and the men who had taken up arms against the tyranny of King George III. The mood throughout the South was jubilant as its people faced the coming conflict; newspapers from Charleston to New Orleans predicted a glorious future for the Confederacy and a grim fate for any Northern troops that invaded southern soil.

Wasting no time, Davis launched into the task of organizing the Confederacy. His first objective was to fill his administration's six cabinet posts, and he astutely chose a man from each of the Confederate states except his own, Mississippi, thus further uniting the separate states. Among his selections were Judah P. Benjamin of Louisiana as attorney general, South Carolina financier Christopher G. Memminger as treasury secretary, and Florida naval expert Stephen R. Mallory as secretary of the navy.

We feel that our cause is just and holy; we protest solemnly in the face of mankind that we desire peace at any sacrifice save that of honor and independence.
—JEFFERSON DAVIS

Jefferson Davis (seated) and his generals (left to right): Raphael Semmes, John B. Hood, James E. B. ("Jeb") Stuart, Thomas J. ("Stonewall") Jackson, Robert E. Lee, Nathan Bedford Forrest, Joseph E. Johnston, and Pierre G. T. Beauregard.

The positions of secretary of state and secretary of war were to remain in constant flux throughout Davis's presidency, and from the beginning he assumed almost all of the responsibility for drawing up war plans and overseeing the Confederacy's military preparations.

Davis understood the importance of obtaining diplomatic recognition from Great Britain and France, and he sent commissioners to the European nations in an effort to win their support and arrange trade agreements. These diplomatic missions were a disappointment, however, for Davis soon learned that the North's wheat meant more to Europe than the South's cotton. He was somewhat more successful at organizing efforts to spur the domestic production of sorely needed war materials, especially gunpowder, artillery, and naval craft. He also kept his eye on the efforts of governors and military commanders to arm and equip the state militias that would form the nucleus of the Confederate army.

On Friday, April 12, 1861, at 4:30 A.M., Confederate guns opened fire on Ft. Sumter, located at the mouth of Charleston Harbor. As the citizens of Charleston cheered from rooftops, federal gunners returned fire, and the Civil War began.

Responding to an order from Jefferson Davis to "reduce" Ft. Sumter before it could be reinforced by federal troops, General Beauregard of Louisiana initiated a bombardment. After 33 hours had passed and 4,000 shells had fallen, Beauregard accepted the surrender of the beleaguered Union garrison.

Davis's most pressing challenge during the spring of 1861 was represented by the eight slave states that were still part of the United States; Davis desperately needed to persuade these states to join the Confederacy. Torn both ways, the states of the Upper South resisted the secessionist calls while they waited to see what Lincoln would do after he assumed office. In his inaugural address in early March, the president offered the hand of friendship to the seceding states and assured them that he was not contemplating an invasion of the South. But he was firm in his resolve that the Union must be restored and that no U.S. property in the South be seized by the Confederacy. One of those pieces of federal property — Fort Sumter, in Charleston Harbor, South Carolina — was the flint that ignited the Civil War.

Confederate volunteers pose for a photograph in Warrington Navy Yard, Pensacola, Florida. "Every man must be for the United States or against it," Stephen Douglas declared. "There can be no neutrals, only patriots — or traitors."

The U.S. garrison at Fort Sumter commanded the entrance to one of the South's most important ports, and its presence was a threat to the Confederacy's self-proclaimed "sovereign" status. When news reached Davis that a Union naval convoy was about to land supplies at Sumter, he sent a telegram ordering General Pierre G. T. Beauregard of the South Carolina militia to take the fort. On April 13, after more than a day of artillery bombardment, the federal garrison surrendered.

The fall of Fort Sumter sparked war fever in the North and South and signaled the beginning of official hostilities. Lincoln immediately declared that the Confederate states were in a state of illegal rebellion against the U.S. government, and he issued a call for 75,000 volunteers to fight the insurrection. Tennessee, North Carolina, Arkansas, and Virginia then seceded from the Union and joined the Confederacy. Although cruelly divided by their conflicting ties to the North and South, Delaware, Maryland, Kentucky, and Missouri remained in the Union. Many men from these four so-called border states enlisted in the South's armies, however.

The entrance of Virginia, the traditional leader of the South, into the Confederacy brought about a change in capitals. Knowing that it was vital for the government to be in Virginia, where, because of its location, much of the fighting was bound to occur, Davis and the Confederate congress moved to Richmond in early June 1861. As he traveled north by train from Montgomery, the popular president was greeted in Atlanta and other cities by throngs of chéering citizens. When he reached Richmond, the largest industrial center in the South, the core of the proud new gray-clad Confederate army welcomed him with a 15-gun salute.

With the help of a few trusted military advisers, including the distinguished general Robert E. Lee and the president's longtime friend Albert Sidney Johnston, Davis mapped out the Confederacy's war strategy. Like Lee, Davis preferred to fight a defensive war that would conserve the South's strength and force the North to hammer away at Confederate strongholds. Recent advances in the accuracy and

A slave market in Atlanta, Georgia. Although slavery was the primary issue in the conflict between the states, blacks were not allowed to fight in the Union armies until the passage of the 1862 Militia Act authorized the president to enroll them "in any military or naval service for which they may be found competent."

General Robert E. Lee of Virginia, commander of the Army of Northern Virginia and top military adviser to President Davis. Like many Southerners, Lee abhorred slavery and opposed secession, but ultimately, his loyalties lay with his home state and the South.

firing rate of weaponry had given a large advantage to defending forces and made the traditional charges of massed infantry an extremely risky proposition. Davis hoped that the South could inflict enough damage on invading Union troops and that its fast fleet of privateer vessels could destroy enough enemy shipping to wear down the North's enthusiasm for the war and force it to sue for peace.

Only 100 miles apart, Davis and Lincoln began their contest of wills and wits. Although slavery was the main issue among the many points of conflict that had pitted them against one another, the official war policies of the two commanders in chief made no reference to slavery. Lincoln stated that the North was fighting to preserve the Union, and Davis asserted that the South was attempting to secure its independence from a hostile government. To Lincoln, however, the war was also a contest to decide whether people could be denied their liberty because of their race; to Davis, the issue was whether the federal government could interfere with a citizen's alleged right to own human property.

The first set battle of the war did not occur until the summer of 1861. Davis had resisted the urging of some of his advisers to launch an attack on Washington because he feared that such an action would further inflame the North and diminish international sympathy for the Confederate cause. In July, Lincoln commanded General Irvin McDowell to march on Richmond with the main Union army. Davis had positioned the Confederate forces under General Beauregard at Manassas Junction in northern Virginia, and he ordered them to meet the invasion. The two armies clashed on July 21, and thanks to a heroic stand by troops under General Thomas J. ("Stonewall") Jackson, the Confederates routed the Union troops and sent them reeling back to Washington.

The victory at Manassas (also known as the First Battle of Bull Run) touched off celebrations throughout the South and convinced many delirious Southerners that the war would soon be won. Davis was proud of the way the Confederate troops had performed, but he also regretted that Beauregard's army had been in too much disarray after the battle to pursue the fleeing enemy into Washington. The U.S. capital had lain open to the South, and the war, Davis believed, might have been ended in a week.

The blockade-runner *Robert E. Lee*, one of the swift steam frigates used by the Confederacy in their attempt to thwart the Anaconda Plan, the Union naval blockade of Southern ports. The *Robert E. Lee* successfully ran the blockade 14 times; it was captured on the 15th try by the USS *Minnesota*.

The Union ironclad, USS *Monitor*, relatively unscathed after a duel with its rebel counterpart, the CSS *Virginia* (also known as the *Merrimac*). The two warships fought to a standstill in a monumental battle off Norfolk, Virginia, March 8, 1862.

The disorganized condition of the armies at Manassas convinced both sides that more preparation was needed before any major campaigns were undertaken. Although he was still flushed with victory, Davis had to face a number of problems that would continue to vex him throughout the war. Some army officers were unhappy that they had not received expected assignments, and the president had an especially bitter row with General Joseph E. Johnston when he refused to give the general higher rank than Robert E. Lee. More troubling was the blockade that the North had imposed on Southern ports. Although it was somewhat porous at the beginning of the war, the blockade was to become progressively tighter, until it threatened to choke off the South's trade and communications abroad. Davis's worries about the blockade were partially offset, however, by the progress that Confederate secretary of the navy Mallory was making in producing ironclad gunboats that could destroy the wooden ships of the Union fleet.

During the period of military preparation, Davis consulted especially closely with General Lee, who in June 1862 would be given command of the largest Confederate force, the Army of Northern Virginia. Davis had complete trust in Lee's judgment, and the two men formed a close working partnership that for a time gave the South a strategic advantage over the Northern armies, which were poorly led initially.

The year 1861 ended with no further large engagements. Davis was disappointed that he was unable to win recognition of the Confederacy from Great Britain, especially after the North infuriated the British by seizing two Confederate diplomats off the British ship *Trent*. But Lincoln's administration repaired relations with Britain, and Davis spent the winter preparing for the coming spring offensive by the Union. The North's plan was to isolate and divide the Confederacy by blockading its ports, seizing control of the Mississippi River, and capturing Richmond and the arms factories near the capital. Davis intended to concentrate his attention on thwarting the Union attack in northern Virginia and left the defense of the vital Mississippi waterway to General Albert Johnston and local military units.

The Union Army of the Potomac, 70,000 men strong, encamped at Cumberland Landing, Virginia, in May 1862. The gigantic force was relatively inactive during the first year of the war, but by September 1862, it stood as the final obstacle between Washington, D.C., and Lee's Army of Northern Virginia.

On February 16, 1862, Confederate general Simon Buckner, in command of Ft. Donelson, Tennessee, realized he was hopelessly surrounded by the army of General Ulysses S. Grant. He asked Grant for terms of surrender; Grant replied that "no terms except unconditional and immediate surrender can be accepted," thus winning the admiration of a victory-starved North.

The spring of 1862 brought a mixture of victory and defeat for the South. In early March, the Confederate ironclad warship *Virginia* (known in the North as the *Merrimac*) sent a shock wave through the North when it sank two Union warships off Hampton Roads, Virginia. Only the arrival of the *Monitor*, the North's own ironclad prototype, saved the Union fleet; after a ferocious battle between the two armored monsters, the *Virginia* withdrew, and the Union blockade was secured. The North continued to dominate American waters, and the losses of the ports of Norfolk, Virginia, and Pensacola and Jacksonville, Florida, were key blows to the Confederate war effort.

Meanwhile, the land war was heating up. In response to a massive assault on Virginia by Northern forces under General George B. McClellan, Davis passed the first conscription law in American history. The arrival of the new troops occurred just in time to stall McClellan short of Richmond, and Lee, Jackson, and Joseph Johnston performed brilliantly in keeping the larger Union army off balance. But despite the repulse of the main Union thrust, critical defeats in the West gave Davis much to worry about. The loss of Fort Henry on the Tennessee River and Fort Donelson on the Cumberland to the forces of Union general Ulysses S. ("Unconditional Surrender") Grant in February had opened the way to Nashville for the Union army, which then occupied western Tennessee. And at Shiloh in southern Tennessee, in a fearsome battle fought on April 6 and 7, 1862, Albert Sidney Johnston came close to crushing Grant's army after a stunning surprise attack at sunrise. Grant's forces survived and mounted a savage counterattack the following day, however, forcing a Confederate retreat, and Johnston bled to death after receiving a leg wound. The loss of his old friend was a severe blow to Davis, and he was never able to find a capable replacement for Johnston in the West.

As the South's casualties increased and supplies decreased, Davis was hard-pressed to find ways to finance the war and keep the ranks of the Confederate armies filled. He had only a limited understanding of how to secure foreign loans and raise taxes for the Confederate treasury, and the South's banking system gradually sank in a sea of inflation under his inept administration. Davis's policy of printing money that was not backed by any hard currency eventually made the Confederate dollar more useful as stuffing for soldiers' boots than as legal tender. The policy of conscripting all able-bodied men for the army also proved harmful because it stripped the South of the men needed to oversee the slaves' production of the food and manufactured goods needed for the war effort.

One thing the South did have was generals in Virginia who could fight and a veteran corps of battle-hardened men. After pushing the Union troops back toward Washington in the summer of 1862, Lee proposed to Davis that he invade Maryland and make an attempt to capture Baltimore and Washington. Davis agreed to the plan, and he hoped that Lee's campaign would bring Maryland into the Confederate fold and force Lincoln to negotiate for peace. But Lee's army was turned back by McClellan's Army of the Potomac at the massive and bloody Battle of Antietam on September 17, 1862.

The bridge over Antietam Creek was at the center of the fearful battle fought on September 17, 1862. A Pennsylvania soldier who survived the fight wrote, "No tongue can tell, no mind conceive, no pen portray the horrible sights I witnessed this morning."

The most significant result of Antietam — aside from the more than 5,000 men killed in the fight — was that Lincoln felt emboldened enough by the victory to issue the Emancipation Proclamation. This decree declared that as of January 1, 1863, the North would consider any slave held in the rebellious Confederate states to be a free person. Lincoln's announcement infuriated the South, and Davis declared that the proclamation was a totally illegal and barbaric act that incited slave uprisings. But the proclamation was a decisive blow in winning international sympathy for the North and isolating the South morally and diplomatically. And because much of the South's manpower was tied up in the army during planting season, the loyalty of its 3 million slaves had become of vital concern.

A Union signal tower on Elk Mountain, Maryland, overlooking the battlefield at Antietam, September 17, 1862. Lieutenant Pierce, atop the tower, observes the movements of the enemy and then reports them, using flag signals, to General McClellan below.

Following the issue of the Emancipation Proclamation, Davis had to contend with a greater threat of slave rebellion and flight of fugitives to the Northern lines. Furthermore, the North had finally decided to begin recruiting black troops, a move that placed the Confederate armies at an even greater manpower disadvantage and spread the fear of an avenging black army throughout the South. Davis could only manage a vindictive and brutal response to Lincoln's tactics: He approved a measure ordering the summary execution of any captured black Union troops.

The defeat of another Union offensive in the freezing mud around Fredericksburg, Virginia, and an unsuccessful stab into Kentucky by Confederate general Braxton Bragg, marked the end of hostilities late in 1862. Exhausted and ill, Davis greeted the winter resting period with a mixture of relief and foreboding. Two years after the formation of the Confederacy, the South was beginning to stagger under the burden of war losses, hunger, and sickness. But the Confederate Stars and Bars still waved defiantly, and a feverish Jefferson Davis firmly believed there was yet a chance that the South could outlast the North.

Guard detail of the 107th U.S. Coloured Infantry. After Lincoln issued the Emancipation Proclamation on September 22, 1862, black soldiers joined the seemingly endless stream of men that Lincoln and Grant hurled against the Confederacy.

32

7

The Darkest Hour

As a haggard Jefferson Davis paced his office in Richmond during the first bitterly cold days of 1863, he had plenty of bad news to occupy his mind. Around him were piles of letters, reports, documents, and newspapers containing a mixture of complaints, threats, condemnations, and pleas. The stacks of paper formed a painful record of how drastically the fortunes of the South and the popularity of its frail president had slipped since the gloriously optimistic days of Fort Sumter. Although Davis had attempted to harden himself against the disappointments of lost opportunities and the attacks of his critics, the inexorable decline of the Confederacy weighed ever more heavily on him as he tried desperately to piece together a strategy that would break the North's anaconda grip on the South.

Davis had just returned from a three-week tour of the western front. The trip had given him a chance to conduct a firsthand investigation of the situation in Tennessee, Mississippi, and Alabama,

A Union arsenal at City Point, Virginia. By 1863, the tide of the war had begun to change in favor of the North. Despite the brilliance of the Southern generals and the courage of the Southern fighting men, the superior man- and firepower of the North was beginning to prevail.

and to speak to General-in-Chief Joseph Johnston and the western commanders. He made public addresses in many of the cities he traveled through to assure the people that they had not been forgotten by the government in Richmond. But the public's mood had grown somber, and his return to his home state was a bitter one: His beloved Brierfield had been seized by the Union forces that controlled most of the Mississippi River.

Davis returned to Richmond knowing that the last links connecting Texas, Arkansas, and Louisiana to the rest of the South were in danger of falling to the federal armies of Grant, William Tecumseh Sherman, and Ambrose Everett Burnside. He could only advise his western commanders to fight on against the enemy's superior forces. If the Confederate armies could hold Virginia, he reasoned, an opportunity might soon arise for a decisive blow against the North. And if that failed, there was still a chance that the growing antiwar sentiment in the North would force Lincoln to negotiate peace. It would have to be soon, however; Davis knew that the starved and battered South could not continue to fight a war of attrition much longer.

President Davis returned to Brierfield in 1863 only to find that it had fallen into the hands of Union troops. The Northerners painted a mocking legend over the front porch: The House Jeff Built.

Major General Ambrose Burnside and the Army of the Potomac faced Lee's army at Fredericksburg, Virginia, in late 1862. Of the failed and costly attempts of Burnside's troops to break the line of entrenched Confederates, a Union soldier remarked, "We might as well have tried to take Hell."

Along with hunger and war weariness had come disillusionment and bitter recrimination. Davis's critics leveled their attacks both at his policies and his personal conduct. Some accused him of being weak; others of being too dictatorial. None could deny that no one labored harder for the Confederate cause, but many said that he busied himself too much with paperwork and details that should have been left to subordinates. The newspapers criticized him for neglecting the war in the West, for giving command positions to certain favorite generals whose abilities were doubtful, for mishandling the diplomatic efforts to secure recognition by European governments, and for not consulting enough with the Confederate congress and his cabinet. He was called cold and arrogant and too conceited to listen to advice.

Newly freed Southern blacks flock to the Union army camp at White House Landing. Known as "contrabands," some would enlist, others would serve as laborers and cooks.

The truth of the matter was that the Southern bid to become an independent slave empire had failed, and at a tremendous cost. The war that the Southerners had believed would be short and glorious had turned into a grueling bloodbath, and as the strength and resolve of Lincoln, Grant, and the North became more apparent with every passing day, the determination and confidence of the South began to wane. Desertion from the military, hoarding, and stealing had become rampant throughout the Confederacy; sizable numbers of able-bodied men enlisted in state militias and remained at home rather than join the active Confederate armies; and many wealthy Southerners took advantage of a rule that exempted owners of 20 or more slaves from military service so that they could guard against slave insurrection. To the small farmers and backwoodsmen who comprised the bulk of the Confederate forces—and who owned no slaves—the conflict had become "a rich man's war, but a poor man's fight." Many of these men simply left their posts and went home.

Davis could order his dwindling armies to fight on, but he was powerless to halt the economic ruin of the Confederacy. As supplies to Southern ports were choked off by the Union naval blockade, industries stopped manufacturing; as men were called into uniform and horses and other livestock were confiscated for army use, the South's agriculture began to fail. Women volunteers performed heroically, keeping farms, hospitals, and factories in operation, but even they became rebellious as inflation spiraled out of control and they could no longer feed their families with nearly worthless Confederate dollars. Bread riots flared in Southern towns and cities.

In May 1863, Robert E. Lee, whose military brilliance had thus far kept the Northern forces in Virginia in check, won a costly victory over the much larger Army of the Potomac, now under the command of General Joseph Hooker, at Chancellorsville. But the loss of the revered general Stonewall Jackson, who was mistakenly shot down by his own troops during the fight, cast a heavy pall over the

The crew of a Union army telegraph wagon awaits news from the front, near Chancellorsville, Virginia, May 1863.

Confederate triumph. Lee was devastated by the death of Jackson, whom he referred to as his "right arm." Davis heard this grim news at the same time he was being told that Vicksburg, Mississippi, the last Confederate stronghold on the Mississippi River, was under heavy siege by General Ulysses S. Grant's forces. The fall of Vicksburg would be a monumental blow to the South's chances in the western theater.

Faced with the possibility that the Union might soon control the West, Davis agreed with Lee that the time had come to gather any resources the South could spare and launch another invasion of the North. The plan was for Lee to sweep through Pennsylvania and threaten Washington. Lee began his invasion of Pennsylvania in June 1863 and was soon a short distance from the state capital at Harrisburg. On July 1, at the small town of Gettysburg, lead Confederate units came into contact with cavalry pickets from General George G. Meade's Army of the Potomac. (Meade had replaced Hooker on June 27.) The conflict soon mushroomed into an epic battle that continued for three days. Lee badly missed the able assistance of Stonewall Jackson, and his attacks on strong Union positions left his regiments decimated. At dawn on July 3, as a spectacular artillery duel raged — the thunderous cannon fire could be heard as far away as Pittsburg — 15,000 Confederate infantrymen under the command of General George E. Pickett launched a final, suicidal assault on the Union center. "Pickett's Charge" was mowed down mercilessly by federal defenders, and Lee was forced to retreat, leaving behind what one eyewitness described as "ghastly heaps of dead men." As the Battle of Gettysburg drew to a close, more than one-third of Lee's proud Army of Northern Virginia were dead, wounded, or captured.

Lee's defeat at Gettysburg, coupled with the surrender of more than 30,000 Confederate troops to Grant at Vicksburg on July 4, 1863, ended whatever hope Davis had of gaining a negotiated peace. He called the twin Confederate defeats "the darkest hour of our political existence" and prepared for

Not the fall of Richmond, nor Wilmington, nor Charleston, nor Savannah, nor Mobile, nor all of the combined, can save the enemy from the constant and exhaustive drain of blood and treasure which must continue until he shall discover that no peace is attainable unless based on the recognition of our indefeasible rights.
—JEFFERSON DAVIS

another torrent of abuse from his critics. Now his only prayer was that the South could somehow fend off Union troops until Lincoln was defeated by the antiwar faction of Northern Democrats known as the Copperheads. But although Lincoln was having serious difficulties with both the Copperheads and the militantly anti-Southern Radical Republicans, his position had become more secure with the victories at Gettysburg and Vicksburg and the emergence of General Grant and a group of experienced and hard-fighting Union commanders.

The wounds of Gettysburg and Vicksburg were deep, but Davis believed that they were not quite fatal. He initiated new steps to arm the Confederacy. With the assistance of Judah Benjamin, now the rebel secretary of state, he began an all-out effort to export cotton, which had previously been held back in an attempt to lure a cotton-hungry Great Britain into the Confederate camp. Recognizing that this tactic had failed, Davis now authorized his trade commissioners to make huge purchases of cotton and ship the crop to neutral ports in the West Indies,

The Gettysburg dead. There were almost 45,000 casualties of the great battle in Pennsylvania, including at least 5,000 killed, and another 10,000 missing.

Three Confederate soldiers captured at Gettysburg. Although President Davis refused to recognize the fact, the decimation of Lee's Army of Northern Virginia at Gettysburg marked the beginning of the end for the Confederacy.

where it could be sold or traded for arms and supplies. Southern blockade-runners enjoyed success evading Union warships and brought back desperately needed supplies to ports at Savannah, Charleston, and Wilmington. At the same time, Captain Raphael Semmes's *Alabama* and other Confederate privateers were taking a heavy toll on Union merchant shipping.

Davis was still faced with the task of protecting the South's long western border. The entire Mississippi River was now in Union hands. In September 1863, he rushed reinforcements to Braxton Bragg's army in southern Tennessee, and the move seemed to work when Bragg routed the Union Army of the Cumberland at the Battle of Chickamauga. Bragg delayed following up the victory, however, and his general staff called for his resignation. The problem became so serious that Davis made a trip to Bragg's headquarters to restore peace between the commander and the mutinous officers. But Bragg's respite was only temporary. In November, he suffered a crushing defeat at the Battle of Chattanooga; he withdrew with his mauled Army of Tennessee into Georgia, opening the way to Atlanta.

Despite the huge losses suffered by the Confederacy in 1863, Davis refused to call a halt to the war, reasoning that the South had already survived the worst of the fighting and that the courage of Dixie would carry it through to victory. But the evidence suggested that Davis was badly deluded and that the South was on its last legs. Stocks of meat and grain were almost exhausted, and the gnawing emptiness of the Confederate soldier's belly was matched by the ragged condition of his uniform. Southern hospitals were unable to handle the masses of wounded and sick carried in from the battle lines, and they were little better than morgues. Throughout the South, flames from burning cotton bales marked the scene of another retreat as Confederate troops destroyed the crop to prevent its capture by the advancing Union juggernaut.

As the size of the Confederacy shrank state by state, Davis retreated into a protective shell. He became obsessed with the details of troop movements and supply reports, slept and ate very little, and stubbornly battled through his recurring bouts of wracking pain and exhaustion. Tragedy mounted upon tragedy: In April 1864, Davis's young son Joseph was killed in a fall from a balcony.

General William Tecumseh Sherman, called by one of his soldiers "the most American-looking man I ever saw." In the spring of 1864, Sherman, at the head of an army of almost 70,000, declared "I can make Georgia howl" and began his destructive march through the South.

A Southern family flees before the approaching army of General Sherman. About the people of the South, Sherman said, "They cannot be made to love us, but they can be made to fear us."

The South's manpower disadvantage really began to tell in 1864. Lincoln's refusal to exchange prisoners of war had greatly decreased the Confederacy's pool of reserves. Davis's answer to the nonexchange policy was to pack tens of thousands of Union prisoners into primitive facilities such as the infamous Andersonville prison in Georgia. As Northerners became aware of the barbaric conditions and horrendous mortality rates associated with the disease-ridden Southern prison camps, they began to develop a contempt for the embattled president of the Confederacy, and Northern support for the war and Lincoln grew even stronger.

In March 1864, Lincoln made Grant lieutenant general (Grant was the first American officer to hold this supreme rank since George Washington) and commander of all the Union armies. Grant was an imperturbable and relentless fighter who was willing to accept heavy casualties as long as the South was beaten thoroughly and finally. In May, the Union commander launched a massive assault on Lee in Virginia while General Sherman attacked Joseph Johnston's forces in Georgia.

The armies of both Lee and Johnston were outnumbered by almost two to one; Davis felt that the Confederacy's only option was to wage a punishing defensive action and hope that Grant would give up. Grant, however, was not the type to give up. Between May and July, Grant and Lee engaged in a series of horrific engagements at the battles of the Wilderness, Spotsylvania, Cold Harbor, and Petersburg. Grant's casualties far exceeded Lee's, but despite the carnage, he kept pressing on, slowly tightening the noose around Richmond. Meanwhile, Sherman was forcing Johnston to retreat step by step toward Atlanta. Frustrated that Johnston could not stop the Union advance, Davis replaced him with the more aggressive general John Bell Hood. The strategy backfired, and on September 2, Sherman's troops marched into Atlanta.

By the fall of 1864, the Confederacy had been sliced into three parts, and Sherman was introducing the South to the concept of total war as he burned and pillaged the South Carolina countryside on his march to Charleston. Clearly, the Confederacy could not continue the fight much longer, but a bitter Davis refused to make more than a halfhearted attempt to negotiate a peace settlement as long as Lincoln demanded that the abolition of slavery and reunification with the North be conditions of a truce. The South's supply and transportation systems were nearly defunct, however, and hungry mobs rioted in the streets of many cities.

The Atlanta perimeter. Despite the elaborate defenses, Atlanta could not resist Sherman's troops forever, and on September 2, 1864, the city fell.

There was a strong public demand for peace at any price. Whether Davis recognized it or not, the Confederacy was doomed, and further fighting could only prolong the agony and the killing.

Obsessively determined to preserve the "honor" of the South, Davis tried to marshal public support for a last stand. In desperation, he proposed that slaves be forced into the Confederate army, but the war was to end before this hideous order could be carried out. In February 1865, Davis finally authorized Vice-president Stephens to meet with Lincoln and attempt to negotiate a truce. Lincoln's terms were the same as before, and once again Davis rejected them. By the end of March, Grant had nearly severed the last route south from Richmond, and the capital had to be abandoned.

On April 2, 1865, Davis and his staff gathered the government records and took one of the last trains out of Richmond. Explosions rocked the capital as Confederate troops tried to destroy anything of value to the enemy. By the next day, the president was in Danville, Virginia, where he temporarily set up his seat of government. On April 10, Davis learned that Lee had been forced to surrender to Grant at Appomattox.

On Sunday, April 9, 1865, at Appomattox Court House in northern Virginia, General Lee formally surrendered the Army of Northern Virginia to General Grant.

An exaggerated cartoon depiction of the capture of Jefferson Davis on May 10, 1865. Davis, for purposes of either disguise, or, as he claimed, protection against the weather, was wearing some of his wife's garments when he was caught.

Only scattered pockets of Confederate resistance remained to carry on the struggle. Davis still could have surrendered with dignity, but he made one last attempt to escape in the hope that he could resume the fight from a stronghold in Texas or New Mexico. His family and a group of cabinet members joined him in a flight southward, during which they learned that Lincoln had been shot on April 14 and died the next day. Davis continued his flight toward Florida on horseback, narrowly escaping Union cavalry patrols on a number of occasions. On May 10, 1865, Davis's luck, and the Confederacy, came to an end. Wearing his wife's overcoat and shawl, the president of the beaten Confederate States of America was captured in a driving rainstorm as he ran from officers of the Fourth Michigan Cavalry in a wooded area outside the town of Irwinville, Georgia.

8

The Lost Cause

The South was shattered. Its agriculture and industries were in ruins, a large proportion of its white male citizenry was dead or maimed, and its millions of newly freed slaves were impoverished and landless. The power of the planter-class aristocracy that Davis had led — and that had drawn the South into the war in the first place — was broken. Federal administrators and military officers now kept order in the South. These men were in charge of the Reconstruction program that the Radical Republican–dominated Congress had designed to keep an iron grip on the South until its loyalty to the United States was assured. With the help of newly enfranchised black voters, Congress intended to completely restructure the South's social and political order.

Jefferson Davis, too, was shattered. He had spent more than two decades as a respected statesman, shaping the policies that guided his nation's destiny and nurturing dreams of Southern imperialist

> *I feel no regret that I stand before you a man without a country, for my ambition lies buried in the grave of the Confederacy.*
> —JEFFERSON DAVIS
> in his last public address,
> April 1889

The downfall of the Confederacy left Jefferson Davis a broken man. Following his release from federal prison, he traveled, wrote, and became involved in several disastrous business ventures. As Reconstruction policies were implemented in the South, his health steadily declined.

Throughout Jefferson Davis's life, his staunchest ally remained his wife Varina. It was largely through her efforts that Davis was finally released from prison in 1867.

grandeur, but now he was a shackled prisoner reviled throughout much of America. In the North, he was condemned as a traitor whose stubborn defense of slavery had almost destroyed the country, and many Southerners used him as a scapegoat for the Confederacy's defeat.

Davis's two-year term of imprisonment was a devastating blow to his pride. On the orders of Secretary of War Edwin M. Stanton, Davis was manacled and confined in a small, dimly lit cell at Fort Monroe, Virginia, while he waited to be tried for treason against the United States. His humiliating ordeal further damaged his health and fading eyesight. He kept his spirits up by reading the Bible and writing to his wife, who was confined on a farm in Georgia.

Varina lobbied vigorously for her husband's release from prison, and she was finally successful after she enlisted the influential New York newspaper publisher Horace Greeley to her cause. On May 11, 1867, Davis was freed on $100,000 bail, which was paid by Greeley and a group of Northerners who wanted to speed national reconciliation. The treason charges against Davis were dropped the next year when President Andrew Johnson pardoned all former officers of the Confederacy.

Once tall and elegant, Davis was now a fragile, ghostly, and pathetic figure. He was free once more to travel through his beloved South, but the land and the times had changed, and he no longer felt comfortable in the states he had once governed. States' rights, Southern imperialism, and the rights of slaveholders — the principles he had spent his life

Davis traveled to Quebec, Canada, in 1867. Many of his Confederate cohorts had taken refuge there following the war, and they were shocked at his appearance. War and imprisonment had taken their toll.

The jury that convicted Davis on charges of treason against the United States. Davis was pardoned in 1868, but he steadfastly refused to take an oath of allegiance to the United States.

fighting for in Washington, Montgomery, and Richmond — were now relics of the past. It was painful for Davis to see the blue-coated U.S. troops enforcing Reconstruction statutes in the heart of what was once the Confederacy. He himself was not an entirely welcome sight to people who wanted to forget the war. Moreover, because he flatly refused to take an oath of allegiance to the United States, he was a man without a country.

After his release from prison, Davis spent a year in Quebec, Canada, where many former Confederates had taken refuge. Glad to be rejoined there with his family, he nonetheless felt morose about his lack of prospects and money. He briefly considered taking the position of president of Randolph-Macon College in Virginia, but he was afraid that his name would hurt the school's reputation. In early 1868, he and Varina made a trip to the South and visited Brierfield; it was their first time home since the beginning of the Civil War. The sight of their ruined estate and the generally miserable condition of their old friends and relatives in Mississippi convinced Davis that he was not yet ready to return permanently to the South.

Hearing about a possible job opportunity as an agent for a cotton importing firm in England, Davis moved his family to London in the summer of 1868. Although he was still burdened by financial worries and bouts of deep depression, the warm reception he received from the British nobility and such Confederate exiles as Judah Benjamin helped to restore his spirits for a while. But the glory days of the South were long gone, and Davis's own star had faded. Unable to find a job in England worthy of the former president of the Confederacy, he finally sailed back to the United States in 1869. Soon after his return, he accepted the position of president of the Carolina Life Insurance Company in Memphis, Tennessee.

The Civil War had receded far enough into the past for Davis to live in peace in the South again, but the region was hardly quiet. More blood was shed during the Reconstruction period as white supremacist groups, such as the Ku Klux Klan, employed terror tactics to fight the rise of black political

In an 1885 woodcut, Klansmen inflict torture on victims. Violent resistance to Reconstruction was spearheaded by racist organizations such as the Ku Klux Klan.

power in the South. By 1874, the southern state legislatures were once more in the hands of white Democrats, and the enactment of strict segregation laws had stripped blacks of many of their civil rights. The South's hateful racial divisions were in place once again.

The reemergence of racist Democratic power in the South in the mid-1870s helped to rekindle white pride in the Confederacy and to restore some of the lost luster to Davis's reputation. His revived popularity was the single bright spot in an otherwise grim period. In 1874, the Carolina Life Insurance Company collapsed and Davis lost much of his remaining savings. After this disaster he became embroiled in a legal battle with the heirs of his deceased brother Joseph for the possession of Brierfield. Although Joseph had given the plantation to Jefferson 40 years earlier, the deed to the land had never been officially transferred. Davis finally won the legal rights to his old home, but he no longer had the energy to manage the estate, and without any slaves to work for him, he was unable to wring any profits from the cotton fields.

Davis reclines on the porch of the library cottage at the Beauvoir estate in Mississippi. Sarah Anne Dorsey, the owner of Beauvoir, invited Davis to live on the estate in 1877; when she died in 1879, she left him the estate in her will.

Varina Anne Davis looked after her father in his last years. In 1886, she accompanied him on a final tour of his beloved South.

Davis's financial woes subsided in 1877 after a friend, the widow Sarah Anne Dorsey, invited him to stay in a cottage at Beauvoir, her estate on the Gulf Coast of Mississippi. The friendship between Davis and his wealthy admirer put some strain on his marriage, but the freedom from financial worries allowed him the time to set to work on a long-planned project, a history of the Confederacy. This period was marred in 1878 by the death of Jefferson, Jr., his only remaining son, and by the death of Sarah Dorsey the following year. Dorsey was extremely generous to Davis in her will, leaving him the stately Beauvoir mansion so that he could live out his final years in comfort.

Like the Confederacy itself, Davis's attempt to chronicle its history was a failure. Published in 1881, *The Rise and Fall of the Confederate Government* was criticized for being dry, tedious, and too polemical. Davis rehashed much of the involved argument about whether a state had the right to secede, and he provided little insight into the major decisions he made as president and commander in chief of the South. The volume was dismissed or ignored by critics and historians and quickly fell into obscurity.

The debate over Davis's performance as president of the Confederacy figured prominently in the histories of the Civil War written before his death. Many of his detractors came from the ranks of the newspaper editors and politicians who had hounded him during the war, and they remained convinced that he had provided neither the military nor administrative leadership that the South needed to win the war. But Davis also had many supporters. Robert E. Lee praised him as a brilliant counselor to his generals and as a leader whose indomitable will had kept the Confederacy on its feet. As the passions aroused by the war subsided, many observers voiced their belief that Davis had done remarkably well to keep the South's cause alive for four tumultuous years. But although Davis's performance may have been laudable in some respects, the cause for which he and his fellow southerners fought so stubbornly can only be viewed as an ugly and perverted version of America's democratic ideals.

Funeral procession for Jefferson Davis in New Orleans, December 1889. Thousands turned out to mourn the passing of the man who led the Confederacy.

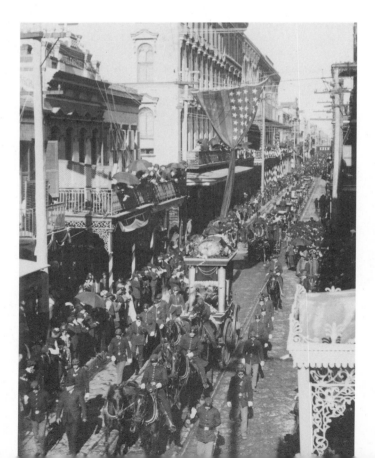

During Davis's last years, scores of Confederate veterans made pilgrimages to Beauvoir to speak with their old leader. For these stalwarts, the bitterness of the South's defeat had given rise to an almost religious reverence for the Lost Cause, the name given to the Confederacy's attempt to secede from the Union. No longer scorned as the architect of the South's defeat, Davis once again enjoyed the admiration of many of his fellow southerners. In 1886, he made a trip through the South with his daughter Varina Anne and was toasted by crowds in Montgomery, Atlanta, and Savannah.

Davis never finished the autobiography he started writing late in his life. In November 1889, he developed a bronchial infection during a final visit to Brierfield. He died on December 6, in New Orleans. Throughout the Cotton Belt, testimonials and eulogies were given for the man who had dedicated his life to the South. He was given a temporary burial in New Orleans, but Varina Anne later decided to have him permanently interred at Richmond, not far from the battlefields where the Confederate armies had waved the Stars and Bars for the last time.

Jefferson Davis was originally buried in New Orleans, but his body was later given permanent interment at Richmond, Virginia, the seat of the once-proud Confederacy.

107

Further Reading

Catton, Bruce. *The Civil War.* Boston: Houghton Mifflin, 1987.

———. *A Stillness at Appomattox.* New York: Washington Square Press, 1970.

Dodd, William E. *Jefferson Davis.* New York: Russell & Russell, 1966.

Eaton, Clement. *Jefferson Davis.* New York: The Free Press, 1977.

———. *The Mind of the Old South.* Baton Rouge: Louisiana State University Press, 1967.

McPherson, James M. *Battle Cry of Freedom: The Civil War Era.* New York: Oxford University Press, 1988.

———. *Ordeal by Fire: The Civil War & Reconstruction.* New York: Knopf, 1982.

Patrick, Rembert W. *Jefferson Davis and His Cabinet.* Baton Rouge: Louisiana State University Press, 1944.

Thomas, Emory M. *The Confederate Nation: 1861–1865.* New York: Harper & Row, 1979.

Vandiver, Frank E. *Their Tattered Flags: The Epic of the Confederacy.* New York: Harper & Row, 1970.

Warren, Robert Penn. *Jefferson Davis Gets His Citizenship Back.* Lexington: University Press of Kentucky, 1980.

Chronology

June 3, 1808	Jefferson Davis born in Christian County, Kentucky
1824	Enters West Point
1828	Begins term of service as officer in the U.S. army
1835	Resigns from army and marries Sarah Knox Taylor
1836	Moves to Mississippi after his wife's death
1845	Marries Varina Howell; elected to first term in the U.S. House of Representatives
1846–47	Commands a Mississippi regiment during the Mexican War and is acclaimed a war hero
Dec. 1847	Begins first term in the Senate
1853	Appointed U.S. secretary of war
1857	Returns to Senate
Dec. 1860	South Carolina secedes from the Union
Jan. 1861	Davis resigns from Senate in support of Mississippi's secession from the Union
March 1861	Named president of the Confederacy
Jan. 1863	Lincoln issues Emancipation Proclamation
July 1863	Confederacy suffers decisive defeat at Gettysburg; Vicksburg falls
April 9, 1865	Lee's army surrenders at Appomattox
May 10, 1865	Davis captured by Union troops
May 1867	Released from prison
Dec. 6, 1889	Dies of pneumonia in New Orleans

Index

Perry Scott King is a Brooklyn-based writer and the author of *Pericles* in the Chelsea House series WORLD LEADERS–PAST & PRESENT. A former Chelsea House editor, he is a graduate of Drew University, where he majored in history.

Arthur M. Schlesinger, jr., taught history at Harvard for many years and is currently Albert Schweitzer Professor of the Humanities at City University of New York. He is the author of numerous highly praised works in American history and has twice been awarded the Pulitzer Prize. He served in the White House as special assistant to Presidents Kennedy and Johnson.

PICTURE CREDITS

Alabama Department of Archives and History, Montgomery: p. 32; Barker Texas History Center, Prints and Photographs Collection, University of Texas at Austin: p. 33; Beauvoir, the Jefferson Davis Shrine: pp. 20, 98, 101, 104; Bettmann: pp. 14, 17, 23, 28, 29, 31, 34, 41, 44, 58, 63, 70, 73, 93, 97, 103; California State Library, Sacramento: pp. 48, 49; Kansas State Historical Society: pp. 56–57; Library of Congress: pp. 2, 12, 15, 22, 24, 25, 26, 37, 38, 40, 42, 43, 46, 51, 53, 60, 61, 65, 67, 69, 72, 74, 75, 76, 77, 78, 79, 80, 82, 83, 84, 87, 89, 91, 92, 95, 96, 106; Louisiana Collection, Howard Tilton Memorial Library, Tulane University: p. 64; Courtesy of the Mississippi Department of Archives & History: pp. 36, 100; Courtesy of the Missouri Historical Society: neg. portraits L-60, p. 16, neg. portraits S-10, p. 62; National Archives: pp. 81, 88, 94; Old Courthouse Museum, Vicksburg: pp. 39, 86; The Valentine Museum, Richmond, Virginia: pp. 102, 105; Virginia State Library and Archive: pp. 18, 107; Courtesy of the West Point Museum Collection, USMA, West Point, New York: p. 30

Making Hard Decisions
with DecisionTools®

THIRD EDITION

Making Hard Decisions
with DecisionTools®

Robert T. Clemen
Fuqua School of Business Duke University

Terence Reilly
Babson College

With contributions by Samuel E. Bodily and
Jeffery Guyse

and

Cases by Samuel E. Bodily, Dana Clyman,
Sherwood C. Frey, Jr., and Phillip E. Pfeifer

SOUTH-WESTERN
CENGAGE Learning·

Australia • Brazil • Japan • Korea • Mexico • Singapore • Spain • United Kingdom • United States

SOUTH-WESTERN
CENGAGE Learning

Making Hard Decisions
with DecisionTools®, 3rd Edition
Robert T. Clemen and Terence Reilly

Senior Vice President, LRS/Acquisitions &
Solutions Planning: Jack W. Calhoun

Editorial Director, Business & Economics:
Erin Joyner

Editor-in-Chief: Joe Sabatino

Senior Acquisitions Editor:
Charles McCormick, Jr.

Developmental Editor: Julie Anderson

Editorial Assistant: Anne Merrill

Brand Manager: Kristen Hurd

Associate Market Development Manager:
Roy Rosa

Art Director: Stacy Shirley

Production Management, and Composition:
PreMediaGlobal

Media Editor: Chris Valentine

Senior Manufacturing Planner:
Ron Montgomery

Rights Acquisition Specialist, Text and Image:
Deanna Ettinger

Inventory Manager: Terina Bradley

Cover Designer: Stuart Kunkler/triARTis
Communications

Cover Image: © Laughing Stock/Corbis

Library of Congress Control Number: 2012955508

ISBN-13: 978-0-538-79757-3

ISBN-10: 0-538-79757-6

South-Western
5191 Natorp Boulevard
Mason, OH 45040
USA

Cengage Learning is a leading provider of customized learning solutions
with office locations around the globe, including Singapore, the United
Kingdom, Australia, Mexico, Brazil, and Japan. Locate your local office at:
www.cengage.com/global

Cengage Learning products are represented in Canada by
Nelson Education, Ltd.

For your course and learning solutions, visit **www.cengage.com**

Purchase any of our products at your local college store or at our preferred
online store **www.cengagebrain.com**

Printed in the United States of America
3 4 5 6 7 18 17 16

To the memory of Ward Edwards,
whose work continues to inspire us.

BRIEF CONTENTS

CONTENTS

6   Organizational Use of Decision Analysis   233

Section 1 Cases   261

17 Conflicting Objectives II: Multiattribute Utility Models with Interactions   760

PREFACE

This book provides a one-semester overview of decision analysis for advanced undergraduate and master's degree students. The inspiration to write it has come from many sources, but perhaps most important was a desire to give students access to up-to-date information on modern decision analysis techniques at a level that could be easily understood by those without a strong mathematical background. At some points in the book, the student should be familiar with basic statistical concepts normally covered in an undergraduate applied statistics course. In particular, some familiarity with probability and probability distributions would be helpful in Chapters 7 through 12. Chapter 10 provides a decision-analysis view of data analysis, including regression, and familiarity with such statistical procedures would be an advantage when covering this topic. Algebra is used liberally throughout the book. Calculus concepts are used in a few instances as an explanatory tool. Be assured, however, that the material can be thoroughly understood, and the problems can be worked, without any knowledge of calculus.

The objective of decision analysis is to help a decision maker think hard about the specific problem at hand, including the overall structure of the problem as well as his or her preferences and beliefs. Decision analysis provides both an overall paradigm and a set of tools with which a decision maker can construct and analyze a model of a decision situation. Above all else, students need to understand that the purpose of studying decision-analysis techniques is to be able to represent real-world problems using models that can be analyzed to gain insight and understanding. It is through that insight and understanding—the hoped-for result of the modeling process—that making hard decisions can be improved.

NEW IN THIS EDITION

This revision has been a long time in the works, and we thank our readers for their patience. As you scan the book, we think you will agree that it has had a major overhaul, and we hope you find the result worth the wait.

The book has been thoroughly revised. Every chapter has been carefully rewritten and brought up-to-date, including new references where appropriate. Chapters 5, Sensitivity Analysis, and Chapter 11, Monte Carlo Simulation, have been completely rewritten. Jeff Guyse contributed material on behavioral decision theory in order to bring Chapters 8, 14, 15, and 16 up-to-date on behavioral issues in probability and utility assessment.

Perhaps the most noticeable additions are two new chapters contributed by Sam Bodily. Under his electronic pen, the previous Chapter 6 on Creativity has been transformed into a new chapter on Organizational Decision Making. He has also contributed the completely new Chapter 13 on Real Options.

Many of the examples, problems, and cases have been updated, and many new ones have been added. In particular, we are fortunate to be able to include 15 cases from Darden's extensive collection. We have grouped appropriate cases at the end of each of the three major sections of the book.

The Palisade DecisionTools Suite is the up-to-date version 6, and all of the tutorials and screen shots in the text have been updated to reflect the new software. It is our intention to modify the tutorials as needed in the future to keep abreast of changes and improvements that Palisade makes in the software.

Finally, you will discover two things missing. First, much of the material that was previously labeled "Optional" is no longer in the book, but available as online content. Three sections that were labeled optional in the previous edition are no longer optional: Constructing an Influence Diagram in Chapter 3; Two-Way Sensitivity Analysis for Three Alternatives in Chapter 5; and Decreasing and Constant Risk Aversion in Chapter 14. Second, the book no longer includes appendices containing pages of numbers for the various probability distributions. Between Microsoft Excel® and the Palisade software included with the book, probabilities for all of those distributions (and many more besides) can be easily found.

GUIDELINES FOR STUDENTS

Along with instructions on using the DecisionTools software, this version of *Making Hard Decisions* covers most of the concepts we consider important for a basic understanding of decision analysis. Although the text is meant to be an elementary introduction to decision analysis, this does not mean that the material is itself elementary. In fact, the more we teach decision analysis, the more we realize that the technical level of the math required for decision analysis is low, whereas the level of the analysis is high. Students must be willing to think clearly and analytically about the problems and issues that arise in decision situations. Good decision analysis requires clear thinking; sloppy thinking results in worthless analysis.

Of course, some topics are more demanding than others. As mentioned previously, for this edition a number of "optional" (i.e., more difficult) sections from previous editions are now available only as online supplements. Our faith in students and readers compels us to say that anyone who can handle the material in the new edition can, with a bit more effort and thought, also handle the online supplements.

In general, we believe that serious learning happens when one tackles problems on one's own. We have included a wide variety of exercises, questions, problems, and case studies. The exercises are relatively easy drills of the material. The questions and problems often require thinking beyond the material in the text. Some concepts are presented and dealt with only in the problems. Do not shy away from the problems! You can learn a lot by working through them.

Many case studies are included in *Making Hard Decisions*. A few of the many successful applications of decision analysis show up as case studies in the book. In addition, many issues are explored in the case studies in the context of current events. In addition to the real-world cases, the book contains many hypothetical cases and examples, as well as fictional historical accounts, all of which have been made as realistic as possible.

Some cases and problems are realistic, but not all the factual information is presented. In these cases, appropriate assumptions are required. On one hand, this may cause some frustration. On the other hand, incomplete information is typical in the real world. Being able to work with problems that are "messy" in this way is an important skill.

Finally, many of the cases and problems involve controversial issues. For example, the material on AIDS (Chapter 7) or medical ethics (Chapter 16) may evoke strong emotional responses from some readers. In writing a book like this, there are two choices: We can avoid the hard social problems that might offend some readers, or we can face these problems that need careful thought and discussion. The text adopts the second approach because we believe these issues require society's attention. Moreover, even though decision analysis may not provide the answers to these problems, it does provide a useful framework for thinking about the difficult decisions that our society must make.

A WORD TO INSTRUCTORS

Many instructors will want to supplement *Making Hard Decisions* with their own material. In fact, topics that we cover in our own courses are not included here. But, in the process of writing the book and obtaining comments from colleagues, it has become apparent that decision-making courses take on many different forms. Some instructors prefer to emphasize behavioral aspects, whereas others prefer analytical tools. Other dimensions have to do with competition, negotiation, and group decision making. *Making Hard Decisions* does not aim to cover everything for everyone. Instead, we have tried to cover the central concepts and tools of modern decision analysis with adequate references (and occasionally cases or problems) so that instructors can introduce their own material where appropriate. For example, in several places we discuss judgmental aspects of probability assessment and decision making, and an instructor can introduce more behavioral material at these points. Similarly, Chapter 16 delves into the additive utility function for decision making. Some instructors may wish to present goal programming or the analytic hierarchy process here.

Regarding the DecisionTools software, we wrote the instructions as a self-contained tutorial. Although the tutorial approach works well, we also believe that it must be supplemented by guidance from the course instructor. One possible way to supplement the instructions is to walk the students through the instructions in a computer lab. This will allow the instructor to answer questions as they arise and will allow students to learn the software in a controlled environment. No new material need be prepared for the computer-lab session, and in the text the students have a written copy of the instructions for later reference.

KEEPING UP WITH CHANGES

The world changes quickly, and decision analysis is changing with it. The good news is that the Internet helps us keep abreast of new developments. We encourage both students and instructors to visit the website of the Decision Analysis Society at www.informs.org/Community/DAS. This organization provides a focus for decision analysts worldwide and many others with interests in all aspects of decision making. On the Society's web page you will find links to many related resources and websites.

While you are keeping up with changes, we hope that you will help us do the same. Regarding the software or instructions in using the software, please send your comments to Terence Reilly at reilly@babson.edu. For all other non-software matters, please send comments to either Terence Reilly or Robert Clemen at clemen@duke.edu. Please send information about (hopefully the few) mistakes or typos that you may find in the book, innovative ways to teach decision analysis, new case studies, or interesting applications of decision analysis.

INSTRUCTOR RESOURCES

Instructor's Resource and Solutions Manual

The Instructor's Resource and Solutions Manual contains teaching notes, a topical cross reference for problems, and answers to all exercises, questions, problems and case studies, including the Darden cases. This supplement is available for convenient download for instructors only at http://login.cengage.com.

PowerPoint® Slides

Exceptional new PowerPoint slides have been created specifically for this edition by Patrick Wheeler at the University of South Florida. Liven up your classroom with engaging PowerPoint slides that contain an excellent summary of each chapter, numerous examples, figures and lively animation. You can modify or customize the slides for your specific course. PowerPoint slides are available for convenient download for instructors only at http://login.cengage.com.

ADDITIONAL SUPPLEMENTS FOR BOTH STUDENTS AND INSTRUCTORS

Chapter Supplements

Due to the variance in how instructors teach the course, many additional supplements will be made available online for students and instructors. All online materials for students can be found at www.cengagebrain.com. Instructors can access the materials at http://login.cengage.com. Online supplemental reading materials include:

Chapter 4: Solving Influence Diagrams: The Details

Chapter 6: Blocks to Creativity and Additional Creativity Techniques

Chapter 7: Correlation and Covariance for Measuring Dependence

Chapter 8: Coherence and the Dutch Book

Chapter 10: Natural Conjugate Distributions

Chapter 17: Three or More Attributes

In addition to the above, data sets and selected Excel models from each chapter can be found at www.cengagebrain.com.

Palisade's DecisionTools Suite, 6.0

The DecisionTools Suite is an integrated set of programs for risk analysis and decision making under uncertainty that runs in Microsoft Excel. The DecisionTools Suite includes @RISK for Monte Carlo simulation, PrecisionTree for decision trees and influence diagrams, StatTools for statistical analysis and forecasting, and RISKOptimizer for stochastic optimization. The programs work together better than ever before, and all integrate completely with Microsoft Excel for ease of use and maximum flexibility. The programs are backward compatible, with models created under older versions seamlessly updated to version 6.0. Additional resources, such as example models and instructional videos are available at www.palisade.com. With purchase of the book, students have complimentary access to the software at www.cengagebrain.com.

ACKNOWLEDGMENTS

It is a pleasure to acknowledge the help we have had with the preparation of this text.

First mention goes to our students, who craved the notes from which the text has grown. For resource support, thanks to the institutions that have supported our work on this and previous editions: The Lundquist College of Business at the University of Oregon; Decision Research of Eugene, Oregon; Applied Decision Analysis, Inc., of Menlo Park, California; the Fuqua School of Business of Duke University; Babson College; and the Board of Research at

Babson College for financial support. Additionally, thanks go to the Darden School of Business at the University of Virginia and the California State Polytechnic University, Pomona for supporting Sam Bodily and Jeff Guyse with their contributions.

Many individuals have provided comments at various stages on portions of this or earlier editions. Thanks to Deborah Amaral, Sam Bodily, Adam Borison, Cathy Barnes, George Benson, Dave Braden, Bill Burns, Peter Farquhar, Ken Gaver, Andy Golub, Gordon Hazen, Max Henrion, Don Keefer, Ralph Keeney, Robin Keller, Craig Kirkwood, Don Kleinmuntz, Irv LaValle, George MacKenzie, Allan Murphy, Bob Nau, Roger Pfaffenberger, Steve Powell, Gordon Pritchett, H.V. Ravinder, Gerald Rose, Sam Roy, Rakesh Sarin, Ross Shachter, Jim Smith, Bob Winkler, and Wayne Winston. Special thanks to Timothy Reilly for sharing his expertise on oil spills in the Larkin Oil case of Chapter 2; Deborah Amaral for guidance in writing the Municipal Solid Waste case in Chapter 9; to Dave Braden for outstanding feedback as he and his students used manuscript versions of the first edition; to Susan Brodt for guidance and suggestions regarding the creativity material in Chapter 6; and to Kevin McCardle for allowing the use of numerous problems from his statistics course. Vera Gilliland and Sam McLafferty of Palisade Corporation have been very helpful. Thanks also to all of the editors who have worked closely with us on this and previous editions over the years: Patty Adams, Marcia Cole, Mary Douglas, Anne and Greg Draus, Keith Faivre, Curt Hinrichs, Charles McCormick, Michael Payne, and Julie Anderson.

Finally, we sincerely thank our families and loved ones for their understanding of the times we were gone and the hours we have spent on this text.

Robert T. Clemen
Terence Reilly

CHAPTER 1

Introduction to Decision Analysis

Have you ever had a difficult decision to make? If so, did you wish for a straightforward way to keep all of the different issues clear? Did you end up making the decision based on your intuition or on a "hunch," but wondered if you were leaving out important details? Although difficult decisions are a common fact of life, understanding how to rigorously analyze decisions is not so common. Rigorous analysis is not as daunting as it sounds and provides unique and helpful insights that can greatly clarify the decision. This chapter introduces decision analysis, a process that provides a structured method with analytical tools designed to improve one's decision-making skills.

The introduction opens with a contentious decision faced by the Board of Regents of Rice University about the status of their college football program. For those who don't know, Rice is located in the state of Texas, a state known for passionate football allegiances and rivalries.

Don't Mess with Texas Football	In 2004, The Board of Regents of Rice University knew that something had to be done about their costly football program. They also knew that their actions would be closely scrutinized by various groups, and unpopular but fiscally sound measures could spark a firestorm of protests. At the center of the decision sat a $4 million deficit, an amount that was expected to grow and that Rice could ill afford year after year. On the one hand, the problem was simple enough: Rice's Board had a fiduciary responsibility to reduce the football program's sizable deficit. On the other hand, football's value extended beyond simple cost accounting to include important, but intangible benefits, such as boosting school spirit and pride, improving alumni relations, and supporting local businesses. Thus, the Board needed to understand and preserve the value of these intangible benefits to the school while coming up with cost-cutting proposals. Throw in the intense emotions

surrounding college football, and Rice's Board was indeed facing a hard decision.

Part of the problem—but also a source of pride—was the fact that Rice was the smallest university in Division I-A, the most prestigious division of the NCAA (National Collegiate Athletics Association). Not all Division I-A schools are created equal, and Rice was discovering that size does matter. For example, ticket receipts of other Division I-A schools averaged $6.5 million annually, whereas Rice could only expect a paltry $900,000. Also, Rice received little of its revenues from the highly profitable bowl games. Although Rice spent $18.4 million annually on athletics, placing them in the lower half of spending by Division I-A schools, they spent the most per undergraduate student at $6,809, more than four times the median spending per student at other Division I-A schools. Clearly, the Board had to address these financial difficulties, but what were their options?

An interesting option that the Board considered was to drop out of Division 1-A, and move to a lower division. They viewed Division III as a better alternative than Division II because the universities belonging to Division III, such as University of Chicago, New York University, and Carnegie Melon were on par with Rice academically. The expectation was that Division III would be lower cost, Rice would gain prestige by association, and, for the student athletes, the emphasis would move toward academic achievement and away from the nearly professional status of many collegiate-sports programs.

While changing divisions held some promise, it was also controversial. Fans, supporters, and alumni formed an advocacy group called Friends of Rice Athletics. They argued through a letter-writing campaigns and rallies that not every university program had to make a profit. They cited an NCAA report claiming that less than a dozen football programs nationwide generated more revenue than costs. Why should Rice's program be required to meet a standard so few other schools met?

Clearly, Rice's Board of Regents faced a particularly complex problem. They could not lightly dismiss the years of support by fans and alumni, nor could they ignore the annual $4 million deficit. Before deciding exactly what course of action to take, the Board needed to carefully consider and balance many issues, including the values of the different constituent groups—but how? There is no escaping the problem: This hard decision requires hard thinking. Add to this complex mix the inherent uncertainty in the situation regardless of the action they took, and you can see the need for clarity and insight when making hard decisions.

The good news is that decision analysis adds clarity and insight in several ways. First, it provides a conceptual framework for thinking systematically through hard decisions. For example, decision analysis allows us to break the problem down into smaller, more easily understood pieces that can be analyzed individually. Second, decision analysis supplies analytical tools that lead to insights and a deeper understanding of the problem. For example, sensitivity analysis tells us which inputs are most important and hence deserve our time and attention. Decision analysis not only helps with our decisions, but instills a sense of confidence in actions we choose.

The bad news is that decision analysis cannot make hard decisions easy. The fact is that hard decisions are just that–hard. Decision analysis is not a magic wand; we cannot simply feed our inputs into a computer and expect the answer to pop out. We must think through all the various aspects of the decision, often from competing viewpoints. We still need to think about all future events and their resulting consequences. While a decision maker can take action with confidence earned through a clear understanding of the issues, this comes only from doing the work needed to find the insights and understand the issues.

WHY ARE DECISIONS HARD?

What makes decisions hard? Viewed from the perspective of a specific decision, each problem is unique and carries its own special difficulties. With experience, however, we begin to see the uniqueness disappear. What looked special in one case may turn out to be a common difficulty across many problems. For example, while Rice's Board was in the unique position of having to balance financial responsibilities with the interests of the fans, alumni, and boosters, they were actually facing the more general problem of decision making with multiple and competing objectives. It is worthwhile to understand how our own unique decision fits into a broader picture, because doing so will help us choose appropriate tools for analysis and may lead us to examine how others have solved similar problems.

Four broad sources of difficulty commonly appear: complexity, uncertainty, multiple objectives, and competing viewpoints. Decision analysis can help with all four.

First, a decision can be hard simply because of its complexity. In the case of Rice's football program, the Board of Regents must consider many different issues: reducing the deficit, balancing the opposing values of the various stakeholders, understanding the value of intangible benefits such as school pride, and so on. In addition, there is uncertainty; no matter what the Board of Regents might decide, future events beyond their control could result in good or bad consequences for the school. Complexity can quickly overwhelm a decision maker, making it nearly impossible to guarantee that each critical component of the decision is appropriately considered in the analysis.

A powerful aspect of decision analysis is its ability to reduce complexity. We will see many examples in which decision analysis picks off pieces one-by-one in a complex problem, allowing the decision maker to think hard about each piece. Although investigating isolated parts of the problem simplifies it, doing so runs the risk of ignoring important connections or relationships between the pieces. Thus, after carefully thinking through the individual pieces, we reassemble them into an overall structure. For example, we will see how to use decision trees and influence diagrams to structure and analyze decisions and to answer "what if" questions. These tools provide effective methods for organizing a complex problem into a structure that can be analyzed.

Second, a decision can be difficult because of the inherent uncertainty in the situation. In a situation that has a lot of uncertainty, there is no way to know precisely how all the factors not under your control will play out. Who hasn't wished they could see into the future? Yet we often have to make a decision before the uncertainty is resolved. For example, imagine a firm deciding whether or not to introduce a new product. The size of the market, the market price, eventual competition, manufacturing costs, and distribution costs all may be uncertain, and all impact the firm's eventual profit. Yet the decision must be made without knowing the outcomes of each of these uncertainties. Worse, because uncertainty clouds the future, as a decision maker one may have to "play the odds," something many people are not accustomed to doing. Or we might try to find an alternative that provides flexibility for adapting as those uncertainties play out.

Decision analysis requires us to think through the uncertainties of our decisions. First, we break each uncertainty down by listing the different outcomes that could occur. Then, for each outcome, we determine both the consequence and the likelihood of that outcome occurring. This is a lot of work, and it is one of the reasons why hard decisions are difficult. But the benefits include knowing which option gives you the best chance at what you want, which option has the most risk, and which uncertainties have the most impact. While understanding uncertainties will not lead to immediate clarity, it can provide decision makers with a richer understanding of the decision problem and help them determine which option best matches their preferences.

Third, a decision maker may be interested in working toward multiple objectives, but progress in one direction may impede progress in others. In such a case, a decision maker must trade off benefits in one area against benefits in another. In the Rice football example, important trade-offs must be made: Are the cost savings from dropping down to Division III worth the potential damage to school pride and alumni relations? Investment decisions usually require us to make a trade-off between risk and return. Decision analysis again provides both a framework and specific tools for dealing with multiple objectives. These tools have the decision maker think about trade-offs in a variety of ways, thereby requiring them to think deeply about what they really want and what might be given up.

Fourth, and finally, a problem may be difficult if different perspectives lead to different conclusions. Or, even from a single perspective, slight changes in particular inputs may lead to different choices. This source of difficulty is especially pertinent when more than one person is involved in making the decision. Different individuals may look at the problem from different perspectives, or they may disagree on the likelihood or value of the various outcomes. The use of the decision-analysis framework and tools can help sort through and resolve these differences, whether the decision maker is an individual or a group of stakeholders with diverse opinions.

A natural question to ask is whether the effort expended in applying decision analysis is worthwhile. The difficulty in answering this question is that once we have chosen and acted on a decision, we cannot go back and choose a different alternative to see how it would have compared. Thus, it is very hard to know how much difference decision analysis can make. There are many published reports of successful applications of decision analysis, but this evidence is self-reported and testimonial. One study, however, was able to estimate the value of using decision analysis to guide the decision process. An analyst at a large U.S. corporation kept records from 1990 to 1998 on projects in which he used decision analysis techniques. An analysis of these records led Clemen and Kwit (2001) to estimate that the projects were worth about $1 billion to the company. In addition, there were many nonmonetary benefits such as improved communication among project team members and increased commitment to chosen alternatives.

WHY STUDY DECISION ANALYSIS?

The obvious reason for studying decision analysis is that carefully applying its techniques can lead to better decisions. But what is a good decision? A simple answer might be that it is the one that gives a good outcome. This answer, however, confuses the idea of a lucky outcome with a good decision. Suppose an inheritance left us with $100,000 to invest. After carefully considering all the options available and consulting with investment specialists and financial planners, we decide to invest in stocks. Was the investment decision a good one? If we were to answer this question based solely on whether we followed a logical and coherent process that matched our needs with the options, then yes, it was a good decision. If, however, we were to answer this question based solely on the resulting ROI (return on investment), then the quality of the decision would have a lot to do with events beyond our control. For example, if we were unlucky enough to invest in October 2007, when the stock market reached its peak just before plunging into the financial crisis of 2008 to 2009, then most likely we would have done poorly.

All this is to say that good decisions can have unlucky outcomes. Of course, you may prefer to have lucky outcomes rather than make good decisions! Although decision analysis cannot prevent unlucky events, it can help improve the decision you make, in the sense of carefully considering and understanding all the issues. That understanding must include the structure of the problem as well as the uncertainties and trade-offs inherent in the alternatives. You may then improve your chances of enjoying a better outcome; more important, you will be less likely to experience unpleasant surprises in the form of unlucky outcomes that were either unforeseen or not fully understood. One way to offset the impact of unfortunate events is to employ hedging strategies, but we can only do so if we have first identified the potential pitfalls. Decision analysis provides the structure and tools to better understand all aspects of the problem, and, if necessary, the opportunity to take preemptive corrective actions.

Even though decision analysis opens our eyes to what could happen, we can still run into a brick wall of unfortunate events. This happened to Robert Rubin, Secretary of the Treasury under President Bill Clinton. Early in his career at Goldman Sachs, Rubin took a position that not only proved costly, but his hedge also went the wrong way.

Risk Arbitrage at Goldman Sachs	Robert Rubin was hired in the late sixties to run Goldman Sachs' fabled risk-arbitrage department, which had annual profits in the millions. Essentially, risk arbitrage amounts to buying securities whose prices might change in the near future due to some event, such as a merger or bankruptcy. In this example, Becton Dickinson, a medical equipment manufacturer, announced a friendly takeover of Univis, an eyeglass maker. A share of Univis was selling for $24, and if the merger went through it would be worth $33.50. The decision to engage in risk arbitrage involved intensive research into the companies to determine the odds of the merger happening, the amount of money to be made if it did occur, and the amount put at risk if the deal fell apart. Research involved not only examining the financial reports of each company, but also making personal judgments about the future fit of the two companies, the trustworthiness of the executives, and a general sense of the proposed deal. After all this careful and sophisticated analysis, Goldman Sachs did invest, but after unfavorable earnings by Univis, Becton Dickinson pulled out and Goldman Sachs lost $675,000— more money than they made on any other arbitrage deal that year! Even the hedge Rubin used to protect against loses backfired causing deeper loses.

Was Rubin's decision to invest bad? Rubin states: "While the result may have been bad, the investment decision wasn't necessarily wrong. After a deal broke up, we'd always reexamine it, looking for clues we might have missed. But even a large and painful loss didn't mean that we misjudged anything. As with any actuarial business, the essence of [risk-]arbitrage is that if you calculate the odds correctly, you will make money on the majority of the deals and on the sum total of all your deals." (Rubin and Weisberg, 2003, p. 46).

The preceding discussion suggests that decision analysis allows people to make effective decisions more consistently. This idea itself warrants discussion. Decision analysis is intended to help people deal with *difficult* decisions. It is a "prescriptive approach designed for normally intelligent people who want to think hard and systematically about some important real problems" (Keeney and Raiffa 1976, p. vii).

This prescriptive view is the most appropriate way to think about decision analysis. It gets across the idea that although we are not perfect deci-

makers, we can do better through using more structure and guidance. We will see that decision analysis is not an idealized theory designed for superrational and omniscient beings. Nor does it describe how people actually make decisions. In fact, ample experimental evidence from psychology shows that people generally do not process information and make decisions in ways that are consistent with the decision-analysis approach. If they did, there would be no need for decision analysis. Based on fundamental principles, and informed by knowledge of human frailties in judgment and decision making, decision analysis offers guidance to the average person working on a hard decision.

Although decision analysis provides structure and guidance for systematic thinking in difficult situations, it does not claim to produce an alternative that must be blindly accepted. Indeed, after the hard thinking that decision analysis fosters, there should be no need for blind acceptance; the decision maker should understand the situation thoroughly. Instead of providing solutions, decision analysis is perhaps best thought of as simply an information source, providing insights about the situation, uncertainties, objectives, and trade-offs, and possibly yielding a recommended course of action. Thus, decision analysis does not usurp the decision maker's job. According to author Derek W. Bunn

"The basic presumption of decision analysis is not at all to replace the decision maker's intuition, to relieve him or her of the obligations in facing the problem, or to be, worst of all, a competitor to the decision maker's personal style of analysis, but to complement, augment, and generally work alongside the decision maker in exemplifying the nature of the problem. Ultimately, it is of most value if the decision maker has actually learned something about the problem and his or her own decision-making attitude through the exercise." (Bunn 1984, p. 8)

We have been discussing decision analysis as if it were always used to help an individual make a decision. Indeed, this is what it is designed for, but its techniques have many other uses. For example, one might use decision-analysis methods to solve complicated inference problems (i.e., answering questions such as "What conclusions can be drawn from the available evidence?"). Structuring a decision problem may be useful for understanding its precise nature, for generating alternative courses of action, and for identifying important objectives and trade-offs. Understanding trade-offs can be crucial for making progress in negotiation settings. Finally, decision analysis can be used to justify why a previously chosen action was appropriate.

SUBJECTIVE JUDGMENTS AND DECISION MAKING

Clearly, a decision maker's beliefs and personal judgments should be part of the decision process. Even in situations where hard data are available, personal judgments and individual attitudes about risk are important inputs for decision analysis. For example, Robert Rubin used both the financial reports and personal judgments in all his risk-arbitrage deals. It will become clear through this text that thinking hard and systematically about important aspects of a decision naturally help us discover and develop these judgments.

Managers and policy makers frequently complain that analytical procedures from management science and operations research ignore subjective judgments. Such procedures often purport to generate "optimal" actions on the basis of purely objective inputs. But the decision-analysis approach allows the inclusion of subjective judgments. In fact, decision analysis *requires* personal judgments; they are important ingredients for making good decisions.

At the same time, it is important to realize that human beings are imperfect information processors. Personal insights about uncertainty and preferences can be both limited and misleading, even when the individual making the judgments is completely confident. (In fact, we will see that one of our most common pitfalls is overconfidence.) An awareness of human cognitive limitations is critical in developing the necessary judgmental inputs, and a decision maker who ignores these problems can magnify rather than adjust for human frailties.

Much current psychological research has a direct bearing on the practice of decision-analysis techniques. In the chapters that follow, many of the results from this research will be discussed and related to decision-analysis techniques. The spirit of the discussion is that understanding the problems people face and carefully applying decision-analysis techniques can lead to better judgments and improved decisions.

THE DECISION ANALYSIS PROCESS

Figure 1.1 shows a flowchart for the decision analysis process. The first step is for the decision maker to identify the decision situation and to understand his or her objectives in that situation. Although we usually do not have trouble finding decisions to make or problems to solve, we do sometimes have trouble identifying the exact problem, and thus we sometimes treat the wrong problem. Careful identification of the decision at hand is always important. Sometimes a surface problem hides the real issue. Hypothetically, perhaps the issue for Rice's board is not the $4 million deficit, but regaining control over an ever increasingly powerful athletic program that has been flouting school policies.

Understanding one's objectives in a decision situation is also an important first step and involves some introspection. What is important? What are the objectives? Minimizing cost? Maximizing profit or market share? What about minimizing risks? Does risk mean the chance of a monetary loss, or does it refer to conditions potentially damaging to health and the environment? One must develop a clear understanding of the crucial objectives in a decision situation before much more can be accomplished. In the next step, knowledge of objectives can help in identifying alternatives, and beyond that the objectives indicate how outcomes must be measured and what kinds of uncertainties should be considered in the analysis.

Many authors argue that the first step is to identify the problem and then figure out the appropriate objectives to be used in addressing the problem. But Keeney (1992) argues the opposite; it is far better, he claims, to spend a lot of effort understanding one's central values and objectives, and then looking for ways—decision opportunities—to achieve those objectives. The debate

FIGURE **1.1**
A decision analysis
process flowchart.

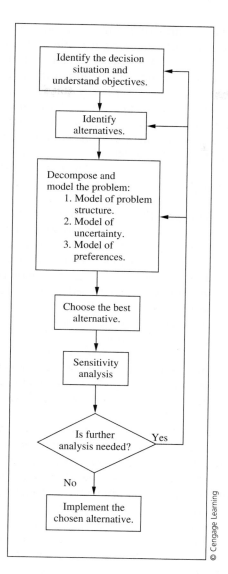

notwithstanding, the fact is that decisions come in many forms. Sometimes we are lucky enough to shape our decision-making future in the way Keeney suggests, and other times we find ourselves in difficult, unanticipated situations. In either case, establishing the precise nature of the decision situation (which we will call the *decision context*) goes hand-in-hand with identifying and understanding one's objectives in that situation.

With the decision situation and pertinent objectives established, we turn to the discovery and creation of alternatives. Often a careful examination and analysis of objectives can reveal alternatives that were not obvious at the outset. This is an important benefit of a decision analysis approach. In addition, research in the area of creativity has led to a number of techniques that can improve the chance of finding new alternatives.

The next two steps, which might be called modeling and solution, form the heart of most textbooks on decision analysis, including this one. Much of this book will focus on decomposing problems to understand their structures and to measure uncertainty and value; indeed, decomposition is the key to decision analysis. The approach is to "divide and conquer." The first level of decomposition calls for structuring the problem in smaller and more manageable pieces. Subsequent decomposition by the decision maker may entail careful consideration of elements of uncertainty in different parts of the problem or careful thought about different aspects of the objectives.

The idea of *modeling* is critical in decision analysis, as it is in most quantitative or analytical approaches to problems. As indicated in Figure 1.1, we will use models in several ways. We will use influence diagrams or decision trees to create a representation or model of the decision problem. Probability will be used to build models of the uncertainty inherent in the problem. Hierarchical and network models will be used to understand the relationships among multiple objectives, and we will assess utility functions in order to model the way in which decision makers value different outcomes and trade off competing objectives. These models are mathematical and graphical in nature, allowing one to find insights that may not be apparent on the surface. Of course, a key advantage from a decision-making perspective is that the mathematical representation of a decision can be subjected to analysis, which can help us understand key drivers in the problem, for example, or identify a preferred alternative,

Decision analysis is typically an iterative process. Once a model has been built, *sensitivity analysis* is performed. Such analysis answers "what if" questions: "If we make a slight change in one or more aspects of the model, does the optimal decision change?" If so, the decision is said to be sensitive to these small changes, and the decision maker may wish to reconsider more carefully those aspects to which the decision is sensitive. Virtually any part of a decision is fair game for sensitivity analysis. The arrows in Figure 1.1 show that the decision maker may return to any aspect of the decision model, even to the problem-identification step. It may be necessary to refine the definition of objectives or include objectives that were not previously included in the model. New alternatives may be identified, the model structure may change, and the models of uncertainty and preferences may need to be refined. The term *decision-analysis cycle* best describes the overall process, which may go through several iterations before a satisfactory solution is found.

During this iterative process, the decision maker's perception of the problem changes, beliefs about the likelihood of various uncertain eventualities may develop and change, and preferences for outcomes not previously considered may mature with reflection. Decision analysis not only provides a structured way to think about decisions, but also more fundamentally provides a structure within which a decision maker can develop beliefs and feelings, those subjective judgments that are critical for a good solution.

REQUISITE DECISION MODELS

Phillips (1982, 1984) has introduced the term *requisite decision modeling*. This marvelous term captures the essence of the modeling process in decision analysis. In Phillips's words, "a model can be considered requisite only when no new intuitions emerge about the problem" (1984, p. 37), or when it contains everything that is essential for solving the problem. That is, a model is requisite when the decision maker's thoughts about the problem, beliefs regarding uncertainty, and preferences are fully developed. For example, consider a first-time mutual-fund investor who finds high, overall long-term returns appealing. Imagine, though, that in the process of researching the funds the investor begins to understand and become wary of highly volatile stocks and mutual funds. For this investor, a decision model that selected a fund by maximizing the average return in the long run would not be requisite. A requisite model would have to incorporate a trade-off between long-term returns and volatility.

A careful decision maker may cycle through the process shown in Figure 1.1 several times as the analysis is refined. Appropriately timed sensitivity analysis can help the decision maker choose the next modeling steps to take in developing a requisite model. Successful decision analysts artistically use sensitivity analysis to manage the iterative development of a decision model. An important goal of this book is that you begin to acquire this artistic ability through familiarity and practice with the concepts and tools of decision analysis.

WHERE IS DECISION ANALYSIS USED?

Decision analysis is widely used in business and government decision making. Perusing the literature reveals applications that include managing research- and development programs, negotiating for oil and gas leases, managing a pharmaceutical research-and-development pipeline, understanding the world oil market, deciding whether to launch a new product or new venture, and developing ways to respond to environmental risks, to name a few. And some of the largest firms make use of decision analysis, including General Motors, Chevron, and Eli Lilly. A particularly important arena for decision analysis applications has been in public utilities, especially electric power generation. In part this is because the problems utilities face (e.g., site selection, power generation methods, waste cleanup and storage, and pollution control) are particularly appropriate for treatment with decision-analysis techniques; they involve long time frames and hence a high degree of uncertainty. In addition, multiple objectives must be considered when a decision affects many different stakeholder groups.

In the literature, many of the reported applications relate to public-policy problems and relatively few to commercial decisions, partly because public-policy problems are of interest to such a wide audience. The reason is perhaps more closely related to the fact that commercial applications often are proprietary; a good decision analysis can create a competitive advantage for a firm, which may not appreciate having its advantage revealed in the open literature. Important public-policy applications have included regulation in the energy (especially nuclear) industry and standard setting in a variety of different situations ranging from regulations for air and water pollution to standards for safety features on new cars.

Another important area of application for decision analysis has been in medicine. Decision analysis has helped doctors make specific diagnoses and individuals to understand the risks of different treatments. Institutional-level studies have included examining the optimal inventory or usage of blood in a blood bank, or the decision of a firm regarding different kinds of medical insurance to provide its employees. On a grander scale, studies have examined policies such as widespread testing for various forms of cancer or the impact on society of different treatment recommendations.

This discussion is by no means exhaustive; the intent is to give you only a feel for the breadth of possible applications of decision analysis and a glimpse at some of the things that have been done. Many other applications are described in cases and examples throughout the book; by the time you have finished, you should have a good understanding of how decision analysis can be (and is) used in many different arenas. And if you feel the need for more, articles by Corner and Kirkwood (1991) and Keefer, Kirkwood, and Corner (2004) describe many different applications.

WHERE DOES THE SOFTWARE FIT IN?

Included with the text is Palisade's DecisionTools® suite, which is a set of computer programs designed to help us complete the modeling and solution phase of the decision process. The suite consists of six programs (Precision-Tree, Evolver, NeuralTools, StatTools, TopRank, and @RISK), two of which (PrecisionTree and @RISK) we we will discuss extensively. As we work our way through the text learning the different steps, we introduce the program that will help that step. We supply detailed instructions on how to use the program and how to interpret the output at the end of the chapters. Table 1.1 shows where in the decision process we use PrecisionTree, @RISK, and RiskOptimizer and the chapter where the instructions appear.

PrecisionTree was specifically designed for the decision-analysis process, and, as shown in Table 1.1, we use it throughout the whole text. PrecisionTree not only helps with the analytical aspects of solving decision models, but it also creates the graphical representations (trees or influence diagrams) of these models. The program @RISK was designed to run simulation models, which we do in Chapters 11 and 13. We also use @RISK to explore different ways to model uncertainties. RISKOptimizer, a subprogram of @RISK, uses genetic algorithms to optimize simulation models, as discussed in Chapter 13.

One of the more convenient aspects about the DecisionTools® suite is that the programs work together seamlessly within Microsoft Excel®. Instead of having to learn a new system, these programs operate within the familiar spreadsheet environment by adding toolbars and menus directly to Excel's® interface. They extend the analytical and graphical capabilities of Excel® to handle the specialized models used in decision analysis. Because they all operate within Excel®, we can easily move from one program to another, even

TABLE **1.1**
The DecisionTools®
Programs

DecisionTools® Program	Where It Is Used in the Decision Process	Where in Text
PrecisionTree	Structuring the decision	Chapter 3
	Solving the decision	Chapter 4
	Sensitivity analysis	Chapter 5
	Value of information	Chapter 12
	Modeling preferences	Chapter 14
@RISK	Modeling uncertainty	Chapters 8 and 9
	Using data to model uncertainty	Chapter 10
	Simulation modeling	Chapters 11 and 13
RISKOptimizer	Optimizing Simulation Models	Chapter 13

using the results of one program as the inputs into another. The integration of the programs with Excel® is seamless, and those familiar with Excel® will have little difficulty using the DecisionTools® suite.

There is also a strong interconnection between the DecisionTools® programs and Excel®. These programs do more than use the spreadsheet as an analytical engine. For example, you can link your decision tree to a spreadsheet model. The links will be dynamic; changes made in the spreadsheet are immediately reflected in the decision tree. These dynamic links will pull input values from the tree to the spreadsheet, calculate an output value, and send the output back to the tree.

Linking is one of many ways that Excel® and the DecisionTools® programs work together. In future chapters we will see other connections. We will also see how flexible and useful electronic spreadsheets can be when constructing decision models. Much of what we will learn about using Excel® will extend beyond decision analysis. It is hard to overemphasize the power of modern spreadsheets; these programs can do virtually anything that requires calculations. Spreadsheets have become one of the most versatile and powerful quantitative tools available to business managers. Virtually all managers now have personal computers on their desks with the ability to run these sophisticated spreadsheet programs, which suggests that aspiring managers would be well advised to become proficient in the use of this flexible tool.

The software can help you learn and understand the concepts presented in the chapter. Reading about the concepts and examples will provide a theoretical understanding. The programs will test your understanding when you apply the theory to actual problems. You will find that your understanding of the concepts greatly increases because the programs force you to think carefully throughout the construction and analysis of the model.

WHERE ARE WE GOING FROM HERE?

This book is divided into three main sections. The first is titled "Modeling Decisions," and it introduces influence diagrams and decision trees as methods for building models of decision problems. The process is sometimes called *structuring* because it specifies the elements of the decision and how the elements are interrelated (Chapters 2 and 3). We also introduce ways to organize a decision maker's values into hierarchies and networks; doing so is useful when multiple objectives must be considered. We will find out how to analyze our decision models (Chapter 4) and how to conduct sensitivity analysis (Chapter 5). Chapter 6 takes a look at how decision analysis is used in organizations.

The second section is "Modeling Uncertainty." Here we delve into the use of probability for modeling uncertainty in decision problems. First we review basic probability concepts (Chapter 7). Because subjective judgments play a central role in decision analysis, subjective assessments of uncertainty are the topic of Chapter 8. Probability can also be used in theoretical probability models (Chapter 9), data-based models (Chapter 10), and simulation (Chapter 11). Chapters 12 and 13 close the section with a discussion of how to value information (how much should we be willing to pay for additional information) and how to value flexibility (real options).

"Modeling Preferences" is the final section. Here we turn to the development of a mathematical representation of a decision maker's preferences, including the identification of desirable objectives and trade-offs between conflicting objectives. A fundamental issue that we often must confront is how to trade off risk and expected value. Typically, if we want to increase our chances at a better outcome, we must accept a simultaneous increase in the risk of loss. Chapters 14 and 15 delve into the problem of modeling a decision maker's attitude toward risk. Chapters 16 and 17 complete the section with a treatment of other conflicting objectives. In these chapters we will complete the discussion of multiple objectives begun in Section 1, showing how to construct a mathematical model that reflects subjective judgments of relative importance among competing objectives.

By the end of the book, you will have learned all of the basic techniques and concepts that are central to the practice of modern decision analysis. This does not mean that your hard decisions will suddenly become easy! But with the decision-analysis framework, and with tools for modeling decisions, uncertainty, and preferences, you will be able to approach your difficult decisions systematically. The understanding and insight gained from such an approach will give you confidence in your actions and allow for better decisions in difficult situations. That is what the book is about—an approach that will help you improve the way you make hard decisions.

SUMMARY

The purpose of decision analysis is to help a decision maker think systematically about complex problems and to improve the quality of the resulting decisions. In this regard, it is important to distinguish between a good decision and a lucky outcome. A good decision is one that is made on the basis of a thorough understanding of the problem and careful thought regarding the important issues. Outcomes, on the other hand, may be lucky or unlucky, regardless of decision quality.

In general, decision analysis consists of a framework and a tool kit for dealing with difficult decisions. The incorporation of subjective judgments is an important aspect of decision analysis, and to a great extent mature judgments develop as the decision maker reflects on the decision at hand and develops a working model of the problem. The overall strategy is to decompose a complicated problem into smaller chunks that can be more readily analyzed and understood. These smaller pieces can then can be brought together to create an overall representation of the decision situation. Finally, the decision-analysis cycle provides the framework within which a decision maker can construct a requisite decision model, one that contains the essential elements of the problem and from which the decision maker can take action.

QUESTIONS AND PROBLEMS

1.1 Give an example of a good decision that you made in the face of some uncertainty. Was the outcome lucky or unlucky? Can you give an example of a poorly made decision whose outcome was lucky?

1.2 Explain how modeling is used in decision analysis. What is meant by the term "requisite decision model"?

1.3 What role do subjective judgments play in decision analysis?

1.4 At a dinner party, an acquaintance asks whether you have read anything interesting lately, and you mention that you have begun to read a text on decision analysis. Your friend asks what decision analysis is and why anyone would want to read a book about it, let alone write one! How would you answer?

1.5 Your friend in Question 1.4, upon hearing your answer, is delighted! "This is marvelous," she exclaims. "I have this very difficult choice to make at work. I'll tell you the facts, and you can tell me what I should do!" Explain to her why you cannot do the analysis for her.

1.6 Give an example in which a decision was complicated because of difficult preference trade-offs. Give one that was complicated by uncertainty.

1.7 In the Rice University football example, what are some of the issues that you would consider in making this decision? What are the alternative courses of action? What issues involve uncertainty, and how could you get information to help resolve that uncertainty? What are the values held by opposing groups? How might your decision make tradeoffs among these values?

1.8 Can you think of some different alternatives that Rice's board might consider for controlling the $4 million deficit?

1.9 Describe a decision that you have had to make recently that was difficult. What were the major issues? What were your alternatives? Did you have to deal with uncertainty? Were there important trade-offs to make?

1.10 "Socially responsible investing" first became fashionable in the 1980s. Such investing involves consideration of the kinds of businesses that a firm engages in and selection of investments that are as consistent as possible with the investor's sense of ethical and moral business activity. What trade-offs must the socially responsible investor make? How are these trade-offs more complicated than those that we normally consider in making investment decisions?

1.11 Many decisions are simple, preprogrammed, or already made. For example, retailers do not have to think long to decide how to deal with a new customer. Some operations research models provide "ready-made" decisions, such as finding an optimal inventory level using an order-quantity formula or determining an optimal production mix using linear programming. Contrast these decisions with unstructured or strategic decisions, such as choosing a career or locating a nuclear power plant. What kinds of decisions are appropriate for a decision-analysis approach? Comment on the statement, "Decision making is what you do when you don't know what to do." (For more discussion, see Howard 1980.)

1.12 The argument was made that beliefs and preferences can change as we explore and learn. This holds true even for learning about decision analysis. For example, what was your impression of this book before reading the first chapter? Have your beliefs about the value of decision analysis changed? How might this affect your decision about reading more of the book?

CASE STUDIES

COMMERCIAL SPACE TRAVEL

On October 4, 2004, at nearly 400,000 feet (70 miles) above the Mojave Desert, history and $10 million dollars were made. SpaceShipOne had completed its third required flight to claim the $10 million X Prize. The Ansari X Prize was created to jump start interest in commercial space travel and was similar to the hundreds of aviation-incentive prizes created in the early 20th century to help develop today's $300 billion commercial aviation industry. The X prize achieved its goal with 26 teams from seven countries spending over $100 million to make commercial space travel a future reality. Once inconceivable for non-governmental agencies, there are now several for-profit companies looking to enter the space-travel market. Sir Richard Branson created a new company, Virgin Galactic, and has ordered five spaceships from the creators of SpaceShipOne. Branson's ships will be larger, holding five passengers and one pilot. Virgin Galactic has already had 5,000 people make serious inquiries about tickets, which are currently running at $190,000 apiece. Another company, Space Adventures, is selling space-travel tickets for less than $100,000 and has advanced deposits of $10,000 from 100 customers. Not only did SpaceShipOne make history in being the first non-governmental group to launch people into space, but it may also have made history by launching a new industry. Only time will tell!

Questions

1. Clearly, there are potentially great risks associated with being blasted into space and then gliding back to earth. Many systems must work almost flawlessly for day-in and day-out space travel. This is rocket science after all. From your perspective, would you be an early adopter and want to be one of the first to fly into space? Or would you wait until the industry

was more mature? What factors would you include when thinking about commercial space travel?

2. The economics of space travel raises some interesting questions. These space-travel entrepreneurs believe that they can control costs better than governmental organizations. By being smaller and leaner, they can react quickly to changes in the marketplace. Peter Diamandis, the organizer of the X Prize,

summed up this sentiment by stating that these entrepreneurs were the "furry mammal(s) among the dinosaurs of the aerospace industry." Do you agree with this thinking, or do you believe that for-profit companies might cut corners to keep costs down and thereby be riskier?

Sources: Alan Boyle (2004), "SpaceShipOne wins $10 million X Prize," http://www.msnbc.msn.com/id/6167761/, Jan 14, 2009; http://space.xprize.org/ansari-x-prize, Jan 12, 2009.

DUPONT AND CHLOROFLUOROCARBONS

Chlorofluorocarbons (CFCs) are chemicals used as refrigerants in air conditioners and other cooling appliances, propellants in aerosol sprays, and in a variety of other applications. Scientific evidence has been accumulating for some time that CFCs released into the atmosphere can destroy ozone molecules in the ozone layer 15 miles above the earth's surface. This layer shields the earth from dangerous ultraviolet radiation. A large hole in the ozone layer above Antarctica has been found and attributed to CFCs, and a 1988 report by 100 scientists concluded that the ozone shield above the mid-Northern Hemisphere had shrunk by as much as 3% since 1969. Moreover, depletion of the ozone layer appears to be irreversible. Further destruction of the ozone layer could lead to crop failures, damage to marine ecology, and possibly dramatic changes in global weather patterns.

Environmentalists estimate that approximately 30% of the CFCs released into the atmosphere come from aerosols. In 1978, the U.S. government banned their use as aerosol propellants, but many foreign governments still permit them.

Some $2.5 billion of CFCs are sold each year, and DuPont Chemical Corporation is responsible for 25% of that amount. In early 1988, DuPont announced that the company would gradually phase out its production of CFCs and that replacements would be developed. Already DuPont claims to have a CFC substitute for automobile air conditioners, although the new substance is more expensive.

Questions

Imagine that you are a DuPont executive charged with making the decision regarding continued production of CFCs.

1. What issues would you take into account?
2. What major sources of uncertainty do you face?
3. What corporate objectives would be important for you to consider? Do you think that DuPont's corporate objectives and the way the company views the problem might have evolved since the mid-1970s when CFCs were just beginning to become an issue?

Sources: "A Gaping Hole in the Sky," *Newsweek*, July 11, 1988, pp. 21–23; A. M. Louis (1988), "DuPont to Ban Products That Harm Ozone," *San Francisco Chronicle*, March 25, p. 1.

CHOOSING A VICE-PRESIDENTIAL CANDIDATE

A presidential candidate in the U.S. chooses his own running mate (the vice-presidential candidate) and although the person chosen does not typically have a major impact on the election, the decision itself is scrutinized for insights into the candidate's leadership style. This was particularly true in 2008, when John McCain chose Sarah Palin. Senator McCain's decision astonished almost everyone; Palin was a little-known governor in Alaska and not on

any pundit's short list of candidates. As a woman, Palin could appeal to female voters. At the same time, although evangelicals and social conservatives were wary of McCain and his politics, Palin was a down-to-earth "hockey mom" who energized this central base of the Republican Party. In these ways, McCain's choice was shrewd.

As much as Palin complemented McCain, his decision entailed considerable risk. For example, by choosing Palin, McCain appeared to be contradicting one of his central arguments against his opponent Barack Obama, that Obama did not have the necessary experience to be president, particularly in foreign policy. While McCain repeatedly attacked Obama's lack of experience, he also repeatedly claimed that his running mate had the qualifications to step into the role of commander-in-chief immediately. The extent of Palin's foreign policy experience was famously summed up by her statement that one could see Russia from Alaska. Not a comforting endorsement for being one heartbeat away from the president! Choosing Palin as his running mate certainly raised questions about McCain's judgment.

Of course, at the time McCain chose Palin, he could not know exactly what effect the choice would have on his candidacy. But it is clear that, although the effect might be positive in some ways, if the negative effect turned out to be greater than expected, his chance of winning the election could be greatly reduced.

Questions

1. What do you think were the objectives of Senator McCain in choosing his vice-presidential running mate?

2. At 72, McCain would have been the oldest first-term president in U.S. history. In addition, he had had several bouts with the most serious form of skin cancer. How do you think these facts might have affected McCain's thinking about whom to choose as a running mate?

3. McCain described himself as a maverick and was known to have a quick temper and to be somewhat unpredictable in his politics. Although McCain's popularity stemmed partly from his independent streak, his choice of Palin sent a message that when making hard decisions, he might follow his gut as opposed to a more reasoned and well-thought-out analysis. What kinds of decisions might a president have to make based on his gut or intuition, and which ones might benefit from careful thought and analysis?

4. A central theme of McCain's campaign was to put "country first" above political considerations. Do you think McCain's choice of Sarah Palin reflects the objective of putting the country first over politics? Why or why not?

REFERENCES

The decision-analysis view is distinctly *prescriptive*. That is, decision analysis helps people make better decisions; in contrast, a *descriptive* view of decision making focuses on how people actually make decisions. Keeney and Raiffa (1976) explain the prescriptive view as well as anyone. For an excellent summary of the descriptive approach, see Hogarth (1987). Bell, Raiffa, and Tversky (1988) provide many readings on these topics.

A fundamental element of the prescriptive approach is discerning and accepting the difference between a good decision and a lucky outcome. This issue has been discussed by many authors, both academics and practitioners. An excellent reference is Vlek et al. (1984).

Many other books and articles describe the decision-analysis process, and each seems to have its own twist. This chapter has drawn heavily from Ron Howard's thoughts; his 1988 article summarizes his approach. Other books worth consulting include Behn and Vaupel (1982), Brown (2005), Bunn (1984), Hammond, Keeney, and Raiffa (1999), Holloway

(1979), Keeney (1992), Lindley (1985), Raiffa (1968), Samson (1988), Skinner (1999), and von Winterfeldt and Edwards (1986). Phillips's (1982, 1984) idea of a requisite decision model is a fundamental concept that we will use throughout the text. For a related view, see Watson and Buede (1987).

Behn, R. D., and J. D. Vaupel (1982) *Quick Analysis for Busy Decision Makers*. New York: Basic Books.

Bell, D., H. Raiffa, and A. Tversky (1988) *Decision Making: Descriptive, Normative, and Prescriptive Interactions*. Cambridge, MA: Cambridge University Press.

Brown, R. (2005) *Rational Choice and Judgment: Decision Analysis for the Decider*. Hoboken, NJ: Wiley.

Bunn, D. (1984) *Applied Decision Analysis*. New York: McGraw-Hill.

Clemen, R. T., and R. C. Kwit (2001) "The Value of Decision Analysis at Eastman Kodak Company, 1990–1999." *Interfaces*, 31, 74–92.

Corner, J. L., and C. W. Kirkwood (1991) "Decision Analysis Applications in the Operations Research Literature, 1970–1989." *Operations Research*, 39, 206–219.

Hammond, J. S., R. L. Keeney, and H. Raiffa (1999) *Smart Choices: A Practical Guide to Making Better Decisions*. Boston, MA: Harvard Business School Press.

Hogarth, R. (1987) *Judgments and Choice*, 2nd ed. New York: Wiley.

Holloway, C. A. (1979) *Decision Making under Uncertainty: Models and Choices*. Englewood Cliffs, NJ: Prentice-Hall.

Howard, R. A. (1980) "An Assessment of Decision Analysis." *Operations Research*, 28, 4–27.

Howard, R. A. (1988) "Decision Analysis: Practice and Promise," *Management Science*, 34, 679–695.

Keefer, D., C. Kirkwood, and J. Corner (2004). "Perspective on Decision Analysis Applications, 1990–2001." *Decision Analysis*, 1, 4–22.

Keeney, R. (1992) *Value-Focused Thinking*. Cambridge, MA: Harvard University Press.

Keeney, R., and H. Raiffa (1976) *Decisions with Multiple Objectives*. New York: Wiley.

Lindley, D. V. (1985) *Making Decisions*, 2nd ed. New York: Wiley.

Phillips, L. D. (1982) "Requisite Decision Modelling." *Journal of the Operational Research Society*, 33, 303–312.

Phillips, L. D. (1984) "A Theory of Requisite Decision Models." *Acta Psychologica*, 56, 29–48.

Raiffa, H. (1968) *Decision Analysis*. Reading, MA: Addison-Wesley.

Rubin, R. E., and J. Weisberg (2003) *In an Uncertain World*, New York, NY: Random House.

Samson, D. (1988) *Managerial Decision Analysis*. Homewood, IL: Irwin.

Skinner, D. C. (1999) *Introduction to Decision Analysis, 2nd Edition*. Gainesville, FL: Probabilistic Publishing.

Vlek, C., W. Edwards, I. Kiss, G. Majone, and M. Toda (1984) "What Constitutes a Good Decision?" *Acta Psychologica*, 56, 5–27.

von Winterfeldt, D., and W. Edwards (1986) *Decision Analysis and Behavioral Research*. Cambridge: Cambridge University Press.

Watson, S., and D. Buede (1987) *Decision Synthesis*. Cambridge: Cambridge University Press.

EPILOGUE

What did Rice's Board of Regents decide? In short, they decided to keep their football program in Division I-A. But that is not all. A problem of this magnitude required a multifaceted solution. They also recommended that the athletic department's deficit be reduced, while a new basketball arena and a new student-faculty fitness center be built. This would pull funds away from football toward the more general needs of the campus. In addition, they required all athletes to go through the same admissions process used for nonathletes.

To meet these new economic and recruiting requirements, Rice Athletic Director Bobby May enlisted volunteers and football players to canvass the area with phone calls selling season tickets. As a result, season ticket sales increased 14% in 2005.

A new director of fund raising was also hired and immediately increased revenues at the annual black-tie dinner to nearly $500,000.

For the first two years, the football team itself struggled in Division I-A. Rice had a 14-game losing streak from 2004 to 2005 and went 1–10 in 2005. It was not until 2006 that Rice's football team qualified for its first lucrative bowl game, their first bowl appearance since 1961. The 2007 and 2008 seasons were also successful for Rice football; in 2008 they won their first bowl game in 55 years.

Source: Amy Merrick (2004, September 20). Football (A Special Report); Another Money-Losing Season: College football: Can't live with it, can't live without it; Just ask Rice University. Wall Street Journal (Eastern Edition); http://en.wikipedia.org/wiki /Rice_University, January 14, 2009.

SECTION 1

Modeling Decisions

This first section is about modeling decisions. Chapter 2 presents a short discussion on the elements of a decision. Through a series of simple examples, the basic elements are illustrated: values and objectives, decisions to be made, upcoming uncertain events, and consequences. The focus is on identifying the basic elements. This skill is necessary for modeling decisions as described in Chapters 3, 4, and 5.

In Chapter 3, we learn how to create graphical structures for decision models. First we consider values and objectives, discussing in depth how multiple objectives can be organized in hierarchies and networks that can provide insight and help to generate creative alternatives. We also develop both influence diagrams and decision trees as graphical modeling tools for representing the basic structure of decisions. An influence diagram is particularly useful for developing the structure of a complex decision problem because it allows many aspects of a problem to be displayed in a compact and intuitive form. A decision-tree representation provides an alternative picture of a decision in which more of the details can be displayed. Both graphical techniques can be used to represent single-objective decisions, but we show how they can be used in multiple-objective situations as well. We end Chapter 3 with a discussion of measurement, presenting concepts and techniques that can be used to ensure that we can adequately measure achievement of our objectives, whether those objectives are straightforward (e.g., maximizing dollars or saving time) or more difficult to quantify (e.g., minimizing environmental damage).

Chapters 4 and 5 present the basic tools available to the decision maker for analyzing a decision model. Chapter 4 shows how to solve decision trees and influence diagrams. The basic concept presented is *expected value*. When we are concerned with monetary outcomes, we call this *expected monetary value* and abbreviate it as EMV. In analyzing a decision, EMV is calculated for each of the available alternatives. In many decision situations it is reasonable to choose the alternative with the highest EMV. In addition to the EMV criterion, Chapter 4 also looks briefly at the idea of risk analysis and the uses of a stochastic-dominance criterion for making decisions. Finally, we show how expected value and risk analysis can be used in multiple-objective decisions.

In Chapter 5 we learn how to use sensitivity-analysis tools in concert with EMV calculations in the iterative decision-structuring and analysis process. After an initial basic model is built, sensitivity analysis can tell which of the input variables really matter in the decision and deserve more attention in the model. Thus, with Chapter 5 we bring the discussion of modeling decisions full circle, showing how structuring and analysis are intertwined in the decision-analysis process.

Finally, Chapter 6 delves into issues relating to organizational decision making and using decision analysis in organizations.

CHAPTER **2**

Elements of Decision Problems

When facing a hard decision, the difficulty is not in thinking about particular aspects of the elements; rather the difficulty lies in making sure all the important issues are thought through. Difficult decisions are by their very nature attention grabbers, and without any structure to follow, the tendency is to jump around from issue to issue. Instead of a haphazard approach, decision analysis starts by identifying the components or elements of the decision. In this chapter, we show how to identify the four decision elements: (1) values and objectives, (2) decisions, (3) uncertain events, and (4) consequences. Later chapters delve into the details of defining these elements precisely and incorporating them into decision analysis models.

VALUES AND OBJECTIVES

Imagine a farmer whose trees are laden with fruit that is nearly ripe. Even without an obvious problem to solve or decision to make, we can consider the farmer's objectives. Certainly one objective is to harvest the fruit successfully. This may be important because the fruit can then be sold, providing money to keep the farm operating, and the profit can be spent for the welfare of the family. The farmer may have other objectives as well, such as minimizing harvest costs, maximizing produce quality, or obtaining an organic certificate for his farm.

Our values and objectives determine to a great extent what it is we want to achieve, and thus which alternatives are attractive to us as individuals. For example, if our farmer were facing possible bankruptcy, he would have little interest in long-term payoffs such as a 5-year preparatory period for organic certification. The better we understand what is important and exactly what it is we want to achieve, the easier it is to know which alternative is best. Thus, the first decision element is determining exactly what it is the decision maker wishes to achieve in the context of the decision.

Although it seems natural to align our actions with our goals, when making decisions most people do not do this explicitly. The usual reaction someone has when facing a difficult decision is to focus on the available alternatives and try to choose the best one. However, it may not be clear exactly what "best" means without some serious thought. By stepping back and determining what is important in the particular decision situation, we can develop a deeper understanding of how the alternatives might help us achieve our objectives, and so we can make better decisions.

Before proceeding, let's take a moment to clarify what we mean by "values and objectives." The term *values* is often overused and can be ambiguous; here we use it in a general sense to mean the things that matter to us. For example, new graduates may have to choose from among a number of job opportunities, and their values are the things they care about in choosing a job. Typical values of graduates include compensation, prestige, healthy work-place environment, housing, and cost-of-living, with time off to spend with family and friends. A scientist may be interested in developing a deep understanding of the basic principles in her discipline. An investor wants to earn a high return on her investments. A manager, like our farmer, wants to run a successful business.

An *objective* is something specific we want to achieve and further defines our values. For example, maximizing salary, maximizing medical benefits, and maximizing retirement savings further defines compensation. The farmer's objective of maximizing profit defines his value of running a successful business. Of course, some objectives are related. The farmer may want profits to purchase food and housing for his family, to fund capital improvements for his farm, or to take a vacation.

An individual's objectives taken together make up his or her values. They define what is important in the context of a specific decision. We can make an even bolder statement: A person's values are the reason for making decisions in the first place! If we did not care about anything, there would be no reason to make decisions at all, because we would not care how things turned out. Moreover, we would not be able to choose from among different alternatives. Without objectives, it would not be possible to tell which alternative would be the best choice.

Making Money: A Special Objective

In modern society, most adults work for a living, and if we ask them why, they will all include in their answers something about the importance of making money. It would appear that making money is an important objective, but a few simple questions—Why is money important? What would you do if you had a million dollars?—quickly reveal that money is important because it helps us do things that we want to do. For many people, money is important because it allows us to eat, afford housing and clothing, travel, engage in activities with friends, and generally live comfortably. Many people spend money on insurance because they have an objective of avoiding risks. For very few individuals is money important in and of itself. Unlike King Midas, most of us do not want to earn money simply to have it; money is important because it provides the means by which we can work toward more basic objectives.

Money's special role as a trading mechanism allows us to use money as a *proxy objective* in many situations. In other words, even though money is typically not an objective in its own right, it can stand in as an objective. For example, imagine a young couple who wants to take a vacation. They will probably need to save money before achieving this goal, and they will face many choices regarding just how to go about saving their money. In many of these decisions, even though their objective is the vacation, their main concern will be how much money they will have when they are ready for the holiday. Thus, money provides an easily understood and measurable way to achieve certain objectives.

For corporations, money, or more precisely increasing shareholders' wealth, is often the primary objective and is measured in terms of earnings per share, dividends, and increased company value. The shareholders themselves can, of course, use their wealth for their own welfare in any way they want. Because the shareholders have the opportunity to trade their wealth to achieve specific objectives, the company need not be concerned with those objectives but can focus on making its shareholders as wealthy as possible.

Using money as an objective has advantages; money is universally understood, measurable, and greatly simplifies making trade-offs because it allows different objectives to be put on the same scale. For example, when purchasing a new car, how much more would we be willing to pay for side air bags? How much more for a premium stereo system? If we wanted to keep the cost down and were deciding between air bags and a stereo, how would we choose between such disparate items? These questions may be difficult to answer, but everyone makes related decisions all the time as we decide whether a product or service is worth its price. The process of placing a monetary value on different objectives is called *pricing out*. It allows us to put different objectives on the same scale, making comparisons and trade-offs easier. Thus, if the stereo costs $1,200 and airbags cost $400, the comparison is much easier; is the stereo system worth three times as much as the airbags?

While pricing out is helpful, it is not always reasonable. Consider the ethical problems faced by a hospital that performs organ transplants. Wealthy individuals can pay more for their operations, and are often willing to do so in order to move up in the queue. The additional money may permit the hospital to purchase new equipment or perform more transplants for needy individuals. But moving the wealthy patient up in the queue will delay surgery for other patients, perhaps with fatal consequences. What if the other patients include young children? Pricing out lives and risks seems like a cold-hearted way to make this decision; rather, the hospital managers might be better off focusing on the hospital's fundamental objectives and how to accomplish them with or without the wealthy patient's fee.

Values and the Current Decision Context

Suppose you have carefully thought about all of your objectives. Among other things you want to do what you can to reduce homelessness in your community, learn to identify birds, send your children to college, and retire at age 55. Having spent the morning figuring out your objectives, you have become hungry and are ready for a good meal. Your decision is where to go for lunch, and it is obvious that the large scale, overall objectives that you have spent all morning thinking about will not be much help.

You can still think hard about your objectives, though, as you consider your lunch decision. It is just that different objectives are appropriate for this particular decision. Do you want a lot to eat or a little? Do you want to save money? Are you interested in a particular type of ethnic food, or would you like to try a new restaurant? If you are going out with friends, what are their preferences? What about a picnic instead of a restaurant meal?

Each specific decision situation calls for specific objectives. We call the setting in which the decision occurs the *decision context*. In one case, a decision context might be deciding where to go for lunch, in which case the appropriate objectives involve satisfying hunger, spending time with friends, and so on. In another case, the context might be what to choose for a career, which would call for consideration of more global or fundamental objectives, such as what do we want to accomplish in our lifetime?

Values and decision context go hand in hand. Every decision situation involves a specific context, and that context determines which objectives need to be considered. The idea of a requisite model comes into play here. A requisite decision model includes all of the objectives that matter, and only those that matter, to the decision context at hand. Without all the appropriate objectives considered, we are left with a gnawing concern that "something is missing," and considering superfluous or inappropriate objectives can distract us from the truly important issues.

When facing a difficult decision, it is worthwhile spending time on thinking about which objectives are appropriate to the specific context. Aside from clarifying what is important in that context, being clear about the relevant objectives can help avoid focusing on irrelevant issues. When the decision context is specified and appropriate objectives aligned with the context, the decision maker knows what the situation is and exactly why he or she cares about making a decision in that situation.

Finding realistic examples in which individuals or companies use their objectives in decision making is easy. In the following example, the Boeing Company found itself needing to acquire a new supercomputer.

Boeing's Supercomputer	As a large-scale manufacturer of sophisticated aircraft, Boeing needs computing power for tasks ranging from accounting and word processing to computer-aided design, inventory control and tracking, and manufacturing support. When the company's engineering department needed to expand its high-power computing capacity by purchasing a supercomputer, the managers faced a huge task of assembling and evaluating massive amounts of information. There were systems requirements and legal issues to consider, as well as price and a variety of management issues.

Source: D. Barnhart, (1993) "Decision Analysis Software Helps Boeing Select Supercomputer." *OR/MS Today*, April, 62–63.

FIGURE **2.1**
Objectives for
Boeing's
supercomputer.

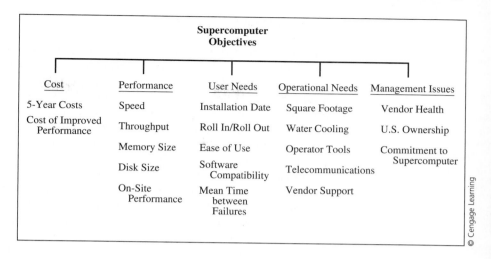

**Supercomputer
Objectives**

Cost	Performance	User Needs	Operational Needs	Management Issues
5-Year Costs	Speed	Installation Date	Square Footage	Vendor Health
Cost of Improved Performance	Throughput	Roll In/Roll Out	Water Cooling	U.S. Ownership
	Memory Size	Ease of Use	Operator Tools	Commitment to Supercomputer
	Disk Size	Software Compatibility	Telecommunications	
	On-Site Performance	Mean Time between Failures	Vendor Support	

© Cengage Learning

Boeing's decision context is acquiring supercomputing capacity for its engineering needs. Even though the company undoubtedly has global objectives related to aircraft production, maximizing shareholder wealth, and providing good working conditions for its employees, in the current decision context the appropriate objectives are specific to the company's computing requirements.

Organizing all of Boeing's objectives in this decision context is complex because of the many different computer users involved and their needs. With careful thought though, management was able to specify five main objectives: minimize costs, maximize performance, satisfy user needs, satisfy organizational needs, and satisfy management issues. Each of these main objectives can be further broken down into different aspects, as shown in Figure 2.1.

DECISIONS TO MAKE

With the decision context understood and values well in hand, the decision maker can identify the second of the four decision elements: decisions to make. Consider our farmer whose fruit crop will need to be harvested soon. If the weather report forecasts mild weather, the farmer has nothing to worry about, but if the forecast is for freezing weather, he might be willing to spend some money on protective measures that will save the crop. In such a situation, the farmer has a decision to make, and that decision is whether or not to take protective action. This is a decision that must be made with the available information.

Many situations have as the central issue a decision that must be made right away. There would always be at least two alternatives; if there were no alternatives, then it would not be a matter of making a decision! In the case of the farmer, the alternatives are to take protective action or to leave matters as they are. Of course, there may be a wide variety of alternatives. For example, the farmer may have several strategies for saving the crop, and it may be possible to implement one or more.

In addition to specifying the alternatives, we also need to know when the decision must be made. For example, our intrepid farmer might need to make his decision first thing in the morning or might be able to wait and obtain more information. If the current weather report suggests the possibility of freezing weather depending on exactly where a weather system travels, then it may be reasonable to wait to determine the storm's direction. Such a strategy, however, may entail a cost. The farmer may have to pay his hired help overtime if the decision to protect the crop is made late in the day. Some measures may take time to set up; if the farmer waits, there may not be enough time to implement some of these procedures.

Other possible alternatives are taking out insurance or hedging. For example, the farmer might be willing to pay the harvesting crew a small amount to be available at night if quick action is needed. Insurance policies also may be available to protect against crop loss (although these typically are not available at the last minute). Any of these alternatives might give the farmer more flexibility but would probably cost something up front.

Identifying the immediate decision to be made is a critical step in understanding a difficult decision situation. Moreover, no model of the decision situation can be built without knowing exactly what the decision problem at hand is. In identifying the central decision, it is important to specify the possible alternatives and understand the timing. Some decisions will have specific alternatives (protect the crop or not), while others may involve choosing a specific value out of a range of possible values (deciding on an amount to bid for a company you want to acquire). Timing is important because the information available to us changes over time as do the set of viable alternatives. Other than the obvious alternative courses of action, a decision maker should always consider the possibilities of doing nothing, of waiting to obtain more information, or of somehow hedging against possible losses.

Sequential Decisions

In many cases, there simply is no single decision to make, but several sequential decisions. The orchard example will demonstrate this. Suppose that several weeks of the growing season remain. Each day the farmer will get a new weather forecast, and each time there is a forecast of adverse weather, it will be necessary to decide once again whether to protect the crop.

The example shows clearly that the farmer has a number of decisions to make, and the decisions are ordered sequentially. If the harvest is tomorrow, the decision is fairly easy, but if several days or weeks remain, the farmer really has to think about the upcoming decisions. For example, it might be worthwhile to adopt a policy whereby the amount spent on protection is less than the value of the crop. One good way to do this would be not to protect during the early part of the growing season; instead, wait until the harvest is closer, and then protect whenever the weather forecast warrants such action. In other words, "If we're going to lose the crop, let's lose it early."

It is important to recognize that in many situations one decision leads eventually to another in a sequence. The orchard example is a special case because the decisions are almost identical from one day to the next: Take protective

FIGURE **2.2**
Sequential
decisions.

A decision maker needs
to consider decisions to
be made now and in the
future.

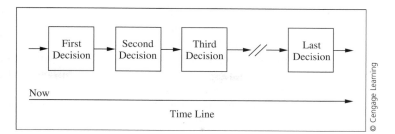

action or not. In many cases, however, the decisions are radically different. For example, a manufacturer considering a new product might first decide whether or not to introduce it. If the decision is to go ahead, the next decision might be whether to produce it or subcontract the production. Once the production decision is made, there may be marketing decisions about distribution, promotion, and pricing.

When a decision situation is complicated by sequential decisions, a decision maker will want to consider future decisions when making the immediate decision. Furthermore, a future decision may depend on exactly what happened before. For this reason, we refer to these kinds of problems as *dynamic* decision situations. In identifying elements of a decision situation, we want to know not only what specific decisions are to be made, but the sequence in which they will arise. Figure 2.2 shows graphically a sequence of decisions, represented by squares, mapped along a time line.

UNCERTAIN EVENTS

In Chapter 1 we saw that decision problems can be complicated because of uncertainty about what the future holds. Many important decisions have to be made without knowing exactly what will happen in the future or exactly what the ultimate outcome will be. A classic example is that of investing in the stock market. An investor may be in a position to buy some stock, but in which company? Some share prices will go up and others down, but it is difficult to tell exactly what will happen. Moreover, the market as a whole may move up or down, depending on economic forces. The best the investor can do is to think very carefully about the chances associated with each different security's price as well as the market as a whole.

The possible ways an uncertain event can turn out are called *outcomes*. Considering the decision context in the orchard example, the key uncertain event is the weather, with outcomes of crop damage or no crop damage. With some situations, such as with the orchard, there are only a few possible outcomes. In other cases, such as the stock market, the outcome is a value within some range. That is, next year's price of the security bought today for $50 per share may be anywhere between, say, $0 and $100. (It certainly could never be worth less than zero, but the upper limit is not so well defined; various individuals might consider different upper limits for the same stock.)

The point is that the outcome of the uncertain event that we call "next year's stock price" comes from a range of possible values and may fall anywhere within that range.

Many different uncertain events might be considered in a decision situation, but only some are relevant. How can you tell which are relevant? The answer is straightforward; the outcome of the event must have some impact on at least one of your objectives. That is, it should matter to you what actually comes to pass. Although this seems like common sense, in a complex decision situation it can be all too easy to concentrate on uncertain events that we can get information about rather than those that really have an impact in terms of our objectives. For example, unsophisticated investors may focus on short-term price fluctuations because these are easy to see day-to-day, whereas the overall market trend and company performance are more difficult to determine, but are more relevant.

Of course, a decision situation often involves more than one uncertain event. The larger the number of uncertain but relevant events in a given situation, the more complicated the decision. Moreover, some uncertain events may depend on others. For example, the price of the specific stock purchased may be more likely to go up if the economy as a whole continues to grow or if the overall stock market increases in value. Thus there may be interdependencies among the uncertain events that a decision maker should consider.

How do uncertain events relate to the decisions in Figure 2.2? They must be dovetailed with the time sequence of the decisions to be made; it is important to know at each decision exactly what information is available and what remains unknown. At the current time ("Now" on the time line), all of the uncertain events are just that; their outcomes are unknown, although the decision maker can look into the future and specify which uncertainties will be resolved prior to each upcoming decision. For example, in the dynamic orchard decision, on any given day the farmer knows what the weather has been in the past but not what the weather will be in the future.

Sometimes an uncertain event that is resolved before a decision provides information relevant for future decisions. Consider the stock market problem. If the investor is considering investing in a company that is involved in a lawsuit, one alternative might be to wait until the lawsuit is resolved. Note that the sequence of decisions is (1) wait or buy now, and (2) if waiting, then buy or do not buy after the lawsuit. The decision to buy or not may depend crucially on the outcome of the lawsuit that occurs between the two decisions.

What if there are many uncertain events that occur between decisions? There may be a natural order to the uncertain events, or there may not. If there is, then specifying that order during modeling of the decision problem may help the decision maker. But the order of events between decisions is not nearly as crucial as the dovetailing of decisions and events to clarify what events are unknown and what information is available for each decision in the process. It is the time sequence of the decisions that matters, along with the information available at each decision. In Figure 2.3, uncertain events, represented by circles, are dovetailed with a sequence of decisions. An arrow from a group of uncertain events to a decision indicates that the outcomes of

FIGURE **2.3**
Dovetailing
uncertain events
and sequential
decisions.

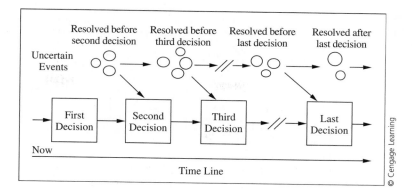

those events are known at the time the decision is made. Of course, the decision maker is like the proverbial elephant and never forgets what has happened. For upcoming decisions, he or she should be able to recall (possibly with the aid of notes and documents) everything that happened up to that point including decisions made and event outcomes.

CONSEQUENCES

After the last decision has been made and the last uncertain event has been resolved, the decision maker's fate is finally determined. It may be a matter of profit or loss as in the case of the farmer. It may be a matter of increase in value of the investor's portfolio. In some cases the final consequence may be a "net value" figure that accounts for both cash outflows and inflows throughout the process. This might happen in the case of the manufacturer deciding about a new product; certain costs must be incurred (development, raw materials, advertising) before any revenue is obtained.

If the decision context requires consideration of multiple objectives, the consequence is what happens for each objective. For example, when deciding which job offer to accept, there is a consequence for salary, for cost of living, for advancement opportunities, and so on. For each objective we feel is important, we will have a consequence that measures the extent to which that objective is achieved.

In our graphical scheme, we must think about the consequence at the end of the time line after all decisions are made and all uncertain events are resolved. For example, the consequence for the farmer after deciding whether to protect his crop and then experiencing the weather might be a profit of $15,000 or a loss of $3,400. For the job offers it might be a salary of $70,000, high cost of living, and high level of stress; or $48,000, low cost of living, and moderate stress. Thus, the end of the time line is reached when the decision maker knows all of the results. Looking forward from the current time and current decision, the end of the time line is called the *planning horizon*. Figure 2.4 shows how consequences fit into our graphical scheme.

FIGURE **2.4**
Including the
consequence.

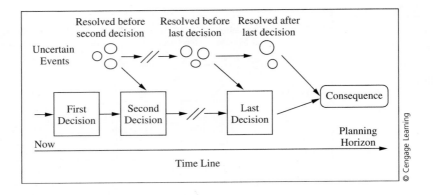

Time Line

What is an appropriate planning horizon? For the farmer, the answer is relatively easy; the appropriate planning horizon is at the time of the harvest. But for the job offers, this question may not be so simple. Is the appropriate horizon the following year, during which we can pay off student loans? Or is it a several years down the road so that we can include future career directions? For the investor, how far ahead should the planning horizon be? A week? A month? Several years? For individuals planning for retirement, the planning horizon may be years in the future. For speculators making trades on the floor of a commodity exchange, the planning horizon may be only minutes into the future.

Thus, one of the fundamental issues with which a decision maker must come to grips is how far into the future to look. It is always possible to look farther ahead; there will always be more decisions to make, and earlier decisions may have some effect on the availability of later alternatives. Even death is not an obvious planning horizon because the decision maker may be concerned with effects on future generations; environmental policy decisions provide perfect examples. At some point the decision maker has to stop and say, "My planning horizon is there. It's not worthwhile for me to think beyond that point in time." For the purpose of constructing a requisite model, the idea is to choose a planning horizon such that the events and decisions that would follow after are not essential parts of the immediate decision problem. To put it another way, choose a planning horizon that is consistent with your decision context and the relevant objectives.

Once the dimensions of the consequences and the planning horizon have been determined, the next step is to figure out how to value the consequences. As mentioned, in many cases it will be possible to work in terms of monetary values. That is, the only relevant objective in the decision context is to make money, so all that matters at the end is profit, cost, or total wealth. Or it may be possible to price out nonmonetary objectives as discussed previously. For example, a manager might be considering whether to build and run a day care center for the benefit of the employees. One objective might be to enhance the goodwill between the company and the workforce. Enhanced goodwill would in turn affect the operations of the company in certain ways, including reduced absenteeism, improved ability to recruit, and a better image in the community. Some of these, such as the reduced absenteeism and improved recruiting, could easily be translated into dollars. Improving the company's image may be more difficult to translate, but the manager might assess its value subjectively by estimating how much money it would cost in terms of public relations work to improve the firm's image by the same amount.

In some cases, however, it will be difficult to determine exactly how the different objectives should be traded off. In the hospital case discussed earlier, how should the administrator trade off the risks to patients who would be displaced in the queue versus the fee paid by a wealthy patient? How much more are you willing to pay, and how much additional CO_2 are you willing to put into the atmosphere in order to drive a higher-performance car? To fight terrorism, how much are we willing to curtail civil liberties? How much damage to the environment are we willing to accept in order to increase the U.S. supply of domestic oil? How much in the way of health risks are we willing to accept in order to have blemish-free fruits and vegetables? Many decisions, especially governmental policy decisions, are complicated by trade-offs like these. Even personal decisions, such as taking a job or purchasing a home, require a decision maker to think hard about the trade-offs involved.

The Time Value of Money: A Special Kind of Trade-Off

One of the most common consequences in personal and business decisions is a stream of cash flows. For example, an investor may spend money on a project (an initial cash outflow) in order to obtain revenue in the future (cash inflows) over a period of years. In such a case, there is a special kind of trade-off: spending dollars today to obtain dollars tomorrow. If a dollar today were worth the same as a dollar next year, then we would trade dollars equally between dollars today and dollars in the future. However, this is not the case. A dollar today can be invested in a savings account or other interest-bearing security; at the end of a year, one dollar invested now would be worth one dollar plus the interest paid. Thus, a dollar today is worth more than a dollar tomorrow.

Trade-offs between current and future dollars (and between future dollars at different points in time) refer to the fact that the value of a dollar depends on when it is available to the decision maker. Because of this, we often refer to the "time value of money." Fortunately, there is a straightforward way to collapse a stream of cash flows into a single number. This number is called the *present value*, or value in present dollars, of the stream of cash flows.

Suppose, for example, that you have $100 in your pocket. If you put that money into a savings account that earns 10% per year, paid annually, then you would have $100 × 1.1 = $110 at the end of the year. At the end of 2 years, the balance in the account would be $110 plus another 10%, or $110 × 1.1 = $121. In fact, you can see that the amount you have is just the original $100 multiplied by 1.1 twice: $121 = $100 × 1.1 × 1.1 = $100 × 1.1^2. If you keep the money in the account for 5 years, say, then the interest compounds for 5 years. The account balance would be $100 × 1.1^5 = $161.05.

We can also use this idea of interest rates to work backward. Suppose, for example, that someone promises that you can have $110 next year. What is this worth to you right now? If you have available some sort of investment like a savings account that pays 10% per year, then you would have to invest $100 in order to get $110 next year. Thus, the present value of the $110 that arrives next year is $110/1.1 = $100. Similarly, the present value of $121 dollars promised at the end of 2 years is $121/(1.1^2) = $100.

In general, we will talk about the present value of an amount x that will be received at the end of n time periods. Of course, we must know the appropriate interest rate. Let r denote the interest rate per time period in decimal form; that is, if the interest rate is 10%, then $r = 0.10$. With this notation, the formula for calculating present value (PV) is:

$$PV(x, n, r) = \frac{x}{(1 + r)^n}$$

The denominator in this formula is a number greater than 1. Thus, dividing x by $(1 + r)^n$ will give a present value that is less than x. For this reason, we often say that we "discount" x back to the present. You can see that if you had the discounted amount now $(x/(1 + r)^n)$ and could invest it at the interest rate r, then after n time periods (days, months, years, and so on) the value of the investment would be the discounted amount times $(1 + r)^n$, which is simply x.

When computing the present value, be careful to keep the interest rate consistent with the time periods. For example, a savings account may pay 10% "compounded monthly." A year is actually 12 time periods, and so $n = 12$. The monthly interest rate is 10%/12, or 0.8333%. Thus, the value of $100 deposited in the account and left for a year would be $100 × (1 + 10%/12)^{12} = $100 × (1.00833)^{12} = $110.47. Notice that compounding helps because the interest itself earns interest during each time period. Thus, if you have a choice among savings accounts that have the same interest rate, the one that compounds more frequently will have a higher eventual payoff.

We can now talk about the present value of a stream of cash flows. Suppose that a friend is involved in a business deal and offers to let you in on it. For $425 paid to him now, he says, you can have $110.00 next year, $121.00 the following year, $133.10 the third year, and $146.41 at the end of Year 4. This is a great deal, he says, because your payments will total $510.51.

What is the present value of the stream of payments? (You probably can guess already!) Let us suppose you put your money into a savings account at 10%, compounded annually. Then we would calculate the present value of the stream of cash flows as the sum of the present values of the individual cash flows:

$$PV = \frac{110.0}{(1.1)^1} + \frac{121.0}{(1.1)^2} + \frac{133.10}{(1.1)^3} + \frac{146.41}{(1.1)^4}$$

$$= \$100 + \$100 + \$100 + \$100 = \$400$$

Thus, the deal is not so great. You would be paying $425 for a stream of cash flows that has a present value of only $400. The *net present value* (NPV) of the cash flows is the present value of the cash flows ($400) minus the cost of the deal ($425), or −$25; you would be better off keeping your $425 and investing it in the savings account.

The formula for calculating NPV for a stream of cash flows $x_0, x_1, ..., x_n$ over n periods at interest rate r is:

$$NPV = \frac{x_0}{(1+r)^0} + \frac{x_1}{(1+r)^1} + \cdots + \frac{x_n}{(1+r)^n}$$

$$= \sum_{i=0}^{n} \frac{x_i}{(1+r)^i}$$

In general, we can have both outflows (negative numbers) and inflows. In the example, we could include the cash outflow of $425 as a negative number in calculating NPV:

$$NPV = \frac{-425.00}{(1.1)^0} + \frac{100.00}{(1.1)^1} + \frac{121.0}{(1.1)^2} + \frac{133.10}{(1.1)^3} + \frac{146.41}{(1.1)^4}$$

$$= -\$425 + \$400$$

$$= -\$25$$

(Recall that raising any number to the zero power is equal to 1, and so $(1.1)^0 = 1$.) Clearly, we can use NPV to deal with any stream of cash flows. There could be one big inflow and then a bunch of outflows (such as obtaining and then repaying a loan), or there could be a large outflow (buying a machine), then some inflows (revenue), another outflow (maintenance costs), and so on. When NPV is calculated, it reveals the value of the stream of cash flows. A negative NPV for a project indicates that the money would be better invested elsewhere to earn interest rate r.

We began our discussion by talking about trade-offs. You can see how calculating present values establishes trade-offs between dollars at one point in time and dollars at another. That is, you would be indifferent between receiving $1 now or $1(1 + r)$ at the end of the next time period. More generally, $1 now is worth $1(1 + r)^n$ at the end of n time periods. NPV works by using these trade-off rates to discount all the cash flows back to the present.

Knowing the interest rate is the key in using present-value analysis. What is the appropriate interest rate? In general, it is the interest rate that you could get for investing your money in the next best opportunity. Often we use the interest rate from a savings account, a certificate of deposit, or short-term (money market) securities. For a corporation, the appropriate interest rate might be the interest rate they would have to pay in order to raise money by issuing bonds. If a firm is considering a project that is typical for them (for example, an electric utility that runs wind farms and is considering adding another 20 wind turbines), the firm will use its weighted average cost of capital (WACC). The firm's WACC is the amount of interest it must pay for every dollar it finances, including interest on debt and dividends on equity shares, and thus represents the overall required return for the firm. Often the interest rate used is called the *hurdle rate*, indicating that an acceptable investment must earn at least this rate.

We have talked about the elements of decision problems: objectives, decisions to make, uncertain events, and consequences. The discussion of the time value of money showed how a consequence that is a stream of cash flows can be valued through the trade-offs implicit in interest rates. Now it is time to put all of this together and try it out in an example. Imagine the problems that an oil company might face in putting together a plan for dealing with a major oil spill. Here are managers in the fictitious "Larkin Oil" struggling with this situation.

Larkin Oil	Pat Mills was restless. The Oil Spill Contingency Plan Committee was supposed to develop a draft Facility Response Plan (FRP) for review and approval by top management of Larkin Oil, Inc. An FRP is mandated under federal law and, among other items, provides a contingency plan in case there is an oil spill. The committee had lots of time; the CEO had asked for a draft FRP within three months. This was their first meeting.

Over the past hour, Sandy Wilton and Marty Kelso had argued about exactly what level of resources should be committed to planning for a major oil spill in the company's main shipping terminal bay.

"Look," said Sandy, "We've been over this so many times. If an oil spill actually occurs, we will have to move fast to clean it up. To do that, we have to have dedicated equipment ready to go along with the qualified individuals ready to manage the developing situation."

"But having equipment and personnel on standby like that means tying up a lot of capital," Chris Brown replied. As a member of the financial staff, Chris was sensitive to committing capital for equipment that would be idle all the time and might actually have to be replaced before it was ever used. "We'd be better off keeping extensive records, maybe just a long list of equipment that would be useful in a major cleanup. We need to know where it is, what it's capable of, what its condition is, and how to transport it. We will also need to ensure that our dedicated personnel are adequately leveraged for other tasks to economize staffing costs."

"Come to think of it, our list will also have to include information on transportation equipment and strategies," Leslie Taylor added.

Pat finally stirred. "You know what bothers me? We're talking about these alternatives, and the fact that we need to do thus and so in order to accomplish such and such. We're getting the cart before the horse. We just don't have our hands on the problem yet. I say we go back to basics. First, how could an oil spill happen?"

"Easy," said Sandy. "Most likely something would happen at the pipeline terminal. Something goes wrong with a coupling, or an operator error occurs, or equipment malfunctions, while loading oil on the ship. The other possibility is that a tanker's hull fails for some reason, probably from running aground because of weather or navigational error."

"Weather may not be the problem," suggested Leslie. "What about incompetence? What if the pilot gets drunk?"

Marty Kelso always was able to imagine the unusual scenarios. "And what about the possibility of sabotage? What if a terrorist decides to wreak environmental havoc?"

"OK," said Pat, "In terms of the actual cleanup, the more likely terminal spill would require a different kind of response than the less likely event of a hull failure. In planning for a terminal accident, we need to think about having equipment at the terminal. Given the higher probability of such an accident, we should probably spend money on cleanup equipment that would be right there and available. Also, the U.S. Coast Guard, as reviewer and approver of our FRP, will want to ensure that we have considered the most likely events, necessitating some equipment on-hand at the terminal."

"I suppose so," conceded Chris. "At least we would be spending our money on the right kind of thing."

"You know, there's another problem that we're not really thinking about," Leslie offered. "An oil spill at the terminal can be easily contained with relatively little environmental damage given the industrial nature of the water body where the terminal is located. On the other hand, if we ever have a hull failure, we have to act fast. If we don't, and mind you, we may not be able to because of the weather, Larkin Oil will have a terrible time trying to clean up the public relations as well as the beaches. And think about the difference in the PR problem if the spill is due to incompetence on the part of a pilot rather than weather or sabotage. The Federally-required Vessel Response Plan (VRP) will have to address these unique issues."

"Even if we act fast, a huge spill could still be nearly impossible to contain," Pat pointed out. "So what's the upshot? Sounds to me as if we need to clearly designate qualified personnel in the FRP and VRP who could make a decision immediately about how to respond; this would be consistent with federal law as well. We need to recover as much oil as possible, minimize environmental damage, and manage the public relations problem."

"And do this all efficiently," growled Chris Brown. "We still have to do it without having tied up all of the company's assets for years waiting for something to happen."

The committee at Larkin Oil has a huge problem on its hands. The effects of its work now and the resource planning that is eventually implemented for coping with possible future accidents will substantially affect the company resources and possibly the environment. We cannot solve the problem entirely, but we can apply the principles discussed so far in the chapter. Let us look at the basic elements of the decision situation.

First, what is the committee's decision context, and what are Larkin's objectives? The context is making recommendations regarding plans for possible future oil spills, and the immediate decision is what policy to adopt for dealing with oil spills. Exactly what alternatives are available is not as clear. The company's objectives are well stated by Pat Mills and Chris Brown at the end of the example: (1) recover as much oil as possible, (2) minimize environmental damage, (3) minimize damage to Larkin's public image, (4) minimize cost, and (5) comply with appropriate federal regulations. These regulations govern requirements for Facility and Vessel Response Plans, including dedicating response resources, naming qualified staff with their contact information, and retaining spill response contractors (i.e., Oil Spill Response Organizations, OSROs). Recovering as much oil as possible is perhaps best viewed as a means to minimize environmental damage as well as the impact on Larkin's image. It also appears that a fundamental issue is how much of the company's resources should be committed to standby status while waiting for an accident to occur. In general, the more resources committed, the faster the company could respond and the less damage would be done. Having these objectives on the table immediately and understanding the inherent trade-offs will help the committee organize their efforts as they explore potential policy recommendations.

Is this a sequential decision problem? Based on Pat's last statement, the immediate decision must anticipate future decisions about responses to specific accident situations. Thus, in figuring out an appropriate policy to adopt now, they must think about possible appropriate future decisions and what resources must be available at the time so that the appropriate action can be taken.

The scenario is essentially about uncertain, but rare events. Of course, the main uncertain event is whether an oil spill will ever occur. From Chris Brown's point of view, an important issue might be how long the cleanup equipment sits idle, requiring periodic maintenance, until an accident occurs; and how to effectively leverage his staff so that he is not wasting corporate resources on personnel with little to do. Also important are events such as the kind of spill, the location, the weather, the cause, the public and natural resources at risk of injury, and the extent of the damage. At the present time, imagining the first (facility-based) accident, all of these are unknowns, but if and when a decision must be made, some information will be available (location, current weather, cause), while other factors—actual volume of oil spilled, chemical makeup of the oil (directly affecting the toxicity of the oil), extent of the eventual damage, and total cleanup cost—probably will not be known.

What is an appropriate planning horizon for Larkin? No indication is given in the case, but the committee members may want to consider the planning horizon. How far into the future should they look? How long will their policy recommendations be active? Understanding relevant regulatory requirements for FRPs and VRPs can help direct the committee's decision making. For example, the federal government requires that FRPs and VRPs be updated on pre-determined schedules, necessitating another committee be charged with reviewing and updating the these plans, considering, for example, scientific and technological advances.

The problem also involves fundamental issues about how the different consequences are valued. As indicated, the fundamental trade-off is whether to save money by committing fewer resources or to provide better protection against future possible accidents. In other words, just how much is insurance against damage worth to Larkin Oil? The committee can imagine some possible consequences and the overall "cost" (in generic terms) to the company: (1) committing substantial resources and never needing them; (2) committing considerable resources and using them effectively to contain a major spill; (3) committing few resources and never needing them (the best possible outcome); and (4) committing few resources and not being able to clean up a spill effectively (the worst possible outcome, potentially jeopardizing Larkin's future operations).

Just considering the dollars spent, there is a time-value-of-money problem that Chris Brown eventually will want the spill contingency planning committee to address. To some extent, dollars can be spent for protection now instead of later on. Alternative financing schemes can be considered to pay for the equipment required. Different strategies for acquiring and maintaining equipment may have different streams of cash flows. Calculating the present value of these different strategies for providing protection may be an important aspect of the decision, minimum federally-mandated resources notwithstanding.

Finally, the committee members also need to think about exactly how to allocate resources in terms of the other objectives stated by Pat Mills. They need to recover oil, minimize environmental damage, and handle public relations problems. Of course, recovering oil and minimizing environmental damage are linked to some extent. Overall, though, the more resources committed to one of these objectives, the less available they are to satisfy the others. The committee may want to specify some guidelines for resource allocation in its recommendations, but for the most part this allocation will be made at the time of future decisions that are in turn made in response to specific accidents.

Can we put all of this together? Figure 2.5 shows the sequence of decisions and uncertain events. This is only a rough picture, intended to capture the elements discussed here, a first step toward the development of a requisite decision model. Different decision makers most likely would have different representations of the situation, although most would probably agree on the essential elements of the values, decisions, uncertain events, and consequences.

FIGURE **2.5**
A graphical representation of Larkin Oil's situation.

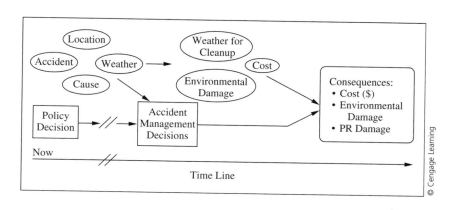

SUMMARY

Hard decisions often have many different aspects. The basic elements of decision situations include values and objectives, decisions to be made, uncertain events, and consequences. This chapter discussed identification of the immediate decision at hand as well as subsequent decisions. We found that uncertain future events must be dovetailed with the sequence of decisions, showing exactly what is known before each decision is made and what uncertainties still remain. We discussed valuing consequences in some depth, emphasizing the specification of a planning horizon and the identification of relevant trade-offs. The discussion about the time value of money showed how interest rates imply a special kind of trade-off between cash flows at different points in time. Finally, the Larkin Oil example served to illustrate the identification of the basic elements of a major (and messy) decision problem.

QUESTIONS AND PROBLEMS

2.1 Suppose you are in the market for a new car to be used mainly for commuting to work, shopping, running errands, and visiting friends.
   a. What are your objectives in this situation? What are some different alternatives?
   b. Suppose you broaden the decision context. Instead of deciding on a car for commuting purposes, you are interested in other means of transportation. In this new decision context, how would you describe your objectives? What are some alternatives that you might not have considered in the narrower decision context?
   c. How might you broaden the decision context further? (There are many ways to do this!) In this broader context, what new objectives must you consider? What new alternatives are available?
   d. Does your planning horizon change when you broaden the decision context in Question b? Question c?

2.2 Explain in your own words why it is important in some situations to consider future decisions as well as the immediate decision at hand. Can you give an example from your own experience of an occasion in which you had to make a decision while explicitly anticipating a subsequent decision? How did the immediate decision affect the subsequent one?

2.3 Sometimes broadening the decision context can change the planning horizon. For example, many companies face specific technical problems. Framed in a narrow decision context, the question is how to solve the specific problem, and a reasonable solution may be to hire a consultant. On the other hand, if the decision context is broadened to include solving related problems as well as the current one, the company might want to develop in-house expertise by hiring one or more permanent employees or training an existing employee in the required skills. What is the planning horizon in each case, and why does it change with the broader context? What objectives must be considered in the broader context that can be ignored in the narrower one?

2.4 Explain in your own words why it is important to keep track of what information is known and what events are still uncertain for each decision.

2.5 What alternatives other than specific protection strategies might Larkin Oil consider (e.g., insurance)?

2.6 Imagine the difficulties of an employer whose decision context is choosing a new employee from a set of applicants whom he will interview. What do you think the employer's objectives should be? Identify the employer's specific decisions to make and uncertainties, and describe the relevant uncertain events. How does the problem change if the employer has to decide whether to make an offer on the spot after each interview?

2.7 Identify the basic elements of a real-estate investor's decision situation. What are the investor's objectives? Is the situation dynamic, that is, are there sequential decisions? What are some of the uncertainties that the investor faces? What are the crucial tradeoffs? What role does the time value of money play for this investor?

2.8 Describe a decision problem that you have faced recently (or with which you are currently struggling). Describe the decision context and your objectives. What were the specific decisions that you faced, and what were the relevant uncertainties? Describe the possible consequences.

2.9 Calculate the net present value of a business deal that costs $2,500 today and will return $1,500 at the end of this year and $1,700 at the end of the following year. Use an interest rate of 13%.

2.10 Find the net present value of a project that has cash flows of −$12,000 in Year 1, +$5,000 in Years 2 and 3, −$2,000 in Year 4, and +$6,000 in Years 5 and 6. Use an interest rate of 12%. Find the interest rate that gives a net present value of zero.

2.11 A friend asks you for a loan of $1,000 and offers to pay you back at the rate of $90 per month for 12 months.
   a. Using an annual interest rate of 10%, find the net present value (to you) of loaning your friend the money. Repeat, using an interest rate of 20%.
   b. Find an interest rate that gives a net present value of 0. The interest rate for which NPV = 0 is often called the *internal rate of return.*

2.12 Terry Martinez is considering taking out a loan to purchase a desk. The furniture store manager rarely finances purchases, but will for Terry "as a special favor." The rate will be 10% per year, and because the desk costs $600, the interest will come to $60 for a 1-year loan. Thus, the total price is $660, and Terry can pay it off in 12 installments of $55 each.
   a. Use the interest rate of 10% per year to calculate the net present value of the loan. (Remember to convert to a monthly interest rate.) Based on this interest rate, should Terry accept the terms of the loan?
   b. Look at this problem from the store manager's perspective. Using the interest rate of 10%, what is the net present value of the loan to the manager?
   c. What is the net present value of the loan to the manager if an interest rate of 18% is used? What does this imply for the real rate of interest that Terry is being charged for the loan?

This kind of financing arrangement was widely practiced at one time, and you can see why from your answers to Question c. By law, lenders in the United States now must clearly state the actual annual percentage rate in the loan contract.

2.13   Lynn Rasmussen is deciding what sports car to purchase. In reflecting about the situation, it becomes obvious that after a few years Lynn may elect to trade in the sports car for a new one, although the circumstances that might lead to this choice are uncertain. Should trading in the car count as an uncertain event or a future decision? What are the implications for building a requisite model of the current car-purchase decision if trading in the car is treated as an uncertain event? Treated as a decision?

2.14   Vijay is feeling much better these days. A year ago he took a big risk and opened a cafeteria style restaurant next to a major university. He knew that college students were as interested in quantity as they were in quality when it came to eating. He figured that the rice, beans, and legumes of his native Indian would be an inexpensive way to fill the plates of his customers, and fill the plates he did. After a slow start, word got out that Rising Moon was the place to go for inexpensive, but decent food when you were hungry.

Now, with his business running successfully, he is considering applying for a liquor license to serve beer and wine. Although the license is expensive, he know that the high margins on alcohol would cover his expenses. As a matter of fact, he expects profits to increase over 30% if he serves beer and wine. However, Vijay is concerned that serving alcohol could introduce many problems, such as rowdiness, possibly fighting, and a host of legal issues. What are the four decision elements of Vijay's decision? Are there any hedging strategies he can employ to avoid the downside risks?

CASE STUDIES

THE VALUE OF PATIENCE

Robin Briggs, a wealthy private investor, had been approached by Union Finance Company on the previous day. It seemed that Union Finance was interested in loaning money to one of its larger clients, but the client's demands were such that Union could not manage the whole thing. Specifically, the client wanted to obtain a loan for $385,000, offering to repay Union Finance $100,000 per year over 7 years.

Union Finance made Briggs the following proposition. Since it was bringing Briggs business, its directors argued, they felt that it was only fair for Briggs to put up a proportionately larger share of the money. If Briggs would put up 60% of the money ($231,000), then Union would put up the remaining 40% ($154,000). They would split the payments evenly, each getting $50,000 at the end of each year for the next 7 years.

Questions

1. Union Finance can usually earn 18% on its money. Using this interest rate, what is the net present value of the client's original offer to Union?

2. Robin Briggs does not have access to the same investments as Union. In fact, the best available alternative is to invest in a security earning 10% over the next 7 years. Using this interest rate, what is Briggs's net present value of the

offer made by Union? Should Briggs accept the offer?

3. What is the net present value of the deal to Union if Briggs participates as proposed?

4. The title of this case study is "The Value of Patience." Which of these two investors is more patient? Why? How is this difference exploited by them in coming to an agreement?

EARLY BIRD, INC.

The directors of Early Bird, Inc. were considering whether to begin a sales promotion for their line of specialty coffees earlier than originally planned. Over the last two quarters, they had worked out an extensive deal with the Fair-Trade Coffee Association for shade-grown, hand-picked beans. To promote this high-quality coffee, they planned to discount their regular coffee beans as a loss leader, that is, as a way to bring more customers into their stores. The fair-trade label would show that they care about the coffee growers by paying a fair price, and care about the environment by supporting sustainable growing practices. "I think we should go ahead with an early promotion and price cuts," Tracy Brandon said. "After all, it couldn't hurt! At the very worst, we'll sell some coffee cheap for a little longer than we had planned, and on the other side we could beat New Morning to the punch."

"That's really the question, isn't it?" replied Jack Santorini. "If New Morning really is planning their own promotion, and we start our promotion now, we would beat them to the punch. On the other hand, we might provoke a price war. And you know what a price war with that company means. We spend a lot of money fighting with each other. There's no real winner. We both just end up with less profit."

Janice Wheeler, the finance VP for Early Bird, piped up, "The consumer wins in a price war. They get to buy things cheaper for a while. We ought to be able to make something out of that."

Ira Press, CEO for Early Bird, looked at the VP thoughtfully. "You've shown good common sense in situations like these, Janice. How do you see it?"

Janice hesitated. She didn't like being put on the spot like this. "You all know what the projections are for the 6-week promotion as planned. The marketing group tells us to expect sales of 10 million dollars. Our objective is to gain first-mover advantage with this premium high-margin coffee. The fair-trade label will continue our strategy of differentiating ourselves from New Morning as the coffee shop for connoisseurs. If all goes well, we expect to gain at least two percentage points of market share, but our actual gain could be anywhere from nothing to 3, 4, maybe even 5 points.

Profits during the promotion are expected to be down by 10%, but after the promotion ends, our increased market share and differentiation strategy should result in more sales, higher margins, and more profits."

Tracy broke in. "That's assuming New Morning doesn't come back with their own promotion in reaction to ours. And you know what our report is from Pete. He says that he figures New Morning is up to something."

"Yes, Pete did say that. But you have to remember that Pete works for our advertising agent. His incentive is to sell advertising. And if he thinks he can talk us into spending more money, he will. Furthermore, you know, he isn't always right. Last time he told us that New Morning was going to start a major campaign, he had the dates right, but it was for a different product line altogether."

Ira wouldn't let Janice off the hook. "But Janice, if New Morning does react to our promotion, would we be better off starting it early?"

Janice thought for a bit. Her immediate concern was the extra pressure that an earlier-than-expected promotion would put on their supply chain. If sales of their fair trade coffees took off, then they might not have a sufficient supply to meet demand. The last thing she wanted was to disappoint consumers. Add to this the downward pressure on profits from a promotion by New Morning, and Janice was starting to realize the complexities of their situation. If she were working at New Morning and saw an unexpected promotion begin, how would she react? Would she want to cut prices to match the competition? Would she try to stick with the original plans? Finally she said, "Look, we have to believe that New Morning also has some common sense. They would not want to get involved in a price war if they could avoid it. At the same time, they aren't going to let us walk away with the market. I think that if we move early, there's about a 30% chance that they will react immediately, and we'll be in a price war before we know it."

"We don't have to react to their reaction, you know," replied Ira.

"You mean," asked Jack, "we have another meeting like this to decide what to do if they do react?"

"Right."

"So," Janice said, "I guess our immediate options are to start our promotion early or to start it later as planned. If we start it now, we risk the possibility of not meeting consumer demand and a strong reaction from New Morning. There is only a small chance, say 10%, of demand outpacing supply. If New Morning does react, then we can decide at that point whether we want to cut our prices further."

Jack spoke up, "But if New Morning reacts strongly and we don't, we would probably end up just spending our money for little financial gain. While we would further differentiate ourselves, we would gain no market share at all. We might even lose some market share. If we were to cut prices further, it would hurt profits, but at least we would be able to preserve what market share gains we had made before New Morning's initial reaction."

At this point, several people began to argue among themselves. Sensing that no resolution was immediately forthcoming, Ira adjourned the meeting, asking everyone to sleep on the problem and to call him with any suggestions or insights they had.

Questions

1. Based on the information in the case, what are Early Bird's objectives in this situation? Are there any other objectives that you think they should consider?

2. Given your answer to the previous question, what do you think Early Bird's planning horizon should be?

3. Identify the basic elements (values, decisions, uncertain events, consequences) of Early Bird's decision problem.

4. Construct a diagram like Figure 2.5 showing these elements.

REFERENCES

Identifying the elements of decision situations is implicit in a decision-analysis approach, although most textbooks do not explicitly discuss this initial step in decision modeling.

The references listed at the end of Chapter 1 are all appropriate for discussions of values, objectives, decisions, uncertain events, and consequences.

The idea of understanding one's values as a prerequisite for good decision making is Ralph Keeney's thesis in his book *Value-Focused Thinking* (1992). A good summary is Keeney (1994). In the conventional approach, espoused by most authors on decision analysis, one finds oneself in a situation that demands a decision, identifies available alternatives, evaluates those alternatives, and chooses the best of those alternatives. Keeney argues persuasively that keeping one's values clearly in mind provides the ability to proactively find new decision opportunities and creative alternatives. Of course, the first step, and sometimes a difficult one, is understanding one's values, which we will explore in depth in Chapter 3.

Dynamic decision situations can be very complicated, and many articles and books have been written on the topic. A basic-level textbook that includes dynamic decision analysis is Buchanan (1982).

DeGroot (1970) covers many dynamic decision problems at a somewhat more sophisticated level. Murphy et al. (1985) discuss the orchardist's dynamic decision problem in detail.

The time value of money is a standard topic in finance courses, and more complete discussions of net present value, internal rate of return (the implied interest rate in a sequence of cash flows), and related topics can be found in most basic financial management textbooks.

Buchanan, J. T. (1982) *Discrete and Dynamic Decision Analysis*. New York: Wiley.

DeGroot, M. H. (1970) *Optimal Statistical Decisions*. New York: McGraw-Hill.

Keeney, R. L. (1992) *Value-Focused Thinking*. Cambridge, MA: Harvard University Press.

Keeney, R. L. (1994) "Creativity in Decision Making with Value-Focused Thinking." *Sloan Management Review*, Summer, 33–41.

Murphy, A. H., R. W. Katz, R. L. Winkler, and W.-R. Hsu (1985) "Repetitive Decision Making and the Value of Forecasts in the Cost-Loss Ratio Situation: A Dynamic Model." *Monthly Weather Review*, 113, 801–813.

EPILOGUE

On March 24, 1989, the Exxon *Valdez* tanker ran aground on a reef in Prince William Sound after leaving the Valdez, Alaska, pipeline terminal. Over 11 million gallons of oil spilled into Prince William Sound, the largest spill in the United States. In the aftermath, it was revealed that Alyeska, the consortium of oil companies responsible for constructing and managing the Trans-Alaska Pipeline, had instituted an oil spill contingency plan that was inadequate to the task of cleaning up a spill of such magnitude. As a result of the inadequate plan and the adverse weather immediately after the spill, little oil was recovered. This lack of spill contingency planning and response spawned the Federal Oil Pollution Act of 1990 (OPA). Among its other functions, OPA mandates FRP and VRP standards.

Hundreds of miles of environmentally delicate shoreline were contaminated. Major fisheries were damaged, leading to specific economic harm to individuals who relied on fishing for a livelihood, as well as multiple tribal villages which subsist on marine resources (fish, invertebrates, etc.). In addition, the spill proved an embarrassment for all of the major oil companies and sparked new interest in environmental issues, especially upcoming leases for offshore oil drilling. Even though the risk of a major oil spill was very small, in retrospect one might conclude that the oil companies would have been better off with a much more carefully thought out contingency plan and more resources invested in it.

Source: "Dead Otters and Silent Ducks," *Newsweek*, April 24, 1989, p. 70.

CHAPTER 3

Structuring Decisions

Having identified the elements of a decision problem, how should one begin the modeling process? Creating a decision model requires three fundamental steps. First is identifying and structuring the values and objectives. Structuring values requires identifying those issues that matter to the decision maker, as discussed in Chapter 2. Simply listing objectives, however, is not enough; we also must separate the values into fundamental objectives and means objectives, and we must specify ways to measure accomplishment of the objectives.

The second step is structuring the elements of the decision situation into a logical framework. To do this we have two tools: influence diagrams and decision trees. These two approaches have different advantages for modeling difficult decisions. Both approaches are valuable and, in fact, complement one another nicely. Used in conjunction with a carefully developed value structure, we have a complete model of the decision that shows all of the decision elements: relevant objectives, decisions to make, uncertainties, and consequences.

The final step is the refinement and precise definition of all of the elements of the decision model. For example, we must be absolutely clear on the precise decisions that are to be made and the available alternatives, exactly what the uncertain events are, and how to measure the consequences in terms of the objectives that have been specified. Although many consequences are easily measured on a natural scale (e.g., NPV can be measured in dollars), nonquantitative objectives such as increasing health or minimizing environmental impact are more problematic. We will discuss ways to create formal scales to measure achievement of such objectives.

STRUCTURING VALUES

Our first step is to structure values. In Chapter 2 we discussed the notion of objectives. In many cases, a single objective drives the decision; a manager might want to maximize profits next year, say, or an investor might want to maximize the financial return of an investment portfolio. Often, though, there are multiple objectives that conflict; for example, the manager might want to maximize profits but at the same time minimize the chance of losing money. The investor might want to maximize the portfolio's return while at the same time minimize the volatility of the portfolio's value.

If a decision involves a single objective, that objective is often easily identified. Careful thought may be required, however, to define the objective in just the right way. For example, you might want to calculate NPV, but over what time frame? A 3-year NPV would favor short-term gains, whereas a 10-year NPV takes a long-term perspective. The discussion of structuring values that follows can help in the identification and clarification of the objective in a single-objective decision situation.

Even though many pages in this book are devoted to the analysis of single objective decisions, for many decisions the real problem lies in balancing multiple conflicting objectives. The first step in dealing with such a situation is to understand just what the objectives are. Specifying objectives is not always a simple matter, as we will see in the following example.

Suppose you are an employer with an opening for a summer intern in your marketing department. Under the supervision of a senior employee, the intern would assist in the development of a market survey relating to a line of your company's consumer products.

Hiring a Summer Intern

Many businesses hire students for short-term assignments. Such jobs often are called *internships,* and the employee—or intern—gets a chance to see what a particular kind of job and a specific company are like. Likewise, the company gets to try out a new employee without making a long-term commitment.

In this example, the fictional PeachTree Consumer Products has an opening for a summer intern. Working under the supervision of a senior employee in the marketing group, the intern would focus primarily on the development of a market survey for certain company products. The problem is how to find an appropriate individual to fill this slot. Where should the company go to locate good candidates, which ones should be interviewed, and on the basis of what criteria should a particular candidate be chosen?

Imagine that you are the manager charged with finding an appropriate intern for PeachTree. Your first step is to create a list of all the things that matter to you in this decision context. What objectives would you want to accomplish in filling this position? Certainly you would want the market survey to be done well. You might want to use the summer as a trial period for the intern, with an eye toward a permanent job for the individual if the internship worked out. You might want to establish or cement a relationship

TABLE **3.1**
Objectives for hiring
summer intern.

- Maximize quality of market survey.
- Sell more consumer products.
- Build market share.
- Identify new market niches for company's products.
- Minimize cost of survey design.
- Try out prospective permanent employee.
- Establish relationship with local college.
- Provide assistance for senior employee.
- Free up an employee to be trained for new assignment.
- Learn updated techniques from intern:
    Self
    Supervisor
    Market research department
    Entire company
- Expose intern to real-world business experience.
- Maximize profit.
- Improve company's working environment by bringing in new and
    youthful energy.
- Provide financial assistance for college student.

with a college or university placement service. Table 3.1 shows a list of objectives (in no special order) that an employer might write down.

How would you go about generating a list like Table 3.1? Keeney (1994) gives some ideas. For example, think about some possible alternatives and list their pros and cons. Or think about what you would like if you could have anything. Table 3.2 gives eight suggestions for generating your list of objectives.

Once you have a list of objectives, what's next? Structuring the objectives means organizing them so that they describe in detail what you want to achieve and can be incorporated in an appropriate way into your decision model. We start by separating the list into items that pertain to different kinds of objectives. In the summer intern example, objectives can be sorted into several categories:

- Business performance (sell more products, maximize profit, increase market share, identify market niches)
- Work environment improvement (bring in new energy, assist senior employee)
- Improvement of the quality and efficiency of marketing activities (maximize survey quality, minimize survey cost)
- Personnel and corporate development (learn updated techniques, free up employee for new assignment, try out prospective employee)
- Community service (provide financial aid, expose intern to real world, build relationship with local college).

Of course, there are other ways to organize these objectives; the idea is to create categories that reflect the company's overall objectives.

TABLE **3.2**
Techniques for identifying objectives.

1. **Develop a wish list.** What do you want? What do you value? What should you want?
2. **Identify alternatives.** What is a perfect alternative, a terrible alternative, some reasonable alternative? What is good or bad about each?
3. **Consider problems and shortcomings.** What is wrong or right with your organization? What needs fixing?
4. **Predict consequences.** What has occurred that was good or bad? What might occur that you care about?
5. **Identify goals, constraints, and guidelines.** What are your aspirations? What limitations are placed on you?
6. **Consider different perspectives.** What would your competitor or your constituency be concerned about? At some time in the future, what would concern you?
7. **Determine strategic objectives.** What are your ultimate objectives? What are your values that are absolutely fundamental?
8. **Determine generic objectives.** What objectives do you have for your customers, your employees, your shareholders, yourself? What environmental, social, economic, or health and safety objectives are important?

Before continuing with the value structuring, we must make sure that the objectives are appropriate for the decision context. Recall that the decision context is hiring a summer intern for the marketing department. This is a relatively narrow context for which some of the listed objectives are not especially relevant. For example, selling more consumer products and maximizing profit, although indeed important objectives, are too broad to be essential in the current decision context. Although hiring the best individual should have a positive impact on overall company performance, more crucial in the specific context of hiring the best intern are the objectives of enhancing marketing activities, personnel development, community service, and enhancing the work environment. These are the areas that hiring an intern may directly affect.

FUNDAMENTAL AND MEANS OBJECTIVES

With a set of objectives that is consistent with the decision context, the next step is to separate *means* from *fundamental* objectives. This is a critical step, because here we indicate those objectives that are important because they help achieve other objectives and those that are important simply because they reflect what we really want to accomplish.

For example, working fewer hours may appear to be an important objective, but it may be important only because it would allow an individual to spend more time with his or her family or to pursue other activities that represent fundamental interests. Thus, "minimize hours worked" is a means objective, whereas "maximize time with family" is a fundamental objective.

Fundamental objectives are organized into *hierarchies*, as shown in Figure 3.1. The upper levels in a hierarchy represent more general objectives, and the lower levels explain or describe important elements of the more general levels. For example, in the context of defining vehicle regulations, a higher-level fundamental objective might be "Maximize Safety," below which one might find "Minimize Loss of Life," "Minimize Serious Injuries," and "Minimize Minor Injuries." The three lower-level objectives are fundamental objectives that explain what is meant by the higher-level objective "Maximize Safety." The three lower-level objectives are also fundamental; each one describes a specific aspect of safety, and as such each one is inherently important. This hierarchy could be expanded by including another level. For example, we might include the objectives "Minimize Loss of Child Lives" and "Minimize Loss of Adult Lives" as aspects of the loss-of-life objective and similarly distinguish between serious injuries to children and adults.

Means objectives are organized into *networks*, as shown in Figure 3.2. In the vehicle safety example, some means objectives might be "Minimize Accidents" and "Maximize Use of Vehicle-Safety Features." Both of these are important because they help to maximize safety. Beyond these two means objectives might be other means objectives such as "Maximize Driving Quality," "Maintain Vehicles Properly," and "Maximize Purchase of Safety Features on Vehicles." A key difference between this network and the fundamental-objectives hierarchy in Figure 3.1 is that means objectives can be connected to several objectives, indicating that they help accomplish these objectives. For example, "Have Reasonable Traffic Laws" affects both "Maximize Driving Quality" and "Maintain Vehicles Properly."

Structuring the fundamental-objectives hierarchy is crucial for developing a multiple-objective decision model. As we will see, the lowest-level fundamental objectives will be the basis on which various consequences will be measured. Distinguishing means and fundamental objectives is important at this stage of the game primarily so that the decision maker is certain that the appropriate objectives—fundamental, not means—are specified in the decision model. But the means network has other uses as well. We will see in the last portion of the chapter that an easily measured means

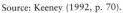

FIGURE **3.1**
A fundamental-objectives hierarchy.

Source: Keeney (1992, p. 70).

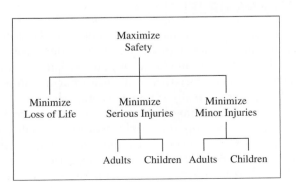

FIGURE **3.2**
A means-objectives
network.

Source: Keeney (1992, p. 70).

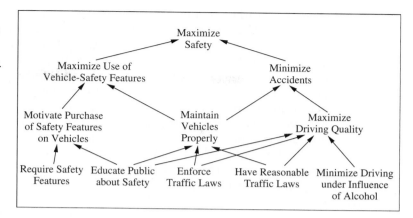

objective can sometimes substitute for a fundamental objective that is more difficult to measure.

How do we first separate means and fundamental objectives and then construct the fundamental-objectives hierarchy and the means-objectives network? A number of guiding questions are used to accomplish these tasks.

The first question to ask regarding any objective is, "Why Is That Important?" Known as the WITI test, this question does two things: distinguishes between means and fundamental objectives and reveals connections among the objectives. If the answer to the question is, "This objective is important because it helps accomplish X," then you know that the original objective is a means objective and that it has an impact on X. Moreover, a decision maker can continue by asking, "Why is X important?" By continuing to ask why the next objective is important, we can trace out the connections from one means objective to the next until we arrive at an objective for which the answer is, "This objective is important just because it is important. It is one of the fundamental reasons why I care about this decision." In this case, we have identified a fundamental objective.

As an example, look again at Figure 3.2. We might ask, for example, "Why is it important to maintain vehicles properly?" The answer is that doing so helps to minimize accidents and maximize the use of vehicle-safety features. Asking why minimizing accidents is important reveals that it helps maximize safety. The same is true if we ask why maximizing use of safety features is important. Finally, why is safety important? Maximizing safety is fundamentally important; it is what we care about in the context of establishing regulations regarding vehicle use. The answers to the questions trace out the connections among these four objectives and appropriately identify "Maximize Safety" as a fundamental objective.

The WITI test is useful for moving from means objectives to fundamental objectives. What about going the other way? The obvious question to ask is, "How can this objective be achieved?" For example, in the vehicle-regulation context we would ask, "How can we maximize safety?" The answer might give any of the upstream means objectives that appear in Figure 3.2.

Sequentially asking "How can this objective be achieved?" can help to identify means objectives and establish links among them.

What about constructing the fundamental-objectives hierarchy? Starting at the top of the hierarchy, the question to ask is, "What do you mean by that?" In our vehicle example, we would ask, "What does maximize safety mean?" The answer is that we mean minimizing lives lost, serious injuries, and minor injuries. In turn we could ask, "What do you mean by minimizing lives lost?" The answer might be minimizing child lives lost and adult lives lost; that is, it might be useful in this decision context to consider safety issues for children and adults separately, perhaps because different kinds of regulations would apply to these two groups.

Finally, we can work upward in the fundamental-objectives hierarchy, starting at a lower-level objective. Ask the question, "Of what more general objective is this an aspect?" For example, if we have identified saving adult lives as a fundamental objective—it is a fundamental reason we care about vehicle regulations—then we might ask, "Is there a more general objective of which saving adult lives is an aspect?" The answer would be the more general objective of saving lives, and asking the question again with respect to saving lives would lead us to the overall fundamental objective of maximizing safety.

Figure 3.3 summarizes these four techniques for organizing means and fundamental objectives. It is important to realize that one might ask these questions in any order, mixing up the sequence, jumping from the means network to the fundamental-objectives hierarchy and back again. Be creative and relaxed in thinking about your values!

Let us look again at PeachTree's summer-intern decision. Figure 3.4 shows both a fundamental-objectives hierarchy and a means network with appropriate connections between them. The means objectives are shown in italics. Note that some objectives have been added, especially criteria for the intern, such as ability to work with the senior employee, ability to demonstrate new techniques to the staff, and a high level of energy. In the decision context, choosing the best intern for the summer position, these criteria help define what "best" means in terms that relate directly to the company's fundamental objectives.

FIGURE **3.3**
How to construct mean objectives networks and fundamental objectives hierarchies.

	Fundamental Objectives	**Means Objectives**
To Move:	*Downward in the Hierarchy:*	*Away from Fundamental Objectives:*
Ask:	"What do you mean by that?"	"How could you achieve this?"
To Move:	*Upward in the Hierarchy:*	*Toward Fundamental Objectives:*
Ask:	"Of what more general objective is this an aspect?"	"Why is that important?" (WITI)

© Cengage Learning

FIGURE **3.4**
Fundamental and
means objectives
for PeachTree's
summer intern
decision.

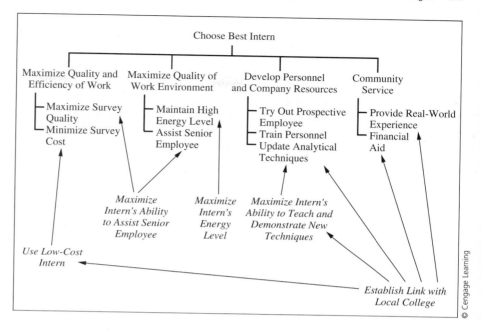

Insights can be gleaned from Figure 3.4. First, the means objectives give some guidance about what kind of intern to hire; up-to-date technical skills, good "people skills" for working with the senior employee, an ability (and willingness) to demonstrate new techniques for the firm, and a high energy level. In addition, establishing a link with the local college is a very important step. Although this is a means objective and hence not important in and of itself, it has an impact on many other objectives, both means and fundamental.

The fundamental-objectives hierarchy and the means-objectives network can provide a lot of insight even at this initial level. The fundamental objectives tell you why you care about the decision situation and what criteria you should be looking at in evaluating options. For the summer-intern situation, the company cares about the main-level fundamental objectives, and the lower-level objectives provide more detail. Having sorted out the means objectives, we can rest assured that we will be able to evaluate candidates (and perhaps even develop a strategy for finding good candidates) whose qualities are consistent with the company's concerns. Finally, as we mentioned previously, the means network can suggest creative new alternatives. For example, a great strategy would be to become acquainted with professors or career counselors at the local college and to explain to them exactly what the company is looking for in a summer intern.

GETTING THE DECISION CONTEXT RIGHT

Recall that the context for PeachTree's decision has been to hire the best intern. What would happen if we were to broaden the context? Suppose we were to set the context as enhancing the company's marketing activities.

First, we would want to consider far more options than just hiring an intern. The broader context also suggests looking for permanent new hires or training current employees in new methods. One of the results would be that the means objectives might change; some of the means objectives might broaden from optimizing characteristics of the intern to optimizing characteristics of the marketing group as a whole. "Maximize Intern's Energy Level" might become "Maximize Marketing Group's Energy Level," which might suggest means objectives such as hiring new high-energy employees or sending employees to a workshop or retreat. You can see that as we broaden the decision context, the objectives change in character somewhat. The more the context is broadened, the greater the change. If we were to go all the way to a *strategic*—broadest possible—context of "maximize profit" or "build market share," for example, then many of the fundamental objectives in Figure 3.4 would become means objectives, and alternatives affecting all parts of the company would have to be considered.

At this point you may be wondering how you know when you have identified the appropriate decision context and its corresponding fundamental-objectives hierarchy and means network. As in Chapter 2, we can invoke the notion of a requisite model to ensure that all appropriate but no superfluous objectives have been included, given the decision context. The real question, though, is the decision context itself. How do you know how broad or narrow to make the context? This question is absolutely fundamental, and unfortunately there is no simple answer. As a decision maker, you must choose a context that fits three criteria. The first is straightforward: ask whether the context you have set really captures the situation at hand. Are you addressing the right problem? For example, searching for a job of the same type as your present one but with a different company is the wrong decision context if your real problem is that you do not enjoy the kind of work required in that job; you should broaden the context to consider different kinds of jobs, careers, or lifestyles. On the other hand, if you really love what you do but are dissatisfied with your current job for reasons related to that particular position or your firm (low salary, poor working conditions, conflicts with fellow workers, and so on), then looking for another similar job with another firm is just the right context.

The second criterion might be called *decision ownership*. Within organizations especially, the broader the decision context, the higher up the organizational ladder you must go to find the authority to make the decision and assume the responsibility for its consequences. Do you have the authority to make decisions within the specified context (or will you be reporting the results of your analysis to someone with that authority)? If you conclude that you do not have this authority, then look for a narrower context that matches the authority you do have.

Feasibility is the final issue; in the specified context, will you be able to do the necessary study and analysis in the time allotted with available resources? Broader contexts often require more careful thought and more extensive analysis. Addressing a broad decision context with inadequate time and resources can easily lead to dissatisfaction with the decision process.

It would be better in such a situation to narrow the context in some way until the task is manageable.

Like most aspects of decision analysis, setting the context and structuring objectives may not be a once-and-for-all matter. After initially specifying objectives, you may find yourself refining the context and modifying the objectives. Refining the context several times and iterating through the corresponding sets of objectives are not signs of poor decision making. Instead, they indicate that the decision situation is being taken seriously, and that many different possibilities and perspectives are being considered.

In Chapter 1, a flow chart was used to describe the decision-analysis process, particularly, its iterative nature. As we cycle through the process, we refine the objectives, set the decision context to match, and hopefully, create new and innovative alternatives to our hard decision. There is no better example of the interrelations among the decision context, the objectives, and the alternatives than the Maliau Basin situation.

Maliau Basin

The government of Malaysia faced a difficult decision and had vocal constituents lobbying for their various points of view. The decision was whether to allow mining in the remote Maliau Basin, a largely unexplored wilderness with several rare species including the Sumatran Rhino and the Rafflessia, the world's largest flower. Without examining the objectives of each group, that is, without investigating what was important to each group and why, the officials found themselves in a narrow decision context framed by two polarized alternatives. On one hand, environmentalists argued that the pristine Maliau Basin would be severely damaged by mining and its uniqueness lost forever. On the other hand, proponents of mining argued that the environmental impact of mining would be minor and offset by the influx of much needed foreign currency. To break through the narrow "Us–vs–Them" decision context, with the unimaginative alternatives (to mine or not mine), the government officials needed to take a step back and examine the objectives of all constituent groups.

A three-day workshop on the Maliau Basin brought together all the different constituents to elicit and structure their objectives. Robin Gregory and Ralph Keeney, the analysts who led the workshop, describe the process and explain how learning about objectives helped the groups make progress. One of the first discoveries was that the two alternatives were not even well defined. The assumption that not mining would preserve the pristine basin was not true. At that time, squatters and poachers were encroaching on the basin, burning and slashing the land to clear it. Nor would mining endanger all the wildlife in the basin. The officials were already discovering some middle ground; perhaps there were other alternatives available?

As is often the case, the participants were surprised to find that their opponents shared many of their own objectives. For example, the environmentalist also wanted to increase prosperity for the local population, and the miners did not want to destroy the natural beauty of the basin. Certainly, the different groups had different opinions on which objectives were the most important, but understanding that they had the same objectives helped to create shared understanding and common ground for discussion. Instead of a rancorous Us-vs-Them debate, the groups started to come to a common understanding, and thereby increased the chance of negotiating a solution.

With the objectives understood and the context widened to include every group's values, new, previously unthought-of alternatives were created. Six alternatives were generated during the workshop based on the values and objectives of the participants. Possibilities, such as ecotourism were raised as a way to bring in foreign currency, or combining underground mining with tourism as a way to preserve the basin and stop encroachment by squatters. Perhaps the most interesting alternative was to allow underground mining in the southern half of the basin, leaving untouched the northern section, which held most of the unique ecological features. Moreover, the mining company would be able to, and have an interest in, securing the perimeter of the basin, thereby protecting both the basin and their operations.

Source: Gregory and Keeney (1994).

STRUCTURING DECISIONS: INFLUENCE DIAGRAMS

With the fundamental objectives specified, structured, and sorted out from the means objectives, we can turn now to the process of structuring the various decision elements—decisions and alternatives, uncertain events and outcomes, and consequences. We begin with influence diagrams, which can provide simple graphical representations of decision situations. Different decision elements show up in the influence diagram as different shapes. These shapes are then linked with arrows in specific ways to show the relationships among the elements.

In an influence diagram, rectangles represent decisions, ovals represent chance events, and diamonds represent the final consequence or payoff node. A rectangle with rounded corners is used to represent a mathematical calculation or a constant value; these rounded rectangles will have a variety of uses, but the most important is to represent intermediate consequences. The four shapes are generally referred to as *nodes*: decision nodes, chance nodes, payoff nodes, and consequence or calculation nodes. Nodes are put together in a *graph*, connected by arrows, or *arcs*. We call a node at the beginning of an arc a *predecessor* and a node at the end of an arc a *successor*.

Consider a venture capitalist's situation in deciding whether to invest in a new business. For the moment, let us assume that the capitalist has only one objective in this context—to make money (not an unreasonable objective for a person in this line of work). The entrepreneur seeking the

FIGURE **3.5**
Influence diagram
of venture
capitalist's
decision.

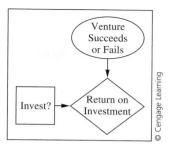

investment has impeccable qualifications and has generally done an excellent job of identifying the market, assembling a skilled management and production team, and constructing a suitable business plan. In fact, it is clear that the entrepreneur will be able to obtain financial backing from some source whether the venture capitalist decides to invest or not. The only problem is that the proposed project is extremely risky—more so than most new ventures. Thus, the venture capitalist must decide whether to invest in this highly risky undertaking. If she invests, she may be able to get in on the ground floor of a very successful business. On the other hand, the operation may fail altogether. Clearly, the dilemma is whether the chance of getting in on the ground floor of something big is worth the risk of losing the investment entirely. If she does not invest in this project, she may leave her capital in the stock market or invest in other less risky ventures. Her investment situation appears as an influence diagram in Figure 3.5.

Note that both "Invest?" and "Venture Succeeds or Fails" are predecessors of the final consequence "Return on Investment." The implication is that the consequence depends on both the decision and the chance event. In general, consequences depend on what happens or what is decided in the nodes that are predecessors of the consequence node. Moreover, as soon as the decision is made *and* the uncertain event is resolved, the consequence is determined; there is no uncertainty about the consequence at this point. Note also that no arc points from the chance node to the decision node. The absence of an arc indicates that when the decision is made, the venture capitalist does not know whether the project will succeed. She may have some feeling for the chance of success, and this information would be included in the influence diagram as probabilities of possible levels of success or failure. Thus, the influence diagram as drawn captures the decision maker's current state of knowledge about the situation.

Also note that no arc points from the decision to the uncertain event. The absence of this arrow has an important and subtle meaning. The uncertainty node is about the success of the venture. The absence of the arc from "Invest?" to "Venture Succeeds or Fails" means that the venture's chances for success are not affected by the capitalist's decision. In other words, the capitalist need not concern herself with her impact on the venture.

It is possible to imagine situations in which the capitalist may consider different levels of investment as well as managerial involvement. For example, she may be willing to invest $100,000 and leave the entrepreneur alone. But if she invests $500,000, she may wish to be more active in running the company. If she believes her involvement would improve the company's chance of success, then it would be appropriate to include an arrow from the decision node to the chance node; her investment decision—the level of investment and the concomitant level of involvement— would be relevant for determining the company's chance of success. In our simple and stylized example, however, we are assuming that her choice simply is whether to invest and that she has no impact on the company's chance of success.

INFLUENCE DIAGRAMS AND THE FUNDAMENTAL OBJECTIVES HIERARCHY

Suppose the venture capitalist actually has multiple objectives. For example, she might wish to focus on a particular industry, such as personal computers, obtaining satisfaction by participating in the growth of this industry. Thus, in addition to the objective of making money, she would have an objective of investing in the personal computer industry.

Figure 3.6 shows a simple two-level objectives hierarchy and the corresponding influence diagram for the venture capitalist's decision. You can see in this figure how the objectives hierarchy is reflected in the pattern of consequence nodes in the influence diagram; two consequence nodes labeled "Return

FIGURE **3.6**
The venture capitalist's decision with two objectives.

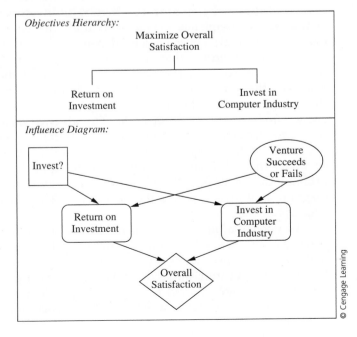

on Investment" and "Invest in Computer Industry" represent the lower-level objectives and in turn are connected to the "Overall Satisfaction" consequence node. This structure indicates that in some situations the venture capitalist may have to make a serious trade-off between these objectives, especially when comparing a computer-oriented business startup with a noncomputer business that has more potential to make money. The rounded rectangles for "Invest in Computer Industry" and "Return on Investment" are appropriate because these consequences are known after the decision is made and the venture's level of success is determined. The diamond for "Overall Satisfaction" indicates that it is the final consequence. Once the two individual consequences are known, its value can be determined.

Figure 3.7 shows the influence diagram for another multiple-objective decision. In this situation, the Federal Aviation Administration (FAA) must choose from among a number of bomb detection systems for commercial air carriers (Ulvila and Brown, 1982). In making the choice, the agency must try to accomplish several objectives. First, it would like the chosen system to be as effective as possible at detecting various types of explosives. The second objective is to implement the system as quickly as possible. The third is to maximize passenger acceptance, and the fourth is to minimize cost. To make the decision and solve the influence diagram, the FAA would have to score each candidate system on how well it accomplishes each objective. The measurements of time and cost would naturally be made in terms of days and dollars, respectively. Measuring detection effectiveness and passenger acceptance might require experiments or surveys and the development of an appropriate measuring device. The "Overall Perfor- mance" node would contain a formula that aggregates the individual scores, incorporating the appropriate trade-offs among the four objectives. Assessing the trade-off rates and constructing the formula to calculate the overall score is demonstrated in an example in Chapter 4 and is discussed thoroughly in Chapters 15 and 16.

FIGURE **3.7**
Multiple objectives in selecting a bomb detection system.

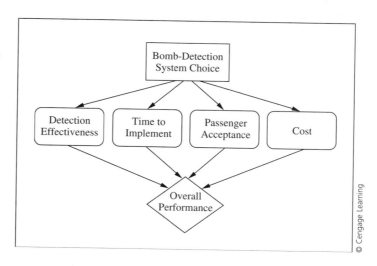

© Cengage Learning

USING ARCS TO REPRESENT RELATIONSHIPS

The rules for using arcs to represent relationships among the nodes are shown in Figure 3.8. In general, an arc can represent either *relevance* or *sequence*. The context of the arrow indicates the meaning. For example, an arrow pointing to a chance node designates relevance, indicating that the predecessor is relevant for assessing the chances associated with the uncertain event. In Figure 3.8 the arrow from Event A to Event C means that the chances (probabilities) associated with C may be different for different outcomes of A. Likewise, an arrow pointing from a decision node to a chance node means that the specific chosen decision alternative is relevant for assessing the chances associated with the succeeding uncertain event. For instance, the chance that a person will become a millionaire depends to some extent on the choice of a career. In Figure 3.8 the choice taken in Decision B is relevant for assessing the chances associated with Event C's possible outcomes.

Relevance arcs can also point to consequence or calculation nodes, indicating that the consequence or calculation depends on the specific outcome of the predecessor node. In Figure 3.8, consequence F depends on both Decision D and Event E. Relevance arcs in Figure 3.6 point to the "Computer Industry Growth" and "Return on Investment" nodes. This indicates that the decision made and the success of the venture are relevant for determining these two consequences. Likewise, relevance arcs point from the two individual consequence nodes to the "Overall Satisfaction" node.

When the decision maker has a choice to make, that choice would normally be made on the basis of information available at the time. What information is available? Everything that happens before the decision is made. Arrows that point to decisions represent information available at the time of the decision and hence represent *sequence*. Such an arrow indicates that the decision is made knowing the outcome of the predecessor node. An arrow from a chance node to a decision means that, from the decision maker's point of view, all uncertainty associated with a chance event is resolved and the outcome known when the decision is made. Thus, information is available to the decision maker regarding the event's outcome. This is the case with Event H and Decision I in Figure 3.8; the decision maker is

FIGURE 3.8
Representing influence with arrows.

Arrows pointing to chance and consequence nodes represent relevance, and arrows pointing to decision nodes represent sequence.

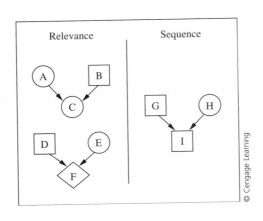

© Cengage Learning

waiting to learn the outcome of H before making Decision I. An arrow from one decision to another decision simply means that the first decision is made before the second, such as Decisions G and I in Figure 3.8. Thus, the sequential ordering of decisions is shown in an influence diagram by the path of arcs through the decision nodes.

The nature of the arc—relevance or sequence—can be ascertained by the context of the arc within the diagram. To reduce the confusion of overabundant notation, all arcs have the same appearance in this book. For our purposes, the rule for determining the nature of the arcs is simple; an arc pointing to a decision represents sequence, and all others represent relevance.

Properly constructed influence diagrams have no *cycles;* regardless of the starting point, there is no path following the arrows that leads back to the starting point. For example, if there is an arrow from A to B, there is no path, however tortuous, that leads back to A from B. Imagine an insect traveling from node to node in the influence diagram, always following the direction of the arrows. In a diagram without cycles, once the insect leaves a particular node, it has no way to get back to that node.

SOME BASIC INFLUENCE DIAGRAMS

In this section, several basic influence diagrams are described. Understanding exactly how these diagrams work will provide a basis for understanding more complex diagrams.

The Basic Risky Decision

This is the most elementary decision under uncertainty that a person can face. The previous venture-capital example is a basic risky decision; there is one decision to make and one uncertain event.

Many decision situations can be reduced to a basic risky decision. For example, imagine that you have $2,000 to invest, with the objective of earning as high a return on your investment as possible. Two opportunities exist, investing in a friend's business or keeping the money in a savings account with a fixed interest rate. If you invest in the business, your return depends on the success of the business, which you figure could be wildly successful, earning you $3,000 beyond your initial investment (and hence leaving you with a total of $5,000), or a total flop, in which case you will lose all your money and have nothing. On the other hand, if you put the money into a savings account, you will earn $200 in interest (leaving you with a total of $2,200) regardless of your friend's business.

The influence diagram for this problem is shown in Figure 3.9. This figure also graphically shows details underlying the decision, chance, and consequence nodes. The decision node includes the choice of investing in either the business or the savings account. The chance node represents the uncertainty associated with the business and shows the two possible outcomes. The consequence node includes information on the dollar return for different decisions (business investment versus savings) and the outcome of the chance event. This table shows clearly that if you invest in the business, your return depends on what the business does. However, if you put your

FIGURE **3.9**
Basic risky decision
with displayed
choices, outcomes,
and consequences.

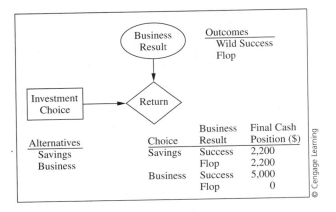

money into savings, your return is the same regardless of what happens with the business.

You can see that the essential question in the basic risky decision is whether the potential gain in the risky choice (the business investment) is worth the risk that must be taken. The decision maker must, of course, make the choice by comparing the risky and riskless alternatives. Variations of the basic risky choice exist. For example, instead of having just two possible outcomes for the chance event, the model could include a range of possible returns, a much more realistic scenario. The structure of the influence diagram for this range-of-risk dilemma, though, would look just the same as the influence diagram in Figure 3.9; the difference lies in the details of the chance event, which are not shown explicitly in the diagram.

Imperfect Information

Another basic kind of influence diagram reflects the possibility of obtaining imperfect information about some uncertain event that will affect the eventual payoff. This might be a forecast, an estimate or diagnosis from an acknowledged expert, or information from a computer model. In the investment example, you might subscribe to a service that publishes investment advice, although such services can never predict market conditions perfectly.

Imagine a manufacturing-plant manager who faces a string of defective products and must decide what action to take. The manager's fundamental objectives are to solve this problem with as little cost as possible and to avoid letting the production schedule slip. A maintenance engineer has been dispatched to do a preliminary inspection on Machine 3, which is suspected to be the source of the problem. The preliminary check will provide some indication as to whether Machine 3 truly is the culprit, but only a thorough and expensive series of tests—not possible at the moment—will reveal the truth. The manager has two alternatives. First, a replacement for Machine 3 is available and could be brought in at a certain cost. If Machine 3 *is* the problem, then work can proceed and the production schedule will not fall behind. If Machine 3 is not the source of the defects, the problem will still exist, and the workers will have to change to another product while the problem is tracked down. Second, the workers could be changed immediately to the other product. This action would certainly cause the production schedule for the current product to fall behind but would avoid the risk (and cost) of unnecessarily replacing Machine 3.

Without the engineer's report, this problem would be another basic risky decision; the manager would have to decide whether to take the chance of replacing Machine 3 based on personal knowledge regarding the chance that Machine 3 is the source of the defective products. However, the manager is able to wait for the engineer's preliminary report before taking action. Figure 3.10 shows an influence diagram for the manager's decision problem, with the engineer's report shown as an example of imperfect information. The diagram shows that the consequences depend on the choice made (replace Machine 3 or change products) and whether Machine 3 actually turns out to be defective. There is no arrow from "Engineer's Report" to the consequence nodes because the report does not have a direct effect on the consequence.

The arrow from "Engineer's Report" to "Manager's Decision" is a sequence arc; the manager will hear from the engineer before deciding. Thus, the engineer's preliminary report is information available at the time of the decision, and this influence diagram represents the situation while the manager is waiting to hear from the engineer. Analyzing the influence diagram will tell the manager how to interpret this information; the appropriate action will depend not only on the engineer's report but also on the extent to which the manager believes the engineer to be correct. The manager's assessment of the engineer's accuracy is reflected in the chances (not shown) associated with the "Engineer's Report" node. Note that a relevance arc points from "Machine 3 OK?" to "Engineer's Report," indicating that Machine 3's state is relevant for assessing the chances associated with the engineer's report. For example, if the manager believes the engineer is very good at diagnosing the situation and Machine 3 really is OK, the chances should be near 100% that the engineer will say so. Likewise, if Machine 3 is causing the defective products, the engineer should be very likely to indicate 3 is the problem. On the other hand, if the manager does not think the engineer is very good at diagnosing the problem—because of lack of familiarity with this particular

FIGURE **3.10**
Influence diagram for manufacturing plant manager's imperfect information.

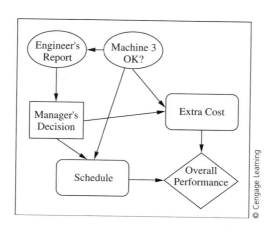

© Cengage Learning

piece of equipment—then there might be a substantial chance that the engineer will make a mistake.

Weather forecasting provides another example of imperfect information. Suppose you live in Miami. A hurricane near the Bahama Islands threatens to cause severe damage; as a result, the authorities recommend that everyone evacuate. Although evacuation is costly, it ensures safety. On the other hand, staying is risky. You could be injured or even killed if the storm comes ashore within 10 miles of your home. If the hurricane's path changes, however, you would be safe without having incurred the cost of evacuating. Clearly, two fundamental objectives are to maximize your safety and to minimize your costs.

Undoubtedly, you would pay close attention to the weather forecasters who would predict the course of the storm. These weather forecasters are not perfect predictors, however. They can provide some information about the storm, but they may not accurately predict its path because not everything is known about hurricanes.

Figure 3.11 shows the influence diagram for the evacuation decision. The relevance arc from "Hurricane Path" to "Forecast" means that the actual weather situation is relevant for assessing the uncertainty associated with the forecast. If the hurricane is actually going to hit Miami, the forecaster is more likely to predict a hit rather than a miss. Conversely, if the hurricane really will miss Miami, the forecaster should be likely to predict a miss. In either case, though, the forecast may be incorrect because the course of a hurricane is not fully predictable. In this situation, although the forecast actually precedes the hurricane's landfall, it is relatively straightforward to think about the forecaster's tendency to make a mistake based on (or conditioned on) what direction the hurricane takes. (The modeling choice is up to you, though! If you would feel more confident in assessing the chance of the hurricane hitting Miami by conditioning on the forecast—that is, have the arrow pointing the other way—then by all means do so!)

The consequence node in Figure 3.11 encompasses both objectives of minimizing cost and maximizing safety. An alternative representation might explicitly include both consequences as separate nodes as in Figure 3.10.

FIGURE **3.11**
Influence diagram for the evacuation decision.

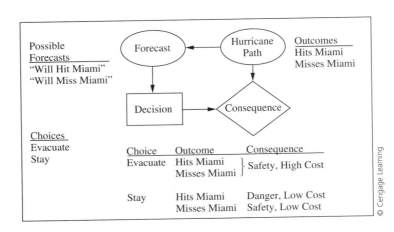

© Cengage Learning

Moreover, these two objectives are somewhat vaguely defined, as they might be in an initial specification of the model. A more complete specification would define these objectives carefully, giving levels of cost (probably in dollars) and a scale for the level of danger. In addition, uncertainty about the possible outcomes—ranging from no injury to death—could be included in the influence diagram. You will get a chance in Problem 3.14 to modify and improve on Figure 3.11.

As with the manufacturing example, the influence diagram in Figure 3.11 is a snapshot of your situation as you wait to hear from the forecaster. The sequence arc from "Forecast" to the decision node indicates that the decision is made knowing the imperfect weather forecast. You might imagine yourself waiting for the 6:00 p.m. weather report on the television, and as you wait, considering what the forecaster might say and what you would do in each case. The sequence of events, then, is that the decision maker hears the forecast, decides what to do, and then the hurricane either hits Miami or misses. As with the manufacturing example, analyzing this model will result in a strategy that recommends a particular course of action for each of the possible statements the forecaster might make.

Sequential Decisions

The hurricane-evacuation decision can be thought of as part of a larger picture.

Suppose you are waiting anxiously for the forecast as the hurricane is bearing down. Do you wait for the forecast or leave immediately? If you wait for the forecast, what you decide to do may depend on that forecast. In this situation, you face a sequential decision situation as diagrammed in Figure 3.12.

The order of the events is implied by the arcs. Because there is no arc from "Forecast" to "Wait for Forecast" but there is one to "Evacuate," it is clear that the sequence is first to decide whether to wait or leave immediately. If you wait, the forecast is revealed, and finally you decide, based on the forecast, whether to evacuate.

In an influence diagram sequential decisions are strung together via sequence arcs, in much the same way as in Chapter 2. (In fact, now you can see that the figures in Chapter 2 use essentially the same graphics as influence diagrams!) For another example, let us take the farmer's decision from

FIGURE 3.12
A sequential version of the evacuation decision.

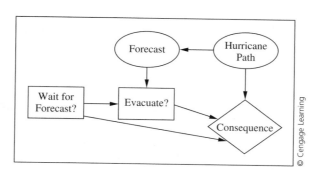

© Cengage Learning

FIGURE **3.13**
Influence diagram
for farmer's
sequential decision
problem.

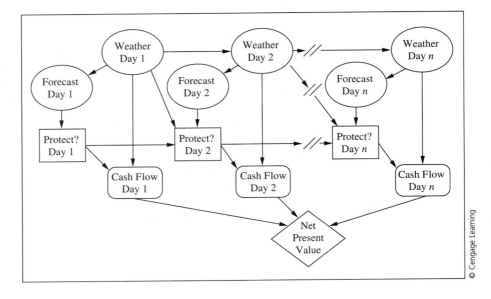

Chapter 2 about protecting his trees against adverse weather. Recall that the
farmer's decision on whether the fruit crop should be protected replayed itself
each day, based on the next day's weather forecast. Let us assume that the
farmer's fundamental objective is to maximize the NPV of the investment,
including the costs of protection. Figure 3.13 shows that the influence diagram essentially is a series of imperfect information diagrams strung together.
Between decisions (to protect or not) the farmer observes the weather and
obtains the forecast for the next day. The arcs from one decision to the next
show the time sequence.

The arrows among the weather and forecast nodes from day to day indicate that the observed weather and the forecast both have an effect. That is,
yesterday's weather is relevant for assessing the chance of adverse weather
today. Not shown explicitly in the influence diagram are arcs from forecast
and weather nodes before the previous day. Of course, the decision maker
observed the weather and the forecasts for each prior day. These arcs are not
included in the influence diagram but are implied by the arcs that connect the
decision nodes into a time sequence. The missing arcs are sometimes called
no-forgetting arcs to indicate that the decision maker would not forget the
outcomes of those previous events. Unless the no-forgetting arcs are critical
in understanding the situation, it is best to exclude them because they tend to
complicate the diagram.

Finally, although we indicated that the farmer has a single objective, that
of maximizing NPV, Figure 3.13 represents the decision as having multiple-
objectives, the objectives being to maximize the cash inflow (and hence minimize outflows or costs) each day. The individual cash flows, of course, are
used to calculate the farmer's NPV. As indicated in Chapter 2, the interest
rate defines the trade-off between earlier and later cash flows.

Intermediate Calculations

In some cases it is convenient to include an additional node that simply aggre-gates results from certain predecessor nodes. Suppose, for example, that a firm is considering introducing a new product. The firm's fundamental objec-tive is the profit level of the enterprise, and so we label the consequence node "Profit." At a very basic level, both cost and revenue may be uncertain, and so a first version of the influence diagram might look like that shown in Figure 3.14.

On reflection, the firm's chief executive officer (CEO) realizes that substantial uncertainty exists for both variable and fixed costs. On the reve-nue side, there is uncertainty about the number of units sold, and a pricing decision will have to be made. These considerations lead the CEO to consider a somewhat more complicated influence diagram, which is shown in Figure 3.15.

Figure 3.15 is a perfectly adequate influence diagram. Another represen-tation is shown in Figure 3.16. Intermediate nodes have been included in Figure 3.16 to calculate cost on one hand and revenue on the other; we will call these *calculation nodes,* because they calculate cost and revenue given the predecessors. (In some discussions of influence diagrams, the term *deter-ministic node* is used to denote a node that represents an intermediate calcula-tion or a constant).

FIGURE **3.14**
Simple influence diagram for new product decision.

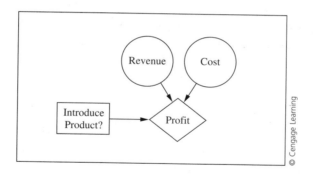

FIGURE **3.15**
New product decision with additional detail.

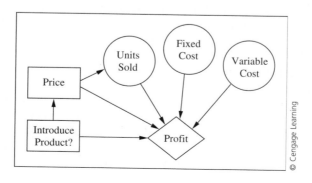

© Cengage Learning

FIGURE **3.16**
New product decision with calculation nodes for intermediate calculation of cost and revenue.

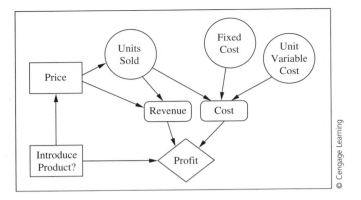

Calculation nodes behave just like consequence nodes; given the inputs from the predecessor nodes, the value of a calculation node can be found immediately. No uncertainty exists after the conditioning variables—decisions, chance events, or other calculation nodes—are known. Of course, there is no uncertainty only in a conditional sense; the decision maker can look forward in time and know what the calculation node will be for any possible combination of the conditioning variables. Before the conditioning variables are known, though, the value that the node will eventually have is uncertain.

In general, calculation nodes are useful for emphasizing the structure of an influence diagram. Whenever a node has many predecessors, it may be appropriate to include one or more intermediate calculations to define the relationships among the predecessors more precisely. In Figure 3.16, the calculation of cost and revenue is represented explicitly, as is the calculation of profit from cost and revenue. The pricing decision is clearly related to the revenue side, uncertainty about fixed and variable costs are clearly on the cost side, and uncertainty about sales is related to both.

Another example is shown in Figure 3.17. In this situation, a firm is considering building a new manufacturing plant that may create some incremental pollution. The profitability of the plant depends on many things, of course, but highlighted in Figure 3.17 are the impacts of other pollution sources. The calculation node "Regional Pollution Level" uses information on the number of cars and local industry growth to determine a pollution-level index. The pollution level in turn has an impact on the chances that the new plant will be licensed and that new regulations (either more or less strict) will be imposed.

With the basic understanding of influence diagrams provided in the preceding paragraphs, you should be able to look at any influence diagram (including any that you find in this book) and understand what it means. Understanding an influence diagram is an important decision-analysis skill. On the other hand, actually creating an influence diagram from scratch is considerably more difficult and takes much practice. The following section gives an example of the construction process for an influence diagram and discusses some common mistakes. If you wish to become proficient in

FIGURE **3.17**
Using a calculation
node to determine
pollution level.

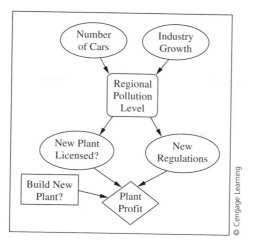

constructing influence diagrams, the next section is highly recommended.
Working through the reading and exercises, however, is just one possibility;
in fact, practice with an influence-diagram program (like PrecisionTree) is the
best way to develop skill in constructing influence diagrams. At the end of
this chapter, there are instructions on how to construct the influence diagram
for the basic risky decision using PrecisionTree.

CONSTRUCTING AN INFLUENCE DIAGRAM

There is no set strategy for creating an influence diagram. Because the task is
to structure a decision that may be complicated, the best approach may be to
put together a simple version of the diagram first and add details as necessary
until the diagram captures all of the relevant aspects of the problem. In this
section, we will demonstrate the construction of an influence diagram for the
classic toxic-chemical problem.

**Toxic Chemicals and
The EPA**

The Environmental Protection Agency (EPA) often must decide whether to
permit the use of an economically beneficial chemical that may be carcinogenic
(cancer-causing). Furthermore, the decision often must be made without perfect information about either the long-term benefits or health hazards. Courses
of action include permitting the use of the chemical, restricting its use, or
banning it altogether. Tests can be run to learn something about the
carcinogenic potential of the material, and survey data can indicate the extent
to which people are exposed when they do use the chemical. These pieces
of information are both important in making the decision. For example, if the
chemical is only mildly toxic and the exposure rate is minimal, then restricted
use may be reasonable. On the other hand, if the chemical is only mildly toxic
but the exposure rate is high, then banning its use may be imperative.

Source: Howard and Matheson (1984).

FIGURE **3.18**
Beginning the toxic-chemical influence diagram.

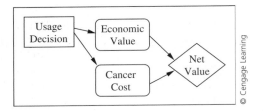

FIGURE **3.19**
Intermediate influence diagram for the toxic-chemical decision.

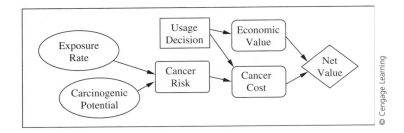

The first step should be to identify the decision context and the objectives. In this case, the context is choosing an allowed level of use, and the fundamental objectives are to maximize the economic benefits from the chemicals and at the same time to minimize the risk of cancer. These two objectives feed into an overall consequence node ("Net Value") that aggregates "Economic Value" and "Cancer Cost" as shown in Figure 3.18.

Now let us think about what affects "Economic Value" and "Cancer Cost" other than the usage decision. Both the uncertain carcinogenic character of the chemical and the exposure rate have an effect on the cancer cost that could occur, thus yielding the diagram shown in Figure 3.19. Because "Carcinogenic Potential" and "Exposure Rate" jointly determine the level of risk that is inherent in the chemical, their effects are aggregated in an intermediate calculation node labeled "Cancer Risk." Different values of the predecessor nodes will determine the overall level of "Cancer Risk."

Note that no arrow runs from "Usage Decision" to "Exposure Rate," even though such an arrow might appear to make sense. "Exposure Rate" refers to the extent of contact when the chemical is actually used and would be measured in terms of an amount of contact per unit of time (e.g., grams of dust inhaled per hour). The rate is unknown, and the usage decision does not influence our beliefs concerning the likelihood of various possible rates that occur when the chemical is used.

The influence diagram remains incomplete, however, because we have not incorporated the test for carcinogenicity or the survey on exposure. Presumably, results from both the test (called a *bioassay*) and the survey would be available to EPA at the time the usage decision is made. Furthermore, it should be clear that the actual degrees of carcinogenic potential and exposure will influence the test and survey results, and thus "Carcinogenic Potential" and "Exposure Rate" are connected to "Test" and "Survey," respectively, in

FIGURE **3.20**
Complete influence
diagram for the
toxic-chemical
decision.

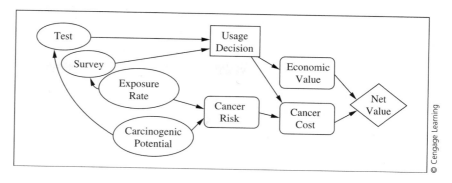

Figure 3.20. Note that "Test" and "Survey" each represent imperfect information; each one provides some information regarding carcinogenicity or exposure. These two nodes are connected to the decision node. These are sequence arcs, indicating that the information is available when the decision is made. This completes the influence diagram.

This example demonstrates the usefulness of influence diagrams for structuring decisions. The toxic-chemicals problem is relatively complex, and yet its influence diagram is compact and, more important, understandable. Of course, the more complicated the problem, the larger the influence diagram. Nevertheless, influence diagrams are useful for creating easily understood overviews of decision situations.

Some Common Mistakes

First, an easily made mistake in understanding and constructing influence diagrams is to interpret them as flowcharts, which depict the sequential nature of a particular process where each node represents an event or activity. For example, Figure 1.1 is a flowchart of a decision-analysis system, displaying the different things a decision analyst does at each stage of the process.

Even though they look a little like flowcharts, influence diagrams are very different.

An influence diagram is a snapshot of the decision situation at a particular time, one that must account for all the decision elements that play a part in the immediate decision. Putting a chance node in an influence diagram means that although the decision maker is not sure exactly what will happen, he or she has some idea of how likely the different possible outcomes are. For example, in the toxic-chemical problem, the carcinogenic potential of the chemical is unknown, and in fact will never be known for sure. That uncertainty, however, can be modeled using probabilities for different levels of carcinogenic potential. Likewise, at the time the influence diagram is created, the results of the test are not known. The uncertainty surrounding the test results also can be modeled using probabilities. The informational arrow from "Test" to "Usage Decision," however, means that the decision maker will learn the results of the test before the decision must be made.

The metaphor of a picture of the decision that accounts for all of the decision elements also encompasses the possibility of upcoming decisions that must be considered. For example, a legislator deciding how to vote on a given issue may consider upcoming votes. The outcome of the current issue might affect the legislator's future voting decisions. Thus, at the time of the immediate decision, the decision maker foresees future decisions and models those decisions with the knowledge on hand.

A second common mistake, one related to the perception of an influence diagram as a flowchart, is building influence diagrams with many chance nodes having arrows pointing to the primary decision node. The intention usually is to represent the uncertainty in the decision environment. The problem is that the arrows into the decision node are sequence arcs and indicate that the decision maker is waiting to learn the outcome of these uncertain events, which may not be the case. The solution is to think carefully when constructing the influence diagram. Recall that only sequence arcs are used to point to a decision node. Thus, an arrow into a decision node means that the decision maker will have a specific bit of information when making the decision; something will be known for sure, with no residual uncertainty. Before drawing an arrow into a decision node, ask whether the decision maker is waiting for the event to occur *and* will learn the information before the decision is made. If so, the arrow is appropriate. If not, don't draw the arrow!

So how should you include information that the decision maker has about the uncertainty in the decision situation? The answer is simple. Recall that the influence diagram is a snapshot of the decision maker's understanding of the decision situation at a particular point in time. When you create a chance node and connect it appropriately in the diagram, you are explicitly representing the decision maker's uncertainty about that event and showing how that uncertainty relates to other elements of the decision situation.

A third mistake is the inclusion of cycles (circular paths among the nodes). As indicated previously, a properly constructed influence diagram contains no cycles. Cycles are occasionally included in an attempt to denote feedback among the chance and decision nodes. Although this might be appropriate in the case of a flowchart, it is inappropriate in an influence diagram. Again, think about the diagram as a picture of the decision that accounts for all of the decision elements at an instant in time. There is no opportunity for feedback at a single point in time, and hence there can be no cycles.

Influence diagrams provide a graphical representation of a decision's structure, a snapshot of the decision environment at one point in time. All of the details (alternatives, outcomes, consequences) are present in tables that are contained in the nodes, but usually this information is suppressed in favor of a representation that shows off the decision's structure.

Multiple Representations and Requisite Models

Even though your influence diagram may be technically correct in the sense that it contains no mistakes, how do you know whether it is the "correct" one for your decision situation? This question presupposes that a unique correct diagram exists, but for most decision situations, there are many ways in which an influence diagram can appropriately represent a decision. Consider the decision modeled in Figures 3.14, 3.15, and 3.16; these figures represent three possible approaches. With respect to uncertainty in a decision problem, several sources of uncertainty may underlie a single chance node. For example, in Figure 3.16, units sold may be uncertain because the CEO is uncertain about the timing and degree of competitive reactions, the nature of consumer tastes, the size of the potential market, the effectiveness of advertising, and so on. In many cases, and certainly for a first-pass representation, the simpler model may be more appropriate. In other cases, more detail may be necessary to capture all of the essential elements of a situation. In the farmer's problem, for example, a faithful representation of the situation may require consideration of the sequence of decisions rather than looking at each decision as being independent and separate from the others. Thus, different individuals may create different influence diagrams for the same decision problem, depending on how they view the problem. The real issue is determining whether a diagram is appropriate. Does it capture and accurately reflect the elements of the decision problem that the decision maker thinks are important?

How can you tell whether your influence diagram is appropriate? The representation that is the most appropriate is the one that is *requisite* for the decision maker along the lines of our discussion in Chapter 1. That is, a requisite model contains everything that the decision maker considers important in making the decision. Identifying all of the essential elements may be a matter of working through the problem several times, refining the model on each pass. The only way to get to a requisite decision model is to continue working on the decision until all of the important concerns are fully incorporated. Sensitivity analysis (Chapter 5) will be a great help in determining which elements are important.

STRUCTURING DECISIONS: DECISION TREES

Influence diagrams are excellent for displaying a decision's basic structure, but they hide many of the details. To display more of the details, we can use a *decision tree*. As with influence diagrams, squares represent decisions to be made, while circles represent chance events. The branches emanating from a square correspond to the choices available to the decision maker, and the branches from a circle represent the possible outcomes of a chance event. The last decision element, the consequence, is specified at the ends of the branches.

Again consider the venture-capital decision (Figure 3.5). Figure 3.21 shows the decision tree for this problem. The decision tree flows from left to right, and so the immediate decision is represented by the square at the left side. The two branches represent the two alternatives, invest or not. If the venture capitalist invests in the project, the next issue is whether the venture succeeds or fails. If the venture succeeds, the capitalist earns a substantial return. However, if the venture fails, then the amount invested in the project will be lost. If the capitalist decides not to invest in this particular risky project, then she would earn a more typical return on another less risky project. These outcomes are shown at the ends of the branches at the right.

FIGURE **3.21**
Decision tree
representation of
venture-capital
decision.

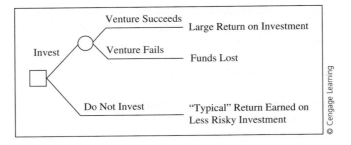

The interpretation of decision trees requires explanation. First, the options represented by branches from a decision node must be such that the decision maker can choose only one option. For example, in the venture-capital decision, the decision maker can either invest or not, but not both. In some instances, combination strategies are possible. If the capitalist were considering two separate projects (A and B), for instance, it may be possible to invest in Firm A, Firm B, both, or neither. In this case, each of the four separate alternatives would be modeled explicitly, yielding four branches from the decision node.

Second, each chance node must have branches that correspond to a set of *mutually exclusive* and *collectively exhaustive* outcomes. *Mutually exclusive* means that only one of the outcomes can happen. In the venture-capital decision, the project can either succeed or fail, but not both. *Collectively exhaustive* means that no other possibilities exist; one of the specified outcomes has to occur. Putting these two specifications together means that when the uncertainty is resolved, one and only one of the outcomes occurs.

Third, a decision tree represents all of the possible paths that the decision maker might follow through time, including all possible decision alternatives and outcomes of chance events. Three such paths exist for the venture capitalist, corresponding to the three branches at the right side of the tree. In a complicated decision situation with many sequential decisions or sources of uncertainty, there may be many potential paths.

Finally, it is almost always useful to think of the nodes as occurring in a time sequence. Beginning on the left side of the tree, the first thing to happen is typically a decision, followed by other decisions or chance events in chronological order. In the venture-capital problem, the capitalist decides first whether to invest, and the second step is whether the project succeeds or fails.

As with influence diagrams, the dovetailing of decisions and chance events is critical. Placing a chance event before a decision means that the decision is made conditional on the specific chance outcome having occurred. Conversely, if a chance node is to the right of a decision node, the decision must be made in anticipation of the chance event. The sequence of decisions is shown in a decision tree by order in the tree from left to right. If chance events have a logical time sequence between decisions, they may be appropriately ordered. If no natural sequence exists, then the order in which they appear in the decision tree is not critical, although the order used does suggest the conditioning sequence for modeling uncertainty. For example, it may be easier to think about the chances of a stock price increasing given that the Dow Jones average increases rather than the other way around.

DECISION TREES AND THE OBJECTIVES HIERARCHY

Including multiple objectives in a decision tree is straightforward; at the end of each branch, simply list all of the relevant consequences. An easy way to do this systematically is with a *consequence matrix* such as Figure 3.22, which shows the FAA's bomb-detection decision in decision-tree form. Each column of the matrix represents a fundamental objective, and each row represents an alternative, in this case a candidate detection system. Evaluating the alternatives requires "filling in the boxes" in the matrix; each alternative must be measured on every objective. Thus every detection system must be evaluated in terms of detection effectiveness, implementation time, passenger acceptance, and cost.

Figure 3.23 shows a decision-tree representation of the hurricane example. The initial "Forecast" branch at the left indicates that the evacuation decision would be made conditional on the forecast made—recall the imperfect-information decision situation shown in the influence diagram in Figure 3.11. This figure demonstrates that consequences must be considered for every possible endpoint at the right side of the decision tree, regardless of whether those endpoints represent a decision alternative or an uncertain outcome. In addition, Figure 3.23 shows clearly the nature of the risk that the

FIGURE **3.22**
Decision tree representation of FAA's multiple-objective bomb-detection decision.

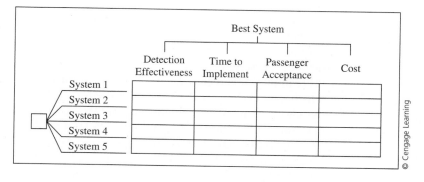

FIGURE **3.23**
Decision tree representation of evacuation decision.

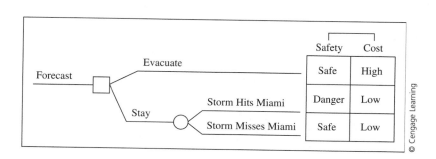

decision to stay entails, and that the decision maker must make a fundamental trade-off between the sure safety of evacuating and the cost of doing so. Finally, the extent of the risk may depend heavily on what the forecast turns out to be!

BASIC DECISION TREES

In this section we will look at some basic decision-tree forms. Many correspond to the basic influence diagrams discussed previously.

The Basic Risky Decision

Just as the venture-capital decision was the prototypical basic risky decision in our discussion of influence diagrams, so it is here as well. The capitalist's dilemma is whether the potential for large gains in the proposed project is worth the additional risk. If she judges that it is not, then she should not invest in the project.

Figure 3.24 shows the decision-tree representation of the investment decision given earlier in influence-diagram form in Figure 3.9. In the decision tree you can see how the sequence of events unfolds. Beginning at the left side of the tree, the choice is made whether to invest in the business or savings. If the business is chosen, then the outcome of the chance event (wild success or a flop) occurs, and the consequence—the final cash position—is determined. As before, the essential question is whether the chance of wild success and ending up with $5,000 is worth the risk of losing everything, especially in comparison to the savings account that results in a bank balance of $2,200 for sure.

For another example, consider a politician's decision. The politician's fundamental objectives are to have a career that provides leadership for the country and representation for her constituency, and she can do so to varying degrees by serving in Congress. The politician might have the options of (1) running for reelection to her U.S. House of Representatives seat, in which case reelection is virtually assured, or (2) running for a Senate seat. If the choice is to pursue the Senate seat, there is a chance of losing, in which case she could return to her old job as a lawyer (the worst possible outcome). On the other hand, winning the Senate race would be the best possible outcome in terms of her objective of providing leadership and representation. Figure 3.25 diagrams the decision. The dilemma in the basic risky decision arises because the riskless alternative results in an outcome that, in terms of

FIGURE **3.24**
The investor's basic risky decision.

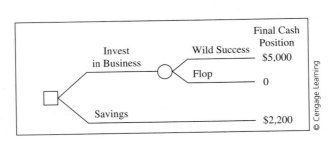

FIGURE **3.25**
The politician's
basic risky decision.

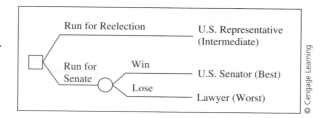

FIGURE **3.26**
Double-risk decision
dilemma.

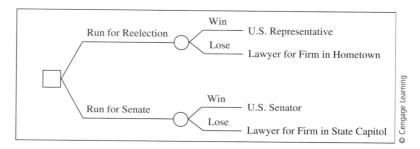

desirability, falls between the outcomes for the risky alternatives. (If this were not the case, there would be no problem deciding!) The decision maker's task is to figure out whether the chance of "winning" in the risky alternative is great enough relative to the chance of "losing" to make the risky alternative more valuable than the riskless alternative.

A variation of the basic risky decision might be called the *double-risk decision dilemma*. Here the problem is deciding between two risky prospects. On one hand, you are "damned if you do and damned if you don't" in the sense that you could lose either way. On the other hand, you could win either way. For example, the political candidate may face the decision represented by the decision tree in Figure 3.26, in which she may enter either of two races with the possibility of losing either one.

In our discussion of the basic risky decision and influence diagrams, we briefly mentioned the *range-of-risk dilemma,* in which the outcome of the chance event can take on any value within a range of possible values. For example, imagine an individual who has sued for damages of $450,000 because of an injury. The insurance company has offered to settle for $100,000. The plaintiff must decide whether to accept the settlement or go to court; the decision tree is shown as Figure 3.27. The crescent shape indicates that the uncertain event—the court award—may result in any value between the extremes of zero and $450,000, the amount claimed in the lawsuit.

Imperfect Information

Representing imperfect information with decision trees is a matter of showing that the decision maker is waiting for information prior to making a decision. For example, the evacuation decision problem is shown in Figure 3.28. Here

FIGURE **3.27**
A range-of-risk
decision dilemma.

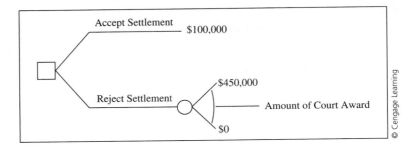

FIGURE **3.28**
Evacuation decision
represented by
decision tree.

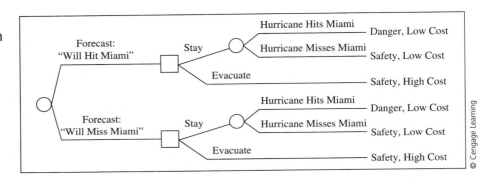

is a decision tree that begins with a chance event, the forecast. The chronological sequence is clear; the forecast arrives, then the evacuation decision is made, and finally the hurricane either hits or misses Miami.

Sequential Decisions

As we did in the discussion of influence diagrams, we can modify the imperfect information decision tree to reflect a sequential decision situation in which the first choice is whether to wait for the forecast or evacuate immediately. Figure 3.29 shows this decision tree.

At this point, you can imagine that representing a sequential decision problem with a decision tree may be very difficult if there are many decisions and chance events because the number of branches can increase dramatically under such conditions. Although full-blown decision trees work poorly for this kind of problem, it is possible to use a *schematic* approach to depict the tree.

Figure 3.30 shows a schematic version of the farmer's sequential decision problem. This is the decision-tree version of Figure 3.13. Even though each decision and chance event has only two branches, we are using the crescent shape to avoid having the tree explode into a bushy mess. With only the six nodes shown, there would be 2^6, or 64, branches.

We can string together the crescent shapes sequentially in Figure 3.30 because, regardless of the outcome or decision at any point, the same events and decisions follow in the rest of the tree. This ability is useful in many

FIGURE **3.29**
Sequential version of evacuation decision in decision-tree form.

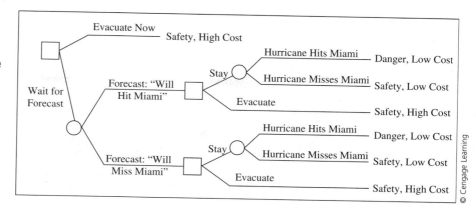

FIGURE **3.30**
Schematic version of farmer's sequential decision: decision-tree form.

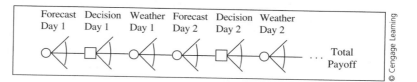

FIGURE **3.31**
An investment decision in schematic form.

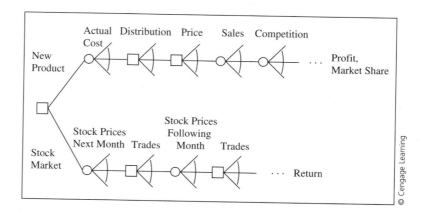

kinds of situations. For example, Figure 3.31 shows a decision in which the immediate decision is whether to invest in an entrepreneurial venture to market a new product or invest in the stock market. Each alternative leads to its own set of decisions and chance events, and each set can be represented in schematic form.

DECISION TREES AND INFLUENCE DIAGRAMS COMPARED

It is time to step back and compare decision trees with influence diagrams. The discussion and examples have shown that, on the surface at least, decision trees display considerably more information than do influence diagrams.

It should also be obvious, however, that decision trees get "messy" much faster than do influence diagrams as decision problems become more complicated. One of the most complicated decision trees we constructed was for the sequential decision in Figure 3.31, and it really does not show all of the intricate details contained in the influence-diagram version of the same problem. The level of complexity of the representation is not a small issue. When it comes time to present the results of a decision analysis to upper-level managers, their understanding of the graphical presentation is crucial. Influence diagrams are superior in this regard; they are especially easy for people to understand regardless of mathematical training.

Should you use decision trees or influence diagrams? Both are worthwhile, and they complement each other well. Influence diagrams are particularly valuable for the structuring phase of problem solving and for representing large problems. Decision trees display the details of a problem. The ultimate decision made should not depend on the representation, because influence diagrams and decision trees are *isomorphic*; any properly built influence diagram can be converted into a decision tree, and vice versa, although the conversion may not be easy. One strategy is to start with an influence diagram to help understand the major elements of the situation and then convert to a decision tree to fill in details. This strategy is made even easier with the software program that comes with the text; PrecisionTree can convert any influence diagram into a decision tree.

Influence diagrams and decision trees provide two approaches for modeling a decision. Because the two approaches have different advantages, one may be more appropriate than the other, depending on the modeling requirements of the particular situation. For example, if it is important to communicate the overall structure of a model to other people, an influence diagram may be more appropriate. Careful reflection and sensitivity analysis on specific probability and value inputs may work better in the context of a decision tree. Using both approaches together may prove useful; the goal, after all, is to make sure that the model accurately represents the decision situation. Because the two approaches have different strengths, they should be viewed as complementary techniques rather than as competitors in the decision-modeling process.

DECISION DETAILS: DEFINING ELEMENTS OF THE DECISION

With the overall structure of the decision understood, the next step is to make sure that all elements of the decision model are clearly defined. Beginning efforts to structure decisions usually include some rather loose specifications. For example, when the EPA considers regulating the use of a potentially cancer-causing substance, it would have a fundamental objective of minimizing the social cost of the cancers. (See, for example, Figure 3.20 and the related discussion.) But how will cancer costs be measured? In incremental lives lost? Incremental cases of cancer, both treatable and fatal? In making its decision, the EPA would also consider the rate at which people are exposed to the toxin while the chemical is in use. What are possible levels of exposure? How will we measure exposure? Are we talking about the number of people exposed to the chemical per day or per hour? Does exposure consist of breathing dust particles, ingesting some critical quantity, or skin contact? Are we concerned about contact over a period of time? Exactly how will we know if an individual has had a high or low level of exposure? The decision maker must give unequivocal answers to these questions before the decision model can be used to resolve the EPA's real-world policy problem.

Much of the difficulty in decision making arises when different people have different ideas regarding some aspect of the decision. The solution is to refine the conceptualizations of events and variables associated with the decision enough so that it can be made. How do we know when we have refined enough? The *clarity test* (Howard 1988) provides a simple and understandable answer. Imagine a clairvoyant who has access to all future information: newspapers, instrument readings, technical reports, and so on. Would the clairvoyant be able to determine unequivocally what the outcome would be for any event in the influence diagram? No interpretation or judgment should be required of the clairvoyant. Another approach is to imagine that, in the future, perfect information will be available regarding all aspects of the decision. Would it be possible to tell exactly what happened at every node, again with no interpretation or judgment? The decision model passes the clarity test when these questions are answered affirmatively. At this point, the problem should be specified clearly enough so that the various people involved in the decision are thinking about the decision elements in exactly the same way. There should be no misunderstandings regarding the definitions of the basic decision elements.

The clarity test is aptly named. It requires absolutely clear definitions of the events and variables. In the case of the EPA considering toxic substances, saying that the exposure rate can be either high or low fails the clarity test; what does "high" mean in this case? On the other hand, suppose exposure is defined as high if the average skin contact per person-day of use exceeds an average of 10 milligrams of material per second over 10 consecutive minutes. This definition passes the clarity test. An accurate test could indicate precisely whether the level of exposure exceeded the threshold.

Although Howard originally defined the clarity test in terms of only chance nodes, it can be applied to all elements of the decision model. Once the problem is structured and the decision tree or influence diagram built, consider each node. Is the definition of each chance event clear enough so that an outside observer would know exactly what happened? Are the decision alternatives clear enough so that someone else would know exactly what each one entails? Are consequences clearly defined and measurable? All of the action with regard to the clarity test takes place within the tables in an influence diagram, along the individual branches of a decision tree, or in the tree's consequence matrix. These are the places where the critical decision details are specified. Only after every element of the decision model passes the clarity test is it appropriate to consider solving the influence diagram or decision tree, which is the topic of Chapter 4.

The next two sections explore some specific aspects of decision details that must be included in a decision model. In the first section we look at how chances can be specified by means of probabilities and, when money is an objective, how cash flows can be included in a decision tree. These are rather straightforward matters in many of the decisions we make. However, when we have multiple fundamental objectives, defining ways to measure achievement of each objective can be difficult; it is easy to measure costs, savings, or cash flows in dollars or pounds sterling, but how does one measure damage to an ecosystem? Developing such measurement scales is an important aspect of attaining clarity in a decision model and is the topic of the second section.

MORE DECISION DETAILS: CASH FLOWS AND PROBABILITIES

Many decision situations, especially business decisions, involve some chance events, one or more decisions to make, and a fundamental objective that can be measured in monetary terms (maximize profit, minimize cost, and so on). In these situations, once the decisions and chance events are defined clearly enough to pass the clarity test, the last step is to specify the final details: specific chances associated with the uncertain events and the cash flows that may occur at different times. What are the chances that a particular outcome will occur? What does it cost to take a given action? Are there specific cash flows that occur at different times, depending on an alternative chosen or an event's outcome?

Specifying the chances for the different outcomes at a chance event requires us to use probabilities. Although probability is the topic of Section 2 of the book, we will use probability in Chapters 4 and 5 as we develop some basic analytical techniques. For now, in order to specify probabilities for outcomes, you need to keep in mind only a few basic rules. First, probabilities must fall between 0 and 1 (or equivalently between 0% and 100%). There is no such thing as a 110% chance that some event will occur. Second, recall that the outcomes associated with a chance event must be such that they are mutually exclusive and collectively exhaustive; only one outcome can occur (you can only go down one path), but one of the set must occur (you must go down some path). The implication is that the probability assigned to any given chance outcome (branch) must be between 0 and 1, and for any given chance node, the probabilities for its outcomes must add up to 1.

Indicating cash flows at particular points in the decision model is straightforward. For each decision alternative or chance outcome, indicate the associated cash flow, either as part of the information in the corresponding influence-diagram node or on the appropriate branch in the decision tree. For example, in the toxic-chemical example, there are certainly economic costs associated with different possible regulatory actions. In the new-product decision (Figure 3.16), different cash inflows are associated with different quantities sold, and different outflows are associated with different costs. All of these cash flows must be combined (possibly using net present value if the timing of the cash flows is substantially different) at the end of each branch in order to show exactly what the overall consequence is for a specific path through the decision model.

FIGURE **3.32**
A research-
and-development
decision.

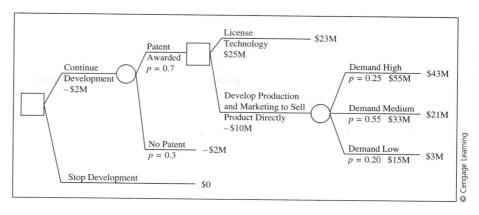

Figure 3.32 shows a decision tree with cash flows and probabilities fully specified. This is a research-and-development decision. The decision maker is a company that must decide whether to spend $2 million to continue with a particular research project. The success of the project (as measured by obtaining a patent) is not assured, and at this point the decision maker judges only a 70% chance of getting the patent. If the patent is awarded, the company can either license the patent for an estimated $25 million or invest an additional $10 million to create a production and marketing system to sell the product directly. If the company chooses the latter, it faces uncertainty of demand and associated profit from sales.

You can see in Figure 3.32 that the probabilities at each chance node add up to 1. Also, the dollar values at the ends of the branches are the net values. For example, if the company continues development, obtains a patent, decides to sell the product directly, and enjoys a high level of demand, the net amount is $43 million = $(-2) + (-10) + 55 million. Also, note that cash flows can occur anywhere in the tree, either as the result of a specific choice made or because of a particular chance outcome.

DEFINING MEASUREMENT SCALES FOR FUNDAMENTAL OBJECTIVES

Many of our examples so far (and many more to come!) have revolved around relatively simple situations in which the decision maker has only one easily measured fundamental objective, such as maximizing profit, as measured in dollars. But the world is not always so accommodating. We often have multiple objectives, and some of those objectives are not easily measured on a single, natural numerical scale. What sort of measure should we use when we have fundamental objectives like maximizing our level of physical fitness, enhancing a company's work environment, or improving the quality of a theatrical production? The answer, not surprisingly, relates back to the ideas embodied in the clarity test; we must find unambiguous ways to measure achievement of the fundamental objectives.

Before going on to the nuts and bolts of developing unambiguous scales, let us review briefly why the measurement of fundamental objectives is crucial in the decision process. The fundamental objectives represent the reasons why the decision maker cares about the decision and, more importantly, how the available alternatives should be evaluated. If a fundamental objective is to build market share, then it makes sense explicitly to estimate how much market share will change as part of the consequence of choosing a particular alternative. The change in market share could turn out to be good or bad depending on the choices made (e.g., bringing a new product to the market) and the outcome of uncertain events (such as whether a competitor launches an extensive promotional campaign). The fact that the decision maker cares about market share, though, indicates that it must be measured.

It is impossible to overemphasize the importance of tying evaluation directly to the fundamental objectives. Too often decisions are based on the wrong measurements because inadequate thought is given to the fundamental objectives in the first place, or certain measurements are easy to make or are made out of habit, or the experts making the measurements have different objectives than the decision maker. An example is trying to persuade the public that high-tech endeavors like nuclear power plants or genetically engineered plants for agricultural use are not risky because few fatalities are expected; the fact is that the public appears to care about many other aspects of these activities as well as potential fatalities! (For example, laypeople are very concerned with technological innovations that may have unknown long-term side effects, and they are also concerned with having little personal control over the risks that they may face because of such innovations.) In complex decision situations many objectives must be considered. The fundamental-objectives hierarchy indicates explicitly what must be accounted for in evaluating potential consequences.

The fundamental-objectives hierarchy starts at the top with an overall objective, and lower levels in the hierarchy describe important aspects of the more general objectives. Ideally, each of the lowest-level fundamental objectives in the hierarchy would be measured. Thus, one would start at the top and trace down as far as possible through the hierarchy. Reconsider the summer-intern example, in which PeachTree Consumer Products is looking for a summer employee to help with the development of a market survey. Figure 3.4 shows the fundamental-objectives hierarchy (as well as the means network). Starting at the top of this hierarchy ("Choose Best Intern"), we would go through "Maximize Quality and Efficiency of Work" and arrive at "Maximize Survey Quality" and "Minimize Survey Cost." Both of the latter require measurements to know how well they are achieved as a result of hiring any particular individual. Similarly, the other branches of the hierarchy lead to fundamental objectives that must be considered. Each of these objectives will be measured on a suitable scale, and that scale is called the objective's *attribute scale* or simply *attribute*.

As mentioned, many objectives have natural attribute scales: hours, dollars, percentage of market. Table 3.3 shows some common objectives with natural attributes. In the intern decision, "Minimize Survey Cost" would be

TABLE **3.3**
Some common
objectives and their
natural attributes.

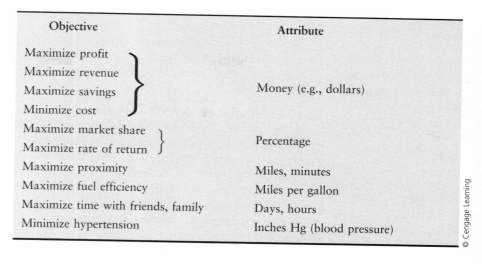

Objective	Attribute
Maximize profit Maximize revenue Maximize savings Minimize cost	Money (e.g., dollars)
Maximize market share Maximize rate of return	Percentage
Maximize proximity	Miles, minutes
Maximize fuel efficiency	Miles per gallon
Maximize time with friends, family	Days, hours
Minimize hypertension	Inches Hg (blood pressure)

easily measured in terms of dollars. How much must the company spend to complete the survey? In the context of the decision situation, the relevant components of cost are salary, fringe benefits, and payroll taxes. Additional costs to complete the survey may arise if the project remains unfinished when the intern returns to school or if a substantial part of the project must be reworked. (Both of the latter may be important uncertain elements of the decision situation.) Still, for all possible combinations of alternatives chosen and uncertain outcomes, it would be possible, with a suitable definition of cost, to determine how much money the company would spend to complete the survey.

While "Minimize Survey Cost" has a natural attribute scale, "Maximize Survey Quality" certainly does not. How can we measure achievement toward this objective? When there is no natural scale, two other possibilities exist. One is to use a different scale as a proxy. Of course, the proxy should be closely related to the original objective. For example, we might take a cue from the means-objectives network in Figure 3.4; if we could measure the intern's abilities in survey design and analysis that might serve as a reasonable proxy for survey quality. One possibility would be to use the intern's grade point average in market research and statistics courses. Another possibility would be to ask one of the intern's instructors to provide a rating of the intern's abilities. (Of course, this latter suggestion gives the instructor the same problem that we had in the first place: how to measure the student's ability when there is no natural scale!)

The second possibility is to construct an attribute scale for measuring achievement of the objective. In the case of survey quality, we might be able to think of a number of levels in general terms. The best level might be described as follows:

> **Best survey quality:** State-of-the-art survey. No apparent crucial issues left unaddressed. Has characteristics of the best survey projects presented at professional conferences.

The worst level might be:

> **Worst survey quality:** Many issues left unanswered in designing survey. Members of the staff are aware of advances in survey design that could have been incorporated but were not. Not a presentable project.

We could identify and describe fully a number of meaningful levels that relate to survey quality. Table 3.4 shows five possible levels in order from best to worst. You can see that the detailed descriptions define what is meant by quality of the survey and how to determine whether the survey was well done. According to these defined levels, quality is judged by the extent to which the statistical and methodological techniques were up to date, whether any of the company still has unresolved questions about its consumer products, and a judgmental comparison with similar survey projects presented at professional meetings.

Constructing scales can range from straightforward to complex. The key to constructing a good scale is to identify meaningful levels, including best, worst, and intermediate, and then describe those levels in a way that fully reflects the objective under consideration. The descriptions of the levels must be elaborate enough to facilitate the measurement of the consequences. In thinking about possible results of specific choices made and particular uncertain outcomes, it should be easy to use the constructed attribute scale to specify the corresponding consequences.

TABLE **3.4**
A constructed scale for survey quality.

Best. State-of-the-art survey. No apparent substantive issues left unaddressed. Has characteristics of the best survey projects presented at professional conferences.

Better. Excellent survey but not perfect. Methodological techniques were appropriate for the project and similar to previous projects, but in some cases more up-to-date techniques are available. One substantive issue that could have been handled better. Similar to most of the survey projects presented at professional conferences.

Satisfactory. Satisfactory survey. Methodological techniques were appropriate, but superior methods exist and should have been used. Two or three unresolved substantive issues. Project could be presented at a professional conference but has characteristics that would make it less appealing than most presentations.

Worse. Although the survey results will be useful temporarily, a follow-up study must be done to refine the methodology and address substantive issues that were ignored. Occasionally similar projects are presented at conferences, but they are poorly received.

Worst. Unsatisfactory. Survey must be repeated to obtain useful results. Members of the staff are aware of advances in survey design that could have been incorporated but were not. Many substantive issues left unanswered. Not a presentable project.

The scale in Table 3.4 actually shows two complementary ways to describe a level. First is in terms of specific aspects of survey quality, in this case the methodology and the extent to which the survey successfully addressed the company's concerns about its line of products. The second way is to use a comparison approach; in this case, we compare the survey project overall with other survey projects that have been presented at professional meetings. There is nothing inherently important about the survey's presentability at a conference, but making the comparison can help to measure the level of quality relative to other publicly accessible projects.

Note also from Table 3.4 that we could have extended the fundamental objectives hierarchy to include "Methodology" and "Address Company's Issues" as branches under the "Maximize Survey Quality" branch, as shown in Figure 3.33. How much detail is included in the hierarchy is a matter of choice, and here the principle of a requisite model comes into play. As long as the scale for "Maximize Survey Quality" can adequately capture the company's concerns regarding this objective, then there is no need to use more detailed objectives in measuring quality. If, on the other hand, there are many different aspects of quality that are likely to vary separately depending on choices and chance outcomes, then it may be worthwhile to create a more detailed model of the objective by extending the hierarchy and developing attribute scales for the subobjectives.

Developing the ability to construct meaningful attribute scales requires practice. In addition, it is helpful to see examples of scales that have been used in various situations. We have already seen one such scale in Table 3.4 relating to the summer intern example. Tables 3.5 and Tables 3.6 show two other constructed attribute scales for biological impacts and public attitudes, respectively, both in the context of selecting a site for a nuclear power generator.

FIGURE **3.33**
An expanded fundamental objectives hierarchy for the summer intern example.

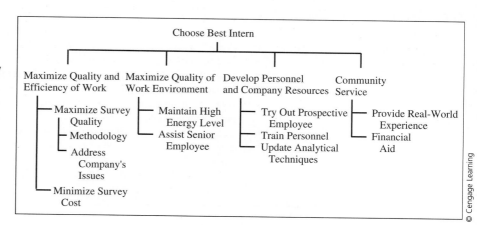

© Cengage Learning

TABLE **3.5**
A constructed attribute scale for biological impact.

Best	• Complete loss of 1.0 square mile of land that is entirely in agricultural use or is entirely urbanized; no loss of any "native" biological communities.
	• Complete loss of 1.0 square mile of primarily (75%) agricultural habitat with loss of 25% of second-growth forest; no measurable loss of wetlands or endangered- species habitat.
	• Complete loss of 1.0 square mile of land that is 50% farmed and 50% disturbed in some other way (e.g., logged or new second growth); no measurable loss of wetlands or endangered-species habitat.
	• Complete loss of 1.0 square mile of recently disturbed (e.g., logged, plowed) habitat plus disturbance to surrounding previously disturbed habitat within 1.0 mile of site border; or 15% loss of wetlands or endangered-species habitat.
	• Complete loss of 1.0 square mile of land that is 50% farmed (or otherwise disturbed) and 50% mature second-growth forest or other undistubed community; 15% loss of wetlands or endangered-species habitat.
	• Complete loss of 1.0 square mile of land that is primarily (75%) undisturbed mature "desert" community; 15% loss of wetlands or endangered-species habitat.
	• Complete loss of 1.0 square mile of mature second-growth (but not virgin) forest community; or 50% loss of big game and upland game birds; or 50% loss of wetlands and endangered-species habitat.
	• Complete loss of 1.0 square mile of mature community or 90% loss of productive wetlands and endangered-species habitat.
Worst	• Complete loss of 1.0 square mile of mature virgin forest and/or wetlands and/or endangered-species habitat.

Source: Adapted from Keeney (1992, p. 105).

TABLE **3.6**
A constructed attribute scale for public attitudes.

Best	• *Support.* No groups are opposed to the facility, and at least one group has organized support for the facility.
	• *Neutrality.* All groups are indifferent or uninterested.
	• *Controversy.* One or more groups have organized opposition, although no groups have action-oriented opposition (e.g., letter-writing, protests, lawsuits). Other groups may either be neutral or support the facility.
	• *Action-oriented opposition.* Exactly one group has action-oriented opposition. The other groups have organized support, indifference, or organized opposition.
Worst	• *Strong action-oriented opposition.* Two or more groups have action-oriented opposition.

Source: Adapted from Keeney (1992, p. 102).

USING PRECISIONTREE FOR STRUCTURING DECISIONS

Decision analysis has benefited greatly from innovations in computers and computer software. Not only have the innovations led to increased computing power allowing for fast and easy analysis of complex decisions, but they have also given rise to user friendly graphical interfaces that have simplified and enhanced the structuring process. Palisade's Decision-Tools®, included with this book, consists of six programs. Throughout the text, as we introduce specific decision analysis concepts, we will also present the corresponding DecisionTools® software and a step-by-step guide on its use. In this chapter, we explain how to use the program PrecisionTree to construct decision trees and influence diagrams.

The PrecisionTree component of DecisionTools® allows you to construct and solve diagrams and trees quickly and accurately. As you build your model, PrecisionTree creates the underlying mathematical representation of the model. PrecisionTree provides the mathematical formulas, allowing you to concentrate on accurately structuring the decision. Features such as pop-up dialog boxes and one-click deletion or insertion of nodes greatly facilitate the structuring process. Visual cues make it easy to distinguish node types: Red circles represent chance nodes, green squares are decision nodes, blue triangles are payoff nodes, and blue rounded rectangles are calculation nodes. Let's put PrecisionTree to work by creating a decision tree for the research-and-development decision (Figure 3.32) and an influence diagram for the basic risky decision (Figure 3.9).

In the instructions in this and subsequent chapters, items in *italics* are words shown on your computer screen. Items in **bold** indicate actions you take, such entering text or clicking the mouse. The boxes you see in the text that follows highlight actions you take as the user, with explanatory text between the boxes. Several steps may be described in any given box, so be sure to read and follow the instructions carefully.

Constructing a Decision Tree for the Research-and-Development Decision

In this chapter we concentrate on PrecisionTree's graphical features, which are specifically designed to help construct decision trees and influence diagrams. Figure 3.34 shows the decision tree for the research-and-development decision that you will generate using the PrecisionTree software.

FIGURE **3.34**

Decision tree for the research-and-development problem created in PrecisionTree.

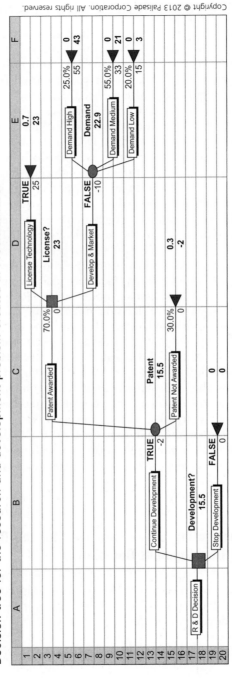

FIGURE **3.35**
PrecisionTree's
toolbar in Excel®

PrecisionTree Toolbar

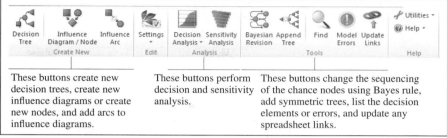

These buttons create new
decision trees, create new
influence diagrams or create
new nodes, and add arcs to
influence diagrams.

These buttons perform
decision and sensitivity
analysis.

These buttons change the sequencing
of the chance nodes using Bayes rule,
add symmetric trees, list the decision
elements or errors, and update any
spreadsheet links.

STEP 1 *Starting the Decision Tree Model.*

1.1 Start by opening both Excel® and PrecisionTree. If prompted, choose **Enable Macros**. If you open PrecisionTree first, Excel® will automatically be launched. However, opening Excel® does not launch PrecisionTree. PrecisionTree's toolbar is shown in Figure 3.35.

1.2 Help is always just one click away. You can access a variety of help features by clicking on the **Help** button shown in Figure 3.35. Under *Documentation*, click on *Help* for a searchable database of Precision-Tree or click on *Manual* for the pdf file of the actual manual. In addition, you can view examples via *Example Spreadsheets* or watch training videos along with a guided tour by clicking on *Welcome to PrecisionTree*.

1.3 The first step is simple; click on the **Decision Tree** button and indicate where you want your tree started in the pop-up dialog box. For this example, we choose cell **A1** and clicked **OK**. When deciding where to start the decision-tree model, do not fret about where to place the tree due to its size. Every time we add nodes, PrecisionTree automatically inserts rows into the spreadsheet to accommodate the addition. Thus, if you have data above or below the model, the tree will not disturb the data. Be careful, however, about whether you have data to the left or right of the model, as the inserted rows could separate the data rows from one another.

1.4 Change the tree name in the *Model Settings* dialog box from *New Tree* to **R & D Decision**. Click **OK**. At any point, you can access the *Model Settings* dialog box by clicking directly on the tree's name. Note that a pointing hand appears when the cursor is in position to access the dialog box. The tree's root appears in A1 along with a single end node (blue triangle).

Two numbers appear at the end of the decision tree, 100% in cell B1 and 0 in B2. Throughout the model, the top number (in this case 100%) always

FIGURE **3.36**
Naming branches of
the "Development?"
decision node.

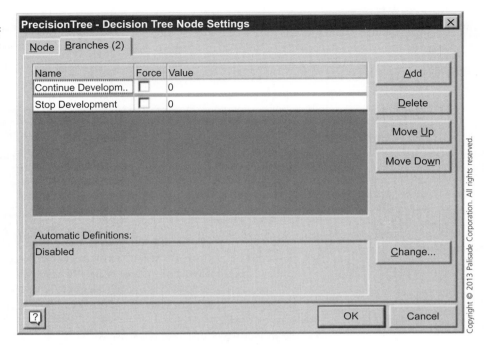

represents the probability of reaching the end node and the bottom number
(in this case 0) always represents the value attained upon reaching this node.
We'll return in the next chapter for a more complete discussion of these
values and probabilities. For now, let's focus our attention on structuring
the decision.

STEP 2 Adding the "Development?" Decision Node.

2.1 To add a node, click directly on the **end node** (blue triangle) where the new
node is to be placed, and the *Node Settings* dialog box pops up. Alternatively,
right-click on the **end node**, and choose *Node Settings* in the pop-up menu.

2.2 Click on the **Decision** button (green square, second from the top) and
change the name from *Decision* to **Development?** We discuss the *Use
of Branch Values* in later chapters.

2.3 Click on the **Branches** (2) tab along the top of the *Node Settings* dialog
box. In this tab, branches can be named, added, deleted, or moved
around via the buttons to the right. Leave the number of branches at 2
because there are two alternatives, and name these alternatives:
Continue Development and **Stop Development**. Your node settings
dialog box should now look like Figure 3.36. Click **OK**.

2.4 Nodes can also be named by directly typing over the current name in
the spreadsheet cell (cell B3 in our example). Branches can be named
by clicking directly on their labels, and typing the new name in the
pop-up dialog box. *Warning*: Do not delete or type over any of
the spreadsheet formulas created by PrecisionTree. For example,

the formula in B4 is part of the PrecisionTree mathematical model, and deleting it will break the model requiring that you start over from the beginning. PrecisionTree formulas are easily identified as they are in bold lettering and colored red, green, or blue.

Each alternative or branch of the decision tree can have an associated value, often representing monetary gains or losses. Gains are expressed as positive values, and losses are expressed as negative values. If there is no gain or loss, the value is zero. In PrecisionTree you enter values by simply typing in the appropriate number below the corresponding branch.

2.5 Enter −2 in the spreadsheet cell below the *Continue Development* branch (B2 for us) because it costs $2 million to continue developing the research project.

2.6 Alternatively, pull up the *Node settings* dialog box by clicking directly on the **decision node** (green square), then click on the **Branches (2)** tab, and enter −2 for the value of *Continue Development*.

2.7 We need not enter zero for the *Stop Development* branch, as zero is the default value.

Working with a spreadsheet gives you the option of entering formulas or numbers in the cells. For example, instead of entering a number directly into one of PrecisionTree's value cells, you might refer to a cell that calculates a net present value. The flexibility of referring to other spreadsheet calculations will be useful in later chapters when we model more complex decisions.

STEP 3 *Adding the "Patent Chance" Node.*

If you decide to stop development, no further modeling is necessary and the tree ends for this alternative. On the other hand, if the decision is to continue development, the future uncertainty regarding the patent requires further modeling. The uncertainty is modeled as the "Patent" chance node shown in Figure 3.34.

3.1 To add a chance node, click on the **end node** (blue triangle) that follows the *Continue Development* branch.

3.2 In the *Node Settings* box that appears, choose the **Chance** node button (red circle, first from the top) and change the name from *Chance* to **Patent.**

3.3 Click on the **Branches (2)** tab. Change the names of the branches to **Patent Awarded** and **Patent Not Awarded** by clicking on the labels and typing in the new names. Click **OK**.

Whereas each branch of a decision node has only an associated value, each branch (outcome) of a chance node has both an associated value and a probability. For PrecisionTree, the probabilities are positioned above the branch and the values below the branch. Looking at the diagram you are constructing, you see that PrecisionTree has placed 50.0% above each branch, and has given each branch a value of zero. These are default values and need to be changed to agree with the judgments of the decision maker, as shown in Figure 3.34.

3.4 Click in the spreadsheet cell (C1) above *Patent Awarded* and type **70%** to indicate that there is a 70% chance of the patent being awarded.

3.5 Select the cell (C5) above *Patent Not Awarded* and enter **=1– C1,** where C1 is the cell that contains 70%. In general, it is better to use cell references than numbers when constructing a model so that any changes will automatically be propagated throughout the model. In this case, using the formula =1–C1 will guarantee that the probabilities add to one even if the patent-awarded probability changes.

3.6 The values remain at zero because there are no direct gains or losses that occur at the time of either outcome.

3.7 Alternatively, we can enter all the previously stated probabilities and values via the *Node Settings* dialog box. To access the *Node Settings* dialog box, click directly on the **Patent** chance node created in Steps 3.1–3.3, click on the **Branches (2)** tab, enter **70%** for the probability of the Patent Awarded branch, and enter **=1–C1** for the probability of Patent Not Awarded. Figure 3.37 shows the completed action for this step.

FIGURE **3.37**
Naming and assigning probabilities to the outcomes of the "Patent" chance node.

Note that probabilities are entered as percentages. Thus, entering 0.70 would result in a probability of 0.7% not the desired 70%. Also, the formula: 1 – C1, where C1 is the 70%, guarantees the 2 probabilities always sum to one, even when the probability values are altered.

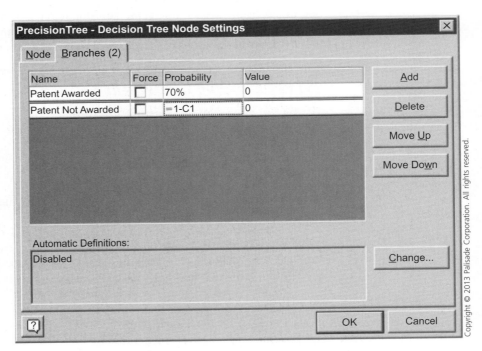

STEP 4 Adding the "License Decision" Node.

Once you know the patent outcome, you must decide whether to license the technology or develop and market the product directly.

4.1 Click the **end node** (blue triangle) of the *Patent Awarded* branch.
4.2 Choose **decision node** (green square) in the *Node Settings* dialog box.
4.3 Name the decision **License?**
4.4 Click on the **Branches (2)** tab and rename the new branches **License Technology** and **Develop & Market**.
4.5 PrecisionTree defaults to a value of zero for each branch. Change the value to **25** for the *License Technology* branch, because the value of licensing the technology is $25 million, given that the patent has been awarded.
4.6 Similarly, enter **–10** for the value of the *Develop & Market* branch, because a $10 million investment in production and marketing is needed, again assuming we have the patent.
4.7 Click **OK.**

PrecisionTree calculates the end-node values by summing the values along the path that lead to that end node. For example, the end value of the "License Technology" branch is 23 because the values along the path that lead to "License Technology" are –2, 0, and 25, which sum to 23. In Chapter 4 we explain how to input your own specific formula for calculating the end-node values.

STEP 5 Adding the "Market Demand" Uncertainty.

Developing the product in-house requires us to model market demand, the final step in the structuring process.

5.1 Click on the **end node** of the *Develop & Market* branch.
5.2 Select **Chance** as the node type.
5.3 Enter the name **Demand.**
5.4 Click on the **Branches (2)** tab, and because we have three outcomes for this uncertainty, click the **Add** button to add our third outcome. Note that the tab's label is now *Branches (3)*. See Figure 3.38.
5.5 Name the branches **Demand High, Demand Medium,** and **Demand Low.**
5.6 Enter **25%**, **55**, and **=1–(E5+E9)** for the probabilities of the *Demand High, Demand Medium,* and *Demand Low* branches respectively.
5.7 Enter **55, 33, 15** for the values of the *Demand High, Demand Medium,* and *Demand Low* branches respectively. Click **OK.**

Congratulations! You have just completed structuring the research-and-development decision tree. You can compare your tree with Figure 3.34.

FIGURE **3.38**
Adding a third
branch with the
probabilities and
values for the De-
mand uncertainty.

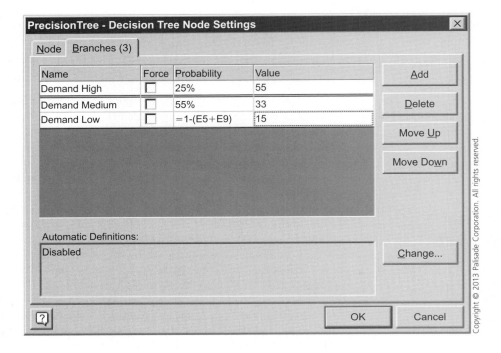

Notice that PrecisionTree has placed a formula above each alternative that reads either TRUE or FALSE. The TRUE identifies the alternative with the maximum expected payout. Thus, for each decision node, there will always be exactly one TRUE (one maximum) and the remaining branches will be labeled FALSE. You can override PrecisionTree's TRUE label by using the *Force* option in the *Node Settings* dialog box, as shown in Figure 3.36. By clicking on a decision node's *Force* checkbox, a TRUE will be placed on that branch identifying that alternative as your most preferred. You can tell when the *Force* option has been chosen as the branch itself turns red.

There are several common spreadsheet or word processing functions that are useful when constructing decision trees. For example, whole sections of a tree can be copied and pasted. If you place the cursor over any node, including end nodes, and right-click, a context-specific submenu appears. The submenu items pertaining to structuring trees and their functions are listed here:

Submenu Command	Function
Node Settings	Accesses the Node Settings dialog box for the chosen node.
Add Branch	Adds one branch to the node.
Collapse Child Branches	Hides, but does not delete, all branches following the node.

Expand Child Branches	Unhides or shows all branches following the node.
Insert Node	Inserts a two-branch decision node before the one selected. Use editing tools to change as needed.
Copy/Paste/Delete SubTree	Copies/Pastes/Deletes node and all branches following node.

You can use the *Copy* and *Paste* command for duplicating nodes. When a node is copied, the entire subtree following it is also copied, making it easy to replicate entire portions of the tree. Similarly, *Delete* removes not only the chosen node, but all downstream nodes and branches as well. For example, to delete the entire tree, simply delete the first branch where the tree's name resides. The *Collapse* button hides all the downstream details but does not delete them; a *boldface plus sign* next to a node indicates that the subtree that follows has been collapsed. New to PrecisionTree is the *Insert* command which inserts nodes anywhere, even between existing nodes. A decision node will be inserted, but this can then be changed to any node type.

PrecisionTree provides two additional node types: logic and reference nodes. The logic node (purple square) is a decision node that determines the chosen alternative by applying a user-specified logic formula to each option. See the PrecisionTree user's manual for more details. The reference node (gray diamond) allows you to repeat a portion of the tree that has already been constructed without manually reconstructing that portion. Reference nodes are especially useful when constructing a large and complex decision tree because they allow you to prune the tree graphically while retaining all the details. See Chapter 4 for an example that uses reference nodes.

Constructing an Influence Diagram for the Basic Risky Decision

PrecisionTree also provides the ability to structure decisions using influence diagrams.

Follow the step-by-step instructions below to create an influence diagram for the basic risky decision (Figure 3.39). Unlike decision trees, you can create nodes in an influence diagram in any order. It is the arcs in an influence diagram that determine their sequence. Our starting point in the text that follows assumes that PrecisionTree is open and your Excel® worksheet is empty. If not, see Step 1 (1.1) above.

STEP 6 *Starting the Influence Diagram.*

6.1 Start by clicking on the **Influence Diagram/Node** button (PrecisionTree toolbar, second button from the left).

6.2 Although an influence diagram may be started by clicking on any cell, for this example start the diagram by clicking on cell **B10**. Click **OK**.

FIGURE **3.39**
Influence diagram for basic risky decision created in PrecisionTree.

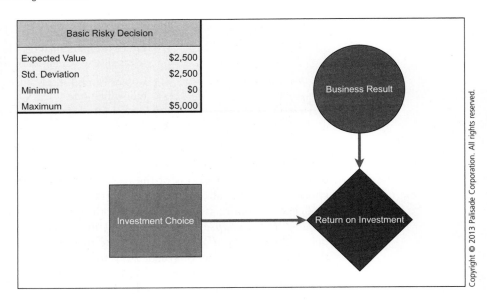

Basic Risky Decision	
Expected Value	$2,500
Std. Deviation	$2,500
Minimum	$0
Maximum	$5,000

The spreadsheet is altered in three ways:

1. A payoff node appears.
2. A dialog box titled *PrecisionTree Model Settings* opens.
3. A gray box labeled *Diagram #1* appears, displaying four summary statistics: expected value, standard deviation, minimum, and maximum. The #N/A appearing for each statistic reflects that we have yet to add values and probabilities to the model.

6.3 Name the influence diagram **Basic Risky Decision** in the *PrecisionTree Model Settings* dialog box, and click **OK**. You can access the model settings at any point by clicking directly on the model's name in cells A1 and B1. Next, we change the payoff node to a decision node with two alternatives: invest $2,000 in a friend's business or $2,000 in a savings account.

6.4 Click directly on the name **Payoff** and the *Influence Node Settings* dialog box appears. The cursor changes into a pointing hand when you are in position to access the *Settings* dialog box. Change to a decision node by clicking on the **Decision** button (green square, second from the top), and enter **Investment Choice** as the node name.

6.5 Click on the **Outcomes (2)** tab along the top of the *Node Settings* box. Rename the alternatives by replacing *Outcome # 1* with **Savings** and *Outcome # 2* with **Business Investment**. The *Up, Down, Delete,* and *Add* buttons in the *Node Settings* dialog box affect only the

Outcomes list and are not used when renaming the outcomes from the list.

6.6 Click on the **Exit to Value Table** button along the bottom of the *Influence Node Settings* dialog box. Figure 3.40 shows the Value Table that pops up.

6.7 Enter **0 (zero)** for the *Value when skipped*. The Value when skipped is usually zero and is the value used in the payoff node (final calculation) if and when the node is skipped. The typical reason for skipping a node is that the model is asymmetric, *e.g.*, if we decide to place our money in a savings account, then we would skip the chance node Business Results because it has no impact on our savings account.

6.8 Enter **–2000** for the value of the savings account; hit the **Enter** key on your keyboard; enter **–2000** for the value of Business investment; and hit **Enter**. These numbers are negative as it costs $2,000 for either investment.

6.9 When you are finished, your *Value Table* should look like Figure 3.40. Click **OK**.

Note that the Value Table shown in Figure 3.40 is actually an Excel® mini-spreadsheet. Thus, we can place numerical values, formulas, or even cell references in the Value Table. This can be very handy as a Value Table requires a value for each possible combination of outcomes from the

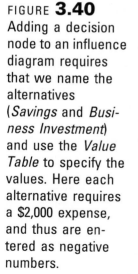

FIGURE **3.40**
Adding a decision node to an influence diagram requires that we name the alternatives (*Savings* and *Business Investment*) and use the *Value Table* to specify the values. Here each alternative requires a $2,000 expense, and thus are entered as negative numbers.

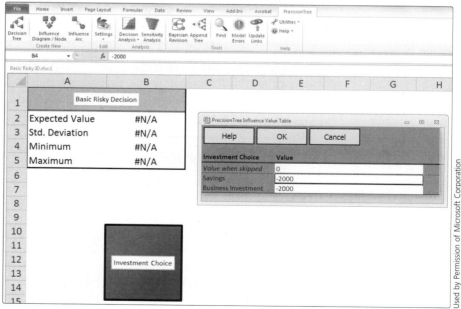

proceeding nodes, and this list can be quite large. Referring to cells in the spreadsheet or even referring to cells in preceding nodes can greatly reduce the tedium of filling out the Value Table. You can also use the drag-down feature of Excel® in a Value Table! We provide examples of the flexibility of Value Tables in Step 11 below.

As with decision trees, right-clicking on the node brings up a context-specific submenu which allows us to rename the node, delete the node, or pull up the Node Settings or the Value Table. In general, you can right-click on any object and the corresponding submenu provides most of the editing features you need. For example, to delete the whole influence diagram, not just a node, right-click on the diagram's name in cells A1 and B1, choose *Model*, then choose *Delete*.

STEP 7 Adding the "Business Result" chance node.

7.1 Click on the **Influence Diagram/Node** button on the PrecisionTree toolbar.

7.2 Click in cell **E2**. Click **OK**.

7.3 To make this a chance node, click on the **Chance** node icon (red circle) in the *Influence Node Settings* dialog box.

7.4 Following the same procedure as before, name the node **Business Result** and the two outcomes **Wild Success** and **Flop.**

7.5 Click on the **Exit to Value Table** button, enter **7000** for the value of *Wild Success* and enter **0.50** for the corresponding probability. Enter **2000** for the value of *Flop* and enter **0.50** for its probability. Finally, enter **0 (zero)** for *Value when skipped* and click **OK**.

Notice that for *Wild Success* we entered $7,000 and upon adding that to −$2,000, we end up at the desired $5,000. Similarly, $2,000 for *Flop* plus the invested $2,000 results in a final cash position of $0.

STEP 8 Adding the payoff node.

The last node to be added to our diagram is the payoff node. Every influence diagram has one and only one payoff node. Creating a payoff node is similar to creating the other types of nodes except that naming the node is the only available option.

8.1 Start by clicking the **Influence Diagram/Node** button.

8.2 Click on cell **E10**. Click **OK**.

8.3 Click on the **payoff node** icon (blue diamond) in the *Influence Node Settings* dialog box, enter the name **Return on Investment,** and click **OK**.

If your payoff node is a bit undersized, you can click on the graphic, not the name, and resize the graphic using the sizing box that surrounds the graphic. Recall that clicking on the name accesses the Settings dialog box.

Now, we add the arcs between the nodes. Arcs in PrecisionTree are somewhat more elaborate than what we've described in the text, and so a brief discussion is in order before proceeding.

PrecisionTree and the text slightly differ on terminology: What we refer to as relevance arcs, PrecisionTree calls value arcs, and what we know as sequence arcs, PrecisionTree calls timing arcs. We are able to tell by context whether the arc is a relevance (value) or a sequence (timing) arc, but the program cannot. Hence, for each arc that you create in PrecisionTree, you must indicate whether it is a value arc, a timing arc, or both. This means that PrecisionTree forces you to think carefully about the type of influence for each arc as you construct your influence diagram. Let's examine these arc types and learn how to choose the right characteristics to represent the desired relationship between two nodes.

The value arc option is used when the possible outcomes or any of the numerical details (probabilities or numerical values associated with outcomes) in the successor node are influenced by the outcomes of the predecessor node. Ask yourself if knowing the outcome of the predecessor affects the outcomes, probabilities, or values of the successor node. If you answer yes, then use a value arc. Conversely, if none of the outcomes has an effect, a value arc is not indicated. (Recall that this is the same test for relevance that we used in the text.) Let's demonstrate with some examples. The arc from *Investment Choice* to *Return on Investment* is a value arc if any of the investment alternatives (*Savings* or *Business*) affect the returns on your investment. Because they clearly do, you would make this a value arc. Another example from the hurricane problem is the arc connecting the chance node *Hurricane Path* with the chance node *Forecast*. This is also a value arc; we presume that the weather forecast really does bear some relationship to the actual weather and hence that the probabilities for the forecast are related to the path the hurricane takes.

Use a timing arc when the predecessor occurs chronologically prior to the successor. An example, again from the hurricane problem, is the arc from the chance node *Forecast* to the decision node *Decision*. It is a timing arc because the decision maker knows the forecast before deciding whether or not to evacuate.

Use both the value and timing options when the arc satisfies both conditions. For example, consider the arc from the *Investment Choice* node to the *Return on Investment* node. To calculate the return, you need to know that the investment decision has been made (timing), and you need to know which alternative was chosen (value). In fact, any arc that terminates at the payoff node must be both value and timing, and so the arc from *Business Result* to *Return on Investment* also has both characteristics.

Arcs in influence diagrams are more than mere arrows; they actually define mathematical relationships between the nodes they connect. It is necessary to think carefully about each arc so that it correctly captures the relationship between the two nodes. PrecisionTree not only forces you to decide the arc type, but it also supplies feedback on the effect each arc has when values are added to the influence diagram. If you add an arc and you do not see the desired results in the Value Table, then simply modify your arc. At first, choosing the correct arc type can be difficult, but with some practice, it becomes much easier. Don't be afraid to experiment!

STEP 9 Adding an arc from Investment Choice to Return on Investment.

9.1 Click on the **Influence Arc** button on the PrecisionTree toolbar (Figure 3.35, third button from the left). Up pops the *Create New Influence Arc* dialog box.

9.2 Choose **Investment Choice** as the *Source Node* and **Return on Investment** as the Destination Node. Click **OK** and click **OK** again.

An arc or arrow appears between the nodes along with the *Influence Arc Settings* dialog box. Because the arc terminates into the payoff node, we have no choice as to its settings. It must be both a Value arc (because the investment decision influences the payoff) and a Timing arc (because the investment decision comes before the payoff). There is a third influence type—structure arcs—that will not be discussed. See the PrecisionTree manual or on-line help about structure arcs.

STEP 10 Adding an arc from Business Result to Return on Investment.

10.1 Click on the **Influence Arc** button on the PrecisionTree toolbar. Up pops the *Create New Influence Arc* dialog box.

10.2 In the *Create New Influence Arc* dialog box, choose **Business Result** as the *Source Node* and **Return on Investment** as the Destination Node. Click **OK** twice.

The last step is to enter the payoff formulas, which are defined in the *Influence Value Table* (Figure 3.41). For each row, we start with an equal sign (=) in the value cell, and define a formula that reflects the decisions and outcomes of that row. For example, reading from right to left in the first row, we see that we invested in the savings account, and the business was (or would have been) a wild success. Because we chose the certain return guaranteed by the savings account, the value of our investment is $2,000 plus 10%, or $2,200. In this case, the value does not depend on whether the business was a success or a flop. Hence, the payoff formula includes only the investment choice and not the business result. In the third row, however, we hit the jackpot with our investment in the business when it becomes a wild success. Thus, the formula for this case will include both the investment choice and the business result.

FIGURE **3.41**
The final payoff
amounts are
determined by using
the outcome table
along the right-hand
side. By clicking
on the name in the
outcome table, the
corresponding
value is accessed.
For example, clicking
on *Business
Investment* pulls
up E6, which is the
$2,000 expense.
Clicking on *Wild
Success* pulls up
D6, the $7,000
payout. Thus,
E6 + D6 = $5,000.

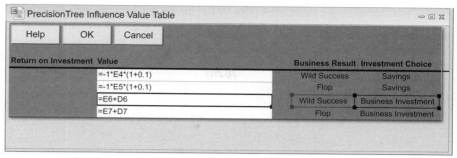

PrecisionTree Influence Value Table			– ⊡ ⌧
Help	OK	Cancel	

Return on Investment Value	Business Result	Investment Choice
=-1*E4*(1+0.1)	Wild Success	Savings
=-1*E5*(1+0.1)	Flop	Savings
=E6+D6	Wild Success	Business Investment
=E7+D7	Flop	Business Investment

STEP 11 *Defining the payoff formulas.*

11.1 Open the *Influence Value Table* by clicking directly on the name **Return on Investment**, then click the **Exit to Value Table ...** button.

11.2 Type an **equal sign** (=) into the first value cell.

11.3 Move the cursor to the right to the word **Savings** below the *Investment Choice* heading, and click. "E4" appears in the value cell next to the equal sign. E4 references the −$2,000 value we assigned to *Savings* in Step 11.

11.4 To complete this cell, we need to compute the final cash position of the savings account. As the accounts pays 10% interest, the payout is $2,200. Starting with E4, which equals −2000, we enter: = E4*(−1)*(1 + 0.1). Multiplying E4 by negative one merely shifts the negative 2000 to positive 2,000, then multiplying by (1 + 0.1) is the principle plus the 10% interest.

11.5 In the next row down, type another = into the value cell.

11.6 Click on **Savings** to the cell's right and two rows below the heading *Investment Choice*. "E5" appears in the cell. Finish by entering = E5*(−1)*(1 + 0.1). Alternatively, you can drag down the formula from Step 11.4; simply highlight the previous cell, move the cursor to the lower right-corner, and drag down. Try it!

11.7 In the third value cell, type =, click on **Business Investment** (to access the $2,000 investment), type +, and click on **Wild Success** (to access the $7,000 earnings) to the cell's right and three rows below the heading *Business Result*.

11.8 Using Figure 3.41 as a guide, enter the final set of values, and click **OK**. Note that you use the cells to the right and always in the *same row* as the value cell you are defining.

Congratulations! You have just completed the influence diagram for the basic risky decision. The summary statistics box should now display the expected value ($2,500), standard deviation ($2,500), minimum ($0), and maximum ($5,000).

The nodes in an influence diagram can be modified in three ways. Clicking directly on the node's name allows us to modify the attributes of the node, such as node type, outcome names, and numerical information. Clicking on the node itself rather than the name allows us to edit the graphics, such as resizing the node or dragging it to a new location. Finally, right-clicking on the node (either on the name or on the graphic) brings up a sub-menu with specific editing features, such as deleting nodes or converting the influence diagram into a decision tree. The conversion feature (from influence diagram to tree) of PrecisionTree is very helpful as it provides feedback on the structure of the diagram. See Problem 3.26 for instructions on how to perform this conversion.

This concludes our instructions for building an influence diagram. Additional influence-diagram structuring tools are available in Precision-Tree that we have not covered. For example, we mentioned that calculation nodes are helpful in emphasizing a decision's structure. These are available in PrecisionTree and are found in the *Node Settings* dialog box as the blue, rounded hexagon. In addition, structure arcs can be used if you wish to skip a node or force a particular outcome or alternative to be chosen. We highly recommend that you spend a few minutes experimenting with the program, trying new options to understand the capabilities of PrecisionTree.

SUMMARY

This chapter has discussed the general process of structuring decision problems. It is impossible to overemphasize the importance of the structuring step, because it is here that one really understands the problem and all of its different aspects. We began with the process of structuring values, emphasizing the importance of identifying underlying fundamental objectives and separating those from means objectives. Fundamental objectives, structured in a hierarchy, are those things that the decision maker wants to accomplish, and means objectives, structured in a network, describe ways to accomplish the fundamental objectives.

With objectives specified, we can begin to structure a decision's specific elements. A decision maker may use both influence diagrams and decision trees as tools in the process of modeling decisions. Influence diagrams provide compact representations of decision problems while suppressing many of the details, and thus they are ideal for obtaining overviews, especially for complex problems. Influence diagrams are especially appropriate for communicating decision structure because they are easily understood by individuals with little technical background. In contrast, decision trees display all of the minute details. Being able to see the details can be an advantage, but in complex decisions, trees may be too large and "bushy" to be of much use in communicating with others.

The clarity test is used to ensure that the problem is defined well enough so that everyone can agree on the definitions of the basic decision elements, and we also discussed the specification of probabilities and cash flows at different points in the problem. We also discussed the notion of attribute scales for measuring the extent to which fundamental objectives are accomplished, and we showed how scales can be constructed to measure achievement of those objectives that do not have natural measures. Finally, we introduced PrecisionTree for structuring decisions with both decision trees and influence diagrams.

EXERCISES

3.1 Describe in your own words the difference between a means objective and a fundamental objective. Why do we focus on coming up with attribute scales that measure accomplishment of fundamental objectives, but not means objectives? What good does it do to know what your means objectives are?

3.2 What are your fundamental objectives in the context of renting an apartment while attending college? What are your means objectives? Create a fundamental-objectives hierarchy and a means-objectives network.

3.3 In the context of renting an apartment (Exercise 3.2), some of the objectives may have natural attribute scales. Examples are minimizing rent ($) or minimizing the distance to campus (kilometers or city blocks). But other attributes, such as ambiance, amount of light, or neighbors, have no natural scales. Construct an attribute scale with at least five different levels, ranked from best to worst, for some aspect of an apartment that is important to you but has no natural scale.

3.4 Before making an unsecured loan to an individual a bank orders a report on the applicant's credit history. To justify making the loan, the bank must find the applicant's credit record to be satisfactory. Describe the bank's decision. What are the bank's objectives? What risk does the bank face? What role does the credit report play? Using PrecisionTree, create an influence diagram of this situation. (*Hint:* Your influence diagram should include chance nodes for a credit report and for eventual default. Also, PrecisionTree can convert influence diagrams into decision tress and this can be helpful in checking your work. See Problem 3.26 for instructions on conversion.) Finally, be sure to specify everything (decisions, chance events, objectives) in your model clearly enough to pass the clarity test.

3.5 When a movie producer decides whether to produce a major motion picture, the main question is how much revenue the movie will generate. Draw a decision tree of this situation, assuming that there is only one fundamental objective, to maximize revenue. What must be included in revenue to be sure that the clarity test is passed?

3.6 You have met an acquaintance for lunch, and he is worried about an upcoming meeting with his boss and some executives from his firm's headquarters. He has to outline the costs and benefits of some alternative investment strategies. He knows about both decision trees and influence diagrams but cannot decide which presentation to use. In your own words, explain to him the advantages and disadvantages of each.

3.7 Reframe your answer to Exercise 3.6 in terms of objectives and alternatives. That is, what are appropriate fundamental objectives to consider in the context of choosing how to present the investment information? How do decision trees and influence diagrams compare in terms of these objectives?

3.8 Create an influence diagram for the politician's decision in Figure 3.25 using PrecisionTree. Include the tables showing decision alternatives, chance-event outcomes, and consequences.

3.9 A dapper young decision maker has just purchased a new suit for $200. On the way out the door, the decision maker considers taking an umbrella. With the umbrella on hand, the suit will be protected in the event of rain. Without the umbrella, the suit will be ruined if it rains. However, if it does not rain, carrying the umbrella is an unnecessary inconvenience.

   a. Create a decision tree of this situation.

   b. Create an influence diagram of the situation using PrecisionTree.

   c. Before deciding, the decision maker considers listening to the weather forecast on the radio. Using PrecisionTree, Create an influence diagram that takes into account the weather forecast.

3.10 When patients suffered from hemorrhagic fever, M*A*S*H doctors replaced lost sodium by administering a saline solution intravenously. However, headquarters (HQ) sent a treatment change disallowing the saline solution. With a patient in shock and near death from a disastrously low sodium level, B. J. Hunnicut wanted to administer a low-sodium-concentration saline solution as a last-ditch attempt to save the patient. Colonel Potter looked at B. J. and Hawkeye and summed up the situation. "O.K., let's get this straight. If we go by the new directive from HQ and don't administer saline to replace the sodium, our boy will die for sure. If we try B. J.'s idea, then he may survive, and we'll know how to treat the next two patients who are getting worse. If we try it and he doesn't make it, we're in trouble with HQ and may get court-martialed. I say we have no choice. Let's try it." (*Source:* "Mr. and Mrs. Who." Written by Ronny Graham, directed by Burt Metcalfe, 1980.)

     Structure the doctors' decision. What are their objectives? What risks do they face? Draw a decision tree for their decision.

3.11 Here is an example that provides a comparison between influence diagrams and decision trees.

   a. Suppose you are planning a party, and your objective is to have an enjoyable party for all the guests. An outdoor barbecue would be the best, but only if the sun shines; rain would ruin the barbecue. On the other hand, you could plan an indoor party. This would be a good party, not as nice as an outdoor barbecue in the sunshine but better than a barbecue in the rain. Of course, it is always possible to forego the party altogether! Construct an influence diagram and a decision tree using PrecisionTree for this problem.

   b. You will, naturally, consult the weather forecast, which will tell you that the weather will be either "sunny" or "rainy." The forecast is not perfect, however. If the forecast is "sunny," then sunshine is more likely than rain, but there still is a small chance that it will rain. A forecast of "rainy" implies that rain is likely, but the sun may still shine. Now draw an influence diagram using PrecisionTree for the decision, including the weather forecast. (There should be four nodes in your diagram, including one for the forecast, which will be available at the time you decide what kind of party to have, and one for the actual weather. Which direction should the arrow point between these two nodes? Why?) Now draw a decision tree for this problem. Recall that the events and decisions in a decision tree should be in chronological order.

3.12 The clarity test is an important issue in Exercise 3.11. The weather obviously can be somewhere between full sunshine and rain. Should you include an outcome like "cloudy"? Would it affect your satisfaction with an outdoor barbecue? How will you define rain? The National Weather Service uses the following definition: Rain has occurred if "measurable precipitation" (more than 0.004 inch) has occurred at the official rain gauge. Would this definition be suitable for your purposes? Define a set of weather outcomes that is appropriate relative to your objective of having an enjoyable party.

3.13 Draw the machine-replacement decision (Figure 3.10) as a decision tree.

QUESTIONS AND PROBLEMS

3.14 Modify the influence diagram in Figure 3.11 (the hurricane-forecast example) so that it contains nodes for each of the two objectives (maximize safety and minimize cost). Cost has a natural attribute scale, but how can you define safety? Construct an attribute scale that you could use to measure the degree of danger you might encounter during a hurricane.

3.15 Decision analysis can be used on itself! What do you want to accomplish in studying decision analysis? Why is decision analysis important to you? In short, what are your fundamental objectives in studying decision analysis? What are appropriate means objectives? Is your course design consistent with your objectives? If not, how could the course be modified to achieve your objectives?

3.16 Facebook is a free social-network website that allows you to find groups of people with similar interests and then befriend them virtually. Facebook provides a "public" area where you can post a profile of yourself along with pictures and links, and a "private" area where you can share more intimate details about your life. Access to the private area is by invitation only, but as many unhappy users have discovered, their privacy can be violated. Stories abound of pictures or comments meant only for a select group of friends being seen by a much wider audience, including potential or current employers. For example, two MIT students used an automated script to download over 70,000 Facebook profiles. Also, unauthorized strangers can search the Facebook site and discover the preferences you record (religious, sexual, political, etc). Wired News searched for women in a major U.S. city who were interested in random hookups with men and found the names and photos of two high school girls! While Facebook allows you to find out what your friends did last night, are doing right now, and plan on doing tomorrow, it also can blindside you when your private area is made public.

Consider setting up your own Facebook profile or modifying the one you already have. You can think of Facebook and other social-network sites as a means to obtain certain objectives. What exactly are *your* objectives in setting up your public and private areas? Using Table 3.2, develop your own fundamentals objective hierarchy. What is it you want to accomplish and why? How does knowing that your private area can be broken into change your objectives? (Sources: http://www.wired.com/software/webservices/news/2007/06 /facebookprivacysearch; Wikipedia: Facebook, January 27, 2009)

3.17 When an amateur astronomer considers purchasing or building a telescope to view deep sky objects (galaxies, clusters, nebulae, etc.), the three primary considerations are minimizing cost, having a stable mounting device, and maximizing the *aperture* (diameter of the main lens or mirror). The aperture is crucial because a larger aperture gathers more light. With more light, more detail can be seen in the image, and what the astronomer wants to do is to see the image as clearly as possible. As an example, many small telescopes have lenses or mirrors up to 8 inches in diameter. Larger amateur telescopes use concave mirrors ranging from 10 to 20 inches in diameter. Some amateurs grind their own mirrors large as 40 inches.

Saving money is important, of course, because the less spent on the telescope, the more can be spent on accessories (eyepieces, star charts, computer-based astronomy programs, warm clothing, flashlights, and so on) to make viewing as easy and comfortable as possible.

Money might also be spent on an observatory to house a large telescope or on trips away from the city (to avoid the light pollution of city skies and thus to see images more clearly).

Finally, a third issue is the way the telescope is mounted. First, the mount should be very stable, keeping the telescope perfectly still. Any vibrations will show up dramatically in the highly magnified image, thus reducing the quality of the image and the detail that can be seen. The mount should also allow for easy and smooth movement of the telescope to view any part of the sky. Finally, if the astronomer wants to use the telescope to take photographs of the sky (astrophotos), it is important that the mount include some sort of tracking device to keep the telescope pointing at the same point in the sky as the earth rotates beneath it.

Based on this description, what are the amateur astronomer's fundamental objectives in choosing a telescope? What are the means objectives? Structure these objectives into a fundamental-objectives hierarchy and a means-objectives network. (*Hint:* If you feel the need for more information, look in your library for recent issues of *Astronomy* magazine or *Sky and Telescope*, two publications for amateur astronomers.)

3.18   Consider the following situations that involve multiple objectives:
a.   Suppose you want to go out for dinner. What are your fundamental objectives? Create a fundamental-objectives hierarchy.
b.   Suppose you are trying to decide where to go for a trip over spring break. What are your fundamental objectives? What are your means objectives?
c.   You are about to become a parent (surprise!), and you have to choose a name for your child. What are important objectives to consider in choosing a name?
d.   Think of any other situation where choices involve multiple objectives. Create a fundamental-objectives hierarchy and a means-objectives network.

3.19   Thinking about fundamental objectives and means objectives is relatively easy when the decision context is narrow (buying a telescope, renting an apartment, choosing a restaurant for dinner). But when you start thinking about your strategic objectives—objectives in the context of what you choose to do with your life or your career—the process becomes more difficult. Spend some time thinking about your fundamental strategic objectives. What do you want to accomplish in your life or in your career? Why are these objectives important?

Try to create a fundamental-objectives hierarchy and a means-objectives network for yourself.

If you succeed in this problem, you will have achieved a deeper level of self-knowledge than most people have, regardless of whether they use decision analysis. That knowledge can be of great help to you in making important decisions, but you should revisit your fundamental objectives from time to time; they might change!

3.20   Occasionally a decision is sensitive to the way it is structured. The following problem shows that leaving out an important part of the problem can affect the way we view the situation.
a.   Imagine that a close friend has been diagnosed with heart disease. The physician recommends bypass surgery. The surgery should solve the problem. When asked about the risks, the physician replies that a few individuals die during the operation, but most recover, and the surgery is a complete success. Thus, your friend can (most likely) anticipate a longer and healthier life after the surgery. Without surgery, your friend will have a shorter and gradually deteriorating life. Assuming that your friend's objective is to maximize the quality of her life, using PrecisionTree diagram this decision with both an influence diagram and a decision tree.
b.   Suppose now that your friend obtains a second opinion. The second physician suggests that there is a third possible outcome: Complications from surgery can develop which will require long and painful treatment. If this happens, the eventual outcome can be either a full recovery, partial recovery (restricted to a wheelchair until death), or death within a few months. How does this change the decision tree and influence diagram that you created in part a? Draw the decision

tree and influence diagram using PrecisionTree that represent the situation after hearing from both physicians. Given this new structure, does surgery look more or less positive than it did in part a? [For more discussion of this problem, see von Winterfeldt and Edwards (1986, pp. 8–14).]

c. Construct an attribute scale for the patient's quality of life. Be sure to include levels that relate to all of the possible outcomes from surgery.

3.21 Create an influence diagram and a decision tree using PrecisionTree for the difficult decision problem that you described in Problem 1.9. What are your objectives? Construct attribute scales if necessary. Be sure that all aspects of your decision model pass the clarity test.

3.22 To be, or not to be, that is the question:

Whether 'tis nobler in the mind to suffer
The slings and arrows of outrageous fortune
Or to take arms against a sea of troubles,
And by opposing end them. To die—to sleep—
No more; and by a sleep to say we end
The heartache, and the thousand natural shocks
That flesh is heir to. 'Tis a consummation
Devoutly to be wished. To die—to sleep.
To sleep—perchance to dream: ay, there's the rub!
For in that sleep of death what dreams may come
When we have shuffled off this mortal coil,
Must give us pause. There's the respect
That makes calamity of so long life.
For who would bear the whips and scorns of time,
The oppressor's wrong, the proud man's contumely,
The pangs of despised love, the law's delay,
The insolence of office, and the spurns
That patient merit of the unworthy takes,
When he himself might his quietus make
With a bare bodkin? Who would these fardels bear,
To grunt and sweat under a weary life,
But that the dread of something after death—
The undiscovered country, from whose bourn
No traveler returns—puzzles the will,
And makes us rather bear those ills we have
Than fly to others that we know not of?

—*Hamlet*, Act III, Scene 1

Describe Hamlet's decision. What are his choices? What risk does he perceive? Construct a decision tree for Hamlet.

3.23 On July 3, 1988, the USS *Vincennes* was engaged in combat in the Persian Gulf. On the radar screen a blip appeared that signified an incoming aircraft. After repeatedly asking the aircraft to identify itself with no success, it appeared that the aircraft might be a hostile Iranian F-14 attacking the *Vincennes*. Captain Will Rogers had little time to make his decision. Should he issue the command to launch a missile and destroy the plane? Or should he wait for positive identification? If he waited too long and the plane was indeed hostile, then it might be impossible to avert the attack and danger to his crew.

Captain Rogers issued the command, and the aircraft was destroyed. It was reported to be an Iranian Airbus airliner carrying 290 people. There were no survivors.

What are Captain Rogers's fundamental objectives? What risks does he face? Draw a decision tree representing his decision.

3.24 Reconsider the research-and-development decision in Figure 3.32. If you decide to continue the project, you will have to come up with the $2 million this year (Year 1). Then there will be a year of waiting (Year 2) before you know if the patent is granted. If you decide to license the technology, you would receive the $25 million distributed as $5 million per year beginning in Year 3. On the other hand, if you decide to sell the product directly, you will have to invest $5 million in each of Years 3 and 4 (to make up the total investment of $10 million). Your net proceeds from selling the product, then, would be evenly distributed over Years 5 through 9.

Assuming an interest rate of 15%, calculate the NPV at the end of each branch of the decision tree.

3.25 When you purchase a car, you may consider buying a brand-new car or a used one. A fundamental trade-off in this case is whether you pay repair bills (uncertain at the time you buy the car) or make loan payments that are certain.

Consider two cars, a new one that costs $15,000 and a used one with 75,000 miles for $5,500. Let us assume that your current car's value and your available cash amount to $5,500, so you could purchase the used car outright or make a down payment of $5,500 on the new car. Your credit union is willing to give you a five-year, 10% loan on the $9,500 difference if you buy the new car; this loan will require monthly payments of $201.85 per month for 5 years. Maintenance costs are expected to be $100 for the first year and $300 per year for the second and third years.

After taking the used car to your mechanic for an evaluation, you learn the following. First, the car needs some minor repairs within the next few months, including a new battery, work on the suspension and steering mechanism, and replacement of the belt that drives the water pump. Your mechanic has estimated that these repairs will cost $150. Considering the amount you drive, the tires will last another year but will have to be replaced next year for about $200. Beyond that, the mechanic warns you that the cooling system (radiator and hoses) may need to be repaired or replaced this year or next and that the brake system may need work. These and other repairs that an older car may require could lead you to pay anywhere from $500 to $2,500 in each of the next 3 years. If you are lucky, the repair bills will be low or will come later. But you could end up paying a lot of money when you least expect it.

Draw a decision tree for this problem. To simplify it, look at the situation on a yearly basis for 3 years. If you buy the new car, you can anticipate cash outflows of 12 × $201.85 = $2,422.20 plus maintenance costs. For the used car, some of the repair costs are known (immediate repairs this year, tires next year), but we must model the uncertainty associated with the rest. In addition to the known repairs, assume that in each year there is a 20% chance that these uncertain repairs will be $500, a 20% chance they will be $2,500, and a 60% chance they will be $1,500. (*Hint:* You need three chance nodes: one for each year!)

To even the comparison of the two cars, we must also consider their values after 3 years. If you buy the new car, it will be worth approximately $8,000, and you will still owe $4,374. Thus, its net salvage value will be $3,626. On the other hand, you would own the used car free and clear (assuming you can keep up with the repair bills!), and it would be worth approximately $2,000.

Include all of the probabilities and cash flows (outflows until the last branch, then an inflow to represent the car's salvage value) in your decision tree. Calculate the net values at the ends of the branches.

3.26 PrecisionTree will convert any influence diagram into the corresponding decision tree with the click of a button. This provides an excellent opportunity to explore the meaning of arrows in an influence diagram because you can easily see the effect of adding or deleting an arrow in the corresponding decision tree. Because we are only concerned with the structural effect of arrows, we will not input numerical values.

a. Construct the influence diagram in Exercise 3.11(a) in PrecisionTree. Convert the influence diagram to a decision tree by right-clicking on the influence diagram's name (straddling cells A1 and B1) to pull up a menu, then choose **Model** and finally click on **Convert To Decision Tree.**

b. Add an arrow from the "Weather" chance node to the "Party" decision node and convert the influence diagram into a decision tree. Why would the decision tree change in this way?

c. Construct the influence diagram in Exercise 3.11(b) in PrecisionTree. Convert the influence diagram to a decision tree. How would the decision tree change if the arrow started at the "Party" decision node and went into the "Forecast" node? What if, in addition, the arrow started at the "Forecast" chance node and went into the "Weather" chance node?

3.27 Jameson is a 32-year-old father of three who thought he had finally found a career. While working as an assistant manager at a local shoe store, a customer, Vijay, befriended Jameson and invited him to join his financial services firm. Excited by the new opportunity, Jameson studied, took the required exams, and became a certified financial advisor. With all the connections he had established over the years at the shoe store, Jameson started to build up a clientele. Then the credit markets froze, and his client base dried up; nobody wanted to move their assets during the down market. Luckily, Jameson had kept his position as assistant manager and now takes home $2,000 per month, but even with that, his family of five still needs an additional $400 each month to make ends meet. With bleak economic forecasts continuing through the next year and perhaps even longer, he is wondering if he should stay the course with Vijay or go back to school for a Masters of Social Work (MSW), something he has always wanted.

Over the next year, Jameson assesses only a 20% chance that he will average $400/month as a financial advisor. His net, however, would only be $300/month, as there is a $100/month charge for Vijay's services. He assesses a 70% chance of averaging $100/month and a 10% chance of bringing in no revenue, all the while paying Vijay for services. Jameson expects the second year to be better, with a 30% chance of averaging $600/month, a 50% chance of $400/month, and a 20% chance of $200/month. Finally, Jameson expects dividends in the third year with a 20% chance of averaging $1,200/month, a 70% chance of $700/month, and 10% chance of $500/month. Vijay has indicated no change in fees for the first 3 years.

An MSW takes 2 years to complete as a full-time student and would necessitate his taking out a student loan for $30,000. Upon graduation in 2 years, Jamison is nearly assured of a position with a 17% chance of earning $40,000 annually, 66% chance of earning $50,000 annually, or 17% chance of earning $60,000 annually. He figures his monthly loan payment would be $175 and he would pay 40% in federal and state taxes.

Structure Jameson's decision using a decision tree. What would you recommend he do? Why?

3.28 Susan Cooper currently works as an assistant manager at Joe's Coffee and Tea, a national chain of over 200 coffee shops. Susan has worked at Joe's for 4 years. Feeling that her career was stalling, she enrolled part time ago at a local beauty college to earn a beautician license. She was planning to leave Joe's to attend college full time, but the recession hit, and her husband, Denzel, found his job as a personal banker to be in jeopardy. If Denzel loses his job while she is attending school full time, they are concerned that their $10,000 in savings will run out. Without recourse to any other funds, running out of money could result in dire consequences, including eviction from their rented apartment.

Susan and Denzel's expenses amount to $5,000/month, of which $2,000 is rent. Susan contributes $2,000 to their monthly expenses, while Denzel contributes $3,000. Denzel believes there is a 40% chance of losing his position. If that happens, unemployment would provide $2,000 for 6 months. Denzel plans to become a mortgage broker if he loses his job, and has every reason to believe that he will earn at least $3,000 per month after 6 months.

If either Susan or Denzel is not earning income they can apply for housing assistance, which is $1,000/month for 6 months. If Susan quits and Denzel is laid off, they assess an 80% chance of obtaining the assistance. If however, only Susan is without an income, then they believe there is a 50-50 chance of assistance. If Susan does not quit, but Denzel is laid off, the probability of obtaining assistance increases a bit to 60%.

If Susan stays at Joe's, it will take her 18 months to finish school. If, however, she attends school full time, then she will finish in 3 months. She believes that it will take her another 3 months to build up her clientele to match her $2,000/month contribution.

Structure Susan and Denzel's decision as an influence diagram using PrecisionTree. Structure it using a decision tree using PrecisionTree. What would you recommend they do? Why?

CASE STUDIES

PRESCRIBED FIRE

Using fire in forest management sounds contradictory. Prescribed fire, however, is an important tool for foresters, and a recent article describes how decision analysis is used to decide when, where, and what to burn. In one example, a number of areas in the Tahoe National Forest in California had been logged and were being prepared for replanting. Preparation included prescribed burning, and two possible treatments were available: burning the slash as it lay on the ground, or "yarding of unmerchantable material" (YUM) prior to burning. The latter treatment involves using heavy equipment to pile the slash. YUM reduces the difficulty of controlling the burn but costs an additional $100 per acre. In deciding between the two treatments, two uncertainties were considered critical. The first was how the fire would behave under each scenario. For example, the fire could be fully successful, problems could arise which could be controlled eventually, or the fire could escape, entailing considerable losses. Second, if problems developed, they could result in high, low, or medium costs.

Questions

1. What do you think the U.S. Forest Service's objectives should be in this decision?
   In the article, only one objective was considered, minimizing cost (including costs associated with an escaped fire and the damage it might do). Do you think this is a reasonable criterion for the Forest Service to use? Why or why not?

2. Develop an influence diagram and a decision tree using PrecisionTree for this situation. What roles do the two diagrams play in helping to understand and communicate the structure of this decision?

Source: D. Cohan, S. Haas, D. Radloff, and R. Yancik (1984) "Using Fire in Forest Management: Decision Making under Uncertainty." *Interfaces*, 14, 8–19.

THE SS *KUNIANG*

In the early 1980s, New England Electric System (NEES) was deciding how much to bid for the salvage rights to a grounded ship, the SS *Kuniang*. If the bid were successful, the ship could be repaired and fitted out to haul coal for its power generation stations. The value of doing so, however, depended on the outcome of a Coast Guard judgment about the salvage value of the ship. The Coast Guard's judgment involved an obscure law regarding domestic shipping in coastal waters. If the judgment indicated a low salvage value, then NEES would be able to use the ship for its shipping needs. If the judgment were high, the ship would be considered ineligible for domestic shipping use unless a considerable amount of money was spent in fitting her with fancy equipment. The Coast Guard's judgment would not be known until after the winning bid was chosen, so there was considerable risk associated with actually buying the ship as a result of submitting the winning bid. If the bid failed, the alternatives included purchasing a new ship for $18 million or a tug/barge combination for $15 million. One of the major issues was that the higher the bid, the more likely that NEES would win. NEES judged that a bid of $3 million would definitely not win, whereas a bid of $10 million definitely would win. Any bid in between was possible.

Questions

1. Draw an influence diagram and a decision tree using PrecisionTree for NEES's decision.
2. What roles do the two diagrams play in helping to understand and communicate the structure of this decision? Do you think one representation is more appropriate than the other? Why?

Source: David E. Bell (1984) "Bidding for the SS *Kuniang.*" *Interfaces*, 14, 17–23.

THE HILLBLOM ESTATE, PART I

Larry Hillblom was an interesting man while alive, but even more fascinating in death. Hillblom was the "H" in DHL—he was one of the founders of the company, and, after buying out his two partners ("D" and "L"), he oversaw DHL's growth into the world's largest courier delivery company. To avoid taxes, Hillblom moved from San Francisco to the tropical, tax-haven island of Saipan, part of the Commonwealth of Northern Mariana Islands (CNMI) located a thousand miles off the southeast coast of Japan. He started dozens of businesses and financed projects in the Philippines, Hawaii, and Vietnam. While alive, Hillblom was an influential and powerful person in Micronesia.

In 1995, Larry Hillblom died in a plane crash and left behind an estimated $750 million. For all intents and purposes, it appeared that his story would end there, as he had executed a legally-binding will that left the bulk of his estate to a trust with the primary beneficiary being the medical schools of the University of California system. Hillblom had never married and made no provisions in his will, either pro or con, for any children he might have had.

Shortly after Hillblom's death, Junior Larry Hillbroom, came forward and filed a lawsuit claiming to be Hillblom's illegitimate child and hence a share of the Hillblom estate. (Yes, it was Junior Larry *Hillbroom*; Junior Larry's mother misspelled Hillblom on the birth certificate.) Both Hillblom and Junior Larry were residents of CNMI and, under Section 2702 of the CNMI probate code, a child born after a will was executed was entitled to receive a share of the estate unless the will explicitly disallowed such claims.

Junior Larry's claim to a share of the Hillblom estate faced several impediments. First, Junior Larry was born 2 years after the will was executed and had to await a decision by the CNMI legislature regarding a proposed law (the "Hillblom law") that would require children born after a will was executed to have legally established paternity prior to the death of the father in order to have a valid claim on the estate. If the law passed, it would invalidate Junior Larry's claim to a share of the Hillblom estate. Junior Larry's lawyers estimated a 0.65 probability of the law being approved.

Second, if the Hillblom Law failed, Junior Larry would still have to present evidence that he was, in fact, the son of Larry Hillblom. Such claims are routinely proven or disproven by matching DNA. However, Hillblom disappeared with virtually no trace—his body was never found. His mansion in Saipan had been antiseptically cleaned shortly after his death, and no Hillblom DNA was recovered. Searches of his other properties turned up no useful DNA evidence. Nevertheless, Junior Larry's lawyers assigned a probability of 0.80 that they would be able to obtain some useful DNA.

Third, if a useful sample of Hillblom's DNA were found, there was the possibility that the DNA evidence would show that Junior Larry was not actually Hillblom's son. Junior Larry's lawyers assigned a probability of 0.70 to the event that a DNA test would provide definitive evidence that Junior Larry was indeed Hillblom's offspring.

Finally, even if paternity could be established, there was uncertainty about how large a share of Hillblom's estate Junior Larry would win in court. The uncertainty stemmed largely from the possibility that other illegitimate children might come forward and prove eligible to receive a share. Before distributing anything to heirs or other beneficiaries, the estate would first pay a 55% estate tax, leaving $337.5 million to distribute. Junior Larry's lawyers estimated a probability of 0.04 that Junior Larry would receive the full $337.5 million. They considered three intermediate possibilities as well, estimating probabilities of 0.20, 0.40, and 0.16 that Junior Larry would receive 5%, 10%, or 20% (respectively) of the after-tax value of the estate. Finally, even though paternity had been established, there was always the possibility that the case would be dismissed, and Junior Larry would receive nothing. Junior Larry's lawyers estimated a 0.20 probability of this outcome.

In 1996, before the outcome of the Hillblom law was known, the Hillblom estate trustees offered Junior Larry a settlement of $8 million dollars. (Of course, they did so while vigorously denying that Junior Larry was Hillblom's son.) Junior Larry and his lawyers had to decide whether to accept the settlement offer or proceed with the case.

Junior Larry's lawyers would take 45% of any settlement or awards paid to Junior Larry in exchange for covering all of the legal expenses associated with the case.

Questions

1. Structure the decision that Junior Larry Hillbroom faces by constructing a decision tree.
2. The amounts involved in this case are huge sums for Junior Larry, a 12-year-old boy living in near poverty on a small island in the Pacific Ocean. If you were advising Junior Larry, would you recommend that he take the settlement or have the lawyers continue the case?

Source: S. Lippman, K. McCardle, (2004). "Sex, Lies and the Hillblom Estate," *Decision Analysis* 1 (2004), 149–166. Jim Smith created the original version of this case. The numbers are fictitious, made up for the purposes of the problem, and are not those of Junior Larry, his lawyers, or anyone involved in the case.

REFERENCES

Decision structuring as a topic of discussion and research is relatively new. Traditionally the focus has been on modeling uncertainty and preferences and solution procedures for specific kinds of problems. Recent discussions of structuring include von Winterfeldt and Edwards (1986, Chapter 2), Humphreys and Wisudha (1987), and Keller and Ho (1989).

The process of identifying and structuring one's objectives comes from Keeney's (1992) *Value-Focused Thinking*. Although the idea of specifying one's objectives clearly as part of the decision process has been accepted for years, Keeney has made this part of decision structuring very explicit. Value-focused thinking captures the ultimate in common sense; if you know what you want to accomplish, you will be able to make choices that help you accomplish those things. Thus, Keeney advocates focusing on values and objectives first, before considering your alternatives. For a more compact description of value-focused thinking, see Keeney (1994).

Relatively speaking, influence diagrams are brand-new on the decision-analysis circuit. Developed by Strategic Decisions Group in the seventies, they first appeared in the decision-analysis literature in Howard and Matheson (1984; reprinted in 2005). Bodily (1985) presents an overview of influence diagrams. For more technical details, consult Shachter (1986, 1988) and Oliver and Smith (1989).

The idea of representing a decision with a network has spawned a variety of different approaches beyond influence diagrams. Two in particular are valuation networks (Shenoy, 1992) and sequential decision diagrams (Covaliu and Oliver, 1995). A recent overview of influence diagrams and related network representations of decisions can be found in Matzkevich and Abramson (1995).

Decision trees, on the other hand, have been part of the decision-analysis tool kit since the discipline's inception. The textbooks by Holloway (1979) and Raiffa (1968) provide extensive modeling using decision trees. This chapter's discussion of basic decision trees draws heavily from Behn and Vaupel's (1982) typology of decisions.

The clarity test is another consulting aid invented by Ron Howard and his associates. It is discussed in Howard (1988).

Behn, R. D., and J. D. Vaupel (1982) *Quick Analysis for Busy Decision Makers*. New York: Basic Books.

Bodily, S. E. (1985) *Modern Decision Making*. New York: McGraw-Hill.

Covaliu, Z., and R. Oliver (1995) "Representation and Solution of Decision Problems Using Sequential Decision Diagrams." *Management Science*, 41, in press.

Gregory, R., and R. L. Keeney (1994) "Creating Policy Alternatives Using Stakeholder Values."

Management Science, 40, 1035–1048. DOI: 10.1287/mnsc.40.8.1035

Holloway, C. A. (1979) *Decision Making under Uncertainty: Models and Choices.* Englewood Cliffs, NJ: Prentice Hall.

Howard, R. A. (1988) "Decision Analysis: Practice and Promise." *Management Science, 34*, 679–695.

Howard, R. A., and J. E. Matheson (1984) "Influence Diagrams." In R. Howard and J. Matheson (eds.) *The Principles and Applications of Decision Analysis*, Vol. II, pp. 719–762. Palo Alto, CA: Strategic Decisions Group. Reprinted in *Decision Analysis, Volume II*, 127–147.

Humphreys, P., and A. Wisudha (1987) "Methods and Tools for Structuring and Analyzing Decision Problems: A Catalogue and Review." Technical Report 87-1. London: Decision Analysis Unit, London School of Economics and Political Science.

Keeney, R. L. (1992) *Value-Focused Thinking.* Cambridge, MA: Harvard University Press.

Keeney, R. L. (1994) "Creativity in Decision Making with Value-Focused Thinking." *Sloan Management Review*, Summer, 33–41.

Keller, L. R., and J. L. Ho (1989) "Decision Problem Structuring." In A. P. Sage (ed.) *Concise Encyclo-pedia of Information Processing in Systems and Organizations.* Oxford, England: Pergamon Press.

Matzkevich, I., and B. Abramson (1995) "Decision-Analytic Networks in Artificial Intelligence." *Management Science, 41*, 1–22.

Oliver, R. M., and J. Q. Smith (1989) *Influence Diagrams, Belief Nets and Decision Analysis* (Proceedings of an International Conference 1988, Berkeley). New York: Wiley.

Raiffa, H. (1968) *Decision Analysis.* Reading, MA: Addison-Wesley.

Shachter, R. (1986) "Evaluating Influence Diagrams." *Operations Research, 34*, 871–882.

Shachter, R. (1988) "Probabilistic Inference and Influence Diagrams." *Operations Research, 36*, 389–604.

Shenoy, P. (1992) "Valuation-Based Systems for Bayesian Decision Analysis." *Operations Research, 40*, 463–484.

Ulvila, J., and R. B. Brown (1982) "Decision Analysis Comes of Age." *Harvard Business Review*, Sept–Oct, 130–141.

von Winterfeldt, D., and W. Edwards (1986) *Decision Analysis and Behavioral Research.* Cambridge: Cambridge University Press.

EPILOGUE

The Hillblom law was, in fact, passed by the CNMI legislature. Before the law was challenged, the Hillblom estate reached a settlement with Junior Larry and three other of Larry Hillblom's (alleged) illegitimate children. A total of eight children had come forward to claim a share of the estate, each accompanied by their own team of lawyers. Although some of Hillblom's DNA was found, there was possible contamination, and the sample was not used. Rather, the lawyers used a novel approach to establish paternity – they compared the DNA of the children with each other and concluded that four of them (including Junior Larry) had the same father. The DNA matches were confirmed with DNA from Larry Hillblom's mother, for which her grandchildren paid her $1 million and deeded her title to a villa in France.

The settlement amounts were not publicly revealed, and press reports varied widely, saying that the children received $10 to $50 million each. In 2005, 21-year-old Junior Larry Hillbroom was arrested on drug possession and bribery charges in Guam. The magistrate's complaint states that Hillbroom reportedly told police, "I have enough money to own you." The 21-year-old also allegedly attempted to bribe the officer with money in return for letting him go and returning the methamphetamine.

CHAPTER **4**

Making Choices

In this chapter, we learn how to use the details in a structured problem to find the preferred alternative. "Using the details" typically means analyzing: performing calculations, creating graphs, and examining the results to gain insight into the decision.

We begin by studying the analysis of decision models that involve only one objective or attribute. Although most of our examples use money as the attribute, it could be anything that can be measured as discussed in Chapter 3. After discussing the calculation of expected values and the use of risk profiles for single attribute decisions, we turn to decisions with multiple attributes and present some simple analytical approaches. The chapter concludes with a discussion of software for doing decision-analysis calculations on personal computers.

Our main example for this chapter is from the famous Texaco-Pennzoil court case.

Texaco versus Pennzoil	In early 1984, Pennzoil and Getty Oil agreed to the terms of a merger. But before any formal documents could be signed, Texaco offered Getty a substantially better price, and Gordon Getty, who controlled most of the Getty stock, reneged on the Pennzoil deal and sold to Texaco. Naturally, Pennzoil felt as if it had been dealt with unfairly and immediately filed a lawsuit against Texaco alleging that Texaco had interfered illegally in the Pennzoil-Getty negotiations. Pennzoil won the case; in late 1985, it was awarded $11.1 billion, the largest judgment ever in the United States at that time. A Texas appeals court reduced the judgment by $2 billion, but interest and penalties drove the total back up to $10.3 billion. James Kinnear, Texaco's chief executive officer, had said that Texaco would file for bankruptcy if Pennzoil obtained court permission to secure the judgment by filing liens against Texaco's

assets. Furthermore, Kinnear had promised to fight the case all the way to the U.S. Supreme Court if necessary, arguing in part that Pennzoil had not followed Security and Exchange Commission regulations in its negotiations with Getty. In April 1987, just before Pennzoil began to file the liens, Texaco offered to pay Pennzoil $2 billion to settle the entire case. Hugh Liedtke, chairman of Pennzoil, indicated that his advisors were telling him that a settlement between $3 and $5 billion would be fair.

What do you think Liedtke (pronounced "lid-key") should do? Should he accept the offer of $2 billion, or should he refuse and make a firm counteroffer? If he refuses the sure $2 billion, he faces a risky situation. Texaco might agree to pay $5 billion, a reasonable amount in Liedtke's mind. If he counteroffered $5 billion as a settlement amount, perhaps Texaco would counter with $3 billion or simply pursue further appeals. Figure 4.1 is a decision tree that shows a simplified version of Liedtke's problem.

The decision tree in Figure 4.1 is simplified in a number of ways. First, we assume that Liedtke has only one fundamental objective: maximizing the amount of the settlement. No other objectives need be considered. Also, Liedtke has a more varied set of decision alternatives than those shown. He could counteroffer a variety of possible values in the initial decision, and in the second decision, he could counteroffer some amount between $3 and $5 billion. Likewise, Texaco's counteroffer, if it makes one, need not be exactly $3 billion. The outcome of the final court decision could be anything between zero and the current judgment of $10.3 billion. Finally, we have not included in our model of the decision anything regarding Texaco's option of filing for bankruptcy.

FIGURE **4.1**
Hugh Liedtke's decision in the Texaco-Pennzoil affair.

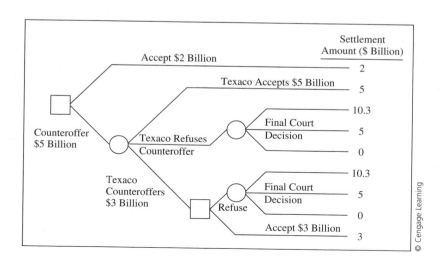

Why all of the simplifications? A straightforward answer (which just happens to have some validity) is that for our purposes in this chapter we need a relatively simple decision tree to work with. But this is just a pedagogical reason. If we were to try to analyze Liedtke's problem in all of its glory, how much detail should be included? As you now realize, all of the relevant information should be included, and the model should be constructed in a way that makes it easy to analyze. Does our representation accomplish this? Let us consider the following points.

1. *Liedtke's objective.* Certainly maximizing the amount of the settlement is a valid objective. The question is whether other objectives, such as minimizing attorney fees or improving Pennzoil's public image, might also be important. Although Liedtke may have other objectives, the fact that the settlement can range all the way from zero to $10.3 billion suggests that this objective will swamp any other concerns.

2. *Liedtke's initial counteroffer.* The counteroffer of $5 billion could be replaced by an offer for another amount, and then the decision tree reanalyzed. Different amounts may change the chance of Texaco accepting the counteroffer. At any rate, other possible counteroffers are easily dealt with.

3. *Liedtke's second counteroffer.* Other possible offers could be built into the tree, leading to a Texaco decision to accept, reject, or counter. The reason for leaving these out reflects an impression from the media accounts (especially *Fortune*, May 11, 1987, pp. 50–58) that Kinnear and Liedtke were extremely tough negotiators and that further negotiations were highly unlikely.

4. *Texaco's counteroffer.* The $3 billion counteroffer could be replaced by a fan representing a range of possible counteroffers. It would be necessary to find a "break-even" point, above which Liedtke would accept the offer and below which he would refuse. Another approach would be to replace the $3 billion value with other values, recomputing the tree each time. Thus, we have a variety of ways to deal with this issue.

5. *The final court decision.* We could include more branches, representing additional possible outcomes, or we could replace the three branches with a fan representing a range of possible outcomes. For a first-cut approximation, the possible outcomes we have chosen do a reasonably good job of capturing the uncertainty inherent in the court outcome.

6. *Texaco's bankruptcy option.* A detail left out of the case is that Texaco's net worth is much more than the $10.3 billion judgment. Thus, even if Texaco does file for bankruptcy, Pennzoil probably would still be able to collect. In reality, negotiations can continue even if Texaco has filed for bankruptcy; the purpose of filing is to protect the company from creditors seizing assets while the company proposes a financial reorganization plan. In fact, this is exactly what Texaco needs to do in order to figure out a way to deal with Pennzoil's claims.

In terms of Liedtke's options, however, whether Texaco files for bankruptcy appears to have no impact.

The purpose of this digression has been to explore the extent to which our structure for Liedtke's problem is requisite in the sense of Chapter 1. The points above suggest that the main issues in the problem have been represented in the problem. While it may be necessary to rework the analysis with slightly different numbers or structure later, the structure in Figure 4.1 should be adequate for a first analysis. The objective is to develop a representation of the problem that captures the essential features of the problem so that the ensuing analysis will provide the decision maker with insight and understanding.

One small detail remains before we can solve the decision tree. We need to specify the chances or probabilities associated with Texaco's possible reactions to the $5 billion counteroffer, and we also need to assess the chances of the various court awards. The probabilities that we assign to the outcome branches in the tree should reflect Liedtke's beliefs about the uncertain events that he faces. As a matter of fact, one of the strengths of decision analysis is the ability to model or represent the knowledge and beliefs of the decision maker, in this case Hugh Liedtke. Instead of using preset probability values (such as equal probability values for all outcomes), we customize the probabilities to match Liedtke's beliefs. For this reason, any numbers that we include to represent these beliefs should be based on what Liedtke has to say about the matter or on information from individuals whose judgments in this matter he would trust. For our purposes, imagine overhearing a conversation between Liedtke and his advisors. Here are some of the issues they might raise:

- Given the tough negotiating stance of the two executives, it could be an even chance (50%) that Texaco will refuse to negotiate further. If Texaco does not refuse, then what? What are the chances that Texaco would accept a $5 billion counteroffer? How likely is this outcome compared to the $3 billion counteroffer from Texaco? Liedtke and his advisors might figure that a counteroffer of $3 billion from Texaco is about twice as likely as Texaco accepting the $5 billion. Thus, because there is already a 50% chance of refusal, there must be a 33% chance of a Texaco counteroffer and a 17% chance of Texaco accepting $5 billion.

- What are the probabilities associated with the final court decision? In the *Fortune* article cited previously, Liedtke is said to admit that Texaco could win its case, leaving Pennzoil with nothing but lawyer bills. Thus, there is a significant possibility that the outcome would be zero. Given the strength of Pennzoil's case so far, there is also a good chance that the court will uphold the judgment as it stands. Finally, the possibility exists that the judgment could be reduced somewhat (to $5 billion in our model). Let us assume that Liedtke and his advisors agree that there is a 20% chance that the court will award the entire $10.3 billion and a

FIGURE **4.2**
Hugh Liedtke's decision tree with chances (probabilities) included.

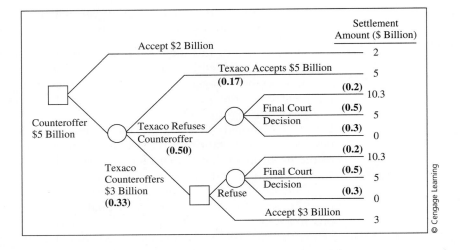

slightly larger, or 30%, chance that the award will be zero. Thus, there must be a 50% chance of an award of $5 billion.

Figure 4.2 shows the decision tree with these chances included. The chances have been phrased in terms of probabilities rather than percentages.

DECISION TREES AND EXPECTED MONETARY VALUE

One way to choose among risky alternatives is to pick the one with the highest *expected value* (EV). When the decision's consequences involve only monetary gains or losses, we call the expected value the *expected monetary value* (EMV), sometimes called the mean. Finding EMVs when using decision trees is called "folding back the tree" for reasons that will become obvious. (The procedure is called "rolling back" in some texts.) We start at the endpoints of the branches on the far-right side and move to the left, (1) calculating expected values (to be defined in a moment) when we encounter a chance node, or (2) choosing the branch with the highest value or expected value[1] when we encounter a decision node. These instructions sound rather cryptic. It is much easier to understand the procedure through a few examples. We will start with a simple example, the double risk dilemma shown in Figure 4.3.

Recall that a double-risk dilemma is a matter of choosing between two risky alternatives. The situation is one in which you choose between Ticket A and Ticket B, each of which allows you participate in a game of chance.

---

[1] Usually our objective is to maximize EV or EMV, but there are times when we wish to minimize EV, such as minimizing costs. In such cases, we choose the branch with the smallest expected value.

FIGURE **4.3**
A double-risk dilemma.

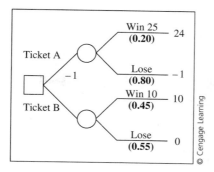

With Ticket A, there is a 20% chance of winning $25 and an 80% chance of winning $0; with Ticket B, there is a 45% chance of winning $10 and a 55% chance of winning $0. Ticket B is free for the asking, but Ticket A costs $1. You must choose one or the other, either A for $1 or B for free. Ticket A has the higher payoff, but is it worth the $1?

Figure 4.3 displays your decision situation. In particular, notice that the dollar consequences at the ends of the branches are the net values as discussed in Chapter 3. Thus, if you chose Ticket A and win, you will have gained a net amount of $24, having paid one dollar for the ticket.

To solve or fold back the decision tree, begin by calculating the expected value of Ticket B, that is, playing for $10. The expected value of Ticket B is simply the weighted average of the possible outcomes of the lottery, the weights being the chances with which the outcomes occur. The calculation is:

$$\text{EMV(Ticket B)} = 0.45 \times \$10 + 0.55 \times \$0$$
$$= \$4.50$$

This formula states that 45% of the time, Ticket B pays $10, and 55% of the time, it pays zero dollars. Thus, the EMV tells us that playing this lottery many times would yield an average of $4.50 per game.

Next, we compare the EMV of Ticket B to the EMV of Ticket A. Calculating EMV for Ticket A gives us the following:

$$\text{EMV(Ticket A)} = 0.20 \times \$24 + 0.80 \times \$-1$$
$$= \$4.00$$

Now we can replace the chance nodes in the decision tree with their expected values, as shown in Figure 4.4. Finally, choosing between the two tickets amounts to choosing the branch with the highest expected value. As Ticket B pays $0.50 more on average, the EMV calculations show that on average it is better to select Ticket B. The double slash through the "Ticket A" branch indicates that this branch would not be chosen.

This simple example is only a warm-up exercise. Now let us see how the solution procedure works when we have a more complicated decision

FIGURE **4.4**
Replacing chance
nodes with EMVs.

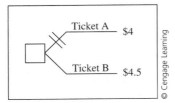

problem. Consider Hugh Liedtke's situation as diagrammed in Figure 4.2. Our strategy, as indicated, will be to work from the right side of the tree. First, we will calculate the expected value of the final court decision. The second step will be to decide whether it is better for Liedtke to accept a $3 billion counteroffer from Texaco or to refuse and take a chance on the final court decision. We will do this by comparing the expected value of the judgment with the sure $3 billion. The third step will be to calculate the expected value of making the $5 billion counteroffer, and finally we will compare this expected value with the sure $2 billion that Texaco is offering now.

The expected value of the court decision is the weighted average of the possible outcomes:

$$\begin{aligned}
\text{EMV}(\textit{Court Decision}) &= [P(\textit{Award} = \$10.3) \times \$10.3] \\
&\quad + [P(\textit{Award} = \$5) \times \$5] \\
&\quad + [P(\textit{Award} = \$0) \times \$0] \\
&= [0.2 \times \$10.3] + [0.5 \times \$5] + [0.3 \times \$0] \\
&= \$4.56 \, \text{Billion}
\end{aligned}$$

We replace both uncertainty nodes representing the court decision with this expected value, as in Figure 4.5. Now, comparing the two alternatives of accepting and refusing Texaco's $3 billion counteroffer, it is obvious that the expected value of $4.56 billion is greater than the certain value of $3 billion, and hence the slash through the "Accept $3 Billion" branch.

To continue folding back the decision tree, we replace the decision node with the preferred alternative. The decision tree as it stands after this replacement is shown in Figure 4.6. The third step is to calculate the expected value of the alternative "Counteroffer $5 Billion." This expected value is:

$$\begin{aligned}
\text{EMV}(\textit{Counteroffer } \$5 \text{ Billion}) &= [P(\textit{Texaco Accepts}) \times \$5] \\
&\quad + [P(\textit{Texaco Refuses}) \times \$4.56] \\
&\quad + [P(\textit{Texaco Counteroffers}) \times \$4.56] \\
&= [0.17 \times \$5] + [0.5 \times \$4.56] + [0.33 \times \$4.56] \\
&= \$4.63 \, \text{Billion}
\end{aligned}$$

Replacing the chance node with its expected value results in the decision tree shown in Figure 4.7. Comparing the values of the two branches, it is clear

FIGURE **4.5**
Hugh Liedtke's decision tree after calculating expected value of court decision.

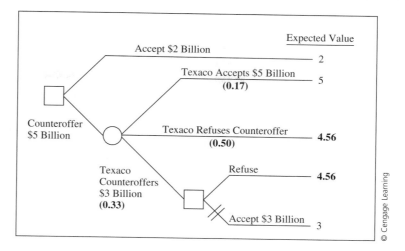

FIGURE **4.6**
Hugh Liedtke's decision tree after decision node replaced with expected value of preferred alternative.

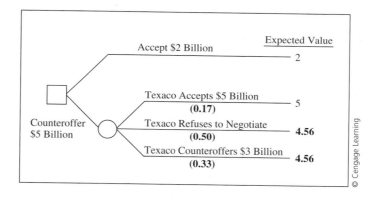

FIGURE **4.7**
Hugh Liedtke's decision tree after original tree completely folded back.

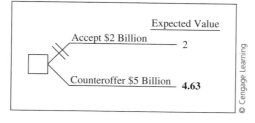

that the expected value of $4.63 billion is preferred to the $2 billion offer from Texaco. According to this solution, which implies that decisions should be made by comparing expected values, Liedtke should turn down Texaco's offer but counteroffer a settlement of $5 billion. If Texaco turns down the $5 billion and makes another counteroffer of $3 billion, Liedtke should refuse the $3 billion and take his chances in court.

FIGURE **4.8**
Hugh Liedtke's
solved decision
tree.

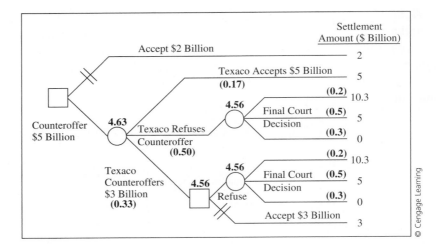

We went through this decision in gory detail so that you could see clearly the steps involved. In fact, when solving a decision tree, we usually do not redraw the tree at each step, but simply indicate on the original tree what the expected values are at each of the chance nodes and which alternative is preferred at each decision node. The solved decision tree for Liedtke would look like the tree shown in Figure 4.8, which shows all of the details of the solution. Expected values for the chance nodes are placed above the nodes. The 4.56 above the decision node indicates that if Liedtke gets to this decision point, he should refuse Texaco's offer and take his chances in court for an expected value of $4.56 billion. The decision tree also shows that his best current choice is to make the $5 billion counteroffer with an expected payoff of $4.63 billion.

The decision tree shows clearly what Liedtke should do if Texaco counteroffers $3 billion: He should refuse. This is the idea of a contingent plan, which we call a *strategy*. A strategy is a particular immediate alternative, as well as specific alternatives in future decisions. For example, if Texaco counteroffers, there is a specific course of action to take (refuse the counteroffer). We denote this strategy by: "Counteroffer $5 Billion; Refuse Texaco Counteroffer." In deciding whether to accept Texaco's current $2 billion offer, Liedtke must know what he will do in the event that Texaco returns with a counteroffer of $3 billion. This is why the decision tree is solved backwards. In order to make a good decision at the current time, we have to know what the appropriate contingent strategies are in the future.

The folding-back procedure highlights one of the great strengths of decision models. Both decision trees and influence diagrams require us to think carefully about the future, in particular the outcomes that could occur and the consequences that might result from each outcome. Because we cannot predict exactly what will happen in the time horizon of the decision context, we think about and model a representative or requisite set of future scenarios. If we have done a good job, then our model adequately portrays the range of possible future events.

SOLVING INFLUENCE DIAGRAMS: OVERVIEW

Solving decision trees is straightforward, and EMVs for small trees can be calculated by hand relatively easily. The procedure for solving an influence diagram, though, is somewhat more complicated. Fortunately, computer programs such as PrecisionTree are available to do the calculations. In this short section we give an overview of the issues involved in solving an influence diagram. For interested readers, we have provided a complete solution of the influence diagram of the Texaco-Pennzoil decision at our website. Please go to www.cengagebrain.com to access the solution.

While influence diagrams appear on the surface to be rather simple, much of the complexity is hidden. Our first step is to take a close look at how an influence diagram translates information into an internal representation. An influence diagram "thinks" about a decision in terms of a symmetric expansion of the decision tree from one node to the next.

For example, suppose we have the basic decision tree shown in Figure 4.9, which represents the "umbrella problem" (see Exercise 3.9). The issue is whether or not to take your umbrella. If you do not take the umbrella, and it rains, your good clothes (and probably your day) are ruined, and the consequence is zero (units of satisfaction). However, if you do not take the umbrella and the sun shines, this is the best of all possible consequences with a value of 100. If you decide to take your umbrella, your good clothes will not get soaking wet. However, it is a bit of a nuisance to carry the umbrella around all day. Your consequence is 80, between the other two values.

If we were to represent this problem with an influence diagram, it would look like the diagram in Figure 4.10. Note that it does not matter whether the sun shines or not if you take the umbrella. If we were to reconstruct exactly

FIGURE **4.9**
Umbrella problem.

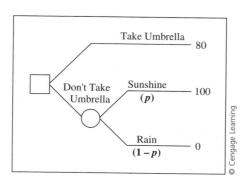

FIGURE **4.10**
Influence diagram
of the umbrella
problem.

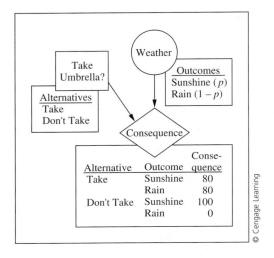

FIGURE **4.11**
How the influence
diagram "thinks"
about the umbrella
problem.

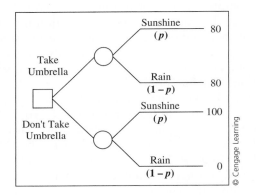

how the influence diagram "thinks" about the umbrella problem in terms of a decision tree, the representation would be that shown in Figure 4.11. Note that the uncertainty node on the "Take Umbrella" branch is an unnecessary node. The payoff is the same regardless of the weather. In a decision-tree model, we can take advantage of this fact by not even drawing the unnecessary node. Influence diagrams, however, use the symmetric decision tree, even though this may require unnecessary nodes (and hence unnecessary calculations).

With an understanding of the influence diagram's internal representation, we can talk about how to solve an influence diagram. The procedure essentially solves the symmetric decision tree, although the terminology is somewhat different. Nodes are *reduced;* reduction amounts to calculating expected values for chance nodes and choosing the largest expected value at decision nodes, just as we did with the decision tree. Moreover, also parallel with the decision-tree procedure, as nodes are reduced, they are removed from the diagram. Thus, solving the influence diagram in Figure 4.10 would require first reducing the

"Weather" node (calculating the expected values) and then reducing the "Take Umbrella?" node by choosing the largest expected value.

RISK PROFILES

Up to this point, we have discussed only one way to choose the best alternative. That is, choose the alternative that maximizes EMV (or minimizes EMV if we are calculating costs). This decision rule is both straightforward and appealing. Straightforward because it is easy to implement and appealing because the EMV is a useful measure for comparing different alternatives.

However, the EMV alone does not tell us the whole story; it does not inform us about how much variation there is in the consequences. For example, Liedtke's expected values are $2 billion and $4.63 billion for his two immediate alternatives. But this does not mean that if Liedtke chooses to counteroffer, he can expect a payment of $4.63 billion. Rather the expected value is a weighted average, and thus summarizes the set of possible consequences. It does not specify the exact amount or consequence that will occur for Liedtke. Thus, to help us choose the best alternative, we should consider both the EMV and the set of possible consequences for each alternative. Table 4.1 shows the EMV and consequences for Liedtke's two immediate alternatives, thereby providing a more in-depth look into what actually could happen than the EMV alone.

That Liedtke could come away from his dealings with Texaco with nothing indicates that choosing to counteroffer is a risky alternative. In later chapters we will look at the idea of risk in more detail. For now, however, we can investigate and discuss the relative riskiness of each alternative by studying the set of possible consequences for each alternative. For Liedtke, there is only one possible consequence for "Accept $2 Billion," which, of course, is a $2 billion payment, showing that there is no risk if he accepts. In contrast, the possible consequences for "Counteroffer" range from zero to over ten billion dollars, indicating much more risk. If, in addition, we know the probability of each consequence value, as in Table 4.2, then we have a more complete picture of what could happen for each alternative.

TABLE **4.1** The EMVs and possible consequences facing Hugh Liedtke when deciding to accept the $2 billion offer or to counteroffer $5 billion.

Alternative	EMV	Possible Consequences
Accept $2 Billion	$2 Billion	$2 Billion
Counteroffer	$4.65 Billion	$0 $5 Billion $10.3 Billion

© Cengage Learning 2014

© Cengage Learning 2014

TABLE **4.2**
Liedtke's two alternatives along with their associated EMVs, consequence values, and probabilities.

Alternative	EMV	Consequence Values	Consequence Prob.
Accept $2 Billion	$2 Billion	$2 Billion	100%
Counteroffer	$4.65 Billion	$0	24.9%
		$5 Billion	58.5%
		$10.3 Billion	16.6%

Table 4.2 shows that there is only a one out of six chance that the consequence would be $10.3 billion. Knowing the probability values can be very helpful when choosing the best strategy. For example, Liedtke would evaluate the "Counteroffer" alternative more favorably if the probability of the $10.3 billion consequence were to jump from 16.6% to 80%.

Note that the probabilities for the two sets of consequences in the above table sum to one. Interestingly, the probabilities for a given alternative or a strategy must always sum to one. Problem 4.21 asks you to show that the probabilities associated with the consequences of each alternative must always add to one.

For any alternative, the consequence values together with their associated probabilities constitute the risk profile for that alternative. The risk profile provides a complete picture of what could happen when we choose an alternative or strategy. We typically display a risk profile as a graph with the consequence values along the x-axis and their associated probabilities along the y-axis.

Risk profiles are very helpful when deciding which alternative we most prefer. Whereas the EMV summarizes each alternative into a single number, risk profiles graphically display the range of possible results, and as such, convey more of the complexity of the alternative. We will see that we can compare the relative merits of each alternative by comparing risk profiles, and that there is special meaning when two risk profile graphs do not cross each other. For now, we know that a risk profile graphs the consequences and their probabilities, providing a comprehensive snapshot of an alternative.

The risk profile for the "Accept $2 Billion" alternative is shown in Figure 4.12 and the risk profile for the "Counteroffer $5 Billion; Refuse Texaco Counteroffer" strategy is shown in Figure 4.13. Figure 4.13 shows there is a 58.5% chance that the eventual settlement is $5 billion, a 16.6% chance of $10.3 billion, and a 24.9% chance of nothing. These probabilities are easily calculated. For example, take the $5 billion amount. This can happen in three different ways. There is a 17% chance that it happens because Texaco accepts. There is a 25% chance that it happens because Texaco refuses and the judge awards $5 billion. (That is, there is a 50% chance that Texaco refuses times a 50% chance that the award is $5 billion.) Finally, the chances are 16.5% that the settlement is $5 billion because Texaco counteroffers $3 billion, Liedtke refuses and goes to court, and the judge awards $5 billion. That is, 16.5% equals 33% times 50%. Adding up, we get the chance of $5 billion = 17% + 25% + 16.5% = 58.5%.

In constructing a risk profile, we collapse a decision tree by multiplying out the probabilities on sequential chance branches. At a decision node, only

FIGURE **4.12**
Risk profile for the "Accept $2 Billion" alternative.

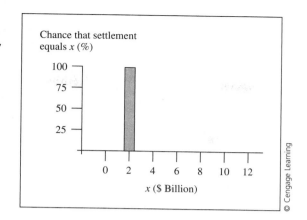

FIGURE **4.13**
Risk profile for the "Counteroffer $5 Billion; Refuse Texaco Counteroffer" strategy.

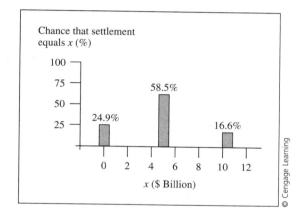

one branch is taken; in the case of "Counteroffer $5 Billion; Refuse Texaco Counteroffer," we use only the indicated alternative for the second decision, and so this decision node need not be included in the collapsing process. You can think about the process as one in which nodes are gradually removed from the tree in much the same sense as we did with the folding-back procedure, except that in this case we keep track of the possible outcomes and their probabilities. Figures 4.14, 4.15, and 4.16 show the progression of collapsing the decision tree in order to construct the risk profile for the "Counteroffer $5 Billion; Refuse Texaco Counteroffer" strategy.

By looking at the risk profiles, the decision maker can tell a lot about the riskiness of the alternatives. In some cases a decision maker can choose among alternatives on the basis of their risk profiles. Comparing Figures 4.12 and 4.13, it is clear that the worst possible consequence for "Counteroffer $5 Billion; Refuse Texaco Counteroffer" is less than the value for "Accept $2 billion." On the other hand, the largest amount ($10.3 billion) is much higher than $2 billion. Hugh Liedtke has to decide whether the risk of perhaps coming away empty-handed is worth the possibility of getting more

FIGURE **4.14**
First step in collapsing the decision tree to make a risk profile for "Counteroffer $5 Billion; Refuse Texaco Counteroffer" strategy.

The decision node has been removed to leave only the outcomes associated with the "Refuse" branch.

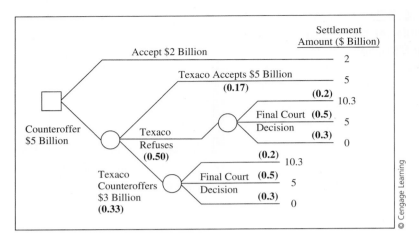

FIGURE **4.15**
Second step in collapsing the decision tree to make a risk profile.

The three chance nodes have been collapsed into one chance node. The probabilities on the branches are the product of the probabilities from sequential branches in Figure 4.14.

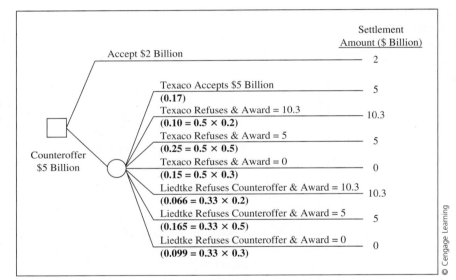

FIGURE **4.16**
Third step in collapsing the decision tree to make a risk profile.

The seven branches from the chance node in Figure 4.15 have been combined into three branches.

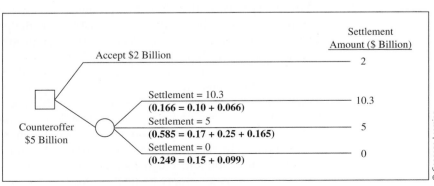

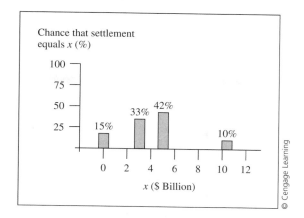

than $2 billion. This is clearly a case of a basic risky decision, as we can see from the collapsed decision tree in Figure 4.16.

Risk profiles can be calculated for strategies that might not have appeared as optimal in an expected-value analysis. For example, Figure 4.17 shows the risk profile for "Counteroffer $5 Billion; Accept $3 Billion," which we ruled out on the basis of EMV. Comparing Figures 4.17 and 4.13 indicates that this strategy yields a smaller chance of getting nothing, but also less chance of a $10.3 billion judgment. Compensating for this is the greater chance of getting something in the middle: $3 or $5 billion.

Although risk profiles can in principle be used as an alternative to EMV to check every possible strategy, for complex decisions it can be tedious to study many risk profiles. Thus, a compromise is to look at risk profiles only for the first one or two decisions, on the assumption that future decisions would be made using a decision rule such as maximizing expected value, which is itself a kind of strategy. (This is the approach used by many decision-analysis computer programs, PrecisionTree included.) Thus, in the Texaco-Pennzoil example, one might compare only the "Accept $2 Billion" and "Counteroffer $5 Billion; Refuse Texaco Counteroffer" strategies.

Cumulative Risk Profiles

We also can present the risk profile in cumulative form. Figure 4.18 shows the *cumulative risk profile* for "Counteroffer $5 Billion; Refuse Texaco Counteroffer." In the cumulative format, the vertical axis is the chance that the payoff is less than or equal to the corresponding value on the horizontal axis. This is only a matter of translating the information contained in the risk profile in Figure 4.13. There is no chance that the settlement will be less than zero. At zero, the chance jumps up to 24.9%, because there is a substantial chance that the court award will be zero. The graph continues at 24.9% across to $5 billion. (For example, there is a 24.9% chance that the settlement is less than or equal to $3.5 billion; that is, there is the 24.9% chance that the settlement is zero, and that is

FIGURE **4.18**
Cumulative risk profile for "Counteroffer $5 Billion; Refuse Texaco Counteroffer."

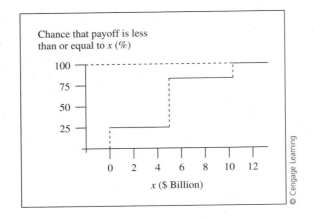

less than $3.5 billion.) At $5 billion, the line jumps up to 83.4% (which is 24.9% + 58.5%), because there is an 83.4% chance that the settlement is less than or equal to $5 billion. Finally, at $10.3 billion, the cumulative graph jumps up to 100%: The chance is 100% that the settlement is less than or equal to $10.3 billion. Thus, you can see that creating a cumulative risk profile is just a matter of adding up, or accumulating, the chances of the individual payoffs.

For any specific value along the horizontal axis, we can read off the chance that the payoff will be less than or equal to that specific value. For example, we can read the following statements from the cumulative risk profile in Figure 4.18:

P(Payoff ≤ $3 billion) = 24.9%, or there is a 24.9% that the payoff is $3 billion or less;

P(Payoff ≤ $4 billion) = 24.9 %, or there is a 24.9% that the payoff is $4 billion or less; and

P(Payoff ≤ $6 billion) = 83.4 %, or there is a 83.4% that the payoff is $6 billion or less.

Notice that the probability of the settlement being $3 billion or less equals the probability of being $4 billion or less. At first, this may seem incorrect. It seems as if an extra $1 billion dollars just appeared. Don't forget that these are cumulative probabilities. As there is a zero probability of the consequence being between $3 and $4 billion, we add this zero probability when going from $3 billion or less to $4 billion or less. In probability notation:

$$
\begin{aligned}
\text{P(Payoff} \leq \ \$4 \text{ billion)} \\
&= \text{P(Payoff} \leq \$3 \text{ billion)} + \text{P(\$3 billion} < \text{Payoff} \leq \$4 \text{ billion)} \\
&= 24.9\% + 0\%.
\end{aligned}
$$

Later in this chapter, we show how to generate risk profiles and cumulative risk profiles in PrecisionTree. Cumulative risk profiles will be very helpful in the next section in our discussion of dominance.

DOMINANCE: AN ALTERNATIVE TO EMV

When it comes down to making the decision, actually choosing which alternative or strategy to pursue, we sometimes have no clear winner, that is, no strategy is clearly the best. Sometimes, it isn't even clear which strategy is the worst! For example, it commonly happens that the strategies with the higher EMVs are also the strategies with the higher levels of risk. Although, we prefer more EMV than less, we shy away from risk, particularly if the risks involve losing money. While taking both the risks and the rewards into consideration provides a more complete understanding of the decision, it does not always produce a clearly identified best solution.

In later chapters, we will present a rigorous approach for assessing the trade-off between risk and reward. There is, however, a relatively easy way to determine if one strategy is head-and-shoulders better than all the other strategies. In such a case, we say that the strategy *dominates* all the other strategies. Let's consider an example to see what it means for one strategy to dominate another and how dominance can be determined.

Suppose through an inheritance, you had $1,000 that you wanted to invest over 5 years. One alternative available to you is a relatively low risk municipal bond. Another alternative is investing the $1,000 in a biotech stock that has recently had promising results. From an expected-value standpoint, you find the biotech stock is a clear winner as its EMV after 5 years is $3,000 and the bond's EMV after the same 5 years is only $1,500. However, you also find that the stock is riskier than the bond in that the stock's value could be anywhere between zero and $5,500, whereas the bond's value ranges from zero to $2,500. From this information, it appears that the biotech stock is the better choice as its EMV is twice as large and the increased risk is due mainly to its upside potential. But, it also appears possible that the bond could be worth more in 5 years, for example, the biotech company could fail and be worth nothing. We next show that by examining the cumulative risk profiles, the biotech stock actually dominates the bond. That is, under all circumstances the stock is a better investment than the bond.

(Incidentally, we are using continuous risk profiles here. That is, we are considering outcomes for the bond and the stock that can take any value within a certain range. We haven't seen these before; all of the risk profile we have seen so far have been associated with decision trees, and because decision trees have specific, discrete end points, the risk profiles are discrete, which displays the "stair-step" shape, as shown previous in Figure 4.18. We will cover continuous distributions in detail in Chapter 8. For now, though, the continuous cumulative risk profiles for the bond and stock will be useful and easy enough to interpret.)

Figure 4.19 shows the cumulative risk profiles associated with our two alternatives. We see that the cumulative risk profile of the biotech stock lies entirely to the right of the cumulative risk profile of the bond. This means that the "Biotech Stock" alternative dominates the "Municipal Bond" alternative. To see why, choose any probability value from the y axis. For

FIGURE **4.19**
Comparing the risk profiles of the two investments, noting that they do not cross.

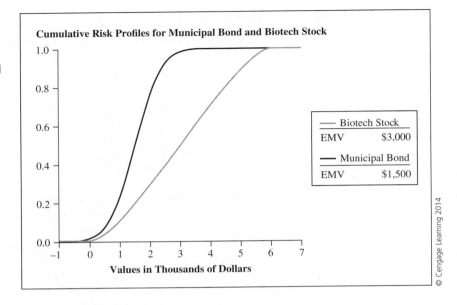

example, we choose 40% as shown in Figure 4.20. Calculating the cumulative probabilities:

$$P(\text{Bond} \leq \$1{,}200) = 40\%, \text{ and}$$

$$P(\text{Stock} \leq \$2{,}300) = 40\%.$$

Hence, there is a 40% chance that the bond will be worth $1,200 or less and a 40% chance that the stock will be worth $2,300 or less. We can make these statements easier to understand and more transparent if we

FIGURE **4.20**
The biotech stock dominates the bond because for any probability, the stock offers a better gamble. For example, with the bond we have a 40% chance of $1,200 or less, but the stock offers a 40% chance of $2,300 or less.

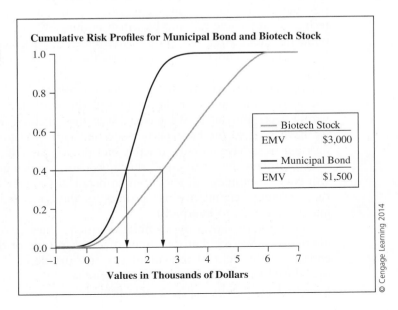

change the "or less" into "or more." For example, $P(Bond \leq \$1,200) = 40\%$ is equivalent to $P(Bond > \$1,200) = 60\%$, that is, there is a 60% chance that the bond will be worth $1,200 or more and similarly a 60% chance that the stock will be worth $2,300 or more. Clearly, we prefer having a 60% chance of making $2,300 or more compared to making $1,200 or more. We have similar statements for any probability we choose. As long as the cumulative risk profile of the stock lies entirely to the right of the cumulative risk profile for the bond, the stock's monetary value will always be larger for any given probability value. No matter what outcome occurs (probability value chosen), the stock will always produce a larger monetary value, and thus dominates the bond.

Actually, dominance is a bit more subtle than simply having one cumulative risk profile lie entirely to the right of another risk profile. If the risk profiles coincide (are identical) for a portion of the graph, and at the points where the risk profiles do not coincide one graph is always positioned to the right, this is also dominance. For example, the stock would still dominate the bond if the stock's risk profile sometimes coincided with the bond's risk profile (meaning they have the same probability of being worth the same amount), and when they do not coincide, the stock's risk profile lies to the right (meaning the stock is worth more). Another way of saying this is that the stock is never worse than the bond and sometimes it is better.

There are also varying degrees of dominance. The type of dominance we have discussed so far is called *stochastic dominance*[2] (also called *probabilistic dominance*). An even stronger type of dominance is called *deterministic dominance*. Deterministic dominance occurs when the maximum payout of one alternative is less than the minimum payout of another alternative. For example, if the most the bond could be worth is $1,100 and the least the stock could be worth is $1,500, then we would conclude that the stock deterministically dominates the bond. The word deterministically refers to the fact that we do not have to take the probabilities into account. No matter what the probabilities are, as long as the minimum of one alternative is larger than the maximum of the other alternative, we have deterministic dominance.

Be careful when analyzing risk profiles to determine dominance. It is easy to make the mistake of viewing dominance starting from the x axis as opposed to the y axis. For example, choosing the x-axis value $2,000 in Figure 4.21, we have $P(Bond \leq \$2,000) = 80\%$ and $P(Stock \leq \$2,000) \approx 30\%$. From this point of view, students sometimes erroneously think that the bond dominates the stock, reasoning incorrectly that the bond has a larger chance of being worth $2,000. Actually, the bond has an 80% chance of being worth $2,000 *or less*, whereas the stock has approximately a 70% chance of being worth $2,000 *or more*. We can also see how the original

---

[2] Strictly speaking, this is first-order stochastic dominance. Higher-order stochastic dominance comes into play when we consider preferences regarding risk.

FIGURE **4.21**
The risk profiles show that the probability of the bond being worth $2,000 or less is 80%, whereas the probability of the stock being worth $2,000 or less is approximately 30%.

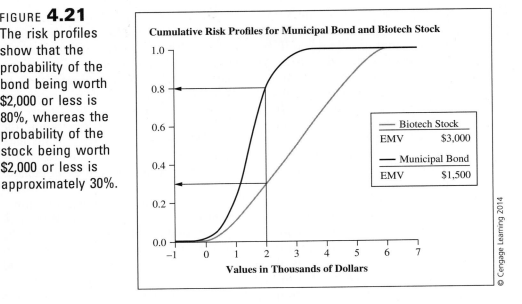

Cumulative Risk Profiles for Municipal Bond and Biotech Stock

Biotech Stock
EMV $3,000
Municipal Bond
EMV $1,500

Values in Thousands of Dollars

© Cengage Learning 2014

reasoning is erroneous if we flip the two probabilities statements. If there is an 80% chance the bond is worth $2,000 or less, then there is a 20% chance the bond is worth more than $2,000. Similarly, there is approximately a 70% chance the stock is worth more than $2,000. Thus, the stock is the better gamble.

Another common mistake is to conclude that one strategy partially dominates another strategy. For example, if the risk profiles of the bond and stock were to cross each other as in Figure 4.22, then students are tempted to state that the bond dominates the stock up to $2,800, and after that the stock dominates the bond. The definition of dominates states that one alternatively always has an equal or higher value for any probability value between zero and one. Thus, it is not possible for one alternative to dominate another for a part of the time or for just some probability values. Dominance cannot be partial.

Dominance clearly helps identify when an alternative is head-and-shoulders better, but it can also identify a strategy that can be eliminated from consideration. Indeed, screening alternatives on the basis of dominance begins implicitly in the structuring phase of decision analysis, and, as alternatives are considered, they usually are at least informally compared to other alternatives. Formal screening of alternatives on the basis of dominance is an important decision-analysis tool. If an alternative can be eliminated early in the selection process using dominance, considerable cost may be saved when analyzing large problems. For example, suppose that the decision involves where to build a new electric power plant. Analysis of proposed sites can be very expensive. If a potential site can be eliminated in an early phase of the analysis on the grounds that another dominates it, that site need not undergo full analysis.

FIGURE **4.22**
The risk profiles cross at $2,800 showing the neither alternative dominates.

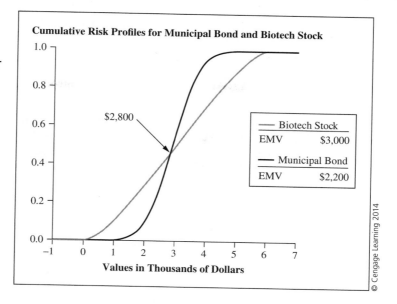

Cumulative Risk Profiles for Municipal Bond and Biotech Stock

	Biotech Stock	
	EMV	$3,000
	Municipal Bond	
	EMV	$2,200

Values in Thousands of Dollars

© Cengage Learning 2014

MAKING DECISIONS WITH MULTIPLE OBJECTIVES

So far we have learned how to analyze a single-objective decision; in the Texaco-Pennzoil example, we have focused on Liedtke's objective of maximizing the settlement amount. How would we deal with a decision that involves multiple objectives? In this section, we learn how to extend the concepts of expected value and risk profiles to multiple-objective situations. In contrast to the grandiose Texaco-Pennzoil example, consider the following down-to-earth example of a young person deciding which of two summer jobs to take.

The Summer Job

Sam Chu was in a quandary. With two job offers in hand, the choice he should make was far from obvious. The first alternative was a job as an assistant at a local small business; the job would pay a bit above minimum wage ($9.25 per hour), it would require 30 to 40 hours per week, and the hours would be primarily during the week, leaving the weekends free. The job would last for three months (13 weeks), but the exact amount of work, and hence the amount Sam could earn, was uncertain. However, the free weekends could be spent with friends.

The second alternative was to work as a member of a trail-maintenance crew for a conservation organization. This job would require 10 weeks of hard work, 40 hours per week at $11.45 per hour, in a national forest in a neighboring state. The job would involve extensive camping and backpacking. Members of the maintenance crew would come from a large geographic area and spend the entire 10 weeks together, including weekends. Although Sam had no doubt about the earnings this job would provide, the real uncertainty was what the staff and other members of the crew would be like. Would new friendships develop? The nature of the crew and the leaders could make for 10 weeks of a wonderful time, 10 weeks of misery, or anything in between.

TABLE **4.3**
A constructed scale for summer fun.

Level	Description
5	(Best) A large, congenial group. Many new friendships made. Work is enjoyable, and time passes quickly.
4	A small but congenial group of friends. The work is interesting, and time off work is spent with a few friends in enjoyable pursuits.
3	No new friends are made. Leisure hours are spent with a few friends doing typical activities. Pay is viewed as fair for the work done.
2	Work is difficult. Coworkers complain about the low pay and poor conditions. On some weekends it is possible to spend time with a few friends, but other weekends are boring.
1	(Worst) Work is extremely difficult, and working conditions are poor. Time off work is generally boring because outside activities are limited or no friends are available.

From the description, it appears that Sam has two objectives in this context: earning money and having fun this summer. Both are reasonable, and the two jobs clearly differ in these two dimensions; they offer different possibilities for the amount of money earned and the possibilities of summer fun.

The amount of money to be earned has a natural scale (dollars), and like most of us Sam prefers more money to less. The objective of having fun has no natural scale, though. Thus, a first step is to create such a scale. After considering the possibilities, Sam has created the scale in Table 4.3 to represent different levels of summer fun in the context of choosing a summer job. Although living in town and living in a forest camp pose two very different scenarios, the scale has been constructed in such a way that it can be applied to either job (as well as to any other prospect that might arise). The levels are numbered so that the higher numbers are preferred.

With the constructed scale for summer fun, we can represent Sam's decision with the influence diagram and decision tree shown in Figures 4.23 and 4.24, respectively. The influence diagram shows the uncertainty about fun and amount of work, and that these have an impact on their corresponding consequences. The tree reflects Sam's belief that summer fun with the in-town job will amount to Level 3 in the constructed scale, but there is considerable uncertainty about how much fun the forest job will be. This uncertainty has been translated into probabilities based on Sam's understanding and beliefs; how to make such judgments is the topic of Chapter 8. Likewise, the decision tree reflects uncertainty about the amount of work available at the in-town job.

Analysis: One Objective at a Time

One way to approach the analysis of a multiple-objective decision is to calculate the expected value and create the risk profile for each alternative, one objective at a time. In the summer job example, it is easy enough to do these things for salary, because salary's scale is dollars. For the forest job, in which

FIGURE **4.23**
Influence diagram
for summer-job
example.

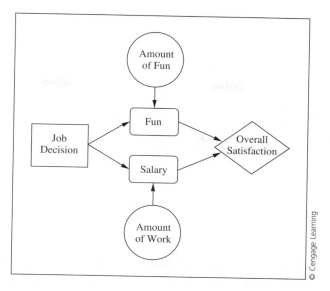

FIGURE **4.24**
Decision tree
for summer-job
example.

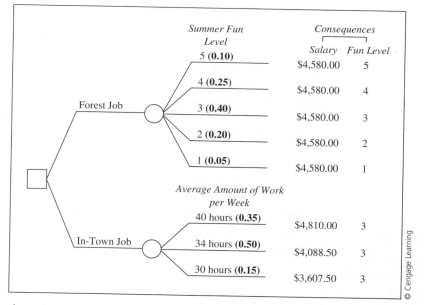

there is no uncertainty about salary, the expected value is $4,580, and the risk profile is a single bar at $4,580, as in Figure 4.25. For the in-town job, the expected salary is:

$$\text{EMV(In Town)} = 0.35(\$4,810.00) + 0.50(\$4,088.50) + 0.15(\$3,607.50)$$
$$= \$4,268.88$$

Thus, considering only the monetary objective, EMV(Forest) > EMV(In Town). The risk profiles of salary for the in-town job and the forest job are shown in Figure 4.25.

FIGURE **4.25**
Risk profiles for
salary in the
summer-job
example.

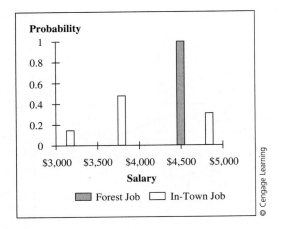

Subjective Ratings for Constructed Attribute Scales

For the summer-fun constructed attribute scale in Table 4.3, risk profiles can be created and compared (Figure 4.26), but expected-value calculations are not meaningful because no meaningful numerical measurements are attached to the specific levels in the scale. The levels are indeed ordered, but the meaning of the ordering is limited. The labels do not mean, for example, that going from Level 2 to Level 3 would give Sam the same increase in satisfaction as going from Level 4 to Level 5, or that Level 4 has twice the satisfaction of Level 2. Thus, before we can do any meaningful analysis, Sam must *rate* the different levels in the scale, indicating how much each level is worth (to Sam) relative to the other levels. This is a subjective judgment on Sam's part. Different people with varying preferences would be expected to give different ratings for the possible levels of summer fun.

To make the necessary ratings, we begin by setting the endpoints of the scale. Let the best possible level (Level 5 in the summer-job example) have a value of 100 and the worst possible level (Level 1) a value of 0. Now all Sam must do is indicate how the intermediate levels rate on this scale

FIGURE **4.26**
Risk profiles for
summer fun in the
summer-job
example.

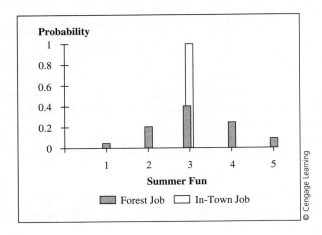

from 0 to 100 points. For example, Level 4 might be worth 90 points, Level 3, 60 points, and Level 2, 25 points. Sam's assessments indicate that going from Level 3 to Level 4, with an increase of 30 points, is three times as good as going from Level 4 to Level 5 with an increase of only 10 points. Note that there is no inherent reason for the values of the levels to be evenly spaced; in fact, it would be surprising to find perfectly even spacing.

This same procedure can be used to create meaningful measurements for any constructed scale. The best level is assigned 100 points, the worst 0 points, and the decision maker must then assign rating points between 0 and 100 to the intermediate levels. A scale like this assigns more points to the preferred consequences, and the rating points for intermediate levels should reflect the decision maker's relative preferences for those levels.

With Sam's assessments, we can now calculate and compare the expected values for the amount of fun in the two jobs. For the in-town job, this is trivial because there is no uncertainty; the expected value is 60 points. For the forest job, the expected value is:

$$E(\text{Fun in Forest Job}) = 0.10(100) + 0.25(90) + 0.40(60) + 0.20(25) + 0.05(0)$$
$$= 61.5 \text{ points.}$$

Considering only the fun objective, the expected value for the forest job is slightly better than the expected value for the in-town job.

With individual expected values and risk profiles, alternatives can be compared. In doing so, we can hope for a clear winner, that is an alternative that dominates all other alternatives on all attributes. Unfortunately, comparing the forest and in-town jobs does not produce a clear winner. Considering salary, the forest job looks good, having no risk and a higher expected value. Considering summer fun, the news is mixed. The in-town job has less risk but a lower expected value. It is obvious that going from one job to the other involves trading risks. Would Sam prefer a slightly higher salary that is predictable and take a risk on how much fun the summer will be? Or would the in-town job be better, playing it safe with the amount of fun and taking a risk on how much money will be earned?

Assessing Trade-Off Weights

The summer-job decision requires Sam to make an explicit trade-off between the objectives of maximizing fun and maximizing salary. How can Sam make this tradeoff? Although this seems like a formidable task, a simple thought experiment is possible that will help Sam understand the relative value of salary and fun.

In order to make the comparison between salary and fun, it is helpful to measure these two on similar scales, and the most convenient arrangement is to put salary on the same 0 to 100 scale that we used for summer fun[3]. As before, the best ($4,810) and worst ($3,607.50) take values of 100 and 0,

---

[3] Alternatively, we could put fun on a monetary scale, assigning a dollar value to each fun level. We discuss how to do this more thoroughly in Chapter 15.

FIGURE **4.27**
Decision tree with
ratings for conse-
quences.

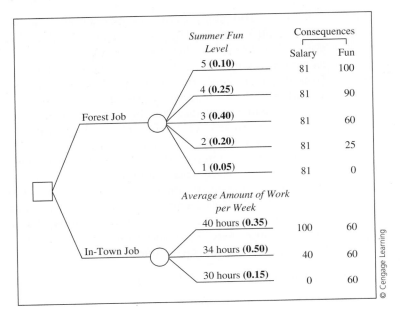

respectively. To get the values for the intermediate salaries ($4,088.50 and $4,580), a simple approach is to calculate them proportionately. Thus, we find that $4,088.50 is 40% of the way from $3,607.50 to $4810, and so it gets a value of 40 on the converted scale. (That is, [$4,088.50 − $3,607.50]/ [$4810 − $3,607.50] = 0.40) Likewise, $4,580 is 81% of the way from $3,607.50 to $4,810, and so it gets a value of 81. (In Chapter 15, we will call this approach *proportional scoring*.) With the ratings for salary and summer fun, we now can create a new consequence matrix, giving the decision tree in Figure 4.27.

Now the trade-off question can be addressed in a straightforward way. The question is how Sam would trade points on the salary scale for points on the fun scale. To do this we introduce the idea of *weights*. What we want to do is assign weights to salary and fun to reflect their relative importance to Sam. Call the weights k_s and k_f, where the subscripts s and f stand for salary and fun, respectively. We will use the weights to calculate a weighted average of the two ratings for any given consequence in order to get an overall score. For example, suppose that $k_s = 0.70$ and $k_f = 0.30$, reflecting a judgment that salary is a little more than twice as important as fun. The overall score (U) for the forest job with fun at Level 3 would be:

$$U(\text{Salary} = 81, \text{Fun} = 60) = 0.70(81) + 0.30(60) = 74.7$$

It is up to Sam to make an appropriate judgment about the relative impor-tance of the two attributes. Although details on making this judgment are in Chapter 15, one important issue in making this judgment bears discussion here. Sam *must* take into consideration the ranges of the two attributes. Strictly speaking, the two weights should reflect the relative value of going from best to worst on each scale. That is, if Sam thinks that improving salary from \$3,607.50 to \$4,810 is three times as important as improving fun from Level 1 to Level 5, this judgment would imply weights $k_s = 0.75$ and $k_f = 0.25$.

Paying attention to the ranges of the attributes in assigning weights is crucial. Too often we are tempted to assign weights on the basis of vague claims that Attribute A (or its underlying objective) is worth three times as much as Attribute B. Suppose you are buying a car, though. If you are looking at cars that all cost about the same amount but their features differ widely, why should price play a role in your decision? It should have a low weight in the overall score. In the Texaco-Pennzoil case, we argued that we could legitimately consider only the objective of maximizing the settlement amount because its range was so wide; any other objectives would be overwhelmed by the importance of moving from worst to best on this one. In an overall score, the weight for settlement amount would be near 1, and the weight for any other attribute would be near zero.

Suppose that, after carefully considering the possible salary and summer-fun outcomes, Sam has come up with weights of 0.6 for salary and 0.4 for fun, reflecting a judgment that the range of possible salaries is 1.5 times as important as the range of possible summer-fun ratings. With these weights, we can collapse the consequence matrix in Figure 4.27 to get Figure 4.28. For example, if Sam chooses the forest job and the level of fun turns out to be Level 4, the overall score is $0.6(81) + 0.4(90) = 84.6$. The other endpoint values in Figure 4.28 can be found in the same way.

In these last two sections we have discussed some straightforward ways to make subjective ratings and trade-off assessments. These topics are treated more completely in Chapter 16. For now you can rest assured that the techniques described here are fully compatible with those described in later chapters.

Analysis: Expected Values and Risk Profiles for Two Objectives

The decision tree in Figure 4.28 is now ready for analysis. The first thing we can do is fold back the tree to calculate expected values. Using the overall scores from Figure 4.28, the expected values are:

$$E(\text{Score for Forest Job}) = 0.10(88.6) + 0.25(84.6) + 0.40(72.6)$$
$$+ 0.20(58.6) + 0.05(48.6)$$
$$= 73.2$$
$$E(\text{Score for In-Town Job}) = 0.35(84) + 0.50(48) + 0.15(24)$$
$$= 57$$

Can we also create risk profiles for the two alternatives? We can; the risk profiles would represent the uncertainty associated with the overall weighted score Sam will get from either job. To the extent that this weighted score is meaningful to Sam as a measure of overall satisfaction, the risk profiles will represent the uncertainty associated with Sam's overall satisfaction. Figures 4.29

FIGURE **4.28**
Decision tree with
overall scores
for summer-job
example.

Weights used are $k_s =$
0.60 and $k_r = 0.40$. For
example, consider the
forest job that has an
outcome of Level 4 on the
fun scale. The rating for
salary is 81, and the rating
for fun is 90. Thus, the
overall score is $0.60(81) +$
$0.40(90) = 84.6$.

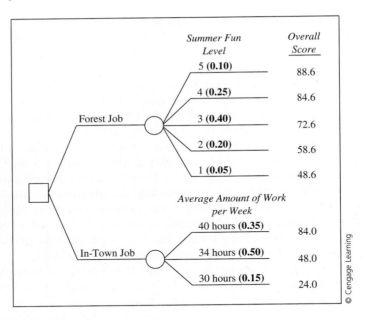

	Summer Fun Level	Overall Score
	5 (**0.10**)	88.6
	4 (**0.25**)	84.6
Forest Job	3 (**0.40**)	72.6
	2 (**0.20**)	58.6
	1 (**0.05**)	48.6

	Average Amount of Work per Week	
	40 hours (**0.35**)	84.0
In-Town Job	34 hours (**0.50**)	48.0
	30 hours (**0.15**)	24.0

© Cengage Learning

FIGURE **4.29**
Risk profiles for
summer jobs.

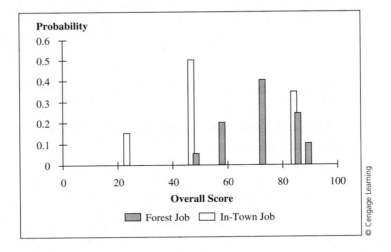

© Cengage Learning

and 4.30 show the risk profiles and cumulative risk profiles for the two jobs.
Figure 4.30 shows that, given the ratings and the trade-off between fun and salary, the forest job stochastically dominates the in-town job in terms of the overall score. Thus, the decision may be clear for Sam at this point; given Sam's
assessed probabilities, ratings, and the trade-off, the forest job is a better risk.
(Before making the commitment, though, Sam may want to do some *sensitivity
analysis*, the topic of Chapter 5; small changes in some of those subjective judgments might result in a less clear choice between the two.)

FIGURE **4.30**
Cumulative risk
profiles for summer
jobs.

The forest job
stochastically domi-
nates the in-town job.

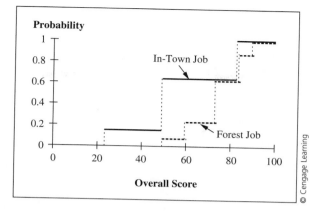

Two final caveats are in order regarding the risk profiles of the overall score. First, it is important to understand that the overall score is something of an artificial outcome; it is an amalgamation in this case of two rating scales. As indicated above, Figures 4.29 and 4.30 only make sense to the extent that Sam is willing to interpret them as representing the uncertainty in the overall satisfaction from the two jobs.

Second, the stochastic dominance displayed by the forest job in Figure 4.30 is a relatively weak result; it relies heavily on Sam's assessed trade-off between the two attributes. A stronger result—one in which Sam could have confidence that the forest job is preferred regardless of his trade-off—requires that the forest job stochastically dominate the in-town job on each individual attribute. (Technically, however, even individual stochastic dominance is not quite enough; the risk profiles for the attributes must be combined into a single two-dimensional risk profile, or *bivariate probability distribution,* for each alternative. Then these 2 two-dimensional risk profiles must be compared in much the same way we did with the single-attribute risk profiles.) The good news is that as long as amount of work and amount of fun are *independent* (no arrow between these two chance nodes in the influence diagram in Figure 4.31), then finding that the same job stochastically dominates the other on each attribute guarantees that the same relationship holds in terms of the technically correct two-dimensional risk profile. Independence and stochastic dominance for multiple attributes will be discussed in Chapter 7.

DECISION ANALYSIS USING PRECISIONTREE

In Chapter 3, we used PrecisionTree to structure influence diagrams and decision trees. Now, we are ready to unlock the analytical capabilities of PrecisionTree. With the click of a button, any tree or influence diagram can be analyzed, various calculations performed, and risk profiles generated. Because it is so easy to run an analysis, however, there can be a temptation to build a quick model, analyze it, and move on. As you learn the steps for running an analysis using PrecisionTree, keep in mind that the insights you are working toward come from careful modeling, then analysis, and perhaps iterating

FIGURE **4.31**

Texaco-Pennzoil decision tree.

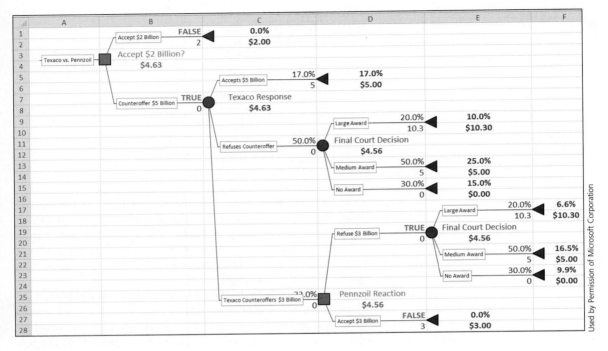

through the model-and-analysis cycle several times. We encourage you to "play" with your model, searching for different insights using a variety of approaches. Take advantage of the time and effort you've saved with the automated analysis by investing it in building a requisite model.

Decision Trees

Figure 4.31 shows the Texaco-Pennzoil decision tree created in PrecisionTree. Notice that at each node, PrecisionTree calculates the value for that node. The expected value for each chance node appears in red in the cell below the node's name. Likewise, at each decision node, the largest branch value (for the preferred alternative) can be seen in the cell below the decision node's name in green. The word "TRUE" identifies the most preferred alternative for that decision node, with all other alternatives labeled "FALSE" for that node. (You can define other decision criteria besides maximizing the expected value. For instructions, see the on-line help manual, Chapter 4: Settings Command.)

In this section, we will first learn how to analyze decision trees and influence diagrams, and then we will learn how to model multiple-objective decisions in a spreadsheet. Although this chapter concludes our discussion of PrecisionTree's basic capabilities, we will revisit PrecisionTree in later chapters to introduce other features, such as sensitivity analysis (Chapter 5), simulation (Chapter 11), and utility curves (Chapter 14).

STEP 1 Build the decision-tree model.

1.1 Start the tree in cell **A1** by clicking on the **Decision Tree** button, and name the tree **Texaco vs. Pennzoil**.

1.2 Add a **Decision** node (by clicking on the end node, blue triangle);
Name the node **Accept $2 Billion?**;
Name the branches **Accept $2 Billion** and **Counteroffer $5 Billion**; and
Enter 2 and 0 for the values of the branches respectively.

1.3 Add a **Chance** node following the *Counteroffer $5 Billion* branch;
Name the node **Texaco Response**;
Add a branch;
Name the branches **Accepts $5 Billion, Refuses Counteroffer** and **Texaco Counteroffers $3 Billion**;
Enter the probabilities **17%, 50%**, and =1−(C5+C9); and
Enter 5, 0, and 0 for the values of the branches respectively. Remember that we use formulas (such as =1−(C5+C9)) to guarantee the probabilities sum to one, even if we alter their values.

1.4 Add a **Chance** node following the *Refuses Counteroffer* branch;
Name the node **Final Court Decision**;
Add a branch;
Name the branches **Large Award, Medium Award** and **No Award**;
Enter the probabilities **20%, 50%**, =1−(D9+D13);
Enter 10.3, 5, and 0 for the values of the branches respectively

1.5 Add a **Decision** node following the *Texaco Counteroffers $3 Billion*;
Name the node **Pennzoil Reaction**;
Name the branches **Refuse $3 Billion** and **Accept $3 Billion**; and
Enter 0 and 3 for the values of the branches respectively.

The decision-tree model is nearly complete; we need only add the *Final Court Decision* when Pennzoil refuses the $3 billion counteroffer from Texaco. But, as we have already added an identical node in Step 1.4, we can use one of two shortcuts. The first is simply to copy the existing node and paste. The second shortcut uses reference nodes. Try both methods described in the text that follows to acquaint yourself with these features.

STEP 2 Replicating nodes.
Method 1: Copy and paste.

2.1 Right-click on the **Final Court Decision** node (on the circle itself when the cursor changes to a hand).

2.2 In the pop-up submenu, choose **Copy Subtree**.

2.3 Right-click on the **Refuse $3 Billion** end node (blue triangle), and choose **Paste Subtree** in the submenu. The program warns us that the current node (the blue triangle) and all successors (there are none in this case) will be deleted. Click **Yes**. Notice that PrecisionTree is smart enough to change the formula for the probability of *No Award*.

Whereas previously, we defined the probability to be 1−(D9+D13), after pasting, the formula becomes 1−(E17+E21).

Method 2: Reference nodes.

2.4 Click on the end node of the **Refuse $3 Billion**.

2.5 Choose **Reference** for the Node Type (gray diamond, fourth button down).

2.6 Name node **Final Court Decision**.

2.7 Under *Reference Options:* choose **Node of this Tree**. There is only one option available—*Final Court Decision (D12)*—as any other choice would lead to a circular reference. Click **OK**.

The dotted line that runs between the reference node (gray diamond at the end of the "Refuse $3 Billion" branch) and the "Final Court Decision" chance node indicates that the tree will be analyzed as if there were an identical "Final Court Decision" chance node at the position of the reference node. PrecisionTree refers back to the "Final Court Decision" chance node for the values and probabilities. If there were additional nodes following the "Final Court Decision" chance node, the reference node would also refer back to all the subsequent downstream structures. In other words, reference nodes are just like copy/paste in that all downstream nodes are utilized. The real difference between reference nodes and copy/paste is that referencing reduces the overall size of the tree, which can be helpful for large, bushy trees.

Now, with the decision tree structured and the appropriate numbers entered, it takes only few clicks of the mouse to run an analysis.

STEP 3 *Analyzing the models.*

3.1 Click on the **Decision Analysis** button (fifth button from the left on the PrecisionTree toolbar). Choose **Risk Profile** in the submenu.

3.2 The *Risk Profile* dialog box pops up and is shown in Figure 4.32. Make sure that the model to be analyzed is the Texaco-Pennzoil model. This is only an issue if you have multiple models opened. Figure 4.32 highlights the choice between analyzing only the optimal alternative (only the path with TRUE values) or analyzing all alternatives. If *Optimal Path Through Model* is chosen, then comparisons between the different alternatives cannot be made. Comparing the expected values of each alternative, and comparing the risks of each alternative can be insightful, thus make sure **All Branches of Starting Node** is chosen. Click **OK**.

PrecisionTree creates a new workbook with three worksheets: one for the statistics report and one each for the two graph types. Figure 4.33 shows the statistics. It is clear that the "Accept $2 Billion" alternative has no uncertainty or risks. The minimum equals both the mean (what we have

FIGURE **4.32**
PrecisionTree will create probability charts and statistical summaries of a decision tree.

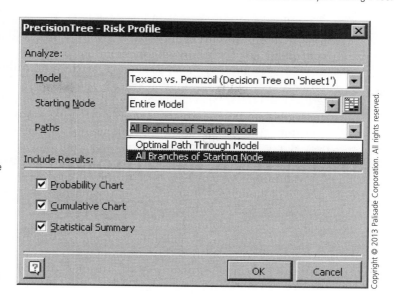

We can analyze the entire model or any subsection of the model. Be careful: If the *Optimal Path Through Model* is chosen; then the analysis is run only on the "TRUE" branches. Typically, *All Branches of Starting Node* is chosen as this allows a comparison of the expected payouts and risks of all the alternatives, not just the optimal alternative.

called the expected value or EMV) and the maximum, because this alternative has a guaranteed $2 billion payout. Ignore the skewness and kurtosis, as these two statistics have no direct bearing on our results. In the next column of Figure 4.33, we see that the "Counteroffer $5 Billion" alternative has a mean of $4.63 billion, or $2.63 billion more than the guaranteed payout. However, the greater EMV of $4.63 billion comes with uncertainty. The statistics report shows that Pennzoil could walk away with nothing[4] (minimum equals zero). If this were to happen, Pennzoil would greatly regret not taking the initial $2 billion offer. The maximum payout is $10.3 billion, and the most likely (mode or modal) payout is $5 billion. Note that the expected value and the most likely value are two different statistics. The expected can be thought

FIGURE **4.33**
Statistics results for the Texaco-Pennzoil decision tree.

Statistics	Accept $2 Billion	Counteroffer $5 Billion
Mean	$2.00	$4.63
Minimum	$2.00	$0.00
Maximum	$2.00	$10.30
Mode	$2.00	$5.00
Std. Deviation	$0.00	$3.28
Skewness	N/A	$0.15
Kurtosis	N/A	2.47

---

[4]The probability charts will give us the probabilities of these different payout amounts.

of as the long-run average of all the possible outcomes, whereas the mode is the one that we would expect to occur most often if we could replicate this situation many times.

The last statistic is the standard deviation. Although we will cover standard deviation in more detail in Chapter 7, it is worth mentioning here. The standard deviation is a measure of the amount of uncertainty in the payout distribution. Whenever the standard deviation equals zero, there is no uncertainty, and the payout is guaranteed. When the standard deviation is not zero, the payouts are uncertain, and the larger the standard deviation, the more uncertain they are. The two main uses of standard deviation are:

1. Measure of uncertainty in the payouts for each alternative
2. Compare the amount of uncertainty between alternatives

For Pennzoil, the standard deviation of $3.28 billion suggests that there is a great deal of uncertainty in counteroffering $5 billion. Clearly, there is more uncertainty in making the counteroffer than accepting the sure $2 billion, which has a standard deviation of $0.

Next, we turn to the probability graphs to determine the probabilities of the different payout amounts. The two remaining worksheets (Probability Chart and Cumulative Chart) provide graphical representations of the risk profiles. Figure 4.34 shows the two risk profiles for the two alternatives "Accept $2 Billion" and "Counteroffer $5 Billion." As there is no uncertainty in accepting $2 billion, there is only one line at $2 billion extending up to

FIGURE **4.34**
The two risk pro-
files produced by
PrecisionTree.

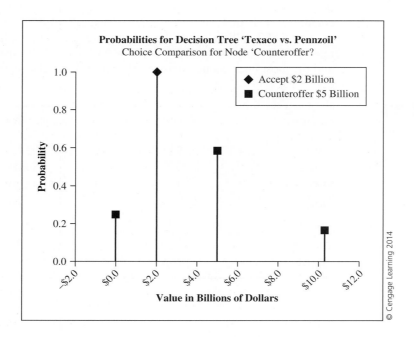

© Cengage Learning 2014

FIGURE **4.35**
The two cumulative risk profiles produced by PrecisionTree.

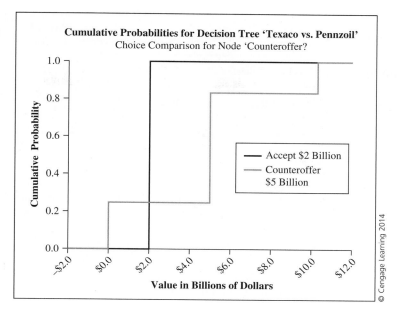

Cumulative Probabilities for Decision Tree 'Texaco vs. Pennzoil'
Choice Comparison for Node 'Counteroffer?'

Value in Billions of Dollars

Cumulative Probability

— Accept $2 Billion
— Counteroffer $5 Billion

probability equal to one. The uncertainty in counter offering is shown by three lines, one for each possible payout. Looking at the chart and the accompanying data table, there is a 24.9% chance of Pennzoil receiving a zero payout, a 58.5% chance of a $5 billion payout, and finally, a 16.6% chance of a $10.3 billion settlement. Thus, if Pennzoil counteroffers, there is approximately a 25% chance of a lower payout than if they took the $2 billion. However, there is a three out of four chance that Pennzoil will do better than $2 billion.

The cumulative chart or risk profile shown in Figure 4.35 has the same probability information, but in cumulative form. For example, the cumulative chart shows that there is a 24.9% chance of Pennzoil receiving zero or less. As zero is the smallest payout, we can drop the "or less" and state there is approximately a 25% chance of receiving zero if Pennzoil refuses the $2 billion settlement. Figure 4.35 shows that there is an 83.4% chance of receiving a $5 billion payout or less. Thus, there is a 58.5% chance of receiving more than zero and no more than $5 billion. Similarly, there is a 100% chance of Pennzoil receiving $10.3 billion or less, and a 16.6% of receiving more than $5 billion.

In addition to the statistical reports and risk profiles, PrecisionTree can also generate a decision table and a policy suggestion. To create these two outputs, click on the **Decision Analysis** button in the PrecisionTree menu, choose **Policy Suggestion**, and click **OK**.

Table 4.4 shows the decision table. The first decision is "Accept $2 Billion?" in cell B4. The Arrival Probability is the probability of making it to that decision node; here there is 100% of making this decision. The

© Cengage Learning 2014

TABLE 4.4
The decision table created by PrecisionTree for the Texaco-Pennzoil decision tree.

Decision	Optimal Choice	Arrival Probability	Benefit of Correct Choice
'Accept 2 Billion?' (B4)	Counteroffer $5 Billion	1.00	$2.635
'Pennzoil Reaction' D26	Refuse $3 Billion	0.33	$1.560

Benefit of Correct Choice is the difference between the optimal (here the maximum expected value) and the worst alternative. Table 4.4 shows that the benefit is $2.635 billion, which means that choosing the "Counteroffer $5 Billion" alternative is optimal and $2.635 billion better than choosing the "Accept $2 Billion" alternative. The second decision is in cell D26, and we have only a 33% chance of making this decision. In other words, there is a 67% chance that we follow a different path through the tree. For this decision, the optimal alternative is to "Refuse $3 Billion" and this is $1.56 billion more than accepting the $3 billion counteroffer from Texaco. Thus, decision tables show what decisions are to be made, which alternative is optimal, the probability of making it to that decision node, and finally the marginal benefit of choosing the optimal over the worst case.

Finally, PrecisionTree also creates the "Optimal Tree." This is just the original decision tree with all FALSE branches removed. The "Optimal Tree" is useful for showing the flow through the decision model when choosing the most preferred alternative. Please note that the "Optimal Tree" is only a graphic, not an actual working decision tree. For example, clicking on a node only highlights the graphic (red circle, green square), and does not access any PrecisionTree dialog box.

One last point before moving on to influence diagrams: How does one copy and paste decision trees and influence diagrams from Excel® into another application, such as Microsoft Word? In Step 2 we showed how to copy sections of a decision tree and then paste it onto an end node. This copy/paste procedure does not work when pasting into a different kind of document. Rather, we need to copy the area of the spreadsheet that surrounds the diagram using the standard Excel® copy command (Ctrl-C or Edit-Copy). Then, to paste the selection into Word, for example, we use the Paste-Special command choosing either Bitmap or Picture. You can turn off the gridlines in Excel® via the Excel® Options menu if you wish to have only the diagram shown.

Influence Diagrams

PrecisionTree analyzes influence diagrams as readily as decision trees, which we demonstrate next with the Texaco-Pennzoil influence diagram. Because the numerical information of an influence diagram is contained in hidden

FIGURE **4.36**
Influence diagram
for Texaco versus
Pennzoil.

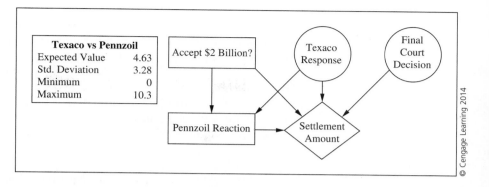

tables, it is important to check carefully that the diagram accurately models the decision before performing any analysis. One simple check is to verify that the values and probabilities are correctly entered (Step 4 in the procedure that follows). Alternatively, PrecisionTree can convert the influence diagram into a decision tree (Step 5), allowing us to easily check the diagram's accuracy. Once satisfied that the influence diagram accurately models the decision, running a complete analysis is as simple as clicking a few buttons.

We need to create the Texaco versus Pennzoil influence diagram, as shown in Figure 4.36 before analyzing it. One option would be to construct the influence diagram from scratch using the skills you learned in the last chapter. If so, be sure that the summary statistics box displays the correct expected value ($4.63 billion), standard deviation ($3.28 billion), minimum ($0 billion), and maximum ($10 billion).

Alternatively, you may open the existing spreadsheet on the website. Please go to www.cengagebrain.com to access the spreadsheet. To encourage you to practice your influence-diagram construction skills, this spreadsheet contains a partially completed model. Step 4 in the procedure that follows describes how to complete this model by adding the values and probabilities, Step 5 describes how to convert the influence diagram into a decision tree, and Step 6 describes how to analyze the influence diagram

As a general rule, numbers are added to a node of an influence diagram by clicking on the name of the node, clicking the *Values* button in the *Influence Node Settings* dialog box, and entering the appropriate numbers in the *Influence Value Editor* dialog box. (Refer to Chapter 3 for a more detailed review if necessary.)

STEP 4 *Entering probabilities and values into an influence diagram.*

4.1 Either open the partially completed influence diagram from website www.cengagebrain.com, or create the diagram (just the nodes and arrows) shown in Figure 4.36. The steps that follow explain how to enter the data into the Value Tables. Thus, you need to create the nodes and joining arrows. If creating the diagram from scratch, use Figure 4.31 to determine the number and name of the branches or outcomes for each node. Specifically, the two decision nodes each have two branches and each chance node has three outcomes.

4.2 Enter the numerical values and probabilities for the nodes "Accept $2 Billion?," "Texaco Response," and "Final Court Decision" nodes using Figure 4.31 as a guide. For example, to enter the values of the "Accept $2 Billion?" node:

Click on **Accept $2 Billion** name

Click on **Exit to Value Table**

Enter **0** for *Value when skipped;* enter **2** if accepted, and enter **0** if $5 billion is counteroffered.

Click **OK.**

Repeat for the "Texaco Response," and "Final Court Decision" nodes.

4.3 Click on the decision node named **Pennzoil Reaction** and click on the **Exit to Value Table** button. A spreadsheet pops up titled *Influence Value Table,* in which we use the entries on the right to specify the values in the *Value* column (Figure 4.37). The *Influence Value Table* is a consequence table similar to Table 4.1 except that the columns are read from right to left.

4.4 Start by typing **0** in the first row (*Value when skipped*) and hit **Enter.**

4.5 Type an equals sign (**=**) in the second row. Reading the rightmost entry, we see that Pennzoil has chosen to accept the $2 billion offer. Hence its value is 2, which is accessed by clicking on the first **Accept $2 Billion** in the column below the *Accept $2 Billion?* heading. Row 2 should now read =E4.

4.6 The next five entries also involve accepting the $2 billion, so repeat Step 4.5 five times; for each row, click on the corresponding **Accept $2 Billion** in the rightmost column. Alternatively, because this is an Excel® spreadsheet, you can use the fill-down command. As a guide, use the outcomes highlighted with white rectangles in Figure 4.37.

4.7 Continuing onto rows 7–12, the rightmost alternative is to counteroffer $5 billion. Since Pennzoil has counteroffered, the values are now determined by Texaco's response. Specify the appropriate value by clicking on the corresponding row under the *Texaco Response* heading. For example, clicking on **Accepts $5 Billion** in row 7, places D10 into the *Value Table.*

4.8 Click **OK** when your *Influence Value Table* matches Figure 4.37.

4.9 Following the same procedure, open the *Influence Value Table* for **Settlement Amount** and enter the appropriate values reading from right to left. Figure 4.38 highlights the cells to click on.

When finished entering the values, the summary statistics box should display the correct expected value (4.63), standard deviation (3.28), minimum (0), and maximum (10.3).

We can also convert the influence diagram into a decision tree.

FIGURE **4.37**
To enter the values
for a specific row,
click on the appro-
priate column entry
in that row.

For example, reading
right-to-left, the first six
rows correspond to ac-
cepting the $2 billion
offer. Thus, for each
row, we click directly on
the "Accept $2 Billion"
entry in that row as
highlighted.

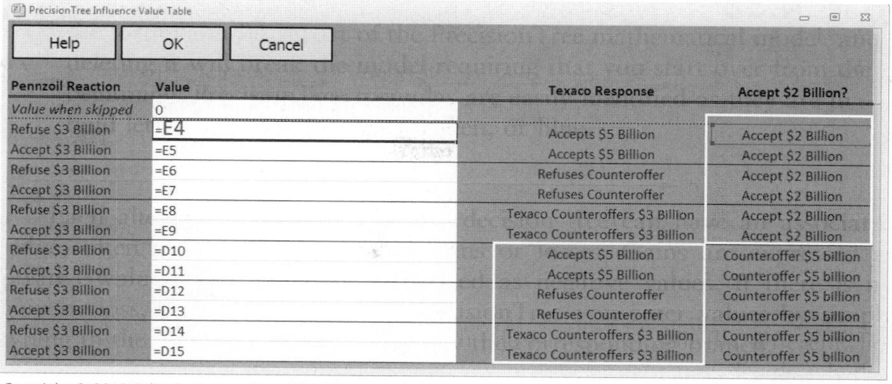

Pennzoil Reaction	Value		Texaco Response	Accept $2 Billion?
Value when skipped	0			
Refuse $3 Billion	=E4		Accepts $5 Billion	Accept $2 Billion
Accept $3 Billion	=E5		Accepts $5 Billion	Accept $2 Billion
Refuse $3 Billion	=E6		Refuses Counteroffer	Accept $2 Billion
Accept $3 Billion	=E7		Refuses Counteroffer	Accept $2 Billion
Refuse $3 Billion	=E8		Texaco Counteroffers $3 Billion	Accept $2 Billion
Accept $3 Billion	=E9		Texaco Counteroffers $3 Billion	Accept $2 Billion
Refuse $3 Billion	=D10		Accepts $5 Billion	Counteroffer $5 billion
Accept $3 Billion	=D11		Accepts $5 Billion	Counteroffer $5 billion
Refuse $3 Billion	=D12		Refuses Counteroffer	Counteroffer $5 billion
Accept $3 Billion	=D13		Refuses Counteroffer	Counteroffer $5 billion
Refuse $3 Billion	=D14		Texaco Counteroffers $3 Billion	Counteroffer $5 billion
Accept $3 Billion	=D15		Texaco Counteroffers $3 Billion	Counteroffer $5 billion

STEP 5 Converting influence diagrams into decision trees.

5.1 Right click on the name of the influence diagram—**Texaco versus Pennzoil**.
5.2 In the submenu, choose **Model**, then **Convert to Decision Tree**.

A new spreadsheet is added to your workbook containing the converted tree. Comparing the converted tree to Figure 4.31 clearly shows the effect of assuming symmetry in an influence diagram, as discussed earlier. For example, the decision tree in Figure 4.31 stops after the "Accept 2" branch, whereas the converted tree has all subsequent chance and decision nodes following the "Accept 2" branch. These extra branches are due to the symmetry assumption and explain why the payoff table for the influence diagram required so many entries. PrecisionTree has the ability to incorporate asymmetry into influence diagrams via structure arcs. Although we do not cover structure arcs, you can learn about structure arcs from the user's manual and the on-line help.

We are now ready to analyze the influence diagram.

STEP 6 Analyzing influence diagrams.

6.1 Right click on the name of the influence diagram—**Texaco versus Pennzoil**.
6.2 In the submenu, choose **Decision Analysis**, then **Risk Profile**.

The only difference in the outputs between analyzing an influence diagram and a decision tree is that the influence diagram reports on only the

FIGURE **4.38**
Value Tables are read right to left.

For example, if Pennzoil accepts the $2 billion offer, the payout value is 2, which is entered by clicking on the "Accept $2 Billion" for that row. If Pennzoil counters $5 billion and Texaco accepts, then click on the "Accept $5 Billion" for that row. Notice that if Texaco refuses the $5 billion counteroffer and does not counter with $3 billion, we jump to the "Final Court Decision."

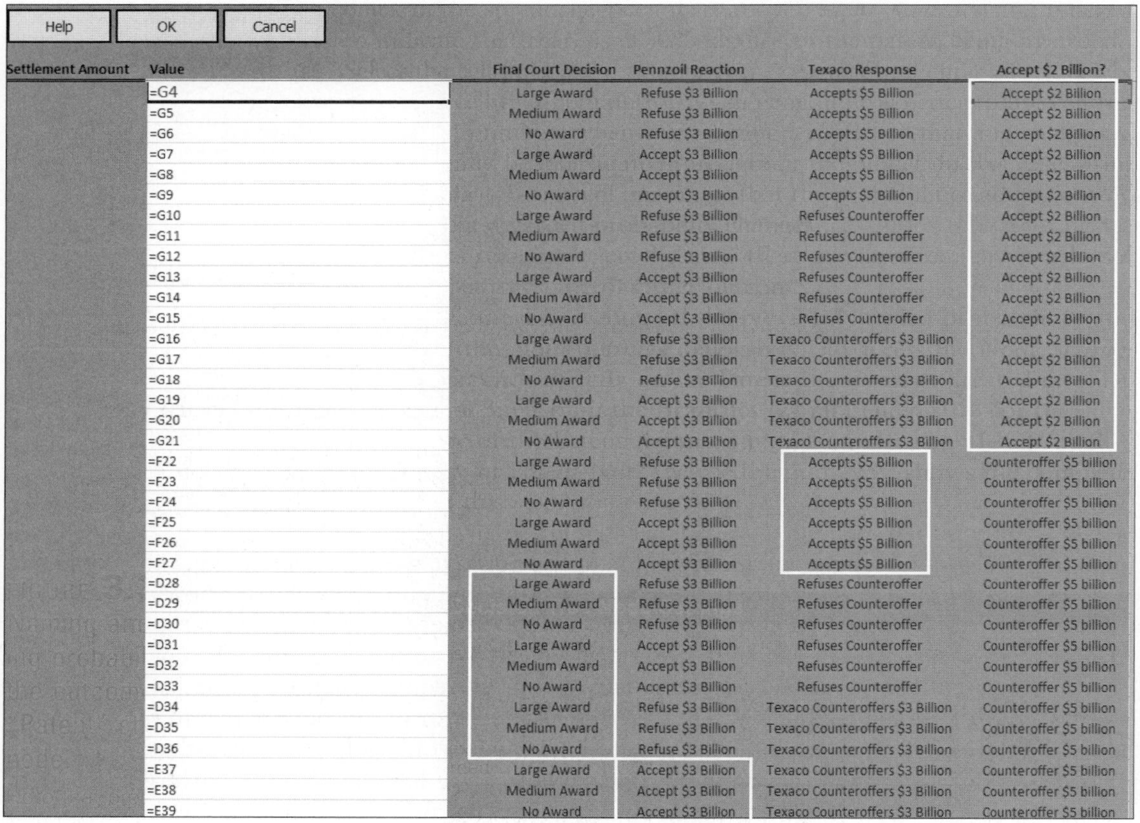

Settlement Amount	Value		Final Court Decision	Pennzoil Reaction	Texaco Response	Accept $2 Billion?
	=G4		Large Award	Refuse $3 Billion	Accepts $5 Billion	Accept $2 Billion
	=G5		Medium Award	Refuse $3 Billion	Accepts $5 Billion	Accept $2 Billion
	=G6		No Award	Refuse $3 Billion	Accepts $5 Billion	Accept $2 Billion
	=G7		Large Award	Accept $3 Billion	Accepts $5 Billion	Accept $2 Billion
	=G8		Medium Award	Accept $3 Billion	Accepts $5 Billion	Accept $2 Billion
	=G9		No Award	Accept $3 Billion	Accepts $5 Billion	Accept $2 Billion
	=G10		Large Award	Refuse $3 Billion	Refuses Counteroffer	Accept $2 Billion
	=G11		Medium Award	Refuse $3 Billion	Refuses Counteroffer	Accept $2 Billion
	=G12		No Award	Refuse $3 Billion	Refuses Counteroffer	Accept $2 Billion
	=G13		Large Award	Accept $3 Billion	Refuses Counteroffer	Accept $2 Billion
	=G14		Medium Award	Accept $3 Billion	Refuses Counteroffer	Accept $2 Billion
	=G15		No Award	Accept $3 Billion	Refuses Counteroffer	Accept $2 Billion
	=G16		Large Award	Refuse $3 Billion	Texaco Counteroffers $3 Billion	Accept $2 Billion
	=G17		Medium Award	Refuse $3 Billion	Texaco Counteroffers $3 Billion	Accept $2 Billion
	=G18		No Award	Refuse $3 Billion	Texaco Counteroffers $3 Billion	Accept $2 Billion
	=G19		Large Award	Accept $3 Billion	Texaco Counteroffers $3 Billion	Accept $2 Billion
	=G20		Medium Award	Accept $3 Billion	Texaco Counteroffers $3 Billion	Accept $2 Billion
	=G21		No Award	Accept $3 Billion	Texaco Counteroffers $3 Billion	Accept $2 Billion
	=F22		Large Award	Refuse $3 Billion	Accepts $5 Billion	Counteroffer $5 billion
	=F23		Medium Award	Refuse $3 Billion	Accepts $5 Billion	Counteroffer $5 billion
	=F24		No Award	Refuse $3 Billion	Accepts $5 Billion	Counteroffer $5 billion
	=F25		Large Award	Accept $3 Billion	Accepts $5 Billion	Counteroffer $5 billion
	=F26		Medium Award	Accept $3 Billion	Accepts $5 Billion	Counteroffer $5 billion
	=F27		No Award	Accept $3 Billion	Accepts $5 Billion	Counteroffer $5 billion
	=D28		Large Award	Refuse $3 Billion	Refuses Counteroffer	Counteroffer $5 billion
	=D29		Medium Award	Refuse $3 Billion	Refuses Counteroffer	Counteroffer $5 billion
	=D30		No Award	Refuse $3 Billion	Refuses Counteroffer	Counteroffer $5 billion
	=D31		Large Award	Accept $3 Billion	Refuses Counteroffer	Counteroffer $5 billion
	=D32		Medium Award	Accept $3 Billion	Refuses Counteroffer	Counteroffer $5 billion
	=D33		No Award	Accept $3 Billion	Refuses Counteroffer	Counteroffer $5 billion
	=D34		Large Award	Refuse $3 Billion	Texaco Counteroffers $3 Billion	Counteroffer $5 billion
	=D35		Medium Award	Refuse $3 Billion	Texaco Counteroffers $3 Billion	Counteroffer $5 billion
	=D36		No Award	Refuse $3 Billion	Texaco Counteroffers $3 Billion	Counteroffer $5 billion
	=E37		Large Award	Accept $3 Billion	Texaco Counteroffers $3 Billion	Counteroffer $5 billion
	=E38		Medium Award	Accept $3 Billion	Texaco Counteroffers $3 Billion	Counteroffer $5 billion
	=E39		No Award	Accept $3 Billion	Texaco Counteroffers $3 Billion	Counteroffer $5 billion

Help   OK   Cancel

optimal alternative. Thus, there is only one set of statistics and one risk profile. The output for influence diagrams is interpreted in the same way as for decision trees.

Multiple-Attribute Models

This section presents two methods for modeling multiple-attribute decisions. Both methods take advantage of the fact that PrecisionTree runs in a spreadsheet and hence provides easy access to side calculations. We will explore these two methods using the summer-job example for illustration.

Method 1

The first method uses the fact that the branch value is entered into a spreadsheet cell, which makes it possible to use a specific formula in the cell to calculate the weighted scores. The formula we use is $U(s, f) = k_s \times s + k_f \times f$ where k_s and k_f are the weights and s and f are the scaled values for "Salary" and "Fun," respectively.

STEP 8 A decision tree for a multiattribute decision.

8.1 Build the decision tree, as shown in Figure 4.39, using the given probabilities.
Leave the values (the numbers below the branches) temporarily at zero.

8.2 Create the weights table by typing **0.6** in cell B3 and **=1−B3** in cell C3.

8.3 Create the consequence table by entering the appropriate scaled salary and scaled fun scores corresponding to the branch values in columns E and **F**, as shown in Figure 4.39.

8.4 Compute the weighted scores for the top branch by clicking in cell C5 and enter **=$B$3*E5+$C$3*F5**. A score of 88.6 should appear in C5.

8.5 Now copy the contents of C5 (either Ctrl-C or Home-Copy).

8.6 Paste contents into cell C7. A score of 84.6 should appear in C7. Continue pasting the formula into the cells corresponding to each of the branches. You can streamline the process by copying the formula once, and then hold down the control key while highlighting each cell into which you want to paste the formula. Now choose paste, and the formula is inserted into each highlighted cell. The weighted scores should be the same as those in Figure 4.39.

Solving the tree and examining the risk profiles demonstrates that the "Forest Job" stochastically dominates the "In-Town Job."

Method 2

The second method is more sophisticated and eliminates the need to enter a separate formula for each outcome. Instead, a link is established between the decision tree and an Excel® table; input values pass from the tree to the table via this link. The endpoint value is calculated by the table for the given input values, and passed back to the corresponding end node. Specifically, for the summer-job example, we will import the salary and fun levels from the tree, compute the weighted score, and export it back into the tree. The table acts as a template for calculating end-node values. Let's try it out.

STEP 9 Building a linked decision tree.

9.1 Construct the "Summer Job" decision tree as shown in Figure 4.40 and name the tree **Linked Tree**. Note: The branch values now correspond to the scaled fun and scaled salary levels. Also, we added extra

FIGURE **4.39**

Modeling multiattribute decisions using the spreadsheet for the calculations.

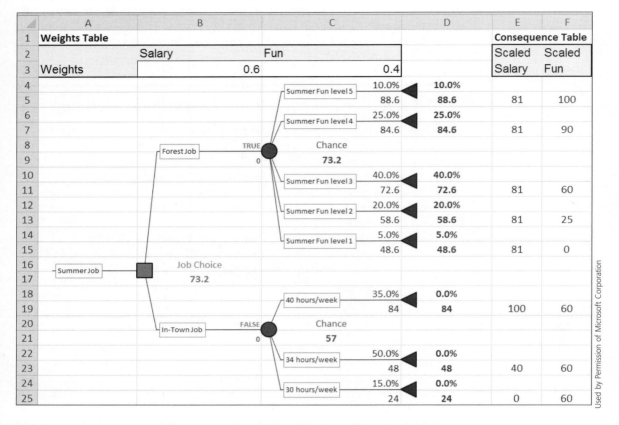

nodes so that each alternative has a node for both the Fun level and the Work level.

9.2 Construct the weights table as shown at the top of Figure 4.40. Enter 0.60 in B3 and =1–B3 in C3. These are the weights for "Fun" and "Salary," respectively.

9.3 Enter the values **100** and **40** the **G** column, and the overall score $U(s,f) = k_s \times s + k_f \times f$ in cell G4 as = **G2*$B$3+G3*$C$3**. This consequence table will act as a template, taking values for the fun and salary levels from the tree, compute the overall score according to the table's formula, and then send the overall value back to the tree's end nodes.

9.4 Link the end nodes to the table's formula by performing these steps:
Click on the **tree's name** to bring up the *Model Settings* dialog box;
Click on the **Calculation** tab;
Choose **Linked Spreadsheet** in the pull-down list for *Method*; choose **Automatic** for *Link Updating*; and finally,
Enter **G4** for the *Default Cell*. Click **OK**.

FIGURE **4.40**

Computing end-node values via linking the tree to a table.

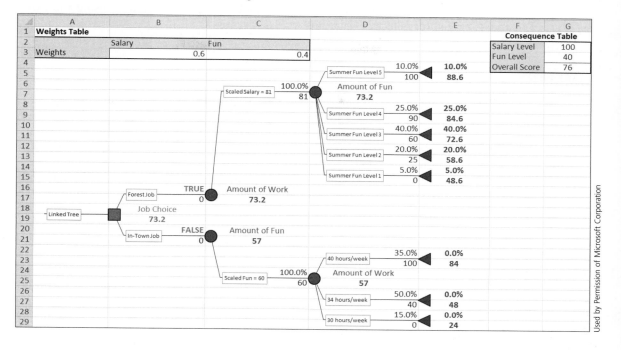

Note that every end-node value is now 76. This is because all end nodes are calculated from cell G4, which currently equals 76.

9.5 Next, we link the salary levels in the tree to their corresponding table cell. Click directly on the chance node *Amount of Work* to bring up the *Node Settings* dialog box. Under *Link Branch Values To*, click on the radio button **Cell**, enter **G2**, and click **OK**. Repeat for the second *Amount of Work* chance node, i.e., both *Amount of Work* chance nodes should be linked to cell **G2**.

9.6 Link the fun levels in the tree to their corresponding table cell, G3. Click directly on the chance node *Amount of Fun*, and under *Link Branch Values To*, click on the radio button **Cell**, enter **G3**, and click **OK**. Repeat for the second *Amount of Fun* chance node. Your tree should now be identical to Figure 4.40. You might need to click on the Update Links button on the PrecisionTree toolbar to update all the node values.

This completes the construction of the linked tree. Analysis of this tree would proceed as described previously. The linked-tree method becomes more advantageous as the decision tree grows in size and complexity. Also, it often happens that a decision is first modeled in a spreadsheet, and later developed into a decision tree. It may be natural in such a case to use the linked-tree method where the end-node values are computed using the existing spreadsheet calculations.

SUMMARY

This chapter has demonstrated a variety of ways to use quantitative tools to make choices in uncertain situations. We first looked at the solution process for decision trees using expected value (or expected monetary value [EMV] when consequences are dollars). This is the most straightforward way to analyze a decision model; the algorithm for solving a decision tree is easy to apply, and expected values are easy to calculate. We also explored the process of solving influence diagrams using expected values. To understand the solution process for influence diagrams, we had to look at their internal structures. In a sense, we had to fill in certain gaps left from Chapter 3 about how influence diagrams work. The solution procedure works out easily once we understand how the problem's numerical details are represented internally. The procedure for reducing nodes involves calculating expected values in a way that parallels the solution of a decision tree.

We have seen that associated with each alternative are a risk profile and the expected value. From these we can get an idea of what to expect if we choose that particular alternative. When the alternative is a certain amount, the expected value and risk profile are elementary: the risk profile is a single line and the expected value is that certain amount. When there are many possible consequences (payoffs) for the alternative, then the risk profile and expected value are more complex. Insights that help determine the preferred alternative come from a thorough comparison of the expected values and risk profiles for all the alternatives analyzed.

EXERCISES

4.1 Is it possible to solve a decision-tree version of a problem and an equivalent influence-diagram version and come up with different answers? If so, explain. If not, why not?

4.2 Explain in your own words what it means when one alternative stochastically dominates another.

4.3 The analysis of the Texaco-Pennzoil example shows that the EMV of counteroffering with $5 billion far exceeds $2 billion. Why might Liedtke want to accept the $2 billion anyway? If you were Liedtke, what is the smallest offer from Texaco that you would accept?

4.4 Solve the decision tree in Figure 4.41.

FIGURE 4.41
Generic decision
tree for
Exercise 4.4.

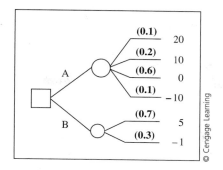

4.5 Use PrecisionTree to create and solve the influence diagram that corresponds to the decision tree in Figure 4.41.

4.6 Solve the decision tree in Figure 4.42. What principle discussed in Chapter 4 is illustrated by this decision tree?

FIGURE 4.42
Generic decision
tree for
Exercise 4.6.

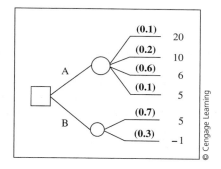

4.7 Which alternative is preferred in Figure 4.43? Do you have to do any calculations? Explain.

FIGURE 4.43
Generic decision
tree for
Exercise 4.7.

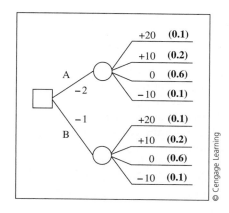

FIGURE **4.44**
Generic decision
tree for
Exercise 4.8.

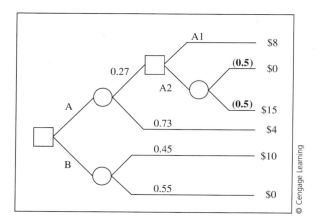

4.8   Solve the decision tree in Figure 4.44.

4.9   Create risk profiles and cumulative risk profiles for all possible strategies in Figure 4.44. Is one strategy stochastically dominant? Explain.

4.10   Use PrecisionTree to create and solve the influence diagram that corresponds to the decision tree in Figure 4.44.

4.11   Explain why deterministic dominance is a special case of stochastic
dominance.

4.12   Explain in your own words why it is important to consider the ranges
of the consequences in determining a trade-off weight.

4.13   Use PrecisionTree to create and solve the influence diagram for the
umbrella problem shown in Figure 4.10.

QUESTIONS AND PROBLEMS

4.14   A real-estate investor has the opportunity to purchase a small apartment
complex. The apartment complex costs $4 million and is expected to gen-
erate net revenue (net after all operating and finance costs) of $60,000 per
month. Of course, the revenue could vary because the occupancy rate is
uncertain. Considering the uncertainty, the revenue could vary from a low
of −$10,000 to a high of $100,000 per month. Assume that the investor's
objective is to maximize the value of the investment at the end of 10 years.

a)   Do you think the investor should buy the apartment complex or invest
the $4 million in a 10-year certificate of deposit earning 9.5%? Why?

b)   The city council is currently considering an application to rezone a
nearby empty parcel of land. The owner of that land wants to build
a small electronics-assembly plant. The proposed plant does not
really conflict with the city's overall land use plan, but it may have a
substantial long-term negative effect on the value of the nearby resi-
dential district in which the apartment complex is located. Because
the city council currently is divided on the issue and will not make a
decision until next month, the real estate investor is thinking about
waiting until the city council makes its decision.

If the investor waits, what could happen? What are the trade-offs that the investor has to make in deciding whether to wait or to purchase the complex now?

c) Suppose the investor could pay the seller $10,000 in earnest money now, specifying in the purchase agreement that if the council's decision is to approve the rezoning, the investor can forfeit the $10,000 and forego the purchase. Draw and solve a decision tree showing the investor's three options. Examine the alternatives for dominance. If you were the investor, which alternative would you choose? Why?

4.15 A stock market investor has $500 to spend and is considering purchasing an option contract on 1,000 shares of Apricot Computer. The shares themselves are currently selling for $28.50 per share. Apricot is involved in a lawsuit, the outcome of which will be known within a month. If the outcome is in Apricot's favor, analysts expect Apricot's stock price to increase by $5 per share. If the outcome is unfavorable, the price is expected to drop by $2.75 per share. The option costs $500, and owning the option would allow the investor to purchase 1,000 shares of Apricot stock for $30 per share. Thus, if the investor buys the option and Apricot prevails in the lawsuit, the investor would make an immediate profit. Aside from purchasing the option, the investor could (1) do nothing and earn about 8% on his money, or (2) purchase $500 worth of Apricot shares.

a) Construct cumulative risk profiles for the three alternatives, assuming Apricot has a 25% chance of winning the lawsuit. Can you draw any conclusions?

b) If the investor believes that Apricot stands a 25% chance of winning the lawsuit, should he purchase the option? What if he believes the chance is only 10%? How large does the probability have to be for the option to be worthwhile?

4.16 Johnson Marketing is interested in producing and selling an innovative new food processor. The decision they face is the typical "make or buy" decision often faced by manufacturers. On one hand, Johnson could produce the processor itself, subcontracting different subassemblies, such as the motor or the housing. Cost estimates in this case are as follows:

Alternative: Make Food Processor	
Cost per Unit	Probability
$35.00	25%
$42.50	25%
$45.00	37%
$49.00	13%

The company also could have the entire machine made by a subcontractor. The subcontractor, however, faces similar uncertainties regarding the costs and has provided Johnson Marketing with the following schedule of costs and probabilities:

Alternative: Buy Food Processor	
Cost per Unit	Probability
$37.00	10%
$43.00	40%
$46.00	30%
$50.00	20%

If Johnson Marketing wants to minimize its expected cost of production in this case, should it make or buy? Construct cumulative risk profiles to support your recommendation. (*Hint:* Use care when interpreting the graph!)

4.17 Analyze the difficult decision situation that you identified in Problem 1.9 and structured in Problem 3.21. Be sure to examine alternatives for dominance. Does your analysis suggest any new alternatives?

4.18 Stacy Ennis eats lunch at a local restaurant two or three times a week. In selecting a restaurant on a typical workday, Stacy uses three criteria. First is to minimize the amount of travel time, which means that close-by restaurants are preferred on this attribute. The next objective is to minimize cost, and Stacy can make a judgment of the average lunch cost at most of the restaurants that would be considered. Finally, variety comes into play. On any given day, Stacy would like to go someplace different than in the past week.

Today is Monday, her first day back from a two-week vacation, and Stacy is considering the following six restaurants:

	Distance (Walking Time)	Average Price
Sam's Pizza	10	$3.50
Sy's Sandwiches	9	$2.85
Bubba's Italian Barbecue	7	$6.50
Blue China Cafe	2	$5.00
The Eating Place	2	$7.50
The Excel-Soaring Restaurant	5	$9.00

a) If Stacy considers distance, price, and variety to be equally important (given the range of alternatives available), where should she go today for lunch? (*Hints:* Don't forget to convert both distance and price to similar scales, such as a scale from 0 to 100. Also, recall that Stacy has just returned from vacation; what does this imply for how the restaurants compare on the variety objective?)

b) Given your answer to part a, where should Stacy go on Thursday?

4.19 The national coffee store Farbucks needs to decide in August how many holiday-edition insulated coffee mugs to order. Because the mugs are dated, those that are unsold by January 15 are considered a loss. These premium mugs sell for $23.95 and cost $6.75 each. Farbucks is uncertain of the demand. They believe that there is a 25% chance that they will sell 10,000 mugs, a 50% chance that they will sell 15,000, and a 25% chance that they will sell 20,000.

a) Build a linked-tree in PrecisionTree to determine if they should order 12,000, 15,000, or 18,000 mugs. Be sure that your model does not allow Farbucks to sell more mugs than they ordered. You can use the IF( ) command in Excel®. If demand is less than the order quantity, the amount sold is the demand. Otherwise, the amount sold is the order quantity. (See Excel's® help or function wizard for guidance.)

b) Now, assume that any unsold mugs are discounted and sold for $5. How does this affect the decision?

4.20 Although the expected value is a straightforward and appealing summary of an alternative, it does have its limitations. We interpret the EMV as the average amount that would be obtained by "playing the game" a large number of times. But is this a worthwhile number to know for unique or one-off decisions? For example, the "game" for Hugh Liedtke amounts to suing Texaco—not a game that Pennzoil will play many times! Discuss the pros and cons of using EMV as a decision selection criterion, especially for one-off decisions.

4.21 We mentioned that the probabilities associated with any risk profile must sum to one. To see why, let's consider the decision modeled in Figure 4.45. Because each uncertainty P, Q, R, and T are probability distributions, we must have:

$$p_1 + p_2 + p_2 = 1; \quad q_1 + q_2 + q_2 = 1; \quad r_1 + r_2 + r_2 = 1; \quad \text{and } t_1 + t_2 + t_2 = 1.$$

Show that the nine end-node probability values $p_1 r_1$, $p_1 r_2$, $p_1 r_3$, $p_2 q_1$, $p_2 q_2$, $p_2 q_3$, $p_3 t_1$, $p_3 t_2$, and $p_3 t_3$ sum to one.

FIGURE **4.45**
Decision tree for
Question 4.21

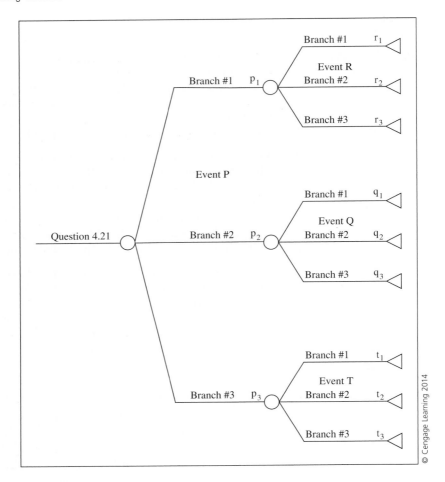

© Cengage Learning 2014

4.22 What is the relationship between stochastic dominance and expected value? If alternative A dominates alternative B, then is it always true that EV(A) is better than EV(B)? Why?

4.23 Consider the decision a contractor faces when bidding on a construction job. The contractor must first decide on the bid amount, then after submitting the bid, waits to see if he won the contract. After winning the contract, he faces additional uncertainties with regards to materials cost, labor costs, delays, etc. Each of these uncertainties influence the final profit, and a summary of this decision is given in Figure 4.46. Build and solve the tree in Figure 4.46 using PrecisionTree. Use this problem to discuss why the most likely value (the mode) is different from the expected value. What conclusions can be drawn based on the mode, and how does this differ from the conclusions based on the expected value?

FIGURE **4.46**
Decision tree for Question 4.23.

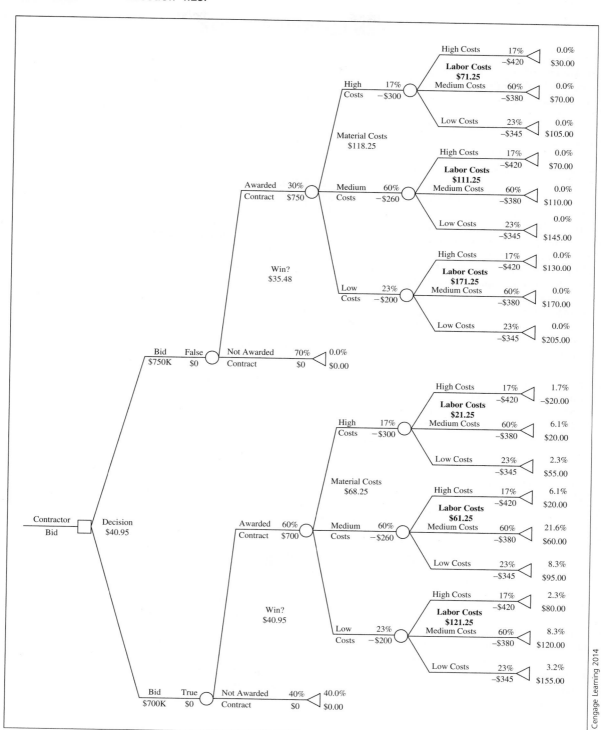

SOUTHERN ELECTRONICS, PART I

Steve Sheffler is president, CEO, and majority stockholder of Southern Electronics, a small firm in the town of Silicon Mountain. Steve faces a major decision: Two firms, Big Red Business Machines and Banana Computer, are bidding for Southern Electronics.

Steve founded Southern 15 years ago, and the company has been extremely successful in developing progressive computer components. Steve is ready to sell the company (as long as the price is right!) so that he can pursue other interests. Last month, Big Red offered Steve $5 million and 100,000 shares of Big Red stock (currently trading at $50 per share and not expected to change substantially in the future). Until yesterday, Big Red's offer sounded good to Steve, and he had planned on accepting it this week. But a lawyer from Banana Computer called last week and indicated that Banana was interested in acquiring Southern Electronics. In discussions this past week, Steve has learned that Banana is developing a new computer, codenamed EYF, that, if successful, will revolutionize the industry. Southern Electronics could play an important role in the development of the machine.

In their discussions, several important points have surfaced. First, Banana has said that it believes the probability that the EYF will succeed is 0.6, and that if it does, the value of Banana's stock will increase from the current value of $30 per share. Although the future price is uncertain, Banana judges that, conditional on the EYF's success, the expected price of the stock is $50 per share. If the EYF is not successful, the price will probably decrease slightly. Banana judges that if the EYF fails, Banana's share price will be between $20 and $30, with an expected price of $25.

Yesterday Steve discussed this information with his financial analyst, who is an expert regarding the electronics industry and whose counsel Steve trusts completely. The analyst pointed out that Banana has an incentive to be very optimistic about the EYF project. "Being realistic, though," said the analyst, "the probability that the EYF succeeds is only 0.4, and if it does succeed, the expected price of the stock would be only $40 per share. On the other hand, I agree with Banana's assessment for the share price if the EYF fails."

Negotiations today have proceeded to the point where Banana has made a final offer to Steve of $5 million and 150,000 shares of Banana stock. The company's representative has stated quite clearly that Banana cannot pay any more than this in a straight transaction. Furthermore, the representative claims, it is not clear why Steve will not accept the offer because it appears to them to be more valuable than the Big Red offer.

Questions

1. In terms of expected value, what is the least that Steve should accept from Banana? (This amount is called his *reservation price*.)
2. Steve obviously has two choices, to accept the Big Red offer or to accept the Banana offer. Create and solve an influence diagram representing Steve's decision.
3. Create and solve a complete decision tree representing Steve's decision.
4. Why is it that Steve cannot accept the Banana offer as it stands?

SOUTHERN ELECTRONICS, PART II

Steve is well aware of the difference between his probabilities and Banana's, and he realizes that because of this difference, it may be possible to design a contract that benefits both parties. In particular, he is thinking about put options for the stock. A put option gives the owner of the option the right to sell an asset at a specific price. (For example, if you own a put option on 100 shares of General Motors (GM) with an exercise price of $75, you could sell 100 shares of GM for $75 per share before the expiration date of the option. This would be useful if the stock price fell below $75.) Steve reasons that if he could get Banana to include a put option on the stock with an exercise price of $30, he would be protected if the EYF failed.

Steve proposes the following deal: He will sell Southern Electronics to Banana for $530,000 plus 280,000 shares of Banana stock and a put option that will allow him to sell the 280,000 shares back to Banana for $30 per share any time within the next year (during which time it will become known whether the EYF succeeds or fails).

Questions

1. Calculate Steve's expected value for this deal. Ignore tax effects and the time value of money.

2. The cost to Banana of their original offer was:

$$\$5,000,000 + 150,000(\$30) = \$9,500,000$$

Show that the expected cost to Banana of Steve's proposed deal is less than $9.5 million, and hence in Banana's favor. Again, ignore tax effects and the time value of money.

STRENLAR

Fred Wallace scratched his head. By this time tomorrow he had to have an answer for Joan Sharkey, his former boss at Plastics International (PI). The decision was difficult to make. It involved how he would spend the next 10 years of his life.

Four years ago, when Fred was working at PI, he had come up with an idea for a revolutionary new polymer. A little study—combined with intuition, hunches, and educated guesses—had convinced him that the new material would be extremely strong for its weight. Although it would undoubtedly cost more than conventional materials, Fred discovered that a variety of potential uses existed in the aerospace, automobile manufacturing, robotics, and sporting goods industries.

When he explained his idea to his supervisors at PI, they had patiently told him that they were not interested in pursuing risky new projects. His appeared to be even riskier than most because, at the time, many of the details had not been fully worked out. Furthermore, they pointed out that efficient production would require the development of a new manufacturing process. Sure, if that process proved successful, the new polymer could be a big hit. But without that process the company simply could not provide the resources Fred would need to develop his idea into a marketable product.

Fred did not give up. He began to work at home on his idea, consuming most of his evenings and weekends. His intuition and guesses had proven correct, and after some time he had worked out a small-scale manufacturing process. With this process, he had been able to turn out small batches of his miracle polymer, which he dubbed Strenlar. At this point he quietly began to assemble some capital. He invested $500,000 of his own, managed to borrow another $500,000, and quit his job at PI to devote his time to Strenlar.

That was 15 months ago. In the intervening time he had made substantial progress. The product was refined, and several customers eagerly awaited the first production run. A few problems remained to be solved in the manufacturing process, but Fred was 80% sure that these bugs could be worked out satisfactorily. He was eager to start making profits himself; his capital was running dangerously low. When he became anxious, he tried to soothe his fears by recalling his estimate of the project's potential. His best guess was that sales would be approximately $35 million over 10 years, and that he would net some $8 million after costs.

Two weeks ago, Joan Sharkey at PI had surprised him with a telephone call and had offered to take Fred to lunch. With some apprehension, Fred accepted the offer. He had always regretted having to leave PI, and was eager to hear how his friends were doing. After some pleasantries, Joan came to the point.

"Fred, we're all impressed with your ability to develop Strenlar on your own. I guess we made a mistake in turning down your offer to develop it at PI. But we're interested in helping you out now, and we can certainly make it worth your while. If you will grant PI exclusive rights to Strenlar, we'll hire you back at, say $80,000 a year, and we'll give you a 2.5% royalty on Strenlar sales. What do you say?"

Fred didn't know whether to laugh or become angry. "Joan, my immediate reaction is to throw my glass of water in your face! I went out on a limb to develop the product, and now you want to capitalize on my work. There's no way I'm going to sell out to PI at this point!"

The meal proceeded, with Joan sweetening the offer gradually, and Fred obstinately refusing. After he got back to his office, Fred felt confused. It would be nice to work at PI again, he thought. At least the future would be secure. But there would never be the potential for the high income that was possible with Strenlar. Of course, he thought grimly, there was still the chance that the Strenlar project could fail altogether.

At the end of the week, Joan called him again. PI was willing to go either of two ways. The company could hire him for $100,000 plus a 6% royalty on Strenlar gross sales. Alternatively, PI could pay him a lump sum of $500,000 now plus options to purchase up to 70,000 shares of PI stock at the current price of $40 any time within the next 3 years. No matter which offer Fred accepted, PI would pay off Fred's creditors and take over the project immediately. After completing development of the manufacturing process, PI would have exclusive rights to Strenlar. Furthermore, it turned out that PI was deadly serious about this game. If Fred refused both of these offers, PI would file a lawsuit claiming rights to Strenlar on the grounds that Fred had improperly used PI's resources in the development of the product.

Consultation with his attorney just made him feel worse. After reviewing Fred's old contract with PI, the attorney told him that there was a 60% chance that he would win the case. If he won the case, PI would have to pay his court costs. If he lost, his legal fees would amount to about $60,000.

Fred's accountant helped him estimate the value of the stock options. First, the exercise date seemed to pose no problem; unless the remaining bugs could not be worked out, Strenlar should be on the market within 18 months. If PI were to acquire the Strenlar project and the project succeeded, PI's stock would go up to approximately $52. On the other hand, if the project failed, the stock price probably would fall slightly to $39.

As Fred thought about all of the problems he faced, he was quite disturbed. On one hand, he yearned for the comradery he had enjoyed at PI 4 years ago. He also realized that he might not be cut out to be an entrepreneur. He reacted unpleasantly to the risk he currently faced. His physician had warned him that he may be developing hypertension and had tried to persuade him to relax more. Fred knew that his health was important to him, but he had to believe that he would be able to weather the tension of getting Strenlar into the market. He could always relax later, right? He sighed as he picked up a pencil and pad of paper to see if he could figure out what he should tell Joan Sharkey.

Question

1. Do a complete analysis of Fred's decision. Your analysis should include at least structuring the problem with an influence diagram, drawing and solving a decision tree, creating risk profiles, and checking for stochastic dominance. What do you think Fred should do? Why? (*Hint:* This case will require you to make certain assumptions in order to do a complete analysis. State clearly any assumptions you make, and be careful that the assumptions you make are both reasonable and consistent with the information given in the case. You may want to analyze your decision model under different sets of assumptions. Do not forget to consider issues such as the time value of money, riskiness of the alternatives, and so on.)

JOB OFFERS

Robin Pinelli is considering three job offers. In trying to decide which to accept, Robin has concluded that three objectives are important in this decision. First, of course, is to maximize disposable income—the amount left after paying for housing, utilities, taxes, and other necessities. Second, Robin wants to spend more time in cold weather climates enjoying winter sports. The third objective relates to the quality of the community. Being single, Robin would like to live in a city with a lot of activities and a large population of single professionals.

Developing attributes for these three objectives turns out to be relatively straightforward.

Disposable income can be measured directly by calculating monthly takehome pay minus average monthly rent (being careful to include utilities) for an appropriate apartment. The second attribute is annual snowfall. For the third attribute, Robin has located a magazine survey of large cities that scores those cities as places for single professionals to live. Although the survey is not perfect from Robin's point of view, it does capture the main elements of her concern about the quality of the singles community and available activities. Also, all three of the cities under consideration are included in the survey.

Here are descriptions of the three job offers:

1. MPR Manufacturing in Flagstaff, Arizona. Disposable income estimate: $1,600 per month. Snowfall range: 150 to 320 cm per year. Magazine score: 50 (out of 100).
2. Madison Publishing in St. Paul, Minnesota. Disposable income estimate: $1,300 to $1,500 per month. (The uncertainty here is because Robin knows there is a wide variety in apartment rental prices and will not know what is appropriate and available until spending some time in the city.)

FIGURE **4.47**
Robin Pinelli's
decision tree.

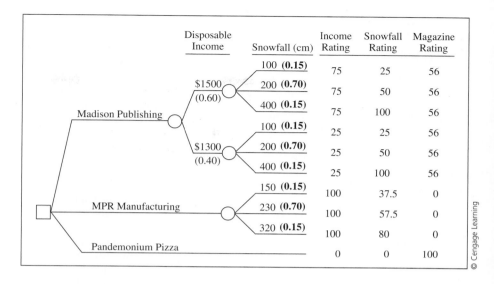

Snowfall range: 100 to 400 cm per year. Magazine score: 75.

3. Pandemonium Pizza in San Francisco, California. Disposable income estimate: $1,200 per month. Snowfall range: negligible. Magazine score: 95.

Robin has created the decision tree in Figure 4.47 to represent the situation. The uncertainty about snowfall and disposable income are represented by the chance nodes as Robin has included them in the tree. The ratings in the consequence matrix are such that the worst consequence has a rating of zero points and the best has 100.

Questions

1. Verify that the ratings in the consequence matrix are proportional scores (i.e., that they were calculated the same way we calculated the ratings for salary in the summer-fun example in the chapter).
2. Comment on Robin's choice of annual snowfall as a measure for the cold-weather–winter-sports attribute. Is this a good measure? Why or why not?
3. After considering the situation, Robin concludes that the quality of the city is most important, the amount of snowfall is next, and the third is income. (Income is important, but the difference between $1,200 and $1,600 is not enough for income to be more important in this context.) Furthermore, Robin concludes that the weight for the magazine rating in the consequence matrix should be 1.5 times the weight for the snowfall rating and three times as much as the weight for the income rating. Use this information to calculate the weights for the three attributes and to calculate overall scores for all of the end branches in the decision tree.
4. Analyze the decision tree using expected values. Calculate expected values for the three measures as well as for the overall score.
5. Do a risk-profile analysis of the three cities. Create risk profiles for each of the three attributes as well as for the overall score. Does any additional insight arise from this analysis?
6. What do you think Robin should do? Why?

SS *KUNIANG*, PART II

This case asks you to find the optimal amount for NEES to bid for the SS *Kuniang* (page 114). Before doing so, though, you need additional details.

Regarding the Coast Guard's (CG) salvage judgment, NEES believes that the following probabilities are an appropriate representation of its uncertainty about the salvage-value judgment:

P(CG judgment = $9 million) = 0.185

P(CG judgment = $4 million) = 0.630

P(CG judgment = $1.5 million) = 0.185

The obscure-but-relevant law required that NEES pay an amount (including both the winning bid and refitting cost) at least 1.5 times the salvage value for the ship in order to use it for domestic shipping. For example, if NEES bid $3.5 million and won, followed by a CG judgment of $4 million, then NEES would have to invest at least $2.5 million more: $3.5 + $2.5 = $6 = $4 × 1.5. Thus, assuming NEES submits the winning bid, the total investment amount required is either the bid or 1.5 times the CG judgment, whichever is greater.

As for the probability of submitting the highest bid, recall that winning is a function of the size of the bid; a bid of $3 million is sure to lose, and a bid of $10 million is sure to win. For this problem, we can model the probability of winning (P) as a linear function of the bid: P=(Bid−$3million)/ ($7 million).

Finally, NEES's values of $18 million for the new ship and $15 million for the tug-barge alternatives are adjusted to reflect differences in age, maintenance, operating costs, and so on. The two alternatives provide equivalent hauling capacity. Thus, at $15 million, the tug-barge combination appears to be the better choice.

Questions

1. Reasonable bids may fall anywhere between $3 and $10 million. Some bids, though, have greater expected values and some less. Describe a strategy you can use to find the optimal bid, assuming that NEES's objective is to minimize the cost of acquiring additional shipping capacity. (*Hint:* This question asks you only to describe an approach to finding the optimal bid.)

2. Use your structure of the problem (or one supplied by the instructor), with the details supplied previously, to find the optimal bid.

MARKETING SPECIALISTS, LTD.

Grace Choi was considering her situation. She had been asked to provide marketing service to Maxim Pharmaceuticals, which wanted to introduce a new product line in Eastern Europe. Grace's company, Marketing Specialists Ltd., had provided such service for a variety of consumer companies since its inception in 1989 and was known for its high-quality and successful marketing plans.

Maxim's new products were a line of over-the-counter consumer drugs aimed at relieving cold and allergy symptoms. The formulation was fully approved by the appropriate agencies of the target countries, and a suitable marketing plan (including development of a brand name appropriate for the product and the target countries) had been developed and approved by Maxim.

Although detailed studies had been done, the cost of the marketing project was uncertain. The best guess seemed to be €4,000,000, but the study team thought the cost could be as low as €3,700,000 or as high as €4,600,000. Grace had asked them to give her probabilities, and they had finally settled on the following probabilities:

Cost	Probability
€3,700,000	0.25
€4,000,000	0.60
€4,600,000	0.15

All that remained was to consider how Marketing Specialists would be paid for its services. Maxim had indicated that it would be willing to consider two possibilities: (1) cost plus 20% of the cost, or (2) a commission on sales over the next 5 years at an agreed-upon rate. The first option would pay 120% of the cost in three equal installments, after 6, 12, and 18 months. The commission is set at 15% and would be paid at the end of each year, based on that year's sales. An additional provision of the commission arrangement was that the total commission could not exceed €7,000,000.

In discussing the issue with other principals at Marketing Specialists, Grace had found considerable support for the commission arrangement on the grounds that, if the marketing plan was successful, the company would be rewarded for its high-quality work. On the other hand, it had been pointed out that the first option avoided the down side; if the product "bombed" (low sales), Marketing Specialists would still have earned back at least its cost.

Analysis of the commission option required some understanding of how sales were likely to develop over the next 5-year period. Taking sales over the entire 5 years as a base, Grace estimated that about 10% would occur in the first year, 15% in the second year, and 25% over each of the last 3 years. The real uncertainty was not what proportion would occur each year, but total sales over the entire 5 years. In consultation with her analysts, Grace had developed the following probabilistic forecast of sales over 5 years:

Sales	Probability
€25,000,000	0.10
€30,000,000	0.34
€50,000,000	0.45
€70,000,000	0.11

However, this was not a complete picture. One of the special features of the plan that Marketing Specialists had developed was that the cost of the marketing project indicated something about the potential sales. If the cost turned out to be low, it suggested that sales were more likely to be low. In contrast, if cost turned out to high, sales were more likely to be high. This feature was appealing to Marketing Specialists' clients because not only was the cost an indication (albeit imperfect) of future sales, it also meant that more would be invested in the marketing of products that were more attractive.

In thinking through the probabilities more carefully, Grace and the analysts came up with the following three probability tables:

If cost equals €3,700,000:

Sales	Probability
€25,000,000	0.10
€30,000,000	0.55
€50,000,000	0.30
€70,000,000	0.05

If cost equals €4,000,000:

Sales	Probability
€25,000,000	0.10
€30,000,000	0.30
€50,000,000	0.50
€70,000,000	0.10

If cost equals €4,600,000:

Sales	Probability
€25,000,000	0.10
€30,000,000	0.15
€50,000,000	0.50
€70,000,000	0.25

In calculating the net present value of cash-flow streams, Marketing Specialists used a discount rate of 12%.

Questions

1. Construct a decision-tree model of the Cost-Plus and Commission options for Grace Choi. Linked trees work well for this problem. For each option, create a table that calculates the net present value given the marketing costs and the 5-year sales.

2. What are the EMVs and standard deviations of both options? Does one option dominate the other? What is the probability that the payments from the Cost Plus option would be higher than the payments from the Commission option? Which option would you recommend to Grace and why?

3. Using either Excel's® Goal Seek function or simple trial-and-error, find the break-even commission rate, that is the commission rate that results in the EMV(Cost Plus) = EMV (Commission). Would you recommend the Commission option at the break-even rate?

REFERENCES

The solution of decision trees as presented in this chapter is commonly found in textbooks on decision analysis, management science, and statistics. The decision-analysis texts listed at the end of Chapter 1 can provide more guidance in the solution of decision trees if needed. For additional basic instruction in the construction and analysis of decisions using influence diagrams, the user's manual for PrecisionTree and other influence-diagram programs can be helpful.

The solution algorithm presented here is based on Shachter (1986). The fact that this algorithm deals with a decision problem in a way that corresponds to solving a symmetric decision tree means that the practical upper limit for the size of an influence diagram that can be solved using the algorithm is relatively small. Recent work has explored a variety of ways to exploit asymmetry in decision models and to solve influence diagrams and related representations more efficiently (Call and Miller 1990; Covaliu and Oliver 1995; Smith et al. 1993; Shenoy 1993).

Hertz (1964) wrote an early and quite readable article on risk profiles. We have developed risk profiles as a way to examine the riskiness of alternatives in a heuristic way and also as a basis for examining alternatives in terms of deterministic and stochastic dominance. Stochastic dominance itself is an important topic in probability. Bunn (1984) gives a good introduction to stochastic dominance. Whitmore and Findlay (1978) and Levy (1992) provide thorough reviews of stochastic dominance.

Our discussion of assigning rating points and trade-off rates is necessarily brief in Chapter 4. These topics are covered in depth in Chapters 13 to 16. In the meantime, interested readers can get more information from Keeney (1992) and Keeney and Raiffa (1976).

Bodily, S. E. (1985) *Modern Decision Making.* New York: McGraw-Hill.

Bunn, D. (1984) *Applied Decision Analysis.* New York: McGraw-Hill.

Call, H., and W. Miller (1990) "A Comparison of Approaches and Implementations for Automating Decision Analysis." *Reliability Engineering and System Safety,* 30, 115–162.

Covaliu, Z., and R. Oliver (1995) "Representation and Solution of Decision Problems Using Sequential Decision Diagrams." *Management Science,* 41.

Hertz, D. B. (1964) "Risk Analysis in Capital Investment." *Harvard Business Review.* Reprinted in *Harvard Business Review,* September–October, 1979, 169–181.

Keeney, R. L. (1992) *Value-Focused Thinking.* Cambridge, MA: Harvard University Press.

Keeney, R., and H. Raiffa (1976) *Decisions with Multiple Objectives.* New York: Wiley.

Levy, H. (1992) "Stochastic Dominance and Expected Utility: Survey and Analysis." *Management Science,* 38, 555–593.

Shachter, R. (1986) "Evaluating Influence Diagrams." *Operations Research,* 34, 871–882.

Shenoy, P. (1995) "Representing and Solving Asymmetric Decision Problems Using Valuation Networks," in D. Fisher and H.-J. Lenz (eds.), *Learning from Data: Artificial Intelligence and Statistics* V, Lecture Notes in Statistics No. 112, pp. 99–108. Springer-Verlag, Berlin.

Smith, J., S. Holtzman, and J. Matheson (1993) "Structuring Conditional Relationships in Influence Diagrams." *Operations Research,* 41, 280–297.

Whitmore, G. A., and M. C. Findlay (1978) *Stochastic Dominance.* Lexington, MA: Heath.

EPILOGUE

What happened with Texaco and Pennzoil? You may recall that in April of 1987 Texaco offered a $2 billion settlement. Hugh Liedtke turned down the offer. Within days of that decision, and only one day before Pennzoil began to file liens on Texaco's assets, Texaco filed for protection from creditors under Chapter 11 of the federal bankruptcy code, fulfilling its earlier promise. In the summer of 1987, Pennzoil submitted a financial reorganization plan on Texaco's behalf. Under their proposal, Pennzoil would receive approximately $4.1 billion, and the Texaco shareholders would be able to vote on the plan. Finally, just before Christmas 1987, the two companies agreed on a $3 billion settlement as part of Texaco's financial reorganization.

CHAPTER 5

Sensitivity Analysis

Sensitivity analysis plays a central role in structuring and analyzing decision models and often provides valuable insights for the decision maker. Conceptually, sensitivity analysis is straightforward: by varying the input values, we determine the potential impact of each input variable in the model. In practice, however, sensitivity analysis can be somewhat complicated, requiring many thoughtful judgments, careful control of probabilities, and interpreting multiple graphs. In this chapter, we will discuss sensitivity-analysis issues, think about how sensitivity analysis relates to the overall decision-modeling strategy, and introduce a variety of graphical sensitivity-analysis techniques.

The main example for this chapter is a common one in which a young couple is deciding between purchasing a single-family home or a multi-family home with the possibility of rental income.

House Hunting

Sanjay Rao and his wife Sarah live south of Boston and, although they are very excited about the arrival of their first child in 5 months, they are also a bit apprehensive. Sarah teaches at a private high school, and most of her free time is spent grading student work or working as the assistant coach for the women's lacrosse team. Sanjay is a sound engineer for a manufacturer of high-end audio equipment, and most of his free time is devoted to finishing his MBA. At his current pace of two classes a term, Sanjay expects to finish in another two years, but his child's arrival could push this out another year or so.

Sarah's pregnancy has been a catalyst, compelling Sanjay and Sarah to discuss and think hard about what they want for their family of three. A major concern is their housing situation. Five years ago, they purchased a modern condominium overlooking the Boston harbor, and while it has been lovely to view the city lights and watch the ships come and go, they knew they wanted a different neighborhood for raising their child. High on their list of values are their child's safety and education. Working with a realtor in one of Boston's suburbs, they are considering three different properties that fit well with their objectives.

The first house under consideration is a traditional single-family house on Astoria Street. The asking price is $499,000, but with the housing market in a slump, they will bid $450,000. The slump has also driven down the selling price of their condominium, but even selling it at a discount, they expect to have $50,000 to cover closing costs and serve as a down payment on the new house. After paying $5,000 in closing costs, their annual mortgage payment for a 30-year fixed rate loan at a 5.5% annual interest rate will be $2,322 monthly or $27,866 annually. Including the other costs of homeownership (homeowners insurance, property taxes, repair and upkeep), their monthly payment will be $2,987 or $35,846 annually. This is a comfortable amount for Sanjay and Sarah, as long as they are both working. They could, if need be, afford this house on Sanjay's salary alone, but it would be tight.

In addition to these costs, there are some monetary advantages to homeownership. The U.S. tax laws allow individuals to deduct the interest payments from their gross income. At a tax rate of 33%, Sanjay and Sarah will have their tax liability reduced by $7,137 annually (averaged over the first 5 years of the loan). In addition, again averaging over the first 5 years, their equity in the house will increase by $6,131 annually as they pay down their loan. Finally, they also hope that the house appreciates over the years, but the amount it will appreciate is uncertain.

The other two properties under consideration are in more desirable neighborhoods (better schools), but also cost considerably more. To offset the additional costs, both properties have apartments that can be rented. The property on Barnard Street has an existing rental that is currently leased. However, the house on Charlotte Street requires considerable renovation of the adjoining apartment before it could be rented. Sarah and Sanjay would bid $750,000 for Barnard and $600,000 for Charlotte. Like the Astoria house, the down payment on Barnard would be $45,000 (the $50,000 from the sale of the condo minus $5,000 for closing costs). The down payment for Charlotte would be only $15,000, reserving $30,000 to cover the renovation costs. Due to the larger loan amounts and relatively smaller down payments, the bank will charge a higher interest rate of 7.0% for these two properties. Table 5.1 shows the annual mortgage payments of $56,813 for Barnard and $47,143 for Charlotte. In addition, homeowner's insurance is proportional to the house's value, and thus costs more for these two houses, and, as these houses are older, Sarah and Sanjay have allotted more for annual repair and upkeep, specifically, $3,200 for Barnard and $4,000 for Charlotte. As shown in Table 5.1, the total annual cost for Barnard is $69,313 and for Charlotte is $58,583.

Clearly, Sanjay and Sarah cannot afford Barnard or Charlotte without the additional income of the rentals. Barnard's apartment currently rents for $2,000/month. Assuming that the apartment would be rented for 10 months per year, this amounts to annual revenue of $20,000. (This revenue would be taxed, and problem 5.12 explores the complete tax ramifications of rental properties.) Charlotte's apartment is expected to rent for $1,500/month, and 10 months of occupancy generates annual revenue of $15,000.

In addition, as with Astoria, they can deduct the interest payment from their taxes, but only in proportion to their living space. Sanjay and Sarah's portion of Barnard is 60% (the apartment taking up the other 40%) allowing them to deduct 60% of their interest payments. Averaging over the first 5 years, their taxes will be reduced by $9,562 for Barnard. For Charlotte the apartment proportion is 35%, so Sanjay and Sarah could deduct $8,595 annually.

Table 5.1 brings together the numbers for all three properties. The Net Annual Cost of Astoria is $28,673. Incorporating the tax deduction and rental income, the Net Annual Cost of Barnard is $39,752, and for Charlotte, the Net Annual Cost is $34,988.

Sanjay and Sarah realize that many of the numbers they are using are only estimates. Furthermore, while the amount of rent is within their control (within limits, of course), the number of months the apartment will be rented is not. How important are these numbers? How much would their Net

TABLE 5.1
A snapshot of the annual financials of three properties in the Boston area, averaged across the first 5 years.

	Astoria St.	Barnard St.	Charlotte St.
Price	$450,000	$750,000	$600,000
Down Payment	$45,000	$45,000	$15,000
Interest Rate	5.5%	7.0%	7.0%
Tax Rate	33%	33%	33%
Property Tax Rate	1%	1%	1%
Percentage Rented	0%	40%	35%
Costs			
Mortgage (30 yr fixed)	$27,866	$56,813	$47,143
Homeowner's Insurance	$1,080	$1,800	$1,440
Repair & Upkeep	$2,400	$3,200	$4,000
Property Taxes	$4,500	$7,500	$6,000
Annual Cost	$35,846	$69,313	$58,583
Rental			
Monthly Rent	$0	$2,000	$1,500
Months Occupied	0	10	10
Rental Income	$0	$20,000	$15,000
Tax Deduction on Interest	$7,173	$9,562	$8,595
Net Annual Cost	$28,673	$39,752	$34,988

© Cengage Learning 2014

Annual Cost change if their estimates were off? Last, but not least, do they really want to move? Perhaps there are other possibilities?

SENSITIVITY ANALYSIS: A MODELING APPROACH

Sensitivity analysis answers the question, "What makes a difference in this decision?" Returning to the idea of requisite decision models discussed in Chapter 1, you may recall that a requisite model is one whose form and content are just sufficient to solve a particular problem. That is, the issues that are addressed in a requisite decision model are the ones that matter, and those issues left out are the ones that do not matter. But how do we know which issues matter and which can be left out? The decision maker's values and objectives help frame the problem and thus help determine what issues are relevant. The decision maker also needs a complete understanding of the mechanics of the problem. For example, Sanjay and Sarah need to understand the tax laws; otherwise, their model might exclude important considerations. But the objectives and problem mechanics only go so far. By incorporating sensitivity analysis throughout the modeling process, we can measure the potential impact of each input, and thereby determine precisely which issues and inputs matter.

No "optimal" sensitivity-analysis procedure exists for decision analysis. To a great extent, model building is an art. Because sensitivity analysis is an integral part of the modeling process, its use as part of the process is also an art. Thus, in this chapter we will discuss the philosophy of model building and how sensitivity analysis helps with model development. Several sensitivity-analysis tools are available, and we will see how they work in the context of the House-Hunting example.

PROBLEM IDENTIFICATION AND STRUCTURE

The flowchart of the decision-analysis process in Figure 1.1 shows that sensitivity analysis can lead the decision maker to reconsider the very nature of the problem. The question that we ask in performing sensitivity analysis at this level is, "Are we solving the right problem?" The answer does not require quantitative analysis, but it does demand careful thought and introspection about the appropriate decision context. Why is this an important sensitivity-analysis concern? The answer is quite simple: Answering a different question, addressing a different problem, or satisfying different objectives can lead to a very different decision.

Solving the wrong problem sometimes is called an "error of the third kind." The terminology parallels Type I and Type II errors in statistics, where incorrect conclusions are drawn regarding a particular question. An error of the third kind, or Type III error, implies that the wrong question was asked; in terms of decision analysis, the implication is that an inappropriate decision context was used, and hence the wrong problem was solved.

Examples of Type III errors abound; we all can think of times when a symptom was treated instead of a cause. Consider lung disease. Researchers and physicians have developed expensive medical treatments for lung disease, the objective being to reduce the suffering of lung-disease patients. If the fundamental objective is to reduce suffering from lung disease in general, however, these treatments might not be as effective as anti-smoking campaigns. We can, in fact, broaden the context further. Is the objective really to reduce patient suffering? Or is it to reduce discomfort in general, including patient suffering as well as the discomfort of nonsmokers exposed to second-hand smoke? Considering the broader problem suggests an entirely different range of options.

For another example, think about a farmer who considers using expensive sprays in the context of deciding how to control pests and disease in an orchard. To a great extent, the presence of pests and disease in orchards result from the practice of monoculture—that is, growing a lot of one crop rather than a smaller amount of many crops. A monoculture does not promote a balanced ecological system in which diseases and pests are kept under control naturally. Viewed from this broader perspective, the farmer might want to consider new agricultural practices rather than relying exclusively on sprays. Admittedly a long-term project, this requires the development of efficient methods for growing, harvesting, and distributing crops that are grown on a smaller scale.

How can one avoid a Type III error? The best solution is simply to keep asking whether the problem on the surface is the real problem. Is the decision context properly specified? What exactly is the "unscratched itch" that the decision maker feels? Sanjay and Sarah appear eager to move to a Boston suburb, but could they "scratch their itch" by moving to a different city, maybe even a different country, or perhaps not moving? Like most parents, they want a yard for their children to play in, and this desire has framed much of their decision. However, a yard in the Boston area also means regular maintenance: shoveling snow in the winter, planting in the spring, mowing in the summer, and raking leaves in the fall. Will Sanjay and Sarah enjoy working in the yard or would they rather spend their time in other pursuits? By taking a step back and asking themselves what they really desire, Sanjay and Sarah can examine which values and objectives are important to them for this decision.

We can also talk about sensitivity analysis in the context of problem structuring. Problem 3.20 gave an example in a medical context in which a decision might be sensitive to the structure. In that situation, the issue was the inclusion of a more complete description of outcomes; coronary bypass surgery can lead to complications that require long and painful treatment. Inclusion of this outcome in a decision tree might make surgery appear considerably less appealing. Von Winterfeldt and Edwards (1986) describe a problem involving the setting of standards for pollution from oil wells in the North Sea. This could have been structured as a standard regulatory problem: Different possible standards and enforcement policies made up the alternatives, and the objective was to minimize pollution while maintaining efficient oil production. The problem, however, was perhaps more appropriately structured as a competitive situation in which the players were the regulatory agency, the industry, and the potential victims of pollution. This is an example of how a decision situation might be represented in a variety of different ways. Sensitivity analysis can aid the resolution of the problem of multiple representations by helping to identify the appropriate perspective on the problem as well as by identifying the specific issues that matter to the decision maker.

Is problem structuring an issue for Sanjay and Sarah? In this case, their alternatives are to purchase Astoria, Barnard, or Charlotte, or remain in the condominium. In narrowing down the list of potential properties, Sanjay and Sarah used their fundamental objectives of maximizing safety and maximizing education quality. In addition, they also considered minimizing commute time, and every property needed to have a private yard. All three properties under consideration satisfy these objectives about equally, and thus they now wish to focus on minimizing costs. Note that Barnard and Charlotte have the better school districts, so Sanjay and Sarah prefer these on the education attribute. On the other hand, there are significant disadvantages, and possibly even safety concerns, with having renters. Sanjay and Sarah feel that the advantages and disadvantages counterbalance each other. Thus, it appears that a straightforward decision tree or influence diagram may do the trick.

Figure 5.1 shows an initial influence diagram for the Barnard St. property. Note that if you drew an influence diagram for Astoria St., it would not have the Rental Income node nor its predecessors. The influence diagram consists almost entirely of rounded rectangles, monthly rent being the only decision. Net Annual Cost is obviously the consequence node, with Mortgage Payment, Annual Cost, Tax Deduction, and Rental Income the intermediate-calculation nodes. All of the other rounded rectangles (Down Payment, Interest Rate, Property Tax Rate, Tax Rate, Repair & Upkeep, Homeowner's Insurance, and Months Occupied) represent inputs to the calculations, and for now we represent these inputs as being constant. (Thus, in Figure 5.1 you can see the different roles—constants and intermediate calculations—that rounded rectangles can play. Although these different roles may seem confusing, the basic idea is the same in each case; for any variable represented by a rounded rectangle, as soon as you know what its inputs are, you can calculate the value of the variable. In the case of the constants, there are no inputs, and so there is no calculation necessary!)

FIGURE **5.1**

Influence diagram representing Sanjay and Sarah's housing decision for the Barnard St. house.

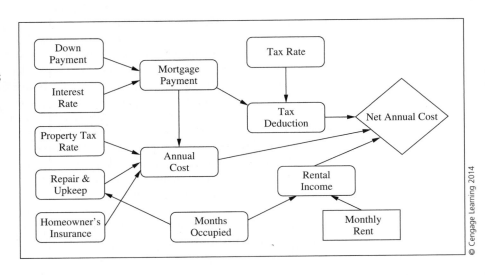

© Cengage Learning 2014

We can actually write down the equation used in Figure 5.1 to calculate Net Annual Cost.

$$Net\ Annual\ Cost = Annual\ Costs - (Rental\ Income + Tax\ Deduction),$$

where

$$Annual\ Cost = Mortgage + Homeowner's\ Insurance + Repair\ \&\ Upkeep$$
$$+ House\ Price \times Property\ Tax\ Rate.$$

$$Rental\ Income = Monthly\ Rent \times Months\ Occupied.$$

$$Tax\ Deduction = Tax\ Rate \times (1 - Percentage\ Rented) \times Interest\ Paid$$
$$= Tax\ Rate \times (1 - Percentage\ Rented) \times (P\% \times Mortgage).$$

Note that the amount of interest paid changes each year. Thus, instead of using a different value for each year, we averaged the interest paid over the first 5 years of the loan and divided by the annual mortgage payment (Mortgage) to get the percentage ($P\%$) of the annual mortgage payment that is interest. For the two-family homes, the interest paid is estimated as $P\% = 85\%$ of the annual mortgage payments over the first 5 years, and for Astoria, the interest paid is estimated as $P\% = 78\%$.

Thus,

$$Interest\ Paid = 85\% \times Mortgage \quad \text{for Barnard and Charlotte, and}$$

$$Interest\ Paid = 78\% \times Mortgage \quad \text{for the single family home.}$$

We use this formula to calculate Sanjay and Sarah's Net Annual Cost over the first 5 years of homeownership for each property. For example, the Net Annual Cost for Charlotte is calculated as:

$$Rental\ Income = Monthly\ Rent \times Months\ Occupied = \$1500 \times 10$$
$$= \$15,000.$$

$$Tax\ Deduction = Tax\ Rate \times (1 - Percentage\ Rented) \times (P\% \times Mortgage)$$
$$= 33\% \times (1 - 35\%) \times (85\% \times \$47,143)$$
$$= \$8,595.$$

$$Annual\ Costs = Mortgage + Homeowner's\ Insurance + Repair\ \&\ Upkeep$$
$$+ House\ Price \times Property\ Tax\ Rate$$
$$= \$47,143 + \$1,440 + 4,000 + \$600,000 \times 1\%$$
$$= \$58,583.$$

$$Net\ Annual\ Cost = \$58,583 - (\$15,000 + \$8,595) = \$34,988.$$

Similarly, this formula is used in Table 5.1 to show the Net Annual Cost of Astoria is $28,673 and the Net Annual Cost of Barnard is $39,752.

Sanjay and Sarah feel that they can afford the Astoria St. house comfortably, even if Sarah were to lose her job or simply take a few years off. The Charlotte St. house costs an additional $6,314 annually, or $526 monthly, and the Barnard St. house costs an additional $11,078 annually, or $923 monthly. Both of these properties are affordable for Sanjay and Sarah, but Sarah would need to work at least half time after her maternity leave. What most worries Sanjay and Sarah are the annual cost values: $59K for Charlotte and $69K for Barnard. Without the additional rental income, these costs could quickly bankrupt them. Thus, they would like to know how much their Net Annual Cost could change if any of their estimates are off. In particular, they want to know which of the input values have the most impact on Net Annual Cost.

Sanjay and Sarah's first step in performing a sensitivity analysis is to list the estimates or variables whose values could change.[1] One such variable is the number of months that the apartment will be occupied. It is easy to imagine that Months Occupied will be one of the more influential inputs to Net Annual Cost. Other variables that Sanjay and Sarah want to know about are: their income tax rate (Tax Rate), the property tax rate (Property Tax Rate), the amount they charge for rent (Monthly Rent), the cost of homeowner's insurance (Homeowner's Insurance), and the repair and upkeep costs (Repair & Upkeep). In addition, Sanjay and Sarah have about $30,000 in stock options that they could cash in and apply to their down payment amount. They have not decided to increase the down payment, but would simply like to know the effect on Net Annual Cost of doing so. Finally, Sanjay and Sarah are curious about changes to the interest rate on their loan. Although their loan is at a fixed rate for 30 years and will not fluctuate, they are concerned that the terms of the loan might change before the house closes and want to know how changes to the interest rate could affect Net Annual Cost.

Next, for each variable in their list Sanjay and Sarah need to choose lower and upper bounds. The lower and upper bounds are specific to the variable, and represent the beliefs of Sanjay and Sarah about the range of values that variable could take on. For example, the lower bound of Months Occupied could be 0 months and the upper bound could be 12 months. The bounds of 0 and 12 are absolute bounds because they are the absolute minimum and maximum. Absolute bounds are not always possible to assess and often are not even desirable. For example, there is an extremely remote possibility that Sanjay and Sarah will need to replace the roof of the house, the water heater, the furnace, the air conditioning unit, the wiring, and the plumbing all in one year, driving Repair & Upkeep into the stratosphere. However, by choosing such a large upper bound for Repair & Upkeep, the sensitivity analysis results will be skewed by extremely unlikely events. Thus, instead of absolute bounds, Sarah and Sanjay can specify bounds such that they would be "very surprised" that the variable would fall outside the bounds. While it is best to be clear about the meaning of very surprised, we need to wait until we cover probability theory in Section 2 before we have the language to provide a precise definition. Until

---

[1] Variables whose values are determined by calculation, such as Mortgage, are not candidates for the sensitivity analysis. Rather, we vary the inputs that feed into the calculation, which then cause the calculated value to change.

then, we can provide some general guidelines to help Sanjay and Sarah determine the lower and upper bounds for each variable.

In establishing the bounds for each variable, we want Sanjay and Sarah to think hard about the different events that could happen that would alter the input value. Staying with Repair & Upkeep, Sanjay and Sarah first need to determine what could cause a low or a high cost; then they need to estimate the potential impact and the likelihood of that event happening. For example, some possible events could be replacing the water heater or roof. Sanjay and Sarah estimate that a water heater will cost $800 and a new roof will cost $10,000. Next, they consider the likelihood of these events. As the water heater is expected to last another three years and the roof is expected to last another 15 years, Sanjay and Sarah would be very surprised to replace the roof, but not the water heater over the next 5 years. Other examples of events that could alter repair and upkeep are: weather (snow removal, rain damage, etc.), house condition (painting, plumbing or electrical repairs, etc.), and yard (fence repairs, tree trimming and removal, etc.). Clearly, coming up with realistic bounds is not a trivial exercise and takes some time and effort. As mentioned in Chapter 4, the decision-analysis process does not make hard decisions easy, but rather breaks the problem down into its components allowing us to think carefully about each component. Here the objective is to assess realistic bounds for the sensitivity analysis, and for Sanjay and Sarah, their effort produced a lower bound of $1,000 and an upper bound of $10,000 for Repair & Upkeep.

Table 5.2 lists the variables that Sanjay and Sarah wish to include in the sensitivity analysis, the lower and upper bound of each variable, with their current best estimate of the value of the variable, which we call the *base case*.

We now have all the required information to run a sensitivity analysis, but before doing so, the model should be checked to ensure that it will report accurate results. When performing a sensitivity analysis, we will determine the impact on Net Annual Cost when the input values of the variables listed in Table 5.2 are changed. However, we must guarantee that

TABLE **5.2**
Sanjay and Sarah's list of inputs, with base-case values and lower and upper bounds.[2]

Variable	Lower Bound	Base Case	Upper Bound
Down Payment	$30,000	$45,000	$70,000
Interest Rate	4%	5.5%	8%
Tax Rate	25%	33%	45%
Property Tax Rate	1%	1%	2%
Monthly Rent	$1,500	$2,000	$2,900
Months Occupied	0	10	12
Homeowner's Insurance	$800	$1,080	$1,600
Repair & Upkeep	$1,000	$2,400	$10,000

© Cengage Learning 2014

[2] An astute reader will realize that not only are the bounds specific to a variable, but also to an alternative. All the variables listed with their bounds are for the Astoria St property except the Monthly Rent and Months Occupied. These latter two variables are for Barnard St.

each variable moves parallel across the alternatives. For example, as Months Occupied changes from 1 to 2 to 3, we must make sure it does so for both Barnard and Charlotte. It would be inaccurate and misleading to compare Net Annual Cost for these two properties if Months Occupied varied for only one of these properties. Similarly, Property Tax Rate is a cost for all three properties, and thus it needs to change simultaneously for all three properties as it swings between 1% and 2%. In other words, if a variable is used in calculating Net Annual Cost, we need to construct the decision model in such a way that its variation occurs across all the appropriate alternatives. While this may seem obvious, it is one of the most common sensitivity analysis mistakes.

How do we construct the model to guarantee that each variable moves parallel across the alternatives? In Excel®, we can use cell referencing. Table 5.3 shows how we used cell referencing to guarantee that the sensitivity analysis accurately reports the effect of changing values across the alternatives. We denoted the variables to be used in the sensitivity analysis with a (*). For example, viewing row 5, we see that Tax Rate will be varied in cell B5, and it will simultaneously vary across all three properties. In addition to guaranteeing that we are comparing like changes across the alternatives, we can also use cell referencing to model certain relationships across the alternatives. For example, Sanjay and Sarah plan to spend $30,000 of the $45,000 down payment on renovating the Charlotte apartment, which is modeled in cell D3 as =B3−E3, where the contents of B3 is $45,000 and E3 is $30,000. Thus, as we vary the down payment amount in B3, the renovation costs are automatically subtracted. Because Down Payment can never be negative, we must take care that the lower bound for Down Payment is not below $30,000. Other examples of relationships modeled in Table 5.3 are:

(1) The interest rate of their loan is 1.5% higher for the two two-family houses (cells C4 and D4);
(2) Sanjay and Sarah plan on charging $500 less for the Charlotte apartment (cell D17) than the Barnard apartment;
(3) Homeowner's insurance is proportional to the price of the house (cells C11 and D11); and
(4) Sanjay and Sarah would also like to compare similar repair and upkeep costs across all three properties. If Astoria has a high repair and upkeep cost, they want to evaluate Barnard with a high repair and upkeep cost. Thus, we have modeled Barnard's repair and upkeep cost (cell C12) to be $800 more than Astoria's and likewise Charlotte's repair and upkeep cost to be $1,600 more than Astoria. See cells C12, B12, and D12 in Table 5.3. Clearly, the repair and upkeep cost for one property does not depend on the repair and upkeep cost of a different property; rather Sanjay and Sarah are taking a modeling shortcut by linking these costs. A more accurate model would be to let repair and upkeep cost vary independently for the three properties. For simplicity, we link these costs and avoid assessing new lower and upper bounds for the repair and upkeep cost for Barnard and Charlotte.

Keep another trick in mind when constructing a decision model—place each constant in its own cell, and use cell referencing when it is needed for a

TABLE **5.3**
Using cell referencing to guarantee that changes in the input values are appropriately reflected across the alternatives.

	A	B	C	D	E
1		Astoria St.	Barnard St.	Charlotte St.	
2	Price	$450,000	$750,000	$600,000	
3	Down Payment (*)	$45,000	$45,000	=B3−E3	30,000
4	Interest Rate (*)	5.5%	=B4+E4	=B4+E4	1.5%
5	Tax Rate (*)	33%	=B5	=B5	
6	Property Tax Rate (*)	1%	=B6	=B6	
7	Percentage Rented	0%	40%	35%	
8					
9	*Costs*				
10	Mortgage (30 yr fixed)	$27,866	$56,813	$47,143	
11	Homeowner's Insurance (*)	$1,080	=(C2/B2)*B11	=(D2/B2)*B11	
12	Repair & Upkeep (*)	$2,400	=B12+E12	=B12+2*E12	$800
13	Property Taxes	$4,500	$7,500	$6,000	
14	**Annual Cost**	$35,846	$69,313	$58,583	
15					
16	*Rental*				
17	Monthly Rent (*)	$0	$2,000	=C17−E17	$500
18	Months Occupied (*)	0	10	=C18	
19	**Rental Income**	$0	$20,000	$15,000	
20					
21	*Tax Deduction on Interest*	$7,173	$9,562	$8,595	
22					
23	**Net Annual Cost**	$28,673	$39,752	$34,988	

computation. By separating out the constants, it is much easier to run a sensitivity analysis as each constant has a location from which it can be varied. For example, we could have used the formula =B3−30000 for the Charlotte down-payment amount instead of =B3−E3. The latter formula requires a bit more effort on our part, but allows the flexibility to vary the $30,000 renovation costs independent of the down-payment value.

It is all too easy to run a quick sensitivity analysis on one's model before accounting for all the necessary relationships or conditions of the model. Before running your sensitivity analysis, take some time and manually vary some of the values. Do the results make sense? Are all the variables changing that should be changing when you vary an input value? It is a rare model that does not need some refinement to guarantee accurate sensitivity analysis results.

ONE-WAY SENSITIVITY ANALYSIS: SENSITIVITY GRAPHS

We are now ready to perform a *one-way sensitivity analysis*, which means that we will vary one and only one of the model inputs at a time. When an input is not being varied, it will be held constant at its base value. (Later in the chapter, we will discuss *two-way sensitivity analysis* where two and only two variables are allowed to vary and the remaining variables are held constant at their base values.) The output for a one-way sensitivity analysis is a series of graphs and tables. The first graphs we consider are called *sensitivity graphs*, which report the input values on the x-axis and the calculated consequence values on the y-axis.

Figure 5.2 illustrates how Net Annual Cost changes for each of the three properties as Sanjay and Sarah's income tax rate varies (or swings) from its lower bound of 25% to its upper bound of 45%. The downward sloping lines in Figure 5.2 show that as Tax Rate increases, Net Annual Cost somewhat surprisingly decreases. This is because the tax rate affects the deduction on interest, and a higher tax rate implies a greater percentage of the interest on the loan can be deducted. For example, averaging over the first 5 years for Astoria, interest constitutes nearly $22,000 of the annual mortgage payment of $27,866. Thus, Sanjay and Sarah's tax deduction is their tax rate times $22,000, and the higher the tax rate, the higher the deduction.

The sensitivity graph provides a few important insights. First, as Tax Rate increases, Net Annual Cost decreases linearly. This is important because this tells us that Net Annual Cost decreases at a constant rate. In fact, the slopes of these lines show that when Tax Rate increases by 1%, such as 33% to 34% or 26% to 27%, then Net Annual Cost decreases by $217 for Astoria, $260 for Charlotte, and $290 for Barnard.

The slopes were computed by referring to Table 5.4, which reports the sensitivity graph data for the tax-rate variable. Each row of Table 5.4 corresponds to one particular tax rate. Row #1 uses a Tax Rate of 25% when

FIGURE **5.2**
The sensitivity graph showing the impact on Net Annual Cost for each of the three properties as the Tax Rate (B5) swings between 25% and 45%.

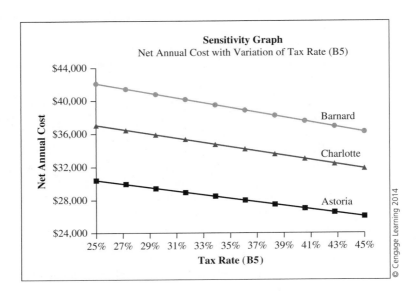

TABLE **5.4**
The sensitivity analysis results showing the impact on Net Annual Cost for each of the three properties as Sanjay and Sarah's income tax rate swings between 25% and 45% in 10 equally spaced steps.

		Sensitivity Graph Data		
		Net Annual Cost		
Steps	Tax Rate	Astoria	Charlotte	Barnard
#1	25.0%	$30,412	$37,071	$42,070
#2	27.2%	$29,929	$36,493	$41,426
#3	29.4%	$29,446	$35,914	$40,782
#4	31.7%	$28,963	$35,335	$40,138
#5	33.9%	$28,480	$34,756	$39,494
#6	36.1%	$27,997	$34,177	$38,850
#7	38.3%	$27,514	$33,599	$38,206
#8	40.6%	$27,031	$33,020	$37,563
#9	42.8%	$26,548	$32,441	$36,919
#10	45.0%	$26,065	$31,862	$36,275

computing Net Annual Cost, row #2 uses 27.2%, and so on. When running a one-way sensitivity analysis, you can either explicitly specify the values for the input variables or use the default, which divides the range into equally-spaced values. Here, the range is from 25% to 45%, which is divided by ten equally-spaced values. Often, these values are referred to as "steps," because they are the steps at which Net Annual Cost is calculated. Figure 5.2 is the graphical representation of Table 5.4.

In addition to the linear effect of the income tax rate, the curves (lines) in Figure 5.2 never cross one another. This is important because this tells us that no matter what the value of Tax Rate (between 25% and 45%), Astoria always costs less than Charlotte, which in turn always costs less than Barnard.

Let us look at one more variable in our one-way sensitivity analysis, namely Monthly Rent, which, of course, is a decision variable. Remember that the amount of rent Sanjay and Sarah plan to charge for the Barnard St. apartment is set to be $500 more than Charlotte's apartment. See Table 5.3. Figure 5.3 shows the sensitivity graph as the rental prices are varied (Barnard is varied from $1,500 to $2,900 while in lock step, Charlotte is varied from $1,000 to $2,400) and Table 5.5 reports the graph data. From these, we can conclude:

- Net Annual Cost for Astoria is constant (a flat line) because rental prices have no impact.
- For both two-family houses, Net Annual Cost steadily decreases as Monthly Rent increases.
- In fact, the slopes of both the Barnard and Charlotte lines equals -10, which means that for every $100 increase in Monthly Rent, Net Annual Cost decreases by $1,000 ($=10 \times \$100$).
- Again, we see that Charlotte is always less costly than Barnard.

FIGURE **5.3**
The sensitivity graph showing the impact on Net Annual Cost for each of the three properties as the Monthly Rent (C17) of Barnard swings between $1,500 and $2,900 with the Monthly Rent of Charlotte being $500 less.

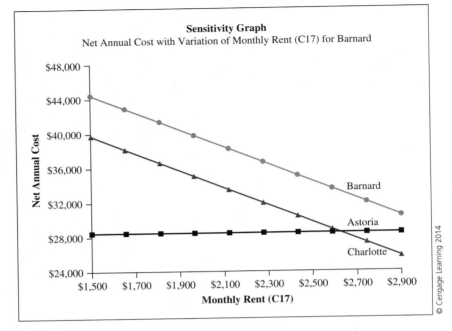

© Cengage Learning 2014

- In fact, for each rental price in the range, Charlotte annually costs $4,764 less than Barnard does.
- Barnard's Net Annual Cost is always higher than Astoria's, even when Monthly Rent is $2,900 per month.

TABLE **5.5**
The sensitivity analysis results showing the impact on Net Annual Cost for each of the three properties as Monthly Rent for Barnard swings between $1,500 and $2,900.

		Sensitivity Graph Data		
		Net Annual Cost		
Steps	Monthly Rent (Barnard)	Barnard	Charlotte	Astoria
#1	$1,500	$44,752	$39,988	$28,673
#2	$1,656	$43,196	$38,432	$28,673
#3	$1,811	$41,641	$36,877	$28,673
#4	$1,967	$40,085	$35,321	$28,673
#5	$2,122	$38,529	$33,765	$28,673
#6	$2,278	$36,974	$32,210	$28,673
#7	$2,433	$35,418	$30,654	$28,673
#8	$2,589	$33,863	$29,099	$28,673
#9	$2,744	$32,307	$27,543	$28,673
#10	$2,900	$30,752	$25,988	$28,673

© Cengage Learning 2014

- When Charlotte's rental price rises above $2,100, Astoria is no longer the cheapest. The sensitivity graphs lines cross when the x-axis value (Monthly Rent) is around $2,600, but remember to subtract $500 from the graph values for Charlotte's rental price.
- In fact, when Charlotte's rental price is $2,400/month, its Net Annual Cost is $25,988, which is approximately $2,700 less annually then Astoria.

The preceding sensitivity graphs and corresponding tables provide Sanjay and Sarah with many insights. For each variable in Table 5.2, the sensitivity graph shows the effect on Net Annual Cost as that variable swings from its lower bound to its upper bound. By looking at the graphs, we can easily determine which alternative is most preferred simply by noting which curve is the lowest (minimum Net Annual Cost). If the curves never cross, then one alternative will always be the most preferred no matter which input value is chosen between the lower and upper bounds. If the curves do cross, the rank ordering of the alternatives changes. Moreover, the value of the input variable at which the curves cross tells us the point at which the rank ordering changes. The corresponding data tables report the exact input values used in the sensitivity analysis and the resulting consequence values.

The previous discussion highlights some of the limitations to a one-way sensitivity analysis. By allowing only one input value at a time to vary, we are tacitly assuming that there is no relationship among the variables. For example, holding Months Occupied at 10 months, and varying Monthly Rent, we are assuming that the occupancy rate is not related to the rental price. Clearly, the more Sanjay and Sarah decide to charge for rent, the smaller the potential pool of renters, which could decrease the number of months the apartment is occupied. This dependence relation between Monthly Rent and Months Occupied should not be ignored, and can be captured later in our decision tree, but for ease in analysis and ease in interpretation, one-way sensitivity analysis ignores all such relationships. In other words, we model relationships in our influence diagrams or decision trees if we believe they are requisite, and we use one-way sensitivity analysis to tell whether the individual variables are influential. If the one-way sensitivity analysis indicates that a variable is influential on its own, then we typically include it and its relationships in our decision model. For example, we saw that Monthly Rent can change the rank ordering of the alternatives, thus we might subsequently model Monthly Rent in our decision model with its relationship to Months Occupied.

ONE-WAY SENSITIVITY ANALYSIS: TORNADO DIAGRAMS

The sensitivity graphs and their corresponding tables provide an excellent indication of the potential impact of each variable individually, but they do not indicate their relative impact. For example, which of the two variables that we just discussed (Tax Rate or Monthly Rent) could cause Net Annual Cost to change most? It would be very useful to know how the variables in our model compare to one another in terms of sensitivity; a *tornado diagram* allows us to make these comparisons.

A tornado diagram is a horizontal bar chart, where each bar represents one variable, and the length of each bar represents the change in the consequence value (Net Annual Cost for Sanjay and Sarah) as that one variable swings from its lower bound to its upper bound. Again, we are allowing only one variable to change at a time, holding the other variables fixed at their base values. The most influential variable (or longest bar) is placed at the top of the tornado diagram, the second most influential variable (or second longest bar) is placed just below, and so on, giving the chart the characteristic shape from which its name is derived.

Figure 5.4 shows the tornado diagram for Net Annual Cost for the Astoria house. We can immediately see that Interest Rate (the interest rate of Sanjay and Sarah's loan) causes the greatest swing or change to Astoria's Net Annual Cost, closely followed by Repair & Upkeep. We see a decreasing impact to Net Annual Cost as we read down the list and both Monthly Rent and Months Occupied are shown to have no effect on Net Annual Cost. The length of each bar represents the change to Astoria's Net Annual Cost, and as Astoria has no apartment, Monthly Rent and Months Occupied have no impact on Net Annual Cost. Thus, for Astoria, Sanjay and Sarah need to keep their eyes on the interest rate for their loan, the repair and upkeep expenses, and the property tax rate, as any one of these three variables can push their annual net cost up substantially. For example, they may want to check with the municipality to find out whether property tax rates may change in the near future.

Table 5.6 shows the data used to create Astoria's tornado diagram. The table ranks the variables by their impact on Astoria's Net Annual Cost, reports at which input value Net Annual Cost is minimized and at which value it is maximized, and the range (maximum minus minimum). For example, Interest Rate is ranked first and causes Astoria's Net Annual Cost to vary

FIGURE **5.4**
Tornado diagram of Net Annual Cost of Astoria.

The chart shows how Net Annual Cost changes as variables in Table 5.2 swing one at a time from their lower bound to their upper bound.

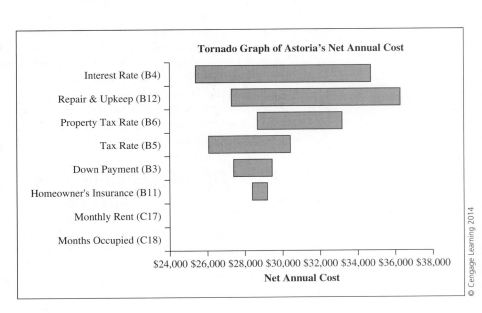

© Cengage Learning 2014

TABLE **5.6**

Data for tornado diagram of Net Annual Cost of Astoria.

The data result from swinging each variable in Table 5.2 one at a time from its lower bound to its upper bound.

		Tornado Diagram Data Net Annual Cost				
		Minimum		Maximum		
Rank	Input Name	Input	Output	Input	Output	Range
1	Interest Rate (B4)	4%	$25,373	8%	$34,695	$9,323
2	Repair & Upkeep (B12)	$1,000	$27,273	$10,000	$36,273	$9,000
3	Property Tax Rate (B6)	1%	$28,673	2%	$33,173	$4,500
4	Tax Rate (B5)	45%	$26,065	25%	$30,412	$4,347
5	Down Payment (B3)	$70,000	$27,396	$30,000	$29,440	$2,044
6	Homeowner's Insurance (B11)	$800	$28,393	$1,600	$29,193	$800
7	Monthly Rent (C17)	$1,500	$28,673	$1,500	$28,673	$0
8	Months Occupied (C18)	0 mos	$28,673	0 mos	$28,673	$0

from $25,373 (when the Interest Rate = 4%) to $34,695 (when the Interest Rate = 8%), a range of $9,323. Table 5.6 shows that the Interest Rate and Repair & Upkeep both can impact the Net Annual Cost by $9,000 or more. Property Tax and Income Tax Rate are ranked #3 and #4, causing Net Annual Cost to vary by $4,500 and $4,347 respectively.

The tornado diagram for Barnard's Net Annual Cost is given in Figure 5.5, and we can see that it reports a different rank ordering of the input variables. For Barnard, the most influential variable is Months Occupied, followed by Interest Rate, and Monthly Rent. In fact, if the Barnard St. apartment is occupied for all 12 months, then the Net Annual Cost for Barnard is $35,752, whereas if it is empty all year, Net Annual Cost is $59,752, a whopping $24,000 range. This means that Sanjay and Sarah's costs can vary by up to $24,000 in any one year depending on rental occupancy. The amount they charge for rent is also influential, but only causes Net Annual Cost to vary by $14 thousand (when Monthly Rent = $1500, then Net Annual Cost = $44,752; when Monthly Rent = $2,900, Net Annual Cost = $30,752). Barnard's tornado diagram also shows that both Down Payment and Homeowner's Insurance have a relatively small effect.

In addition to using tornado diagrams to find insights about the factors influencing each alternative, we can also compare the impact of a factor across the alternatives by comparing the tornado diagrams. For example, comparing the tornado diagrams for Astoria and Barnard, we see that certain variables, such as Months Occupied, can go from having no impact to being the most influential. We also see that the scales for the two diagrams are quite different.

FIGURE **5.5**
Tornado diagram
of Net Annual Cost
of Barnard when
the variables in
Table 5.2 swing
from their lower
bound to their
upper bound.

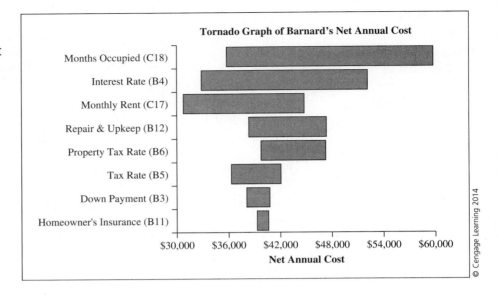

The most influential variables for Astoria only change Net Annual Cost by approximately $9,000, whereas the top three variables for Barnard can alter Net Annual Cost by over $14,000, suggesting that Barnard is somewhat riskier than Astoria. For example, with Astoria, Sanjay and Sarah may have to absorb an extra $7,600 in cost,[3] which would occur if Repair & Upkeep climbs to $10,000. The Barnard St. house, however, could require Sanjay and Sarah to absorb an additional $24,000 in cost if the apartment is never rented.

We have seen that for each variable included in the sensitivity analysis, we might have one sensitivity graph that reports the potential impact of that variable on the consequence measure for each alternative. In the House-Hunting example, there are eight variables listed in Table 5.2, and thus we could have eight sensitivity graphs. We could also have a tornado diagram for each alternative. The House-Hunting example has three alternatives and three tornado diagrams. The sensitivity graphs and tornado diagrams complement one another with the sensitivity graphs showing the impact of one variable across the alternatives and the tornado diagrams showing the relative impact of each variable on one alternative. Often, we look to the tornado diagram first to determine which variables impact the specific alternative most and then turn to the sensitivity graphs to understand the exact nature of the variable's effect.

DOMINANCE CONSIDERATIONS

In our discussion of making decisions in Chapter 4, we learned that alternatives can be screened based on deterministic and stochastic dominance, and inferior alternatives can be eliminated. Sensitivity analysis is not the

---

[3] $7,600 is computed by subtracting the base net annual cost ($28,673) from the maximum Net Annual Cost for Repair & Upkeep in Table 5.6 ($36,273).

FIGURE **5.6** The sensitivity graph shows the impact on Net Annual Cost for each of the three properties as Interest Rate of Astoria swings between 4% and 8%. Interest Rate for the two two-family houses is always 1.5% higher.

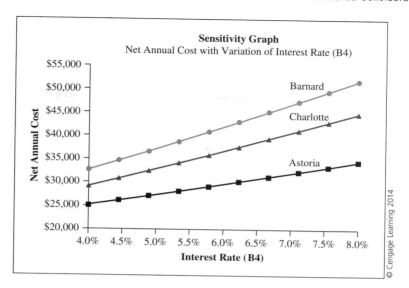

same as identifying dominated alternatives, and while sensitivity analysis can go a long way toward suggesting dominance, it can never provide conclusive proof.

Remember that we say Alternative B is dominated by Alternative A if B is never better than A, and that we determine stochastic dominance by comparing risk profiles of the alternatives. Risk profiles require probability distributions, and we have assessed no probability distributions for the sensitivity analysis. Rather, for the sensitivity analysis, we are stepping through the model with a series of values, one variable at a time. Thus, while sensitivity analysis and dominance are similar, they are not identical and we cannot conclude that an alternative is dominant or dominated by the sensitivity analysis results.

Sensitivity graphs compare the consequence values for each alternative as one particular variable swings from its lower bound to its upper bound. Thus, if the sensitivity graph shows that the consequence values (or curve) for Alternative B are always worse than the consequence values (or curve) for Alternative A, then, for that particular variable, B is never better than A. We do not say, however, that A dominates B. For example, the Interest Rate sensitivity graph in Figure 5.6 shows that Astoria is always better than Charlotte, which in turn is always better than Barnard. This graph only suggests that Astoria might dominate Charlotte, and Charlotte might dominate Barnard. But the graph shows the effects of only one variable. Looking at the Monthly Rent variable, we see that Astoria is not always better than Charlotte, as Charlotte has a lower Net Annual Cost when Charlotte's rent is greater than $2,100/month. However, for all three of the sensitivity graphs we have viewed so far, Charlotte is always better than Barnard. In fact, for all eight variables in Table 5.2, the sensitivity graphs show that Charlotte is always better than Barnard. However, this is still not enough to conclude dominance.

We cannot conclude dominance of Charlotte over Barnard based solely on the sensitivity graphs for three reasons. First, the set of variables we chose to use in Table 5.2 in the sensitivity analysis is not exhaustive and we may have missed a variable that, if included, would show that Barnard is better for some values of that variable. Even if the list in Table 5.2 were exhaustive, we still cannot conclude dominance because we are running a one-way sensitivity analysis. It could be that if we let two, three, or four variables simultaneously change, some combination of values could show that Barnard is better than Charlotte.

The third reason why dominance is not assured is that we have been evaluating these houses on Net Annual Cost alone and have been ignoring one of the main reasons for homeownership. For example, in the original discussion of our example, we noted that Sanjay and Sarah cared about safety and quality of education. Sanjay and Sarah might also want to look at their house as an investment opportunity, in which case they might have as an objective to maximize their equity in their house. An increase in equity can come from principal payments on their mortgage, appreciation in the housing market, and improvements they might make to the property. For the first 5 years, the annual equity gain due to principal payments is $8,522 for Barnard compared to $6,131 for Astoria. The average appreciation in the Boston area over the last 25 years has been 6.25% annually, which translates into an annual appreciation gain of approximately $28,000 for Astoria, $37,000 for Charlotte, and $47,000 for Barnard. Taking into account both the equity gains and the potential appreciation gains (Problem 5.14), Barnard might be better than both Astoria and Charlotte. All of this is to say that a different perspective—that is, a different objective—can lead to a different rank ordering of the alternatives. If they have other objectives like maximizing equity, Sanjay and Sarah should not eliminate any alternative based on the results of a one-way sensitivity analysis in which only one objective is considered.

TWO-WAY SENSITIVITY ANALYSIS

Although one-way sensitivity analysis can provide many insights, those insights are limited to what can be learned by moving only one variable at a time.

In the House-Hunting example, suppose we want to consider the combined impact of changes in two of the more critical variables, Monthly Rent and Interest Rate. We have already assessed the lower and upper bounds of $1,500 to $2,900 for Monthly Rent and 4% to 8% for Interest Rate. We can create a graph with Monthly Rent on the horizontal axis, and Interest Rate on the vertical axis. If we let Monthly Rent range from $1,500 to $2,900 and Interest Rate from 4% to 8%, the graph will cover all possible combinations of rental prices and interest rates that these two variables could take on. Figure 5.7 shows this rectangular space. Our objective is to subdivide the rectangle into three regions, one for each alternative. The Astoria region will consist of all points (rental prices and interest rates) for which Astoria's Net Annual Cost is less than that of the other two alternatives. Similarly, Barnard's region

FIGURE **5.7**
Two-way sensitivity graph for House-Hunting example.

The curve from point A to point B represents the Interest Rates and Monthly Rent values when Astoria's Net Annual Cost equals Charlotte's Net Annual Cost. There is no region for Barnard because it never has the minimum Net Annual Cost in this rectangular space.

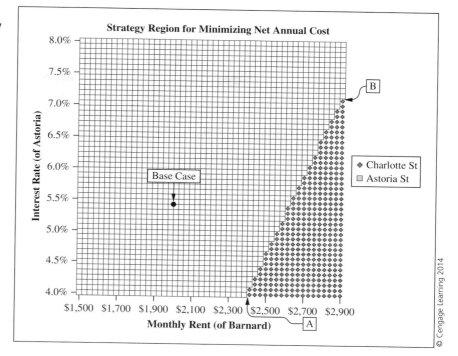

identifies the rental prices and interest rates when Barnard has the minimum Net Annual Cost and the same for Charlotte. The brute force method for identifying these three areas, which we call *strategy regions*, is to calculate the three Net Annual Cost values for a few hundred or even a few thousand points within the space, figure out which property has the minimum Net Annual Cost at each point, and then plot the results on the graph. A computer is the perfect tool for this approach, and we show how Data Tables in Excel® or PrecisionTree can carry out these calculations at the end of the chapter.

Instead of performing thousands of calculations, we can write down the mathematical expressions that define each region and use algebra to solve for the boundaries. For example, Astoria's region is defined to be the rental prices and interest rates when Astoria's Net Annual Cost is the least of the three properties:

Net Annual Cost(Astoria)

$$\leq Min\{\text{Net Annual Cost(Barnard), Net Annual Cost(Charlotte)}\}.$$

Next, we write down the formulas for each expression. Note that Interest Rate is used to calculate Net Annual Cost via the mortgage payment. That is, as we vary Interest Rate, the mortgage payment changes, which in turn, changes Net Annual Cost. To denote this relationship, we write *Mortgage(Interest Rate)* to be the 30-year fixed annual mortgage payment evaluated at a specific interest rate.

Let's begin by comparing Astoria and Charlotte. First we set up the expressions for Net Annual Cost for each property:

Net Annual Cost(Astoria)

$$= Mortgage(Interest\ Rate) + Homeowner's\ Insurance$$
$$+ Repairs\ \&\ Upkeep + House\ Price \times Property\ Tax\ Rate$$
$$- Tax\ Rate \times (P\% \times Mortgage)$$
$$= Mortgage(Interest\ Rate) + \$1,080 + \$2,400 + \$450,000 \times 1\%$$
$$-33\% \times (78\% \times Mortgage(Interest\ Rate))$$
$$= 0.743 \times Mortgage(Interest\ Rate) + \$7,980.$$

Net Annual Cost(Charlotte)

$$= Mortgage(Interest\ Rate + 1.5\%) + Homeowner's\ Insurance$$
$$+ Repairs\ \&\ Upkeep + House\ Price \times Property\ Tax\ Rate$$
$$- ((Monthly\ Rent - 500) \times Months\ Occupied) + Tax\ Rate$$
$$\times (1 - Percentage\ Rented) \times (P\% \times Mortgage)$$
$$= Mortgage(Interest\ Rate + 1.5\%) + \$1,440 + \$4,000 + \$600,000$$
$$\times 1\% - ((Monthly\ Rent - \$500) \times 10 + 33\% \times (1 - 35\%)$$
$$\times (85\% \times Mortgage(Interest\ Rate)))$$
$$= 0.818$$
$$\times Mortgage(Interest\ Rate + 1.5\%) - 10 \times Monthly\ Rent + \$16,440.$$

Thus, Net Annual Cost(Astoria) ≤ Net Annual Cost(Charlotte), when

$$0.743 \times Mortgage(Interest\ Rate) + \$7,980$$
$$\leq 0.818\ Mortgage(Interest\ Rate + 1.5\%) - 10 \times Monthly\ Rent + \$16,440$$

Now, it is a matter of finding the range of values for the two variables—Monthly Rent and Interest Rate—for which the preceding inequality holds.

Because the mortgage payment is a non-linear function of the interest rate, in Figure 5.7 the boundary between Astoria's region (when Astoria is the cheapest) and Charlotte's region is slightly curved. Remember that the boundary is made up of the interest rates and monthly rental rates when Astoria's Net Annual Cost equals that of Charlotte. Thus, to find the boundary, we simply find the values at a point when the two Net Annual Costs are equal. We could solve using algebra or using the Excel® function Goal Seek (which is described in the software instructions at the end of the chapter). For example, letting Interest Rate = 4%, then Astoria's mortgage is $23,421 and Charlotte's mortgage at 5.5% is $40,251. Substituting these values into the previous expression results in:

$$0.743 \times \$23,421 + \$7,980 = 0.818 \times \$40,251 - 10 \times Monthly\ Rent + \$16,440.$$

Solving for Monthly Rent, we have equality at $2,398/month. Therefore point A is (4%, $2,398), and means that when the interest rate is 4% for Astoria, and 5.5%

for Charlotte, and Sanjay and Sarah charge $1,898/month for the Charlotte apartment, then Astoria and Charlotte have the same Net Annual Cost. Choosing additional values for the interest rate, such as, 5%, 6%, 7%, and 8%, it is straightforward to find the corresponding monthly rental price for the Charlotte apartment which results in equality for Astoria's and Charlotte's Net Annual Costs. These break-even values are traced by the boundary between the regions in Figure 5.7. Note that point B was found by letting Monthly Rent = $2,900, and then solving for the interest rate, which was found to be 7.16%. Thus, when the interest rate for Charlotte is 8.66%, the rental price would need to be $2,400/month for Charlotte to have the same Net Annual Cost as Astoria with an interest rate of 7.16%. As Figure 5.7 shows, Astoria's region is above the boundary and Charlotte's region is below it. As it turns out for these two variables, with interest rates between 4% and 8% and rents between $1,500 and $2,900, there are no points for which Barnard's Net Annual Cost is the minimum.

What insights can Sanjay and Sarah draw from Figure 5.7?

- Barnard's absence from Figure 5.7 is quite telling. As we have said, this means that Barnard's Net Annual Cost is always greater than Astoria's and Charlotte's. Coupled with the one-way sensitivity graphs, this goes a long way toward showing that either Astoria or Charlotte is the better choice, at least when the consequence measure is Net Annual Cost.
- The base-case value shown in Figure 5.7 is the point (5.5%, $2,000) and it is not very close to the boundary. This means that Astoria has the lowest Net Annual Cost of the three properties because the base case is located in Astoria's region. That fact that it is not close means that either one or both of the base-case values must change by a considerable amount (more than about 20%) before moving into Charlotte's region. Keeping Interest Rate equal to 5.5% and reading across the graph, we do not enter Charlotte's region until Monthly Rent equals $2,631. Remembering to subtract $500 for Charlotte, Sanjay and Sarah would need to charge $2,131/month for Charlotte's apartment to match Astoria's Net Annual Cost. This is $631 more than the $1,500 anticipated Monthly Rent, an increase of 42%.
- The slope of the boundary at any given point gives an idea of how Monthly Rent and Interest Rate balance each other. For example, in going from 4% to 5%, monthly rent would need increase by $155 to cover the additional interest expense. Going from 7% to 8%, monthly rent would need increase by $165.
- Even though Charlotte shows up on the two-way sensitivity graph, it occupies a relatively small triangular region. Only a combination of a low interest rate and a high monthly rent would lead to Charlotte having the lower Net Annual Cost.
- It is important for Sanjay and Sarah to keep in mind that all variables aside from Monthly Rent and Interest Rate are kept at their base values for this analysis. For example, Months Occupied is held constant at 10 months. If Sanjay and Sarah had a renter for only 9 months, then Charlotte would have an even smaller triangular region, if one at all. Similarly, if Months Occupied increased to 11 or 12 months, then Charlotte's region would grow.

SENSITIVITY TO PROBABILITIES

Our sensitivity analysis of the house-hunting example has focused on variables about which Sanjay and Sarah have some uncertainty. Suppose Sanjay and Sarah want to model those uncertainties with probabilities, but they are reluctant to give any specific values for those probabilities. We can still run a sensitivity analysis on those probabilities.

As we've seen, the house-hunting example is fairly complex, and incorporating probabilities makes it more so. Let's begin our discussion of sensitivity analysis of probabilities with a somewhat simpler example: a stock market–investment problem that involves three alternatives and an uncertainty with three outcomes.

Investing in the Stock Market

An investor has funds available to invest in one of three choices: a high-risk stock, a low-risk stock, or a savings account that pays a sure $500. If he invests in the stocks, he must pay a brokerage fee of $200.

His payoff for the two stocks depends in part on what happens to the market as a whole. If the market goes up (as measured, say, by the Standard and Poor's 500 Index increasing 8% over the next 12 months), he can expect to earn $1,700 from the high-risk stock and $1,200 from the low-risk stock. Finally, if the stock market goes down (as indicated by the index decreasing by 3% or more), he will lose $800 with the high-risk stock but still gain $100 with the low-risk stock. If the market stays at roughly the same level, his payoffs for the high- and low-risk stocks will be $300 and $400, respectively.

Figure 5.8 shows the decision tree. You can see in the decision tree that we have assigned variables to the probabilities, so that P(market up) = t and P(market same) = v. Of course, P(market down) = $1 - t - v$, because the probabilities of each chance node must sum to 1. We will run a sensitiy analysis on t and v.

To construct the two-way sensitivity graph, we first locate the boundaries, remembering that $t + v$ must always be less than or equal to 1. For example, if $t = \frac{1}{4}$, then $v \leq \frac{3}{4}$. Therefore, the complete set of possible values for t and v is the triangular region shown in Figure 5.9. Any point outside this triangle would violate the laws of probability.

To find the strategy regions, we compare the alternatives two at a time. Let's begin by finding the area where the savings account would be preferred to the low-risk stock:

$$\text{EMV(Savings Account)} \geq \text{EMV(Low-Risk Stock)}$$

$$500 \geq 1{,}000t + 200v + (-100)(1 - t - v)$$

Solving for v in terms of t, we get

$$v \leq 2 - \frac{11t}{3}$$

© Cengage Learning 2014

FIGURE **5.8**
Decision tree for
a stock market
investor.

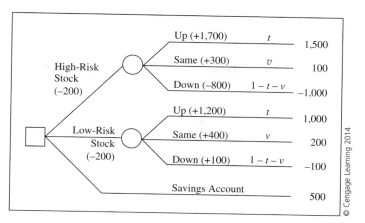

FIGURE **5.9**
Beginning the
analysis of the
stock market
problem.

Note that $t + v$ must be
less than or equal to 1,
and so the only feasible
points are within the
large triangular region.

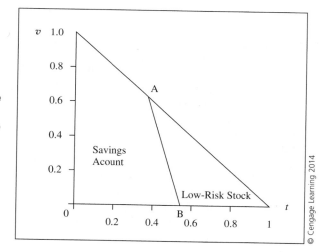

Figure 5.9 shows the regions for the savings account and the low-risk
stock divided by Line AB.

Now let us find the regions for the high- and low-risk stocks. Begin by
setting up the inequality:

$$\text{EMV(Low} - \text{Risk Stock)} \geq \text{EMV(High-Risk Stock)}$$

$$1{,}000t + 200v + (-100)(1 - t - v) \geq 1{,}500t + 100v + (-1{,}000)(1 - t - v)$$

Doing the algebra, this reduces to:

$$v \leq \frac{9 - 14t}{8}$$

FIGURE **5.10**
Second stage in
analysis of the
stock market
problem.

A second inequality has
been incorporated. The
optimal strategy is clear
now for all regions
except CDA.

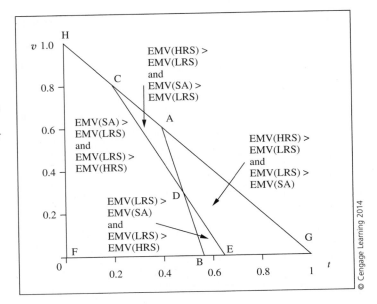

Using this inequality, we can add another line to our graph (Figure 5.10).
Now Line CDE separates the graph into regions in which EMV(Low-Risk
Stock) is greater or less than EMV(High-Risk Stock).

From Figure 5.10 we can tell what the optimal strategy is in all but
one portion of the graph. For example, in region ADEG, we know that
the high-risk stock is preferred to the low-risk stock and that the low-risk
stock is preferred to the savings account. Thus, the high-risk stock would
be preferred overall. Likewise, in HFBDC the savings account would be
preferred, and in DBE the low-risk stock would be preferred. But in
CDA, all we know is that the low-risk stock is worse than the other two,
but we do not know whether to choose the savings account or the high-
risk stock.

If the decision maker is sure that the probabilities t and v do not fall into
the region CDA, then the sensitivity analysis could stop here. If some question
remains, then we can complete the graph by comparing EMV(Savings
Account) with EMV(High-Risk Stock):

$$\text{EMV(Savings Account)} \geq \text{EMV(High-Risk Stock)}$$

$$500 \geq 1{,}500t + 100v + (-1{,}000)(1 - t - v)$$

This inequality reduces to:

$$v \leq \frac{1{,}525t}{11}$$

Incorporating this result into the graph allows us to see that region CDA
actually is split between the high-risk stock and the savings account as indicated by Line ID in Figure 5.11.

FIGURE **5.11**
Completed two-way
sensitivity graph for
the stock market
problem.

Line ID has split region
CDA.

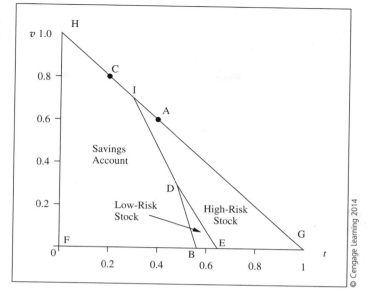

With the analysis completed, the investor now can think about probabilities t and v. If the investor can specify base values and ranges, it
should be possible to tell whether the optimal investment decision is sensitive to these probabilities and whether additional effort should be spent
refining the uncertainty model of the stock market's movements.

SENSITIVITY TO PROBABILITIES—HOUSE-HUNTING

Given the sensitivity analysis above for the house-hunting example, Sanjay
and Sarah might want to model the uncertainty surrounding the more influential variables. For this example, we will develop probability models for
Months Occupied and Repair & Upkeep and run a sensitivity analysis on
the probabilities for those two variables. In an initial attempt to model the
uncertainties, Sanjay and Sarah choose 12 months, 9 months, and 7 months
as possible outcomes for Months Occupied, and two values for Repair &
Upkeep, one representing an optimistic scenario and one representing a pessimistic scenario. An influence diagram representing the model for the Barnard
property, for example, is shown in Figure 5.12, showing Months Occupied
and Repair & Upkeep as chance nodes. The remaining input variables are
set at their base values and hence continue to be represented by rounded rectangles (constants).

From the decision tree in Figure 5.13, you can see what we are up
against. There are three probabilities for Months Occupied (p_1, p_2, and p_3)
and eight for Repair & Upkeep (q_1, q_2, r_1, r_2, s_1, s_2, and t_1, t_2). Why so
many for Repair and Upkeep? The arrow in Figure 5.12 from Months

FIGURE **5.12**
Influence diagram representing Sanjay and Sarah's Housing Decision.

Only two variables, Repair & Upkeep and Months Occupied, are uncertain. Moreover, the relevance arc between them means that the probabilities for Repair & Upkeep may be different depending on Months Occupied.

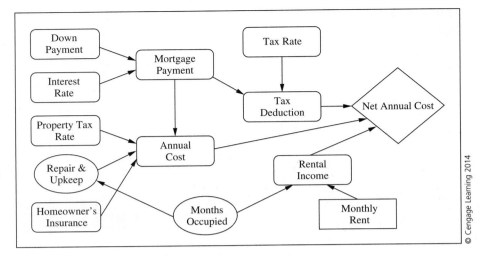

Occupied to Repair & Upkeep means that, for Barnard and Charlotte, the Repair & Upkeep probabilities are judged to depend on Months Occupied; Sanjay and Sarah suspect that an increase in Months Occupied implies a likely increase in Repair & Upkeep. So for Barnard and Charlotte we need different optimistic and pessimistic probabilities for each of the three levels of Months Occupied. That's six probabilities, and we need two more for Astoria, for a total of 11 probabilities! We cannot easily perform an 11-way sensitivity analysis, so we will have to look for some ways to simplify. This is where modeling comes in. We will develop a simple model that will allow us to specify all the probabilities with just two variables, thereby allowing a two-way sensitivity analysis.

We start by recalling that each chance node's probabilities have to sum to one. Thus, we have $p_3 = 1 - (p_1 + p_2); q_2 = 1 - q_1; r_2 = 1 - r_1; s_2 = 1 - s_1;$ and $t_2 = 1 - t_1$. To further reduce the number of variables, we can model relationships among some of them. For example, suppose Sanjay and Sarah believe that it is twice as likely that the apartment will be rented 9 months compared to all 12 months. Thus, $p_2 = 2p_1$, which in turn implies that $p_3 = 1 - (p_1 + p_2) = 1 - 3p_1$. Furthermore, suppose Sanjay and Sarah feel that a reasonable way to model the dependence between Months Occupied and Repair & Upkeep is to let r_1 be 80% of q_1. That is, if the apartment is occupied 9 months, then the probability of high Repair & Upkeep is 80% of the probability of high Repair & Upkeep when the apartment is occupied all 12 months. Thus, $r_1 = 0.80q_1$. By similar reasoning, they conclude that $s_1 = 0.70r_1$, that is, if the apartment is occupied 7 months the probability of high Repair & Upkeep is 70% of the probability of high Repair & Upkeep when the apartment is occupied 9 months.

With no apartment, Astoria has no uncertainty surrounding Months Occupied, but does have pessimistic and optimistic values for Repair & Upkeep. Sanjay and Sarah feel the probability t_1 for high Repair & Upkeep

FIGURE **5.13**
Decision tree for the House-Hunting example with two uncertain variables.

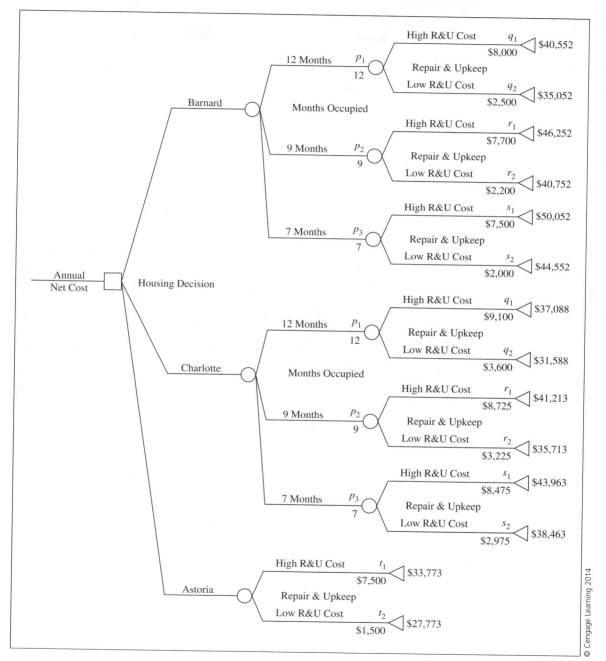

for Astoria is 80% of the probability p_1 of high Repair & Upkeep when the Barnard apartment is occupied all 12 months. Thus, $t_1 = 0.80p_1$. Figure 5.14 shows the modified decision tree, with only p_1 and q_1 left as unknowns; all other probabilities are calculated from these two.

We can now create a two-way sensitivity analysis graph by letting both p_1 and q_1 take values within their respective ranges. As with the previous two-way sensitivity analysis, the graph can potentially be subdivided into three regions. The Astoria region will consist of all values for p_1 and q_1 for which the decision tree in Figure 5.14 reports Astoria as the low cost alternative. Likewise, the Barnard and Charlotte regions will consist of (p_1, q_1) pairs for which Barnard and Charlotte are the low cost alternatives, respectively.

If Sanjay and Sarah cannot provide ranges for p_1 and q_1, we can let them vary over as large a range as possible. For q_1, the possible range is from zero to one, inclusive; as long as it falls in this range, all of the other Repair & Upkeep probabilities will also fall between zero and one. For p_1, the situation is a bit more complicated. Like the investment example, we have to be sure that p_2, and p_3 also fall between zero and one. For example, because we have the condition $p_2 = 2p_1$, p_1 must always be less than one-half. But we also have the condition that $p_3 = 1 - 3p_1$, which implies that p_1 must also be less than one-third. Thus, all possible (p_1, q_1) pairs fall in a rectangle defined by $0 \leq p_1 \leq \frac{1}{3}$, and $0 \leq q_1 \leq 1$.

To create the graph, we first write out the expected Net Annual Cost of each property, substituting in the values and probabilities from the tree in Figure 5.14. For Astoria,

$$E[Net\ Annual\ Cost(Astoria)] = t_1(\$33,773) + t_2(\$27,773).$$

Substituting in $t_1 = 0.8q_1$ and $t_2 = 1 - 0.8q_1$, we have

$$E[Net\ Annual\ Cost(Astoria)] = 0.8q_1(\$33,773) + (1 - 0.8q_1)(\$27,773)$$

$$= \$4,800q_1 + \$27,773$$

Similarly, we write the expected Net Annual Cost expressions for Barnard and Charlotte as functions of p_1 and q_1. For convenience, we calculated the consequence values for Barnard and denote them as follows: $V_{B1} = \$40,522$, $V_{B2} = \$35,052, \cdots, V_{B6} = \$44,522$, where V_{B1} indicates the first (top) consequence value in the tree for Barnard, V_{B2} represents the next one down, and so on. We will do the same for Charlotte: $V_{C1} = \$37,088$, $V_{C2} = \$31,588, \cdots,$ $V_{C6} = \$38,463$. Using this notation allows us to write the expected Net Annual Cost for both properties efficiently as:

$E[Net\ Annual\ Cost(Barnard)]$

$$= p_1q_1V_{B1} + p_1q_2V_{B2} + p_2r_1V_{B2} + p_2r_2V_{B4} + p_3s_1V_{B5} + p_3s_2V_{B6}.$$

$E[Net\ Annual\ Cost(Charlotte)]$

$$= p_1q_1V_{C1} + p_1q_2V_{C2} + p_2r_1V_{C2} + p_2r_2V_{C4} + p_3s_1V_{C5} + p_3s_2V_{C6}.$$

FIGURE **5.14**

Decision tree for the House-Hunting example with two uncertain variables. This tree is now ready for a two-way sensitivity analysis on p_1 and q_1.

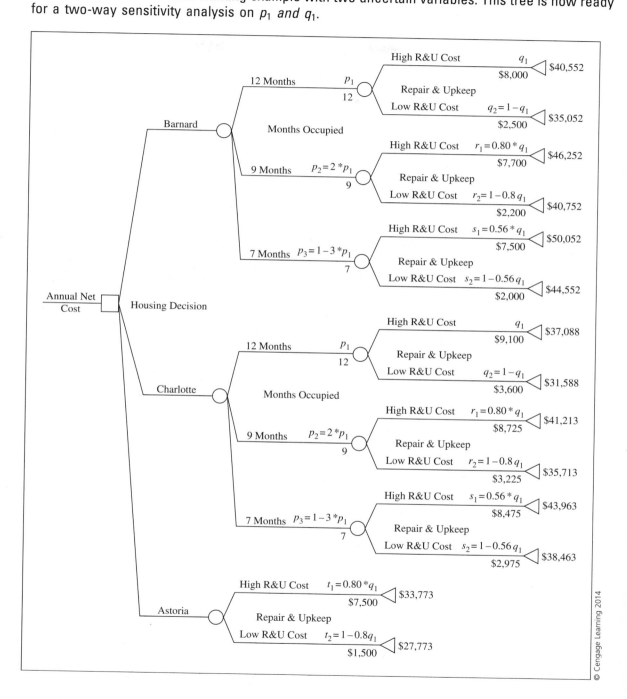

For all of the probabilities except p_1 and q_1, we can substitute in their expressions in terms of p_1 and q_1:

$$p_2 = 2p_1, \qquad r_1 = 0.8q_1, \qquad s_1 = 0.56q_1,$$

$$p_3 = 1 - 3p_1, \quad r_2 = 1 - 0.8q_1, \quad s_2 = 1 - 0.56q_1, \quad \text{and} \quad q_2 = 1 - q_1.$$

For Barnard, for example, we have:

$$E[NetAnnualCost(Barnard)]$$
$$= p_1 q_1 (V_{B1} - V_{B2} + 1.6V_{B3} - 1.6V_{B4} - 1.68V_{B5} + 1.68V_{B6})$$
$$+ p_1(V_{B2} + 2V_{B4} - 3V_{B6}) + q_1(0.56V_{B5} - 0.56V_{B6}) + V_{B6}.$$

Substituting in Barnard's consequence values, we have:

$$E[Net\ Annual\ Cost(Barnard)] = \$5,060p_1q_1 - \$17,100p_1 + \$3,080q_1 + \$44,552.$$

Going through the same process for Charlotte, we get:

$$E[Net\ Annual\ Cost(Charlotte)] = \$5,060p_1q_1 - \$12,375p_1 + \$3,080q_1 + \$38,463.$$

With these algebraic expressions, we can determine the conditions under which each property has the lowest expected Net Annual Cost. It is as simple as plugging values for p_1 and q_1 into the above expressions and identifying the property with the minimum expected Net Annual Cost. First, it is fairly easy to see that the expected Net Annual Cost for Barnard will always be greater than for Charlotte. (Can you see why? Remember that $p_1 \leq \frac{1}{3}$.) Comparing Astoria and Charlotte, it turns out that Astoria always has the lower expected Net Annual Cost, and so the two-way sensitivity analysis graph consists of only one region – Astoria. This tells Sanjay and Sarah that, regardless of the probabilities they use in the model, Astoria will always have the lowest expected Net Annual Cost. If minimizing Net Annual Cost is their objective, Astoria is their best alternative.

One of the benefits of constructing a decision model is that you can try out various scenarios and find out the implications for your decision. This is a type of "What if..?" analysis. To illustrate, suppose Sarah somewhat preferred Barnard to Charlotte and preferred Charlotte to Astoria. In order to make Barnard and Charlotte look more attractive to Sanjay, she could volunteer to keep her teaching job and contribute, say, $700 per month to the housing budget if they were to purchase Charlotte and $800 per month if they were to purchase Barnard. Remember that they could comfortably afford Astoria on Sanjay's salary alone, so this is Sarah's way to incorporate her preferences into the decision.

Turning to the model, we simply subtract $8,400 from the Net Annual Cost of Charlotte and $9,600 from the Net Annual Cost of Barnard. This does not mean that the cost of these properties has dropped. Instead, Sarah's monthly contributions have lowered the cost that Sanjay's salary must cover. Subtracting Sarah's monthly contributions alters the rank ordering with Charlotte's expected Net Annual Cost being the lowest at $26,588, followed by Astoria at $28,673. Barnard is still the highest at $30,152. Rerunning the two-way sensitivity analysis on the probabilities p_1 and q_1 produces Figure 5.15, which shows the graph subdivided into two regions, one for Astoria and one for Charlotte. Barnard's absence tells us that there is no value for p_1 and q_1 for which Barnard's expected Net Annual Cost is the lowest, even with Sarah's $800/month contribution. Figure 5.15 also shows that, regardless of the probability of high Repair & Upkeep (q_1), as the probability of high occupancy (p_1) increases from zero, the expected cost advantage of Astoria gradually diminishes until, at some point, Charlotte becomes the preferred alternative. This result makes sense; Charlotte would have a higher probability of higher revenues, thereby lowering its expected Net Annual Cost.

Figure 5.15 also shows that, for some values of p_1, increasing q_1, the probability of high Repair & Upkeep, can lead to Charlotte being preferred. At first blush, this seems counterintuitive, but we can understand why by looking at the model. Note that there is always a chance ($1 - 3p_1$ to be precise) that Charlotte's occupancy will be only 7 months, which leads to lower probabilities of high Repair & Upkeep. As q_1 increases, Repair & Upkeep plays a greater role in the expected Net Annual Cost for each property, but the possibility of Charlotte's occupancy being less than 7 months means that Repair & Upkeep's increased impact is less for Charlotte than it is for Astoria. For example, suppose $p_1 = 15\%$, and consider an increase in q_1 from 20% to 70%. Astoria's expected Net Annual Cost would increase by $2,400, whereas Charlotte's would increase by only $1,920. So, with a large enough q_1, even though the expected Net Annual Cost would have increased for each property, Astoria's increase might be enough greater than Charlotte's to leave Charlotte with the lower expected Net Annual Cost.

FIGURE **5.15**
Two-way sensitivity graph for the House-Hunting example showing p_1 = probability of High Occupancy vs. q_1 = probability of High R&U Cost with Charlotte's Net Annual Cost reduced by $700/month.

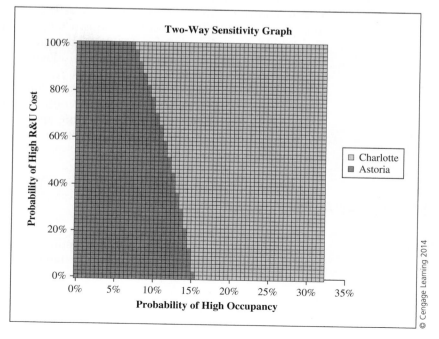

FIGURE **5.16**
Two-way sensitivity graph incorporating annual contributions from Sarah of $700/month for Charlotte and $1,100/month for Barnard.

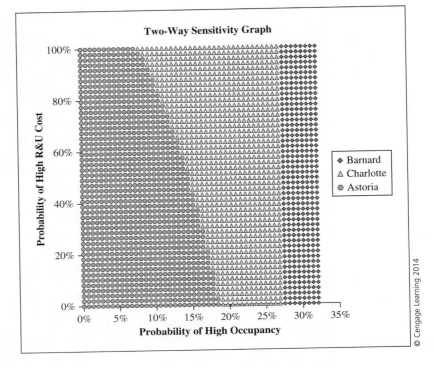

Another What-If question that we could ask is how much Sarah would need to contribute to make Barnard preferred? We saw that a $700/month contribution by Sarah produces scenarios when Charlotte has the minimum Net Annual Cost, but that her $800/month contribution did not result in Barnard ever being the low-cost alternative. Figure 5.16 shows the results of a two-way sensitivity analysis on p_1 and q_1, with Charlotte's Net Annual Cost reduced by Sarah's $700/month contribution and Barnard's Net Annual Cost reduced by a $1,100/month contribution ($13,200 annually). We see that each property has its own region, and that when the probability of high occupancy is greater than 27%, Barnard has the lowest expected Net Annual Cost.

SENSITIVITY ANALYSIS IN ACTION

Is sensitivity analysis ever used in the real world? Indeed it is. Sensitivity analysis is an important tool that is used in scientific studies of all kinds, and it is the source of important insights and understanding. The following example comes from medical decision making, showing how sensitivity-analysis graphs can improve decisions in an area where hard decisions are made even harder by the stakes involved.

Heart Disease in Infants

Macartney, Douglas, and Spiegelhalter used decision analysis to study alternative treatments of infants who suffered from a disease known as coarctation of the aorta. Difficult to detect, the fundamental uncertainty is whether the disease is present at all. Three alternative treatments exist if an infant is suspected of having the disease. The first is to do nothing, which may be appropriate if the disease is not present. The second is to operate. The third alternative is to catheterize the heart in an attempt to confirm the diagnosis, although it does not always yield a perfect diagnosis. Moreover, catheterizing the heart of a sick infant is itself a dangerous undertaking and may lead to death. The difficulty of the problem is obvious; with all of the uncertainty and the risk of death from operating or catheterization, what is the appropriate treatment?

Source: Macartney, F., J. Douglas, and D. Spiegelhalter (1984) "To Catheterise or Not to Catheterise?" *British Heart Journal*, 51, 330–338.

In their analysis Macartney et al. created a two-way sensitivity graph (Figure 5.17) showing the sensitivity of the decision to two probabilities. The two probabilities are (1) the disease is present, which is along the horizontal axis and (2) the mortality rate for cardiac catheterization, which is along the vertical axis. The mortality rate also could be interpreted as the physician's judgment regarding the chance that the infant would die as a result of catheterization.

The graph shows three regions, reflecting the three available alternatives. The location of the three regions makes good sense. If the physician believes that the chances are low that the disease is present and that the risk of

FIGURE **5.17**
Two-way sensitivity analysis for the heart disease treatment decision.

Source: Macartney et al. (1984).
© British Medical Association used by permission

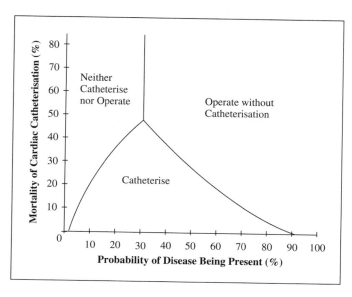

catheterizing the infant is high, the appropriate response is to do nothing. However, if the risk of catheterization is high relative to the chance that the disease is present, operating without catheterizing is the prescribed treatment. Catheterization is recommended only for situations with relatively low risk from the procedure.

SENSITIVITY ANALYSIS: A BUILT-IN IRONY

There is a strange irony in sensitivity analysis and decision making. We begin by structuring a decision problem, part of which involves identifying several alternatives. Then some alternatives are eliminated on the grounds of dominance. Those remaining are difficult to choose from and therefore lead us to unveil our array of decision-analysis tools. They may be difficult to choose from because they probably differ little in expected value; and if so, it does not matter much which alternative one chooses, does it? For the analyst who wants to be quite sure of making the best possible choice, this realization can be terribly frustrating; almost by definition, hard decisions are sensitive to our assessments. For those who are interested in modeling to improve decision making, the thought is comforting; the better the model, the better the decision, but only a small degree of improvement may be available from rigorous and exquisite modeling of each minute detail. Adequate modeling is all that is necessary. The best way to view sensitivity analysis is as a source of guidance in modeling a decision problem. It provides the guidance for each successive iteration through the decision-analysis cycle. You can see now how the cycle is composed of modeling steps, followed by sensitivity analysis, followed by more modeling, and so on. The ultimate objective of this cycle of modeling and analysis is to arrive eventually at a requisite decision model and to analyze it just enough to understand clearly which alternative should be chosen. By the time the decision maker reaches this point, all important issues will be included in the decision model, and the choice should be clear.

SENSITIVITY ANALYSIS USING EXCEL® AND PRECISIONTREE

We now turn to the DecisionTools Suite and use PrecisionTree to carry out sensitivity analyses and create tornado diagrams and sensitivity graphs. In addition, we explain how to use the Excel® functions Goal Seek and Data Tables for sensitivity analysis. The following instructions for Excel® and PrecisionTree explain how to run one-way and two-way sensitivity analyses using the House-Hunting example. (The DecisionTools Suite also includes TopRank for analyzing general spreadsheet models. We do not discuss TopRank here for a number of reasons; readers who wish to try TopRank can find instructions at the Palisade website.)

Often the steps in decision analysis begin with constructing a spreadsheet model, running a sensitivity analysis to determine those inputs for which the decision is sensitive, and then modeling the uncertain influential variables as chance nodes in the decision tree. Thus, we need to discuss how to run a sensitivity analysis on both a spreadsheet model and on a decision tree. The instructions follow these steps by first analyzing the spreadsheet model for the House-Hunting example, and then running one-way and two-way sensitivity analyses on a linked decision tree. The reader may wish to refer back to the discussion of linked trees in Chapter 4 as a refresher.

STEP 1 Model Setup.

1.1 Open Excel® and PrecisionTree, enabling any macros.

1.2 Either **construct the spreadsheet as shown in** Table 5.7 or download the workbook House Hunting.xls from www.cengagebrain.com.

1.3 Construct the decision tree shown in Figure 5.18 and link each end node to the corresponding property's Net Annual Cost spreadsheet cell.

  a) After creating a **three-branch decision node**, click on the tree's name **Net Annual Cost** to access the *Model Settings* dialog box.

TABLE **5.7**

Spreadsheet model for Sanjay and Sarah's Housing Decision. *Note that the annual mortgage payment is found using Excel®'s PMT function.*

	A	B	C	D	E	F	G
1		Astoria St.	Barnard St.	Charlotte St.		Model Parameters	
2	Price	450000	750000	600000			
3	Down Payment	45000	=B3	=B3-G3			
4	Interest Rate	0.055	=B4+G4	=B4+G4		Renovation Cost	30000
5	Tax Rate	0.33	=B5	=B5		Interest Rate Premium	0.015
6	Property Tax Rate	0.01	=B6	=B6			
7	Percentage Rented	0	0.4	0.35			
8							
9	Costs						
10	Mortgage (30 yr fixed)	=-PMT(B4,30,B2-B3)	=-PMT(C4,30,C2-C3)	=-PMT(D4,30,D2-D3)			
11	Homeowner's Insurance	1080	=C2/B2*B11	=D2/B2*B11			
12	Repair & Upkeep	2400	=B12+G12	=B12+2*G12		Additional Upkeep Cost	800
13	Property Taxes	=B6*B2	=C6*C2	=D6*D2			
14	Annual Cost	=SUM(B10:B13)	=SUM(C10:C13)	=SUM(D10:D13)			
15							
16	Rental						
17	Monthly Rent	0	2000	=C17-G17		Monthly Rent Premium	500
18	Months Occupied	0	10	=C18			
19	Rental Income	=B17*B18	=C17*C18	=D17*D18			
20							
21	Tax Deduction on Interest	=0.78*B10*(1-B7)*B5	=0.85*C10*(1-C7)*C5	=0.85*D10*(1-D7)*D5			
22							
23	Net Annual Cost	=B14-B19-B21	=C14-C19-C21	=D14-D19-D21			

As shown in Figure 5.18, choose the **Calculation** tab, for *Method* choose **Linked Spreadsheet**, and enter **B23** (Astoria's Net Annual Cost) for the *Default Cell*. We recommend that **Automatic** be chosen for the *Link Updating* so that any changes to the model are immediately reflected in the decision tree. Also, do not forget to set the *Optimal Path* to **Minimum Payoff** as we prefer lower costs. Click **OK**.

b) The other two branches (Barnard and Charlotte) need to be linked manually to their Net Annual Cost formulas by clicking directly on their **end nodes**, and in the pop-up dialog box choosing the

FIGURE **5.18**

Linking the decision tree to the spreadsheet model for Sanjay and Sarah's Housing Decision allows us to use the spreadsheet model to calculate Net Annual Cost.

Note that we have defined the optimal path to be the minimum net-cost value.

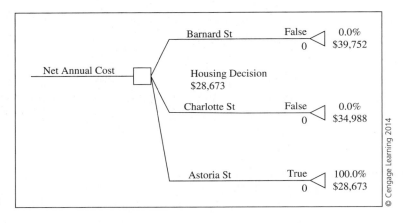

© Cengage Learning 2014

FIGURE **5.19**
Each branch or
alternative of the
decision tree must
be linked to the
appropriate
spreadsheet cell.
Thus, Astoria's
branch is linked to
cell B23, Barnard to
C23, and Charlotte
to D23.

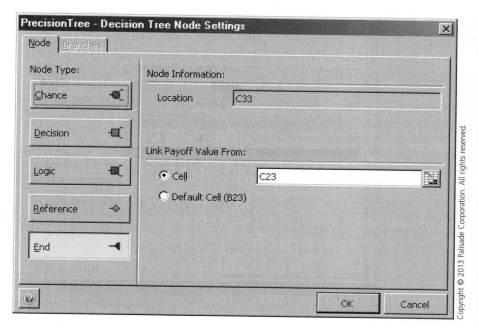

appropriate Net Annual Cost spreadsheet cell. Figure 5.19 shows
how Barnard's Net Annual Cost formula in cell **C23** is linked to
Barnard's branch. Sometimes after linking a spreadsheet to a decision tree, the numerical values do not appear in the tree. If this
happens, simply double click in a cell showing VALUE! and hit
the Enter key.

STEP 2 *Sensitivity Graphs.*

2.1 Open PrecisionTree's sensitivity-analysis dialog box by clicking on the
Sensitivity Analysis button in the PrecisionTree menu. Figure 5.20
shows that we are starting with a **One-Way Sensitivity**.

2.2 Under *Output:* in Figure 5.20, chose **Model Expected Value** for
Type of Value. This means that the sensitivity analysis' output will
be the expected value of the decision tree's Net Annual Cost. The
other option instead of Model Expected Value is Spreadsheet Cell,
which means that the sensitivity analysis output can be any
spreadsheet cell. PrecisionTree can carry out a sensitivity analysis
on a decision tree or a general spreadsheet model.

FIGURE **5.20**
PrecisionTree's
Sensitivity Analysis
dialog box.

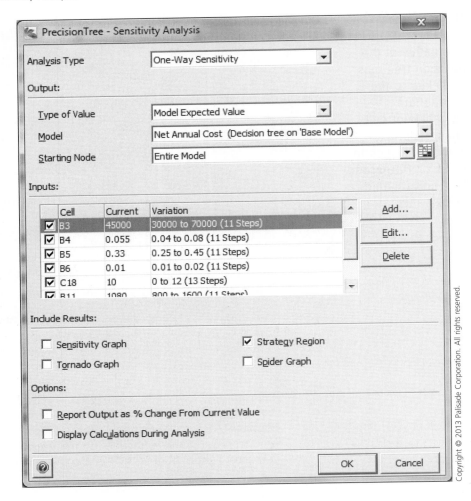

2.3 Under *Inputs:* we enter the cells that correspond to the variables in Table 5.2 with their lower and upper bounds. The first variable in Table 5.2 is Down Payment, and its corresponding cell in the spreadsheet model is B3 as shown in Table 5.7. Thus, click the **Add** button to the right of *Inputs:*, and the *Sensitivity Input Definition* dialog box appears.

a) Enter **B3** as the *Cell* and **Down Payment** as the *Label*.

b) Under *Variation*, choose **Actual Maximum and Minimum** as the *Method*; then enter the bounds of 30000 and 70000.

c) Leave the number of *Steps* at 11, which means that the model will be evaluated at 11 down payment values starting at $30,000 and ending at $70,000. Click **OK**.

> **d)** Repeat for the remaining seven variables in Table 5.2. For Monthly Rent and Months Occupied, be sure to link to C17 and C18, respectively. Note also that we set the number of steps equal to 13 for Months Occupied so that the steps are whole numbers: 0, 1, ..., 12.
>
> **2.4** Finally we see that under *Include Results:* we have chosen **Strategy Region**, leaving out *Tornado Graph, Spider Graph,* and *Sensitivity Graph.* We definitely want to view the sensitivity graphs, but the problem is that PrecisionTree uses a different terminology. What we have been calling sensitivity graphs in this chapter, PrecisionTree calls strategy regions.
>
> **2.5** To run the sensitivity analysis, click the **OK** button as shown in Figure 5.20.

PrecisionTree's one-way sensitivity analysis on our eight variables creates a new workbook that contains eight worksheets, one for each of the eight sensitivity graphs. The sensitivity graphs (or PrecisionTree's strategy region graphs) show the result to the consequence variable as the input variables take on the values between the upper and lower bounds. Figure 5.21 shows the evaluation points as markers with a linear interpolation between each marker. Because we ran our sensitivity analysis on a decision tree with three alternatives, the sensitivity graphs show the results for each alternative using three curves.

FIGURE 5.21
One of the eight sensitivity graphs produced by PrecisionTree.

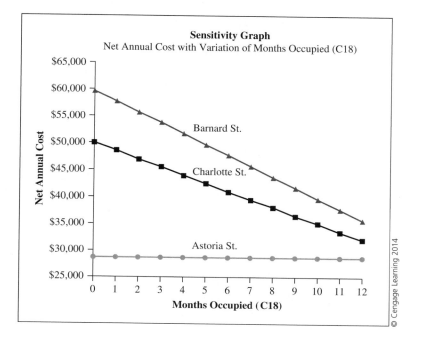

© Cengage Learning 2014

Creating a tornado diagram is straightforward:

STEP 3 Tornado Diagrams.

3.1 Reopen PrecisionTree's sensitivity-analysis dialog box by clicking on the **Sensitivity Analysis** button in the PrecisionTree menu. This time, choose **Spreadsheet Cell** for *Type of Value* and **B23** for *Cell*.
In addition, choose the **Tornado Graph** under *Include Results*.
Now click **OK**, and (assuming you have followed Step 2) Precision-Tree will create the Astoria tornado diagram. Similarly, entering **C23** or **D23** will create tornado diagrams for Barnard and Charlotte respectively.

Running a two-way sensitivity analysis is simple once the variables and their ranges have been input into the sensitivity-analysis window.

STEP 4 Two-Way Sensitivity Analysis.

4.1 To perform a two-way sensitivity analysis in PrecisionTree, click the **Sensitivity Analysis** button in PrecisionTree's toolbar.
4.2 For *Analysis Type*, choose **Two-Way Sensitivity**. Keep the *Output* section the same, as shown in Figure 5.22, and under *Inputs*, choose the two desired variables. We choose Monthly Rent in cell C17 and Interest Rate in cell B4. If you want your graph to look just like Fig 5.7, use the Edit button to change cells B4 and C17 to 50 steps.
4.3 Click on **Sensitivity Graph** and **Strategy Region** for the results, and finally **OK** to run the two-way sensitivity analysis.

The result of running a two-way analysis is again a new workbook, but this time with two worksheets. The sensitivity graph is three-dimensional with the height being the minimum Net Annual Cost across the three alternatives. The strategy region shows the rectangular region of the input variables and a marker at each evaluation point indicating which property has the lowest net cost. Figures 5.7, 5.15 and 5.16 show PrecisionTree's strategy region. Note that for these graphs, we choose 50 as the number of steps. Thus, each of the three net cost formulas were evaluated at 2500 (= 50^2) points.

PrecisionTree certainly helps us build and solve influence diagrams and decision trees. It also will carry out the thousands of calculations necessary for a sensitivity analysis, saving us from this tedium. The sensitivity-analysis feature of PrecisionTree, however, has some limitations. PrecisionTree does not have a special feature for running a two-way sensitivity analysis when

FIGURE **5.22**
Running a two-way
sensitivity analysis
with PrecisionTree
on Monthly Rent
(C17) and Interest
Rate (B4).

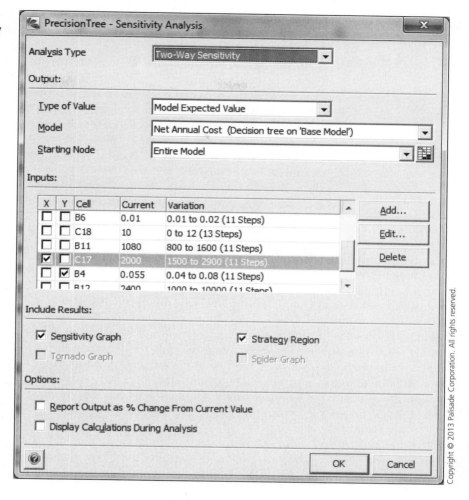

the region over which the two variables are changing is nonrectangular. We
saw that when we wanted to vary two probabilities from the same chance
node with three outcomes, the region was triangular. Thus, for such situations, we recommend that you algebraically solve for the strategy region of
each alternative.

Note that one does not need to use linked trees to carry out a sensitivity
analysis. For many problems, you can simply run the sensitivity analysis
directly on the decision tree. In such cases, you would select the input variables not from a spreadsheet model, but from the tree itself.

Excel® itself has two functions that can be useful in carrying out a sensitivity analysis. Goal Seek is an Excel® function that attempts to find (or seek
out) a specific value for an input cell that results in an output cell equaling a
specific numerical value (or its goal). Goal Seek can be very useful because it
essentially solves algebraic equations. For example, we used Goal Seek in the

two-way sensitivity analysis when we wanted to find the monthly rent value that resulted in the Net Annual Cost of Astoria equaling the Net Annual Cost of Charlotte.

In the next few paragraphs, we explain how to use Goal Seek and look at some of its limitations. We will start with an elementary example, then explore ways to use Goal Seek on more advanced problems. Suppose we wish to use Goal Seek to find the value for X that solves $X + 2 = 5$. To set this up in Excel®, we will use cell A1 for the value of X, A2 will have the value of 2, and A3 will have the formula $=$**A1** $+$ **A2**. If you enter the number 7 into A1, A3 will show 9. To find the value for A1 (our X) for which A3 (our $X + 2$) equals 5, we use Goal Seek by clicking on the **Data** menu tab in Excel®, then clicking on the **What-If Analysis** button, and finally on **Goal Seek**. The Goal Seek dialog box is shown in Figure 5.23, where we specify cell **A3** as the *Set cell*, 5 as the *To value*, and **A1** as the *By changing cell*. For our example, set cell A3 to the value of 5 by changing cell A1. Click OK, and you can see that cell A3 is now equal to 5, and A1 equals 3, just as expected.

Although our example was extremely simple, Goal Seek is based on sophisticated numerical analysis that finds successive approximations with each iteration getting closer and closer to the goal value. Hence, Goal Seek can be used on complex problems with ease. There are, however, limitations to Goal Seek. An important limitation of Goal Seek is that cell references cannot be used for the goal value; rather the goal value must be a numerical value that is typed in, such as our 5. Sometimes this can be problematic because we may not know the actual goal value. For example, suppose you wanted to find the monthly rent values for which the Net Annual Costs of Barnard equals that of Astoria. The problem is that we do not know at what value these are equal. More simply, suppose we wanted to know when $X + Y = X \times Y$, when $Y = 3.5$? We would have trouble using Goal Seek because we do not know what to enter for the goal value. The standard way around this limitation is to use differences, that is, to subtract the two formula cells and use the goal value of zero. Specifically, enter 3.5 in cell A2, enter $=$**A1** $+$ **A2** into cell A3, enter $=$**A1** $\times$ **A2** into cell A4, and enter $=$**A3** $-$ **A4** into cell A5. Here cell A5 contains $X + 3.5 - X \times 3.5$. Now, pull up the Goal Seek dialog box, and set cell **A5** to the value of 0 by changing cell **A1**. The result will be A1 equals 1.4; A2 equals 3.5; and A3 and A4 equal 4.9. By subtracting our two formula cells and setting the difference

FIGURE **5.23**
Excel®'s Goal Seek being used to solve $X + 2 = 5$, where cell $A3 = A1 + 2$.

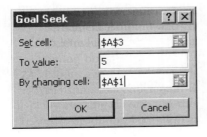

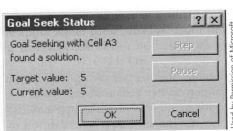

equal to zero, we can find the point where the two formulas are equal without knowing the value at which they are equal.

Beside the limitation that the target cell must be a known numerical value, Goal Seek allows only one unknown cell. Thus, Goal Seek can be helpful in a one-way sensitivity analysis where we allow one and only one variable to alter its value. Goal Seek is often used to find break-even values, such as when revenue equals cost. Finally, Goal Seek can be very helpful when exploring a model for insights, particularly for identifying breakeven points.

An Excel® Data Table can be helpful in carrying out a sensitivity analysis. As the name suggests, Data Table creates a table of output values based on a sequence of input values. For example, we could use Data Table to calculate the Net Annual Cost of Astoria based on a sequence of interest rates, such as 4.5%, 5.0%, 5.5%, 6.0%, and 6.5%. Data Table works much like linked decision trees in that a two-way communication bridge is established between the table of values and the model. First, a value, such as 4.5%, is taken from the table and sent to the model. Care must be taken to ensure that this value is sent to the correct cell, in this case the interest rate cell. The model then calculates Astoria's Net Annual Cost based on the value sent over. Finally, the computed Net Annual Cost is sent back to the table. Thus, Data Table can be used to determine the potential impact on the consequence value as an input value varies.

To create this particular table of values, we first enter the specific interest rate values (**4.5%, 5.0%, 5.5%, 6.0%, 6.5%**) in column J, as shown in Figure 5.24. Next, we enter the formula (or preferably a cell reference to the formula) one column to the right, and one row above the first row of our interest rates. In Figure 5.24, we entered the interest rates from J3 to J7, and in cell K2 we enter =**B23**, because B23 contains the formula for Astoria's Net Annual Cost. Finally, **highlight J2:K7**, click on the **Data** menu tab in Excel®, then click on the **What-If Analysis** button, and finally on **Data Table**. As we have a column of interest rates, we enter **B4** into the *Column input cell*. Why B4? Because B4 is the location of the interest rate used in the formula in B23. Clicking **OK** produces a table of Net Annual Costs for Astoria, each value based on its corresponding interest rate. Figure 5.24 shows that the interest rates that we entered are sent to cell B4, one at a time, and the corresponding Net Annual Cost is sent back to the table. For example, if the interest rate on their 30-year fixed mortgage is 4.5%, the Net Annual Cost will be $26,444 and jumps to $31,011 when the rate is 6.5%. Graphing the table of values produces a sensitivity graph.

A data table can be generalized in two different ways. First, there is no requirement that we have only one consequence measure. For example, if we want to calculate the Net Annual Cost of each property for the given sequence of interest rates, we simply add additional columns, one for each consequence measure. Begin by **selecting K3:K7** and **pressing Delete**. This clears the previous data table. Now insert =**C23** (Barnard's Net Annual Cost formula) in cell L2 and =**D23** (Charlotte's Net Annual Cost formula) in cell M2.

FIGURE **5.24**

Using Excel®'s Data Table to calculate the Net Annual Cost of Astoria for select values of Interest Rate. Steps 1–4 are repeated for each interest rate listed in column J.

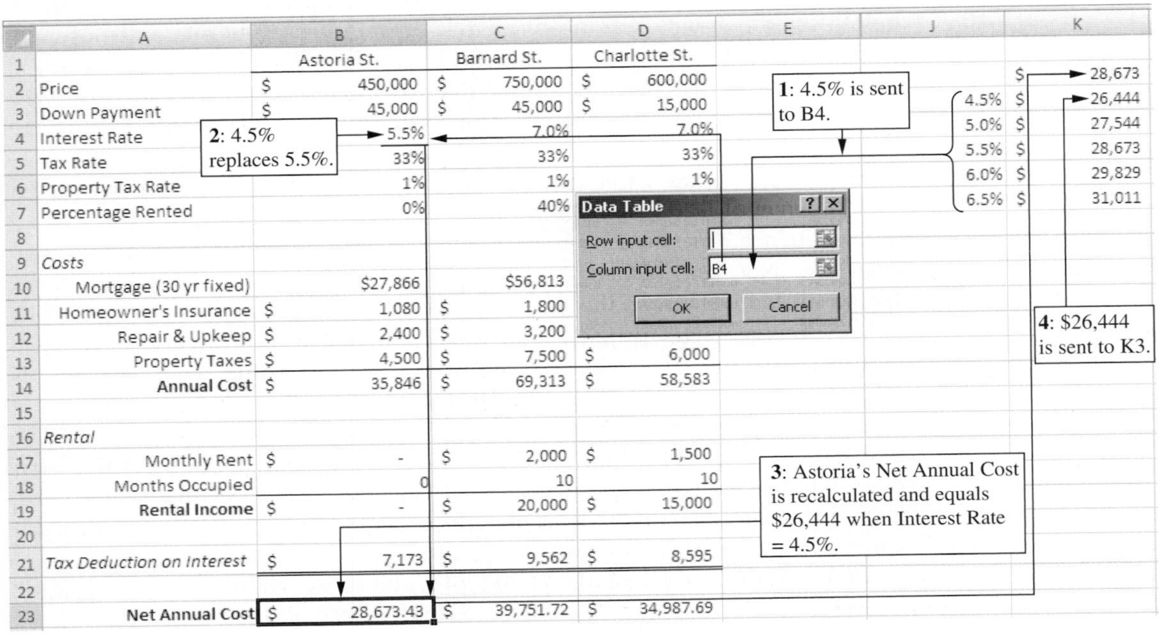

	A	B	C	D	E	J	K
		Astoria St.	Barnard St.	Charlotte St.			$ ➤ 28,673
1							
2	Price	$ 450,000	$ 750,000	$ 600,000	**1: 4.5% is sent to B4.**	4.5% $ ➤ 26,444
3	Down Payment	$ 45,000	$ 45,000	$ 15,000		5.0% $ 27,544
4	Interest Rate	**2: 4.5%** ➤5.5%	7.0%	7.0%		5.5% $ 28,673
5	Tax Rate	**replaces 5.5%.** 33%	33%	33%		6.0% $ 29,829
6	Property Tax Rate	1%	1%	1%		6.5% $ 31,011
7	Percentage Rented	0%	40%	Data Table [?][X]		
8				Row input cell:			
9	Costs			Column input cell: B4		
10	Mortgage (30 yr fixed)	$27,866	$56,813			
11	Homeowner's Insurance	$ 1,080	$ 1,800	OK Cancel		
12	Repair & Upkeep	$ 2,400	$ 3,200		**4: $26,444 is sent to K3.**
13	Property Taxes	$ 4,500	$ 7,500	$ 6,000		
14	Annual Cost	$ 35,846	$ 69,313	$ 58,583		
15						
16	Rental					
17	Monthly Rent	$ -	$ 2,000	$ 1,500		
18	Months Occupied	0	10	10	**3: Astoria's Net Annual Cost is recalculated and equals $26,444 when Interest Rate = 4.5%.**
19	Rental Income	$ -	$ 20,000	$ 15,000		
20						
21	Tax Deduction on Interest	$ 7,173	$ 9,562	$ 8,595		
22						
23	Net Annual Cost	$ 28,673.43	$ 39,751.72	$ 34,987.69		

Highlight J2:M7 and invoke **Data Table** again entering **B4** for the *Column input cell*. The result will be a table with the first column representing the interest rates, and the following three columns representing the Net Annual Costs of Astoria, Barnard, and Charlotte.

Data Tables can also be generalized to two-way sensitivity analysis. For example, if we wanted to determine how Astoria's Net Annual Cost changes for various interest rates (**4.5%, 5%, ..., 6.5%**) and various property tax rates (**1%, 1.5%, 2%**), we would enter a column of the specific interest rate values and a row of the specific property tax rates. The row of property tax rates must start one column to the right and one row above the interest rates. See Figure 5.25. The formula for Astoria's Net Annual Cost *must* be placed immediately above the first interest rate and immediately to the left of the first property tax rate. In Figure 5.25, we entered =B23 into cell J2. Now **highlight J2:M7**. Finally, pull up the **Data Table** dialog box, this time entering **B6** for the row input cell and **B4** for the column input cell. The result is the table of values shown in Figure 5.25, which reports the Net Annual Cost for Astoria for the 15 different combinations of interest rates and property taxes.

FIGURE **5.25**

Using Excel®'s Data Table to calculate a two-way table of Net Annual Cost of Astoria for select values of Interest Rate and Property Tax Rate.

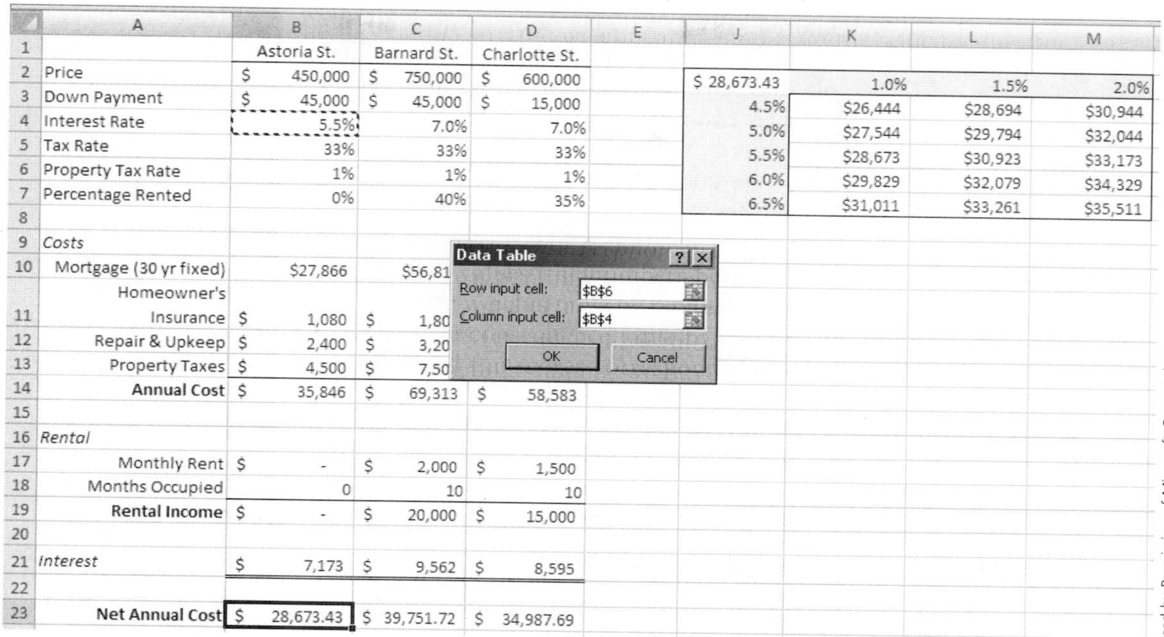

	A	B	C	D	E	J	K	L	M
1		Astoria St.	Barnard St.	Charlotte St.					
2	Price	$ 450,000	$ 750,000	$ 600,000		$ 28,673.43	1.0%	1.5%	2.0%
3	Down Payment	$ 45,000	$ 45,000	$ 15,000		4.5%	$26,444	$28,694	$30,944
4	Interest Rate	5.5%	7.0%	7.0%		5.0%	$27,544	$29,794	$32,044
5	Tax Rate	33%	33%	33%		5.5%	$28,673	$30,923	$33,173
6	Property Tax Rate	1%	1%	1%		6.0%	$29,829	$32,079	$34,329
7	Percentage Rented	0%	40%	35%		6.5%	$31,011	$33,261	$35,511
8									
9	Costs								
10	Mortgage (30 yr fixed)	$27,866	$56,81						
11	Homeowner's Insurance	$ 1,080	$ 1,80						
12	Repair & Upkeep	$ 2,400	$ 3,20						
13	Property Taxes	$ 4,500	$ 7,50						
14	Annual Cost	$ 35,846	$ 69,313	$ 58,583					
15									
16	Rental								
17	Monthly Rent	$ -	$ 2,000	$ 1,500					
18	Months Occupied	0	10	10					
19	Rental Income	$ -	$ 20,000	$ 15,000					
20									
21	Interest	$ 7,173	$ 9,562	$ 8,595					
22									
23	Net Annual Cost	$ 28,673.43	$ 39,751.72	$ 34,987.69					

Data Table dialog box:
Row input cell: $B$6
Column input cell: $B$4
OK   Cancel

One limitation to note regarding Data Tables is that the input cells must be on the same spreadsheet as the table itself. If your model and inputs are on a separate spreadsheet, you can simply move the inputs to the spreadsheet with the table.

SUMMARY

This chapter has presented an approach and several tools for performing sensitivity analysis. We have considered sensitivity analysis in the context of structuring decision models, analyzing dominance among alternatives, and assessing probabilities. Tornado diagrams and one- and two-way sensitivity graphs were developed, and we discussed ways to perform sensitivity analysis using PrecisionTree. The purpose of sensitivity analysis in the decision-analysis cycle is to provide guidance for the development and interpretation of a requisite decision model.

EXERCISES

5.1. What is the fundamental question that sensitivity analysis answers? Describe the role that sensitivity analysis plays in the development of a requisite decision model?

5.2. Some friends of yours have been considering purchasing a new home. They currently live 20 miles from town on a two-acre tract. The family consists of the mother, father, and two small children. The parents also are considering having more children, and they realize that as the children grow, they may become more involved in activities in town. As it is, most of the family's outings take place in town. Describe the role that sensitivity analysis could play in your friends' decision. What variables could be subjected to sensitivity analysis?

5.3. Over dinner, your father mentions that he is considering retiring from real-estate sales. He has found a small retail business for sale, which he is considering acquiring and running. There are so many issues to think about, however, that he has a difficult time keeping them all straight. After hearing about your decision-analysis course, he asks you whether you have learned anything that might help him in his decision. What kinds of issues are important in deciding whether to buy a retail business? Describe how he might use sensitivity analysis to explore the importance of these issues.

5.4. When purchasing a home, one occasionally hears about the possibility of "renting with an option to buy." This arrangement can take various forms, but a common one is that the renter simply pays rent and may purchase the house at an agreed-upon price. Rental payments typically are not applied toward purchase. The owner is not permitted to sell the house to another buyer unless the renter/option holder waives the right to purchase. The duration of the option may or may not be specified.

Suppose that a buyer is considering whether to purchase a house outright or rent it with an option to buy. Under what circumstances would renting with an option be a dominated alternative? Under what circumstances would it definitely not be dominated?

5.5. Explain why the lines separating the three regions in Figure 5.11 all intersect at Point D.

QUESTIONS AND PROBLEMS

5.6. *Cost-to-loss ratio problem.* Consider the decision problem shown in Figure 5.26. This basic decision tree often is called a cost-to-loss ratio problem and is characterized as a decision situation in which the question is whether to take some protective action in the face of possible adverse circumstances. For example, the umbrella problem (Figure 4.9) is a cost-to-loss ratio problem. Taking the umbrella incurs a fixed cost and protects against possible adverse weather. A farmer may face a cost-to-loss ratio problem if there is a threat of freezing weather that could damage a fruit crop. Steps can be taken to protect the orchard, but they are costly. If no steps are taken, the air temperature may or may not become cold enough to damage the crop.

Sensitivity analysis is easily performed for the cost-to-loss ratio problem. How large can the probability p become before "Take Protective Action" becomes the optimal (minimum expected cost) alternative? Given your answer, what kind of information does the decision maker need in order to make the decision? (*Hint:* This is an algebra problem. If that makes you uncomfortable, substitute numerical values for C, L, and p.)

5.7. *The cost-to-loss ratio problem continued.* The cost-to-loss ratio problem as shown in Figure 5.26 may be considered a simplified version of the actual situation. The protective action that may be taken may not provide perfect protection. Suppose that, even with protective action, damage D will be sustained with probability q. Thus, the decision tree appears as Figure 5.27. Explain how sensitivity analysis could be used to determine whether it is important to include the upper chance node with probability q and damage D.

5.8. An orange grower in Florida faces a dilemma. The weather forecast is for cold weather, and there is a 50% chance that the temperature tonight will be cold enough to freeze and destroy his entire crop, which is worth some $50,000. He can take two possible actions to try to alleviate his loss if the temperature drops. First, he could set burners in the

FIGURE **5.26**
Cost-to-loss ratio problem.

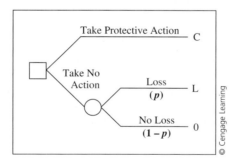

FIGURE **5.27**
More general version of the cost-to-loss problem.

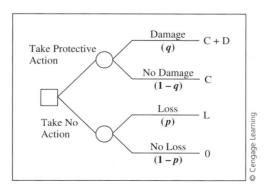

orchard; this would cost $5,000, but he could still expect to incur damage of approximately $15,000 to $20,000. Second, he could set up sprinklers to spray the trees. If the temperature drops, the water would freeze on the fruit and provide some insulation. This method is cheaper ($2,000), but less effective. With the sprinklers he could expect to incur as much as $25,000 to $30,000 of the loss with no protective action.

Compare the grower's expected values for the three alternatives he has, considering the various possible loss scenarios for the burners and the sprinklers. Which alternative would you suggest the grower take? Why?

5.9. An important application of sensitivity analysis occurs in problems involving multiple attributes. Many decision makers experience difficulty in assessing trade-off weights. A sensitivity analysis of the trade-off weight, though, can reveal whether a decision maker must make a more precise judgment. Reconsider the summer-job example described and analyzed in Chapter 4. In the analysis, we used trade-off weights of $k_s = 0.60$ for salary and $k_f = 0.40$ for fun (see Figure 4.28).

Suppose Sam Chu is uncomfortable with the precise assessment that $k_s = 0.60$. Sam does believe, though, that k_s could range from 0.50 up to 0.75. (Recall that k_s and k_f add up to 1, so by implication, k_f can range from 0.50 to 0.25, depending on the value of k_s.) Perform a sensitivity analysis on the expected overall score for the two jobs by varying k_s over this range. Is the forest job preferred for all values of k_s between 0.50 and 0.75?

5.10. A friend of yours can invest in a multiyear project. The cost is $14,000. Annual cash flows are estimated to be $5,000 per year for six years but could vary between $2,500 and $7,000. Your friend estimates that the cost of capital (interest rate) is 11%, but it could be as low as 9.5% and as high as 12%. The basis of the decision to invest will be whether the project has a positive net present value. Construct a tornado diagram for this problem. On the basis of the tornado diagram, advise your friend regarding either (1) whether to invest or (2) what to do next in the analysis.

5.11. Reconsider Hugh Liedtke's decision as diagrammed in Figure 4.2. Note that three strategies are possible: (1) accept $2 billion, (2) counteroffer $5 billion and then accept $3 billion if Texaco counteroffers, and (3) counteroffer $5 billion and then refuse $3 billion if Texaco counteroffers. Suppose that Liedtke is unsure about the probabilities associated with the final court outcome. Let $p = P(10.3 \text{ Billion})$ and $q = P(5 \text{ Billion})$ so that $1 - p - q = P(0 \text{ Billion})$. Create a two-way sensitivity graph that shows optimal strategies for Liedtke for possible values of p and q. (*Hint:* What is the constraint on $p + q$?) If Liedtke thinks that p must be at least 0.15 and q must be more than 0.35, can he make a decision without further probability assessment?

5.12. The tax situation for houses with rentals is a bit more complicated than we presented in the chapter. On one hand, Sanjay and Sarah must pay taxes on any rental income, which will increase their expenses. On the other hand, Sanjay and Sarah can depreciate the percentage of the home rented and can deduct a percentage of expenses for repair and upkeep. For example, 35% of the Charlotte house is rented, thus the depreciation amount (a straight-line depreciation over 27 years) for Charlotte is $\frac{Percentage\ Rented \times Price}{27} = \frac{35\% \times 600,000}{27} = \$7,778$. In addition, 35% of the repair and upkeep cost for Charlotte can be deducted from the rental income before computing the taxes. Incorporating these additional liabilities and deductions into net annual cost gives:

$$Net\ Annual\ Costs = Total\ Costs - (Rental\ Income + Tax\ Deduction).$$

$$Rental\ Income = (Monthly\ Rent \times Months\ Occupied).$$

$$
\begin{aligned}
Tax\ Deduction &= (Tax\ Rate \times (1 - Percentage\ Rented) \times Interest\ Paid) \\
&\quad + Depreciation \\
&= (Tax\ Rate \times (1 - Percentage\ Rented) \times P\% \times Mortgage) \\
&\quad + \frac{Percentage\ Rented \times Price}{27}
\end{aligned}
$$

$$
\begin{aligned}
Total\ Costs &= Mortgage + Home\ Owner's\ Insurance \\
&\quad + Repair\ \&\ Upkeep + (House\ Price \times Property\ Tax\ Rate) \\
&\quad + Taxes\ on\ Rental\ Income \\
&= Mortgage + Home\ Owner's\ Insurance + Repair\ \&\ Upkeep \\
&\quad + (House\ Price \times Property\ Tax\ Rate) + Tax\ Rate \\
&\quad \times (Monthly\ Rent \times Months\ Occupied) \\
&\quad - (Percentage\ Rented \times Repair\ \&\ Upkeep)
\end{aligned}
$$

Using this more complete formula, we can compute the Net Annual Cost of each property. Note that Sanjay and Sarah need only pay the taxes on rental income when there is a renter, but they can deduct depreciation whether the apartment is rented or not. Thus, depreciation provides Sanjay and Sarah with a small buffer when the apartment is vacant.

a) Using the variables and the upper and lower bounds given in Table 5.2 run a one-way sensitivity analysis on Sanjay and Sarah's three housing alternatives. Interpret the results.

b) How do the sensitivity results differ from what we found in the chapter?

c) Choose two variables to run a two-way sensitivity analysis.

5.13. The consequence variable used in the House-Hunting example was Net Annual Cost, but as we mentioned, houses are also purchased as investments, suggesting that it might be useful to include equity and appreciation in the consequence measure.

a) In this problem, we will consider the consequence measure Appreciation + Equity − Net Annual Cost. Sanjay and Sarah will gain equity in each property by paying down the loan. Averaging over the first five years, they will gain $6,131 in Astoria, $8,522 in Barnard, and $7,071 in Charlotte. To model appreciation, add a row to your spreadsheet model labeled Appreciation Percentage and enter 6.25% for Astoria. Then, use cell referencing; we will assume the same appreciation percentage across all three properties. Doing so should result in Appreciation + Equity − Net Annual Cost equaling $5,582 for Astoria, $17,576 for Barnard, and $10,771 for Charlotte. Run a one-way sensitivity analysis on the spreadsheet model using this new consequence measure and Table 5.2. Add Appreciation Percentage to the sensitivity analysis with lower bound −2% and upper bound 10%. Discuss the sensitivity graph of Appreciation Percentage. How important is Appreciation Percentage? Do any of the lines in the sensitivity graphs cross? For which variables do the sensitivity graphs cross and at what value?

b) Create a decision tree for the House-Hunting example by adding a chance node for Appreciation Percentage to the tree in Figure 5.11. Run a two-way sensitivity analysis on p_1 and q_1 from Figure 5.11, but using the consequence measure Appreciation + Equity − Net Annual Cost. How has this changed the results when using Net Annual Cost as the consequence measure?

c) We have looked at two different consequence measures for the House-Hunting example. Discuss the pros and cons of each measure.

DUMOND INTERNATIONAL, PART I

"So that's the simplified version of the decision tree based on what appear to be the critical issues," Nancy Milnor concluded. "Calculating expected values, it looks as though we should introduce the new product. Now, I know that we don't all agree on the numbers in the tree, so why don't we play around with them a little bit. I've got the data in the computer here. I can make any changes you want and see what effect they have on the expected value."

Nancy had just completed her presentation to the board of directors of DuMond International, which manufactured agricultural fertilizers and pesticides. The decision the board faced was whether to go ahead with a new pesticide product to replace an old one or whether to continue to rely on the current product, which had been around for years and was a good seller. The problem with the current product was that evidence was beginning to surface that showed that the chemical's use could create substantial health risks, and there even was some talk of banning the product. The new product still required more development, and the question was whether all of the development issues could be resolved in time to meet the scheduled

introduction date. And once the product was introduced, there was always the question of how well it would be received. The decision tree (Figure 5.28) that Nancy had presented to the board captured these concerns.

The boardroom was beginning to get warm. Nancy sat back and relaxed as she listened to the comments.

"Well, I'll start," said John Dilts. "I don't have much trouble with the numbers in the top half of the tree. But you have the chance of banning the current product fixed or pinned at 30%. That's high. Personally, I don't think there's more than a 10% chance of an out-and-out ban."

"Yeah, and even if there were, the current product ought to be worth $300,000 at least," added Pete Lillovich. "With a smaller chance of a ban and a higher value, surely we're better off with the old product!"

"Well, I don't know about you two," said Marla Jenkins. "I think we have a pretty good handle on what's going on with the current product. But I'd like to play the new product a little more conservatively. I know that the values at the ends of the branches on the top half of the tree are accounting's best guesses based

FIGURE **5.28**
DuMond's new
product decision.

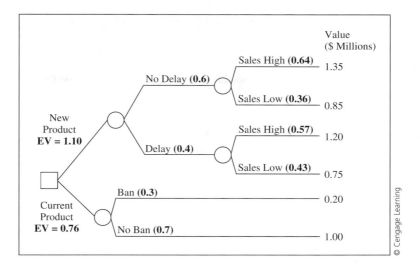

on a complete analysis, but maybe they should all be reduced by $100,000 just to play it safe. And maybe we should just set the probability of high sales equal to 50% regardless of the delay."

Steven Kellogg had been involved in the preliminary development of the new product more than anyone else. He piped up, "And the delay is actually more likely than no delay. I'd just reverse those probabilities so that there's a 60% chance of a delay. But I wouldn't make any changes on the lower part of the tree. I agree with Marla that we have a good idea about the performance of the current product and the prospects for a ban."

"I don't think it matters," countered Lillovich. "The changes John and I suggest make the

current product look better than it does in Nancy's analysis. Marla's and Steven's changes make the new product look worse. Either way, the effect is the same."

Nancy had kept track of the comments and suggested changes. She sat down at the computer and started to enter the changes. After a few moments, she grinned and turned to the board. "In spite of your changes," she said, "I believe I can persuade you that DuMond should go with the new product."

Question

1. Explain why Nancy believes that DuMond should go with the new product.

STRENLAR, PART II

Question

1. The Strenlar case study at the end of Chapter 4 required substantial modeling. Use sensitivity analysis to refine your model. In particular, you might consider (1) the interest rate used to calculate net present value, (2) legal fees, (3) the eventual price of PI's stock, (4) Strenlar's gross sales, (5) Fred's profits if Strenlar is successful (remembering that profits are linked to sales), (6) the probability of Strenlar being successful, and (7) the probability of winning the lawsuit.

Do you think that Fred's decision is sensitive to any of these variables? Try wiggling one variable at a time away from its base value (the value given in the case) while holding everything else at base value. How much can you wiggle the variable before the decision changes? At the end of your analysis, discuss your results and the implications for Fred's decision model. If he were to refine his model, what refinements should he make?

JOB OFFERS, PART II

Questions

1. Reconsider the Job Offers case at the end of Chapter 4. Suppose that Robin is unwilling to give a precise probability for disposable income with the Madison Publishing job. Conduct a sensitivity analysis on the expected value of the Madison Publishing job assuming that the probability of disposable income being $1,500 could range from zero to 1. Does the optimal choice—the job with the highest expected overall score—depend on the value of this probability? [*Hint:* Remember that probabilities must add up to 1, so P(Disposable

Income = $1,300) must equal 1 − P(Disposable Income = $1,500).]

2. Suppose Robin is unable to come up with an appropriate set of trade-off weights. Assuming that any combination of weights is possible as long as all three are positive and add up to 1, conduct a sensitivity analysis on the weights. Create a graph that shows the regions for which the different job offers are optimal (have the highest expected overall score). (*Hint:* Given that the three weights must sum to 1, this problem reduces to a two-way sensitivity analysis like the stock market example.)

THE HILLBLOM ESTATE, PART II

Recall the problem that Junior Larry faced in *The Hillblom Estate* at the end of Chapter 3. Consider the decision from Junior Larry's perspective.

Questions

1. Build a decision tree and calculate the expected value of continuing the case. What is the probability that Junior Larry will end up with nothing?

2. Run one-way and two-way sensitivity analyses on the decision tree. Which variables are the most influential? Why? Does the rank ordering of the alternatives ever change? If so, for which variables and at which values?

3. Based on your analysis, would you recommend that Junior Larry take the settlement or have the lawyers continue the case?

MANPADS

Ever since 9/11, there has been concern about the possibility of attacks on commercial airliners. In particular, man-portable air defense systems (MANPADS)—such as shoulder-launched missiles—have been used in aircraft attacks in Baghdad, Iraq, and Kenya. In this exercise, we will look at a model for evaluating the use of countermeasures against MANPADS on U.S. commercial aircraft.

Even though relatively little is known about the effects of a possible attack, there is some available information, enough to make an effort to address this problem. Below you will find information that can be used to create a simple model.

Specifications, Parameters, and Inputs:

1. Time horizon: 10 years. That is, we will consider the possibility of an attack over the next 10 years.

2. Decision: To use countermeasures or not. The specific type of countermeasure is not specified, but it is safe to say that it is probably an electronic device; such devices have been used by the U.S. military against infrared-guided missiles.

3. Uncertainties. Whether countermeasures are used or not, there are four uncertainties. Probabilities are shown in the tables below.

   a. Attempt/No attempt. Will there be an attempted attack on a U.S. aircraft over the next 10 years?

For this model, we will consider only the possibility of one attempt in ten years.

b. Interdiction/No interdiction. If there is an attempt, will it be interdicted (rendered harmless) or not?

c. Hit/Miss. If there is an attempt that is not interdicted, will the missile hit the aircraft or not?

d. Fatal crash/safe landing. If there is an attempt, not interdicted, that hits the aircraft, will the aircraft crash or be able to land safely?

Probabilities of uncertain events given no countermeasures.

p	P(Attempt)	0.50
q	P(Interdiction | attempt)[4]	0.05
b	P(Hit | attack, no countermeasures)	0.80
r	P(Crash | Hit)	0.25

[4]The probability of interdiction given an attempt.

If countermeasures are employed, they could be more or less effective in a variety of ways. We will model the extent to which countermeasures reduce each of the probabilities shown above:

Effectiveness of countermeasures. These are percentage changes in the probabilities above when countermeasures are used.

d	Deterrence effectiveness	50%
f	Interdiction effectiveness	50%
e	Diversion/destruction effectiveness	80%
g	Crash reduction effectiveness	0%

4. Consequences. We will consider five different kinds of consequences:

LL	Number of fatalities | crash	200
CP	Cost of the aircraft ($ million)	200
EL	Economic loss | fatal crash ($ billion)	100
FA	Number of false alarms per year	10
CC	Cost of countermeasures ($ billion)	10

We will value lives lost and false alarms in terms of dollars:

VOL	Value of a life ($ million)	5
VOF	Cost of a false alarm ($ million)	10

For simplicity, assume that all dollar values are present values, so you can ignore discounting.

Finally, some outcomes that do not involve a crash may result in an economic loss—a loss smaller than if a crash had occurred. We will model two such cases as percentages of the loss in case there is a crash:

a	Percent of economic loss | hit and safe landing	25%
b	Percent of economic loss | miss	10%

All other outcomes (no attack, or an attempt that is successfully interdicted) result in no cost, except the cost of countermeasures if they are used.

Build a decision tree to model this problem. The basic decision is whether to adopt countermeasures. Be sure to use good modeling practice: in the tree or in any formulas, use cell references to any input or constant. This will make it possible to perform sensitivity analysis on the inputs.

Questions

1. Which alternative has the lowest expected cost, countermeasures or no countermeasures?

2. Create a risk profile for each alternative. Based on a comparison of the two risk profiles, how would you describe the effect that countermeasures have on the risk associated with this decision?

3. The preceding inputs are actually pretty soft, and it will be important to perform sensitivity analysis to understand how changes in them might impact the decision. Can you tell anything about which inputs might have the most impact on the expected costs of the alternatives?

Source: D. von Winterfeldt, T. O'Sullivan (2006). "Should We Protect Commercial Airplanes Against Surface-to-Air Missile attacks by Terrorists?" *Decision Analysis*, 3 (2006), 63–75.

REFERENCES

Sensitivity analysis is an important addition to the decision analyst's bag of tricks. As more complicated decision problems have been tackled, it has become obvious that sensitivity analysis plays a central role in guiding the analysis and interpreting the results.

A good general overview of sensitivity analysis can be found in Saltelli, Chan, and Scott (2000). Overviews of sensitivity analysis oriented toward decision analysis can be found in Samson (1988), von Winterfeldt and Edwards (1986), and Watson and Buede (1987). In particular, Watson and Buede use real-world examples to show how sensitivity analysis is a central part of the decision-analysis modeling strategy. Phillips (1982) describes an application in which sensitivity analysis played a central part in obtaining consensus among the members of a board of directors.

Howard (1988) presents tornado diagrams and gives them their name. This approach to deterministic sensitivity analysis, along with other sensitivity-analysis tools, is discussed by McNamee and Celona (1987). The spiderplot, which can be generated using PrecisionTree is described by Eschenbach (1992). The spiderplot is similar to the tornado diagram in that it allows simultaneous comparison of the impact of

several different variables on the consequence or expected value.

Eschenbach, T. G. (1992) "Spiderplots versus Tornado Diagrams for Sensitivity Analysis." *Interfaces*, 22(6), 40–46.

Howard, R. A. (1988) "Decision Analysis: Practice and Promise." *Management Science*, 34, 679–695.

McNamee, P., and J. Celona (1987) *Decision Analysis for the Professional with Supertree*. Redwood City, CA: Scientific Press.

Phillips, L. D. (1982) "Requisite Decision Modelling." *Journal of the Operational Research Society*, 33, 303–312.

Phillips, L. D. (1982) "Requisite Decision Modelling." *Journal of the Operational Research Society*, 33, 303–312.

Saltelli, A., Chan, K. and Scott, M., eds. (2000) *Sensitivity Analysis*. New York: Wiley.

Samson, D. (1988) *Managerial Decision Analysis*. Homewood, IL: Irwin.

von Winterfeldt, D., and W. Edwards (1986) *Decision Analysis and Behavioral Research*. Cambridge: Cambridge University Press.

Watson, S., and D. Buede (1987) *Decision Synthesis*. Cambridge: Cambridge University Press.

CHAPTER 6

Organizational Use of Decision Analysis

SAMUEL E. BODILY

Effective organizational use of decision analysis goes far beyond having individuals in the organization who know how to do decision analysis. In this chapter, we consider how decision analysis may be laced into an organization in such a way that value is created for the organization by helping organization members make choices that have a high chance of improving their strategy and operation. We recommend a process that interweaves a decision board and a strategy team as they work together through six steps. The process focuses on alternative generation, evaluation, and implementation, and is grounded in decision analysis. Tools for structuring of analysis and creativity enhancement are crucial to success, and much of this chapter is about creativity. Collaborative efforts to frame the assessment of risk and make explicit value trade-offs are integral to the process. Risk-management techniques expand the set of alternatives to add value and reduce risk. Companies—in the pharmaceutical, oil-and-gas, and other industries—have been very successful with this process.[1]

Organizations exist to add value to their owners and other stakeholders. Value creation requires leadership in the three areas

---

[1] While many schools and consulting companies have contributed to this process over several decades, Strategic Decisions Group and its predecessors (e.g., SRI International) have been the leader in developing the process we describe here, combining the ideas and work of many individuals.

This chapter was written by Samuel E. Bodily, John Tyler Professor at the Darden Graduate Business School, University of Virginia, Copyright Samuel E. Bodily 2004. It includes parts of the previous chapter 6 of the 2nd Edition of *Making Hard Decisions with Decision tools Suite.*

FIGURE **6.1**
Value creation
requires integrating
three different
management
activities.

Source: Reprinted by
permission, Bodily & Allen,
*A Dialogue Process for
Choosing Value-Creating
Strategies, Interfaces*, 29, 6,
1999. Copyright 1999 the
Institute for Operations
Research and the Manage-
ment Sciences (INFORMS),
7240 Parkway Drive, Suite
300, Hanover, MD 21076
USA.

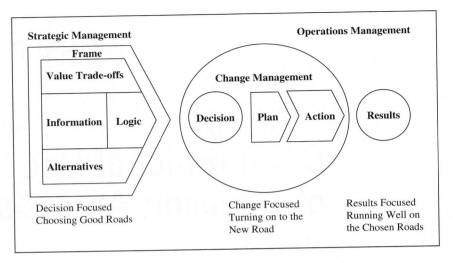

shown in Figure 6.1: strategic management, change management, and operations management. Organizations will be successful to the extent that leaders can select an appropriate path, move onto that path's direction, and then move effectively along that path. Organizational decision analysis succeeds to the extent that it anticipates these needs and provides a process that will flow through all three components.

THE DECISION-MAKING PROCESS

The process for making decisions in an organization should be tailored to the characteristics of the decision problem. For example, many decision analyses, while analytically complex, may be entirely personal: the consequences affect only one person, all the information going into the decision analysis can be assessed by that individual, and the choice can be implemented by the decision maker. Contrast that with family decisions, where various family members contribute assessments of probabilities and consequences, express preference trade-offs, face the consequences together, and jointly implement the ultimate choice. Going further, within organizations, such as a firm, many people will provide expertise in generating alternatives, assessing consequences, implementing various aspects of the choice, and so on. We address the latter end of the spectrum here. We are focusing on those decision situations represented by the upper-right box of Figure 6.2, where high organizational complexity comes together with high analytical difficulty.

A Six-Step Decision Process: The Lacing Diagram

A six-step process (often referred to as the dialogue decision process) has proven effective in conducting strategic decision analyses for companies. A key to the success of this process is the involvement of a decision board,

FIGURE **6.2**
The decision-making process needs to be tailored to the problem's characteristics.

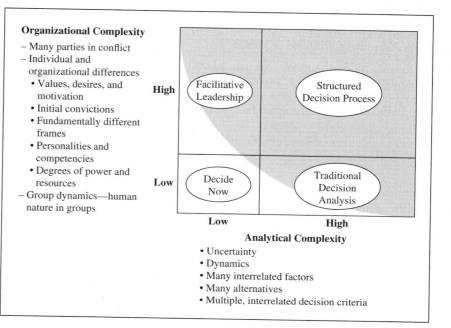

Organizational Complexity

– Many parties in conflict
– Individual and organizational differences
  • Values, desires, and motivation
  • Initial convictions
  • Fundamentally different frames
  • Personalities and competencies
  • Degrees of power and resources
– Group dynamics—human nature in groups

High

Facilitative Leadership

Structured Decision Process

Low

Decide Now

Traditional Decision Analysis

Low   **High**

Analytical Complexity

  • Uncertainty
  • Dynamics
  • Many interrelated factors
  • Many alternatives
  • Multiple, interrelated decision criteria

consisting of those closest to the business unit that is affected by and responsible for implementing the decision. A team of line managers and staff conducts the decision analysis. This team includes those best equipped to collect information and analyze it objectively, and should not be composed entirely of advocates or champions of an alternative. The key to success is to use the steps of the decision process to lace together the decision board and the decision-analysis team (or strategy team). The lacing diagram in Figure 6.3 illustrates how the process pulls together the components and binds the two teams.

The decision board must agree to the decision made and take the lead in implementing the related strategy. The makeup of both boards is critical in ensuring that they are teams that work together well and that they are the actual owners of decisions and results. Dialogue between the decision board and the analysis team is indispensable both for progress along the steps of the process and for knitting together the two teams toward a unified strategy. Contrast this approach with the usual advocacy approach, where factions propose and lobby for their favored choice.

In many cases, a decision analysis is done by someone who has no ownership of the decision and no appreciation of the issues that surround the choice of an alternative and its implementation. And the first time the analyst actually has any interaction with the decision maker(s) is often when the analysis is done and a presentation of a proposed choice is made. Success is much more likely if the decision board has interacted with the analysis team through the entire decision-analysis process. The decision board will charter

FIGURE **6.3**
The dialogue decision process is designed for successful strategy development and implementation.

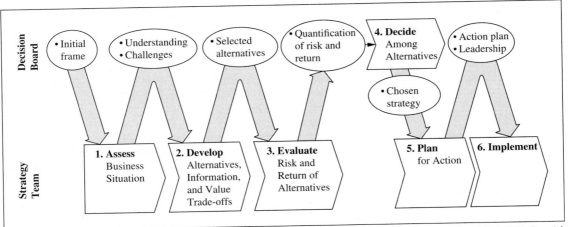

Source: Reprinted by permission, Bodily & Allen, *A Dialogue Process for Choosing Value-Creating Strategies, Interfaces*, 29, 6, 1999. Copyright 1999 the Institute for Operations Research and the Management Sciences (INFORMS), 7240 Parkway Drive, Suite 300, Hanover, MD 21076 USA.

the decision process, approve the progress at various points in the process (providing information, values, and trade-offs), and ultimately make the decision. The analysis team will consist of subject-matter experts and analysts who develop and structure the alternatives and information, evaluate alternatives, and plan implementation. Let's consider the individual steps in the process where these teams interact.

STEP 1 ASSESS *the Business Situation.*

The first step in the process sets the frame. This includes the purpose, the perspective, and the scope of the decision. It may involve a business assessment (Figure 6.4)—an analysis of the organization's formula for success, how it adds value in its value chain (Porter 1998), and how the

FIGURE **6.4**
Step 1, Assess what we need to know and what needs to be delivered.

Source: Bodily & Allen, *Interfaces* 29:6

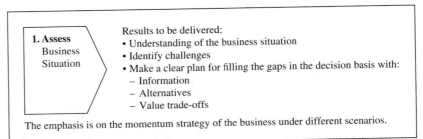

FIGURE **6.5**
Understanding a business-success formula can reveal additional challenges.

Source: Reprinted by permission, Bodily & Allen, *A Dialogue Process for Choosing Value-Creating Strategies, Interfaces*, 29, 6, 1999. Copyright 1999 the Institute for Operations Research and the Management Sciences (INFORMS), 7240 Parkway Drive, Suite 300, Hanover, MD 21076 USA.

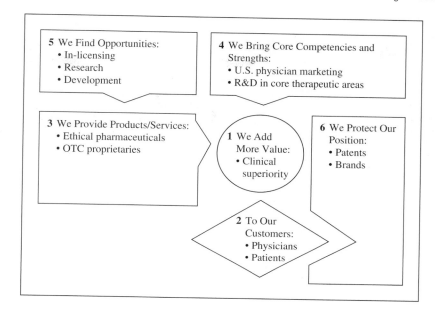

organization competes within its industry. A good business assessment looks forward and considers how external forces will affect the organization in the future. It understands the momentum (status quo) strategy of the business under different scenarios. It identifies the challenges and opportunities of the firm.

Challenges are expressed as statements of specific needs for value creation. A starting point for developing challenges is to examine the success formula for the business. Figure 6.5 is a description of a formula for doing business from a composite pharmaceutical company (Bodily and Allen 1999), which we call Therapharma. The success of this firm relied on strong marketing to U.S. physicians. In discussing the company's success formula, it became apparent that future success would depend on proprietary over-the-counter drugs (OTCs), marketed directly to consumers, not doctors. This ability was missing and needed to be developed. The inability to rush products to market also became apparent.

In the Therapharma case, it was important to frame the decision problem correctly: What will the firm's future success rely on, and how can we ensure that the company has the necessary capabilities? Setting a proper frame is often neglected in a decision analysis. This may result in the scope's being too narrow or too wide. For Therapharma, a broad frame was needed; a narrower frame might have missed the coming changes in the industry and what the company would have to do to cope with those changes.

You can think of framing as similar to what you do when taking a photograph. You compose the elements that you wish to be included in the picture and cut out extraneous features. Just as poor photographic framing can lead to mediocre or even unattractive snapshots, incorrect decision frames can lead to misguided decisions. The frame may be too much of a

FIGURE **6.6**
Nine-Dot Puzzle.

Connect the dots using four straight lines without lifting your pencil.

Source: *Conceptual Blockbusting: A Guide to Better Ideas by* James L. Adams. Copyright © 2001 James L. Adams. Reprinted by permission of Basic Books, a member of the Perseus Books Group.

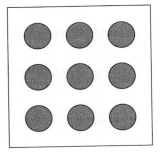

close-up, for example, by focusing on the organization's actions without considering competitors' reactions, which may entirely negate what the organization does. Alternatively, it may be too wide-angle by conducting a comparative analysis of the most attractive industry in which to operate when the salient question is simply whether it is time to upgrade a particular product.

As a little exercise in setting the appropriate frame, consider the classic nine-dot puzzle. Lay out nine dots in a square, three dots per row (Figure 6.6), and then, without lifting your pencil, draw four straight lines that cross all nine dots. Try it before you read on. The epilogue to this chapter gives the standard solution as well as many surprising solutions that Adams (1979) has collected from creative readers.

The nine-dot puzzle is a nice example, but what does this block have to do with framing decisions? People often look at problems with tacitly imposed constraints, which are sometimes appropriate and sometimes not. Suppose you believe you need more warehouse space for your business, so you have your real-estate agent look for warehouses of a specific size to rent. The size, however, may be an inappropriate constraint. Perhaps so much space is unnecessary in a single location, or perhaps the space may be divided among several smaller warehouses. Maybe some characteristic of your product would permit a smaller warehouse to be modified in a clever way to provide adequate storage.

Issue raising is an essential part of framing a decision problem. An "issue" is an aspect of the decision problem having to do with values or objectives (what we want), the bounds or constraints on the problem (what we can do), and information (what we know). Sometimes issue-raising is done using a SWOT analysis (strengths, weaknesses, opportunities, threats). Identifying issues is difficult for many organizations, making it that much more important for organizations to develop the ability and regularly practice identifying important issues.

Clear framing and understanding of issues should make it possible for decision makers in an organization to agree on a simple vision statement. A good statement answers three questions: What are we going to do? Why are we doing this? How will we know if we are successful? Agreement on a vision statement for a project helps ensure that team members understand and accept a shared purpose.

ORGANIZATIONAL ISSUES IN ENHANCING CREATIVITY AND ENABLING CHOICES

While these questions seem simple, coming up with top-quality answers is not. Creativity is necessary. Although creativity is often thought of as important for the process of generating alternatives, it can help with all parts of an organization's decision-making process, especially the first steps of framing, issue-raising, and developing a clear vision statement.

Without a doubt, different organizations have different characteristics or cultures, and organizational culture can have a strong influence on how the organization copes with decision situations. For example, an organization may have a culture that promotes open criticism and judging of ideas or that practices stereotyping in subtle ways. Such company traditions may discourage humor, playfulness, artistic thinking or openness to change, thereby reducing the creative potential of individuals in the organization and limiting the organization's ability to frame its decisions, identify key issues, and ultimately to consider a wide range of available opportunities.

By their very nature, organizations can impede creative thought. As Adams (1979, 143) points out, "The natural tendency of organizations to routinize, decrease uncertainty, increase predictability, and centralize functions and controls is certainly at odds with creativity." Other features of organizations can also hinder creativity. Examples include excessive formal procedures (red tape) or lack of cooperation and trust among coworkers. Hierarchical organizational structures can hinder creativity, which, in turn, can be exacerbated by autocratic supervisors.

While our focus here is on a process for organizational decision, individual and organizational creativity is inextricably tied to its success. "Creativity and Organizations" below summarizes some of the extensive work on organizational creativity as background to our discussion of the organizational decision process.

Creativity and Organizations

Teresa Amabile has studied creativity and organizations for more than 30 years. Her work has led to a detailed model of individual creativity in the organizational context (Amabile 1988, 2011). First, individual creativity requires three ingredients: expertise in the domain, skill in creative thinking, and intrinsic motivation to do the task well. In other words, we need someone who is good at what he or she does, who likes to do it just because it is interesting and fun, and who has some skill in creative thinking, perhaps along the lines of the creativity-enhancing techniques we discuss later in this chapter.

Amabile's work shows how the organizational environment can influence individual creativity. In particular, she warns that expecting detailed and critical evaluation, being closely watched, focusing on tangible rewards, competing with other people, and having limited choices and resources for doing the job can all hinder one's creativity. When she compares high- and low-creativity scenarios in organizations, however, the results depend on maintaining a delicate balance. For example, workers need clear overall goals, but at the same time, they need latitude in how to achieve those goals. Likewise, evaluation must be focused on the work itself (as opposed to the person) and provides informative and constructive help. Such evaluation ideally involves peers as well as supervisors. Although a focus on tangible rewards can be detrimental, knowing that there will be recognition of one's successful creative efforts is important. A sense of urgency can create a challenging atmosphere, particularly if individuals understand the importance of the problem on which they are working. If the challenge is viewed as artificial, however (e.g., competing with another division in the company or having an arbitrary deadline), the effect can be to decrease creativity. Thus, although creativity is essentially an individual phenomenon, managers can have a significant impact on creativity in their organizations through goal setting, evaluation, recognition and rewards, and creating pressure that reflects a genuine need for a creative solution.

Finally, even though managers can help individuals in their organizations be more creative, one can develop a "blind spot" because of a long-term association with a particular firm; it becomes difficult to see things in a new light simply because certain procedures have been followed or perspectives adopted over a long time. The German word for this situation (*betriebsblind*) literally means "company-blind." One of the important roles that consultants play is to bring a new perspective to the client's situation.

Once the organization has framed the decision and uncovered relevant issues, those issues must be sorted into the components of a decision analysis. This is illustrated in Figure 6.7, showing how the issue-raising process results in decisions, uncertainties, and values. In the next stage, the relationships among these components will be refined.

FIGURE **6.7**
Categorizing the issues focuses attention on key decisions, uncertainties, and values.

Source: © *by Strategic Decisions Group.* All rights reserved. Used by permission.

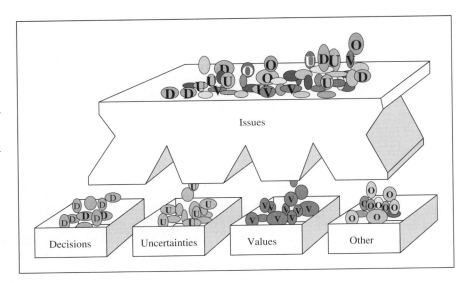

STEP 2 DEVELOP *Information, Value Tradeoffs, and Alternatives.*

The second step of the six-step process is to develop the structure for the issues and challenges identified in Step 1. In particular, the issues that have been identified and sorted in Step 1 are further refined. Individuals with different viewpoints may be brought together to discuss and evaluate each issue that has been raised in order to further understand how best to incorporate the issue into the decision analysis model.

For this chapter, we will focus on developing alternatives. Developing information consists largely of learning more about the uncertainties; in Chapters 7–12, we consider these issues in considerable depth. In the spirit of this chapter, it is interesting to note that creativity techniques can be used to see uncertainties from a variety of perspectives and to identify sources of information that might have been otherwise overlooked. We have already discussed value trade-offs in Chapters 3 and 4 and will return to the topic in Chapters 15–16. However, we will see that we can use Value-Focused Thinking as a useful basis for developing alternatives.

DEVELOPING ALTERNATIVES: UNDERSTANDING THE CREATIVE PROCESS

Individual creativity stems from a capacity for making unusual and new mental associations of concepts (Campbell 1960, Mednick 1962, Staats 1968). Campbell proposes that creative thought is just one manifestation of a general process by which people acquire new knowledge and thereby learn about the world. The first step in this process is the production of "variations," a result of mentally associating elements of a problem in new ways. People who are more creative are better at generating a wider range of variations as they think about the problems they face. Having a broader range of life experiences and working in the right kind of environment can facilitate the production of variations. Finally, some people simply are better at recognizing and seizing appropriate creative solutions as they arise; the ability to come up with creative solutions is not very helpful if one ignores those solutions later. A number of authors have identified phases of the individual creative-thought process. For example, Wallas (1926) identified preparation, incubation, illumination, and verification.

1. **Preparation:** In this first stage, the individual learns about the problem, its elements, and their relation to each other. It may include looking at the problem from different perspectives or asking other people what they know or think about the problem. From a decision-making point of view, this stage is very similar to problem structuring as delineated in Chapters 2 and 3. Spending effort in understanding fundamental objectives, decisions that must be made (along with the immediately available set of alternatives),

uncertainties inherent in the situation, and how these elements relate to each other—all prepare the decision maker for creative identification of new alternatives.

2. **Incubation:** In the second stage, the prepared decision maker explores, directly or indirectly, a multitude of different paths toward different futures. We might also use the term "production" or "generation of issues." The decision maker may do many things that seem to have a low chance of generating a new issue, such as eliminating assumptions or adopting an entirely different perspective. Apparently, frivolous activities may evoke the idea of the decision maker's "playing" with the decision. Many authors have included in this phase unconscious processing of information known about the decision. The literature on creativity contains several well-known and oft-quoted examples of this unconscious process, including Kekule's dream that led to the discovery of the chemical structure of the benzene ring and Poincaré's discovery of the fuchsian family of groups and functions in mathematics.

One explanation of unconscious incubation as a valid element of the creative process has been suggested by researchers in artificial intelligence. The explanation is based on a "blackboard" model of memory in the human brain. When the brain is in the process of doing other things—when a problem is incubating—parts of the blackboard are erased and new items put up. Every so often, the new information just happens to be pertinent to the original problem, and the juxtaposition of the new and old information suggests a creative solution; in other words, the process of coming up with a new and unusual association can result simply from the way the brain works. An attractive feature of this theory is that it explains why incubation works only a small percentage of the time. Too bad it works so infrequently!

Beyond the literature's examples and the speculation described previously about how the brain works, however, there is little hard evidence that unconscious processes are at work searching for creative solutions (Baron 1988). Still, it is a romantic thought, and if it provides an excuse for many of us to relax a little, perhaps the reduced stress and refocusing of our attention is enough to help us be more creative when we are trying to be.

3. **Illumination:** This is the instant of becoming aware of a new candidate solution to a problem, that flash of insight when all the pieces come together, either spontaneously (Aha!) or as the result of careful study and work. Wallas described illumination as a separate stage, but you can see that illumination is better characterized as the culmination of the incubation stage.

4. **Verification:** In the final step, the decision maker must verify that the candidate solution does, in fact, have merit. (How many times have you thought you had the answer to a difficult problem, only to realize later—sometimes moments, sometimes much later—that your "dream solution" turned out to be just that: an impossible dream?) The verification stage requires the careful thinker to turn back to the hard logic of the problem at hand to evaluate the quality of the candidate solution. In our decision-making context, this means looking very carefully at a newly

invented alternative in terms of whether it satisfies the constraints of the problem and how well it performs relative to the fundamental objectives.

Although there are many ways to think about the creative-thought process, the cognitive approach, which was described previously, including the stages of creativity, can help us identify issues related to a decision. An online supplement for this chapter provides other techniques for enhancing creativity as well as tips for removing common mental blocks to creativity.

Brainstorming techniques may play an important role in developing alternatives with a team. The team can conduct an idea-generation session involving participants with different viewpoints. In order to promote creative thinking, de Bono (1992) suggests these rules for a brainstorming session:

- Suspend judgment as ideas are proposed.
- Avoid criticism.
- Focus on a quantity of ideas.
- Encourage people to build on each other's ideas.
- Challenge the conventional wisdom of the business.
- Keep a clear record of all ideas.
- Have fun/be creative.

VALUE-FOCUSED THINKING FOR CREATING ALTERNATIVES

Another important technique for generating alternatives, mentioned in Chapter 3, is the use of Value-Focused Thinking. Keeney (1992) stresses that an individual, group, or organization that understands its values and objectives clearly is perfectly positioned to look for decision opportunities proactively rather than merely reacting to decision problems served up by life. As you may agree, life does not always generously provide decision situations with many attractive options, but instead often seems to pose difficult decision problems that must be addressed, often under trying circumstances.

Keeney (1992, Chapters 7 and 8) describes a number of different ways in which fundamental and means objectives can be used as a basis for creating new alternatives for decision problems. In this section, we review some of these techniques.

Fundamental Objectives

The most basic techniques use the fundamental objectives directly. For example, take one fundamental objective and, ignoring the rest, invent an alternative (possibly hypothetical) that is as good as it could be for that one objective. Do this for each fundamental objective, one at a time, and keep track of all the alternatives you generate. Now go back and consider pairs of objectives. What are good alternatives that balance these two objectives? After doing this for various combinations of objectives, look at the alternatives you have listed. Could you modify any of them so that they would be feasible or perhaps satisfy the remaining objectives better? Can you combine any of the alternatives?

A related approach is to consider all the fundamental objectives at once and imagine what an alternative would look like that is perfect in all dimensions; call this the ideal alternative. Most likely, it is impossible. What makes it impossible? If the answer is constraints, perhaps you can remove or relax some of those constraints.

Still another possibility is to go in the opposite direction. Find a good alternative and think of ways to improve it. The fact that the alternative is a good one in the first place can reduce the pressure of finding a better one. In searching for a better one, examine the alternative carefully in terms of the objectives. On which objectives does it perform poorly? Can it be improved in these dimensions? For example, Keeney (1992) describes an analysis of possible sites for a hydroelectric-power plant. One of the potential sites was very attractive economically but had a large environmental impact, which made it substantially less desirable. On further study, however, the design of the facility at the site was modified to reduce the environmental impact while maintaining the economic advantage.

Means Objectives

We mentioned back in Chapter 3 that the means objectives can provide a particularly fruitful hunting ground for new alternatives. The reason for this is simply that the means objectives provide guidance on what to do to accomplish the fundamental objectives. In complicated problems with many fundamental objectives and many related means objectives, this approach can generate many possible courses of action. As an illustration of many alternatives generated by examining the means objectives, see the nuclear waste decision situation below.

Transportation of Nuclear Waste

One of the problems with the use of fission reactors for generating electricity is that the reactors generate substantial amounts of radioactive waste that can be highly toxic for extremely long periods of time. Thus, management of the waste is necessary, and one possibility is to place it in a storage facility of some sort. Transporting the waste, however, is itself hazardous. In describing the problem, Keeney (1992) notes that the decision situation includes the selection of a type of storage cask in which the material will be shipped, followed by the selection of a transportation route and a choice as to how many casks to ship at once. The uncertainties include whether an accident occurs, the amount of radiation released, and whether an efficient evacuation plan exists if an accident occurs.

Means objectives are associated with each of the decisions and uncertainties. For example, a means objective is to select the best possible cask, which might include designing a special kind of cask out of a particular material with appropriate size and wall-thickness specifications. Selecting a transportation route that travels through a sparsely populated area is a means objective to reduce potential exposure in the case of an accident. In selecting the number of casks to ship at once, one would want to balance the chance of smaller accidents that could occur with more frequent but smaller shipments against the chance of a larger accident that could occur with larger and less frequent shipments.

In examining the uncertainties, obvious means objectives come to mind. For example, an important means objective is to reduce the chance of an accident, which, in turn, suggests strict rules for nuclear-waste transportation (slow speeds, driving during daylight hours, special licensing of drivers, additional maintenance of roads along the route, and so on). Reducing the amount of radiation released in an accident and increasing the chance of an efficient evacuation plan's being in place suggest the development of special emergency teams and procedures at all points along the transportation route (Keeney 1992, 205–7).

Source: Keeney 1992, 205–7

In another example, we can use a means network directly. Take the automotive-safety example that we discussed in Chapter 3; the problem is to find ways to maximize safety of automotive travel and, according to the fundamental objectives (Figure 3.1), maximizing safety means minimizing minor injuries, serious injuries, and deaths of both adults and children. The means-objectives network is reproduced here as Figure 6.8. You can see that each node in the network suggests particular alternatives. The objective of maximizing use of vehicle-safety features suggests that currently available features might be mandated or incentives might be provided to manufacturers. Likewise, incentives (e.g., a reduced insurance premium) might be given to automobile drivers who use safety features. Further down in the network we find the objective of educating the public. We already have widespread driver-education programs for new drivers—what about providing incentives for adult drivers to take periodic refresher courses? To combat drunken driving in particular, many U.S. states have implemented a combination of tougher traffic laws and public-education programs.

You can see from these examples how useful the means objectives can be for identifying new alternatives. Moreover, using a means-objectives network can ensure that as many aspects of the decision problem as possible are covered; the decision maker can see exactly what the new alternatives help achieve, and perhaps can further develop the alternatives to attain a level of balance among the fundamental and means objectives. For example,

FIGURE **6.8**
A means-objective network for improving automotive safety.

Source: Adapted from Keeney (1992 p. 70).

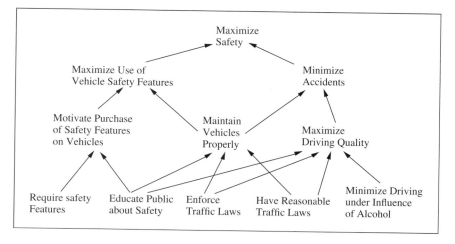

in examining a set of safety proposals, matching the proposals against means and fundamental objectives might reveal that safety of children has not been explicitly addressed or that the set of proposals currently under consideration do nothing to encourage proper vehicle maintenance.

STRATEGY TABLES

In some cases, alternatives are complex and numerous enough to warrant the use of a strategy table. In a strategy table, such as that shown in Figure 6.9 for Thera-pharma, the first column contains a list of strategies. For purposes of this table, a strategy is a path of choices made in various areas of activity, each area associated with the other columns in the table. For example, the focused-reallocation strategy (indicated by solid-line ovals) includes the following choices in the five areas:

- Build or acquire companies or joint venture to achieve critical sales-force mass in Germany, Japan, etc.
- Maintain current sales-force levels and increase advertising.
- Limit out-licensing to low-potential drugs and focused in-licensing with joint research agreements.
- Stay out of generics and promote trademarks to prevent share erosion.

FIGURE **6.9**
Each alternative strategy comprises a consistent set of choices—one option under each decision.

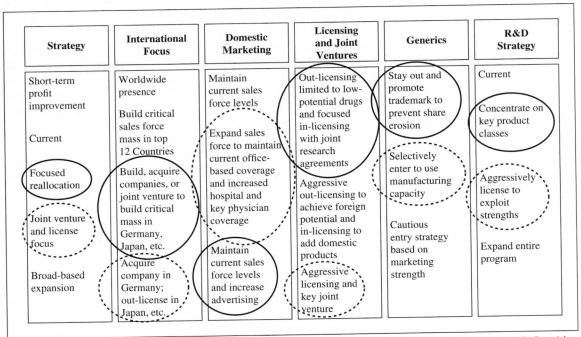

Source: Reprinted by permission, Bodily & Allen, *A Dialogue Process for Choosing Value-Creating Strategies, Interfaces*, 29, 6, 1999. Copyright 1999 the Institute for Operations Research and the Management Sciences (INFORMS), 7240 Parkway Drive, Suite 300, Hanover, MD 21076 USA.

- Concentrate R&D on key product classes (including three existing major therapeutic areas).

The joint-venture-and-license-focus strategy (dotted ovals) has different choices in each area.

There are a large number of potential strategy alternatives, specifically $4 \times 3 \times 3 \times 3 \times 4 = 432$. While many of these combinations would be infeasible or obviously unwise, thinking about various combinations may raise innovative possibilities that would otherwise be overlooked. It is especially useful to look for so-called *hybrid* strategies that take the best column choices for two or more attractive strategies and combine them into a strategy that may be even more attractive.

The Therapharma example is a good one for understanding how Step 2 in the organizational decision process contributes to the development of information, values, and alternatives. During Step 2, the tools of previous chapters, including decision trees and influence diagrams are used to structure the uncertainties and decisions. Any information gaps are identified and filled. For Therapharma, one information challenge was to better understand when and with what probability pharmaceuticals under development would be registered for sale. This challenge led to a pilot decision analysis of each of the major development programs in the clinic, and these analyses were based on the best information available, including the latest clinical information and attitudes of the registration authorities such as the U.S. Food and Drug Administration.

It is important to note that the decision process relies on the strategy team working with each other on this structuring—and together with others on the decision board or approved by the decision board. As the structure of the decision takes form, the strategy team asks for buy-in from the decision board, which serves to lace together the two teams.

STEP 3 EVALUATE *the Risk and Return of Alternatives.*

In Step 3, the strategy team evaluates the alternatives by using the tools discussed in previous chapters to quantify the probabilities and consequences and the timing of consequences. They conduct sensitivity analysis, both deterministic and probabilistic. They estimate, by assessing subject-matter experts' probability distributions for each alternative. Spreadsheets and other software tools provide economic measures for possible outcomes. Figure 6.10 illustrates the tools used in this evaluation.

The decision board receives from the strategy team a report of the total uncertainty of each alternative as a cumulative-distribution function or a frequency curve of relevant measures of performance. Sensitivity analysis is reported through tornado diagrams and other tools discussed in Chapter 5. Decision-board members are responsible for asking questions in order to understand the risks fully, so that when they select alternatives, they know what they are betting on.

FIGURE **6.10**
A variety of tools assists in the decision analysis cycle.

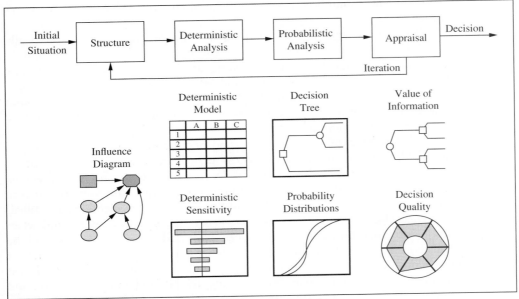

In the Therapharma example, sensitivity analysis revealed that a critical uncertainty that could affect overall shareholder value was efficacy of their products relative to major competitors' products. The global variable, annual real price growth/decline, which is a surrogate for governmental and other managed care price pressures, could affect all the current and potential pharmaceuticals in Therapharma's product portfolio. Probability distributions were assessed in more detail for the critical uncertainties.

Step 3 of the process includes the largest portion of the analysis work done by the strategy team. As you can see from Figure 6.10, many of the tools we have already discussed—and more that we will cover in future chapters—provide the methodological platform for analyzing the alternatives.

STEP 4 DECIDE among Alternatives.

Of course the decision board makes the decision among alternatives. The strategy team supports the decision with explanations of the results of their analysis, together with additional sensitivity analysis and answers to questions. The board weighs organizational issues and the strategic fit of alternatives, as well as economic measures of value added.

FIGURE **6.11**

Actions to add value and reduce risk.

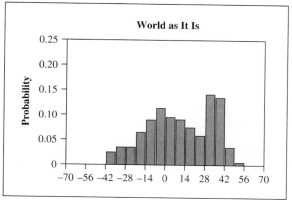

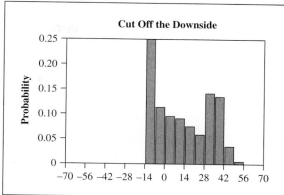

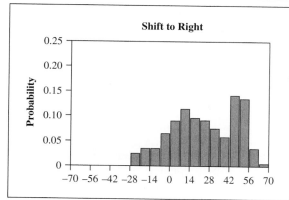

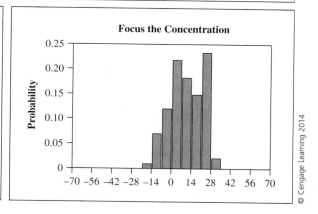

This is the time for the decision board, with the help of the strategy team, to consider ways to reduce risk. Too often, organizations accept the risk offered by *the world as it is*, only working hard to reduce risk when that risk is totally unacceptable. Superior organizations do not accept the world as it is, but instead proactively seek to improve the world by reducing risk and adding value.

Suppose the result of the decision analysis is the risk profile for net present value shown at the top of Figure 6.11. In general, we would like to improve the world as it is to the extent possible. The other distributions in Figure 6.11 illustrate three possible ways to mitigate the risk:

- Shift the entire distribution to the right (the second distribution in Figure 6.11). How could you do this? Perhaps you could by reducing costs across the board, raising revenues through higher market penetration, higher price, etc.

- Cut off the downside (the third distribution in Figure 6.11). For example, losses can be cut by buying insurance. Or create a contingent contract with a partner who would bear responsibility for factors involved in poor performance. The contract language may state that, if the outcome is below some level, the partner reimburses the organization. Keep in mind, though, that risk mitigation, through insurance or other agreements, is rarely free. Generally, reducing the downside risk also entails reducing the expected monetary value either through increased cost or a concomitant reduction in upside potential.

- Focus the distribution. Risk sharing, among other possibilities, might do this. For example, you might sell half of the opportunity to an investor. Essentially, the investor is taking half of the risk and in exchange gives you a sure amount, greatly reducing the range of possible outcomes.

Once the leading alternative is identified in Step 4, the decision board and strategy team can conduct a brainstorming session to identify opportunities for adding value and reducing risk in the ways we have described. Chelst and Bodily (2000) offer suggestions on structuring this discussion.

The opportunities available will depend on the nature of the leading alternative, characteristics of the organization, and the competitive environment in which the organization finds itself. Figure 6.12 provides a list of possible risk-management activities that could be used in a brainstorming

FIGURE **6.12**
Management activities that add value and reduce risk.

Internal Management of Firm	External Arrangements
• Cost controls Setting milestones Monitoring outflows Quick response • Productivity increases Incentive systems Labor coordination • Technological innovation Computer simulation of performance Extensive prototype testing Use of proven designs Pilot plant • Product improvements Marketing studies Field tests Shared development Tried and true fallback systems • Manufacturing capacity Flexible machines Commonality of product design Agile workforce Globally integrated planning Spare capacity (machines, parts)	• Controls Reduce accounts receivable Increase accounts payable Improve delivery times Supplier cooperation • Contract arrangements Take or pay clauses Penalty/incentive clause Performance-based contingent claim Match exposure to interests Length of contract commitment Reliability requirements Termination option Variable usage option Staged investing • Financial Markets Hedges Options Derivatives Shared ownership Risk sharing Alliance Joint venture • Insurance against contingencies • Targeted Marketing

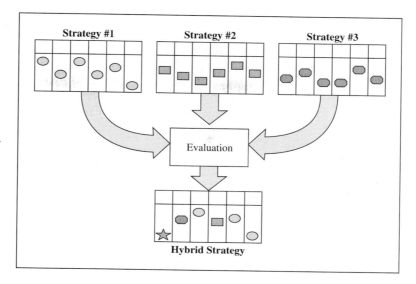

session. The tornado sensitivity diagram produced in earlier steps of the decision process will be invaluable for suggesting "low-hanging fruit"—inexpensive changes in some variables that add a large amount of value. A useful exercise is to start at the top of the tornado diagram and consider each variable, thinking about how one could easily change that variable to gain value.

New strategies may be identified by going back to the strategy table and looking for a hybrid strategy. As illustrated in Figure 6.13, the hybrid strategy consists of the best component choices from each of several already-identified strategies. Very often, the hybrid strategy is feasible and better than any other previously identified strategy.

After new strategies or risk-reduction schemes have been identified, the strategy team must update its analysis. As always, the goal is not just to provide numbers, but to generate insight into the strengths and weaknesses of each alternative and how each one contributes to the organization. Finally, the decision board makes the call as to which alternative to adopt. In making this choice, the board must consider the difficulty of implementing the choice as well as its desirability.

As the decision board makes a decision, it is a good time for them, together with the strategy team, to reflect on the success of the process through the first four steps. Psychological research on decision making has shown that people tend to make the same kinds of errors in making decisions. This research has produced insights about how to prevent those mistakes.

The 10 most dangerous "decision traps" were summarized by Russo and Schoemaker (1989) as follows:

1. **Plunging in**—Beginning to gather information and reach conclusions without first taking a few minutes to think about the crux of the issue you're facing or to think through how you believe decisions like this one should be made.

2. **Frame blindness**—Setting out to solve the wrong problem because you have created a mental framework for your decision, with little thought. This causes you to overlook the best options or lose sight of important objectives.
3. **Lack of frame control**—Failing to define the problem consciously in more ways than one or being unduly influenced by the frames of others.
4. **Overconfidence in your judgment**—Failing to collect key factual information because you are too sure of your assumptions and opinions.
5. **Shortsighted shortcuts**—Relying inappropriately on "rules of thumb" such as implicitly trusting the most readily available facts or anchoring too much on convenient facts.
6. **Shooting from the hip**—Believing you can keep straight in your head all the information you've discovered, and therefore "winging it" rather than following a systematic procedure when making the final choice.
7. **Group failure**—Assuming that, with many smart people involved, good choices will follow automatically, and therefore failing to manage the group decision-making process.
8. **Fooling yourself about feedback**—Failing to interpret the evidence from past outcomes for what it really says, either because you are protecting your ego or because you are tricked by hindsight.
9. **Not keeping track**—Assuming that experience will make its lessons available automatically, and therefore failing to keep systematic records to track the results of your decisions and failing to analyze those results in ways that reveal their key lessons.
10. **Failure to audit decision process**—Failing to create an organized approach to understanding your own decision making, so you remain constantly exposed to all the above mistakes.

In significant decisions affecting an organization, the decision traps may cause great damage. Even a good decision maker can be caught in a trap. The key is to realize it and pull out of the trap. These errors afflict different parts of the decision process, and awareness of these pitfalls is helpful throughout the entire decision process. The point when the decision is made at the end of Step 4, though, is the last opportunity to ensure that we haven't been ensnared.

For Therapharma, the *Focused Reallocation* strategy appeared to be better than the *Broad-Based Expansion* or *Joint Venture and License Focus* alternatives partly because of its relatively low risk. This strategy built upon therapeutic areas where they had significant franchises, or could build them (e.g. OTC medicines). The risk of failure in the negotiation and implementation of joint ventures was avoided. Bets were made on products that played to Therapharma's strengths rather than in-licensed products of new therapeutic areas.

The commitment made in Step 4 includes resources and the assignment of responsibility for carrying out implementation. For Therapharma a major expansion of the OTC medicines program and supporting marketing, and the abandonment of three therapeutic areas were part of the new path chosen. The guidance of the decision board to the strategy team was to focus on these critical change areas in developing the action plan in Step 5.

STEP 5 PLAN for Action.

In Step 5, the principal task is to create the image—mentally and on paper—of the organization after the implementation of the chosen alternative. Related tasks are to select those responsible for implementing this alternative and to set the plan of action. The plan delineates organizational changes and improvements in business processes that are related to the alternative selected. Clarity about what will *not* be done in the future that was done in the past is as important as outlining new activities.

During Step 5, it is usually desirable to add personnel to the decision board and/or the strategy team. These are people who will be involved in the implementation and who could not have been identified until the alternative was selected, in Step 4. Having additional people involved in the process at this point expands organizational buy-in and makes it possible to foresee any barriers to implementation.

Therapharma envisioned a company focused on four therapeutic areas plus OTC medicines after implementation. The company quickly realized that substantial advertising capability and additional direct sales force for OTC products would be needed. Therefore, during Step 5 they initiated a joint venture with an OTC medicines company that was a leader in advertising and marketing. They also planned the personnel reassignments and out-licensing of products to carry out the phase-out of three therapeutic areas. The company also anticipated the declogging of the development process and associated improvements in time to market associated with the phaseouts.

STEP 6 IMPLEMENT the Plan.

If the previous five steps have been carried out well and in detail, then implementation is relatively straightforward, though not automatic. This is where the lacing of commitment of key line and staff members of the decision board will pay off. Never assume, however, that implementation will take care of itself. It will take effort and detailed attention by members of the decision board. If the earlier steps are not done well and the ideas and concerns of these people have not been integrated into the decision, the necessary commitment may be missing, and nothing will happen.

At Therapharma, the strategy team was expanded in Step 5 to include key personnel who would, among other things, prioritize and speed pharmaceuticals to market and direct clinical resources. Because Step 3 had established a value on R&D projects that could be monitored and updated, this was substantially easier.

MANAGING AND MONITORING THE SIX-STEP DECISION PROCESS

The six-step decision process fosters effective decision analysis in the way that it

- Focuses on decisions
- Engenders rapid and widespread organizational awareness and commitment, which can be channeled toward further effort
- Ensures that decision makers struggle over explicit alternatives
- Brings together alternatives, uncertainty, and values
- Transforms choices into action

All steps of the process produce definable products.

The typical use of the six-step process involves many people (a dozen or more) often on different continents over many months. The consequences are typically measured in the millions or hundreds of millions of dollars over time spans of years and tens of years. The cost of the decision effort itself can be in the millions of dollars but is typically only a few percent of the overall value added. Many of the decision board and strategy team find time to work on the project by squeezing it into an already full agenda. Needless to say, it is difficult to get a full appreciation for what is required to succeed with this process in a classroom setting.

Different mixes of organizational capabilities are needed as the process proceeds through its various stages (Figure 6.14). Greater success will come from structuring teams with the breadth to provide all the needed skills. Even though there are advantages to having the same teams throughout the entire decision process, asking different team members to facilitate and lead each stage can be helpful.

The difference in value between the strategy that was selected and implanted by Therapharma relative to the momentum strategy, or strategy in place, was over $900 million. Beyond the particular decision made, the six steps knit together the parties involved in strategic development and change.

One thing that helps to ensure success of the decision process is to monitor decision quality throughout. At any point, there are six questions to ask to check whether the approach is complete and balanced. The six questions are shown in Figure 6.15 in what is known as a "spider diagram."

FIGURE **6.14** Mix of skills and effort required in steps of the decision process.

Source: Reprinted by permission, Bodily & Allen, *A Dialogue Process for Choosing Value-Creating Strategies, Interfaces,* 29, 6, 1999. Copyright 1999 the Institute for Operations Research and the Management Sciences (INFORMS), 7240 Parkway Drive, Suite 300, Hanover, MD 21076 USA.

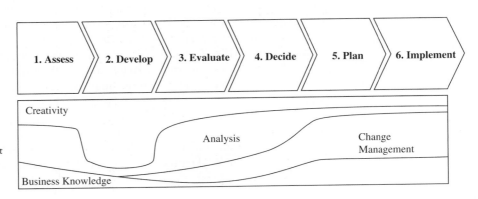

1. Assess 2. Develop 3. Evaluate 4. Decide 5. Plan 6. Implement

Creativity

Analysis

Change Management

Business Knowledge

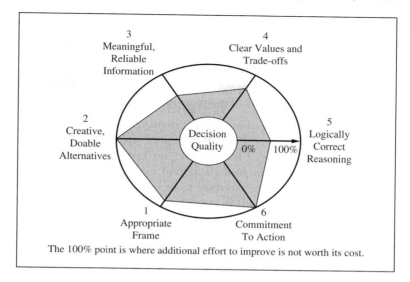

3
Meaningful,
Reliable
Information

4
Clear Values and
Trade-offs

2
Creative,
Doable
Alternatives

Decision
Quality

0%   100%

5
Logically
Correct
Reasoning

1
Appropriate
Frame

6
Commitment
To Action

The 100% point is where additional effort to improve is not worth its cost.

The degree to which a particular aspect is covered is indicated by how far the spider's "web" extends along each radius. Perfection would be a web that completely extends in all six directions. White space along a radius suggests further attention should be given to that aspect. For a deeper discussion of decision quality, see Matheson and Matheson (1998).

Other Examples

The Therapharma example is a good one, but there are many more. Skaf (1999) describes the process used by a major upstream oil-and-gas company for managing its portfolio of assets. The process was designed especially to account for the many uncertainties, some interrelated, about assets that were being developed or were already producing within and across business units in the corporation. Figure 6.16 shows the linking of the portfolio decision team and the asset teams in a very complex and encompassing set of decisions. The decisions were taken over the complete lifecycle of leases and assets and across the business units of the corporation. The six-step process has also been applied to financial institutions and durable goods companies.

Portfolio decisions in the pharmaceutical industry are discussed in Sharpe and Keelin (1998). They describe how the organization can create new alternatives to find better research-and-development (R&D) opportunities by adopting as standard practice the consideration of increased or decreased funding for each proposed project relative to the amount requested. Matheson and Matheson (1998) in *The Smart Organization* provide many examples of the six-step process for R&D decision analysis in organizations. The projects they describe range from bidding to acquire steel plants in Brazilian privatization to managing the portfolio of scripts and movies for a motion picture company.

For another example, consider Syncrude Canada, which produced crude oil from leased oil sands containing 20% more oil than all of Saudi Arabia. The company faced a daunting set of multistate technology choices, environmental challenges, and political decisions. Even though

FIGURE **6.16**

A generic version of the Skaf portfolio management process.

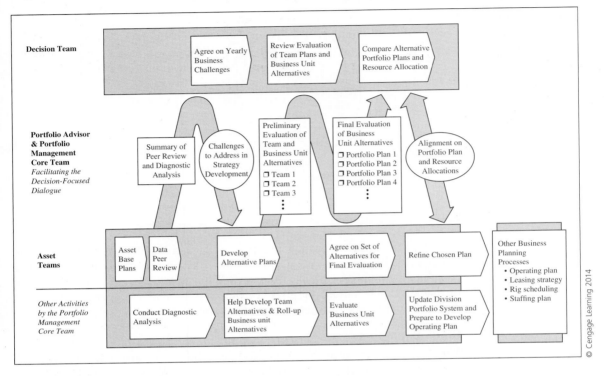

Syncrude was owned by several oil companies—each with its own objectives for Syncrude—the decision process enabled the management committee and strategy team to bring all of the owners and stakeholders together in order to move ahead. The new path selected resulted in an increase in the return on capital from 3.1% to 8.9% over a 5-year period, with additional future gains expected.

SUMMARY

The six-step process can help organizations raise issues and challenges and turn them into actionable alternatives. It also enables managers to use the tools and techniques of decision analysis to create value and reduce risk for the firm, and to lead the company toward a balance between analytical evaluation and organizational acceptance and implementation. The process is grounded in systematic rational reasoning and commitment to action by project leaders, strategy analysts, and managers across the company. The process goes beyond analysis to knit together the relevant parties for managing change and improving operational performance.

Creative thinking is part and parcel of the six-step process and of organizational decision making in general. We discussed stages in the creative process and how the organization can enhance creativity. Value-focused thinking can be a basis for developing creative alternatives, and we showed how means objectives in particular can provide a fertile ground for generation of new alternatives. Another useful tool is the strategy table, providing a way for decision makers to sift through many aspects of an overall strategy. An online supplement for this chapter provides additional techniques for enhancing creativity as well as tips for removing common mental blocks to creativity.

QUESTIONS AND PROBLEMS

6.1 Think about organizations in which you have worked, for whom you worked as consultants, or with which you are familiar. What barriers to the implementation of recommendations did you encounter? How would you overcome these barriers? What changes would you make in the decision-making process in those organizations?

6.2 What are the keys to getting *commitment to action* from the decision-board participants in the six-step process?

6.3 In what quadrant of the grid in Figure 6.2 would you place the following tasks?
   a. Selecting an investment for the funds in your retirement account
   b. Creating an organizational chart for merging two major divisions in an organization
   c. Recommending a direction for an organization regarding geographic expansion, disposition of subsidiaries, and product offerings

6.4 Think of a strategic mistake that you made or that was made by an organization. What do you think caused it? How might the six-step process or the creativity-enhancement ideas in the chapter have improved the situation?

6.5 Invent another hybrid strategy using the strategy table of Figure 6.9, using what you consider to be the best features of the strategies shown in that figure.

6.6 Choose a decision that you currently face. What are your objectives in this situation? List your means objectives, and for each means objective list at least one alternative that could help achieve that objective.

6.7 How would you design an organization so that it could, in Tom Peters's (1998) words, "thrive on chaos"? What characteristics would such an organization have? What kind of people would you try to hire? How would the role of the managers differ from the traditional view of what a manager does?

6.8 The point is often made that formal schooling can actually discourage young children from following their natural curiosity. Curiosity is an important element of creativity, and so it may be the case that schools indirectly and inadvertently cause children to become less creative than they might be. What does this imply for those of us who have attended school for many years? What can you suggest to today's educators as ways to encourage children to be curious and creative?

6.9 Use the means-objectives network in Figure 6.8 to create a list of alternatives for improving automotive safety. Try to create at least one alternative for each objective listed.

6.10 Reconsider the summer-intern decision discussed in Chapter 3. Figure 3.4 shows the fundamental and means objectives. With a group of friends, use these objectives, together with brainstorming, to generate a list of at least 20 things PeachTree can do to help locate and hire a good summer intern.

6.11 Describe a situation in which unconscious incubation worked for you. Describe one in which it did not. Can you explain why it worked in the first case but not in the second?

6.12 Add ideas of your own to the list in Figure 6.12 concerning methods for reducing risk and adding value.

6.13 Score the quality of some personal decision you are making using the spider diagram of Figure 6.15. Does your analysis suggest anything?

CASE STUDY

EASTMAN KODAK

Businesses have life cycles (Figure 6.17), and transitioning from one life-cycle phase to another may not be easy. Firms may become accustomed to managing a mature, steady business, only to find themselves in a turbulent period. Consider the amateur photography business of the now defunct Eastman Kodak Company. Originally, George Eastman developed a success formula for amateur photography based on celluloid film technology and simple, inexpensive cameras. Along came the challenge of electronic imaging and digital cameras. Kodak faced a contraction of their business—or possibly renewal.

Questions

1. Use whatever creativity-enhancing techniques you can to help think about alternatives for Kodak at the time of their first awareness of electronic and digital amateur photography.

2. If an alternative you suggest had been adopted by Kodak as their new path, what would it take for them to turn onto and move down that path? What kinds of organizational barriers do you think Kodak might have encountered?

FIGURE **6.17**
A management style appropriate for mature, steady businesses may not generate alternatives when the business faces turbulent change.

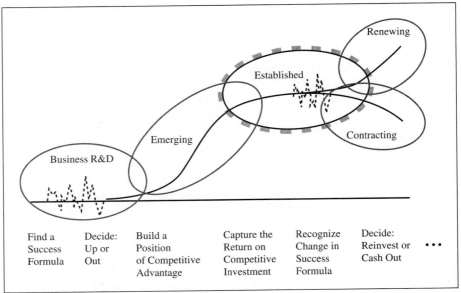

© Cengage Learning 2014

REFERENCES

The main focus of this chapter is the six-step organizational decision process. This process was largely developed by SDG and is best described by Bodily and Allen (1999). Occasionally the process is called the "dialogue decision process," a term coined by Vince Barraba (1995) in reference to a version of the process developed for General Motors. Sharpe and Keelin (1998) provide an example from the pharmaceutical industry, where the process has been adopted by a number of firms.

Very little literature on creativity exists within management science. Keller and Ho (1989) review and summarize this literature. Keeney (1992) devotes many pages to creativity, and Kleindorfer, Kunreuther, and Schoemaker (1993) also discuss creativity from a management-science perspective. Howard (1988) describes strategy tables.

Some of the literature on creativity, like Adams (1979), comes from an engineering/design/inventing perspective. (In fact, a book on creativity by Adams [1986] contains a chapter on decision analysis!) Most of the literature, however, comes from psychology. Baron (1988), Bazerman (1994), and Hogarth (1987) provide good reviews of the creativity literature from a psychological perspective. Johnson, Parrott, and Stratton (1968) provide some insights on the value of brainstorming.

Adams, J. L. (1979) *Conceptual Blockbusting: A Guide to Better Ideas,* 2nd ed. Stanford, CA: Stanford Alumni Association.

Adams, J. L. (1986) *The Care and Feeding of Ideas.* Stanford, CA: Stanford Alumni Association.

Amabile, T. (1988) "A Model of Creativity and Innovation in Organizations." *Research in Organizational Behavior,* 10, 123–167.

Amabile, T., and S. Kramer (2011) *The Progress Principle: Using Small Wins to Ignite Joy, Engagement, and Creativity at Work.* Cambridge, MA: Harvard Business Review Press.

Barraba, V. P. (1995) *Meeting of the Minds: Creating the Market-Based Enterprise.* Cambridge, MA: Harvard Business School Press.

Baron, J. (1988) *Thinking and Deciding.* Cambridge: Cambridge University Press.

Bazerman, M. H. (1994) *Judgment in Managerial Decision Making,* 3rd ed. New York: Wiley.

Bodily, S. E. and M. S. Allen (1999) "A Dialogue Process for Choosing Value-Creating Strategies," *Interfaces,* 29, 16–28.

Campbell, D. T. (1960) "Blind Variation and Selective Retention in Creative Thought as in Other Knowledge Processes," *Psychological Review,* 67, 380–400.

Chelst, K. and S. E. Bodily (2000) "Structured Risk Management: Filling a Gap in Decision Analysis Education," *Journal of the Operational Research Society,* 51, 1420–1430.

de Bono, E. (1992) *Serious Creativity.* New York: Harper Business.

Hogarth, R. (1987) *Judgement and Choice,* 2nd ed. Chichester, England: Wiley.

Howard, R, A. (1988) "Decision Analysis: Practice and Promise," *Management Science,* 34, 679–695.

Johnson, D. M., G. L. Parrott, and R. P. Stratton (1968) "Production and Judgment of Solutions to Five Problems," *Journal of Educational Psychology Monograph Supplement,* 59, 1–21.

Keeney, R. (1992) *Value-Focused Thinking.* Cambridge, MA: Harvard University Press.

Keller, L. R., and J. L. Ho (1989) "Decision Problem Structuring: Generating Options," *IEEE Transactions on Systems, Man, and Cybernetics,* 18, 715–728.

Kleindorfer, P. R., H. C. Kunreuther, and P. J. H. Schoemaker (1993) *Decision Sciences: An Integrated Perspective.* Cambridge: Cambridge University Press.

Matheson, D. and J. Matheson, (1998), *The Smart Organization.* Boston: Harvard Business School Press.

Peters, T. (1988) *Thriving on Chaos.* New York: Knopf.

Porter, M. E. (1998) *Competitive Advantage: Creating and Sustaining Superior Performance.* New York: Free Press.

Russo, J. E. and P. J. H. Schoemaker (1989) *Decision traps: ten barriers to brilliant decision-making and how to overcome them.* New York: Doubleday/Currency.

Sharpe, P. and T. Keelin (1998), "How SmithKline Beecham Makes Better Resource-Allocation Decisions, *Harvard Business Review,* March–April.

Skaf, M. A. (1999), "Portfolio Management in an Upstream Oil and Gas Organization," *Interfaces,* 29, 84–104.

Staats, A. W. (1968) *Learning, Language, and Cognition.* New York: Holt.

Wallas, G. (1926) *The Art of Thought.* New York: Harcourt, Brace.

EPILOGUE

The basic solution to the nine-dot puzzle is shown in Figure 6.18. Many people tacitly assume that the lines may not go beyond the square that is implied by the dots, and so they fail to solve the puzzle. Figure 6.19 shows how to connect nine fat dots with three straight lines, removing the block that the line has to go through the centers of the dots.

It is possible, with enough effort to remove the necessary blocks, to connect the dots with one line. Some solutions include the following:

- Fold the paper in a clever way so that the dots line up in a row. Then just draw one straight line through all nine dots.

- Roll the paper up and tape it so that you can draw connected straight lines through all the dots.

- Cut the paper in strips and tape it together so that the dots are in one row.

- Draw large dots, wad the paper up, and stab it with a pencil. Unfold it and see if the pencil went through all the dots. If not, try again. "Everybody wins!"

- Fold the paper carefully so that the dots are lying one on top of the other. Now stab your pencil through the nine layers of paper. It helps to sharpen your pencil first.

- Draw very small dots very close together in the square pattern and then draw a fat line through all of them at once. This one is courtesy of Becky Buechel when she was 10 years old.

FIGURE **6.18**
The standard solution to the nine-dot puzzle.

Source: From *Conceptual Blockbusting: A Guide to Better Ideas* by James L. Adams. Copyright © 2001 James L. Adams. Reprinted by permission of Basic Books, a member of the Perseus Books Group.

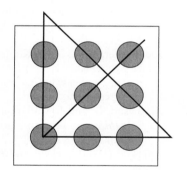

FIGURE **6.19**
An unblocked three-line solution.

Source: From *Conceptual Blockbusting: A Guide to Better Ideas* by James L. Adams. Copyright © 2001 James L. Adams. Reprinted by permission of Basic Books, a member of the Perseus Books Group.

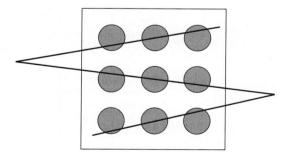

ATHENS GLASS WORKS

DARDEN
BUSINESS PUBLISHING
UNIVERSITY *of* VIRGINIA

In early August 1993, Christina Matthews, the product manager for nonglare glass at the Athens Glass Works (AGW), met with Robert Alexander, the controller of the Specialty Glass Division, to review the product's performance and prepare a pricing recommendation for the coming quarter. Once approved by the division president, the price would be announced and, as was customary in this segment of the glass industry, adhered to for at least 90 days.

The flat-glass industry was a $10-billion industry worldwide, of which $2.7 billion was generated in the United States. Approximately 57 percent of domestic production was for the construction industry, 25 percent for the automotive industry, and the remaining 18 percent for specialty products ranging from the mundane, like mirrors, to a wide variety of high-tech applications. Among the many technical applications of specialty glasses were solar panels, laminated and tempered safety glasses, heat- and bullet-resistant glasses, electrical and insulating glasses, phototechnical and photosensitive glasses, aerospace glass, and cookware. Nonglare glass was a fairly simple specialty product designed to reduce the glare of reflected light. It was used primarily to frame and protect artwork.

With 1992 sales of $195 million, Athens Glass Works was a midsized, regional glass company serving several niche markets in the southeastern United States. For a number of reasons, AGW enjoyed a dominant market position for nonglare glass in its region: (1) AGW was known for its fast, reliable service; it was willing to deliver glass on short notice at no extra charge in any of a variety of cut-to-order sizes, including the industry-standard delivery size (48-by-96-inch sheets) and all of the standard picture-frame sizes; (2) AGW provided an exceptionally high-quality nonglare glass with little light loss and virtually no blemishes; (3) AGW operated its own fleet of delivery vehicles so that delivery times were well managed and shipping charges were kept low; and (4) AGW's salaried sales staff was widely acknowledged for its helpful, courteous service and customer orientation.

The production of nonglare glass, like many other coated-glass products, began with flat glass, the output of one of Specialty Glass's sister divisions. The flat glass was treated by the Specialty Glass Division with a patented coating that provided the desired optical characteristics. This process required specialized equipment that was usable only in the production of nonglare glass. The finished, treated glass was then cut to order and shipped.

The business outlook for nonglare glass, like that for flat-glass products in general, had been flat for the past several years. As a result, last September, in response to increased corporate pressure to improve margins, Christina and Robert increased the price of nonglare glass by slightly less than ten percent, from $2.15 to $2.36 per square foot. This pricing decision was one of many made during the past year in anticipation of the company's considerable capital requirements to fund a recently approved long-term expansion and modernization program. At the time of the price increase, Christina and Robert hoped that competitors would follow AGW's lead and increase their prices as well.

Unfortunately, AGW's competitors held the line on the price of nonglare glass, and Christina believed that AGW's significant loss of market share in the last nine months was due solely to AGW's price change, as little else had changed in the industry during that period. To document the decline, Christina prepared Exhibit 1, which presents the sales-volume and price-history data for nonglare glass in AGW's market region for the past eight quarters. Looking ahead, Christina believed that a reasonable forecast of total regional volume for the fourth quarter of 1993 (usually the best quarter of the year) was 920,000 square feet. Christina believed that if AGW were to return to the $2.15 price, it could regain a major portion of its original market share with sales of 275,000 square feet. On the other hand, if competitive prices were not met, she feared a further decline. Nonetheless, because of AGW's outstanding reputation in the crafts marketplace, she reasoned that a sufficient number of customers would stay with AGW and prevent sales from falling below 150,000 square feet, even at the current price of $2.36 per square foot.

EXHIBIT **1**

Sales-Volume and
Price History of
Nonglare Glass

Year	Quarter	Sales Volume (000 square feet)		Price ($ per square foot)	
		AGW	Competitors	AGW	Competitors
1991	3	241	443	2.05	2.05
1991	4	313	592	2.05	2.05
1992	1	204	381	2.15	2.15
1992	2	269	513	2.15	2.15
1992	3	251	456	2.15	2.15
1992	4	238	672	2.36	2.15
1993	1	139	474	2.36	2.15
1993	2	162	642	2.36	2.15

While reflecting on the upcoming meeting with Christina, Robert realized that price would be the major topic of discussion, so he had his staff prepare a schedule of expected costs to produce nonglare glass over a wide range of production levels. This schedule is presented in Exhibit 2.

During their discussion, Christina and Robert together reviewed the historical sales levels and pricing data as well as the anticipated-cost schedule. They began by discussing the cost schedule. Christina noticed that unit costs grew with increasing volumes, but Robert said that the increasing unit costs were simply the result of the company's cost allocation system. Next, Robert asked whether there was any possibility that competitors might reduce their prices below $2.15 per square foot if AGW returned to that price. Christina replied that she was confident no competitor would do so because all were facing the same general economic conditions resulting from the long recession and several were in particularly tight financial straits. They then discussed whether the pricing decision for nonglare glass would have any repercussions on other Specialty Glass products; both were convinced it would not. Finally, they explored the implications of AGW's

EXHIBIT **2**

Nonglare Glass:
Estimated Cost per
Square Foot at
Various Production
Volumes

Production volume (000 sq. ft.)	150	175	200	225	250	275	300	325
Material	$0.45	$0.45	$0.45	$0.45	$0.45	$0.45	$0.45	$0.45
Energy	0.38	0.36	0.36	0.35	0.35	0.37	0.37	0.38
Labor	0.32	0.31	0.30	0.31	0.33	0.35	0.36	0.38
Shipping	0.11	0.11	0.11	0.11	0.11	0.11	0.11	0.11
General overhead[1]	0.08	0.08	0.08	0.08	0.08	0.09	0.09	0.09
Depreciation	0.27	0.23	0.20	0.18	0.16	0.15	0.14	0.13
Manufacturing cost	1.61	1.54	1.50	1.48	1.48	1.52	1.52	1.54
Selling and admin. costs[2]	0.72	0.69	0.67	0.66	0.67	0.68	0.68	0.69
Total cost	$2.33	$2.23	$2.17	$2.14	$2.15	$2.20	$2.20	$2.23

[1] General overhead includes a variety of corporate expenditures. It is allocated as twenty-five percent of labor.
[2] Selling and administrative costs include the costs of the sales and administrative support staff. It is allocated as forty-five percent of manufacturing cost.

returning to the industry price of $2.15 per square foot. Christina believed recapturing lost market share was essential in order for AGW to maintain its dominant role in the nonglare-glass niche. Robert, however, was concerned that, at $2.15, the product would show a loss, an outcome that would not be welcomed by senior management.

Source: This case was written by Sherwood C. Frey, Jr., Ethyl Professor of Business Administration. Copyright © by the University of Virginia Darden School Foundation, Charlottesville, VA, Rev. 7/94. All rights reserved. *To order copies, send an e-mail to* sales@dardenbusinesspublishing.com. *No part of this publication may be reproduced, stored in a retrieval system, used in a spreadsheet, or transmitted in any form or by any means—electronic, mechanical, photocopying, recording, or otherwise—without the permission of the Darden School Foundation.*

INTEGRATED SITING SYSTEMS, INC.

DARDEN
BUSINESS PUBLISHING
UNIVERSITY of VIRGINIA

After the plentiful years of the Reagan military buildup, the defense industry realized that it would have to diversify into nonmilitary applications if it were to survive the contractions of the 1990s without losing the capabilities of its highly trained and specialized work force. One result was the spin-off of a variety of small firms, each attempting to commercialize some collection of specialized skills and technologies that had been developed for military use. Integrated Siting Systems, Inc. (ISSI), was one such firm.

By February 1992, not only had ISSI successfully navigated the system-development phase of its first commercial product, an integrated, real-time, mobile-vehicle-tracking system, but already it had successfully installed its first several systems. The ISSI tracking system continuously updated and displayed the location of every vehicle in its network on centralized maps at any number of dispatch centers. It was designed for use by emergency-services providers such as ambulance, police, and fire.

By tracking and routing mobile units to emergency sites, response times could be reduced significantly from those of traditional systems that dispatched centrally housed vehicles. When the system was used with vehicles already in motion, performance time could be further improved by automatically tracking both the location and availability of each vehicle (whether available for a call or currently active). The ISSI system had already demonstrated response-time reductions in excess of 10 percent. Because improved 911 response time often meant saved lives, and because many emergency-services providers were paid on the basis of realized response time, interest in the system was high.

Complexity and costs, however, were also high. ISSI's system integrated a wide variety of commercially available components with proprietary software to provide a *real-time*, vehicle-locator system with "pinpoint" accuracy. This system, like other (mostly periodically updated) locator systems, was built on the shoulders of the military's Global Positioning System (GPS).

Over the past decade, the Pentagon had launched (and fully paid for) a constellation of satellites in high low-earth orbit. The satellites were referred to as a constellation because their positions were constantly changing relative to the earth and each other. Each satellite of the constellation transmitted a signal, called the ephemerides, that contained the satellite's position and, most importantly, the precise time of transmission. Upon receipt of the ephemerides from four different satellites, it was possible to locate the receiver in space-time (that is, in the three spatial dimensions and time).[1]

With a military receiver that included a decoder code, the system was accurate (anywhere on or about the earth) to within about 10 meters. To prevent an enemy from taking advantage of the system, however, all satellite transmissions were perturbed to degrade performance.[2] As a result, an enemy (or commercial) receiver lacking the decoder code could only locate vehicles to within 100 meters, which was more than sufficient for most commercial applications like air and sea navigation and the tracking of hazardous cargoes, weather balloons, and buoys at sea.

Such degraded performance was not sufficient, however, for tracking a police car on the streets of a city.[3] To overcome this problem, ISSI implemented a differential GPS. This system required two receivers:

---

[1] The calculations had to be done in space-time because the time delay between transmission and reception determined the distance between the receiver and the satellite. Because satellite positions were known with great accuracy, all that was needed, theoretically, was an identifying signal transmitted on a regular, predetermined basis. However, the entire ephemerides was transmitted because synchronizing clocks sufficiently well was impossible, and because it improved the robustness of the system.

[2] The perturbation was accomplished by introducing a systematic error in the time signal.

[3] One hundred meters is about the length of a city block.

one in the vehicle in motion and the other in a reference center at rest. By correcting for the apparent motion of the reference receiver resulting from the signal perturbations, the receiver in motion could be located to within one meter.

ISSI's system included mobile GPS receivers in each vehicle. These GPS receivers were sophisticated pieces of equipment. At a minimum, they included one or more receivers to look for some number of satellite signals simultaneously; some sort of receiver (FM, cellular, or VHF—very high frequency) to receive signals from the reference center so the reference-point data could be included in the calculations; a high-speed processor to execute the computationally intensive, differential GPS-software algorithms; and a transmitter (cellular or VHF) to send the vehicle's location back to the dispatch centers.

In some configurations, cellular systems were used for communications to (and perhaps from) the centralized site. Cellular communications could occur either through a modem over the voice line or in digitized data packets transmitted during the pauses in the conversations of others.[4] In other systems, a VHF network was used. The VHF alternative was generally preferred whenever there was concern that during a disaster, like an earthquake or a flood, the cellular system might overload and collapse just when it was needed most to dispatch emergency services. A VHF-based system was economically feasible, however, only when the transmission towers required for the network were already in place throughout the area.

In addition to the equipment in the mobile units, there were one or more dispatch centers. The handling and processing of signals from all of the vehicles in the system required a signal processor attached to a very fast workstation, with an exceptionally large and high-quality color-graphics monitor, running a Geographical Information System (GIS). A GIS was a data-management program, coupled with a geographical data base, designed to display data geographically on a digitally encoded map. When working properly, the system could essentially pinpoint and display in real time the location of every vehicle in its system.

In some configurations, ISSI included an additional processor and monitor in each vehicle to update and display continuously the location of the vehicle on its own digitized map. The major advantage of this

addition was that the central station could then send the location of an emergency to the mobile unit, which would in turn display the location and routing instructions on the vehicle's monitor, further reducing response time.

The Contract

Jordeen Scott, chief of engineering, was at her desk early on this brisk February morning preparing her regular 9:00 a.m. briefing for John Luce, president of ISSI. This particular briefing was troublesome because of a recently signed contract to install one of ISSI's systems in a medium-sized city in the Midwest.

Scott had warned Sales that ISSI had little experience in the dense urban environments of midwestern cities, and that everything from the size, shape, and layout of the buildings to the numbers of large trees and the shapes of their leaves could create interference with the line-of-sight reception of satellite transmissions. Because all of ISSI's prior installations had been in the Southwest, the system simply had not had to contend with the amount of foliage and large urban canyons that it was facing here. Scott had pointed out this difficulty prior to contract negotiations and had suggested a more robust system alternative than the standard package that ISSI had installed elsewhere.

System performance depended on a combination of processing power and signal quality. By using a more powerful GPS unit, ISSI could lock onto and track up to 12 satellites simultaneously. Because line-of-sight transmissions faded in and out, the more signals locked onto, the more likely there would be four good signals to use for computation at any one time. Furthermore, with a more powerful processor, ISSI could do more with degraded signals. First, there was simple signal enhancement. Second, there were all sorts of interpolation and inertial-navigation possibilities. In other words, ISSI could try to calculate what the signal would have said had it been heard.

The bottom line was the more capable and discriminating the receivers and the faster the processor, the more robust the system. ISSI could build a near-perfect system if it spent enough money. Unfortunately, fearing loss of the contract, Sales had priced the package at $850,000. Although this amount represented a bit of a premium over the normal markup on a standard system, which would cost $550,000 to deliver and install, it did not represent the full markup for a more robust package that could be guaranteed to work in the urban midwestern environment. To change now, therefore, would erode profitability below normal levels, as the more robust system design that could be

---

[4]Cellular companies charged substantially reduced rates for this form of transmission because the bandwidth was otherwise unused. The data from the reference center could also be sent to the vehicles in data packets in the pauses in standard FM broadcasts. Use of this bandwidth for this purpose had been approved by the Federal Communications Commission.

guaranteed to work would cost $700,000 to deliver and install. Scott wondered whether a recommendation for the more robust system was too risk averse; after all, current simulations still indicated a 90 percent chance that the standard system would meet the performance requirements of the contract.

Nevertheless, contract terms were pretty explicit about ISSI's obligations should the system fail. In addition to prespecified contract penalties, ISSI would have to pull the GPS units from all of the vehicles and replace them with the more powerful processors and receivers. Scott calculated that the incremental cost of upgrading in the field from the standard to the robust system would be $400,000. This figure included her estimates for the net additional cost of the more expensive equipment (assuming the original ones could be salvaged and used on another project), the major rework cost of pulling and replacing the GPS units in each vehicle, and the contracted penalty for the resulting one-month delay in the system launch.

Scott's calculations accounted for all of the costs associated with an in-field system replacement, except for any associated with the fact that the company would have experienced its first major failure. Moreover, because of the "whiz-bang" nature of the technology, news coverage was prominent, and any such failure would be highly visible. Scott wondered how Luce would react to such a possibility and whether she could offer any useful analytical counsel for evaluating such an important, yet intangible, outcome.

The Test

Scott turned next to the recommendation of the System Design team for further tests to improve their estimates of the environmental parameters that drive the simulation models. Their report reiterated that every specific environment has its own peculiarities. As a result, ISSI's assumptions about signal quality and the periodicity of degradation could be very wrong, and errors have a tendency to compound. Given their prior evaluation of this particular environment, they generated signal-strength distributions for the simulation models. None of these estimates were perfect, however, and in their prior installations in the Southwest they had never had to deal with the degree of urban density that were facing here.

The report noted that the current 90 percent success-rate assessment for the standard system was based on the current set of environmental parameter estimates. Better estimates could be obtained and a new series of simulations run for about $50,000. This would cover the costs of sending a team to the city to collect information on street layout and building size and to map the trees (estimating foliage, because it was winter) and other obstructions. The $50,000 would also enable the System Design team to customize the computer-simulation models that they used to assesses the distributions of signal intensities to vehicles moving about the city as the satellites changed positions overhead. Because the entire operation could be accomplished over the next several months, before the GPS units had to be installed in the vehicles, there would be no delay in the contract.

The report also noted, however, that the proposed test, like all tests, was imperfect. No matter how much was spent to develop the test, there would always be a chance that a bad system would pass the test or that a good system would fail it. Knowing that Luce would scrutinize the numbers, Scott turned to the probability assessments provided by the Systems Design team for the test they recommended.

After collecting the data and running the test, the standard system would either pass or fail. The System Design team assessed the odds as 24 to 1 that a standard system would work if it passed the test, a substantial improvement over the current unconditional assessment of 90 percent. Nevertheless, even if the standard system failed the test, the System Design team assessed the chance that a standard system would work to be 72 percent. (These numbers, along with almost every other conceivable conditional probability, were presented by the design team and are replicated in Exhibit 1. The design team prepared all such combinatorial estimates as a matter of course to enable them to check the consistency of the conditional probabilities. Note that the vertical bar in the table is mathematical shorthand—the last line of the table is read like this: If the system fails the test, there is a 28 percent chance that the system is bad.)

Scott knew that Luce's natural inclination would be to forego the test. With barely fifteen minutes left until the briefing, she was deeply engaged in thought.

Source: This case was prepared by Dana R. Clyman, Assistant Professor of Business Administration, and Sherwood C. Frey, Ethyl Professor of Business Administration. It was written as a basis for class discussion rather than to illustrate effective or ineffective handling of an administrative situation. Copyright © by the University of Virginia Darden School Foundation, Charlottesville, VA, Rev. 7/97. All rights reserved. To order copies, send an e-mail to sales@dardenbusinesspublishing.com. *No part of this publication may be reproduced, stored in a retrieval system, used in a spreadsheet, or transmitted in any form or by any means— electronic, mechanical, photocopying, recording, or otherwise— without the permission of the Darden School Foundation.*

EXHIBIT **1**
System Design
Team's Probability
Assessments Pre-
suming Standard
GPS Units

P(System Good)	0.90
P(System Bad)	0.10
P(Passes Test)	0.75
P(Fails Test)	0.25
P(Passes Test I System Good)	0.80
P(Passes Test I System Bad)	0.30
P(Fails Test I System Good)	0.20
P(Fails Test I System Bad)	0.70
P(System Good I Passes Test)	0.96
P(System Bad I Passes Test)	0.04
P(System Good I Fails Test)	0.72
P(System Bad I Fails Test)	0.28

INTERNATIONAL GUIDANCE AND CONTROLS

Time was running out on the $20 million CARV (Confined Aquatic Recovery Vehicle) project, and Project Manager Thomas Stearns was concerned about meeting schedule. With ten months left, considerable portions of the software remained to be developed, and he was by no means certain that all necessary development work would be completed on time.

Software Development

Stearns had had his project team working all-out in recent months on the software development for CARV's command and guidance system. His headcount (the number of full-time-equivalent workers assigned to the project) had been increased recently, so total development costs were running at $300,000 per month, 25 percent over budget. Stearns believed there was but an 80 percent chance that the necessary software would be completed in the remaining ten months. Despite this risk of not meeting schedule, he could not increase the headcount on the project or increase the rate of software development in any way.

If the software were not completed on time, Stearns was fairly certain that one or two extra months of work would suffice to complete the project. Unfortunately, each month's delay in project completion meant a 2.5 percent ($500,000) reduction in the price of the contract. In

addition to this precisely defined cost of not meeting schedule, a hard-to-quantify but no less significant cost of lost reputation was associated with not completing a project as scheduled.

Hardware Expansion

Part of the difficulty in developing the software for CARV was a result of the original design for the hardware. This somewhat underdesigned hardware was making the software development much more difficult and time consuming than originally planned.

One remedy that would virtually eliminate schedule risk would be to immediately begin an expansion of the hardware portion of the system. This expansion would require five months of effort at a total cost to the project of $1.5 million. In addition, this action would significantly reduce the software-development effort, to a point where software-development costs would decrease to $200,000 per month for the remaining ten months of the project.

Delaying the Hardware Expansion

Because the hardware expansion could be completed in five months, Stearns thought continuing with the all-out development of the software for the next five months would be prudent before committing to the hardware expansion. The software progress of the next five months would certainly give him a better idea of the chances of completing the project on schedule. If the five-month progress were favorable, then Stearns reasoned that the chances of completing the project on time would rise to 90 percent. If the progress were unfavorable, the chances would decrease to something like 40 percent. However, the distinct possibility also existed that the progress over the next five months would leave him in the same position in which he now found himself, with an 80 percent probability of completing the project as scheduled. Stearns believed that this latter event (not learning anything new in the next five months) had a probability of about 30 percent. He thought carefully about how to distribute the remaining 70 percent probability between the "favorable progress" and "unfavorable progress" events and soon realized that, in order to remain consistent with all of his earlier assessments, the probability of "favorable progress" had to be 56 percent and the probability of "unfavorable progress" had to be 14 percent.

If he decided to expand the hardware at the end of five months, he would again eliminate all the risk of not meeting the schedule and would also alleviate much of the software-development burden. He reasoned that the remaining five months of software development would cost only $150,000 per month, because much of the previous five months of developed software would be usable.

Source: This case was written by Professor Phillip E. Pfeifer as a basis for class discussion rather than to illustrate effective or ineffective handling of an administrative situation. Copyright © by the University of Virginia Darden School Foundation, Charlottesville, VA, Rev. 8/93. All rights reserved. *To order copies, send an e-mail to sales@dardenbusinesspublishing.com. No part of this publication may be reproduced, stored in a retrieval system, used in a spreadsheet, or transmitted in any form or by any means—electronic, mechanical, photocopying, recording, or otherwise—without the permission of the Darden School Foundation.*

GEORGE'S T-SHIRTS

For the last six years, George Lassiter, a project engineer for a major defense contractor, had enjoyed an interesting and lucrative side business—designing, manufacturing, and hawking "special event" t-shirts. He had created shirts for a variety of rock concerts, major sporting events, and special fund-raising events. Although his t-shirts were not endorsed by the event sponsors and were not allowed to be sold within the arenas at which the events were held, they were cleverly designed, well produced, and reasonably priced (relative to the official shirts). They were sold in the streets surrounding the arenas and in the nearby parking lots, always with the appropriate licenses from the local authorities. Lassiter had a regular crew of vendors to whom he sold the shirts on consignment for $100 per dozen. These vendors then offered the shirts to the public at $10 apiece.

A steady stream of t-shirt business came to Lassiter, and he was generally working on several designs in various stages of development. His current problem centered around the number of shirts he should have stenciled for a rock concert that was scheduled to be staged in two months.

This concert was almost certain to be a huge success. Lassiter had no doubt that the 20,000 tickets for the standing area around the stage would be instantly bought by the group's devoted fans. The major unknown was the number of grandstand seats that would be sold. It could be anywhere from a few thousand to more than double the number of standing tickets. Given the popularity of the performing group and the intensity of the advance hype, Lassiter believed the grandstand sales were more likely to be at the high rather than the low end of the spectrum. He decided to think in terms of three possibilities (a high, a medium, and a low value), specifically, 80,000, 50,000, and 20,000 grandstand seats. Despite his optimism, he believed that 50,000 was as likely as either of the other two possibilities combined. The two extreme numbers were about equally likely; maybe 80,000 was a little more likely than 20,000.

A second unknown was the percentage of the attendees who would buy one of his shirts. To the credit of his designs and the quality of the shirts, the number generally (about 6 times out of 10) ran about 10 percent of the attendance, but sometimes it was in the range of 5 percent. On a rare occasion, sales would be in the vicinity of 15 percent (maybe 1 time out of 10, if Lassiter's memory served him right).

Several weeks ago, Lassiter had requested a cost estimate for this concert's design from the silk screener/ shirt supply house with which he had been working for several years. He used this particular firm almost exclusively, because he had found it to be reliable in both quality and schedule and to have reasonable prices. The estimate had arrived yesterday. It was presented in the usual batches of 2,500 shirts with the usual volume discounts:

Order Size	Cost
10,000	$32,125
7,500	$25,250
5,000	$17,750

The order had to be one of the quoted multiples of 2,500 shirts.

On the basis of his volume estimates, Lassiter was prepared to place an order for 5,000 shirts. With his sales generally about 10 percent of attendance, he didn't believe he could justify an order for 7,500 shirts. Such an order would require the concert's attendance to be 75,000, and while he was optimistic about the popularity of the event, he wasn't quite that optimistic. Also, in the past, he had taken the conservative route and it had served him well. He had never had an appreciable number of shirts left over, but those that were left were sold to a discount clothing chain for $1.50 per shirt.

Source: This case was written by Sherwood C. Frey, Jr., Ethyl Professor of Business Administration, and Professor Phillip E. Pfeifer, as a basis for discussion rather than to illustrate effective or ineffective handling of an administrative situation. Copyright © by the University of Virginia Darden School Foundation, Charlottesville, VA, Rev. 1/93. All rights reserved. *To order copies, send an email to sales@dardenbusinesspublishing.com. No part of this publication may be reproduced, stored in a retrieval system, used in a spreadsheet, or transmitted in any form or by any means— electronic, mechanical, photocopying, recording, or otherwise— without the permission of the Darden School Foundation.*

SECTION 2

Modeling Uncertainty

As we have seen, uncertainty is a critical element of many of the hard decisions that we face. In the next five chapters we will consider a variety of ways to use probability to model uncertainty in decision problems. We begin with a brief introduction to probability in Chapter 7. This introduction has three objectives: to remind you of probability basics, to show some ways that probability modeling is used in decision problems, and to give you a chance to polish your ability to manipulate probabilities. The problems and cases at the end of Chapter 7 are recommended especially to help you accomplish the last goal.

Chapter 8 introduces the topic of subjective probability. Subjective probabilities are not simply made up numbers or guesses. Subjective probabilities come from working carefully with experts to encode their knowledge in terms of probabilities. Subjective probabilities increase our flexibility when modeling uncertainties, as they allow us to incorporate our beliefs along with the most up-to-date trends and information into our models. Chapter 8 discusses various methods to assess probability values, and with contributions from Jeff Guyse, we discuss some common problems that occur when dealing with subjective probabilities.

In many cases the uncertainty that we face has characteristics that make it similar to certain prototypical situations (such as measurement errors or customer arrival rates). In these cases, it is possible to represent the uncertainty with a standard mathematical model and then derive probabilities on the basis of the mathematical model. Chapter 9 presents a variety of theoretical probability models that are useful for representing uncertainty in many typical situations.

Chapter 10 discusses the use of historical data as a basis for developing probability distributions. If data about an uncertainty in a decision situation are available, a decision maker would surely want to use them. Chapter 10 shows how to use data alone to estimate discrete and continuous distributions, and we also discuss the use of data to model relationships or dependency among variables.

Chapter 11 introduces a very interesting and useful modeling procedure—Monte Carlo simulation. We use simulation to determine characteristics of a system. The system could be specific, such as pricing an option, or could be quite general, such as the social security system or markets as a whole. Simulation allows us to mimic the system under normal circumstances and under potential changes to the system. By comparing the results, we can predict the potential impact when changes are made to the system. During the financial crisis in 2008–2009, the U.S. Federal Reserve Bank used simulation to perform stress tests on major U.S. banks to determine their vulnerability to possible future losses and the required capital to absorb these losses. By simulating the system tens of thousands of times, we can obtain of good approximation of the probabilities associated with different outcomes.

Chapter 12 discusses the value of information; how much would you pay to reduce your uncertainty? It can be surprising how much (or how little!) information can be worth when considered in the context of a specific decision. Chapter 13, written by Sam Bodily, introduces the important topic of real options. Where Chapter 12 provides insight into the value of information, Chapter 13 goes further by showing how much value can be obtained through active management of projects in response to information received.

The next few chapters are technical and at times difficult, but we encourage to the reader to master the concepts. The rigor is needed to appropriately model real-life uncertainties and discover subtle insights in our hard decisions.

CHAPTER **7**

Probability Basics

In the previous chapters, we have used probabilities in an intuitive way to model the uncertainties we face in our hard decisions. We shied away from a rigorous discussion of probability theory because we wanted to focus on structuring and solving decision models. If, however, we want to accurately model complex uncertainties, we need a more complete understanding of probability theory. This chapter presents the basic principles for working with probability and probability models.

After reading the chapter and working the problems and cases, you should be (1) reasonably comfortable with probability concepts, (2) comfortable in the use of probability to model simple uncertain situations, (3) able to interpret probability statements in terms of the uncertainty that they represent, and (4) able to manipulate and analyze the models you create.

A LITTLE PROBABILITY THEORY

A quick note on terminology: We use the term *chance event* to refer to something about which a decision maker is uncertain. In turn, a chance event has more than one possible *outcome*. When we talk about probabilities, we are concerned with the chances associated with the different possible outcomes. For convenience, we will refer to chance events with boldface letters (e.g., Chance Events **A** and **B**), and to outcomes with lightface letters (e.g., Outcomes A_1, B_j, or C). Thus Chance Event **B**, for example, might represent a particular chance node in an influence diagram or decision tree, and Outcomes B_1, B_2, and B_3 would represents **B**'s possible outcomes.[1]

---

[1] The terminology we adopt in this book is slightly unconventional. Most authors define an *outcome space* that includes all possible elemental outcomes that may occur. For example, if the uncertain event is how many orders arrive at a mail-order business in a given day, the outcome space is composed of the integers 0, 1, 2, 3, ... , and each integer is a possible elemental outcome (or simply an outcome). An *event* is then defined as a set of possible outcomes. Thus, we might speak of the event that the number of orders equals zero or the event that more than 10 orders arrive in a day.

Probabilities must satisfy the following three requirements.

1 Probabilities Must Lie Between 0 and 1 Every probability (p) must be a non-negative number between 0 and 1 inclusive ($0 \leq p \leq 1$). This is a sensible requirement. In informal terms it simply means nothing can have more than a 100% chance of occurring or less than a 0% chance.

2 Probabilities Must Add Up Suppose two outcomes are mutually exclusive (only one can happen, not both). The probability that one or the other occurs is then the sum of the individual probabilities. Mathematically, we write $P(A_1 \text{ or } A_2) = P(A_1) + P(A_2)$ if A_1 and A_2 cannot both happen simultaneously. For example, consider the stock market. Suppose there is a 30% chance that the market will go up and a 45% chance that it will stay the same (as measured by the Dow Jones average). It cannot do both at the same time, and so the probability that it will either go up or stay the same must be 75%.

3 Total Probability Must Equal 1 Suppose a set of outcomes is mutually exclusive and collectively exhaustive. This means that one (and only one) of the possible outcomes must occur. The probabilities for this set must sum to 1. Informally, if we have a set of outcomes such that one of them has to occur, then there is a 100% chance that one of them will indeed come to pass.

We have seen this in decision trees; the branches emanating from a chance node must be such that one and only one of the branches occurs, and the probabilities for all the branches must add to 1. Consider the stock market example again. If we say that the market can go up, down, or stay the same, then one of these three outcomes must happen. The probabilities for these outcomes must sum to 1—that is, there is a 100% chance that one of them will occur.

VENN DIAGRAMS

Venn diagrams provide a graphic interpretation of probability. Figure 7.1 shows a simple Venn diagram in which two Outcomes, A_1 and A_2, are displayed. Think of the diagram as a whole representing a chance event (**A**) and areas representing possible outcomes. The circle labeled A_1 thus represents Outcome A_1. Because the areas of A_1 and A_2 do not overlap, A_1 and A_2 cannot both occur at the same time; they are mutually exclusive.

We can use Figure 7.1 to interpret the three requirements of probability previously mentioned. The first requirement is that a probability must lie between 0 and 1. Certainly an outcome cannot be represented by a negative area. Furthermore, an outcome cannot be represented by an area larger than the entire rectangle. For the second requirement, we see that A_1 and A_2 are mutually exclusive because they do not overlap. Thus, the probability of A_1

In this book we use the term *outcome* to refer to what can occur as the result of an uncertain event. Such occurrences, which we represent as branches from chance nodes in decision trees, can be either events or elemental outcomes in the conventional terminology. Thus, our usage of the term *outcome* includes the conventional *event* as well as *outcome*. Why the change? For our purposes it is not necessary to distinguish between elemental outcomes and sets of outcomes. Also, we avoid the potential confusion that can arise by using the term *uncertain event* to refer to a process and *event* to refer to a result of that process.

FIGURE **7.1**
A Venn diagram.

Outcomes A_1 and A_2
are mutually exclusive
events.

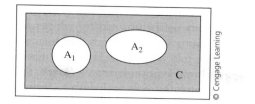

or A_2 occurring must be the sum of the probability of A_1 plus the probability of A_2. For the third requirement, label the shaded portion of the rectangle as C. This is what must occur if neither A_1 nor A_2 happens. Because A_1, A_2, and C together make up the whole rectangle, one of the three must occur. Moreover, only one of them can occur. The upshot is that their probabilities must sum to 1. Alternatively, there is a 100% chance that A_1, A_2, or C will occur.

MORE PROBABILITY FORMULAS

The following definitions and formulas will make it possible to use probabilities in a wide variety of decision situations.

4 Conditional Probability Suppose that you are interested in whether a particular stock price will increase. You might use a probability P(Up) to represent your uncertainty. If you find out that the Dow Jones Industrial Average increased, you would probably want to modify your probability of P(Up) if you felt there was a relationship between your stock and the Dow Jones. Figure 7.2 represents the situation with a Venn diagram. Now the entire rectangle actually represents two chance events; what happens with the Dow Jones index and what happens with the stock price? For the Dow Jones event, one possible outcome is that the index goes up, represented by the circle. Likewise, the oval represents the possible outcome that the stock price goes up. Because these two outcomes can happen at once, the two areas overlap in the diagonally shaded area. When both outcomes occur, this is called the *joint outcome* or *intersection*, and we indicate joint outcomes by (*A* and *B*), which in this case is (*Stock Price Up and Dow Jones Up*). It also is

FIGURE **7.2**
A Venn-diagram
representation
of conditional
probability.

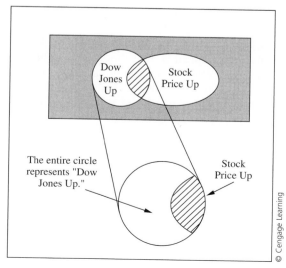

possible for one to rise while the other does not, which is represented in the diagram by the non-overlapping portions of the "Dow Jones Up" and "Stock Price Up" areas. And, of course, the gray area surrounding the circle and oval represents the joint outcome that neither the Dow Jones index nor the stock price goes up.

Once we know that the Dow Jones has risen, we know that no event or outcome outside the Dow Jones circle can occur, and we can restrict our attention to the "Dow Jones Up" circle. We want to know what the probability is that the stock price will increase given that the Dow Jones average is up, and so we are interested in the probability associated with the area "Stock Price Up" within the restricted space ("Dow Jones Up" circle).

Given that we are only looking at the restricted space, the conditional probability of "Stock Price Up given Dow Jones Up" is represented by the joint outcome "Stock Price Up" *and* "Dow Jones Up" (the diagonally shaded area). Thus, the conditional probability must be the proportion of the joint outcome area relative to the "Dow Jones Up" circle. This intuitive approach leads to the conclusion that:

$$P(Stock\ Price\ Up\ given\ Dow\ Jones\ Up) = \frac{P(Stock\ Price\ Up\ and\ Dow\ Jones\ Up)}{P(Dow\ Jones\ Up)}.$$

Mathematically, we write $P(A|B)$ to represent the conditional probability of A given that B occurs. Read it as "Probability of A given B." The definition is

$$P(A|B) = \frac{P(A\ and\ B)}{P(B)}$$

Informally, knowing that Outcome B has already occurred, $P(A|B)$ is the proportion of those times that Outcome A also occurs. The probability $P(A\ and\ B)$ is often called a *joint* probability.

We have actually seen and been using conditional probabilities in our decision models already. For example, in a decision tree with consecutive chance nodes **B** followed by **A**, the probability values of the outcomes for **A** are conditioned on which outcome for **B** has occurred. Remember, the branches for **B** are the outcomes for **B**. By placing the chance node **A** following B_1, B_2, *etc*, we are giving a sequence to the events, and thus the appropriate branch probability is the probability of A_1 given B_1, A_2 given B_1, and so on. The preceding formula for conditional probability provides a rigorous way to calculate the very probability values we need in our decision models.

If it turns out that the probability values for the outcomes of **A** stay the same no matter which outcome of **B** has occurred, we call this *independence* or *probabilistic independence*.

5 Independence The definition of probabilistic independence is as follows:

Chance Events A (with Outcomes A_1, A_2, ..., A_n) and B (with Outcomes B_1, B_2, ..., B_m) are *independent* if and only if

$$P(A_i|B_j) = P(A_i)$$

for all possible Outcomes A_1, A_2, ..., A_n and B_1, B_2, ..., B_m.

In words, knowing which of **B**'s outcomes occurred doesn't alter the probabilities for **A**'s outcomes. Note that the asymmetry in the definition of independence stated previously makes it look as if **A** is independent of **B**, but Problem 7.28 asks you to show that if $P(A_i|B_j) = P(A_i)$ for all possible Outcomes $A_1, A_2, \ldots, A_n$ and $B_1, B_2, \ldots, B_m$ then $P(B_i|A_i) = P(B_i)$ for all possible Outcomes $A_1, A_2, \ldots, A_n$ and $B_1, B_2, \ldots, B_m$ Thus, independence in one direction implies independence in the other direction, allowing us to say the Chance Events **A** and **B** are independent.

Independence simplifies our decision models because we need only determine the probability values of the outcomes, and not the probability value of the outcomes dependent on a variety of conditions. Furthermore, if Chance Events **A** and **B** are independent, then for any $i = 1, 2, \ldots, n$ and $j = 1, 2, \ldots, m$ we can write

$$P(A_i) = P(A_i|B_j) = \frac{P(A_i \ and \ B_j)}{P(B_j)}$$

From this we can see that $P(A_i \ and \ B_j) = P(A_i)P(B_j)$. Thus, when two events are independent, we can find the probability of a joint outcome by multiplying the probabilities of the individual outcomes.

Independence between two chance events is shown in influence diagrams by the absence of an arrow between chance nodes. This is fully consistent with the definitions given in Chapter 3. If one event is not relevant in determining the chances associated with another event, there is no arrow between the chance nodes. An arrow from chance node **B** to chance node **A** would mean that the probabilities associated with **A** are conditional probabilities that depend on the outcome of **B**.

As an example of independent chance events, consider the probability of the Dow Jones index increasing and the probability of the Dow Jones increasing *given* that it rains tomorrow. It seems reasonable to conclude that:

$$P(\text{Dow Jones Up}) = P(\text{Dow Jones Up} \mid \text{Rain})$$

because knowing about rain does not help to assess the chance of the index going up.

Independent chance events are not to be confused with mutually exclusive outcomes. Two outcomes are mutually exclusive if only one can happen at a time. Clearly, however, independent chance events can have outcomes that happen together. For example, it is perfectly possible for the Dow Jones to increase and for rain to occur tomorrow. Rain and No Rain constitute mutually exclusive outcomes; only one occurs at a time.

Finally, if two chance events are probabilistically dependent, this does *not* imply a causal relationship. As an example, consider economic indicators. If a leading economic indicator goes up in one quarter, it is unlikely that a recession will occur in the next quarter; the change in the indicator and the occurrence of a recession are dependent events. But this is not to say that the indicator going up causes the recession not to happen, or vice versa. In some cases there may be a causal chain linking the events, but it may be a very convoluted one. In general, dependence does not imply causality.

Conditional Independence. This is an extension of the idea of independence. Conditional independence is best demonstrated with an influence

© Cengage Learning

FIGURE **7.3**
Conditional independence in an influence diagram.

In these influence diagrams, A and B are conditionally independent given C. As shown, the conditioning event can be either (a) a chance event or (b) a decision.

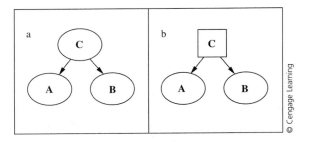

diagram. In Figure 7.3, Events **A** and **B** are conditionally independent given Event **C**. Note that **C** can be a chance event or a decision, as in Figure 7.3b. The only connection between **A** and **B** goes through **C**; there is no arrow directly from **A** to **B**, or vice versa. Mathematically, we would write

> Events **A** and **B** are conditionally independent given **C** if and only if
>
> $$P(A_i | B_j, C_k) = P(A_i | C_k)$$
>
> for all possible Outcomes. A_i, B_j, and C_k

In words, suppose we are interested in Event **A**. If **A** and **B** are conditionally independent given **C**, then learning the outcome of **B** adds no new information regarding **A** if the outcome of **C** is already known. Alternatively, conditional independence means that:

$$P(A_i \text{ and } B_j | C_k) = P(A_i | C_k) P(B_i | C_k)$$

Conditional independence is the same as normal (unconditional) independence except that every probability has the same conditions to the right side of the vertical bar. When constructing influence diagrams or decision trees, identification of conditional independence can ease the burden of finding probabilities for the chance events.

As an example of conditional independence, consider a situation in which you wonder whether or not a particular firm will introduce a new product. You are acquainted with the CEO of the firm and may be able to ask about the new product. But one of your suppliers, who has chatted with the CEO's assistant, reports that the company is on the brink of announcing the new product. Your probability that the company will indeed introduce the product thus would change:

P(Introduce Product | Supplier's Report) ≠ P (Introduce Product)

Thus, these two events are not independent when considered by themselves. Consider, however, the information from the CEO. Given that information, the supplier's report might not change your probability:

P(Introduce Product | Supplier's Report, Information from CEO)

= P(Introduce Product | Information from CEO)

Thus, given the information from the CEO, the supplier's report and the event of the product introduction are conditionally independent.

Conditional independence is an important concept when thinking about causal effects and dependence. As mentioned previously, dependence between two events does not necessarily mean that one causes the other. For example, more drownings tend to be associated with more ice cream consumption, but it seems unlikely that these two are causally related. The explanation lies in a common cause; both tend to happen during summer, and it might be reasonable to assume that drownings and ice cream consumption are conditionally independent given the season. Another example is that high skirt hemlines tend to occur when the stock market is advancing steadily (a bull market), although no one believes that hemlines cause the stock market to advance, or vice versa. Perhaps both reflect a pervasive feeling of confidence and adventure in our society. If we had an adequate index of "societal adventuresomeness," hemline height and stock market activity might well be conditionally independent given the index.

6 Complements Let $\overline{B}$ ("Not B" or "B-bar") represent the outcome that is the complement of B. This means that if B does not occur, then $\overline{B}$ must occur. Because probabilities must add to 1 (requirement 3 as shown previously),

$$P(\overline{B}) = 1 - P(B)$$

The Venn diagram in Figure 7.4 demonstrates complements. If the area labeled B represents Outcome B, then everything outside of the oval must represent what occurs if B does not happen. For another example, the lightly shaded area in Figure 7.2 represents the complement of the Outcome "Dow Jones Up *or* Stock Price Up," the union of the two individual outcomes.

7 Total Probability of an Event A convenient way to calculate P(A) is with this formula:

$$P(A) = P(A \text{ and } B) + P(A \text{ and } \overline{B})$$
$$= P(A|B)P(B) + P(A|\overline{B})P(\overline{B})$$

To understand this formula, examine Figure 7.5. Clearly, Outcome A is composed of those occasions when A and B occur and when A and $\overline{B}$ occur. Because the joint Outcomes "A and B" and "A and $\overline{B}$" are mutually exclusive, the probability of A must be the sum of the probability of "A and B" plus the probability of "A and $\overline{B}$."

As an example, suppose we want to assess the probability that a stock price will increase. We could use its relationship with the Dow Jones index (Figure 7.2) to help make the assessment:

P(Stock Price Up) = P(Stock Price Up | Dow Jones Up) × P(Dow Jones Up)

+ P(Stock Price Up | Dow Jones Not Up)

× P(Dow Jones Not Up)

Although it may appear that we have complicated matters by requiring three probabilities instead of one, it may be quite easy to think about (1) the

FIGURE **7.4**
Venn diagram illustrating the idea of an outcome's complement.

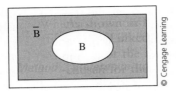

FIGURE **7.5**
Total probability.

Outcome A is made up of Outcomes "A and B" and "A and $\overline{B}$."

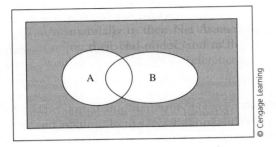

probability of the stock price movement conditional on the change in the Dow Jones index and (2) the probabilities associated with changes in the index.

Note that the formula for total probability can be expanded. For example, "Dow Jones Not Up" can be further decomposed into the mutually exclusive events "Dow Jones Stays Even" and "Dow Jones Down." Thus:

$$P(\text{Stock Price Up}) = P(\text{Stock Price Up} \mid \text{Dow Jones Up}) \times P(\text{Dow Jones Up})$$
$$+ P(\text{Stock Price Up} \mid \text{Dow Jones Stays Even})$$
$$\times P(\text{Dow Jones Stays Even})$$
$$+ P(\text{Stock Price Up} \mid \text{Dow Jones Down})$$
$$\times P(\text{Dow Jones Down})$$

Notice the symmetry in the formula and how the conditioning events need to be collectively exhaustive and mutually exclusive.

8 Bayes' Theorem Because of the symmetry of the definition of conditional probability, we can write

$$P(B|A)P(A) = P(A|B)P(B)$$

from which we can derive:

$$P(B|A) = \frac{P(A|B)P(B)}{P(A)}$$

Now expanding $P(A)$ with the formula for total probability, we obtain

$$P(B|A) = \frac{P(A|B)P(B)}{P(A|B)P(B) + P(A|\overline{B})P(\overline{B})}$$

This formula often is referred to as *Bayes' theorem*. It is extremely useful in decision analysis, especially when using information. We will see numerous applications of Bayes' theorem in the examples at the end of this chapter, as well as in Chapters 9 and 12.

Bayes' theorem is indispensible if you want to reorder the chance nodes in a decision tree or influence diagram. For example, in 2008, you might have had a model structured with two chance events: "General Motors (GM) introduces plug-in hybrid car (yes/no)" followed by "GM declares bankruptcy." You might legitimately have viewed the probability of GM going bankrupt to vary depending on whether they introduce the plug-in hybrid. However, in 2009, GM did declare bankruptcy, and then you might want to know the probability of their introducing the plug-in hybrid, given bankruptcy, effectively reversing the order of the chance nodes.

If chance node **B** is followed by chance node **A**, then we use the probabilities $P(B_1)$, $P(B_2)$ and so on, followed by $P(A_1|B_1)$, $P(A_1|B_2)$, $P(A_2|B_1)$, $P(A_2|B_2)$ and so on. To reorder the nodes, we need the probabilities $P(A_1)$, $P(A_2)$ as A is now first, followed by $P(B_1|A_1)$, $P(B_1|A_2)$, $P(B_2|A_1)$, $P(B_2|A_2)$, because **B** is now second and conditioned on **A**'s outcomes. Looking at Bayes theorem, we see that to compute $P(B_1|A_1)$ we need $P(A_1|B_1)$ and $P(B_1)$, which are exactly the probabilities we have. It is almost as if Bayes' theorem was invented for reordering chance nodes! At the end of the chapter we present more examples of chance-node reordering, demonstrating the use of Bayes' theorem

PRECISIONTREE® AND BAYES' THEOREM

PrecisionTree includes a feature to reorder chance nodes and apply Bayes' theorem automatically. Begin by creating a simple decision tree, starting with a chance node (labeled B), with branches B_1 and B_2. Each branch has a probability of 50%. At the end of both B_1 and B_2 comes chance node A, also with two branches, A_1 and A_2. The conditional probabilities are different, though depending on whether the previous outcome is B_1 or B_2. Set $P(A_1|B_1) = 0.90$ and $P(A_1|B_2) = 0.40$. [Can you calculate $P(A_2|B_1)$ and $P(A_2|B_2)$?] When you are ready, point to chance node B, **right-click**, and choose **Bayesian Revision**. In the dialog box, by default PrecisionTree lists the nodes in the revised order; you should see A listed first, indicating that PrecisionTree will move A to the beginning of the tree. Click **OK**. The new tree shows A first, followed by B, and PrecisionTree has applied Bayes' theorem to calculate the revised probabilities.

UNCERTAIN QUANTITIES

For the remainder of the chapter, we assume all of our uncertain events have quantitative outcomes, that is numerical values. Many uncertain events have natural quantitative outcomes. For example, we already have mentioned stock prices and the level of the Dow Jones index. If an event is not quantitative in the first place, we might define a variable that has a quantitative outcome based on the original event. For example, if we were concerned about precipitation, we could measure the amount of precipitation or we could define an uncertain quantity X: Let $X = 1$ if precipitation occurs, and $X = 0$ if not. By assuming quantitative outcomes, we gain the ability to mathematically model and analyze uncertainties.

The set of probabilities associated with all possible outcomes of an uncertain quantity is called its *probability distribution*. For example, consider the probability distribution for the number of raisins in an oatmeal cookie, which we could denote by Y. We might have: $P(Y = 0) = 0.2$, $P(Y = 1) = 0.05$, $P(Y = 2) = 0.20$, $P(Y = 3) = 0.40$, and so on. Of course, the probabilities in a probability distribution must add to 1 because the events—numerical outcomes—are collectively exhaustive. Uncertain quantities (often called *random variables*) and their probability distributions play a central role in decision analysis.

In general, we will use capital letters to represent uncertain quantities. Thus, we will write: $P(X = 3)$ or $P(Y > 0)$, for example, which are read as "the probability that the uncertain quantity X equals 3," and "the probability that the uncertain quantity Y is greater than 0." Occasionally we will need to use a more general form. Lowercase letters will denote outcomes or realizations of an uncertain quantity. An example would be $P(X = x)$, where capital X denotes the uncertain quantity itself and lowercase x represents the actual outcome.

It is helpful to distinguish between *discrete* and *continuous* uncertain quantities because the diagrams and formulas are different for discrete *versus* continuous distributions. The next section focuses on discrete uncertain quantities, their probability distributions, and certain characteristics of those distributions. Then we turn to some continuous quantities and show how their probability distributions and their characteristics are analogous to the discrete case.

Discrete Probability Distributions

The discrete probability distribution case is characterized by an uncertain quantity that can assume a finite or countable number of possible values. We already have seen two examples. The first was the precipitation example; we defined a discrete uncertain quantity that could take only the values 0 and 1. The other example was the number of raisins in an oatmeal cookie. Other examples might be the number of vehicles passing through a tollbooth per hour or the number of games that will be won by the Chicago Cubs next year. Strictly speaking, future stock prices quoted on the New York Stock Exchange are discrete uncertain quantities because they can take only values that are in dollars and cents. Even though stock prices are discrete, they have so many possible values that we model them as continuous distributions.

When we specify a probability distribution for a discrete uncertain quantity, we can express the distribution in several ways. Two approaches are particularly useful. The first is to give the *probability mass function*. This function lists the probabilities for each possible discrete outcome. For example, suppose that you think that no cookie in a batch of oatmeal cookies

FIGURE **7.6**
A probability mass function for the number of raisins per oatmeal cookie displayed as a bar chart.

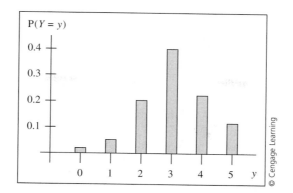

could have more than five raisins or any fractional pieces of raisins. A possible probability mass function would be:

$$P(Y = 0 \; raisins) = 0.02 \qquad\qquad P(Y = 3 \; raisins) = 0.40$$
$$P(Y = 1 \; raisin) = 0.05 \qquad\qquad P(Y = 4 \; raisins) = 0.22$$
$$P(Y = 2 \; raisins) = 0.20 \qquad\qquad P(Y = 5 \; raisins) = 0.11$$

This mass function can be displayed in graphical form (Figure 7.6), where the height of each bar is the probability the outcome.

The second way to express a probability distribution is as a *cumulative distribution function* (CDF). A cumulative distribution gives the probability that an uncertain quantity is less than or equal to a specific value: $P(Y \leq x)$. For our example, the CDF is given by:

$$P(Y \leq 0 \; raisins) = 0.02 \qquad\qquad P(Y \leq 3 \; raisins) = 0.67$$
$$P(Y \leq 1 \; raisin) \; = 0.07 \qquad\qquad P(Y \leq 4 \; raisins) = 0.89$$
$$P(Y \leq 2 \; raisins) = 0.27 \qquad\qquad P(Y \leq 5 \; raisins) = 1.00$$

Cumulative probabilities can be graphed; the CDF for the oatmeal cookie is graphed in Figure 7.7. To read probabilities from a CDF graph, the height at the value y_0 is the cumulative probability value $P(Y \leq y_0)$

FIGURE **7.7**
Cumulative distribution function (CDF) for number of raisins in an oatmeal cookie.

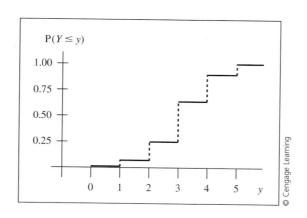

Note that the graph actually covers all the points along the horizontal axis. That is, we can read from the graph not only $P(Y \leq 3)$, but also $P(Y \leq 4.67)$, for example. In fact, $P(Y \leq 4.67) = P(Y \leq 4) = 0.89$, because it is not possible for a cookie to have a fractional number of raisins (assuming whole raisins, of course).

You may recognize this idea of a probability mass function and a CDF. When we constructed risk profiles and cumulative risk profiles in Chapter 4, we were working with these two representations of probability distributions.

Expected Value

A discrete uncertain quantity's *expected value* is the probability-weighted average of its possible values. That is, if X can take on any value in the set $\{x_1, x_2, \ldots, x_n\}$, then the expected value of X is simply the weighted sum of x_1 through x_n, each weighted by the probability of its occurrence. Mathematically,:

$$Expected\ Value\ of\ X = x_1 P(X = x_1) + x_2 P(X = x_2) + \cdots + x_n P(X = x_n)$$

$$= \sum_{i=1}^{n} x_i P(X = x_i)$$

The expected value of X also is referred to as the average or mean of X and is denoted by $E(X)$ or occasionally μ_x (Greek mu).

The expected value can be thought of as the "best guess" for the value of an uncertain quantity or random variable. If it were possible to observe many outcomes of the random variable, the average of those outcomes would be very close to the expected value. We already have encountered expected values in calculating EMVs to solve influence diagrams and decision trees. The expected monetary value is the expected value of a random variable that happens to be the monetary outcome in a decision situation.

Portfolio Example

The motivation for this chapter is to put our understanding of probability and probability distributions on a rigorous foundation so that we may appropriately model complex uncertainties, which in turn can lead us to further insights into our hard decisions. Let's apply what we have learned so far about probability distributions to portfolio management.

Consider a portfolio with three assets: AB, CD, and EF. For each asset, we define the uncertain quantities: R_{AB}, R_{CD}, and R_{EF} to be the respective returns on AB, CD, and EF one year from today. Thus, $R_{AB} = 15\%$ means that in one year, the price of a share of AB has risen by 15% (or is 115% times today's price). Figure 7.8 shows the probability distributions for the returns of each of the three assets; note that not all returns are positive.

A portfolio is a mixture of assets. Specifically, let W_{AB}, W_{CD}, and W_{EF} represent the percentage of our total investment that is invested in AB, CD,

FIGURE **7.8**
The probability
distributions for the
returns of the three
stocks AB, CD,
and EF.

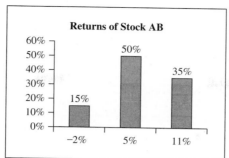

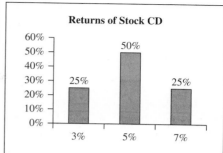

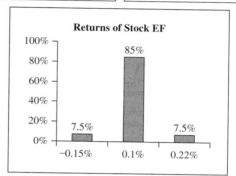

and EF respectively. We have only three assets in the portfolio, so $W_{AB} + W_{CD} + W_{EF} = 1$, which means that 100% of our total is invested. Our fourth random variable is R_p which is the return of our portfolio P one year from today. Thus, $R_p = 10\%$ means that the total value of the portfolio has increased by 10%.

Given the probability mass distributions for AB, CD, and EF in Figure 7.8, we can calculate the expected return of each stock.

$$E(R_{AB}) = -2\% \times (0.15) + 5\% \times (0.50) + 11\% \times (0.35) = 6.1\%$$

$$E(R_{CD}) = 3\% \times (0.25) + 5\% \times (0.50) + 7\% \times (0.25) = 5.0\%$$

$$E(R_{EF}) = -15\% \times (0.075) + 10\% \times (0.85) + 22\% \times (0.075) = 9.0\%$$

Although we do not know the exact return of EF one year from now, our expectation is that EF will give a 9% return on our investment. EF has approximately a 50% higher return on average than either AB or CD. CD has the lowest expected return at 5%, and AB is slightly better at 6.1%.

Calculating the return of the portfolio is a bit more involved. Each of our three assets has three possible return values generating up to 27 different returns for the portfolio. If we were to use the preceding expected value formula, we would need not only to calculate all 27 possible returns, but also the corresponding 27 probability values. Luckily, there is a short cut. Because R_P is a linear function of R_{AE}, R_{CD}, and R_{EF}, the formulas that follow show that $E(R_P)$ is a linear function of $E(R_{AB})$, $E(R_{CD})$, and $E(R_{EF})$.

More generally, suppose that X is used to calculate some other quantity, say Y. Then it is possible to talk about the expected value of Y, or the expected value of this function of X:

$$If \ Y = f(X), then$$

$$E(Y) = E[f(X)].$$

The preceding formula can be made more specific when Y is a linear function of X, that is one in which X is multiplied by a constant and has a constant added to it. If Y is a linear function of X, then $E(Y)$ is particularly easy to find:

$$If \ Y = a + bX, then$$

$$E(Y) = a + bE(X).$$

That is, plug $E(X)$ into the linear formula to get $E(Y)$. Unfortunately, this does not hold for nonlinear functions (log, square root, and so on). Suppose you have the function $f(X)$ and you want to find the expected value of $E[f(X)]$. In general, you cannot plug $E(X)$ into the function and get the correct answer: $E[f(X)] \neq f[E(X)]$, unless $f(X)$ is a linear function like $a + bX$.

To go one step further, suppose we have several uncertain quantities, $X_1, X_2, \ldots, X_n$ and we add them to get uncertain quantity Y. Then the expected value of Y is the sum of the expected values:

$$If \ Y = X_1 + X_2 + \cdots + X_n, then$$

$$E(Y) = E(X_1) + E(X_2) + \cdots + E(X_n)$$

For instance, if we know the expected amount of precipitation for each of the next seven days, the expected amount of precipitation for the entire week is simply the sum of the seven daily expected values.

Returning to our portfolio, we can now easily calculate the expected return of P:

$$E(R_P) = E(W_{AB}R_{AB} + W_{CD}R_{CD} + W_{EF}R_{EF})$$

$$= E(W_{AB}R_{AB}) + E(W_{CD}R_{CD}) + E(W_{EF}R_{EF})$$

$$= W_{AB}E(R_{AB}) + W_{CD}E(R_{CD}) + W_{EF}E(R_{EF})$$

$$= W_{AB}(6.1\%) + W_{CD}(5\%) + W_{EF}(9\%).$$

It is important to point out that the weights are constants and not random variables, thus they slide out of the expected value: $E(W_{AB}R_{AB}) = W_{AB}E(R_{AB})$.

This formula is quite important to the portfolio manager as it shows that the expected portfolio return is the weighted sum of the individual returns. If the sole goal of the manager was to maximize expected return of P, then all the funds should be invested in EF, because EF has the highest expected return. Alternate weighting schemes would give lower expected returns. An equally weighted portfolio P has expected return equal to 6.7%. If two-thirds of the fund were placed in EF, and one-sixth in AB and CD, then P has expected return equal to 7.85%.

Portfolio managers need not only manage the expected return of the portfolio, but also the variability or risk of the portfolio, trying to carefully balance the two. While the expected return is a simple weighted average, portfolio risk is a more complex concept. In the next section, we develop the formulas needed to measure risk and discuss the subtleties of managing risk.

Variance and Standard Deviation

Another useful measure of a probability distribution is the *variance*. The variance of uncertain quantity X is denoted by $Var(X)$ or σ_X^2 (Greek sigma) and is calculated mathematically by

$$Var(X) = [x_1 - E(X)]^2 P(X = x_1) + \cdots + [x_n - E(X)]^2 P(X = x_n)$$

$$= \sum_{i=1}^{n} [x_i - E(X)]^2 P(X = x_i)$$

In words, first calculate the difference between the expected value and x_i, then square that difference. Do this for each: x_i, $i = 1, \ldots, n$. Finally, the variance is the probability weighted sum of these n squared differences. Note that any probability weighted sum is an expected value. Thus, the variance can be interpreted as the expected value of the squared differences:

$$Var(X) = E[(X - E(X))^2]$$

As with expected values, we can find variances of functions for X. In particular, the variance of a linear function of X is easily found:

$$If\ Y = a + bX,\ then$$

$$Var(Y) = b^2 Var(X).$$

For example, suppose that a firm will sell an uncertain number (X) of units of a product. The expected value of X is 1000 units, and the variance is 400. If the price is \$3 per unit, then the revenue (Y) is equal to $3X$. This is a linear function of X, so

$$E(Y) = E(3X) = 3E(X) = \$3,000 \text{ and}$$

$$Var(Y) = Var(3X) = 3^2 Var(X) = 9(400) = 3600.$$

We also can calculate the variance of a sum of independent uncertain quantities. *As long as the uncertain quantities are probabilistically independent*—the probability distribution for one does not depend on the others—then the variance of the sum is the sum of the variances:

> If $X_1, X_2, \ldots, X_n$ are probabilistically independent, then
>
> $Y = X_1 + X_2 + \cdots + X_n$ implies
>
> $Var(Y) = Var(X_1) + Var(X_2) + \cdots + Var(X_n)$.

So, if our firm sells two products, one for $3 and another for $5, and the variance for these two products is 400 and 750, respectively, and if the two products' sales are independent, then the variance of the firm's revenue is $Var(Y) = 3^2 Var(X_1) + 5^2 Var(X_2) = 9(400) + 25(750) = 22{,}350$. If however, there was a dependence relation between these two products, the preceding calculation is in error. To derive the formula when there is dependency, we need to know the relationship between X_1 and X_2, a topic covered in the online supplement at www.cengagebrain.com.

The *standard deviation* of X, denoted by σ_X is just the square root of the variance. Because the variance is the expected value of the squared differences, the standard deviation can be thought of as a "best guess" as to how far the outcome of X might lie from E(X). A large standard deviation and variance means that the probability distribution is quite spread out; a large difference between the outcome and the expected value is anticipated. For this reason, the variance and standard deviation of a probability distribution are used as measures of variability; a large variance or standard deviation indicates more variability in the outcomes.

To illustrate the ideas of expected value, variance, and standard deviation, consider the double-risk dilemma depicted in Figure 7.9. Choices A and B both lead to uncertain dollar outcomes. Given Choice A, for example, there are three possible profit outcomes having probability mass function P(Profit = $20 | A) = 0.24, P(Profit = $35 | A) = 0.47, and P(Profit = $50 | A) = 0.29. Likewise, for B we have P(Profit = −$9 | B) = 0.25, P(Profit = $0 | B) = 0.35, and P(Profit = $95 | B = 0.40. Now we can calculate the expected profits conditional on choosing A or B:

$$E(\text{Profit} \mid A) = 0.24(\$20) + 0.47(\$35) + 0.29(\$50) = \$35.75$$

$$E(\text{Profit} \mid B) = 0.25(-\$9) + 0.35(\$0) + 0.40(\$95) = \$35.75$$

FIGURE **7.9**
A choice between two uncertain prospects.

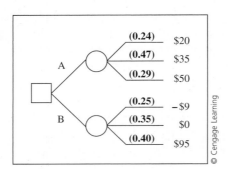

© Cengage Learning

These two uncertain quantities have exactly the same expected values. (Note that the expected profit does not have to be one of the possible outcomes!)

We also can calculate the variances and standard deviations (σ) for A and B:

$$\text{Var}(\text{Profit} \mid A) = (20 - 35.75)^2(0.24) + (35 - 35.75)^2(0.47)$$
$$+ (50 - 35.75)^2(0.29)$$
$$= 118.69 \text{ "dollars squared"}$$
$$\sigma_A = \$10.89$$

$$\text{Var}(\text{Profit} \mid B) = (-9 - 35.75)^2(0.25) + (0 - 35.75)^2(0.35)$$
$$+ (95 - 35.75)^2(0.40)$$
$$= 2352.19 \text{ "dollars squared"}$$
$$\sigma_B = \$48.50$$

The variance and standard deviation of B are much larger than those for A. The outcomes in B are more spread out or more variable than the outcomes for A, which are clustered fairly closely around the expected value.

The example also points out the fact that variance, being a weighted sum of squared terms, is expressed in squared units. In this case, the variance is in "dollars squared" because the original outcomes are in dollars. Taking the square root to find the standard deviation brings us back to the original units, or, in this case, dollars. For this reason, the standard deviation is interpreted more easily as a measure of variability.

The standard deviation is often used as a measure of the amount of uncertainty in a distribution. In finance, one speaks of the volatility of an asset or a portfolio, and volatility is simply the standard deviation. A standard deviation of zero corresponds to no uncertainty, and the distribution is simply a 100% chance of some particular number. A standard deviation that is not zero indicates that there is uncertainty; the larger the magnitude of the standard deviation, the greater the uncertainty. For example, in the double-risk dilemma, B has nearly five times the amount of uncertainty that A has; compare $\sigma_B = \$48.50$ to $\sigma_A = \$10.89$.

Be careful when interpreting the standard deviation. Students often jump to the conclusion that 68% of the distribution's values are within one standard deviation of the mean and 95% are within two standard deviations. Although this property sometimes is mentioned in statistics courses, it is only true for symmetric, bell-shaped distributions. For example, in the double-risk dilemma, we had the expected profit for A equal to $35.75 and the standard deviation equal to $10.89. Adding and subtracting one standard deviation from the mean produces the interval ($24.86, $46.64). According to the distribution of profit of A given in Figure 7.9, there is only a 47% chance, not a 68% chance, of A's profit being in this interval. Our use of the standard deviation is more nuanced than the 68–95% rule.

Because we know the distribution values, we can actually calculate the exact probability of the distribution falling within one or two standard deviation of the mean. As shown previously, there is a 47% chance of A's profit being between $24.86 and $46.64. Adding and subtracting two standard deviations, results in the interval ($13.97, $57.53), and referring to A's distribution in Figure 7.9, we see that there is a 100% chance that A's profit will be in that range. For B, there is a 60% chance of B's profit being within one standard deviation and 100% chance of being within two standard deviations.

In addition to the standard deviation as a measure of risk, cumulative probabilities can also be used to gauge the riskiness of an option. For example, we have $P(Profit \leq 0|A) = 0$, but $P(Profit \leq 0|B) = 0.6$, and B thus looks somewhat riskier than A. At the other extreme, of course, B looks better. Project A cannot produce a profit greater than $50: $P(Profit \leq \$50|A) = 1.00$, For B, however, $P(Profit \leq \$50|B) = 0.60$. Whereas the standard deviation provides a simple single-number summary of the risk, the CDF provides a more comprehensive description of the risk.

Continuous Probability Distributions

The preceding discussion has focused on discrete uncertain quantities. Now we turn briefly to continuous uncertain quantities. In this case, the uncertain quantity can take any value within some range. For example, the temperature tomorrow at O'Hare Airport in Chicago at noon is an uncertain quantity that can be anywhere between, say, $-50°F$ and $120°F$. The length of time until some anticipated event (e.g., the next major earthquake in California) is a continuous uncertain quantity, as are locations in space (the precise location of the next earthquake), as well as various measurements such as height, weight, and speed (e.g., the peak "ground acceleration" in the next major earthquake).

Surprisingly, when working with continuous uncertain quantities, the probability of a particular value occurring is equal to zero: $P(Y = y) = 0$. How can $P(Y = y) = 0$ for every single value y? Because there are infinitely many possible values for y, and so the probability of any particular value must be infinitely small. Rather, we typically speak of interval probabilities: $P(a \leq Y \leq b)$, for example, the probability that temperature tomorrow at O'Hare Airport in Chicago at noon is between 45 and 60 degrees. Next, we construct a CDF for a continuous uncertain quantity on the basis of interval probabilities.

Suppose you are interested in buying a particular duplex as income property, and you want to understand the distribution of yearly profits (revenues minus costs). You determine that if there were no vacancies (maximum revenue) and no upkeep costs, the maximum profit would be $24,000. If there were no renters and many repairs were necessary, then the minimum profit would be $-$25,000$ (i.e., a loss of $25,000). Thus, $P(-\$25,000 \leq Yearly\ Profit \leq \$24,000) = 1$. Then considering various vacancy rates (20%, 30%, etc.) and various upkeep costs and repairs, you determine that there is only a 10% chance that profits will be below $-$10,000$, that is $P(-\$25,000 \leq Yearly\ Profit \leq -\$10,000) = 0.10$, and that there is a 25% that profits will be above $15,000 or $P(\$15,000 \leq Yearly\ Profit \leq \$24,000) = 0.25$. Profit is of particular interest when above zero, which you determine has probability 70%, $P(\$0 \leq Yearly$

$Profit \leq \$24,000) = 0.70$. Because $P(\$15,000 \leq Yearly\ Profit \leq \$24,000) = 0.25$, we can calculate that $P(\$0 \leq Yearly\ Profit \leq \$15,000) = 0.45$.

At this point, we can construct a CDF based on these interval probabilities. First, we rewrite previous probability values as cumulative probabilities:

Interval Probability	Cumulative Probability
$P(Yearly\ Profit \leq -\$25,000) = 0.00$	$P(Yearly\ Profit \leq -\$25,000) = 0.00$
$P(-\$25,000 \leq Yearly\ Profit \leq -\$10,000) = 0.10$	$P(Yearly\ Profit \leq -\$10,000) = 0.10$
$P(-\$10,000 \leq Yearly\ Profit \leq \$0) = 0.20$	$P(Yearly\ Profit \leq \$0) = 0.30$
$P(\$0 \leq Yearly\ Profit \leq \$15,000) = 0.45$	$P(Yearly\ Profit \leq \$15,000) = 0.75$
$P(\$15,000 \leq Yearly\ Profit \leq \$24,000) = 0.25$	$P(Yearly\ Profit \leq \$24,000) = 1.00$

Then, we display these probabilities on a graph, with dollars along the horizontal axis and $P(Yearly\ Profit \leq y\ dollars)$ along the vertical axis. The graph, shown in Figure 7.10, allows you to select a dollar value on the horizontal axis and the resulting height of the graph is the probability that your yearly profit is less than or equal to that dollar value. As with the discrete case, this graph represents the cumulative distribution function, or CDF.

As before, the CDF allows us to calculate the probability of any interval. For example, $P(\$0 < Yearly\ Profit \leq \$10,000) = P(Yearly\ Profit \leq \$10,000) - (Yearly\ Profit \leq \$0) = 0.58 - 0.30 = 0.28$. If we were to make more assessments, we could refine the curve in Figure 7.10, but it should always slope upward. If it ever were to slope downward, it would imply that some interval had a negative probability!

FIGURE 7.10
Cumulative distribution of yearly profit for a rental property.

The five assessed values are shown as squares and the CDF is approximated by passing a smooth curve through the five points.

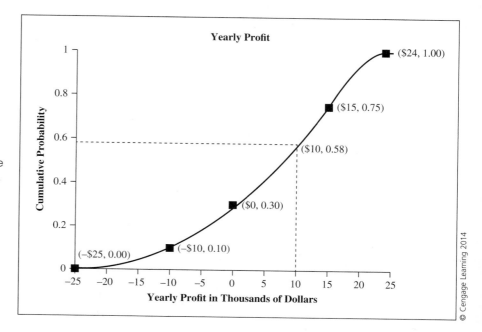

FIGURE **7.11**
CDFs for three
investment
alternatives.

Investment B
stochastically
dominates
Investment A.

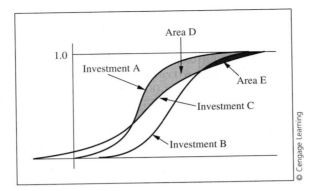

Stochastic Dominance Revisited

Figure 7.11 shows CDFs for three investment alternatives, each of which is modeled as a continuous uncertain quantity. Investment B stochastically dominates Investment A because the CDF for B lies entirely to the right of the CDF for A. On the other hand, Investment C neither dominates nor is dominated by the other two alternatives. For instance, Area E represents the portion of B's CDF that lies to the left of the CDF for Investment C. Because C's CDF crosses the other two, no decision can be made between C and B (or between C and A) on the basis of stochastic dominance. There is a sense in which B dominates C, however. Imagine an investor who is averse to risk; such an investor would gladly trade any risky prospect for its expected value. B is better than C for such an investor because it has less risk (the distribution is less spread out) and a greater expected value (the distribution is shifted to the right).

Probability Density Functions

The CDF for a continuous uncertain quantity corresponds closely to the CDF for the discrete case. Is there some representation that corresponds to the probability mass function? The answer is yes, and that representation is called a *probability density function*, which, if we are speaking of uncertain quantity X, would be denoted typically as $f(x)$. The density function $f(x)$ can be built up from the CDF. It is a function in which the area under the curve within a specific interval represents the probability that the uncertain quantity will fall in that interval. Whereas height represents probability for discrete distributions, it is area that represents probability for continuous distributions.

For example, the density function $f(Yearly\ Profit)$ for the yearly profit of the duplex might look something like the graph in Figure 7.12. The total area under the curve equals 1 because the uncertain quantity must take on some value. The middle area in Figure 7.12 corresponds to $P(\$0 < Yearly\ Profit \leq \$18,000)$ and the corresponding probability is given above the graph and equals 57%. We can also read from the graph that $P(Yearly\ Profit \leq \$0) = 30\%$ and

FIGURE **7.12**
Probability density
for yearly profit of
a rental property
showing a 57%
chance that profit
will be between
$0 and $18,000.

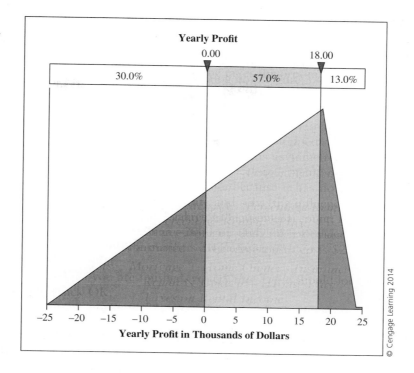

$P(\$18,000 < Yearly\ Profit) = 13\%$. Note that any shape, even triangles, can be a probability density function as long as the area under the curve is one and the curve never drops below the x-axis.

Expected Value, Variance, and Standard Deviation: The Continuous Case

As in the discrete case, a continuous probability distribution can have an expected value, variance, and standard deviation. But the definition is not as easy as it was before because now we do not have probabilities for specific values, only probabilities for intervals. Without going into a lot of detail, these characteristics of a continuous probability distribution are defined by using calculus. The definitions for a continuous uncertain quantity X correspond to the discrete case, except that the summation sign is replaced with an integral sign and the density function is used in place of the probabilities:

$$E(X) = \int_{x^-}^{x^+} x f(x)\,dx$$

$$Var(X) = \sigma_x^2 = \int_{x^-}^{x^+} [x - E(X)]^2 f(x)\,dx$$

FIGURE **7.13**
A density function
$f(x)$ divided into
narrow, equal-
width intervals.

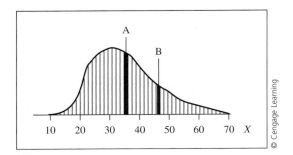

The probability that
X falls in interval A is
about twice as great
as for B because $f(x)$
is about twice as high in
A as it is in B.

where x^- and x^+ represent the lower and upper bounds for the uncertain quantity X. As before, the standard deviation σ_X is the square root of the variance.

The interpretation of these formulas also corresponds closely to the summation in the discrete case. It turns out that integration is really the continuous equivalent of the summing operation. Consider the formula for the expected value, for example. Each possible value x between x^- and x^+ is multiplied by (weighted by) the height of the density function $f(x)$. The integration then adds all of these $xf(x)$ products to find $E(X)$. It is as if we had carved up the density function into a very large number of quite narrow but equally wide intervals (Figure 7.13). The relative likelihood of X falling in these different intervals corresponds to the relative height of the density function in each interval. That is, if the density function is (on average) twice as high in one interval as in another, then X is twice as likely to fall into the first interval as the second. As the intervals become infinitesimally narrow, the height of the interval becomes equal to the value $f(x)$. In the limit, as the width of each interval approaches 0, we take each x, multiply by $f(x)$, add these products (by integration), and—bingo!—we get $E(X)$.

Rest assured—you will not be required to perform any integration (in this book anyway). In general, the integration of density functions to obtain expected values and variances is a difficult task and beyond the technical scope of this textbook. Fortunately, mathematicians have studied many different kinds of probability distributions and have performed the integration for you, providing you with formulas for the expected values and variances. We will encounter several of these in Chapter 9.

What about all of those formulas for the expected value and variance of Y, a function of X, or for linear combinations of random variables? Fortunately, *all of those formulas carry over to the continuous case.* If you know the expected value and variance of several uncertain quantities, you can apply the preceding formulas regardless of whether the uncertain quantities are continuous or discrete. For example, if $Y = a + bX$, then $E(Y) = a + bE(X)$. If $Y = aX_1 + bX_2$, and X_1 and X_2 are independent, then $Var(Y) = a^2 Var(X_1) + b^2 Var(X_2)$. It does not matter whether the X's are discrete or continuous.

OIL WILDCATTING

An oil company is considering two sites for an exploratory well. Because of budget constraints, only one well can be drilled. Site 1 is fairly risky, with substantial uncertainty about the amount of oil that might be found. On the other hand, Site 2 is fairly certain to produce a low level of oil. The characteristics of the two sites are as follows:

Site 1: Cost to Drill $100,000	
Outcome	Payoff
Dry	−$100,000
Low producer	$150,000
High producer	$500,000

If the rock strata underlying Site 1 are characterized by what geologists call a "dome" structure (see Figure 7.14), the chances of finding oil are somewhat greater than if no dome structure exists. The probability of a dome structure is $P(Dome) = 0.6$. The conditional probabilities of finding oil at Site 1 are given in Table 7.1.

Site 2 is considerably less complicated. A well there is not expected to be a high producer, so the only outcomes considered are a dry hole and a low producer. The cost, outcomes, payoffs, and probabilities are as follows:

Site 2: Cost to Drill $200,000		
Outcome	Payoff	Probability
Dry	−$200,000	0.2
Low producer	$50,000	0.8

The decision tree is shown in Figure 7.15. The problem with it as drawn, however, is that we cannot assign probabilities immediately to the outcomes

FIGURE **7.14**
Rock strata forming a dome structure.

Oil tends to pool at the top of the dome in an oilbearing layer if the layer above is impermeable.

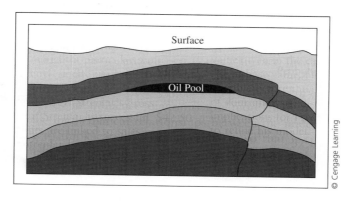

© Cengage Learning

TABLE **7.1**
Conditional
probabilities of
outcomes at Site 1.

If Dome Structure Exists	
Outcome	P(Outcome | Dome)
Dry	0.600
Low	0.250
High	0.150
	1.000

If No Dome Structure Exists	
Outcome	P(Outcome | No Dome)
Dry	0.850
Low	0.125
High	0.025
	1.000

© Cengage Learning

FIGURE **7.15**
Decision tree for
oil wildcatting
problem.

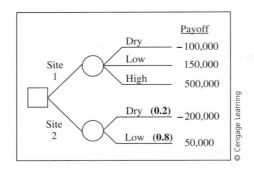

© Cengage Learning

for Site 1. To find these probabilities, we must use the conditional probabilities and the law of total probability to calculate P(Dry), P(Low), and P(High):

$$P(Dry) = P(Dry \mid Dome)\, P(Dome) + P(Dry \mid No\ Dome)\, P(No\ Dome)$$

$$= 0.6(0.6) + 0.85(0.4) = 0.70$$

$$P(Low) = P(Low \mid Dome)\, P(Dome) + P(Low \mid No\ Dome)\, P(No\ Dome)$$

$$= 0.25(0.6) + 0.125(0.4) = 0.20$$

$$P(High) = P(High \mid Dome)\, P(Dome) + P(High \mid No\ Dome)\, P(No\ Dome)$$

$$= 0.15(0.6) + 0.025(0.4) = 0.10$$

Everything works out as it should. The three probabilities are for mutually exclusive and collectively exhaustive outcomes, and they add to 1, just as they should. Folding back the decision tree, we find that Site 1 has the higher EMV (expected payoff):

$$\text{EMV(Site 1)} = 0.7(-100K) + 0.2(150K) + 0.1(500K)$$
$$= \$10K$$
$$\text{EMV(Site 2)} = 0.2(-200K) + 0.8(50K)$$
$$= \$0$$

We also can calculate the variance and standard deviation of the payoffs for each site:

$$\sigma_1^2 = 0.7(-100 - 10)^2 + 0.2(150 - 10)^2 + 0.1(500 - 10)^2$$
$$= 0.7(-110)^2 + 0.2(140)^2 + 0.1(490)^2$$
$$= 36{,}400K^2$$
$$\sigma_1 = \$190.79K$$

$$\sigma_2^2 = 0.2(-200 - 0)^2 + 0.8(50 - 0)^2$$
$$= 0.2(-200)^2 + 08(50)^2$$
$$= 10{,}000K^2$$
$$\sigma_2 = \$100.00K$$

If we treat these numbers as measures of variability, it is clear that Site 1, with its higher variance and standard deviation, is more variable than Site 2. In this sense, Site 1 might be considered to be riskier than Site 2.

Note that we could have drawn the decision tree as in Figure 7.16, with "stacked" probabilities. That is, we could have drawn it with a first chance node indicating whether or not a dome is present, followed by chance nodes for the amount of oil. These chance nodes include the conditional probabilities from Table 7.1.

FIGURE **7.16**
An alternative decision tree for the oil wildcatting problem.

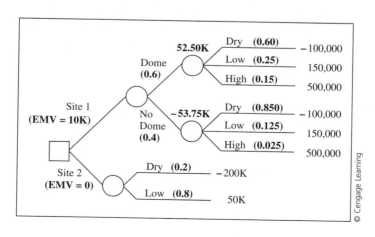

TABLE **7.2**
Calculating the
probabilities for
Site 1.

	Dome	No Dome	
Dry	0.36	0.34	0.70
Low	0.15	0.05	0.20
High	0.09	0.01	0.10
	0.60	0.40	1.00

© Cengage Learning

We also could have created a probability table as in Table 7.2. The probabilities in the cells of the table are the joint probabilities of both outcomes happening at the same time. Calculating the joint probabilities for the table requires the definition of conditional probability. For example:

$$P(\text{Low and Dome}) = P(\text{Dome})\, P(\text{Low} \mid \text{Dome})$$

$$= 0.60\,(0.25)$$

$$= 0.15$$

The probability table is easy to construct and easy to understand. Once the probabilities of the joint outcomes are calculated, the probabilities of the individual outcomes then are found by adding across the rows or down the columns. For example, from Table 7.2, we can tell that $P(Dry) = 0.36 + 0.34 = 0.70$. (You may remember that these are called *marginal* probabilities because they are found in the margins of the table!)

Suppose that the company drills at Site 1 and the well is a high producer. In light of this evidence, does it seem more likely that a dome structure exists? Can we figure out P(Dome | High)? This question is part of a larger problem. Figure 7.17 shows a "probability tree" (a decision tree without decisions) that reflects the information that we have been given in the problem. We know P(Dome) and P(No Dome), and we know the conditional probabilities of the amount of oil given the presence or absence of a dome. Thus, our probability tree has the chance node representing the presence or absence of a dome on the left and the chance node representing the amount of oil on the right. Finding P(Dome | High) is a matter of "flipping the tree" so that the chance node for the amount of oil is on the left and the node for the presence or absence of a dome is on the right, as in Figure 7.18.

FIGURE **7.17**
Probability tree for
the uncertainty
faced at Site 1.

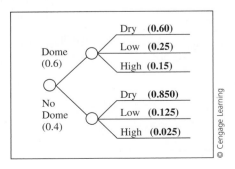

© Cengage Learning

FIGURE **7.18**
Flipping the probability tree in Figure 16.

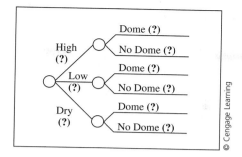

© Cengage Learning

FIGURE **7.19**
Reversing arrows between chance nodes in an influence diagram.

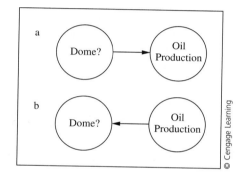

© Cengage Learning

Flipping a probability tree is the same as reversing an arrow between two chance nodes in an influence diagram. In Figure 7.19a, the direction of the arrow represents the probabilities as they are given in Table 7.1. Because the arrow points to the "Oil Production" node, the probabilities for the level of oil production are conditioned on whether or not there is a dome. Figure 7.19b shows the arrow reversed. Now the probability of a dome or no dome is conditioned on the amount of oil produced. Changing the direction of the arrow has the same effect as flipping the probability tree.

Simply flipping the tree or turning the arrow around in the influence diagram is not enough. The question marks in Figure 7.18 indicate that we do not yet know what the probabilities are for the flipped tree. The probabilities in the new tree must be consistent with the probabilities in the original version. Consistency means that if we were to calculate P(Dome) and P(No Dome) using the probabilities in the new tree, we would get 0.60 and 0.40, the probabilities we started with in Figure 7.17. How do we ensure consistency?

We can find P(High), P(Low), and P(Dry) by using the law of total probability. When we did the preceding calculations for Figure 7.15, we found that P(High) = 0.10, P(Low) = 0.20, and P(Dry) = 0.70. How about finding the new conditional probabilities? Bayes' theorem provides the answer. For example:

$$P(Dome \mid High) = \frac{P(High \mid Dome)P(Dome)}{P(High)}$$

$$= \frac{P(High \mid Dome)P(Dome)}{P(High \mid Dome)P(Dome) + P(High \mid No\ Dome)P(No\ Dome)}$$

$$= \frac{0.15(0.6)}{0.15(0.6) + 0.025(0.4)}$$

$$= \frac{0.15(0.6)}{0.10} = 0.90$$

Probabilities that have the same conditions must add to 1, and so P(No Dome | High) must be equal to 0.10. Likewise, we can calculate the conditional probabilities of a dome or no dome given a dry hole or a low producer. These probabilities are shown in Figure 7.20.

If you did not enjoy using Bayes' theorem directly to calculate the conditional probabilities required in flipping the tree, you may be pleased to learn that the probability table (Table 7.2) has all the information needed. Recall that the entries in the cells inside the table are the joint probabilities. For example, P(High and Dome) = 0.09. We need P(Dome | High) = P(High and Dome)/P(High), which is just 0.09/0.10 = 0.90. That is, we take the joint probability from inside the table and divide it by the probability of the outcome on the right side of the vertical bar. This probability is found in the margin of the probability table.

Whether we use Bayes' theorem directly or the probability-table approach to flip the probability tree, the conditional probabilities that we obtain have an interesting interpretation. Recall that we started with P(Dome) = 0.60. After finding that the well was a high producer, we were able to calculate P(Dome | High). This probability sometimes is called a *posterior* probability, indicating that it is the result of revising the original probability after gathering data. In contrast, the probability with which we started, in this case P(Dome) = 0.60, sometimes is called the *prior* probability. One way to think about Bayes' theorem is that it provides a mechanism to update prior probabilities when new information becomes available. [*Source:* The oil-wildcatting

FIGURE **7.20**
The flipped probability tree with new probabilities.

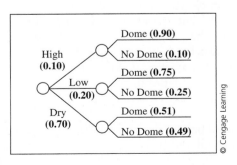

© Cengage Learning

example and analysis are adapted from C. A. Holloway (1979) *Decision Making under Uncertainty: Models and Choices,* pp. 195–200. Englewood Cliffs, NJ: Prentice-Hall.]

JOHN HINCKLEY'S TRIAL

In 1982 John Hinckley was on trial, accused of having attempted to kill President Reagan. During Hinckley's trial, Dr. Daniel R. Weinberger told the court that when individuals diagnosed as schizophrenics were given computerized axial tomography (CAT) scans, the scans showed brain atrophy in 30% of the cases compared with only 2% of the scans done on normal people. Hinckley's defense attorney wanted to introduce as evidence Hinckley's CAT scan, which showed brain atrophy. The defense argued that the presence of atrophy strengthened the case that Hinckley suffered from mental illness.

We can use Bayes' theorem easily to analyze this situation. We want to know the probability that Hinckley was schizophrenic given that he had brain atrophy. Approximately 1.5% of people in the United States suffer from schizophrenia. This is the *base rate,* which we can interpret as the prior probability of schizophrenia before we find out about the condition of an individual's brain. Thus, $P(S) = 0.015$, where S means schizophrenia. We also have $P(A \mid S) = 0.30$ (A means atrophy) and $P(A \mid \bar{S}) = 0.02$. We want $P(S \mid A)$. Bayes' theorem provides the mathematical mechanism for flipping the probability from $P(A \mid S)$ to $P(S \mid A)$:

$$P(S \mid A) = \frac{P(A \mid S)P(S)}{P(A \mid S)P(S) + P(A \mid \bar{S})P(\bar{S})}$$

$$= \frac{0.30(0.015)}{0.30(0.015) + 0.02(0.985)}$$

$$= 0.186$$

Thus, given that his brain showed such atrophy, Hinckley still has less than a 1-in-5 chance of being schizophrenic. Given the situation, this is perhaps a surprisingly low probability. The intuition behind this result is that there are many false-positive tests. If we tested 100,000 individuals, some 1,500 of them would be schizophrenic and 98,500 would be normal (or at least not schizophrenic). Of the 1,500, only 30%, or approximately 450, would show atrophy. Of the 98,500, 2% (some 1,970) would show brain atrophy. If a single individual has atrophy, is he one of the 450 with schizophrenia or one of the 1,970 without? Note that:

$$0.186 = \frac{450}{450 + 1,970}$$

The real question is whether this is good news or bad news for Hinckley. The prosecution might argue that the probability of schizophrenia is too small to make any difference; even in light of the CAT-scan evidence,

Hinckley is less than one fourth as likely to be schizophrenic as not. On the other hand, the defense would counter, 0.186 is much larger than 0.015. Thus, the CAT-scan results indicate that Hinckley was more than 12 times as likely to be schizophrenic as a randomly chosen person on the street.

Now, however, consider what we have done in applying Bayes' theorem. We have used a prior probability of 0.015, which essentially is the probability that a randomly chosen person from the population is schizophrenic. *But Hinckley was not randomly chosen.* In fact, it does not seem reasonable to think of Hinckley, a man accused of attempted assassination, as the typical person on the street.

If 0.015 is not an appropriate prior probability, what is? It may not be obvious what an appropriate prior probability should be, so let us consider a sensitivity analysis approach and see what different prior probabilities would imply. Imagine a juror who, before encountering the CAT-scan evidence, believes that there is only a 10% chance that Hinckley is schizophrenic. For most of us, this would be a fairly strong statement; Hinckley is nine times as likely to be normal as schizophrenic. Now consider the impact of the CAT-scan evidence on this prior probability. We can calculate this juror's posterior probability:

$$P(S \mid A) = \frac{0.30(0.10)}{0.30(0.10) + 0.02(0.90)}$$

$$= 0.63$$

$P(S \mid A) = 0.63$ is a substantial probability. We can do this for a variety of values for the prior probability. Figure 7.21 shows the posterior probability

FIGURE **7.21**
Graph of the posterior probability that Hinckley was schizophrenic plotted against the prior probability.

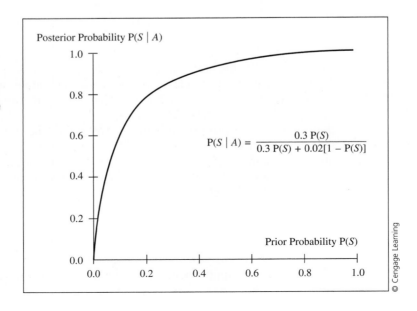

Posterior Probability P(S | A)

$$P(S \mid A) = \frac{0.3\,P(S)}{0.3\,P(S) + 0.02[1 - P(S)]}$$

Prior Probability P(S)

© Cengage Learning

P(S | A) graphed as a function of the prior probability that Hinckley was schizophrenic.

As a result of this discussion, it is clear that a juror need not have a very strong prior belief for the CAT-scan evidence to have an overwhelming effect on his or her posterior belief of Hinckley's mental illness. Furthermore, no matter what the juror's prior belief, the CAT-scan result must increase the probability that Hinckley was schizophrenic. [*Source:* A. Barnett, I. Greenberg, and R. Machol (1984) "Hinckley and the Chemical Bath." *Interfaces,* 14, 48–52.]

SUMMARY

The definitions and formulas at the beginning of the chapter are the building blocks of probability theory. Venn diagrams provide a way to visualize these probability "laws." We also discussed uncertain quantities, their probability distributions, and characteristics of those distributions such as expected value, variance, and standard deviation. The use of probability concepts and the manipulation of probabilities were demonstrated in the oil-wildcatting and Hinckley trial examples.

EXERCISES

7.1. Explain why probability is important in decision analysis.

7.2. Explain in your own words what an uncertain quantity or random variable is. Why is the idea of an uncertain quantity important in decision analysis?

7.3. You are given the following probability table:

	A	$\overline{A}$	
B	0.12	0.53	0.65
$\overline{B}$	0.29	0.06	0.35
	0.41	0.59	1.00

Use the probability table to find the following:

P(A and B), P(A and $\overline{B}$), P(A), P(B), P($\overline{B}$), P(B | A), P(A | B), P($\overline{A}$ | $\overline{B}$)

7.4. Use the probability table in Exercise 7.3 to find P(A or B), or the outcome where either A occurs or B occurs (or both).

7.5. The Outcome (A or B) sometimes is called the union of A and B. The union event occurs if either Outcome A or Outcome B (or both) occurs. Suppose that both A and B can happen at the same time (i.e., their areas overlap in a Venn diagram). Show that P(A or B) = P(A) + P(B) − P(A and B). Use a Venn diagram to explain. Why is this result consistent with the second requirement that probabilities add up?

7.6. Often it is difficult to distinguish between the probability of an intersection of outcomes (joint probability) and the probability of a conditional outcome (conditional probability). Classify the following as joint probability statements or conditional probability statements. [If in doubt, try to write down the probability statement; for example, P(Crash Landing | Out of Fuel) or P(Dow Jones Up and Stock Price Up).]

   a. Eight percent of the students in a class were left-handed and red-haired.
   b. Of the left-handed students, 20% had red hair.
   c. If the Orioles lose their next game, then the Cubs have a 90% chance of winning the pennant.
   d. Fifty-nine percent of the people with a positive test result had the disease.
   e. For 78% of patients, the surgery is a success and the cancer never reappears.
   f. If the surgery is a success, the cancer is unlikely to reappear.
   g. Given the drought, food prices are likely to increase.
   h. There is an even chance that a farmer who loses his crop will go bankrupt.
   i. If the temperature is high and there is no rain, farmers probably will lose their crops.
   j. John probably will be arrested because he is trading on insider information.
   k. John probably will trade on insider information and get caught.

7.7. Calculate the variance and standard deviation of the returns of stocks AB, CD, and EF in the portfolio example of this chapter. See Figure 7.8.

7.8. $P(A) = 0.42$, $P(B \mid A) = 0.66$, and $P(B \mid \overline{A}) = 0.25$. Find the following:

$$P(\overline{A}), \; P(\overline{B} \mid A), \; P(\overline{B} \mid \overline{A}), \; P(B), \; P(A \mid B), \; P(\overline{A} \mid B), \; P(A \mid \overline{B}), \; P(\overline{A} \mid \overline{B})$$

7.9. $P(A) = 0.10$, $P(B \mid A) = 0.39$, and $P(B \mid \overline{A}) = 0.39$. Find the following:

$$P(\overline{A}), \; P(\overline{B} \mid A), \; P(\overline{B} \mid \overline{A}), \; P(B), \; P(\overline{B}), \; P(A \mid B), \; P(\overline{A} \mid B), \; P(A \mid \overline{B}), \; P(\overline{A} \mid \overline{B})$$

How would you describe the relationship between Outcomes A and B?

7.10. Consider the following joint probability distribution for uncertain quantities X and Y:

$$P(X = -2 \text{ and } Y = 2) = 0.2$$

$$P(X = -1 \text{ and } Y = 1) = 0.2$$

$$P(X = 0 \text{ and } Y = 0) = 0.2$$

$$P(X = 1 \text{ and } Y = 1) = 0.2$$

$$P(X = 2 \text{ and } Y = 2) = 0.2$$

    a. Calculate

        $P(Y = 2)$, $P(Y = 2 \mid X = 2)$, $P(Y = 2 \mid X = 2)$, $P(Y = 2 \mid X = 0)$

    b. Calculate $P(X = 2)$, $P(X = 2 \mid Y = 2)$, $P(X = 2 \mid Y = 0)$

    c. Are X and Y dependent or independent? How would you describe the relationship between X and Y?

7.11. Write probability statements relating hemline height, stock market prices, and "adventuresomeness" that correspond to the following description of these relationships:

> Another example is that high skirt hemlines tend to occur when the stock market is advancing steadily (a bull market), although no one believes that hemlines cause the stock market to advance, or vice versa. Perhaps both reflect a pervasive feeling of confidence and adventure in our society. If we had an adequate index of "societal adventuresomeness," hemline height and stock market activity might well be conditionally independent given the index.

7.12. Even though we distinguish between continuous and discrete uncertain quantities, in reality everything is discrete if only because of limitations inherent in our measuring devices. For example, we can only measure time or distance to a certain level of precision. Why, then, do we make the distinction between continuous and discrete uncertain quantities? What value is there in using continuous uncertain quantities in a decision model?

7.13. $P(A) = 0.68$, $P(B \mid A) = 0.30$, and $P(B \mid \overline{A}) = 0.02$. Find $P(A)$, $P(A \text{ and } B)$, and $P(\overline{A} \text{ and } B)$. Use these to construct a probability table. Now use the table to find the following:

    $P(\overline{B} \mid A)$, $P(\overline{B} \mid \overline{A})$, $P(B)$, $P(\overline{B})$, $P(\overline{A} \mid B)$, $P(A \mid \overline{B})$, $P(\overline{A} \mid \overline{B})$.

7.14. Julie Myers, a graduating senior in accounting, is preparing for an interview with a Big Four accounting firm. Before the interview, she sets her chances of eventually getting an offer at 50%. Then, on thinking about her friends who have interviewed and gotten offers from this firm, she realizes that of the people who received offers, 95% had good interviews. On the other hand, of those who did not receive offers, 75% said they had good interviews. If Julie Myers has a good interview, what are her chances of receiving an offer?

7.15. Find the expected value, variance, and standard deviation of X in the following probability distributions:

    a. $P(X = 1) = 0.05$, $P(X = 2) = 0.45$, $P(X = 3) = 0.30$, $P(X = 4) = 0.20$

    b. $P(X = -20) = 0.13$, $P(X = 0) = 0.58$, $P(X = 100) = 0.29$

    c. $P(X = 0) = 0.368$, $P(X = 1) = 0.632$

7.16. If $P(X = 1) = p$ and $P(X = 0) = 1-p$, show that $E(X) = p$ and $Var(X) = p(1-p)$.

7.17. If $P(A \mid B) = p$, must $P(A \mid \overline{B}) = 1-p$? Explain.

7.18. Suppose that a company produces three different products. The sales for each product are independent of the sales for the others. The information for these products is given in the table that follows:

Product	Price ($)	Expected Unit Sales	Variance of Unit Sales
A	3.50	2,000	1,000
B	2.00	10,000	6,400
C	1.87	8,500	1,150

a. What are the expected revenue and variance of the revenue from Product A alone?
b. What are the company's overall expected revenue and variance of its revenue?

7.19. A company owns two different computers, which are in separate buildings and operated entirely separately. Based on past history, Computer 1 is expected to break down 5.0 times a year, with a variance of 6, and costing $200 per breakdown. Computer 2 is expected to break down 3.6 times per year, with a variance of 7, and costing $165 per breakdown. What is the company's expected cost for computer breakdowns and the variance of the breakdown cost? What assumption must you make to find the variance? Is this a reasonable assumption?

7.20. A firm is negotiating with a local club to supply materials for a party. The firm's manager expects to sell 100 large bags of pretzels for $3 each or 300 for $2 each; these two outcomes are judged to be equally likely. The expected number of bags sold is $200 = (100 + 300)/2$, and expected price is $2.50 = (\$3 + \$2)/2$. The manager then calculates expected revenue as the expected number sold times the expected price: E(Revenue) = 200($2.50) = $500. What is wrong with the manager's calculation?

7.21. Flip the probability tree shown in Figure 7.22.

7.22. Figure 7.23 shows part of an influence diagram for a chemical that is considered potentially carcinogenic. How would you describe the relationship between the test results and the field results?

7.23. Let CP denote carcinogenic potential, TR test results, and FR field results. Suppose that for Figure 7.23 we have the following probabilities:

$$P(CP\ High) = 0.27 \qquad P(CP\ Low) = 0.73$$

$$P(TR\ Positive \mid CP\ High) = 0.82 \qquad P(TR\ Positive \mid CP\ Low) = 0.21$$

$$P(TR\ Negative \mid CP\ High) = 0.18 \qquad P(TR\ Negative \mid CP\ Low) = 0.79$$

$$P(FR\ Positive \mid CP\ High) = 0.95 \qquad P(FR\ Positive \mid CP\ Low) = 0.17$$

$$P(FR\ Negative \mid CP\ High) = 0.05 \qquad P(FR\ Negative \mid CP\ Low) = 0.83$$

FIGURE **7.22**
A probability tree representing the diagnostic performance of a medical test.

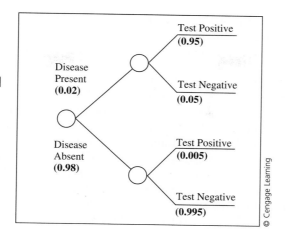

FIGURE **7.23**
An influence diagram for a potentially carcinogenic chemical.

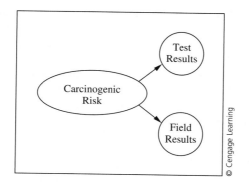

Find the following:

$$P(\text{TR Positive and FR Positive} \mid \text{CP High})$$

$$P(\text{TR Positive and FR Negative} \mid \text{CP High})$$

$$P(\text{TR Negative and FR Negative} \mid \text{CP Low})$$

$$P(\text{TR Negative and FR Positive} \mid \text{CP Low})$$

QUESTIONS AND PROBLEMS

7.24. Linda is 31 years old, single, outspoken, and very bright. She majored in philosophy. As a student, she was deeply concerned with issues of discrimination and social justice and also participated in antinuclear demonstrations. Use your judgment to rank the following statements by their probability, using 1 for the most probable statement and 8 for the least probable:

a. Linda is a teacher in an elementary school.
b. Linda works in a bookstore and takes Yoga classes.
c. Linda is active in the feminist movement.
d. Linda is a psychiatric social worker.
e. Linda is a member of the League of Women Voters.
f. Linda is a bank teller.
g. Linda is an insurance salesperson.
h. Linda is a bank teller and is active in the feminist movement.

[*Source:* Amos Tversky and Daniel Kahneman (1982) "Judgments of and by Representativeness." In D. Kahneman, P. Slovic, and A. Tversky (eds.), *Judgment under Uncertainty: Heuristics and Biases,* pp. 84–98. Cambridge: Cambridge University Press.]

7.25. The description and statements given in Problem 7.24 often elicit responses that are not consistent with probability requirements. If you are like most people, you ranked statement h (Linda is a bank teller and is active in the feminist movement) as more probable than statement f (Linda is a bank teller).

a. Explain why you ranked statements h and f as you did.
b. Statement h is actually a compound event. That is, for h to be true, Linda must be both a bank teller (Outcome A) and active in the feminist movement (Outcome B). Thus, statement h is represented by the Outcome "A" *and* "B." Use a Venn diagram to explain why statement h must be less probable than statement f.
c. Suppose that you have presented Problem 1 to a friend, who ranks statement h as more probable than statement f. Your friend argues as follows: "Well, it's not very likely that Linda is a bank teller in the first place. But if she is a bank teller, then she is very likely to be active in the feminist movement. So h would appear to be more likely than f." How is your friend interpreting statement h? Explain why this is not an appropriate interpretation.

7.26. Suppose you are a contestant on the television game show, *Let's Make a Deal.* You must choose one of three closed doors, labeled A, B, and C, and you will receive whatever is behind the chosen door. Behind two of the doors is a goat, and behind the third is a new car. Like most people, you have no use for a goat, but the car would be very welcome. Suppose you choose Door A. Now the host opens Door B, revealing a goat, and offers to let you switch from Door A to Door C. Do you switch? Why or why not? [*Hint:* What can you assume about the host's behavior? Would it ever be the case that the host would open a door to reveal the car before asking if you want to switch?]

7.27. On the fictitious television game show, "Marginal Analysis for Everyone," the host subjects contestants to unusual tests of mental skill. On one, a contestant may choose one of two identical envelopes labeled A and B, each of which contains an unknown amount of money. The host reveals, though, that one envelope contains twice as much as the other. After choosing A, the host suggests that the contestant might want to switch.

"Switching is clearly advantageous," intones the host persuasively. "Suppose you have amount x in your Envelope A. Then B must contain either $x/2$ (with probability 0.5) or $2x$ (also with probability 0.5). Thus, the expected value of switching is $1.25x$. In fact now that I think about it, I'll only let you switch if you give me a 10% cut of your winnings. What do you say? You'll still be ahead."

"No deal," replies the contestant. "But I'll be happy to switch for free. In fact, I'll even let you choose which envelope I get. I won't even charge you anything!"

What is wrong with the host's analysis?

[*Source:* This problem was suggested by Ross Shachter.]

7.28. Show that if A is independent of B, that is, $P(A_i \mid B_j) = P(A_i)$ for all possible Outcomes $A_1, A_2, \ldots, A_n$ and $B_1, B_2, \ldots, B_m$ then B is independent of A, that is, $P(B_j \mid A_i) = P(B_j)$ for all possible Outcomes $A_1, A_2, \ldots, A_n$ and $B_1, B_2, \ldots, B_m$

7.29. Calculate the variance and standard deviation of the payoffs in the final court decision in the Texaco-Pennzoil case as diagrammed in Figure 4.2.

7.30. In the oil-wildcatting problem, suppose that the company could collect information from a drilling core sample and analyze it to determine whether a dome structure exists at Site 1. A positive result would indicate the presence of a dome, and a negative result would indicate the absence of a dome. The test is not perfect, however. The test is highly accurate for detecting a dome; if there is a dome, the test shows a positive result 99% of the time. On the other hand, if there is no dome, the probability of a negative result is only 0.85. Thus, $P(+ \mid \text{Dome}) = 0.99$ and $P(- \mid \text{No Dome}) = 0.85$. Use these probabilities, the information given in the example, and Bayes' theorem to find the posterior probabilities $P(\text{Dome} \mid +)$ and $P(\text{Dome} \mid -)$. If the test gives a positive result, which site should be selected? Calculate expected values to support your conclusion. If the test result is negative, which site should be chosen? Again, calculate expected values.

7.31. In Problem 7.30, calculate the probability that the test is positive and a dome structure exists $[P(+ \text{ and Dome})]$. Now calculate the probability of a positive result, a dome structure, and a dry hole $[P(+ \text{ and Dome and Dry})]$. Finally, calculate $P(\text{Dome} \mid + \text{ and Dry})$.

7.32. Referring to the oil-wildcatting decision diagrammed in Figure 7.16, suppose that the decision maker has not yet assessed $P(\text{Dome})$ for Site 1. Find the value of $P(\text{Dome})$ for which the two sites have the same EMV. If the decision maker believes that $P(\text{Dome})$ is between 0.55 and 0.65, what action should be taken?

7.33. Again referring to Figure 7.16, suppose the decision maker has not yet assessed P(Dry) for Site 2 or P(Dome) for Site 1. Let P(Dry) = p and P(Dome) = q. Construct a two-way sensitivity analysis graph for this decision problem.

7.34. Refer to Exercises 7.22 and 7.23. Calculate P(FR Positive) and P(FR Positive | TR Positive). [*Hints:* P(FR Positive) is a fairly simple calculation. To find P(FR Positive | TR Positive), first let B = FR Positive, C = TR Positive, A = CP High, and $\overline{A}$ = CP Low. Now expand P(FR Positive | TR Positive) using the law of total probability in this form:

$$P(B \mid C) = P(B \mid A, \ C)P(A \mid C) + P(B \mid \overline{A}, \ C)P(\overline{A} \mid C)$$

Now all of the probabilities on the right side can be calculated using the information in the problem.]

Compare P(FR Positive) and P(FR Positive | TR Positive). Would you say that the test results and field results are independent? Why or why not? Discuss the difference between conditional independence and regular independence.

7.35. The return of an asset is defined to be the ratio of the change in price to the initial price. For example, if we denote the initial price of AB as $ABPrice_0$ and the price after one period as $ABPrice_1$ the return after one period is:

$$R_{AB} = \frac{(ABPrice_1 - ABPrice_0)}{ABPrice_0}.$$

Given the beginning and ending prices of the three assets, AB, CD, and EF, calculate the beginning and ending price of the portfolio P. Then show $R_P = W_{AB}R_{AB} + W_{CD}R_{CD} + W_{EF}R_{EF}$.

CASE STUDIES

DECISION ANALYSIS MONTHLY

Peter Finch looked at the numbers for the renewals of subscriptions to *Decision Analysis Monthly* magazine. For both May and June he had figures for the percentage of expiring subscriptions that were gift subscriptions, promotional subscriptions, and from previous subscribers. Furthermore, his data showed what proportion of the expiring subscriptions in each category had been renewed (see Table 7.3).

Finch was confused as he considered these numbers. Robert Calloway, who had assembled the data, had told him that the overall proportion of renewals had dropped from May to June. But the figures showed clearly that the proportion renewed had increased in each category. How could the overall proportion possibly have gone down? Peter got a pencil and pad of paper to check Calloway's figures. He had to report to his boss that afternoon and wanted to be able to tell him whether these figures represented good news or bad news.

Question

1. Do the data represent good news or bad news regarding renewal trends? Why?

TABLE **7.3**
Subscription data for *Decision Analysis Monthly.*

May Subscription Data	Expiring Subscriptions, %	Proportion Renewed
Gift Subscriptions	70	0.75
Promotional Subscriptions	20	0.50
Previous Subscribers	10	0.10
Total	100	

June Subscription Data	Expiring Subscriptions, %	Proportion Renewed
Gift Subscriptions	45	0.85
Promotional Subscriptions	10	0.60
Previous Subscribers	45	0.20
Total	100	

SCREENING FOR COLORECTAL CANCER

The fecal occult blood test, widely used both in physicians' offices and at home to screen patients for colon and rectal cancer, examines a patient's stool sample for blood, a condition indicating that the cancer may be present. A recent study funded by the National Cancer Institute found that of 15,000 people tested on an annual basis, 10% were found to have blood in their stools. These 10% underwent further testing, including *colonoscopy,* the insertion of an optical-fiber tube through the rectum in order to inspect the colon and rectum visually for direct indications of cancer. Only 2.5% of those having colonoscopy actually had cancer. Additional information in the study suggests that, of the patients who were tested, approximately five out of 1,000 tested negative (no blood in the stool) but eventually did develop cancer.

Questions

1. Create a probability table that shows the relationship between blood in a stool sample and colorectal cancer. Calculate P(Cancer | Blood) and P(Cancer | No Blood).
2. The study results have led some medical researchers to agree with the American Cancer Society's long-standing recommendation that all U.S. residents over 50 years of age be tested annually. On the other hand, many researchers claim the costs of such screening, including the cost of follow-up testing on 10% of the popula-

tion, far exceeds its value. Assume that the test can be performed for as little as $10 per person, that colonoscopy costs $750 on average, and that about 60 million people in the United States are over age 50. What is the expected cost (including follow-up colonoscopy) of implementing a policy of screening everyone over age 50? What is the expected number of people who must undergo colonoscopy? What is the expected number of people who must undergo colonoscopy only to find that they do not have cancer after all?

3. Over 13 years of follow-up study, 0.6% (6 out of 1,000) of those who were screened annually with the fecal occult blood test died from colon cancer anyway. Of those who were not screened, 0.9% (nine out 1,000) died of colon cancer during the same 13 years. Thus, the screening procedure saves approximately three lives per 1,000 every 13 years. Use this information, along with your calculations from Questions 1 and 2, to determine the expected cost of saving a life by implementing a policy requiring everyone over 50 to be screened every year.

4. What is your conclusion? Do you think everyone over 50 should be screened? From your personal point of view, informed now by your preceding calculations, would the saved lives be worth the money spent and the inconvenience, worry, discomfort, and potential complications of

subjecting approximately 6 million people each year to colonoscopy even though relatively few of them actually have detectable and curable cancer?

Source: J. S. Mandel, J. H. Bond, T. R. Church, D. C. Snover, G. M. Braley, L. M. Schuman, and F. Ederer (1993) "Reducing Mortality from Colorectal Cancer by Screening for Fecal Occult Blood. (Minnesota Colon Cancer Control Study)." *New England Journal of Medicine,* 328(19), 1365–1371.

AIDS

Acquired immune deficiency syndrome (AIDS) was perhaps the most frightening disease of the late twentieth century. The disease attacks and disables the immune system, leaving the body open to other diseases and infection. It is almost always fatal, although years may pass between infection and the development of the disease. In 2007, there were 14,561 deaths of persons with AIDS in the United States, and cumulatively, there have been 583,298 deaths due to AIDS.

Even more frightening is the process by which the disease travels through the population. AIDS is caused by a virus (human T-lymphotropic virus, Type III, or HTLV-III, although more commonly listed as HIV). The virus is transmitted through blood, semen, and vaginal secretions, and may attack virtually anyone who engages in any of several risky behaviors. The extent of the concern about AIDS among public health officials is reflected in the fact that the U.S. Surgeon General's office mailed brochures on AIDS to 107 million households in May and June 1988, the largest single mailing undertaken by the federal government to that time.

When an individual becomes infected, the body produces a special antibody in an effort to counteract the virus. But it can be as long as 12 weeks before these antibodies appear, and it may be years before any signs or symptoms of AIDS infection appear. During this time the individual may not be aware that he or she is infected and thus can spread the disease inadvertently.

Because of the delayed reaction of the virus, there are many more infected individuals than reported AIDS cases. Epidemiologists estimate that about 1 million people in the United States are infected with HIV and thus are potentially infectious of others. Worldwide, the estimate is that over 13 million people are infected. Because of this and because of the way the disease is transmitted, the best way to avoid AIDS simply is to avoid risky behavior. Do not share drug needles. Use a latex condom during intercourse unless you are certain that your partner is not infected. To help reduce the rate at which AIDS is spread, a number of local (and often controversial) programs have sprung up to provide condoms to sexually active teenagers and clean needles to intravenous drug users.

Figure 7.24 illustrates the distribution of AIDS across the United States broken down by state. We can also break down new cases by race or ethnicity. The majority of new cases (46%) occur in non-Hispanic whites, with African Americans accounting for 35% of the new cases, and Hispanics for 18%. However, when accounting for the size of each subpopulation, we see that there are 36 new cases per million Hispanics, 65 new cases per million African American, and only 14 new cases per million non-Hispanic Caucasians. Thus, even though non-Hispanic Caucasians account for nearly half of the new cases, African Americans and Hispanics have more than twice the likelihood for contracting AIDS on a per person basis.

The best tests available for AIDS detect the antibodies rather than the virus. Two such tests are generally available and widely used. The first is the *enzyme-linked immunosorbent assay* (ELISA). An individual is considered to have a positive result on the ELISA test only if both of two separate trials yield positive results. The performance of such a diagnostic test can be measured by the probabilities associated with correct diagnosis. The probability that an infected individual tests positive, P(ELISA+ | Infected), is called the *sensitivity* of the test. The probability that an uninfected individual tests negative, P(ELISA− | Not Infected), is called the *specificity* of the test. A negative result for an infected individual is called a *false-negative,* and a positive result for someone who is not infected is called a *false-positive.* An ideal test would have 100% sensitivity and 100% specificity, giving correct diagnoses all the time with neither false-negatives nor false-positives. In 1990, the Centers for Disease Control (CDC) reported a study indicating that the sensitivity and specificity of the ELISA test are 0.997 and 0.985, respectively.

FIGURE **7.24**
The distribution of AIDS across the United States.

Source: From http://www.cdc.gov/hiv/topics/surveillance/resources/slides/2009report_tables/slides/hasr_22.pdf

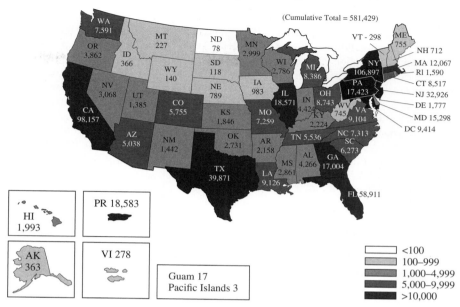

Total AIDS Cases Reported through December 1996

(Cumulative Total = 581,429)

TABLE **7.4**
Performance of ELISA and Western blot tests.

Test	Sensitivity P(+ | Inf)	False-Negative Rate P(− | Inf)	Specificity P(− | Not Inf)	False-Positive Rate P(+ | Not Inf)
ELISA	0.997	0.003	0.985	0.015
Western blot	0.993	0.007	0.916	0.084

© Cengage Learning

The *Western blot* test generally is used to confirm or disconfirm a positive ELISA result. For some time the Western blot was considered to be a perfect test, but this may not be true. The Western blot is a labor-intensive test, the results of which require interpretation by a skilled laboratory technician. The same CDC study indicated sensitivity and specificity of the Western blot to be 0.993 and 0.916, respectively.

Table 7.4 summarizes the performance characteristics of the two tests.

Questions

1. Given that the tests are not perfect, it is worthwhile to calculate the probability of being infected, given the various combinations of results on the tests. Calculate the probability of being infected given a positive ELISA test result, P(Inf | ELISA+). Use as your prior probability the P(Inf) = 0.0038, the estimated overall rate of infection in the United States. For P(ELISA + | Inf) and P(ELISA +| Not Inf), use the numbers from Table 7.4.

2. Create a graph like Figure 7.21 that shows P(Inf | ELISA+) as a function of P(Inf), the prior probability. Indicate on your graph the appropriate prior and posterior probabilities for female military recruits in New Jersey, gay men in Providence, Rhode Island, and intravenous drug users in New York City.

3. Repeat Questions 1 and 2, but this time find the probability of being infected given a negative ELISA result, P(Inf | ELISA−).

4. Calculate the probability of being infected given a positive ELISA test result and a positive Western blot, P(Inf | ELISA+, WB+) and the probability of being infected given a positive ELISA and negative Western blot, P(Inf | ELISA+, WB−). [*Hint: All* of the information in the case regarding the performance of the Western blot assumes a positive ELISA. The calculations required here can be done with Bayes' theorem, using as the prior probability P(Inf | ELISA+), the quantity calculated in Question 1.]

5. Create graphs like those for Questions 2 and 3 that show P(Inf | ELISA+, WB+) and P(Inf | ELISA+, WB−) as functions of the prior probability P(Inf). [*Hint:* Note that this prior probability enters the calculations through P(Inf | ELISA+).]

6. Some public health officials have called for widespread testing for HIV infection. Certainly there is considerable value to society in identifying HIV carriers, although there are costs inherent in incorrect diagnoses. For example, suppose that you were forced to be tested, and both ELISA and Western blot tests gave a positive result. Imagine that a later tissue culture revealed no HIV exposure. Thus, for some time you would have been falsely labeled as an AIDS carrier. On the other hand, suppose that the tests had been falsely negative. Then you may have engaged in risky behavior under the assumption that you had no infection. Discuss the social trade-offs of costs and benefits that are involved in using imperfect screening tests for AIDS.

Source: This case study was prepared using several publications available from the Centers for Disease Control National AIDS Clearinghouse, P.O. Box 6003, Rockville, MD 20849. The key publications used were "Surgeon General's Report to the American Public on HIV Infection and AIDS" (1994); "Serologic Testing for HIV–1 Antibody—United States, 1988 and 1989"; *Morbidity and Mortality Weekly Report* (1990), 39, 380–383 (abstracted in *Journal of the American Medical Association,* July 11, 1990, 171–173); and "National HIV Serosurveillance Summary: Results Through 1992," HIV/NCID/11-93/036.

DISCRIMINATION AND THE DEATH PENALTY

Is there a relationship between the race of convicted defendants in murder trials and the imposition of the death penalty on such defendants? This question has been debated extensively, with one side claiming that white defendants are given the death sentence much less frequently than nonwhites. This case can help you understand one reason for the debate. Table 7.5 shows information regarding 326 cases.

Questions

1. On the basis of Table 7.5, estimate P(Death Penalty | Defendant White) and P(Death Penalty | Defendant Black). What is your conclusion on the basis of these calculations?

2. Table 7.6 shows the same data disaggregated on the basis of the race of the victim. Use Table 7.6 to estimate the following probabilities:

   P(Death Penalty | Defendant White, Victim White)

   P(Death Penalty | Defendant Black, Victim White)

   P(Death Penalty | Defendant White, Victim Black)

   P(Death Penalty | Defendant Black, Victim Black)

   Now what is your conclusion?

3. Explain the apparent contradiction between your answers to Questions 1 and 2.

TABLE **7.5**
Death-penalty and racial status for 326 convicted murderers.

Race of Defendant	Death Penalty Imposed		Total Defendants
	Yes	No	
White	19	141	160
Black	17	149	166
Total	36	290	326

Source: M. Radelet (1981) "Racial Characteristics and Imposition of the Death Penalty." *American Sociological Review,* 46, 918–927.

TABLE **7.6**
Death-penalty and racial status for 326 convicted murderers, disaggregated by victim's race.

Race of Victim	Race of Defendant	Death Penalty Imposed		Total Defendants
		Yes	No	
White	White	19	132	151
	Black	11	52	63
	Total	30	184	214
Black	White	0	9	9
	Black	6	97	103
	Total	6	106	112
	Total	36	290	326

Source: M. Radelet (1981) "Racial Characteristics and Imposition of the Death Penalty." *American Sociological Review*, 46, 918–927.

REFERENCES

Probability basics appear in a wide variety of books on probability and statistics, presenting the material at various levels of sophistication. Good lower-level introductions can be found in elementary statistics textbooks such as McClave and Benson (1988), Mendenhall et al. (1989), Sincich (1989), and Wonnacott and Wonnacott (1984). Two excellent resources written at higher levels are Olkin, Gleser, and Derman (1980) and Feller (1968).

All decision-analysis textbooks seem to have at least one example about oil wildcatting. True, this is the quintessential decision-analysis problem, and it includes many sources of uncertainty, concerns about attitudes toward risk, and opportunities for gathering information. But many problems have these characteristics. Probably the real reason for the oil-wildcatting scenario is that, in 1960, C. J. Grayson published one of the first applied dissertations using decision theory, and its area of application was oil drilling. Decision theorists ever since have used oil drilling as an example!

Feller, W. (1968) *An Introduction to Probability Theory and Its Applications*, Vol. 1, 3rd ed. New York: Wiley.

Grayson, C. J. (1960) *Decisions under Uncertainty: Drilling Decisions by Oil and Gas Operators*. Cambridge, MA: Division of Research, Harvard Business School.

McClave, J. T., and P. G. Benson (1988) *Statistics for Business and Economics*, 4th ed. San Francisco: Dellen.

Mendenhall, W., J. Reinmuth, and R. Beaver (1989) *Statistics for Management and Economics*, 6th ed. Boston: PWS-KENT.

Olkin, I., L. J. Gleser, and C. Derman (1980) *Probability Models and Applications*. New York: Macmillan.

Sincich, T. (1989) *Business Statistics by Example*, 3rd ed. San Francisco: Dellen.

Wonnacott, T. H., and R. J. Wonnacott (1984) *Introductory Statistics for Business and Economics*. New York: Wiley.

EPILOGUE

John Hinckley Hinckley's defense attorney was not permitted to introduce the CAT scan of Hinckley's brain. In spite of this, the jury's verdict found Hinckley "not guilty by reason of insanity" on all counts, and he was committed to Saint Elizabeth's Hospital in Washington, D.C. The trial caused a substantial commotion among the public, many people viewing the insanity plea and the resulting verdict as a miscarriage of justice. Because of this, some lawmakers initiated efforts to tighten legal loopholes associated with the insanity plea.

AIDS New diagnostic tests for AIDS are under continual development as research on this frightening disease continues. For example, in December 1994, the U.S. Food and Drug Administration approved an AIDS diagnostic test that uses saliva instead of blood. This test may be easier to use, and the hope is that more people will be willing to be tested. The ELISA and Western blot tests described in the case study are typical of medical diagnostic tests in general, and the analysis performed shows how to evaluate such tests.

CHAPTER 8

Subjective Probability

All of us are used to making judgments regarding uncertainty, and we make them frequently. Often our statements involve informal evaluations of the uncertainties that surround an event. Statements such as "The weather is likely to be sunny today," "I doubt that the Republicans will win the next presidential election," or "The risk of cancer from exposure to cigarette smoke is small" all involve a personal, subjective assessment of uncertainty at a fundamental level. As we have seen, subjective assessments of uncertainty are an important element of decision analysis. A basic tenet of modern decision analysis is that subjective judgments of uncertainty can be made in terms of probability. In this chapter we will explore how to make such judgments and what they imply.

Although most people can cope with uncertainty informally, it is not clear perhaps that it is worthwhile to develop a more rigorous approach to measure the uncertainty that we feel. Just how important is it to deal with uncertainty in a careful and systematic way? The following vignettes demonstrate the importance of uncertainty assessments in a variety of public-policy situations.

UNCERTAINTY AND PUBLIC POLICY

Fruit Frost Farmers occasionally must decide whether to protect a crop from potentially damaging frost. The decision must be made on the basis of weather forecasts that often are expressed in terms of probability (U.S. National Weather Service is responsible for providing these forecasts). Protecting a crop can be costly, but hopefully less so than the potential damage. Because of such potential losses, care in assessing probabilities is important.

Jeffery Guyse, Professor of Technology and Operations Management at Cal Poly Pomona contributed to the behavioral and psychological aspects of this chapter.

Earthquake Prediction Geologists have developed ways to assess the probability of major earthquakes for specific locations. In 2008 the U.S. Geological Survey published Fact Sheet 2008–3027 that estimated the probability of a major earthquake (magnitude 6.7 or larger) occurring in California within the next 30 years to be greater than 99%. Such an earthquake could cause catastrophic damage. The probability of an even more powerful earthquake (magnitude 7.5 or larger) is 46% and most likely to happen in Southern California.

Environmental Impact Statements Federal and state regulations governing environmental impact statements typically require assessments of the risks associated with proposed projects. These risk assessments often are based on the probabilities of various hazards occurring. For example, in projects involving pesticides and herbicides, the chances of cancer and other health risks are assessed.

Public Policy and Scientific Research Often scientists learn of the possible presence of conditions that may require action by the government. But without absolute certainty that a condition exists, the government may delay action. For example, scientists in 1988 reported that the earth had begun to warm up because of the greenhouse effect, resulting from various kinds of pollution and the destruction of tropical forests. In testimony that year before the U.S. Congress, James Hansen of NASA expressed his beliefs in probabilistic terms, saying that he was 99% certain that the greenhouse effect was upon us.

Medical Diagnosis Many physicians in hospital intensive-care units (ICUs) have access to a complex computer system known as APACHE III (Acute Physiology, Age, and Chronic Health Evaluation). Based on information about a patient's medical history, condition, treatment, and lab results, APACHE III evaluates the patient's risk as a probability of dying either in the ICU or later in the hospital.

Some of the preceding examples include more complicated and more formal probability assessments as well as subjective judgments. For example, the National Weather Service forecasts are based in part on a large-scale computer model of the global atmospheric system. The computer output is just one bit of information used by a forecaster to develop an official forecast that involves his or her subjective judgment regarding the uncertainty in local weather. Some risk assessments are based on cancer studies performed on laboratory animals. The results of such studies must be extrapolated subjectively to real-world conditions to derive potential effects on humans. Because of the high stakes involved in these examples and others, it is important for policy makers to exercise care in assessing the uncertainties they face.

At a reduced scale, personal decisions also involve high stakes and uncertainty. Personal investment decisions and career decisions are two kinds of decisions that typically involve substantial uncertainty. Perhaps even harder to deal with are personal medical decisions in which the outcomes of possible treatments are not known in advance. If you suffer from chronic chest pain, would you undergo elective surgery in an attempt to eliminate the pain? Because of the risks associated with open heart surgery, this decision must be made under a condition of uncertainty. You would want to think carefully about your chances on the operating table, considering not only statistics regarding the operation but also what you know about your own health and the skills of your surgeon and the medical staff.

PROBABILITY: A SUBJECTIVE INTERPRETATION

Many introductory textbooks present probability in terms of long-run frequency. For example, if a six-sided die is thrown many times, it would land with the five on top approximately one-sixth of the time; thus, the probability of a five on a given throw of the die is one-sixth. In many cases, however, it does not make sense to think about probabilities as long-run frequencies. For example, in assessing the probability that the California condor will be extinct by the year 2030 or the probability of a major nuclear power plant failure in the next 10 years, thinking in terms of long-run frequencies or averages is not reasonable because we cannot rerun the "experiment" many times to find out what proportion of the times the condor becomes extinct or a power plant fails. We often hear references to the chance that a catastrophic nuclear holocaust will destroy life on the planet. Let us not even consider the idea of a long-run frequency in this case!

Even when a long-run frequency interpretation might seem appropriate, there are times when an event has occurred, but we remain unsure of the final outcome. For example, consider the following:

1. You have flipped a coin that has landed on the floor. Neither you nor anyone else has seen it. What is the probability that it is heads?
2. What is the probability that Oregon beat Stanford in their 1970 football game?
3. What is the probability that the coin flipped at the beginning of that 1970 football game came up heads?
4. What is the probability that Millard Fillmore was President in 1850?

For most of us the answers to these questions are not obvious. In every case the actual event has taken place. But unless you know the answer, you are uncertain.

The point of this discussion is that we can view uncertainty in a way that is different from the traditional long-run frequency approach. In the preceding Examples 1 and 3, there was a random event (flipping the coin), but the randomness is no longer in the coin. You are uncertain about the outcome because you do not know what the outcome was; the uncertainty is in your mind. In all of the examples, the uncertainty lies in your own brain cells. When we think of uncertainty and probability in this way, we are adopting a subjective interpretation, with a probability representing an individual's *degree of belief* that a particular outcome will occur.

Decision analysis requires numbers for probabilities, not phrases such as "common," "unusual," "toss-up," or "rare." In fact, there is considerable evidence from the cognitive psychologists who study such things that the same phrase has different connotations to different people in different contexts. For example, in one study (Beyth-Marom, 1982), individuals gave the phrase "there is a non-negligible chance ..." specific probability interpretations that ranged from below 0.36 to above 0.77. Furthermore, it may be the case that we interpret such phrases differently depending on the context. The phrase "a slight chance that it will rain tomorrow" may carry a very different probability interpretation from the phrase "a slight chance that the space shuttle will explode."

The problems with using verbal representations of uncertainty can be seen in the following financial-accounting policy.

Accounting for Contingent Losses	When a company prepares its financial statements, in some instances it must disclose information about possible future losses. These losses are called *contingent* because they may or may not occur contingent on the outcome of some future event (e.g., the outcome of a lawsuit or a subsidiary's default on a loan that the parent company guaranteed). In their *Statement of Financial Accounting Standards No. 5*, "Accounting for Contingencies," the Financial Accounting Standards Board provides guidelines for different accounting treatments of accounting losses, depending on whether the contingent loss is judged to be "probable," "remote," or "reasonably possible." In defining these verbal terms of uncertainty, "probable" is taken to mean that the future event is likely to occur. "Remote" means that the chance the event will occur is slight. Finally, "reasonably possible" means that the chance of the event occurring is somewhere between slight and likely.

Source: Financial Accounting Standards Board (1991). *Original Pronouncements: Accounting Standards. Vol. 1: FASB Statement of Standards.* Homewood, IL: Irwin. |

In this example, verbal terms of uncertainty are defined using other verbal terms; no precise guidance is provided. The wording of the standard moves us from wondering about the meaning of "probable" and "remote" to a concern with "likely to occur" and "slight." How much more straightforward the accountant's job would be if the standard specified the different degrees of risk in terms of quantitative judgments made by a knowledgeable person!

One of the main topics of this chapter is how to assess probabilities—the numbers—that are consistent with one's subjective beliefs. Of the many concepts in decision analysis, the idea of subjective probability is one that seems to give students trouble. Some are uncomfortable assessing a degree of belief, because they think there must be a "correct" answer. There are no universally agreed upon correct answers when it comes to subjective judgment; different people have different degrees of belief and hence will assess different probabilities.

If you disagree with a friend about the probability that your favorite team will win a game, do you try to persuade your friend that your probability is better? You might discuss different aspects of the situation, such as which team has the home advantage, which players are injured, and so forth. But even after sharing your information, the two of you still might disagree. Then what? You might place a bet. For many people, betting reflects their personal subjective probabilities. Some people bet on anything even if the outcome is based on some "objectively" random event (flipping a coin, playing cards, and so on). One of the most common bets might be investing —betting—in the stock market. For example, you might be willing to purchase a stock now if you think its value is likely to increase.

We will begin with the assessment of probabilities. We will show how you can view different situations in terms of the bets you might place involving small cash amounts or in terms of hypothetical lotteries. Following the discussion of the assessment of discrete probabilities, we will see how to deal with continuous probability distributions (the fan or crescent shape in the range-of-risk dilemma that was introduced in Chapter 3). Special psychological phenomena are associated with probability assessment, and we will explore the cognitive heuristics that we tend to use in probability assessment. The next section discusses procedures for decomposing probability assessments. We end the chapter with a real-world example and ways to use @RISK® in assessing subjective probabilities.

ASSESSING DISCRETE PROBABILITIES

There are three basic methods for assessing probabilities. The first is simply to have the decision maker assess the probability directly by asking, "What is your belief regarding the probability that event such and such will occur?" The decision maker may or may not be able to give an answer to a direct question like this and may place little confidence in the answer given.

The second method is to ask about the bets that the decision maker would be willing to place. The idea is to find a specific amount to win or lose such that the decision maker is indifferent about which side of the bet to take. If he or she is indifferent about which side to bet, then the expected value of the bet must be the same regardless of which is taken. Given these conditions, we can then solve for the probability.

As an example, suppose that the Los Angeles Lakers are playing the Boston Celtics in the NBA finals this year. We are interested in finding the decision maker's probability that the Lakers will win the championship. Thus, we set up two bets where one bet is the opposite side of the other bet. In general the bets[1] are:

Bet 1	Win $X if the Lakers win.
	Lose $Y if the Lakers lose.
Bet 2	Lose $X if the Lakers win.
	Win $Y if the Lakers lose.

---

[1] In these bets, X and Y can be thought of as the amounts that each person puts into the pot. The winner of the bet takes all of the money therein.

FIGURE **8.1**
Decision-tree representation for assessing subjective probability via the betting method.

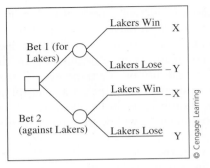

The assessor's problem is to find X and Y so that he or she is indifferent about betting for or against the Lakers.

For instance:

Bet 1	Win \$250 if the Lakers win.
	Lose \$380 if the Lakers lose.
Bet 2	Lose \$250 if the Lakers win.
	Win \$380 if the Lakers lose.

Because the bets take opposite sides, the decision maker will prefer one bet to the other. Then through adjusting the values of X and Y, we can find two opposite bets for which the decision maker is indifferent; that is, both bets are equally attractive. Once we find these values of X and Y, we can compute the probability the Lakers win the championship. Figure 8.1 displays the decision tree that the decision maker faces.

If the decision maker is indifferent between Bets 1 and 2, then in his or her mind their expected values must be equal:

$$X\, P(\text{Lakers Win}) - Y[1 - P(\text{Lakers Win})]$$
$$= -X\, P(\text{Lakers Win}) + Y[1 - P(\text{Lakers Win})],$$

which implies that

$$2\big\{X\, P(\text{Lakers Win}) - Y[1 - P(\text{Lakers Win})]\big\} = 0.$$

We can divide through by 2 and expand the left side to get

$$X\, P(\text{Lakers Win}) - Y + Y\, P(\text{Lakers Win}) = 0.$$

Collecting terms gives

$$(X + Y)\, P(\text{Lakers Win}) - Y = 0,$$

which reduces to

$$P(\text{Lakers Win}) = \frac{Y}{X+Y}.$$

For example, if our friend is indifferent between the two preceding specific bets, his subjective probability that the Lakers win, as implied by his betting behavior, is $380/(250 + 380) = 0.603$. Thus, he believes there is a 60% chance the Lakers will win the NBA Championship and a 40% chance that the Celtics will win.

Finding the pair of bets for which a decision maker would be willing to take either side is fairly straightforward. Begin by offering a bet that is highly favorable to one side or the other, and note which side of the bet she would take. Then offer a bet that favors the opposite side, and ask which side of this new bet she would prefer. Continue offering bets that first favor one side and then the other, gradually adjusting the payoffs on each round. By adjusting the bet appropriately, making it more or less attractive depending on the response to the previous bet, the indifference point can be found.

The betting approach to assessing probabilities appears straightforward enough, but it does suffer from a number of problems. First, many people simply do not like the idea of betting (even though most investments can be framed as a bet of some kind). For these people, casting the judgment task as a bet can be distracting. Most people also dislike the prospect of losing money; they are *risk averse*. Thus, the bets that are considered must involve small enough amounts of money that the issue of risk aversion does not arise. Some people, however, may be risk averse even for very small amounts. Finally, the betting approach also presumes that the individual making the bet cannot make any other bets on the specific event (or even related events). That is, the individual cannot protect himself or herself from losses by "hedging" one bet with another.

To get around the problems with direct assessment or with the betting approach, a third approach adopts a thought-experiment strategy in which the decision maker compares two lottery-like games. We would ask the decision maker to compare the lottery

Win Prize A if the Lakers win.

Win Prize B if the Lakers lose.

with the lottery

Win Prize A with known probability p.

Win Prize B with probability $1 - p$.

For convenience, set it up so that the decision maker prefers A to B. (Prize A might be a fully paid two-week vacation in Hawaii, and Prize B a coupon for a free beer.) The decision-tree representation is shown in Figure 8.2. The second lottery is called the *reference lottery,* for which the probability mechanism must be well specified. A typical mechanism is drawing a colored ball from an urn in which the proportion of colored balls is known to be p. Another mechanism is to use a "wheel of fortune" with a known area that represents "win"; if the wheel were spun and the pointer landed in the win area, the decision maker would win Prize A.

Once the mechanism is understood by the decision maker, the trick is to adjust the probability of winning in the reference lottery until the decision maker is indifferent between the two lotteries. Indifference in this case means

FIGURE **8.2**
Decision-tree representation for assessing subjective probability with equivalent-lottery method.

The assessor's problem is to find a value of p so that the two lotteries are equivalent.

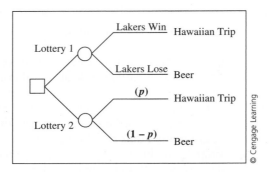

that the decision maker has no preference between the two lotteries, but slightly changing probability p makes one or the other lottery clearly preferable. If the decision maker is indifferent, then her subjective probability that the Lakers win must be the p that makes her indifferent.

How do we find the p that makes the decision maker indifferent? The basic idea is to start with some p_1 and ask which lottery she prefers. If she prefers the reference lottery, then p_1 must be too high; she perceives that the chance of winning in the reference lottery is higher. In this case, choose p_2 less than p_1 and ask her preference again. Continue adjusting the probability in the reference lottery until the indifference point is found. It is important to begin with extremely wide brackets and to converge on the indifference probability slowly. Going slowly allows the decision maker plenty of time to think hard about the assessment, and she probably will be much happier with the final result than she would be if rushed. This is an important point for finding your own probability assessments. Be patient, and hone in on your indifference point gradually.

The wheel of fortune is a particularly useful way to assess probabilities. By changing the setting of the wheel to represent the probability of winning in the reference lottery, it is possible to find the decision maker's indifference point quite easily. Furthermore, the use of the wheel avoids the bias that can occur from using only "even" probabilities (0.1, 0.2, 0.3, and so on). With the wheel, a probability can be any value between 0 and 1. Figure 8.3 shows the probability wheel corresponding to the probability assessments of Texaco's reaction to Pennzoil's $5 billion offer.

The lottery-based approach to probability assessment is not without its own shortcomings. Some people have a difficult time grasping the hypothetical game that they are asked to envision, and as a result they have trouble making assessments. Others dislike the idea of a lottery or carnival-like game. These same people, though, do make trade-offs with their own money whenever they purchase insurance, invest in a small business, or purchase shares of stock in a company. In some cases it may be better to recast the assessment procedure in terms of risks that are similar to the kinds of financial risks an individual might take.

The last step in assessing probabilities is to check for consistency. Many problems will require the decision maker to assess several interrelated

FIGURE **8.3**
The Texaco reaction
chance node and
the corresponding
probability wheel.

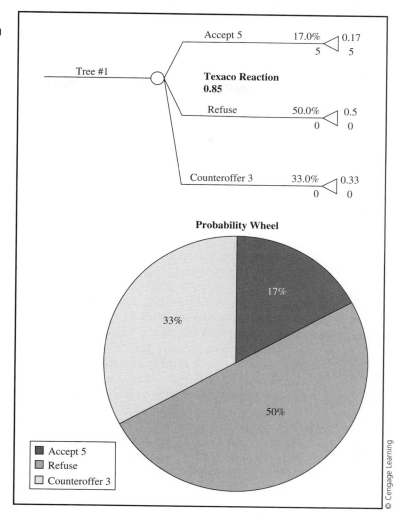

FIGURE **8.3**
The Texaco reaction chance node and the corresponding probability wheel.

probabilities. It is important that these probabilities be consistent among themselves; they should obey the probability laws introduced in Chapter 7. For example, if $P(A)$, $P(B \mid A)$, and $P(A \text{ and } B)$ were all assessed, then it should be the case that

$$P(A)P(B \mid A) = P(A \text{ and } B)$$

If a set of assessed probabilities is found to be inconsistent, the decision maker should reconsider and modify the assessments as necessary to achieve consistency.

ASSESSING CONTINUOUS PROBABILITIES

The premise of this chapter is that it always is possible to model a decision maker's uncertainty using probabilities. How would this be done in the case

FIGURE **8.4**
Decision-tree
representation for
assessing *Profit* ≤
$10,000 in the rental
property example.

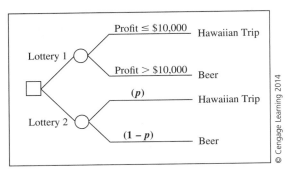

of an uncertain but continuous quantity? We already have learned how to assess individual probabilities; we will apply this technique to assess several cumulative probabilities and then use these to plot a rough CDF. We will discuss two strategies for assessing a subjective CDF.

Let us re-examine the Chapter 7 example of yearly profits resulting from buying a duplex as an income property. As you recall, the problem was to derive a probability distribution representing the distribution of yearly profits based on the assessments. In that example, several probabilities were found, and these were transformed into cumulative probabilities.

A typical cumulative assessment would be to assess $P(Yearly\ Profit \leq a)$, where a is a particular value. For example, consider $P(Yearly\ Profit \leq \$10,000)$. The outcome $Yearly\ Profit \leq \$10,000$ is an outcome just like any other, and so a decision maker could assess the probability of this event by using any of the three techniques previously discussed. For example, a wheel of fortune might be used as an assessment aid to find the probability p that would make the decision maker indifferent between the two lotteries shown in Figure 8.4.

Using this technique to find a CDF amounts to assessing the cumulative probability for a number of points, plotting them, and drawing a smooth curve through the plotted points. Suppose the following assessments were made:

$$P(Yearly\ Profit \leq -\$25,000) = 0.00$$

$$P(Yearly\ Profit \leq -\$10,000) = 0.10$$

$$P(Yearly\ Profit \leq \$0) = 0.30$$

$$P(Yearly\ Profit \leq \$15,000) = 0.75$$

$$P(Yearly\ Profit \leq \$24,000) = 1.00$$

Plotting these cumulative probabilities would result in the graph that we originally drew in Figure 7.10, and which is reproduced here as Figure 8.5.

The strategy that we have used here is to choose a few values from the horizontal axis (some yearly profit values) and then to find the cumulative probabilities that correspond to those profit values. This is a perfectly reasonable

FIGURE **8.5**
Cumulative distribution of yearly profit for a rental property created by fitting a smooth line to the five assessed points shown.

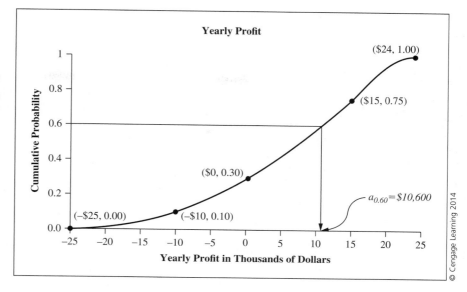

FIGURE **8.6**
Decision tree for assessing the 0.60 fractile of a continuous distribution for an uncertainty quantity X.

The decision maker's task is to find the value of x in Lottery A that results indifference between the two lotteries.

strategy for assessing a CDF. Another strategy builds up the graph the other way around. That is, we pick a few cumulative probabilities from the vertical axis and find the corresponding profit values. For example, suppose we pick probability 0.60. Now we want the profit value $a_{0.60}$ such that $P(Yearly\ Profit \leq a_{0.60}) = 0.60$. The number $a_{0.60}$ is called the 0.60 *fractile* of the distribution. In general, the p fractile of a distribution for X is the value x_p such that $P(X \leq x_p) = p$. We can see from Figure 8.5 that the 0.60 fractile of the distribution is approximately \$10,600. We know from the assessments that were made that the 0.10 fractile is −\$10,000, the 0.30 fractile is \$0, and the 0.75 fractile is \$15,000.

How could you go about assessing a fractile? Figure 8.6 shows a decision tree that represents the process for assessing the 0.60 fractile. In Lottery B, or the reference lottery, the probability of winning is fixed at 0.60. The assessment task is to adjust the number x in Lottery A until indifference

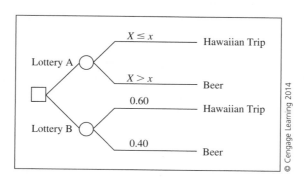

between the lotteries is achieved. Indifference would mean that the probability of winning in Lottery A must be 0.60. Hence, there must be a 0.60 chance that X is less than or equal to the assessed x. By definition, then, x must be the 0.60 fractile of the distribution.

It is important to recognize the difference between Figures 8.4 and 8.6. In Figure 8.4 we adjusted the probability value p in the reference lottery to find indifference. To assess the 0.60 fractile in Figure 8.6, we fix the probability in the reference lottery at 0.60, and we adjust the consequence value x in the upper lottery.

The term *fractile* is a general one, but other similar terms are useful for referring to specific fractiles. The idea of a *median* may be familiar. If we can find an amount such that the uncertain quantity is as likely to be above as below that amount, then we have found the median. The median is defined as the 0.50 fractile, and for yearly profit the median is approximately $7,000. We also can speak of *quartiles*. The first quartile is an amount such that $P(X \leq first\ quartile) = 0.25$, or the 0.25 fractile. In our example, the first quartile appears to be around a negative $1,200. Likewise, the third quartile is defined as the 0.75 fractile. The third quartile of our example is $15,000 because $P(Yearly\ Profit \leq \$15,000)$ equals 0.75. The second quartile is, of course, the median. Fractiles also can be expressed as *percentiles*. For example, the 90th percentile is defined as the 0.90 fractile of a distribution.

As previously mentioned, we can exploit this idea of fractiles to assess a continuous distribution. In general, the strategy will be to select specific cumulative probabilities and assess the corresponding fractiles. The first step might be to find the uncertain quantity's extreme values. How small or large could this quantity be? Because it often is difficult, and sometimes even misleading, to think in terms of extreme probabilities values of 0 or 1, we take the 0.05 and 0.95 fractiles (or the 5th and 95th percentiles). In our yearly profit example, the 0.05 fractile is a value $a_{0.05}$ such that there is only a 5% chance that the yearly profit would be less than or equal to $a_{0.05}$. Likewise, the 0.95 fractile is the value $a_{0.95}$ such that there is a 95% chance that the profit would be less than or equal to $a_{0.95}$. Informally, we might think of these as the smallest and largest values that the uncertain quantity could reasonably assume. Anything beyond these values would be quite surprising. This terminology may sound familiar as it was used when describing the lower and upper limits for a sensitivity analysis.

After assessing the extreme points, the median might be assessed. For example, Figure 8.7 shows the decision tree that corresponds to the assessment for the median in our example. The task would be for the decision maker to find a profit value $a_{0.50}$ that makes the two lotteries equivalent in the judgment of the decision maker. The value of $a_{0.50}$ that leaves the decision maker indifferent is the median of the distribution and can be plotted as a point on the decision maker's subjective CDF.

Next, assess the first and third quartiles. These assessments can be made using a lottery setup similar to that in Figure 8.6. Another way to think of the quartiles is that they "split" the probability intervals above and below the median. For example, the first quartile is a value x such that the uncertain quantity is just as likely to fall below x as between x and the median.

FIGURE **8.7**
Decision tree for assessing the median of the distribution for the yearly profit of the rental property.

The assessment task is to adjust the profit value *a* in Lottery A to achieve indifference.

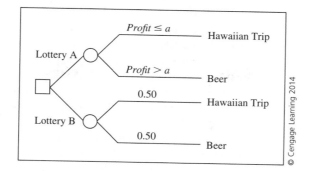

Having assessed the extreme points, the median, and the quartiles, we have five points on the cumulative distribution function. These points can be plotted on a graph, and a smooth curve drawn through the points.

As an example, suppose you have developed a new soft pretzel that you are thinking about marketing through sidewalk kiosks. You are interested in assessing the annual demand for the pretzels as a continuous quantity. You might make the following assessments:

- 0.05 fractile for demand = 5,000.
- 0.95 fractile for demand = 45,000.
- Demand is just as likely to be above 23,000 as below or equal to 23,000.
- There is a 0.25 chance that demand will be below 16,000.
- There is a 0.75 chance that demand will be below 31,000.

The last three assessments establish the median to be 23,000, the first quartile to be 16,000, and the third quartile to be 31,000. Plotting the points, we obtain the graph in Figure 8.8. A smooth curve drawn through the five points represents your subjective cumulative probability distribution of demand for the new pretzels.

Once we assess a continuous distribution, how can we use it? Apparently, our motivation for assessing it in the first place was that we faced uncertainty in the form of a range-of-risk dilemma. In our example, we may be deciding

FIGURE **8.8**
A subjectively assessed CDF for pretzel demand.

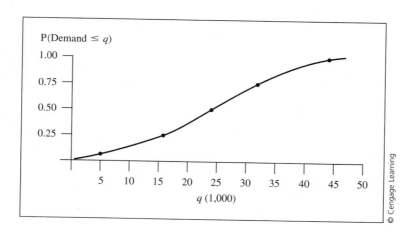

whether to go ahead and market the pretzels. We need the probability distribution to fill out our decision tree, calculate expected values, and find an optimum choice. But how will we calculate an expected value for this subjectively assessed distribution? There are several possibilities, some of which we will explore in later chapters. At the end of this chapter, we will learn how to use the program @RISK to fit distribution curves to the subjective assessments. We need only type in the assessed probabilities and their corresponding values, and @RISK does the rest. It draws a distribution curve through the points; it calculates the expected value, the standard deviation, and the various other statistics; and it provides a simple method for calculating any fractile. Once satisfied with the fitted distribution, @RISK will export the formula to Excel, where it can be used in our decision models. Also, in the next chapter, we will see how to fit a theoretical distribution to an assessed one; we then can use the mathematical properties of the theoretical distribution. Advanced simulation and numerical integration techniques also are possible. At this point, however, we will content ourselves with some simple and useful approximation techniques.

The easiest way to use a continuous distribution in a decision tree or influence diagram is to replace it with a discrete distribution. Not any discrete distribution will do, of course; we need a specifically constructed distribution that approximates the continuous distribution as closely as possible. We next discuss two methods for constructing discrete approximations to continuous distributions. For both of these methods, we need to assess specific fractiles from the decision maker, and then assign preset probabilities to those fractiles. Both methods are three-point approximations, meaning that we need only assess three fractiles. At first blush, three points do not seem sufficient to adequately replace a continuous distribution, but Keefer and Bodily (1983) showed that these particular methods are surprisingly accurate for a wide range of different continuous distributions.

The two methods are the Extended Swanson-Megill (ES-M) and the Extended Pearson-Tukey (EP-T) approximations methods. Both methods are three-point approximations, and they differ from one another in which fractiles are assessed and in the preset probability values assigned to those fractiles. ES-M requires the median along with the 0.10 and 0.90 fractiles. EP-T also requires the median, but pushes the assessments out to the 0.05 and 0.95 fractiles. Because it is more difficult to assess values for low probability events, the ES-M could be easier for the decision maker. On the other hand, accurate knowledge of the tails of a distribution provides opportunities for more accurate approximations.

Figure 8.9 shows the ES-M approximation for the pretzel demand distribution. It is important to notice that the preset probability assigned to the 0.10 fractile is not 0.10. Rather, the ES-M always assigns the probability value of 1/6 to the 0.10 fractile. In fact, 1/6 is assigned to both the 0.10 and to the 0.90 fractiles and 2/3 is assigned to the median. These assigned probability values were derived to minimize error when approximating continuous distributions. From Figure 8.9, we see that at some points ES-M

FIGURE **8.9**

The Extended Swanson-Megill three-point approximation to the pretzel demand distribution.

Extended Swanson-Megill Approximation Method

X (Pretzels)	Fractile	Probability
7,750	0.10	0.167
23,000	0.50	0.666
41,500	0.90	0.167

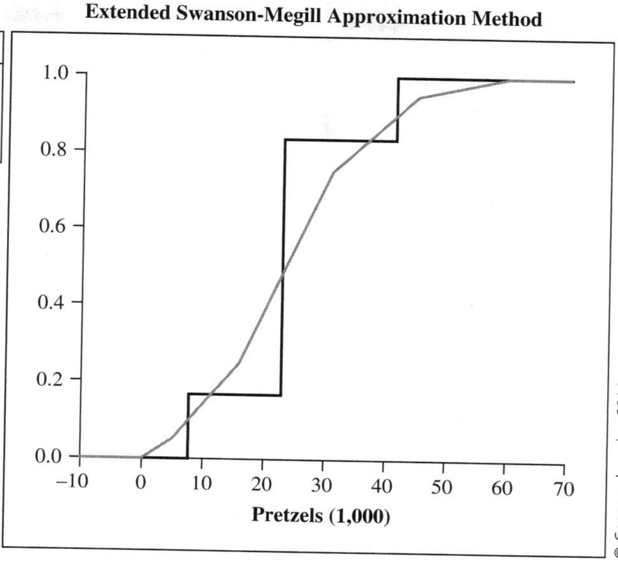

© Cengage Learning 2014

overestimates the continuous distribution and at other points, it underestimates the distribution. The same sort of thing occurs with EP-T approximation. The over/under estimation results in compensating errors that effectively cancel each other out, making both the ES-M and EP-T excellent discrete approximations.

The EP-T method requires the decision maker to assess the median with the 0.05 and 0.95 fractiles. Again, we have preset probability values for the assessed fractiles. The EP-T assigns the probability value of 0.185 to both the 0.05 and 0.95 fractiles and 0.630 to the median. Notice that both the ES-W and EP-T are symmetric in that they assign the same probability values to the extreme fractiles. The EP-T approximation is shown in Figure 8.10.

One way to determine how well the discrete approximation fits the original distribution is to compare the statistics of the two distributions. The two most important statistics are the mean and the standard deviation. Both EP-T and ES-M match the mean of the pretzel demand distribution rather well. The mean of the pretzel demand is 24,075 pretzels and the EP-T approximation has a mean of 23,740 pretzels (difference of 335) and the ES-M approximation has a mean of 23,542 pretzels (difference of 533). Comparing the standard deviations, we find the ES-M underestimated the standard deviation quite a bit. The standard deviation of pretzel demand is 12,464 pretzels and the EP-T has a standard deviation of 12,204 pretzels, but the ES-M has a standard deviation of 9,773 pretzels. Thus, for this example, the EP-T is the better fitting approximation.

Figure 8.11 depicts replacing the continuous pretzel demand distribution with the three-point Extended Pearson-Tukey discrete approximation.

FIGURE **8.10**
The Extended Pearson-Tukey three-point approximation to the pretzel demand distribution.

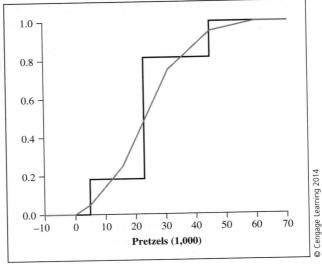

X (Pretzels)	Fractile	Probability
5,000	0.05	0.185
23,000	0.50	0.630
45,000	0.95	0.185

© Cengage Learning 2014

FIGURE **8.11**
Replacing a continuous distribution with a three-branch discrete uncertainty node in a decision tree.

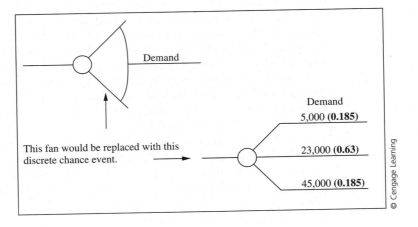

© Cengage Learning

HEURISTICS AND BIASES IN PROBABILITY ASSESSMENT

The methods presented above make probability assessment sound easy. As you probably realize, however, thinking in terms of probabilities is not easy. It takes considerable practice before one is comfortable making probability assessments. Even then, we tend to use rather primitive cognitive techniques to make our probability assessments. Tversky and Kahneman (1974) have labeled these techniques *heuristics*. In general, heuristics can be thought of as rules of thumb for accomplishing tasks. For example, an inventory-control heuristic might be to keep 10% of total yearly demand for any given item on hand. When placing an order for an item that sells some 200 units per year, one then would check the stock and order enough to have 20 units on hand. Heuristics tend to be simple, are easy to follow, and usually do not give optimal answers.

Heuristics for assessing probabilities operate in basically the same way. They are easy and intuitive ways to deal with uncertain situations, but they can result in probability assessments that are biased in different ways depending on the heuristic used. For example, when individuals tend to ignore or significantly discount the level of uncertainty in order to simplify an otherwise very complex decision problem, the result can be a subjective probability distribution that is too narrow (Remus and Kotteman, 1986).

What does it mean for a subjective probability to be biased? There are two different ways to think about it. First, suppose you could compare an individual's probability distributions with probabilities based on real-world observations. In that case, bias could be interpreted as any systematic differences between the subjective probabilities and the data-based distributions. For example, each year for several years an investor might assess the probability that her stock portfolio increases in value. Let's say that each year her probability of an increase in value is 90%. Now suppose we look at how the portfolio has performed over each of the past 10 years, and we find that it has increased in value in five of those 10 years, as opposed to the nine or ten that we would have expected from her assessments. In this case, we would say that the investor is biased—in particular, she is overoptimistic.

The second interpretation of probability bias is somewhat more general. Instead of thinking about the comparison with observed data, consider how the process works. When an individual makes a probability judgment, he or she has some knowledge and information about the world and uses that information to form a probability and then express it. To the extent that those probabilities are systematically affected in spurious ways because of the heuristics, the probabilities are biased. In this case, the bias can be thought of as the extent to which the probabilities are different from what they would be in the absence of the spurious effects. For example, when an individual thinks about how likely someone is to die from different kinds of accidents, he might be influenced by the fact that he can imagine or visualize some kinds of accidents (being struck by lightning) much more easily than others (lawnmower accident).

In this section we will look at a variety of heuristics and biases that occur in subjective probability assessment. Before we begin, however, consider the case of Tom W.

TOM W.

"Tom W. is of high intelligence, although lacking in true creativity. He has a need for order and clarity, and for neat and tidy systems in which every detail finds its appropriate place. His writing is rather dull and mechanical, occasionally enlivened by somewhat corny puns and by flashes of imagination of the sci-fi type. He has a strong drive for competence. He seems to have little feel and little sympathy for other people and does not enjoy interacting with others. Self-centered, he nonetheless has a deep moral sense."

The preceding personality sketch of Tom W. was written during his senior year in high school by a psychologist on the basis of projective tests. Tom W. is now a graduate student. Please rank the following nine fields of graduate specialization in order of the likelihood that Tom W. is now a graduate student in that field:

a. Business administration
b. Computer science
c. Engineering
d. Humanities and education
e. Law
f. Library science
g. Medicine
h. Physical and life sciences
i. Social science and social work.

Write down your rankings before you read on.

Source: Kahneman and Tversky (1973).

If you are like most people, you wrote down your ranks on the basis of how similar the description of Tom W. is to your preconceived notions of the kinds of people in the nine different fields of study. Specifically, Tom W.'s description makes him appear to be a "nerd," and so most people think that he has a relatively high chance of being in engineering or computer science. But judging the probability of membership in a group on the basis of similarity ignores important information. There are many more graduate students in humanities and education and in social science and social work than in computer science or engineering. Information relating to the incidence or *base rate* of occurrence in the different fields is ignored however, when we make probability judgments on the basis of similarity.

Making such judgments on similarity is one example of a kind of heuristic that Kahneman and Tversky (1973) call *representativeness*. In its most fundamental form, the representativeness heuristic is used to judge the probability that someone or something belongs to a particular category. Using the representativeness heuristic means that the judgment is made from memory by comparing the information known about the person or thing with the stereotypical member of the category. The closer the similarity between the two, the higher the judged probability of membership in the category.

Biases can also arise from sources other than an individual's memory. There are also statistical, confidence, adjustment, and motivational biases (Arnott, 2006).

Memory Biases

Along with representativeness, the *availability heuristic* operates as a memory-related process and can have an impact on our subjective probabilities. According to the availability heuristic, we judge the probability of an event by the ease with which we can retrieve similar events from memory. In general, this makes sense; the more likely an event is, the more often we might have heard about such a thing happening or the more often we would have thought about it. As with representativeness, the availability of events in memory arises from many different sources, not all relevant to the judgment of probability. External events and influences, for example, can have a substantial effect on the availability of similar incidents. Seeing a traffic accident can increase one's estimate of the chance of being in an accident; thus, you might judge the probability of being in a traffic accident much higher immediately after seeing an accident than, say, a week later, even though nothing has changed about your driving habits or circumstances. Being present at a house fire can have more effect on the retrievability of fire incidents than reading about the fire in the newspaper. Furthermore, differential attention by the news media to different kinds of incidents can affect the availability of items in memory. Suppose the local newspaper plays up deaths resulting from homicide but plays down traffic deaths; such unbalanced reporting can affect readers' judgments of the relative incidence of homicides and traffic fatalities. To the extent that this effect extends to many people in a community, it might actually lead to wasteful community decisions, for example having the police department put more effort into reducing violent crime and postponing the installation of needed traffic lights.

Bias from availability arises in other ways as well. For example, as suggested previously, some situations are simply easier to imagine than others. The *imaginability bias* occurs when an event is judged more (or less) probable if can be easily (or not easily) imagined. For example, one who has never driven across the United States may underestimate the likelihood of mishaps along the way due to changes in the environment, from tornadoes in the Midwest to snow on the Rockies and eventually the desolation of the Arizona and California deserts. Similarly, before 2008 it might have been difficult for many investors to imagine the effect on the world economy of a crisis in the financial world. However, that was one of the key reasons for the recession of 2009; as banks began to fail—especially large ones, like Lehman Brothers—banks stopped lending to other banks, and money simply was not flowing as it normally would in the world economy. The effect was a lack of liquidity; without the cash to operate, many firms struggled to stay in business. Facing less available credit, fewer jobs, and falling housing prices, consumers in the United States sharply cut back on purchases.

Another bias is called *illusory correlation*. If a pair of events is perceived as happening together frequently, this perception can lead to an incorrect judgment regarding the strength of the relationship between the two events. In general, the probability of the two events occurring together can be overestimated. In fact, the two events can be falsely correlated in the mind of the assessor even when only experienced *once*! For example, let's say that the flu was going around. You visited your 3-year-old nephew who, you learned afterward, developed flu symptoms later the same day. Two days later, after a nice evening out with friends at a new restaurant, you became violently ill. Even though you had been careful about washing your hands and not sharing food with your nephew, you believe your illness to be the flu, and you decide to stay home for the next few days to avoid exposing anyone else. You made the connection between your nephew's illness and your own, but you actually had a case of food poisoning.

The ease of recall can also bias the assessed probability of an event occurring *after* it has actually occurred. This is known as the *hindsight bias*. "I knew this would happen" or "I saw that coming" are conversational indications of individuals' overestimation of their internal subjective probabilities. Why do individuals overestimate the probability of a past event occurring? Psychologists hypothesize that the new information (outcome of the event) is more readily recalled from memory and therefore given more weight over past, less recallable information.

Statistical Biases

Statistical biases are associated with the findings that individuals are not very adept at processing information about uncertainty in accordance with probability theory and statistics. The representativeness heuristic discussed previously surfaces in many different situations and can lead to a variety of different statistical biases. For example, as in the Tom W. problem at the beginning of this section, people can be *insensitive to base rates* or prior probabilities. If one were to consider base rates carefully in the Tom W. problem, humanities and education may well be recognized as the most likely category.

Chance Bias

The chance bias occurs when individuals assess independent random events as having some inherent (non-random) pattern. For example, when visiting a casino, the roulette tables will "publish" the last 10 outcomes. Gamblers may see a string of red outcomes and think that "black is due." They are therefore overestimating the probability of a black outcome given a string of red outcomes. However, in roulette these probabilities are independent. Casino managers know this, and by publishing the previous outcomes, they are able to exploit the fact that many of their customers are subject to the chance bias. Next time you visit a casino, notice that the electronic board where the string of outcomes is displayed tends to be updated much more quickly (and with more consistency) when an unusual string (like 9 reds in a row, or a string of red-black-red-blacks) than when the outcomes appear somewhat random. Research on the chance bias has revealed that individuals are generally poor at perceiving randomness.

Conjunction Bias: The "AND" in Probability Theory

If two or more events are independent, we have seen that multiplication of the independent probabilities is the correct way to determine the likelihood of the intersection. The conjunction bias occurs when individuals overestimate the probability of the intersection of two (or more) events. This can help explain the often excessive optimism displayed by project managers for the completion time of a project. Managers tend to overestimate the likelihood that all of the critical activities in the project will finish on time. Another example of the conjunction bias is known as the *subset bias* which is directly related to representativeness. Individuals may judge a subset to be more probable than its set. To illustrate, Tversky and Kahneman (1982) asked participants in a survey to rank the most likely of the following match possibilities for a famous tennis player:

a. The player will win the match.
b. The player will lose the match.
c. The player will win the first set and then go on to lose the match.
d. The player will lose the first set and then go on to win the match.

Overall, participants indicated that they believed option "d" to be more probable than option "a", which cannot be the case since "d" is a special case (subset) of "a."

Disjunction Bias: The "OR" in Probability Theory

We also saw in Chapter 7 that the likelihood of disjunctive events should be assessed using the addition rule of probability theory. The disjunction bias occurs when individuals underestimate the probability of disjunctive events. For example, for your car to fail to get you to your destination the next time you drive, only one of a large number of mechanical and/or electrical functions has to fail. Individuals tend to not take into account all of these different possibilities when assessing the probability that the car will break down.

Sample Bias

Insensitivity to sample size is another statistical bias that could be the result of the representativeness heuristic. Sometimes termed the *law of small numbers,* people (even scientists!) sometimes draw conclusions from highly representative small samples even though inferences from small samples are subject to considerably more statistical error than those from large samples. For example, you might notice that there were fewer hot days last summer than there were the previous summer, and on the basis of that one sample you might conclude that global climate change is not leading to warmer temperatures in your locale. In fact, climate scientists base climate change on data collected over many years from around the world. One particularly acute example of the small-sample bias occurred in 2007–2008. In the summer of 2007, scientists saw that the Arctic ice pack melted at an alarming rate, and they claimed that this was one indication of Arctic warming, one of the anticipated effects of global climate change. Making the claim on the basis of only one extreme observation would indeed be an example of the sample bias; fortunately, the conclusion that the Arctic is warming is based on many years of observations. However, in 2008, the melting of the ice pack was more along historical lines. The sample bias might have led you, on the basis of observing just the two summers, to question whether the Arctic is really warming as claimed. Interestingly, the explanation is that an extreme year of ice-pack melt is expected to be followed by a much less extreme one; with less ice covering it, the Arctic Ocean radiates more heat into space, resulting in colder water temperatures—and more ice the following year.

Confidence Biases

Sometimes individuals assess probabilities with an aim to increase their perceived skill as decision makers. In particular, probability assessments can be subject to the desire and selectivity biases.

Desire Bias

The desire bias occurs when the probability of a desired outcome is overestimated. Some might just classify this as "wishful thinking," but individuals systematically overestimate the probability of desired outcomes in decision problems. For example, an avid fan of a particular NBA team may overestimate the probability of the team making the playoffs. A marketing manager may overestimate the success of a new product because he or she wants to be successful, and a candidate may overestimate her likelihood of being elected because of the desire to hold office. From evangelists to CEOs, the desire bias surfaces and has been shown to greatly reduce decision quality (Hogarth, 1987; Olsen, 1997).

Selectivity Bias

The selectivity bias results in discounting (or completely excluding) information that is inconsistent with the decision maker's personal experience. Although this is primarily a bias that reduces the amount of information used in the decision problem, it can also bias a decision maker's probabilities. Individuals may ignore information that is inconsistent with experience, even though this information may be important to consider when considering particular events and their probabilities. For example, in the 2004 NBA Playoffs, it was believed that if the Los Angeles Lakers were to defeat the San Antonio Spurs in the Western Conference Semi-Finals, the Lakers would win all subsequent playoff series. This is due to recent past experience when the Spurs were the only team to defeat the Lakers in the postseason, and the Eastern-Conference teams historically did not offer much competition. The Lakers did defeat the Spurs and also subsequently the Minnesota Timberwolves in the Western-Conference Finals. To everyone's surprise, though, (including the odds-makers in Las Vegas) the Detroit Pistons overwhelmed the Lakers in the NBA Finals and took the series easily in five games. All current information about the success the Detroit Pistons were having in their playoff series seemed to be ignored, because the expectation was for the Lakers to prevail.

Adjustment Heuristics and Biases

This set of heuristics refers to the notion that individuals tend to under-adjust their initial judgments in face of uncertainty or randomness. The most well-known is the *anchoring and adjustment heuristic*. In making estimates we often choose an initial anchor of some sort and then adjust from that anchor based on our knowledge of the specific event in question. An excellent example is sales forecasting. Many people make such forecasts by considering the sales figures for the most recent period and then adjusting those values based on new circumstances. The problem is that the adjustment usually is insufficient.

The anchor-and-adjust heuristic affects the assessment of probability distributions for continuous uncertain quantities more than it affects discrete assessments. When asked to assess ranges, we appear to begin with some default range and then adjust the endpoints. Because of the tendency to adjust insufficiently, most such ranges (and many assessed probability distributions) are too narrow, poorly reflecting the inherent variability in the uncertain quantity. One of the consequences is that we tend to be overconfident, having underestimated the probability of extreme outcomes, often by a substantial amount (Capen 1976).

Another bias in this class is the *partition dependence* bias. This bias arises when an individual is asked to assess probabilities for n different possible outcomes of an uncertain event. In doing so, the individual begins with a default distribution that assigns equal probability of $1/n$ to each of the n events, and then adjusts those equal probabilities based on what he or she knows. For example, if you were asked to predict NASDAQ index closings 2 years from now—below 2,000, between 2,000 and 2,200, or above 2,200—you would tend to start with default probabilities of 1/3, 1/3, and 1/3, and then adjust. However, in a case like this where you may know very little, you will tend not to adjust very much, so your probability that the index closes below 2,000 will be biased toward 1/3. In fact, if you were asked the probability that the NASDAQ closed below 1,600, between 1,600 and 1,800, between 1,800 and 2,000, or above 2,000, the total of the first three probabilities (i.e., the probability of closing below 2,000) would be biased toward 3/4. Fox and Clemen (2005) show that this bias can be quite severe, and that even professional decision analysts are subject to it!

Another example of an anchoring bias comes from the field of behavioral finance. Some investors tend to anchor on recent highs or lows and make investment decisions by comparing the current price with the anchor. For example, if a stock had a recent high of $80 and has fallen to $40, it may appear to be a bargain, and the investor may snap it up, thinking it to be undervalued. However, the stock's fundamentals—the economic conditions of the firm—may have deteriorated. If this is the case, the low price may be quite appropriate, and the investor has made a mistake that stems from the anchoring bias (and, one might add, a failure to consider all relevant information).

Beyond anchoring and adjustment, other biases in this class include the *conservatism and regression biases.*

Conservatism Bias

One can think of the conservatism bias as having the opposite effect from ignoring the base rate. With the base-rate bias, new information is weighted more heavily than old information. With conservatism, new information is discounted or even ignored, because the decision maker has anchored on previous information, and thus does not adjust his or her probability sufficiently.

Regression Bias

The idea that an isolated extreme outcome in a series of events is just randomness in the system can be hard for individuals to comprehend. As mentioned, we are not very good at perceiving randomness. When assessing the probability of success of, say, a research project, a recent overwhelming success can lead to a probability that is overly optimistic. Likewise, a recent catastrophic failure can lead to an overly pessimistic judgment of future success. This bias is related, to some extent, to memory biases, because the most recent event is given more weight.

One of the most important managerial implications of the regression bias relates to changes over time and misunderstanding the extent to which a process can be controlled. For example, Kahneman and Tversky relate their experience with a flight instructor in Israel. The instructor had been in the habit of praising students for good landings and scolding them for poor ones. He observed that after receiving praise for a good landing, a pilot's subsequent landing tended to be worse. Conversely, after a pilot received a scolding, his next landing tended to be better. The instructor concluded that scolding was effective feedback and that praise was not. In fact, this phenomenon is more easily explained by what is known as the statistical phenomenon *regression toward the mean*. If performance or measurements are random, then extreme cases will tend to be followed by less extreme ones. Landing a jet is not an easy task, and the pilot must deal with many different problems and conditions on each landing. It is perfectly reasonable to assume that performance for any pilot will vary from one landing to the next. Regression toward the mean suggests that a good landing probably will be followed by one that is not as good, and that a poor one will most likely be followed by one that is better.

Motivational Bias

The cognitive biases previously described relate to the ways in which we as human beings process information. But we also must be aware of motivational biases. Incentives often exist that lead people to report probabilities or forecasts that do not entirely reflect their true beliefs. For example, a salesperson asked for a sales forecast may be inclined to forecast low so that he will look good (and perhaps receive a bonus) when he sells more than the amount forecasted. Occasionally incentives can be quite subtle or even operate at a subconscious level. For example, some evidence suggests that weather forecasters, in assessing the probability of precipitation, persistently err on the high side; they tend to overstate the probability of rain. Perhaps they would rather people were prepared for bad weather (and were pleasantly surprised by sunshine) instead of expecting good weather and being unpleasantly surprised. Even though forecasters generally are good probability assessors and strive for accurate forecasts, their assessments may indeed be slightly affected by such implicit incentives.

Heuristics and Biases: Implications

The heuristics we use have evolved with human nature, and in most situations they allow us to process information "well enough" to achieve good outcomes. One might worry, though, whether these heuristics are up to coping with the complexity of modern society and the decisions we have to make. If we really are subject to such deficiencies in assessing probabilities, is there any hope? There is indeed. First, some evidence suggests that individuals can learn to become good at assessing probabilities. As mentioned, weather fore-casters are good probability assessors; in general, they provide accurate prob-abilities. For example, on those occasions when a forecaster says the probability of rain is 0.20, rain actually occurs very nearly 20% (or slightly less) of the time. Weather forecasters have three advantages; they have a lot of specialized knowledge about the weather, they make many forecasts, and they receive immediate feedback regarding the outcome. All of these appear to be important in improving probability-assessment performance.

Second, awareness of the heuristics and biases may help individuals make better probability assessments. If nothing else, knowing about some of the effects, you now may be able to recognize them when they occur. For exam-ple, you may be able to recognize regression toward the mean, or you may be sensitive to availability effects that result from unbalanced reporting in the news media. Moreover, when you obtain information from other individuals, you should realize that their judgments are subject to these same problems.

Third, the techniques we have discussed for assessing probabilities involve thinking about lotteries and chances in a structured way. These contexts are quite different from the way that most people think about uncertainty. By thinking hard about probabilities using these methods, it may be possible to avoid some heuristic reasoning and attendant biases. At the very least, thinking about lotteries provides a new perspective in the assessment process.

Finally, some problems simply cannot be addressed well in the form in which they are presented. In many cases it is worthwhile to decompose a chance event into other events. The result is that more assessments must be made, although they may be easier. In the next section we will see how decomposition may improve the assessment process.

DECOMPOSITION AND PROBABILITY ASSESSMENT

In many cases it is possible to break a probability assessment into smaller and more manageable chunks. This process is known as *decomposition*. There are at least three different scenarios in which decomposition of a probability assessment may be appropriate. In this section, we will discuss these different scenarios.

In the simplest case, decomposition involves thinking about how the event of interest is related to other events. A simple example might involve assessing the probability that a given stock price increases. Instead of consid-ering only the stock itself, we might think about its relationship to the market as a whole. We could assess the probability that the market goes up (as mea-sured by the Dow Jones average, say), and then assess the conditional proba-bilities that the stock price increases given that the market increases and given that the market does not increase. Finding the probability that the stock price increases is then a matter of using the law of total probability:

$$P(\text{Stock Price Up}) = P(\text{Stock Price Up} \mid \text{Market Up}) \, P(\text{Market Up})$$

$$+ \, P(\text{Stock Price Up} \mid \text{Market Not Up}) \, P(\text{Market Not Up})$$

The reason for performing the assessment in this way is that it may be more comfortable to assess the conditional probabilities and the probability about

FIGURE **8.12**
Decomposing the
probability assess-
ment for stock-
price movement.

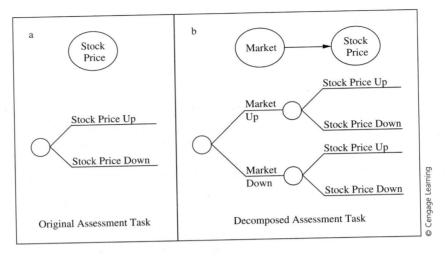

Original Assessment Task

Decomposed Assessment Task

© Cengage Learning

the market rather than to assess P(Stock Price Up) directly. In terms of
an influence diagram or a probability tree, we are adding a chance node that
is relevant to the assessment of the probabilities in which we are interested.
Figure 8.12 shows the decomposition of the stock-price assessment.

In the second scenario, it is a matter of thinking about what kinds of
uncertain outcomes could eventually lead to the outcome in question. For
example, if your car will not start, there are many possible causes. The
decomposition strategy would be to think about the chances that different
things could go wrong and the chance that the car will not start given each
of these specific underlying problems or some combination of them.

For a more complicated example that we can model, suppose that you
are an engineer in a nuclear power plant. Your boss calls you into his office
and explains that the Nuclear Regulatory Commission has requested safety
information. One item that the commission has requested is an assessment of
the probability of an accident resulting in the release of radioactive material
into the environment. Your boss knows that you have had a course in decision analysis, and so you are given the job of assessing this probability.

How would you go about this task? Of course, one way is to sit down
with a wheel of fortune and think about lotteries. Eventually you would be
able to arrive at a probability assessment. Chances are that as you thought
about the problem, however, you would realize that many different kinds of
situations could lead to an accident. Thus, instead of trying to assess the
probability directly, you might construct an influence diagram that includes
some of the outcomes that could lead to an accident. Figure 8.13 shows the
simple influence diagram that you might draw.

The intuition behind Figure 8.13 is that an accident could result
from a failure of the cooling system or of the control system. The cooling
system could either spring a leak itself, thus spilling radioactive material,
or its pumps could fail, allowing the reactor core to overheat, and thus
resulting in a possible accident. The control system also is critical. If the
control system fails, it may become impossible to maintain safe operation

FIGURE **8.13**
Simple influence diagram for assessing the probability of a nuclear power plant accident.

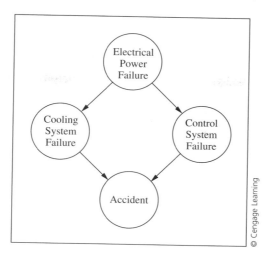

of the reactor, and thus possibly result in an accident. Furthermore, the control system and the cooling system do not operate independently; they both depend on the electrical power system within the plant. Thus, failure of the electrical system would make failure of both the cooling and the control systems more likely. (Many other relationships also are possible. An influence diagram to assess the probability of an accident in an actual nuclear power plant would be considerably more complicated than Figure 8.13.)

In our simplified model, each chance node in Figure 8.13, has two possible outcomes, failure or no failure. Because failures of both the cooling and control systems are relevant to the assessment of an accident, we have four conditional probabilities to assess. Let A denote the outcome of an accident, L the outcome of a cooling system failure, N the outcome of a control system failure, and E the outcome of an electrical system failure. The four conditional probabilities we must assess for outcome A are $P(A \mid L, N)$, $P(A \mid \overline{L}, N)$, $P(A \mid L, \overline{N})$, and $P(A \mid \overline{L}, \overline{N})$. For the cooling system node, probabilities $P(L \mid E)$ and $P(L \mid \overline{E})$, must be assessed. Likewise, for the control system node $P(N \mid E)$ and $P(N \mid \overline{E})$ must be assessed. Finally, $P(E)$ must be assessed for the electrical system node.

There are nine assessments in all. Again, the reason for decomposing the assessment task into multiple assessments is that you may be more comfortable with the assessments that are required in the decomposed version. For example, you may be able to conclude that $P(A \mid \overline{L}, \overline{N}) = 0$; if neither the cooling system nor the control system fails, then the probability of an accident is essentially zero.

Assembling the probabilities in this case again is a matter of using the law of total probability, although it must be used more than once. Start out by using the law of total probability to expand $P(A)$:

$$P(A) = P(A|L, N)P(L, N) + P(A|\overline{L}, N)P(\overline{L}, N)$$
$$+ P(A|L, \overline{N})P(L, \overline{N}) + P(A|\overline{L}, \overline{N})P(\overline{L}, \overline{N})$$

Now the problem is to find P(L, N), P($\overline{L}$, N), P(L, $\overline{N}$), and P($\overline{L}$, $\overline{N}$). Each in turn can be expanded using the law of total probability. For example, consider P(L, N):

$$P(L, N) = P(L, N|E)P(E) + P(L, N|\overline{E})P(\overline{E})$$

Now we must find P(L, N | E) and P(L, N|$\overline{E}$). From the influence diagram, the only connection between the cooling system (L) and the control system (N) is through the electrical system. Thus, cooling and control failures are conditionally independent given the state of the power system. From the definition of conditional independence in Chapter 7, we can write

$$P(L, N|E) = P(L|E)P(N|E)$$

and

$$P(L, N|\overline{E}) = P(L|\overline{E})P(N|\overline{E})$$

Thus, by expanding out the probabilities, it is possible to build up the probability P(A) from the nine assessments and their complements.

The third scenario is related to the second. In this case, however, it is not a matter of different possible underlying causes but a matter of thinking through all of the different events that must happen before the outcome in question occurs. For example, in assessing the probability of an explosion at an oil refinery, an engineer would have to consider the chances that perhaps some critical pipe would fail, that all of the different safety measures also would fail at the same time, and that no one would notice the problem before the explosion occurred. Thus, many different individual outcomes would have to occur before the explosion. In contrast, the nuclear power plant example involved alternative paths that could lead to a failure. Of course, the second and third scenarios can be combined. That is, there may be alternative paths to a failure, each requiring that certain individual outcomes occur. This kind of analysis often is called *fault-tree analysis* because it is possible to build a tree showing the relationship of prior outcomes to the outcome in question, which often is the failure of some complicated system.

As you may have noticed in the nuclear power plant example, the probability manipulations can become somewhat complicated. Fortunately, in complicated assessment problems, computer programs can perform the probability manipulations for us. Using such a program allows us to focus on thinking hard about the assessments rather than on the mathematics.

As with many decision-analysis techniques, there may be more than one way to decompose a probability assessment. The whole reason to use decomposition is to make the assessment process easier. The best decomposition to use is the one that is easiest to think about and that gives the clearest view of the uncertainty in the decision problem.

As previously indicated, decomposition in decision-analysis assessment of probabilities is important for many reasons. Perhaps most important, though, is that it permits the development of large and complex models of

FIGURE **8.14**
Influence diagram for a decision analysis of alternative sites for a nuclear-waste repository.

Source: Springer and D. Reidel Publishing Company, 1987, p. 352, Merkhofer, M. W., Figure 8.15, © D. Reidel Publishing Company with kind permission from Springer Science + Business Media B.V.

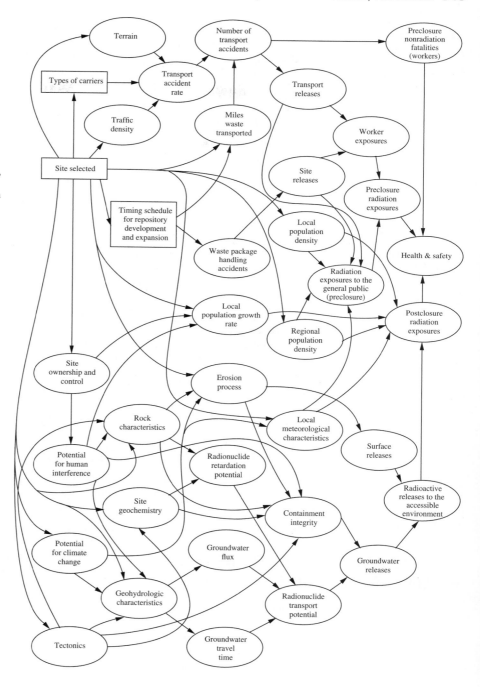

uncertainty. Examples are given in Figures 8.14, 8.15, and 8.16. The influence diagram in Figure 8.14 was constructed as part of an analysis of alternative sites for a nuclear-waste repository in the United States (Merkhofer 1987b). Figures 8.15 and 8.16 show parts of the influence diagram for a probabilistic

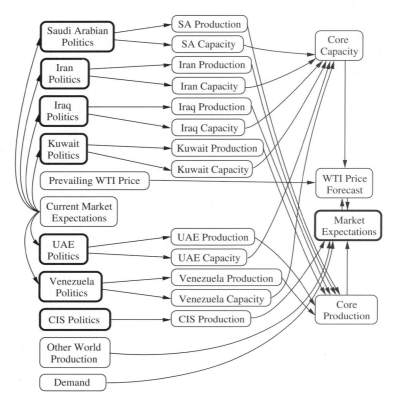

FIGURE **8.15**
Influence diagram
(or belief network)
for forecasting crude
oil prices.

Rounded rectangles are
used instead of ovals
to represent chance
nodes. Nodes with bold
outlines represent
entire submodels.

Source: Abramson and
Finizza (1995). International
Journal of Forecasting, 11,
Bruce Abramson and
Anthony Finizza, Probabilistic
Forecasts from Probabilistic
Models: A Case Study in
the Oil Market, pp. 63–72,
© 1995, with permission
from Elsevier.

model for forecasting crude oil prices (Abramson and Finizza, 1995). In Figures 8.15 and 8.16 the authors have used rounded rectangles to represent chance nodes. In addition, each of the nodes with bold outlines in Figure 8.15 actually represents an entire submodel. For example, Figure 8.16 shows the generic structure for each of the "Politics" nodes. In all, this model of the oil market includes over 150 chance nodes.

EXPERTS AND PROBABILITY ASSESSMENT: PULLING IT ALL TOGETHER

Our discussion thus far has taken a conventional decision-analysis approach; the decision maker makes the probability assessments that are required in the decision model. In practice, though, decisions are often quite complex, and the decision maker must rely on experts to provide information—in the form of probability assessments—regarding crucial uncertainties. For example, all of the probability assessments required in the influence diagrams in Figures 8.14, 8.15, and 8.16 regarding nuclear-waste technology and the world oil market, respectively, were provided by experts.

FIGURE **8.16**
Details of the "Politics" submodels in Figure 8.15.

Source: Abramson and Finizza (1995). International Journal of Forecasting, 11, Bruce Abramson and Anthony Finizza, Probabilistic Forecasts from Probabilistic Models: A Case Study in the Oil Market, pp. 63–72, © 1995, with permission from Elsevier.

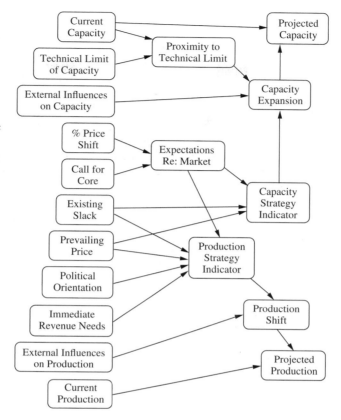

In such complex problems, expert risk assessment plays a major role in the decision-making process. As such, the process by which the expert information was acquired must stand up to professional scrutiny, and thus policy makers who acquire and use expert information must be able to document the assessment process. In general, this is no different from standard scientific principles of data collection; scientists who run experiments or conduct surveys are expected to adhere to standards that ensure the scientific validity of their data. Adherence to these standards is necessary if the conclusions drawn on the basis of the data are to have any validity.

The assessment of expert judgments must also adhere to standards. Not surprisingly, though, the standards for experts are quite different from those for data collection; whereas there are well-established norms for data collection, subjective assessments from experts require additional considerations due to the unique circumstances and even due to the quirks of the experts. There are important parallels between the two situations, however. For example, the definition of an expert in any given situation is not always without controversy. Thus, the policy maker must be able to document and justify the expert-selection process, just as the data-collecting scientist must be able to document and justify the process by which specific data points were selected. Also, as we have mentioned, experts can be subject to numerous biases. Thus, policy makers must be able to show that the environment in which the judgments were made did as much as possible to reduce or avoid these biases. The counterpart in data collection is that the scientist must be able to show that measurements were taken without bias. If judgments from multiple experts are combined to obtain a single probability distribution, then issues of relative expertise and redundancy among the experts must be taken into account. The corresponding situation in data collection occurs when a scientist combines multiple data sets or uses results from multiple studies to draw conclusions.

Over the past 20 years, as the use of expert information has grown in importance, procedures have been developed for acquiring expert probability assessments. In general, the approach requires the creation of a *protocol* for expert assessment that satisfies the need for professional scrutiny. Thorough discussions of protocol development are found in Merkhofer (1987a) and Morgan and Henrion (1990). Although procedures vary (e.g., Morgan and Henrion describe three different approaches), every assessment protocol should include the following steps:

1 Background The first step is to identify those variables for which expert assessment is needed. Although this sounds obvious, it is an important first step. Relevant scientific literature should be searched to determine the extent of scientific knowledge. The objectives of stakeholders should be examined to be sure that information is being obtained about pertinent concerns. For example, if stakeholders in an environmental-management situation care about habitat for endangered species, ecosystem viability, extraction of natural resources for economic purposes, recreation opportunities, and saving wilderness for future generations, then information on all five of these issues must be acquired. Some may require expert assessment, while others may be better addressed by conventional scientific studies. In many cases, experts may be required to make issue-specific probabilistic judgments based on their knowledge.

2 Identification and Recruitment of Experts Identification of appropriate experts can range from straightforward to very difficult. Often an organization can find in-house expertise. In some cases, experts must be recruited externally. Recommendations by peers (e.g., through professional associations) can help to justify the selection of specific experts.

3 Motivating Experts Experts often are leery of the probability-assessment process. Typically they are scientists themselves and prefer to rely on the process of science to generate knowledge. Their opinions may or may not be "correct," and hence they hesitate to express those opinions. The fact remains, though, that a decision must be made with the limited information available, and the choice was made in Step 1 that expert opinion is the appropriate way to obtain that information. Thus, it is important to establish rapport with the experts and to engender their enthusiasm for the project.

4 Structuring and Decomposition This step might be called *knowledge exploration*. This step identifies specific variables for which judgments are needed and explores the experts' understanding of causal and statistical relationships among the relevant variables. The objective is to develop a general model (expressed, for example, as an influence diagram) that reflects the experts' thinking about the relationships among the variables. The resulting model may be an elaborate decomposition of the original problem, showing which probability distributions must be assessed conditional on other variables. The model thus gives an indication of the order in which the probability assessments must be made.

5 Probability-Assessment Training Because many experts do not have specific training in probability assessment, it is important to explain the principles of assessment, to provide information on the inherent biases in the process and ways to counteract those biases, and to give the experts an opportunity to practice making probability assessments.

6 Probability Elicitation and Verification In this step the experts make the required probability assessments, typically under the guidance of an individual trained in the probability-elicitation process. The expert's assessments are checked to be sure they are consistent (probabilities sum to 1, conditional probabilities are consistent with marginal and joint probability assessments, and so on). As part of this process, an expert may provide detailed chains of reasoning for the assessments. Doing so can help to establish a clear rationale for specific aspects of the assessed distributions (e.g., a variable's extreme values or particular dependence relationships). At the same time, encouraging a thorough examination of the expert's knowledge base can help to counteract the biases associated with the psychological heuristics of availability, anchoring, and representativeness. Thus, as output this step produces the required probability assessments and a documentation of the reasoning behind the assessments.

7 Aggregation of Experts' Probability Distributions If multiple experts have assessed probability distributions, it may be necessary to aggregate their assessed probability distributions into a single distribution for the use of the decision maker. Another reason for aggregation is that a single distribution may be needed in a probabilistic model of a larger system. In general, two approaches are possible. One is to ask the experts themselves to generate a consensus distribution. Doing so may require considerable sharing of information, clarification of individual definitions, and possibly compromise on the parts of individuals. Unfortunately, the necessary interactions can also lead to biases in the consensus opinion. For this reason, several methods have been proposed to control the interaction among the individual experts.

If the experts are unable to reach a consensus, either because of irreconcilable differences or because convening the group is logistically inconvenient, one can aggregate their individual distributions using a mathematical formula. Simply averaging the distributions is a straightforward (and intuitively appealing) aggregation approach, but it ignores the relative expertise among the experts as well as the extent to which their information is redundant or dependent.

The seven steps described above give a feel for the process of obtaining expert probability assessments. In a full-blown risk assessment, this process can involve dozens of people and may take several months to complete. The following example describes a risk assessment in which expert climatologists provided probability assessments regarding possible future climate changes at the site of the proposed nuclear-waste repository in Nevada.

Climate Change at Yucca Mountain, Nevada	In 1987 the U.S. government proposed construction of a long-term nuclear-waste repository at Yucca Mountain, about 100 miles northwest of Las Vegas, Nevada. Spent fuel rods from nuclear reactors around the nation would be sealed in large steel casks, shipped to Yucca Mountain, and stored in a large cavern carved out of solid rock about 300 meters below the surface. When full, the repository would be sealed, but the nuclear waste would remain dangerous for millennia. Thus, requirements for licensing the facility included showing that the repository could safely contain the radioactive material for 10,000 years.
	One of several risks that the repository would face was that the local climate was expected to change over time as the global climate changed. In broad-brush terms, one might expect that increased human activity would lead to some warming but that natural climate cycles would lead to a global cooling or even another ice age. Climatologists have studied general climate trends over long periods of time and have produced global climate-change forecasts. What does the future hold for Yucca Mountain, Nevada, though? One of the attractions of Yucca Mountain was the dry climate; it experiences an annual average precipitation of about 15 centimeters. If the future climate changed enough, groundwater could enter the repository. How much future precipitation is likely at Yucca Mountain over the next 10,000 years?

To address this question, the Center for Nuclear Waste Repository Analyses (CNWRA) undertook a project to obtain the opinions of expert climatologists. The seven steps described above helped to provide a framework for the project, during which the experts assessed subjective probability distributions for a variety of different climatological variables (average annual rainfall, average temperature, amount of cloud cover, and others) at several different points in time over the next 10,000 years.

Although the exceptionally long forecast horizon suggested that forecasting would be difficult if not impossible, the experts found this to be an interesting project, and they were able to develop carefully thought-out rationales for different scenarios and assess probability distributions that reflected their reasoning. In general, the experts agreed that the Yucca Mountain area would warm up slightly in the short term due to atmospheric buildup of greenhouse gases such as carbon dioxide and water vapor, followed by slight cooling as the earth enters a "mini ice age," but they disagreed regarding the extent and persistence of the global-warming effect. This disagreement showed up, for example, in Figure 8.17a, which shows the medians of the experts' CDFs for average temperature traced over time. Some experts thought the effect of global warming would be short-lived, followed quickly by global cooling, whereas others believed it would last longer and be more pronounced. This disagreement is also seen in their assessed CDFs. Figures 8.17b and c, for example, show the experts' CDFs for change in average temperature (°C) and change in average annual precipitation (mm) 3,000 years in the future.

The Yucca Mountain climate forecast is just one example of a probabilistic risk analysis that assessed expert opinions in the form of probability distributions. Other examples of such analyses involve sales forecasting, research-and-development decisions, analysis of health risks due to ozone,

FIGURE **8.17**
Some assessments of climate change at Yucca Mountain.

(a) Medians of CDFs for average temperature over time. (b) CDFs for change in average temperature 3,000 years in future. (c) CDFs for change in average annual precipitation 3,000 years in future.

Source: DeWispelare et al. (1993). *Expert elicitation of future climate in the Yucca Mountain vicinity*, Technical Report CNWRA 93–016. Prepared for Nuclear Regulatory Commission. San Antonio, TX: Southwest Research Institute.

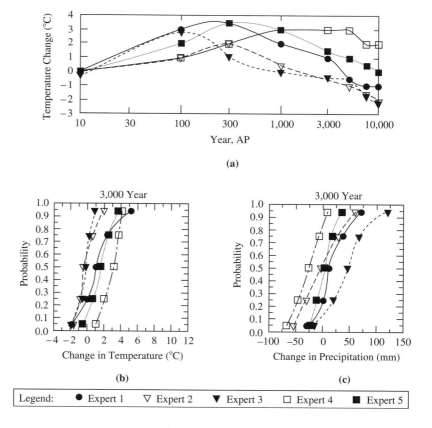

policy making regarding hazardous waste, power plant design analysis, and many others. Risk analyses are performed by both government agencies and private corporations and are becoming more important over time as decision makers, both public and private, face important decisions with substantial uncertainty and imperfect information.

CONSTRUCTING DISTRIBUTIONS USING @RISK

Having spent the time and energy to carefully and coherently assess probability values, we now turn to the program @RISK to fit probability distributions to the subjective assessments. Keep in mind that our goal is to construct a distribution, based on our assessments, that accurately captures the underlying uncertainty. @RISK helps us by translating the assessments into a graph of the distribution. The graph provides a visual check of our assessments and highlights properties that may not be apparent from a list of numerical values. The pitfalls of probability assessment that we discussed are hard to avoid, and sometimes we do not realize our assessments need to be modified until we see the resulting graph. For example, the graph may reveal that we overstated the probability of certain outcomes at the expense of others. We demonstrate @RISK using the assessed values from the pretzel problem. Along with the data previously give, we also need minimum and maximum values for demand. For this example, let's assume the minimum equals 0 and the maximum equals 60,000.

Monthly Demand X	Cumulative Probability P(Monthly Demand ≤ X)
5,000	0.05
16,000	0.25
23,000	0.50
31,000	0.75
45,000	0.95
0	Min
60,000	Max

STEP 1 *Opening @RISK.*

1.1 Open Excel and then @RISK, enabling any macros if requested.
1.2 You can access a variety of help features by clicking on the **Help** button in the @RISK ribbon. Under *Documentation*, the *Manual* is a

pdf file of the actual manual, and *@RISK Help* is a searchable database. In addition, you can view examples via *Example Spreadsheets* or video tutorials via Videos.

STEP 2 *Selecting the Cumulative Distribution.*

2.1 Enter the monthly demand values given in the preceding table into cells **A2** to **A8** and the probabilities into cells **B2** to **B8**.

2.2 Highlight cell **E3** in Excel. This is the cell where we will place the fitted distribution.

2.3 Either click the **Define Distributions** button (first from the left in the *@RISK* toolbar) or **right-click** the mouse and choose **@RISK**, then **Define Distributions**. An *@RISK-Define Definition: E3* window is opened, as shown in Figure 8.18. This window shows the variety of distributions available for modeling uncertainties, many of which we discuss in the next chapter.

2.4 Select the **Cumul** distribution found along the top row, and click the **Select Distribution** button at the bottom right.

2.5 The pop-up window shows a cumulative distribution curve in the center, summary statistics, such as the minimum, maximum, mean, and

FIGURE **8.18**
@RISK's distribution palette showing the variety of distributions available.

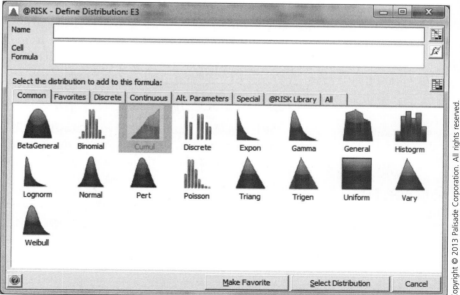

standard deviation of the distribution to the right, and various ways to customize the distribution on the left. Next, we show how to customize the cumulative distribution to match the assessments.

STEP 3 Customizing the CDF.

3.1 We start by naming the distribution **Monthly Demand** in the *Name* text box on top.

3.2 We have two options for entering the *Min, Max, X-Table* and *P-Table* values. We can manually type the Min and Max values directly into their cells, then click in the *X-Table* and then click again on the pull-down triangle to access the *Table Editor*. The second option is better because it references the Excel spreadsheet, and any changes made to the spreadsheet are automatically reflected in the distribution. Click on the **Assign Excel References** button (shown in Figure 8.20) and the data entry window pops up as shown in Figure 8.19. Enter **A7** for the *Min*, **A8** for the *Max*, **A2:A6** for the *X-Table*, and **B2:B6** for the *P-Table* and return to the *Define Distribution* window by clicking the upper-right corner of the data entry table.

3.3 Your *Define Distribution* window should now be the same as Figure 8.20. Click **OK** and the formula is placed in cell E3.

Now that we have created a distribution that matches the assessments, we have a variety of options. The first is to check with our experts to make sure that the fitted distribution is correct (Step 4). We can also format and export the graph (Step 5).

STEP 4 Checking Fitted CDF for Accuracy.

4.1 @RISK reports various summary statistics to help us understand the fitted distribution. Thus, we should share these statistics with our experts as a check of the accuracy of the assessments.

FIGURE **8.19**
The data entry window in @RISK.

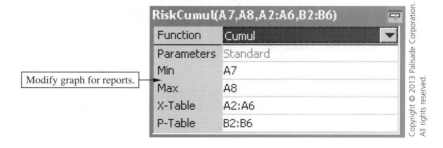

Modify graph for reports.

4.2 The two delimiters (black vertical lines overlaying the graph) are markers that allow us to determine the cumulative probability of any x value. In Figure 8.20, the leftmost delimiter is at the 5th percentile, as shown by the 5.0% in the bar above the curve. The graph shows that the x value equals 5,000. Therefore, there is a 5% probability that the monthly quantity demand for pretzels will be less than or equal to 5,000. The 90.0% shown indicates that there is a 90% probability that demand will be greater than 5,000 but less than 45,000. The rightmost delimiter shows that there is a 95% probability that the monthly quantity demand for pretzels will be less than or equal to 45,000, or equivalently a 5% probability that the monthly demand will be greater than 45,000 pretzels.

4.3 Using the delimiters, we can easily read off any cumulative probability value corresponding to an x value or conversely, any x value corresponding to a cumulative probability value. It is as simple as opening the *Define Distribution: E3* window (Step 2), placing the cursor over the delimiter line, and while holding the mouse button down, sliding the cursor. The delimiter line moves in accordance while the probabilities and x values change instantly. For example, to find the probability that demand will be between 10,000 and 40,000, simply move the left delimiter to **10,000** on the x-axis and the right delimiter

FIGURE **8.20**

The Define Distribution window in @RISK showing the fitted distribution to the pretzel demand assessments.

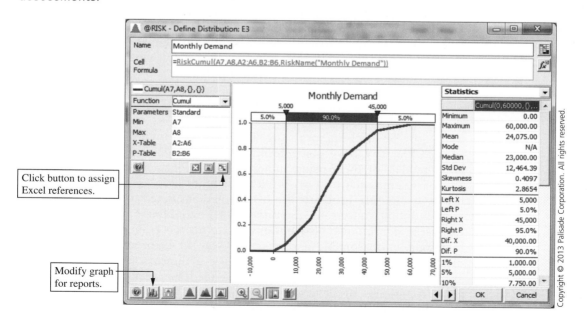

Click button to assign Excel references.

Modify graph for reports.

to 40,000. The probability equals 73.8% as shown in the bar above the graph.

The delimiters allow us to report back to the expert the implied probabilities for any range. Doing so allows the expert to revise his original assessments to ensure complete consistency with his or her beliefs.

STEP 5 *Formatting Options.*

5.1 This last step provides instruction on how to create professional graphs for reports. Click on the **Graph Options** button shown along the bottom left of Figure 8.20. The *Graph Options* window pops up, and each tab along the top of the window provides formatting options. Here you change the style of the distribution shown, the title, customize the x and y axes, modify the legend adding other statistics, and remove the delimiters if you wish.

5.2 To export or copy the graph, simply right-click while the cursor is over graph and choose the desired option in the pop-up submenu.

We end this section with a word of caution: @RISK provides the opportunity to modify the distribution in many ways. Be careful that any changes accurately reflect your expert's beliefs about the variable that you are modeling. @RISK makes it easy and tempting to play around with the numbers, but unless you have a good reason and sound data for making changes—DON'T! Distributions are subtle, and small changes can have big effects. Always check the summary statistics when you make changes to ensure that they match your expert's judgment.

SUMMARY

Many of the decision problems that we face involve uncertain future events. We may have some feeling for such uncertainties, and we can build models of them using subjective probability-assessment techniques. The basic approach to assessing a probability involves either setting up a bet or comparing lotteries. We also have considered assessment methods for continuous uncertain quantities and found that it is straightforward to assess continuous distributions in terms of cumulative distribution functions. A reasonable and practical way to incorporate a continuous distribution into a decision tree is to use a discrete approximation such as the Extended Pearson-Tukey or Extended Swanson-Megill three-point approximations.

Our discussion also touched on the pitfalls of probability assessment. Individuals tend to use cognitive heuristics to judge probabilities. Heuristics such as representativeness, availability, and anchoring and adjustment can lead to bias in probability assessment. Some ideas for improving probability assessments were discussed, including decomposition of the assessment task. We also presented a protocol-based approach to obtaining expert probability assessments and showed how this approach was used in a risk assessment for a proposed nuclear waste repository.

In the online supplement at www.cengagebrain.com, we discuss the idea of coherence—that is, that subjective probabilities must obey the same probability laws that "long-run frequency" probabilities do. Being coherent in probability assessment means being sure that one cannot be exploited through a series of bets known as a Dutch book.

EXERCISES

8.1. Explain in your own words the idea of subjective probability.

8.2. An accounting friend of yours has gone to great lengths to construct a statistical model of bankruptcy. Using the model, the probability that a firm will file for bankruptcy within a year is calculated on the basis of financial ratios. On hearing your explanation of subjective probability, your friend says that subjective probability may be all right for decision analysis, but his model gives objective probabilities on the basis of real data. Explain to him how his model is, to a great extent, based on subjective judgments. Comment also on the subjective judgments that a bank officer would have to make in using your friend's model.

8.3. Explain in your own words the difference between assessing the probability for a discrete event and assessing a probability distribution for a continuous unknown quantity.

8.4. For each of the following phrases write down the probability number that you feel is represented by the phrase. After doing so, check your answers to be sure they are consistent. (For example, is your answer to e less than your answer to j?)
   a. "There is a better than even chance that ..."
   b. "A possibility exists that ..."
   c. "... has a high likelihood of occurring."
   d. "The probability is very high that ..."
   e. "It is very unlikely that ..."
   f. "There is a slight chance ..."
   g. "The chances are better than even ..."
   h. "There is no probability, no serious probability, that ..."
   i. "... is probable."
   j. "... is unlikely."
   k. "There is a good chance that ..."
   l. "... is quite unlikely."
   m. "... is improbable."
   n. "... has a high probability."

    o.   "There is a chance that ..."
    p.   "... is very improbable."
    q.   "... is likely."
    r.   "Probably ..."

8.5. Suppose your father asked you to assess the probability that you would pass your decision-analysis course. How might you decompose this probability assessment? Draw an influence diagram to represent the decomposition.

QUESTIONS AND PROBLEMS

8.6. Assess your probability that the following outcomes will occur. Use the equivalent lottery method as discussed in the chapter. If possible, use a wheel of fortune with an adjustable win area, or a computer program that simulates such a wheel. What issues did you account for in making each assessment?
    a.   It will rain tomorrow in New York City.
    b.   You will have been offered a job before you graduate.
    c.   The women's track team at your college will win the NCAA championship this year.
    d.   The price of crude oil will be more than $200 per barrel on January 1, 2030.
    e.   The Dow Jones industrial average will go up tomorrow.
    f.   Any other uncertain outcome that interests you.

8.7. Consider the following two outcomes:
    a.   You will get an A in your most difficult course.
    b.   You will get an A or a B in your easiest course.
Can you assess the probability of these outcomes occurring? What is different about assessing probabilities regarding your own performance as compared to assessing probabilities for outcomes like those in Problem 8.6.?

8.8. Describe a decomposition strategy that would be useful for assessing the probabilities in Problem 8.7.

8.9. Many people deal with uncertainty by assessing odds. For example, in horse racing different horses' odds of winning are assessed. Odds of "a to b for Outcome E" means that $P(E) = a/(a + b)$. Odds of "c to d against Outcome E" means that $P(\overline{E}) = c/(c + d)$. For the outcomes in Problem 8.6, assess the odds for that outcome occurring. Convert your assessed odds to probabilities. Do they agree with the probability assessments that you made in Problem 8.6?

8.10. It is said that Napoleon assessed probabilities at the Battle of Waterloo in 1815. His hopes for victory depended on keeping the English and Prussian armies separated. Believing that they had not joined forces on the morning of the fateful battle, he indicated his belief that he had a

90% chance of defeating the English; P(Napoleon Wins) = 0.90. When told later that elements of the Prussian force had joined the English, Napoleon revised his opinion downward on the basis of this information, but his posterior probability was still 60%; P(Napoleon Wins | Prussian and English Join Forces) = 0.60.

Suppose Napoleon were using Bayes' theorem to revise his information. To do so, he would have had to make some judgments about P(Prussian and English Join Forces | Napoleon Wins) and P(Prussian and English Join Forces | Napoleon Loses). In particular, he would have had to judge the ratio of these two probabilities. Based on the previously stated prior and posterior probabilities, what is that ratio?

8.11. Should you drop your decision-analysis course? Suppose you faced the following problem: If you drop the course, the anticipated salary in your best job offer will depend on your current GPA:

Anticipated Salary | Drop = ($4,000 × Current GPA) + $16,000

If you take the course, the anticipated salary in your best job offer will depend on both your current GPA and your overall score (on a scale of 0 to 100) in the course:

Anticipated Salary | Do Not Drop = 0.6($4,000 × Current GPA)

+ 0.4($170 × Course Score)

+ $16,000

The problem is that you do not know how well you will do in the course. You can, however, assess a distribution for your score. Assuming that 90–100 is an A, 80–89 is a B, 70–79 a C, 60–69 a D, and 0–59 an F, assess a continuous probability distribution for your numerical score in the course. Use that distribution to decide whether or not to drop the course. Figure 8.21 shows your decision tree.

FIGURE **8.21**
Decision tree for Question 8.11.

Should you drop your decision-analysis course?

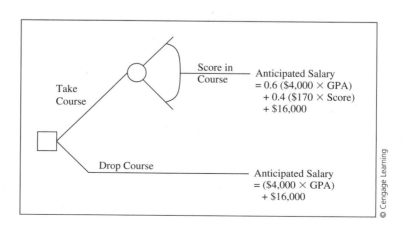

© Cengage Learning

8.12. Assess these fractiles for the following uncertain quantities: 0.05 fractile, 0.25 fractile (first quartile), 0.50 (median), 0.75 fractile (third quartile), and 0.95 fractile. Plot your assessments to create graphs of your subjective CDFs.

a. The closing Dow Jones industrial average (DJIA) on the last Friday of the current month.

b. The closing DJIA on the last Friday of next year.

c. The exchange rate, in Japanese yen per dollar, at the end of next Monday.

d. The official high temperature at O'Hare International Airport tomorrow.

e. The number of fatalities from airline accidents in the United States next year.

f. The number of casualties from nuclear power plant accidents in the United States over the next 10 years.

g. The value of the next jackpot won in the California state lottery.

8.13. For each of the following 10 items, assess the 0.05 and 0.95 fractiles based only on your current knowledge. That is, choose upper and lower estimates such that you are 90% sure that the actual value falls between your estimates. Your challenge is to be neither too narrow (i.e., overconfident) nor too wide (underconfident).

	0.05 Fractile (Low)	0.95 Fractile (High)
1. Martin Luther King's age at death	_____	_____
2. Length of the Nile River	_____	_____
3. Number of countries that are members of OPEC	_____	_____
4. Number of books in the Old Testament	_____	_____
5. Diameter of the moon	_____	_____
6. Weight of an empty Boeing 747	_____	_____
7. Year of Wolfgang Amadeus Mozart's birth	_____	_____
8. Gestation period of an Asian elephant	_____	_____
9. Air distance from London to Tokyo	_____	_____
10. Depth of deepest known point in the oceans	_____	_____

If you have done a good job, most of your intervals contain the actual value (given in the online supplement at www.cengagebrain.com—no peeking!). If three or more of your intervals missed the actual value, though, you have demonstrated overconfidence. Given your results in this question, would you adjust your assessments in Problem 8.12? [*Source:* Adapted from J. E. Russo and P. J. H. Schoemaker (1989) *Decision Traps: The Ten Barriers to Brilliant Decision Making and How to Overcome Them.* New York: Fireside. Reprinted by permission.]

8.14. Forecasters often provide only point forecasts, which are their best guesses as to an upcoming event. For example, an economic forecaster might predict that U.S. gross national product (GNP) will increase at a 3% annual rate over the next three months. Occasionally a forecaster also will provide an estimate of the degree of confidence in the point forecast to indicate how sure (or unsure) the forecaster is.

In what sense can your answers to Problem 8.12 be interpreted as forecasts? What advantages do subjective probability distributions have over typical point forecasts? What disadvantages? How could a decision maker use probabilistic forecasts such as those in Problem 8.12?

8.15. Choose a course that you are currently taking in which the final exam is worth 100 points. Treating your score on the exam as if it were a continuous uncertain quantity, assess the subjective probability distribution for your score. After you have finished, check your assessed distribution for consistency by:

a. Choosing any two intervals you have judged to have equal probability content, and

b. Determining whether you would be willing to place small even-odds bets that your score would fall in one of the two intervals. (The bet would be called off if the score fell elsewhere.)

c. After assessing the continuous distribution, construct a three-point approximation to this distribution with the extended Pearson-Tukey method. Use the approximation to estimate your expected exam score.

d. Now construct an approximation using the extended Swanson-Megill method. Use this approximation to estimate your expected exam score. How does your answer compare with the estimate from part c?

8.16. Compare the discrete-approximation methods by doing the following:

a. Use the extended Pearson-Tukey method to create three-point discrete approximations for the continuous distributions assessed in Problem 8.12. Use the approximations to estimate the expected values of the uncertain quantities.

b. Repeat part a, but construct the extended Swanson-Megill approximations. Compare your estimated expected values from the two methods.

8.17. Assess the probability that the New York Mets will win the World Series (WS) next year. Call this probability p. Now assess the following probabilities: P(Win WS | Win Pennant) and P(Win Pennant). Use these to calculate q = P(Win WS) = P(Win WS | Win Pennant) P(Win Pennant) = P(Win WS and Win Pennant). (To play in the World Series, the team must first win the pennant.)

a. Does $p = q$? Which of the two assessments are you more confident about? Would you adjust your assessments to make $p = q$? Why or why not?

b. If you do not like the Mets, do this problem for your favorite major league baseball team.

8.18. Assess the probability that you will be hospitalized for more than one day during the upcoming year. In assessing this probability, decompose the assessment based on whether or not you are in an automobile accident. With this decomposition, you must assess P(Hospitalized | Accident), P(Hospitalized | No Accident), and P(Accident). In what other ways might this assessment be decomposed?

8.19. Choose a firm in which you are particularly interested, perhaps one where you might like to work. Go to the library and read about this firm, about its industry, and about the relationship of this firm and the industry to the economy as a whole. After your reading, assess a subjective CDF for the firm's revenue over the next fiscal year. Discuss the assessment process. In particular, what did you learn in your research that had an impact on the assessment? What kinds of decomposition helped you in your assessment process?

8.20. After observing a long run of red on a roulette wheel, many gamblers believe that black is bound to occur. Such a belief often is called the *gambler's fallacy* because the roulette wheel has no memory. Which probability-assessment heuristic is at work in the gambler's fallacy? Explain.

8.21. Look again at Problems 7.24 and 7.25. These problems involve assessments of the relative likelihood of different statements. When an individual ranks "Linda is a bank teller and is active in the feminist movement" as more probable than the statement "Linda is a bank teller," which of the three probability-assessment heuristics may be at work? Explain.

8.22. Suppose that you are a solid B student. Your grades in your courses have always been B's. In your statistics course, you get a D on the midterm. When your parents express concern, what statistical phenomenon might you invoke to persuade them not to worry about the D?

8.23. When we assess our subjective probabilities, we are building a model of the uncertainty we face. If we face a range-of-risk problem, and we begin to assess a continuous distribution subjectively, then clearly it is possible to perform many assessments, which would make the sketched CDF smoother and smoother. How do we know when to stop making assessments and when to keep going? When is the model of our uncertainty adequate for solving the problem, and when is it inadequate?

8.24. Most of us have a hard time assessing probabilities with much precision. For instance, in assessing the probability of rain tomorrow, even carefully considering the lotteries and trying to adjust a wheel of fortune to find the indifference point, many people would eventually say something like this: "If you set $p = 0.2$, I'd take Lottery A, and if $p = 0.3$, I'd take Lottery B. My indifference point must be somewhere in between these two numbers, but I am not sure where."

How could you deal with this kind of imprecision in a decision analysis? Illustrate how your approach would work using the umbrella problem (Figure 4.9). (*Hint:* The question is *not* how to get more precise assessments. Rather, given that the decision maker refuses to make precise assessments, and you are stuck with imprecise assessments, what kinds of decision-analysis techniques could you apply to help the individual make a decision?)

8.25. **Ellsberg Paradox** A barrel contains a mixture of 90 red, blue, and yellow balls. Thirty of the balls are red, and the remaining 60 are a mixture of blue or yellow, but the proportion of blue and yellow is unknown. A single ball will be taken randomly from the barrel.

a. Suppose you are offered the choice between gambles A and B:
   A: Win $1,000 if a red ball is chosen.
   B: Win $1,000 if a blue ball is chosen.
   Would you prefer A or B? Why?

b. Now suppose that you are offered a choice between gambles C and D:
   C: Win $1,000 if either a red or a yellow ball is chosen.
   D: Win $1,000 if either a blue or a yellow ball is chosen.
   Would you prefer C or D? Why?

c. Many people prefer A in the first choice and D in the second. Do you think this is inconsistent? Explain.

CASE STUDIES

ASSESSING CANCER RISK—FROM MOUSE TO MAN

Cancer is a frightening disease. The biological process that creates cancerous cells from healthy tissue is poorly understood at best. Much research has been conducted into how external conditions relate to cancer. For example, we know that smoking leads to substantially higher incidence of lung cancer in humans. Cancer appears spontaneously, however, and its onset seems to be inherently probabilistic, as shown by the fact that some people smoke all their lives without developing lung cancer.

Some commentators claim that the use of new and untested chemicals is leading to a cancer epidemic. As evidence they point to the increase in cancer deaths over the years. Indeed, cancer deaths have increased, but people generally have longer life spans, and more elderly people now are at risk for the disease. When cancer rates are adjusted for the increased life span, cancer rates have not increased substantially. In fact, when data are examined this way, some cancer rates (liver, stomach, and uterine cancer) are less common now than they were 50 years ago (1986 data of the American Cancer Society). Nevertheless, the public fears cancer greatly. The Delaney Amendment to the Food, Drug, and Cosmetics Act of 1954 outlaws residues in processed foods of chemicals that pose any risk of cancer to animals or humans. One of the results of this fear has been an emphasis in public policy on assessing cancer risks from a variety of chemicals.

Scientifically speaking, the best way to determine cancer risk to humans would be to expose one group of people to the chemical while keeping others away from it. But such experiments would not be ethical. Thus, scientists generally rely on experiments performed on animals, usually mice or rats. The laboratory animals in the experimental group are exposed to high doses of the substance being tested. High doses are required because low doses probably would not have a statistically noticeable effect on the relatively small experimental group. After the animals die, cancers are identified by autopsy. This kind of experiment is called a *bioassay*. Typical cancer bioassays involve 600 animals, require 2 to 3 years to complete, and cost several hundred thousand dollars.

When bioassays are used to make cancer risk assessments, two important extrapolations are made. First, there is the extrapolation from high doses to low doses. Second, it is necessary to extrapolate from effects on test species to effects on humans. On the basis of data from laboratory experiments and these extrapolations, assessments are made regarding the incidence of cancer when humans are exposed to the substance.

Questions

1. Clearly, the extrapolations that are made are based on subjective judgments. Because cancer is viewed as being an inherently probabilistic phenomenon, it is reasonable to view these judgments as probability assessments. What kinds of assessments do you think are necessary to make these extrapolations? What issues must be taken into account? What kind of scientific evidence would help in making the necessary assessments?

2. It can be argued that most cancer risk assessments are weak evidence of potential danger or lack thereof. To be specific, a chemical manufacturer and a regulator might argue different sides of the same study. The manufacturer might claim that the study does not conclusively show that the substance is dangerous, while the regulator might claim that the study does not conclusively demonstrate safety. Situations like these often arise, and decisions must be made with imperfect information. What kind of strategy would you adopt for making these decisions? What trade-offs does your strategy involve?

3. In the case of risk assessment, as with many fields of scientific inquiry, some experiments are better than others for many reasons. For example, some experiments may be more carefully designed or use larger samples. In short, some sources of information are more "credible."

   For a simple, hypothetical example, suppose that you ask three "experts" whether a given coin is fair. All three report that the coin is fair; for each one the best estimate of P(Heads) is 0.50. You learn, however, that the first expert flipped the coin 10,000 times and observed heads on 5,000 occasions. The second flipped the coin 20 times and observed 10 heads. The third expert did not flip the coin at all, but gave it a thorough physical examination, finding it to be perfectly balanced, as nearly as he could measure.

   How should differences in credibility of information be accounted for in assessing probabilities? Would you give the same weight to information from the three examiners of the coin? In the case of putting together information on cancer risk from multiple experiments and expert sources, how might you deal with the information sources' differential credibility?

Source: D. A. Freedman and H. Zeisel (1988) "From Mouse-to-Man: The Quantitative Assessment of Cancer Risks." *Statistical Science*, 3, 3–56. Includes discussion.

BREAST IMPLANTS

The controversy surrounding breast implants is a good example of scientific uncertainty. Yanked from the market by the Food and Drug Administration in 1991 because of some evidence of dangerous side effects, breast implants received a reprieve in 1994 when the *New England Journal of Medicine* published an article that found no evidence of danger. An editorial in the *San Jose Mercury News* opined regarding the controversy:

> The wisdom of letting science settle this question [regarding breast implants] will win the ready assent of everyone. "Scientific certainty" has such a reassuring ring to it.
>
> But the implant case is a sterling example of the limits of science. Regarding long-term harm, science often can't provide definitive answers within the time a decision needs to be made.
>
> And many policy decisions are out of the realm of science. What level of risk is reasonable for a woman who's lost a breast to cancer? What about reasonable risk for a woman who wants a fuller figure? Who decides what's reasonable? Is cosmetic breast enhancement a misuse of medicine to reinforce outdated notions of female beauty?

Questions

1. What kinds of information should a jury consider when deciding whether a plaintiff's claims of damages are reasonable? Anecdotes? The number of plaintiffs filing similar lawsuits? Scientific studies? What does a juror need to know in order to evaluate the quality of a scientific study? Do you think the average juror (or judge for that matter!) in the United States has the ability to critically evaluate the quality of scientific studies?

2. Discuss the questions asked in the last paragraph of the preceding quote. Do these questions relate to uncertainty (scientific or otherwise) or to values? Given the imperfect information available about breast implants, what role should the

manufacturers play in deciding what risks are appropriate for which women? What role should government agencies play? What role should individual consumers play?

Source: "Uncertain Science," *San Jose Mercury News,* June 17, 1994, p.10B.

THE SPACE SHUTTLE *CHALLENGER*

On January 28, 1986, the space shuttle *Challenger* lifted off from an ice-covered launch pad. Only 72 seconds into the flight, the shuttle exploded, killing all seven astronauts aboard. The United States and the rest of the world saw the accident firsthand as films from NASA were shown repeatedly by the television networks.

Before long the cause of the accident became known. The shuttle's main engines were fueled by liquid hydrogen and oxygen stored in a large tank carried on the shuttle's belly. Two auxiliary rockets that used solid fuel were mounted alongside the main fuel tank and provided additional thrust to accelerate the shuttle away from the launch pad. These boosters used their fuel rapidly and were jettisoned soon after launch.

The solid rocket boosters were manufactured in sections by Morton Thiokol, Inc. (MTI), in Utah. The sections were shipped individually to Kennedy Space Center (KSC) in Florida where they were assembled. The joints between sections of the rocket were sealed by a pair of large rubber O-rings, whose purpose was to contain the hot gases and pressure inside the rocket. In the case of the *Challenger,* one of the joint seals failed. Hot gases blew past the O-rings and eventually burned through the large belly tank, igniting the highly explosive fuel inside. The resulting explosion destroyed the spacecraft.

Before long it also became known that the launch itself was not without controversy. MTI engineers had been aware of the problems with the O-rings for some time, having observed eroded O-rings in the boosters used on previous flights. A special task force was formed in 1985 to try to solve the problem, but ran into organizational problems. One memo regarding the task force began, "Help! The seal task force is constantly being delayed by every possible means." The problem came to a head when, on the evening before the launch, MTI engineers recommended not launching the shuttle because of the anticipated cold temperatures on the launch pad. After a teleconference involving officials at KSC and the Marshal Space Flight Center (MSFC) in Alabama, management officials at MTI reversed their engineers' recommendation and approved the launch.

Questions

1. To a great extent, the engineers were concerned about the performance of the O-ring under anticipated cold weather conditions. The coldest previous flight had been 53°F, and, knowing of the existing problems with the seals, the engineers hesitated to recommend a launch under colder conditions. Technically, the problem was that an O-ring stiffens as it gets colder, thus requiring a longer time to seal a joint. The real problem, however, was that the engineers did not know much about the performance of the O-rings at cold temperatures. Robert K. Lund, vice president of engineering for MTI, testified to the presidential commission investigating the accident, "We just don't know how much further we can go below the 51 or 53 degrees or whatever it was. So we were concerned with the unknown.... They [officials at MSFC] said they didn't accept that rationale" (*Report of the Presidential Commission on the Space Shuttle* Challenger *Accident,* p. 94).

   The MTI staff felt as if it were in the position of having to prove that the shuttle was unsafe to fly instead of the other way around. Roger Boisjoly, an MTI engineer, testified, "This was a meeting where the determination was to launch, and it was up to us to prove beyond a shadow of a doubt that it was not safe to do so. This is in total reverse to what the position usually is in a preflight conversation or a flight readiness review. It is usually exactly opposite that" (*Report,* p. 93).

   NASA solicited information regarding ice on the launch pad from Rockwell International, the shuttle's manufacturer. Rockwell officials told NASA that the ice was an unknown condition. Robert Glaysher, a vice president at Rockwell, testified that he had specifically said to NASA, "Rockwell could not 100% assure that it is safe to fly" (*Report,* p. 115). In this case, the presidential commission also found that "NASA appeared to be requiring a contractor to prove that it was not safe to launch, rather than proving it was safe" (*Report,* p. 118).

   The issue is how to deal with unknown information. What do you think the policy should be regarding situations in which little or no information is available? Discuss the problems faced by both MTI and NASA. What incentives and pressures might they have faced?

2. Professor Richard Feynman, Nobel Laureate in physics, was a member of the commission. He issued his own statement, published as an appendix to the report, taking NASA to task for a variety of blunders. Some of his complaints revolved around assessments of the probability of failure.

Failure of the solid rocket boosters. A study of 2,900 flights of solid-fuel rockets revealed 121 failures, or approximately 1 in 25. Because of improved technology and special care in the selection of parts and in inspection, Feynman is willing to credit a failure rate of better than 1 in 100 but not as good as 1 in 1,000. But in a risk analysis prepared for the Department of Energy (DOE) that related to DOE radioactive material aboard the shuttle, NASA officials used a figure of 1 in 100,000. Feynman writes:

> If the real probability is not so small [as 1 in 100,000], flights would show troubles, near failures, and possibly actual failures with a reasonable number of trials, and standard statistical methods could give a reasonable estimate. In fact, previous NASA experience had shown, on occasion, just such difficulties, near accidents, and accidents, all giving warning that the probability of flight failure was not so very small. (*Report*, p. F–1)

Failure of the liquid fuel engine. In another section of his report, Feynman discussed disparate assessments of the probability of failure of the liquid fuel engine. His own calculations suggested a failure rate of approximately 1 in 500. Engineers at Rocketdyne, the engine manufacturer, estimated the probability to be approximately 1 in 10,000. NASA officials estimated 1 in 100,000. An independent consultant for NASA suggested that a failure rate of 1 or 2 per 100 would be a reasonable estimate.

How is it that these probability estimates could vary so widely? How should a decision maker deal with probability estimates that are so different?

3. To arrive at their overall reliability estimates, NASA officials may have decomposed the assessment, estimated the reliability of many different individual components, and then aggregated their assessments. Suppose that, because of an optimistic viewpoint, each probability assessment had been slightly overoptimistic (that is, a low assessed probability of failure). What effect might this have on the overall reliability estimate?

4. In an editorial in *Space World* magazine, editor Tony Reichhardt commented on the accident:

> One person's safety is another's paranoia. How safe is safe? What is acceptable risk? It's no small question, in life or in the space program. It's entirely understandable that astronauts would come down hard on NASA policies that appear to be reckless with their lives. But unless I'm misreading the testimony [before the commission], at the end of the teleconference that night of January 27, most of the participating engineers believed that it was safe to go ahead and launch. A few argued that it was not safe *enough*. There was an element of risk in the decision, and in many others made prior to *Challenger's* launch, and seven people were killed.
>
> Whether this risk can be eliminated is a question of monumental importance to the space program. Those who have put the blame squarely on NASA launch managers need to think hard about the answer. If no Shuttle takes off until everyone at every level of responsibility is in complete agreement, then it may never be launched again. No single person can be absolutely sure that the whole system will work. On this vehicle, or on some other spacecraft next year or 30 years from now—even if we ease the financial and scheduling pressures—something will go wrong again. [*Source*: T. Reichhardt (1986) "Acceptable Risk," *Space World*, April, p. 3. Reprinted by permission.]

Comment on Reichhardt's statement. What is an acceptable risk? Does it matter whether we are talking about risks to the general public from cancer or risks to astronauts in the space program? Would your answer change if you were an astronaut? A NASA official? A manufacturer of potentially carcinogenic chemicals? A cancer researcher? How should a policy maker take into account the variety of opinions regarding what constitutes an acceptable risk?

Source: Information for this case was taken from many sources, but by far the most important was the report by the Rogers Commission (1986) *Report of the Presidential Commission on the Space Shuttle Challenger Accident.* Washington, DC: U.S. Government Printing Office.

REFERENCES

The subjective interpretation of probability is one of the distinguishing characteristics of decision theory and decision analysis. This interpretation was presented first by Savage (1954) and has been debated by probabilists and statisticians ever since. Winkler (2003) provides an excellent introduction to subjective probability and Bayesian statistics (so called because of the reliance on Bayes' theorem for inference), as well as extensive references to the literature.

Although we argued that verbal expressions of uncertainty are by nature less precise than numerical probabilities, Wallsten, Budescu, and Zwick (1993) show how to *calibrate* a set of verbal probability labels so that the meaning of each label is precisely understood.

Spetzler and Staël von Holstein (1975) is the standard reference on probability assessment. Winkler (2003) also covers this topic. Wallsten and Budescu (1983) review the field from a psychological perspective.

The construction of an appropriate discrete distribution is an interesting problem that has occupied a number of decision-analysis researchers. Many different approaches exist; the extended Pearson-Tukey and Swanson-Megill approximations are two of the more straightforward methods that perform well. More complicated (and more precise) approaches create discrete distributions with mathematical characteristics that match those of the continuous distribution (e.g., Miller and Rice 1983, Smith 1993); such approaches are difficult to use "by hand" but are easily implemented in computer software. Studies that report on the relative performance of different discrete-approximation methods include Keefer and Bodily (1983), Keefer (1994), and Smith (1993).

The literature on heuristics and biases is extensive. One reference that covers the topic at an introductory level is Tversky and Kahneman (1974). Hogarth (1987) provides a unique overview of this material in the context of decision analysis. Kahneman, Slovic, and Tversky (1982) and Gilovich, Griffin, and Tversky (2002) have collected key research papers in the area. Arnott (1998) provides the basis for how we have classified the various biases. With respect to the issue of overconfidence in particular, Capen (1976) reports an experiment that demonstrates the extent of overconfidence in subjective probability assessments and possible ways to cope with this phenomenon. The partition dependence bias is a relative newcomer to the heuristics and biases literature; Fox and Clemen (2005) describe

the bias, show how it affects probability judgment, and suggests methods decision analysts can use to reduce the bias.

Probability decomposition is a topic that has not been heavily researched, although there are many applications. For example, see Bunn (1984) and von Winterfeldt and Edwards (1986) for discussions and examples of fault trees. A paper by Ravinder, Kleinmuntz, and Dyer (1988) discusses when decomposition is worth doing. Fault-tree analysis is widely used in reliability engineering and risk analysis. It is described in Gottfried (1974), Bunn (1984), and Merkhofer (1987b). Covello and Merkhofer (1993) provide additional references regarding fault trees.

Abramson, B., and A. J. Finizza (1995) "Probabilistic Forecasts from Probabilistic Models Case Study: The Oil Market." *International Journal of Forecasting*, 11, 63–72.

Arnott, D. (2006) "Cognitive Biases and Decision Support Systems Development: A Design Science Approach." *Information Systems Journal*, 16, 55–78.

Beyth-Marom, R. (1982) "How Probable Is Probable? A Numerical Translation of Verbal Probability Expressions." *Journal of Forecasting*, 1, 257–269.

Bunn, D. (1984) *Applied Decision Analysis*. New York: McGraw-Hill.

Capen, E. C. (1976) "The Difficulty of Assessing Uncertainty." *Journal of Petroleum Technology*, August, 843–850. Reprinted in R. Howard and J. Matheson (eds.) (1983) *The Principles and Applications of Decision Analysis*. Menlo Park, CA: Strategic Decisions Group.

Covello, V. T., and M. W. Merkhofer (1993) *Risk Assessment Methods: Approaches for Assessing Health and Environmental Risks*. New York: Plenum.

Ellsberg, D. (1961) "Risk, Ambiguity, and the Savage Axioms." *Quarterly Journal of Economics*, 75, 643–669.

Fox, C., and R. T. Clemen (2005). "Subjective Probability Assessment in Decision Analysis: Partition Dependence and Bias Toward the Ignorance Prior." *Management Science*, 51, 1417–1432.

Gilovich, T., D. Griffin, and A. Tversky (2002) *Heuristics and Biases: The Psychology of Intuitive Judgment*. Cambridge: Cambridge University Press.

Gottfried, P. (1974) "Qualitative Risk Analysis: FTA and FMEA." *Professional Safety*, October, 48–52.

Hogarth, R. M. (1987) *Judgment and Choice*, 2nd ed. New York: Wiley.

Kahneman, D., P. Slovic, and A. Tversky (eds.) (1982) *Judgment under Uncertainty: Heuristics and Biases.* Cambridge: Cambridge University Press.

Kahneman, D., and A. Tversky (1973) "On the Psychology of Prediction." *Psychological Review*, 80, 237–251.

Keefer, D. L. (1994) "Certainty Equivalents for Three-Point Discrete-Distribution Approximations." *Management Science*, 40, 760–773.

Keefer, D., and S. E. Bodily (1983) "Three-Point Approximations for Continuous Random Variables." *Management Science*, 29, 595–609.

Merkhofer, M. W. (1987a) "Quantifying Judgmental Uncertainty: Methodology, Experiences, and Insights." *IEEE Transactions on Systems, Man, and Cybernetics*, 17, 741–752.

Merkhofer, M. W. (1987b) *Decision Science and Social Risk Management.* Dordrect, Holland: Reidel.

Miller, A. C., and T. R. Rice (1983) "Discrete Approximations of Probability Distributions." *Management Science*, 29, 352–362.

Morgan, M. G., and M. Henrion (1990) *Uncertainty: A Guide to Dealing with Uncertainty in Quantitative Risk and Policy Analysis.* Cambridge: Cambridge University Press.

Olsen, R. A. (1997) "Desirability bias among professional investment managers: Some evidence from experts." *Journal of Behavioral Decision Making*, 10, 65–72.

Ravinder, H. V., D. Kleinmuntz, and J. S. Dyer (1988) "The Reliability of Subjective Probabilities Obtained Through Decomposition." *Management Science*, 34, 186–199.

Remus, W. E., and J. Kotteman (1986) "Toward Intelligent Decision Support Systems: An Artificially Intelligent Statistician." *MIS Quarterly*, 10, 413–418.

Savage, L. J. (1954) *The Foundations of Statistics.* New York: Wiley.

Smith, J. E. (1993) "Moment Methods for Decision Analysis." *Management Science*, 39, 340–358.

Spetzler, C. S., and C. A. Stael von Holstein (1975) "Probability Encoding in Decision Analysis." *Management Science*, 22, 340–352.

Tversky, A., and D. Kahneman (1974) "Judgments under Uncertainty: Heuristics and Biases." *Science*, 185, 1124–1131.

von Winterfeldt, D., and W. Edwards (1986) *Decision Analysis and Behavioral Research.* Cambridge: Cambridge University Press.

Wallsten, T. S., and D. V. Budescu (1983) "Encoding Subjective Probabilities: A Psychological and Psychometric Review." *Management Science*, 29, 151–173.

Wallsten, T. S., D. V. Budescu, and R. Zwick (1993) "Comparing the Calibration and Coherence of Numerical and Verbal Probability Judgments." *Management Science*, 39, 176–190.

Winkler, R. L. (2003) *Introduction to Bayesian Inference and Decision*, 2nd Ed. Gainesville, FL: Probabilistic Publishing.

EPILOGUE

The Yucca Mountain repository was originally scheduled to begin accepting shipments of nuclear waste in 1998. After decades of research and construction, billions of dollars spent beyond what was projected, and extended delays due to legal challenges and political wrangling, President Obama cut all funding to the project in 2010. Court battles over the facility continue, however, because utilities made payments toward construction on the promise that they would be able to dispose of their waste at Yucca Mountain.

Without the repository, the utilities are stuck with the cost of storing the waste on site.

At this writing, the U.S. remains without a long-term nuclear waste storage strategy. However, the U.S. Department of Energy has developed a new timeline and expects to have an underground storage facility open in 2048!

Source: Many online sources provide information and links to documents on the history and current status of Yucca Mountain. The information here was gleaned from www.yuccamountin.org.

CHAPTER 9

Theoretical Probability Models

In the previous chapter, we focused on developing a rigorous assessment process that we could use to elicit probabilities for any general probability distribution. We now focus on specific types of quantitative uncertainties—those that occur often in decision models, often enough that they have been named and fully developed into models of uncertainty. The quintessential example is the normal probability model which is used to describe particular phenomena such as test scores or measurement errors. Another example is the exponential distribution which is often used to model the arrival times of customers. We call these ready-made distributions theoretical probability models. Being able to use them saves us from having to build distributions from scratch. Once we find a theoretical distribution that matches the specific properties of the uncertainty we are modeling, we estimate the distribution's parameters, and incorporate it into the decision model. This chapter introduces six theoretical probability models that together cover a wide variety of common types of uncertainty.

Theoretical probability models can also be used in conjunction with subjective assessments. Given the probability assessments, we can determine which theoretical model most closely matches the assessed values. A decision maker might do this simply to make the probability and expected-value calculations easier or to use more common and recognizable distributions.

As you read through the chapter notice that we need to make a number of subjective judgments as to the nature of the uncertainty, and ultimately as to which theoretical probability model to use. Although it may appear that theoretical models are more objective, subjective judgments still play an important role.

How important are theoretical probability distributions for decision making? To answer this question, consider the following applications of theoretical models.

Theoretical Models Applied	**Educational Testing** Most major educational and intelligence tests generate distributions of scores that can be well represented by the normal distribution, or the familiar bell-shaped curve. Many colleges and universities admit only individuals whose scores are above a stated criterion that corresponds to a specific percentile of the normal distribution of scores.
	Market Research In many market research studies, a fundamental issue is whether a potential customer prefers one product to another. The uncertainty involved in these problems often can be modeled using the binomial or closely related distributions.
	Quality Control How many defects are acceptable in a finished product? In some products, the occurrence of defects, such as bubbles in glass or blemishes in cloth, can be modeled quite nicely with a Poisson process. Once the uncertainty is modeled, alternative quality-control strategies can be analyzed for their relative costs and benefits.
	Predicting Election Outcomes How do the major television networks manage to extrapolate the results of exit polls to predict the outcome of elections? Again, the binomial distribution forms the basis for making probability statements about who wins an election based on a sample of results.
	Capacity Planning Do you sometimes feel that you spend too much time standing in lines waiting for service? Service providers are on the other side; their problem is how to provide adequate service when the arrival of customers is uncertain. In many cases, the number of customers arriving within a period of time can be modeled using the Poisson distribution. Moreover, this distribution can be extended to the placement of orders at a manufacturing facility, the breakdown of equipment, and other similar processes.
	Environmental Risk Analysis In modeling the level of pollutants in the environment, scientists often use the lognormal distribution, a variant of the normal distribution. With uncertainty about pollutant levels modeled in this way, it is possible to analyze pollution-control policies to understand the relative effects of different policies.

There are many theoretical probability distributions and they cover a wide variety of quantitative uncertainties. We will be scratching only the surface here, introducing a few of the more common distributions. For discrete probability situations, we will discuss the binomial and Poisson distributions, both of which are commonly encountered and easily used. Continuous distributions that will be discussed are the triangular, exponential, normal, and beta distributions. We also have access to over 30 theoretical distributions via @RISK.® References at the end of this chapter will direct you to sources on other distributions.

For each distribution that we discuss in this chapter, we describe the properties of that particular theoretical distribution. Knowing the properties of the theoretical distribution is important in order to correctly match the distribution with the uncertainty. When deciding on whether a theoretical distribution should be used, we compare the properties of our uncertainty to that of the theoretical distribution. If they match reasonably well, we can use that theoretical model with some assurance that the model does a good job of representing the uncertainty. Essentially, we want to choose the right tool for the job.

We have altered the structure of this chapter a bit by placing the software (@RISK) instructions not at the chapter's end, but after the description of each theoretical probability model. The format for each section in this chapter is: (1) introduce a theoretical model, (2) show how to use @RISK to compute probability values for that model, and (3) describe an example. The software will greatly simplify our calculations and is needed for the examples.

THE BINOMIAL DISTRIBUTION

The *binomial* distribution is based on the simplest of all uncertainties: those that have only two outcomes, one having probability p and the other having probability $1 - p$. Suppose, for example, that you were in a race for mayor of your hometown, and you wanted to find out how you were doing with the voters. You might take a sample, count the number of individuals who indicated a preference for you, and then, based on this information, judge your chances of winning the election. In this situation, the binomial makes sense; each voter is either for you or not.

Do not let the simplicity of the binomial fool you. Because many situations can be broken down into two outcomes (success vs. failure; hit vs. miss; on vs. off), the binomial is of fundamental importance and widely applicable. The binomial is used in quality control where an item may or may not be defective, in market research, and in many other situations. The binomial option-pricing model is widely used in finance, as it is more flexible and can handle a wider variety of conditions than other option-pricing models.

The binomial distribution arises from a situation that has the following characteristics:

1. *Dichotomous outcomes*. Uncertain events occur in a sequence, each one having one of two possible outcomes—success/failure, heads/tails, yes/no, true/false, on/off, and so on.
2. *Constant probability*. Each event, or *trial* has the same probability of success. Call that probability p.

3. *Independence.* The outcome of each trial is independent of the outcomes of the other trials. That is, the probability of success does not depend on the preceding outcomes[1].

When deciding whether to use the binomial, check to make sure that the uncertainty being modeled has the three characteristics previously listed. The typical setting for the binomial is modeling the number of successes (yeses, trues, 1s, etc.) in *n* trials. For example, if your friend Ray makes, on average, 80% of his free-throw basketball shots, we might use the binomial to model the number of free-throw shots made by Ray out of *n* shots. To use the binomial, we would have to conclude that the probability of making a shot remains constant from shot to shot (Condition 2) and that making or missing a shot does not impact the outcome of the next shot (Condition 3). If any one of these conditions is not met, the binomial may produce misleading probability estimates.

Let *R* denote the uncertain quantity or random variable of the number of free-throw shots made by Ray in the sequence of *n* trials. *R* could equal zero, meaning he misses all his shots; or *R* could equal one, meaning he makes one and only one shot; and so on up to *R* equal to *n*, where every shot goes into the hoop. Assuming Ray has a $p = 80\%$ success rate, Figure 9.1 shows the graph of the binomial probability distribution of *R* for $n = 10$ trials. Not surprisingly, the most likely (highest probability) event is that exactly 8 shots are made. The bar above the graph in Figure 9.1 shows that there is only a 3.3% chance that five or fewer shots are made in 10 tries; there is an 86% chance that between 6 and 9 shots will go in out of ten tries; and there is a 10.7% chance that Ray will make all ten shots. (Remember, for discrete probability distributions, the height of the bar at *r* is the probability that $R = r$.)

FIGURE **9.1**
The binomial distribution with $n = 10$ trials and the probability of success is $p = 80\%$.

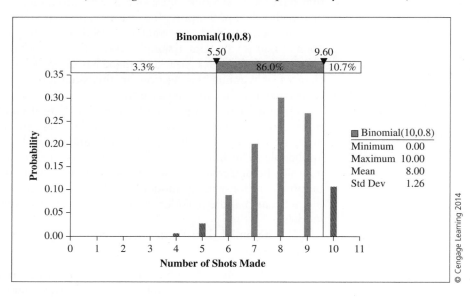

---

[1] The *gambler's fallacy* is that there is some dependence from outcome to outcome. A roulette wheel that has come up red 5 or 50 consecutive times is not "due" to come up black. Given independence from one spin to the next, the probability of black still is 0.5, regardless of the previous outcomes.

In probability notation, we write $P_B(R|10, 0.8)$ to denote the binomial probability distribution with $n = 10$ and $p = 0.8$. Both n and p are called parameters, and by specifying values for n and p, we determine the shape of the distribution and the probability values for R. The probabilities we gave previously can be written as:

$$P_B(R < 6|10, 0.8) = 3.3\%,$$

$$P_B(6 \leq R \leq 9|10, 0.8) = 86\%, \text{ and}$$

$$P_B(R = 10|10, 0.8) = 10.7\%.$$

The probabilities for the binomial are calculated in a straightforward way. To demonstrate, let's compute the probability that Ray will make all four shots in four tries, i.e., $P_B(R = 4|4, 0.8)$. Four baskets in four shots can happen in only one way: S_1, S_2, S_3, S_4 where S_k means the kth shot was a success and F_k means the kth shot was a failure. Thus, using the rules of probability, we have:

$$P_B(R = 4|4, 0.8) = P(S_1, S_2, S_3, S_4)$$
$$= P(S_1)\,P(S_2|S_1)\,P(S_3|S_2, S_1)\,P(S_4|S_3, S_2, S_1) \text{ Conditional Probabilities}$$
$$= P(S_1)\,P(S_2)\,P(S_3)\,P(S_4) \text{ Independence (Condition 3)}$$
$$= p^4 \quad \text{Constant probability (Condition 2)}$$
$$= (0.80)^4 \quad P = 0.80 \text{ for Ray}$$
$$= 0.41$$

What is the probability of Ray making three shots in four tries? In this case, Ray can make three shots in any one of four ways:

Sequences	Probability
S_1, S_2, S_3, F_4	$ppp(1-p) = p^3(1-p)$
S_1, S_2, F_3, S_4	$pp(1-p)p = p^3(1-p)$
S_1, F_2, S_3, S_4	$p(1-p)pp = p^3(1-p)$
F_1, S_2, S_3, S_4	$(1-p)ppp = p^3(1-p)$

We see that the probability of each sequence is $p^3(1-p)$, and because these four sequences are mutually exclusive, the probability of three made shots is simply the sum of the individual probabilities, or

$$P_B(R = 3|4, 0.8) = 4p^3(1-p) = 4(0.80^3)(0.20) = 0.41.$$

In general, the probability of obtaining r successes in n trials is given by

$$P_B(R = r|n, p) = \frac{n!}{r!(n-r)!}p^r(1-p)^{n-r} \quad \text{for } r = 0, 1, 2, \ldots, \text{n}, \qquad (9.1)$$

The term with the factorials is called the *combinatorial term*. It counts the number of ways that a sequence of n trials can have r successes. The second term is just the probability associated with a particular sequence with r successes in n trials.

The expected number of successes is simply $E(R) = np$. (If I have n trials, I expect proportion p of them to be successes.) The variance of the number of successes is $\text{Var}(R) = np(1 - p)$.

Binomial probabilities are not difficult to calculate using Formula 9.1, but the graphical feature of @RISK, allows us to calculate the probabilities by simply sliding the cursor across the screen.

STEP 1 *Binomial Calculations.*

1.1 With @RISK opened, **right click** in any spreadsheet cell to pull up the submenu. Choose **@RISK**, then **Define Distribution.**

1.2 Choose the **Binomial** (the second distribution) and click on the **Select Distribution** button.

1.3 In this chapter we will discuss only the minimum, maximum, mean, and standard deviation, but you can see that PrecisionTree® gives you many more statistics. To make your figures match ours, click on the **Graph Options** button (bottom left, second from left), choose the **Legend** tab, and replace *Statistics Grid* with **Legend with Statistics Table.**

1.4 Figure 9.2 shows that the default binomial has $n = 10$ and $p = 0.5$ Either type in your specific parameter values for n and p or click on the **Assign Excel® References** button.

1.5 To calculate the probability of any interval, drag the two **delimiter bars** to the desired x-axis values. Hold the **mouse button down** to move the bars.

FIGURE **9.2**

The @RISK Define Distribution window showing the binomial distribution with $n = 10$ and $p = 0.5$.

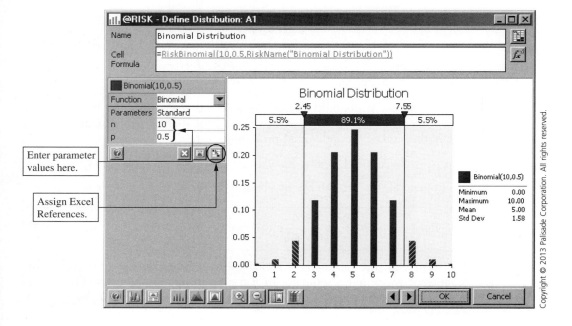

For example, to calculate $P_B(R = 3|4, 0.8)$:
> Enter $n = 4$ and $p = 0.8$, and slide the left and right delimiter bars to cover only $R = 3$, as shown in Figure 9.3. Thus $P_B(R = 3|4, 0.8) = 41\%$.

For example, to calculate $P_B(2 \leq R \leq 3|12, 0.2)$:
> Enter $n = 12$ and $p = 0.2$, and slide the left and right delimiter bars to cover only $R = 2$ and $R = 3$, as shown in Figure 9.4. Thus $P_B(2 \leq R \leq 3|12, 0.2) = 52\%$.

Note that the @RISK window actually reports three different probability values. For example, from Figure 9.4 we have $P_B(R < 2|12, 0.2) = 27.5\%$ and $P_B(R > 3|12, 0.2) = 20.5\%$ in addition to $P_B(2 \leq R \leq 3|12, 0.2) = 52\%$. It is important to make sure that the delimiter bars are correctly placed when calculating the probabilities, especially for discrete distributions. With discrete distributions, the probability remains constant until the delimiter passes over one of the outcome values, at which point, the probability values change. Thus, we have some flexibility in where to place the delimiters, but make sure that their placement corresponds to the desired interval.

An Example: Melissa Bailey

It is the beginning of winter term at the College of Business at Eastern State. Melissa Bailey says she is eager to study, but she has plans for a ski trip each weekend for 12 weeks. She will go only if there is good weather. The probability of good weather on any weekend during the winter is approximately 0.65. What is the probability that she will be gone for eight or more weekends?

FIGURE **9.3**
The binomial distribution with $n = 4$ and $p = 0.8$, showing that $P_B(R = 3|4, 0.8) = 41.0\%$.

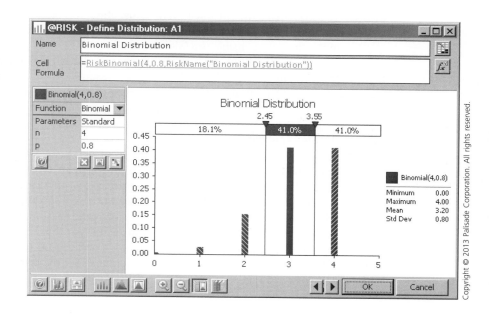

FIGURE **9.4**
The binomial distri-
bution with $n = 12$
and $p = 0.2$,
showing that
$P_B(2 \leq R \leq 3|12, 0.2)$
$= 52.0\%$.

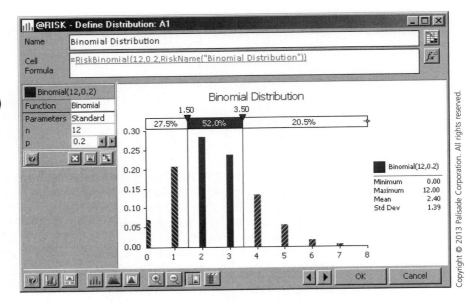

Are all of the requirements satisfied for the binomial distribution? Weekend weather is good or bad, satisfying the dichotomous outcomes property. We will assume that the probabilities are the same from one weekend to the next, and moreover it seems reasonable to assume that the weather on one weekend during the winter is independent of the weather on previous weekends. Given these assumptions, the binomial distribution is an appropriate model for the uncertainty in this problem. Keep in mind that we are building a model of the uncertainty. Although our assumptions may not be exactly true, the binomial distribution should provide a good approximation.

To solve the problem, we must find $P_B(R \geq 8|n = 12, p = 0.65)$. Of course, it is always possible to calculate this probability directly using the formula; however, using @RISK, we enter $n = 12$ and $p = 0.65$, and slide the right delimiter all the way to the right and the left delimiter to 7.5. Figure 9.5 shows that $P_B(R < 8|12, 0.65) = 41.7\%$ and $P_B(R \geq 8|12, 0.65) = 58.3\%$. Thus, there is more than a 50% chance that Melissa will be home on four or fewer weekends and gone on eight or more weekends.

Another Example: eKnow

Having just completed your first year of a 2-year MBA program, you have opted to forgo a summer internship and instead work on your new product idea. You are eager to apply the entrepreneurial skills you learned over the past year to what you hope is an ingenious new product idea. Your product, which you are calling eKnow, is an electronic dictionary the size of a typical bookmark (1.5 × 6 inches) and is ultra thin so that it can be carried between the pages of a book. The eKnow has a small digital screen for displaying the definitions of words which can be entered using the mini keyboard with a stylus, such as a pen or pencil, or can be entered by voice command. Thus, if you come across a word you do not know, you need only say the word out loud

FIGURE **9.5**
The number of ski
weekends for
Melisa modeled as
binomial showing
that $P_B(R \geq 8|12, 0.2)$
= 58.3%.

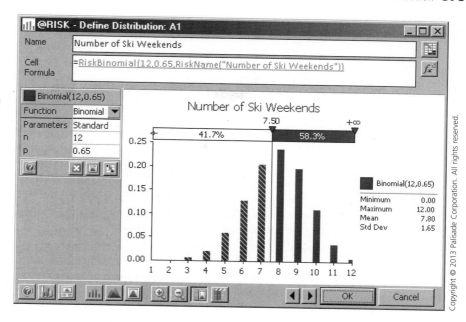

into eKnow and its definition appears on the screen. You are excited about eKnow because you feel there is a large market for such a product, and because you can envision a number of product extensions, such as flash cards, a thesaurus option, and if the technology becomes available, a wireless capability.

Your school has a business incubator program specifically designed to help students and companies work on various issues around product development. From the initial design to product launch, the incubator program provides the physical space to work on the product, access to local experts, such as engineers and marketers, and even access to venture capital funding. With the support of the incubator program you have designed and built a dozen working prototypes of eKnow and are currently trying to secure funding. After careful research and discussion with some experts, you conclude that the eKnow might be a hit, in which case it will capture 30% of the U.S. market by the fifth year. On the other hand, it may be a flop, in which case the market share will be only 10% after five years. You judge these outcomes to be equally likely: P(Hit) = P(Flop) = 0.5.

To gather some data, you decide to test market the eKnow with 20 readers from your target market to gauge their reaction to eKnow. At first blush, the test results appear discouraging; only 5 out of the 20 people responded that they would purchase eKnow. Then, you remembered that eKnow would be a hit if it captured 30% of the market and 5 out of 20 is 25%, close to the 30%. So, what is the probability[2] eKnow will be a hit based on the test market results?

The question we are asking is this: What is P(eKnow is a Hit | 5 of 20 would purchase eKnow)? How can we get a handle on this probability? A problem like this that involves finding a probability given some new

_____

[2] Because it takes time for a product to gain recognition, we are taking the test market results as an estimate of the market share in 5 years.

evidence almost certainly requires an application of Bayes' theorem. Let us use some notation to make our life simpler. Let "Hit" and "Flop" denote the outcomes that eKnow is a hit or a flop, respectively. Let R be the number of people (out of 20) who would purchase eKnow. Now we can write Bayes' theorem using this notation:

$$P(\text{eKnow is a Hit} \mid 5 \text{ of } 20 \text{ would purchase eknow})$$

$$= P(\text{Hit} \mid R = 5)$$

$$= \frac{P(R = 5 \mid \text{Hit})P(\text{Hit})}{P(R = 5 \mid \text{Hit})P(\text{Hit}) + P(R = 5 \mid \text{Flop})P(\text{Flop})}$$

Next we must fill in the appropriate probabilities on the right side of the Bayes' theorem equation. The probabilities P(Hit) and P(Flop) are easy. Using the judgment that the two outcomes are considered to be equally likely, we insert 0.5 for P(Hit) and P(Flop).

What about $P(R = 5 \mid \text{Hit})$ and $P(R = 5 \mid \text{Flop})$? These are a bit trickier. Consider $P(R = 5 \mid \text{Hit})$. This is the binomial probability that 5 out of 20 people would purchase eKnow, given that 30% ($p = 0.30$) of the target market would purchase eKnow. That is, if eKnow is a hit, you will capture 30% of the market. How does this idea of 30% across the entire target market relate to the chance of 5 out of a sample of 20 would purchase eKnow? Provided that we can view the 20 people in our test as "randomly selected," we can apply the binomial distribution. ("Randomly selected" means that each member of the target market had the same chance of being chosen. That is, each potential customer has the same chance of being willing to purchase your product, thus satisfying the independence and constant probabilities for the binomial distribution.) We have $p = 0.30$ (Hit) and $n = 20$ (the sample size), and so $P(R = 5 \mid \text{Hit}) = P_B(R = 5 \mid n = 20, p = 0.30)$. We can use Formula (9.1) or @RISK to find $P_B(R = 5 \mid n = 20, p = 0.30) = 0.179$.

The same argument can be made regarding $P(R = 5 \mid \text{Flop})$. Now the condition is that eKnow is a flop, which means that only 10% of the target market would purchase eKnow in 5 years. Thus, we have $p = 0.10$ in this case. This gives us $P(R = 5 \mid \text{Flop}) = P_B(R = 5 \mid n = 20, p = 0.10)$, which equals 0.032.

We now have everything we need to do the calculations that are required by Bayes' theorem:

$$P(\text{eKnow is a Hit} \mid 5 \text{ of } 20 \text{ would purchase eKnow})$$

$$= P(\text{Hit} \mid R = 5)$$

$$= \frac{P(R = 5 \mid \text{Hit})P(\text{Hit})}{P(R = 5 \mid \text{Hit})P(\text{Hit}) + P(R = 5 \mid \text{Flop})P(\text{Flop})}$$

$$= \frac{0.179(0.50)}{0.179(0.50) + 0.032(0.50)}$$

$$= 0.848$$

Thus, this evidence (5 out of 20 people would purchase eKnow) is good news. Your posterior probability that eKnow will be a hit is almost 85%.

Of course, we did the analysis on the basis of prior probabilities being P(Hit) = P(Flop) = 0.50. If you had assessed different prior probabilities, your answer would be different, although in any case, the posterior probability that eKnow is a hit increases with the given evidence.

THE POISSON DISTRIBUTION

While the binomial distribution is particularly good for representing successes in several trials, the *Poisson* distribution is good for representing occurrences of a particular event over time or space. Suppose, for example, that you are interested in the number of customers who arrive at a bank in one hour. Clearly this is an uncertain quantity; there could be none, one, two, three, and so on. The Poisson distribution also may be appropriate for modeling the uncertainty surrounding the number of machine breakdowns in a factory over some period of time. Other Poisson applications include modeling the uncertain number of blemishes in a bolt of fabric or the number of chocolate chips in a chocolate chip cookie.

The Poisson distribution requires the following:

1. Events can happen at any of a large number of places within the unit of measurement (hour, square yard, and so on), and preferably along a continuum.
2. At any specific point, the probability of an event is small. This simply means that the events do not happen too frequently. For example, we would be interested in a steady flow of customers to a bank, not a run on the bank.
3. Events happen independently of other events. In other words, the probability of an event at any one point is the same regardless of the time (or location) of other events.
4. The average number of events over a unit of measure (time or space) is constant no matter how far or how long the process has gone on.

Let K represent the uncertain number of events in a unit of time or space. Under the conditions given above, the probability that $K = k$ events is given by

$$P_P(K = k|m) = \frac{e^{-m}m^k}{k!} \qquad \text{for } k = 0, 1, 2, \ldots. \qquad (9.2)$$

where the subscript P indicates this is a Poisson probability, e is the constant 2.718 ... (the base of the natural logarithms), and m is a parameter that characterizes the distribution.

The Poisson distribution is different from the binomial distribution in two ways. First, it has no maximum value; that is, the number of events K could equal 0, 1, 2, 3, ... with no upper bound. Second, the Poisson has only one parameter, which is m. The binomial had two parameters (n and p), whereas Poisson's one parameter means we can modify the Poisson only by our choice of m. The parameter m turns out also to be the expected number of events, i.e., $E(K) = m$. Thus, we need only determine or estimate the expected number of events, and this is our choice for m, which in turn completely specifies the

Poisson. Note that the Poisson random variable K, must be a nonnegative integer, but m need not be an integer.

It is easy to calculate Poisson probabilities using Formula (9.2). For example,

$$Pp(K = 2|m = 1.5) = \frac{e^{-1.5}(1.5)^2}{2!}$$

$$= 0.251.$$

@RISK makes our calculations easy and also provides the graph of the probability distribution. Figure 9.6 shows the Poisson distribution with $m = 1.5$. We see that $P_p(K < 2|1.5) = 55.8\%$, $P_p(K = 2|1.5) = 25.1\%$, and $P_p(K > 2|1.5) = 19.1\%$ An astute reader will notice from Figure 9.6 that the parameter m is labeled λ (lambda) in @RISK. Both m and λ are common symbols used for the Poisson parameter, and they represent the same value, namely the mean value of the distribution. Thus $m = \lambda$.

STEP 2 Poisson Calculations.

2.1 With @RISK opened, **right-click** in any spreadsheet cell to pull up the submenu. Choose **@RISK**, then **Define Distribution.**

2.2 Choose the **Poisson** (second row, fourth distribution) and click on the **Select Distribution** button.

2.3 Either type in your specific parameter value for m or click on the **Assign Excel References** button.

2.4 To calculate the probability of any interval, drag the two **delimiter bars** to the desired x-axis values.

For example, to calculate $P_p(K \leq 8|7.4)$:

Enter $m = 7.4$, and slide the left delimiter bar past 8 but before 9, as shown in Figure 9.7. Thus $P_p(K \leq 8|7.4) = 67.6\%$.

An Example: Blemishes in Fabric

As an example, suppose that you are interested in estimating the number of blemishes in 200 yards of cloth. Based on earlier experience with the cloth manufacturer, you estimate that a blemish occurs (on average) every 27 yards. At a rate of 1 blemish per 27 yards, this amounts to approximately 7.4 blemishes in the 200 yards of cloth.

Is the Poisson distribution appropriate? Condition 1 is satisfied—we are looking at a continuous 200 yards of fabric. Condition 2 also is satisfied; apparently there are only a few blemishes in the 200 yards. Conditions 3 and 4 both should be satisfied unless blemishes are created by some machine malfunction that results in many blemishes occurring together. Thus, the

FIGURE **9.6**
The Poisson
distribution with
$m = 1.5$ showing
that $P_p(K = 2|1.5)$
$= 25.1\%$.

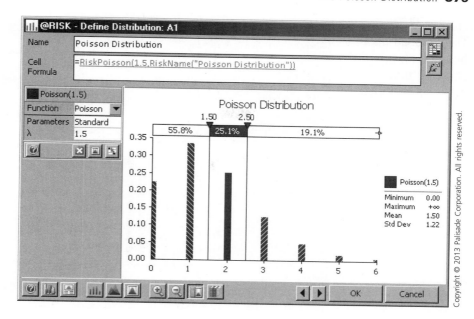

Poison distribution appears to provide an appropriate model of the uncertainty in this problem.

The expected value of 7.4 indicates that we should use a Poisson distribution with $m = 7.4$. Figure 9.7 shows the probability histogram for this distribution. Although it is theoretically possible for there to be a very large number of blemishes, we can see that the probability of more than 16 is extremely low. In fact, the probability that the number of blemishes is less than 15 is 99.6%, leaving 0.4% for the probability of having 16 or more blemishes per 200 yards. Figure 9.7 shows that the probability of having between 9 and 15 blemishes per 200 yards inclusive is 32%, i.e., $P_p(9 \leq K \leq 15|1.5) = 32\%$. Note that if you were using Formula 9.2 to calculate $P_p(9 \leq K \leq 15|1.5) = 32\%$, then you would need to calculate the probability of each value $K = 9$, 10, 11, 12, 13, 14, and 15 separately, and then add up the probabilities.

eKnow, Continued

Let us continue with the development of eKnow. As luck would have it, the National Book Conference is being held in Boston just a few miles from your school. You believe that the conference is a perfect opportunity to test the market's reaction to eKnow, and although it took some effort and resourcefulness, you were able to find a vendor to split booth space with you. From Thursday to Saturday, you will be witnessing people's reactions to eKnow, both positive and negative, and you would like to use this information to

FIGURE **9.7**
The Poisson distribution with $m = 7.4$ showing that $P_p(9 \leq K \leq 15|7.4) = 32\%$.

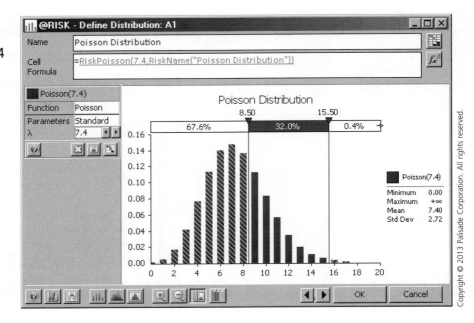

refine your estimate of potential sales. Thus, you have designed a short questionnaire to be handed out. As the questionnaires are returned, you will be able to use Bayes' theorem to update your estimate of future sales during the conference.

You have been told that you can expect about 100 visitors per hour to your booth during the busy hours from 10 a.m. to 3 p.m. From 10 a.m. to 11 a.m. you plan to count the number of "Definitely Purchase" responses to the question: "If available today, would you purchase an eKnow for $29.95?" For this simple model, you are considering three possibilities based on average market acceptance. Failure corresponds to 10% market share, Potential to 15% market share, and Success to 20% market share. Because you expect 100 visitors per hour, these percentages correspond to expected values of 10, 15, and 20 Definitely-Purchase responses for Failure, Potential, and Success, respectively. Finally, you judge that these three possibilities are equally probable: P(Failure) = P(Potential) = P(Success) = 1/3.

After one hour there had been exactly 100 responses, including 18 Definitely-Purchase responses. Given these results, we can use Bayes theorem to update the probabilities of Failure, Potential, and Success. We use the Poisson distribution; we are counting the number of occurrences within a specified time period. Thus, we will use the Poisson with $m = 10$ if Failure, with $m = 15$ if Potential, and with $m = 20$ if Success. Letting D be the number of Definitely-Purchase responses in a hour, we wish to compute P(Failure|$D = 18$), P(Potential|$D = 18$) and P(Success|$D = 18$).

Using Bayes theorem,

$P(\text{Failure}|D = 18)$

$$= \frac{P(D = 18|\text{Failure})P(\text{Failure})}{P(D = 18|\text{Failure})P(\text{Failure}) + P(D = 18|\text{Potential})P(\text{Potential}) + P(D = 18|\text{Success})P(\text{Success})}$$

$$= \frac{P_p(D = 18|m = 10)(1/3)}{P_p(D = 18|m = 10)(1/3) + P_p(D = 18|m = 15)(1/3) + P_p(D = 18|m = 20)(1/3)}$$

$$= \frac{0.007(1/3)}{0.007(1/3) + .071(1/3) + 0.084(1/3)}$$

$= 0.04.$

Similarly,

$P(\text{Potential}|D = 18)$

$$= \frac{P(D = 18|\text{Potential})P(\text{Potential})}{P(D = 18|\text{Failure})P(\text{Failure}) + P(D = 18|\text{Potential})P(\text{Potential}) + P(D = 18|\text{Success})P(\text{Success})}$$

$$= \frac{0.071(1/3)}{0.007(1/3) + .071(1/3) + 0.084(1/3)}$$

$= 0.44.$

Therefore, with 18 Definitely-Purchase responses, the probability of Failure drops from 33.3% to 4% while the probability of Potential increases to 44% and the probability of Success increases to 52%.

Figure 9.8 shows how the $P(\text{Success}|K = k)$ and $P(\text{Potential}|K = k)$ change for $k = 1, 2, \ldots, 30$. As expected: the probability of Success steadily increases as the number of Definitely-Purchase responses increases. It is a little more surprising that the probability of Potential first increases as the number of Definitely-Purchase responses increases, but then it starts to decrease when $k > 15$. Why? Because, for each value of k, the three probabilities must sum to one:

$$P(\text{Success}|K = k) + P(\text{Potential}|K = k) + P(\text{Failure}|K = k) = 1.$$

Thus, when the number of Definitely-Purchase responses is low, $k < 9$, then the $P(\text{Failure}|K = k)$ is high, forcing the probability of Success and Potential to be low. As k increases from 9 to 15, the $P(\text{Potential}|K = k)$ increases from 20% to 54% and $P(\text{Success}|K = k)$ increases from 2% to 27%, while $P(\text{Failure}|K = k)$ decreases from 78% to 18%. Thus, as more Definitely-Purchase responses come in, the probabilities of Potential and Success both increase, but after some point, which is represented by $(k = 15)$ the probability of Potential starts to decrease while the probability of Success continues to increase. The $P(\text{Potential}|K = k)$ attains its maximum value at $k = 15$ which makes sense as $m = 15$ is the mean of the Poisson that describes the probability of Potential.

FIGURE **9.8**

The posterior probabilities of Success and Potential as a function of the number of Definitely-Purchase responses.

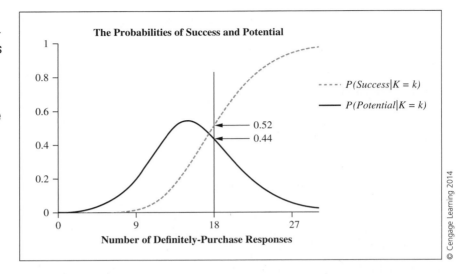

The Poisson and binomial distributions are examples of discrete probability distributions because an outcome can only be specific "discrete" values. What about continuous uncertain quantities? For continuous uncertainties, we do not model the probability of a single value occurring, but rather the probability of a value falling within an interval. For example, we might be interested in the probability of tomorrow's high temperature being over 100°F or the probability that the per-barrel price of crude oil in 6 months is between $100 and $130. Continuous distributions are defined over an interval, such as from zero to one or from negative infinity to positive infinity, and probabilities are calculated as the area under the probability density curve bounded by the interval. Let's begin with a very common distribution, the exponential.

THE EXPONENTIAL DISTRIBUTION

In this section, we will look briefly at the *exponential* distribution for a continuous random variable. In fact, the exponential distribution is closely related to the Poisson. If in the Poisson we were considering the number of arrivals within a specified period of time, then the uncertain time between arrivals (T) has an exponential distribution. The two go hand in hand; if the four conditions listed for the Poisson hold, then the time (or space) between events follows an exponential distribution.

For the exponential, the density function is:

$$f_E(t|m) = \frac{1}{m} e^{-(1/m)t} \qquad \text{for any } t \geq 0. \tag{9.3}$$

where m is the same average rate that we used in the Poisson and t represents the possible values for the uncertain quantity T. An exponential density function with $m = 2$ is illustrated in Figure 9.9. Note that @RISK uses the parameter value of β while we used $1/m$. If m is the Poisson mean value,

FIGURE **9.9**
The exponential distribution with parameter $\beta = \frac{1}{2}$.

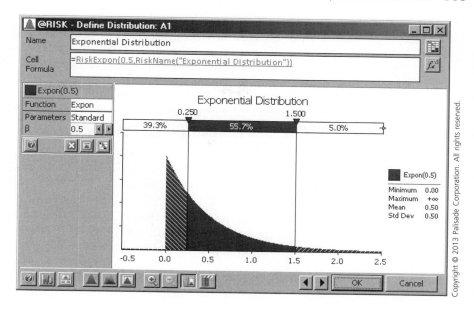

then $\beta = 1/m$ as shown in Figure 9.9 with $\beta = 1/2$. It makes sense that $\beta = 1/m$ because if m equals 6 arrivals per hour, then the expected time between arrivals is 10 minutes or 1/6 of an hour.

Previously, we used the Poisson distribution with $m = 7.4$ to model the number of blemishes per 200 yards of cloth. Thus, if we wanted to model the number of yards between blemishes, we could use the exponential distribution with $\beta = 200/7.4 = 27.03$ yards/blemish. Figure 9.10 shows this distribution and shows that there is a 50.5% probability that there will be less than

FIGURE **9.10**
The exponential distribution with parameter $\beta = 200/7.4 = 27.03$, modeling the number of yards between blemishes.

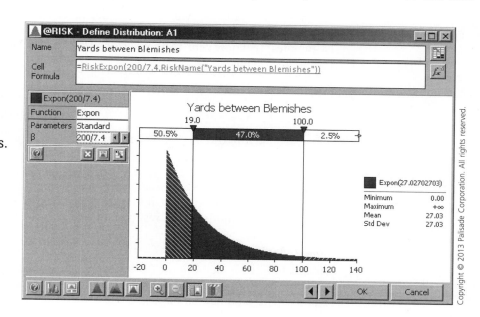

19 yards between blemishes. In probability notation, if we let Y denote the number of yards between blemishes, then $P_E(Y < 19\,yards\,|\,\beta = 27.03\,yards/blemish) = 50.5\%$. Figures 9.9 and 9.10 both show that the parameter of the exponential distribution (β) is not only the mean of the exponential, but is also its standard deviation.

STEP 3 *Exponential Calculations.*

3.1 With @RISK opened, **right-click** in any spreadsheet cell to pull up the submenu. Choose **@RISK**, then **Define Distribution**.

3.2 Choose the **Exponential** (first row) and click on the **Select Distribution** button.

3.3 Either type in your specific parameter value for β or click on the **Assign Excel References** button.

3.4 To calculate the probability of any interval, drag the two **delimiter bars** to the desired x-axis values.

For example, to calculate $P_E(T \le 1.5\,|\,\beta = 0.5)$:

Enter $\beta = 0.5$, drag the right delimiter bar to **1.5**, and drag the left delimiter bar all the way to the left. From the top, read $P_E(T \le 1.5\,|\,\beta = 0.5) = 95\%$.

Be careful to keep your units straight when working with the Poisson and exponential distributions. For example, suppose the mean arrival rate is two arrivals per hour, then to calculate the probability of the next arrival being longer than 15 minutes, we must convert all units into hours: $P_E(T > 15\,min\,|\,m = 2\,arrivals\,per\,hr) = P_E(T > 0.25\,hr\,|\,\beta = 0.5\,hr)$.

For example, Figure 9.9 shows that $P_E(T > 0.25\,hr\,|\,\beta = 0.5\,hr) = 55.7\% + 5\% = 60.7\%$. Moreover, we can check this particular probability by using the Poisson. The outcome "The time until the next arrival is greater than 15 minutes" is equivalent to the outcome "There are no arrivals in the next 15 minutes." Thus,

$$P_E(T > 15\,min\,|\,m = 2\,arrivals\,per\,hr)$$

$$= P_p(X = 0\,arrivals\,in\,15\,min\,|\,m = 2\,arrivals\,per\,hr)$$

$$= P_p(X = 0\,arrivals\,in\,15\,min\,|\,m = 0.5\,arrivals\,per\,15\,min)$$

$$= 60.7\%$$

To reiterate: The exponential distribution's parameter is β, which is its mean value; the Poisson distribution's parameter is m, which is its mean value; and when modeling corresponding uncertainties, $\beta = 1/m$.

eKnow, Again

Let's continue with the National Book Conference. At 11 o'clock you start to wonder how much time you can expect to pass before the next Definitely-Purchase response. This is somewhat difficult because we do not know whether the eKnow will be a Failure, a Potential, or a Success. If it is a Failure, then the expected time between Definitely-Purchase responses is $\beta = 1/m = 0.1\, hours = 6\, minutes$. Likewise, we expect a Definitely-Purchase response approximately every 4 minutes if eKnow is labeled Potential and every 3 minutes if labeled Success. At 11:00 o'clock, after counting the 18 Definitely-Purchase responses, the expected time would be $0.04 \times (6\ minutes) + 0.44 \times (4\ minutes) + 0.52 \times (3\ minutes) = 3.6\ minutes$.

Encouraged by the first hour of observations, you are a bit anxious to see what the second hour of observations delivers. Instead of waiting until the end of the second hour, you start monitoring the time between Definitely-Purchase responses. Hoping that the eKnow is a success, you hope that the time between Definitely-Purchase responses is less than 3 minutes. We can now calculate the probability of waiting less than 3 minutes between Definitely-Purchase responses. Again, we do not know exactly the future sales of eKnow, but have three possibilities: Failure, meaning $m = 10$ favorable responses per hour, Potential, meaning $m = 15$ favorable responses per hour, and Success, meaning $m = 20$ favorable responses per hour. As we have three possibilities for the rate m, we can expand $P(T > 3\ Min)$ by using the total probability formula:

$$P(T > 3\ Min) = P_E(T > 3\ Min | m = 10/Hr)P(m = 10)$$

$$+ P_E(T > 3\ Min | m = 15/Hr)P(m = 15)$$

$$+ P_E(T > 3\ Min | m = 20/Hr)P(m = 20)$$

$$= P_E(T > 0.05\ Hr | \beta = \frac{1}{10}\ Hr)P(m = 10)$$

$$+ P_E(T > 0.05\ Hr | \beta = \frac{1}{15}\ Hr)P(m = 15)$$

$$+ P_E(T > 0.05\ Hr | \beta = \frac{1}{20}\ Hr)P(m = 20)$$

$$= 0.607\, P(m = 10) + 0.472\, P(m = 15) + 0.368\, P(m = 20)$$

Now we substitute in the posterior probabilities that we calculated previously, $P(\text{Failure}|D = 18) = 0.004$, $P(\text{Potential}|D = 18) = 0.44$, and $P(\text{Success}|D = 18) = 0.52$:

$$P(T > 3\ Min) = 0.607(0.004) + 0.472(0.44) + 0.368(0.52) = 0.424.$$

Thus, the probability is 42% that the time between arrivals is greater than 3 minutes. Put another way, because $P(T \leq 3\ min) = 1 - 0.424 = 57.6\%$, we can see that almost 60% of the time the next Definitely-Purchase response will arrive before 3 minutes pass.

The Normal Distribution

Another useful continuous distribution is the *normal* distribution, which has the familiar bell-shaped curve. The normal distribution is particularly good for modeling situations in which the uncertain quantity is subject to many different sources of uncertainty or error. For example, in measuring something, errors may be introduced by a wide range of environmental conditions—equipment malfunctions, human error, and so on. Many measured biological phenomena (height, weight, length) often follow a bell-shaped curve that can be represented well with a normal distribution.

FIGURE **9.11**
Normal density function. The shaded area represents $P_N(a \leq Y \leq b|\mu, \sigma)$.

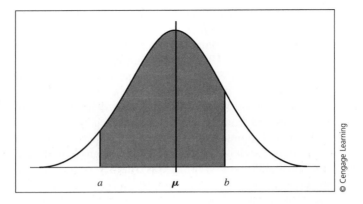

We will let Y represent an uncertain quantity that follows a normal distribution. If this is the case, the density function for Y is:

$$f_N(y|\mu, \sigma) = \frac{1}{\sigma\sqrt{2\pi}} e^{-(y-\mu)^2/2\sigma^2} \quad \text{for} \quad -\infty < y < \infty, \qquad (9.4)$$

where μ and σ are the parameters of the distribution and y represents the possible values that Y can take. Again, the parameters have an interpretation, namely $E(Y) = \mu$ and $Var(Y) = \sigma^2$. Figure 9.11 illustrates a normal density function and the shaded area represents $P_N(a \leq Y \leq b|\mu, \sigma)$. Strictly speaking, a normal random variable can take values anywhere between plus and minus infinity. But the probabilities associated with values more than four standard deviations from the mean are negligible, so we often use the normal to represent values that have a restricted range (e.g., weight or height, which can only be positive) as long as the extreme points are several standard deviations from the mean.

STEP 4 Normal Calculations.

4.1 With @RISK open, **right click** in any spreadsheet cell to pull up the submenu. Choose **@RISK**, then **Define Distribution.**

4.2 Choose the **Normal** (second row, second column) and click on the **Select Distribution** button.

4.3 Either type in your specific parameter values for μ and σ or click the **Assign Excel References** button. Be careful when entering the parameter values, as it is the standard deviation and not the variance which is the second parameter for the normal distribution.

4.4 To calculate the probability of any interval, drag the two **delimiter bars** to the desired x-axis values.

For example, to calculate $P_N(Y \leq 35|10, 20)$:
Enter $\mu = 10$ and $\sigma = 20$, and drag the right delimiter bar to **35** as shown in Figure 9.12. Thus $P_N(Y \leq 35|10, 20) = 89.4\%$.

FIGURE **9.12**
The normal distri-
bution with mean
equal to 10 and
standard deviation
equal to 20.

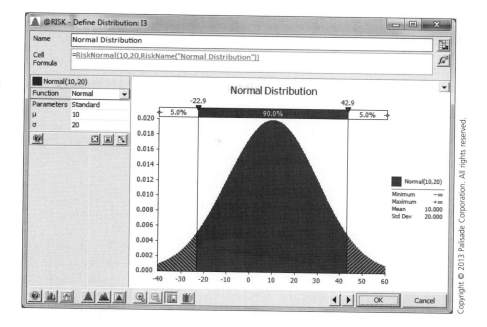

You can now check the so-called *Empirical Rule* that there is a 68% chance that a random variable falls within one standard deviation of the mean, and a 95% chance that it falls within two standard deviations of the mean. This rule derives from the normal distribution. In symbols:

$$P_N(\mu - \sigma \le Y \le \mu + \sigma) \approx 0.68$$

$$P_N(\mu - 2\sigma \le Y \le \mu + 2\sigma) \approx 0.95$$

These are useful approximations for many real-world random variables. However, keep in mind that they work best for bell-shaped distributions and can be very far off for other distributional shapes.

An Investment Example

Consider three alternative investments, A, B, and C. Investing in C yields a sure return of $40. Investment A has an uncertain return (X), which is modeled in this case by a normal distribution with mean $50 and standard deviation $10. Investment B's return (represented by Y) also is modeled with a normal distribution having a mean of $59 and a standard deviation of $20. On the basis of expected values, B is the obvious choice because $59 is greater than $50 or $40. The decision tree is shown in Figure 9.13.

While it is obvious that the expected payoffs for both Investment A and B are greater than the sure $40 for C, we would like to know the probability that either A's or B's payoff will be less than $40. @RISK has an overlay feature that allows us to place more than one distribution in the graph, thereby allowing us

FIGURE **9.13**
Decision tree for
three alternative
investments.

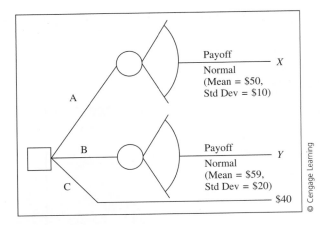

to calculate the probability of both events at one time. (Overlaying is easy; construct the first distribution, click on the **Overlay** button—5th from the left along the bottom—and construct the second distribution.) Figure 9.14 shows the two normal distributions for Investments A and B and the probability that either one is less than $40. Specifically, we see that $P_N(A \leq 40|50, 10) = 15.9\%$ and $P_N(B \leq 40|59, 20) = 17.1\%$. Thus, even though Investment A has a lower expected value than does B, A has a smaller probability of having a return of less than $40. Why? The larger variance for B means that the distribution for B is spread out more than is the distribution for A.

Example: Quality Control

Suppose that you are the manager for a manufacturing plant that produces disk drives for personal computers. One of your machines produces a part that is used in the final assembly. The width of this part is important to the disk drive's operation; if it falls below 3.995 or above 4.005 millimeters (mm), the disk drive will not work properly and must be repaired at a cost of $10.40.

The machine can be set to produce parts with a width of 4 mm, but it is not perfectly accurate. In fact, the actual width of a part is normally distributed with mean 4 mm and a variance that depends on the speed of the machine. If the machine is run at a slower speed, the width of the produced parts has a standard deviation of 0.0019 mm. At the higher speed, however, the machine is less precise, producing parts with a standard deviation of 0.0026 mm.

Of course, the higher speed means that more parts can be produced in less time, thus reducing the overall cost of the disk drive. In fact, it turns out that the cost of the disk drive when the machine is set at high speed is $20.45. At low speed, the cost is $20.75.

The question that you as plant manager face is whether it would be better to run the machine at high or low speed. Is the extra expense of lower speed more than offset by the increased precision and hence the lower defect rate?

FIGURE **9.14**
Overlaying the normal distributions that model the Investment A and Investment B showing that there is a 15.9% chance that A returns less than $40 and a 17.1% chance that B returns less than $40.

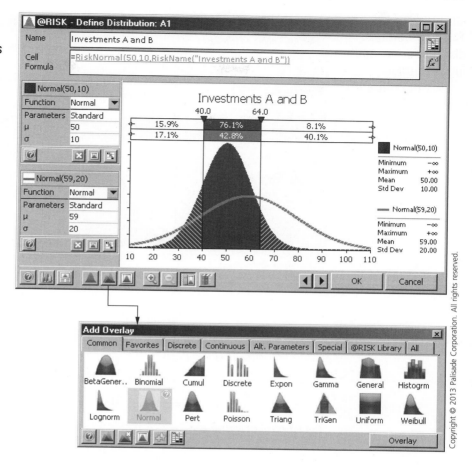

FIGURE **9.15**
Decision tree for a quality-control problem.

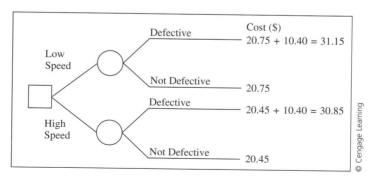

You would like to choose the strategy with the lower expected cost. Your decision tree is shown in Figure 9.15.

To decide, we need to know the probability of a defective unit under both machine settings. Again, using the overlay feature, Figure 9.16

FIGURE **9.16**
The two normal distributions modeling disk-drive widths at high and low speeds.

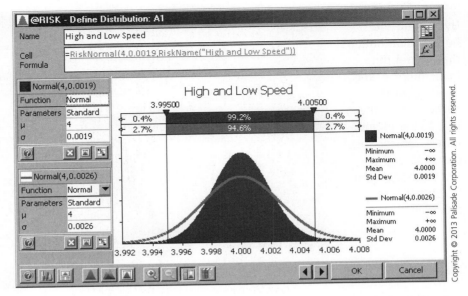

shows the two normal distributions for the two speeds and the following probabilities:

$$P(Defective|Low\ speed) = P_N(Y \le 3.995\ or\ Y \ge 4.005|4, 0.0019)$$

$$= P_N(Y \le 3.995|4, 0.0019) + P_N(Y \ge 4.005|4, 0.0019)$$

$$= 0.4\% + 0.4\% = 0.8\%$$

$$P(Defective|High\ speed) = P_N(Y \le 3.995\ or\ Y \ge 4.005|4, 0.0026)$$

$$= P_N(Y \le 3.995|4, 0.0026) + P_N(Y \ge 4.005|4, 0.0026)$$

$$= 2.7\% + 2.7\% = 5.4\%$$

With these probabilities, it now is possible to calculate the expected cost for each alternative:

$$E(Cost|Low\ Speed) = 0.992(\$20.75) + 0.008(\$31.15)$$

$$= \$20.83$$

$$E(Cost|High\ Speed) = 0.946(\$20.45) + 0.054(\$30.85)$$

$$= \$21.01$$

Thus, in this case the increased cost from the slower speed is more than offset by the increased precision and lower defect rate, and you would definitely choose the slower speed.

THE TRIANGULAR DISTRIBUTION

Our next distribution was not created to model a specific type of uncertainty as much as to be both easily assessed and to model many types of uncertainties. It is called the *triangular* distribution, and, not surprisingly, it has a triangular

FIGURE **9.17**
The triangular distribution with *Min* = 0, *Most Likely* = 8, and *Max* = 10.

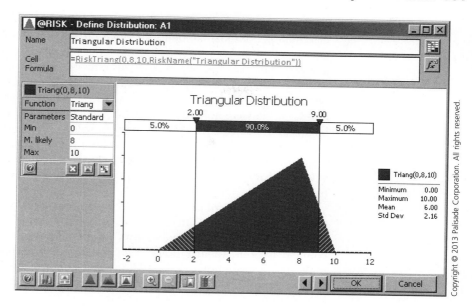

shape. Just as three points determine a triangle, three assessments or three parameters are required to specify the triangular distribution. The three parameters required are the minimum, the most likely (mode), and the maximum. For example, Figure 9.17 shows the triangular distribution with *Min* = 0, *Most Likely* = 8, and *Max* = 10. To denote the probability of a triangular distribution, we write $P_T(Y \leq y | Min, Most\ Likely, Max)$, and from Figure 9.17 we see that $P_T(Y \leq 2|0, 8, 10) = 5\%$.

The density function for triangular distribution Y is

$$f_T(y|Min, Most\ Likely, Max) = \begin{cases} \dfrac{2(y - Min)}{(Max - Min)(Most\ Likely - Min)}, & for\ Min \leq y \leq Most\ Likely \\[2ex] \dfrac{2(Max - y)}{(Max - Min)(Max - Most\ Likely)}, & for\ Most\ Likely \leq y \leq Max \\[2ex] 0, & otherwise \end{cases} \tag{9.5}$$

Two common misunderstandings about the triangular center around the most-likely value. First, the most-likely value can be any number between the minimum and maximum, including the minimum and maximum. If the most-likely value equals either extreme, we end up with a right triangle. Second, the most likely is not the same as the mean value. Figure 9.17 shows that the mean equals six while the most likely equals eight. Thus, care needs to be taken when assessing the most likely: It is not the expected value (mean) nor is it the middle probability value (median), but the value that is expected to occur most frequently (mode).

The triangular distribution is often used as a compromise between finding the best theoretical distribution and one that is easily assessed. For example, one of us (Reilly) used the triangular distribution when helping a liquidation company determine the value of a company's assets in bankruptcy. Even healthy companies may need to know their bankrupt value as banks use this value in determining both loan amounts and loan rates. Historically, the liquidation company sent assessors to determine the value of unsold merchandise, and these assessors produced point estimates of each item, such as 300 T-shirts assessed at $4.25 each. By asking the assessors to produce three assessments for each item, such as 300 T-shirts at a low of $3.75, a most likely of $4.25 and a high of $4.55, we were able to create a more comprehensive picture of a company's bankrupt value. Instead of a company having a single bankrupt value, the new method produced a distribution describing a company's bankrupt value. The triangular was important here because the assessors could easily produce the three values and no further calculations were required; we simply plugged the assessments into the triangular distribution.

Triangular distributions can also be used to quickly and easily incorporate the uncertainty of the different components of a system. For example, to value a company, typically the company's future cash flows are estimated and discounted back to today's dollars. Instead of using a single point estimate for each future cash flow, we could use a triangular distribution, and thereby provide a more complete analysis of the company's value. Here, the triangular distribution is being used not because it is the best or most accurate distribution, but because it is conceptually easy to understand and is easily implemented.

THE BETA DISTRIBUTION

Our next and final distribution is the *beta* distribution. The beta is remarkable in its flexibility. As we show in this section, the beta distribution can assume a wide variety of shapes, and as each shape represents a specific uncertainty, the beta can be used to model a wide variety of uncertain quantities. The beta is confined to the interval zero to one, and thus typically is used to model uncertainty of a percentage, or a proportion, such as a firm's market share. Suppose you are interested in the proportion of voters who will vote for the Republican candidate in the next presidential election; as that proportion must be between zero and one, the beta is a candidate.

We use Q to denote a beta random variable. Its density function is

$$f_\beta(q|\alpha_1, \alpha_2) = \frac{(\alpha_1 + \alpha_2)!}{(\alpha_1 - 1)!(\alpha_2 - 1)!} q^{\alpha_1 - 1}(1 - q)^{\alpha_2 - 1} \text{ for any } 0 \le q \le 1. \quad (9.6)$$

The parameters of the beta distribution are α_1 and α_2. So far, the parameters of all the distributions we have discussed have had interpretations, such as m being the mean of the Poisson distribution, but unfortunately, the parameters of the beta distribution do not have a standard interpretation. For example, the mean of the beta distribution is $\alpha_1/(\alpha_1 + \alpha_2)$, which makes interpreting α_1 and α_2 difficult. Without an interpretation, how do we choose the values for α_1 and α_2? We next provide some general guidelines along with numerous examples to help you determine values for α_1 and α_2. Then, we discuss an alternative method for choosing the parameter values that relies on subjective assessments.

FIGURE **9.18**
The beta distribution with $\alpha_1 = 1$ and $\alpha_2 = 1$, showing that beta can be constant between zero and one.

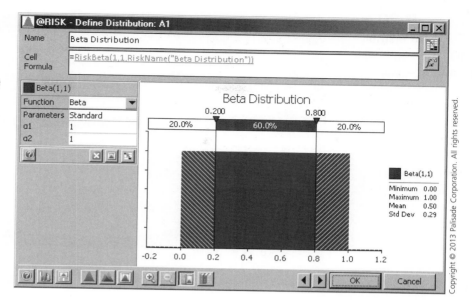

Let's take a look at the variety of shapes that a beta distribution can have. Starting with $\alpha_1 = 1$ and $\alpha_2 = 1$, Figure 9.18 shows a beta distribution that is constant. That is, $f_\beta(q|\alpha_1 = 1, \alpha_2 = 1) = 1$. In this case, all values between zero and one are equally likely (see Problems 9.27–9.29). Certain triangular distributions are special cases of the beta ($\alpha_1 = 1$, $\alpha_2 = 2$ and $\alpha_1 = 2$, $\alpha_2 = 1$). Increasing α_1 to be greater than one and decreasing α_2 below one, the beta distribution takes on a "J" shape as shown in Figure 9.19 where $\alpha_1 = 1.5$ and $\alpha_2 = 0.8$. The "J" shape means that the probability increases as the x value moves toward one, and we can see from the figure that values

FIGURE **9.19**
The beta distribution with $\alpha_1 = 1.5$ and $\alpha_2 = 0.8$, showing a skewed beta distribution with larger values being more probable than smaller values.

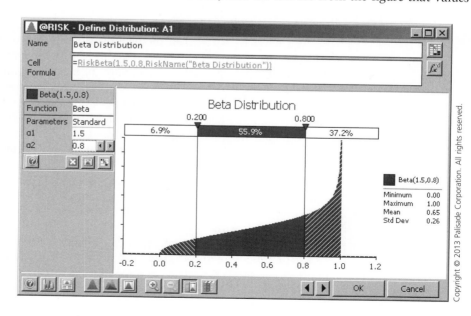

FIGURE **9.20**
The beta distribution with $\alpha_1 = 0.5$ and $\alpha_2 = 0.5$, showing a symmetric beta distribution with values close to zero and one being more probable than values close to ½.

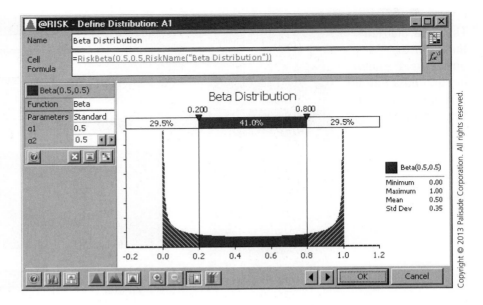

above 0.8 are five times more likely than values below 0.2. Flipping the parameter values, that is choosing $\alpha_1 < 1$ and $\alpha_2 > 1$, results in flipping the distribution, placing most of the probability towards zero instead of towards one. If both $\alpha_1 < 1$ and $\alpha_2 < 1$, the density takes on a "U" shape as shown in Figure 9.20, placing more probability towards the endpoints of zero and one than in the middle. Figure 9.20 shows that 59% of the probability lies towards the extremes while only 41% is in the middle values. An example of a "U" shaped uncertainty is consumer preference for a product that is mainly either hated (values toward zero) or loved (values toward one) with relatively few people being indifferent (values in the middle).

Whenever $\alpha_1 = \alpha_2$, then the beta distribution is symmetric about its mean value of ½. Figure 9.21 shows that as the parameter values increase, the standard deviation decreases. As a matter of fact, the variance of the beta distribution is $(\alpha_1\alpha_2)/(\alpha_1 + \alpha_2)^2(\alpha_1 + \alpha_2 + 1))$. This formula shows that if either α_1 or α_2 increases, then the standard deviation decreases. Finally, beta distributions are skewed when either $\alpha_1 < \alpha_2$ or $\alpha_1 > \alpha_2$ as shown in Figure 9.22.

Although the preceding helps us understand the relationship between the shape of the distribution and the values of the parameters α_1 and α_2, we still need to know how to select the precise values of α_1 and α_2. Because α_1 and α_2 do not have a direct interpretation, we need to indirectly determine their values. We do this by assessing two percentiles of the uncertainty. Input these values into @RISK, and @RISK will compute the corresponding values for α_1 and α_2 based on the assessed percentiles. For example, suppose you assessed 0.29 and 0.52 as the 25th and 75th percentiles, respectively: $P(Q \leq 0.29) = 0.25$ and $P(Q \leq 0.52) = 0.75$. Then, following the instructions given in the text that follows, @RISK finds $\alpha_1 = 3.5$ and $\alpha_2 = 5.0$ is the best fitting beta distribution that matches these two percentiles. We will call this indirect method

FIGURE **9.21**
Two beta distributions, one with $\alpha_1 = 5$ and $\alpha_2 = 5$, and the other with $\alpha_1 = 25$ and $\alpha_2 = 25$ showing that the standard deviation decreases as the parameter values increase.

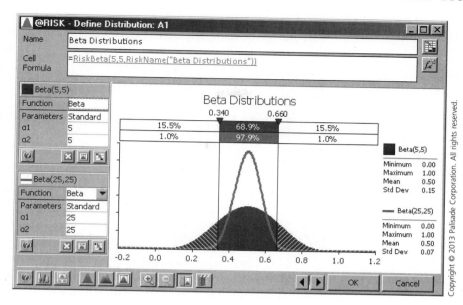

FIGURE **9.22**
Two beta distributions, one with $\alpha_1 = 3$ and $\alpha_2 = 6$, and the other with $\alpha_1 = 10$ and $\alpha_2 = 5$.

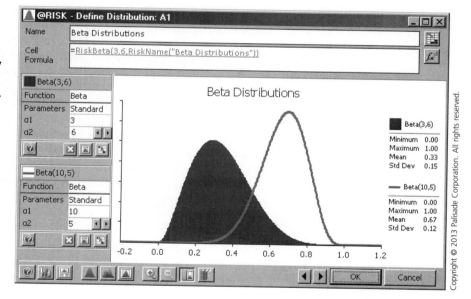

(using assessments of fractiles instead of the parameters) the alternative-parameter method.

Before describing how to use @RISK, we note that @RISK has two beta distributions in its library. The *BetaGeneral* distribution in @RISK differs from the *Beta* in that the BetaGeneral has two additional parameters, which are *Min* and *Max*. The BetaGeneral removes the restriction that the minimum must be zero and maximum must be one; rather we specify the values for the minimum and maximum. The BetaGeneral greatly increases the adaptability of the beta distribution allowing us to model many uncertainties with fixed boundaries.

STEP 5 Beta Calculations.

5.1 With @RISK opened, **right-click** in any spreadsheet cell to pull up the submenu. Choose **@RISK**, then **Define Distribution.**

5.2 Choose the **BetaGeneral** (the first distribution), and click on the **Select Distribution** button.

5.3 Enter 0 for the *Min*, and **1** for the *Max*. Now the BetaGeneral is identical to the Beta.

5.4 To calculate the probability of any interval, drag the two **delimiter bars** to the desired x-axis values.

For example, to calculate $P_B(Q \leq 0.34|5, 5)$:

Enter $\alpha_1 = 5$ and $\alpha_2 = 5$, and drag the left delimiter bar to **0.340** as shown in Figure 9.21. Thus $P_B(Q \leq 0.34|5, 5) = 15.5\%$.

5.5 The alternative-parameter method for determining α_1 and α_2 works similarly:

5.5.1 Choose **BetaGeneral**, set *Min* = 0, and *Max* = 1.

5.5.2 Click on the word **Standard** as shown in Figure 9.23, and in the pop-up menu, choose **Alternate Parameters.**

5.5.3 In the *Alternate Parameter Options* section, click on **Percentile** for α_1 and **Percentile** for α_2 as shown in Figure 9.23. Change the default percentiles from 5% and 25% if you have different percentiles. Select **Min** and **Max.** Click **OK.**

5.5.4 Finally, enter the two assessed values for the percentiles.

For example, to find the beta that matches the two assessments:

$$P(Q \leq 0.29) = 0.25 \text{ and } P(Q \leq 0.52) = 0.75$$

Select the **BetaGeneral** setting *Min* = 0 and *Max* = 1.

Choose **Alternative Parameters** and enter **25** and **75**, as we assessed the 25th and 75th percentiles. Select **Min** and **Max**, and click **OK.**

Enter **0.29** for the 25th percentile and **0.52** for the 75th, as shown in Figure 9.24.

If you wish to know the parameter values of α_1 and α_2 that @RISK computes based on the two assessments, click on the *Parameters: Alternate* (left of the graph), and uncheck the Alternate Parameters checkbox.

We can employ the alternative-parameter method that uses assessed values to determine the parameter values for continuous distributions other than the beta. For example, instead of inputting the mean and standard deviation of the normal, we can give two assessed values. You may have noticed that there is a one-to-one correspondence between the number of parameters and the number of assessments. For the beta, we have two parameters, and thus needed two assessments. You may have even noticed that for the BetaGeneral, we could also replace the minimum and maximum parameters with two additional assessments. If you have more assessments than parameters, then there may not

FIGURE **9.23**
To use assessments of percentiles as a method for choosing parameter values, choose the Alternate Parameters as shown.

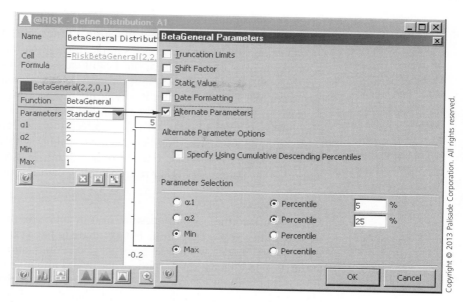

be any single distribution of a specific type that matches all the assessments. For example, there is no beta distribution that exactly matches the three assessments: $P(Q \leq 0.36) = 0.25$, $P(Q \leq 0.40) = 0.50$, and $P(Q \leq 0.52) = 0.75$. In this case, we would have three choices. We could be satisfied with an approximation, use another type of distribution or use our subjective assessment directly via one of @RISK's custom distribution, such as Cumul, General, or Histogram.

The two additional options shown in Figure 9.23 are *Truncation Limits* and *Shift Factor*. A Shift Factor of 5 means that the distribution is shifted right 5 units. Truncation Limits of -2 and 5 mean that between -2 and 5 the distribution is defined in its standard form, and outside those bounds

FIGURE **9.24**
Specifying a beta distribution using the 25th and 75th percentiles.

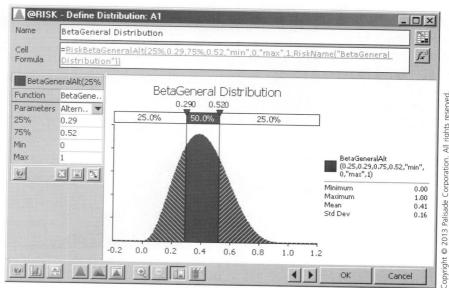

it is defined to equal zero. The idea behind truncation is that a particular distribution may model the uncertainty well within a range, but the variable cannot take on values outside that range. For example, the normal distribution is often used to model heights of individuals, but height cannot be negative. Thus, we might use the truncated normal distribution with a lower bound of zero. Truncation may seem like a good idea, but it is typically not necessary if the boundary limits are sufficiently far away from the mean. For example, if you are using a normal distribution to model height with mean 5 feet and standard deviation 1 foot, the probability of a negative number (negative height) with this distribution is less than 0.000000287 (less than one out of a million). This is a small enough probability that we might not bother to truncate the distribution.

eKnow, One Last Time

Let us return to the original question of how much market share the eKnow will capture in five years. Denote the market share in five years by Q; unlike our original binomial model, we will let Q be an uncertain quantity that must be between 0 and 1. You might want to model your beliefs about Q with a beta distribution. As you think about eKnow's market share, you know that Q is not likely to be close to 1. Suppose also that you think that the median is approximately 0.20 and the upper quartile is 0.35. Figure 9.25 shows the unique beta distribution that matches these two percentiles. Returning to the standard parameters, we see that $\alpha_1 = 1.10$ and $\alpha_2 = 3.48$. The mean or expected value of Q is 24% with a standard deviation of 18%. This beta has a large standard deviation because we have a large amount of uncertainty in eKnow's market share in five years.

Let's take a look at the possible financial outcomes of going ahead with eKnow. Doing so should help in the decision of whether to become an eKnow entrepreneur. You have chosen $19.95 as the wholesale price of the eKnow and the total annual market is estimated to be 200,000 units. You figure that the total annual fixed cost of the project amounts to $300,000 for

FIGURE **9.25**
Market share of eKnow modeled as a beta distribution based on the 50th and 75th percentiles.

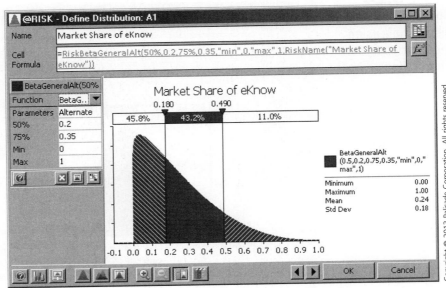

marketing, finance costs, and overhead. The variable cost of each eKnow is $11.55, so the marginal contribution of each eKnow sold is $19.95 − $11.55 = $8.40.

The question is how profitable and how risky the overall eKnow project will be. Begin by writing the equation for net contribution as the difference between total revenue and total costs:

$$\text{Net Contribution} = 200{,}000(\$19.95)Q - 200{,}000(\$11.55)Q - \$300{,}000$$
$$= 200{,}000(\$8.40)Q - \$300{,}000$$
$$= \$1{,}680{,}000Q - \$300{,}000.$$

The expected net contribution is found by substituting the expected market share, $E(Q) = 24\%$ for market share:

$$E(\text{Net Contribution}) = \$1{,}680{,}000E(Q) - \$300{,}000$$
$$= \$1{,}680{,}000(0.24) - \$300{,}000$$
$$= \$403{,}200 - \$300{,}000$$
$$= \$103{,}200.$$

On the basis of expected value, eKnow is a good idea! But it also is a pretty risky proposition. What is the probability, for instance, that eKnow could result in a loss? To answer this, we can find the specific value for Q (call it q^*) that would make the net contribution equal to zero:

$$0 = \$1{,}680{,}000q^* - \$300{,}000$$

$$q^* = \frac{300{,}000}{1{,}680{,}000} = 0.179.$$

If Q turns out to be less than 0.179, you would have been better off with a savings account. Figure 9.25 shows that there is about a 45% chance that Q will be less than 0.179, in which case the project will result in a loss. Are you willing to go ahead with eKnow?

SUMMARY

In this chapter we examined ways to use theoretical probability distributions in decision-analysis problems. The distributions we considered were the binomial, Poisson, exponential, normal, triangular, and beta. These are only a few of the simpler ones; many other theoretical distributions are available. Each is appropriate in different situations, and a decision analyst must develop expertise in recognizing which distribution provides the best model of the uncertainty in a decision situation. Table 9.1 summarizes the distributions we covered by listing the parameters required to specify each distribution, a brief explanation of the parameters and also the formula for the mean in terms of the parameters.

We conclude by noting that there are many sources that provide probability calculations in addition to @RISK. For example, Excel has its own built in formulas that will calculate probability values. In some ways, the Excel formulas are more convenient as you do not need to read the probability from a

TABLE **9.1**
An overview of distributions discussed in this chapter.

Distribution	Parameters	Alternate Parameters?	Mean Value
Binomial	n = number of trials p = probability of success	No	np
Poisson	m = expected value	No	m
Exponential	β = expected value	Yes	β
Normal	μ = mean value σ = standard deviation	Yes	μ
Triangular	Min = minimum Most Likely = mode Max = maximum	Yes	$\dfrac{Min + Most\ Likely + Max}{3}$
Beta	α_1 α_2	No	$\dfrac{\alpha_1}{\alpha_1 + \alpha_2}$
BetaGeneral	α_1 α_2 Min = minimum Max = maximum	Yes	$Min + \dfrac{\alpha_1}{\alpha_1 + \alpha_2}(Max - Min)$

graph. Phillip Stark, University of California-Berkeley, has created an easy-to-use on-line probability calculator at www.stat.berkeley.edu/~stark/Java/Html/ProbCalc.htm. Stat Trek (http://stattrek.com/) has on-line probability calculators along with free tutorials on theoretical probability distributions. Finally, Wolfram Mathematica (http://demonstrations.wolfram.com/) has over five thousand interactive live demonstrations, many showing the relationship between the parameter choice and the theoretical distribution.

EXERCISES

9.1. In the binomial example with Melissa Bailey, what is the probability that she will be gone six or more weekends?

9.2. Suppose you are interested in an investment with an uncertain return. You think that the return could be modeled as a normal random variable with mean $2,000 and standard deviation $1,500. What is the probability that the investment will end with a loss? What is the probability that the return will be greater than $4,000?

9.3. If the number of chocolate chips in a chocolate-chip cookie follows a Poisson where the average is 3.6 chocolate chips per cookie, what is the probability of finding no chocolate chips in a given cookie? Fewer than 5 chocolate chips? More than 10 chips?

9.4. Refer to the discussion of eKnow in the section on the beta distribution. Find the probability that the net contribution of eKnow would be greater than $600,000. What is the probability the net contribution will be less than $100,000?

9.5. Use the probability statements that follow to find the value of the random variable.

a. $P_B(R \leq r|n = 12, \; p = 0.85) = 0.024$; find r.
b. $P_P(K > k|m = 3.2) = 0.62$; find k.
c. $P_E(T \leq t|\beta = 32) = 0.952$; find t.
d. $P_N(Y \geq y|\mu = 30, \sigma = 8) = 0.10$; find y.
e. $P_T(Y \leq y|Min = 10, \; Most\ Likely = 10, \; Max = 18) = 0.75$; find y
f. $P_B(Q \leq q|\alpha_1 = 6, \alpha_2 = 20) = 0.40$; find q.

9.6. Using the alternative-parameter method, determine the parameters of the following distributions based on the given assessments. Refer to Step 5.5 if necessary.

a. Find the parameter value β for the exponential distribution given $P_E(T \leq 15|\beta) = 0.50$.
b. Find the parameters μ and σ for a normal distribution given $P_N(Y \leq 125|\mu, \sigma) = 0.25$ and $P_N(Y \leq 125|\mu, \sigma) = 0.75$.
c. Find the *Min, Most Likely,* and *Max* for the triangular distribution given
$$P_T(Y \leq 15|Min, Most\ Likely, Max) = 0.15,$$
$$P_T(Y \leq 50|Min, Most\ Likely, Max) = 0.50, \text{ and}$$
$$P_T(Y > 95|Min, Most\ Likely, Max) = 0.05.$$
d. Find the parameter values α_1 and α_2 for the beta distribution given $P_B(Q \leq 0.3|\alpha_1, \alpha_2) = 0.05$ and $P_B(Q \leq 0.5|\alpha_1, \alpha_2) = 0.25$.

9.7. An exponential distribution has $P_E(T \geq 5|m) = 0.24$. Find m.
9.8. A Poisson distribution has $P_P(X \geq 12|m) = 0.01$ and $P_P(X \leq 2|m) = 0.095$. Find m.
9.9. A Poisson distribution has $P_P(X = 0|m) = 0.175$. Calculate m.
9.10. Typically, the more information we have, the better estimates we can make. However, we mentioned that when using the alternative-parameter method, if we have more assessments than parameters then there may be no single distribution of that type which exactly matches all the assessments. Discuss how having more information (assessments) can lead to ambiguity in the distribution choice instead of identifying a unique distribution. In this case, is having more information bad?
9.11. Make the necessary calculations to verify the Empirical Rule for normal distributions, which states that the probability is approximately 0.68 that a normal random variable is within one standard deviation of the mean μ and the probability is approximately 0.95 that the random variable is within two standard deviations of the mean.

QUESTIONS AND PROBLEMS

9.12. The amount of time that a union stays on strike is judged to follow an exponential distribution with a mean of 10 days.
a. Find the probability that a strike lasts less than one day.
b. Find the probability that a strike lasts less than six days.
c. Find the probability that a strike lasts between six and seven days.
d. Find the conditional probability that a strike lasts less than seven days, given that it already has lasted six days. Compare your answer to part a.

9.13. A photographer works part-time in a shopping center, two hours per day, four days per week. On the average, six customers arrive each hour, and the arrivals appear to occur independently of one another. Twenty minutes after she arrives one day, the photographer wonders what the chances are that exactly one customer will arrive during the next 15 minutes. Find this probability (i) if two customers just arrived within the first 20 minutes and (ii) if no customers have come into the shop yet on this particular day.

9.14. A consumer is contemplating the purchase of a new smart phone. A consumer magazine reports data on the major brands. Brand A has lifetime (T_A), which is exponentially distributed with $m = 0.2$; and Brand B has lifetime (T_B), which is exponentially distributed with $m = 0.1$. (The unit of time is one year.)

   a. Find the expected lifetimes for A and B. If a consumer must choose between the two on the basis of maximizing expected life-time, which one should be chosen?

   b. Find the probability that A's lifetime exceeds its expected value. Do the same for B. What do you conclude?

   c. Suppose one consumer purchases Brand A, and another consumer purchases Brand B. Find the mean and variance of (i) the average lifetime of the two devices and (ii) the difference between their lifetimes.(*Hint:* You must use the rules about means and variances of linear transformations discussed in Chapter 7.)

9.15. On the basis of past data, the owner of an automobile dealership finds that, on average, 8.5 cars are sold per day on Saturdays and Sundays during the months of January and February, with the sales rate relatively stable throughout the day. Moreover, purchases appear to be independent of one another. The dealership is open for 10 hours per day on each of these days. There is no reason to believe that sales for the upcoming year will be any different from sales in the past.

   a. On the first Saturday in February, the dealership will open at 9 a.m. Find the probability that the time until the first sale is more than two hours, $P_E(T \geq 2\,hours|m = 8.5\,cars\,per\,10\,hours)$.

   b. Find the probability that the number of sales before 11 a.m. is equal to zero, $P_P(X = 0\,in\,2\,hours|m = 8.5\,cars\,per\,10\,hours)$. Compare your answer with that from part a. Can you explain why the answers are the same?

   c. The owner of the dealership gives her salespeople bonuses, depending on the total number of cars sold. She gives them $200 whenever exactly 13 cars are sold on a given day, $300 whenever 14 cars are sold, $500 whenever 15 cars are sold, and $700 whenever 16 or more cars are sold. On any given Saturday or Sunday in January or February, what is the expected bonus that the dealer will have to pay?

   d. Consider the bonus scheme presented in part c. February contains exactly four Saturdays and four Sundays. What is the probability that the owner will have to pay the $200 bonuses exactly twice in those days?

9.16. Reconsider your assessed 0.05 and 0.95 fractiles in Problem 8.13. If you are perfectly *calibrated* when judging these fractiles, then you would expect that in any given situation the actual value has a 0.90 chance of falling between your assessed fractiles (for that variable).

　　a. Assuming you are perfectly calibrated, what is the probability that 0, 1, or 2 of the 10 actual values fall between the assessed fractiles?

　　b. To justify using the binomial distribution to answer part a, you must assume that the chance of any particular value falling between its fractiles is the same regardless of what happens with the other variables. Do you think this is a reasonable assumption? Why or why not?

9.17. In the first eKnow example in which we used binomial probabilities, suppose the results had been that 4 out of the 20 people responded that they would purchase the eKnow. Use Bayes' theorem to find your posterior probability $P(Hit|r = 4, n = 20)$ for the following pairs of prior probabilities:

　　a. $P(Hit) = 0.2, P(Flop) = 0.8$
　　b. $P(Hit) = 0.4, P(Flop) = 0.6$
　　c. $P(Hit) = 0.5, P(Flop) = 0.5$
　　d. $P(Hit) = 0.75, P(Flop) = 0.25$
　　e. $P(Hit) = 0.90, P(Flop) = 0.10$
　　f. $P(Hit) = 1.0, P(Flop) = 0$

Create a graph of the posterior probability as a function of the prior probability.

9.18. In a city, 60% of the voters are in favor of building a new park. An interviewer intends to conduct a survey.

　　a. If the interviewer selects 20 people randomly, what is the probability that more than 15 of them will favor building the park?

　　b. Instead of choosing 20 people as in part a, suppose that the interviewer wants to conduct the survey until he has found exactly 12 who are in favor of the park. What is the probability that the first 12 people surveyed all favor the park (in which case the interviewer can stop)? What is the probability that the interviewer can stop after interviewing the thirteenth subject? What is the probability that the interviewer can stop after interviewing the eighteenth subject?

9.19. In bottle production, bubbles that appear in the glass are considered defects. Any bottle that has more than two bubbles is classified as "nonconforming" and is sent to recycling. Suppose that a particular production line produces bottles with bubbles at a rate of 1.1 bubbles per bottle. Bubbles occur independently of one another.

　　a. What is the probability that a randomly chosen bottle is nonconforming?

    b.   Bottles are packed in cases of 12. An inspector chooses one bottle from each case and examines it for defects. If it is nonconforming, she inspects the entire case, replacing nonconforming bottles with good ones. This process is called rectification. If the chosen bottle conforms (has two or fewer bubbles), then she passes the case. In total, 20 cases are produced. What is the probability that at least 18 of them pass?

    c.   What is the expected number of nonconforming bottles in the 20 cases after they have been inspected and rectified using the scheme described in part b?

9.20. In our discussion of the Poisson distribution, we used this distribution to represent the distribution of positive responses (Definitely Purchase) to the eKnow per hour at the convention booth. Is it reasonable to assume that the Poisson distribution is appropriate for finding the probabilities that we need? Why or why not?

9.21. You are the mechanical engineer in charge of maintaining the machines in a factory. The plant manager has asked you to evaluate a proposal to replace the current machines with new ones. The old and new machines perform substantially the same jobs, and so the question is whether the new machines are more reliable than the old. You know from past experience that the old machines break down roughly according to a Poisson distribution, with the expected number of breakdowns at 2.5 per month. When one breaks down, $1,500 is required to fix it. The new machines, however, have you a bit confused. According to the distributor's brochure, the new machines are supposed to break down at a rate of 1.5 machines per month on average and should cost $1,700 to fix. But a friend in another plant that uses the new machines reports that they break down at a rate of approximately 3.0 per month (and do cost $1,700 to fix). (In either event, the number of breakdowns in any month appears to follow a Poisson distribution.) On the basis of this information, you judge that it is equally likely that the rate is 3.0 or 1.5 per month.

    a.   Based on minimum expected repair costs, should the new machines be adopted?

    b.   Now you learn that a third plant in a nearby town has been using these machines. They have experienced 6 breakdowns in 3.0 months. Use this information to find the posterior probability that the breakdown rate is 1.5 per month.

    c.   Given your posterior probability, should your company adopt the new machines in order to minimize expected repair costs?

    d.   Consider the information given in part b. If you had read it in the distributor's brochure, what would you think? If you had read it in a trade magazine as the result of an independent test, what would you think? Given your answers, what do you think about using sample information and Bayes' Theorem to find posterior probabilities? Should the source of the information be taken into consideration somehow? Could this be done in some way in the application of Bayes' theorem?

9.22. When we calculated the expected net contribution for the eKnow example, we first showed that Net Contribution = $1,680,000Q − $300,000, where Q is the market share. We then substituted the expected market share ($E(Q)$) into the net-contribution formula:

$$E(\text{Net Contribution}) = \$1,680,000E(Q) − \$300,000.$$

Why can we do this? In other words, the expected net contribution is the sum of all possible contribution values times their associated probability value, that is

$$E(\text{Net Contribution}) = \sum Cont\,Value \times P(Cont\,Value).$$

The question is why does $\sum Cont\,Value \times P(Cont\,Value) = \$1,680,000\ E(Q) − \$300,000$?

9.23. Sometimes we use probability distributions that are not exact representations of the physical processes that they are meant to represent. (For example, we might use a normal distribution for a distribution of individuals' weights, even though no one can weigh less than zero pounds.) Why do we do this?

9.24. You are an executive at Procter and Gamble and are about to introduce a new product. Your boss has asked you to predict the market share (Q, a proportion between 0 and 1) that the new product will capture. You are unsure of Q, and you would like to communicate your uncertainty to the boss. You have made the following assessments: There is a 1-in-10 chance that Q will be greater than 0.22, and also a 1-in-10 chance that Q will be less than 0.08. The value for Q is just as likely to be greater than 0.14 as less than 0.14.

a. What should your subjective probabilities $P(0.08 < Q < 0.14)$ and $P(0.14 < Q < 0.22)$ be in order to guarantee consistency?

b. Use @RISK to find a beta distribution for Q that closely approximates your subjective beliefs.

c. The boss tells you that if you expect that the market share will be less than 0.15, the product should not be introduced. Write the boss a memo that gives an expected value and also explains how risky you think it would be to introduce the product. Use your beta approximation.

9.25. Suppose you are considering two investments, and the critical issues are the rates of return (R_1 and R_2). For Investment 1, the expected rate of return (μ_1) is 10%, and the standard deviation (σ_1) is 3%. For the second investment, the expected rate of return (μ_2) is 20%, and the standard deviation (σ_2) is 12%.

a. Does it make sense to decide between these two investments on the basis of expected value alone? Why or why not?

b. Does it make sense to represent the uncertainty surrounding the rates of return with normal distributions? What conditions do we need for the normal distribution to provide a good fit?

c. Suppose you have decided to use normal distributions (either because of or in spite of your answer to part b). Use @RISK to find the following probabilities:

$$P(R_1 < 0\%)$$

$$P(R_2 < 0\%)$$

$$P(R_1 > 20\%)$$

$$P(R_2 < 10\%)$$

d. Suppose R_1 and R_2 are correlated (as they would be if, say, both of the investments were stocks). Then the random variable $\Delta R = R_1 - R_2$ is normal with mean $\mu_1 - \mu_2$ and variance $\sigma_1^2 + \sigma_2^2 - 2\rho\sigma_1\sigma_2$ where ρ is the correlation between R_1 and R_2. If $\rho = 0.5$, find $P(R_1 > R_2)$. Find the probability that $R_1 > R_2$.

e. How could you use the information from the various probabilities developed in this problem to choose between the two investments?

9.26. Your inheritance, which is in a blind trust, is invested entirely in McDonald's or in U.S. Steel. Because the trustee owns several McDonald's franchises, you believe the probability that the investment in McDonald's is 0.8. In any one year, the return from an investment in McDonald's is approximately normally distributed with mean 14% and standard deviation 4%, while the investment in U.S. Steel is approximately normally distributed with mean 12% and standard deviation 3%. Assume that the two returns are independent.

a. What is the probability that the investment earns between 6% and 18% (i) if the trust is invested entirely in McDonald's, and (ii) if the trust is invested entirely in U.S. Steel?

b. Without knowing how the trust is invested, what is the probability that the investment earns between 6% and 18%?

c. Suppose you learn that the investment earned more than 12%. Given this new information, find your posterior probability that the investment is in McDonald's.

d. Suppose that the trustee decided to split the investment and put one-half into each of the two securities. Find the expected value and the variance of this portfolio.

9.27. A continuous random variable X has the following density function:

$$f(x) = \begin{cases} 0.5, & for\ 3 \leq x \leq 5 \\ 0, & otherwise \end{cases}$$

a. Draw a graph of this density. Verify that the area under the density function equals 1.

b. A density function such as this one is called a *uniform* density, or sometimes a *rectangular* density. It is extremely easy to work with because probabilities for intervals can be found as areas of rectangles. For example, find $P_U(X \leq 4.5|Min = 3, Max = 5)$. (The parameters *Min* and *Max* are used to denote the lower and upper extremes, respectively.)

c. Find the following uniform probabilities:

$$P_U(X \leq 4.3|Min = 3, Max = 5)$$
$$P_U(X > 3.4|Min = 0, Max = 10)$$
$$P_U(0.25 \leq X \leq 0.75|Min = 0, Max = 1)$$
$$P_U(X < 0|Min = -1, Max = 4)$$

d. Plot the CDF for the uniform distribution where $Min = 0$ and $Max = 1$.

e. The expected value of a uniform distribution is $E(X) = (Min + Max)/2$, and the variance is $Var(X) = (Max - Min)^2/12$. Calculate the expected value and variance of the uniform density with $Min = 3, Max = 5$.

9.28. The length of time until a strike is settled is distributed uniformly from 0 to 10.5 days. (See the previous problem for an introduction to the uniform density.)

a. Find the probability that a strike lasts less than 1 day.

b. Find the probability that a strike lasts less than 6 days.

c. Find the probability that a strike lasts between 6 and 7 days.

d. Find the conditional probability that a strike lasts less than 7 days, given that it already has lasted 6 days.

e. Compare your answers with those from Problem 9.12.

9.29. In a survey at a shopping center, the interviewer asks customers how long their shopping trips have lasted so far. The response (T) given by a randomly chosen customer is uniformly distributed from 0 to 1.5 hours.

a. Find the probability that a customer has been shopping for 36 minutes or less.

b. The interviewer surveys 18 customers at different times. Find the probability that more than one-half of these customers say that they have been shopping for 36 minutes or less.

9.30. Phillip Sheridan frequently flies between Washington, D.C. and Raleigh, North Carolina, and as the distance is short, the airline uses turboprop airplanes. He often has a choice between flying on a two-engine or a four-engine airplane. Phillip's intuition is that the four-engine plane is safer as he knows that a plane needs at least one half of its engines working properly to land the plane safely. Thus, if one engine failed, both planes could land safely, but if two engines failed, then the four-engine plane would be okay and the two-engine plane would crash. Is Phillip's intuition correct? Assume that each engine has the same probability p of not failing and that the engines are independent of one another.

a. Explain why $P_B(R \geq 1|n = 2, p)$ is the probability of the two-engine plane landing safely and $P_B(R \geq 2|n = 4, p)$ is the probability of the four-engine plane landing safely.

b. Compute the probability of a safe arrival for both plane types when the probability of an engine not failing is $p = 0.95$, $p = 0.80$, $p = 0.67$, and $p = 0.10$. Comment on which plane is safer as the probability of engine failure increases (that is, as p decreases).

9.31. To help counselors identify teenagers who may become problem drinkers, a psychologist created a written test and individuals with scores above 75 on this test are flagged as potential problem drinkers. The test was administered to two groups of people: those who have problems with drinking and those who do not. The problem drinkers scored a mean of 80 with a standard deviation of 5, while the non-problem drinkers scored a mean of 60 with a standard deviation of 10. Assuming that the test scores follow a normal distribution, what is the percentage of problem drinkers identified as not having a problem? Also, what percentage of non-problem drinkers are identified as having a problem?

9.32. A greeting card shop makes cards that are supposed to fit into 6-inch (in.) envelopes. The paper cutter, however, is not perfect. The length of a cut card is normally distributed with mean 5.9 in. and standard deviation 0.0365 in. If a card is longer than 5.975 in., it will not fit into a 6-in. envelope.

a. Find the probability that a card will not fit into a 6-in. envelope.

b. The cards are sold in boxes of 20. What is the probability that in one box there will be two or more cards that do not fit in 6-in. envelopes?

9.33. You are the maintenance engineer for a plant that manufactures consumer electronic goods. You are just about to leave on your vacation for two weeks, and the boss is concerned about certain machines that have been somewhat unreliable, requiring your expertise to keep them running. The boss has asked you how many of these machines you expect to fail while you are out of town, and you have decided to give him your subjective probability distribution. You have made the following assessments:

1. There is a 0.5 chance that none of the machines will fail.

2. There is an approximate 0.15 chance that two or more will fail.

3. There is virtually no chance that four or more will fail.

Being impatient with this slow assessment procedure, you decide to try to fit a theoretical distribution.

a. Many operations researchers would use a Poisson distribution in this case. Why might the Poisson be appropriate? Why might it not be appropriate?

b. Find a Poisson distribution that provides a good representation of your assessed beliefs. Give a specific value for the parameter m.

c. Given your answer to b, what is the expected number of machines that will break down during your absence?

9.34. After you have given your boss your information in Problem 9.33, he considers how accurate you have been in the past when you have made such assessments. In fact, he decides you are somewhat optimistic (and he believes in Murphy's Law), so he assigns a Poisson distribution with $m = 1$ to the occurrence of machine breakdowns during your two-week vacation. Now the boss has a decision to make. He either can close the part of the plant involving the machines in question, at a cost of $10,000, or he can leave that part up and running. Of course, if there are no machine failures, there is no cost. If there is only one failure, he can work with the remaining equipment until you return, so the cost is effectively zero. If there are two or more failures, however, there will be assembly time lost, and he will have to call in experts to repair the machines immediately. The cost would be $15,000. What should he do?

9.35. When we used Bayes' theorem to update the probabilities that eKnow would be a Success, Potential, or Failure by counting the number of Definitely-Purchase responses at the National Book Conference, we showed the impact of counting 18 Definitely-Purchase responses in the first hour. Now, suppose that in the second hour you counted 17 Definitely-Purchase responses.

    a. Use Bayes' theorem a second time to update the posterior probabilities that incorporate the 18 Definitely-Purchase responses.

    b. Suppose you did not have time to update the equal probability values of 1/3, 1/3, 1/3 for Success, Potential, and Failure after the first hour. Starting with these equal probability values, show that having 35 Definitely-Purchase responses in two hours produces the same updated probabilities as computing the updated probabilities after each hour.

9.36. A factory manager must decide whether to stock a particular spare part. The part is absolutely essential to the operation of certain machines in the plant. Stocking the part costs $10 per day in storage and cost of capital. If the part is in stock, a broken machine can be repaired immediately, but if the part is not in stock, it takes one day to get the part from the distributor, during which time the broken machine sits idle. The cost of idling one machine for a day is $65. There are 50 machines in the plant that require this particular part. The probability that any one of them will break and require the part to be replaced on any one day is only 0.004 (regardless of how much time has elapsed since the part was previously replaced). The machines break down independently of one another.

    a. If you wanted to use a probability distribution for the number of machines that break down on a given day, would you use the binomial or Poisson distribution? Why?

    b. Whichever theoretical distribution you chose in part a, what are the appropriate parameters? That is, if you chose the binomial, what are the values for p and n? If you chose the Poisson, what is the value for m?

c. If the plant manager wants to minimize his expected cost, should he keep zero, one, or two parts in stock? Draw a decision tree and solve the manager's problem. (Do not forget that more than one machine can fail in one day!)

9.37. Another useful distribution that is based on the normal is the *lognormal* distribution. Among other applications, this distribution is used by environmental engineers to represent the distribution of pollutant levels, by economists to represent the distribution of returns on investments, and by actuaries to represent the distribution of insurance claims.

Finding probabilities from a lognormal distribution is "as easy as falling off a log"! If X is lognormally distributed with parameters μ and σ, then $Y = ln(X)$ is normally distributed and has mean μ and variance σ^2. Thus, the simplest way to work with a lognormal random variable X is to work in terms of $Y = ln(X)$. It is easy to obtain probabilities for Y using @RISK. The expected value and variance of X are given by the following formulas:

$$E(X) = e^{\mu+0.5\sigma^2} \text{ and } Var(X) = (e^{2\mu})(e^{\sigma^2} - 1)(e^{\sigma^2}).$$

For example, if X is lognormally distributed with parameters $\mu = 0.3$ and $\sigma = 0.2$, then Y is normal with mean 0.3 and standard deviation 0.2. Finding probabilities just means taking logs:

$$P_L(X \geq 1.4 | \mu = 0.3, \sigma = 0.2) = P_N(Y \geq ln(1.4) | \mu = 0.3, \sigma = 0.2)$$
$$= P_N(Y \geq 0.336 | \mu = 0.3, \sigma = 0.2)$$
$$= P_N(Z \geq 0.18)$$
$$= 0.4286$$

The mean and expected value of X are

$$E(X) = e^{0.3+0.5(0.2)^2} = 1.38$$

$$Var(X) = (e^{2(0.3)})(e^{(0.2)^2} - 1)(e^{(0.2)^2}) = 0.077$$

After all that, here is a problem to work. After a hurricane, claims for property damage pour into the insurance offices. Suppose that an insurance actuary models noncommercial property damage claims (X, in dollars) as being lognormally distributed with parameters $\mu = 10$ and $\sigma = 0.3$. Claims on different properties are assumed to be independent.

a. Find the mean and standard deviation of these claims.
b. Find the probability that a claim will be greater than $50,000.
c. The company anticipates 200 claims. If the state insurance commission requires the company to have enough cash on hand to be able to satisfy all claims with probability 0.95, how much money

should be in the company's reserve? [*Hint:* The total claims can be represented by the variable $Q = \sum_{1}^{200} x_i$. Q is approximately normally distributed with mean equal to $200E(X)$ and variance $200Var(X)$.]

CASE STUDIES

OVERBOOKING

Most airlines practice *overbooking*. That is, they are willing to make more reservations than they have seats on an airplane. Why would they do this? The basic reason is simple; on any given flight a few passengers are likely to be "no-shows." If the airline overbooks slightly, it still may be able to fill the airplane. Of course, this policy has its risks. If more passengers arrive to claim their reservations than there are seats available, the airline must "bump" some of its passengers. Often this is done by asking for volunteers. If a passenger with a reserved seat is willing to give up his or her seat, the airline typically will provide incentives of some sort. The fundamental trade-off is whether the additional expected revenue gained by flying an airplane that is nearer to capacity on average is worth the additional expected cost of the incentives. To study the overbooking policy, let us look at a hypothetical situation. Mockingbird Airlines has a small commuter airplane that seats 16 passengers. The airline uses this jet on a route for which it charges $225 for a one-way fare. Every flight has a fixed cost of $900 (for pilot's salary, fuel, airport fees, and so on). Each passenger costs Mockingbird an additional $100. Finally, the no-show rate is 4%. That is, on average approximately 4% of those passengers holding confirmed reservations do not show up. If Mockingbird must bump a passenger, the passenger receives a refund on his or her ticket ($225) plus a $100 voucher toward another ticket.

How many reservations should Mockingbird sell on this airplane? The strategy will be to calculate the expected profit for a given number of reservations. For example, suppose that the Mockingbird manager decides to sell 18 reservations. The revenue is $225 times the number of reservations:

$$R = \$225(18)$$
$$= \$4050$$

The cost consists of two components. The first is the cost of flying the plane and hauling the passengers who arrive (but not more than the airplane's capacity of 16):

$$C_1 = \$900 + \$100 \times Min(Arrivals, 16)$$

The second component is the cost of refunds and free tickets that must be issued if 17 or 18 passengers arrive:

$$C_2 = (\$225 + \$100) \times Max(0, Arrivals - 16)$$

In this expression for C_2, the $225 represents the refund for the purchased ticket, and the $100 represents the cost of the free ticket. The Max ( ) expression calculates the number of excess passengers who show up (zero if the number of arrivals is 16 or less.

Questions

1. Find the probability that more than 16 passengers will arrive if Mockingbird sells 17 reservations (Res = 17). Do the same for 18 and 19.

2. Find:

   $E(R|Res = 16)$
   $E(C_1|Res = 16)$
   $E(C_2|Res = 16)$

   Finally, calculate

   $E(Profit|Res = 16) = E(R|Res = 16)$
   $\quad - E(C_1|Res = 16) - E(C_2|Res = 16)$

3. Repeat Question 2 for 17, 18, and 19 reservations. What is your conclusion? Should Mockingbird overbook? By how much?

EARTHQUAKE PREDICTION

Because of the potential damage and destruction that earthquakes can cause, geologists and geophysicists have put considerable effort into understanding when and where earthquakes occur. The ultimate aim is the accurate prediction of earthquakes on the basis of movements in the earth's crust, although this goal appears to be some way off. In the meantime, it is possible to examine past data and model earthquakes probabilistically.

Fortunately, considerable data exist on the basis of which to model earthquakes as a probabilistic phenomenon. Gere and Shah (1984) provide the information shown in Table 9.2. Richter magnitude refers to the severity of the earthquake. For example, if an earthquake is in the 8.0–8.9 category, by definition the ground would shake strongly for 30 to 90 seconds over an area with a diameter of 160 to 320 kilometers. Earthquakes of magnitude less than 4.0 are not dangerous and, for the most part, are not noticed by laypeople.

An earthquake of magnitude 8.0 or greater could cause substantial damage and a great many deaths if it were to occur in a highly populated part of the world. In fact, the San Francisco earthquake of April 6, 1906, was calculated later as measuring 8.3 on the Richter scale. The resulting fire burned much of the city, and some 700 people died. California is particularly susceptible to earthquakes because the state straddles two portions of the earth's crust that are slipping past each other, primarily along the San Andreas Fault. For this reason, we will consider the probability of a severe earthquake happening again in California in the near future.

Questions

1. We can model the occurrence of earthquakes using a Poisson distribution. Strictly speaking, the independence requirement for the Poisson is not met for two reasons. First, the geologic processes at work in California suggest that the probability of a large earthquake increases as time elapses following an earlier large quake. Second, large earthquakes often are followed by aftershocks. Our model will ignore these issues and hence can be viewed only as a first-cut approximation at constructing a probabilistic model for earthquakes.

The data from Gere and Shah indicate that, on average, 2,493 earthquakes with magnitude 4.0 or greater will occur in California over a 100-year period. Thus, we might consider using a Poisson distribution with $m = 24.93$ to represent the probability distribution for the number of earthquakes (all magnitudes greater than 4.0) that will hit California during the next year. Use this distribution to find the following probabilities:

$P_P(X \le 10 \text{ in Next Year} | m = 24.93 \text{ Earthquakes per Year})$

$P_P(X \le 7 \text{ in Six Months} | m = 24.93 \text{ Earthquakes per Year})$

$P_P(X > 3 \text{ in Next Month} | m = 24.93 \text{ Earthquakes per Year})$

2. We also can model the probability distribution for the magnitude of an earthquake. For example, the data suggest that the probability of an earthquake in California of magnitude 8.0 or greater is 1/2493, or approximately 0.0004. If we use an exponential distribution to model the distribution of magnitudes, assuming that 4.0 is the least possible, then we might use the following model. Let M denote the magnitude, and let $M' = M - 4$. Then, using the exponential formula, we have $P(M \ge 8) = P(M' \ge 4) = e^{-4m} = 0.0004$. Now we can solve for m:

TABLE **9.2**
Earthquake frequency data for California.

Richter Magnitude	Average Number of Earthquakes per 100 Years in California
8.0–8.9	1
7.0–7.9	12
6.0–6.9	80
5.0–5.9	400
4.0–4.9	2000

$$e^{-4m} = 0.0004$$

$$ln(e^{-4m}) = ln(0.0004)$$

$$-4m = -7.824$$

$$m = 1.96$$

Thus, the density function for M is given by

$$f(M) = 1.96e^{-1.96(M-4)}$$

Plot this density function.

We now can find the probability that any given earthquake will have a magnitude within a specified range on the Richter scale. For example, use this model to find

$$P_E(M \leq 6.0|m = 1.96)$$

$$P_E(5.0 \leq M \leq 7.5|m = 1.96)$$

$$P_E(M \leq 6.4|m = 1.96)$$

You may find it instructive to use this distribution to calculate the probability that an earthquake's magnitude falls within the five ranges of magnitude shown in Table 9.2. Here is a sensitivity-analysis issue: How might you find other reasonable values for m? What about a range of possible values for m?

3. We now have all of the pieces in the puzzle to find the probability of at least one severe (8.0 magnitude or more) earthquake occurring in California in the near future, say, within the next six months. Our approach will be to find the probability of the complement

$$P(X_{8+} \geq 1) = 1 - P(X_{8+} = 0)$$

where X_{8+} is used to denote the number of earthquakes having magnitude 8.0 or greater. Now expand $P(X_{8+} = 0)$ using total probability:

$$P(X_{8+} \geq 1) = 1 - P(X_{8+} = 0|X = 0)$$

$$+ P(X_{8+} = 0|X = 1)P(X = 1)$$

$$+ P(X_{8+} = 0|X = 2)P(X = 2)$$

$$+ \dots + P(X_{8+} = 0|X = k)P(X = k)$$

$$= \sum_{k=0}^{\infty} P(X_{8+} = 0|X = k)P(X = k)$$

The probabilities $P(X = k)$ are just the Poisson probabilities from Question 1:

$$P(X = k) = P_P(X = k|m = 12.5)$$

where $m = 12.5$ because we are interested in a 6-month period. The probability of no earthquakes of magnitude 8.0 out of the k that occur is easy to find. If $k = 0$, then $P(X_{8+} = 0|X = 0) = 1$. If $k = 1$ then

$$P(X_{8+} = 0|X = 1) = P_E(M < 8.0|m = 1.96)$$

$$= 1 - e^{-1.96(8-4)}$$

$$= 0.9996$$

Likewise, if $k = 2$ then

$$P(X_{8+} = 0|X = 2) = (0.9996)2 = 0.9992$$

because this is just the probability of two independent earthquakes each having magnitude less than 8.0. Generalizing,

$$P(X_{8+} = 0|X = K) = (0.9996)^k$$

Now we can substitute these probabilities into the formula:

$$P(X_{8+} \geq 0) = 1 - P(X_{8+} = 0)$$

$$= 1 - \sum_{k=0}^{\infty} P(X_{8+} = 0|X = k)P(X = k)$$

$$= 1 - \sum_{k=0}^{\infty} (0.9996)^K P_P(X = k|m = 12.5)$$

To calculate this, you must calculate with k until the Poisson probability is so small that the remaining probabilities do not matter. It turns out that the probability of at least one earthquake of magnitude 8.0 or more within six months is approximately 0.005.

Now that you have seen how to do this, try calculating the probability of at least one earthquake of magnitude 8.0 or more (i) within the next year and (ii) within the next five years. For these, you may want to use a computer program to calculate the Poisson probabilities. How does the probability of at least one severe earthquake vary as you use the different reasonable values for m from your exponential model in Question 2? [*Hint:* Calculating the Poisson probabilities may be

TABLE **9.3**
Probabilities for major earthquakes in California from two different probability models.

Time	USGS Probability	Poisson Model Probability
Next 5 years	0.27	0.29
Next 10 years	0.49	0.50
Next 20 years	0.71	0.75
Next 30 years	0.90	0.87

Source for USGS probabilities: U.S. Geological Survey (1988) "Probabilities of Large Earthquakes Occurring in California on the San Andreas Fault," by the Working Group on California Earthquake Probabilities. USGS Open-File Report No. 88-398, Menlo Park, CA.

difficult, even with Excel, because of the large exponential and factorial terms. An easy way to calculate these probabilities is to use the recursive equation

$$P_P(X = k + 1 | m) = \frac{m}{k+1} P_P(X = k | m)$$

[Using this equation avoids having to calculate large factorial and exponential terms.]

4. Using the probability model previously described, it turns out that the probability of at least one earthquake of magnitude 8.0 or more within the next 20 years in California is approximately 0.2 (or higher, depending on the value used for m in the exponential distribution for the magnitude, M). That is a 1-in-5 chance. Now imagine that you are a policy maker in California's state government charged with making recommendations regarding earthquake preparedness. How would this analysis affect your recommendations? What kinds of issues do you think should be considered? What about the need for more research regarding precise earthquake prediction at a specific location? What about regulations regarding building design and construction? What other issues are important?

The probabilistic model that we have developed using the information from Gere and Shah is based on a very simplistic model and does not account for geologic processes. Geologists do, however, use probability models in some cases as a basis for earthquake predictions. For example, as mentioned at the beginning of Chapter 8, a recent U.S. Geological Survey report concluded that the probability of an earthquake of 7.5–8.0 magnitude along the southern portion of the San Andreas Fault within the next 30 years is approximately 60%. The authors of the report actually constructed separate probability models for the occurrence of large quakes in different segments of major faults using data from the individual segments. Rather than a Poisson model, they used a lognormal distribution to model the uncertainty about the time between large earthquakes. Although their approach permits them to make probability statements regarding specific areas, their results can be aggregated to give probabilities for at least one major earthquake in the San Francisco Bay Area, along the southern San Andreas Fault in Southern California, or along the San Jacinto Fault. Table 9.3 compares their probabilities, which were developed for "large" earthquakes with expected magnitudes of 6.5–8.0, with our Poisson model probabilities of at least one earthquake having a magnitude of 7.0 or greater. It is comforting to know that our model, even with its imperfections, provides probabilities that are not radically different from the geologists' estimates.

MUNICIPAL SOLID WASTE

Linda Butner considered her task. As the risk analysis expert on the city's Incineration Task Force (ITF), she was charged with reporting back to the ITF and to the city regarding the risks posed by constructing an incinerator for disposal of the city's municipal solid waste (MSW).

It was not a question of whether such an incinerator would be constructed. The city landfill site would be full within three years, and no alternative sites were available at a reasonable cost.

In particular, the state Department of Environmental Quality (DEQ) required information regarding levels of pollutants the incinerator was expected to produce. DEQ was concerned about organic compounds, metals, and acid gases. It was assumed that the plant would incorporate appropriate technology and that good combustion practices would be followed. Residual emissions were expected, however, and the officials were interested in obtaining close estimates of these. Linda's task was to provide an analysis of anticipated emissions of dioxins and furans (organic compounds), particulate matter (PM, representing metals), and sulfur dioxide (SO_2, representing the acid gases). She figured that a thorough analysis of these substances would enable her to answer questions about others.

The current specifications called for a plant capable of burning approximately 250 tons of waste per day. This placed it at the borderline between small- and medium-sized plants according to the Environmental Protection Agency's (EPA) guidelines. In part, this size was chosen because the EPA had proposed slightly different permission levels for these two plant sizes, and the city would be able to choose the plant size that was most advantageous. A smaller (less than 250 tons/day) plant would be expected to have an electrostatic precipitator for reducing particulate matter but would not have a specified SO_2 emission level. A larger plant would have a fabric filter instead of an electrostatic precipitator and would also use dry sorbent injection—the injection of chemicals into the flue—to control the SO_2 level.

A summary of the EPA's proposed emission levels is shown in Table 9.4.

Standard practice in environmental risk analysis called for assessment and analysis of "worst case" scenarios. But to Linda's way of thinking, this kind of approach did not adequately portray the uncertainty that might exist. Incineration of municipal solid waste (MSW) was particularly delicate in this regard, because the levels of various pollutants could vary dramatically with the content of the waste being burned. Moreover, different burning conditions within the incineration chamber (more or less oxygen, presence of other gasses, different temperatures, and so on) could radically affect the emissions. To capture the variety of possible emission levels for the pollutants, Linda decided to represent the uncertainty about a pollutant-emission level with a probability distribution.

The lognormal distribution makes sense as a distribution for pollutant-emission levels. (See Problem 9.37 for an introduction to the lognormal.) After consulting the available data for the content of pollutants in MSW and the pollutant-emission levels for other incinerators, Linda constructed a table (Table 9.5) to show the parameters for the lognormal distributions for the three pollutants in question. Figure 9.26 illustrates the lognormal distribution for the SO_2 emissions.

As Linda looked at this information, she realized that she could make certain basic calculations. For example, it would be relatively straightforward to calculate the probability that the plant's emissions

TABLE **9.4**
Proposed pollutant emission levels.

Pollutant	Plant Capacity (Tons of Waste per Day)	
	Small (Less than 250)	Medium (250 or More)
Dioxins/furans (ng/Nm^3)	500	125
PM (mg/dscm)	69	69
SO_2 (ppmdv)	—	30

© Cengage Learning

TABLE **9.5**
Lognormal distribution parameters μ and σ for pollutants.

Pollutant	μ	σ
Dioxins/furans	3.13	1.20
PM	3.43	0.44
SO_2	3.20	0.39

© Cengage Learning

FIGURE **9.26**
Lognormal density
function for SO$_2$
emissions from
incineration plant.

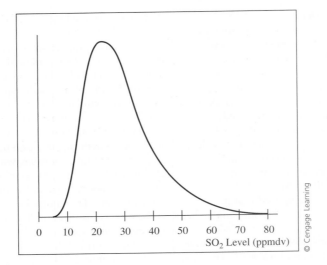

SO$_2$ Level (ppmdv)

© Cengage Learning

would exceed the proposed levels in Table 9.4. Having these figures in hand, she felt she would be able to make a useful presentation to the task force.

Questions

1. The plant will be required to meet established emission levels for dioxins/furans and PM on an annual basis. Find the probabilities for exceeding the small-plant levels specified in Table 9.4 for these two pollutants. Repeat the calculations for the medium-plant emission levels.

2. If the plant is subject to SO$_2$ certification, its emissions of this pollutant will be monitored on a continual basis and the average daily emission level must remain below the specified level in Table 9.4. The numbers in Table 9.5, however, refer to the probability distribution of a single observation. That is, we could use the specified lognormal distribution to find the probability that a single reading of the SO$_2$ level exceeds the specified level. Finding the probability that an average daily emission exceeds the specified level, though, requires more analysis.

   Let us assume that the average emission level will be calculated by taking n observations and then calculating the *geometric mean*. To do

this, we multiply the n observations together and then take the nth root of the product. In symbols, let G denote the geometric mean:

$$G = \left(\prod_{i=1}^{n} X_i \right)^{\frac{1}{n}}$$

It turns out that if each X_i is drawn independently from a distribution that is lognormal with parameters μ and σ, then G has a lognormal distribution with parameters μ and $\sigma/\sqrt{n}$,. In our case we will take the 24th root of a product of 24 hourly observations of emission levels. Find the probability that the geometric mean of the 24 hourly emission observations exceeds the SO$_2$ limit specified in Table 9.4. Compare this with the probability that a single observation will exceed the same limit.

3. Discuss the issues that the city should consider in deciding whether to build a small- or medium-sized plant.

Sources: J. Marcus and R. Mills (1988) "Emissions from Mass Burn Resource Recovery Facilities," *Risk Analysis*, No. 8, 315–327; and (1989) "Emission Guidelines: Municipal Waste Combustors," *Federal Register*, 54 (243), 52209.

REFERENCES

In this chapter we have only scratched the surface of theoretical probability distributions, although we have discussed most of the truly useful probability models.

Theoretical distributions are widely used in operations research and in the construction of formal models of dynamic and uncertain systems. For additional study as well as many illustrative examples, consult the texts by DeGroot (1970); Feller (1968); Olkin, Gleser, and Derman (1980); or Winkler (1972). Johnson and Kotz (1969, 1970a, 1970b, and 1972) have compiled encyclopedic information on a great variety of probability distributions.

DeGroot, M. (1970) *Optimal Statistical Decisions.* New York: McGraw-Hill.

Feller, W. (1968) *An Introduction to Probability Theory and Its Applications, Vol. 1,* 3rd ed. New York: Wiley.

Johnson, N. L., and S. Kotz (1969) *Distributions in Statistics: Discrete Distributions.* New York: Houghton Mifflin.

Johnson, N. L., and S. Kotz (1970a) *Distributions in Statistics: Continuous Univariate Distributions I.* Boston: Houghton Mifflin.

Johnson, N. L., and S. Kotz (1970b) *Distributions in Statistics: Continuous Univariate Distributions II.* Boston: Houghton Mifflin.

Johnson, N. L., and S. Kotz (1972) *Distributions in Statistics: Continuous Multivariate Distributions.* New York: Wiley.

Olkin, I., L. J. Gleser, and C. Derman (1980) *Probability Models and Applications.* New York: Macmillan.

Winkler, R. L. (1972) *Introduction to Bayesian Inference and Decision.* New York: Holt.

EPILOGUE

The initial version of the case study on earthquake prediction was written in early October 1989, just two weeks before the Loma Prieta earthquake of magnitude 7.1 occurred near Santa Cruz, California, on the San Andreas Fault. Strong ground shaking lasted for approximately 15 seconds. The results were 67 deaths, collapsed buildings around the Bay Area, damage to the Bay Bridge between San Francisco and Oakland, and the destruction of a one-mile stretch of freeway in Oakland. This was a small earthquake, however, relative to the 8.3 magnitude quake in 1906. The "big one" is still to come and may cause even more damage.

CHAPTER 10

Using Data

The last two chapters described methods for constructing probability distributions, which, of course, is what we use to model uncertainties in our decision problems. Chapter 8 used subjective assessments for the source of the probabilities, and Chapter 9 introduced theoretical distributions. We now discuss a variety of ways to construct probability distributions using data. First, we show how data can be used either to select a theoretical distribution or to build an *empirical distribution* (a distribution based only on observations). Second, we use data to model relationships, and then use these relationships to build more precise distributions. For example, data can help determine the relationship between a company's profit and its sales force size, thereby helping to predict future profits more precisely. Although we touch upon many topics in Chapter 10, the focus is always on building useful probability models for the uncertainties in our decision problem.

USING DATA TO CONSTRUCT PROBABILITY DISTRIBUTIONS

In this section, we show how historical data can be used in two different ways to construct probability distributions. Either we can directly construct a distribution based solely on the data or we can use the data to select a theoretical distribution that fits the data. Both of these methods are conceptually straightforward, but can be computationally intensive. Luckily for us, @RISK will do all the computations. The @RISK instructions appear at the end of this section rather than at the end of the chapter.

Data for decision models come in essentially two forms: *sample data*, which are observations of the uncertain quantity, or subjectively assessed data. Sample data are usually of the form of n observations and denoted $x_1, x_2, ..., x_n$, where each x_i is a known number. For example, if we were interested in a particular stock's performance, we might gather a sample of the stock's monthly returns: 1.2%, 0.8%, ..., −0.3%. In contrast, subjectively assessed probabilities might be in the form of n pairs of values and denoted $(x_1, p_1), (x_2, p_2), ..., (x_n, p_n)$, where p_i is the cumulative probability associated with x_i, that is $P(X \le x_i) = p_i$, $i = 1, 2, ..., n$. For example, using an analyst's reports on the stock, we might assess future performance: $(-0.9\%, 0.25)$, $(1.0\%, 0.75)$, and $(1.5\%, 1.0)$. Here, the probability that the monthly return is less than or equal to a loss of 0.9% equals 0.25. Both types of data (sample or assessed) can be used to either directly construct a probability distribution or to find the best fitting theoretical distribution.

When using data to construct distributions, we often need to know if the distribution we wish to model is discrete or continuous. Typically, this is an easy determination, but not always. It turns out that if there are many categories for the discrete distribution, it may actually be easier to model it as a continuous distribution. For example, when working with currency variables (Price, Cost, etc.), it is much easier to model the discrete dollar and cents values as a continuous distribution because the number of categories is large. Even in cases when there are as few as a dozen or so categories, a continuous approximation to the discrete variable might simplify the decision model and expected-value calculations. A common example is using the normal distribution to approximate the binomial distribution. While it may seem counterintuitive that continuous distributions can be easier to work with than discrete distributions, we show in this chapter that the data requirements are less stringent for continuous distributions and the fitting procedures can be more robust.

Constructing a discrete distribution based on sample data is rather simple, and most likely you have done something like this in the past, at least informally. Suppose, for example, that you are interested in planning a picnic at the Portland Zoo on an as-yet undetermined day during February. Obviously, the weather is a concern in this case, and you want to assess the probability of rain. If you were to ask the National Weather Service for advice in this regard, forecasters would report that the probability of rain in Portland, Oregon on any given day in February is approximately 0.47. They base this estimate on analysis of weather during past years; on 47% of the days in February over the past several years, rain has fallen in Portland. Thus, your discrete distribution is 47% chance of Rain and 53% chance of No Rain.

Constructing a discrete distribution amounts to counting the number of occurrences of each category, and the probabilities are the relative frequencies. Imagine that you are in charge of a manufacturing plant, and to develop a maintenance policy for your machines, you examine the frequency of machine failures. You found that there were no machine failures for 217 of the past 260 days. For 32 of the past 260 days, exactly one of the machines in the plant had failed, and for 11 of the past 260 days, exactly two machines had failed. There were no days on which three or more machines failed. The discrete distribution for the number of machine failures is shown in Table 10.1 and Figure 10.1. The decision-tree representation of this uncertainty is a chance node with three branches like that in Figure 10.2.

Constructing a discrete distribution requires that we assign probabilities to the categories, and we can either use sample or subjectively assessed data.

TABLE **10.1**
Probabilities
of discrete
distributions are
estimated as
the relative
frequencies.

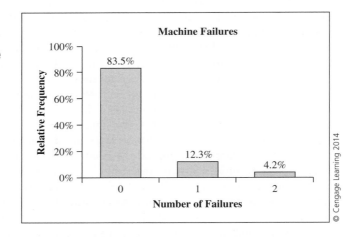

Event: Number of Machine Failures	Count: Number of Days	Probability: Relative Frequency
Zero Failures	217	217/260 = 83.5%
One Failure	32	32/260 = 12.3%
Two Failures	11	11/260 = 4.2%

© Cengage Learning 2014

FIGURE **10.1**
Relative frequency
for machine failure
data.

Machine Failures

© Cengage Learning 2014

FIGURE **10.2**
The decision-tree
representation
of uncertainty
regarding
machine failures.

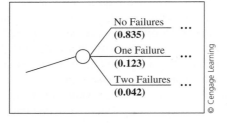

© Cengage Learning

If the data are sample values, the discrete probabilities are the relative frequencies. If the data are subjective assessments, the discrete probabilities are simply the assessments. As discussed in Chapter 8, we can either directly assess the discrete probabilities or use lotteries to estimate the probabilities. Our discussion of using data to estimate discrete probabilities is brief precisely because the task is simply a matter of counting.

One concern is that we must have enough data to make reliable estimates. When constructing discrete distributions using sample data, we suggest having at least five observations for each category. If, for example, there was one day in the past 260 when four machines failed, this one observation, while accurate, is not sufficient to create a completely new category. Rather, we would place this day into the Two Failure category and now have 12 days of the past 260 with two or more machine failures.

Whenever we work with data of any kind, there are several important considerations or judgments. These judgments can be straightforward (Is the sample sufficiently large?) or more nuanced (Are the data representative of the uncertainty?). We cannot cover all such considerations in this text, but we will discuss some of the more important judgments. Many, if not all, data considerations can be dealt with by applying common sense. Simply approaching the data set knowing that there are most likely errors and misrepresentations compels us to search out and fix these errors. Likewise, casting a critical eye on how well the data match or fit our circumstances can help ferret out potential problems.

Errors can enter a data set in a myriad of ways, from data collection blunders to data entry mistakes to data corruption. Sometimes these errors are easily found, such as an entry of 10 for a 0/1-variable or a house price of $20. The best way to fix these errors is to refer back to the original survey and determine if a simple transcription error occurred. Other times, the errors in the data set are more subtle, and can be more difficult to identify and fix. We recommend spending a few minutes searching through the data using summary statistics and graphs to find potential errors. If you find a potential error, but no clear solution presents itself, you may want to delete the entry to preserve the integrity of the data.

In addition to correcting any data errors, the data itself may not accurately represent the uncertainty being modeled. In the previous example, what if the plant had been closed for two weeks for maintenance? For those two weeks, clearly no machines failed. We should then remove those two weeks from the data (reducing the count from 260 to 246 days) for a more accurate representation of the distribution of machine failures. What if you had recently replaced the machine that was responsible for over half of the machine failures recorded in your sample? Then, based on the data as is, the preceding probability estimates would be too high, resulting in too much scheduled maintenance. These two examples point out that the better you understand the data, the better your judgments will be on how well the data represents the uncertainty. Finding out how the data were collected, who collected it, where, when, and why it was collected all help flesh out the data and how it can be used to represent the uncertainty.

Because we need to make a series of judgments about the accuracy of the data, we see that the line between objective data and subjective assessments can be rather blurry. Clearly, we should not use a data set without checking its accuracy and determining if it represents the uncertainty. But once we start making judgments about the data, we are incorporating our beliefs into the data set. For example, suppose it is 2007 and you are viewing data on single-family house prices. Your data show that the mean annual growth in prices over the previous 5 years is 15% annually. As an investment opportunity, this looks promising. If however, you had a strong belief that this growth has led to a bubble (unsustainable growth) and that prices are likely to drop, perhaps precipitously, in the near future, you would not want to use 15% as the estimated growth in the future. Your actual estimate will be an amalgamation of the data and your beliefs.

Data by its very nature is historical as it was collected in the past. If you believe that the future will resemble the past, there is no temptation to make any modifications to the estimates. If, however, the data or sections of the data do not reflect future conditions, modifications may be appropriate. If you are not satisfied with the applicability of the data, you may need to model your uncertainty using subjective assessment methods. We are not suggesting that you modify the dataset itself according to your beliefs. Data are facts, and you should not change the facts to fit your beliefs. Rather, clean the data of any errors, create your estimates, and then construct your probability distributions using subjective judgments as needed.

Empirical CDFs

Having seen how to construct a discrete distribution based on data, we now turn our attention to continuous distributions. It turns out that constructing a continuous distribution directly from data is almost as easy as counting. Say we have a sample of 10 observations.[1] To construct the empirical distribution based on the sample, we first sort the sample from lowest to highest value, and then assign equal probabilities to each value. That is it; we just constructed the empirical distribution. Table 10.2 shows the ten sample values sorted from lowest to highest and their corresponding probabilities, while Figure 10.3 shows the empirical CDF of these ten observations.

TABLE **10.2**
Constructing an empirical distribution based on 10 observations.

Observation	Assigned Probability	Cumulative Probability
0.6	1/10	1/10
2.0	1/10	2/10
3.5	1/10	3/10
4.0	1/10	4/10
5.7	1/10	5/10
7.1	1/10	6/10
10.6	1/10	7/10
14.1	1/10	8/10
19.2	1/10	9/10
23.7	1/10	1.00

© Cengage Learning 2014

[1] Note that a sample size of 10 could be too small for a discrete distribution, but it is not too small for a continuous distribution. Of course, we would prefer more data to less, but as this example shows, it is not unreasonable to have only 10 observations.

FIGURE **10.3**
An empirical
distribution
based on 10
observations.

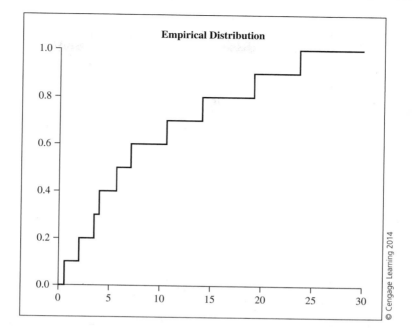

Empirical Distribution

The most striking feature of the empirical CDF is its staircase appearance. Each step up occurs at the sampled or observed value (0.6, 2.0, ..., 23.7) and the height of each step is 1/10. The steps are not equally spaced because the data are not equally spaced. We have seen this staircase type of graph before when viewing risk profiles in Chapter 4. An astute reader will realize that the empirical distribution is simply a discrete distribution with each sampled value given equal probability. Thus, the risk profiles from Chapter 4 along with empirical distributions are discrete distributions, which always have staircase-shaped CDFs.

How well does the empirical distribution approximate the underlying continuous distribution? Given the simplicity of the empirical distribution, it may come as a surprise that the empirical distribution is an excellent approximation. This is easy to test and show. We start by assuming we know the true underlying distribution. We assume this so that we can measure how close our approximation is to the true values. For ease, we choose an exponential distribution with parameter $\beta = 10$. Second, we draw a sample[2] of n observations $x_1, x_2, ..., x_n$ from this distribution and construct the empirical distribution based only on the sample. Next, we compare the empirical to the exponential distribution from which the sample came. Figure 10.4 shows how well the empirical and underlying distributions match. The over/

---

[2] We explain in the next chapter how one can draw a sample from a known distribution.

FIGURE **10.4**
An empirical
distribution based
on 10 observations
is compared to
its underlying
distribution,
an exponential
with $\beta = 10$.

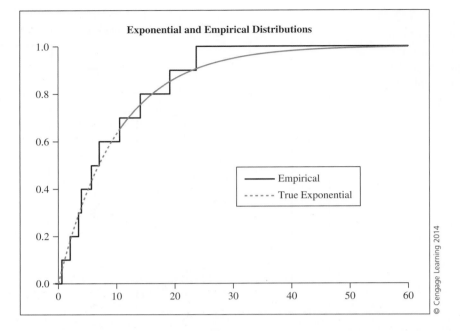

underestimating that we saw with the Extended Pearson-Tukey and Extended Swanson-Megill distributions is also evident here. Increasing the sample size produces an even better approximation as shown in Figure 10.5, where 30 observations were used.

FIGURE **10.5**
An empirical
distribution
based on 30
observations is
compared to its
underlying
distribution,
an exponential
with $\beta = 10$.

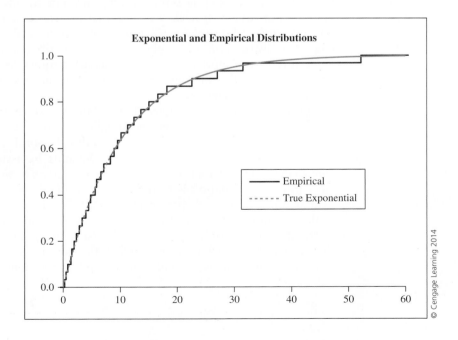

Clearly, the empirical distribution based on 30 values is the better approximation, but how much better? How do we measure the quality or closeness of the approximation? We could measure how far apart the two distributions are by measuring the vertical distance between the distributions, but the distance is not constant and changes depending where the measurement is taken. Because the distance varies, we need to settle on a well-defined way to measure the distance between two distributions. One possibility is to define the distance between two distributions to be the maximum vertical distance between the two distributions. This distance is called the *Kolmogorov-Smirnov distance*. Often abbreviated *K-S* distance, this measure reports the greatest vertical distance between the two CDFs. For both preceding samples, the empirical distribution was the furthest away from the true distribution with a *K-S* distance of 0.095 in Figure 10.4 and a *K-S* distance of 0.033 in Figure 10.5. Thus, as measured by the *K-S* distance, the fit is almost three times better with 30 observations than with 10. We will encounter the *K-S* distance again in the next section when choosing the theoretical distribution that best fits the data.

Another way to measure the quality of the approximation is to compare the mean and standard deviation of the fitted distribution to the underlying distribution. The closer the fitted values are to the true values, the better the approximation. The mean and standard deviation of the empirical distribution are called the sample mean and sample standard deviation. The sample mean is denoted $\bar{x}$ and is the arithmetic average:

$$\bar{x} = \frac{1}{n}(x_1 + x_2 + \cdots + x_n)$$

The sample standard deviation is denoted s and is the square root of the average of the squared deviations:

$$s = \sqrt{\frac{(x_1 - \bar{x})^2 + (x_2 - \bar{x})^2 + \cdots + (x_n - \bar{x})^2}{n - 1}}$$

Table 10.3 compares the sample values to the true values, and again we see that having more data produces a better fit.

TABLE **10.3**
Determining the quality of an approximation by comparing means and standard deviations.

Comparing True Mean to Sample Means			
	True	10 Observations	30 Observations
Mean	10	9.05	10.37
Comparing True Standard Deviation to Sample Standard Deviations			
Standard Deviation	10	7.73	11.20

The following example illustrates using data to construct discrete and continuous distributions, and is loosely based on an actual business.

Solar Trash Compactors	Jim Swanson was very pleased to see his start-up company doing well. While in graduate school, he had invented and patented solar-powered trash compactors. Designed for high-use areas such as parks, campuses, and resorts, his trash compactors held up to five times the amount of trash of similar sized trashcans. Jim's design used solar power to monitor the trash level, compact it when it reached a specified level, and even sent out a radio signal when ready for emptying. Although his units cost more than a simple trashcan, they typically paid for themselves within the first 2 to 3 years of operation due to lower maintenance costs. In addition, being solar powered, the compactors were more desirable for green-minded institutions such as cities and universities.

Sources: www.bigbellysolar.com http://pwmag.com/industry-news.asp?sectionID=760&articleID=1221666 www.manta.com/c/mmgtvnt/big-belly-solar-inc

As an entrepreneur, Jim faced many uncertainties from financing to distribution, from costs of operations to sales levels, and so on. For example, Jim experienced uncertainty in the demand for his different products, which made it hard to control inventory costs. He sold three sizes of solar trash compactors: Baby Bertha (10 gallons); Bertha (30 gallons), and Big Bertha (50 gallons). Looking over his sales records for the past year, Jim had sold 300 Baby Berthas, 750 Berthas, and 450 Big Berthas. Although Jim expected to sell more compactors in the upcoming year, for a typical sale he could expect 20% (=300/1,500) of his sales to be Baby Berthas; 50% (=750/1,500) to be Berthas, and 30% (=450/1,500) to be Big Berthas.

Armed with this discrete product-mix distribution, Jim could better control inventory costs. However, exploring the data in more depth suggested some modifications. For example, Jim believed that larger cities and universities tended to buy more of the larger sizes of compactors. Segmenting the data into organizations with 300 or less employees and organizations with more than 300 employees, Jim discovered that the discrete distributions describing product mix were quite different for the two segments. He found that over the past year the smaller organizations had purchased 225 Baby Berthas, 300 Berthas, and 200 Big Berthas; whereas the larger organizations had purchased 75 Baby Berthas, 450 Berthas, and 550 Big Berthas. Figure 10.6 shows the refined distributions. Thus, knowing the product-mix distribution and that it changed based on the size of the client could help Jim control inventory even better, improve his sales pitch, and even predict future sales volume.

A continuous uncertainty that Jim faced was annual operating costs. On the one hand, the solar trash compactors needed to be emptied less often than conventional trashcans, thereby reducing their operating costs. On the other hand, the solar trash compactors were much more complicated, requiring regular maintenance and occasional repairs. Jim needed to know the distribution of total operating costs to be able to make comparisons with regular trashcans. The annual operating cost of an ordinary trash receptacle turns out to be surprisingly high. For example, in 2008, Philadelphia spent

FIGURE **10.6**
Relative frequencies of units sold for the three sizes of solar trash compactors.

The top panel shows all organizations, while the lower panel shows smaller organizations (300 or less employees) and larger organizations (over 300 employees).

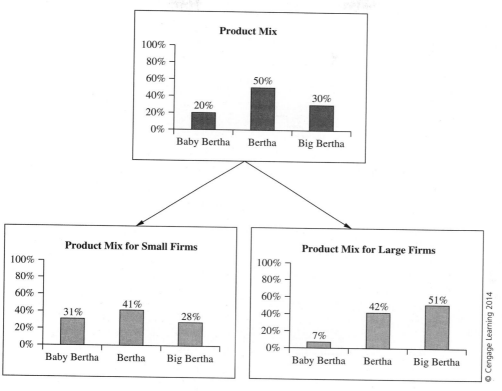

$2.3 million annually servicing 700 regular trash receptacles, which is over $3,200/receptacle.[3] Table 10.4 shows a random sample of 20 annual operating costs for the Big Bertha. From the table, we can see that the minimum observed annual cost is $656.47 and the maximum is $1,355.78. Thus, even though there is considerable uncertainty in the operating cost of any one Big Bertha, each sampled value is less than half the cost of an ordinary trash receptacle.

TABLE **10.4**
Annual operating costs of a random sample of 20 Big Berthas.

$1,166.18	$1,151.96	$1,263.38	$1,069.56
$1,322.22	$973.79	$902.52	$1,203.83
$966.34	$1,042.95	$836.08	$1,016.73
$874.40	$693.54	$945.76	$781.05
$737.74	$1,103.81	$656.47 (min value)	$1,355.78 (max value)

© Cengage Learning 2014

---

[3] Garbage Terminators, *Public Works Magazine*, March 1, 2010.

FIGURE **10.7**
The empirical
distribution of
annual operating
costs based on a
random sample of
20 Big Bertha solar
trash compactors.

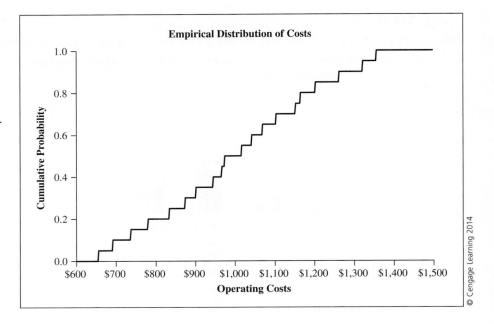

FIGURE **10.8**
Extended Pearson-
Tukey three-point
approximation for
the operating costs
of Big Bertha.

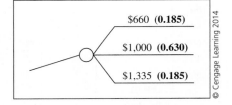

The empirical distribution based on this sample of 20 annual operating costs is given in Figure 10.7. Jim could use the empirical distribution to make probability statements such as this: 90% of the time, the annual operating costs were between $660 and $1,335; or 75% of the time, the annual operating costs were less than $1,160. Jim could also summarize the empirical distribution by stating that the sample mean operating cost is $1,005 per Big Bertha, significantly less than the $3,200. Finally, for inclusion into a decision tree, Jim could approximate the empirical distribution with either the Extended Swanson-Megill or Extended Pearson-Tukey distribution, as shown in Figure 10.8. (Note that there is no uniquely defined fifth percentile as every value between $656.47 and $693.54 is a valid choice.)

USING DATA TO FIT THEORETICAL PROBABILITY MODELS

Instead of constructing a distribution from scratch using only the data, we can look for a theoretical distribution that closely matches the data. If a particular theoretical distribution and the data match, we could choose to model our uncertainty using that particular theoretical distribution. For example, if your data were the arrival times of customers, it would be natural to choose the exponential distribution as it is often used to model arrival times. In this section, we investigate different ways to measure how well the data and a distribution match and how to determine which of several potential distributions provides the best match.

We rely heavily on the program @RISK in this section, as @RISK can run a series of sophisticated algorithms to determine how well each of the distributions in its library matches the data. After we input the data, @RISK generates a report with graphs and statistics describing the match between data and distribution both visually and numerically. @RISK even rank orders the theoretical distributions putting the best matching distribution first in the list, the second best matching second, and so on. Before jumping into the @RISK instructions, we take a moment to understand how theoretical distributions are fitted to data.

Each theoretical distribution has its own parameters, and the values of those parameters determine the exact specification for the distribution. For example, the exponential distribution has only one parameter, which we denote β, and once the value of β is determined, this completely specifies the exponential. Fitting a theoretical distribution to data amounts to finding the values of the parameters such that the theoretical distribution matches the data as closely as possible. Think of the parameters as dials, and as you adjust each dial, the theoretical distribution changes shape. @RISK knows how to adjust the dials to provide the best match possible. For example, when @RISK is fitting a normal distribution to data, there are two parameters—the mean and the standard deviation—to adjust. Researchers have shown that the best fitting normal always occurs when the mean is set equal to the sample mean of the data and the standard deviation is set equal to the sample standard deviation. Thus, @RISK uses the data to determine the parameter values, and with the parameter values set, it creates a report detailing how well each theoretical distribution fits the data.

Typically, we are unsure of which distribution will fit best, and so we let @RISK run the fit on all of its distributions in its library. @RISK systematically works through its store of theoretical distributions, choosing one distribution at a time, fitting that distribution to the data through specification of the parameters, and after fitting the last distribution, will rank order the distributions with the best fitting distribution first in the list and the worst fitting distribution last.

With the fitted distributions rank ordered from best to worst, it would seem natural that we automatically choose the best fitting theoretical distribution to use in our decision model. However, it is not quite that simple. For example, suppose your data were customer arrival times and the exponential distribution did not appear first in the list. We are still likely to choose the exponential because the properties of the exponential match the properties of the uncertainty. It is often important that the properties of the distribution match the properties of the uncertainty. Also, as we show next, the top few fitting distributions are usually very close to one another (as one would expect), and there is little difference in the final results based on which you choose. Thus, it makes sense to choose the distribution with the properties that are the most appropriate for the uncertainty in question.

It is natural to assume that if a theoretical distribution and the uncertainty have the same properties, they should closely match. While for the most part this is true, it does not mean that the particular theoretical distribution will always be the overall best fitting distribution. Why? Because, there are certain distributions that have extra flexibility in shifting their shape to match the data. We saw in Chapter 9 that the beta distribution could assume many different shapes. Because of the beta's flexibility, it often matches the data well. The generalized beta distribution (which @RISK calls the "beta general") has even more flexibility than the beta, as it is not confined to be between zero and one, and thus the generalized beta often appears near the top of the @RISK list of fitted distributions. A simple rule of thumb is that the more parameters a distribution has, the better it can dial in its fit to match the data. The exponential has only one parameter, the beta has two parameters, and the generalized beta has four parameters.

Another reason we do not automatically choose the first, or best-fitting distribution is that there are different ways to measure the fit. For each different method of measuring the fit, we have a different rank ordering of the distributions. For example, the exponential might be the best fit (#1) under one measure, but only be #4 under a second method of measuring fit. Thus, there is not necessarily such a thing as *the* best fitting distribution, because it depends on how the fit is measured.

We discussed the Kolmogorov-Smirnov distance, which is one of the six different ways @RISK measures the fit. Thus, if you choose the *K-S* distance, then @RISK rank orders the fitted distributions by their maximum vertical distance. The distribution listed first is the best fitting, according to the *K-S* distance.

Another measure of fit is the *Anderson-Darling distance* or *A-D* distance. Although a deep dive into the details would take us too far afield, suffice it to say that the *A-D* distance is similar to the *K-S* distance in that it measures the vertical distance between two distributions, but the *A-D* distance adds a penalty when the tails or extremes of the two distributions do not match well. For many applications, modeling the extreme values well is important, and for these situations the *A-D* distance is preferred over the *K-S* distance. For example, in many financial situations (option pricing, valuations, etc.), extreme payoffs occur in the tails and can bankrupt the firm unless properly modeled and hedged. (In fact, this is one of the problems with the mathematical models that the investment banks were using prior to the financial collapse in 2008; the distributions used in the models did not give enough probability to extreme events.)

A third measure of fit determines how well the fractiles of the theoretical distribution match the fractiles of the data and is called the Chi-Squared distance. This measure works by first dividing the data into segments, called bins, and comparing the number of observations to the predicted number of values in each bin. If the number of observations equals the number of predicted values, then the Chi-Square distance is zero. Note that Chi-Square is based not on matching the observed values to the predicted values, but matching the number of observed values in each bin to the number of predicted values in the bin. Thus, the Chi-Square distance depends on the location of the bins, and for this reason different bin choices can lead to different results.

The final measures of fit between two distributions are the Akaike Information Criterion (AIC) and the Bayesian Information Criterion (BIC). Although we will not discuss these measures in detail, the general idea is that they level the playing field by penalizing the fitted distribution for each of its parameters. For example, the exponential distribution only has one parameter, and thus it is less likely to fit a data set as well as a more flexible distribution such as the beta. The extra flexibility provided by an additional parameter is neutralized when using AIC or BIC measures.

USING @RISK TO FIT DISTRIBUTIONS TO DATA

This section provides the instructions for using @RISK to fit distributions to data. We start by showing how to fit theoretical discrete distributions to discrete sample data, then continuous distributions to continuous sample data, and finally continuous distributions to subjectively assessed data. For each data type, we will cheat a little, by which we mean that we start by knowing what distribution created the data. Knowing the answer will allow us to see well @RISK fits the distributions to the data.

We start with a sample of size 20 from a Poisson distribution with $\lambda = 2$. The values are given in Table 10.5. Note that there are not five observations in every category. Thus, if we were to construct this distribution using relative frequencies, we would need to combine categories, such as combining the zero and one categories and calling it "One or Less" because there are only two zeros.

STEP 1 *Open @RISK.*

1.1 Open Excel® and then @RISK, enabling any macros if requested.

1.2 You can access a variety of help features by clicking on the **Help** button. The *Online Manual* is a pdf file of the actual manual, and *@RISK Help* is a searchable database. In addition, you can view examples via *Example Spreadsheets* or video tutorials via the *Getting Started Tutorial*.

1.3 Enter the data in Table 10.5 into D3:D22.

TABLE **10.5**
A random sample of 20 observations from a Poisson distribution with $\lambda = 2$.

1	4	5	2	1	1	3	2	2	0
2	1	0	3	2	2	1	3	1	4

© Cengage Learning 2014

STEP 2 *Fitting Discrete Distributions to a Discrete Sample.*

2.1 Open the *@RISK – Fit Distributions to Data* window by clicking on the **Distribution Fitting** menu button and in the submenu choosing **Fit**.

2.2 Figure 10.9 shows the *@RISK – Fit Distributions to Data* window where we named the data **Poisson Dataset**. We entered the range **D3: D22**, and the *Type* (of data) is **Discrete Sample Data**. Note that sample data must be in a single spreadsheet column.

2.3 Now, we need only click the **Fit** button, and @RISK will fit each of its five discrete distributions to determine which fits the best.

2.4 Figure 10.10 shows the *@RISK – Fit Results* window with the Poisson distribution fitting the data the best and the binomial fitting the second best as shown on the left-hand side under *Fit Ranking*. The two discrete distributions in the center are the fitted Poisson (shaded bars) and the input data (lines). Above the graph, we see that according to the data the probability of being less than 0.15 is 10%, but for the fitted Poisson, the probability is 13.5%. Finally, various statistics are reported to the right of the graph, such as the minimums, maximums, means, standard deviations, and select percentiles for the data (Input) and the Poisson. Although the fit is not exact, the input data and fitted Poisson have identical mean values and nearly identical standard deviation values (1.3377 versus 1.4142).

2.5 Typically, it is easier to compare fits by viewing the CDFs. We do this now by clicking the **Graph Options** button, second from the left along the bottom of the *Fit Results* window, and choosing **Cumulative Ascending**. Now, to see the fit of the binomial distribution to the data check the box for the binomial on the left under *Fit Ranking*. The fitted binomial is now added to the graph along with its statistics. Figure 10.11 shows CDFs of the input data and the two fitted distributions. To remove a distribution from the graph, clear its checkbox. Note that between the graph's title and the graph, @RISK reports the parameters of the fitted distributions. Figure 10.11 shows that the best fitting Poisson has $\lambda = 2$, which is excellent as it is identical to the distribution that created the data. The best fitting binomial has $n = 13$ and $p = 0.15385$.

2.6 The default measure of fit is the AIC measure, for which smaller numbers indicate better fits. To see how the rank order of the fitted distributions changes when a different measure (BIC or Chi-Squared distance) is used, click on the **Black Triangle** next to *Fit Ranking*. For example, choosing **Chi-Squared** results in the binomial being ranked first and the Poisson ranked second.

2.7 To view the fit of the IntUniform (a discrete uniform distribution with integer values), deselect the **Poisson** and **binomial** distributions and click on **IntUniform**. Figure 10.12 shows that the IntUniform is not a good fit. We can see this in different ways. Visually, we see a lot of separation between the CDFs showing a disagreement in probability values, and thus a poor fit. For example, with the data there is only a 5% chance of a value being greater than 4.15, but with the IntUniform there is a 16.7% chance. The statistics show a greater difference between the fitted IntUniform and the input data than either the binomial or Poisson.

FIGURE **10.9**
Setting up @RISK to run its fitting procedure for discrete distributions on a sample of discrete data.

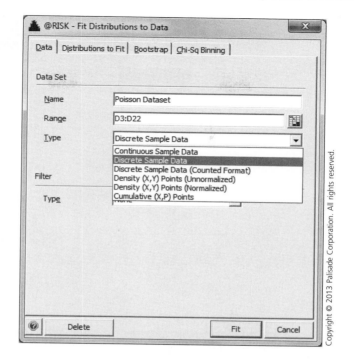

FIGURE **10.10**
The @RISK report showing that the Poisson matches the data the best with the binomial distribution coming in second. The graph in the center compares the input distribution (shown as thin lines) to the best fitting Poisson distribution (shaded bars).

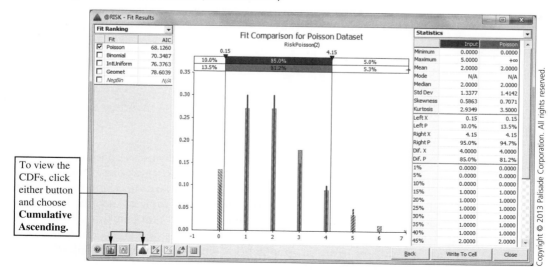

FIGURE **10.11**
The @RISK – fit results showing the fit of the Poisson and binomial distributions to the discrete data using CDFs.

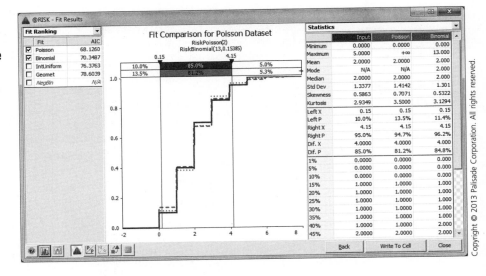

FIGURE **10.12**
The @RISK – fit results showing that the IntUniform does *not* fit the data well.

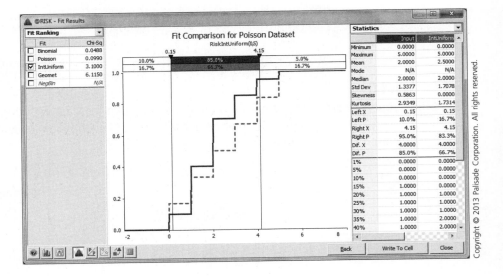

Next, let's see how to fit continuous distributions to continuous sample data. To start, we take a random sample of 20 observations from a lognormal distribution with mean equal to 60 and standard deviation equal to 40. The lognormal is often used to model the distribution of income, because it has a lower bound of zero and no upper bound. You can think of the random sample given in Table 10.6 as a sample of annual incomes in thousands of dollars from a population with mean income $60,000 and standard deviation $40,000.

TABLE **10.6**
A random sample of 20 observations from a lognormal distribution with mean equal to 60 and standard deviation equal to 40.

155.28	44.97	105.97	31.96
110.20	47.54	83.73	39.35
62.24	19.78	14.70	51.44
25.15	76.72	66.46	55.41
28.82	70.46	39.72	35.81

STEP 3 *Fitting Distributions to a Continuous Sample.*

3.1 First, enter the data from Table 10.6 into your spreadsheet, then open the *@RISK – Fit Distributions to Data* window by clicking on the **Distribution Fitting** menu button and in the submenu choosing **Fit Distributions to Data.**

3.2 In the *@RISK – Fit Distributions to Data* window, name the fit **Lognormal Dataset,** enter the data range and choose **Continuous Sample Data** as the type of data. Note that you can first highlight the data, then open the *@RISK – Fit Distributions to Data* window, and the range is automatically entered. Again, the data must be entered into one column.

3.3 Click the **Fit** button.

3.4 The extreme value (ExtValue) distribution fits best by the AIC measure. The lognormal is the seventh best fitting, which is shown by holding the cursor over the lognormal name. Doing so, shows that the lognormal is ranked 7th for both the AIC and BIC measures, 1st for both the Chi-Square and Anderson-Darling measures, and 2nd for the Kolmogorov-Smirnov measure. To see how well the lognormal fits the data, check the **Lognormal** and uncheck **ExtValue** under *Fit Ranking* along the left. Figure 10.13 shows the resulting *@RISK – Fit Results* window, after choosing **Cumulative Ascending (CDF)** in **Graph Options.** The statistics show that the fitted mean (58.57) is close to the sample mean (58.29), and the fitted standard deviation (36.96) is a bit higher than the sample value of (34.94). The parameters for the lognormal are listed below the graph's title in Figure 10.13, with the mean equal to 58.92, the standard deviation equal to 36.96, and the shift equal to −0.35. The shift means that the whole graph is shifted left (because of the negative sign) by 0.35. Shifting left is equivalent to subtracting 0.35 from each value and thus moves the stated mean value of 58.92 to the actual mean value of $58.92 - 0.35 = 58.57$. Shifting is somewhat like a parameter in that it can help dial in a closer fit. Here, however, shifting has not helped. Why? Because an important property of an income distribution is that income can never be negative; it can be zero, but not below zero. Thus, we want our fitted distributions also to have this property, and we need to rerun @RISK's fitting procedure with this property specified. Click **Close.**

3.5 Return to the *@RISK – Fit Distributions to Data* window by clicking on the **Distribution Fitting** button, choosing **Fit Manager**, highlighting the **Lognormal Dataset** in the *Fit Manager* window, and finally clicking on the **Goto** button. We had to go through the Fit Manager because the fitting procedure has already been run on this data.

3.6 Click on the **Distributions to Fit** tab along the top of the *@RISK – Fit Distributions to Data* window. Figure 10.14 shows that we can specify the upper and lower limits of the distributions used in the fitting procedure. For this dataset, we set the *Lower Limit* to be a **Fixed Bound** at 0, and the *Upper Limit* to be **Open (Extends to +Infinity)**. With the properties specified, click **Fit**.

3.7 With these constraints, the inverse Gaussian (InvGauss) is the best fitting and the lognormal a close second by the AIC measure. **Holding the cursor over lognormal** shows the rank of the fitted lognormal by each of the five fit measures as shown in Figure 10.15. Notice that there is no shift and the estimated parameters are quite close to the parameters we chose to create the data. We used a mean of 60, and @RISK estimated the lognormal mean to be 58.6. We used a standard deviation of 40, and @RISK estimated the lognormal standard deviation to be 37.1.

3.8 To see the ranking for the *A-D* distance, click on the **Black Triangle** next to *Fit Ranking* and choose the **Anderson-Darling Statistic**. Now the Pearson6 is the best fitting distribution with the lognormal a close second. See Figure 10.16.

FIGURE **10.13**
The @RISK – Fit Results window for the lognormal dataset showing how well the fitted lognormal distribution matches the data.

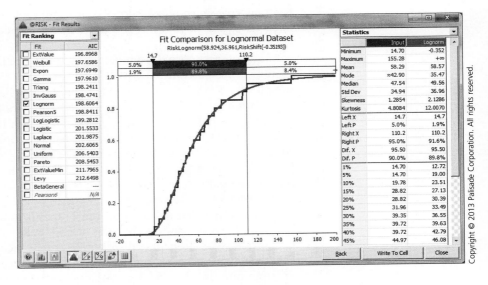

FIGURE 10.14
Specifying the properties (upper and lower bounds) of the distributions to be fitted to match the properties of our data, namely a fixed lower bound of zero and no upper bound.

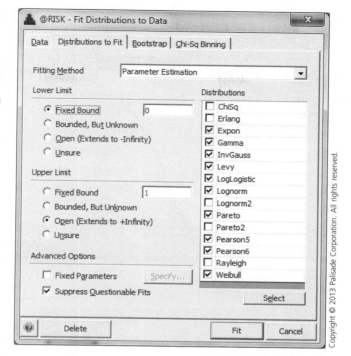

FIGURE 10.15
After specifying the properties (upper and lower bounds) of the distributions to be fitted, the lognormal fits the best as measured by the *K-S* distance.

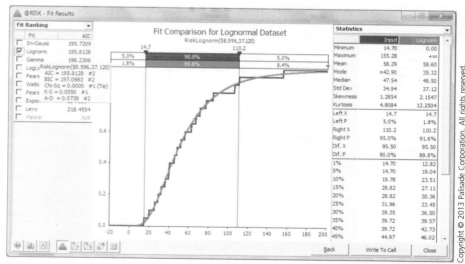

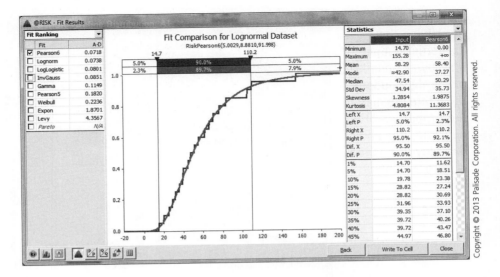

Our next and last dataset demonstrates how to fit theoretical distributions to subjectively assessed values. Whereas with sample data we wanted the fitted distribution to match or mimic the data as closely as possible, with assessed values we want the fitted distribution to match the assessments. Think of the assessed values as known points or targets on the CDF; the fitted distribution should come as close as possible to each of the target points. Thus, @RISK will manipulate the parameters of the theoretical distributions to make each one pass as closely as possible to the assessed values. The distribution type that fits best is the one that most closely matches the assessed values.

To measure how closely the fitted theoretical distribution is to the assessed values we (and @RISK) use *Euclidean distance*, which is simply a generalization of the Pythagorean Theorem. More precisely, let $(x_1, p_1), (x_2, p_2), ...,$ (x_n, p_n) be the assessed values where p_i is the cumulative probability associated with x_i, that is $P(X \leq x_i) = p_i, i = 1, 2, ..., n$. For each assessed value (x_i, p_i), @RISK measures the vertical distance from the fitted curve to (x_i, p_i), as shown in Figure 10.17. The Euclidean distance is then the square root of the sum of the squared distances: $\sqrt{(Distance1^2 + Distance2^2 + Distance3^2)}$. The actual measure used by @RISK is the square root of the average of the squared distances: $\sqrt{\dfrac{(Distance1^2 + Distance2^2 + Distance3^2)}{3}}$ and is called the *RMSE*, for Root Mean Square Error. Note that if the fitted curve passes through an assessment value, the distance is zero, and if the fitted curve passes through all the assessed values, the *RMSE* equals zero.

The data we use for this example are the five assessed values from Chapter 7 and 8 for yearly profit of a rental duplex, repeated here in Table 10.7. These five assessed are very close to that what one would

FIGURE **10.17**
Measuring the distance from the fitted distribution to the three assessed values requires measuring the vertical distance from the assessed value to the fitted curve.

RMSE is the square root of the average of squared vertical distances.

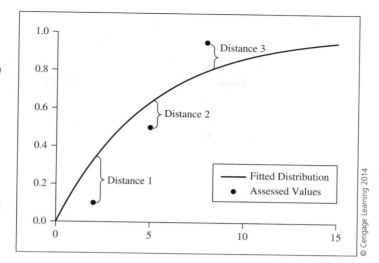

TABLE **10.7**
Assessed yearly profits of an income property.

$P(Yearly\ Profit \leq -\$25,000) = 0.00$
$P(Yearly\ Profit \leq -\$10,000) = 0.10$
$P(Yearly\ Profit \leq \$0) = 0.30$
$P(Yearly\ Profit \leq \$15,000) = 0.75$
$P(Yearly\ Profit \leq \$24,000) = 1.00$

© Cengage Learning 2014

obtain from a triangular distribution with *minimum* equal to −$25,000, *most likely* equal to $18,300, and *maximum* equal to $24,000. Using *RSME* to measure fit, let's see which distributions fit best, and especially how well the triangular distribution fits.

STEP 4 *Fitting Distributions to Assessed Values.*

4.1 First, we need to put the data into the correct format by entering the values −**25000**, −**10000, 0, 15000,** and **24000** into a column and their corresponding cumulative probabilities **0.00, 0.10, 0.30, 0.75,** and **1.00** in the column next to the values. We entered the values in C3:C7 and the probabilities in D3:D7.

4.2 Open the @RISK – *Fit Distributions to Data* window by clicking on the **Distribution Fitting** menu button and in the submenu choosing **Fit**.

4.3 Figure 10.18 shows the @RISK – *Fit Distributions to Data* window where we named the data **Assessed Profits**, entered the range **C3:D7**, and specified the type of data as **Cumulative (X, P) Points**.

4.4 Click the **Fit** button.

4.5 Figure 10.19 shows that the BetaGeneral distribution (as discussed in Chapter 9) fits the assessed profit values most closely. With *RSME* of nearly zero, the flexible BetaGeneral with its four parameters nearly hits or matches all five assessed values. Note that even though this BetaGeneral is nearly perfect in hitting its target values, this does not necessarily mean that its mean and standard deviation match the mean and standard deviation of the assessed values. As a matter of fact, the BetaGeneral's mean of $5,917 is $417 higher than the assessed distribution's mean of $5,500 and its standard deviation of $11,010 is $797 less than the standard deviation of $11,807 from the assessed distribution. Thus, this particular BetaGeneral overestimates yearly profit by over 7% and underestimates variability by over 6%.

4.6 The triangular distribution has the second best fit, which can be seen by deselecting the **BetaGeneral** and selecting **Triang** below *Fit Ranking* as shown in Figure 10.20. Knowing that our assessed values were actually pulled from a triangular distribution, we can compare how well @RISK estimated the three parameters of the triangular. We used a *minimum* value of −25,000, which was estimated at −25,045; we used a *most likely* value of 18,300, which was estimated at 18,587; and we used a *maximum* value of 24,000, which was estimated at 23,860.

4.7 As mentioned earlier, it is reasonable to choose a theoretical distribution for our decision model even if it does not appear first in the list. Click on the sixth best fitting distribution (**Normal**) under *Fit Ranking*. Figure 10.21 shows that the normal distribution fits the five assessed values reasonably well; its estimated mean is within 5.5% of the mean of the assessed distribution, and the standard deviation is within 1% of the standard deviation of the assessed distribution. Thus, the normal would be a reasonable choice, even though it is the fifth best fit.

4.8 Not every distribution listed is viable. Click on **Expon**, the second lowest ranked distribution, and we see that the exponential shape is not a good match, even though @RISK has found the best fitting exponential among all exponential distributions. (Figure 10.22). In trying to come as close as possible to the assessed values, the exponential passes through two of the five assessments and splits the difference between the other three.

We conclude the @RISK instructions with a brief description of some of the fitting options available to refine your fitted distribution.

First, a maxim of distribution fitting is to match the properties of the theoretical distribution to those of the uncertainty being modeled. For example, setting the upper and lower bounds, as we did in Step 3, can have a dramatic impact on the quality of the fitted distributions. @RISK provides a number of

FIGURE **10.18**
Setting up @RISK
to run its fitting
procedure for
continuous
distributions on
assessed values.

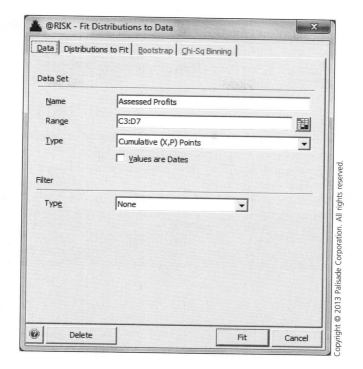

FIGURE **10.19**
The @RISK – Fit Results window showing that the BetaGeneral distribution matches the assessed
profits values the best with the smallest RSME.

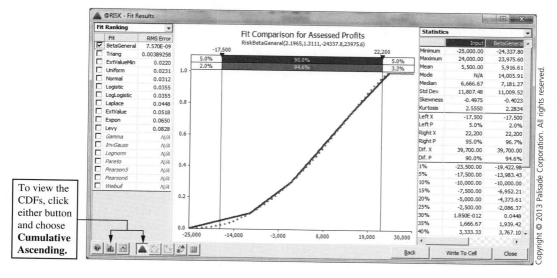

To view the
CDFs, click
either button
and choose
**Cumulative
Ascending.**

FIGURE **10.20**
The @RISK – Fit
Results window
showing that the
Triang (triangular)
distribution
matches the
assessed profits
values second best.

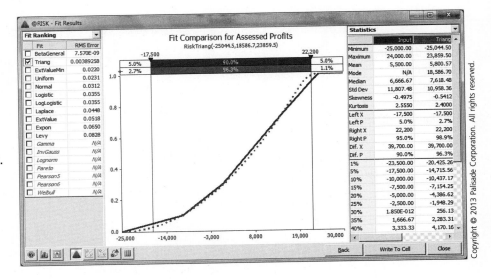

FIGURE **10.21**
The normal distri-
bution fits the
assessed values
rather closely even
though it is listed as
the fifth best fitting
distribution.

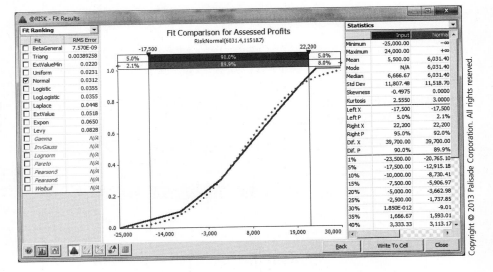

ways to specify which properties you want for the fitted distributions. First,
you can specify if the data should be filtered. If you believe the data includes
extreme values that misrepresent the uncertainty, you can filter the data by
removing values that are either outside a range you specify or beyond a fixed
number of standard deviations. In the *@RISK – Fit Distributions to Data*

FIGURE **10.22**
The exponential
distribution fits the
assessed values
rather poorly.

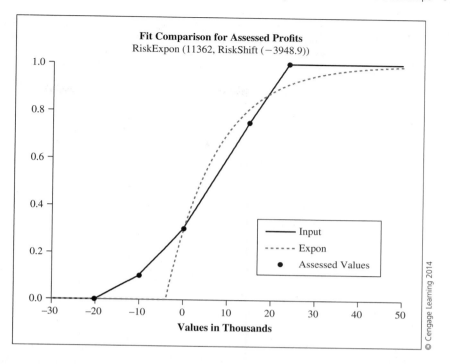

window, choose **Absolute** and enter in your range values, such as zero and one, if you want all data below zero and greater than one to be ignored or filtered out. Alternatively, you can choose **Relative** and enter in the number of standard deviations, such as three if you want all data beyond three standard deviations in either direction of the mean to be filtered out.

We can also specify the upper and lower bounds of the theoretical distributions that are to be fit. As explained in Steps 3.4 and 3.5, go to the *@RISK – Fit Distributions to Data* window, click the **Distributions to Fit** tab, and specify the upper and lower limits of the distribution. Figure 10.15 shows that each limit has four options. *Fixed Bound* is used when you know the value; otherwise choose *Bounded, But Unknown*. If there is no bound, choose *Open (Extends to ±Infinity)*. The last option is self explanatory: *Unsure*.

Finally, we note that there are numerous graphing options (modifying labels, axes, line styles, and so on) available for the @RISK – Fit results. These options are accessed by clicking the Graph Options button, second from the left along the bottom of the *@RISK – Fit Results* window.

USING DATA TO MODEL RELATIONSHIPS

In this section we show how to use data to model relationships and then use the relationships to construct more precise models of uncertainty. We have seen an example of this process already when we divided the sales data for the solar trash compactors into smaller and larger organizations. We found that knowing whether the firm was small or large resulted in a more complete model of the product mix.

One of the most important things that we do with data is to try to understand the relationships that exist among different phenomena in our world. The following list includes just a few examples:

Causes of Cancer. Our smoking habits, diet, exercise, stress level, and many other aspects of our lives have an impact on our overall health, including the risk of having cancer. Scientists collect data from elaborate experiments to understand the relationships among these variables.

Sales Revenue. For a business, perhaps the most crucial issue is understanding how various economic conditions, including its own decisions, can impact demand for products and, hence, revenue. Firms try to understand the relationships among sales revenue, prices, advertising, and other variables.

Economic Conditions. Economists develop statistical models to study the complex relationships among macroeconomic variables like disposable income, gross domestic product, unemployment, and inflation.

Natural Processes. Much scientific work is aimed at understanding the relationships among variables in the real world. A few examples include understanding the relationships among weather phenomena, movements in the earth's crust, changes in animal and plant populations due to ecological changes, and causes of violence in society.

Understanding the full scope of the interactions among phenomena can help immensely when making decisions. However, it is often impossible for any one person to account for all the interactions using only subjective judgments. This is one of the reasons we create models—so that we can incorporate complex relationships into the decision analysis. Failure to model critical relationships can lead to spectacular failures, such as that of Long Term Capital Management (LTCM). Founded in 1994, LTCM was a hedge fund that used complex financial models and intricate trading strategies. At first, LTCM was exceptionally successful, giving its investors annualized returns of over 40% after fees. In 1998, the Russian financial crisis occurred, and like one domino knocking the next domino down, a series of dependent events unfolded whose interactions were not accounted for in LTCM's model. The fund lost $4.6 billion in less than 4 months. By ignoring some critical relationships (particularly between foreign currency exchange rates), LTCM's model lead to disastrous decisions, and the fund folded in 2000.

In most cases, the motivation for studying relationships among phenomena that we observe is either to make accurate predictions or to gain some degree of control over our world. In many cases we hope to make changes in those areas where we have direct control in order to accomplish a change in another area. For example, the U.S. Federal Reserve Board may buy or sell securities in order to have an impact on interest rates in the U.S. money market. Doing so requires an understanding of how its operations in the market can affect interest rates. Firms want to set prices and advertising budgets so that they result in an optimal level of profits, but doing so requires an understanding of what affects demand for their products and services. Scientific studies of natural processes often are used as inputs in government policy and regulation decisions.

The setting for this section is that we have an uncertain quantity Y that we want to model for our decision problem. We have data not only on Y, but also on a number of auxiliary variables, which we will denote as $X_1, ..., X_k$. We can either use the data on Y alone to construct the probability distribution of Y as we did in the first part of this chapter, or we can use all the data to construct the conditional probability distribution of Y, conditioned on the values of the auxiliary variables. Y is often called the *response variable,* because its conditional probability distribution changes in response to changes in the X's. Likewise, the X's are often called *explanatory variables,* a descriptive label that we will adopt from here on, because they can be used to help explain the changes in Y.[4]

How do we know if we should bother with the explanatory variables? Essentially, the stronger the relationship is between response and explanatory variables, the more precise the conditional probability distribution of Y will be. The precision comes from three sources:

1. We know both the direction and strength between the response and each explanatory variable giving us some potential control.
2. We can more accurately predict values for Y.
3. We can reduce the uncertainty in our predictions.

For example, suppose you are developing a probability distribution of home prices, and you have data on the following variables: Price (Y), Bedrooms (X_1), and Square Footage (X_2), where Price is the sales price of homes in thousands of dollars. Ignoring any relationship with Bedrooms or Square Footage, Price is roughly bell-shaped with a sample mean of $300,000 and a sample standard deviation of $100,000. Hence, one possibility would be to model Price as a normal distribution with the mean equal to $300,000 and standard deviation equal to $100,000.

Looking to the explanatory variables, we can segment Price by the number of bedrooms. Our belief is that knowing the number of bedrooms in the house allows us to refine our estimate of Price, resulting in more accurate predictions. In addition, we hope that by segmenting the data, the uncertainty in Price as measured by the standard deviation will also decrease. Figure 10.23 shows the probability distribution for Price along the top with the mean $300,000 and standard deviation $100,000. The next row down shows the conditional distribution of Price given Bedrooms. We see that for one-bedroom houses, the mean Price is $200,000, for two-bedroom houses the mean Price is $230,000, and for six-bedroom houses, the mean Price is $500,000. In addition, the overall uncertainty in Price has decreased from a standard deviation of $100,000 across all houses to a standard deviation of $50,000 when we know the number of bedrooms in the house. The decrease

---

[4] Y and the X's are also sometimes called *dependent* and *independent* variables, although this terminology can be misleading. Y does not necessarily *depend* on the X's in a causal sense, and the X's can be highly dependent—in a probabilistic sense—among themselves.

FIGURE **10.23**
The distribution of Price can be refined and made more precise by leveraging the relationship between Price and Bedrooms (second row) or between Price and both Bedrooms and Square Footage (third row).

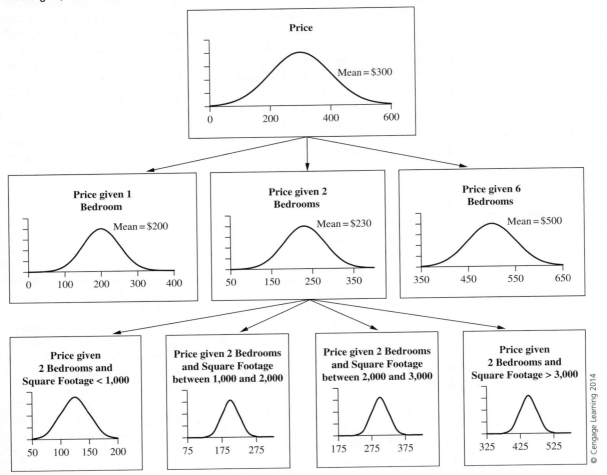

in the standard deviation indicates that Bedrooms is a strong explanatory variable.

Continuing in the same fashion, we now condition Price on both Bedrooms and Square Footage, with the intention of further improving our predictions and decreasing the overall uncertainty in house prices. For illustration, Figure 10.23 shows only four of the conditional distributions out of many that are possible. The bottom row of Figure 10.23 shows four conditional distributions given Bedrooms equals 2 and Square Footage in one of four intervals. Again, we see that the conditional mean varies, ranging from a low of $125,000 for the smallest houses to $450,000 for the largest. In addition, the standard deviation has decreased to $25,000. Thus, by incorporating what we know about the number of bedrooms and the house's square footage, we have greatly reduced the overall uncertainty, thereby increasing the precision of our estimates.

The use of data to understand relationships is not trivial. Not only will we be using sophisticated algorithms to estimate the relationships, but also we need to be clever in pulling as much information out of the data as we can. In the housing example, there are many ways to define conditional distributions of Price. Following this approach, though, the number of conditional distributions could explode. In our example, we would need to come up with twelve different conditional probability distributions for Price based on the three possible scenarios for Bedrooms and four categories for Square Footage. (Some of these distributions may not be meaningful, though. For example, there probably are very few 1-bedroom houses that have 3,000 square feet!).

THE REGRESSION APPROACH

Our objective is to construct a conditional probability distribution for Y conditioned on explanatory variables $X_1, ..., X_k$. To do this, we will make two simplifying assumptions. First, we will make an assumption about the mean of the conditional distributions, $E(Y \mid X_1, ..., X_k)$. Second, we make an assumption about the type or shape of the conditional probability distribution. Statisticians refer to this general modeling approach as *regression*.

We focus here on the simplest regression model, whose assumptions naturally lead it to be called *linear regression*. Beginning with the conditional expected value:

Assumption 1

The conditional expected value of Y is linear in $X_1, ..., X_k$. In symbols,

$$E(Y \mid X_1, ..., X_k) = \beta_0 + \beta_1 X_1 + \cdots + \beta_k X_k.$$

This formula greatly simplifies using data to model relationships, because it states that the expected value of Y given explanatory variables $X_1, ..., X_k$ is linear in terms of these variables. This means that the rate of change in the conditional mean stays the same over the range of the explanatory variables. For example, if we had found that $E(Price|Bedrooms) = $180,000 + $50,000 \times Bedrooms$, then each additional bedroom increases expected Price by $50,000. The assumption is that this increase is constant for each additional bedroom no matter whether the change is from 1 to 2 bedrooms or from 5 to 6 bedrooms. When making predictions, though, it is important to stay within the range of the data. If in the data the number of bedrooms ranged from 1 to 6 bedrooms, the conditional expected value equation would be valid only when predicting the expected selling price for houses with 1 to 6 bedrooms. We could not say, for example, that an additional bedroom in a 20-bedroom house would increase the expected selling price by $50,000.

Why do these assumptions simplify the problem? Essentially, we are saying that there is a linear relationship between Y and the Xs. We can see this in the interpretation of the conditional expected value: $E(Y \mid X_1, ..., X_k) = \beta_0 + \beta_1 X_1 + \cdots + \beta_k X_k$. If there is only one explanatory variable, then $E(Y \mid X_1) = \beta_0 + \beta_1 X_1$, where β_0 (beta zero) is the y-axis intercept and β_1 (beta one) is the slope or rate of change. Often β_0 has no interpretation, but the interpretation of β_1 is always helpful. The slope tells us both the direction and magnitude change in Y for a unit change in X_1. For example, if $E(Price \mid Square\,Footage) = \$120,000 + \$85 \times Square\,Footage$, then for each additional square foot, the expected selling price increases (because $85 is positive) by $85. It is important to note that we are not saying that each additional square foot always increases the selling price by $85. The actual impact of each additional square foot depends on the house, its location, its size, and so on. Rather, we are saying that on average, the selling price increases by $85 for each additional square foot. For some houses, the selling price will increase more than $85, some less than $85, but averaging across all the houses results in an $85 increase per square foot.

If there is more than one explanatory variable, we will have a slope for each one. As before, each slope tells us the marginal change in Y for a unit change in the explanatory variable, but now with an important caveat. To understand the caveat, let's look at another example:

$$E(Price \mid Bedrooms, Square\,Footage)$$
$$= \$100,000 + \$5,000 \times Bedrooms + \$85 \times Square\,Footage.$$

If we compare two houses (A and B), each with 2 bedrooms, and House A is 2,000 sq. ft. while House B is 2,100 sq. ft, then

$$E(Price\;of\,A \mid Bedrooms, Square\,Footage)$$
$$= \$100,000 + \$5,000(2) + \$85(2,000) = \$280,000$$

and

$$E(Price\;of\,B \mid Bedrooms, Square\,Footage)$$
$$= \$100,000 + \$5,000(2) + \$85(2,100) = \$288,500$$

The difference in expected selling prices is $8,500, which can be directly attributed to House B having an additional 100 sq. ft. at $85/sq. ft. Note that the number of bedrooms is still 2 for both houses. Whenever we interpret any one slope, we must always add the caveat that all other variables are held constant. Hence, we would state that the expected selling price increases by $85 per additional square foot while holding the number of bedrooms constant, and the expected selling price increases by $5,000 per additional bedroom, holding square footage constant.

Another common mistake is ignoring the units of the explanatory variables. Consider the case of a manager exploring the relationship between sales, advertising expenses, the company's price for an item, and a competitor's price for a similar item. Suppose the conditional expected value of Sales is given by

$$E(Sales|Advertising, Price, Competition\,Price)$$
$$= \$2,000 + 1.48\,Advertising - 500\,Price + 500\,Competition\,Price$$

where Sales is the regional sales (in \$1,000s) of a high-volume consumer electronics item (say, a cell phone); Advertising is the amount of money spent on advertising in that region also in \$1,000s; Price is the retail price set forth for that item in the ads (in \$1s); and Competition Price is the current price of a competitive product (in \$1s). It is easy to conclude incorrectly that each additional \$1 increase in Competition Price increases the expected sales by \$500, assuming Advertising and Price remain unchanged. The interpretation is incorrect because the units for Sales are in thousands of dollars, which implies that an increase of 500 units is actually an increase of \$500,000. The correct statement is that for every \$1 increase in Competition Price, we can expect Sales to increase by \$500,000, assuming that Advertising and Price remain unchanged.

An influence diagram portraying the relationship of Sales with Advertising, Price, and Competition Price is shown in Figure 10.24. Note that we have placed the coefficients on the arrows, indicating the effect that each variable has on the expected value of Sales. For example, every additional \$1,000 spent on Advertising leads to an increase in expected Sales of \$14,800 (14.8 times \$1,000), given that Price and Competition Price stay the same. The opposite signs on the coefficients for Price and Competition Price indicate that these variables are expected to have opposite effects; an increase in Price decreases expected Sales (everything else being equal), as indicated by the negative coefficient (−500). However, an increase in Competition Price (again, with everything else held constant) is good news for us and increases our expected sales, as indicated by the positive coefficient (+500) on Competition Price. Moreover, the price effects are quite strong, reflecting the competitive nature of the market; an increase in Price of \$1 leads to a \$500,000 decrease in expected Sales. Likewise, a \$1 increase in the Competition Price leads to an increase in expected Sales of \$500,000.

It is important to remember that the conditional expected value equation defines a relationship between the explanatory variables and the *expected*

FIGURE **10.24**
Relating sales to three explanatory variables.

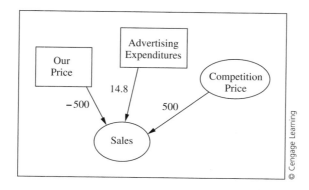

© Cengage Learning

Y (Sales). The *actual* Y value will be above or below this expected value to some extent; this is where the uncertainty and the conditional probability distribution of Y come into play. The regression approach makes the following assumption about this distribution:

Assumption 2

The distribution around the conditional expected value has the same shape regardless of the particular values of the explanatory variables.

Thus, the shape of the conditional distribution is always the same; for example, it always has the same standard deviation. In fact, everything is the same except the expected value, which is given by Assumption 1.

A convenient way to think about this is in terms of random errors (or "noise") added to the conditional expected value. Denote a random error as ϵ and let us say that these errors are, on average, equal to zero: $E(\epsilon) = 0$. Now we can write an expression for an actual Y value as follows:

$$Y = E(Y \mid X_1, ..., X_k) + \epsilon$$

This implies that the conditional distribution has the same shape as the distribution of the errors. Thus, by specifying the distribution of errors with mean equal to zero, we are in fact specifying the shape of the conditional distribution of Y.

Take the Sales example. Suppose that the errors—the unexplainable factors that make Sales fall above or below its conditional expected value—have a CDF as shown in Figure 10.25. Now, suppose we decide to spend $40,000 on Advertising ($X_1$) and to set Price ($X_2$) at $97.95, and Competition Price (X_2) turns out to be $94.99. Then expected Sales (Y), conditional on these values, would be

$$E(Y \mid X_1, X_2, X_3) = 2,000 + 14.8(40) - 500(97.95) + 500(94.99)$$

$$= 1,112 \ (\$1,000s)$$

$$= \$1,112,000.$$

FIGURE **10.25**
A CDF for errors in the Sales example.

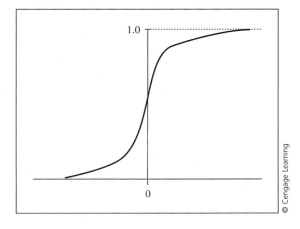

© Cengage Learning

Suppose in an entirely different scenario we had Advertising equal to $70,000, Price equal to $93.95, and Competition Price equal to $98.99. Then conditional expected Sales would be:

$$E(Y \mid X_1, X_2, X_3) = 2,000 + 14.8(70) - 500(93.95) + 500(98.99)$$

$$= 5,556 \ (\$1,000s)$$

$$= \$5,556,000.$$

The conditional CDFs for Sales, given the three conditioning variables in each scenario and the distribution for errors, are displayed in Figure 10.26. As you can see, the distributions have the same shape as the distribution for the errors shown in Figure 10.25. In Figure 10.26, though, the location or center of each distribution is different, and this is due entirely to differences in the explanatory variables.

Our two assumptions—a linear expression for conditional expected value and the constant shape for the conditional distributions—take us quite a long way toward being able to use data to study relationships among variables. You should keep in mind, however, that this is only one way to model the relationships and that it is quite possible for the expected-value relationships to be nonlinear or for the distributions to change shape. An example of a nonlinear relationship would be the degree of acidity in a lake and the number of microorganisms. If the lake is highly acidic, reducing the acidity can lead to an increase in microorganisms up to a point, beyond which further changes are detrimental to the microorganisms' population. Changes in the distribution can be somewhat more subtle. Consider house prices versus square footage again. Often there is more variation in prices for larger houses than smaller houses. If the variation in price does indeed increase as the square footage increases, this violates Assumption 2.

Although our approach has some limitations, it provides an excellent base that can be extended via additional modeling techniques. We will mention some of these techniques later. For now, though, let us turn to the problem of using data within the regression framework we have established.

FIGURE **10.26** Conditional CDFs for sales in two scenarios.

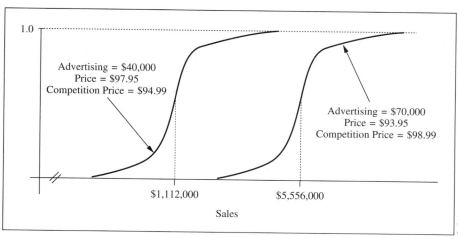

© Cengage Learning

Estimation: The Basics

The discussion in the previous section has assumed that we know the values of the β coefficients and the distribution of the errors. Of course, we may be able to make subjective judgments of these quantities, but if data are available, we may want to use that information in a systematic way to estimate the β's and to construct a data-based distribution of errors. To understand the process, let us simplify the sales example that we have been using. Suppose that we have data only for Sales and Advertising, and we want to study the relationship between these two variables alone. The data, observations of Advertising and Sales during 36 different promotions in the eastern United States, are shown in Table 10.8. Figure 10.27 shows a *scatterplot* of these data; each point on the graph represents one of the observations.

Using the linear-regression assumptions from the previous section, we establish the equation relating expected Sales (Y) and Advertising (X_1):

$$E(Y|X_1) = \beta_0 + \beta_1 X_1$$

We will use the data to estimate β_0 and β_1. Estimating β_0 and β_1 amounts to finding a line that passes through the cloud of points in the scatterplot; Figure 10.28 shows two different candidates with their corresponding expressions. The expressions show what those particular lines use as estimates of β_0 and β_1. The dashed line, for example, estimates β_0 to be 1900 and β_1 to be 15. Clearly, no single line can pass precisely through all of the points at once, but we would like to find one that in some sense is the "best fitting" line. And, as you can see from the graph, there are many reasonable estimates for β_0 and β_1.

How will we choose the best-fitting line through the data points? Although there are many possible answers to this question, we will choose a way that many statisticians have found convenient and useful. In simple terms, we will choose the line that minimizes the sum of the squared vertical distances between the line and each point. Figure 10.29 shows how this will work for two sample points, A and B. Between the line and any given point (x_i) there is a certain vertical distance, which we will call the *residual* (e_i). For any given line, we can calculate the residuals for all of the points. Then we square each residual and add up the squares. Finally, we choose the unique line that minimizes the sum of squared residuals.[5]

In symbols, let b_0 and b_1 represent the estimates of β_0 and β_1, respectively. With this we can calculate the ith residual as:

$$e_i = y_i - (b_0 + b_1 x_i)$$

Squaring and summing over the n residuals gives the total (which we denote by SSE for the sum of squared errors):

$$SSE = \sum_{i=1}^{n} [y_i - (b_0 + b_1 x_i)]^2$$

---

[5] The decision to minimize squared residuals is somewhat arbitrary. We could just as well choose estimates that minimize the sum of the absolute values of residuals, for example. Any error measure that penalizes large errors above or below the line will work. Mathematicians have focused on the sum of squared residuals because this sum is easy to work with mathematically.

TABLE **10.8**
Data for sales example.

Promotion	Advertising ($1,000s)	Sales ($1,000s)
1	366	10,541
2	377	8,891
3	387	5,905
4	418	8,251
5	434	11,461
6	450	6,924
7	457	7,347
8	466	10,972
9	467	7,811
10	468	10,559
11	468	9,825
12	475	9,130
13	479	5,116
14	479	7,830
15	481	8,388
16	490	8,588
17	494	6,945
18	502	7,697
19	505	9,655
20	529	11,516
21	532	11,952
22	533	13,547
23	542	9,168
24	544	11,942
25	547	9,917
26	554	10,666
27	556	9,717
28	560	13,457
29	561	10,319
30	566	9,731
31	566	10,279
32	582	7,202
33	609	12,103
34	612	11,482
35	617	11,944
36	623	9,188

FIGURE **10.27**
A scatterplot of
Advertising versus
Sales.

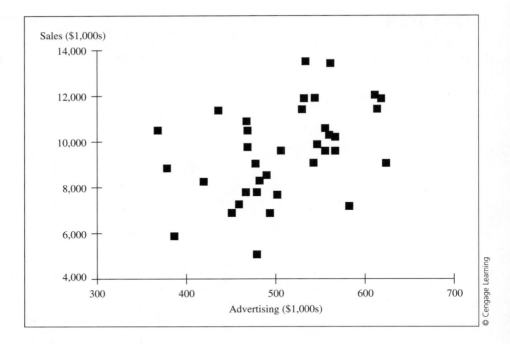

FIGURE **10.28**
Two possible lines
relating expected
sales and
advertising.

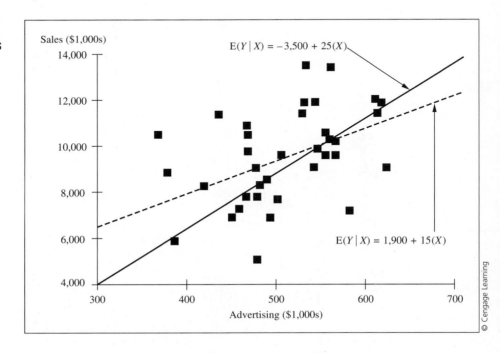

FIGURE **10.29**
Calculating
residuals.

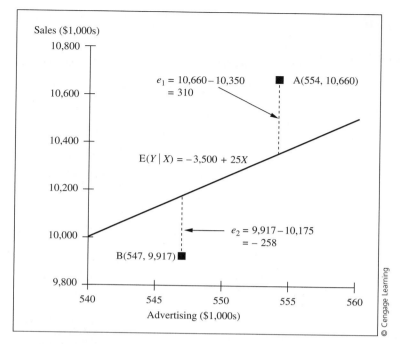

We want to choose b_0 and b_1 so that SSE is minimized. While this sounds like a complicated problem, it turns out to be a rather straightforward calculus problem. And even more good news is that you will never need to do the calculations yourself! Many computer programs are available that do the calculations for you automatically.

Figure 10.30 shows the Excel spreadsheet that results from doing the calculations using Excel's built-in "Regression" procedure in the Sales-Advertising example. The figure highlights Excel's estimates $b_0 = 3,028.18$ and $b_1 = 12.95$. These are the coefficients that produce the minimum-SSE line. (In fact, SSE = 117,853,513 and is shown in the column labeled "Sum of Squares.") Excel does many other calculations that are useful in drawing inferences from the data. For our current purposes of modeling relationships among variables, we will stick to the basics. All we require at this point are the values b_0 and b_1, which are the estimates of β_0 and β_1. At the end of the chapter we will briefly discuss the idea of statistical inference and how it relates to decision-analysis modeling.

We can write out the expression for the line defined by the estimates b_0 and b_1:

$$E(Y \mid X_1) = 3,028.18 + 12.95X_1, \text{ or}$$

$$E(Sales \mid Advertising) = 3,028.18 + 12.95Advertising.$$

This equation makes sense. In general, we expect Sales to increase when we spend more on Advertising, as indicated by the positive coefficient 12.95. In particular, this coefficient can be interpreted as follows: For every additional $1,000 spent on advertising, Sales are expected to increase by $12,950. (Recall that Advertising and Sales are both measured in $1,000s.)

FIGURE **10.30**
Using Excel to
estimate regression
coefficients.

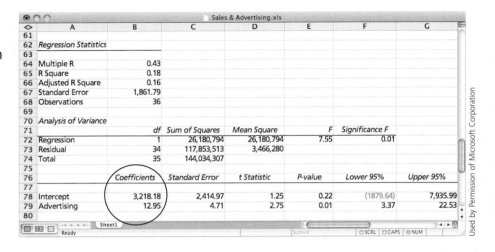

For our simple model, we now have an indication of how expected Sales changes as Advertising changes. How can we use the data to construct a model of the distribution of errors? This step is straightforward; for every data point we have a residual, which can be thought of as an estimate of the error associated with that particular point. Thus, the distribution of the residuals should be a good approximation to the distribution of the errors. Table 10.9 shows the calculation of the residuals, and Figure 10.31a displays the empirical cumulative distribution constructed from the residuals. Figure 10.31b shows a histogram of the residuals.

The CDF can be used to make probability statements about the errors. For example, the quartiles are approximately −1,300 and +1,300, so there is approximately a 50% chance that the actual Sales is within plus/minus $1.3 million (=1,300 ×1,000) of the predicted Sales. Or we can use the CDF to construct a discrete approximation. From the residuals in Figure 10.31, we see that the 0.05 fractile is approximately −3,000, the 0.50 fractile is approximately 0, and 0.95 fractile is approximately 3,000, which are the three fractiles required for the three-point extended Pearson-Tukey approximation as shown in Figure 10.32.

The CDF can also be used as a basis for representing the uncertainty in Sales given Advertising. To create a conditional distribution for Sales given Advertising, simply add the conditional expected Sales value to each residual value, which shifts the distribution along the horizontal scale. For example, if Advertising = $110,000, then E(Sales|Advertising) = $4,452,680; add this amount to the horizontal scale to get the distribution for Sales given Advertising = $110,000 as shown in Figure 10.33. This distribution can in turn be used to generate conditional probability statements about Sales. Or we could create a discrete approximation of the distribution for use in an influence diagram or decision tree. Finally, we could also fit a theoretical distribution. Typically in regression analysis, a normal distribution is fit to the residuals, but virtually any continuous distribution that makes sense for the situation could be used. For example, the residuals could be used as data in @RISK to find the best-fitting distribution.

TABLE **10.9**
Residuals for the
sales example.

Observation	Sales (Y)	Advertising (X)	E(Y|X) = 3028.18 +12.95X	Residual = Y − E(Y|X)
1	10,541	366	7,768	2,773
2	8,891	377	7,911	980
3	5,905	387	8,040	2,135
4	8,251	418	8,442	−191
5	11,461	434	8,649	2,812
6	6,924	450	8,856	1,932
7	7,347	457	8,947	−1,600
8	10,972	466	9,063	1,909
9	7,811	467	9,076	−1,265
10	10,559	468	9,089	1,470
11	9,825	468	9,089	736
12	9,130	475	9,180	−50
13	5,116	479	9,232	4,116
14	7,830	479	9,232	1,402
15	8,388	481	9,258	−870
16	8,588	490	9,374	−786
17	6,945	494	9,426	2,481
18	7,697	502	9,530	1,833
19	9,655	505	9,568	87
20	11,516	529	9,879	1,637
21	11,952	532	9,918	2,034
22	13,547	533	9,931	3,616
23	9,168	542	10,048	−880
24	11,942	544	10,074	1,868
25	9,917	547	10,112	−195
26	10,666	554	10,203	463
27	9,717	556	10,229	−512
28	13,457	560	10,281	3,176
29	10,319	561	10,294	25
30	9,731	566	10,358	−627
31	10,279	566	10,358	−79
32	7,202	582	10,566	−3,364
33	12,103	609	10,915	1,188
34	11,482	612	10,954	528
35	11,944	617	11,019	925
36	9,188	623	11,097	−1,909

FIGURE **10.31**

Empirical CDF and histogram of the residuals from regressing Sales on Advertising.

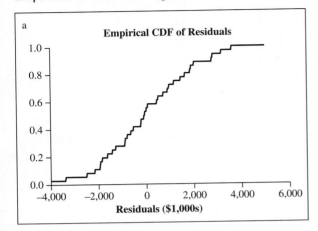 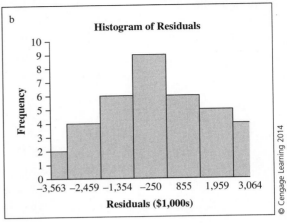

FIGURE **10.32**
Extended Pearson-
Tukey three-point
approximation
for the residual
distribution.

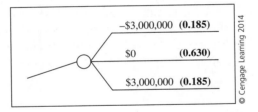

FIGURE **10.33**
CDF for Sales given
Advertising =
$110,000.

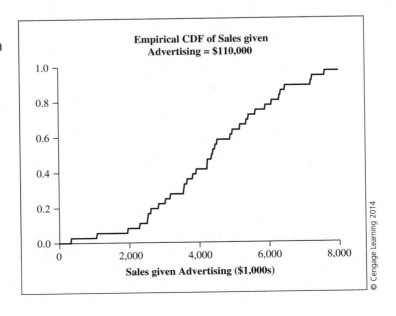

FIGURE **10.34**
Influence diagram
model showing
relationship
between sales and
advertising.

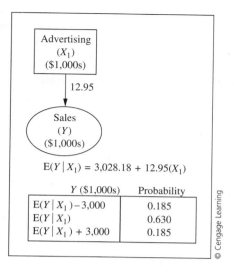

$$E(Y \mid X_1) = 3{,}028.18 + 12.95(X_1)$$

Y ($1,000s)	Probability
$E(Y \mid X_1) - 3{,}000$	0.185
$E(Y \mid X_1)$	0.630
$E(Y \mid X_1) + 3{,}000$	0.185

© Cengage Learning

With the coefficient estimates and the distribution of errors, we have a complete, if simplified, model of the uncertainty in Sales given its conditioning variable, Advertising. Figure 10.34 shows an influence diagram that represents the simple model we have created, including a three-point approximation for Sales given Advertising. Again, we note the importance of limiting the regression equation to the range of the explanatory variables.

Estimation: More than One Conditioning Variable

The advertising-and-sales example in the previous section demonstrated the basics. The model that we came up with, though, really is quite simplistic. In fact, with Advertising as the only explanatory variable, we implicitly assume that nothing else matters. But that clearly is too simple, and we have already argued that both the price of our product and our competitor's price also matter.

An augmented data set is shown in Table 10.10. For each of the 36 occasions, we now also have information on Price (X_2) and Competition Price (X_2). Can we incorporate these data into our analysis? The answer is yes, and the procedure is essentially the same as it was before.

We want to come up with estimates for $\beta_0, \beta_1, \beta_2$, and β_3 in the following expression:

$$E(Y \mid X_1, X_2, X_3) = \beta_0 + \beta_1 X_1 + \beta_2 X_2 + \beta_3 X_3$$

As before, we will let b_0, b_1, b_2, and b_3 denote the estimates of the corresponding β coefficients. Analogous to the one-variable version of the problem, we can calculate expected Sales, given the values of the conditioning variables. In turn, we can calculate each of the 36 residuals by subtracting

TABLE **10.10**
Augmented data set for sales example.

Promotion	Advertising ($1,000s)	Price ($)	Competition Price ($)	Sales ($1,000s)
1	366	90.99	96.95	10,541
2	377	90.99	93.99	8,891
3	387	94.99	90.99	5,905
4	418	96.99	97.95	8,251
5	434	92.99	97.95	11,461
6	450	95.95	93.95	6,924
7	457	93.95	90.99	7,347
8	466	91.95	96.95	10,972
9	467	96.95	94.99	7,811
10	468	92.95	96.95	10,559
11	468	97.99	98.95	9,825
12	475	91.95	90.99	9,130
13	479	99.95	91.95	5,116
14	479	96.99	95.95	7,830
15	481	91.95	90.95	8,388
16	490	96.99	96.99	8,588
17	494	96.95	91.95	6,945
18	502	98.95	95.95	7,697
19	505	94.99	96.99	9,655
20	529	93.99	97.95	11,516
21	532	91.99	95.99	11,952
22	533	92.99	97.99	13,547
23	542	93.99	92.95	9,168
24	544	90.95	95.95	11,942
25	547	94.99	93.95	9,917
26	554	89.95	90.95	10,666
27	556	96.95	95.95	9,717
28	560	91.99	97.95	13,457
29	561	98.99	97.95	10,319
30	566	93.95	91.99	9,731
31	566	94.99	94.99	10,279
32	582	98.99	91.99	7,202
33	609	89.95	92.99	12,103
34	612	92.95	92.99	11,482
35	617	92.95	94.95	11,944
36	623	94.99	91.99	9,188

FIGURE **10.35**
Regression analysis
for full model.

	A	B	C	D	E	F	G
128							
129	*Regression Statistics*						
130							
131	Multiple R	0.98					
132	R Square	0.95					
133	Adjusted R Square	0.95					
134	Standard Error	459.10					
135	Observations	36					
136							
137	*Analysis of Variance*						
138		df	Sum of Squares	Mean Square		F	Significance F
139	Regression	3	137,289,638	45,763,213		217.12	0.00
140	Residual	32	6,744,669	210,771			
141	Total	35	144,034,307				
142							
143		Coefficients	Standard Error	t Statistic	P-value	Lower 95%	Upper 95%
144							
145	Intercept	2199.34	3839.74	0.57	0.57	-5621.94	10020.62
146	Advertising	15.05	1.17	12.83	0.00	12.66	17.44
147	Price	-503.76	28.34	-17.77	0.00	-561.50	-446.03
148	Comp Price	499.67	30.56	16.35	0.00	437.42	561.92

the expected sales calculation from the actual sales for that observation. And, as before, we choose the values of the b's so that the sum of the squared residuals is minimized. Accomplishing this is just a slightly more general version of the one-variable problem previously described.

Figure 10.35 shows the Excel screen with the results of the regression analysis with all three conditioning variables. As before, b_0, b_1, b_2, and b_3 are in the column labeled "Coefficients." With these values, we can now write out the formula for expected Sales, given the three conditioning variables:

$$E(Y \mid X_1, X_2, X_3) = 2,199.34 + 15.05X_1 - 503.76X_2 + 499.67X_3 \text{ or}$$

$$E(Sales \mid Ad, Price, CPrice) = 2,199.34 + 15.05Ad - 503.76Price + 499.67CPrice$$

where we abbreviated Advertising as Ad and Competition Price as CPrice. We now have a more comprehensive model of Sales and can predict how expected Sales changes as the explanatory variables change. We see that an additional $1,000 spent on Advertising increases expected Sales by $15,050 holding Price and Competition Price constant. Increasing our price by $1 would lead to a decrease in expected Sales by $503,760 if Advertising and Competition Price both remain constant. An increase in our competitor's price by $1 would bring expected Sales up by $499,670 assuming neither Advertising nor Price changes.

Also as before, we can calculate the residuals and use them to construct a CDF for the errors. Table 10.11 gives the residuals for our full model, and Figure 10.36 displays the CDF of the residuals from both regression models. From the graph, we can see that the distribution of errors is much tighter in

TABLE **10.11**
Residuals for the
full model.

Observation	Sales (Y)	$E(Y \mid X_1, X_2, X_3)$	Residual
1	10,541	10,312	229
2	8,891	8,999	−108
3	5,905	5,635	270
4	8,251	8,572	−321
5	11,461	10,827	634
6	6,924	7,578	−654
7	7,347	7,212	135
8	10,972	11,333	−361
9	7,811	7,850	−39
10	10,559	10,859	−300
11	9,825	9,320	505
12	9,130	8,490	640
13	5,116	5,000	116
14	7,830	8,490	−660
15	8,388	8,561	−173
16	8,588	9,175	−587
17	6,945	6,737	208
18	7,697	7,849	−152
19	9,655	10,408	−753
20	11,516	11,753	−237
21	11,952	11,826	126
22	13,547	12,337	1,210
23	9,168	9,450	−282
24	11,942	12,511	−569
25	9,917	9,521	396
26	10,666	10,667	−1
27	9,717	9,669	48
28	13,457	13,227	230
29	10,319	9,716	603
30	9,731	9,352	379
31	10,279	10,327	−48
32	7,202	7,054	148
33	12,103	12,514	−411
34	11,482	11,047	435
35	11,944	12,102	−158
36	9,188	9,686	−498

FIGURE **10.36**
Residuals of two regressions showing that the uncertainty in Sales has been greatly reduced when regressing on all three explanatory variables.

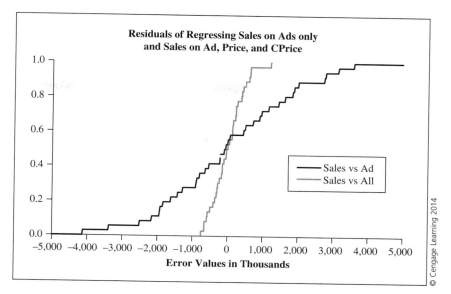

Not only does the SE estimate the standard deviation of the conditional distributions, but it also provides an easy way to determine if the explanatory variables are helpful in producing probability distributions that are more precise. For example in Figure 10.30, when Advertising is the only explanatory variable, SE = $1.86 million. We see nearly a fourfold decrease in the

the full model than it was in the previous model in which we used only Advertising. For example, we saw that 50% of the time, the actual sales level would be within $1.3 million of the predicted sales level when using only Advertising, but when using all three explanatory variables, 50% of the time actual sales will be within approximately $300,000. Thus, the full regression model has substantially reduced the amount of uncertainty we have in Sales, which in turn leads to a more precise probability model of Sales.

Instead of creating the CDF of the residuals, there is a shortcut, or summary number that tells us how much uncertainty remains in our response variable (Y) after accounting for the linear effects of the explanatory variables. The *Standard Error* (SE) is an estimate of the standard deviation of the conditional distributions, and as such, the SE indicates the amount of uncertainty there is when we use the regression model for predictions. For example, cell B134 in Figure 10.35 shows that the SE equals 459.10. The units for SE are always the same as the units for the response variable (Y); hence SE = $459,100. Now, using the regression, we predict that expected Sales would be $4,562,600 when Advertising is set at $110,000, Price at $94.50, and Competition Price at $96.69. If we assume that the residuals are normally distributed (a common assumption), then we could state that 68% of the time actual sales will fall within $4,562,600 \pm \$459,100$ and 95% of the time actual sales will fall within $4,562,600 \pm 2 \times \$459,100$.

Not only does the SE estimate the standard deviation of the conditional distributions, but it also provides an easy way to determine if the explanatory variables are helpful in producing probability distributions that are more precise. For example in Figure 10.30, when Advertising is the only explanatory variable, SE = $1.86 million. We see nearly a fourfold decrease in the uncertainty in our predictions when Price and Competitive Price are added to the model because the SE = $459,100.

In general, the standard deviation of the response variable (before any regressions) determines the overall uncertainty, which we compare to the SE (after a regression) to determine whether knowing the explanatory variables helps decrease the uncertainty. For example, the standard deviation of Sales is $2.029 million. Conditioning on only Advertising decreases the uncertainty to $1.86 million, which is not a great improvement. However, conditioning on all three explanatory variables reduces the uncertainty to $459,000, which is a remarkable improvement and shows that, taken together, all three variables are relevant and useful for understanding Sales.

The tightness of the distribution, as indicated by the CDF of the errors and the standard deviation of that distribution, is the best available indication of the value of the model. For example, a product manager might look at the $1.8 million standard deviation for the previous single-variable model and scoff. Such a broad distribution makes planning difficult at best. However, the $459,100 standard deviation of the residuals in the full model may represent enough accuracy that this model could be used for planning production and distribution for a major promotion. And further model enhancements (adding other variables or improved modeling through advanced techniques) might reduce the uncertainty even further, thereby making the model that much more useful as a forecasting and planning tool.

The influence diagram in Figure 10.37 shows the entire model, including a three-point approximation of the error distribution to represent the conditional uncertainty about Sales.

FIGURE **10.37**
Influence diagram model of sales given advertising, price, and competition price.

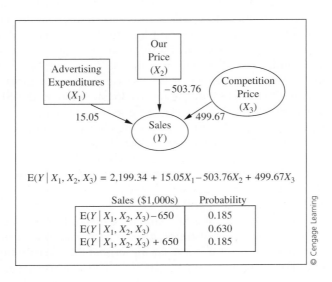

$$E(Y \mid X_1, X_2, X_3) = 2{,}199.34 + 15.05X_1 - 503.76X_2 + 499.67X_3$$

Sales ($1,000s)	Probability
$E(Y \mid X_1, X_2, X_3) - 650$	0.185
$E(Y \mid X_1, X_2, X_3)$	0.630
$E(Y \mid X_1, X_2, X_3) + 650$	0.185

© Cengage Learning

Regression Analysis and Modeling: Some Do's and Don't's

The preceding examples and discussion give you a good idea of how regression analysis can be used to create models in decision analysis. However, you should be aware that we have barely scratched the surface of this powerful statistical technique. Complete coverage of regression is beyond the scope of this text, but many excellent statistical textbooks are available. This section provides a brief survey of some of the issues in regression modeling, especially as they relate to decision analysis.

We have seen a number of approaches to creating uncertainty models, including subjective assessment, the use of theoretical distributions, and data. The use of data can be very powerful; a statistical model and analysis, when based on an appropriate data set of adequate size, is very persuasive. The drawback is that data collection can take time and resources and may not always be feasible. In such cases, an analyst might be better off relying on theoretical distributions and expert subjective judgments. Still, when data are available, they can be valuable.

Although you should by now have an understanding of regression basics (which will improve with practice on some problems), there is much more to learn. Many courses in statistics are available, as are innumerable textbooks, some of which are listed in this chapter's reference section. In addition, becoming familiar with statistical software greatly facilitates understanding of regression and its limitations. Regression software not only calculates the estimated slopes and the standard error, but also provides users with a variety of graphs and diagnostics that help interpret the results completely. Excel provides only the basics of regression, and we suggest a more robust program. One such program actually is included in the DecisionTools® Suite and is called StatTools. Like Precision Tree and @RISK, StatTools is an Excel add-in and increases Excel's statistical capabilities greatly.

Creating an uncertainty model with regression can be quite powerful. It does have some important limitations, however. Two in particular warrant consideration in the context of decision analysis. First, the data set must have an adequate number of observations. Just what "adequate" means is debatable; many rules of thumb have been proposed, and some work better than others. The approach for decision-analysis modeling we have previously described will perform poorly without enough data to estimate the coefficients and the error distribution. Although "enough data" may mean different things in different contexts, a conservative rule of thumb would be to have at least 10 observations for each explanatory variable and never less than 30 observations total.

The main reason for having adequate data is that many data points may be necessary to fully represent all of the different ways in which the variables can occur together. You would like to have as good a representation as possible of all the possible combinations. In the sales example, we would like to have occasions when prices are high, low, and in between, and for each different price level, advertising expenditures should range from high to low. Note that there is no guarantee that a large data set will automatically provide adequate coverage of all possibilities. (Inadequate coverage can result in nonsensical coefficient estimates. Advanced techniques can diagnose this situation and provide ways to get around it to some extent.) On the other hand, very small data sets almost by definition will not provide adequate coverage.

Another way to view this problem is to realize that a small number of observations means that we cannot be very sure that the b's are accurate or reliable estimates of the β's. When we use the b's to calculate the conditional expected value, however, we are in essence assuming that the b's are good estimates and that virtually all of the uncertainty in the response variable comes from the error term. In fact, with a small data set, we may also be very unsure about what the conditional expected value itself should be. In some cases you might want to model the uncertainty about the estimates explicitly and incorporate this additional uncertainty by an appropriate broadening of Y's conditional probability distribution. Statistical procedures for generating appropriate probability intervals under these circumstances are included in most computer regression programs.

Even with an adequate data set and a satisfactory model and analysis, there remains an important limitation. Recall that the regression model has a particular form; it is a linear combination of the explanatory variables. And the coefficient estimates are based on the particular set of observations in the data set. The upshot is that your model may be a terrific approximation of the relationship for the variables in the neighborhood of the data that you have. But if you try to predict the response variable outside of the range of your data, you may find that your model performs poorly. For example, our preceding sales example was based on prices that ranged from about $89 to $100. If the product manager were contemplating reducing the price to $74.95, it is unlikely that an extrapolation of the model would give an accurate answer; there is no guarantee that the linear approximation used in the first place would extend so far outside of the range of the data. The result can be an inaccurate conditional expected value and a poor representation of the uncertainty, usually in the form of a too-narrow distribution, resulting in turn in poor planning. In practical terms, this means that the company could be taken by surprise by how many (or how few) units are sold during the promotion.

The limitation with the range of the data goes somewhat further yet when we use multiple explanatory variables, and this is related to the discussion of the data requirement discussed previously. You may try to predict the response variable for a combination of the explanatory variables that is poorly represented in the data. Even though the value of each explanatory variable falls within its own range, the combination for which you want to create a forecast could be very unusual. In the sales example, it would not be unreasonable to find in such a competitive situation that both Price and Competition Price move together. Thus, it might be unlikely to observe these prices more than a few dollars apart. Using Price = $89.99 and Competition Price = $99.95 (or visa versa) could turn out to be a situation poorly represented by the data, and in this case the analysis may provide a very misleading representation of the expected Sales and the uncertainty. Although there is no simple way to avoid this problem, one helpful step is to prepare scatterplots of all pairs of explanatory variables and to ensure that the point for which you wish to predict the response variable lies within the data cloud in each of the scatterplots. Thus, in the sales example, we would be sure that the combination of prices and advertising that we wanted to analyze fell within the data clouds for each of three different scatterplots: Price versus Competition Price, Price versus Advertising, and Competition Price versus Advertising.

Regression Analysis: Some Bells and Whistles

As mentioned, our coverage of regression is necessarily limited. In this section, we look briefly at some of the ways in which regression analysis can be extended.

Nonlinear Models

First, we can easily get past the assumption that the conditional expected value is a linear function of the explanatory variables. For example, suppose an analyst encounters the scatterplot in Figure 10.38, which relates average temperature (X) and energy consumption (Y), measured in kilowatt-hours, for small residences. A linear relationship between these two quantities clearly would not work well, and the reason is obvious: When the temperature deviates from a comfortable average temperature (around 20°C), we consume additional energy for either heating or air conditioning. To model this, a quadratic expression of the form $E(Y|X) = \beta_0 + \beta_1 X + \beta_2 X^2$ might work well.

FIGURE **10.38**
A nonlinear relationship between temperature and energy consumption.

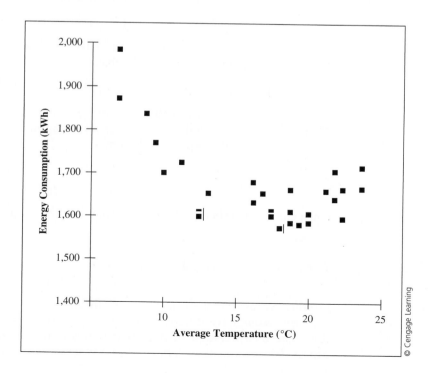

© Cengage Learning

Implementation is easy: For each observation calculate X^2, thereby creating a second explanatory variable. Now run the regression with two explanatory variables, X and X^2. The coefficient estimates obtained define a parabolic curve that fits the data best in a least-squares sense. A similar approach works for fitting exponential or logarithmic functional forms, some of which have very compelling and useful economic interpretations. A textbook on regression modeling such as Kutner, Nachtsheim, and Neter (2004) discusses such modeling techniques in depth.

Categorical Explanatory Variables

Up to this point, all of the explanatory variables have been quantitative, but what about qualitative variables? For example, curb appeal or location can be excellent explanatory variables when predicting a house's sale price. These variables are often qualitative, such as location being coded as Neighborhood 1, Neighborhood 2, etc. or Boston, New York, etc. Another common qualitative variable is Gender, coded as Male or Female. Or it might be useful to classify people into different age categories (child, adolescent, young adult, middle age, senior citizen) for marketing purposes. Is it possible to include qualitative variables in a regression model?

The answer is yes, and the technique is straightforward. Suppose we have marketing data $(X_1, ..., X_k)$ for both men and women, but we would like to treat them separately. We can create a categorical variable (X_{k+1}) that equals 1 for men and 0 for women:

$$X_{k+1} = \begin{cases} 1 & \text{if male} \\ 0 & \text{if female} \end{cases}$$

This adds an extra column to the data matrix, and in the regression equation we include the new (categorical) variable:

$$E(Y \mid X_1, ..., X_k, X_{k+1}) = \beta_0 + \beta_1 X_1 + \cdots + \beta_k X_k + \beta_{k+1} X_{k+1}$$

Now consider how this equation works for men and women separately. Women have X_{k+1} coded as a 0, so the last term on the right side drops out. Thus, for women the expression becomes

Women:

$$E(Y \mid X_1, ..., X_k, X_{k+1} = 0) = \beta_0 + \beta_1 X_1 + \cdots + \beta_k X_k$$

For men, on the other hand, $X_{k+1} = 1$, and so the last term becomes β_{k+1}.

Men:

$$\begin{aligned} E(Y \mid X_1, ..., X_k, X_{k+1} = 1) &= \beta_0 + \beta_1 X_1 + \cdots + \beta_k X_k + \beta_{k+1} X_{k+1} \\ &= (\beta_0 + \beta_{k+1}) + \beta_1 X_1 + \cdots + \beta_k X_k \end{aligned}$$

In other words, the coefficients for X_1 through X_k are exactly the same, but the expressions have different constant terms to represent the different genders. The interpretation of β_{k+1} is that this is the incremental difference in expected Y for a man as compared to a woman. For example, if Y represents mail-order clothing purchases per year, then $\beta_{k+1} = -\$50$ means that, everything else (age, income, and so on) being equal, a man is expected to spend $50 less per year on mail-order clothing than a woman.

Actually doing the analysis is easy. Create the categorical variable, include it as one of the explanatory variables in the regression analysis, and obtain the coefficient for the categorical variable from the computer printout. The rest is the same as before: To generate a prediction for a particular person, plug in the appropriate demographic data for all of the variables (including gender), calculate $E(Y \mid X_1, ..., X_k, X_{(k+1)})$, and use the error distribution to construct the conditional probability distribution for Y.

Note that we had two categories (male and female), and we were able to distinguish between them with just one categorical variable. What if you have more than two categories? The rule is that you should use *one less categorical variable than there are categories*. For example, take the age example that we mentioned. There are five categories: child, adolescent, young adult, adult, and senior citizen. (These categories must, of course, be defined clearly enough so that any individual can be placed unambiguously into one of the categories.) Now define four categorical variables:

$$X_{k+1} = \begin{cases} 1 & \text{if child} \\ 0 & \text{otherwise} \end{cases}$$

$$X_{k+2} = \begin{cases} 1 & \text{if adolescent} \\ 0 & \text{otherwise} \end{cases}$$

$$X_{k+3} = \begin{cases} 1 & \text{if young adult} \\ 0 & \text{otherwise} \end{cases}$$

$$X_{k+4} = \begin{cases} 1 & \text{if adult} \\ 0 & \text{otherwise} \end{cases}$$

Each individual will have a 1 or a 0 for each of these variables. Imagine reviewing the values of these variables for some particular person. If you see that $X_{k+3} = 1$ and the others are zero, you know that this person is a young adult, and likewise for the other variables. In fact, there will never be more than one nonzero value, and that nonzero value will be a 1, indicating the person's category. But what if you see zeros for all four of these variables? Simple: This person falls into none of the four categories associated with the variables and therefore must be a senior citizen.

The rule of having one less categorical variable than you have categories is easy to forget. It may seem natural to set up one variable for each category. There is a failsafe mechanism, however. Your computer program will not run with the extra categorical variable! It will most likely produce some cryptic error message like ANALYSIS FAILED—MATRIX SINGULAR, which is its way of indicating that it is unable to solve the required equations. Although this type of message can indicate other problems, if you have categorical variables, it almost surely means that you have one too many.

Categorical Response Variable (Y)

The regression procedure we have presented is designed especially for situations in which Y is a continuous variable. Often, though, you want to use data to predict whether an observation falls into a particular category (e.g., whether a particular customer will place another order or whether a particular individual will develop cancer). In decision-analysis terms, you would want to specify the conditional probability of falling into that category, given the values of the conditioning variables.

Statistical procedures are available to use data for this very purpose. However, these procedures have special requirements, and it is beyond the scope of this short introduction to describe how to use them. Suffice it to say that the standard approach we have laid out for continuous variables is *not* appropriate for categorical response variables. If you would like to use data to model conditional probabilities for such variables, consult one of the advanced regression texts mentioned at the end of this chapter.

Regression Modeling: Decision Analysis versus Statistical Inference

Our approach in this section has very much reflected the decision-analysis paradigm. We have used data as a basis for constructing a model of the uncertainty surrounding a response variable. Our focus has been on coming up with a conditional probability distribution for Y, given values of conditioning variables. The motivation has been that understanding and modeling the relationships among the explanatory and response variables can be of use in making decisions.

If you have been exposed to regression analysis before, perhaps in a statistics course, you no doubt realize that the perspective taken here is somewhat different from the conventional approach. Although our approach is not inconsistent with conventional thinking, there are some key differences:

- Statistical inference often focuses on various types of *hypothesis tests* to answer questions like, "Is a particular coefficient equal to zero?" Or, "Is this set of explanatory variables able to explain any of the variation in Y?" As decision analysts, such questions would more likely be framed as, "Is it reasonable to include X as an explanatory variable, or should it be left out?" A decision analyst might answer such a question with standard sensitivity-analysis techniques, which would permit consideration of the context of the current decision, including costs, benefits, and other risks. The conventional hypothesis-testing approach ignores these issues.

- Conventional regression modeling and the inference that is typically done (including hypothesis tests and the calculation of confidence and prediction intervals for Y) rely on the assumption that the errors follow a normal distribution. While the analysis can be quite powerful when this condition is met, it can be limiting or even misleading for situations in which normality is inappropriate. As decision analysts, we have focused on using the data to create a useful model of the uncertainty for forecasting and decision-making purposes, which includes coming up with a suitable error distribution.

- The standard regression approach leaves unaddressed the question of how to model uncertainty in the explanatory variables. For those variables that are themselves uncertain (like Competition Price in our example), it may be important from a decision-analysis point of view to model that uncertainty. The influence-diagram approach that we have shown in this chapter provides the basis for such modeling. Either historical data or subjective judgments can be used to assign a probability distribution to an uncertain explanatory variable. Thus included in the model, that uncertainty becomes an integral part of any further analysis that is done.

An Admonition: Use with Care

With a little knowledge of regression, you are using a very powerful data-analysis tool. It is tempting to apply the tool indiscriminately to a wide variety of situations. Part of its appeal is that it is using "objective" data, and hence the analysis and results are free of subjective judgments and bias. This is far from true! In fact, you should appreciate the broad range of judgments and assumptions that we made: linear expected values, the error probability distribution that does not change shape, and the inclusion of particular explanatory variables in the model. More fundamentally, we implicitly make the judgment that the past data we use are appropriate for understanding current and future relationships among the variables. When we use a conditional probability distribution based on regression analysis, all of these judgments are implicit. Thus, the admonition is to use regression with care (especially with regard to its data requirements) and to be cognizant of its limitations and implicit assumptions. Regression is a rich and complex statistical tool. This section has provided only a brief introduction: further study of regression analysis will be especially helpful for developing your skill in using data for modeling in decision analysis.

SUMMARY

In this chapter we have seen some ways in which data can be used in the development of probabilities and probability distributions for decision analysis. We began with the basics of constructing discrete and continuous distributions based solely on data. We then discussed how to use data to estimate parameters for theoretical distributions. The last half of the chapter discussed using data via regression analysis to model relationships among variables. Although many of the basic calculations are the same as what you might encounter in a statistics course, we emphasized a decision-analysis approach to regression analysis.

EXERCISES

10.1. Explain in your own words the role that data can play in the development of models of uncertainty in decision analysis.

10.2. Why might a decision maker be reluctant to make subjective probability judgments when historical data are available? In what sense does the use of data still involve subjective judgments?

10.3. Suppose that an analyst for an insurance company is interested in using regression analysis to model the damage caused by hurricanes when they come ashore. The response variable is Property Damage, measured in millions of dollars, and the explanatory variables are Diameter of Storm, Barometric Pressure, Wind Speed, and Time of Year.

    a. What subjective judgments, both explicit and implicit, must the analyst make in creating and using this model?

    b. If X_1, Diameter of Storm, is measured in miles, what is the interpretation of the coefficient β_1?

    c. Suppose the analyst decides to introduce a categorical variable X_5, which equals 1 if the eye of the hurricane comes ashore within 20 miles of the center of a large city (defined as a city with population $\geq 500,000$) and 0 otherwise. How would you interpret β_5?

10.4. Estimate the 0.65 and 0.35 fractiles of the distribution of yearly operating costs of the Big Bertha solar trash compactors, based on the CDF in Figure 10.7.

10.5. Choose appropriate intervals and create a relative frequency histogram based on the annual operating costs of the Big Bertha data in Table 10.4.

10.6. Figure 10.36 shows two empirical CDFs of the residuals of Sales for two regressions. Estimate (roughly) the 0.20 and 0.80 fractiles of both of these empirical CDFs. What do these two intervals say about predicting future sales amount?

QUESTIONS AND PROBLEMS

10.7. It was suggested that five is the minimum number of data points for the least likely category when constructing discrete distributions. In many cases, however, we must estimate probabilities that are extremely small or for which relatively few data are available. For example, the probability of bankruptcy for a firm is (hopefully) quite small, but it is important for both borrowers and lenders to know this small probability value. Typically, either expert opinion or proxy measures are used to determine these small probability values instead of using data, What makes us reluctant to use data to estimate small probability values?

10.8. As discussed in the text, it often is possible to use a theoretical distribution as an approximation of the distribution of some sample data. It is always important, however, to check to make sure that your data really do fit the distribution you propose to use.

    Consider the solar trash compactor data again. We calculated the sample mean $\bar{x} = \$1,005$ and the sample standard deviation $s = \$204$. Taking these as approximately equal to μ and σ, find the normal cumulative probabilities for operating costs of $700, $800, $900, $1,000, $1,200, and $1,400. How do these theoretical normal probabilities compare with the data-based probabilities from the CDF in Figure 10.7? Do you think that the normal distribution is an appropriate distribution to use in this case? Compare the fit of the normal distribution CDF to the empirical CDF by superimposing them onto one graph.

10.9. A scientist collected the following weights (in grams) of laboratory animals:

9.79	9.23	9.11	9.62
8.73	11.93	10.39	8.68
9.76	9.59	11.49	9.86
11.41	9.60	7.24	

Run @RISK's distribution fitting procedure on the weights of the laboratory animals.

a. The normal distribution is often used with measurement variables such as height and weight. Compare the normal distribution to the empirical distribution by computing the following probability values for both distributions:

$$P(Weight \leq 8\,gms), P(Weight \leq 9.5\,gms), \; and \; P(Weight \leq 11.5\,gms).$$

b. Do you think the normal distribution is a good choice for a theoretical distribution to fit these data? Why or why not?

10.10. A plant manager is interested in developing a quality-control program for an assembly line that produces light bulbs. To do so, the manager considers the quality of the products that come from the line. The light bulbs are packed in boxes of 12, and the line produces several thousand boxes of bulbs per day. To develop baseline data, workers test all the bulbs in 100 boxes. They obtain the following results:

No. of Defective Bulbs/Box	No. of Boxes
0	68
1	27
2	3
3	2

Run @RISK's distribution fitting procedure on the preceding data choosing Discrete Sample Data (Counted Format) for the type of data.

a. The Fit Results window shows that the Poisson is the best fitting theoretical distribution. Is the Poisson a good choice? Why or why not? What is the interpretation of the parameter for the Poisson in this setting?

b. Noticing that there are only two boxes with three defective bulbs, you combine the last two categories in the preceding data. Rerunning @RISK's fitting procedure, we see that the binomial now fits best according to the Chi-Square measure, with the Poisson coming in a close second. How much has the parameter (m) for the Poisson changed from the case with four categories? Is there a reasonable interpretation of the parameters n and p for the binomial in this setting?

c. Which distribution would you use if you were the plant manager? Why?

10.11. A retail manager in a discount store wants to establish a policy of the number of cashiers to have on hand and also when to open a new cash register. The first step in this process is to determine the rate at which customers arrive at the cash register. One day, the manager observes the following times (in minutes) between arrivals of customers at the cash registers:

0.1	2.6	2.9	0.5
1.2	1.8	4.8	3.3
1.7	0.2	1.5	2.0
4.2	0.6	1.0	2.6
0.9	3.4	1.7	0.4

a. What kind of theoretical distribution do you think would be appropriate for these data? Why?

b. Run @RISK's fitting procedure on the data. Is the distribution that you choose in part a the best fitting distribution? Does the distribution you choose in part a fit the data closely enough to be chosen?

c. We did not use all the information we had when we ran the preceding fitting procedure. Waiting times can never be negative. Therefore, rerun @RISK's fitting procedure setting the lower bound to be fixed at zero. See Steps 3.5 and 3.6 for instructions on how to modify the fit. Does this improve the fit of the distribution you choose in part a? How do the mean values compare?

10.12. An ecologist studying the breeding habits of birds sent volunteers from the local chapter of the Audubon Society into the field to count nesting sites for a particular species. Each team was to survey five acres of land carefully. Because she was interested in studying the distribution of nesting sites within a particular kind of ecological system, the ecologist was careful to choose survey sites that were as similar as possible. In total, 24 teams surveyed 5 acres each and reported the following numbers of nesting sites in each of the 5-acre parcels:

7	12	6	9
5	2	9	9
7	3	9	9
5	1	7	10
1	8	6	3
4	5	3	13

a. What kind of theoretical distribution might you select to represent the distribution of the number of nesting sites? Why?

b. Run @RISK's fitting procedure to determine how well your distribution choice in part a fits the data. Compare the sample mean and sample standard deviation to those of the fitted theoretical distribution.

c. Each of the discrete distributions in @RISK's library has trouble matching the probability of nine nesting sites per 5-acre parcel. For example, the data show a 20.8% probability of nine nesting sites, but all the theoretical distributions show only a 4–8% probability of finding nine nesting sites per five-acre parcels. Is this a problem? If so, what might you do? Explain.

10.13. Decision analyst Sandy Baron has taken a job with an up-and-coming consulting firm in San Francisco. As part of the move, Sandy will purchase a house in the area. There are two houses that are especially attractive, but their prices seem high. To study the situation a bit more, Sandy obtained data on 30 recent real-estate transactions involving properties roughly similar to the two candidates. The data are shown in Table 10.12. The Attractiveness Index measure is a score based on several aspects of a property's character, including overall condition and features (e.g., swimming pool, view, seclusion).

a. Run a regression analysis on the data in Table 10.12 with Sale Price as the response variable and House Size, Lot Size, and Attractiveness as explanatory variables. What are the coefficients for the three explanatory variables? Write out the expression for the conditional expected Sale Price given House Size, Lot Size, and Attractiveness.

TABLE **10.12**
Data for 30 real-estate transactions in Problem 10.13.

Property	House Size (Sq. Ft.)	Lot Size (Acres)	Attractiveness Index	Sale Price ($1,000s)
1	3,000	3.6	64	550
2	2,300	1.2	69	461
3	3,300	1.3	72	501
4	2,100	3.2	71	455
5	3,900	1.1	40	503
6	3,100	2.0	74	529
7	3,600	1.6	69	478
8	2,900	2.5	85	562
9	2,000	2.6	70	417
10	3,500	1.3	74	566
11	3,100	2.3	79	494
12	3,200	1.5	75	515
13	2,800	1.3	62	490
14	3,300	3.3	62	537
15	3,000	3.9	70	527
16	3,400	2.4	81	577
17	2,800	1.7	77	490
18	2,000	3.4	67	486
19	2,400	2.9	68	450
20	3,600	2.9	84	674
21	2,400	1.9	75	454
22	3,000	2.8	63	523
23	2,200	3.6	78	469
24	3,600	2.4	73	628
25	2,900	1.1	85	570
26	3,000	4.4	69	564
27	3,100	1.8	54	444
28	2,200	2.1	75	494
29	2,500	3.9	61	479
30	2,900	1.1	74	477

b. Create a CDF based on the residuals from the regression in part a.

c.   The two properties that Sandy is considering are as follows:

House	List Price	House Size	Lot Size	Attractiveness
1	575	2700	1.6	75
2	480	2000	2.0	80

What is the expected Sale Price for each of these houses according to the regression analysis from part a?

d.   Create a probability distribution of the Sale Price for each house in part c. Where does the List Price for each house fall in its respective distribution? What advice can you give Sandy for negotiating on these houses?

10.14. Ransom Global Communications (RGC), Inc., sells communications systems to companies that have worldwide operations. Over the next year, RGC will be instituting important improvements in its manufacturing operations. The CEO and majority stockholder, Thomas Ransom, has been extremely optimistic about the outlook for the firm and made the statement that sales will certainly exceed $6 million in the first half of next year.

Semiannual data for RGC over the past 19 years are presented in Table 10.13. The Spending Index is related to the amount of disposable income that consumers have, adjusted for inflation and averaged over the industrial nations. System Price is the average sales price of systems that RGC sells, Capital Investment refers to net capital investment in the business, and Advertising and Marketing and Sales are self-explanatory.

a.   Use the data in Table 10.13 to run a regression analysis with Sales as the response variable and the other four variables as explanatory variables. Write out the expression for Expected Sales, conditional on the other variables. Interpret the coefficients.

b.   The forecast for the Spending Index in the first half of next year is 45.2. The company has committed $145,000 for capital improvements during this time. In order to make his goal of $6 million in sales, Ransom has indicated that the company will offer discounts on systems (to the extent that the average system price could be as low as $70,000) and will spend up to $90,000 on advertising and various marketing programs. If the firm drops the price as much as possible and spends the full $90,000 on Advertising and Marketing, what is the expected value for Sales over the next 6 months? Estimate the probability that Sales will exceed $6 million.

c.   Given that the company spends the full $90,000 on Advertising and Marketing, how low would Price have to be in order to ensure a 90% chance that Sales will exceed $6 million? What advice would you give Thomas?

TABLE **10.13**
Twenty years
of data for
Ransom Global
Communications,
Inc.

Year	Spending Index	System Price ($1,000s)	Net Capital Investment ($1,000s)[6]	Advertising and Marketing ($1,000s)	Sales ($1,000s)
1994	39.8	56.2	49.9	76.9	5,540
	36.9	59.0	16.6	88.8	5,439
1995	26.8	56.7	89.2	51.3	4,290
	48.4	57.8	106.7	39.6	5,502
1996	39.4	59.1	142.6	51.7	4,872
	33.2	60.1	61.3	20.5	4,708
1997	33.6	59.8	–30.4	40.2	4,628
	38.3	60.1	–44.6	31.6	4,110
1998	28.5	63.1	–28.4	12.5	4,123
	27.7	62.3	75.7	68.3	4,842
1999	45.6	64.9	144.0	52.5	5,740
	35.5	64.9	112.9	76.7	5,094
2000	36.4	63.4	128.3	96.1	5,383
	32.0	65.6	10.1	48.0	4,888
2001	31.1	67.0	–24.8	27.2	4,033
	36.2	66.9	116.7	72.7	4,942
2002	40.8	66.2	120.4	62.3	5,313
	43.3	67.9	121.8	24.7	5,140
2003	35.9	68.9	71.1	73.9	4,397
	47.6	71.4	–4.2	63.3	5,149
2004	41.5	69.3	–46.9	28.7	5,151
	42.0	69.7	7.6	91.4	4,989
2005	53.6	73.2	127.5	74.0	5,927
	43.2	73.4	–49.6	16.2	4,704
2006	43.6	73.1	100.1	43.0	5,366
	41.5	74.9	–40.2	41.1	4,630
2007	46.2	73.2	68.2	92.5	5,712
	42.9	74.2	88.0	83.3	5,095
2008	51.7	74.3	27.1	74.9	6,124
	32.8	77.1	59.3	87.5	4,787
2009	41.8	78.6	142.0	74.5	5,036
	51.5	77.1	126.4	21.3	5,288
2010	41.2	78.2	29.6	26.5	4,647
	45.5	77.9	18.0	94.6	5,316
2011	55.4	81.0	42.4	92.5	6,180
	44.1	79.9	–21.6	50.0	4,801
2012	41.7	80.6	148.4	83.2	5,512
	46.1	82.3	–17.6	91.2	5,272

[6]Net Capital Investment can be negative when depreciation exceeds the amount of investment.

TACO SHELLS

Martin Ortiz, purchasing manager for the True Taco fast food chain, was contacted by a salesperson for a food service company. The salesperson pointed out the high breakage rate that was common in the shipment of most taco shells. Martin was aware of this fact, and noted that the chain usually experienced a 10% to 15% breakage rate. The salesperson then explained that his company recently had designed a new shipping container that reduced the breakage rate to less than 5%, and he produced the results of an independent test to support his claim.

When Martin asked about price, the salesperson said that his company charged $25 for a case of 500 taco shells, $1.25 more than True Taco currently was paying. But the salesperson claimed that the lower breakage rate more than compensated for the higher cost, offering a lower cost per usable taco shell than the current supplier. Martin, however, felt that he should try the new product on a limited basis and develop his own evidence. He decided to order a dozen cases and compare the breakage rate in these 12 cases with the next shipment of 18 cases from the current supplier. For each case received, Martin carefully counted the number of usable shells. The results are shown below.

Questions

1. Martin Ortiz's problem appears to be which supplier to choose to achieve the lowest expected cost per usable taco shell. Draw a decision tree of the problem, assuming he orders one case of taco shells. Should you use continuous fans or discrete chance nodes to represent the number of usable taco shells in one case?

2. Develop CDFs for the number of usable shells in one case for each supplier. Compare these two CDFs. Which appears to have the highest expected number of usable shells? Which one is riskier?

3. Create discrete approximations of the CDFs found in Question 2. Use these approximations in your decision tree to determine which supplier should receive the contract.

4. Based on the sample data given, calculate the average number of usable tacos per case for each supplier. Use these sample means to calculate the cost per usable taco for each supplier. Are your results consistent with your answer to Question 3? Discuss the advantages of finding the CDFs as part of the solution to the decision problem.

5. Should Martin Ortiz account for anything else in deciding which supplier should receive the contract?

Source: This case was adapted from W. Mendenhall, J. Reinmuth, and R. Beaver (1989) *Statistics for Management and Economics*, 6th ed. Boston: PWS-KENT.

Usable Shells				
New Supplier		Current Supplier		
468	467	444	441	450
474	469	449	434	444
474	484	443	427	433
479	470	440	446	441
482	463	439	452	436
478	468	448	442	429

REFERENCES

Using data as the basis for probability modeling is a central issue in statistics. Some techniques that we have discussed, such as creating histograms, are basic tools; any basic statistics textbook will cover these topics. The text by Vatter et al. (1978) contains an excellent discussion of the construction of a data-based CDF. Fitting a theoretical distribution using sample statistics such as the mean and standard deviation is also a basic and commonly used technique (e.g, Olkin, Gleser, and Derman 1994), although it is worth noting that statisticians have many different mathematical techniques for fitting distributions to empirical data.

Virtually every introductory statistics text covers regression analysis at some level. More advanced texts include Chatterjee and Price (2006), Draper and Smith (1981), and Kutner, Nachtsheim, and Neter (2004).

The treatment in Chapter 9 of Vatter et al. (1978) is similar to the one presented here.

Chatterjee, S., and B. Price (2006) *Regression Analysis by Example*. 4th ed., New York: Wiley.

Draper, N., and H. Smith (1981) *Applied Regression Analysis*, 3rd ed. New York: Wiley.

Kutner, M., Nachtsheim, C., and Neter, T., (2004) *Applied Linear Statistical Models*, 5th ed. Homewood, IL: McGraw Hill/Irwin.

Olkin, I., L. J. Gleser, and C. Derman (1994) *Probability Models and Applications*. 2nd ed. New York: Macmillan.

Vatter, P., S. Bradley, S. Frey, and B. Jackson (1978) *Quantitative Methods in Management: Text and Cases*. Homewood, IL: Irwin.

EPILOGUE: SOLAR TRASH COMPACTORS

Solar-powered trash compactors were the brainchild of Jim Poss when he was a graduate student at Babson College. Jim started out as an entrepreneur in the renewable energy sector, and his eureka moment happened when he was walking by an overflowing, smelly trashcan near Fenway Park. He started to think about all the inefficiencies in trash collection, and became motivated to create a solar-powered trash compactor, which he did and named Big Belly. Big Bellies not only keep the trash from smelling bad and overflowing, but also reduce many of the resources required for maintenance. For example, in 2008, downtown Philadelphia had 700 trash receptacles that required 17 weekly collections by 33 employees. In 2009, after installing 500 Big Bellies and 210 solar-powered recycling units, their weekly collections dropped down to five, requiring only nine employees. Philadelphia saved over $1 million on trash collection in 2009 and expects to save over $13 million in the next 10 years.

The Big Belly appears to dominate the traditional trashcan both environmentally and economically. Judging by the quickly rising sales of the Big Belly, cities and universities agree with its superiority. Jim sold his first Big Belly to Vail, Colorado in 2004, and now has over 40 distributors and expects annual sales of $2.2 million in 2010 (as reported by Manta.com). Big Belly Solar represents a new breed of green companies that are not only environmentally friendly, but also provide economically viable solutions.

Sources: www.bigbellysolar.com http://pwmag.com/industry-news.asp?sectionID=760&articleID=1221666 www.manta.com/c/mmgtvnt/big-belly-solar-inc

CHAPTER 11

Simulation

The decision-analysis process uses decision trees and influence diagrams to help us structure and analyze hard decisions. Decision trees and influence diagrams are particularly helpful in computing expected values and structuring conditional relationships between uncertainties. When a model includes many random variables, and especially when some are continuous, the methods we have seen for analyzing such models become cumbersome. In this chapter, we show how to analyze complex decision models using a technique called *Monte Carlo simulation*, or simply simulation.

The essence of simulation can be grasped with a simple example. Suppose you have a coin that is bent. Although you would expect flipping a normal coin would produce heads about half of the time, with the bent coin you might suspect the probability of heads is different from one-half but you are not sure. To find out, the most natural thing to do would be to flip the coin many times, keeping track of the number of times it comes up heads. The more flips, the more accurate would be your estimate of *P(Heads)*. Simulation does essentially the same thing with more complex computer-based models: Values are chosen for uncertain variables according to specified probability distributions; consequences are calculated based on the values chosen; and those consequences are tracked to understand how they are distributed—what risk profile they produce. Each round of choosing new values and calculating consequences is called an *iteration* or *trial*. You can see why the process is called Monte Carlo simulation— the simulation process chooses random outcomes each time, just like playing roulette or rolling dice in a casino.

Simulation is becoming more and more prevalent because it allows us to analyze complex decisions with many uncertainties. This chapter introduces the mechanics of simulation, discusses how to build a simulation model and interpret its output, and concludes with instructions on using @RISK for simulation models. Along the way, we will present some practical examples of simulation.

Our main example shows that interesting insights can come from a simulation model even when there is only one uncertainty.

Simulating Seasonal Sales	Leah Sanchez dreaded the Christmas holiday season, not because of the holiday itself, but because the season carried with it the pressure of whether her bookstore made a profit for the year. Leah was in her second year as a manager of a college bookstore, and she was hoping that she would end the year in the black, unlike last year's dismal numbers. As she looked over last year's sales records, she realized that she fell short of her revenue goals due to her decisions on how much merchandise to order for seasonal items. For many items, such as books, notebooks, pens, and so on, she had the opportunity to adjust her order quantity month by month. If she ordered too much in one month, she could cut back on next month's order, or if she ordered too little, she could up her order next month or put in a rush order to replenish inventory. For seasonal items, such as ornaments, greeting cards, and calendars, however, she could only place one order each year and there was no opportunity to adjust her order quantity as the season progressed. Last year, Leah watched in dismay as certain items sold out quickly while others languished on the shelves and there was little she could do about it. This year, she was determined to do better. She decided to focus first on calendar sales.

The calendars cost $5.95 apiece and Leah sold them for $14.95 each. She would place her order for the calendars on October 1st, they would arrive November 1st, and any unsold calendars on February 1st would be returned to the publisher for a $1.95 refund. Thus, for every calendar purchased, she would make $9.00, and for every calendar left unsold, she would lose $4.00. Last year, Leah ordered 650 calendars and sold them all by January 15th. This year, she planned to increase her order amount by 5%, to 680 calendars, but due to the current downturn in the economy and high unemployment rates, she wondered if perhaps she should order less than 680.

Leah is facing a tricky inventory-management decision, where ordering too many calendars results in a $4.00 loss on each unsold calendar, but ordering too few means turning away willing customers. Moreover, Leah has minimal experience with making this kind of decision and does not know if she should err on the high or low side. Whereas each unsold calendar will erode her profits, she also knows that unmet demand could turn willing customers into unsatisfied customers, and dissatisfaction could push her customers to shop at other stores in the future.

To help Leah gain experience and develop her understanding of the range of possible consequences that could occur depending on the number of calendars ordered, we will build a simulation model that simulates one year of calendar sales at her bookstore. The simulation model will be interactive and fast, allowing Leah to test different order quantities. For each order quantity, she can see how many calendars are sold, how many are left over, and her resulting profit. More precisely, she will be able to examine the probability distributions for number sold, number left over, and profit. The simulation model will not only provide Leah with essential insights into her order decision, but will also help her determine the optimal order quantity.

MECHANICS OF SIMULATION

Before jumping into the details of how to build a simulation model, we will first discuss what a simulation model is and how simulation works. Once we understand the mechanics, we will turn our attention to a variety of models.

A simulation model is a mathematical model in which a probability distribution is used to represent the possible values of an uncertain variable. This is similar to decision trees and influence diagrams where we use chance nodes to represent uncertain variables. In a decision tree, chance nodes are typically modeled using discrete distributions, allowing us to list every possible outcome, one outcome per branch. Simulation models allow for continuous as well as discrete distributions. Rather than listing all of the possible outcomes—clearly impossible with continuous distributions—we embed the probability distribution into the model. (We explain in the @RISK instructions at the end of the chapter exactly how we insert a whole probability distribution into a single spreadsheet cell.) In our example, Leah's uncertainty is the quantity of calendars demanded. After constructing a model showing how an order quantity and a particular level of demand leads to a profit or loss for Leah, we will replace the constant value for quantity demanded with a probability distribution that matches Leah's beliefs about this season's sales.

For our example, suppose Leah has assessed the following probabilities for Sales:

1. The probability that sales could be less than 600 or greater than about 900 is virtually zero.
2. The median value for sales is about 670. That is $P(\text{Sales} \leq 670) = 0.5$.

FIGURE **11.1**

A continuous distribution representing the uncertainty in number of calendars demanded. This is a shifted and scaled beta distribution with minimum at 600, maximum at 1400, $\alpha_1 = 2$, and $\alpha_2 = 18$.

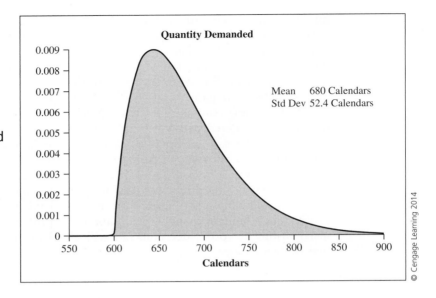

3. The 5th and 95th percentiles are about 615 and 780, respectively. That is, P(Sales ≤ 615) = 0.05 and P(Sales ≤ 780) = 0.95.
4. The lower and upper quartiles are about 640 and 710, respectively. That is, P(Sales ≤ 640) = 0.25 and P(Sales ≤ 710) = 0.75.

Based on these statements, we can use the (shifted and scaled) beta distribution shown in Figure 11.1 as a good approximation to her beliefs about sales. For this distribution we have the minimum at 600, maximum at 1,400, $\alpha_1 = 2$, and $\alpha_2 = 18$. Recall that Chapter 8 discusses how to elicit Leah's beliefs about sales uncertainty and then translate those beliefs into a probability distribution.

Simulation models are dynamic; for every iteration (i.e., every time the model is recalculated), a new value is chosen for each uncertainty according to the corresponding probability distribution, and this value is used in the calculations for that particular iteration. The values are chosen to match their frequency in the probability distribution. For example, according to Figure 11.1, Sales between 600 and 700 calendars occurs about 71% of the time, but Sales between 800 and 900 calendars occurs much less frequently, about 3% of the time. Even though we do not know which value will be chosen for any one iteration, we do know that over hundreds or thousands of iterations, the sampled values will mimic the distribution. Increasing the number of iterations results in sampled values more closely aligned with the distribution, just as more flips of the bent coin produce better estimates of *P(Heads)*.

Figure 11.2 illustrates the dynamic nature of simulation models and shows how the model produces a distribution of consequence values. Figure 11.2 shows a generic model on the left with two embedded probability distributions. As shown, the model is recalculated over and over, each time with values chosen from the probability distributions. For each given set of values, a consequence value is computed by the model. Thus, if we recalculate

FIGURE **11.2**

In a spreadsheet, the simulation process starts with a deterministic model, one that has no probability distributions specified.

Specific cells that contain uncertain inputs are identified, and in these cells appropriate probability distributions are embedded. On each iteration, each probability distribution is used to supply a value to its corresponding cell. The simulation process iterates through the model many times—often thousands of times—and on each iteration, a new value is pulled from each distribution. The resulting consequence values themselves form a distribution of possible consequences, which we call a risk profile.

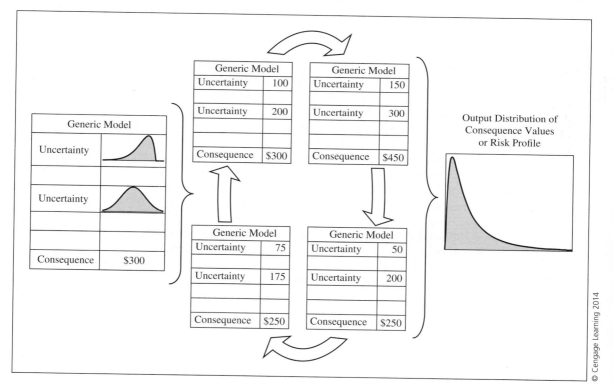

the model 1,000 times based on 1,000 pairs of values drawn from the two distributions, we will have 1,000 consequence values. Note that some of the 1,000 consequence values can be repeated, as shown in Figure 11.2, where the same consequence value ($250) can come about from different input values. Taken together, the set of consequence values themselves form a probability distribution, which we call a risk profile. The simulation-based risk profile is analogous to the risk profiles we saw with decision trees; each one shows the likelihood of possible consequence values.

Note that when a model contains two or more probability distributions, we need to think about the nature of the relationship between the uncertainties. In many cases probabilistic independence, as discussed in Chapter 7, makes good sense, but not always. Independence means that values will be chosen for each uncertainty without regard to the values chosen for the other uncertainties. We have seen plenty of examples so far where one uncertain variable's value does depend on another's. Later in this chapter, we will discuss ways to model relationships among uncertain variables in simulation models.

SAMPLING FROM PROBABILITY DISTRIBUTIONS

Simulation models work by brute force by drawing hundreds or thousands of values from each probability distribution and using these values as inputs. The process of drawing values from a distribution is called *sampling*, and the set of values drawn is called the *sample*. The goal, of course, is for the sampling procedure to produce a sample that closely matches the distribution, but how do we guarantee that it does? For example, consider the probability distribution of an uncertain variable X shown in Figure 11.3. How should we draw a sample of 100 values so that the frequency of the sample closely approximates the probabilities given by the distribution? A direct approach would be to choose values along the x-axis of Figure 11.3, and then check to see if the sample frequencies match the specified probabilities. Here, it turns that an indirect approach works much better. Rather than first choosing the x-axis values, we choose probability values and then we use these probabilities to compute the desired x-axis values. We must be careful in choosing the probability values. A rather simple mathematical theorem states that as long as we choose the probability values uniformly (every possible value is equally likely) from the interval [0, 1], then the x values will have approximately the desired distribution. This simple theorem has tremendous impact as it allows all simulation programs to run effectively and efficiently.

Figure 11.4 illustrates how an x-axis value is computed from a given probability value. We start with a probability value chosen from the uniform[1] distribution, which we denote as $U[0, 1]$. Figure 11.4(a) shows that

FIGURE **11.3**
Continuous probability distribution for uncertain variable *X*, from which we wish to draw a representative sample.

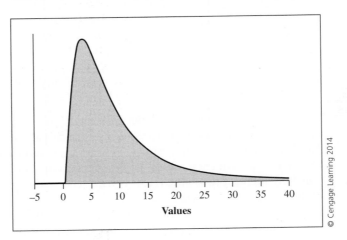

Values

© Cengage Learning 2014

---

[1] The uniform distribution $U[0, 1]$ is shown in Figure 11.4(a). The uniform is unique in that its shape is flat, which means that every interval of the same width has the same probability. See Problems 9.27–9.29.

FIGURE **11.4**

Drawing a random value from a distribution begins by first drawing a probability value using a uniform distribution between zero and one, and then computing its corresponding x-axis values.

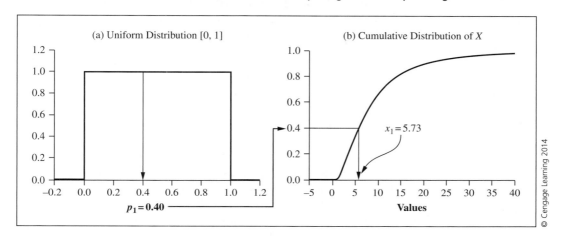

$p_1 = 0.40$ is the chosen probability value. Note that the uniform distribution $U[0, 1]$ must be used as every probability value between zero and one must have the same chance of being chosen. Once the probability value is chosen, we compute the x-axis value x_1 as shown in Figure 11.4(b). Algebraically, x_1 is defined as the unique x-axis value that satisfies $P(X \leq x_1) = p_1$. Here, we see that the x-axis value of 5.73 corresponds to the cumulative probability 0.40. Given any value between zero and one, we can always calculate the unique x value whose cumulative probability equals the given value. This approach works for any probability distribution—continuous, discrete, or even a mixture of the two.

To draw a representative sample of size n from a given probability distribution for an uncertain variable X, we repeat the process n times. First draw a uniform sample of n probability values: $p_1, p_2, \ldots, p_n$. For each probability value p_k, compute x_k, by $P(X \leq x_k) = p_k$ for $k = 1, \ldots, n$. As long as the probability values were chosen uniformly over the interval $[0, 1]$, the theorem guarantees that $x_1, x_2, \ldots, x_n$ will have approximately the same distribution as X. The approximation improves as the size of the sample increases. To draw a representative sample from two or more probability distributions, we draw one sample of uniform probabilities for each distribution. Specifically, if we have two independent uncertainties X and Y, we draw two samples: $p_1, p_2, \ldots, p_n$ and $q_1, q_2, \ldots, q_n$. These two samples are drawn independently of one another, both from $U[0, 1]$. Then, for each pair of values (p_k, q_k), we compute (x_k, y_k), by $P(X \leq x_k) = p_k$ and $P(Y \leq y_k) = q_k$ for $k = 1, \ldots, n$. Finally, each pair of values (x_k, y_k) is used as a pair of input values, and a single consequence value is computed based on these input values.

An astute reader will realize that we have replaced the problem of drawing a representative sample from an arbitrary probability distribution with the problem of drawing a representative sample from the uniform distribution $U[0, 1]$. Essentially, all we need to do is to create a series of random numbers between zero and one and we have an effective method for drawing a representative sample of any size from any distribution. Creating a series of random numbers between zero and one is a well-known problem, and methods for doing so are aptly called *random number generators*. Computers use pseudo-random number generators because they are fast, effective, and produce outcome distributions that are virtually indistinguishable from those of true random number generators. As the name implies, pseudo-random numbers are not truly random, but in fact are based on a starting value and an algorithm that calculates the subsequent numbers in the sequence. True random number generators[2] are typically based on measuring some physical phenomenon such as radio noise and are impractical for computer-based simulation. For our simulation models, we need be able to create dozens of sequences of random values, each one typically a thousand or more numbers long. Today's computer-based pseudo-random number generators can do this accurately and nearly instantaneously.

SIMULATION MODELS

We have seen that simulation models are simply models that use probability distributions to model specific uncertain variables. Because decision trees and influence diagrams also incorporate uncertainties, they can be helpful in the process of constructing a simulation model. For example, influence diagrams not only help identify which variables are decisions, which are computations, and which are uncertain, but they also determine the relationships among the variables. For example, in Leah's case, we know that she has one decision (Order Quantity), one uncertainty (Quantity Demanded), and that her objective is to maximize profit (Profit). The influence diagram in Figure 11.5 shows a graphical representation of the simulation model we wish to build. It is important to note that no arrow exists between the Quantity–Demanded and the Order–Quantity nodes; Quantity Demanded is not known when the order is placed, nor does Order Quantity affect the probability distribution of the Quantity Demanded.

Using the influence diagram in Figure 11.5 as a guide, we can build a model for simulating one year of calendar sales. The first step is to build a *deterministic* model, that is, a static model whose consequence value is completely determined by the input values. For Leah, her consequence is Profit, so we need a model that calculates Profit based on specific values for Order Quantity and Quantity Demanded. Remember, we will be running this model through thousands of iterations, and on each iteration, the model must calculate Profit correctly. In particular, it must do so for every possible

---

[2] The website random.org of Trinity College, Dublin, Ireland offers true random numbers based on atmospheric noise along with information on number generators.

FIGURE **11.5**
Influence diagram
of Leah's inventory
decision.

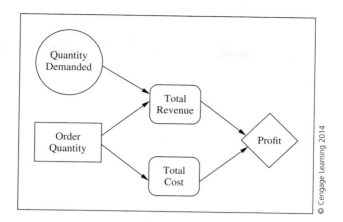

© Cengage Learning 2014

combination of Quantity Ordered and Quantity Demanded. Hence, it is always important to test the model to be sure that it is correct.

Unless you are meticulous, precise, and thorough, it is easy to build a model that produces incorrect values, even for a simple model like Leah's. Two mistakes in this particular problem are common, and both stem from the fact that students build the model to handle special cases instead of calculating Profit correctly for *all possible* values. The most common mistake is shown in Figure 11.6. Each value in Figure 11.6 is correct; even the consequence value (Profit of $5,455) is correct. How can the model be wrong when every value is correct? Because there are possible or potential values for the Quantity-Demanded cell that would produce incorrect Profit values. According to cell B11, Leah's Sales Revenue equals Quantity Demanded (B8) times Retail Price per Calendar (B4), even when Quantity Demanded rises above 700. The error is that Leah has only ordered 700 calendars, as indicated in cell B7, and so, in this case, 700 is the upper limit of sales. The mistake the student made in constructing this model is the assumption that Quantity Demanded can never be greater than Order Quantity, although it could be the case that customers ask for more calendars than Leah ordered. Not only is the formula for Sales Revenue incorrect, but so is the formula for Refund Revenue. The formula (=(B7−B8)∗B5) fails miserably when B8 (Quantity Demanded) is greater than B7 (Order Quantity); in such a case the formula calculates a negative refund amount, even though there would be no calendars to return and hence no refund.

Often, students jump to fix the error shown in Figure 11.6 by changing the formula for Sales Revenue to =B7∗B4, that is, =Order Quantity × Retail Price per Calendar, but this is another error. Again, this formula will only be correct for special cases, specifically those cases in which Quantity Demanded is greater than Order Quantity. The problem here is that we need two different formulas to calculate revenue, one when Quantity Demanded exceeds Order Quantity (Sales Revenue = Order Quantity × Retail Price per Calendar) and the other when Quantity Demanded is less than Order Quantity (Sales Revenue = Quantity Demanded × Retail Price per Calendar). Excel offers a variety of ways to handle such situations.

© Cengage Learning 2014

FIGURE **11.6**
An INCORRECT model of annual calendar sales that assumes all merchandise demanded will be sold regardless of quantity ordered.

	A	B
1	Annual Calendar Sales	
2		
3	Cost per Calendar	$5.95
4	Retail Price per Calendar	$14.95
5	Refund per Calendar	$1.95
6		
7	Order Quantity	700
8	Quantity Demanded	635
9		
10	Revenue	
11	Sales	$9,493.25 =B8 * B4
12	Refund	$126.75 =(B7−B8) * B5
13	Total Revenue	$9,620.00 =SUM(B11:B12)
14		
15	Total Cost	$4,165.00 =B7 * B3
16	Profit	$5,455.00 =B13−B15

Figure 11.7 shows a correct deterministic model for annual calendar sales. Now in cell B13 we have the formula

$$\text{Sales Revenue} = \text{MIN}(\text{Order\_Quantity},\ \text{Quantity\_Demanded}) * \text{Price\_per\_unit}.$$

Thus, the number of calendars Leah sells is the minimum of Order Quantity and Quantity Demanded. We could also use an IF statement here. An example of Excel's IF statement is shown in Figure 11.7, cell B10, where we calculate the number of leftover calendars. If you have any questions concerning your spreadsheet program's functions, you can always check the program's help facility. (You may have also noticed in Figure 11.7 that instead of referring to the cells as B4 or A5, we have named the cells—a feature in Excel—for ease in reading.)

Clearly, it is important to check your deterministic model for accuracy before running the simulation for thousands of iterations. One way to verify that your model is correct is the brute-force method of entering a variety of potential values, and checking that the consequence values are always calculated correctly. Another way is to build in redundant calculations, such as calculating the consequence using different methods or formulas. If the results differ from one formula to the next, there is an error somewhere in the model. One of the best ways to avoid mistakes is to practice good modeling

FIGURE **11.7**
A CORRECT model
of annual calendar
sales.

	A	B	
1	Annual Calendar Sales		
2			
3	Cost per Calendar	$5.95	
4	Retail Price per Calendar	$14.95	
5	Refund per Calendar	$1.95	
6			
7	Order Quantity	700	
8	Quantity Demanded	635	
9			
10	Leftovers	65	=IF(Order_Quantity > Quantity_Demanded, Order_Quantity-Quantity_Demanded, 0)
11			
12	Revenue		
13	Sales	$9,493.25	=MIN(Order_Quantity, Quantity_Demanded)*Price_per_unit
14	Refund	$126.75	=Leftovers*Resale_per_unit
15	Total Revenue	$9,620.00	=SUM(B13:B14)
16			
17	Total Cost	$4,165.00	=Order_Quantity*Cost_per_unit
18			
19	Profit	$5,455.00	=Total_Revenue-Cost

techniques and to construct specific quality-assurance checks into the model. Good modeling techniques include the following:

1. The model is organized in a coherent and natural way.
2. Each constant has its own cell location. Often constants are grouped in a "data area" in the upper left corner of the spreadsheet.
3. Constants are never entered directly into formulas. Any formula should contain only cell references.
4. Formulas are broken down into logical pieces, each piece with its own cell location. It is easy for anyone to make mistakes when entering a long formula.
5. Quality checks such as redundant calculations are built in.
6. The model is verified.
7. The model is fully documented.

By quality checks we mean side calculations in which you know hard facts about the possible results. For example, in the model in Figure 11.7, we have added a formula to calculate the number of leftover calendars. Clearly, this number can never be negative. Thus, after running a simulation, we can check the lower bound of Leftovers, and if it has been negative on any iteration, the model must have mistakes. There are many possible quality checks, such as to add the number of calendars sold to the number of leftovers and subtract the number of calendars ordered; this calculation should always equal zero. Using such quality checks cannot prove your model is 100% correct, but doing so can help you avoid mistakes.

SIMULATING THE MODEL

The next step is to model each uncertain variable with its chosen probability distribution. Substituting probability distributions for unknown inputs transforms the deterministic model into a probabilistic or *stochastic* model, that is, a model whose values are indeterminate and governed by probability distributions. Clearly, the goal of incorporating probability distributions is to create a more realistic model. In Leah's case, the realism comes from mimicking calendars sales at her bookstore; she orders in October without knowing the exact demand, then waits until February to see how many calendars she sold, how many are left over, and her final profit. Our model follows the same progression; she orders now not knowing the demand level, then demand is simulated (over fractions of a second rather than months), after which Leah will know her profit value. Running the simulation through many iterations will give Leah a distribution or risk profile of possible profit values. Not only will Leah gain realistic insights into her sales and profits, but she can also compare the results of different order quantities and choose the best one.

Substituting the distribution in Figure 11.1 for the constant of 635 in the Quantity-Demanded cell creates a stochastic model, and we are almost ready to simulate the model. First, though, we need to choose the number of iterations. For Leah, one iteration is one season of calendar sales. In a simulation, we typically run the model for fixed[3] number of iterations. Thousands of iterations are typical, but how many iterations are necessary to achieve reliable results? The answer depends on the complexity of the model, the number of uncertain variables, and the overall objective of the analysis. For most problems in this text, we recommend at least 1,000 iterations, and 10,000 is not at all unreasonable.

The next step is to run the simulation model and interpret the results. Leah's first choice for how many calendars to order is the expected demand number, which is 680 calendars. It only seems natural that she should order 680 calendars if on average 680 calendars will be demanded. Running the model for 5,000 iterations produces the risk profile for Profit shown in

---

[3] Instead of setting a fixed value for the number of iterations, one can specify that the simulation process should stop once the results converge (or stop changing) within a specified tolerance level. See your simulation software for more details.

FIGURE **11.8**

(a) The risk profile for Profit when 680 calendars are ordered and (b) the cumulative risk profile for Profit when 680 calendars are ordered.

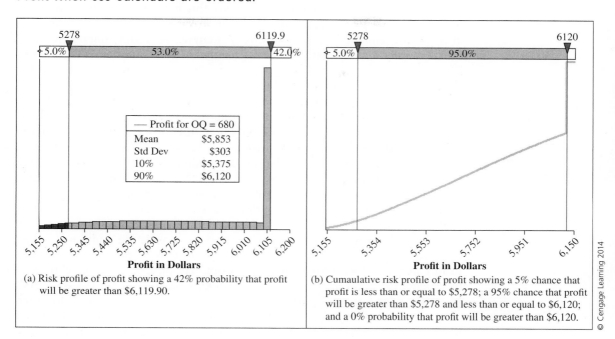

(a) Risk profile of profit showing a 42% probability that profit will be greater than $6,119.90.

(b) Cumaulative risk profile of profit showing a 5% chance that profit is less than or equal to $5,278; a 95% chance that profit will be greater than $5,278 and less than or equal to $6,120; and a 0% probability that profit will be greater than $6,120.

Figure 11.8. The legend shows that if Leah orders 680 calendars, her expected profit is $5,853. The standard deviation is $303, the 10th percentile is $5,375, and the 90th percentile is $6,120. Thus, according to our model, when Leah orders 680 calendars, then on average her profit will be $5,853, with a 10% chance that it will be $5,375 or lower and a 10% chance that her profit will be $6,120 or higher.

The risk profile in Figure 11.8(a) and its corresponding cumulative form in Figure 11.8(b) look different from others we have seen. A major difference is that these risk profiles have a smooth shape compared to the discrete or staircase shape of the risk profiles for decision trees and influence diagrams. The difference is a result of using continuous distributions instead of the discrete distributions used in decision-tree models. A continuous distribution allows all values in a range to be possible, and by sampling 5,000 values, we get a comparatively smooth risk profile.

Also note that the risk profiles shown in Figures 11.8 are not the typical bell-shaped curves. Both figures show a jump in the probability in the $6,120 vicinity. This bump in probability is an unusual feature and deserves our attention. Figure 11.8 shows that the probability suddenly jumps 42% from when Profit = $6,119.90 to when Profit = $6,120. To see this jump, focus on the shaded region of the bars along the top of Figure 11.8. We see that the probability of Profit being less than or equal to $6,119.90 is 58% (= 5% + 53%) and the probability of Profit being less than or equal to $6,120 is 100% (= 5% + 95%). To determine why this happens, we can turn to the model and look for scenarios that result in Profit equaling $6,120. There are also specific simulation tools (sensitivity analysis, scenarios, filters, etc.) that can be used to investigate the risk profiles. In this situation, the value of $6,120 is the maximum profit value, and a moment's reflection reveals that the jump occurs whenever Leah sells all of her inventory.

One way to understand why the risk profile has a jump at $6,120 is to turn to the Quantity-Demanded distribution in Figure 11.1. Given that Leah ordered 680 calendars, we want to know the probability that Quantity Demand is 680 or more. Not surprisingly, when we calculate this probability, it is 42%. Thus, in the simulation, approximately 42% of the time the demand distribution will produce Quantity-Demanded values above 680, and for each of these values Profit equals $6,120. In other words, if Leah orders 680 calendars, 42% of the time she will sell out by Feb 1st, resulting in Profit equaling $6,120.

Leah can go further in her investigation by considering additional values for Order Quantity. By comparing the risk profiles of the different orders, Leah can find which Order Quantity is optimal. Suppose she has chosen to investigate the additional eight values of 600, 650, 700, 750, 800, 850, 900, and 950 calendars. After running eight separate simulations, one for each of the values, there will be eight Profit distributions. In Figure 11.9, we have graphed the expected Profit for the Order-Quantity values, that is, $E[Profit \mid Order\ Quantity = 600]$, $E[Profit \mid Order\ Quantity = 650]$, etc.

For an order of 600 calendars, the simulation results show that Leah's expected profit is $5,400. If Leah were to order 650 calendars, expected profit increases to $5,763. Hence, the simulation shows that based on the objective of maximizing expected profit, 650 calendars is a better order quantity than 600 calendars. The maximum expected profit occurs at 700, with an expected profit of $5,865. However, 700 is not necessarily the optimal order

FIGURE **11.9**
Eight simulations were run, each one for 5,000 iterations.

Expected profit increases for order quantities up to 700 calendars, then decreases.

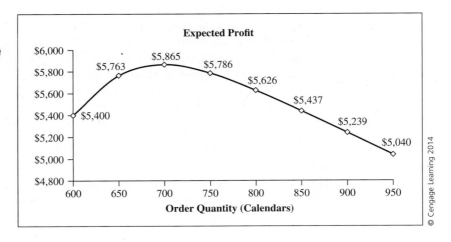

© Cengage Learning 2014

© Cengage Learning 2014

FIGURE **11.10**
The expected profit of eight simulations, each with 5,000 iterations, are shown for Order-Quantity values 660, 670, 680, 690, 700, 710, 720, and 730 calendars.

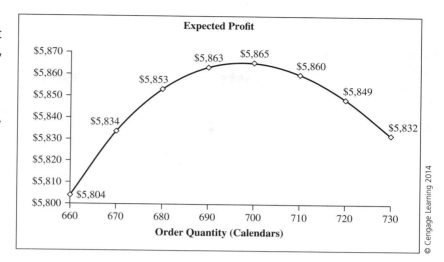

quantity. We only know that the order quantity that maximizes expected profit is in the neighborhood of 700 calendars. We can run another set of simulations, this time with order quantities more closely spaced around 700. Let's try 660, 670, 680, 690, 700, 710, 720, and 730.

The results from the second set of simulations are shown in Figure 11.10. Expected Profit is again maximized when Order Quantity is 700. In both Figures 11.9 and 11.10, it appears that the expected Profit drops off somewhat more quickly for lower values of Order Quantity than for higher ones. In other words, it is more costly to Leah to order too few than too many. This makes sense—remember from the original problem that Leah buys the calendars for $5.95 each, sells what she can for $14.95, and gets a $1.95 refund for any leftovers. So if she orders too many, she loses $4.00 for every one left over, but if she orders too few, she misses out on $9.00 in profit for every missed sale. So it makes sense that she would err on the high side, ordering more than the expected demand of 680.

One additional thing to note about Figure 11.10 is that there is not a lot of difference in the expected values. All are between $5,800 and $5,865, and if we look at the expected values for order quantities 680 to 720, all of the expected values are within a $16 band. Of course, 700 is the optimal quantity, and that's what Leah should order, but it's interesting to note that her expected value would not be much less if she were to order 680, the expected demand. This is an example of what is known as the *flat maximum*; when optimizing an expected value, it is often the case that the expected value in the neighborhood of the optimal decision is not highly sensitive. This is good news, because it means that you can make small mistakes—be slightly non-optimal—and your expected value will still be close to optimal. In other words, if your model is solid (i.e., correct and requisite) and gives you an optimal choice, you don't have to sweat the details.

The eight Profit risk profiles (one for each value of Order Quantity) report more than the expected values; they also report the risks associated

© Cengage Learning 2014

FIGURE **11.11**
The middle 90% of profit values of eight simulations, each with 5,000 iterations.

The graph shows that as the quantity ordered increases, so does the risk.

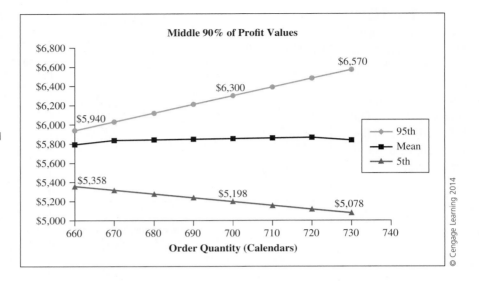

with each Order Quantity. Figure 11.11 shows the middle 90% of the Profit values (5th to 95th percentile) for each Order Quantity. We clearly see that with an increase in the number of calendars ordered, there is greater variability in profit. For example, ordering 660 calendars results in a 90% chance that Profit will be between $5,358 and $5,940, whereas ordering 730 nearly triples the width of the middle 90% of profits from $5,078 to $6,570. The wider range for ordering 730 calendars shows that there are greater risks. At the 700-calendar order, where expected Profit is maximized, the range is $5,198 to $6,300. Thus, if Leah were to order 700 calendars, she will be choosing the order quantity that maximizes expected Profit, but she will be taking on more risk than she would if she ordered fewer calendars.

Note that instead of investigating the middle 90% of Profit values, we could have considered the complete range, that is, from the minimum to the maximum. While the range is an important consideration when making hard decisions, the range can be greatly influenced simply by which values were chosen from the probability distribution for the simulation. Remember that simulation is based on choosing probability values and then using them to derive the sample values. Suppose that in one run of the simulation, the smallest probability value chosen is 0.01, and for the next running, the smallest probability value chosen is 0.0001 or even 0.00000001. While the difference between these probability values is relatively small, the difference in their corresponding sample values can be quite large and, furthermore, these extreme sample values can have considerable impact on the consequence function. Thus, the minimum and maximum of the consequence variable can be greatly affected by the mechanics of simulation, which is generally not true for less extreme percentiles, such as the 5th and 95th.

Standard deviation is also used to measure risk; the larger the standard deviation, the greater the associated risks. The standard-deviation measure of risk and the 5th to 95th percentile range almost always agree, as they do in this example. Here, the least risky alternative is ordering 660 calendars, as it has the narrowest 90% interval and the smallest standard deviation of $204. The riskiest alternative is ordering 730 calendars as it has the widest 90% interval and greatest standard deviation of $503. Finally, the riskiness of 700-calendar order is somewhere between these two with a standard deviation of $394. Note that maximizing expected profit puts upward pressure on the number of calendars to order, whereas minimizing risk puts a downward pressure on how many calendars to order. Leah could either use utility theory (Chapter 13) to make trade-offs between risk and return or she could use her judgment to decide on the best order quantity, now that she knows the risks and returns.

Leah has discovered an important inventory-management fact through this relatively simple simulation model. For her, expected Profit is maximized by an Order Quantity that is greater than the expected Quantity Demanded. Remember, she stated that she believed 680 calendars would be demanded for the upcoming season, and thus, the mean of the Quantity-Demanded distribution in Figure 11.1 is 680 calendars. A common misconception is that ordering the expected demand (long-run average of demand) will be the order amount that minimizes leftovers and maximizes expected profit. In fact, in this model, expected Profit is maximized when ordering 700 calendars, which is 20 calendars more than Leah expects to sell. Why? The reason is that it costs more for Leah to miss out on a sale than to have a calendar left over; when she misses out on a sale because of having too few calendars, she "loses" (could have had) $9.00, but a leftover calendar only costs $4 ($5.95 cost minus $1.95 refund) when she sends it back. As a result, she would rather err on the side of having too many calendars on hand.

Leah now has a much greater understanding of the distribution of Profit for each value of Order Quantity she is considering. She may go with the alternative that maximizes expected Profit or she may choose another alternative, particularly if she wants to reduce risks.

SIMULATION VS. DECISION TREES

What is the relationship between simulation and decision-tree models? That is, if we construct a simulation model using continuous distributions and a decision-tree model using discrete distributions, should we expect the same results? To answer this for the bookstore example, we need to construct a decision tree using all the same parameters, but substituting a discrete distribution for the shifted beta distribution. Which discrete distribution should we use? In Chapter 8 we discussed two methods for constructing a discrete distribution that approximates a continuous distribution: the extended Swanson-Megill (ES-M) and the extended Pearson-Tukey (EP-T) approximations. Remember that both of these are three-point distributions, so we will be comparing our simulation model using a continuous beta distribution with a model based on a simple three-point discrete distribution. The results may surprise you!

We will substitute the EP-T approximation (leaving the ES-M to an exercise) for the beta and compare the results. Remember that the EP-T is constructed by assigning the probability values of 0.185 to the 5th percentile, 0.63 to the 50th percentile, and again 0.185 to the 95th percentile. When

FIGURE **11.12**
The (a) probability density graphs and the (b) cumulative distribution graphs for the continuous beta distribution shown in Figure 11.1 and its extended Pearson-Tukey approximation.

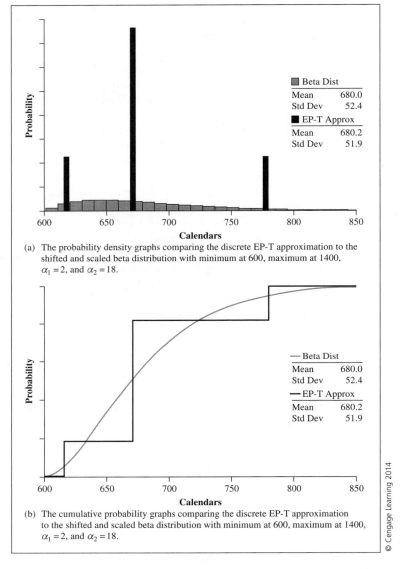

(a) The probability density graphs comparing the discrete EP-T approximation to the shifted and scaled beta distribution with minimum at 600, maximum at 1400, $\alpha_1 = 2$, and $\alpha_2 = 18$.

(b) The cumulative probability graphs comparing the discrete EP-T approximation to the shifted and scaled beta distribution with minimum at 600, maximum at 1400, $\alpha_1 = 2$, and $\alpha_2 = 18$.

© Cengage Learning 2014

Leah made her original probability assessments at the beginning of the chapter, she gave us exactly what we need: her 5th, 50th, and 95th percentiles for demand were 615, 670, and 780[4] calendars, respectively. The EP-T approximation for the shifted beta distribution in Figure 11.1 is shown in Figure 11.12. It doesn't look much like that beta distribution, does it?

_____

[4] We are using 780 because it is Leah's assessed 95th percentile, although the astute reader may notice that the shifted and scaled beta distribution that approximates Leah's beliefs has its 95th percentile at 781. Strictly speaking, if we wanted to approximate the shifted and scaled beta distribution itself, we would have used 781; see Problem 11.12.

Even though the EP-T distribution looks quite different from the beta distribution, the statistics reported to the right of each graph show that the two distributions have nearly identical means (680 vs. 680.2) and close standard deviations (52.4 vs. 51.9). This is no accident. Both the EP-T and ES-M were developed specifically to closely match the mean and standard deviation.

Figure 11.13 shows the decision-tree model for Leah's decision with the discrete approximation representing uncertainty about demand. Only two different values for Order Quantity are shown, but we will evaluate several possible values, just as we did in the simulation model.

To compare the results from the continuous simulation model and discrete decision-tree model, we use each model to calculate the expected Profit for Order Quantities ranging from 600 to 850 calendars. Figure 11.14 shows the expected Profits for both the continuous and discrete models, and we see

FIGURE **11.13**

Decision tree of calendar sales, where the consequence values are the associated profit values.

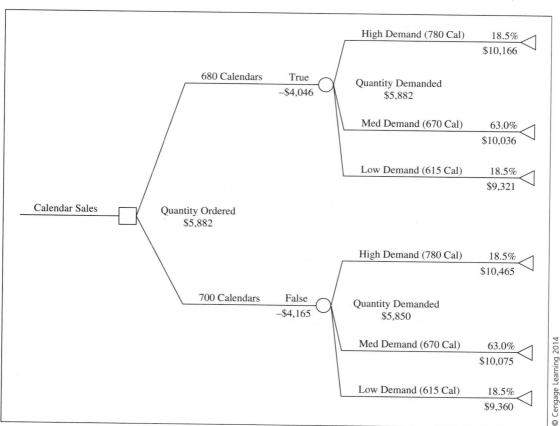

© Cengage Learning 2014

FIGURE **11.14**
Comparing the
expected Profit for
a discrete versus a
continuous distri-
bution used to
describe quantity
demanded.

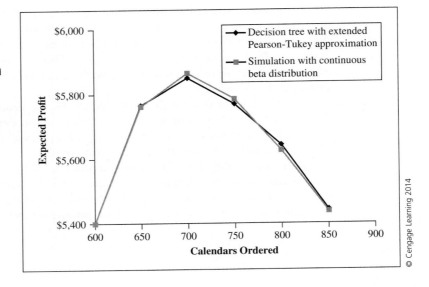

that there is very little difference. The maximum difference in the expected
Profits is only $17 and occurs at the 800-calendar order. Similarly, but not
shown, the standard deviations for the continuous and discrete models are
nearly identical, with the maximum difference being $49 at the 700-calendar
order.

The lesson we want you to draw from this example is that decision trees
and simulation models can produce very similar results, even though they use
two very different processes to calculate the risk profiles. Of course, care must
be taken in the choice of the distributions for both model types. In particular,
if a discrete distribution is substituted for a continuous distribution, we recommend using one of the discrete-approximation approaches discussed in
Chapter 8.

We conclude our discussion of Leah's order-quantity decision with a
few observations. First, there is no requirement that there be only one output or consequence measure. Leah's main objective is to maximize expected
profit, but she might also be concerned about the number of leftover
(unsold) calendars and/or concerned about unmet demand. She can easily
create risk profiles of these secondary concerns using simulation. Exercise
11.8 investigates what is the optimal order quantity when the consequence
includes an additional $3.00 penalty (due to loss of goodwill, for example)
for each calendar that could have been sold if inventory was sufficient.
Thus, simulation models allow us to easily investigate additional variables,
such as leftover calendars, or include additional concerns such as goodwill
or opportunity costs.

Second, note also how the idea of requisite models was used in Leah's
decision. For example, we included only calendar sales in the model,

even though a customer typically will purchase more items than just calendars. Of course, we can always cycle back through the modeling process as described in Figure 1.1 to include more items if this becomes an important aspect of Leah's decision. We have also ignored the fact that the calendars can only be sold in whole units. While it is unrealistic to sell fractional amounts, our goal is not to build the most realistic model, but a requisite model. The question is: Does including fractional sales materially impact the model results? Exercise 11.10 asks you to answer this question. The point is that no amount of modeling can ever produce a completely realistic model, but deep insights into the decision problem can be found by using a requisite model.

Finally, as a manager, Leah can take certain actions to manage calendar demand. Through advertising and promotions, she can potentially increase demand. The model in Figure 11.7 can be modified to include marketing campaigns, which will have associated costs and may change the Quantity-Demanded distribution. Determining exactly how marketing affects the demand distribution is tricky, but analysis of past campaigns may be helpful. Leah can then use the revised model to determine whether marketing would be cost effective.

EXAMPLES OF SIMULATION MODELS

Now that we understand the mechanics of simulation, let's look at how simulation can help us make hard decisions. Our first example demonstrates how simulation can solve probability questions easily. We then discuss how simulation can help with budget decisions, and the last example shows how simulation can help in the evaluation of financial assets.

Probability Models

Two well-known problems in probability are the Monty Hall Problem and the Birthday Problem. One reason these problems are well known is that they are easily stated, but their solutions go against our intuition. Many people, even trained statisticians, have difficulty solving these problems. We will tackle the Birthday Problem here, leaving the Monty Hall Problem as Problem 11.15 at the end of the chapter.

The Birthday Problem asks the question, "What is the probability that, out of 30 people, at least two will have the same birthday (that is, they were born on the same day of the year)?" Our intuition is that it is unlikely that two people out of a random group of 30 would have the same birthday, but surprisingly the probability is about 70%.

To use simulation to solve the Birthday Problem, we first construct a deterministic model. As shown in Figure 11.15, we simply list 30 people in Column A and in Column B, and assign a number between 1 and 365 inclusive to each person, representing the day of the year they were born. Then in Column D, we compare the birthday assigned to Person 1 (138 in this case)

FIGURE **11.15**
Spreadsheet model of Birthday Problem.

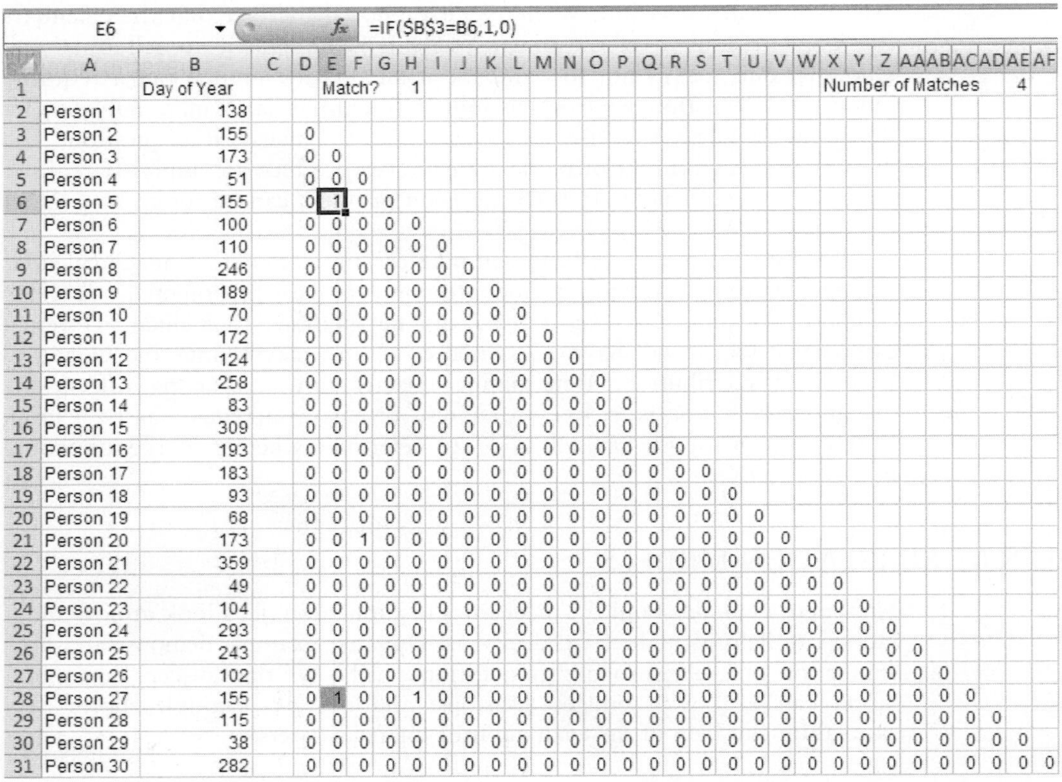

E6		f_x	=IF($B$3=B6,1,0)

	A	B	C	D	E	F	G	H	I	J	K	L	M	N	O	P	Q	R	S	T	U	V	W	X	Y	Z	AA	AB	AC	AD	AE	AF
1		Day of Year			Match?				1																Number of Matches							4
2	Person 1	138																														
3	Person 2	155		0																												
4	Person 3	173		0	0																											
5	Person 4	51		0	0	0																										
6	Person 5	155		0	1	0	0																									
7	Person 6	100		0	0	0	0	0																								
8	Person 7	110		0	0	0	0	0	0																							
9	Person 8	246		0	0	0	0	0	0	0																						
10	Person 9	189		0	0	0	0	0	0	0	0																					
11	Person 10	70		0	0	0	0	0	0	0	0	0																				
12	Person 11	172		0	0	0	0	0	0	0	0	0	0																			
13	Person 12	124		0	0	0	0	0	0	0	0	0	0	0																		
14	Person 13	258		0	0	0	0	0	0	0	0	0	0	0	0																	
15	Person 14	83		0	0	0	0	0	0	0	0	0	0	0	0	0																
16	Person 15	309		0	0	0	0	0	0	0	0	0	0	0	0	0	0															
17	Person 16	193		0	0	0	0	0	0	0	0	0	0	0	0	0	0	0														
18	Person 17	183		0	0	0	0	0	0	0	0	0	0	0	0	0	0	0	0													
19	Person 18	93		0	0	0	0	0	0	0	0	0	0	0	0	0	0	0	0	0												
20	Person 19	68		0	0	0	0	0	0	0	0	0	0	0	0	0	0	0	0	0	0											
21	Person 20	173		0	0	1	0	0	0	0	0	0	0	0	0	0	0	0	0	0	0	0										
22	Person 21	359		0	0	0	0	0	0	0	0	0	0	0	0	0	0	0	0	0	0	0	0									
23	Person 22	49		0	0	0	0	0	0	0	0	0	0	0	0	0	0	0	0	0	0	0	0	0								
24	Person 23	104		0	0	0	0	0	0	0	0	0	0	0	0	0	0	0	0	0	0	0	0	0	0							
25	Person 24	293		0	0	0	0	0	0	0	0	0	0	0	0	0	0	0	0	0	0	0	0	0	0	0						
26	Person 25	243		0	0	0	0	0	0	0	0	0	0	0	0	0	0	0	0	0	0	0	0	0	0	0	0					
27	Person 26	102		0	0	0	0	0	0	0	0	0	0	0	0	0	0	0	0	0	0	0	0	0	0	0	0	0				
28	Person 27	155		0	1	0	0	1	0	0	0	0	0	0	0	0	0	0	0	0	0	0	0	0	0	0	0	0	0			
29	Person 28	115		0	0	0	0	0	0	0	0	0	0	0	0	0	0	0	0	0	0	0	0	0	0	0	0	0	0	0		
30	Person 29	38		0	0	0	0	0	0	0	0	0	0	0	0	0	0	0	0	0	0	0	0	0	0	0	0	0	0	0	0	
31	Person 30	282		0	0	0	0	0	0	0	0	0	0	0	0	0	0	0	0	0	0	0	0	0	0	0	0	0	0	0	0	0

with the remaining 29 people. We use an IF() statement, shown in the formula bar of Figure 11.16, to make the comparison, assigning a 1 if there is a match and a 0 if not. Because there are no 1's in Column D, Person 1 is the only person in the group born on day 138. In Column E, we compare Person 2's assigned birthday of 155 to the remaining 28 people. We see that not only does Person 5 have the same birthday as Person 2, but so does Person 27. So there are two 1's in Column E.

Building this model gives us an immediate insight as to why the probability of finding a match is higher than our initial impression. We need to compare not just one person to the rest, but compare all possible pairs of people, and there are a surprisingly large number of distinct pairs among 30 people. A quick calculation shows that there are 435 distinct pairs, and each and every one of these is a potential match. Clearly, the more potential matches, the higher the probability of observing a match.

Finally, we need to compute the consequence value. As shown on the far right of Figure 11.15, we have the "Number of Matches," which is the sum

FIGURE **11.16**
Simulation results for the Birthday Problem showing the probability of no matches (about 30.4%) and at least one match (69.6%).

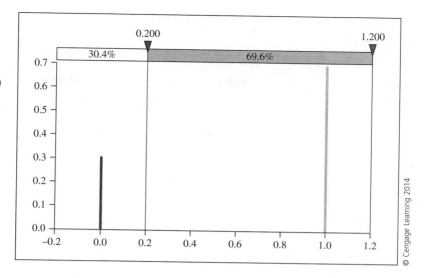

of all the comparisons, SUM(D3:AF31). If this number is zero, no birthdays matched. If the sum is one or greater, two or more people have a shared birthday. The formula for "Match?" in H1 is an IF() statement and reports a one when the total number of matches is one or more, and reports zero if there are no matches at all. Thus, our consequence measure is H1 and we want to know what is the probability that cell H1 = 1.

To simulate this model, we need to incorporate 30 probability distributions, one for each person. We assume birthdays are uniformly distributed across the calendar year. (There is research showing that there are actually more births than expected in the months July–October, and fewer in March–May. Problem 11.16 asks you to solve the Birthday Problem using a distribution based on the actual data of births by day of year.) Assuming uniformly distributed births across the year, we assign 30 discrete uniform distributions (minimum = 1, maximum = 365) to the values in cells B2 to B31. (For simplicity we are assuming that no one was born on Feb 29, although that could be incorporated into the model quite easily. Can you see how?) Each iteration of the model will assign a birthday to each of the 30 people, and because we have assumed independence, the assignment of a birthday for one person does not depend on the assignment for the other people. Thus, it is by the luck of the draw whether two or more people share a birthday. This is equivalent to choosing a different set of 30 people in each iteration; a simulation of 1,000 iterations is equivalent to 1,000 groups of 30 people.

As the simulation runs, it keeps track of the number of times the consequence value, H1, equals one (at least one match), and likewise the number of times the consequence value equals zero (no matches). The simulation results in Figure 11.16 show that zero or no matches occurred in 30.4% of the 1,000 iterations. Thus, according to this model, the probability of at least 2 people out of 30 sharing the same birthday is approximately 70%.

A Capital Budgeting Model

Our next example is a capital budgeting example showing how a simple simulation model can help with management decisions. Suppose you are VP of marketing, and divisions report to you. For the upcoming fiscal year, you need to know the total capital requirements for the launch of a new product, and so you have asked the 10 division heads to report their forecasts. Let's further assume that each division head reports the same forecast of $100,000. In addition, each one reports that he or she is 90% confident that the actual amount will be between $90,000 and $110,000. Given these estimates, how much should you budget for the upcoming year? Clearly, the expected total capital requirement is $1 million (10 times $100,000), but how much variation should you plan for?

The model is quite simple and is shown in Figure 11.17. We have placed the triangular distribution shown in Figure 11.17 in each of the division's annual budget cells, and the total budget is simply the sum of the divisions' budgets. Each triangular distribution has a mean of $100,000, and a 90% probability of returning a cost between $90,000 and $100,000, in line with each division's projections.

A common business practice used to determine the range of possible outcomes is to carry out a best-worst case analysis where the model is calculated twice, once for the best-case scenario and once again for the worst-case scenario. In this budget example, we will take the best case to be when division

FIGURE **11.17**

Annual budget model based on the projections of 10 divisions, where each division's costs are modeled as a triangular distribution.

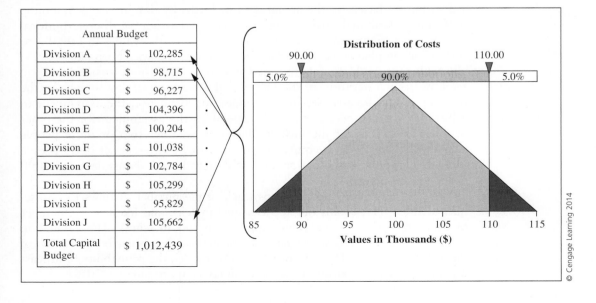

Annual Budget		
Division A	$	102,285
Division B	$	98,715
Division C	$	96,227
Division D	$	104,396
Division E	$	100,204
Division F	$	101,038
Division G	$	102,784
Division H	$	105,299
Division I	$	95,829
Division J	$	105,662
Total Capital Budget	$ 1,012,439	

Distribution of Costs

© Cengage Learning 2014

costs are at the 5th percentile, or $90,000.[5] Substituting $90,000 for each division into our model produces a total capital budget of $900,000. Similarly, the worst case is taken to be the 95th percentile, or $110,000, for each division, resulting in a total capital budget of $1.1 million. Thus, our best-worst case analysis reports that the total capital requirement could be anywhere from $900,000 to $1.1 million. Based on this, a conservative VP would budget $1.1 million for the upcoming year.

The best-worst case analysis can be seriously flawed, though. Why? Because it ignores how the system (in this case, the company) actually functions. In general, some divisions will have higher costs than forecast, and some will have lower costs. Rarely will every division simultaneously exceed the forecasts to the same extent (i.e., all best cases or all worst cases). Figure 11.17 shows one realization of costs for each of the 10 divisions; notice that some of the costs are above the forecast and some are below. As a matter of fact, only three of the 10 divisions in Figure 11.17 fall below the forecast, and still the total capital requirement is closer to $1 million than it is to the worst case of $1.1 million.

Simulation produces much different results when compared to the best-worst case analysis. Figure 11.18 shows the risk profile of the total capital requirement. Naturally, the mean is $1 million. The 5th and 95th percentiles, however, are $0.96 and $1.04 million, respectively. Thus, we can be 90% sure that the total capital requirement will fall between $0.96 and $1.04 million, a

FIGURE **11.18**
Distribution of total capital budget based on capital requirement forecasts from 10 divisions.

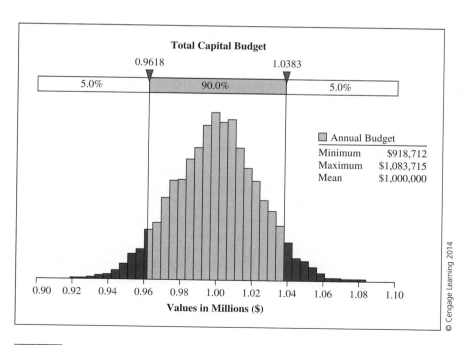

---

[5] Clearly, the best case would be zero costs, but that is unreasonable. And although our triangular distribution indicates that the lowest possible cost is around $85,000, we are taking the 5th percentile as a more reasonable lower bound. Similarly, we will take the 95th percentiles as a reasonable upper bound.

range of only $42,000, compared to the $200,000 range from the best-worst case analysis. Our conservative VP needs to set aside only $1.04 million to be 95% confident of covering the entire capital requirement for this particular project, freeing up $96,000 for other investments. You can see how simulation gives a more precise and realistic picture of the variation in the actual capital required, which in turn can help in determining an appropriate capital budget.

Remember that a simulation analysis draws from the input distributions independently unless the model is explicitly created with dependencies among the uncertainties. There are a number of ways to handle dependencies, which we discuss in the @RISK instructions at the end of the chapter. For the capital budget problem, how would dependencies arise and be modeled? Because we are dealing 10 divisions within one firm, we might think there would be a positive relationship among the divisions. In this case, if one division has costs that are higher than forecasted, we would expect the other nine divisions also to exceed their forecasts. To determine if this is a reasonable assumption, we would need to know more about the workings of the firm, but for now, let's assume there is a positive correlation among all 10 divisions.

Figure 11.19 shows the impact of incorporating a positive correlation among all 10 divisions. Figure 11.19(a) shows the case where the correlation between any two divisions is 0.50 and Figure 11.19(b) shows a more extreme case where the correlation between any two divisions is 0.90. In both cases, the expected total capital requirement is unchanged at $1 million. The correlations affect the spread of the distributions, and we see that the higher the correlation, the wider apart are the 5th and 95th percentiles. In the independent case previously analyzed, the difference between the 5th and 95th percentiles is $42,000, but when the correlation is 0.50, the difference is $177,000, and when the correlation is 0.90, the difference is $230,000. The increased spread makes sense because the more highly correlated the costs are, the more likely a high cost in one division would be associated with similar high costs in the other divisions.

Stock Price Model

One way to think of a Monte Carlo simulation, and for that matter a decision tree, is that they both model, in an explicit fashion, all possible future outcomes and the resulting consequences. Often the goal of such a model is to leverage the knowledge of what could happen to one's advantage. Nowhere is this more readily apparent as when we turn to models of stock prices. There are a variety of ways to model future stock prices (bootstrapping, binomial trees, and factor models), and one of the more sophisticated is the lognormal pricing model. The lognormal model is based on the lognormal distribution, and, not by accident, stock prices tend to follow a lognormal distribution. In Figure 11.20, we show the results of 5,000 iterations of the lognormal pricing model forecasting stock prices 6 months into the future. The distribution shown in Figure 11.20 is a lognormal distribution, and before discussing the details of the model, we note two important points about the lognormal distribution. First, zero is the lower bound, so prices can never be negative. Second, Figure 11.20 shows that the distribution is skewed right, which shows that prices can climb and climb,

FIGURE **11.19**
Distribution of total
capital budget
based on forecasts
from 10 divisions
when (a) the
correlation
between any two
divisions is 0.50 and
(b) the correlation
between any two
divisions is 0.90.

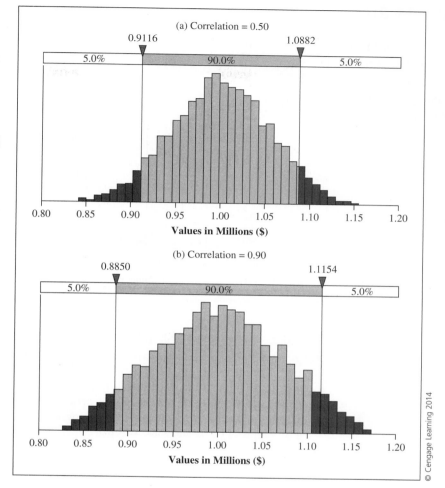

but with increasingly smaller probabilities. For example, we see that there is a
5% chance that the stock price will be greater than $158.40 and the maximum
of the 5,000 iterations extends all the way to $317.41.

The lognormal pricing model requires three parameters or inputs: the current or today's stock price (*TP*), the stock's annual growth rate (*Rate*), and
the stock's annual volatility (*Vol*). Letting FP_k represent the future price of
the asset after *k* years, the lognormal model is:

$$FP_k = TP \times \exp\left(\left(Rate - \frac{1}{2} \times Vol^2\right) \times k + Vol \times \sqrt{k} \times N(0,1)\right)$$

where $N(0,1)$ represents a standard normal random variable (mean zero and
standard deviation one). Note that we are constructing a lognormal random
variable from the standard normal. Although the math behind doing so is
beyond the scope of this text, you can see that we are essentially multiplying

FIGURE **11.20**
Lognormal pricing
model results for a
stock with a current
price of $100,
annual growth rate
of 7%, and annual
volatility of 40%.

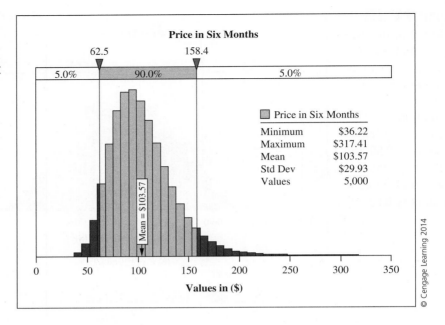

the standard normal variable times a constant ($Vol \times \sqrt{k}$), adding a constant ($Rate - \frac{1}{2} \times Vol^2$), and then exponentiating the result. As you know from Chapter 7, multiplying a normal random variable by a constant and adding a constant yields a random variable that is still normal, albeit with different mean and standard deviation. It is the process of exponentiation that transforms the normal random variable into a lognormal one.

For Figure 11.20, we want the price in 6 months ($k = 0.5$). Substituting our input values (current price of $100, annual growth rate of 7%, and annual volatility of 40%) into Formula 11.1 gives

$$FP_{0.5} = \$100 \times \exp\left(\left(0.07 - \frac{1}{2} \times (0.40)^2\right) \times 0.5 + 0.40 \times \sqrt{0.5} \times N(0,1)\right)$$

To simulate the future price in 6 months ($FP_{0.5}$), we begin by sampling from a standard normal distribution, and then substitute that number into Formula 11.2 to calculate $FP_{0.5}$. Simulating $FP_{0.5}$ in this way for 5,000 iterations produced Figure 11.20, the distribution for this stock's price in 6 months.

How can we leverage this information to our advantage? By knowing the distribution of prices, we can calculate the distribution of cash flows on financial derivatives based on that asset. For example, in Chapter 13, we use the lognormal pricing model to model the cash flows from an option, and then price that option. The derivatives market is a multi-trillion-dollar market just in the United States, and knowing how to price a derivative is valuable information. In addition, portfolio managers are very interested in the possible distribution of their assets, particularly as these assets can move in tandem, exposing their portfolios to great risk. Using the lognormal pricing model

© Cengage Learning 2014

FIGURE **11.21**
Four possible future price paths for a stock whose current price is $100 as predicted by the lognormal pricing model.

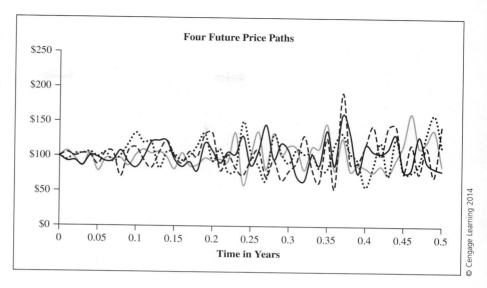

together with correlations can help managers develop insights about their portfolios. In addition, it allows the manager to investigate modifications to the makeup of the portfolio and investigate possible hedging strategies. These two examples show that the lognormal pricing model used in conjunction with simulation can be very useful in quantitative finance.

We conclude by noting that while the lognormal model does not tell us what the stock price will be in 6 months, it provides the distribution of prices based on all possible future price paths for the underlying asset or stock. For example, Figure 11.21 shows four possible price paths of the stock over the 6-month period. The figure shows that as we go further into the future, the price becomes more uncertain. Also, if you were to look at the distribution of prices at any point in Figure 11.21, the prices would follow a lognormal distribution. In others words, MC simulation does not tell us the exact future, but does tell us which prices are probable and which are unlikely. Even though we don't know the exact future price path, knowing the future price distribution can help us make better financial decisions.

**Monte Carlo
Simulation
in the Wild**

Monte Carlo simulation is a widely used research tool. Applications can be found in fields ranging from physics to life sciences, from finance and economics to archaeology. We have chosen a few interesting examples to highlight the various ways people have used Monte Carlo to help make difficult decisions.

- **TB Alliance.** Each year, tuberculosis (TB) infects some 10 million people around the world, and about 2 million die. Treatment of TB is difficult, and many strains of the microbe have become resistant to existing drugs. The Global Alliance for TB Drug Development (TB Alliance) is a partnership among pharmaceutical companies, governmental agencies, and academia to jointly manage a number of promising anti-tuberculosis drugs at various stages of development. When the study began, a stated goal of the TB Alliance was to bring a novel anti-tuberculosis drug to market by 2010 (a goal which was not achieved). A 2006 analysis used a spreadsheet-based Monte Carlo simulation model to determine the likelihood that the TB Alliance's goal would be reached by considering the various drugs under development and the chances of each one succeeding as they moved through the drug development-and-approval process. The analysis showed a chance of less than 5% that the goal would be reached by 2010 with the portfolio of compounds under development in 2005. However, the probability of at least one new TB drug reaching the market by 2019 jumped to over 70%. The model also indicated that, in order to succeed by 2019, the TB Alliance would need more than $100 million in additional funding, a tall order given that they had only $36 million at the time (Glickman et al., 2006).

- **Renewable Energy.** Many researchers, companies, and consultants are using Monte Carlo simulation as part of the planning process for renewable energy projects. For example, a recent study (Marmidis et al., 2008) used Monte Carlo to solve the problem of optimal placement of wind turbines on a wind farm. By simulating the wind characteristics across the wind farm, the authors were able to show how one could place wind turbines optimally, choosing wind turbines with appropriate specifications at each location. In another example, scientists from Argonne National Laboratories in Chicago used Monte Carlo to estimate the levelized cost of energy for solar power produced by photovoltaic panels (Darling et al., 2011). The levelized cost is calculated by dividing the lifecycle cost of the facility by the lifetime energy produce. Although that sounds simple, it becomes a complicated calculation when all of the aspects of cost and energy production are incorporated. Many of the inputs, such as energy production, are uncertain, but that uncertainty can be modeled using probability distributions. Estimated levelized costs ranged from 6.9 cents/kilowatt-hour in Sacramento to 9.7 cents/kilowatt-hour in Chicago. The uncertainty was high, though: standard deviations were 2.0 and 2.8 cents/kilowatt-hour for Sacramento and Chicago, respectively. Even so, these cost estimates are encouraging and suggest that solar power may become a cost-competitive source of energy relative to coal, natural gas, and wind.

- **SS Central America.** "Nerds Haul Ocean Riches" was the headline in *The Miami Herald* newspaper on October 6, 1989. As Bob Evans, project director for the Columbus America Discovery Group, opined, "You don't mind being called a nerd if the next words are 'hauls ocean riches'."[6] The headline announced the discovery of the wreck of the *SS Central America* off the coast of South Carolina. The ship was carrying a full load of passengers and an estimated $400 million in gold from the California gold fields when it sank in a hurricane on September 12, 1857.

---

[6] "Search for the *SS Central America*: Mathematical Treasure Hunting." Presentation at Edelman Prize Competition, ORSA/TIMS meeting, Anaheim, CA, 1991.

The ship and its treasures languished at the bottom of the sea until Tommy Thompson and the Columbus America Discovery group found the sunken vessel and recovered much of its treasure.

How did Thompson and his crew go about locating the *SS Central America*? Based on a variety of historical documents, mathematical models of wind and ocean currents, with a few subjective probability judgments, the team created a Monte Carlo simulation model that allowed them to create a "probability map" of the sea floor covering a region where the ship sank. Based on the probability map, which gave an indication of the relative likelihood of the ship's location over more than 140 square miles, they then developed an optimal search strategy based on the ship and sonar equipment they were using to scan the ocean floor. The strategy worked; the ship was located and by the end of summer, 1989, the group had recovered over a ton of gold bars and gold coins from the wreck. Maybe being a nerd isn't so bad after all! (Source: Kinder et al, 1998)

SIMULATING SPREADSHEET MODELS USING @RISK

This section provides the instructions for building and running simulation models using Palisade's @RISK software. @RISK provides the power to run full-scale simulations within the familiar and flexible spreadsheet environment. We take this opportunity to simulate a classic cash-flow model (an initial cash outlay followed by a series of cash payments) to demonstrate how to embed probability distributions into individual spreadsheet cells and how to run a simulation. We will also demonstrate some more advanced features of @RISK, such as sequential simulations and correlated random variables.

STEP 1 Open @RISK.

1.1 Open Excel and @RISK, enabling any macros if prompted.

1.2 You can access a variety of help features by clicking on the **Help** button. The *Online Manual* is a pdf file of the actual manual, and *@RISK Help* is a searchable database. In addition, you can view examples via *Example Spreadsheets* or video tutorials via the *Getting Started Tutorial*.

STEP 2 Construct the Deterministic Model.

2.1 Build the cash-flow spreadsheet as shown in Figure 11.22. Enter the numerical values shown for the initial investment, the seven cash flows, and the discount rate. Enter the formulas shown for Present Value and Net Present Value.

FIGURE **11.22**
Model of discounted cash flows.

◢	A	B	C	D	E	F
1				Discounted Cash Flow		
2						
3	Initial Investment	$500,000				
4						
5	Cash Flows			Low (10th Percentile)	Most Likely	High (90th Percentile)
6	Yr 1	$30,000		$24,000	$30,000	$36,000
7	Yr 2	$60,000		$48,000	$60,000	$72,000
8	Yr 3	$90,000		$72,000	$90,000	$108,000
9	Yr 4	$120,000		$96,000	$120,000	$144,000
10	Yr 5	$150,000		$120,000	$150,000	$180,000
11	Yr 6	$180,000		$144,000	$180,000	$216,000
12	Yr 7	$210,000		$168,000	$210,000	$252,000
13						
14	Discount Rate	10%				
15						
16	Present Value	$528,946.16	=NPV(B14,B6:B12)			
17	Net PV	$28,946.16	=B16-B3			

The deterministic model in Figure 11.22 is a typical net present value calculation where there is an initial investment, $500,000 in this case, followed by a sequence of cash flows over time, which in this case is a payment of $30,000 at the end of year 1, and so on, until the final payment of $210,000 at the end of year 7. Each of the seven payments are discounted by 10% annually back to today's dollars, and the sum of the discounted values is $528,946. Subtracting the initial $500,000 produces a positive net present value (NPV) implying that the investors will earn their required 10% interest and more.

The next instruction step shows how to make this model stochastic by inserting probability distributions for the future cash flows. We will insert one probability distribution for each of the seven cash flows, and, as these cash flows happen over time, we will assume future payments have greater uncertainty. Specifically, we will insert a triangular distribution for each future cash flow and, by choosing a wider and wider range for successive years, we effectively increase the uncertainty over time. Table 11.1 shows the widening range, where the reported low value is the 10th percentile and the high is the 90th percentile.

TABLE **11.1**
The 10th and 90th percentiles for each of the seven cash flow distributions.

Year	Cash Flow	Low (10th Percentile)	Most Likely Value	High (90th Percentile)
1	$30,000	$24,000	$30,000	$36,000
2	$60,000	$48,000	$60,000	$72,000
3	$90,000	$72,000	$90,000	$108,000
4	$120,000	$96,000	$120,000	$144,000
5	$150,000	$120,000	$150,000	$180,000
6	$180,000	$144,000	$180,000	$216,000
7	$210,000	$168,000	$210,000	$252,000

STEP 3 Embed Probability Distributions.

3.1 Highlight cell **B6** and either click the **Define Distributions** button in the @RISK toolbar as shown in Figure 11.23 or **right-click** when the cursor is over B6, and in the pop-up menu, select **@RISK**, and then **Define Distributions**. A window pops up, titled *@RISK – Define Distribution: B6*, from which any of the @RISK probability distributions can be chosen. Click on the **TriGen** distribution (second row, third from the right). Note that a faint "?" appears in the highlighted area in the upper right corner. Clicking on the question mark opens the *@RISK Help* to the page that explains that particular distribution's behavior and common uses. Click on the **Select Distribution** button.

3.2 The window for defining the TriGen distribution appears and is shown in Figure 11.24. Starting with the *Name*, at the top of the window, we rename the distribution **Yr 1 Cash Flow**. (You can also use a cell reference to A6 to establish the name. If you do so, use a relative cell reference; you'll see why in a moment!) Skipping the *Cell Formula*, enter the parameters for the TriGen distribution on the left side. Notice that we are following good-modeling techniques by using cell references for our parameter values. Click on the **Assign Excel References** button, as highlighted in Figure 11.24, enter the *Bottom, Most Likely,* and *Top* values using the tenth, most likely value, and ninetieth values given in Table 11.1. Also, enter the most likely value for the static entry, which is the value used when this cell is not allowed to vary its value. Note that the TriGen is a triangular distribution, but instead of entering the minimum and maximum values, we will enter the 10th and 90th percentiles. Click **OK**, and the TriGen formula =RiskTrigen(D6,E6,F6,10,90,RiskStatic(E6),RiskName("Yr 1 Cash Flow")) is placed in cell B6. (You can edit the formula just like any Excel formula. In particular, you can use references to refer to static values and absolute references for the percentiles. You can also access the @RISK functions via Excel's function wizard; click on the *fx* button in the formua bar.)

3.3 Continue to enter the remaining cash flow distributions, one for each of the remaining years. You can either enter each distribution one at a time using the 10th and 90th percentiles from Table 11.1 or you can simply use the drag-down feature of Excel. Either way, you should now have seven TriGen distributions in your model. If the *Random/Static* button (the button with two dice) is selected, pressing the **F9 Key** will select and display a new iteration of the model.

@RISK provides considerable flexibility in defining an input distribution. You can select from among the 50 theoretical distributions in @RISK's library, or you can construct custom distributions, such as discrete or cumulative distributions. Chapters 8 and 10 both discussed how we can

FIGURE **11.23**
Inserting probability distributions into Excel spreadsheet cells using @RISK.

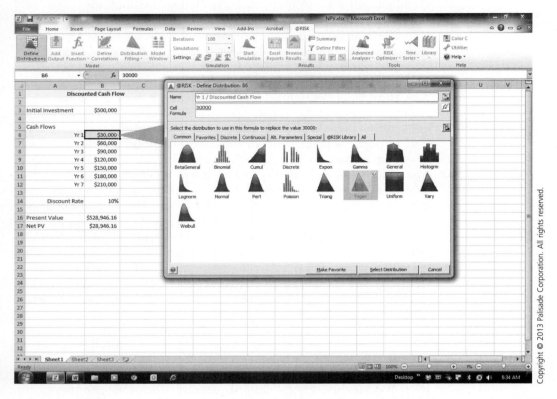

FIGURE **11.24**
Enter cell locations for a distribution's parameters by clicking on the circled button.

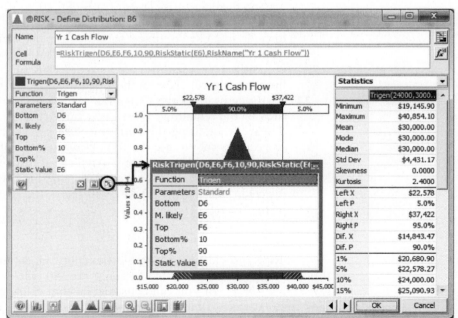

use subjective assessments or data to construct a probability distribution that has the same properties as the underlying uncertainty. We even used @RISK in these chapters to run sophisticated algorithms that match theoretical distributions to data.

Many students fret over choosing the "correct" distribution, believing that there is a single right answer. Typically, there are quite a few distributions that adequately model the uncertainty. If you are trying to decide which of a couple of different distributions to use in your model, then try them all! Once the simulation model has been created, it takes very little time to insert a new distribution, re-run the simulation, and compare the results with those using the original distribution. This is like a sensitivity analysis, but instead of changing a constant's value, we change a whole probability distribution. Not surprisingly, if you are choosing between two input distributions that are similar, the output distribution often does not differ very much. We recommend that you experiment with different distributions in your model. You will find that in many cases simulation is rather forgiving, and so you do not have to worry too much about getting the distributions "just right."

Recall that the point of running a simulation is to learn about the output risk profile. Thus, at least one cell must be identified as an output variable. After each simulation run, @RISK generates reports and graphs for each output variable. Our output variable is Net Present Value (B17).

STEP 4 *Define Consequence.*

4.1 **Right-click** when the cursor is over B17, highlight **@RISK**, and click on **Add Output**.

4.2 A small naming box pops up, which allows us to name the output **Net Present Value**. Click **OK**.

STEP 5 *Run Simulation.*

5.1 In the middle of @RISK's toolbar is a pull-down menu titled *Iterations*. Set the number of iterations to **1,000**.

5.2 Click the **Start Simulation** button (middle of @RISK's toolbar), and @RISK will simulate the model for 1,000 iterations. The histogram shown in Figure 11.25 should pop up upon completion of the 1,000 iterations. Note that your results may differ somewhat as different values can be chosen from simulation to simulation. If the histogram does not pop up, click on the **Browse Results** button on the @RISK toolbar.

Not only can the histogram shown in Figure 11.25 be customized, it is also interactive. The buttons along the bottom of the graph allow you to

FIGURE **11.25**
Histogram of Net
Present Value
based on 1,000
iterations of the
model.

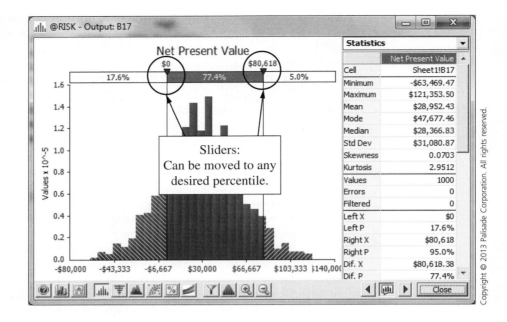

change the graph type or format the graph. The graph is interactive in that
the two sliders shown in Figure 11.25 can be moved to display any percentile.
Here, the sliders are displaying the 17.6th and 95th percentiles. The 17.6th
percentile is particularly important because it is zero, meaning there is a
17.6% chance that the NPV is less than zero. According to this model, the
investor has nearly an 18% chance of not making the desired 10% return.
How do your results compare to these? They should be close!

CORRELATIONS AMONG RANDOM VARIABLES

There are essentially two ways to introduce dependency between two or more
uncertain variables. One way is to develop algebraic equations to model the
relationship. In developing an algebraic equation, you should be trying to
mimic the way the process works. For example, suppose that for the first
year of our cash flow model the payout is uncertain, but then the payout in
year 2 is $30K plus year 1's payout. If this is actually the way the process
works, we would model year 1 stochastically (as a probability distribution)
and add $30K to year 1's value for year 2. Clearly, there are many ways,
from simple to sophisticated, to develop equations that provide a dependency
between two or more distributions.

The second way to model dependencies between uncertain variables is to
use *correlations*. A correlation is a measure of dependency between two random variables. It is a unitless measure and must be between 1 and –1. A positive correlation means that the two random variables tend to move in the
same direction, while a negative correlation indicates that they tend to move

in opposite directions. For example, if Year 1 and Year 2 cash flows had a correlation of 0.50, then the cash flows would tend to move in the same way; larger than expected cash flows in Year 1 would tend to be followed by larger than expected cash flows in Year 2, and likewise smaller than expected cash flows in Year 1 would tend to be followed by smaller than expected cash flows in Year 2. Correlations closer to 1 or −1 indicate stronger relationships, while correlations near zero indicate weak relationships. As described below, @RISK allows you to enter a correlation value for any two random variables in your model.

STEP 6 *Define Correlations.*

6.1 To correlate a group of uncertain variables, first highlight the variables in the spreadsheet. Specifically, we wish to correlate the cash flows over years 1 to 7; thus highlight cells **B6:B12**.

6.2 Click on the **Define Correlations** button on the @RISK toolbar.

6.3 A *Define Correlations* dialog box appears similar to that shown in Figure 11.26. Because we choose to correlate 7 uncertain variables, a 7×7 matrix is created in the dialog box, in which we are to enter the desired correlation values. Enter **0.80** for the correlation between year 1 and year 2 cash flows. Please note that a correlation matrix is symmetric, meaning that a value above the diagonal must equal its corresponding value below the diagonal. Thus, upon entering 0.80 into the second row, first column, the program automatically inserts 0.80 into the first row, second column. Notice also that the diagonal entries are all one, with no option to alter their value.

6.4 Next, enter a correlation value of **0.50** for year 1 and year 3 as shown in Figure 11.26. The implication is that there is a stronger dependency between year 1 and year 2 than there is between year one and year 3.

6.5 Continue in this fashion, entering a correlation value of *0.80* between year *n* and year *n + 1*, and a correlation value of *0.50* between year *n* and year *n + 2*. We leave all the remaining correlations set at zero.

6.6 To view a sample scatterplot of the relationship between year 1 and year 2, click on the **Show Scatterplots for Correlation Matrix** button, third button from the left at the bottom of the window. Figure 11.26 shows the two-way scatterplots for our matrix. Note that you can use the slider along the bottom of Figure 11.26 to vary the correlation value and immediately view the corresponding scatterplot.

6.7 While it is true that the correlation between two probability distributions can be any value between −1 and 1, it is not true that when correlating a group of variables that any value between −1 and 1 can be chosen. It turns out that correlations among groups of variables are much more complex than simply choosing values between −1 and 1. This is because along with the primary relationship, there are secondary relationships, tertiary relationships, and so on. In other

FIGURE **11.26**
Using correlations to model dependence among the cash flows.

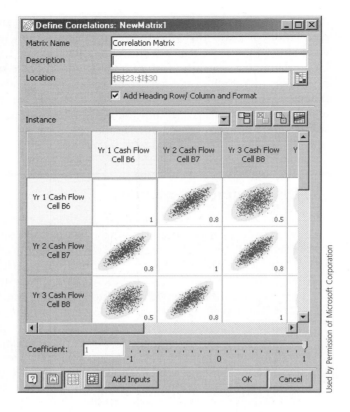

words, simply entering numbers between −1 and 1 into the correlation matrix is no guarantee that all the various relationships are consistent. Click the **Check Matrix Consistency** button (fourth from the left along the bottom of the window) and you can see that the matrix that was entered is not consistent. @RISK helps out here by creating a matrix "as close as possible" to the entered matrix, but one that is consistent. If you wish to use the matrix that @RISK proposes, click **OK.** You will see that @RISK replaced each 0.8 with 0.69 and each 0.5 with 0.43. Finally, click the **OK** button. When asked for the matrix location, enter a cell reference for the upper left corner of the matrix.

Now that the correlation matrix has been constructed, @RISK will sample the probability distributions so that the random variables will reflect the specified correlations. Figure 11.27 shows the Net Present Value distribution using the correlations, and you can see that the results have

FIGURE **11.27**
Net Present Value
distribution when
the cash flows
are positively
correlated.

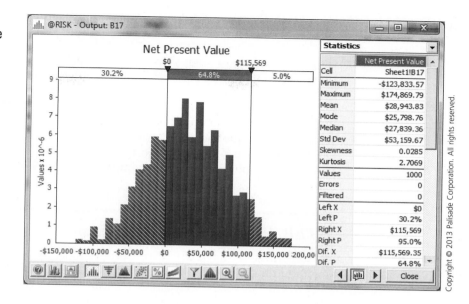

dramatically changed when compared to the previous uncorrelated model. With the cash flows positively correlated, the probability of not meeting the 10% return has jumped from 17.6% to 30.2%. Also, the range and standard deviation both increased compared to the uncorrelated model. The reason is because if the cash flow in year 1 was low, this started a cascade of subsequent low values. This also happens on the high side, thus increasing both the range and standard deviation. The only value that did not change is the expected Net Present Value.

We conclude our discussion of correlating uncertain variables by noting that correlations should be used only when the relationship between the variables is monotonic—that is, when the relationship does not change direction throughout their ranges. Correlations do a very good job of modeling monotonic relationships, as shown in the correlation scatterplots in Figure 11.26. If the relationship is non-monotonic, though, correlations can be misleading. For example, consider the two variables crop yield and fertilizer used. We all know that as you increase the amount of fertilizer used, typically, your crop yield will increase. However, the relationship is not monotonic, because after some point additional fertilizer does not increase yield. In fact, adding still greater amounts can decrease crop yield as the fertilizer becomes toxic. Thus, the scatterplot of the relationship would show a change in direction; it would look something like an upside-down "U." If we were to calculate the sample correlation, we might get something close to zero, but clearly, modeling this relationship with a zero (or any) correlation value would be misleading. Thus, we advise some investigation into the nature of the relationship before using correlations.

SEQUENTIAL SIMULATIONS

In exploring which order quantity was best for Leah, we ran multiple simulations, one for each order quantity. Specifically, we ran 5,000 iterations with 700 calendars fixed as the order quantity, and then we ran another 5,000 iterations with 750 as the fixed order quantity. By comparing the results of the two simulation runs, we are able to gain a better understanding of the impact of the different choices. In general, we often wish to run sequential simulations, where only one value is allowed to change from one simulation run to the next. @RISK makes it easy to run sequential simulations and compare the results of the different simulations.

STEP 7 *Sequential Simulations.*

7.1 Figure 11.7 shows the correct profit model for Leah. To this model, add the order quantities 680, 690, 700, 710, 720, and 730, in cells D1 to D6. These are six possible choices.

7.2 Highlight cell B7 (Order Quantity) and enter **=RiskSimTable(D1:D6)**. Alternatively, you can use Excel's *Insert Function* feature (the *fx* button in the toolbar).

7.3 Immediately below *Iterations* in the @RISK toolbar is *Simulations*. Because we want to run six sequential simulations, we must change the *Simulations* from 1 to **6**. Click **OK**.

7.4 Click the **Run Simulation** button.

As shown in Figure 11.28, a histogram automatically appears after the six simulations are completed. The title of the histogram is *Profit (Sim #1)*. Sim #1 refers to the first of our six calendar order sizes, namely 680 calendars. Figure 11.28 shows that if 680 calendars are ordered, the expected profit is approximately $5,853. You may wish to give your sequential simulations descriptive names instead of @RISK's uncreative Sim #1, Sim #2, and so on. To name the sequential simulations, simply open the *Simulation Settings* dialog box, and click on the **Simulation Names** button.

If you wish to view the profit distribution when the order quantity is any one of the other five table values used, click on the **Select Simulation# to Display** button. See Figure 11.28 for the location of this button. You can either choose to view the six distributions one at a time or view all six together. When viewing multiple distributions on one graph, we highly recommend that you change the graph shape to cumulative ascending graphs (CDF). Typically, we do not want to view all the graphs together, but rather a select subset. For example, we might want to compare the profit distribution when the 690 calendars are ordered (Sim #2) to distribution when 710 are ordered (Sim #4). In this case, we use the **Add Overlay to Graph** button highlighted in Figure 11.28. Please note that

FIGURE **11.28**
After running sequential simulations, @RISK shows the histogram of profit for the first value in the table, in this case an order of 680 calendars.

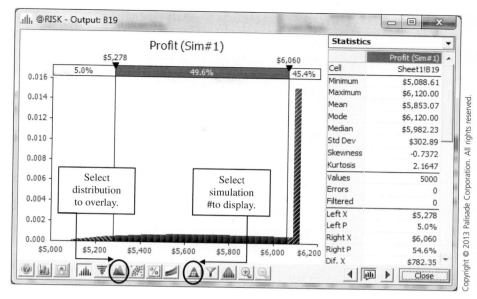

FIGURE **11.29**
The profit distribution for Sim #2 (690 calendars, dashed line) overlaid on the profit distribution for Sim #4 (710 calendars, solid line).

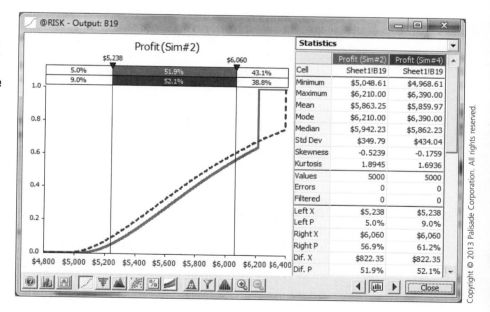

after clicking on the *Add Overlay to Graph* button, you will be asked to select the cell to overlay, and here the cell is B19, profit. Figure 11.29 shows the two CDFs for profit when the number of calendars ordered is 680 (Sim #2) and 710 (Sim #4).

SIMULATION, DECISION TREES, AND INFLUENCE DIAGRAMS

Monte Carlo simulation provides a useful modeling tool for decision analysis. Indeed, simulation has become widely used because of the ease with which simulations can be performed in a spreadsheet environment. Because of this, it is worthwhile to spend a bit of time thinking about how simulation relates to the other modeling tools in decision analysis.

Simulation is an excellent tool for developing a model of uncertainty. We have used it here to develop risk profiles for decision alternatives; with risk profiles for different alternatives in hand, a decision maker would have some basis for choosing one alternative over the other. As mentioned previously, however, simulation also could be used as a subsidiary modeling tool to construct a probability model for a particularly messy part of a problem. For example, if a policy maker is attempting to evaluate alternatives regarding chemical spills, he or she may ask an analyst to develop a probability model for accidents that lead to spills. Such a model can be developed in the context of a simulation, and once an appropriate overall probability distribution for accidents has been constructed, it can be used within a larger analysis.

The ease with which simulation can be performed, along with the flexibility of the simulation environment, makes it an attractive analytical tool. But this ease of use and flexibility does not mean that the decision maker can get away with less effort. In fact, subtle issues in simulation require careful thought. For example, we typically build the simulation in such a way that many of the random numbers are independent draws from their respective distributions. We saw in the previous section that incorporating dependence in a simple cash-flow model can have a dramatic effect on the results. The analyst may even model uncertainty about parameters through the specification of distributions on those parameters, but still have the parameters independent from one another. But would they be? If the analyst has been optimistic in assessing one parameter, perhaps other estimates have been subject to the same optimism.

A somewhat less subtle issue in simulation modeling is that an analyst may be tempted to include all possible sources of uncertainty in the model. This is relatively easy to do, after all, whereas effort is required to perform the sensitivity analysis to determine whether an uncertain quantity really matters in the analysis of the model. Hence, there may be a tendency with simulation not to take certain analytical steps that might lead to real insights as to what matters in a model, what issues should be considered more fully, or what uncertainties may demand more attention.

A key question that many students ask is, "When should I use simulation, and when should I use decision trees?" In many cases both approaches will work fine. However, there are two key issues that can help you decide. First, if your decision situation involves a large number of uncertainties, the necessarily large decision tree can be very clumsy to work with. In contrast, a simulation model, especially one built using a spreadsheet, can be a very compact and easily understood model.

The second issue is whether your decision situation involves future or "downstream" decisions. If not, simulation will work like a charm. If so, a decision tree might be easier to work with. In a spreadsheet, you can program simple decision rules using IF statements, but the more complicated the decision rule, the harder it is to program these rules—and do so correctly—in your simulation model.

So what do you do if you have lots of uncertainties AND multiple downstream decisions? Well, the first thing is to realize that this probably is one of those hard decisions that deserves careful thought and modeling. If you find yourself in such a situation, take your time, perhaps try each approach—or even a hybrid of the two—to identify the approach that makes the most sense, given the situation. At this point you are into the art of modeling, and many modeling choices will have to be made. There are no cut-and-dried procedures, but you are always allowed to ask for help!

In short, constructing a Monte Carlo simulation model requires the same careful thought that is required in any decision modeling. Simulation does have its own advantages (flexibility and ease of use) as well as disadvantages (a tendency toward rampant independence assumptions and brute force solution procedures). But the same is true of decision modeling in general. The decision maker and the decision analyst still are required to think clearly about the problem at hand and to be sure that the decision model addresses the important issues appropriately. Clear thinking is the key, not fancy quantitative modeling. The objective with any decision-analysis tool is to arrive at a requisite model of the decision, one that appropriately addresses all essential elements of the decision problem. It is through the process of constructing a requisite model, which includes careful thought about the issues, that the decision maker will gain insight and understanding about the problem.

SUMMARY

As we have seen in this chapter, Monte Carlo simulation is another approach to dealing with uncertainty in a decision situation. The basic approach is to construct a model that captures all of the relevant aspects of the uncertainty, and then to translate this model into a form that a computer can use. We focused on the development of such models within the environment of spreadsheets using @RISK to perform the simulation and analyze the results. We discussed the possibility of including dependence among probability distributions and the role of simulation in creating a requisite decision-analysis model.

EXERCISES

11.1. Explain in your own words how Monte Carlo simulation may be useful to a decision maker.

11.2. Explain how the simulation process works to produce results that are helpful to a decision maker.

11.3. If you were to make Leah Sanchez's decision of how many calendars to order, what order amount would you chose? Why?

11.4. A friend of yours has just learned about Monte Carlo simulation methods and has asked you to do a simulation of a complicated decision problem to help her make a choice. She would be happy to have you solve the problem and then recommend what action she should take. Explain why she needs to be involved in the simulation modeling process and what kind of information you need from her.

11.5. Explain why a simulation model with only discrete probability distributions produces the same results as the corresponding decision tree model even though it uses very different solution methods.

11.6. Consider the statement "In simulation models, the values for the uncertain cells are chosen randomly." Why is this statement incorrect, strictly speaking?

11.7. Why should you not model a decision variable as a random variable with a probability distribution?

QUESTIONS AND PROBLEMS

11.8. Leah Sanchez is concerned that if she orders too few calendars, customers' disappointment in not finding a calendar might drive them to shop elsewhere, resulting in more of a loss over the long term than just the $9.00 of lost profit on the calendar. Modify the model in Figure 11.7 by adding a row that calculates unmet demand (number of calendars not sold, but could have been if a sufficient number were ordered). Assume Leah assigns $3.00 to each unmet-demand calendar as the additional opportunity cost due to future lost sales. For example, if Leah ordered 650 calendars and 700 are demanded, 50 calendars is the unmet demand and $150 is the additional opportunity cost. Incorporate this additional cost into your model. How many calendars would you recommend that Leah order based on this new model?

11.9. Leah Sanchez might have a different objective than maximizing expected profit. How does her optimal order quantity change if her objective is to minimize leftovers? What if her objective is to maximize the probability of making a profit of at least $5,200? What if her objective is to minimize leftovers given that the 5th percentile of profit is at least $5,200?

11.10. Insert the continuous beta distribution given in Figure 11.1 as the input distribution for quantity demanded in Figure 11.7. In addition, modify the model so that only whole calendars are sold. How do these changes impact Leah's optimal choice?

11.11. Modify the decision-tree model in Figure 11.13 to use the extended Swanson-Megill (ES-M) approximation for demand instead of the EPT approximation.
   a. Use your ES-M model to calculate expected profit for Order-Quantity values 600, 650, 700, 750, and 800. How do your results compare to those in Figure 11.14?

11.12. Use your ES-M model to calculate the standard deviation of Profit for Order-Quantity values 600, 650, 700, 750, and 800. Compare those with the corresponding standard deviations using the extended Pearson-Tukey (EP-T) approximation and the standard deviations from the simulation model using the continuous beta distribution. (You will have to calculate the standard deviations from all three models.) How do the standard deviations from the ES-M model compare to those from the EP-T and simulation models? Repeat problem 11.11, but using the EP-T approximation with 781 as the 95th percentile instead of 780 as we did in the text. How much difference is there between the results using 780 versus 781?

11.13. Your boss has asked you to work up a simulation model to examine the uncertainty regarding the success or failure of five different investment projects. He provides probabilities for the success of each project individually: $p_1 = 0.50$, $p_2 = 0.35$, $p_3 = 0.65$, $p_4 = 0.58$, $p_5 = 0.45$. Because the projects are run by different people in different segments of the investment market, you both agree that it is reasonable to believe that, given these probabilities, the outcomes of the projects are independent. He points out, however, that he really is not fully confident in these probabilities and that he could be off by as much as 0.10 in either direction on any given probability.

  a. How can you incorporate his uncertainty about the probabilities into your simulation?

  b. Now suppose he says that if he is optimistic about the success of one project, he is likely to be optimistic about the others as well. For your simulation, this means that if one of the probabilities increases, the others also are likely to increase. How might you incorporate this information into your simulation?

11.14. A decision maker is working on a problem that requires her to study the uncertainty surrounding the payoff of an investment. There are three possible levels of payoff—$1,000, $5,000, and $10,000. As a rough approximation, the decision maker believes that each possible payoff is equally likely. But she is not fully comfortable with the assessment that each probability is exactly 1/3, and so would like to conduct a sensitivity analysis. In fact, she believes that each probability could range from 0 to 1/2.

  a. Show how a Monte Carlo simulation could facilitate a sensitivity analysis of the probabilities of the payoffs.

  b. Suppose the decision maker is willing to say that each of the three probabilities could be chosen from a uniform distribution between 0 and 1. Could you incorporate this information into your simulation? If so, how? If not, explain why not, or what additional information you would need.

11.15. In the Monty Hall Problem, the host (Monty Hall) asks a contestant to choose one of three curtains. Behind one and only one of these curtains is a fabulous prize, such as an all-expense paid vacation, and behind the other two curtains are much less valuable prizes; let's suppose donkeys. At this point, the contestant has no reason to prefer one curtain over the other two. After the contestant chooses, Monty opens one of the remaining two curtains to reveal a donkey and gives the contestant the opportunity to switch from his original (and still unopened) curtain to the remaining one. What should the contestant do, stay with the original choice or switch to the unopened curtain? Set up a simulation model to determine whether it is better to stay or switch.

11.16. Use simulation to solve the Birthday Problem using the data file ObservedBirthDays.xls at www.cengagebrain.com. The first three rows of the data are shown in the table that follows. The dataset begins with the number 101 representing Jan 1st and ends with 1231 representing Dec 31, and includes leap day. There were a total of 481,040 births reported, and relative frequency is used to calculate probability. For example, the probability of being born on Jan 1st is $0.31\% = 1,482/481,040 \times 100\%$.

Date	Probability	Count
101	0.31%	1482
102	0.25%	1213
103	0.25%	1220

CASE STUDIES

CHOOSING A MANUFACTURING PROCESS

AJS, Ltd. is a manufacturing company that performs contract work for a wide variety of firms. It primarily manufactures and assembles metal items, and so most of its equipment is designed for precision machining tasks. The executives of AJS currently are trying to decide between two processes for manufacturing a product. Their main criterion for measuring the value of a manufacturing process is net present value (NPV). The contractor will pay AJS $8 per unit. AJS is using a three-year horizon for its evaluation (the current year and the next 2 years).

Process 1

Under the first process, AJS's current machinery is used to make the product. The following inputs are used:

Demand   Demand for each of the three years is unknown. These three quantities are modeled as

discrete random variables denoted $D0$, $D1$, and $D2$ with the following probability distributions:

D_0	$P(D_0)$	D_1	$P(D_1)$	D_2	$P(D_2)$
11K	0.2	8K	0.2	4K	0.1
16K	0.6	19K	0.4	21K	0.5
21K	0.2	27K	0.4	37K	0.4

Variable Cost   Variable cost per unit changes each year, depending on the costs for materials and labor. Let V_0, V_1, and V_2 represent the three variable costs. The uncertainty surrounding each variable is represented by a normal distribution with mean $4 and standard deviation $0.40.

Machine Failure   Each year, AJS's machines fail occasionally, but obviously it is impossible to predict when or how many failures will occur during the year. Each time a machine fails, it costs the firm $8,000. Let Z_0, Z_1, and Z_2 represent the number of machine failures in each of the 3 years, and assume that each is a Poisson random variable with parameter $\lambda = 4$.

Fixed Cost   Each year a fixed cost of $12,000 is incurred.

Process 2

The second process involves scrapping the current equipment (it has no salvage value) and purchasing new equipment at a cost of $60,000. Assume that the firm pays cash for the new machine, and ignore tax effects.

Demand   Because of the new machine, the final product is slightly altered and improved, and consequently demand is likely to be higher than before, although more uncertain. The new demand distributions are:

D_0	$P(D_0)$	D_1	$P(D_1)$	D_2	$P(D_2)$
14K	0.3	12K	0.36	9K	0.4
19K	0.4	23K	0.36	26K	0.1
24K	0.3	31K	0.28	42K	0.5

Variable Cost   Variable cost still changes each year, but this time V_0, V_1, and V_2 are each judged to be normal with mean $3.50 and standard deviation $1.00.

Machine Failures   With the new equipment, failures are less likely, occurring each year according to a Poisson distribution with parameter $\lambda = 3$. They also tend to be less serious, costing only $6,000.

Fixed Cost   The fixed cost of $12,000 is unchanged.

Questions

1. Draw an influence diagram for this decision problem. Do you think it would be feasible to solve this problem with an influence diagram? Explain.
2. Write out the formula for the NPV for both processes previously described. Use the variable names as specified, and assume a 10% interest rate.
3. For Process 1, construct a model and perform 1,000 simulation trials. Estimate the mean and standard deviation of NPV for this process. Print a histogram of the results, and estimate the probability of a negative NPV occurring.
4. Repeat Question 3 for Process 2.
5. Compare the distribution of NPV for each of the two alternatives. Which process would be better for AJS? Why?

Source: This case was provided by Tom McWilliams.

LA HACIENDA MUSA[7]

La Hacienda Musa in Costa Rica was a long way from Leuven, Belgium. But for Maria Keller, the transition was as natural as it could be. She had spent 20 years in Leuven studying banana genetics at the Catholic University of Leuven's Laboratory of Tropical Crops, the world center of banana research. She had learned about the challenges the banana-growing industry faced from a variety of diseases, why bananas seemed to be especially susceptible, and how difficult it is to develop new strains of the world's most popular fruit. But after two decades of study, Maria was ready for something new. She did her homework, packed her few possessions, and headed to her newly purchased Costa Rican banana plantation.

To say that La Hacienda Musa was already a banana plantation was overstating the case. In fact, Maria owned 100 hectares of previously cleared land on which bananas had never been grown. Because this plot was isolated from established banana-growing operations in Costa Rica, the land was expected to be reasonably free from the most important and virulent of banana diseases, Black Sigatoka, a fungal leaf blight. The isolation, coupled with Maria's expert knowledge of banana culture, and especially the new varieties she

[7]Although the case is entirely fictitious, much of the information is taken from *Banana: The Fate of the Fruit that Changed the World*, by Dan Koeppel, New York: Hudson Street Press (2008).

had brought with her from Belgium, suggested that she ought to be able to make a success of her new venture.

The question that faced Maria at the moment was how much, if any, of her 100 hectares should be dedicated to organic bananas. There were good reasons to go organic: top-quality organic produce would command a premium, and her isolated location would be ideal for growing organic bananas. In 2007, Costa Rica had announced its intention to become the first fully carbon-neutral country. As part of its efforts to offset all Costa Rican carbon emissions, tourists and businesses would pay a voluntary "tax" that would be used to fund conservation, reforestation, and other enterprises that would help move the country toward carbon neutrality. Some of those tax revenues would support organic farming in order to reduce the use of petrochemical-based fertilizers. Although Maria did not expect any rebates that would reduce her costs, she knew that if she went organic, she would receive support in a variety of small ways, such as special soil analyses, access to compost, and help locating workers with organic farming experience.

Any land that was not planted in organic bananas would be used to grow bananas conventionally. Under conventional growing methods, La Hacienda Musa would produce an expected yield of 10 metric tonnes of bananas per hectare. Because of the vagaries of the weather, pests, and diseases, the actual yields were uncertain. Maria had good access to historical data, and so she knew that, with conventional growing methods, the actual yield on her plantation would be approximately normally distributed with mean 10 tonnes per hectare and a standard deviation of 0.8 tonnes per hectare.

The uncertainty associated with organic farming was greater than conventional methods because the methods were less established in general and particularly because less was known about how to mitigate diseases and insect infestations using organic means. Maria estimated that yields would be normally distributed with a mean of 9.2 tonnes per hectare and a standard deviation of 2.4 tonnes per hectare. Because of their common dependence on the weather, the yields for organic and conventional bananas were positively correlated, with a correlation coefficient of 0.70.

The prices for bananas were also uncertain. The price (paid to the grower) for conventional bananas was normally distributed with a mean of $220 per tonne and a standard deviation of $28 per tonne. Because large yields for La Hacienda Musa tended to occur at the same time as large yields from other banana plantations, large yields tended to correspond to lower market prices. Thus the market price was negatively correlated with Maria's yields for conventionally grown bananas, having a correlation coefficient of -0.50.

Organic bananas would sell at a premium over conventional bananas, but how much this premium would be was uncertain. Maria thought the percentage premium would have a lognormal distribution with a mean of 15% and standard deviation of 2.5%. (A premium of 5%, for example, meant that the price paid for organic bananas would be 5% more than the price for conventional bananas.) This premium depended mainly on market factors—how many growers were in the organic business, consumer demand for organic produce—and was independent of all of the other uncertainties Maria faced.

Finally, the costs associated with growing bananas were uncertain and approximately normally distributed with a mean of $1,800 per hectare and a standard deviation of $300 per hectare. Because the uncertainty in growing costs was primarily due to labor rates and water use, the growing costs were identical under the two growing methods. These costs were uncorrelated with the other uncertainties.

Maria smiled to herself as she realized that her dilemma was actually quite simple to state: how much of her land should she plant in organic bananas and how much in conventional? Although the question seemed straightforward, the answer was not obvious!

Questions

1. Construct a simulation model of Maria Keller's decision.

   a. Suppose that Maria Keller planted all 100 hectares in organic bananas. What is the expected profit? What is the probability of a loss (i.e., negative profit)?

   b. What is the probability that organically grown bananas will be more profitable per hectare than conventionally grown bananas?

   c. Suppose that Keller planted 50 hectares in organic and 50 in conventional bananas. What is the expected profit in this scenario? What are the 10th, 50th, and 90th percentiles for profit?

   d. How would the distribution for profit change as the area planted in organic varies? Describe the change in words and support your statements with appropriate documentation. (It will suffice to consider the cases where the area planted in organic is 0, 25, 50, 75, or 100 hectares.)

2. To help stimulate growth in the supply of organic produce, a major fruit and vegetable company is contemplating giving growers like Maria Keller a guaranteed minimum price (GMP) for organic bananas. For example, if the GMP were $260 per tonne, Maria would get $260 per tonne or the market price, whichever was greater. The company's hope is that such a price guarantee would help overcome growers' concerns about the risks of growing bananas organically.

a. If the GMP were $260 per tonne, what would be the optimal percentage for Maria to plant in organic? Assume that Maria is risk averse with a risk tolerance of $150,000. (Again, it will suffice to consider the cases where the area planted in organic is 0, 25, 50, 75, or 100 hectares.)

b. Suppose the company will buy all of Maria's organic bananas, regardless of the amount she grows.

  i. If the GMP is set to $260 per tonne, what is the company's expected incremental cost (i.e., incremental relative to paying the market price for Keller's organic bananas)?

  ii. Suppose that the company's objective is to get Maria to plant all of her land in organic bananas. What is the smallest GMP that would accomplish this?

  iii. What do you think of the GMP strategy? Can you think of a better approach that the company might consider?

OVERBOOKING, PART II

Consider again Mockingbird Airlines' problem as described in the overbooking case study in Chapter 9.

Questions

1. Construct a simulation model of the system, and use it to find Mockingbird's optimal policy regarding overbooking. Compare this answer with the one based on the analysis done in Chapter 9.

2. Suppose that you are uncertain about the no-show rate. It could be as low as 0.02 or it could be as high as 0.06, and all values in between are equally likely. Furthermore, the cost of satisfying the bumped passengers may not be constant. That is, the airline may in some cases be able to entice a passenger or two to relinquish their seats in exchange for compensation that would be less than a refund and another free ticket. Alternatively, in some cases the total cost, including loss of goodwill, might be construed as considerably higher. Suppose, for example, that the cost of satisfying an excess customer is normally distributed with mean $300 and standard deviation $40.

Modify the simulation model constructed in Question 1 to include the uncertainties about the no-show rate and the cost. Do these sources of uncertainty affect the optimal overbooking policy?

3. How else might Mockingbird's analysts address the uncertainty about the no-show rate and the cost?

REFERENCES

Hertz's (1964) article in *Harvard Business Review* extolled the virtues of simulation for the decision-analysis community early on. Hertz and Thomas (1983, 1984) provide discussion and examples of the use of simulation for decision analysis. More recently, simulation and its uses have been reported in a number of books written for general audiences. Taleb's (2008) *Fooled by Randomness* explores the role of simulation in equities trading. Savage's (2009) *Flawed by Averages* is a readable and entertaining account explaining how to incorporate uncertainty in an analysis via simulation. Winston's two texts (2008) *Financial Models using Simulation and Optimization I* and *II* provide over 100 example models fully worked out for practitioners. More technical introductions to Monte Carlo simulation at a moderate level are provided by Law and Kelton (2000).

Darling, S., F. You, T. Veselka, and A. Velosa (2011) "Assumptions and the levelized cost of energy for photovoltaics." *Energy and Environmental Science*, DOI:10.1039/c0ee00698.

Glickman, S., E. Rasiel, C. Hamilton, A. Kubataev, and K. Schulman (2006) "A portfolio model of drug development for tuberculosis." *Science* 311, 1246–1247. DOI:10.1126/science.1119299.

Hertz, D. B. (1964) "Risk Analysis in Capital Investment." *Harvard Business Review*. Reprinted in *Harvard Business Review*, September–October 1979, 169–181.

Hertz, D. B., and H. Thomas (1983) *Risk Analysis and Its Applications*. New York: Wiley.

Hertz, D. B., and H. Thomas (1984) *Practical Risk Analysis*. New York: Wiley.

Kinder, G. (1998). *Ship of Gold in the Deep Blue Sea*. Atlantic Monthly Press, New York.

Law, A. M., and D. Kelton (2000) *Simulation Modeling and Analysis*, 3rd ed. New York: McGraw-Hill.

Marmidis, G., S. Lazarou, and E. Pyrgioti (2008). Optimal placement of wind turbines in a wind park using Monte Carlo simulation. *Renewable Energy* 33, pp. 1455–1460.

Savage, S. L. (2009) *Flaw of Averages: Why We Underestimate Risk in the Face of Uncertainty*. New York: Wiley.

Stone, L. (1992). Search for the *SS Central America*: Mathematical Treasure Hunting. *Interfaces* 22(1), 32–54.

Taleb, N. N. (2008) *Fooled by Randomness: The Hidden Role of Chance in Life and Markets*, 2nd ed. New York: Random House.

Winston, W. (2008) *Financial Models Using Simulation and Optimization I*. New York: Palisade Corp.

Winston, W. (2008) *Financial Models Using Simulation and Optimization II*. New York: Palisade Corp.

EPILOGUE

The name of the Monty Hall problem is actually somewhat misleading. Monty Hall was the host of *Let's Make a Deal*, a television show that aired in the United States. in the 1960s and 1970s. Contestants were offered the opportunity to choose one of three doors, and Monty Hall did open a wrong door to generate excitement. However, contestants were not offered the option to switch doors. Instead, they could opt out of the game for a known prize—typically a specified amount of cash worth much less than the big prize. So it wasn't so much a probability problem, but a matter of comparing the known cash amount with the uncertain prospect of winning the big prize.

In a 1975 issue of *American Statistician*, Steve Selvin introduced the problem as we have stated it in problem 11.15, and he showed that it is indeed beneficial to switch doors. Fifteen years later the problem appeared in Marilyn vos Savant's column in *Parade* magazine and instantly created a furor, because the optimality of switching is counterintuitive for many people. The magazine received about 10,000 letters from readers, including many from mathematicians and scientists who claimed that the answer should be that it doesn't matter whether the contestant switches. The debate has led to many academic articles on the problem along with several write-ups in the popular press.

At this point, there are numerous websites devoted to the Monty Hall problem, and we encourage the reader to follow up by Googling "Monty Hall Problem." The good news is that when you click on one of the links that Google produces, no one will ask you if you would like to switch to a different link!

CHAPTER 12

Value of Information

Decision makers who face uncertain prospects often gather information with the intention of reducing uncertainty. Information gathering includes consulting experts, conducting surveys, performing mathematical or statistical analyses, doing research, or simply reading books, journals, and newspapers. The intuitive reason for gathering information is straightforward; to the extent that we can reduce uncertainty about future outcomes, we can make choices that give us a better chance at a good outcome.

In this chapter, we will work through a few examples that should help you understand the principles behind information valuation. Naturally, the examples also will demonstrate the techniques used to calculate information value. At the end of the chapter we will consider a variety of issues, including information in complex decisions, the use of information evaluation as an integral part of the decision-analysis process, what to do in the case of multiple nonmonetary objectives, and the problem of evaluating and selecting experts for the information they can provide.

The main example for this chapter is the stock market example that we introduced in Chapter 5 in our discussion of sensitivity analysis. For convenience, the details are repeated here.

Investing in the Stock Market	An investor has some funds available to invest in one of three choices: a high-risk stock, a low-risk stock, or a savings account that pays a sure $500. If he invests in the stocks, he must pay a brokerage fee of $200.
	His payoff for the two stocks depends on what happens to the market. If the market goes up, he will earn $1,700 from the high-risk stock and $1,200 from the low-risk stock. If the market stays at the same level, his payoffs for the high- and low-risk stocks will be $300 and $400, respectively. Finally, if the stock market goes down, he will lose $800 with the high-risk stock but still gain $100 with the low-risk stock.

FIGURE **12.1**
(a) Influence-
diagram and
(b) decision-tree
representations of
the investor's
problem.

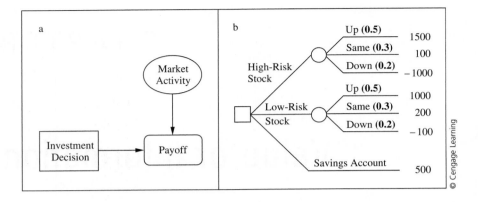

The investor's problem can be modeled with either an influence diagram or a decision tree. These two representations are shown in Figure 12.1.

VALUE OF INFORMATION: SOME BASIC IDEAS

Before we begin an in-depth study of information from a decision-analysis perspective, let us consider certain fundamental notions. What does it mean for an expert to provide perfect information? If the expert's opinion is not perfect, how can we think about imperfect information? How does probability relate to the idea of information? What is an appropriate basis on which to evaluate information in a decision situation? This section addresses these questions and thus sets the stage for a complete development of the value of information in the rest of the chapter.

Probability and Perfect Information

An expert's information is said to be perfect if it is always correct. Thus, to capture the idea of perfect information using probability, we need to describe the relationship between what the expert says and what actually occurs. Conditional probability is tailor-made to model perfect information. Remember, $P(A|B)$ is the conditional probability that outcome A will occur given that outcome B has occurred. With regard to perfect information, this translates into statements of the form:

$$P(Outcome\ A \mid Expert\ Says\ ``Outcome\ A\ Occurs") = 1$$

This conditional probability states that given the expert has said Outcome A will occur, we have a 100% chance that it will occur. Now that's perfect.

For our stock market example, we are interested in two types of conditional probability statements: $P(Market\ Goes\ Up \mid Expert\ Says\ ``Market\ Goes\ Up")$, which measures the likelihood that the market will follow what the expert says; and $P(Expert\ Says\ "Market\ Goes\ Up"\ |\ Market\ Goes\ Up)$, which measures the likelihood that the expert will state what the market will do given a particular outcome of the market (up in this case). One way to understand the difference in these statements is that when incorporating an expert's opinion in our decision model, we will need to consult the expert *before* the event has happened, and thus we will be using statements of the form: $P(Outcome\ A\ Occurs\ |\ Expert\ Says\ "Outcome\ A")$. This statement reports the likelihood of an outcome occurring when an expert says it will. The other conditional statement, $P(Expert\ Says\ "Outcome\ A"\ |\ Outcome\ A)$, can be thought of as a calibration statement that indicates the expert's accuracy in identifying Outcome A when it will actually occur. We often start with such calibration statements, and then use Bayes' theorem to flip the order of the conditioning to produce a more directly useful statement like $P(Outcome\ A\ |\ Expert\ Says\ "Outcome\ A\ Occurs")$.

When discussing perfect information, not only must the perfect-information expert correctly identify what will happen, but also what will not happen. For example, if the market really does go up, then we have not only:

$$P(Expert\ Says\ "Market\ Goes\ Up"\ |\ Market\ Goes\ Up) = 1$$

but also:

$$P(Expert\ Says\ "Market\ Stays\ Flat"\ |\ Market\ Goes\ Up) = 0$$

$$P(Expert\ Says\ "Market\ Goes\ Down"\ |Market\ Goes\ Up) = 0$$

Probability theory helps out here because the first conditional probability being equal to one implies that the following two conditional probabilities must equal zero.

But this is only half the story. The expert also must never say that Outcome A will occur if any other outcome will occur. There must be no chance of our expert saying that the market will rise when it really will not:

$$P(Expert\ Says\ "Market\ Stays\ Flat"\ |\ Market\ Stays\ Flat) = 1$$

$$P(Expert\ Says\ "Market\ Goes\ Down"\ |\ Market\ Goes\ Down) = 1$$

In other words, our perfectly calibrated expert needs to be 100% accurate for all possible outcomes.

For the Stock Market example, perfect information is represented by the nine conditional probability statements given in Table 12.1.

If the expert's information is perfect, then upon hearing the expert's report, no doubt about the future remains; if the expert says the market will rise, then we know that the market really will rise. Having used conditional probabilities to model the expert's perfect information, we can use Bayes' theorem to "flip" the probabilities as we did in Chapter 7 and show that there is no uncertainty after we have heard the expert. We want to know

TABLE **12.1** Conditional probability is used to show the expert provides perfect information.

Actually Happens	Expert States	Conditional Probability
Market Goes Up	"Market Goes Up"	$P(Expert\ Says\ "Market\ Goes\ Up"\ |\ Market\ Goes\ Up) = 1$
	"Market Stays Flat"	$P(Expert\ Says\ "Market\ Stays\ Flat"\ |\ Market\ Goes\ Up) = 0$
	"Market Goes Down"	$P(Expert\ Says\ "Market\ Goes\ Down"\ |\ Market\ Goes\ Up) = 0$
Market Stays Flat	"Market Goes Up"	$P(Expert\ Says\ "Market\ Goes\ Up"\ |\ Market\ Stays\ Flat) = 0$
	"Market Stays Flat"	$P(Expert\ Says\ "Market\ Stays\ Flat"\ |\ Market\ Stays\ Flat) = 1$
	"Market Goes Down"	$P(Expert\ Says\ "Market\ Goes\ Down"\ |\ Market\ Stays\ Flat) = 0$
Market Goes Down	"Market Goes Up"	$P(Expert\ Says\ "Market\ Goes\ Up"\ |\ Market\ Goes\ Down) = 0$
	"Market Stays Flat"	$P(Expert\ Says\ "Market\ Stays\ Flat"\ |\ Market\ Goes\ Down) = 0$
	"Market Goes Down"	$P(Expert\ Says\ "Market\ Goes\ Down"\ |\ Market\ Goes\ Down) = 1$

$P(Market\ Goes\ Up | Expert\ Says\ "Market\ Goes\ Up")$. Some notation to make our lives easier:

$$Up = The\ market\ goes\ up$$

$$"Market\ Up" = Expert\ says\ "Market\ goes\ up"$$

$$Flat = The\ market\ stays\ flat$$

$$"Market\ Flat" = Expert\ says\ "Market\ stays\ flat"$$

$$Down = The\ market\ goes\ down$$

$$"Market\ Down" = Expert\ says\ "Market\ goes\ down"$$

Now we can apply Bayes' theorem:

$P(Up|"Market\ Up")$

$$= \frac{(P("Market\ Up"|Up)P(Up))}{(P("Market\ Up"|Up)P(Up) + P("Market\ Up"|Flat)P(Flat) + P("Market\ Up"|Down)P(Down))}$$

$$= \frac{1 * P(Up)}{1 * P(Up) + 0 * (Flat) + 0 * P(Down)}$$

$$= \frac{P(Up)}{P(Up)}$$

$$= 1$$

Observe that the posterior probability $P(Up|"Market\ Up")$ is equal to 1 regardless of the prior probability $P(Up)$. This is because of the conditional probabilities that we used to represent the expert's perfect performance. Of course, this situation is not typical of the real world. In real problems we rarely can eliminate uncertainty altogether. If the expert sometimes makes mistakes, these conditional probabilities would not be 1's and 0's and the posterior probability would not be 1 or 0; some uncertainty about what would actually happen would remain.

This exercise may seem a bit arcane. Its purpose is to introduce the idea of thinking about information in a probabilistic way. We can use conditional probabilities and Bayes' theorem to evaluate all kinds of information in virtually any decision setting.

The Expected Value of Information

How can we place a value on information in a decision problem? For example, how could we decide whether to hire the expert described in the last section? Does it depend on what the expert says? In the investment decision, the optimal choice is to invest in the high-risk stock. Now imagine what could happen. If the expert says that the market will rise, the investor still would choose the high-risk stock. In this case, the information has no value in the sense that the investor would have taken the same action regardless of the expert's information. On the other hand, the expert might say that the market will fall or remain the same, in which case the investor would be better off with the savings account. In this second case, the information has value because it leads to a different action, one with a higher expected value than what would have been experienced without the expert's information. Thus, from the decision analytic perspective, information has no value when it leads to the same action we would have taken without the information, and it has value when it leads to an action different from the one we would have taken without the information.

We can think about information value after the fact, as we have done in the preceding paragraph, but it is much more useful to consider it before the fact—that is, before we actually get the information or before we hire the expert. What effects do we anticipate the information will have on our decision? We will talk about the *expected value of information*. By considering the expected value, we can decide whether an expert is worth consulting, whether a test is worth performing, or which of several information sources would be the best to consult.

The worst possible case would be that, regardless of the information we hear, we make the same choice that we would have made in the first place. In this case, the information has zero expected value! If we would take the same action regardless of what an expert tells us, then why hire the expert in the first place? We are just as well off as we would have been without the expert. Thus, at the worst, the expected value of information is zero. But if there are certain cases—things an expert might say or outcomes of an experiment—on the basis of which we would change our minds and make a different choice, then the expected value of the information must be positive. In those cases, the information may lead to a different action (depending on exactly what the information turns out to be). Taking a different action implies that the expected value of that action, given the information, is greater than the expected value of the original action, given the information. Thus, the expected value with the information must be greater than the expected value without. So the expected value can either remain the same (i.e., the information is worthless) or increase due to the information. The expected value of information can be zero or positive, but never negative.

At the other extreme, perfect information is the best possible situation. Nothing could be better than resolving all of the uncertainty in a problem. When all uncertainty is resolved, we no longer have to worry about unlucky outcomes; for every choice, we know exactly what the outcome will be. Thus, the expected value of perfect information provides an upper bound for the expected value of information in general. Putting this together with the argument in the previous paragraph, the expected value of any information source must be somewhere between zero and the expected value of perfect information.

Finally, you might have noticed that we continue to consider the expected value of information in terms of the particular choices faced. Indeed, the expected value of information is critically dependent on the particular decision problem at hand. For this reason, different people in different situations may place different values on the same information. For example, General Motors may find that economic forecasts from an expensive forecaster may be a bargain in helping the company refine its production plans. The same economic forecasts may be an extravagant waste of money for a restaurateur in a tourist town.

EXPECTED VALUE OF PERFECT INFORMATION

Now we will see how to calculate the expected value of perfect information (EVPI) in the investment problem. For an expected value-maximizing investor, the optimal choice is the high-risk stock because it has the highest EMV ($580); however, this is partly because the investor is optimistic about what the market will do. How much would he be willing to pay for information about whether the market will move up, down, or sideways?

Suppose he could consult an expert with perfect information—a clairvoyant—who could reveal exactly what the market would do. By including an arrow from "Market Activity" to "Investment Decision," the influence diagram in Figure 12.2 represents the decision situation in which the investor has access to perfect information. Remember, an arrow leading from an uncertainty node to a decision node means that the decision is made knowing the outcome of the uncertainty node. This is exactly what we want to represent in the case of perfect information; the investor knows what the market will do before he invests his money.

With a representation of the decision problem including access to perfect information, how can we find the EVPI? Easy. Solve each influence diagram, Figures 12.1a and 12.2. Find the EMV of each situation. Now subtract the EMV for Figure 12.1a ($580) from the EMV for Figure 12.2 ($1,000). The difference ($420) is the EVPI. We can interpret this quantity as the maximum amount that the investor should be willing to pay the clairvoyant for perfect information. PrecisionTree further simplifies EVPI calculations because

© Cengage Learning

FIGURE **12.2**
Perfect information
in the investor's
problem.

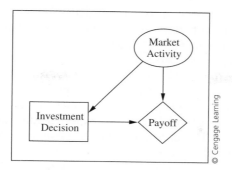

it solves influence diagrams automatically. To calculate the EVPI from Figure 12.1a, we need only add an arc from the chance node to the decision node, and PrecisionTree reports the new EMV of $1,000.

It also is useful to look at the decision-tree representation. To do this, draw a decision tree that includes the opportunity to obtain perfect information (Figure 12.3). As in the influence-diagram representation, the EMV for consulting the clairvoyant is $1,000. This is $420 better than the EMV obtained by acting without the information. As before, EVPI is the difference, $420.

FIGURE **12.3**
Investment
decision tree
with the perfect-
information
alternative.

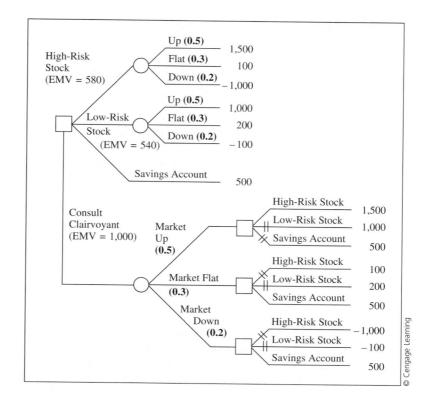

Recall that in a decision tree the order of the nodes conforms to a chronological ordering of the events. Is this what happens in the perfect-information branch in Figure 12.3? Yes and no. Yes in the sense that the uncertainty regarding the stock market's activity is resolved before the investment decision is made. This is the important part. But once the decision is made, the market still must go through its performance. It is simply that the investor knows exactly what that performance will be.

This points out a useful aspect of expected-value-of-information analysis with decision trees. If a decision maker faces some uncertainty in a decision, which is represented by those uncertainty nodes that come after his decision in a decision tree, redrawing the tree to capture the idea of perfect information is easy. Simply reorder the decision and uncertainty nodes! That is, redraw the tree so that the uncertainty nodes for which perfect information is available come before the decision node. This is exactly what we did in the perfect-information branch in Figure 12.3; along this branch, the "Market Activity" and "Investment Decision" nodes are reversed relative to their original positions. Reordering the nodes of a decision tree is simple in Precision-Tree because of its copy and paste features. At the end of this chapter, we show that a few clicks of the mouse are all that is needed to calculate EVPI in PrecisionTree.

It is worth reiterating that the way we are thinking about the value of information is in a strictly *a priori* sense. The decision-tree representation reinforces this notion because we actually include the decision branch that represents the possibility of consulting the clairvoyant. The investor has not yet consulted the clairvoyant; rather, he is considering whether to consult the clairvoyant in the first place. That action increases the expected value of the decision. Specifically, in this case there is a 50% chance that the clairvoyant will say that the market is not going up, in which case the appropriate choice would be the savings account rather than the high-risk stock.

EXPECTED VALUE OF IMPERFECT INFORMATION

We rarely have access to perfect information. In fact, our information sources usually are subject to considerable error. Thus, we must extend our analysis to deal with imperfect information.

The analysis of imperfect information parallels that of perfect information. We still consider the expected value of the information before obtaining it, and we will call it the *expected value of imperfect information* (EVII). (In some texts, you may see EVSI, which stands for expected value of sample information. It is essentially the same thing, but is generally used in cases where the information amounts to the collection of sample data.)

In the investment example, suppose that the investor hires an economist who specializes in forecasting stock market trends. The economist can make mistakes, though, so his information is imperfect. For example, suppose his track record shows that if the market actually will rise, he says "up" 80% of the time, "flat" 10%, and "down" 10%. We construct a table (Table 12.2) to characterize his performance in probabilistic terms. The probabilities therein

TABLE **12.2**
Conditional
probabilities
characterizing
economist's
forecasting abilities.

Economist's Prediction	True Market State		
	Up	Flat	Down
"Up"	0.80	0.15	0.20 = P(Economist Says "Up" | Down)
"Flat"	0.10	0.70	0.20 = P(Economist Says "Flat" | Down)
"Down"	0.10	0.15	0.60 = P(Economist Says "Down" | Down)
	1.00	1.00	1.00

© Cengage Learning 2014

are conditional; for example, P(Economist Says "Flat" | Flat) = 0.70. The table shows that he is better when times are good (market up) and worse when times are bad (market down); he is somewhat more likely to make mistakes when times are bad.

How should the investor use the economist's information? Figure 12.4 shows an influence diagram that includes an uncertainty node representing the economist's forecast. The structure of this influence diagram should be familiar from Chapter 3; the economist's information is an example of imperfect information. The arrow from "Market Activity" to "Economic Forecast" means that the probability distribution for the particular forecast is conditioned on what the market will do. This is reflected in the distributions in Table 12.2. In fact, the distributions contained in the "Economic Forecast" node are simply the conditional probabilities from that table.

Solving the influence diagram in Figure 12.4 gives the EMV associated with obtaining the economist's imperfect information before action is taken. The EMV turns out to be $822. As we did in the case of perfect information, we calculate EVII as the difference between the EMVs from Figures 12.4 and 12.1a, or the situation with no information. Thus, EVII equals $822 − $580 = $242.

The influence-diagram approach is easy to discuss because we do not see the detailed calculations. On the other hand, the decision-tree approach shows the calculation of EVII in its full glory. Figure 12.5 shows the decision-tree representation of the situation, with a branch that represents the alternative of consulting the economist. Look at the way in which the nodes are ordered in the "Consult Economist" alternative. The first event is the economist's forecast. Thus, we need probabilities *P(Economist Says "Up")*,

FIGURE **12.4**
Imperfect
information in
the investor's
problem.

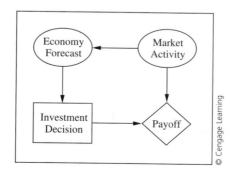

© Cengage Learning

FIGURE **12.5**
Incomplete
decision tree for
the investment
example, including
the alternative for
consulting the
economist.

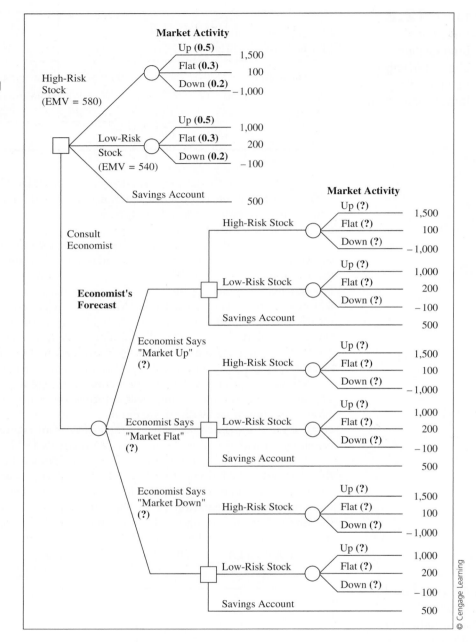

P(*Economist Says "Flat"*), and P(*Economist Says "Down"*). Then the investor decides what to do with his money. Finally, the market goes up,
down, or sideways. Because the "Market Activity" node follows the "Economists Forecast" node in the decision tree, we must have conditional
probabilities for the market such as P(*Market Up | Economist Says "Up"*)
or P(*Market Flat | Economist Says "Down"*). What we have, however, is

the opposite. We have probabilities such as $P(Market\ Up)$ and conditional probabilities such as $P(Economist\ Says\ "Up"\ |\ Market\ Up)$.

As we did when we first introduced the notion of the value of an expert's information at the beginning of this chapter, we use Bayes' theorem to find the posterior probabilities for the actual market outcome. For example, what is $P(Market\ Up\ |\ Economist\ Says\ "Up")$? It stands to reason that after we hear him say "Up," we should think it more likely that the market actually will go up than we might have thought before.

We used Bayes' theorem to "flip" probabilities in Chapter 7. There are several ways to think about this situation. First, applying Bayes' theorem is tantamount to reversing the arrow between the nodes "Market Activity" and "Economic Forecast" in Figure 12.4. In fact, reversing this arrow is the first thing that must be done when solving the influence diagram (Figure 12.6). Or we can think in terms of flipping a probability tree as we did in Chapter 7. Figure 12.7a represents the situation we have, and Figure 12.7b represents what we need.

Whether we think of the task as flipping a probability tree or reversing an arrow in an influence diagram, we still must use Bayes' theorem to find the probabilities we need. For example,

$$P(Market\ Up\ |\ Economist\ Says\ "Up") = P(Up\ |\ "Up")$$

$$= \frac{P("Up"\ |\ Up)P(Up)}{P("Up"\ |\ Up)P(Up) + P("Up"\ |\ Flat)P(Flat) + P("Up"\ |\ Down)P(Down)}$$

$P(Up)$, $P(Flat)$, and $P(Down)$ are the investor's prior probabilities, while $P(Economist\ Says\ "Up"\ |\ Up)$, and so on, are the conditional probabilities shown in Table 12.2. From the principle of total probability, the denominator is $P(Economist\ Says\ "Up")$.

Substituting in values for the conditional probabilities and priors from Figure 12.7a,

$$P(Market\ Up\ |\ Economist\ Says\ "Up") = \frac{0.8(0.5)}{0.8(0.5) + 0.15(0.3) + 0.2(0.2)}$$

$$= \frac{0.400}{0.485}$$

$$= 0.8247$$

$P(Economist\ Says\ "Up")$ is given by the denominator and is equal to 0.485.

© Cengage Learning

FIGURE **12.6**
First step in solving the influence diagram.

We reverse the arrow between "Economic Forecast" and "Market Activity."

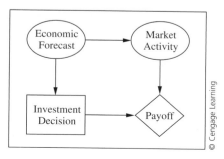

FIGURE **12.7**
Flipping the
probability tree
to find posterior
probabilities
required for value-
of-information
analysis.

In (a) we see what we
have; in (b) we see what
we need.

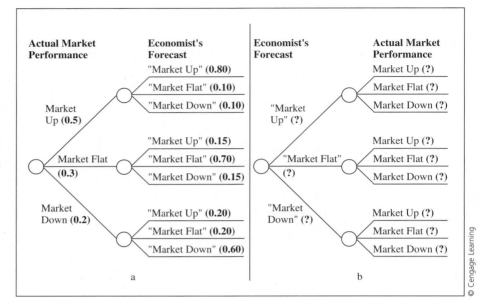

Of course, we need to use Bayes' theorem to calculate nine different posterior probabilities to fill in the gaps in the decision tree in Figure 12.5. Table 12.3 shows the results of these calculations; these probabilities are included on the appropriate branches in the completed decision tree (Figure 12.8).

We also noted that we needed the marginal probabilities $P("Up")$, $P("Flat")$, and $P("Down")$. These probabilities are $P("Up") = 0.485$, $P("Flat") = 0.300$, and $P("Down") = 0.215$; they also are included in Figure 12.8 to represent our uncertainty about what the economist will say. As usual, the marginal probabilities can be found in the process of calculating the posterior probabilities because they simply come from the denominator in Bayes' theorem.

From the completed decision tree in Figure 12.8 we can tell that the EMV for consulting the economist is $822, while the EMV for acting without consulting him is (as before) only $580. The EVII is the difference between the two EMVs. Thus, EVII is $242 in this example, just as it was when we solved

TABLE **12.3**
Posterior
probabilities for
market trends
depending on
economist's
information.

Economist's Prediction	Posterior Probability for:		
	Up	Flat	Down
"Up"	0.8247	0.0928	0.0825 = P(Down | Economist Says "Up")
"Flat"	0.1667	0.7000	0.1333 = P(Down | Economist Says "Flat")
"Down"	0.2325	0.2093	0.5581 = P(Down | Economist Says "Down")

FIGURE **12.8**
Completed decision
tree for the
investment
example.

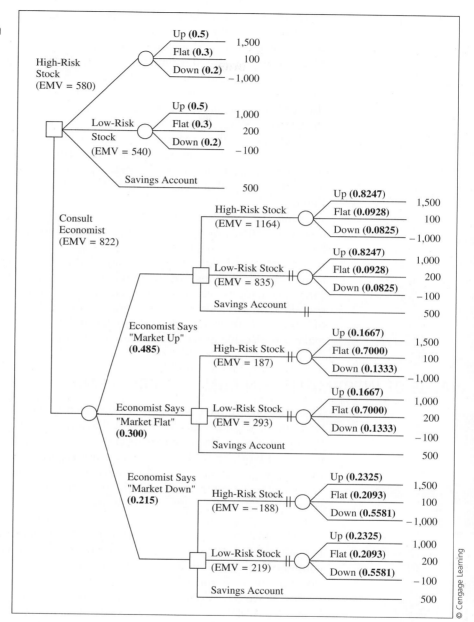

the problem using influence diagrams. Given this particular decision situation, the investor would never want to pay more than $242 for the economic forecast.

As with perfect information, $242 is the value of the information only in an expected-value sense. If the economist says that the market will go up, then we would invest in the high-risk stock, just as we would if we did not consult him. Thus, if he does tell us that the market will go up, the information turns out to do us no good. But if he tells us that the market will be flat or go down, we would put our money in the savings account and avoid the relatively low expected value associated with the high-risk stock. In those two cases, we would "save" $500 − $187 = $313 and $500 − (−$188) = $688, respectively, with the savings in terms of expected value. Thus, EVII also can be calculated as the "expected incremental savings," which is $0(0.485) + $313(0.300) + $688(0.215) = $242.

Such probability calculations can make value-of-information analysis tedious and time-consuming. This is where computers can play a role. PrecisionTree can perform all of the necessary probability calculations and thus make finding EVII a simple matter. See the instructions at the end of the chapter.

One last note regarding value-of-information calculations. If you have used your calculator to work through the examples in this chapter, you may have found that your answers differed slightly from those in this book. This is because calculations involving Bayes' theorem and value of information tend to be highly sensitive to rounding error. The appropriate strategy is to carry calculations out to many decimal places throughout a given problem, rounding off to dollars or cents only at the end of the problem. Rounding off intermediate results that are used in later calculations sometimes can make a noticeable difference in the final answer.

VALUE OF INFORMATION IN COMPLEX PROBLEMS

The example we have looked at in this section has been fairly simple. There was only one uncertain event, the behavior of the market, and we modeled the uncertainty with a simple discrete distribution. As we know, however, most real-world problems involve considerably more complex uncertainty models. In particular, we need to consider two specific situations. First, how can we handle continuous probability distributions? Second, what happens when there are many uncertain events and information is available about some or all of them?

The answer to the first question is straightforward conceptually, but in practice the calculation of EVPI or EVII may be difficult when dealing with continuous probability distributions. The principle is the same. Evaluate decision options with and without the information, and find the difference in the EMVs, as we have done in the discrete case. The problem, of course, is calculating the EMVs. Obviously, it is always possible to construct a discrete approximation as discussed in Chapter 8. Another possibility is to construct a Monte Carlo simulation model. Finally, for some theoretical probability models, analytical results are possible. The mathematics for such analysis, however, tend to be somewhat complicated and are beyond the scope of this introductory textbook. References for interested readers are included at the end of the chapter.

The second question asks how we handle value-of-information problems when there are many uncertain events. Again, in principle, the answer is easy, and is most transparent if we think in terms of influence diagrams. Perfect information about any particular event simply implies the presence of an informational arc from the event to the decision node. Naturally, it is possible to include such arcs for a subset of events. The only requirement is that the event not be downstream in the diagram from the decision node, because the inclusion of the information arc would lead to a cycle in the influence diagram. Solving the influence diagram with the informational arcs in place provides the EMV with the information, and this then may be compared to the EMV without the information to obtain the EVPI for the particular information sought.

Consider the same problem when the model is in decision-tree form. In the decision tree in Figure 12.3, the information branch was constructed by reversing the event node and the decision node. The same principle can apply if there are many sources of uncertainty; simply move those chance nodes for which information is to be obtained so that they precede the decision node. Now calculating EMV for the information branch will give the EMV in the case of perfect information for those events that precede the decision node in the decision tree.

For imperfect information, the same general principles apply. For influence diagrams, include an imperfect-information node that provides information to the decision maker. An excellent example is the toxic-chemicals influence diagram in Figure 3.20. Two sources of imperfect information are included in that model, the exposure survey and the lab test. In a decision-tree model, it would be a matter of constructing a tree having the appropriate informational chance nodes preceding the decision node. Unfortunately, if there are more than one or two such chance nodes, the decision tree can become extremely unwieldy. Moreover, it may be necessary to calculate and track the marginal and posterior probabilities for the decision tree; these calculations are done automatically in the influence diagram.

VALUE OF INFORMATION, SENSITIVITY ANALYSIS, AND STRUCTURING

Our motivation for studying value of information has been to examine situations in which information is available and to show how decisions can be made systematically regarding what source of information to select and how much an expert's information might be worth. Strictly speaking, this is precisely what value-of-information analysis can do. But it also can play an elegant and subtle role in the structuring of decisions and in the entire decision-analysis process of developing a requisite decision model. Recall the ideas of sensitivity analysis from Chapter 5. In that chapter we talked about a process of building a decision structure. Using a tornado diagram, the first step is to find those variables to which the decision was sensitive; these variables require probabilistic modeling. The second step, after constructing a probabilistic model, may be to perform sensitivity analysis on the probabilities.

A third step in the structuring of a probabilistic model would be to calculate the EVPI for each uncertain event. This analysis would indicate where the analyst or decision maker should focus subsequent efforts in the decision-modeling process. That is, if EVPI is very low for an event, then there is little sense in spending a lot of effort in reducing the uncertainty by collecting information. But if EVPI for an event is relatively high, it may indeed be worthwhile to put considerable effort into the collection of information that relates to the event. Such information can have a relatively large payoff by reducing uncertainty and improving the decision maker's EMV. In this way, EVPI analysis can provide guidance to the decision analyst as to what issues should be tackled next in the development of a requisite decision model.

We will end this chapter with a short description of a rather unusual application of value-of-information analysis. Although few applications are as elaborate as this one, this example does provide an idea of how analysis based on the value of information can be used to address real-world concerns.

Seeding Hurricanes	Hurricanes pack tremendous power in their high winds and tides. Storms such as Camille (1969) and Hugo (1989) caused damage in excess of a billion dollars and amply demonstrated the destructive potential of large hurricanes. In the 1960s, the U.S. government experimented with the seeding of hurricanes—the practice of dropping silver iodide into the storm to reduce peak winds by forcing precipitation. After early limited experiments, Hurricane Debbie was seeded in 1969 with massive amounts of silver iodide on two separate occasions. Each seeding was followed by substantial drops in peak wind speed. Given these results, should hurricanes that threaten highly populated areas be seeded on the basis of current knowledge? Should the government pursue a serious research program on the effects of hurricane seeding?

Howard, Matheson, and North (1972) addressed these specific questions about hurricane seeding. They asked whether it would be appropriate to seed hurricanes, undertake a research program, or whether the federal government should simply not pursue this type of weather modification? To answer these questions, they adopted a decision-analysis framework. On the basis of a relatively simple probabilistic model of hurricane winds, along with the relationships among wind speed, damage, and the effect of seeding, they were able to calculate expected dollar losses for two decision alternatives—seeding and not seeding a typical threatening hurricane. On the basis of their model, they concluded that seeding would be the preferred alternative if the federal government wanted to reduce expected damage.

The authors realized that the government might be interested in more than the matter of reducing property damage. What would happen, for example, if the decision was made to seed a hurricane, the wind speed subsequently increased, and increased damage resulted? The government most likely would become the target of many lawsuits for having taken action that appeared to have adverse effects. Thus, the government also faced an issue of responsibility if seeding were undertaken. On the basis of the authors' analysis, however, the government's "responsibility cost" would have to be relatively high in order for the optimal decision to change.

To address the issue of whether further research on seeding would be appropriate, the authors used a value-of-information approach. They considered the possibility of repeating the seeding experiment that had been performed on Hurricane Debbie and the potential effects of such an experiment. By modeling the possible outcomes of this experiment and considering the effect on future seeding decisions, the authors were able to calculate the expected value of the research. Including reasonable costs for government responsibility and anticipated damage over a single hurricane season, the expected value of the experiment was determined to be approximately $10.2 million. The authors also extended their analysis to include all future hurricane seasons, discounting future costs by 7% per year. In this case, the expected value of the research was $146 million. To put these numbers in perspective, the cost of the seeding experiment would have been approximately $500,000.

VALUE OF INFORMATION AND NONMONETARY OBJECTIVES

Throughout this chapter we have calculated the expected value of information on the basis of EMVs, implicitly assuming that the only objective that matters is making money. This has been a convenient fiction; as you know, in many decision situations there are multiple objectives. For example, consider the Federal Aviation Administration (FAA) bomb-detection example again (Chapter 3). Recall that the FAA was interested in maximizing the detection effectiveness and passenger acceptance of the system while at the same time minimizing the cost and time to implementation. For any given system, there may be considerable uncertainty about the level of passenger acceptance, for example, but this uncertainty could be reduced in many ways. A less expensive, but highly imperfect, option would be to run a survey. A more expensive test would be to install some of the systems at a few airports and try them out. But how much should be spent on such efforts?

With the FAA example, the answer is relatively straightforward, because minimizing cost happens to be one of the objectives. The answer would be to find the additional cost that makes the net expected value of getting the information equal to the expected value without the information (and, naturally, without the cost). If there is a clear trade-off rate that can be established for, say, dollars of cost per additional point on the passenger-acceptance scale, the increase in expected passenger acceptance level that results from additional information can be translated directly into dollars of cost. (Any increase in the expected value of the other objectives—which may happen due to choosing different options under different information scenarios—would also have to be included in the calculations. Doing so can also be accomplished through the specification of similar trade-offs between cost and the other objectives. Understanding such trade-offs is not complex and is treated in more detail in Chapter 16.)

When a decision situation does not involve a monetary objective, the same techniques that we have developed in this chapter can still be used. Suppose one objective is to minimize the decision maker's time; different choices and different outcomes require different amounts of time from the decision maker. Information can be valued in terms of time; the expected value of perfect information might turn out to be, say, five days of work. If resolving some uncertainty would take more time than that, it would not be worth doing!

VALUE OF INFORMATION AND EXPERTS

In Chapter 8 we discussed the role of experts in decision analysis. Issues that analysts face in using experts include how to set a value on them, how to choose the number of experts needed, and which experts to consult. In general, the valuation is not a practical concern; the high stakes involved in typical public-policy risk analyses typically warrant the use of experts who may charge several thousand dollars per day in consulting fees. What is less obvious, however, is that experts typically provide information that is somewhat interrelated. Because experts tend to read the same journals, go to the same conferences, use the same techniques in their studies, and even communicate with each other, it comes as no surprise that the information they provide can be highly redundant. The real challenge in expert use is to recruit experts who look at the same problem from very different perspectives. Recruiting experts from different fields, for example, can be worthwhile if the information provided is less redundant. It can even be the case that a highly diverse set of less knowledgeable (and less expensive) experts can be much more valuable than the same number of experts who are more knowledgeable (and cost more) but give redundant information!

CALCULATING EVPI AND EVII WITH PRECISIONTREE

We have seen in this chapter that calculating EVPI is relatively simple and involves nothing more than adding an arc to an influence diagram or, equivalently, reordering the nodes in a decision tree, but it can be tedious if done by hand. We will demonstrate how PrecisionTree simplifies the process with its one-click copying and pasting of decision trees. EVII calculations are more complex in that they require additional nodes and a Bayesian revision of the probabilities. PrecisionTree greatly simplifies EVII calculations for influence diagrams because the probabilities are automatically revised using Bayes' theorem. We will demonstrate how to perform both EVPI and EVII calculations in PrecisionTree using the investment problem.

EVPI

EVPI is usually calculated after the decision problem has been structured, so our starting point is a constructed decision tree and influence diagram of the investor's problem.

STEP 1 Open PrecisionTree.

1.1 Open Excel® and PrecisionTree.

1.2 Either construct both the influence diagram and decision tree for the investor's problem, as shown in Figure 12.1, or open the workbook titled Stock Market at www.cengagebrain.com. The decision tree is in the worksheet titled "Base Tree" and the influence diagram is in the worksheet titled "Base ID."

Influence Diagrams

It is very simple to compute EVPI with an influence diagram; merely add an arc from the specified chance node to the appropriate decision node. Precision-Tree updates the expected value and displays it in the upper left corner of the spreadsheet. EVPI is the difference between the updated expected value and the original expected value. We demonstrate for the investor's problem.

STEP 2 Add Perfect-Information Arc.

2.1 Open the influence-diagram worksheet titled **Base ID**.

2.2 To add an arc, click on the **Influence Arc** button, choose **Market Activity** as the *Source Node* and **Investment Decision** as the *Destination Node*. The arc is drawn after clicking on **OK**.

2.3 Choose **Value** and **Timing** (Implied by Value) for the arc's influence type, and click **OK**.

PrecisionTree solves the new influence diagram and reports the summary information in the upper left-corner of the spreadsheet. Table 12.4 lists the summary statistics for the two influence diagrams: the diagram shown in Figure 12.1 without perfect information and the diagram shown in Figure 12.2 with perfect information.

Let's examine what we can learn from this table. First, EVPI equals $1,000, which is found by subtracting the expected values: $1,000 − $580. Second, the standard deviation is cut nearly in half (compare $996 to $500) and downside risks are reduced (compare the two minimums, −$1,000 and $500) when you know the market activity before choosing your investment.

TABLE **12.4**
Comparing summary statistics for the influence diagrams in Figures 12.1 and 12.2.

	No Information	Knowing Market Activity
Expected Value	$580	$1,000
Standard Deviation	$996	$500
Minimum	−$1,000	$500
Maximum	$1,500	$1,500

© Cengage Learning

Decision Trees

Calculating the expected value of perfect information is more cumbersome for decision trees because the nodes must be reordered. In our investment problem tree (Figure 12.1b), we need to move the "Market Activity" chance node in front of the "Investment Decision" node.

STEP 3 Building a Perfect-Information Decision Tree.

3.1 Open the Base Tree worksheet as described in Step 1.1. In a new worksheet start a decision tree by clicking the **Decision Tree** button and clicking in cell **A1**.

3.2 Name the tree **EVPI(Market Activity)**.

3.3 The first node in the tree will be the chance node "Market Activity." Go back to the Base Tree and **right-click** directly on the chance node **Market Activity** (not the name, but the red circle). Choose **Copy Sub-Tree** in the pop-up menu.

3.4 Return to the new tree, **right-click** on the only end node, and choose **Paste SubTree**. The chance node, its three outcome branches, and their associated values and probabilities are added to the first position of the new tree.

3.5 Change the values for each branch to **0**, but do not change the probabilities.

Forgetting to set the branch values to zero is a common mistake for students. Because we have not yet chosen an investment (stocks or savings), we have no cash flows at this point.

STEP 4 Copy and Paste Subtrees.

4.1 We now paste a copy of the Base Tree at each of the three end nodes (one for each of the three outcomes). Return to the Base Tree and **right-click** directly on the decision node **Investment Decision** (not the name, but the green square). Choose **Copy SubTree**.

4.2 Return to the new tree, **right-click** on an end node, and choose **Paste SubTree**. Repeat for the remaining two end nodes.

STEP 5 Update Probabilities.

5.1 Complete the tree by updating the probabilities of the second "Market Activity" chance node to reflect that the market activity outcome is known. For example, at first, there is a 50% chance that the market will go up, but once we find out for sure that it *will* go up, the probability is 100%. To incorporate this change in probability, delete the branches that do not occur in the second "Market Activity" chance node and give the one remaining branch a probability of 100%. Use Figure 12.9 as a guide. Branches are deleted by right-clicking directly on the branch name

FIGURE **12.9**
Investment decision tree showing perfect information.

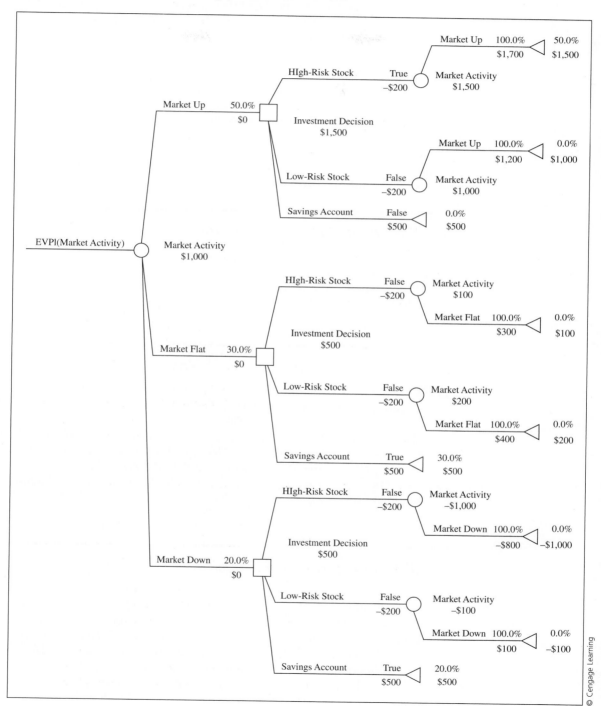

and choosing **Delete**. (Of course, it is not necessary to delete the zero-probabiliy arcs; you can simply set their probabilities to zero. Deleting the extra branches, though, removes some clutter from the diagram.)

Your completed diagram should look exactly like Figure 12.9 and should have an expected value of $1,000. Hence, the EVPI is $1,000 − $580 = $420, which agrees with the influence diagram. Running a decision analysis on this tree will produce the summary statistics listed in Table 12.3.

EVII

We show here how to use PrecisionTree to calculate EVII in an influence diagram, including the automatic application of Bayes' theorem.

STEP 6 *Open Influence Diagram.*

6.1 Open the **Base ID** worksheet. Our goal is to create the influence diagram found in Figure 12.4. (If necessary, remove the arc between Market Activity and Investment Decision that was added in Step 2.2. Delete an arc by right-clicking on the arc.)

STEP 7 *Add Economic Forecast Node.*

7.1 We include the economic forecast by inserting a chance node. Click on the **Influence Diagram/Node** button (second from the left, PrecisionTree toolbar), then click in cell **D6**.

7.2 Choose **Chance** node, change the node name to **Economic Forecast**, and name the outcomes **Says Up, Says Flat,** and **Says Down**. Outcomes are added by clicking the *Outcomes* tab and then the *Add* button.

7.3 Click **OK**. We will return to this node to add the values and probabilities after adding the arcs.

STEP 8 *Add Information Arcs.*

8.1 Add two arcs. Add the first by clicking on the **Influence Arc** button (third from left) and choosing **Market Activity** as the *Source Node* and **Economic Forecast** as the *Destination Node*. In the pop-up dialog box, choose both the **Value** and **Timing** checkboxes and click **OK**. Value was chosen because we believe that the future market outcomes and the expert's forecast are related.

8.2 Add the second arc from **Economic Forecast** to **Investment Decision** by following the same procedure. Choose both the **Value** and **Timing** (implied by Value checkboxes).

FIGURE **12.10**
Probabilities and
values for the
Economic Forecast
chance node of
the investment
problem.

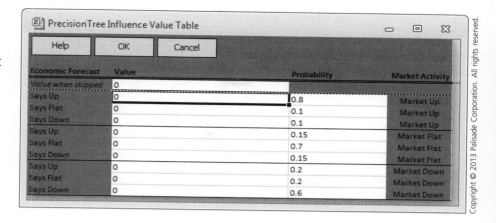

Economic Forecast	Value	Probability	Market Activity
Value when skipped	0		
Says Up	0	0.8	Market Up
Says Flat	0	0.1	Market Up
Says Down	0	0.1	Market Up
Says Up	0	0.15	Market Flat
Says Flat	0	0.7	Market Flat
Says Down	0	0.15	Market Flat
Says Up	0	0.2	Market Down
Says Flat	0	0.2	Market Down
Says Down	0	0.6	Market Down

STEP 9 *Include Probabilities and Values.*

9.1 Click on the **Economic Forecast** name, and then the **Exit to Value Table** button in the *Settings* dialog box.

9.2 Enter the values and probabilities into the *Influence Value Table,* as shown in Figure 12.10. Click **OK**.

9.3 Click on the **Investment Decision** name, and then the **Exit to Value Table** button in the *Settings* dialog box. Enter −200 for the High-Risk and Low-Risk Stocks, enter 0 for the Savings Account, and click **OK**.

The updated summary statistics show that the expected value of the influence diagram is $822, so, EVII = $822 − $580, or $242. By converting this influence diagram into a decision tree (right-click on any node, choose **Model**, and **Convert to Decision Tree**), you will see that the chance node "Economic Forecast" comes first and the revised probabilities match those in Figure 12.8. We leave it to the reader to construct a decision tree for computing EVII for the investor's problem. Use Figure 12.8 as a guide and the copy/paste feature to expedite structuring. Note that the *Bayesian Revision* button reorders chance nodes and updates the probabilities using Bayes' theorem.

SUMMARY

By considering the expected value of information, we can make better decisions about whether to obtain information or which information source to consult. We saw that the expected value of any piece of information must be zero or greater, and it cannot be more than the expected value of perfect information. Both influence diagrams and decision trees can be used as frameworks for calculating expected values. Influence diagrams provide the neatest representation because information available for a decision can be represented through appropriate use of arcs and, if necessary, additional uncertainty nodes representing imperfect information. In contrast, representing the expected value of imperfect information with decision trees is more complicated, requiring the calculation of posterior and marginal probabilities. The expected value of information is simply the difference between the EMV calculated both with and without the information.

The final sections in the chapter discussed generally how to solve value-of-information problems in more complex situations. We concluded with discussions of the role that value-of-information analysis can play in the decision-analysis process of developing a requisite decision model, how to value information related to nonmonetary objectives, and evaluation and selection of experts.

EXERCISES

12.1. Explain why in decision analysis we are concerned with the *expected* value of information.

12.2. Calculate the EVPI for the decision shown in Figure 12.11.

12.3. What is the EVPI for the decision shown in Figure 12.12? Must you perform any calculations? Can you draw any conclusions regarding the relationship between value of information and deterministic dominance?

12.4. For the decision tree in Figure 12.13, assume Chance Events **E** and **F** are independent.
   a. Draw the appropriate decision tree and calculate the EVPI for Chance Event **E** only.
   b. Draw the appropriate decision tree and calculate the EVPI for Chance Event **F** only.
   c. Draw the appropriate decision tree and calculate the EVPI for both Chance Events **E** and **F**: that is, perfect information for both **E** and **F** is available before a decision is made.

12.5. Draw the influence diagram that corresponds to the decision tree for Exercise 12.4. How would this influence diagram be changed in order to answer parts a, b, and c in Exercise 12.4?

FIGURE **12.11**
Generic decision tree for Exercise 12.2.

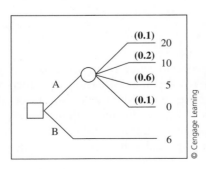

© Cengage Learning

FIGURE **12.12**
Generic decision
tree for Exercise
12.3.

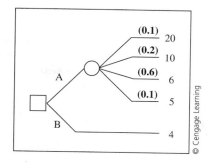

FIGURE **12.13**
Generic decision
tree for Exercise
12.4.

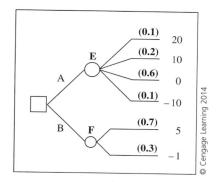

QUESTIONS AND PROBLEMS

12.6. The claim was made in the chapter that information always has positive value. What do you think of this? Can you imagine any situation in which you would prefer *not* to have some unknown information revealed?

a. Suppose you have just visited your physician because of a pain in your abdomen. The doctor has indicated some concern and has ordered some tests whose results the two of you are expecting in a few days. A positive test result will suggest that you may have a life-threatening disease, but even if the test is positive, the doctor would want to confirm it with further tests. Would you want the doctor to tell you the outcome of the test? Why or why not?

b. Suppose you are selling your house. Real-estate transaction laws require that you disclose what you know about significant structural defects. Although you know of no such defects, a buyer insists on having a qualified engineer inspect the house. Would you want to know the outcome of the inspection? Why or why not?

c. Suppose you are negotiating to purchase an office building. You have a lot of experience negotiating commercial real-estate deals, and your agent has explained this to the seller, who is relatively new to the business. As a result, you expect to do very well in this negotiation. Because of the unique circumstance of the building, your agent has suggested obtaining an appraisal of the property by a local expert. You know exactly how you would use this information; it would provide an upper bound on what you are willing to pay. This fact is also clear to the seller, who will know whether you obtained the appraisal but will only find out the appraised value if you elect to reveal it. Would you obtain the appraisal? Why or why not?

12.7. Consider another oil-wildcatting problem. You have mineral rights on a piece of land that you believe may have oil underground. There is only a 10% chance that you will strike oil if you drill, but the payoff is $200,000. It costs $10,000 to drill. The alternative is not to drill at all, in which case your profit is zero.

    a. Draw a decision tree to represent your problem. Should you drill?

    b. Draw an influence diagram to represent your problem. How could you use the influence diagram to find EVPI?

    c. Calculate EVPI. Use either the decision tree or the influence diagram.

    d. Before you drill you might consult a geologist who can assess the promise of the piece of land. She can tell you whether your prospects are "good" or "poor." But she is not a perfect predictor. If there is oil, the conditional probability is 0.95 that she will say prospects are good. If there is no oil, the conditional probability is 0.85 that she will say poor. Draw a decision tree that includes the "Consult Geologist" alternative. Be careful to calculate the appropriate probabilities to include in the decision tree. Finally, calculate the EVII for this geologist. If she charges $7,000, what should you do?

12.8. Consider the preceding oil-wildcatting problem. The basic tree is shown in Figure 12.14.

Based on Figure 12.14, work through these steps:

    a. Change P(Strike Oil) from 0.1 to 1.0 and P(No Oil) to 0.0. What is the EMV for the decision tree? Record this as EMV | Strike Oil.

    b. Now change P(Strike Oil) to 0.0 and P(No Oil) to 1.0. What is the EMV for the decision tree? Record this as EMV | No Oil.

    c. Calculate 0.1 EMV | Strike Oil + 0.9 EMV | No Oil. How would you explain the meaning of the resulting value?

    d. Finally, from the result in part c, subtract the original EMV of the tree ($10,000) as shown in Figure 12.14. The answer you get is the EVPI for whether you strike oil. Explain why this approach gives the same result as calculating EVPI by moving the chance node before the decision node as described in the chapter.

FIGURE **12.14**
The Basic
Oil-Wildcatting
Decision Tree.

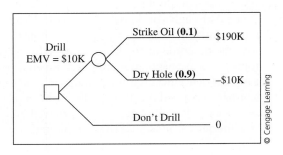

© Cengage Learning

12.9. In Problem 4.16, find:
   a. EVPI for the cost of making the processor.
   b. EVPI for the cost of subcontracting the processor.
   c. EVPI for both uncertain events.

12.10. Look again at Problem 8.11, which concerns whether you should drop your decision analysis course. Estimate EVPI for your score in the course.

12.11. In Problem 9.34, the issue is whether or not to close the plant. If your boss knew exactly how many machines would fail during your absence; he would be able to decide what to do without the fear of making a mistake.
   a. Find his EVPI concerning the number of machine failures during your absence over the next 2 weeks.
   b. Suppose that the cost of repairing the broken machines is $30,000. Then what is EVPI?
   c. Suppose that the cost of repairing the machines is $15,000 but the cost of closing the plant is $20,000. Now calculate EVPI.

12.12. Consider the Texaco–Pennzoil example from Chapter 4.
   a. What is EVPI to Hugh Liedtke regarding Texaco's reaction to a counteroffer of $5 billion? Can you explain this result intuitively?
   b. The timing of information acquisition may make a difference.
      (i) For example, suppose that Liedtke could obtain information about the final court decision before making his current decision (take the $2 billion or counteroffer $5 billion). What would be EVPI of this information?
      (ii) Suppose that Liedtke knew he would be able to obtain perfect information only after he has made his current decision but before he would have to respond to a potential Texaco counteroffer of $3 billion. What would be EVPI in this case?
   c. In part b, EVPI for (ii) should be less than EVPI calculated in (i). Can you explain why? (Incidentally, if your results disagree with this, you should check your calculations!)

12.13. In the Texaco–Pennzoil case, what is EVPI if Liedtke can learn both Texaco's reaction and the final court decision before he makes up his mind about the current $2 billion offer? (*Hint:* Your answer should be more than the sum of the EVPIs for Texaco's reaction and the court decision calculated separately in Problem 12.12.) Can you explain why the interaction of the two bits of information should have this effect?

12.14. In Problem 5.8, assume that the grower's loss incurred with the burners would be $17,500 and that the loss incurred with the sprinklers would be $27,500.
   a. Find EVPI for the weather conditions (freeze or not).
   b. Now assume that the loss incurred with the burners is uniformly distributed between $15,000 and $20,000. Also assume that the loss

incurred with the sprinklers is uniformly distributed between $25,000 and $30,000. Now estimate EVPI regarding these losses, under the assumption that a better weather forecast cannot be obtained.

c. Do you think the farmer should put more effort into learning his costs more precisely or should he concentrate on obtaining better weather forecasts?

12.15. In Exercise 12.4, is it necessary to assume that the events are independent? What other assumption could be made?

CASE STUDIES

TEXACO–PENNZOIL REVISITED

Often when we face uncertainty, we would like to know more than simply the outcome; it would be nice to control the outcome and bring about the best possible result! A king might consult his wizard as well as his clairvoyant, asking the wizard to cast a spell to cause the desired outcome to occur. How much should such a wizard be paid for these services? The expected value of his wizardry naturally depends on the decision problem at hand, just as the expected value of information does. But the way to calculate the "expected value of wizardry" (to use Ron Howard's term) is very similar to solving the calculations for the expected value of perfect information.

To demonstrate this idea, let's look again at Hugh Liedtke's decision situation as diagrammed in

Figure 4.2. Now consider the entirely hypothetical possibility that Liedtke could pay someone to influence Texaco's CEO, James Kinnear.

Questions

1. What would be the most desirable outcome from the "Texaco Reaction" chance node?

2. Construct the decision tree now with three alternatives: "Accept $2 Billion," "Counteroffer $5 Billion," and "Counteroffer $5 Billion and Influence Kinnear."

3. Solve your decision tree from Question 2. What is the maximum amount that Liedtke could pay in order to influence Kinnear?

MEDICAL TESTS

One of the principles that arises from a decision-analysis approach to valuing information is that information is worthless if no possible informational outcome will change the decision. For example, suppose that you are considering whether to make a particular investment. You are tempted to hire a consultant recommended by your Uncle Jake (who just went bankrupt last year) to help you analyze the decision. If, however, you think carefully about the things that the consultant might say and conclude that you would (or would not) make the investment regardless of the consultant's recommendation, then you should not hire the consultant. This principle makes perfectly good sense in the light of our approach; do not

pay for information that cannot possibly change your mind.

In medicine, however, it is standard practice for physicians to order extensive batteries of tests for patients. Although different kinds of patients may be subjected to different overall sets of tests, it is nevertheless the case that many of these tests provide information that is worthless in a decision-analysis sense; the doctor's prescription would be the same regardless of the outcome of a particular test.

Questions

1. As a patient, would you be willing to pay for such tests? Why or why not?

2. What incentives do you think the doctor might have for ordering such tests, assuming he realizes that his prescription would not change?

3. How do his incentives compare to yours?

DUMOND INTERNATIONAL PART II

Refer back to the DuMond International case study at the end of Chapter 5. Nancy Milnor had returned to her office, still concerned about the decision. Yes, she had persuaded the directors that their disagreements did not affect her analysis; her analysis still showed the new product to be the appropriate choice. The members of the board, however, had not been entirely satisfied. The major complaint was that there was still too much uncertainty. Could she find out more about the likelihood of a ban, or could she get a better assessment from engineering regarding the delay? What about a more accurate sales forecast for the new product?

Nancy gazed at her decision tree (Figure 5.29). Yes, she could address each of those questions, but where should she start?

Questions

1. Calculate EVPI for the three uncertain events in DuMond's decision as diagrammed in Figure 5.29.
2. Based on the EVPI values, where should Nancy Milnor begin her investigation?

REFERENCES

This chapter has focused primarily on the technical details of calculating the value of information.

The most complete, and most highly technical, reference for this kind of analysis is Raiffa and Schlaifer (1961). Winkler (1972) provides an easily readable discussion of value of information. Both texts contain considerably more material than what is included here, including discussion of EVPI and EVII for continuous distributions. Another succinct and complete reference is Chapter 8 in LaValle (1978).

Three articles by LaValle (1968a, b, c) contain many results regarding the expected value of information, including the result that the expected value of information about multiple events need not equal the sum of the values for individual events. Ponssard (1976) and LaValle (1980) show that expected value of information can be negative in some competitive situations. Clemen and Winkler (1985) discuss the value of information from experts, especially focusing on the effect of probabilistic dependence among experts.

At the end of the chapter, we discussed the way in which the value of information can be related to sensitivity analysis and the decision-analysis process. These ideas are Ron Howard's and have been part of his description of decision analysis since the early 1960s. Many of the articles in Howard and Matheson (1983) explain this process, and illustrative applications show how the process has been applied in a variety of real-world decision problems.

Felli and Hazen (1998) show that EVPI can be thought of as combining into a single measure the probability of changing the most preferred alternative and the marginal benefit of changing. The articles by Yokota and Thompson (2004a, 2004b) review the use of VOI in environmental health risk management decisions.

Clemen, R., and R. Winkler (1985) "Limits for the Precision and Value of Information from Dependent Sources." *Operations Research*, 33, 427–442.

Felli, J.C., and G.B. Hazen (1998) "Sensitivity Analysis and the Expected Value of Perfect Information." *Medical Decision Making*, 18, 95–109.

Howard, R. A., and J. E. Matheson (eds.) (1983) *The Principles and Applications of Decision Analysis* (2 volumes). Palo Alto, CA: Strategic Decisions Group.

Howard, R. A., J. E. Matheson, and D. W. North (1972) "The Decision to Seed Hurricanes." *Science*, 176, 1191–1202.

LaValle, I. (1968a) "On Cash Equivalents and Information Evaluation in Decisions under Uncertainty; Part I. Basic Theory." *Journal of the American Statistical Association*, 63, 252–276.

LaValle, I. (1968b) "On Cash Equivalents and Information Evaluation in Decisions under Uncertainty; Part II. Incremental Information Decisions." *Journal of the American Statistical Association, 63,* 277–284.

LaValle, I. (1968c) "On Cash Equivalents and Information Evaluation in Decisions under Uncertainty; Part III. Exchanging Partition-*J* for Partition-*K* Information." *Journal of the American Statistical Association, 63,* 285–290.

LaValle, I. (1978) *Fundamentals of Decision Analysis.* New York: Holt.

LaValle, I. (1980) "On Value and Strategic Role of Information in Semi-Normalized Decisions." *Operations Research, 28,* 129–138.

Ponssard, J. (1976) "On the Concept of the Value of Information in Competitive Situations." *Management Science, 22,* 737–749.

Raiffa, H., and R. Schlaifer (1961) *Applied Statistical Decision Theory.* Cambridge, MA: Harvard University Press.

Winkler, R. L. (1972) *Introduction to Bayesian Inference and Decision.* New York: Holt.

Yokota, F. and K.M. Thompson (2004a) "Value of Information Literature Analysis: A Review of Applications in Health Risk Management." *Medical Decision Making, 24,* 287–298.

Yokota, F. and K.M. Thompson (2004b) "Value of Information Analysis in Environmental Health Risk Management Decisions: Past, Present, and Future." *Risk Analysis, 24,* 635–650.

CHAPTER 13

Real Options

SAMUEL E. BODILY

"All business decisions are real options, in that they confer the *right* but not the *obligation* to take some initiative in the future."

—Judy Lewent, CFO, Merck

Although you may not go as far as Ms. Lewent, who claims that "all business decisions are real options," you will likely agree that options are critically important in decision making. Understanding how to create them and to value them are vital skills for personal, business, and policy decisions. Decision analysis is an ideal approach to provide insight into options.

We have all created options at some time in our lives. We create an option when we make a nonrefundable deposit to hold a hotel room for the first night of a four-night ski vacation or to save a seat in the entering class of a college. The deposit is the price we pay for the right to decide at a later date whether we will rent the room or attend the college. If we eventually decide to use the hotel room, we are said to have exercised our option. If, instead, we decide not to use the hotel room, for example because there is no snow at that time, we are said to have let our option expire.

Suppose the hotel deposit is $100, nonrefundable. In order to decide whether we should pay the $100 deposit, we would consider several characteristics of the option. These would include the chance that we would actually exercise the option to stay in the hotel, how much we would value staying in the room, and how we value the scenario in which we don't use it.

This chapter was written by Samuel E. Bodily, John Tyler Professor at the Darden Graduate Business School, University of Virginia. Copyright 2004 by Samuel E. Bodily.

In this chapter, we will consider how to use decision trees and Monte Carlo simulation to structure the analysis of options decisions and to value them. We start with simple examples and move to richer and multifaceted examples. By the end of the chapter, we will have developed tools that can be used on a wide range of option situations, limited only by our ability to model the underlying uncertainties and clarify the nature of the option.

With many business options, the structure of the decision situation can be complicated. Consider the Chris Wireless Service and Proteiz examples:

Chris Wireless Service	Chris, an entrepreneur, is thinking about starting a company that will operate a wireless network service. She will operate within her city, providing she is granted a city license, and in the surrounding county, where she has a license. If she can operate in both the city and the county, the business will be worth substantially more than if she serves only the county.
	Because she doesn't know if the city license will be awarded, she may want to take action now to enable a *switch* option. In the switch option, she would invest in the preparation of certain technologies that will run the wireless service in the city without requiring a city license. These technologies are somewhat more expensive to operate. In the event that the license is not granted, however, Chris may then switch to the alternative technology.
	In contrast, Chris could make the minimum investment necessary to apply for the license and wait until the announcement of whether the license is approved before launching the business. This is a *defer* or *learn* option.

Proteiz	Proteiz is a start-up venture that will develop a new protein for use in laboratories. This opportunity will require upfront capital to discover and protect the appropriate protein. The protein will be produced by biological processes that have the following:
	• High variable cost with an uncertain initial value
	• A significant learning curve for variable cost with an uncertain rate of learning
	• Uncertain unit sales volume with an uncertain growth
	• Annual operating costs that follow a random walk from an uncertain initial level
	• A random process for the price per unit of the protein

Some real options have been identified for this venture. One option is to set up flexibility to *abandon* the start-up to the ownership of others once its performance looks unfavorable. On the other hand, an alternative option can

be arranged to go in the opposite direction: if the early performance is stellar, *scale up* the business by proceeding to develop a second protein.

The timing of exercising these options must be determined. It will be necessary to understand and carefully model how the uncertain performance of the company will unfold. Finally, we will need to consider how to anticipate exercising these options.

OPTION BASICS

The option on the ski hotel, like any option, is the right, not the obligation, to choose an action in the future. This option can be exercised any time within an *exercise window*—in this instance, stretching up to the night of arrival. There is a price to pay, the *option premium*—in this instance, the $100 deposit. The option premium may be some action or commitment rather than a cash outlay. There is a price to exercise the option, the *exercise price*. If, as the time draws close and we do go on the ski vacation, we will spend a $300 exercise price to stay the four nights. Or we may choose to stay home, forfeiting the $100 option premium.

In valuing an option, we will need to clarify several attributes of the option:

- What is the option premium (or what action must we value to estimate the premium)?
- What is the exercise price (or what action must we value to estimate it)?
- What is the exercise date (or window in which we can exercise the option)?
- What are the related uncertainties?

Usually, it will be apparent what specific right is given by an option. It may be useful to clarify what the underlying asset is on which the option is based. In the ski hotel example, the underlying asset is the use of the room for the stated four nights, a nontransferable right. The worth of this asset may not be readily apparent, nor how its value will change (with the weather) as we draw closer to the exercise date. In order to make the original deposit (buy the option), we must believe that, at the time of exercise, the asset might be worth at least the future value of $100 (which is paid today) plus $300.

Related to the value of the underlying asset is the value of the option itself. Its value will depend on characteristics of the uncertainty, more specifically, in this case, the probability of skiable snow by the exercise date. How would we use these characteristics to think about whether the $100 is justified?

Suppose that the chance of skiable snow is 0.4, and that we would be willing to pay as much as $600 for the 4-day hotel expense of the ski vacation if there is skiable snow. This implies that if we pay the $100 deposit plus the $300 for the next 3 nights, the net gain of consumer surplus would be $200 in the event of skiable snow. A simple decision tree for the option is shown in Figure 13.1. There we see that the EMV of the option is $20, after

FIGURE **13.1**

Decision Tree for Ski Hotel Deposit Option.

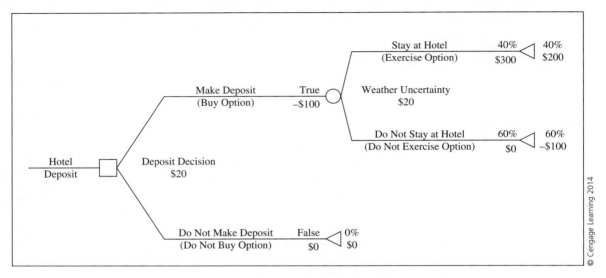

© Cengage Learning 2014

the option premium has been paid. Because the EMV is positive, the deposit option would be attractive to a risk-neutral decision maker.

In some cases, it may be possible to sell an option or to sell the underlying asset on which the option is based (i.e., four nights in the hotel). There may be a market where the asset or the option could be traded at any time. For example, in the case of financial options, at least the underlying asset can be traded in a financial market, and often the option itself can be traded. For instance, an option to buy a share of IBM common stock for $90 next September 18 is an example of a financial option (in particular, a "call" option).

Financial Options: A Brief Tutorial

In order to understand real options, it helps to have a basic understanding of financial options. The approach to valuing a financial option, which can be found in many standard texts (for example, Hull 2005), is based on what the option price must be to be consistent with the asset price. It is an arbitrage-free value. In other words, if the option were not priced in such a manner, arbitrageurs could trade shares of the option and shares of the asset in such a way that they would be guaranteed to make money with no risk. Factors that play a role in valuing financial options are the volatility of the underlying stock, whether dividends are paid by the stock, and the risk-free discount rate.

To get started on valuing options, let's consider how one might value the IBM $90 call option. Suppose the current price is $85, and we have an entire year before the exercise date of the call option. Let's assume that the option is a *European call option* that can be exercised only on one date, rather than an *American call option*, which may be exercised at any time until the end of the exercise window.

The crucial question for the European call option is: What will be the price of the IBM stock in 1 year? (The American call would be harder because we would have to think about exercising the option at every moment during the year.) In Chapter 11, the lognormal model was introduced specifically to model the future path of a stock's price. The lognormal model actually arises from a random process called geometric Brownian motion (GBM) in which the path of a stock's price over time is modeled with what is called a random walk. A random walk is exactly what its name implies—the price moves in a series of random steps, at each step moving from where it is by an uncertain amount. The standard approach to valuing a European call option is called the Black-Scholes model (Black 1973), which uses the GBM and the lognormal model:

Stock Price in One Year = Current Stock Price × [exp(Risk Free Rate

$$- 0.5 \times \text{Volatility}^2 + \text{Volatility} \times \text{Standard Normal})],$$

where volatility is the standard deviation of percentage price fluctuation in a year; Standard Normal is a normal random variable with mean 0 and standard deviation 1.0; and exp(x) denotes the exponential function e^x.

For this option, we have the Current Stock Price = $85, Exercise Price = $90, and let's assume that the Risk Free Rate = 5% and Volatility = 20%. This option is "out of the money," because the current price of $85 is lower than the strike or exercise price of $90. Because the expected price in 1 year, $87.59($= e^{0.03} \times 85) is also less than $90, more often than not the option would also be "out of the money" in 1 year. Sometimes, however, the stock price will exceed $90 in a year and owning the option will have value at that time. In general, we calculate for the option

Payoff at Maturity = MAX(Stock Price in One Year − Exercise Price, 0).

Then the payoff in current dollars would be given by

Present Value of Payoff = Payoff at Maturity/(1 + Risk Free Rate).

We could use the Black-Scholes assumptions and formula to calculate the value of the option. Or we can use Monte Carlo simulation to get a distribution of the Present Value of Payoff using the preceding formulas. The simulation needs only one uncertainty, a standard normal random variable.

Figure 13.2 shows the risk profile and expected value from a 50,000-trial Monte Carlo simulation of the Present Value of Payoff. Notice that more often than not (55.5% of the time) the option has a value that lands in the bucket at zero, because the stock price never reaches the exercise price. Sometimes the stock price is well above the exercise price, even more than $35 above the exercise price (in present-value terms). Figure 13.2 shows that 3.2% of the time the stock price is more than $35 above the exercise price, and even went as high as $111.30 above the exercise price. The expected value of the option is $6.50. For a traded option, this would make the value of the option $6.50; if it were any other price, an arbitrageur could take a

FIGURE **13.2**
Simulation Results for Value of IBM $90 Call Option.

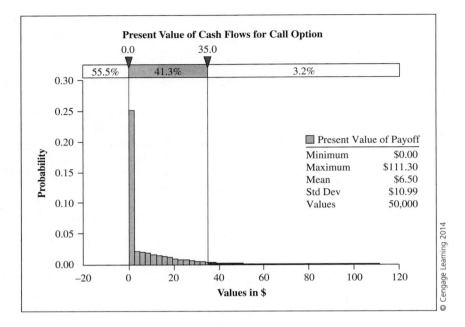

position involving some number of shares of the stock and another number of shares of the option and make money risk free.

We could also value a put option. A put option is the right to *sell* an asset at some time in the future. Suppose we want to value a put option with the same exercise price of $90. Then we would write the payoff of the put option in 1 year as

Put Option Payoff at Maturity

= MAX(Exercise Price − Stock Price in One Year, 0).

In other words, if our exercise price of $90 is above the stock price in a year, we'll buy the stock and immediately exercise the option to sell it, pocketing the difference between the $90 and the stock price. Or if the exercise price is equal to or below the stock price, the put option is worthless.

With a current stock price of $85, the put option is in the money, and would remain so even if the stock price increases over the coming year. Would you expect this put option to have greater value than the call option? Because it is in the money, it should be valued more highly than the out-of-the-money call option. The picture of the risk profile for the put option (Figure 13.3) shows that less than half the time (44.7%), the option has zero value. As a result, compared to the call option it has higher probabilities of positive values, and a higher mean, $7.11.

Let's consider how the values of the call and put options might change under different circumstances. First, suppose the exercise price of the call option and the put option are set to be equal. What happens to the price of the call option and the price of the put option when the exercise price

FIGURE **13.3**
Risk Profile for the
Present Value of a
$90 Put Option.

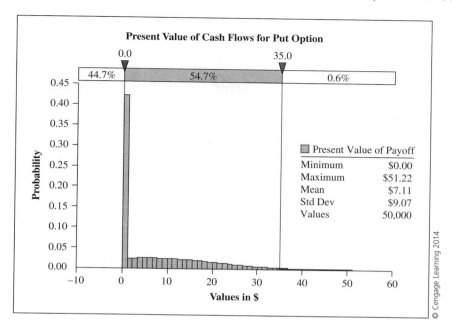

increases? The value of the call option would decrease (get further out of the money), and the value of the put option would increase. Another question has to do with the uncertainty or volatility of the IBM stock price. It's tempting to think that adding more uncertainty would make the option more risky and hence less valuable. But is that true? Let's say we increase the volatility from 20% to 40%. In other words, we double the standard deviation of Stock Price in 1 year. What does it do to our call option? It makes it more likely that IBM stock will be above $90 in a year, making it more likely that we would exercise the call option. It also widens the distribution of prices so that, if we do exercise the call option, we are likely to get more money. When changing the volatility from 20% to 40%, the simulation reports the mean of the call option value to be $13.24, compared to the earlier value of $6.50. The same reasoning applies to the put option; because the downside tail is also stretched out, the mean of the put-option value would also increase. The simulation gave a mean of $13.85, compared to the previous value of $7.11.

Because we adopted assumptions that are consistent with the Black-Scholes model, we can use that approach to calculate the values of the call and put options. For example, for the call option the Black-Scholes model gives a value of $6.49. In fact the difference between the simulated value of $6.50 and the Black-Scholes calculation of $6.49 is due entirely to sampling error in the simulation.

Formulas like Black-Scholes are easy to use—input the parameters and out pops the option value. Such formulas are very good for a financial option based on an asset like a stock that is traded on financial markets.

When an option is based on an underlying asset that is not traded on financial markets, it is known as a "real option." Holding a reservation at the ski hotel is an example; there is no public marketplace where one can buy or sell the underlying asset, nights spent at the hotel. Some real options are mixed; they involve some uncertainties that are based on traded assets, and some that are not. For example, an oil-drilling right is a real option that is based in part on relevant prices for traded assets (gas and oil prices) and in part on nontraded uncertainties (oil discovery, volume of oil, production flow rate).

The valuation of real options is inherently more difficult than the valuation of financial options. We must first consider what the underlying asset (an oil well, a drug in development) is worth; we can't look up the price of the asset in the financial pages of the newspaper. A large part of the task is to value the underlying asset, both now and its uncertain value in the future. Only then can we move to the valuation of the option. Because we often use a pro forma spreadsheet model of cash flow and NPV to value an asset, it is a natural setting for valuing the option. And we will often find that the assumptions of closed-form models like Black-Scholes are too restrictive for real options.

Finance theory has also been applied to real assets in an analogous way—so-called real options. Because the underlying asset is not traded, the approach asks what value the option would have if the underlying asset were to be traded. What volatility would such an asset have and how could we apply the same arbitrage arguments to value it?

Abundant references are available on using finance theory to value real options (Dixit and Pindyck, 1993, Trigeorgis, 1996, Copeland and Antikarov, 2001). Our intent here is not to duplicate these approaches, but rather to use the tools of decision analysis and simulation to value an option.

REAL OPTIONS

There are many kinds of real options in business strategy. Think of the real option as something that adds flexibility, as illustrated in Figure 13.4. Each of these flexibilities is available in the future if certain actions are taken now. For example, if a start-up business introduces a new product, scaling up to a second product later is made possible. Or, if the sales and manufacturing infrastructures have been put in place, switching to a different product may be possible.

In a decision-analysis context, additional flexibility comes from choosing an alternative that enables a downstream decision, which can be represented as an additional decision node later in a decision tree. We must do something now to enable that alternative or choice in the future. For example, if we want to have the flexibility to use a tire jack to fix a flat tire, we need to carry the jack in the trunk of our car. If we want to have the flexibility to add a product to our product line in the future, we must set up the product line (and perhaps the manufacturing flexibility) to accommodate an additional product.

FIGURE **13.4**

Flexibilities in Business Strategy Viewed as Real Options.

Category	Flexibility	Description	Examples
Grow	Scale Up	By laying the ground work, businesses can scale up early success with cost-effective sequential investments as market grows.	• High technology • R & D intensive • Multinational • Strategic acquisition
	Switch	With early investment, an opportunity to switch products, processes, or plants is enabled by a shift in underlying price or demand of inputs or outputs.	• Small-batch goods producers • Utilities • Farming
	Enlarge Scope	Investments in proprietary assets in one location or industry enables company to enter another industry or location cost-effectively-link-synergies and leverage are exploited.	• Multinationals • Companies with lock-in • De facto standard bearers
Defer/Learn	Study	Delay investment until more information or skill is acquired, reducing uncertainty, and cost.	• Natural resource companies • Real estate development
Shrink	Scale Down	Shrink or shut down a project when new information reduces the expected payoffs.	• Capital-intensive industries • Financial services • New product introduction • Airframe order cancellations
	Downshift	Switch to more cost-effective and flexible assets as new information is obtained.	• Small-batch goods producers • Utilities
	Reduce Scope	Limit the scope of (or abandon) operations in a related industry or location when there is no further potential in a business opportunity.	• Conglomerates • Multinationals

Sources: This figure incorporates ideas from Lenos Trigeorgis (1998) *Real Options*, Cambridge, MA: The MIT Press; and Martha Amram and Nalin Kulatilaka (1999) *Real Options*, Cambridge, MA: Harvard Business School Press.

Not all flexibilities give exclusive private value. The flexibility must be yours and no one else's to provide exclusive value to you. If free tire jacks were made available to anyone on any highway, you would not find value in carrying one. For an option to have exclusive value, there must be some commitment of resources to acquire the option, and there must be a particular window of time in which the options can be used.

The ability to create option opportunities is as useful as the ability to value them. Part of recognizing good options, of course, is being able to know when they are valuable. Here are some aspects of options that generally lead to higher value:

- Greater uncertainty in the variable(s) related to exercising the option
- A longer window in which to exercise the option
- A lower exercise price
- Higher value for the underlying asset
- More range of action in exercising the option (e.g., there can be more value in the flexibility to scale up to two additional products as compared with just one).

Succinctly said, we are looking for greater "flexibility." The ideas for valuing different kinds of information from the previous chapter carry over into option value. If an uncertain quantity has high information value, it is also likely that real options associated with that uncertainty will have high value. For example, if a particular market test has high information value, then preserving options to serve a market until after the market uncertainties are resolved will also have high value.

Figure 13.4 might be used as a kind of template or checklist for generating real options. All the ideas on creativity related to generating alternatives and framing decision problems from Chapter 6 would also come into play in identifying sources of optionality.

AN APPROACH TO VALUING REAL OPTIONS

Our approach to valuing real options can be applied to simple and complex options alike, and to any value model and uncertainty structure that fits the situation. It consists of three steps:

1. Estimate what the underlying opportunity, excluding the option, is worth (because it is not traded) with a decision tree or a spreadsheet simulation.
2. Estimate the value of the opportunity with the option included.
3. Calculate the value of the option itself as the difference between the value of the opportunity with the option and the value without it.

We'll develop this approach for discrete uncertainties, where we can use decision trees, and for continuous uncertainties, where we will use spreadsheet models and Monte Carlo simulation.

Discrete Uncertainties and Choices: Decision Trees

First, we will illustrate how a decision tree can be used to value an option with discrete uncertain outcomes and discrete choices. Let's use the Chris Wireless example. Recall that Chris, an entrepreneur, plans to operate a wireless network service within her city and surrounding county. Operating within the city requires a license from the city, which she has a reasonable chance of obtaining (60%). It will cost her $80,000 to launch the business, including the cost to apply for the city license. If she can operate in both the city and county, the business will be worth $120,000, and if she operates in the county only (because the city refuses to give her the license), the business will be worth $10,000. Her base decision tree is shown in Figure 13.5. Because the expected monetary value of the business is −$4,000, the opportunity does not look attractive.

Now let's think about some sources of flexibility. One is a *switch* option: Certain technologies for running the wireless service may be operated without a city license, although they are somewhat more expensive. If the license is not granted, Chris may switch to the alternative technology. If she does so, the business will be worth $90,000, accounting for the additional operational expense of the alternative technology.

FIGURE **13.5**
Base Decision Tree for Launching Wire Service.

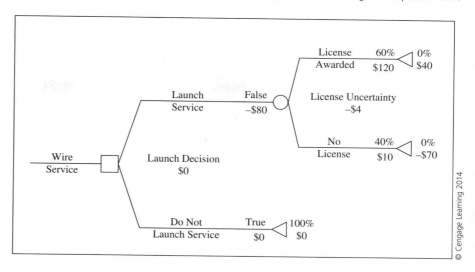

FIGURE **13.6**
Decision Tree with Switch Option.

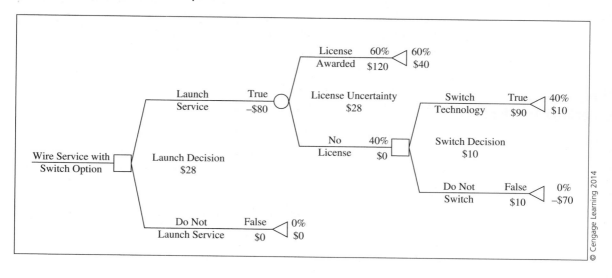

The decision tree with the switch option included is given in Figure 13.6, which shows an improved EMV of $28,000, making it a viable opportunity. Because the EMV of the base decision was 0—Chris would not have undertaken the business opportunity in Figure 13.5—the incremental option value for the switch is calculated as the difference between the EMV of the switch-option tree ($28,000) and the EMV without the option ($0), giving a net value for the option of $28,000. Some of this gain could be used to make the contingent arrangements in the system design to enable the use of these technologies later. The cost of these contingent arrangements, if put in dollar terms, becomes the option premium, to be compared to the option value of $28,000.

There are other possible options, such as a *defer/learn* option: Chris could make the minimum investment necessary to apply for the license and wait until the announcement of whether the license is approved before launching the business. The decision tree for this option is shown in Figure 13.7. It takes $10,000 to apply for the license. If the license is granted, the business is launched. And if the license is not granted, there is less money on the table to be lost. This option also makes for a viable business, this time with an EMV of $20,000, relative to the do nothing base.

What about doing both options together? Because each option is mitigating the same risk, though, the value of doing the second option may not cover its premium. In this example, doing both options would not be better than doing the best of the options (the switch option) alone. You may wish to draw the tree and check it for yourself. (See Problem 13.12.)

Many of the decision-analysis examples in this book have the attributes of options. These examples generally include a decision downstream from an uncertainty. By exercising the option after realizing the outcome of the uncertainty, we can reduce the effects of the risk. Building in the flexibility to allow such a downstream decision usually entails some additional cost (the option premium). We can value the option with the decision-tree tools we already know, gaining additional insight in the process.

FIGURE **13.7**
Decision Tree for the Defer/Learn Option.

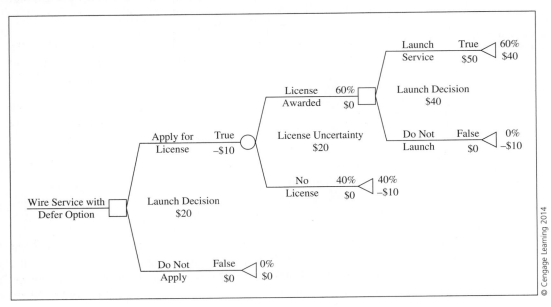

Continuous Uncertainties and Discrete Choices: Spreadsheet Simulation

When we move beyond simple options involving discrete uncertainties and discrete choices, the complexity can increase dramatically. Uncertain quantities can take on any value within some range, and there may be many uncertainties that are interrelated. As the window of time increases, modeling the dynamics of the variables can require complicated structures. Especially challenging is the task of projecting how downstream decisions will be made in the face of many dynamically varying variables. Fortunately, Monte Carlo simulation can meet all these challenges.

Consider the case of Proteiz, described at the beginning of the chapter. This opportunity will have high and uncertain variable costs and a learning curve with an uncertain rate of learning. Unit sales volume has an uncertain initial value and uncertain growth. Annual operating costs (salaries, utilities, and other fixed costs) are a random walk from an uncertain initial level—that is we can express a probability distribution for how the price will move in each time period and sum these incremental movements when we want to see where the cost is after some period of time. The price per unit of the protein will also follow a random walk; in this case we'll assume discrete geometric Brownian motion.

While valuing the opportunity itself without options poses challenges, it can be done by incorporating uncertainties into a spreadsheet model. Figure 13.8 shows a 10-year spreadsheet for the start-up. The relationships among the variables initially (at time 0) and in years 1, 2, and 10 are shown in Figure 13.9. It is clear that many variables are changing dynamically over time: Price, Unit Volume, Unit Cost, and Operating Cost. These variables will continue to evolve as time unfolds.

Many of the initial values of variables are assumed to have triangular distributions. For example, Initial Cost/Unit has an uncertain starting value that is modeled as the triangular distribution with minimum $75/unit, most likely $95/unit, and maximum $110/unit. In our spreadsheet model, the seven variables listed in columns D to K are each triangular distributions with their respective three parameters listed immediately below the variable. See Figures 13.8 and 13.9.

Because we expect cost/unit to decrease over time, we use a learning curve model. In this model, the initial cost/unit is a function of the cumulative volume and a learning parameter that controls the rate of adjustment:

$$\text{Cost/Unit} = \text{Initial Cost Per Unit} \times \text{Cumulative Unit Volume}^{-\text{Learning Parameter}}.$$

For example, if the Learning Parameter is 0.23, then every time the Cumulative Unit Volume doubles, the Cost/Unit drops by the same percentage to a cost that is $85\% = 2^{-0.23}$ of the initial cost. The rate of learning is itself uncertain, which we model with a Learning Parameter that has a triangular (0.05, 0.25, 0.39) distribution.

Unit Volume starts from an uncertain initial value and grows at an uncertain rate. Price Per Unit is a random walk—in fact, geometric Brownian

FIGURE **13.8**

Base Spreadsheet for Proteiz Venture.

	A	B	C	D	E	F	G	H	I	J	K	L
1						Proteiz Model						
2	Parameters											
3	Capital Investment	$500			Initial Values					Learning Rate	23%	
4	Income Tax Rate	40%								Minimum	5%	
5	CapGain Tax Rate	10%		Price	$	48.33	Cost/Unit	$	93.33	Most Likely	25%	
6	OpCost Sigma	$18		Minimum $	25		Minimum $	75		Maximum	39%	
7	Hurdle Rate	12%		Most Likely $	45		Most Likely $	95				
8	Risk-Free Rate	6.00%		Maximum $	75		Maximum $	110		Volume Growth	3%	
9	Price Growth	10%								Minimum	-15%	
10	Price Sigma	0.25		Unit Volume (000)	7.33		Operating Cost ($000)	$	180.00	Most Likely	5%	
11				Minimum	2		Minimum	160		Maximum	18%	
12				Most Likely	6		Most Likely $	180				
13				Maximum	14		Maximum $	200		Volume Growth P2	4%	
14										Minimum	-10%	
15										Most Likely	5%	
16										Maximum	18%	
17												
18												
19		Initial		Year 1	Year 2	Year 3	Year 4	Year 5	Year 6	Year 7	Year 8	Year 9	Year 10
20	Price		$	53.17 $	58.48 $	64.33 $	70.76 $	77.84 $	85.63 $	94.19 $	103.61 $	113.97 $	125.36
21	Cost/Unit		$	58.67 $	49.87 $	45.29 $	42.26 $	40.02 $	38.26 $	36.81 $	35.59 $	34.53 $	33.59
22	Unit Volume (000)			7.53	7.73	7.94	8.15	8.36	8.59	8.82	9.05	9.29	9.54
23												
24						All numbers below in thousands of dollars ($000)						
25	Operating Cost		$	180.00 $	180.00 $	180.00 $	180.00 $	180.00 $	180.00 $	180.00 $	180.00 $	180.00 $	180.00
26	Cash Flow after tax		$	(133) $	(68) $	(17) $	31 $	82 $	136 $	196 $	261 $	335 $	417
27	Cumulative NPV	$ (500.00) $		(619) $	(673) $	(685) $	(665) $	(619) $	(550) $	(461) $	(356) $	(235) $	(101)
28											NPV ($000)	$ (100.73)	

motion (see Figure 13.9). Operating Cost per year is a simple additive random walk (the equation is shown in Figure 13.9).

The spreadsheet shows the NPV for the project to be −$100,730 evaluated at the means of all the uncertainties. What we really want to know, however, is the expected NPV, which considers the effects of the uncertainties. This is shown in Figure 13.10 to be −$2,860, the mean of the simulation of NPV. The expected NPV is negative, so Proteiz does not appear to be an attractive investment.

The distribution for NPV is not normal, having a long tail on the right. Indeed, it does not necessarily have the shape of any recognizable standard distribution. In addition, the random process for the cash flows over time (or the value of the Proteiz business, for that matter) would not follow any standard distribution. Simulation brings richness to modeling a business opportunity in all its generality that cannot be captured in a standard analytical process that might be amenable to a closed-form solution, such as the Black-Scholes model.

OPTIONALITY AND PROTEIZ

What options are possible in the Proteiz opportunity? One flexibility not currently treated in the spreadsheet is the option to abandon the start-up if its initial performance is unfavorable. If, on the other hand, the initial

FIGURE **13.9**

Proteiz Spreadsheet Formulas.

Price	
Minimum	= RiskTriang(E6,E7,E8)
Most Likely	25
Maximum	45
	75

Cost/Unit	
Minimum	= RiskTriang(H6,H7,H8)
Most Likely	75
Maximum	95
	110

	Initial	Year 1	Year 2	Year 10
Price		= Initial_Price * (1 + RiskNormal(Price_Growth, Price_Sigma))	= C20 * (1 + RiskNormal (Price_Growth,Price_Sigma))	= K20 * (1 + RiskNormal (Price_Growth,Price_Sigma))
Cost/Unit		= Initial_Cost_Unit * C22^(−1 * Learning_parameter)	= $H$5 * (SUM($C$22:D22))^ (−1 * Learning_parameter)	= $H$5 * (SUM($C$22:L22))^ (−1 * Learning_parameter)
Unit Volume (000)		= Initial_Unit_Volume * (1 + Volume_growth)	= C22 * (1 + Volume_growth)	= K22 * (1 + Volume_growth)
Operating Cost		= Initial_Operating_Cost + RiskNormal (0,OpCost_Sigma)	= C25 + RiskNormal (0,OpCost_Sigma)	= K25 + RiskNormal (0,OpCost_Sigma)
Cash Flow after tax		= ((C20−C21) * C22−C25) * (1−Income_Tax_Rate)	= ((D20−D21) * D22−D25) * (1−Income_Tax_Rate)	= ((L20−L21) * L22−L25) * (1−Income_Tax_Rate)
Cumulative NPV	= −1 * Capital_ Investment	= NPV(Hurdle_Rate,C26) + $B$27	= NPV(Hurdle_Rate,$C$26: D26) + $B$27	= NPV(Hurdle_Rate,$C$26:L26) + $B$27
				= RiskOutput("NPV") + L27

FIGURE **13.10**
Base Case Simulation of Proteiz Opportunity Showing Mean NPV = −$2,860.

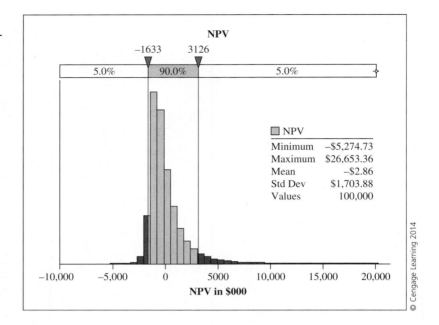

performance is stellar, an alternative option is to scale up the business by moving into a second protein.

To get started, we need to ask about the timing of these decisions. The principal parties suggest that these decisions would best be taken 2 years after startup. Two years would provide enough experience with the first protein to decide whether to call it quits or expand the business. (Deciding when to exercise a real option can be part of the analysis, but for now we will assume that the principals have already decided on 2 years.)

This leads to the question, what uncertainties will be resolved before the decision about exercising each option is made? This evaluation will be much more challenging for this real option than it would be for a typical financial option. For a financial option, it is necessary only to project the future price of the asset. And the decision is also easy, being simply a matter of whether that projected price will be greater than the contracted exercise price (for a call option).

In this case, we must think about what information we might use in the future to make the decision (to abandon or to scale up/expand), as well as how we would use that information. Price, Unit Volume, Unit Cost, and Operating Cost will continue to change as time unfolds, so their values are never entirely settled, but they will also be observed each period. By the end of year 2, when the decisions will be made as to whether to exercise the options, much will be known about the path that will have been taken by these variables. This information can be used to make the best decision we can about the real options.

A Trigger Value for Deciding

It is not always apparent how to anticipate the decision to exercise a real option. In a financial option—a call, for example—the decision to exercise the option and buy the asset is triggered by the actual price exceeding the exercise price. In a real option, we can decide to exercise however we wish, although we do want to make that decision the best way we can. Let's think about developing a trigger of some sort, on the basis of which we decide whether to exercise the options.

The set point on a thermostat is a familiar trigger. When the temperature in the room goes above the set point, the thermostat triggers the air conditioning to come on (or vice versa for heating). It's easy to define the trigger for the thermostat, because ultimately our comfort is related to the difference between the temperature and the target. Many investors leave "limit orders" with their brokers; if the price of a the specified security reaches a particular value—the trigger—the broker executes a transaction as instructed by the investor. In real options in general, it may take some effort to identify what variable or variables are related to ultimate value. And even then, further work will be required to choose the optimal set point for when to pull the trigger.

Consider the trigger for deciding to abandon an investment opportunity. Ultimately, what we care about is the NPV of the business. So it might make sense to construct the trigger using one or more variables that are closely associated with NPV over the life of the project. Or perhaps we would use a function of several variables as the triggering mechanism. Once we know the best triggering variable or function, we also need to consider the threshold (like an exercise price for a stock option) for that variable or function. Again, we want to set the threshold at a level that maximizes expected NPV.

How would we use the variables that we know at the end of year 2 to make the exercise decision on abandonment? Let's refer to these variables as candidate-triggering variables and think about which of them we should use. The best triggering variable will be the variable most associated with the ultimate success of the business. Because we have the spreadsheet model of the business, we can use it to gauge which variable is the best predictor. One way to do that is to run a simulation of the business, capturing the realizations of the venture's NPV for years 3 through 10, assuming it continues through year 10, along with the realizations of the various candidate-triggering variables known by the end of year 2. Then we can calculate the correlation of each of the candidate-triggering variables with the NPV.

Table 13.1 shows such correlations calculated from 10,000 trials of the Monte Carlo simulation. Note that Price, Volume, and Cash Flow Year 2 are positively correlated, while the cost variables are negatively correlated, as we would expect. The variable most highly correlated with NPV is the Cash Flow Year 2, with a correlation of 0.651 (As an aside, we have not included Cash Flow Year 1 or Cumulative Cash Flow, because the learning curve would reduce their correlation with NPV.) While Cash Flow Year 2 may be

TABLE 13.1
Correlations of Year 2 Candidate-Triggering Variables with NPV Years 3–10.

Price Year 2	0.495
Cost/Unit Year 2	−0.276
Unit Volume Year 2	0.399
Operating Cost Year 2	−0.034
Cash Flow Year 2	0.651

the best single triggering variable, there is, of course, some additional information contained in the other variables. We will see later how to construct a trigger using more than one variable. For now, let's use Cash Flow Year 2 as the triggering variable.

VALUING THE ABANDON OPTION

The next step in valuing the abandon option is to model the effects of exercising the option. We must include the cost to exercise the option and the effects of exercising the option on the opportunity. This is easy to do in this instance:

- We assume that it costs nothing to abandon.
- The effect on the opportunity at the time of exercise is simply to cancel future cash flows.

Therefore, we must modify the Proteiz model such that if the simulated Cash Flow Year 2 is less than the trigger value, we abandon the project; whereas if the simulated value is greater than the trigger value, we continue the project to year 10. Figure 13.11 shows that we added three rows to the previous Proteiz model. The first row is simply a constant trigger value of −$400 in cell D29. The next two rows will be identical to the previous model whenever the value of cell D26 (simulated Cash Flow Year 2) is greater than the trigger value. Thus, the formula in cell E30 is "=IF(D29<D26,E26,0)." Note that

FIGURE **13.11**
Proteiz model in which the project is abandoned whenever the simulated Cash Flow in year 2 is less than the trigger value.

	A	B	C	D	E	F	G	H	I	J	K	L
18												
19		Initial	Year 1	Year 2	Year 3	Year 4	Year 5	Year 6	Year 7	Year 8	Year 9	Year 10
20	Price		$ 53.17	$ 58.48	$ 64.33	$ 70.76	$ 77.84	$ 85.63	$ 94.19	$ 103.61	$ 113.97	$ 125.36
21	Cost/Unit		$ 58.67	$ 49.87	$ 45.29	$ 42.26	$ 40.02	$ 38.26	$ 36.81	$ 35.59	$ 34.53	$ 33.59
22	Unit Volume (000)		7.53	7.73	7.94	8.15	8.36	8.59	8.82	9.05	9.29	9.54
23												
24					All numbers below in thousands of dollars ($000)							
25	Operating Cost		$ 180.00	$ 180.00	$ 180.00	$ 180.00	$ 180.00	$ 180.00	$ 180.00	$ 180.00	$ 180.00	$ 180.00
26	Cash Flow after tax		$ (133)	$ (68)	$ (17)	$ 31	$ 82	$ 136	$ 196	$ 261	$ 335	$ 417
27	Cumulative NPV	$ (500.00)	$ (619)	$ (673)	$ (685)	$ (665)	$ (619)	$ (550)	$ (461)	$ (356)	$ (235)	$ (101)
28											NPV	$ (100.73)
29	Trigger Value - CF Yr2			$ (400)								
30	CF after tax (Abandon)		$ (133)	$ (68)	$ (17)	$ 31	$ 82	$ 136	$ 196	$ 261	$ 335	$ 417
31	Cumulative NPV (Abandon)		$ (619)	$ (673)	$ (685)	$ (665)	$ (619)	$ (550)	$ (461)	$ (356)	$ (235)	$ (101)
32											NPV (Abandon)	$ (100.73)

cell E30 is the third year cash flow because when the abandonment option kicks in, there will be no cash flows starting in year 3. The only additional change required is to zero out all future cash flows whenever the simulated Cash Flow Year 2 is less than the trigger value. This is accomplished by inserting "=IF(E30=0,0,F26)" into cell F30 (CF after tax (Abandon) in year 4) and dragging the formula to year 10. The modified model will now report all cash flows for years 3–10 to be zero whenever the simulated cash flow in year 2 is less than the trigger value.

Now that we know that Cash Flow Year 2 is our trigger variable and how to model the effects of exercising the option, we need to determine the optimal threshold level of the triggering variable, the point at which we decide to exercise the option. We can search for the best triggering threshold in a couple of ways:

- In our spreadsheet model, we can use @RISK's RiskSimTable function to calculate the risk profile of NPV for a sequence of threshold levels. Our simulation then tracks the NPV for each threshold level. After the simulation has run, we can review the risk profiles and statistics and decide which threshold is the best, typically the one with the highest expected NPV. (We can also use this approach iteratively on sets of more narrowly spaced thresholds, gradually homing in on the optimal threshold, just as we did to find the optimal calendar order in Chapter 11.)
- We can use the program RISKOptimizer to search for the optimal threshold level. RISKOptimizer generates candidate threshold levels, simulates the expected NPV, then uses genetic algorithms to generate and test other threshold levels that show promise of being even better. After a set amount of time, or after reaching a set level of accuracy, the optimizer reports the best threshold level it has found. The instructions at the end of this chapter show how to use RISKOptimizer.

For this first example, we will use the RiskSimTable[1] approach. First, we enter 11 potential trigger threshold levels from −$400,000 to +$600,000, in increments of $100,000. Then we run 11 simulations on the modified model, each with 100,000 trials; the results are shown in Figure 13.12. The trigger thresholds of −$200,000 and −$100,000 have the highest expected NPVs and, most importantly, have positive expected NPVs. For example, if the project is abandoned whenever the cash flow in year 2 is less than −$200,000, then the expected NPV is $48,000, which is an improvement over the $2,860 loss, the expected NPV without the abandon option.

Figure 13.12 shows that the curve is fairly flat near the maximum—there is a significant range of the threshold where the expected NPV is similar. On one hand, this can make it difficult to identify the precise optimal trigger threshold. On the other hand, however, it suggests that it may not be terribly important to find the precise threshold; as long as you are reasonably close, your expected NPV will not differ much from the expected NPV at the exact optimum. As mentioned in Chapter 11, this phenomenon of the "flat

---

[1] See instructions in Chapter 11 for RiskSimTable.

FIGURE **13.12**
Eleven simulations were run to determine the impact on expected NPV ($000) for trigger threshold values between −$400,000 and $600,000.

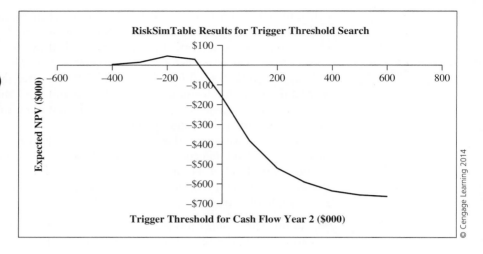

maximum" is not unusual; in many decision analyses where we compare a sequence of decision values or thresholds, the curve is relatively flat near the optimum. Although it is tempting to try to identify the precise optimum, remember that the model itself is imperfect, and so the "precise" optimum you find is probably not the actual optimum. However, if your model is a reasonable reflection of the real decision situation, you can have some confidence that choosing a value somewhere in the relatively flat range near the optimum in your results will be close to the actual optimum and will give you an EMV that is also close to the maximum EMV you could have achieved.

Next, a finer-grained RiskSimTable was created with the 11 trigger threshold values of −$250,000, −$225,000, ..., −$25,000, $0, and the 11 simulations were run, each with 100,000 trials. The best threshold for Cash Flow Year 2 was found to be −$150,000. Thus, if the after-tax cash flow in year 2 is below –$150,000, then Proteiz should abandon the business; otherwise, they should continue. By using the trigger value of −$150,000, the expected NPV has jumped to $65,000.

The fact that the optimal threshold for Cash Flow Year 2 is a negative number suggests it is advisable to continue to operate even if the business is still losing money at the end of year 2. The cash flow can eventually turn positive as the learning curve brings the costs down or as the price and/or unit volume grow to profitable levels, providing the cash flow is near enough to positive. The optimal value of –$150,000 shows that it is OK to be losing some money at the end of year 2 (up to $150,000), but if we are losing more than that, we should exercise the abandonment option. In other words, cut your losses if the second year cash flow is worse than a $150,000 loss.

Comparing the risk profile with the abandonment threshold set at −$150,000 (Figure 13.13), against the base risk profile (Figure 13.10) shows that the Proteiz business opportunity is greatly improved with the abandonment

FIGURE **13.13**
Risk Profile for the
Best Abandonment
Threshold Level of
−$150,000.

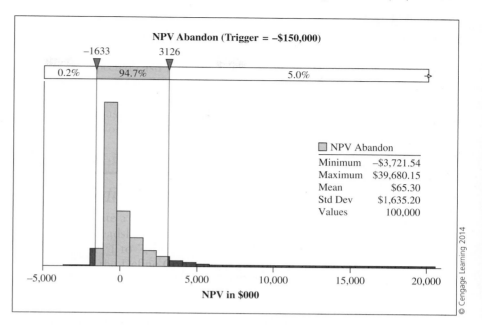

option. The mean NPV increases to $65,300 from −$2,860 and the downside is significantly reduced. In particular, without the abandonment option, there is a 5% chance the Proteiz will lose $1.63 million or more, but with the option, there is only a two-tenths of one percent chance that the project will lose $1.63 million or more. As expected, we see no change on the upside, as witnessed by the 95th percentiles being identical values, namely $3.13 million; abandoning the business protects us from losing more money in the future and doesn't take away from the upside potential.

Although the option to abandon seems obvious in the context of this example, in real-world settings the option to abandon is often overlooked. Decision makers frequently feel compelled to continue with a poor opportunity because much effort, time, and expense have already been expended on the project. This is called the sunk cost bias and discussed in Chapter 15.

VALUING THE SCALE-UP OPTION

Our other Proteiz example option is to scale up the business: go on to the development of a second similar protein if the first protein is successful. We will need to carefully model how this option affects performance. Figure 13.14 shows the spreadsheet model for the scale-up option and the corresponding formulas are given in Figure 13.15. We next discuss the rationale in developing the scale-up option.

- The initial year for the second protein will be year 2. As shown in Figures 13.14 and 13.15, the initial year for the second protein (P2) is column D, which corresponds to year 2 of the first protein. While there

FIGURE **13.14**

Spreadsheet for Scale-Up Option of the Proteiz Venture.

	A	B	C	D	E	F	G	H	I	J	K	L	M	N
33														
34				Initial	Year 1	Year 2	Year 3	Year 4	Year 5	Year 6	Year 7	Year 8	Year 9	Year 10
35	Price - P2			$ 58.48	$ 64.33	$ 70.76	$ 77.84	$ 85.63	$ 94.19	$ 103.61	$ 113.97	$ 125.36	$ 137.90	$ 151.69
36	Cost/Unit - P2			$ 49.87	$ 30.85	$ 26.18	$ 23.73	$ 22.10	$ 20.89	$ 19.93	$ 19.14	$ 18.46	$ 17.88	$ 17.36
37	Unit Volume - P2 (000)			7.73	8.06	8.41	8.78	9.16	9.56	9.97	10.40	10.85	11.32	11.81
38														
39								All numbers below in thousands of dollars ($000)						
40	Yearly Operating Cost - P2			$ 135.00	$ 135.00	$ 135.00	$ 135.00	$ 135.00	$ 135.00	$ 135.00	$ 135.00	$ 135.00	135.00	$ 135.00
41	Cash Flow after tax - P2				$ 81	$ 144	$ 204	$ 268	$ 339	$ 420	$ 511	$ 615	734	$ 871
42	Cumulative NPV - P2			-100	$ (22)	$69.50	$185.27	$321.10	$474.57	$644.03	$828.25	$1,026.30	$1,237.43	$1,461.04
43													NPV ("Protein 2")	$1,461.04
44	Trigger Value - Reg Yr2			$ 1,519	$ (200)									
45	CF after tax - P2 (Scale Up)				$ 81	$ 144	$ 204	$ 268	$ 339	$ 420	$ 511	$ 615	734	$ 871
46	Cumulative NPV - P2 (Scale Up)			-100	$ (22)	$69.50	$185.27	$321.10	$474.57	$644.03	$828.25	$1,026.30	$1,237.43	$1,461.04
47													NPV ("P2 Scale Up")	$1,461.04
48														
49														
50													Total NPV	$1,360.31

is great uncertainty before the launch of the business, information and experience gained with the first protein over the 2 years will carry over to the second protein. Thus, the initial values for many of the variables for the second protein are related to second-year levels for the first protein.

- We assume that the capital investment will be $100,000, whereas the original capital investment was $500,000. See cell D42. The first protein paves the way for the second protein, which will be reflected in how that protein is included in the spreadsheet model. The second protein will have a lower capital requirement because some infrastructure needed to discover the protein will already be in place.

- Price for second protein is a random walk starting at the second-year price of the first protein. This anticipates that the second protein would have functionality and customers very similar to the first protein, except that it would satisfy a different specialized need. Specifically, the initial price of the second protein (cell D35) is "=D20*RiskNormal (1,0.1)." Then, as we did with the first protein, the price of the second protein in subsequent years follows the same growth and volatility. The price in year 1 of the second protein is given by "=D35*(1+Risk Normal(Price_Growth,Price_Sigma))."

- The unit cost of the second protein is initially the same as the second-year price of the first protein, and proceeds from there down a learning curve at the same rate as the first protein. This follows from the similarity in the manufacturing process of the proteins. See Figures 13.14 and 13.15 for exact relationships.

- Unit volume varies around the second-year unit volume of the first protein, modeled by multiplying second-year unit volume by a triangular distribution with a low of 0.9, most likely 1.0, and a high of 1.1. While the amount of use of a protein is unclear prior to the launch of the first protein, the second protein would follow in line with the experience observed with the first, inasmuch as it goes to the same labs and similar uses. However, the second protein will have a slightly different growth

FIGURE **13.15**
Proteiz Spreadsheet Formulas.

	Initial	Year 1	Year 10
Price – P2	=D20 * RiskNormal(1,0.1)	=D35 * (1 + RiskNormal(Price_Growth,Price_Sigma))	=M35 * (1 + RiskNormal(Price_Growth, Price_Sigma))
Cost/Unit – P2	=D21	=$D$36 * E37^(–1 * Learning_parameter)	=$D$36 * SUM($E$37:N37)^(–1 * Learning_parameter)
Unit Volume – P2 (000)	=D22 * RiskTriang (0.9,1,1.1)	=D37 * (1 + Volume_Growth_P2)	=M37 * (1 + Volume_Growth_P2)
All numbers below in thousands of dollars ($000)			
Yearly Operating Cost – P2	=D25 * 0.75	=D40 + RiskNormal(0,OpCost_Sigma)	=M40 + RiskNormal(0,OpCost_Sigma)
Cash Flow after tax – P2		=((E35–E36) * E37–E40) * (1 – Income_Tax_Rate)	=((N35–N36) * N37 – N40) * (1 –Income_Tax_Rate)
Cumulative NPV – P2	–100	=(NPV(Hurdle_Rate,E41) + $D$42)/ (1 + Hurdle_Rate)^2	=(NPV(Hurdle_Rate,$E$41:N41) + $D$42)/(1 + Hurdle_Rate)^2
Trigger Value – Reg Yr2	=B58 + B59 * D20 + B60 * D21 + B61 * B22 + B62 * D25 + B63 * D26	–200	**=RiskOutput("Protein 2") + N42**
CF after tax – P2 (Scale Up)		=IF(AND(D44 > E44,D26 > D29), E41,0)	=IF(M45=0,0,N41)
Cumulative NPV – P2 (Scale Up)	=IF(E45=0,0,D42)	=(NPV(Hurdle_Rate,E45) + $D$46)/ (1 + Hurdle_Rate)^2	=(NPV(Hurdle_Rate,$E$45:N45) + $D$46)/(1 + Hurdle_Rate)^2
			=RiskOutput("P2 Scale Up") + N46
			=RiskOutput("Total NPV") + N47 + L32

rate. Specifically, it will follow a triangular distribution with minimum of −10%, most likely of 5%, and maximum of 18%. See cell K13 for the volume growth distribution of the second protein and cell E37 for its use.

- Annual operating costs start at a lower level, 75% of the second-year operating costs of the first protein, inasmuch as many of the fixed salaries and facilities would be shared. Each subsequent year, the operating cost varies around this number, with a normal distribution having a mean of zero and a standard deviation of $18,000. See cells D40 and E40.
- Finally, the NPV of the second protein in its first year is given by "=NPV(Hurdle_Rate,E41)+$D$42." However, we need to know today's value. Thus, in cell E42, we have "=(NPV(Hurdle_Rate,E41)+$D$42)/(1+Hurdle_Rate)^2." Continuing in the same fashion, we compute the cumulative NPV across 10 years.

The preceding assumptions represent reasonable modeling choices for this example, and other applications of the simulation real option methodology will use other assumptions. The model illustrates the usability of the simulation methodology in a reasonably complicated situation.

These characteristics of the second protein suggest that the option to scale up would be attractive. Much, though not all, of the uncertainty has been resolved in the first protein. And the capital, operating, and unit costs are reduced, on average. However, if the characteristics of the first option are highly unfavorable, we would not wish to scale up our losses.

How should we make the decision to scale up? Once again, the same set of variables will be potentially useful for triggering a positive exercise decision. As with the abandon option, we can extend the model to include the second protein, simulate the NPV from the second protein, and see how well the possible triggering variables correlate with the NPV from the second protein. Table 13.2 shows the resulting correlation from a simulation of 10,000 trials.

As before, Price, Volume, and Cash Flow Year 2 are positively correlated with NPV from the second protein, while the cost variables are negatively correlated. The numbers are different from those in Table 13.1 because we are using NPV for the second protein, not the NPV to go for the first protein. Cash Flow Year 2 is the most highly correlated, at 0.565; however, it is not far ahead of several other variables.

While we could use any one of these variables successfully, suppose we use the information in all of them together. If we wanted to make the best possible use of these variables, we would try to find the region in the

TABLE **13.2**
Correlations between Candidate-Triggering Variables and NPV for Second Protein.

Price Year 2	0.448
Cost/Unit Year 2	−0.257
Unit Volume Year 2	0.348
Operating Cost Year 2	−0.023
Cash Flow Year 2	0.565

multi-dimensional space of all these variables for which it is better to scale up than not. This would be very difficult to do and beyond the scope of the text. However, we can accomplish something close to this by assuming a linear triggering function and estimating that triggering function using regression techniques from Chapter 10.

Using the same data from the 10,000-trial simulation that was used to create Table 13.2, we use regression to estimate NPV, using the set of five variables listed in Table 13.2 as independent variables. The results are shown in Table 13.3.

The numbers in the "Coefficients" column in the lower part of Table 13.3 are what we need to construct our trigger function on which to base the decision to exercise the scale-up option. Therefore our Trigger Function is:

$$Estimated\ NPV\ (P2) = -646.28 + 4.05 \times Price\ Year\ 2 + 9.8 \times Cost/Unit$$
$$Year\ 2 + 196.07 \times Unit\ Volume\ Year\ 2 + 2.81$$
$$\times Operating\ Cost\ Year\ 2 + 8.56 \times Cash\ Flow\ Year\ 2.$$

Recall that an expression like this gives the expected value for the response variable—in this case NPV for the second protein—conditioned on the Year 2 explanatory variables (Price, Cost/Unit, Volume, Operating Cost, and Cash Flow). So you can see what we are doing; we are essentially trying to predict the NPV for the second protein using variables we have observed at the time we make the decision about exercising the scale-up option. There's no guarantee, of course, that the prediction will be accurate, but we are getting its conditional expected value, and we will use that as a basis for deciding whether to exercise the option to expand with the second protein.

Now that we have a trigger function, the next problem is to find the best threshold; how high does the conditional expected NPV have to be before we decide to exercise the option? Rather than focus on just the scale-up option, though, it is worthwhile to reconsider the abandonment option. If there is a possibility of expansion, might that imply that the threshold for abandoning would change? Intuitively, we might think that the abandonment threshold might drop. That is, the possibility of expanding in the future might make it attractive to continue the business with the first protein even if the second year cash flow were less than −$150,000. Following this thinking, we will look for two optimal thresholds at once, one for the abandonment option, and one for the scale-up option.

As before, we could use either a data table (this time a 2-way data table, because we are optimizing on two variables) or an optimizer; this time we will demonstrate the use of RISKOptimizer. The two decision variables to be optimized are:

- Best threshold for the triggering function for the scale-up option
- Best threshold for the level of Cash Flow Year 2 to trigger the abandon option

In the software instructions at the end of this chapter, we show how to set up RISKOptimizer. For this example, it was set to run 100,000 trials for each of 100 candidate threshold levels to find the optimal threshold values that maximize the expected NPV for the two proteins.

TABLE **13.3**
Regression of NPV vs. Five Triggering Variables for Scale-Up Option.

Regression Statistics

Multiple R	0.6092678
R Square	0.3712072
Adjusted R Square	0.3708926
Standard Error	1795.203
Observations	10000

ANOVA

	df	SS	MS	F	Significance F
Regression	5	19014080529	3.8E + 09	1179.99	0
Residual	9994	32208200432	3222754		
Total	9999	51222280962			

	Coefficients	Standard Error	t Stat	P-value	Lower 95%	Upper 95%
Intercept	−646.28	176.05	−3.67	0.00	−991.37	−301.19
Price Year 2	4.05	2.01	2.02	0.04	0.12	7.99
Cost/Unit Year 2	9.80	2.52	3.89	0.00	4.86	14.74
Unit Volume Year 2	196.07	7.01	27.96	0.00	182.32	209.81
Operating Cost Year 2	2.81	0.71	3.96	0.00	1.42	4.21
Cash Flow Year 2	8.56	0.40	21.34	0.00	7.78	9.35

The best threshold value for the triggering function for the scale-up option turns out to be $60,749 (although again the curve is fairly flat for thresholds in the neighborhood of $60,749). This suggests that when the expected NPV for the second protein is calculated to be above $60,749, then Proteiz should develop that protein. This number may seem surprisingly high, but remember that many instances of poor performance are culled out by the abandon trigger. Interestingly, the threshold value for the triggering function for the abandon option is −$223,437 and changed only somewhat from the previous value we found, −$150,000. In this case, the explanation is that the two decisions are made at exactly the same time, and one (abandon) affects only the lower tail of the distribution of NPV, and the second (scale up) affects only the upper tail. In other situations, the two decisions may interact, so it can be important to optimize the two thresholds jointly as we did here.

Figure 13.16 shows the risk profile for the business when both options are incorporated into the analysis using the optimal thresholds. Significant value was added by the scale-up option; the mean NPV is $1,583,000, or $1,518,000, on average, above the value including only the abandon option. This comes from the additional probability of high values, especially when the decision is to scale up and both proteins are successful.

This example illustrates how to put teeth into growth judgments often made in practice. Real-world decision makers may push ahead on a poor project by claiming that the project has "strategic value" above and beyond the project itself. The strategic value to which they refer certainly includes the kind exhibited by the scale-up/expand option we have just explored. The approach used in this example can provide an actual number for that strategic value, transforming the decision-making process from a "gut feel" to a clearly articulated quantitative analysis of the value added.

FIGURE 13.16
Risk Profile of Total NPV Incorporating Abandon and Scale-Up Options.

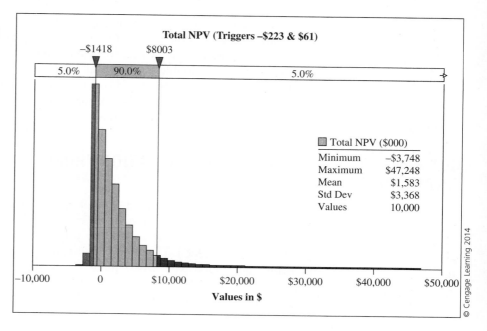

REVIEW OF THE APPROACH FOR CONTINUOUS UNCERTAINTIES

The approach we have developed builds on skills developed elsewhere in this book. It includes the following tasks:

- Build the basic spreadsheet model as would be done for valuing the underlying opportunity:
  - Add uncertainty. It may be helpful to describe the structure with an influence diagram.
  - Include dynamic changes of variables over time.
  - Include relationships and correlations among the variables.
- Clarify the optionality:
  - What must be done now to enable the option later? How much will it cost, or what resources must be committed?
  - What is the timing of exercising the option?
  - What is the cost of exercise and how will it be modeled?
- Propose alternative triggering variables and functions of triggering variables:
  - Look for leading indicators of ultimate success.
  - The triggering variables must be observed at the time of option exercise.
- Compare triggering variables:
  - Look for higher correlation with the ultimate objective (NPV to go, for example).
  - Regression techniques, where the response variable is the ultimate objective, can provide a triggering function of multiple independent triggering variables.
- Find the best triggering cutoff levels:
  - Data-table simulation.
  - Search with a simulation optimizer.

It is possible to consider options (e.g., scale-up or abandon options) that occur at any and every time period. By simply putting in a trigger or triggering function for each year, multiple decision points could be analyzed. Each trigger could use the same variable(s) (observed at a different time) and the same threshold level, or it could employ distinct triggering functions and thresholds for each year. The point is that the approach is general; it could be used for virtually any model structure and virtually any kind of option structure.

COMPARISON WITH REAL OPTION VALUATION FROM FINANCIAL THEORY

The approach to real options described here differs from that found in finance textbooks and articles based on financial theory. In those treatments, the intent is to value the option itself in a way that is consistent with how the underlying asset is valued. Those approaches are based on price and arbitrage arguments that work well when there is an active market in which the underlying asset is traded. They would be inadequate for an example such as Proteiz, which has the following complications:

- Multiple uncertain factors: volume, price, variable cost, operating cost. Financial approaches to real options have difficulty with even two factors.
- The factors do not follow standard assumptions typical in financial options theory. For example:
  - Unit cost depends on cumulative units produced (which is built into the learning curve).
  - The value of the underlying asset, in this case the value of Proteiz as a business, is a complicated combination of volume, price, variable cost, and operating cost. While the random process for an individual factor such as price/unit may be familiar, the issue is the random process for the value of the business which, as we have seen, is complicated and does not follow any of the standard random processes.
- The volatility of the asset would be needed in the typical real-option-valuation approach from financial theory, and a simulation model would most likely be needed to generate it. This volatility would then be used in some kind of lattice model that approximates the valuation. Given that one is creating a simulation to value the underlying asset and its volatility, why not use the simulation to value the asset plus option, without the loss of accuracy introduced by the approximations?

WHAT DISCOUNT RATE?

Real options almost always involve cash flows over significant periods of time. As a result, there is a question as to what discount rate to use in valuing the option. Because most real options involve numerous uncertainties that are not associated with traded financial assets, as is the case in our examples, there are three possible approaches. The key is to be consistent with how risk is incorporated into the valuation:

1. If the decision is based on just the expected cash flows or mean NPV, then use the business' weighted average cost of capital (WACC). Here, the risk adjustment is made through the discount rate, and only the mean of the NPV (or cash flow) is used, not the standard deviation or volatility. This is the traditional approach as typically used by financial analysts, and it essentially assumes that all projects being evaluated have similar risk levels. If the project being considered has a different risk profile/distribution relative to the other projects in the company, this approach may result in a misleading value.

2. If virtually all the risk is included in the model, including nonsystematic project-specific risk, and you use the risk profile—in the sense that the decision maker may reject an opportunity with a significant downside, even though it has a mean NPV > 0—then use a risk-free discount rate (e.g., a Treasury fixed rate having a duration similar to that of the opportunity). Incorporating the risk into the model and then basing the decision on the risk profile accounts for the risk. If you also risk-adjusted the discount rate in computing NPV, you would be double-counting the risk.

3. As we will see in the next chapter, it is also possible to directly model a decision maker's risk preference by means of a "utility function." Doing so incorporates into the model an implicit valuation of the risk, and so the risk-free discount rate would be used.

In practice, a hybrid of methods 1 and 2 is often used. A large part of the risk is included in the model, the discount rate is adjusted somewhat for risk, to the extent that not all risk is in the model, and decision makers consider the risk profile, especially for rejecting opportunities. As we have seen throughout the book, examining the risk profile before accepting an opportunity or an option is an important step in decision analysis, especially when the risk is large and could threaten the viability of the organization.

FINDING OPTIMAL DECISION VALUES USING RISKOPTIMIZER

This section provides the instructions for optimizing simulation models using Palisade's RISKOptimizer. Naively optimizing a simulation model seems as simple as running Solver on the model, but then one realizes that Solver will return the optimal decision value for only one iteration. As a matter of fact, change the input values, and the optimal value changes. In addition, for each possible decision value, there isn't only one output value—there is a whole distribution of values. Remember in the Proteiz example, we had to run 11 simulations for each trigger value? We did this to find the risk profile and the corresponding expected net present value for each trigger value. The more we think about how to optimize a stochastic model, the more complexities we come across, and thus, require a more sophisticated tool than Solver.

RISKOptimizer uses genetic algorithms, which are amazingly clever and based on the idea of the survival of the fittest. While we will not provide a detailed explanation of genetic algorithms, we will cover the basic ideas so that you can make effective use of RISKOptimizer.

First, RISKOptimizer starts with a population of 50 "individuals." By individuals, we mean potential solutions. For example, in the Proteiz example, we want to find the best trigger value for the abandonment option and simultaneously the best trigger value for the scale-up option. Thus, our population of 50 would be 50 pairs of trigger values, one for each option. Next, we determine the "fitness" level of each population member. Here fitness is measured by the objective of the optimization problem, which in the Proteiz example is maximizing the expected Total NPV. Thus, to determine the fitness level, we must determine the expected NPV for each population member, that is we must run 50 simulations. These two steps, choosing the population and measuring the fitness of each member, sets up the optimization.

Next, we want the fittest to survive and become stronger, that is, give us even better (near optimal) decision values. Genetic algorithms use techniques inspired by natural evolution, such as inheritance, mutation, and crossover to produce offspring from the previous generation (population) that are more fit. Although the exact details are beyond our scope, suffice it to say that, genetic algorithms keep improving from one generation to the next by producing more and more fit successive populations.

Genetic algorithms are very powerful, and given enough time the optimal decision values will be found. However, genetic algorithms can easily require hours if not days to find the optimal values. This is where we often invoke the flat-maximum principle. As we demonstrate in the material that follows, RISKOptimizer provides a view of its progress, which helps us determine when we are close to a flat maximum. As time progresses, if the estimated maximum value changes very little, it is safe to assume that we are close to the maximum.

STEP 1 Open RISKOptimizer via @RISK.

1.1 Open Excel® and @RISK, and enable any macros if prompted. RISKOptimizer is accessed via the Tools section of @RISK's menu ribbon.

1.2 You can access a variety of help features by clicking on the **Help** button. The *Manual* is a PDF file of the actual manual, while @RISK *Help* is a searchable database and both are found under *Documentation*. In addition, you can view examples via *Example Spreadsheets* or video tutorials via *Videos*.

STEP 2 Open the Proteiz Model.

2.1 Open the file **Proteiz Handout.xlsx** found at www.cengagebrain.com. Explore the model by finding the trigger values and the input distributions.

2.2 Choose **Total NPV** (cell N50) as an *Output Cell*.

STEP 3 RISKOptimizer Set Up.

3.1 Click on the **RISKOptimizer** button, then on **Settings**.

3.2 The *RISKOptimizer – Optimization Settings* dialog box pops up and is shown in Figure 13.17.

3.3 Because RISKOptimizer can run for an indefinite time, we have a number of stopping conditions. We have clicked the **Time** checkbox and entered **30 Minutes**. Other possibilities include setting the total number of simulations (trials) to be run at a fixed number (such as 1,000) or by progress. Click **OK**.

3.4 In addition, we need to set the number of iterations for each of our simulations or trials. In the @RISK ribbon, enter **10,000** for *Iterations*. This means that each simulation or trial will run for 10,000 iterations to estimate the expected value, then run another 10,000 iterations for the next trial value.

FIGURE **13.17**
RISKOptimizer's
setting dialog box
showing that the
optimization will run
for 30 minutes.

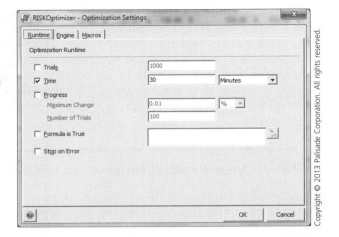

STEP 4 RISKOptimizer Model Definition.

4.1 Click on the **RISKOptimizer** button, then click on **Model Definition**.

4.2 The *RISKOptimizer – Model* dialog box pops up as shown in Figure 13.18. In the pull-down menu, choose **Maximum** for the *Optimization Goal*.

4.3 For the *Cell*, enter the location of the objective function, which for us is Total NPV and resides in N50.

4.4 For *Statistic*, you can choose the mean value, the standard deviation (such as in minimizing portfolio volatility), or any of a half dozen other summary statistics of the risk profile. We entered **Mean** in the pull-down menu. Thus, we are looking for the combination of trigger values that produces the highest mean (or expected) Total NPV.

4.5 For the *Adjustable Cell Ranges*, we enter a range for each trigger variable, and it is within this range that RISKOptimizer will search for the optimal value. Specifically, the trigger value for the abandonment option is in cell D29, thus click on the **Add** button, click in cell **D29**, click **OK**, and enter **–500** and **200** for the lower and upper bounds. Similarly, enter the trigger value for the scale-up option cell **E44** with **–100** as the lower bound and **400** as the upper bound.

4.6 Finally, we see that RISKOptimizer allows you to enter constraints for your optimization problem. Both hard and soft constraints are allowed, and we refer the interested reader to RISKOptimizer's online manual for additional information.

4.7 Click **OK**.

FIGURE **13.18**
Specifying the
model for
RISKOptimizer.

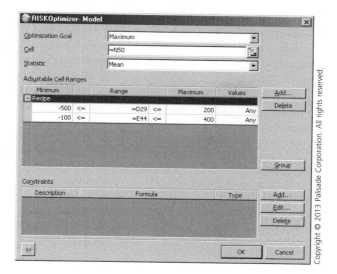

FIGURE **13.19**
RISKOptimizer's
progress window
showing that 10,000
iterations are being
run for each simu-
lation; that 1,014
trials have been
run; that 1 hour of a
5 hour time limit has
passed; and that
the original
expected Total NPV
was $1,447,538 and
the best expected
Total NPV found is
$1,592,945.

STEP 5 RISKOptimizer Results.

5.1 In the RISKOptimizer menu, click on the **Start** button.

5.2 After initializing the model, the *RISKOptimizer Progress* pop-up window appears in lower left corner. See Figure 13.19. The second button
from the left shows a magnifying glass and is the *Watcher* button.
Click on the **Watcher** button.

5.3 *RISKOptimizer's Watcher* window pops up and is shown in Figure 13.20.
Here we see that over the last 100 trials there has been no increase found
in the expected Total NPV. Across all the simulations, we saw the biggest
gains to expected Total NPV during the early stages of the optimization
and then only slow gains, just as one would expect with a flat maximum.

5.4 Click on the **Summary** tab of the *RISKOptimizer's Watcher* window. Figure 13.21 shows that the best solution found so far (the fittest individual) was found on trial number 596, with an expected Total NPV of $1,592,945 occurring when D29 (abandon trigger) equals −$223.44 (000) and E44 (scale-up trigger) equals $60.75 (000).

FIGURE 13.20
RISKOptimizer's Watcher window showing successive maximum expected Total NPV values found after 1 hour, when 1,014 trials were run, and the best result occurred at trial 596.

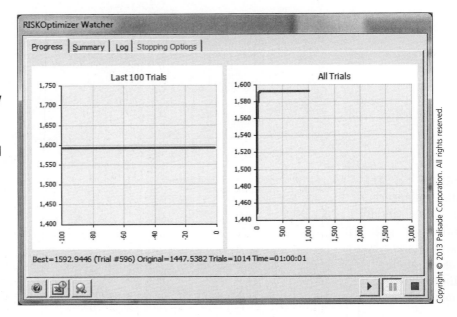

FIGURE 13.21
Under the Summary tab, we see the results and corresponding threshold values for 3 trials: Best, Orginal, and Last.

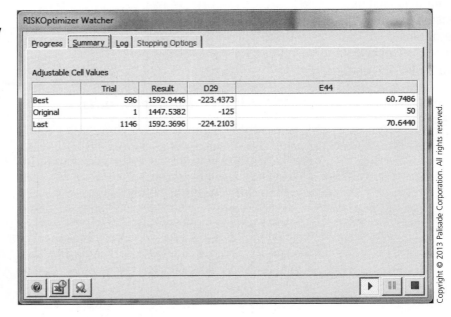

This concludes the RISKOptimizer instructions. As we have mentioned, genetic algorithms are powerful, but can take an inordinate amount of time. For example, we set the number of iterations at 100,000 and ran RISKOptimizer for 16 hours for the results in this chapter.

SUMMARY

There are many reasons for understanding options. Strategic choices by firms and individuals create options. These may be options to add related businesses or make product-line extensions. For example, an electronics hardware business has the option of selling software. By being careful to enable later choices, a firm can use its high market value to acquire other businesses. The value of these other businesses should include the options owned by those businesses, the value the new business gives to the acquiring company's own options, and opportunities to create new options.

More uncertainty only enhances the value of options and options thinking. Uncertainty only hurts you if you have no options. The greater the uncertainty, the greater the options portion of the value of an opportunity.

Options do not fall into your lap; they must be created, often at some expense. For this reason, it is crucial to look for optionality and to be able to value an option, rather than hope one will appear. Even if an option will be obvious to you when you get to it, you must be able to see it early in order to correctly evaluate the venture. Options are more attractive when the upfront cost is lower, when the exercise cost is lower, when there is a longer window in which to exercise the option, when the cash flows, if exercised, are higher, and, again, when there is more uncertainty that can be exploited by the option. Thinking with an options framework, recognizing option opportunities, and estimating their approximate value (even when time to do the formal valuation analysis is limited) are important skills.

Without dynamic analysis, managers tend to assign zero value to flexibility (by ignoring it) or assign "infinite" value by choosing more-flexible projects for vague "strategic" reasons. Thinking with options requires being proactive, in both thinking ahead and acting in advance. Flexibility can be valuable, but it comes at a cost that may never be recovered. Dynamic analysis of options enables managers to develop insights about the value of flexibility relative to its costs.

EXERCISES

13.1. Perhaps at some point in your life you have taken each of the actions a–e that follow. In doing so, you exhibited "options thinking." For each, explain how the option value arises. Additional questions you might consider: What constitutes the option cost, the exercise window, the trigger strategy? How could you estimate the value it gives you?

   a. Double-booking: You make a partially refundable airplane reservation and a refundable train reservation for the same trip because you are concerned about an impending major storm that would ground airplanes.

b. Lease versus buy: When moving to a new place, you rent an abode on a month-to-month basis rather than buying a house before moving.

c. Contingency: You are going to spend three months in Southeast Asia, working and traveling. You plan to visit a number of countries, in some parts of which malaria is prevalent. You may decide to go to these areas when you are in the country. You obtain a prescription for malaria pills from your physician and plan to fill the prescription and take the pills with you, even though you don't know if you will use them.

d. Capacity planning: There is a big concert coming up and you are online to buy tickets. You must decide in real time how many to buy because they will be sold out in a few moments. You believe your partner would like to go and possibly a couple of friends and maybe a couple of family members. You think that maybe you should buy four tickets and worry about what to do with them later.

e. Sequencing: You have two tasks to do. One is a group project with a classmate that can't be done until that classmate provides some information. The other one is to edit video for the student newspaper's Web site, a project that requires three video components that will come by e-mail. Characteristically, your classmate will arrive late for any scheduled meeting and may not have prepared all that he promised. And the video components may not arrive by the deadline. The group project and video project will each take two hours. You decide to schedule in the same window of time (1) a four-hour project meeting with your classmate and (2) a four-hour reservation for the video equipment you will need for your editing. You'll decide later the sequence in which you will do the two projects.

13.2. Do real options always have a nonnegative incremental value? Justify and explain why or why not.

13.3. A hybrid automobile has two motors, gasoline and electric. It switches between motors for power, sometimes using both motors. When accelerating, both electricity and gasoline are providing power to the wheels. When cruising, the electric motor is not being used. The gasoline engine provides power to the wheels and uses excess power to slowly charge the batteries. When going downhill or braking, the wheels drive the generator, slowing the car and charging the battery.

a. How could two engines possibly make for a more efficient automobile? What does this have to do with real options?

b. What must be true of the various capital and operating costs for the option to switch/mix two motors (which also includes cost) to add value to the car?

13.4. Ruined Mound Properties is in final negotiations for the rights to mine copper on a tract of land in Indonesia. They must decide about adding an option in their agreement with the government of Indonesia. This option would allow them to develop an identical adjacent tract of land, beginning no later than 4 years after they break ground on the original development. By that time, they will have 4 years of experience with a number of variables in their model of the performance of the original development, the key variables being the volume of ore on the tract of land, the yield of the ore (pounds of copper in a ton of ore), the price per pound of copper, and the cost per ton of processing the ore. Suggest some good possibilities for a triggering function for the exercise of the option to develop the second tract of land.

13.5. Staged investment: The development of a drug requires Food and Drug Administration (FDA) approval at five stages (a preclinical phase; clinical phases I, II, and III; and a final approval). A pharmaceutical company could commit a lump-sum amount upfront to acquire a prospective compound from another firm and then follow it through these stages. Or it could enter into a staged contract wherein the acquirer pays an amount at each of the approvals. Assume that, in present-value terms, the lump-sum payment is equivalent to the expected total of the staged payments. What is the advantage to the acquirer of the contract for staged commitment?

QUESTIONS AND PROBLEMS

13.6. Pierre, a book broker, is about to sign a contract to buy the rights to a book about twin teenage computer-security sleuths titled *Nan and Dan vs. the Monika Worm.* His offer to advance $50,000 for the book has been verbally accepted. Pierre plans to immediately turn over his rights to a publisher with whom he has a standing agreement, netting $20,000 for his efforts in searching through hundreds of leads and manuscripts to find this book. The possibility of a sequel to the book has occurred to him (having just read the latest Harry Potter book), so he is considering adding language to the contract giving him rights to a sequel. It is reasonable to assume that the sequel, should it be written, would bring him $75,000 from a publisher, 18 months from now. Determine if it would be attractive to Pierre to add language to the contract that would secure the rights to a sequel involving the same characters, under the following conditions:

- Pay an additional $10,000 now for a right of first refusal on the first sequel to *Nan and Dan vs. the Monika Worm*, and...
- The exercise price in 2 years is again a $50,000 advance on the sequel.

Assume Pierre's hurdle rate is 10% per year and that the probability of an acceptable sequel in 18 months is 0.6. Suppose you thought you could negotiate a 20% reduction in one, but not both, of the amounts in (a) and (b). Which one should he most like to change? Should Pierre be willing to increase the option offers? To what level? (Extra credit) How would you structure the analysis of an option on a series of *Nan and Dan* books flowing from the first?

13.7. Shu Mei Wang is going to start a new business to provide a geographical-information system (GIS) to be used by small businesses in selecting promotions and for other marketing applications.[2] She will provide her service to on-line subscribers via a sophisticated Internet server. She is considering two alternative servers: the GZ1000, which will cost $21,000, and the GZ1450, priced at $33,000. The choice of server depends on the peak number of subscribers she will have. Standard practice is to plan the server capacity to be 10% of the number of subscription accounts. The GZ1000 has capacity for 80 connections and the GZ1450 for 140 connections.

The number of subscriptions for the year will be settled within the first month of the year and continue for the entire year, but will not be settled before the server must be ordered. Shu Mei expects that it is equally likely that her business will attract 400 or 800 accounts in the first year of operation. In the second year, there is a 50% chance that there will be 1,200 accounts and a 50% chance that accounts will stay at 800, if the number in the first year is 800. On the other hand, if there are 400 first-year accounts, Shu Mei assesses a 50% chance that accounts will remain at 400 and a 50% chance that they will go up to 800 in the second year.

The price per month per GIS client account will be $30 regardless of usage. The operating cost per account amounts to $13.50. Total fixed overhead for the business will be $9,000 per month. For simplicity, ignore time value of money and taxes for each option.

a. Should Shu Mei buy one GZ1000 or one GZ1450, based on expected profit over the first 2 years of operation? (Either server will have a useful life of 2 years and zero salvage value.)

b. *Expand option:* Shu Mei can decide in 1 year to expand the server operation. Suppose that the same GIS servers will be available 1 year from now at 40% of the original price on the resale market. Does her initial decision change?

c. *Switch option:* It might be a good idea for Shu Mei to sell her GZ1000 after 1 year and buy the discounted GZ1450, rather than buy another server. Would Shu Mei want to do this? What is the expected monetary value of this option? Assume resale value is 40% of original price.

d. *Exit option:* In the event that demand is low after one year, Shu Mei may just want to get out of the business. If she does, the original server would be salvageable at 40% of the original price. Does this option affect the initial investment decision?

e. *Delay option:* All these options and the inherent uncertainty have made Shu Mei nervous about the business. Perhaps she should delay for a year, observe the demand for her service, and then buy a used server (at the 40% discounted price) to capture the second-year demand. Is this option attractive when compared with the other options?

---

[2] Adapted from an exercise in Harvard Business School case 9-396-308.

13.8. The lead time for delivery of the largest offshore platforms for oil and gas drilling and collecting is now 2 years. ConExoco Petroleum is thinking about putting down a $15 million nonrefundable deposit on one in the Gulf of Mexico. This deposit is 15% of what the purchase price would be in 2 years. ConExoco will want this structure badly in 2 years if (1) the exploratory drilling on their newly leased tracts shows substantial oil and gas reserves when completed in 2 years and (2) the price of oil is high enough at that time to put the equipment into imme-diate use ($45/barrel would do it). Because ConExoco would be in a much better position than anyone else to use this specialized platform in 2 years, if they don't take it, no one else would want it and ConExoco would forfeit its deposit. Structure a real-options approach for deciding whether to make such a deposit. What variables would you include in your analysis? What value would you need to compute using those variables? What would the triggering formula look like using those variables? What approach would you use to value the asset?

13.9. A biopharma project being pursued by Hopfer Pharmaceutical has a negative NPV of −$28 million Still, Hopfer may participate in this project as a "pioneer" option, giving the company an option to partic-ipate later in a large project that could have an attractive NPV. The large follow-on project will require $750 million in cash in 4 years. The current NPV of that project is estimated to be $270 million, and it has annual volatility of 35%. Assume a risk-free rate of 10%. Should Hopfer take the pioneer option?

13.10. Underwater partnership. You are acting in a consulting capacity advising a limited partner in a real-estate partnership. The partnership has nega-tive income because of high vacancy rates and discounts on lease rates in the current soft market. The general partner would like to consolidate ownership, and is asking your client to give up his interest in the part-nership; in return, the general partner will not ask him to contribute cap-ital to the partnership. The general partner claims that the value of the partnership real estate is negative and that your client should be happy to turn his interest over to him. In fact, he has threatened that if your client doesn't cooperate, he will sue him in order to close out the limited part-nership and convert the properties to another use. In addition, the gen-eral partner has threatened to discontinue his recent practice of making up the mortgage shortfall. In that event, the bank (on whose board he sits) would foreclose on the property. Your client would perhaps be will-ing to fund his share of the mortgage shortfall, in the interest of main-taining his share in a property that he believes will come back to profitability. The vacancy rates and discounts are likely to change when the local economy improves—some leading indicators of improvement seem to have already appeared. If this case goes to court, how would you argue before the judge that your client's share is worth some positive amount? How would you structure the analysis of the value of your share? Just lay out the approach, rather than look for a specific number, but do argue convincingly that the property is not worthless.

13.11. A start-up venture owns the rights to new technology for a coated stent. The company is about to begin animal trials that could lead to FDA approval of the use of the stent in humans. The company could conduct those trials in two different ways (for coronary applications and for neurological applications) at some individual cost over just coronary applications. That would allow the company the option, later in the FDA process, to split the technology and go forward with two separate stents, to proceed with either of the two separate stents, or to proceed with a stent that could be used in both applications (and thus a lower likelihood of approval). If the option were taken later to split into two separate stents, each stent would have independent paths to approval. Structure how the company should think about the worth of pursuing the early studies for both applications.

13.12. Two options are evaluated separately in Figures 13.6 and 13.7. Do the analysis for both options together, calculate the option value for the two options together, and explain your results.

13.13. Acquisition: The board of directors of Quickercom Inc. is considering an acquisition of Honest Communication Inc. (HCI) for a total price of $3 billion, to be finalized January 1, 2016. After thorough due diligence, the financial experts at Quickercom are concerned that HCI's value could decrease significantly in the next year and make the deal unprofitable. To make sure they receive a gain on the deal, they put an exit clause into the contract. The exit clause states that if the earnings before interest, taxes, depreciation, and amortization (EBITDA) falls below $80 million for the fourth quarter of 2015, this will be considered a material adverse change in the position of HCI, and Quickercom can exit the contract and not have to complete the deal.

HCI is a 19-year-old telecommunications firm specializing in long-distance service. Revenues have been steadily declining at HCI over the past six years because many customers are going to cell phones for their long-distance service, prices have been steadily declining, and the number of minutes per month per customer is decreasing. From 2008 to 2014, the yearly EBITDA at HCI has fallen from $633 million to $418 million, which represents a decrease of more than 50%. Industry analysts believe that revenues will continue to fall for at least the next 3 years. Experts believe that HCI, on average, will continue to lose customers at a rate of 0.6% per quarter, with a quarterly volatility of 0.07. They also think that HCI will continue to see a decrease of 1.4% per quarter in the total minutes used per customer per quarter, at a quarterly volatility of 0.10. Finally, those same experts believe strongly that HCI will continue to decrease its prices per minute charged at a rate of 1.2% per quarter, with a quarterly volatility of 0.09. The price per minute includes sign-up fees and any other revenue HCI will make each quarter.

Because we are already more than halfway through the first quarter of 2015, financial experts have a better idea of HCI's first-quarter 2015 numbers. Their best guess for the average number of customers is 17.1 million, with a minimum of 16.5 million and a maximum of 18.3 million.

They believe that the average number of minutes used per customer for the quarter will be 259, the least amount of minutes will be 250, and the most will be 269. Lastly, they believe that the average price HCI will charge per minute for the quarter will be 13.1 cents, with a minimum of 12.7 cents and a maximum of 13.9 cents. The cost of goods sold (COGS) has remained steady for the past 6 years at 56% of total revenue, and the cost of SG&A has been constant at 27% of total revenue.

The following represents the EBITDA for HCI for the fourth quarter of 2014:

	Q4 2014
# of customers (millions)	17.2
Total minutes used per customer	259.0
$ per minute	$0.132
Total revenue ($millions)	$588.0
COGS ($millions)	$329.3
SG&A ($millions)	$158.8
Q4 EBITDA ($millions)	$100.0
Effective yearly EBITDA ($million)	$399.9
HCI value ($millions)	$2,979.0

To find out the current value of HCI, the financial experts used 7.45 for the EBITDA multiple, which, when multiplied by the effective yearly EBITDA of $399.9 million, gave them a current company value of $2,979 million. Quickercom's financial experts believe that this deal will develop synergies worth at least $616 million for Quickercom, making the total deal worth $3,595 million today. Because the value of HCI has been steadily declining, for Quickercom to have any chance of making a profit, the EBITDA must not fall below $80 million per quarter; hence, the need for the exit clause.

The board of directors of Quickercom has asked you to develop a simple Monte Carlo simulation to model the uncertainties associated with this deal. For simplicity, ignore the time value of money.

Do the following:

a. Develop a continuous model to find the expected EBITDA for each quarter of 2015 and the deal value for Quickercom for the fourth quarter of 2015, using the effective yearly EBITDA and $616 million for the synergies.

b. For the fourth quarter of 2015, calculate the expected value of the deal while including the exit clause at an EBITDA of less than $80 million.

    c.   What is the value of the exit clause for Quickercom and how likely is the company to invoke it?

    d.   How would *HCI* value this deal using the same model?

Note: This problem was inspired by the press releases concerning the failed attempt by Qwest to acquire MCI in 2005.

REFERENCES

For a general introduction to real options, any standard finance text will have some sections or chapters about financial options and, nowadays, real options. Hull (2000) provides an excellent introduction to the Black-Scholes model. The Dixit and Pindyck (1993) and Luenberger (1998) texts are more specialized towards uncertainty and options. The article by Black and Scholes (1973) started the development of pricing models for financial options. Trigeorgis (1996) provides a book-length treatment of extensions of finance options theory to real options. Smith and Nau (1995) provide a basis for using decision analysis to value projects, including those with embedded real options. Amram and Kulatilaka (1999) and Copeland and Antikarov (2001) provide a more accessible discussion of real options concepts and uses.

Amram, M., and N. Kulatilaka (1999) "Disciplined Decisions: Aligning Strategy with the Financial Markets," *Harvard Business Review*, Jan–Feb, 95–109.

Black, F., and M. Scholes (1973) "The Pricing of Options and Corporate Liabilities," *Journal of Political Economy*, 81, 637–654.

Copeland, T., and V. Antikarov (2001) *Real Options: A Practitioner's Guide*. London: Texere.

Dixit, A. K., and R. S. Pindyck (1993) *Investment under Uncertainty*. Princeton, N.J.: Princeton University Press.

Hull, J. C. (2005) *Options, Futures, and Other Derivative Securities*, 6th ed. Englewood Cliffs, N.J.: Prentice Hall.

Luenberger, D. G. (1998) *Investment Science*. New York, N.Y.: Oxford University Press.

Smith, J. E., and R. F. Nau (1995) "Valuing Risky Projects—Option Pricing Theory and Decision-Analysis," *Management Science*, 41, 795–816.

Trigeorgis, L. (1996) *Real Options: Managerial Flexibility and Strategy in Resource Allocation*. Cambridge, Mass.: MIT Press.

LAC LEMAN FESTIVAL DE LA MUSIQUE (A)

DARDEN
BUSINESS PUBLISHING
UNIVERSITY *of* VIRGINIA

A beautiful idea came to Carla Monte, director of the Lac Leman Festival de la Musique, as she took a long bicycle ride around the east end of Lac Leman. Her idea was as lofty as the Swiss Alps she saw in the distance. She realized that, because the festival ran for two nights, she could videotape Friday's performance, which included every performer in the festival, and sell DVDs at Saturday's performance. As she pushed her bike onto the ferry to return from St. Gingolph, her mind and spirit rejuvenated by the crisp alpine air, she fleshed out the project's process and logistics.

Her contracts with the performers gave her the right to record and sell the video at the festival site only; come Sunday, any unsold DVDs would be worthless. The contractual limitations made an investment in a DVD risky. Worse yet, it was difficult for Monte to know in advance how many concertgoers would attend the festival on Saturday, or what percentage of the attendees might purchase the DVD.

With the festival only a month away, Monte asked her assistant for business development, Hekka Fyno, to collect some data and do a preliminary analysis. Fyno had just completed an Executive MBA program in Scandinavia and was excited by this new project. He produced the data (Exhibit 1), which showed Saturday attendance for the festival's entire 15-year run, and delivered it to Monte, commenting:

> After thinking about it for a while, I don't believe that attendance at the festival this year will be different from any of the prior years. People don't really make their decision to come until just before the event, and our grassy hillside is large enough so that we never sell out. Saturday's ticket is a separate admission at the same price as Friday—30 Swiss francs [SFr30].

Fyno also had an idea about doing some market research to gauge whether attendees would buy a DVD:

EXHIBIT 1
Historical data for Saturday attendance.

Year	Saturday Attendance[1]
1	6,510
2	43,580
3	39,360
4	28,590
5	33,560
6	13,710
7	15,410
8	24,190
9	14,240
10	19,310
11	17,470
12	34,250
13	33,910
14	20,990
15	17,000
Mean	24,139
Standard deviation	10,818

[1] Attendance numbers represent customers who paid for their seat and attended the performance.

> Let's send a survey to a random subset of people who came to the festival last year and ask them whether they would purchase the proposed DVD if they were to come this year. We have an e-mail address for about half of the people who bought an on-line ticket to Saturday's event last year, and we know who actually attended. We could easily send an electronic survey to some of those who were in attendance.

Monte approved the idea, and two weeks later, the information was available (Exhibit 2).

EXHIBIT **2**
Survey results with
annotations by
Hekka Fyno.

A survey was sent electronically to 150 attendees at last year's Saturday night concert.

After describing the DVD idea in all its particulars, including the price, the survey asked a single yes or no question: "If you were in attendance on Saturday night, would you buy the DVD?"

Of the 150 attendees who received the survey, 37 responded, of whom 7 stated that they would purchase the DVD.

Fyno's notes:

My estimate of the mean probability of an individual attendee's choice to buy the DVD is

$$\text{mean } p = 7/37 = 0.1892.$$

I have concerns about non-response bias here and that the decisions of buyers may not be independent of each other when it comes to their actual behavior. Even so, this number can serve as a starting point forecast to use for the portion of those who attend the concert that would buy the DVD.

Of course, we are not sure that this percentage is exactly 0.1892. After all, we have only 37 responses. If we had more responses, then I would be more confident in this number. I looked up in the notes from one of my MBA classes, where I had written the following:

The standard deviation of an individual's choice (with a probability p of observing 1 and a probability $1 - p$ of observing 0) would be equal to $\text{sqrt}(p * (1 - p)) = 0.3917$.

What we need is the uncertainty in the average proportion for the 37 responders, which would be lower than this. However, I can't find it in my notes. Once I recall that formula, I should check the sensitivity to this uncertainty, since non-response bias and lack of independence can drive the uncertainty higher.

Creating and Producing a DVD

Two weeks before the festival, Fyno was preparing a recommendation about whether to pay the nonrefundable fee of SFr11,740 to engage a video crew to record Friday's performance digitally. If Monte and Fyno wished to go ahead with the video recording, they were to deliver a check that afternoon to the video company.

At the end of Friday's concert, an editing crew would work through the night to edit the video into a master DVD, at a cost of SFr3,000. At 7:00 a.m. the next morning, Monte would deliver the master DVD and her desired order quantity to a production company. The production company charged SFr1,250 for setup and SFr0.86 per unit to burn, print labels, and pack up to 5,300 DVDs in jewel cases. If Monte's order exceeded 5,300 units, the production company would pull capacity from other jobs to process the excess units, at an additional cost of SFr0.20 per excess unit. The production company assured Monte

that the DVDs would be ready for sale no later than two hours before Saturday's performance. Finally, the festival would pay a royalty to the performers of SFr1.02 per unit (only for DVDs sold, not for the number that were burned).

Fyno and Monte had agreed on a price of SFr18 for the DVD. The festival's contracts with the performers required that any DVDs not sold on Saturday night be shredded.

Source: This case was prepared by Samuel E. Bodily, John Tyler Professor of Business Administration, and Robert Jenkins, Research Assistant (MBA '06). It was written as a basis for class discussion rather than to illustrate effective or ineffective handling of an administrative situation. The numbers used in the case are disguised. Copyright © 2007 by the University of Virginia Darden School Foundation, Charlottesville, VA. All rights reserved. *To order copies, send an e-mail to* sales@dardenbusinesspublishing.com. *No part of this publication may be reproduced, stored in a retrieval system, used in a spreadsheet, or transmitted in any form or by any means— electronic, mechanical, photocopying, recording, or otherwise— without the permission of the Darden School Foundation.*

LAC LEMAN FESTIVAL DE LA MUSIQUE (B)

DARDEN
BUSINESS PUBLISHING
UNIVERSITY *of* VIRGINIA

Early Saturday Morning

It was now five o'clock Saturday morning. The Friday night concert had been glorious, and the weather had been clear and nearly perfect for making an exceptional master DVD. Attendance had been 18,394, a little better than average. Just as Hekka Fyno was thinking about how many would attend that evening's concert and how many DVDs they might sell, he saw the weather forecast on his office computer. There was an 80% chance of rain for Saturday night at the venue. This news prompted him to check the files for the festival's entire 15-year run, where he found a complete record of attendance for both Friday and Saturday nights and whether it had rained or not each night (Exhibit 1). Fyno mused to himself: "There is a lot of variability in attendance for both nights. It is lucky that I found complete attendance and rain records for all the years of the festival. Now, what does it mean about how many will come to our open-air venue tonight?"

Epilogue

At 7:00 a.m., Fyno's phone rang. Simultaneously, Carla Monte blurted out, "How many DVDs do we want?" and Fyno answered the phone automatically the way he always did, "Hekka Fyno."

Source: This case was prepared by Samuel E. Bodily, John Tyler Professor of Business Administration, and Robert Jenkins, Research Assistant (MBA '06). It was written as a basis for class discussion rather than to illustrate effective or ineffective handling of an administrative situation. The numbers used in the case are disguised. Copyright © 2007 by the University of Virginia Darden School Foundation, Charlottesville, VA. All rights reserved. *To order copies, send an e-mail to* sales@dardenbusinesspublishing. com. *No part of this publication may be reproduced, stored in a retrieval system, used in a spreadsheet, or transmitted in any form or by any means—electronic, mechanical, photocopying, recording, or otherwise—without the permission of the Darden School Foundation.*

EXHIBIT **1**
Complete
historical data.[1]

Year	Friday Rain	Friday Attendance	Saturday Rain	Saturday Attendance
1	1	3,960	1	6,510
2	1	26,920	0	43,580
3	0	25,430	0	39,360
4	1	17,750	0	28,590
5	0	24,910	0	33,560
6	1	10,210	1	13,710
7	1	8,910	0	15,410
8	0	27,080	1	24,190
9	0	14,140	1	14,240
10	0	12,740	0	19,310
11	0	11,110	0	17,470
12	0	18,750	0	34,250
13	0	20,390	0	33,910
14	0	13,440	0	20,990
15	0	11,570	0	17,000
Mean	0.333	16,487	0.267	24,139
Standard deviation	0.488	7,219	0.458	10,818

[1] Attendance numbers represent customers who paid for their seat and attended the performance. Rain is 1 if there was measurable precipitation during the concert and 0 if not.

SPRIGG LANE (A)

May 19, 1988, was a beautiful day in Charlottesville, Virginia. Tom Dingledine could see some cows grazing in the pasture on the rolling hillside outside his window. He was grateful for the bucolic setting, which was made possible by his doing well with the projects he managed, one of which now required some concentration. Dingledine was the president of Sprigg Lane Natural Resources, a subsidiary of the Sprigg Lane Investment Corporation (SLIC). The decision at hand was whether to invest in the Bailey Prospect natural gas opportunity.

The Company

Founded in 1961, Sprigg Lane was a privately held investment corporation. It had become a diversified corporation comprising two major groups. The first was devoted to manufacturing high-quality home furnishings. Its masthead company was Virginia Metalcrafters, which produced handcrafted brass giftware. Other companies in the group included an outdoor-lantern company in Maine and an antique-reproduction furniture company in Maryland. With the establishment of the National Legal Research Group in 1970, another major group, the Research Group, was started. Since then, four other research companies had been added in the fields of consumer-product marketing, computer software, tax research, and investment financial analysis.

The recent formation of the Sprigg Lane Development Corporation, which was involved in the purchase and development of real estate, brought the total number of Sprigg Lane's subsidiaries to nine. SLIC sales for 1987 approximated $30 million, and it employed more than 525 people.

Drilling and Developing a Well[1]

The cost to drill an "average" well in Doddridge County, West Virginia, location of the Bailey Prospect, was $160,000. There was some uncertainty, however, regarding the cost from well to well because of factors such as the differing depths of wells and the different types of terrain that had to be drilled into.

Experts in Doddridge County said that there was a 95% chance that the cost for any given well would be within $5,400 of the average cost, assuming a normal distribution.

SLIC's Entry into Natural Gas

In January 1987, Tom Dingledine, the CFO of a private oil-and-gas exploration and development company, met SLIC's president and decided to join the company to help it find some investment opportunities. Dingledine became convinced that the company could enjoy higher potential returns (30%–40% after tax) from natural-resource exploration than from other investment opportunities, including real estate, which were yielding 15%–20%. Although natural-resource exploration was clearly riskier, Dingledine believed the risk could be managed by drilling only on sites that were surrounded on three or four sides by existing wells. Through further research, he found two other factors that helped reduce the risk: (1) contracts with the pipeline distributors typically locked in the natural gas selling prices for four years, and (2) well operating-expenses were covered by contracts that only allowed increases every three years, with the increase capped at 15% per three-year period. Dingledine thought that the annual increase in the total well cost would be equivalent to half the rate of inflation.

The president of SLIC was so impressed with Dingledine's presentation on the entire subject that he offered him the presidency of a new division to be called Sprigg Lane Natural Resources (SLNR). Dingledine accepted the offer, and in his first year on the job (1987), SLNR drilled four wells. Although it had not been difficult operationally to drill the four wells, it had been challenging to find enough high-quality investment opportunities. Dingledine considered wells to be "good" if they met all the following criteria: (l) payback of initial cash investment in 42 months or less, (2) at least 25% internal rate of return (IRR) on an after-tax basis, and (3) at least 15% IRR on a pretax basis.

In the first five months of production, one of the wells had already paid back 52% of its initial investment—well ahead of its target 28-month payout. The other wells were also doing well, and all of them were at least on schedule for meeting their targeted return on investment. Even though things had gone favorably for Dingledine so far, he knew

---

[1] U.S. Department of Energy, *The Oil and Gas Drilling Industry* (1981), 13–16.

the pressure was still on him to make good decisions because SLNR was planning to drill 20 more wells in 1988.

Investment Strategy

SLNR acted as the managing general partner in the gas-drilling ventures it formed, which gave it full responsibility for choosing sites and managing the well if gas were found. SLNR gathered information from the state of West Virginia and from other companies drilling in the vicinity (if they were willing to engage in "information trading"). Dingledine would then put together a package of 10 wells that he considered good investments based on all the information he had gathered. The total initial investment for a typical package would be around $1.6 million. SLNR would retain about 25% ownership and sell the rest to several other general partners.

As managing general partner, SLNR was responsible for hiring a general contractor who would actually hire an outside firm to do the drilling, and SLNR's geologist, Brad Thomas, would determine whether there really was enough gas to make it worthwhile to complete a well. If the decision was made to go ahead, the general contractor would also be in charge of the day-to-day operations of the well. SLNR had entered into a joint venture with Excel Energy of Bridgeport, West Virginia, in which they agreed that Excel would act as the general contractor for all the wells that SLNR managed as general partner.

The first-year production level varied significantly from well to well. Dingledine found that the uncertainty could be described with a lognormal probability distribution having a mean of 33 million cubic feet and a standard deviation of 4.93 million cubic feet.

The Bailey Prospect

Exhibit 1 (available as an Excel spreadsheet at www .cengagebrain.com) is a copy of the spreadsheet Dingledine developed to analyze one well, called the Bailey Prospect, as a potential member of the package of 10 wells he was currently putting together. The Bailey Prospect was typical of the 10 wells that would be in the package offered to investors. As Dingledine thought about the realization of this one well, he knew the Bailey Prospect was surrounded by producing wells from the target gas-producing formation. It was virtually certain, therefore, that SLNR would hit the formation and decide to

complete the well, but there was a 10% chance that an operational failure would cause zero production or that the gas formation would be depleted because of the surrounding wells, resulting in essentially zero production. In either of those cases, the pretax loss would be $160,000. In the more likely case, gas would be produced and Dingledine would then find out how much the well would produce in the first and subsequent years. He would also learn what the gas's BTU content was, which would affect the total revenue generated by the well (see Exhibit 2 for an explanation of the more commonly used abbreviations and terms in the well-drilling business).

Revenues and expenses

The spreadsheet was basically an income statement over the well's life. The price per mcf was calculated by multiplying the contracted price per MMBTU times the BTU content divided by 1,000. The production in mcf was then estimated for the first year and calculated for each succeeding year, based on the percentage decline values given in the assumptions. The gross revenue was the product of the price per mcf times the mcf of gas produced in a given year. Out of the gross revenue came a 15.23% royalty payment to the owner of the mineral rights, leaving the net revenue. Several expenses were deducted from net revenue to arrive at the pretax profit:

1. Monthly operating costs of $300 were paid to Excel Energy in addition to a budgeted amount of $3,000 for other operating expenses that might occur on an annual basis. Those costs were increased annually by the well-expense inflation factor.

2. Local taxes of 4.5% times the gross revenue were paid to the county, and a severance tax (see Exhibit 2) of 3.4% times the gross revenue was paid to the state of West Virginia.

3. Depreciation expense for year 0 equaled the intangible drilling cost, which was 72.5% of the total well cost. The remainder of the initial drilling cost was depreciated on a straight-line basis over seven years. To compute after-tax profit , the following equations applied:

$$\text{Profit after tax} = \text{Profit before tax} - \text{Depletion}$$
$$- \text{ State income tax}$$
$$- \text{ Federal income tax}$$

EXHIBIT **1**
Bailey Prospect base-case spreadsheet.

ECONOMIC ENVIRONMENT		
GNP DEFLATOR		3.50%

WELL		TAXES		RESULTS	
TOTAL WELL COST	$160,000	FEDERAL TAX RATE	34.00%	EQUITY PAYOUT (AFTER-TAX) =	23.26 MONTHS
INTANGIBLE COST(%OFTOTAL)	72.50%	STATE TAX RATE	9.75%		
		SEVERANCE TAX RATE	3.40%	INTERNAL RATE OF RET. (CF AFTER-TAX) =	41.07%
MONTHLY OPERATING COSTS	$300	COUNTY TAX RATE	4.50%	INTERNAL RATE OF RET. (PBT) =	16.65%
ANNUAL LEASE EXPENSE	$3,000	SECTION 29 TAX CREDIT($/MMBTU)	$0.7600		
INFLTION FACTOR-WELL EXPENSE	1.75%	% QUALIFIED	100.00%	NET PRESENT VALUE (CFAT) @ 15% =	$110,263
PRODUCTION DATA		GAS CHARACTERISTICS		CUMULATIVE CASH FLOW AFTER-TAX =	$432,235
ENOUGH(0=NO,1=YES)?	1	ROYALTIES	15.2344%		
1st YEAR Mcf	33,000				
DECLINE MULTIPLIER	1.000	GAS PRICE DATA			
PRODUCTION DECLINE AFTER …		INFLATION	3.50%		
YEAR 1 =	22.50%	CURRENTPRICE($/MMBTU)	$1.90		
YEAR 2 =	17.50%	BTUCONTENT(BTU/FT3)	1,155		
YEAR 3-5 =	12.50%				
YEAR 6-14 =	10.00%	1ST YEAR OF			
YEAR 15-24 =	5.00%	PRICE INCREASE	5		

YEAR	0	1	2	3	4	5	6	7	8	9	10	11	12
INITIAL INVESTMENT	($160,000)												
PRICE PER MCF		2.19	2.19	2.19	2.19	2.27	2.35	2.43	2.52	2.61	2.70	2.79	2.89
PRODUCTION(MCF)		33,000	25,575	21,099	18,462	16,154	14,135	12,721	11,449	10,304	9,274	8,347	7,512
GROSS REVENUE		$72,419	$56,124	$46,303	$40,515	$36,691	$33,228	$30,952	$28,832	$26,857	$25,017	$23,304	$21,707
LESS: ROYALTIES		11,033	8,550	7,054	6,172	5,590	5,062	4,715	4,392	4,092	3,811	3,550	3,307
NET REVENUE		$61,386	$47,574	$39,249	$34,343	$31,101	$28,166	$26,237	$24,440	$22,766	$21,206	$19,753	$18,400
OPERATING EXPENSES		6,600	6,716	6,833	6,953	7,074	7,198	7,324	7,452	7,583	7,715	7,850	7,988
SEVERANCE & COUNTY TAX		5,721	4,434	3,658	3,201	2,899	2,625	2,445	2,278	2,122	1,976	1,841	1,715
DEPRECIATION	116,000	6,286	6,286	6,286	6,286	6,286	6,286	6,286					
PROFIT BEFORE TAX	($116,000)	$42,779	$30,139	$22,472	$17,904	$14,843	$12,057	$10,182	$14,710	$13,061	$11,514	$10,062	$8,698
DEPLETION		9,208	7,136	5,887	5,151	4,665	4,225	3,936	3,666	3,415	3,181	2,963	2,760
STATE INC. TAX	(11,310)	2,042	1,289	830	555	369	199	83	587	484	387	296	210
FEDERAL INC. TAX	(35,595)	(18,247)	(15,853)	(14,484)	(13,821)	(12,937)	(12,141)	(11,631)	(9,231)	(8,796)	(8,393)	(8,022)	(7,679)
PROFIT AFTER TAX	($69,095)	$49,777	$37,567	$30,238	$26,018	$22,746	$19,775	$17,795	$19,688	$17,958	$16,339	$14,825	$13,407
AFTER TAX CASH FLOW	($113,095)	$65,270	$50,989	$42,411	$37,455	$33,697	$30,285	$28,016	$23,354	$21,373	$19,520	$17,788	$16,167
CUMUL. AFT TAX CASH FLOW	($113,095)	($47,825)	$3,164	$45,575	$83,030	$116,727	$147,013	$175,029	$198,383	$219,756	$239,276	$257,064	$273,232
NPV THROUGH YEAR N	($113,095)	($56,339)	($17,784)	$10,102	$31,518	$48,271	$61,364	$71,896	$79,531	$85,606	$90,432	$94,255	$97,277

YEAR	13	14	15	16	17	18	19	20	21	22	23	24	25
INITIAL INVESTMENT													
PRICE PER MCF	2.99	3.10	3.20	3.32	3.43	3.55	3.68	3.81	3.94	4.08	4.22	4.37	4.52
PRODUCTION(MCF)	6,761	6,085	5,476	5,202	4,942	4,695	4,460	4,237	4,025	3,824	3,633	3,451	3,279
GROSS REVENUE	$20,220	$18,835	$17,545	$17,251	$16,962	$16,678	$16,399	$16,124	$15,854	$15,588	$15,327	$15,071	$14,818
LESS: ROYALTIES	3,080	2,869	2,673	2,628	2,584	2,541	2,498	2,456	2,415	2,375	2,335	2,296	2,257
NET REVENUE	$17,140	$15,966	$14,872	$14,623	$14,378	$14,137	$13,901	$13,668	$13,439	$13,214	$12,992	$12,775	$12,561
OPERATING EXPENSES	8,127	8,270	8,414	8,414	8,414	8,414	8,414	4,207	4,207	4,207	4,207	4,207	4,207
SEVERANCE & COUNTY TAX	1,597	1,488	1,386	1,363	1,340	1,318	1,296	1,274	1,252	1,231	1,211	1,191	1,171
DEPRECIATION													
PROFIT BEFORE TAX	$7,415	$6,208	$5,072	$4,846	$4,624	$4,405	$4,191	$8,187	$7,979	$7,775	$7,574	$7,377	$7,183
DEPLETION	2,571	2,395	2,231	2,193	2,157	2,121	2,085	2,050	2,016	1,982	1,949	1,916	1,884
STATE INC. TAX	129	52	(21)	(35)	(48)	(61)	(73)	324	312	300	288	276	265
FEDERAL INC. TAX	(7,364)	(7,074)	(6,808)	(6,737)	(6,668)	(6,599)	(6,532)	(5,175)	(5,110)	(5,046)	(4,983)	(4,921)	(4,860)
PROFIT AFTER TAX	$12,080	$10,836	$9,670	$9,424	$9,182	$8,945	$8,711	$10,987	$10,761	$10,539	$10,320	$10,105	$9,894
AFTER TAX CASH FLOW	$14,651	$13,231	$11,901	$11,618	$11,339	$11,065	$10,796	$13,037	$12,777	$12,521	$12,269	$12,022	$11,778
CUMUL. AFT TAX CASH FLOW	$287,882	$301,113	$313,014	$324,632	$335,971	$347,036	$357,832	$370,869	$383,646	$396,166	$408,435	$420,457	$432,235
NPV THROUGH YEAR N	$99,658	$101,528	$102,990	$104,232	$105,286	$106,180	$106,938	$107,735	$108,414	$108,992	$109,485	$109,905	$110,263

Where:

$$\text{Depletion} = \text{Minimum of } \{0.5 \times (\text{Profit before tax})$$
$$\text{or } 0.15 \times (\text{Net revenue})\}$$

State income tax
$$= \text{State tax rate} \times (\text{Profit before tax} - \text{Depletion})$$
$$- 0.5 \times (\text{Severance tax})$$

Federal income tax
$$= \text{Federal tax rate} \times (\text{Profit before tax} - \text{depletion}$$
$$- \text{State income tax}) - \text{Section 29 credit}$$

In 1978, Congress passed section 29 of the Federal Tax Code to stimulate drilling for a particular kind of natural gas that was especially difficult to extract from the ground, namely, that found in rock called Devonian shale, which composed the Bailey Prospect. Devonian

EXHIBIT **2**
Explanation of
commonly used
terms.

BTU	British Thermal Unit—amount of heat required to raise the temperature of 1 pound of water by 1° Fahrenheit.
MMBTU	1 million BTUs.
Decatherm	1 MMBTU.
FT³	1 cubic foot.
mcf	1,000 cubic feet.
Intangible well costs	Any expense for something that could not be used again (e.g., fees to the drilling crew, cement costs). A purchase of metal pipe, however, would represent a tangible cost.
Severance	Sales tax to state on gas or oil withdrawn and sold.
Depletion	Generally, the concept is similar to depreciation. It compensated the company for the money spent to acquire the right to drill. Generally accepted accounting principles only recognized cost depletion, which amortized the cost on a unit-of-production basis (e.g., number of mcf produced this year divided by the total mcf in the ground times the cost). The IRS, however, allowed the company to calculate depletion under the more favorable of two methods: cost depletion or percentage depletion. The latter was in the spreadsheet and was almost always more favorable.

shale consisted of many very small pockets where the gas resided until it was ferreted out. In 1988, the law provided a tax credit of $0.76 per decatherm. This tax-credit rate was increased each year for inflation, but its future value was in the hands of Congress and thus far from certain.

Initial results and investment considerations

To find the net present value (NPV), Dingledine added back the depreciation and depletion to the after-tax profit to come up with the yearly cash flows, which were then discounted at the company's hurdle rate of 15% for projects of that risk (see Exhibit 3 for a table listing the rates of return for investments of varying maturities and degrees of risk) to calculate the NPV through any given year of the well's life. His pro forma analysis indicated that the project had an IRR of 41.1% and an NPV of $110,263.

Dingledine was feeling good about the Bailey Prospect, even though he knew he had made many assumptions. He had used 1155 BTU/FT³ to estimate the heat content of the gas because it was the expected (mean) value, even though he knew it could

be as low as 1055 or as high as 1250, with the most likely value (mode) being 1160. He also guessed that inflation, as measured by the Gross National Product (GNP) Deflator (a measure similar to the Consumer Price Index, or CPI), would average 3.5% over the 25-year project life, but he thought he needed to check a couple of forecasts and look at the historical trends. See Exhibit 4 for forecasts of GNP Deflator values as well as historical GNP Deflator values and historical natural gas prices. Dingledine's idea was to use the GNP Deflator to forecast natural gas prices after the four-year contract expired and to increase the value of the natural gas tax credit on an annual basis.

Further questions and uncertainties

When Dingledine showed the results to Henry Ostberg, a potential partner, Ostberg was impressed with the "expected" scenario, but asked, "What is the downside on an investment such as this?" Dingledine had done his homework and produced Exhibits 5 and 6. Exhibit 5 shows the results if there were not enough gas to develop. Exhibit 6 shows

EXHIBIT **3**
Interest rates
and yields.

		Treasuries						Moody's[1]	
		Bills	Notes and Bonds						
		1-Yr	3-Yr	5-Yr	7-Yr	10-Yr	30-Yr	Aaa	Baa
1985		7.81	9.64	10.12	10.5	10.62	10.79	11.37	12.72
1986		6.08	7.06	7.30	7.54	7.68	7.78	9.02	10.39
1987		6.33	7.68	7.94	8.23	8.39	8.59	9.38	10.58
1988	Jan	6.52	7.87	8.18	8.48	8.67	8.83	9.88	11.07
	Feb	6.21	7.38	7.71	8.02	8.21	8.43	9.40	10.62
	Mar	6.28	7.50	7.83	8.19	8.37	8.63	9.39	10.57
	May 18	7.34	8.23	8.66	8.90	9.20	9.30	10.22	11.45

[1] Based on yields to maturity on selected long-term corporate bonds.

Sources: *Federal Reserve Bulletin* (June 1988); *Wall Street Journal*, 19 May 1988.

what would happen if there were enough gas but all other uncertain quantities were set at their 1 chance in 100 worst level. Ostberg was somewhat disturbed by what he saw, but said, "Hey, Tom, we're businesspeople. We're here to take risks; that's how we make money. What we really want to know is the likelihood of this sort of outcome."

Dingledine realized he had not thought enough about the probabilities associated with potential risks that a project of this kind involved. He also put his

EXHIBIT **4**
Historical and
forecast data.

	Historical Natural Gas Prices		
Year	Wellhead Price ($/MCF)	Year	Wellhead Price ($/MCF)
1987	1.78	1975	0.44
1986	1.94	1974	0.30
1985	2.51	1973	0.22
1984	2.66	1972	0.19
1983	2.59	1971	0.18
1982	2.46	1970	0.17
1981	1.98	1969	0.17
1980	1.59	1968	0.16
1979	1.18	1967	0.16
1978	0.91	1966	0.16
1977	0.79	1965	0.16
1976	0.58	1964	0.15

All years: Mean = $0.976, Standard deviation = $0.922

Last 8 years: Mean = $2.189, Standard deviation = $0.412

Source: *Basic Petroleum Data Book* (January 1988) Section VI, Table 2.

EXHIBIT **4**
(Continued)

Percentage Change from Previous Period in GNP Deflator			
Year	% Chg	Year	% Chg
1987	3.0	1969	5.6
1986	2.6	1968	5.0
1985	3.2	1967	2.6
1984	3.7	1966	3.6
1983	3.9	1965	2.7
1982	6.4	1964	1.5
1981	9.7	1963	1.6
1980	9.0	1962	2.2
1979	8.9	1961	1.0
1978	7.3	1960	1.6
1977	6.7	1959	2.4
1976	6.4	1958	2.1
1975	9.8	1957	3.6
1974	9.1	1956	3.4
1973	6.5	1955	3.2
1972	4.7	1954	1.6
1971	5.7	1953	1.6
1970	5.5		

We can calculate a moving average by first calculating the average of the years 1953–77, then the average of the years 1954–78, and so on, ending with the average of years 1963–87. The 11 25-year moving averages have:
Mean = 4.91%
Standard deviation = 0.46%

Source: *Economic Report of the President* (1988): 253.

Forecasts for Percentage Change in GNP Deflator			
	1988	1989	1990	AVG 1988–90
Data Resources[1]	3.1	3.8	4.5	3.8
Wharton[2]	3.8	4.5	4.5	4.3
UCLA[3]	2.7	2.8	3.9	3.1

[1]*Data Resources, Inc.* (November 1987): 99.

[2]*Wharton Econometrics* (September 1987): 9.7–9.8.

[3]*UCLA National Business Forecast* (December 1987): 47.

mind to work thinking about whether he had considered all the things he had seen that could change significantly from one project to another. The only additional uncertainty he generated was the yearly production decline, which could vary significantly for a given well. He had used what he considered the expected values in this case, but now he realized that he needed to multiply each one by some uncertain

EXHIBIT **5**

Spreadsheet with no gas produced.

		ECONOMIC ENVIRONMENT				
		GNP DEFLATOR		3.50%		
WELL		**TAXES**			**RESULTS**	
TOTAL WELL COST	$160,000	FEDERAL TAX RATE		34.00%	EQUITY PAYOUT (AFTER-TAX) =' #DIV/0! MONTHS	
INTANGIBLE COST(%OFTOTAL)	72.50%	STATE TAX RATE		9.75%		
		SEVERANCE TAX RATE		3.40%	INTERNAL RATE OF RET. (CF AFTER-TAX) =' #NUM!	
MONTHLY OPERATING COSTS	$300	COUNTY TAX RATE		4.50%	INTERNAL RATE OF RET. (PBT) = ' #NUM!	
ANNUAL LEASE EXPENSE	$3,000	SECTION 29 TAX CREDIT($/MMBTU)		$0.7600		
INFLATION FACTOR-WELL EXPENSE	1.75%	% QUALIFIED		100.00%	NET PRESENT VALUE (CFAT) @ 15% =	($95,304)
PRODUCTION DATA		**GAS CHARACTERISTICS**			CUMULATIVE CASH FLOW AFTER-TAX =	($95,304)
ENOUGH(0=NO,1=YES)?	0	ROYALTIES		15.2344%		
1st YEAR Mcf	33,000					
DECLINE MULTIPLIER	1.000	**GAS PRICE DATA**				
PRODUCTION DECLINE AFTER...		INFLATION		3.50%		
YEAR 1 =	22.50%	CURRENTPRICE($/MMBTU)		$1.90		
YEAR 2 =	17.50%	BTUCONTENT(BTU/FT3)		1,155		
YEAR 3-5 =	12.50%					
YEAR 6-14 =	10.00%	1ST YEAR OF				
YEAR 15-24 =	5.00%	PRICE INCREASE		5		

YEAR	0	1	2	3	4	5	6	7	8	9	10	11	12
INITIAL INVESTMENT	($160,000)												
PRICE PER MCF		2.19	2.19	2.19	2.19	2.27	2.35	2.43	2.52	2.61	2.70	2.79	2.89
PRODUCTION(MCF)		0	0	0	0	0	0	0	0	0	0	0	0
GROSS REVENUE		$0	$0	$0	$0	$0	$0	$0	$0	$0	$0	$0	$0
LESS: ROYALTIES		0	0	0	0	0	0	0	0	0	0	0	0
NET REVENUE		$0	$0	$0	$0	$0	$0	$0	$0	$0	$0	$0	$0
OPERATING EXPENSES		0	0	0	0	0	0	0	0	0	0	0	0
SEVERANCE & COUNTY TAX		0	0	0	0	0	0	0	0	0	0	0	0
DEPRECIATION	160,000	0	0	0	0	0	0	0					
PROFIT BEFORE TAX	($160,000)	$0	$0	$0	$0	$0	$0	$0	$0	$0	$0	$0	$0
DEPLETION		0	0	0	0	0	0	0	0	0	0	0	0
STATE INC. TAX	(15,600)	0	0	0	0	0	0	0	0	0	0	0	0
FEDERAL INC. TAX	(49,096)	0	0	0	0	0	0	0	0	0	0	0	0
PROFIT AFTER TAX	($95,304)	$0	$0	$0	$0	$0	$0	$0	$0	$0	$0	$0	$0
AFTER TAX CASH FLOW	($95,304)	$0	$0	$0	$0	$0	$0	$0	$0	$0	$0	$0	$0
CUMUL. AFT TAX CASH FLOW	($95,304)	($95,304)	($95,304)	($95,304)	($95,304)	($95,304)	($95,304)	($95,304)	($95,304)	($95,304)	($95,304)	($95,304)	($95,304)
NPV THROUGH YEAR N	($95,304)	($95,304)	($95,304)	($95,304)	($95,304)	($95,304)	($95,304)	($95,304)	($95,304)	($95,304)	($95,304)	($95,304)	($95,304)

YEAR	13	14	15	16	17	18	19	20	21	22	23	24	25
INITIAL INVESTMENT													
PRICE PER MCF	2.99	3.10	3.20	3.32	3.43	3.55	3.68	3.81	3.94	4.08	4.22	4.37	4.52
PRODUCTION(MCF)	0	0	0	0	0	0	0	0	0	0	0	0	0
GROSS REVENUE	$0	$0	$0	$0	$0	$0	$0	$0	$0	$0	$0	$0	$0
LESS: ROYALTIES	0	0	0	0	0	0	0	0	0	0	0	0	0
NET REVENUE	$0	$0	$0	$0	$0	$0	$0	$0	$0	$0	$0	$0	$0
OPERATING EXPENSES	0	0	0	0	0	0	0	0	0	0	0	0	0
SEVERANCE & COUNTY TAX	0	0	0	0	0	0	0	0	0	0	0	0	0
DEPRECIATION													
PROFIT BEFORE TAX	$0	$0	$0	$0	$0	$0	$0	$0	$0	$0	$0	$0	$0
DEPLETION	0	0	0	0	0	0	0	0	0	0	0	0	0
STATE INC. TAX	0	0	0	0	0	0	0	0	0	0	0	0	0
FEDERAL INC. TAX	0	0	0	0	0	0	0	0	0	0	0	0	0
PROFIT AFTER TAX	$0	$0	$0	$0	$0	$0	$0	$0	$0	$0	$0	$0	$0
AFTER TAX CASH FLOW	$0	$0	$0	$0	$0	$0	$0	$0	$0	$0	$0	$0	$0
CUMUL. AFT TAX CASH FLOW	($95,304)	($95,304)	($95,304)	($95,304)	($95,304)	($95,304)	($95,304)	($95,304)	($95,304)	($95,304)	($95,304)	($95,304)	($95,304)
NPV THROUGH YEAR N	($95,304)	($95,304)	($95,304)	($95,304)	($95,304)	($95,304)	($95,304)	($95,304)	($95,304)	($95,304)	($95,304)	($95,304)	($95,304)

quantity—with a most likely value of 1.0, a low of 0.5, and a high of 1.75—to allow for the kind of fluctuation he had seen.

Dingledine wondered what would be the most effective way to incorporate all six of the uncertainties (total well cost, whether the well produced gas or not, first-year production of gas, the BTU content, rate of production decline, and the average inflation over the next 25 years) into his investment analysis. He remembered doing "what if" tables in the spreadsheet back in business school, but he had never heard of a six-way table. As he skimmed through his quantitative-methods book, he saw a chapter on Monte Carlo simulation and read enough to be convinced that that method was ideally suited to his current situation.

When Dingledine told Ostberg about this new method of evaluation he was contemplating, his partner laughed and said, "Come on, Tom, it can't be that hard. What you're talking about sounds like something they'd teach brand-new MBAs. You and I have been doing this type of investing for years. Can't we just figure it out on the back of an envelope?" When Dingledine tried to estimate the probability of his worst-case scenario, it came out to

EXHIBIT **6**

Spreadsheet with gas found but all other uncertainties set at 1 chance in 100 worst level.

ECONOMIC ENVIRONMENT		
GNP DEFLATOR		2.43%

WELL		TAXES		RESULTS		
TOTAL WELL COST	$166,281	FEDERAL TAX RATE	34.00%	EQUITY PAYOUT (AFTER-TAX)=	65.30	MONTHS
INTANGIBLE COST(%OFTOTAL)	72.50%	STATE TAX RATE	9.75%			
		SEVERANCE TAX RATE	3.40%	INTERNAL RATE OF RET. (CF AFTER-TAX) =	#NUM!	
MONTHLY OPERATING COSTS	$300	COUNTY TAX RATE	4.50%	INTERNAL RATE OF RET. (PBT) =	#DIV/0!	
ANNUAL LEASE EXPENSE	$3,000	SECTION 29 TAX CREDIT($MMBTU)	$0.7600			
INFLATION FACTOR-WELL EXPENSE	1.21%	% QUALIFIED	100.00%	NET PRESENT VALUE (CFAT) @ 15% =	($30,417)	
PRODUCTION DATA		**GAS CHARACTERISTICS**		CUMULATIVE CASH FLOW AFTER-TAX =	($18,740)	
ENOUGH(0=NO,1=YES)?	1	ROYALTIES	15.2344%			
1st YEAR Mcf	24,000					
DECLINE MULTIPLIER	1.653	**GAS PRICE DATA**				
PRODUCTION DECLINE AFTER...		INFLATION	2.43%			
YEAR 1 =	37.20%	CURRENTPRICE($MMBTU)	$1.90			
YEAR 2 =	28.93%	BTUCONTENT(BTU/FT3)	1,060			
YEAR 3-5 =	20.67%					
YEAR 6-14 =	16.53%	1ST YEAR OF				
YEAR 15-24 =	8.27%	PRICE INCREASE	5			

YEAR	0	1	2	3	4	5	6	7	8	9	10	11	12
INITIAL INVESTMENT	($166,281)												
PRICE PER MCF		2.01	2.01	2.01	2.01	2.06	2.11	2.16	2.22	2.27	2.33	2.38	2.44
PRODUCTION(MCF)		24,000	15,072	10,711	8,498	6,741	5,348	4,464	3,726	3,110	2,596	2,167	1,808
GROSS REVENUE		$48,336	$30,355	$21,572	$17,114	$13,907	$11,301	$9,662	$8,260	$7,062	$6,038	$5,162	$4,413
LESS: ROYALTIES		7,364	4,624	3,286	2,607	2,119	1,722	1,472	1,258	1,076	920	786	672
NET REVENUE		$40,972	$25,731	$18,286	$14,507	$11,788	$9,579	$8,190	$7,002	$5,986	$5,118	$4,376	$3,741
OPERATING EXPENSES		6,600	6,680	6,761	6,843	6,927	7,011	7,096	7,182	7,269	7,358	7,447	7,538
SEVERANCE & COUNTY TAX		3,819	2,398	1,704	1,352	1,099	893	763	653	558	477	408	349
DEPRECIATION	120,554	6,532	6,532	6,532	6,532	6,532	6,532	6,532					
PROFIT BEFORE TAX	($120,554)	$24,021	$10,120	$3,288	($221)	($2,769)	($4,857)	($6,202)	($833)	($1,841)	($2,717)	($3,479)	($4,145)
DEPLETION		6,146	3,860	1,644	(111)	(1,385)	(2,428)	(3,101)	(416)	(921)	(1,358)	(1,740)	(2,073)
STATE INC. TAX	(11,754)	921	94	(206)	(302)	(371)	(429)	(467)	(181)	(210)	(235)	(257)	(277)
FEDERAL INC. TAX	(36,992)	(13,570)	(10,341)	(8,424)	(7,292)	(6,323)	(5,538)	(5,049)	(3,631)	(3,277)	(2,977)	(2,723)	(2,508)
PROFIT AFTER TAX	($71,808)	$30,524	$16,507	$10,275	$7,483	$5,309	$3,538	$2,415	$3,396	$2,567	$1,854	$1,241	$712
AFTER TAX CASH FLOW	($117,535)	$43,203	$26,899	$18,451	$13,905	$10,457	$7,642	$5,846	$2,979	$1,646	$496	($499)	($1,361)
CUMUL. AFT TAX CASH FLOW	($117,535)	($74,333)	($47,434)	($28,983)	($15,078)	($4,621)	$3,022	$8,868	$11,847	$13,493	$13,989	$13,490	$12,129
NPV THROUGH YEAR N	($117,535)	($79,968)	($59,628)	($47,497)	($39,546)	($34,347)	($31,043)	($28,845)	($27,872)	($27,404)	($27,281)	($27,388)	($27,643)

YEAR	13	14	15	16	17	18	19	20	21	22	23	24	25
INITIAL INVESTMENT													
PRICE PER MCF	2.50	2.56	2.62	2.69	2.75	2.82	2.89	2.96	3.03	3.10	3.18	3.26	3.33
PRODUCTION(MCF)	1,509	1,260	1,052	965	885	812	745	683	627	575	527	484	444
GROSS REVENUE	$3,773	$3,226	$2,758	$2,591	$2,435	$2,288	$2,150	$2,020	$1,898	$1,783	$1,676	$1,575	$1,479
LESS: ROYALTIES	575	491	420	395	371	349	328	308	289	272	255	240	225
NET REVENUE	$3,198	$2,734	$2,338	$2,197	$2,064	$1,939	$1,822	$1,712	$1,609	$1,512	$1,420	$1,335	$1,254
OPERATING EXPENSES	7,629	7,722	7,816	7,816	7,816	7,816	7,816	3,908	3,908	3,908	3,908	3,908	3,908
SEVERANCE & COUNTY TAX	298	255	218	205	192	181	170	160	150	141	132	124	117
DEPRECIATION													
PROFIT BEFORE TAX	($4,729)	($5,242)	($5,696)	($5,824)	($5,944)	($6,057)	($6,163)	($2,355)	($2,449)	($2,537)	($2,620)	($2,698)	($2,771)
DEPLETION	(2,365)	(2,621)	(2,848)	(2,912)	(2,972)	(3,029)	(3,082)	(1,178)	(1,224)	(1,269)	(1,310)	(1,349)	(1,385)
STATE INC. TAX	(295)	(310)	(325)	(328)	(334)	(337)	(334)	(149)	(152)	(154)	(156)	(158)	(160)
FEDERAL INC. TAX	(2,326)	(2,172)	(2,043)	(1,993)	(1,945)	(1,900)	(1,857)	(1,218)	(1,181)	(1,146)	(1,113)	(1,082)	(1,053)
PROFIT AFTER TAX	$256	($138)	($480)	($591)	($696)	($795)	($887)	$190	$108	$31	($41)	($109)	($173)
AFTER TAX CASH FLOW	($2,109)	($2,760)	($3,328)	($3,503)	($3,668)	($3,823)	($3,969)	($988)	($1,117)	($1,237)	($1,351)	($1,458)	($1,558)
CUMUL. AFT TAX CASH FLOW	$10,021	$7,261	$3,933	$430	($3,239)	($7,062)	($11,031)	($12,019)	($13,136)	($14,373)	($15,724)	($17,182)	($18,740)
NPV THROUGH YEAR N	($27,985)	($28,375)	($28,784)	($29,159)	($29,500)	($29,809)	($30,087)	($30,148)	($30,207)	($30,264)	($30,319)	($30,370)	($30,417)

.00000001%—not very likely! There was no way he could use this method to figure out the expected NPV by hand based on all the uncertainties, regardless of how intuitive his friend thought it should be. And this applied to just one well—it would not give him the uncertainty in a 1/10 share of a package of 10 wells. Consequently, Dingledine thought a little more about how Monte Carlo simulation would work with this decision.

In his current method of evaluating projects, he had used the three criteria mentioned earlier (<42-month payback of initial cash investment, >15%

IRR on pretax basis, and >25% IRR on after-tax basis). He could see that calculating the average IRR after several Monte Carlo trials would not be very meaningful, especially as there was a 10% chance that one could spend $160K on a pretax basis and get no return! It would be impossible to find an IRR in that particular scenario. He did feel he could calculate an average NPV after several trials and even find out how many years it would take until the NPV became positive. As he settled into his chair to finish reading the chapter, which looked vaguely familiar, he looked up briefly at the verdant hillside and wondered for a moment what resources were under the hill.

Source: This case was prepared by Larry Weatherford, research assistant, under the supervision of Professor Samuel E. Bodily, as a basis for class discussion rather than to illustrate effective or ineffective handling of an administrative situation. Copyright © 1988 by the University of Virginia Darden School Foundation, Charlottesville, VA. All rights reserved. *To order copies, send an e-mail to sales @dardenbusinesspublishing.com. No part of this publication may be reproduced, stored in a retrieval system, used in a spreadsheet, or transmitted in any form or by any means—electronic, mechanical, photocopying, recording, or otherwise—without the permission of the Darden School Foundation.* Rev. 8/05.

APPSHOP, INC.

Bonuses, gain-sharing, competitive pricing—these ideas were attractive and simple enough, but they made negotiating a contract much more challenging for Eric Clark, director of the Central Region for Appshop, Inc. Clark was in the throes of settling terms and deciding whether and how to do the OS-7 project, a major implementation of Oracle software in all seven international locations of a large multinational company (the "client"). Appshop had recently completed a successful implementation of Oracle financials in the client's Dallas headquarters. Appshop had met or exceeded all stated objectives, and would continue to support corporate Oracle applications for the client.

Appshop was the largest independent full-service Oracle consulting, applications-management, and outsourcing company. Privately held, Appshop had annual revenues of $25 million. Clark was responsible for growing the client base and selling additional professional services, as well as managing existing clients headquartered within his region. The client had told Clark that it would like Appshop to do all the consulting for the OS-7 project. Clark and a team of consultants spent two weeks working on the strategy, scope, and timeline for the roll-out. Based on that analysis, Appshop calculated that the project would require 1,000 hours of work per month for 24 months from a variety of contracted professionals and support personnel, which would result in a total cost to Appshop of $140 an hour. Because of their wide experience in doing these implementations, Clark and his team were confident that this level of effort would result in a completed and running implementation. How much the implementation would save the client and how pleased the client would be with its performance were yet to be determined.

Clark's team proposed that it bill the client and receive at the end of each month $175,000 in revenue over 24 months, which would provide a contribution of $35,000 a month. This amounted to a present-value contribution of $789,700 for the OS-7 project, using the Appshop discount rate of ½ percent per month (which compounded to 6.17 percent per year).

After lengthy discussions, the client informed Appshop that it was prepared to award the contract to Appshop but not for the $175,000 monthly payment. The client wanted a lower price, and offered two alternatives: equal payments of $155,000 a month over 24 months or $125,000 a month plus a $1.5-million bonus paid at the end of month 24 if the work were completed with commendable performance, using standard measurements against stated benchmarks. Even though a system might work satisfactorily and be tuned to meet a specific benchmark, the multiple benchmarks were much harder to meet simultaneously. Based on previous experience with other implementations and the complexity and uniqueness of this international project, Clark's team arrived at a consensus probability of 0.7 of receiving the bonus.

If Appshop did not accept one of the two pricing alternatives, then the officers of the client company had said they would produce a Request for Proposal (RFP) and distribute it to Appshop's competitors, the so-called Big 4. Upon hearing this, Clark thought for a moment that maybe, just maybe, the multinational was bluffing and would acquiesce to Appshop's original request of $175,000 a month. "I guess that's just fantasy," he said to himself.

The terms of the client's RFP would include payment of the revenue-bid amount to the winning bidder at the end of each month, plus a gain-share reward at the end of the 24th month. The client would base the gain-share on the documented savings it would realize from the new Oracle applications, using precise cost-accounting procedures spelled out in the RFP. This approach was common in the software-consulting industry, and Appshop had successfully used it on some contracts in the past. The winning bidder for the RFP would receive a share of the savings according to the following schedule:

Savings	Winning Bidder's Share of Savings
< $4 million	0
$4 million up to $6 million	20 percent of excess above $4 million
$6 million up to $8 million	$400,000 plus 40 percent of excess above $6 million
> $8 million	$1.2 million plus 60 percent of excess above $8 million

Clark and his team had used their previous experience and judgmental assessment of the OS-7 implementation to forecast the client's savings. They concluded that savings would have a triangular distribution, with a low of $3.2 million, a high of $12.8 million, and a most likely value of $5.6 million.

Appshop would bid $150,000 a month for the RFP, if it were issued. This amount was lower than its original offer because of the gain-sharing reward built into the RFP. Appshop had a reasonable chance of winning inasmuch as it generally priced projects below the typical Big 4 price. The team's consensus estimate of Appshop's chances of winning the RFP at the $150,000 bid was 45 percent.

Clark and his team wanted the firm to do well with the OS-7 project. Clark's own compensation package depended primarily on total contribution in his region, with a secondary small incentive for keeping the region's blended hourly revenue rate high.

Source: This case was prepared by Samuel E. Bodily, John Tyler Professor of Business Administration, and Eric Clark, based in part on a class assignment submitted by Eric Clark to Professor James Dyer, University of Texas. It was written as a basis for class discussion rather than to illustrate effective or ineffective handling of an administrative situation. Cost and revenue numbers are disguised. Copyright © 2003 by the University of Virginia Darden School Foundation, Charlottesville, VA. All rights reserved. *To order copies, send an e-mail to* sales@dardenbusinesspublishing.com. *No part of this publication may be reproduced, stored in a retrieval system, used in a spreadsheet, or transmitted in any form or by any means—electronic, mechanical, photocopying, recording, or otherwise—without the permission of the Darden School Foundation.*

CALAMBRA OLIVE OIL (A)

Frank Lockfeld pushed his chair back from the table and surveyed the remains of the meal he had spent the afternoon preparing. After an appetizer of roasted peppers with caramelized garlic accompanied by a crisp 1982 Roederer champagne, he and his guests sat down to a main course of his own devising, designed to take advantage of the light, yet intense, flavor of Calambra olive oil. In the Chicken Breasts Calambra, he used fresh lemons, thyme, garlic, shallots, cherry tomatoes, and parsley (all from his garden), sixteen green and sixteen black olives, and five tablespoons of Calambra olive oil. (A collection of Frank's Calambra recipes is presented in Exhibit 1.) With the chicken, Frank served fresh zucchini (also from his garden) and a shiitake mushroom risotto, complemented by a superb 1986 Chalone Chardonnay Reserve. This course was followed by an endive salad with his own special vinaigrette—balsamic vinegar, fresh lime juice (from the tree in his garden), freshly ground pepper, and the 1993 vintage Calambra olive oil. Frank took another sip of the Chalone and gazed into its rich amber depths while strains of Mozart's Piano Concerto no. 20 in D Minor played in the background. Turning to his wife, B.J., and friends Marv and Linda White, he said,

How am I supposed to decide how many gallons of olive oil to order for next year? It's only the beginning of August, and we've just begun the first selling season. It was only three months ago, late last April, that we bottled the first crop of Calambra olive oil. This was supposed to be our test year. That's why we bought only 800 gallons of the 1993 vintage oil; if we can't sell that much,

EXHIBIT **1**
A collection
of Frank's
Calambra
recipes.

Chicken Breasts CALAMBRA

4 chicken-breast halves	4 sprigs fresh thyme
5 T CALAMBRA Olive Oil	1 small bay leaf
16 pitted black olives	½ cup chicken broth
16 green olives stuffed with pimento	½ cup dry white wine
16 cherry tomatoes	2 T chopped fresh parsley
2 T chopped shallots	½ t red-pepper flakes
1 T chopped garlic	Ground white pepper
	Lemon juice

Pat chicken with lemon juice and sprinkle with ground pepper. Warm 4 T CALAMBRA Olive Oil in 12″ pan. Sauté chicken, skinside down, over medium-high heat for 5 minutes. Turn, lower heat to moderate, and sauté for 15–20 minutes, turning so chicken browns evenly. Remove to heated serving dish and cover. Add olives and tomatoes to pan; turn in pan until they are warm. Place olives and tomatoes around chicken. Pour off pan contents, retaining approximately 2 T in pan. Add shallots, garlic, thyme, and bay leaf; cook for 2 minutes. Add wine and mix pan scrapings; reduce by half over high heat. Add broth, parsley, and red-pepper flakes; simmer for 10 minutes. Remove from heat and blend in remaining T CALAMBRA Olive Oil. Spoon over chicken and serve. Serves 4.

Lamb Chops CALAMBRA

4 lamb chops (shoulder or round bone)	3 T fresh thyme, or 1 T dried
4 T CALAMBRA Olive Oil	3/8 cup dry red wine
2 T chopped garlic, or to taste	2 T butter
4 T chopped fresh parsley, or 2 T dried	Lemon juice
2 T chopped fresh basil, or 1 T dried	Ground white pepper

Trim chops well. Rub with lemon juice and sprinkle lightly with pepper. Sauté garlic in CALAMBRA Olive Oil over medium-high heat for 1 minute in 12″ pan. Add chops. Cover chops with ½ each of the herbs. Sauté for 4 minutes. Turn, cover with remaining herbs, and sauté for 4 minutes. Turn and sauté for 2 minutes. Remove chops to heated platter and cover. Add wine to pan, stir, and reduce by half over high heat. Remove from heat, whisk in butter and juices from chops. Pour sauce over chops and serve. **Serves 4.**

Spinach CALAMBRA

2 bunches fresh spinach, destemmed and prepared in ½″ chiffonade	1 T chopped garlic, or to taste
	4 T toasted pine nuts
4 T CALAMBRA Olive Oil	1 T freshly grated Parmesan cheese

Preheat broiler to 350 degrees. Blanch spinach in boiling water for 30 seconds; drain well. Sauté garlic in CALAMBRA Olive Oil in 10″ pan over moderate heat for 2 minutes. Fold spinach and pine nuts into oil and garlic; mix well. Cook for 2 minutes. Sprinkle with Parmesan cheese. Place under broiler for 30 seconds. Serves 4.

EXHIBIT **1**
(Continued)

Shiitake and Pasta CALAMBRA

4 T CALAMBRA Olive Oil	1 T chopped fresh parsley
½ pound fresh shitake mushrooms, sliced	2 T chopped fresh chives
1 pound fettucini	1 T chopped garlic, or to taste
2 T finely chopped fresh tarragon	4 T crème fraîche
	Freshly grated Parmesan cheese

In 10″–12″ pan, sauté garlic in CALAMBRA Olive Oil for 1 minute over moderate heat. Add shitake and cook over low heat for 20 minutes. Prepare fettucini al dente; drain. Combine shitake and oil mixture with fettucini. Add and mix tarragon, parsley, and chives. Mix in crème fraîche. Serve with Parmesan cheese on the side. (Note: 3 oz. dried shiitake reconstituted with water may be used if fresh shiitake are not available. If fresh herbs are not available, reconstitute dried herbs in a saucer with a small amount of CALAMBRA Olive Oil. If chanterelles are used, cook for 45 minutes.) **Serves 4 as an entrée, 8–10 as a pasta course.**

Grilled Tomatoes CALAMBRA

4 large tomatoes, halved	2 large cloves of garlic, thinly sliced
2 T CALAMBRA Olive Oil	Lemon juice
2 T finely chopped fresh oregano	Ground white pepper

Preheat broiler at 350 degrees. Oil baking dish just large enough to accommodate tomato halves. Sprinkle tomatoes with lemon juice and pepper lightly. Cover with sliced garlic. Sprinkle with oregano. Drizzle with CALAMBRA Olive Oil. Broil for 7 minutes with heat 4 inches from surface.

Mayonnaise CALAMBRA

¼ cup CALAMBRA Olive Oil	1 T lemon juice
1 cup plus 1 T safflower oil	1 t prepared mustard, such as Provençale or Pommery
1 egg	
1 T shallots	

In processor work bowl, place egg (white and yolk), mustard, shallots, 1 T lemon juice, and 1 T safflower oil. Process for 1 minute. Continue processing and drizzle through feed tube: ½ cup of safflower oil, almost drop by drop; CALAMBRA Olive Oil; remaining safflower oil. (Garlic may be substituted for shallots.)

Pesto CALAMBRA

1 cup CALAMBRA Olive Oil	½ cup grated Parmesan cheese
2 cups firmly packed fresh basil	4 oz. pine nuts
	1 T garlic, or to taste

Place all ingredients in food processor. Process until blended and smooth. Combine with pasta al dente. Yields approximately 2 cups pesto. Unused portion can be covered with CALAMBRA Olive Oil in closed container and kept in refrigerator for up to 3 weeks.

we probably don't have a business. Now it seems we have to make the decision about the 1994 crop before we have any real idea about how this experiment is going to turn out.

What's more, sales so far have been disappointing. But it's been only three months. We're hoping for a big jump in sales when the retail shops stock up in anticipation of holiday buying. What's more, there's the possibility we'll sign contracts with Neiman Marcus and Williams-Sonoma for inclusion in their holiday catalogs. Inclusion in either would provide a real boost to sales. But the fact remains: so far, we've shipped only 24 cases.

Sometimes, I'm very optimistic and tempted to order 3,000 gallons, as originally planned for year two. This is, after all, the best-tasting olive oil on the market. But at other times, I'm concerned that sales may never materialize. I have visions of standing in front of the warehouse filled to the brim with leftover cases of 1993 bottles just as a big truck pulls up with this huge 1994 shipment.

Background

Shortly after Frank Lockfeld moved to California from London in 1968 to work with Wilbur Smith and Associates, a well-known transportation-planning and -consulting firm, he planted two olive trees in the backyard of his house in Palo Alto. Several years later, after the trees began to bear fruit, Frank decided to try to make olive oil from his own olives. As Frank later explained, he was mostly "just curious" and intrigued by the idea of producing his own olive oil.

The first batch of olive oil was simply terrible, and Frank set out to determine why. The answer came in the form of one Gino Ambrano, a seventh-generation olive-oil presser of Sicilian descent. Ambrano's family had relocated to California in the early 1900s, and Ambrano, an independent businessman in Mountain View, California, continued the family tradition by maintaining a small olive-oil press, on which he would press a small quantity of oil that he sold in gallon jugs.

Ambrano explained to Frank that the olives Frank used were the wrong kind for making high-quality olive oil. Most California olives, he explained, were the wrong kind—producing oil that could only be used for such industrial purposes as making soap. The popular hand soap, Palmolive, for example, was aptly named because one of its main ingredients was olive oil.

High-quality olive oil, Ambrano explained, required olives grown in extremes of temperature—hot, dry summers and cold, crisp winters. Palo Alto's moderate climate was neither hot enough, dry enough, nor cold enough. The only good California olives came from the Central Valley in the area surrounding the town of Oroville. There, the high volcanic-ash content of the soil coupled with the temperature extremes provided an ideal environment for growing the kind of olives needed to make high-quality olive oil.

To prove his point, Ambrano offered Frank a taste of his own hand-pressed, extra virgin,[1] olive oil. Ambrano made this oil with Oroville olives using his family's extremely gentle, traditional pressing methods. Upon tasting the latest vintage of Ambrano's olive oil, Frank knew he had met a master. The oil was light and delicate, yet intense. It had a medium-amber color, with a full, rich nose and brilliant, fruity flavor. The taste was distinctly of ripe olives, sweet and pure, with a surprisingly mild aftertaste. Frank had never tasted anything like it and thought that Ambrano's was probably the best-tasting olive oil in America.

Frank was so impressed that he arranged to purchase a small quantity of Ambrano's olive oil to give to his friends as Christmas presents. After funneling the bulk oil into wine bottles, he designed and handinked personalized labels for each of the bottles. These gifts were a big hit; everyone who tried the oil thought its taste was remarkable, and not a few of them suggested that Frank try to find some way to bring it to market.

The Calambra Concept

Frank thought he could gain a distinctive marketing advantage by emphasizing that this oil was from California. Almost all high-quality olive oil sold in the United States was imported from Europe. Just as California wines had won market acceptance in competition with French wines, Frank was convinced that a California olive oil could do the same by winning a reputation for very high quality. He combined "California" with "Ambrano" to come up with the name of his new venture.

---

[1] Olive oil comes in several grades, which denote acidity level. For the highest grade, extra virgin, the acidity level must be less than 1 percent.

To encourage consumers to make the connection between olive oil and fine wine, Frank decided to sell Calambra olive oil in 750-milliliter, "dead-leaf" green wine bottles.[2] In addition, Frank decided to display the bottling year on each label. (Few people know it, but the taste and quality of olive oil vary from year to year. Furthermore, like wine, olive oil ages. If you prefer your olive oil intense, use it while it is fresh; if you prefer a mellower, more understated taste, allow it to age in the bottle.)[3] Frank believed that by dating each bottle, he could encourage consumers to pay attention to both the year-to-year differences and the effects of age, thereby differentiating Calambra from other olive oils and increasing the connection between Calambra Olive Oil and fine wine.

To complete the package, Frank designed a beautiful, high-quality label. The four-color label—a rising sun in gold foil, bicolored olive branches, and the vintage date—was so well done that it later won several design awards.[4]

In keeping with the highest-quality image, Frank saw Calambra carrying a retail price higher than any other olive oil on the market. He expected Calambra to be sold initially in specialty and gourmet-food stores. Access to such stores was provided through "fancy-food" brokers, individuals who sold an array of noncompeting gourmet-food products to retail outlets in return for a fixed-percentage commission. Frank planned to start in Northern California, especially in the Bay Area, and later move on to other major metropolitan areas. Department stores and large supermarkets would follow a successful introduction in specialty stores.

Promotional plans for the introduction of Calambra were modest. Taste tests, magazine articles, and newspaper coverage were the major vehicles Frank would pursue. The primary costs of these efforts were Frank's time and whatever oil was used in marketing promotions, taste tests, and giveaways.

The 1993 Vintage

In August 1992, Frank contracted with Gino Ambrano for delivery during the last week of April 1993 of 800 gallons of olive oil at $22 per gallon. Although most oils are made from olives picked in December or January, Ambrano used only handpicked, extraripe, late-harvest black olives from the April crop. These extraripe fruit, which were restricted to black olives to avoid green-olive bitterness, had to be handled gently to avoid damage and quickly, from picking to pressing, to avoid mold.

As had his grandfather—and *his* grandfather before him—Ambrano, immediately upon receipt of the olives, lightly crushed the extraripe fruit. (This extremely gentle pressing avoided the bitterness of the pit because it ensured that the pit itself was never crushed.) Ambrano then took the resulting mixture of oil and skins and allowed gravity to filter it through cotton twice. This centuries-old process, using no heat, pressure, or chemicals, produced the sweetest, purest olive oil imaginable.

In preparation for delivery, Frank began exploring various ways to bottle the oil. His first surprise came when a local bottler told him that he could expect to lose about 53 of his 800 gallons during the bottling process. This loss was composed of three components. The first was a fixed loss of about 25 gallons that occurred during the setup process as target fill-levels were set, spin speeds were established, and fill apertures were chosen. The speed at which the machine filled the bottles and the apertures from which the product was poured depended on a variety of factors, including the shape, size, and mouth-width of the bottles, and the viscosity and consistency (chunkiness) of the fluid. Next, there was a variable loss of about 3 percent due to spillage during the filling process. Finally, there was a residual loss of about 5 gallons because emptying the machine fully without degrading the product was impossible.[5]

---

[2] Frank chose the expensive "dead-leaf" green bottles because they protected the oil from light. As with fine wines, exposure to light could cause olive oil to break down.

[3] When aging olive oil, it should be stored in a cool, dark place of constant (or, at most, slowly changing) temperature. Just as with wine, quick temperature changes could facilitate chemical reactions that cause the oil to break down.

[4] The label was so expensive relative to the alternatives that, in order to reduce unit costs, Frank purchased 100,000 labels, enough to see him through the first six years of production under even his most optimistic sales forecasts. The labels were printed without the vintage date, which was then overprinted as needed.

---

[5] The bottler explained that these losses were considered minor by his usual customers, who were generally bottling high-volume food products with low unit costs, like soup, vinegar, and chunky salsa. Unfortunately for Frank, this loss meant that his 800 gallons of olive oil would result in only about 314 twelve-bottle cases of 750-milliliter bottles of olive oil. (Without any loss, 800 gallons would result in about 336 cases, as there are 3.7853 liters per gallon.)

EXHIBIT **2**
1993 Calambra Olive
Oil: prices and
costs per case.

Calambra selling price per case		$150.00
Expenses		
Glass	$4.91	
Capsules	0.50	
Closures	0.60	
Labels	0.68	
Bottling expense	0.00	
Oil[1]	$54.15	
Cost of goods		$60.84
Gross margin		89.16
Broker fee		30.00
Gross margin after brokerage		$59.16

[1] 800 gallons at $22 per gallon made 325 cases.

Because setup and cleaning represented major components of the bottler's activity, the cost of using the bottling plant consisted of a correspondingly high fixed cost of $3,000 and a correspondingly low variable cost of only $0.30 per bottle, plus supplies.

To avoid the loss of oil and the huge fixed costs relative to the quantity he was bottling, Frank arranged for friends and family to help him handbottle the 1993 oil over a weekend. From friends in the wine business, he borrowed a six-hole handbottling machine to fill the bottles and a foiler-spinner to put in the capsules and seal the bottles. In return for the help of his friends and the use of the machines, Frank gave away several cases of freshly bottled, first-vintage, 1993 Calambra Olive Oil. Thus, his only costs were the cost of the supplies, gifts, and the food and wine he served during his bottling extravaganza (spillage was negligible). When all was said and done, Frank had 325 cases of oil and a small cadre of friends who fully believed that Calambra was the best olive oil imaginable.[6]

Frank stored the cases of Calambra Olive Oil in space he rented from a local wine wholesaler and began the process of supporting his broker's efforts to sell the product to local specialty retailers in the San Francisco Bay Area. While the broker introduced her clients to Calambra as part of her routine calls to specialty-food stores, Frank used his spare time (mostly weekends) arranging for and conducting taste tests at specialty markets around the Bay Area and contacting editors and writers of various gourmet magazines and newspaper columns.

A case of Calambra Olive Oil was priced to retailers at $150. (See Exhibit 2 for the prices and costs of a case of 1993 Calambra Olive Oil.) The broker made 20 percent on each sale, and product was shipped directly from the warehouse to the retailer. Exhibit 3 contains Frank's projected profit-and-loss statement for the business for the years 1993 through 1999 based on actual oil purchases in 1993 and forecasted purchases of 3,000, 4,500, 6,750, and 10,000 gallons from 1994 on. Frank's original intention was to prove the market in 1993 and then roll out the business per this projection.

August 1993

The introduction of Calambra Olive Oil was an artistic success. Calambra ranked number one in a tasting of 19 Italian, French, Spanish, Greek, and California olive oils sponsored by Narsai's Market, a well-known specialty-food store in Kensington, California (see Exhibit 4 for the judging criteria and a list of the oils tested). The Narsai victory received coverage in *San Francisco Focus*, a slick, monthly magazine covering events in the Bay Area for upscale readers. It also got

---

[6] Frank set aside 25 of the 325 cases for marketing purposes. Of those, five were normal 12-bottle cases. For the other 20 cases, however, Frank chose half-size (375-milliliter) clear-glass wine bottles to highlight the oil's beautiful amber color. These cases consisted of 24 bottles each.

EXHIBIT **3**
Projected profit
and loss:
1993–97.

	1993	1994	1995	1996	1997
Gallons of oil	800	3,000	4,500	6,750	10,000
Net gallons[1]	773	2,881	4,336	6,518	9,671
Cases of oil produced	325	1,211	1,823	2,741	4,067
Marketing cases	25	50	50	75	100
Cases available for sale	300	1,161	1,773	2,666	3,967
Revenue	$45,000	$174,150	$265,950	$399,900	$595,050
Cost of goods					
Oil	$17,600	$62,000	$90,500	$133,250	$195,000
Bottling cost ($3.60/case)	NA	7,360	9,563	12,868	17,641
Material ($6.69/case)	$2,174	$8,102	$12,196	$18,337	$27,208
Selling expenses					
Freight ($4.00/case)	$1,200	$4,644	$7,092	$10,664	$15,868
Broker (20% of sales)	9,000	34,830	53,190	79,980	119,010
Printing ($0.12/case)	39	145	219	329	488
Warehouse ($3.50/case)	1,050	4,064	6,206	9,331	13,885
Advertising	$1,500	$2,250	$5,000	$11,000	$17,500
General and administrative					
Legal	$1,400	$500	$500	$500	$500
Accounting	850	650	650	650	650
Insurance	260	285	325	375	440
Telephone	600	900	1,500	2,400	3,000
Miscellaneous	$750	$1,000	$1,500	$2,000	$3,000
Total costs	$36,423	$126,729	$188,440	$281,684	$414,190
Profit	$8,577	$47,421	$77,510	$118,216	$180,860

[1] Presumes handbottling in 1993 and use of the bottling plant for years 1994 through 1997.

Frank invited back to conduct an instore tasting on July 24. On that Saturday Frank sold 20 bottles. Calambra also received a very favorable review in the article "Liquid Gold: The True Meaning of 'Extra Virgin' and Other Secrets of the Controversial Oil from the Little Black Fruit," which appeared in the "California Living" section of the *Los Angeles Herald*. A list of the selling points and accolades for Calambra Olive Oil are presented in Exhibit 5.

Unfortunately, these successes had yet to translate into shipments. As of July 30, Frank had shipped 24 cases to 17 different customers in the Bay Area, each of whom had initially ordered a single trial case and only four of whom had as yet placed a second order. This was a far cry from the 20 to 30 cases that Frank hoped the average store would sell each year. Nonetheless, Frank was hopeful that many of these stores would soon be placing orders in anticipation of holiday buying.

In addition, Frank was currently in negotiations with Neiman Marcus and Williams Sonoma for inclusion in their Christmas catalogs. Neiman Marcus was thinking of including a bottle of Calambra Olive Oil in each of its Christmas baskets and talking about a

EXHIBIT **4**
Narsai's taste
test, Saturday,
May 29, 1993.

ITALIAN OILS	FRENCH OILS
Antinori Santa Cristina (1991 Extra Virgin Chianti Classico)	Domaine de la Gautiere (N.V. Virgin Buis les Baronnies)
I. Pozzi-Montefollonico (N.V. Extra Virgin, Tuscany)	James Plagniol (N.V. Pure Olive Oil, Marseille)
Poggio at Sole (N.V. Extra Virgin, Val di Pesa, Firenza)	Old Monk (N.V. Extra Virgin, Nice)
Tahoe Sardegna (N.V. Extra Virgin, Foligno)	**SPANISH OIL**
Sasso (N.V. Pure Olive Oil, Oneglia)	Siurana (N.V. Extra Virgin, Priorat, Catalonia)
Badia Coltibuono (1991 Extra Virgin, Chianti Classico)	**GREEK OIL**
Badia Coltibuono (December 1992 Extra Virgin, Unfiltered)	Arethousa (N.V. Pure Olive Oil, Calamata)
Chianti Classico (Special Bottling)	
Castello di Volpaia (1991 Extra Virgin, Chianti Classico)	**CALIFORNIA OILS**
	Kimberly (1993 Extra Virgin, Northern California)
II Castelluzzo (N.V. Extra Virgin, Orvieto)	**Winner: Calambra (April 1993, Extra Virgin, Central Valley)**
Colavita (N.V. Extra Virgin, Campobasso)	Estus Gourmet (N.V. Extra Virgin)

CRITERIA FOR EVALUATION OF HIGH-QUALITY OLIVE OIL

- Bouquet, perfume, aroma of the fresh olive
- Flavor on the tongue; fruitiness versus greasiness
- Degree of acidity and extent of burning and stinging at back of mouth; some degree of pepperiness, but not too much to override the delicate flavor
- Color—deep, rich emerald to golden green, depending on degree of filtering

purchase of 100 cases of oil; Williams Sonoma was thinking of listing Calambra directly in its catalog and was considering 30 cases. Frank believed that either deal would be a great boon for Calambra, more for the enhancement of Calambra's reputation than for the sale of oil. Moreover, Frank thought it was an almost even bet that he would get at least one of the contracts. Specifically, he believed there was about a 10 percent chance that the Neiman deal would come through and about a 40 percent chance for Williams Sonoma. Frank did not think the outcome of either negotiation would affect the other.

The Quantity Decision

Although it was only August, Gino Ambrano was pressing Frank to decide how many gallons of oil he wanted in 1994. Although this urgency seemed premature, Frank realized that producing Calambra-quality oil required that the olives be left to ripen on the trees far longer than if the olives were to be used for any other purpose. Thus, in one sense, Frank was asking Ambrano to contract with the olive growers to "reserve" some portion of their crop for a late-April harvest so that it could be made into Calambra Olive Oil.

EXHIBIT **5**
Selling points and accolades.

- Ranked no. 1 in tasting of 19 Italian, French, Greek, Spanish, and California olive oils at Narsai's Market, Kensington, California
- Praised as "the outstanding olive oil" at the third annual International Gourmet Food and Wine Show, San Francisco, by Harvey Steiman, *San Francisco Examiner* food critic
- Seventh-generation olive-oil master
- Full flavor and aroma of olives
- A very light oil without greasiness (does not stick to the roof of your mouth)
- Smooth, balanced taste without sharpness common to other olive oils
- Made from fully ripe black olives only; no green-olive bitterness
- Olives from selected farms in north Central Valley, where heat brings fruit to ripeness
- April harvesting when the olives are fully developed
- Very lightly cold-pressed, avoiding bitterness near pit (pit is not crushed)
- No "culls" (canned olive rejects); no heat, no chemicals
- Gravity-filtered twice through cotton; no pressure applied

On the other hand, Frank also thought that Ambrano was applying pressure, in his own skillful and gentle way, simply to make Frank commit. Frank believed that, for personal reasons, Ambrano was willing to press only about 6,000 gallons of olive oil in 1994—even though he had a lot more capacity—and that the reason Ambrano wanted to know how much oil Frank wanted was so he could make plans for the rest.

As a result, Ambrano sent Frank the agreement reproduced in Exhibit 6. After several weeks of discussion, Frank came to realize that the proposed price schedule was not negotiable. Frank knew that this agreement was truly a take-it-or-leave-it offer, and that he would have to make up his mind by the end of the month. This situation disturbed Frank because he did not believe he was getting much of a break from Ambrano for committing to buy the oil in advance and in quantity. Nonetheless, he had no other choice. Although low-grade oil was available commercially in 55-gallon drums for about $5 per gallon, and there was some extra virgin oil available in drums for sale to restaurants at $15 to $17 per gallon, none of it tasted like Ambrano's.

In thinking about how many gallons to order, Frank was forced to project where the business might be in April 1994 when the new order would be delivered. Clearly, the events of the next few months would go a long way to help determine just how many gallons he would need next April.

As Marv and Frank began to clear the table, Marv asked Frank if he still thought he would sell all of the 1993 oil. Frank answered,

I'm not giving up hope that all 300 cases of 1993 oil will be sold before the 1994 shipment arrives, but without catalog sales, I'm afraid I'd now have to say it's a little less than an even bet. In fact, while I still think there's some chance we could sell 500 cases or more to the retail stores if we had them, at this point if we don't get the stores to stock up for the holidays, we might sell fewer than 50 cases.

The good news, though, is the catalogs. Closing either deal would be a big boon to 1993 sales in two ways. Not only would we get those extra sales from the catalog purchases, but it would easily increase our total sales to retailers by 20 cases because of the added advertising value.

"Come back to the retail market for a moment," Marv said. "If I understand you correctly—and I'm guessing that your not-quite-an-even bet means your mdipoint is off by about 10 percent—what you're saying is that it's as likely that you'll sell more than 270 cases as it is that you'll sell less. Right?"

"That's about right."

"OK, let's see if we can add a little definition to this forecast. If I told you that you were definitely going to sell less than 270 cases to retailers, where do you think you'd end up? What do you think is the point below 270 that you're as likely to be over as under?"

EXHIBIT **6**
Agreement.

This is an agreement between Calambra Olive Oil (Calambra), a California subchapter S corporation, and Gino Ambrano, Martine Avenue, Mountain View, California.

Gino Ambrano will provide Calambra with olive oil of his own pressing from the 1994 crop according to the following price schedule:

For the first 500 gallons:	$23.00 per gallon
For any of the next 500 gallons:	$22.00 per gallon
For any of the next 500 gallons:	$21.00 per gallon
For any of the next 500 gallons:	$20.00 per gallon
For any additional oil:	$19.00 per gallon

The oil will be received by Calambra at Gino Ambrano's place of business in Mountain View, California, in 55-gallon drums, unless prior written arrangements are mutually agreed upon. Delivery will be made during the last week of April 1994.

All drums delivered to Calambra prior to April 30 will be returned not later than May 5. Calambra may, upon consent of Gino Ambrano, purchase the drums at a price of $50 per drum.

Payment for the oil shall be made by check drawn on the account of Calambra, upon receipt of delivery, excepting the first $5,000.00, which is due upon execution of this contract.

This represents the entire agreement between the parties hereto, notwithstanding any prior or verbal representations by either party. Any amendments to this agreement shall be written and signed by the parties to this agreement.

For Calambra Olive Oil

_____
Frank Lockfeld
President

date:

_____
Gino Ambrano

date:

"I don't know. I've never thought about that. Maybe 175 cases."

"And what about the similar point on the upside, assuming, of course, you had them to sell?"

"That one is easier," Frank responded. "If I knew we were going to sell more than 270 cases, that would mean the product has been at least reasonably well accepted and I'd think that if we had them to sell to the stores, we'd be as likely to sell more than 400 cases as less than 400 cases, though I'd have to add that at this point I think the chance of exceeding 500 cases is no more than one in twenty.

As Frank fired up the cappuccino machine, Linda said that she thought the question was how much oil to buy for the 1994 vintage. "Don't we need to talk about the potential for 1994 sales?" Frank agreed, but added that 1993 was the key:

Selling out in 1993 would have an enormous positive impact on the business. Although some stores might be upset that they weren't able to reorder when they wanted to, most would realize that Calambra is like a small Sonoma Valley vineyard and that to carry the product, they would have to compete to place orders.

In fact, if we sell out in 1993, I believe it would only lead to more, faster sales in 1994, as stores try to increase their inventories to prevent stockouts. These larger orders, plus the accompanying press, would make it very easy to move to other metropolitan areas with the 1994 crop [Los Angeles, New York, and Washington, D.C., were all on Frank's list] and truly launch this business.

But, most importantly, selling out in 1993 provides the signal that there really are enough connoisseurs out there who appreciate the value of a fine olive oil.

As B.J. brought out her famous Linzer torte (a raspberry-and-almond torte made from her own *secret* recipe in the style and tradition of the great bakers of the city of Linz, Austria), Frank continued,

If we sell all of the 1993 oil, whether through specialty shops or catalog sales, the experiment will have been a success and the business will be a "go." In this case, Linda, I'd say the potential for 1994 sales ranges from just matching 1993 sales of 300 cases all the way up to 1,600 cases. In this scenario, I'd be pretty optimistic about our most likely sales level; in fact, I'd stick with my original forecast of about 1,200 cases.

On the other hand, if we don't sell out in 1993, then I'd have to conclude that Calambra is unlikely to realize the consumer acceptance it needs, and I'd have to call the experiment a failure. To me that means there aren't enough olive-oil connoisseurs in the Bay Area to support the venture. What's worse, if we can't make it happen here, it isn't likely to

happen anywhere. So, if we don't sell out in 1993, we don't have a business and we don't order any more oil for 1995.

In this depressing case, I'd have to say that the most likely outcome would be to sell about the same amount of oil in 1994 as we sold in 1993. But it could be a lot worse. If the channel is full and the product isn't selling, we might only sell a quarter as much. On the other hand, there is probably still some upside, as the business could still take off; but it's hard to imagine that we'd sell more than three times as much in 1994 as we sold in 1993. I even have a hard time thinking about this scenario.

As Frank got up to make more cappuccino, B.J. asked him what would happen should sales fail to materialize in either 1993 or 1994 and the business had to be abandoned. "What do we do with all that oil?"

"If we're not in business, we'll simply have to find a way to dispose of it," Frank answered, "but we'll probably take quite a bath. There's always Trader Joe's." (Trader Joe's was a discount chain of fancy-food stores in the Southwest that bought warehouse-sized lots of fancy-food products at distress prices, usually about 10 cents on the dollar, and then resold them in their own stores at deep discounts.) "Painful as it might be, we could always sell the oil to them."

"On the other hand, if we are in business in 1995, we could always sell leftover bottles in later years, although I don't think I'd ever want to sell more of a vintage in the out-years than sales in the year it was introduced. I'd be afraid that having too much older oil on the market could have a negative effect on sales."

"I think you're right." Marv piped in, "In fact, it seems to me you might be better off simply eating any leftover oil rather than risking the possibility of a negative market reaction. Over pasta would be nice; we'll come help."

Source: This case was prepared by Professors Dana R. Clyman and Phillip E. Pfeifer. This case was written as a basis for class discussion rather than to illustrate effective or ineffective handling of an administrative situation. Copyright © by the University of Virginia Darden School Foundation, Charlottesville, VA, Rev. 9/02. All rights reserved. *To order copies, send an e-mail to sales@dardenbusinesspublishing.com. No part of this publication may be reproduced, stored in a retrieval system, used in a spreadsheet, or transmitted in any form or by any means— electronic, mechanical, photocopying, recording, or otherwise— without the permission of the Darden School Foundation.*

CALAMBRA OLIVE OIL (B)

The next morning, while drinking freshly ground coffee and savoring the crisp, almond essence of his chocolate-almond biscotti, Frank's thoughts returned to the previous night's conversation. There ought to be some way, he thought, to use all the added detail that Marv, Linda, and B.J. had elicited from him about his assessments of future sales for Calambra Olive Oil.

After finishing the Sunday paper, Frank decided to try to use his more refined assessments to examine a few scenarios. He remembered from his student days that one could use scenarios to gain insight into decision problems. He also remembered that to evaluate a scenario properly, one had to push it out far enough so that the outcome could be valued.

Sitting down at his computer, Frank began to build a spreadsheet model. In the first cell he entered "Oil ordered for 1994 (gallons)." Then, realizing he could do multiple evaluations at once, he decided to evaluate a total of nine order quantities at one time. In the second column of his spreadsheet he entered a quantity of 1,000 gallons; in the second row, he entered an incremental value of 250 gallons. Then for each successive column, he added the increment to the prior order quantity, thereby obtaining order quantities from 1,000 to 3,000 gallons for evaluation. For convenience, Frank displayed the highest order quantity under the incremental value, where he could see it. (The first four columns of Frank's spreadsheet are presented in Exhibit 1.)

Next, he began to define the scenario. To avoid having to reenter the scenario in more than one place, he entered, in the third and higher columns, a formula referring back to the scenario in the prior column. Frank decided to start with a pessimistic scenario because that would make tracking unsold gallons of oil easier than would an optimistic one. For his pessimistic scenario, Frank reasoned he would obtain no catalog sales, and he assumed a 1993 retail demand of only about 120 cases. With this information, Frank was able to enter an if-statement to calculate the zero-or-twenty-case catalog bonus. He was also able to enter a formula for 1993 retail sales, which could not be greater than his supply of 300 cases. Finally, because in this scenario he would not sell out the 1993 vintage, Frank chose 90 cases for his estimate of 1994 demand, a value somewhat less than 1993 demand.

Frank realized that before calculating 1994 sales, which would be the smaller of demand and the amount of oil he had available, he first had to compute how many cases of oil he could produce given his order quantity. Thus, from the order quantity he subtracted the fixed setup loss of 25 gallons, the variable loss of 3 percent and, finally, the fixed cleaning loss of 5 gallons, which gave him net gallons after bottling. Then, knowing that there are 3.7853 liters per gallon, 0.75 liter per bottle, and 12 bottles per case, Frank calculated the number of cases of oil that he could produce. Finally, after subtracting the 50 cases that he was going to set aside for marketing, he obtained the number of cases of 1994 vintage oil available for sale.

While refilling his coffee cup, Frank decided to do all the case math before doing any financial calculations. He retrieved from above the number of cases sold in 1993 (to have it all in one place), and he calculated the number of cases left over, the number he would consider selling the following year (here, he implemented his out-year rule: the maximum number of cases that could be carried forward as inventory equaled this year's sales), and, finally, the number of unsalable cases that were available for salvage or, he chuckled to himself, dinner.

He then did the same case calculations for 1994. To get the total number of cases available for sale in 1994, he added the number he produced in 1994 to the number of 1993 cases that he had carried forward for sale. (To remind himself that these "94" cases were not all 1994-vintage oil, Frank used quotation marks.) He then retrieved the number of cases sold, and calculated the number left over. Then, once more using his out-year rule, he calculated the number of cases he would be able to carry forward as inventory for the following year. Before he could decide whether to carry this inventory forward or sell it as salvage, however, Frank had to decide whether he would be in business in 1995. Therefore, in the next row he placed an indicator variable that tested whether he would sell out in 1993. Then, using yet another if-statement, Frank carried inventory forward only if he were going to be in business the following year. Finally, he calculated the amount of "94" oil he would have to salvage at the end of 1994.

Having completed the case math, Frank began the financial modeling. Beginning with revenue, Frank calculated sales at $150 per case for 1993 and 1994. He then looked at whether he would be in business in 1995. If 1994 were to be his last year, he realized he

EXHIBIT **1**
Frank's spread-
sheet model
(first four columns).

Oil ordered for 1994 (gallons)	1,000	1,250	1,500
250 Increment			
3,000 Last Column			
Scenario			
Neiman Marcus	0	0	0
Williams Sonoma	0	0	0
93 Retail demand	120	120	120
Retail bonus for catalog	0	0	0
93 Retail sales	120	120	120
94 Retail demand	90	90	90
Oil calculations			
Fixed setup loss	25	25	25
Variable loss	29	37	44
Fixed cleaning loss	5	5	5
Net gallons	941	1,183	1,426
Liters	3,561	4,479	5,397
Bottles	4,748	5,972	7,196
Cases of oil produced	395	497	599
94 Marketing cases	50	50	50
94 Cases available for sale	345	447	549
Case sales summary			
93 Cases sold	120	120	120
93 Cases left over	180	180	180
93 Cases carried as 94 inventory	120	120	120
93 Cases available for salvage	60	60	60
"94" Cases available for sale	465	567	669
"94" Cases sold	90	90	90
"94" Cases left over	375	477	579
Potential inventory carryforward	90	90	90
In business in 95? (1=Yes, 0=No)	0	0	0
"94" Cases carried as 95 inventory	0	0	0
"94" Cases available for salvage	375	477	579
Revenue			
93 Sales	$18,000	$18,000	$18,000
94 Sales	13,500	13,500	13,500
94 Salvage (out of business in 95)	6,525	8,055	9,585
94 Inventory credit (in business in 95)	0	0	0
Total revenue	$38,025	39,555	$41,085

EXHIBIT **1**
(Continued)

Costs			
93 Oil cost	$17,600	$17,600	$17,600
93 Bottling costs	NA	NA	NA
93 Materials costs ($6.69/case)	2,174	2,174	2,174
93 Freight ($4.00/case)	480	480	480
93 Broker (20% of sales)	3,600	3,600	3,600
93 Printing ($0.12/case)	39	39	39
93 Warehouse ($3.50/case)	1,050	1,050	1,050
93 Fixed costs	5,360	5,360	5,360
Subtotal, 93 costs	$30,303	$30,303	$30,303
94 Oil cost	$22,500	27,750	$33,000
94 Bottling costs ($3.60/case)	4,422	4,789	5,156
94 Materials costs ($6.69/case)	2,643	3,325	4,007
94 Freight ($4.00/case)	360	360	360
94 Broker (20% of sales)	2,700	2,700	2,700
94 Printing ($0.12/case)	47	60	72
94 Warehouse ($3.50/case)	1,838	2,195	2,552
94 Fixed costs	5,585	5,585	5,585
Subtotal, 94 costs	$40,094	$46,763	$53,432
Total costs	$70,398	$77,067	$83,735
Two-Year profit	$(32,373)	$(37,512)	$(42,650)

could salvage all leftover oil from 1993 and 1994 by selling it to Trader Joe's at the end of 1994. (Note that by not salvaging any oil at the end of 1993, Frank had decided that he would not salvage oil as long as he was in business.)

Next he considered the more complicated issue of what to do with the cases he was carrying forward for sale in 1995 in those scenarios where Calambra was an ongoing business. Because all that having these cases available for sale would do was prevent him from having to buy and bottle more oil, Frank decided to credit himself with their cost of replacement. Doing so, after all, would make these scenarios comparable to scenarios in which he would not have any oil left over but could still buy and sell it.

He figured it cost him $6.69 per case in bottling materials plus another $3.60 in bottling costs plus about $45.175 for the oil. (To get this last number,

Frank calculated the number of gallons per case and assumed that, at the margin, his replacement cost of oil was $19 per gallon.) Adding this up gave him a total credit of $55.465 per case.

Frank next turned to his costs. Starting in 1993, he knew that it had cost him $22 per gallon to buy the oil and $6.69 in materials for each of the 325 cases he produced. Frank wondered if he should include some charge for the bottling weekend but decided any cost incurred was really irrelevant. For freight, he realized, he should only charge himself for the cases he shipped, in this scenario, 120. Broker fees were computed based on sales, printing, based on production, and warehouse, based only on cases available for sale (because he kept the 25 marketing cases at home where he would have easy access to them). For fixed costs, he added up the costs in his projected profit-and-loss statement (see Exhibit 3 of the A case).

Turning to 1994, Frank thought for a while about how to enter the cost of oil. He finally settled on a fairly complicated, nested if-statement to capture the structure of the quantity discounts that he had been offered by Ambrano. After checking the calculation several times with pencil and paper, Frank decided he had written the if-statement correctly. For the bottling and materials costs, Frank simply multiplied the per-unit costs times the number of cases produced.

For freight, Frank charged himself only for the number of cases sold. Broker fees were also easy: 20 percent of sales revenue. For printing, Frank again referenced cases produced. Warehousing was a little more difficult: Frank decided he had to include not only all cases produced, but also all of the cases he carried forward, either for sale or for salvage, less, of course, the marketing cases he would keep at home for easy access. Finally, he again took the fixed-cost numbers from his projections (see Exhibit 3 of the A case).

At this point, Frank's model building was essentially complete. All that was left was to add up the costs and subtract them from the revenues to obtain a two-year profit figure. Frank knew that he should probably separate the years and do a discounted net-present-value (NPV) analysis, but with only two years and the strange way in which costs and revenues would actually occur over the year, Frank decided that an NPV analysis was simply not worth the effort.

Looking across the bottom of the spreadsheet, Frank was not at all surprised to discover that he was best off with the least amount of oil in this pessimistic scenario.

Frank then decided to try a "best guess" scenario. Reasoning that at least one catalog deal was fairly likely to go through and because Williams Sonoma was far more likely than Neiman Marcus, Frank assumed he sold Williams Sonoma 30 cases for its catalog. He then set retail demand at his median estimate of 270 cases and noted that in this scenario there would be a sellout in 1993. Therefore, he used for his estimate of 1994 demand his most likely assessment of 1,200 cases.

Moving to the bottom of the spreadsheet, he was delighted to find that the contribution continued to grow all the way up through 3,000 gallons. (Maybe 3,000 gallons is too conservative after all, he thought.) Returning to the top of the spreadsheet, he changed the increment from 250 gallons to 500 gallons; returning to the bottom row, he then discovered that, in this scenario, his optimal order quantity was somewhere between 3,000 and 4,000 gallons, as the highest profit figure appeared at 3,500 gallons.

Finally, for an optimistic scenario, Frank assumed he signed both Neiman Marcus and Williams Sonoma, that 1993 demand was 400 cases, and that 1994 demand was 1,500 cases. When he checked the bottom of the spreadsheet this time, Frank found that his optimal order quantity had increased to somewhere between 3,500 and 4,500 gallons, and his two-year profit had gone up by about $17,000 to $74,474.

Source: This case was prepared by Associate Professor Dana R. Clyman and Professor Phillip E. Pfeifer. This case was written as a basis for class discussion rather than to illustrate effective or ineffective handling of an administrative situation. Copyright © by the University of Virginia Darden School Foundation, Charlottesville, VA, Rev. 8/99. All rights reserved. *To order copies, send an e-mail to sales@dardenbusinesspublishing.com. No part of this publication may be reproduced, stored in a retrieval system, used in a spreadsheet, or transmitted in any form or by any means—electronic, mechanical, photocopying, recording, or otherwise—without the permission of the Darden School Foundation.*

SCOR-eSTORE.COM

Scor-eStore.com was not yet a company—it was still simply the ideas and experiments of two budding entrepreneurs. Mark Burgess, a graduate student in computer science, and Chris Madsen, a professional musician, hoped it would become a company. They had both invested a lot of time and creativity in their spare time to get where they were now.

Mark Burgess had created a prototype sheet-music viewer that could display sheet music on a PC screen, play the music through the PC's speakers, and print the music on the PC's printer, all via the Web. For proprietary music, it would print the music only when it was purchased over the Web and all transmissions would be encrypted. This viewer, unlike other viewers currently available, would, when completed, read files created by the popular notation software used by musicians to write and edit music. This capability would give the viewer a competitive edge by accepting music uploaded to it on the Web. Composers could use the viewer to show their music to others, give them a chance to play the music (or a portion of it), and deliver printed sheet music on the Web, without ever giving the user an electronic copy that could be copied to others electronically. By using additional existing software that transcribed pieces played on an instrument into an electronic musical-notation file, a composer could even create the music by playing it on an electronic piano keyboard or other instrument. At this point, however, the viewer was not fully functional, and testing would be needed to confirm that it would do all of these things in practice.

Chris Madsen had used the pilot of the viewer to convert a dozen selections of music into the viewer's format, adding a lot of touch-up work by hand. When perfected, the viewer would do all the conversion automatically, including all the music's diacritical marks. Madsen had created a prototype Web page where invited visitors could browse, play, and print sample pieces of sheet music. From the comments of visitors to the Web site, there was ample reason to think that a dressed-up Web site, endowed with a thousand or so selections and listed in the common search engines, could be successful.

The next steps, if Scor-*e*Store.com was to become a company, were to (1) bring the viewer to full functionality and finish alpha and beta testing and (2) create a first-rate Web site with a collection of at least 1,000 compositions, complete with shopping cart and payment capabilities. About $90,000 would be needed to pay the two principals subsistence wages and to lease computer equipment and use home offices (for about four months) and then to operate the Web site for a couple of months. By then, at the end of six months, they would know whether the business was viable.

Burgess and Madsen had approached a variety of venture capitalists, friends, and friends of friends for funding as they themselves were penniless. For various reasons, they had not managed to find a mutually acceptable deal with an investor, and they were down to their last prospect. Lance Bernard was considering a proposal whereby he would put up the entire $90,000 and take 1/3 ownership of Scor-*e*Store.com.

Bernard had said to Burgess and Madsen that "someone will make a lot of money with an on-line sheet-music business. It's the perfect way to deliver music—no stores, no sales clerks, no inventory; you don't even need to buy paper or do any printing and binding." In the privacy of his office, Bernard made some quick calculations, however, that led him to frown on the investment. Bernard believed that only about four sheet-music Web sites would survive to be worth anything, and that it would be apparent a couple of months after the Web site was officially opened (six months from now) whether Scor-*e* Store.com would be among the top sheet-music Web sites. If it were not in the top group by then, in Bernard's mind, the business would not be worth pursuing further and it should just die. If the Web site were among the top four at that time, he would sell his share for what he thought would be about $500,000 and move on to something new.[1] Assessing a 15 percent chance[2] that the Web-site business would be viable, he multiplied 15 percent by $500,000, obtaining $75,000, discounted it for six months at his usual rate of 20 percent, and concluded that his share of the business should be valued at no more than $68,182. This amount was less than the $90,000 investment, so Bernard planned to pass on the opportunity. He threw the file in his bag and headed for a casual dinner with some of his venture-capital buddies.

At dinner that evening, Bernard mentioned the on-line music opportunity and lamented, "If an idea this good doesn't cut it, why do people invest in Internet start-ups?" Questions about the underlying business model prompted Bernard to describe how the business would work. He told them that two things were required: a competitively functional viewer and a winning Web site with attractive content. After four months he would know about the viewer, and in months five and six he could test the Web site. If this viewer were not functional after four months, his test of the Web site could still be performed by licensing an existing, more-limited viewer and hand-editing the pieces for the music

---

[1] His current appraisal was that, based on projected earnings before interest and taxes (EBITDA), the entire business would be worth about $1.5 million at that time.

[2] This was a composite of a 50 percent chance that the Web site and its content would be a winner and a 30 percent chance that the viewer could be made competitively functional.

collection in the test. Then the others entered the conversation:

Allen: Suppose the viewer is competitively functional and yet, after six months, the Web site is not a winner. Could you abandon the Web business and sell the technology, maybe as software for composers to publish their work on-line?

Bernard: Well I believe that I could, and this would create some additional value to reward the development effort. In fact, the principals told me that, for an additional $25,000 of my money, they could turn a working viewer into a shrink-wrapped software product. But they, and I, wouldn't want to run a software business. They told me that they could sell the software rights for something like $450,000, and I would then get a third of that.

Soares: If you could use the technology separately, what about going ahead with the Web site separately? Suppose the viewer is not functional after four months, but the Web site proves to be a winner with a little extra effort by the end of month six—what could you do with the Web site and the music content?

Bernard: First of all, if the viewer didn't work, I'm sure we could arrange temporary rights with the alternate inferior viewer to test the Web site. If the Web site is successful, we could, after six months, build a Web-site business by switching to a license of the alternate viewer. The value of the Web business would be lower since the licensed viewer would not read files from existing notation software. I think we would sell the business to the owner of the other viewer in that case. We could probably get $300,000 for the sale, and remember, I only get a third of that.

Estes: Do you have any ideas on how to expand on the basic business if both the technology and Web site are successful after six months?

Bernard: One thing that came up in our conversations was to build upon our viewer's ability to read directly the files created by working composers. We thought about adding a capability for composers to upload their compositions to the Web site and earn either free copies of other works or royalties. This capability could be added after six months of operating a viable business. The on-line upload capability would take an additional $450,000 at the time the decision to expand was taken. I would put up my third of this money, and the other owners would find financing for their shares of it as well. The upload expansion would about double the value of the business (by the end of month 12 of operation) from its base level without the expanded capability. I think the decision to finance this expansion would be taken only if the venture showed a good EBITDA.[3] I know if the EBITDA were as much as $18,000 per month we would expand, maybe for less. I would make sure in our start-up agreements that I had the right to make the decision about whether to expand in this particular way.

Bouchek: I've now heard three grand ideas to add value to your venture. Let me add one more before dessert comes. This is based on something I've been wondering since you started talking about this business. Who has control in this business, and to what extent do you think these guys can make the right calls on running the company? Can you find a way to get more ownership and, perhaps, control if it is a viable business?

Bernard: One thing that worries me is that, if Chris and Mark get a working viewer, and quality Web-site content together, they may not have enough business skill to really develop and run the business. The thing is, they realize this also, unlike many founders. I believe they will agree to let me buy out some of their shares if the business works well—at least enough to give me control of the business and pick the management. Let's assume they would accept a clause in our start-up documents that would allow me to pay, say, $250,000, to buy 17 percent more of the company (giving me a controlling 50 1/3 percent share) 18 months from now. They'd be happy to get some cash

---

[3] Earnings before interest, taxes, depreciation, and amortization.

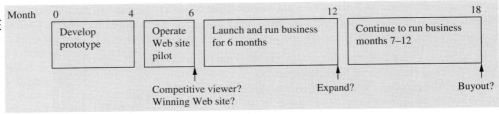

EXHIBIT **1**
SCOR-*e*STORE
timeline.

for their success and, at the same time, retain interest in the business.

Bouchek: That clause could give you a bargain price on what could, at that time, be very valuable shares, even without considering the extra worth of having a controlling interest. You're lucky that they would give you that. I'll tell you what: I'll pay for dinner if you let me have the deal.

Bernard: Well, I'm not going to give the deal away and I want to think more about the value of the ideas the four of you have given me. Let me say thanks to you all by taking care of the check.

Bernard picked up the paper napkin showing the timeline he had drawn while they spoke (Exhibit 1), said goodbye to his friends and drove home thinking that each idea he'd gotten from the dinner conversation could be worth hundreds of times the cost of dinner. Could there be other opportunities that he ought to consider as well? First, he would evaluate the current ideas. Tomorrow he would ask his newly minted MBA hire to develop a model to value a viable base business, starting after the six-month development period, assuming that both the viewer and Web site prove out (see Exhibit 2 for the spreadsheet model[4] that was produced). The two of them could then see how much incremental gain arose from each of the four ideas, over and above the value of the original opportunity he

had been ready to reject. The spreadsheet would be useful for those opportunities that arose after the business became viable. His usual approach was to value companies using a multiple of EBITDA. The analysis he envisioned would only go up to 18 months as he would definitely sell his interest at that point.

He felt confident that he could maintain decision-making control in return for putting up the money needed for each opportunity. The equal share ownership would not change if he actually carried out any of the ideas, except for Bouchek's buyout idea. He wondered whether $18,000 per month EBITDA was the right cutoff point for going ahead with the expansion and about how he would decide whether to purchase additional shares and control of the company. Control of a viable company was worth around $100,000 in and of itself, he thought. The valuation model would allow him to assess the value of each idea so he could revisit the decision about the basic investment opportunity.

Source: This case was prepared by Samuel E. Bodily, John Tyler Professor of Business Administration. It was written as a basis for class discussion rather than to illustrate effective or ineffective handling of an administrative situation. Copyright © by the University of Virginia Darden School Foundation, Charlottesville, VA. Rev. 7/04. All rights reserved. *To order copies, send an e-mail to sales@dardenbusinesspublishing.com. No part of this publication may be reproduced, stored in a retrieval system, used in a spreadsheet, or transmitted in any form or by any means—electronic, mechanical, photocopying, recording, or otherwise—without the permission of the Darden School Foundation.*

---

[4] The initial month of the spreadsheet ended 7 months from now and the final month ended 18 months from now. The spreadsheet used "page views" (the number of times visitors to the Web site viewed the company's home page), "conversion rate" (the percentage of page viewers who bought music), "margin per purchase" (the margin made when a purchase was made), net of all credit-card charges, and other variable costs. Initial page views, conversion rate, and margin were uncertain, and page views followed a random growth pattern over time. The company was valued as a multiple of EBITDA.

EXHIBIT **2**
Spreadsheet model of a viable Web site business, with formulas.

Scor-eStore Dot Com Business

Page Views Growth	60% annual
Page views sigma	0.55 annual volatility
Yearly EBITDA multiple	15.1

All numbers below in 000

	Initial	Month 2	Month 3	Month 4	Month 5	Month 6	Month 7	Month 8	Month 9	Month 10	Month 11	Month 12
Page Views	110.00	115.50	121.28	127.34	133.71	140.39	147.41	154.78	162.52	170.65	179.18	188.14
Conversion Rate	14%	14%	14%	14%	14%	14%	14%	14%	14%	14%	14%	14%
Margin per purchase	$ 0.88	$ 0.88	$ 0.88	$ 0.88	$ 0.88	$ 0.88	$ 0.88	$ 0.88	$ 0.88	$ 0.88	$ 0.88	$ 0.88
Monthly operating cost	5.27	5.27	5.27	5.27	5.27	5.27	5.27	5.27	5.27	5.27	5.27	5.27
EBITDA	$ 8.28	$ 8.96	$ 9.67	$ 10.42	$ 11.20	$ 12.03	$ 12.89	$ 13.80	$ 14.75	$ 15.75	$ 16.80	$ 17.91
Valuation	$ 1,501	$ 1,623	$ 1,752	$ 1,888	$ 2,030	$ 2,179	$ 2,336	$ 2,500	$ 2,673	$ 2,855	$ 3,045	$ 3,245

@RISK formulas

	A	B	C
1	Scor-eStore Dot Com Business		
2	Page Views Growth	0.6	annual
3	Page Views Sigma	0.55	annual volatility
4	Yearly EBITDA multiple	15.1	
5		Initial	Month 2
6	Page Views	=RiskTriang(90,110,130)	=B6+B6*(Page_Views_Growth*(1/12)+Page_views_sigma*SQRT(1/12)* RiskNormal(0,1))
7	Conversion Rate	=RiskTriang(0.08,0.14,0.2)	=$B$7
8	Margin per purchase	0.88	=B8+RiskNormal(0,0.08)
9	Monthly operating cost	=RiskTriang(4.54,5.27,6)	=B9
10	EBITDA	=Page_Views*Conversion_Rate*Margin_per_purchase-Monthly_operating_cost	=Page_Views*Conversion_Rate*Margin_per_purchase-Monthly_operating_cost
11	Valuation	=MAX(0,Yearly_EBITDA_multiple*12*EBITDA)	=MAX(0,Yearly_EBITDA_multiple*12*EBITDA)

SECTION 3

Modeling Preferences

We have come a long way since the first chapters. The first part of the book talked about structuring problems, and the second discussed modeling uncertainty through the use of probability. Now we turn to the problem of modeling preferences.

Why should we worry about modeling preferences? Because virtually every decision involves some kind of trade-off. In decision making under uncertainty, the fundamental trade-off question often is, How much risk is a decision maker willing to assume? After all, expected monetary value is not everything! Often the alternative that has the greatest EMV also involves the greatest risk.

Chapters 14 and 15 look at the role of risk attitudes in decision making. In Chapter 14, basic concepts are presented, and you will learn how to model your own risk attitude. We will develop the concept of a utility function. Modeling your preferences by assessing your utility function is a subjective procedure much like assessing subjective probabilities. Because a utility function incorporates a decision maker's attitude toward risk, the decision maker may decide to choose the alternative that maximizes his or her expected utility rather than expected monetary value.

Chapter 15 discusses some of the foundations that underlie the use of utility functions. The essential reason for choosing alternatives to maximize expected utility is that such behavior is consistent with some fundamental choice and behavior patterns that we call axioms. The paradox is that, even though most of us agree that intuitively the axioms are reasonable, there are cases for all of us when our actual choices are not consistent with the axioms. In many situations these inconsistencies have little effect on a decision maker's choices. But occasionally they can cause trouble, and we will discuss some of these difficulties and their implications.

Dealing with risk attitudes is an important aspect of decision making under uncertainty, but it is only part of the picture. As we discussed in Section 1, many problems involve conflicting objectives. Decision makers must balance many different aspects of the problem and try to accomplish many things at once. Even a simple decision such as deciding where to go for dinner involves trade-offs: How far are you willing to drive? How much should you spend? How badly do you want Chinese food?

Chapters 16 and 17 deal with modeling preferences in situations in which the decision maker has multiple and conflicting objectives. In both chapters, one of the fundamental subjective assessments that the decision maker must make is how to trade off achievement in one dimension against achievement in another. Chapter 16 presents a relatively straight-forward approach that is easy and intuitive, extending the introductory approach presented in Chapters 3 and 4. Chapter 17 extends the discussion to include interactions between objectives. What if what you would prefer on one dimension depends on what you choose on another one? For example, what you would like to have for dinner might depend on where you decide to eat; if you go to a top French restaurant, you might not want to order a hamburger, although that's exactly what you might prefer at a fast-food restaurant. Chapter 17 introduces some ways to model conflicting objectives to account for such preferences, especially when the outcomes are unknown.

CHAPTER 14

Risk Attitudes

WITH CONTRIBUTIONS BY JEFFERY GUYSE

This chapter marks the beginning of our in-depth study of preferences. Before we begin, let us review where we have been and think about where we are going. The first six chapters provided an introduction to the process of structuring decision problems for decision analysis and an overview of the role that probability and preference modeling play in making choices. Chapters 7 through 13 have focused on probability concerns: using probability in a variety of ways to model uncertainty in decision problems, including the modeling of information sources and real options.

At this point, we change directions and look at the preference side of decision analysis. How can we model a decision maker's preferences? This chapter looks at the problems associated with risk and return trade-offs and introduces an approach called *utility theory* that allows us to incorporate the riskiness of an alternative when deciding on the best course of action. For example, in Chapter 11, Leah Sanchez could determine how many calendars to order if she wanted to maximize expected monetary value (EMV), but what if she wanted to minimize her risk as well as maximize her return? As we noted in that example, each order quantity had its own level of risk. For Leah, what order quantity would best balance return—her EMV—against the risk she would take?

Chapter 14 develops the basic tools of utility theory for risky decision making. Chapter 15 briefly explores the axiomatic foundations of utility theory and discusses certain paradoxes from cognitive psychology. These paradoxes generally indicate that people do not make choices that are perfectly consistent with the axioms, even though they may agree that the

---

Jeffery Guyse, Professor of Technology and Operations Management at California State Polytechnic University, Pomona contributed to the behavioral and psychological aspects of this chapter.

axioms are reasonable! Although such inconsistencies generally do not have serious implications for most decisions, there are certain occasions when they can cause difficulty.

The primary motivating example for this chapter comes from the history of railways in the United States. Imagine what might have gone through E. H. Harriman's mind as he considered his strategy for acquiring the Northern Pacific Railroad in March 1901.

E. H. Harriman Fights for the Northern Pacific Railroad

"How could they do it?" E. H. Harriman asked, still angry over the fact that James Hill and J. P. Morgan had bought the Burlington Railroad out from under his nose. "Every U.S. industrialist knows I control the railroads in the West. I have the Illinois Central, the Union Pacific, the Central and Southern Pacific, not to mention the Oregon Railroad and Navigation Company. Isn't that true?"

"Yes, sir," replied his assistant.

"Well, we will put the pressure on Messrs. Hill and Morgan. They will be surprised indeed to find out that I have acquired a controlling interest in their own railroad, the Northern Pacific. I may even be able to persuade them to let me have the Burlington. By the way, how are the stock purchases going?"

"Sir, we have completed all of the purchases that you authorized so far. You may have noticed that our transactions have driven the price of Northern Pacific stock up to more than $100 per share."

Harriman considered this information. If he bought too fast, he could force the stock price up high enough and fast enough that Hill might begin to suspect that Harriman was up to something. Of course, if Harriman could acquire the shares quickly enough, there would be no problem. On the other hand, if he bought the shares slowly, he would pay lower prices, and Hill might not notice the acquisition until it was too late. His assistant's information, however, suggested that his situation was somewhat risky. If Harriman's plan were discovered, Hill could persuade Morgan to purchase enough additional Northern Pacific shares to enable them to retain control. In that case, Harriman would have paid premium prices for the stock for nothing! On the other hand, if Hill did not make the discovery immediately, the triumph would be that much sweeter.

"How many more shares do we need to have control?" asked Harriman.

"If you could purchase another 40,000 shares, sir, you would own 51% of the company."

Another 40,000 shares. Harriman thought about giving Hill and Morgan orders on how to run their own railroad. How enjoyable that would be! Yes, he would gladly increase his investment by that much.

"Of course," his assistant continued, "if we try to purchase these shares immediately, the price will rise very quickly. You will probably end up paying an additional $15 per share above what you would pay if we were to proceed more slowly."

"Well, $600,000 is a lot of money, and I certainly would not want to pay more. But it would be worth the money to be sure that we would be able to watch Hill and Morgan squirm! Send a telegram to my broker in New York right away to place the order. And be quick! It's already Friday. If we are going to do this, we need to do it today. I don't want Hill to have the chance to think about this over the weekend."

RISK

Basing decisions on expected monetary values (EMVs) is convenient, but it can lead to decisions that may not seem intuitively appealing. For example, consider the following two games:

> **Game 1:** Win $30 with probability 0.5
>
> Lose $1 with probability 0.5
>
> **Game 2:** Win $2,000 with probability 0.5
>
> Lose $1,900 with probability 0.5

Imagine that you have the opportunity to play one game or the other, but only one time. Which one would you prefer to play? Your choice also is drawn in decision-tree form in Figure 14.1.

Game 1 has an expected value of $14.50. Game 2, on the other hand, has an expected value of $50. If you were to make your choice on the basis of expected value, you would choose Game 2. Most of us, however, would consider Game 2 to be riskier than Game 1, and it seems reasonable to suspect that most people actually would prefer Game 1. This is an example where what we actually prefer differs from maximizing EMV.

Why this discrepancy? Simply put: The possibility of losing $1,900 in Game 2 is very unappealing, and perhaps even frightening. Using expected values or EMV to make decisions means that the decision maker is considering only the average or expected payoff. If we take a long-run frequency approach, the expected value is the average amount we would be likely to

FIGURE **14.1**
Two lottery games.

Which game would you choose?

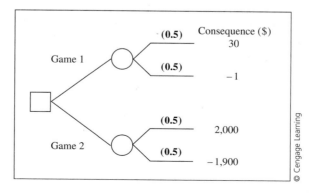

win over many plays of the game. But the long-run average ignores the range of possible values. After all, if we play each game ten times, the worst we could do in Game 1 is to lose $10. On the other hand, the worst we could do in Game 2 is lose $19,000!

Many of the examples and problems that we have considered so far have been analyzed in terms of EMV. However, EMV does not capture risk attitudes. For example, consider the Texaco-Pennzoil example in Chapter 4. If Hugh Liedtke were afraid of the prospect that Pennzoil could end up with nothing at the end of the court case, he might be willing to take the $2 billion that Texaco offered. Or consider the House Hunting example in Chapter 5, where purchasing the Barnard Street property is a much riskier alternative than Astoria. Sarah and Sanjay were quite concerned with the risk associated with the Barnard house, noting that Barnard could "quickly bankrupt them." Even someone like E. H. Harriman considered the riskiness of the situations in which he found himself. In our fictionalized example, Harriman weighed the value of a riskless alternative (immediately purchasing the 40,000 shares that were required to gain control) against the risky alternative of not purchasing the shares and the possible outcomes that might then follow. Even though all of the dollar amounts were not specified, it is clear that Harriman was not thinking solely in terms of EMV.

Individuals who are afraid of risk or are sensitive to risk are said to be *risk-averse*. We can explain risk aversion if we think in terms of a *utility function* (Figure 14.2) that is curved and opening downward (the technical term for a curve with this shape is *concave*). This utility function represents a way to translate dollars into "utility units." That is, if we take some dollar amount (x), we can locate that amount on the horizontal axis. Read up to the curve and then horizontally across to the vertical axis, where we read off the utility value U(x) for the dollars we started with.

A utility function might be specified in terms of a graph, as in Figure 14.2, or given as a table, as in Table 14.1. A third form is a mathematical expression. If graphed, for example, all of the following expressions would have the

FIGURE **14.2**
A utility function that displays risk aversion.

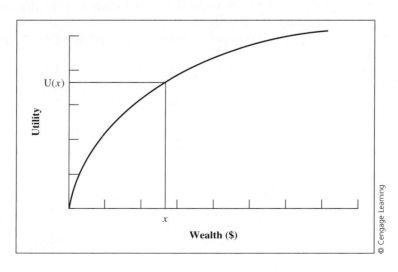

© Cengage Learning

TABLE **14.1**
A utility function
in tabular form.

Wealth ($)	Utility Value
$2,500	1.50
$1,500	1.24
$1,000	0.93
$600	0.65
$400	0.47
$0	0.15

same general concave shape (opening downward) as the utility function graphed in Figure 14.2:

$$U(x) = \log(x)$$
$$U(x) = 1 - e^{1-x/R}$$
$$U(x) = +\sqrt{x} \qquad [\text{or } U(x) = x^{0.5}]$$

Of course, the utility and dollar values in Table 14.1 also could be graphed, as could the functional forms previously shown. Likewise, the graph in Figure 14.2 could be converted into a table of values. The point is that the utility function makes the translation from dollars to utility regardless of its displayed form.

RISK ATTITUDES

We think of a typical utility curve as (1) upward sloping and (2) concave. An upward-sloping utility curve makes fine sense; it means that more wealth is better than less wealth, everything else being equal. Few people will argue with this. Concavity in a utility curve implies that an individual is risk-averse.

Imagine that you are forced to play the following game:

Win $500 with probability 0.5

Lose $500 with probability 0.5

Would you pay to get out of this situation? How much? The game has a zero expected value, so if you would pay something to get out, you are avoiding a risky situation with zero expected value. Generally, if you would trade a gamble for a sure amount that is less than the expected value of the gamble, you are risk-averse.

Purchasing insurance is an example of risk-averse behavior. Insurance companies analyze a lot of data in order to understand the probability distributions associated with claims for different kinds of policies. Of course, this work is costly. To make up these costs and still have an expected profit, an

FIGURE **14.3**
Three different shapes for utility functions.

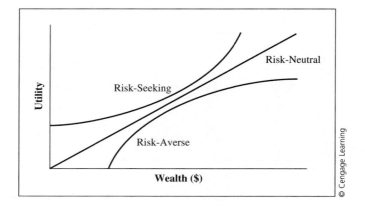

insurance company must charge more for its insurance policy than the policy can be expected to produce in claims. Thus, unless you have some reason to believe that you are more likely than others in your risk group to make a claim, you probably are paying more in insurance premiums than the expected amount you would claim.

Not everyone displays risk-averse behavior all the time, and so utility curves need not be concave. A convex (opening upward) utility curve indicates risk-seeking behavior (Figure 14.3). The risk seeker might be eager to enter into a gamble; for example, he or she might pay to play the game just described. An individual who plays a state lottery exhibits risk-seeking behavior. State lottery tickets typically cost $1 and have an expected value of approximately 50 cents.

Finally, an individual can be risk-neutral. Risk neutrality is reflected by a utility curve that is simply a straight line. For this type of person, maximizing EMV is the same as maximizing expected utility. This makes sense; someone who is risk-neutral does not care about risk and can ignore risk aspects of the alternatives that he or she faces. Thus, EMV is a fine criterion for choosing among alternatives, because it also ignores risk.

Although most of us are not risk-neutral, it often is reasonable for a decision maker to assume that his or her utility curve is nearly linear in the range of dollar amounts for a particular decision. This is especially true for large corporations that make decisions involving amounts which are small relative to their total assets. In many cases, it may be worthwhile to use EMV in a first-cut analysis, and then check to see whether the decision would be sensitive to changes in risk attitude. If the decision turns out to be fairly sensitive (that is, if the decision would change for a slightly risk-averse or slightly risk-seeking person), then the decision maker may want to consider modeling his or her risk attitude carefully.

This discussion makes it sound as though individuals can be reduced to their utility functions, and those utility functions can reveal whether the individual is risk-averse or risk-seeking. Keep in mind, however, that the utility function is only a model of an individual's attitude toward risk. Moreover, our development of utility functions in this chapter is intended to help with the modeling of risk attitudes at a fundamental level, and our model may not be able to capture certain complicated psychological aspects. For example, some individuals may be extremely frightened by risk. Others may find that small wagers greatly increase their enjoyment in watching a sporting event, for example. Still others may find that waiting for the uncertainty to be resolved is a source of excitement and exhilaration, although concern about losing money is a source of anxiety. For some people, figuring out exactly what their feelings are toward risky alternatives may be extremely complicated and may depend on the amount at stake, the context of the risk, and the time horizon.

INVESTING IN THE STOCK MARKET, REVISITED

If we have a utility function that translates from dollars to utility, how should we use it? The whole idea of a utility function is that it should help to choose among alternatives that have uncertain payoffs. Instead of maximizing expected value, the decision maker should maximize expected utility. In a decision tree or influence-diagram payoff table, the net dollar payoffs would be replaced by the corresponding utility values and the analysis performed using those values. The best choice then should be the action with the highest expected utility.

As an example, let us reconsider the stock market–investment example from Chapters 5 and 12. You will recall that an investor has funds that he wishes to invest. He has three choices: a high-risk stock, a low-risk stock, or a savings account that would pay $500. If he invests in the stocks, he must pay a $200 brokerage fee.

With the two stocks, his payoff depends on what happens to the market. If the market goes up, he will earn $1,700 from the high-risk stock and $1,200 from the low-risk stock. If the market stays at the same level, his payoffs for the high- and low-risk stocks will be $300 and $400, respectively. Finally, if the stock market goes down, he will lose $800 with the high-risk stock but still earn $100 from the low-risk stock. The probabilities that the market will go up, stay the same, or go down are 0.5, 0.3, and 0.2, respectively.

Figure 14.4 shows his decision tree, including the brokerage fee and the payoffs for the two stocks under different market conditions. Note that the values at

FIGURE **14.4**
Decision tree for the stock market investor.

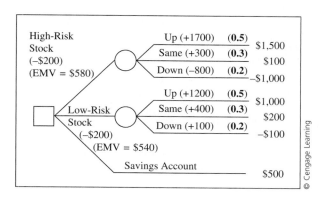

TABLE 14.2
Utility function for the investment problem.

Dollar Value	Utility Value
$1,500	1.00
$1,000	0.86
$500	0.65
$200	0.52
$100	0.46
−$100	0.33
−$1,000	0.00

© Cengage Learning

the ends of the branches are the *net* payoffs, taking into account both the brokerage fee and the investment payoff. Table 14.2 gives his utility function.

We have already calculated the expected values of the three investments in Chapter 12. They are:

EMV(High-Risk Stock) = $580

EMV(Low-Risk Stock) = $540

EMV(Savings Account) = $500

As a result, an expected-value maximizer would choose the high-risk stock.

Figure 14.5 shows the investor's decision tree with the utility values instead of the payoffs. Solving this decision tree, we calculate the expected utility (EU) for the three investments:

EU(High-Risk Stock) = 0.638

EU(Low-Risk Stock) = 0.652

EU(Savings Account) = 0.650

Now the preferred action is to invest in the low-risk stock because it provides the highest EU, although it does not differ much from that for the savings

FIGURE 14.5
Decision tree for stock market investor—utility values instead of dollars.

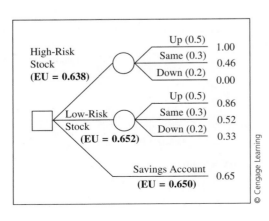

account. You can see how the EUs make it possible to rank these investments in order of preference. According to the utility function we are using, this investor dislikes risk enough to find the high-risk stock the least preferred of his three alternatives.

EXPECTED UTILITY, CERTAINTY EQUIVALENTS, AND RISK PREMIUMS

When working with utility functions, we run into a problem of interpretation. Referring back to the investment example, we found that the low-risk stock had the greatest EU, but what does it mean to say its EU equals 0.652? We do not have a ready interpretation of a unit of utility. Even more problematic is trying to interpret the difference between EUs. We saw that the EU of the savings account was a "close" second at 0.650, only 0.002 utility units less than the low-risk stock. But what does that difference of 0.002 mean?

An elegant solution to interpreting utility is to come full circle and translate the EUs back to dollars. In other words, after calculating EUs, use the utility function to translate each EU back to its corresponding dollar value. The dollar value associated with an EU is called its *certainty equivalent*—some decision analysts use the term *certain equivalent*—because it is the amount of money that is equivalent in your mind to a given situation that involves uncertainty. For example, suppose you face the following gamble:

Win $2,000 with probability 0.50

Lose $20 with probability 0.50

Now imagine that one of your friends is interested in taking your place. "Sure," you reply, "I'll sell it to you." After thought and discussion, you conclude that the least you would sell your position for is $300. If your friend cannot pay that much, then you would rather keep the gamble. (Of course, if your friend were to offer more, you would take it!)

Your certainty equivalent for the gamble is $300. The $300 is a sure thing; no risk is involved. From this, the meaning of certainty equivalent becomes clear. If $300 is the least that you would accept for the gamble, then the gamble must be equivalent in your mind to a sure $300.

In the example at the beginning of the chapter, Harriman decided that he would pay the additional $600,000 simply to avoid the riskiness of the situation. His thinking at the time was that committing the additional money would ensure his control of the Northern Pacific Railroad. He indicated that he did not want to pay more, and so we can think of $600,000 as his certainty equivalent for the gamble of purchasing the shares more slowly and risking detection.

Let us again consider the stock market investor. We can make some inferences about his certainty equivalent for the gambles represented by the low-risk and high-risk stocks because we have information about his utility function. For example, his EU for the low-risk stock is 0.652, which is just a shade more than U($500) = 0.650. Thus, his certainty equivalent (CE) for the low-risk stock must be only a little more than $500. Likewise, his EU for the high-risk stock is 0.638, which is somewhat less than 0.650. Therefore, his CE for the high-risk stock must be less than $500 but not as little as $200, which has a utility of 0.520.

You can see also that we can rank the investments by their CEs. The high-risk stock, having the lowest CE, is the least preferred. The low-risk stock, on the other hand, has the highest CE, and so it is the most preferred. Ranking alternatives by their CEs is the same as ranking them by their EUs. If two alternatives have the same CE, they must have the same EU, and the decision maker would be indifferent between the two.

Closely related to the idea of a CE is the notion of *risk premium*. The risk premium is defined as the difference between the EMV and the CE:

$$\text{Risk Premium} = \text{EMV} - \text{CE}$$

Note that the risk premium is also a dollar value, making it easy to interpret. Consider the gamble between winning $2,000 and losing $20, each with probability 0.50. The EMV of this gamble is $990. On reflection, you assessed your CE to be $300, and so your risk premium is

$$\text{Risk Premium} = \$990 - \$300$$
$$= \$690$$

Because you were willing to trade the gamble for $300, you were willing to "give up" $690 in expected value in order to avoid the risk inherent in the gamble. You can think of the risk premium as the premium you pay (in the sense of a lost opportunity) to avoid the risk.

Figure 14.6 graphically ties together utility functions, CEs, and risk premiums. Notice that the CE and the EU of a gamble are points that are "matched up" by the utility function. That is,

$$\text{EU(Gamble)} = \text{U(CE)}.$$

In words, the utility of the CE is equal to the EU of the gamble. Because these two quantities are equal, the decision maker must be indifferent to the choice between them. After all, that is the meaning of CE.

Now we can put all of the pieces together in Figure 14.6. Imagine a gamble that has EU equal to Y. The value Y is in utility units, so we must first locate Y on the vertical axis. Trace a horizontal line from the EU point until the line intersects the utility curve. Now drop down to the horizontal axis to find the CE. The difference between the expected value of the gamble and the CE is the risk premium.

For a risk-averse individual, the horizontal EU line reaches the concave utility curve before it reaches the vertical line that corresponds to the expected

FIGURE **14.6**
Graphical repre-
sentation of risk
premium.

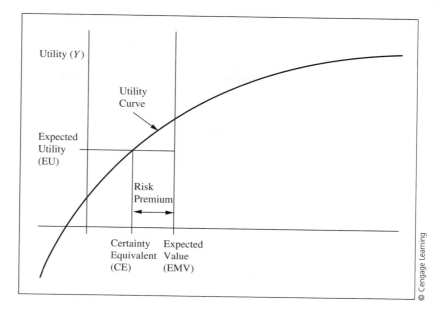

value. Thus, for a risk-averse individual, the risk premium must be positive. If the utility function were convex, the horizontal EU line would reach the expected value before the utility curve. The CE would be greater than the expected value, and so the risk premium would be negative. This would imply that the decision maker would have to be paid to give up an opportunity to gamble.

In any given situation, the CE, expected value, and risk premium all depend on two factors: the decision maker's utility function and the probability distribution for the payoffs. The values that the payoff can take combine with the probabilities to determine the EMV. The utility function, coupled with the probability distribution, determines the EU and hence the CE. The degree to which the utility curve is nonlinear determines the distance between the CE and the expected payoff.

If the CE for a gamble is assessed directly, then finding the risk premium is straightforward—simply calculate the EMV of the gamble and subtract the assessed CE. In other cases, the decision maker may have assessed a utility function and then faces a particular gamble that he or she wishes to analyze. If so, there are four steps in finding the gamble's risk premium:

1. Calculate the EU for the gamble.
2. Find the CE, or the sure amount that has the utility value equal to the EU that was found in Step 1.
3. Calculate the EMV for the gamble.
4. Subtract the CE from the EMV to find the risk premium. This is the difference between the expected value of the risky situation and the sure amount for which the risky situation would be traded.

FIGURE **14.7**
Utility function for
a risk-averse
decision maker.

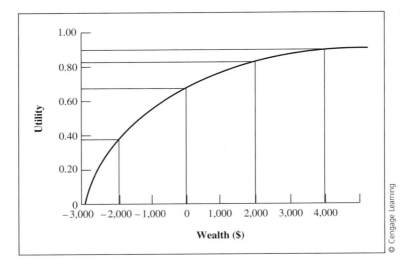

Here is a simple example. Using the hypothetical utility function given in Figure 14.7, we will find the risk premium for the following gamble:

Win $4,000 with probability	0.40
Win $2,000 with probability	0.20
Win $0 with probability	0.15
Lose $2,000 with probability	0.25

The first step is to find the EU:

$$EU = 0.40\ U(\$4,000) + 0.20\ U(\$2,000) + 0.15\ U(\$0) + 0.25\ U(-\$2,000)$$
$$= 0.40(0.90) + 0.20(0.82) + 0.15(0.67) + 0.25(0.38)$$
$$= 0.72$$

The second line is simply a matter of estimating the utilities from Figure 14.7 and substituting them into the equation.

For Step 2, the CE is the sure amount that gives the same utility as the EU of the gamble. Figure 14.8 shows the process of finding the CE for the gamble that has EU = 0.72. We start at the vertical axis with the utility value of 0.72, read across to the utility curve, and then drop down to the horizontal axis. From Figure 14.8, we can see that the CE is approximately $400.

Step 3 calculates the expected payoff or EMV:

$$EMV = 0.40(\$4,000) + 0.20(\$2,000) + 0.15(\$0) + 0.25(-\$2,000)$$
$$= \$1,500$$

Finally, in Step 4, we calculate the risk premium by subtracting the CE from the EMV:

$$Risk\ Premium = \$1,500 - \$400 = \$1,100.$$

FIGURE **14.8**
Finding a certainty
equivalent.

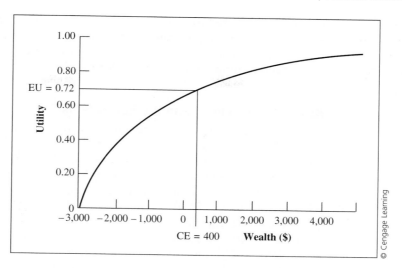

KEEPING TERMS STRAIGHT

Students often confuse the terms we use in utility theory. The basic idea, remember, is to use a utility function to translate dollars into utility units. If we compare two risky projects on the basis of EU, we are working in utility units. When we calculate CEs or risk premiums, however, we are working in dollars. Thus, a CE is not the same as the EU of a gamble. The two measurements provide equivalent information, but only in the sense that the CE for a gamble is the sure amount that gives the same utility as the EU of the gamble. The translation from CE to EU and back again is through the utility function, as depicted in Figures 14.6 and 14.8. Again, a CE is a dollar amount, whereas EU is in utility units. Be careful to use these terms consistently.

UTILITY FUNCTION ASSESSMENT

Different people have different risk attitudes and thus are willing to accept various levels of risk. Some are more prone to taking risks, while others are more conservative and avoid risk. Thus, assessing a utility function is a matter of subjective judgment, just like assessing subjective probabilities. In this section, we will look at two utility-assessment approaches that are based on the idea of CEs. The following section introduces an alternative approach.

It is worth repeating at this point our credo about modeling and decision making. Remember that the objective of the decision-analysis exercise is to help you make a better decision. To do this, we construct a model, or representation, of the decision. When we assess a utility function, we are constructing a mathematical model or representation of preferences. This representation then is included in the overall model of the decision problem and is used to analyze the situation at hand. The objective is to find a way to represent preferences that incorporates risk attitudes. A perfect representation is not necessary. All that is required is a model that represents feelings about risk well enough to understand and analyze the current decision.

Assessment Using Certainty Equivalents

The first assessment method requires the decision maker to assess several CEs. Suppose you face an uncertain situation in which the payoff is $10 in the worst case, $100 in the best case, or possibly something in between. You have a variety of options, each of which leads to an uncertain payoff between $10 and $100. To evaluate the alternatives, you must assess your utility for payoffs from $10 to $100.

We can get the first two points of your utility function by arbitrarily setting U($100) = 1 and U($10) = 0. This may seem a bit strange but is easily explained. The idea of the utility function, remember, is to rank-order risky situations. We can always take any utility function and rescale it—add a constant and multiply by a positive constant—so that the best outcome has a utility of 1 and the worst has a utility of 0. The rank ordering of risky situations in terms of EU will be the same for both the original and rescaled utility functions. What we are doing here is taking advantage of this ability to rescale. We are beginning the assessment process by setting two utility points. The remaining assessments then will be consistent with the scale set by these points. (We could just as well set the endpoints at 100 and 0, or 100 and −50, say. We are using 1 and 0 because this choice of endpoints turns out to be particularly convenient. But we will have to be careful not to confuse these utilities with probabilities!)

Now imagine that you have the opportunity to play the following lottery, which we will call a *reference lottery*:

Win $100 with probability 0.5

Win $10 with probability 0.5

What is the minimum amount for which you would be willing to sell your opportunity to play this game? $25? $30? $110? Your job is to find your CE for this reference gamble. A decision tree for your choice is shown in Figure 14.9.

FIGURE **14.9**
A "reference gamble" for assessing a utility function.

Your job is to find the CE so that you are indifferent between options A and B.

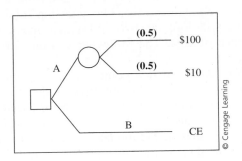

© Cengage Learning

Your subjective judgment comes into play when finding your CE. The CE undoubtedly will vary from person to person. Suppose that for this reference gamble your CE is $30. That is, for $31 you would take the money, but for $29 you would rather play the lottery; $30 must be your true indifference point.

The key to the rest of the analysis is this: *Because you are indifferent between $30 and the risky gamble, the utility of $30 must equal the EU of the gamble.* We know the utilities of $10 and $100, so we can figure out the EU of the gamble:

$$U(\$30) = 0.5 \, U(\$100) + 0.5 \, U(\$10)$$

$$= 0.5(1) + 0.5(0)$$

$$= 0.5$$

We have found a third point on your utility curve. To find another, take a different reference lottery:

Win $100 with probability 0.5

Win $30 with probability 0.5

Now find your CE for this new gamble. Again, the CE will vary from person to person, but suppose that you settle on $50. We can do exactly what we did before, but with the new gamble. In this case, we can find the utility of $50 because we know U($100) and U($30) from the previous assessment.

$$U(\$50) = 0.5 \, U(\$100) + 0.5 \, U(\$30)$$

$$= 0.5(1) + 0.5(0.5)$$

$$= 0.75$$

This is the fourth point on your utility curve.

Now consider the reference lottery:

Win $30 with probability 0.5

Win $10 with probability 0.5

Again you must assess your CE for this gamble. Suppose it turns out to be $18. Now we can do the familiar calculations:

$$U(\$18) = 0.5 \, U(\$30) + 0.5 \, U(\$10)$$

$$= 0.5(0.5) + 0.5(0)$$

$$= 0.25$$

We now have five points on your utility curve, and we can graph and draw a curve through them. The graph is shown in Figure 14.10. A smooth curve drawn through the assessed points should be an adequate representation of your utility function for use in solving your decision problem.

FIGURE **14.10**
Graph of the utility function assessed using the certainty equivalent approach.

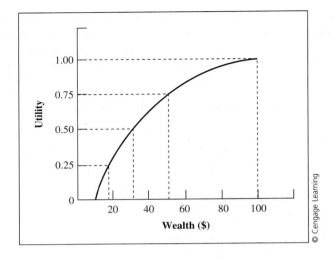

Assessment Using Probabilities

The CE approach described above requires that you find a dollar amount that makes you indifferent between the gamble and the sure thing in Figure 14.9. Another approach involves specifying the sure amount in Alternative B and adjusting the probability in the reference gamble to achieve indifference. We will call this the *probability-equivalent* (PE) assessment technique.

For example, suppose you want to know your utility for $65. This is not one of the CEs that you assessed, and thus U($65) is unknown. You could make an educated guess. Based on the previous assessments and the graph in Figure 14.10, U($65) must be between 0.75 and 1.00; it probably is around 0.85. But rather than guess, you can assess the value directly. Consider the reference lottery:

Win $100 with probability p

Win $10 with probability $(1 - p)$

This gamble is shown in Figure 14.11.

To find your utility value for $65, adjust p until you are indifferent between the sure $65 and the reference gamble. That is, think about various

FIGURE **14.11**
A reference gamble for assessing the utility of $65 using the probability-equivalent method.

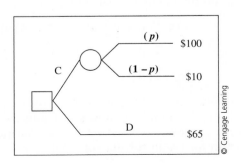

probabilities that make the chance of winning $100 greater or less until you are indifferent between Alternatives C and D in Figure 14.11. Now you can find U($65) because you know that U($100) = 1 and U($10) = 0.

$$U(\$65) = p\, U(\$100) + (1 - p)\, U(\$10)$$

$$= p(1) + (1 - p)(0)$$

$$= p$$

The probability that makes you indifferent just happens to be your utility value for $65. For example, if you chose $p = 0.87$ to achieve indifference, then U($65) = 0.87.

Assessment Using Tradeoffs

We have seen that we can assess a utility function by using the CE and PE methods. Recently, Peter Wakker and Daniel Deneffe (1996) proposed a new method for eliciting utilities, which they call the tradeoff method (TO). Let's apply this method to our current problem, where we choose a pair of "reference" outcomes (let's try $50 and $100) and a minimal outcome, like $10. Now ask yourself what amount of money ($$X_1$) would make you indifferent between the following two gambles:

A₁   Win $50 with probability 0.5

         Win X_1 with probability 0.5

A₂   Win $100 with probability 0.5

         Win $10 with probability 0.5

What value for X_1 would make you indifferent? Not $10, because the second gamble would make you just as well off 50% of the time and better off (by $50) the other 50% of the time. So it must be a number greater than $10, right? By similar reasoning (recall our discussion of dominance from Chapter 4), it must also be less than $100. Let's say you are indifferent between the two lotteries when $X_1 = \$40$.

For the next step, repeat the same procedure, but replacing the minimum outcome of $10 used in A₂ with the $40 elicited previously to get the following:

B₁   Win $50 with probability 0.5

         Win X_2 with probability 0.5

B₂   Win $100 with probability 0.5

         Win $40 with probability 0.5

Now your task is to find the value of X_2 that makes you indifferent between B₁ and B₂. Let's say you are indifferent when $X_2 = \$90$. From this we can infer U($90) = 2U($40). (Can you see why? See Problem 14.34.) Repeat this procedure again to get $U(X_3) = 3U(X_1)$. Continue in the same vein to get $U(X_4) = 4U(X_1)$, $U(X_5) = 5U(X_1)$, and so on, up to $U(X_N) = NU(X_1)$. (N may not be that big – you may need only a few assessments to cover the range.) By setting the utility of the minimum outcome X_0 ($10 in our example) equal to $U(X_0) = 0$, and letting $U(X_1) = 1/N$, we have $U(X_0) = 0, U(X_1) = 1/N, U(X_2) = 2/N, \ldots, U(X_N) = 1$.

Gambles, Lotteries, and Investments

As with the assessment of subjective probabilities, we have framed utility assessment in terms of gambles or lotteries. For many individuals doing so evokes images of carnival games or gambling in a casino, images that may seem irrelevant to the decision at hand or even distasteful. An alternative is to think in terms of investments that are risky. Instead of asking whether you would accept or reject a particular gamble, think about whether you would make a particular investment. Would you agree to invest in a security with a p chance of yielding $1,000 and a $1 - p$ chance of yielding nothing? How much would you be willing to pay for such a security? Framing your utility-assessment questions in this way may help you to think more clearly about your utility, especially for investment decisions.

RISK TOLERANCE AND THE EXPONENTIAL UTILITY FUNCTION

The CE, PE, and TO methods described previously work well for assessing a utility function subjectively, and they can be used in any situation. However, they can involve a fair number of assessments. Another approach is to base the assessment on a particular mathematical function, such as one of those that we introduced early in the chapter. In particular, let us consider the *exponential utility function*:

$$U(x) = 1 - e^{-x/R}$$

This utility function is based on the constant $e = 2.71828\ldots$, the base of natural logarithms, and it has a few useful properties. As mentioned previously, it is concave, and so it can be used to model risk aversion. In addition, as x increases, $U(x)$ approaches 1. The utility of zero, $U(0)$, is equal to 0, and the utility for negative x (being in debt) is negative.

In the exponential utility function, R is the parameter that determines how concave the utility function is, which in turn reflects how risk averse the decision maker is. We call R the *risk tolerance*. Greater values of R make the exponential utility function flatter, while smaller values make it more concave or more risk-averse. Thus, if you are less risk-averse—if you can tolerate more risk—you would assess a greater value for R to obtain a flatter utility function. If you are less toler-ant of risk, you would assess a smaller R and have a more curved utility function.

How can R be determined? A variety of ways exist, but it turns out that R has a very intuitive interpretation that makes its assessment relatively easy. Consider the gamble

Win Y with probability 0.5

Lose $Y/2$ with probability 0.5

Would you be willing to take this gamble if Y were $100? $2,000? $35,000? Or, framing it as an investment, how much would you be willing to risk ($Y/2$) in order to have a 50% chance of tripling your money (winning Y and

FIGURE **14.12**

Assessing your risk tolerance.

Find the greatest value of Y for which you would prefer Alternative E.

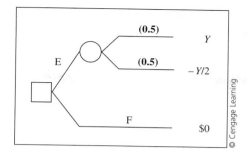

keeping your $Y/2$)? At what point would the risk become intolerable? The decision tree is shown in Figure 14.12.

The greatest value of Y for which you would prefer to take the gamble rather than not take it is approximately equal to your risk tolerance. This is the value that you can use for R in your exponential utility function. For example, suppose that after considering the decision tree in Figure 14.12 you conclude that the greatest Y for which you would take the gamble is $Y = \$900$. Hence, $R = \$900$. Using this assessment in the exponential utility function would result in the utility function

$$U(x) = 1 - e^{-x/900}$$

This exponential utility function provides the translation from dollars to utility units.

Once you have your R value and your exponential utility function, it is fairly easy to find CEs. For example, suppose that you face the following gamble:

Win $2,000 with probability 0.4

Win $1,000 with probability 0.4

Win $500 with probability 0.2

The EU for this gamble is

$$EU = 0.4\ U(\$2{,}000) + 0.4\ U(\$1{,}000) + 0.2\ U(\$500)$$
$$= 0.4(0.8916) + 0.4(0.6708) + 0.2(0.4262)$$
$$= 0.7102$$

To find the CE, we must work backward through the utility function. We want to find the value x such that $U(x) = 0.7102$. Set up the equation

$$0.7102 = 1 - e^{-x/900}$$

Subtract 1 from each side to get

$$-0.2898 = -e^{-x/900}$$

Multiply through to eliminate the minus signs:

$$0.2898 = e^{-x/900}$$

Now we can take natural logs of both sides to eliminate the exponential term:

$$\ln(0.2898) = \ln(e^{-x/900}) = \frac{-x}{900}.$$

The rule (from algebra) is that $\ln(e^y) = y$ for any real number y. Now we simply solve for x:

$$\ln(0.2898) = \frac{-x}{900}$$

$$x = -900[\ln(0.2898)]$$

$$= \$1,114.71$$

This procedure requires that you use the exponential utility function to translate the dollar outcomes into utilities, find the EU, and finally convert back to dollars to find the exact CE. That can be a lot of work, especially if there are many outcomes to consider. Fortunately, an approximation is available from Pratt (1964) and also discussed in McNamee and Celona (1987). Suppose you can figure out the expected value and variance of the payoffs. Then the CE is approximately

$$\text{Certainty Equivalent} \approx \text{Expected Value} - \frac{0.5(\text{Variance})}{\text{Risk Tolerance}}$$

In symbols,

$$\text{CE} \approx \mu - \frac{0.5(\sigma^2)}{R}$$

where μ and σ^2 are the expected value and variance, respectively. For example, in the preceding gamble, the expected value (EMV or μ) equals $1,300, and the standard deviation (σ) equals $600. Thus, the approximation gives

$$\text{CE} \approx \$1,300 - \frac{0.5(\$600^2)}{\$900}$$

$$\approx \$1,100.$$

The approximation is within $15. That's pretty good! This approximation is especially useful for continuous random variables or problems where the expected value and variance are relatively easy to estimate or assess compared to assessing the entire probability distribution. The approximation will be closest to the actual value when the outcome's probability distribution is a symmetric, bell-shaped curve.

What are reasonable R values? For an individual's utility function, the appropriate value for R clearly depends on the individual's risk attitude. As indicated, the less risk-averse a person is, the greater R is. Suppose, however, that an individual or a group (a board of directors, say) has to make a decision on behalf of a corporation. It is important that these decision makers adopt a decision-making attitude based on corporate goals and acceptable risk levels for the corporation. This can be quite different from an individual's personal risk attitude; the individual director may be unwilling to risk $10 million, even though the corporation can afford such a loss. Howard (1988) suggests certain guidelines for determining a corporation's risk tolerance in terms of total sales, net income, or equity. Reasonable values of R appear to be approximately 6.4% of total sales, 1.24 times net income, or 15.7% of equity. These figures are based on observations that Howard has made in the course of consulting with various companies. More research may refine these figures, and it may turn out that different industries have different ratios for determining reasonable Rs.

Using the exponential utility function seems like magic, doesn't it? One assessment, and we are finished! Why bother with all of those CEs that we discussed previously? You know, however, that you never get something for nothing, and that definitely is the case here. The exponential utility function has a specific kind of curvature and implies a certain kind of risk attitude. This risk attitude is called *constant risk aversion.* Essentially it means that no matter how much wealth you have—how much money in your pocket or bank account—you would view a particular gamble in the same way. The gamble's risk premium would be the same no matter how much money you have. Is constant risk aversion reasonable? Maybe it is for some people. Many individuals might be less risk-averse if they had more wealth.

In later sections of this chapter, we will study the exponential utility function in more detail, especially with regard to constant risk aversion. The message here is that the exponential utility function is most appropriate for people who really believe that they would view gambles the same way regardless of their wealth level. But even if this is not true for you, the exponential utility function can be a useful tool for modeling preferences.

PITFALLS IN UTILITY ASSESSMENT: BIASES IN THE CE, PE, AND TO METHODS

According to utility theory, the three different assessment methods (CE, PE, and TO) should all result in the same utility function. That is, the method should not influence (or bias) the shape of the utility function being assessed. Research has shown that this is not the case. The method used can *systematically* influence the shape, as shown by Hershey and Shoemaker (1985). This is a violation of a principle called *procedure invariance*; different procedures to measure the same phenomenon should give the same measurement.

Much of the difference between these methods is due to the characteristics of our preferences, specifically *loss aversion* and *probability transformations.* We will discuss these more in Chapter 15. What we can report here is that the tradeoff method is insensitive to loss aversion and probability transformations; the certainty-equivalent method is insensitive to loss aversion, but biased by probability transformations; and the probability-equivalent method is biased by both (Bleichrodt, Pinto, and Wakker, 2001)! So why not just use the TO method? A disadvantage of the TO method is that, compared to the other two methods, more questions must be asked in order to assess the utility function. If the decision maker is willing to put more effort into the assessment, the TO method should give less biased results.

The Endowment Effect

In our examples, we have described a CE as the amount of money that "makes you indifferent." But indifference might not be the same thing in all cases. For example, think about lottery tickets. On one hand, if someone has a lottery ticket and you are interested in purchasing it, what's the most you would pay for it? On the other hand, suppose you own the lottery ticket—what's the least you would sell it for?

According to utility theory, your minimum selling price should be fairly close to your maximum buying price (and if you have an exponential utility function, they should be equal). However, research by University of Chicago Professor Richard Thaler has shown that this is not the case. In general, individuals tend to inflate their minimum selling price, which Thaler (1980) calls the *endowment effect*: Owners of a good (such as the lottery) may value the good more than those who do not own it. For example, eBay has done research on successful sales of items with and without a *reserve price*. If the online auction does not produce an amount that equals or exceeds the reserve price, the seller does not have to part with the item. Sounds like a minimum selling price! If the endowment effect is prevalent, one would expect sellers to overestimate the value of their goods and set the reserve prices too high, in which case the auction ends without an exchange occurring. This seems to be the case; eBay has found that sellers who don't use a reserve successfully sell their items more frequently than those who do set a reserve price.

Preference Reversals

Even aside from the endowment effect, utility assessment biases can still exist. Let us look more closely at the CE method. As we have argued previously, if your CE for lottery A is greater than your CE for lottery B, then lottery A is preferred to lottery B. Violation of this simple logic is known as a *preference reversal*. That is, for many people, their assessed CE for some lottery A may be greater than their CE for lottery B, but when the individual is asked directly which lottery he or she prefers, it turns out that B is preferred to A! How can this happen? Consider the following lotteries:

A: Win $4 with probability 0.99

Win $0 with probability 0.01

B: Win $16 with probability 0.25

Win $0 with probability 0.75

The expected values of the two gambles are $3.96 and $4, respectively. A large proportion of people will indicate a preference for lottery A when asked to choose between the two, yet give lottery B a greater CE (Grether and Plott, 1979). Earlier experiments run by Lichtenstein and Slovic (1971) revealed this preference reversal phenomenon, even when working with gamblers in Las Vegas using real money! So what is causing these so-called preference reversals?

The results from further research have revealed that much of the cause of preference reversal is due to our old *anchor-and-adjust* heuristic discussed back in Chapter 8 and a violation of so-called procedure invariance.

When individuals are asked to judge a value, they tend to anchor and (insufficiently) adjust from that anchor. In gambles A and B, the $16 payoff in B might anchor you at a higher level than the $4 of lottery A. When asked to choose, though, you might look at some other feature of the gamble, like the relatively large probability of winning in A, and therefore choose it over B. After all, the expected values of the two gambles are similar. So the problem appears to be a bias in the judgment of the CE. Bostic, Herrnstein, and Luce (1990) elicited CEs from their experimental subjects using an approach that did not involve this kind of judgment. They used a computer program known as Parameter Estimation by Sequential Testing (PEST), which had individuals choose between gambles and sure amounts. By the direction of choice the individual indicated and subsequent computer adjustments of the sure amount, they were able to reach true choice indifference. That is, the choice-based CEs do reflect the individual's preferences and therefore are not susceptible to the preference reversal phenomenon.

Implications for Assessing Utilities

If people can make such mistakes in assessing their utilities, what can we do? The first point is to recognize that the biases exist. However, researchers typically have demonstrated these biases using experimental subjects rather than decision makers facing a real (and possibly complex) decision. Higher stakes, such as the future of one's career or major decisions for a company, can motivate a decision maker to think carefully about the judgments he or she must make.

Even with careful thought, though, biases can creep into the judgment process. To cope with this possibility, the analyst can take a two-pronged approach. First, in the judgment phase, we can try to use methods and approaches, like the TO method, that are robust to the biases. Second, in analyzing the decision model, we can use sensitivity analysis. The question to ask is whether the preferred choice—the one with the greatest EU—is robust to changes in the utilities. For example, if we are using the exponential utility function, we can run a sensitivity analysis on the value of the risk tolerance parameter. How much does R have to change before the preferred decision changes? By using care both in the assessment process and in analyzing the model, we can be reasonably sure that we have accounted for any biases that might be present.

MODELING PREFERENCES USING PRECISIONTREE

It is straightforward to model a decision maker's risk preferences in Precision-Tree. You need only choose the utility curve, and PrecisionTree does the rest. It converts all end-node monetary values into utility values and calculates either EUs or CEs, whichever you choose. You can use one of the two built-in utility functions (the exponential or logarithmic), or you can define a custom utility curve. Here are instructions on using the exponential utility function in PrecisionTree, demonstrated using the investment example from the beginning of the chapter.

STEP 1 Construct Decision Tree.

1.1 Open PrecisionTree.
1.2 Click on cell **A8** and construct the decision tree shown in Figure 14.13.

STEP 2 Exponential Function—Expected Utility.

2.1 In cell *B4*, type in $5,000. We have chosen *B4* for the location of the risk tolerance *R* value.
2.2 Click on the name **Investment Example** and the *Model Settings* dialog box opens (Figure 14.14). Choose the **Utility Function** tab.
2.3 Check the **Use Utility Function** checkbox.

FIGURE **14.13**
Investment example using PrecisionTree.

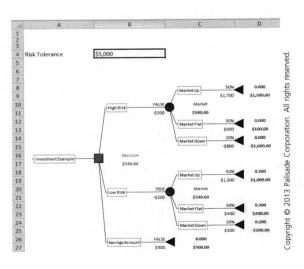

FIGURE **14.14**
Clicking on the tree's name brings up the *Model Settings* dialog box, where we specify the utility function, the *R* value (risk tolerance), and the values to be displayed.

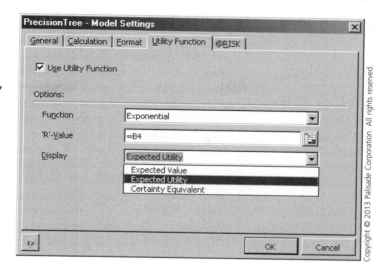

2.4 For the *Function* option, choose the default **Exponential** and for the *R value* enter = **B4**.
2.5 For *Display*, Choose **Expected Utility** and click **OK**.

Figure 14.15 shows that each of the dollar values has been replaced by its exponential utility value when $R = \$5,000$, and for each chance node the EU has been calculated. For the high-risk stock, the utility of $1,500 is 0.259, the utility of $100 is 0.020, and the utility of $-\$1,000$ is -0.221. Remember that the $200 brokerage fee is being subtracted. The EU of the high-risk stock is 0.091. Figure 14.15 shows that when $R = \$5,000$, the high-risk stock is least preferred and the low-risk stock is most preferred with a utility value of 0.098.

Next, we turn to the CEs to more easily interpret the results. We know that the high-risk stock has the greatest EMV at $580, but that when associated risks are included, the low-risk stock has a greater EU. How much greater? In utility values, it is 0.098 compared to 0.091. In dollar values, it is the difference between the CEs. Computing CEs in PrecisionTree is easy.

STEP 3 Exponential Function—Certainty Equivalent.

3.1 Click on the tree's name **Investment Example**, and the *Model Settings* dialog box pops up. Choose the **Utility Function** tab.
3.2 Choose **Certainty Equivalent** for the *Display*, as shown in Figure 14.14.
3.3 Click **OK**.

FIGURE **14.15**
The Investment
example showing
the utility values
and EUs of the
three alternatives.

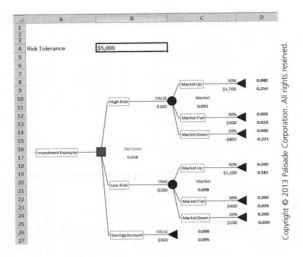

The decision tree in Figure 14.16 now shows the CEs for each node. We see that the CE of the high-risk stock is $478.43, which, as expected, is less than the CE of $517.69 for the low-risk stock. Note that the CE of the savings account is $500, which is the same as its EMV because there is no uncertainty involved. We can also calculate the risk premium for each alternative. The risk premium of the high-risk stock is $580 − $478.43 = $101.57, and the risk premium of the low-risk stock is $540 − $517.69 = $22.31.

Next, we consider the impact of changing the risk tolerance or *R* value on the EU values or CEs. We know that as we become more tolerant of risk

FIGURE **14.16**
The Investment
example showing
the certainty
equivalents of the
three alternatives.

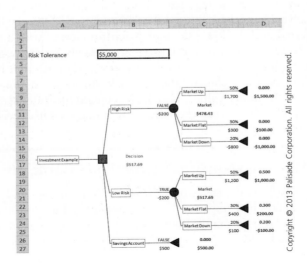

(R increases), eventually the high-risk stock will have the greatest EU, but at what value of R does this happen? And what about going the other way? Is the savings account ever the most preferred? To answer these questions, we use Excel®'s Data Tables to vary R across a range of values. Essentially, we are using Data Tables the same way we did in Chapter 5 as a sensitivity analysis tool.

STEP 4 *Sensitivity Analysis of Risk Tolerance.*

4.1 First, we enter the range of values for R. Starting in cell *E5* enter **100**, then **500** in *E6*, **1000** in *E7*, **2000** in *E8*, and continue by increments of 1000 until entering **15000** in *E21*. See Figure 14.17.

4.2 For Data Tables, the formula you want calculated needs be entered one cell to the right and one cell up from the range of values just entered. In other words, in cell *F4*, enter **=C11**, the cell where PrecisionTree has inserted the formula for the CE of the high-risk stock. To enter the CEs of the other two alternatives, enter **=C21** (CE of low-risk stock) in *G4* and **=C27** (CE of savings account) in *H4*.

4.3 Highlight the whole table, that is, with your cursor, highlight cells from **E4** to **H21**.

4.4 Click on the **Data** tab in the Excel menu, click on **What-If Analysis,** and in the pull-down menu, choose **Data Table.**

4.5 Enter **B4** for the *Column Input Cell*; *B4* is the cell location of R. Leave the *Row Input Cell* field blank. Click **OK**, and the highlighted table is filled in with the CEs for all three alternatives, for each of the risk tolerance values listed on the left.

Figure 14.17 shows the CEs for the three alternatives, and we see that the saving account has the maximum CE for risk tolerance values less than or equal to $2,000; that the low-risk stock has the maximum CE for risk tolerance values between $3,000 and $9,000 inclusive; and that the high-risk stock has the maximum CE for risk tolerance values greater than or equal to $10,000. If we wanted to know the exact risk tolerance value for which two alternatives have equal CEs, we could use Excel's Goal Seek to find the value. For example, when the $R = \$9,779$, then the CE of the low-risk and high-risk stocks are both equal to $528.61.

This concludes the PrecisionTree instructions. If you are interested in using the other built-in utility function, the logarithmic function, you need to guarantee that only positive monetary values are used, because the logarithmic function is not defined for negative values. PrecisionTree allows you to enter a constant value as a way to guarantee that the logarithm is defined. Specifically, PrecisionTree uses $U(x) = \ln(x + R)$, where $\ln(x)$ is the natural

FIGURE **14.17**
Using data tables to determine the effect of choosing a different risk tolerance value (*R*) on the CEs for each alternative, *R* ranging from $100 to $15,000.

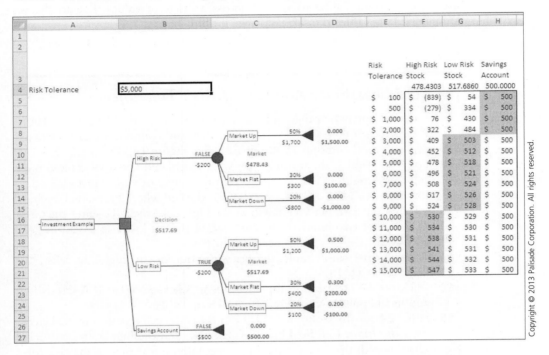

logarithm of *x*, and *R* is chosen so that $x + R > 0$, for all *x* values.[1] Finally, PrecisionTree also allows you to define a customized utility function, but this requires programming in Excel. For those interested, refer to Excel's User Guide for instructions on writing user-defined functions.

DECREASING AND CONSTANT RISK AVERSION

In this section, we will consider how individuals might deal with risky investments. Suppose you have $1,000 to invest. How would you feel about investing $500 in an extremely risky venture in which you might lose the entire $500? Now suppose you have saved more money and have $20,000. Now how would you feel about that extremely risky venture? Is it more or less attractive to you? How do you think a person's degree of risk aversion changes with wealth?

---

[1] Incidentally, PrecisionTree uses R to denote the constant for the logarithmic utility function for a very good reason. It turns out that, when U(*x*) = ln(*x* + R), R can be thought of as your risk tolerance and can be assessed in exactly the same way as for the exponential.

Decreasing Risk Aversion

If an individual's preferences show *decreasing risk aversion,* the risk premium decreases if a constant amount is added to all payoffs in a gamble. Expressed informally, decreasing risk aversion means the more money you have, the less nervous you are about a particular bet.

For example, suppose an individual's utility curve can be described by a logarithmic function:

$$U(x) = \ln(x).$$

Using this utility function, consider the gamble

Win $10 with probability 0.5

Win $40 with probability 0.5

To find the CE, we first find the EU. The utility values for $10 and $40 are

$$U(\$10) = \ln(10) = 2.3026$$
$$U(\$40) = \ln(40) = 3.6889$$

Calculating EU:

$$EU = 0.5(2.3026) + 0.5(3.6889) = 2.9957$$

To find the CE, we must find the dollar value that has $U(CE) = 2.9957$; thus, set the utility function equal to 2.9957:

$$2.9957 = \ln(CE)$$

Now solve for CE. To remove the logarithm, we take antilogs:

$$e^{2.9957} = e^{\ln(CE)} = CE$$

The rule here corresponds to what we did with the exponential function. Here we have $e^{\ln(y)} = y$ for any positive real number y. Finally, we calculate $e^{2.9957}$:

$$CE = e^{2.9957} = \$20$$

To find the risk premium, we need the EMV, which equals $0.5(\$10) + 0.5(\$40) = \$25$. Thus, the risk premium is $EMV - CE = \$25 - \$20 = \$5$.

Using the same procedure, we can find risk premiums for the lotteries shown in Table 14.3. Notice that the sequence of lotteries is constructed so that each is like having the previous one plus $10. For example, the $20–$50 lottery is like having the $10–$40 lottery plus a $10 bill. The risk premium decreases with each $10 addition. The decreasing risk premium reflects decreasing risk aversion, which is a property of the logarithmic utility function.

An Entrepreneurial Example

For another example, suppose that an entrepreneur is considering a new business investment. To participate, the entrepreneur must invest $5,000. There is a 25% chance that the investment will earn back the $5,000, leaving her just as well off as if she had not made the investment. But there is

TABLE **14.3**
Risk premiums from logarithmic utility function.

50–50 Gamble Between ($)	Expected Value ($)	Certainty Equivalent ($)	Risk Premium ($)
10, 40	25	20.00	5.00
20, 50	35	31.62	3.38
30, 60	45	42.43	2.57
40, 70	55	52.92	2.08

© Cengage Learning

also a 45% chance that she will lose the $5,000 altogether, although this is counterbalanced by a 30% chance that the investment will return the original $5,000 plus an additional $10,000. Figure 14.18 shows the entrepreneur's decision tree.

We will assume that this entrepreneur's preferences can be modeled with the logarithmic utility function $U(x) = \ln(x)$, where x is interpreted as total wealth. Suppose that the investor has $10,000. Should she make the investment or avoid it?

The easiest way to solve this problem is to calculate the EU of the investment and compare it with the EU of the alternative, which is to do nothing. The EU of doing nothing simply is the utility of the current wealth, or U($10,000), which is

$$U(\$10,000) = \ln(10,000) = 9.2103$$

The EU of the investment is easy to calculate:

$$EU = 0.30 \; U(\$20,000) + 0.25 \; U(\$10,000) + 0.45 \; U(\$5,000)$$

$$= 0.30(9.9035) + 0.25(9.2103) + 0.45(8.5172)$$

$$= 9.1064$$

Because the EU of the investment is less than the utility of not investing, the investment should not be made.

Now, suppose that several years have passed. The utility function has not changed, but other investments have paid off handsomely, and she currently

FIGURE **14.18**
Entrepreneur's investment decision.

Current wealth is denoted by x.

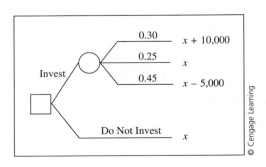

© Cengage Learning

has $70,000. Should she undertake the project now? Recalculating with a base wealth of $70,000 rather than $10,000, we find that the utility of doing nothing is U($70,000) = 11.1563, and the EU for the investment is 11.1630. Now the EU of the investment is greater than the utility of doing nothing, and so she should invest.

The point of these examples is to show how decreasing risk aversion determines the way in which a decision maker views risky prospects. As indicated, the wealthier a decreasingly risk-averse decision maker is, the more comfortable he or she will be about taking a particular gamble. Generally speaking, decreasing risk aversion makes sense when we think about risk attitudes and the way that many people appear to deal with risky situations. Many would feel better about investing money in the stock market if they were wealthier to begin with. For such reasons, utility functions with decreasing risk aversion are often used by economists and decision theorists as a model of typical risk attitudes.

Constant Risk Aversion

An individual displays constant risk aversion if the risk premium for a gamble does not depend on the initial amount of wealth held by the decision maker. Intuitively, the idea is that a constantly risk-averse person would be just as anxious about taking a bet regardless of the amount of money available.

If an individual is constantly risk-averse, the utility function is exponential:

$$U(x) = 1 - e^{-x/R}$$

For example, suppose that the decision maker has assessed a risk tolerance of $35:

$$U(x) = 1 - e^{-x/35}$$

We can perform the same kind of analysis that we did with the logarithmic utility function previously. Consider the gamble

Win $10 with probability 0.5

Win $40 with probability 0.5

As before, the expected payoff is $25. To find the CE, we must find the EU, which requires plugging the amounts $10 and $40 into the utility function:

$$U(\$10) = 1 - e^{-10/35} = 0.2485$$

$$U(\$40) = 1 - e^{-40/35} = 0.6811$$

Thus, EU = 0.5 (0.2485) + 0.5 (0.6811) = 0.4648. To find the CE, set the utility function to 0.4648. The value that gives the utility of 0.4648 is the gamble's CE:

$$0.4648 = 1 - e^{-CE/35}$$

Now we can solve for CE as we did earlier when working with the exponential utility function:

$$0.5352 = e^{-CE/35}$$
$$\ln(0.5352) = \ln(e^{-CE/35})$$
$$-0.6251 = -CE/35$$
$$CE = 0.6251(35) = \$21.88$$

Finally, the expected payoff (EMV) is $25, and so the risk premium is

$$\text{Risk Premium} = \text{EMV} - \text{CE} = \$25 - \$21.88 = \$3.12$$

Using the same procedure, we can find the risk premium for each gamble in Table 14.4. The risk premium stays the same as long as the difference between the payoffs does not change. Adding a constant amount to both sides of the gamble does not change the decision maker's attitude toward the gamble.

Alternatively, you can think about this as a situation where you have a bet in which you may win $15 or lose $15. In the first preceding gamble, you face this bet with $25 in your pocket. In the constant-risk-aversion situation, the way you feel about the bet (as reflected in the risk premium) is the same regardless of how much money is added to your pocket. In the decreasing-risk-aversion situation, adding something to your pocket made you less risk-averse toward the bet, thus resulting in a lower risk premium.

Figure 14.19 plots the two utility functions on the same graph. They have been rescaled so that U($10) = 0 and U($100) = 1 in each case. Note their similarity. It does not take a large change in the utility curve's shape to alter the nature of the individual's risk attitude.

Is constant risk aversion appropriate? Consider the kinds of risks that railroad barons such as E. H. Harriman undertook. Would a person like Harriman have been willing to risk millions of dollars on the takeover of another railroad had he not already been fairly wealthy? The argument easily can be made that the more wealth one has, the easier it is to take larger risks. Thus, decreasing risk aversion appears to provide a more appropriate

TABLE **14.4**
Risk premiums from exponential utility function.

50–50 Gamble Between ($)	Expected Value ($)	Certainty Equivalent ($)	Risk Premium ($)
10, 40	25	21.88	3.12
20, 50	35	31.88	3.12
30, 60	45	41.88	3.12
40, 70	55	51.88	3.12

FIGURE **14.19**
Logarithmic and exponential utility functions plotted over the range of $10 to $100.

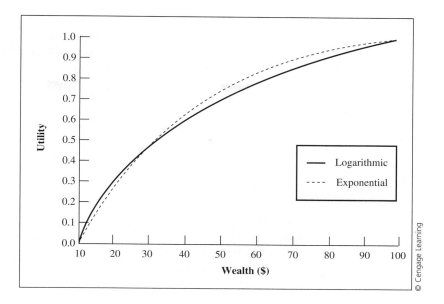

model of preferences than does constant risk aversion. This is an important point to keep in mind if you decide to use the exponential utility function and the risk-tolerance parameter; this utility function displays constant risk aversion.

After all is said and done, while the concepts of decreasing or constant risk aversion may be intriguing from the point of view of a decision maker who is interested in modeling his or her risk attitude, precise determination of a decision maker's utility function is not yet possible. Decision theorists still are learning how to elicit and measure utility functions. Many unusual effects arise from human nature; we have mentioned a few of these previously, and we will study others in the next chapter. It would be an overstatement to suggest that it is possible to determine precisely the degree of an individual's risk aversion or whether he or she is decreasingly risk-averse. It is a difficult enough problem just to determine whether someone is risk-averse or risk-seeking!

Thus, it may be reasonable to use the exponential utility function as an approximation in modeling preferences and risk attitudes. A quick assessment of risk tolerance, and you are on your way. And, as mentioned, it is always possible to use the sensitivity-analysis approach; it may be that a precise assessment of the risk tolerance is not necessary.

SOME CAVEATS

A few things remain to be said about utilities. These are thoughts to keep in mind as you work through utility assessments and use utilities in decision problems.

1. Utilities do not add up. That is, $U(A + B) \neq U(A) + U(B)$. This actually is the whole point of having a nonlinear utility function. Thus, when using utilities in a decision analysis, you must calculate net payoffs or net contributions at the endpoints of the decision tree before transforming to utility values.

2. Utility differences do not express strength of preferences. Suppose that $U(A_1) - U(A_2) > U(A_3) - U(A_4)$. This does not necessarily mean that you would rather go from A_2 to A_1 instead of from A_4 to A_3. Utility only provides a numerical scale for ordering preferences, not a measure of their strengths. Whether this is reasonable is a matter of some debate. For example, von Winterfeldt and Edwards (1986) give the following example: You are first told that you will receive $100, and then told that you actually will receive $500, and then finally told that the actual payment will be $10,000. It would indeed be a pleasant surprise to go from $100 to $500, but for most of us, the delight we would experience from $500 to $10,000 would eclipse the difference between $100 and $500. Von Winterfeldt and Edwards argue that we can make judgments of just this sort. Whether one agrees or not, it is necessary to interpret utility carefully in this regard.

3. Utilities are not comparable from person to person. A utility function is a subjective personal statement of an individual's preferences and so provides no basis for comparing utilities among individuals.

SUMMARY

In this chapter, we have explored some basic concepts that underlie risk and return trade-offs, with the aim of being able to understand how to model a decision maker's risk preferences. We discussed the notion of a risk premium (EMV − CE), which can be thought of as a measure of how risk-averse a decision maker is in regard to a particular risky situation. The basic procedure for assessing a utility function requires comparison of lotteries with risk-less payoffs. Once a utility function has been determined, the procedure is to replace dollar payoffs in a decision tree or influence diagram with utility values and solve the problem to find the option with the greatest EU. We also studied the exponential utility function and the notion of risk tolerance. Because of its nature, the exponential utility function is particularly useful for modeling preferences in decision analysis. The concepts of decreasing and constant risk aversion also were discussed.

EXERCISES

14.1. Why is it important for decision makers to consider their attitudes toward risk?

14.2. We have not given a specific definition of risk. How would you define it? Give examples of lotteries that vary in riskiness in terms of your definition of risk.

14.3. Explain in your own words the idea of a certainty equivalent.

14.4. Explain what is meant by the term *risk premium*.

14.5. Explain in your own words the idea of risk tolerance. How would it apply to utility functions other than the exponential utility function?

14.6. Suppose a decision maker has the utility function shown in Table 14.1. An investment opportunity has EMV = $1,236 and EU = 0.93. Find the CE for this investment and the risk premium.

14.7. A decision maker's assessed risk tolerance is $1,210. Assume that this individual's preferences can be modeled with an exponential utility function.

    a.   Find U($1,000), U($800), U($0), and U(−$1,250).

    b.   Find the EU for an investment that has the following payoff distribution:

$$P(\$1,000) = 0.33$$
$$P(\$800) = 0.21$$
$$P(\$0) = 0.33$$
$$P(-\$1,250) = 0.13$$

    c.   Find the exact CE for the investment and the risk premium.

    d.   Find the approximate CE using the expected value and variance of the payoffs.

    e.   Another investment possibility has expected value $2,400 and standard deviation $300. Find the approximate CE for this investment.

14.8. Many firms evaluate investment projects individually on the basis of expected value and at the same time maintain diversified holdings in order to reduce risk. Does this make sense in light of our discussion of risk attitudes in this chapter?

14.9. A friend of yours, who lives in Reno, has life insurance, homeowner's insurance, and automobile insurance and also regularly plays the quarter slot machines in the casinos. What kind of a utility function might explain this kind of behavior? How else might you explain such behavior?

14.10. Two risky gambles were proposed at the beginning of the chapter:

        Game 1:   Win $30 with probability 0.5

                        Lose $1 with probability 0.5

        Game 2:   Win $2,000 with probability 0.5

                        Lose $1,900 with probability 0.5

Many of us would probably pay to play Game 1 but would have to be paid to participate in Game 2. Is this true for you? How much would you pay (or have to be paid) to take part in either game?

QUESTIONS AND PROBLEMS

14.11. **St. Petersburg Paradox.** Consider the following game that you have been invited to play by an acquaintance who always pays his debts. Your acquaintance will flip a fair coin. If it comes up heads, you win $2. If it comes up tails, he flips the coin again. If heads occurs on the second toss, you win $4. If tails, he flips again. If heads occurs on the third toss, you win $8, and if tails, he flips again, and so on. Your payoff is an uncertain amount with the following probabilities:

Flip Number	Payoff	Probability	
1	$2	$\frac{1}{2} = 0.5$	
2	$4	$\frac{1}{2^2} = 0.25$	
3	$8	$\frac{1}{2^3} = 0.125$	
$\vdots$	$\vdots$	$\vdots$	
n	2^n	$\frac{1}{2^n}$	(where n is the flip number of the first heads)
$\vdots$	$\vdots$	$\vdots$	

This is a good game to play because you are bound to come out ahead. There is no possible outcome from which you can lose. How much would you pay to play this game? $10? $20? What is the expected value of the game? Would you be indifferent between playing the game and having the expected value for sure?

14.12. Assess your utility function in three different ways.
   a. Use the certainty-equivalent approach to assess your utility function for wealth over a range of $100 to $20,000.
   b. Use the probability-equivalent approach to assess U($1,500), U($5,600), U($9,050), and U($13,700). Are these assessments consistent with the assessments made in part a?
   c. Use the trade-off method to assess your utility function for values ranging from $100 to $20,000.
   Plot the assessments from parts a, b, and c on the same graph and compare them. Why do you think they differ? Can you identify any biases in your assessment process?

14.13. Assess your risk tolerance (R). Now rescale your exponential utility function—the one you obtain by substituting your R value into the exponential utility function—so that U($100) = 0 and U($20,000) = 1. That is, find constants a and b so that $a + b(1 - e^{-100/R}) = 0$ and $a + b(1 - e^{-20,000/R}) = 1$. Now plot the rescaled utility function on the same graph with the utility assessments from Problem 14.12. How do your assessments compare?

TABLE 14.5
Utility function for
Liedtke.

Payoff (Billions)	Utility
$10.3	1.00
$5.0	0.75
$3.0	0.60
$2.0	0.45
0.0	0.00

14.14. Let us return to the Texaco-Pennzoil example from Chapter 4 and think about Liedtke's risk attitude. Suppose that Liedtke's utility function is given by the utility function in Table 14.5.
   a. Graph this utility function. Based on this graph, how would you classify Liedtke's attitude toward risk?
   b. Use the utility function in conjunction with the decision tree sketched in Figure 4.2 to solve Liedtke's problem. With these utilities, what strategy should he pursue? Should he still counteroffer $5 billion? What if Texaco counteroffers $3 billion? Is your answer consistent with your response to part a?
   c. Based on this utility function, what is the least amount (approximately) that Liedtke should agree to in a settlement? (*Hint:* Find a sure amount that gives him the same EU that he gets for going to court.) What does this suggest regarding plausible counteroffers that Liedtke might make?
14.15. Of course, Liedtke is not operating by himself in the Texaco-Pennzoil case; he must report to a board of directors. Table 14.6 gives utility functions for three different directors. Draw graphs of these. How would you classify each director in terms of his or her attitude toward risk? What would be the strategies of each? (That is, what would each one do with respect to Texaco's current offer, and how would each react to a Texaco counteroffer of $3 billion? To answer this question, you must solve the decision tree—calculate EUs—for *each* director.)

TABLE 14.6
Utility functions for
the three directors
of Pennzoil.

Payoff (Billions)	Utility Director A	Director B	Director C
$10.3	3.0	100	42.05
$5.0	2.9	30	23.50
$3.0	2.8	15	16.50
$2.0	2.6	8	13.00
0.0	1.0	0	6.00

14.16. How do you think Liedtke (Problem 14.14) and the directors in Problem 14.15 will be able to reconcile their differences?

14.17. Rescale the utility function for Director A in Problem 14.15 so that it ranges between 0 and 1. That is, find constants a and b so that when you multiply the utility function by a and then add b, the utility for $10.30 billion is 1 and the utility for $0 is 0. Graph the rescaled utility function and compare it to the graph of the original utility function. Use the rescaled utility function to solve the Texaco-Pennzoil decision tree. Is the optimal choice consistent with the one you found in Problem 14.15?

14.18. What if Hugh Liedtke were risk-averse? Based on Figure 4.2, find a critical value for Hugh Liedtke's risk tolerance. If his risk tolerance is small enough (very risk-averse), he would accept the $2 billion offer. How small would his risk tolerance have to be for EU(Accept $2 billion) to be greater than EU(Counteroffer $5 billion)?

14.19. The idea of dominance criteria and risk aversion come together in an interesting way, leading to a different kind of dominance. If two risky gambles have the same expected payoff, on what basis might a risk-averse individual choose between them without performing a complete utility analysis?

14.20. This problem is related to the ideas of dominance that we discussed in Chapters 4 and 8. Investment D in the table that follows is said to show "second-order stochastic dominance" over Investment C. In this problem, it is up to you to explain why D dominates C.

You are contemplating two alternative uncertain investments, whose distributions for payoffs are as follows.

	Probabilities	
Payoff	Investment C	Investment D
$50	1/3	1/4
$100	1/3	1/2
$150	1/3	1/4

a. If your preference function is given by $U(x) = 1 - e^{-x/100}$, calculate EU for both C and D. Which would you choose?

b. Plot the cumulative distribution functions (CDFs) for C and D on the same graph. How do they compare? Use the graph to explain intuitively why any risk-averse decision maker would prefer D. (*Hint:* Think about the concave shape of a risk-averse utility function.)

14.21. Utility functions need not relate to dollar values. Here is a problem in which we know little about five abstract outcomes. What is important, however, is that a person who does know what A to E represent should be able to compare the outcomes using the lottery procedures we have studied.

A decision maker faces a risky gamble in which she may obtain one of five outcomes. Label the outcomes A, B, C, D, and E. A is the most preferred, and E is least preferred. She has made the following three assessments.

- She is indifferent between having C for sure or a lottery in which she wins A with probability 0.5 or E with probability 0.5.
- She is indifferent between having B for sure or a lottery in which she wins A with probability 0.4 or C with probability 0.6.
- She is indifferent between these two lotteries:
  1. A 50% chance at B and a 50% chance at D
  2. A 50% chance at A and a 50% chance at E

What are U(A), U(B), U(C), U(D), and U(E)?

14.22. You have considered insuring a particular item of property (such as an expensive camera, your computer, or your Stradivarius violin), but after considering the risks and the insurance premium quoted, you have no clear preference for either purchasing the insurance or taking the risk. The insurance company then tells you about a new scheme called "probabilistic insurance." You pay half the insurance premium quoted but have coverage only in the sense that in the case of a claim there is a probability of one-half that you will be asked to pay the other half of the premium and will be completely covered, or that you will not be covered and will have your premium returned. The insurance company can be relied on to be fair in flipping the coin to determine whether or not you are covered.

　a. Do you consider yourself to be risk-averse?
　b. Would you purchase probabilistic insurance?
　c. Draw a decision tree for this problem.
　d. Show that a risk-averse individual always should prefer the probabilistic insurance.

(*Hint:* This is a difficult problem. To solve it, you must be sure to consider that you are indifferent between the regular insurance and no insurance. Write out the equation relating these two alternatives and see what it implies. Another strategy is to select a specific utility function—the log utility function $U(x) = \ln(x)$, say—and then find values for the probability of a claim, your wealth, the insurance premium, and the value of your piece of property so that the utility of paying the insurance premium is equal to the EU of no insurance. Now use these values to calculate the EU of the probabilistic insurance. What is the result?)

14.23. An investor with assets of $10,000 has an opportunity to invest $5,000 in a venture that is equally likely to pay either $15,000 or nothing. The investor's utility function can be described by the utility function $U(x) = \ln(x)$, where x is his total wealth.

　a. What should the investor do?
　b. Suppose the investor places a bet with a friend before making the investment decision. The bet is for $1,000; if a fair coin lands

heads up, the investor wins $1,000, but if it lands tails up, the investor pays $1,000 to his friend. Only after the bet has been resolved will the investor decide whether or not to invest in the venture. What is an appropriate strategy for the investor? If he wins the bet, should he invest? What if he loses the bet?

c.   Describe a real-life situation in which an individual might find it appropriate to gamble before deciding on a course of action.

Source: D. E. Bell (1988). "Value of Pre-Decision Side Bets for Utility Maximizers." *Management Science*, 34, 797–800.

14.24. A bettor with utility function $U(x) = \ln(x)$, where x is total wealth, has a choice between the following two alternatives:

A   Win $10,000 with probability 0.2

Win $1,000 with probability 0.8

B   Win $3,000 with probability 0.9

Lose $2,000 with probability 0.1

a.   If the bettor currently has $2,500, should he choose A or B?
b.   Repeat a, assuming the bettor has $5,000.
c.   Repeat a, assuming the bettor has $10,000.
d.   Do you think that this pattern of choices between A and B is reasonable? Why or why not?

Source: D. E. Bell (1988) "One-Switch Utility Functions and a Measure of Risk." *Management Science*, 34, 1416–1424.

14.25. Repeat Problem 14.24 with $U(x) = 0.0003x - 8.48e^{-x/2775}$. A utility function of this form is called *linear-plus-exponential*, because it contains both linear ($0.0003x$) and exponential terms. It has a number of interesting and useful properties, including the fact that it switches only once among any pair of lotteries (such as those in Problem 14.24) as wealth increases (see Bell 1995a, b).

14.26. Show that the linear-plus-exponential utility function in Problem 14.25 has decreasing risk aversion. (*Hint:* You can use this utility function to evaluate a series of lotteries like those described in the text and analyzed in Tables 14.3 and 14.4. Show that the risk premium for a gamble decreases as wealth increases.)

14.27. Buying and selling prices for risky investments obviously are related to CEs. This problem, however, shows that the prices depend on exactly what is owned in the first place!

Suppose that Peter Brown's utility for total wealth (A) can be represented by the utility function $U(A) = \ln(A)$. He currently has $1,000 in cash. A business deal of interest to him yields a reward of $100 with probability 0.5 and $0 with probability 0.5.

a.   If he owns this business deal in addition to the $1,000, what is the smallest amount for which he would sell the deal?
b.   Suppose he does not own the deal. What equation must be solved to find the greatest amount he would be willing to pay for the deal?

c.   For part b, it turns out that the most he would pay is $48.75, which is not exactly the same as the answer in part a. Can you explain why the amounts are different?

d.   (*Extra credit for algebra hotshots.*) Solve your equation in part b to verify the answer ($48.75) given in part c.

Source: This problem was suggested by R. L. Winkler.

14.28. We discussed decreasing and constant risk aversion. Are there other possibilities? Think about this as you work through this problem. Suppose that a person's utility function for total wealth is

$$U(A) = 200A - A^2 \quad \text{for } 0 \le A \le 100$$

where A represents total wealth in thousands of dollars.

a.   Graph this preference function. How would you classify this person with regard to her attitude toward risk?

b.   If the person's total assets are currently $10,000 should she take a bet in which she will win $10,000 with probability 0.6 and lose $10,000 with probability 0.4?

c.   If the person's total assets are currently $90,000 should she take the bet given in part b?

d.   Compare your answers to parts b and c. Does the person's betting behavior seem reasonable to you? How could you intuitively explain such behavior?

Source: R. L. Winkler (1972).

14.29. Suppose that a decision maker has the following utility function:

$$U(x) = -0.000156x^2 + 0.028125x - 0.265625$$

Use this utility function to calculate risk premiums for the gambles shown in Tables 14.3 and 14.4; create a similar table but based on this quadratic utility function. How would you classify the risk attitude of a decision maker with this utility function? Does such a risk attitude seem reasonable to you?

14.30. The CEO of a chemicals firm must decide whether to develop a new process that has been suggested by the research division. His decision tree is shown in Figure 14.20. There are two sources of uncertainty. The production cost is viewed as a continuous random variable, uniformly distributed between $1.75 and $2.25, and the size of the market (units sold) for the product is normally distributed with mean 10,300 units and standard deviation 2,200 units.

The firm's CEO is slightly risk-averse. His utility function is given by

$$U(Z) = 1 - e^{-Z/20,000} \quad \text{where } Z \text{ is the net profit}$$

Should the CEO develop the new process? Answer this question by running a computer simulation, using 10,000 trials. Should the decision maker be concerned about the fact that if he develops the new

FIGURE **14.20**
Decision tree for
Problem 14.30.

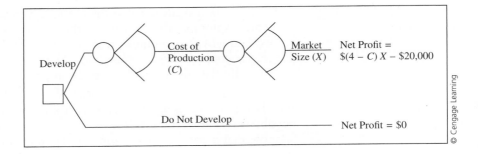

process, the utility could be less than or greater than the utility for $0?
On what basis should he make his decision?

14.31. The year is 2040, and you are in the supercomputer business. Your firm
currently produces a machine that is relatively expensive (list price $6
million) and relatively slow (for supercomputers in the twenty-first century). The speed of supercomputers is measured in calculations, known as
floating point operations ("flops"), per second. Thus, one 1 petaflop per
second = 1 pps, or one quadrillion calculations per second. Your current
machine is capable of 150 pps. If you could do it, you would prefer to
develop a supercomputer that costs less (to beat the competition) and is
faster.

You have a research-and-development (R&D) decision to make a
supercomputer based on two alternatives. You can choose one or the
other of the following projects, or neither, but budget constraints prevent you from engaging in both projects.

A. **The super-supercomputer.** This project involves the development
of a machine that is extremely fast (800 pps) and relatively inexpensive ($5 million). But this is a fairly risky project. The engineers
who have been involved in the early stages estimate that there is
only a 50% chance that this project would succeed. If it fails, you
will be stuck with your current machine.

B. **The better supercomputer.** This project would pursue the development of an $8 million machine capable of 500 gps. This project also

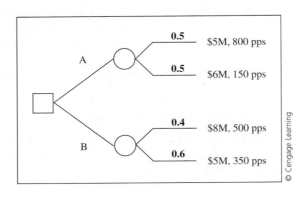

FIGURE **14.22**

Assessments to assist your choice from among the supercomputer R&D projects in Problem 14.31.

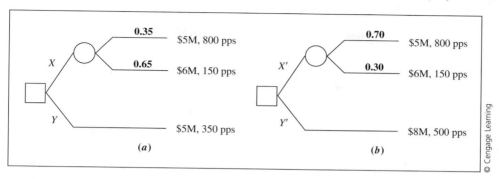

(a)

(b)

© Cengage Learning

is somewhat risky. The engineers believe that there is only a 40% chance that this project will achieve its goal. They quickly point out, however, that even if the $8 million, 500 gps machine does not materialize, the technology involved is such that they would at least be able to produce a $5 million machine capable of 350 gps.

The decision tree is shown in Figure 14.21. To decide between the two alternatives, you have made the following assessments:

   I.   The best possible outcome is the $5 million, 800 gps machine, and the worst outcome is the status quo $6 million, 150 gps machine.

   II. If you had the choice, you would be indifferent between Alternatives X and Y shown in Figure 14.22a.

   III. If you had the choice, you would be indifferent between Alternatives X' and Y' in Figure 14.22b.

  a. Using assessments I, II, and III, decide between Projects A and B. Justify your decision.

  b. Explain why Project A appears to be riskier than Project B. Given that A is riskier than B, would you change your answer to part a? Why or why not?

14.32. Show that the value of Y that yields indifference between the two alternatives in Figure 14.12 is within about 4% of the risk tolerance R.

14.33. We stated that to assess the risk tolerance value of R for the exponential utility function, we should find the greatest value of Y such that the decision maker is indifferent between receiving $0 or a 50-50 gamble with payoffs Y and $-Y/2$. Show why this assessment procedure works. (*Hint:* Show that the EU of the gamble is approximately equal to the EU of $0 when $U(x) = 1 - e^{-x/Y}$.)

14.34. In the trade-off method for assessing utilities, consider the dollar amount X_1 that makes you indifferent between gambles A_1 and A_2, and X_2 that makes you indifferent between gambles B_1 and B_2. Show that $U(X_2) = 2U(X_1)$. (Hint: Write out the equations that reflect indifference between the gambles.)

INTERPLANTS, INC.

Don Newcomb was perplexed. It had been five years since he had founded Interplants, Inc., a research-and-development firm that developed genetically engineered plants for interplanetary space flight. During that five years, he and his scientists had made dramatic advances in developing special plants that could be used for food and air-purification systems in space stations and transports. In fact, he mused, their scientific success had been far greater than he had ever expected.

Five years ago, after the world superpowers had agreed to share space-travel technology, the outlook had been quite rosy. Everyone had been optimistic. Indeed, he was one of many investors who had jumped at the chance to be involved in the development of such technology. But now, after 5 tumultuous years, the prospects were less exciting.

First, there had been the disappointing realization that none of the superpowers had made substantial progress on an ion engine to power space vehicles. Such an engine was absolutely crucial to the success of interplanetary space flight, because—theoretically, at least—it would make travel 10 times as fast as conventionally powered ships. When the importance of such an engine became obvious, the superpowers had generously funded a huge multinational research project. The project had made substantial progress, but many hurdles remained. Don's risk assessors estimated that there was still a 15% chance that the ion engine would prove an infeasible power source. If this were to happen, of course, Don and the many other investors in space travel technology would lose out.

Then there was the problem with the settlement policy. The superpowers could not agree on a joint policy for the settlement of interplanetary space, including the deployment of space stations as well as settlements on planets and their satellites. The United American Alliance urged discretion and long-range planning in this matter, suggesting that a multinational commission be established to approve individual settlement projects. Pacificasia and the Allied Slavic Economic Community were demanding that space be divided now. By immediately establishing property rights, they claimed, the superpowers would be able to develop the optimum space economy in which the superpowers could establish their own economic policies within their "colonies" as well as determine trade policies with the other superpowers. Europa favored the idea of a commission, but also was eager to explore other available economic possibilities.

The discussion among the superpowers had been going on since long before the founding of Interplants. Five years ago, progress was made, and it appeared that an agreement was imminent. But 18 months ago the process stalled. The participants in the negotiations had established positions from which they would not budge. Don had followed the discussions closely and had even provided expert advice to the negotiators regarding the potential for interplanetary agricultural developments. He guessed that there was only a 68% chance that the superpowers would eventually arrive at an agreement. Naturally, until an agreement was reached, there would be little demand for space-traveling plants.

Aside from these external matters, Don still faced the difficult issue of developing a full-scale production process for his plants. He and his engineers had some ideas about the costs of the process, but at this point, all they could do was come up with a probability distribution for the costs. In thinking about the distribution, Don had decided to approximate it with a three-point discrete distribution. Thus, he characterized the three branches as "inexpensive," "moderate," and "costly," with probabilities of 0.185, 0.63, and 0.185, respectively. Of course, his eventual profit (or loss) depended on the costs of the final process.

Don also had thought long and hard about the profits that he could anticipate under each of the various scenarios. Essentially, he thought about the uncertainty in two stages. First was the determination of costs, and second was the outcome of the external factors (the ion-engine research and the negotiations regarding settlement policy). If costs turned out to be "inexpensive," then, in the event that the superpowers agreed and the ion engine was successful, he could expect a profit of 125 billion credits. He would lose 15 billion credits if either the engine or the negotiations failed. Likewise, if costs were "moderate," he could anticipate either a profit of 100 billion credits if both of the external factors resulted in a positive outcome, or a loss of 18 billion if either of the external factors were negative. Finally, the corresponding figures in the case of a "costly" production process were profits of 75 billion credits or a loss of 23 billion.

"This is so confusing," complained Don to Paul Fiester, his chief engineer. "I really never expected to be in this position. Five years ago none of these risks were apparent to me, and I guess I just don't tolerate risk well."

After a pause, Paul quietly suggested, "Well, maybe you should sell the business."

Don considered that. "Well, that's a possibility. I have no idea how many crazy people out there would want it."

"Some of the other engineers and I might be crazy enough," Paul replied. "Depending on the price, of course. At least we'd be going in with our eyes open. We know what the business is about and what the risks are."

Don gave the matter a lot of thought that night. "What should I sell the company for? I hate to give up the possibility of earning up to 125 billion credits. But I don't like the possibility of losing 23 billion either—no

one would!" As he lay awake, he finally decided that he would let the business go—with all its risks—for 20 billion credits. If he could get that much for it, he'd sell. If not, he'd just as soon stick with it, in spite of his frustrations with the risks.

Questions

1. Draw a decision tree for Don Newcomb's problem.
2. What is the significance of his statement that he would sell the business for 20 billion credits?
3. Suppose that Don's risk attitude can be modeled with an exponential utility function. If his certainty equivalent were 15 billion credits, find his risk tolerance. What would his risk tolerance be if his CE were 20 billion?

STRENLAR, PART III

Consider once again Fred Wallace's decision in the Strenlar case study at the end of Chapter 4. What if Fred is risk-averse? Assume that Fred's attitude toward risk in this case can be adequately modeled using an exponential utility function in which the utility is calculated for net present value. Thus,

$$U(NPV) = 1 - e^{-NVP/R}$$

Question

1. Check the sensitivity of Fred's decision to his risk tolerance, R. What is the critical R value for which his optimal decision changes? What advice can you give to Fred?

REFERENCES

For the most part, the material presented in this chapter has been our own version of familiar material. Good basic treatments of EU and risk aversion are available in most decision-analysis textbooks, including Bunn (1984), Holloway (1979), Raiffa (1968), Vatter et al. (1978), von Winterfeldt and Edwards (1986), and Winkler (1972). Keeney and Raiffa (1976) offer a somewhat more advanced treatment that focuses on multiattribute utility models, although it does contain an excellent exposition of the basic material at a somewhat higher mathematical level. The text by von Winterfeldt and Edwards (1986) points out that we tend to think about various kinds of money (pocket money, monthly income, investment capital) in different ways; thus, how utility-assessment questions are framed in terms of these different funds can have a strong effect on the utility function.

The material on the exponential utility function and risk tolerance is based primarily on Holloway (1979) and McNamee and Celona (1987). Both books contain excellent discussion and problems on this material.

For students who wish more detail on decreasing and constant risk aversion, look in the financial economics literature. In financial models, utility functions for market participants are important for modeling the economic system. An excellent starting point is Copeland and Weston (1979). A classic article that develops the idea of a risk-aversion coefficient (the reciprocal of risk tolerance) is Pratt (1964). Bell (1995a, b) discusses the "linear-plus-exponential" utility function $aw - be^{-cw}$, where w is total wealth. This utility function has many desirable properties; see Problems 14.25 and 14.26.

Our discussion of biases in utility assessment has necessarily been cursory. Much research has been done on this topic, and we have just skimmed the surface. For more on this topic, Kahneman and Tversky (2000) provides a compilation of important academic articles. Plous (1993) and Bazerman and Moore (2008) are good general introductions for a layperson.

Our discussion of what to do to mitigate biases was also quite cursory. We saw that there are two general approaches: use assessment methods that reduce the biases in the first place, and use sensitivity analysis during analysis to counteract any errors. A third approach is also possible, and that is to adjust a decision maker's assessments after the fact to account for suspected biases. Clemen (2008) provides an overview of recent research along this line.

Bazerman, M., and D, Moore (2008) *Judgment in Managerial Decision Making, 7th Edition.* New York: Wiley.

Bell, D. (1995a) "Risk, Return, and Utility." *Management Science*, 41, 23–30.

Bell D. (1995b) "A Contextual Uncertainty Condition for Behavior under Risk." *Management Science*, 41, 1145–1150.

Bleichrodt, H., J. Pinto, and P. Wakker (2001) "Making descriptive use of Prospect Theory to improve the prescriptive use of EU." *Management Science*, 11, 1498–1514.

Bostic, R., R. Herrnstein, and R. D. Luce (1990) "The effect on the preference-reversal phenomenon of using choice indifferences." *Journal of Economic Behavior and Organization*, 13, 193–212. Bunn, D. (1984) *Applied Decision Analysis.* New York: McGraw-Hill.

Clemen, R. (2008). "Improving and measuring the effectiveness of decision analysis: Linking decision analysis and behavioral decision research." Book chapter in: T. Kugler, J. C. Smith, T. Connolly, and Y.-J. Son (eds.) *Decision modeling and behavior in complex and uncertain environments.* New York: Springer, 3–31.

Copeland, T. E., and J. F. Weston (1979) *Financial Theory and Corporate Policy.* Reading, MA: Addison-Wesley.

Grether, D., and C. Plott (1979) "Economic theory of Choice and the Preference Theory Phenomenon." *American Economic Review*, 69, 623–638.

Hershey, J., and P. Schoemaker (1985) "Probability versus Certainty Equivalence Methods in Utility Measurement: Are They Equivalent?" *Management Science*, 31, 1213–1231.

Holloway, C. A. (1979) *Decision Making under Uncertainty: Models and Choices.* Englewood Cliffs, NJ: Prentice Hall.

Howard, R. A. (1988) "Decision Analysis: Practice and Promise." *Management Science, 34,* 679–695.

Kahneman, D., and A. Tversky (eds.) (2000) *Choices, Values, and Frames.* Cambridge: Cambridge University Press; Keeney, R., and H. Raiffa (1976) *Decisions with Multiple Objectives.* New York: Wiley.

Lichtenstein, S., and P. Slovic, P. (1971) "Reversals of preference between bids and choices in gambling decisions." *Journal of Experimental Psychology*, 89, 46–55.

McNamee, P., and J. Celona (1987) *Decision Analysis for the Professional with Supertree.* Redwood City, CA: Scientific Press.

Plous, S. (1993) *The Psychology of Judgment and Decision Making.* New York: McGraw-Hill.

Pratt, J. (1964) "Risk Aversion in the Small and in the Large." *Econometrica*, 32, 122–136.

Raiffa, H. (1968) *Decision Analysis.* Reading, MA: Addison-Wesley.

Thaler, R. (1980) "Toward a Positive Theory of Consumer Choice," *Journal of Economic Behavior and Organization*, 1980, 1, 39–60. Vatter, P. A., S. P. Bradley, S. C. Frey, Jr., and B. B. Jackson (1978) *Quantitative Methods in Management.* Homewood, IL: Irwin.

Von Winterfeldt, D., and W. Edwards (1986) *Decision Analysis and Behavioral Research.* Cambridge: Cambridge University Press.

Wakker, P., and D. Deneffe (1996) "Eliciting von Neumann-Morganstern utilities when probabilities are distorted or unknown." *Management Science*, 42, 1131–1150.

Winkler, R. L. (1972) *Introduction to Bayesian Inference and Decision.* New York: Holt.

EPILOGUE

Harriman's broker, Jacob H. Schiff, was at his synagogue when Harriman's order for 40,000 shares was placed; the shares were never purchased. By the following Monday, Hill had cabled Morgan in France, and they had decided to buy as many Northern Pacific shares as they could. The share price went from $114 on Monday to $1,000 on Thursday. In the aftermath, Hill and Morgan agreed that Harriman should be represented on the board of directors. Harriman, however, had little if any influence; James Hill continued to run the Great Northern, Northern Pacific, and Burlington railroads as he saw fit.

Source: S. H. Holbrook (1958) "The Legend of Jim Hill." *American Heritage,* IX(4), 10–13, 98–101.

CHAPTER 15

Utility Axioms, Paradoxes, and Implications

WITH CONTRIBUTIONS BY JEFFERY GUYSE

In this chapter, we will look at several issues. First, we will consider some of the foundations of utility theory. From the basis of a few behavioral axioms, it is possible to establish logically that people who behave according to the axioms should make choices consistent with the maximization of expected utility. But since the early 1950s, cognitive psychologists have noted that people do not always behave according to expected utility theory, and extensive literature now covers these behavioral paradoxes. We review part of that literature here. Because decision analysis depends on foundational axioms, it is worthwhile to consider some implications of these behavioral paradoxes, particularly with regard to the assessment of utility functions.

The following example previews some of the issues we will consider. This one is a participatory example. You should think hard about the choices you are asked to make before reading on.

Preparing for an Influenza Outbreak	The United States is preparing for an outbreak of an unusual Asian strain of influenza. Experts expect 600 people to die from the disease. Two programs are available that could be used to combat the disease, but because of limited resources only one can be implemented.

Program A (Tried and True)	400 people will be saved.
Program B (Experimental)	There is an 80% chance that 600 people will be saved and a 20% chance that no one will be saved.

Which of these two programs do you prefer?

Jeffery Guyse, Professor of Technology and Operations Management at California State Polytechnic University, Pomona contributed to the behavioral and psychological aspects of this chapter.

Now consider the following two programs:

Program C   200 people will die.

Program D   There is a 20% chance that 600 people will die and an 80% chance that no one will die.

Would you prefer C or D?

Source: Reprinted with permission from Tversky, A., and D. Kahneman, "The Framing of Decisions and the Psychology of Choice," *Science*, 211, 453–458. Copyright 1981 by the American Association for the Advancement of Science.

AXIOMS FOR EXPECTED UTILITY

Our first step in this chapter is to look at the behavioral assumptions that form the basis of expected utility. These assumptions, or *axioms,* relate to the consistency with which an individual expresses preferences from among a series of risky prospects. Instead of axioms, we might call these *rules for clear thinking.* In the following discussion, the axioms are presented at a fairly abstract level. Simple examples are given to clarify their meaning. As we put them to work in the development of the main argument, the importance and intuition behind the axioms should become clearer.

1. *Ordering and transitivity.* A decision maker can rank order (establish preference or indifference) any two consequences, and the ordering is transitive. For example, given any two consequences A_1 and A_2, either A_1 is preferred to A_2 (which is sometimes written as $A_1 \succ A_2$), A_2 is preferred to A_1 (denoted $A_1 \prec A_2$), or the decision maker is indifferent between A_1 and A_2 (denoted $A_1 \sim A_2$). Transitivity means that if A_1 is preferred to A_2 and A_2 is preferred to A_3, then A_1 is preferred to A_3. For example, this axiom says that an individual can express his or her preferences regarding, say, cities in which to reside. If that person preferred Amsterdam to London and London to Paris, then he or she would prefer Amsterdam to Paris.

2. *Reduction of compound uncertain events.* A decision maker is indifferent between a compound uncertain event (a complicated mixture of gambles or lotteries) and a simple uncertain event as determined by reduction using standard probability manipulations. Figure 15.1 illustrates the reduction

FIGURE **15.1**

The reduction axiom showing that compound uncertain events can be reduced to simple uncertain events without changing the decision maker's preferences.

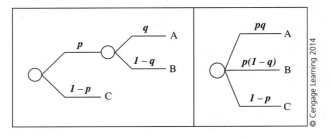

© Cengage Learning 2014

axiom in that going from the compound uncertainty on the left to the uncertainty on the right does not alter the decision maker's preferences; the decision maker should be indifferent between the two. This comes into play when we reduce compound events into reference gambles. The assumption says that we can perform the reduction without affecting the decision maker's preferences. We made use of this axiom in Chapter 4 in our discussion of risk profiles. The progression from Figure 4.14 through Figure 4.16 is a matter of reducing to simpler terms the compound uncertain event that is associated with the counteroffer.

3. *Continuity.* Given three consequences A_1, A, and A_2 where the decision maker's stated preferences are $A_1 \succ A \succ A_2$, then we can always find a probability value p, $0 < p < 1$, such that the decision maker is indifferent between receiving A for sure and a lottery with probability p of receiving A_1 and probability $1 - p$ of receiving A_2. This simply says that we can always construct a reference gamble with some probability p, $0 < p < 1$, for which the decision maker will be indifferent between the reference gamble and A. For example, suppose you find yourself as the plaintiff in a court case. You believe that the court will award you either $5,000 or nothing. Now imagine that the defendant offers to pay you $1,500 to drop the charges. According to the continuity axiom, there must be some probability p of winning $5,000 (and the corresponding $1 - p$ probability of winning nothing) for which you would be indifferent between taking or rejecting the settlement offer. Of course, if your subjective probability of winning happens to be lower than p, then you should accept the proposal.

4. *Substitutability.* A decision maker is indifferent between any original uncertain event that includes outcome A and one formed by substituting for A an uncertain event that is judged to be its equivalent. Figure 15.2 shows how this works. This axiom allows the substitution of uncertain reference gambles into a decision for their certainty equivalents (CEs). For example, suppose you are interested in playing the lottery, and you are just barely willing to pay 50 cents for a ticket. If I owe you 50 cents, then you should be just as willing to accept a lottery ticket as the 50 cents in cash.

FIGURE **15.2**

Two decision trees.

If A is equivalent to a lottery with a p chance at C and $1 - p$ chance at D, then Decision Tree I is equivalent to Decision Tree II.

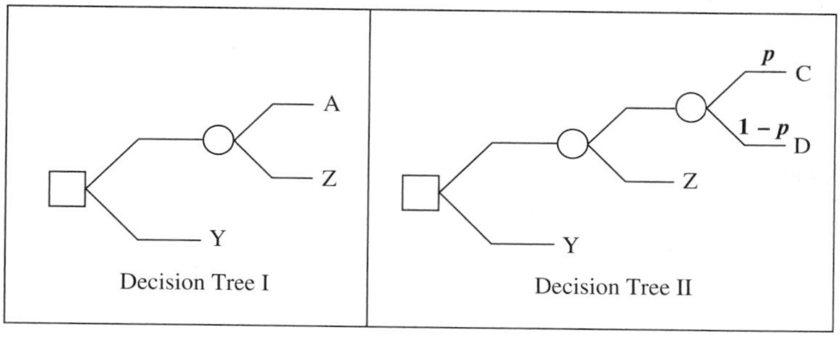

Decision Tree I

Decision Tree II

© Cengage Learning

5. *Monotonicity.* Given two reference gambles with the same possible outcomes, a decision maker prefers the one with the higher probability of winning the preferred outcome. This one is easy to see. Imagine that two different car dealerships each can order the new car that you want. Both dealers offer the same price, delivery, warranty, and financing, but one is more likely to provide good service than the other. To which one would you go? The one that has the better chance of providing good service, of course.

6. *Invariance.* All that is needed to determine a decision maker's preferences among uncertain events are the payoffs (or consequences) and the associated probabilities.

7. *Finiteness.* No consequences are considered infinitely bad or infinitely good.

Most of us agree that these assumptions are reasonable under almost all circumstances. It is worth noting, however, that many decision theorists find some of the axioms controversial! The reasons for the controversy range from introspection regarding particular decision situations to formal psychological experiments in which human subjects make choices that clearly violate one or more of the axioms. We will discuss some of these experiments in the next section.

For example, the substitutability axiom is a particular point of debate. For some decision makers, the fact of having to deal with two uncertain events in Decision Tree II of Figure 15.2 can be worse than facing the single one in Decision Tree I. Moreover, individuals might make this judgment and at the same time agree that in a single-stage lottery, A is indeed equivalent to the risky prospect with a p chance at C and a $1 - p$ chance at D.

As another example, we can pick on the apparently innocuous transitivity axiom. In Figure 15.3, you have two lotteries from which to choose. Each of the six outcomes has probability $\frac{1}{6}$. One way to look at the situation is that the prize in Game B is better than Game A's in five of the six outcomes, and thus it may be reasonable to prefer B, even though the structure of the lotteries is essentially the same. Now consider the games in Figure 15.4. If B was preferred to A in Figure 15.3, then by the same argument, C would be preferred to B, D to C, E to D, F to E, and, finally, A would be preferred to F. Thus, these preferences do not obey the transitivity axiom, because transitivity would never permit A to be preferred to something else that is in turn preferred to A.

FIGURE **15.3**
A pair of lotteries.

Outcomes 1 through 6 each occurs with probability $\frac{1}{6}$. Would you prefer to play Game A or Game B?

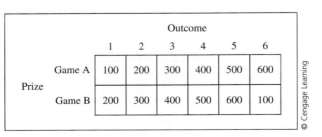

		Outcome					
		1	2	3	4	5	6
Prize	Game A	100	200	300	400	500	600
	Game B	200	300	400	500	600	100

© Cengage Learning

FIGURE **15.4**
More games to consider.

Outcomes 1 through 6 each still has probability $\frac{1}{6}$.

	Outcome 1	2	3	4	5	6
Game B	200	300	400	500	600	100
Game C	300	400	500	600	100	200
Game D	400	500	600	100	200	300
Game E	500	600	100	200	300	400
Game F	600	100	200	300	400	500
Game A	100	200	300	400	500	600

Prize (label at left of table)

© Cengage Learning

The controversy about individual axioms notwithstanding, if you accept axioms 1 through 7, then logically you also must accept the following proposition.

> **Proposition:** Given any two uncertain outcomes B_1 and B_2, if assumptions 1 through 7 hold, there are numbers U_1, U_2, ..., U_n representing preferences (or utilities) associated with the consequences such that the overall preference between the uncertain events is reflected by the expected values of the Us for each consequence. In other words, if you accept the axioms, (1) it is possible to find a utility function for you to evaluate the consequences, and (2) you should be making your decisions in a way that is consistent with maximizing expected utility.

In the following pages, we will demonstrate how the axioms permit the transformation of uncertain alternatives into reference gambles (gambles between the best and worst alternatives) with different probabilities. It is on the basis of this kind of transformation that the proposition can be proved.

Suppose you face the simple decision problem shown in Figure 15.5. For convenience, assume the payoffs are in dollars. The continuity axiom says that we can find reference gambles that are equivalent to the outcomes at the ends of the branches. Suppose (hypothetically) that you are indifferent between $15 and the following reference gamble:

Win $40 with probability 0.36

Win $10 with probability 0.64

Likewise, suppose you are indifferent between $20 and the next reference gamble:

Win $40 with probability 0.60

Win $10 with probability 0.40

FIGURE **15.5**
A simple decision problem under uncertainty.

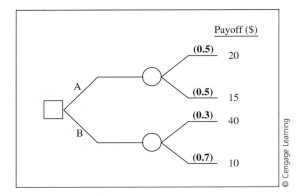

FIGURE **15.6**
Decision tree from Figure 15.5 after substituting reference gambles for outcomes.

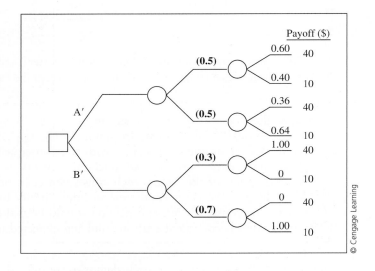

The substitutability axiom says that we can replace the original outcomes with their corresponding reference gambles, as in Figure 15.6. (We have replaced the outcomes in Lottery B with "trivial" lotteries. The reason for doing so will become apparent.) The substitutability axiom says that you are indifferent between A and A′ and also between B and B′. Thus, the problem has not changed.

Now use the reduction-of-compound-events axiom to reduce the decision tree (Figure 15.7). In performing this step, the overall probability of winning $40 in A″ is 0.5(0.60) + 0.5(0.36), or 0.48; it is similarly calculated for winning $10. For the lower half of the tree, we just end up with B again. The monotonicity axiom means we prefer to A″ to B″, and so by transitivity (which says that A″ ~ A′ ~ A and B″ ~ B′ ~ B), we must prefer A to B in the original decision.

To finish the demonstration, we must show that it is possible to come up with numbers that represent utilities so that a greater expected utility implies

FIGURE **15.7**
Reducing the
decision tree to
reference gambles.

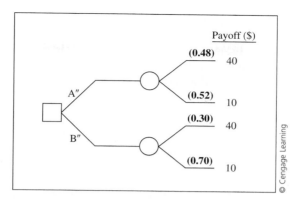

a preferred alternative, and vice versa. In this case, we need utilities that result in a greater expected utility for Alternative A. Use the probabilities assessed previously in the reference gambles as those utilities. (Now you can see the reason for the extension of B in Figure 15.6; we need the probabilities.) We can redraw the original decision tree, as in Figure 15.8, with the utilities in place of the original monetary payoffs. Calculating expected utilities shows that A has the higher expected utility and hence should be preferred:

$$EU(A) = 0.5(0.60) + 0.5(0.36) = 0.48$$

$$EU(B) = 0.3(1.00) + 0.7(0) = 0.30$$

This exercise may seem arcane and academic. But put simply, if you think it is reasonable to behave according to the axioms at the beginning of the section, then (1) it is possible to find your utility values, and (2) you should make decisions that would be consistent with the maximization of expected utility.

In our discussions of utility assessment in Chapter 14, the claim was made that a utility function could be scaled (multiplied by a positive constant and added to a constant) without changing anything. Now you should see

FIGURE **15.8**
Original decision
tree with utility
values replacing
monetary values.

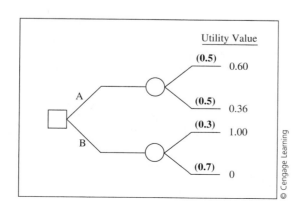

clearly that the whole purpose of a utility function is to rank-order risky prospects. Take Alternatives A and B. We have concluded that A is preferred to B because EU(A) = 0.48, which is greater than EU(B) = 0.30. Suppose that we take the utility numbers, as shown in Figure 15.8, and scale them. That is, let $U'(x)$ be the new utility function:

$$U'(x) = a + bU(x)$$

where $b > 0$ and $U(x)$ is our original utility function (from Figure 15.8). We calculate the expected utilities of A and B on the basis of the new utility function:

$$
\begin{aligned}
EU'(A) &= 0.5[a + bU(20)] + 0.5[a + bU(15)] \\
&= a + b[0.5U(20) + 0.5U(15)] \\
&= a + bEU(A) \\
&= a + b(0.48)
\end{aligned}
$$

$$
\begin{aligned}
EU'(B) &= 0.3[a + bU(40)] + 0.7[a + bU(10)] \\
&= a + b[0.3U(40) + 0.7U(10)] \\
&= a + bEU(B) \\
&= a + b(0.30)
\end{aligned}
$$

It should be clear that $EU'(A) = a + b(0.48)$ will be greater than $EU'(B) = a + b(0.30)$ as long as $b > 0$. As indicated, the implication is that we can scale our utility functions linearly with the constants a and $b > 0$ without changing the rankings of the risky alternatives in terms of expected utility. Specifically, this means that no matter what the scale of a utility function, we always can rescale it so that the largest value is 1 and the smallest is 0. (For that matter, you can rescale it so that the largest and smallest values are whatever you want!)

If you look carefully at our transformations of the original decision problem presented previously, you will see that we never explicitly invoked either the invariance or finiteness axioms. Why are these axioms important? The invariance axiom says that we need nothing but the payoffs and the probabilities; nothing else matters. (In the context of multiattribute utility as discussed in Chapters 16 and 17, we would need consequences on all relevant dimensions.)

The finiteness axiom assures us that expected utility will never be infinite, and so we always will be able to make meaningful comparisons. To see the problem with unbounded utility, suppose that you have been approached by an evangelist who has told you that unless you accept his religion, you will burn in Hell for eternity. If you attach an infinitely negative utility to an eternity in Hell (and it is difficult to imagine a worse fate), then no matter how small your subjective probability that the evangelist is right, as long as it is even slightly positive, you must be compelled to convert. This is simply because any small positive probability multiplied by the infinitely negative utility will result in an infinitely negative expected utility. Similar problems are encountered if an outcome is accorded infinite positive utility; you would do anything at all if doing so gave you even the slightest chance at achieving such a wonderful outcome. Thus, if an outcome in your decision problem has unbounded utility, the expected utility approach does not help much when it comes to making the decision.

PARADOXES

Even though the axioms of expected utility theory appear to be compelling when we discuss them, people do not necessarily make choices in accordance with them. Research into these behavioral deviations from the normative model began almost as early as the original research into utility theory itself, and now a large literature exists for many aspects of human behavior under uncertainty. Much of this literature is reviewed in Bazerman and Moore (2008), Hastie and Dawes (2010), Hogarth (1987), Plous (1993), and von Winterfeldt and Edwards (1986). We will cover a few of the high points.

Most violations of the axioms of expected utility theory are classified as *paradoxes*. Because the axioms appear to be logical indicators of how we *should* choose, deviations from the axioms are viewed by some as "irrational" behavior. We must differentiate between those deviations that are indeed violations of logic and those that are merely induced by the procedure used to elicit these choices. Let us propose that different techniques used to determine an individual's preferred choice from the same set of alternatives should lead to the same choice. That is, if you prefer A over B, it should not matter how you are asked to reveal your preference; you should always prefer A over B. This consistency is known as *procedure invariance,* as discussed in Chapter 14. Violations of the transitivity axiom have been linked directly to violations of procedure invariance, in particular to differences between asessed CEs versus CEs derived from explicit choices; see our discussion of *preference reversals* in Chapter 14.

A violation of procedure invariance is not the only way intransitive preferences can arise. Transitivity can also be violated and procedure invariance holds when individuals cannot distinguish differences between alternatives, or when the differences do not seem significant. For example, turn your radio up just a fraction of a hair and you would not be able to hear the difference in volume right? Now do it again, just a little tiny bit on the knob. No difference again. Repeating this procedure seems to bear fruitless results, but if you compare the starting volume with the ending, one can definitely hear the increase. It was just too gradual to distinguish one decibel at a time. Car salesmen (among others) know this and can use it to your disadvantage. When buying a $25,000 car, what is an additional $250 for a 6-disc CD changer? Only $5 a month. And the sport wheels? Only $12 a month more! Add a sunroof, extended warranty, floor mats, etc., and the next thing you know is that you can barely afford the car payment! How did this happen? Even though the individual additions did not seem significant, their aggregate contribution is. Procedures like this can lead to violations of transitivity, which most of us would view as irrational.

Explicitly induced *framing effects* are among the most pervasive paradoxes in choice behavior that violate procedure invariance. Tversky and Kahneman (1981) show how an individual's risk attitude can change depending on the way the decision problem is posed—that is, on the *frame* in which a problem is presented. The difficulty is that the same decision problem usually can be expressed in different frames. A good example is the influenza-outbreak problem at the beginning of the chapter. You may have noticed that Program A is the same as C and that B is the same as D. It all depends on whether you think in terms of deaths or lives saved. Many people prefer A on one hand, but D on the other.

To a great extent, the reason for the inconsistent choices appears to be that different *points of reference* are used to frame the problem in two different ways. For example, outcomes better than the reference point are thought of as gains, while those worse than the reference point are thought of as losses. That is, in Programs A and B, the reference point is that 600 people are expected to die, but some may be saved. Thus, we think about gains in terms of numbers of lives saved. On the other hand, in Programs C and D, the reference point is that no people would be expected to die without the disease. In this case, we tend to think about lives lost. One of the important general principles that psychologists Kahneman and Tversky and others have discovered is that people tend to be risk-averse in dealing with gains but risk-seeking in deciding about losses. A typical assessed utility function for changes in wealth is shown in Figure 15.9. These results have been obtained in many different behavioral experiments. (For a very early example, see Swalm 1966.)

FIGURE **15.9**
Typical assessed utility function for changes in wealth.

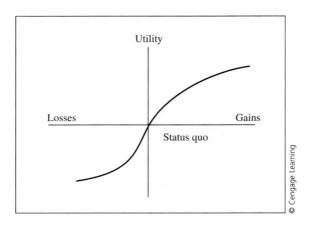

Is a specific axiom being violated when a decision maker's choices exhibit an explicit framing effect? The answer to this question is not exactly clear. Although many possibilities exist, the invariance axiom may be the weak link in this case. It may be that payoffs (or utilities) and probabilities are not sufficient to determine a decision maker's preferences. Some understanding of the decision maker's frame of reference also may be required.

For another example, consider the Allais paradox:

Allais Paradox

You have two decisions to make.

Decision 1: **A** Win \$1 million with probability 1

          B Win \$5 million with probability 0.10

              Win \$1 million with probability 0.89

              Win \$0 with probability 0.01

Before proceeding, choose A or B. Would you give up a sure \$1 million for a small chance at \$5 million and possibly nothing?

Decision 2: **C** Win \$1 million with probability 0.11

              Win \$0 with probability 0.89

          D Win \$5 million with probability 0.10

              Win \$0 with probability 0.90

Now choose C or D in Decision 2.

This is the well-known Allais Paradox (Allais 1953; Allais and Hagen 1979). The decisions are shown in decision-tree form in Figure 15.10. Experimentally, as many as 82% of subjects prefer A over B and 83% prefer D over C. But we can easily show that choosing A on the one hand and D on the other is contrary to expected utility maximization. Let $U(\$0) = 0$ and $U(\$5,000,000) = 1$; they are the best and worst outcomes. Then,

FIGURE 15.10
Choices in the Allais Paradox.

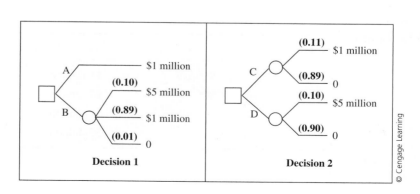

$$EU(A) = U(\$1 \text{ million})$$
$$EU(B) = 0.10 + 0.89\, U(\$1 \text{ million})$$

Thus, A is preferred to B if and only if

$$U(\$1 \text{ million}) > 0.10 + 0.89\, U(\$1 \text{ million})$$

or

$$U(\$1 \text{ million}) > 0.91$$

Now for Decision 2,

$$EU(C) = 0.11\, U(\$1 \text{ million})$$
$$EU(D) = 0.10$$

so D is preferred to C if and only if $U(\$1 \text{ million}) < 0.91$.

U($1 million) cannot be both greater than and less than 0.91 at the same time, so choosing A and D is not consistent with expected utility. Consistent choices are A and C or B and D. Kahneman and Tversky (1981) have attributed this common inconsistency to the *certainty effect*, whereby individuals tend to place too much weight on a certain outcome relative to uncertain outcomes. In the Allais Paradox, the certainty effect would tend to make individuals overvalue A in Decision 1, possibly leading to an inconsistent choice. When confronted with their inconsistency, some individuals revise their choices. Would you revise yours in light of this discussion?

Another way to look at the Allais Paradox is to structure the decision problem using lottery tickets in a hat. Imagine that 100 tickets are numbered sequentially from 1 to 100 and placed in a hat. One ticket will be drawn at random, and you will receive a prize depending on the option you choose and the number on the ticket. Prizes for A and B are described in Table 15.1. For A, you would win $1 million regardless of the ticket chosen, but for B, you would win nothing if Ticket 1 is chosen, $5 million for Tickets 2 through 11, and $1 million for Tickets 12 through 100. Note that you win the same ($1 million) in the two lotteries for Tickets 12 through 100. Thus,

TABLE 15.1 Prizes in the Allais Paradox.

Tickets 1–100 are placed in a hat, and one ticket is drawn randomly. The dollar amounts shown in the table are the prizes for the four options.

Option	Ticket #1	Tickets #2–11	Tickets #12–100
A	$1 million	$1 million	$1 million
B	$0	$5 million	$1 million
C	$1 million	$1 million	$0
D	$0	$5 million	$0

© Cengage Learning

your choice should depend only on your preferences regarding the outcomes or payoffs for Tickets 1 through 11.

The same kind of thing can be done for Options C and D, which also are shown in Table 15.1. If you choose C, you win $1 million for Tickets 1–11 and nothing for Tickets 12–100. In D, you would win nothing for Ticket 1, $5 million for Tickets 2–11, and nothing for Tickets 12–100. Again, you win exactly the same thing (nothing) in both C and D for Tickets 12–100, and so your preferences between C and D should depend only on your preferences regarding Tickets 1–11. As you can see, the prizes associated with Tickets 1–11 are the same for Options A and C on the one hand and B and D on the other. Thus, if you prefer A to B, you also should prefer C to D, and vice versa.

It is intuitively reasonable that your preferences should not depend on Tickets 12–100, because the outcome is the same regardless of the decision made. This is an example of the *sure-thing principle,* which says that our preferences over lotteries or risky prospects should depend only on the parts of the lotteries that can lead to different outcomes. The idea of the sure thing is that, in the choice between A and B, winning $1 million is a sure thing if one of the tickets from 12 to 100 is drawn, regardless of your choice. If, as in the Allais choices, there are possible outcomes that have the same value to you regardless of the option you choose, and these outcomes occur with the same probability regardless of the option chosen, then you can ignore this part of the lottery. The sure-thing principle can be derived logically from our axioms. For our purposes, it is best to think of it as a behavioral principle that is consistent with our axioms; if you agree to behave in accordance with the axioms, you also should obey the sure-thing principle. If your choices in the Allais Paradox were inconsistent, then your preferences violated the sure-thing principle.

In addition to the certainty effect and the sure-thing principle, research has shown that gains are somehow less valued than equivalent losses. That is, losing $5 "hurts" more than finding $5 makes us "feel good." This is shown in the value function in Figure 15.9 as the curve for losses being steeper than that of gains. This asymmetry about the reference point is known as the *reflection effect* or *loss aversion* and can lead to some interesting behavior. For example, for many people, the financial status quo changes as soon as they file their income-tax return in anticipation of a refund; they "spend" their refund, usually in the form of credit, long before the check arrives in the mail. This could be due to the refund being coded as a gain and therefore may be valued less than if it was money earned from immediate labor. In other cases, individuals may maintain a particular reference point far longer than they should. A case in point is that gamblers often try to make up their losses; they throw good money after bad. Here "gamblers" can refer to individuals in casinos as well as to stock market investors or even managers who maintain a commitment to a project that has obviously gone sour. Typically, such a gambler will argue that backing out of a failed project amounts to a waste of the resources already spent.

Finally, the reference point has been shown to be affected by biases, in particular the anchoring and adjustment heuristic discussed in Chapter 8. To illustrate, consider the following:

> You have wanted to purchase a particular couch for your living room. It has not gone on sale since you found it in a department store near your residence six months ago. Finally the department store has a "once-a-year furniture extravaganza sale" and you have the ability to purchase the $700 couch for $400! You code this as a $300 gain since $700 is your reference and anchor. The day after delivery of the couch to your place, your next door neighbor comes over. He sees your new couch and exclaims, "Oh, I see you got that couch! I saw it on sale at the outlet across town for $200. Is that where you got it?"

Blast! Just like that, a $300 gain becomes a $200 loss. See how vulnerable our reference points are? Reference points can also be implicitly formulated, which leads us to *hedonic framing*.

HEDONIC FRAMING

The use of reference points in decision making may lead to more violations of expected utility theory by way of *hedonic framing* or *mental accounting*. Due to the shape of the value function shown in Figure 15.9, individuals may *implicitly* frame decisions to enhance their appeal. Richard Thaler (1985) came up with some nice examples. Let us look at some of them. To illustrate, answer the question: who is happier?

> "A" who is given two lottery tickets that are both winners, one for $25 and the other for $50.

> "B" who is given one lottery ticket that wins $75.

In experimental studies, most participants view A as being happier. We can obviously see that both A and B are better off by $75. Why does it matter the way in which the $75 was received? The shape of the value function indicates that when working with gains, dividing a large gain into smaller ones may be valued more by the receiver. This is known as *segregating gains*. Another way to think about this is to ask yourself whether or not you would like all of your birthday presents wrapped in one box. Would you? If not, you wish to segregate gains.

In addition, individuals also tend to *integrate losses*. Read the following example and ask yourself this time "who feels worse"?

> "A" gets a letter from the Internal Revenue Service saying he made a mistake on his income-tax return, and he owes $150.

> "B" gets two letters, one saying he owes $100 on his federal tax, and another saying he owes $50 on his state income tax.

Once again, you probably consider B to feel worse, even though you realize they are both worse off by $150. Consolidation of debt and including extra options in an automobile purchase are two other examples that may follow this preference pattern.

So although we like to separate gains, we prefer to combine losses. What happens when we mix the two? Well, it depends which is greater, the loss or the gain. Let us look at another example and answer once more who is happier:

"A" wins $100 in a lottery, but on the same day accidentally damages the rug in his apartment, which costs $80 to fix.

"B" wins $20 in the lottery.

Most will probably respond that B is happier. In general, we would rather have a small gain by itself than a larger gain with a (relatively) large loss. One more example illustrates preferences over mixed gains and losses known as the *silver lining principle*:

A's car gets $200 worth of damage in a parking lot. The damage is not covered by his insurance, but he wins a $25 football pool the same day.

B's car gets $175 worth of damage (again not covered), but does not win the pool.

Who was more upset? Must be Mr. B. Why? No "silver lining." We like to offset large losses with a gain, even a small one.

The four previous examples illustrate how we mentally account for gains and losses. Please note that utility theory would not be able to differentiate between any of the pairs in the four examples, because final wealth was the same in each instance. Even though we probably have a preference for which person we would rather be, A or B, can one argue that such a preference is irrational? These are simple examples to illustrate how hedonic framing or mental accounting can lead to seemingly reasonable preferences that are inconsistent with utility theory. Mental accounting *can*, however, lead us to decisions that we ourselves consider irrational, especially when faced with *sunk costs*.

FAILURE TO IGNORE SUNK COSTS

Economists have long argued that costs that cannot be recouped should be ignored in decisions. Richard Thaler (1980) reveals evidence that many times sunk costs are not ignored. For example, one experiment looked at the effects of sunk costs on unknowing diners at a pizza restaurant. Individuals paid $3 for an all-you-can-eat lunch at the door and then ordered from their server as many pieces of pizza as they wanted. Half of the tables in the restaurant were selected at random and given a $3 refund before ordering. The other half did not get the refund. Who ate more pizza? Believe it or not, those who "had to pay" (i.e., who had a real sunk cost of $3) ate more pizza on average than those who received a refund and hence had no sunk cost. It seems reasonable to think that, in an all-you-can-eat setting and when the meal is free, a person would eat until he or she is satisfactorily full. So, when one has to pay for it, they eat until they are *more* than full? It appears so, and the "get my money's worth" argument does not appear to maximize utility in this situation if the individual leaves the restaurant overly full and with the possibility of indigestion!

STATUS QUO BIAS

The search for alternatives may be limited when the decision maker has a bias toward keeping the status quo. Sameulson and Zeckhauser (1988) performed a series of decision-making experiments in which the participants showed a strong bias to sticking with the status quo. That is, individuals may overvalue the incumbent alternative when making iterative choices.

Just because people choose the status quo does not mean that they are making an irrational decision. It could be that a rational decision was made the first time, and if nothing has changed (in terms of alternatives, events, and outcomes with their respective values), the initial decision is again the best. Solve a decision tree twice without changing anything, and you will come to the same conclusion! This can hardly be viewed as irrational. But what if it costs something to change to the other alternative from one decision to the next? If changing is relatively expensive, it may be rational to stick with the status quo, because the marginal gain from the new alternative could be overshadowed by the switching cost.

But there are situations in which the status quo bias can lead to poor decision quality. This can occur if the status quo is given more weight for no other reason than it is the status quo. Decision makers can be averse to change, even if the change leaves them better off. It may be the fear of the unknown that can keep a battered wife with her abusive spouse, a bored employee at his uninteresting job, or a commuter sitting in rush-hour traffic on the freeway because she is unwilling to move closer to work (even after 10 years of commuting!)

IMPLICATIONS

The evidence is clear: People do not always behave according to the behavioral axioms. This fact has distinct implications for the practice of decision analysis. First, there are implications regarding how utility assessments should be made. Second, and perhaps more intriguing, are the implications for managers and policy makers whose jobs depend on how people actually make decisions. It may be important for such managers to consider some of the previously described behavioral phenomena. In this section, we will look at the issues involved in each of these areas.

IMPLICATIONS FOR UTILITY ASSESSMENT

We rely on assessments of CEs and other comparisons to find a utility function. Given the previous discussion, it is clear that, in the assessment process, we ask decision makers to perform tasks that we know they do not always

FIGURE **15.11**
A general framework for assessing utilities.

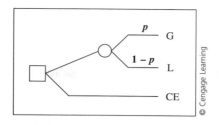

© Cengage Learning

perform consistently according to the axioms! Thus, it is no surprise that the behavioral paradoxes previously discussed may have some impact on the way that utility functions should be assessed.

There are several approaches to the assessment of utilities. In Chapter 14, we introduced the certainty-equivalent approach (find a CE for a specified gamble), the probability-equivalent (PE) approach (find a probability that makes a reference lottery equivalent to a specific certain amount), and the tradeoff (TO) method. If we think of the general case (Figure 15.11) as being indifferent between CE for sure and the reference lottery:

Win G with probability p

Win L with probability $1 - p$

then it is clear that we must preset three out of the four variables p, CE, G, and L. The selection of the fourth, which makes the decision maker indifferent between the two prospects, allows the specification of a utility value. Most practioners use either the CE or PE approaches. (The TO method is a relatively new approach.) Assessing a CE involves fixing G, L, and p and assessing CE; the PE method involves fixing CE, G, and L and assessing p.

The relative merits of the possible assessment techniques have been discussed to some degree. Hershey, Kunreuther, and Shoemaker (1982) report that the use of the CE approach tends to result in more risk-averse responses than does the PE approach when the consequences are gains. On the other hand, when the consequences are losses, the CE approach results in more risk-seeking behavior. When using the PE approach, many people appear to exhibit certain forms of probability distortion. Although the evidence is far from conclusive, it suggests that people deal best with 50–50 chances.

Many of the differences among the CE, PE, and TO methods are due to characteristics of the utility function, specifically *loss aversion* and *probability transformations*. Remember that loss aversion occurs when individuals place higher importance on losses than equivalent gains. The endowment effect discussed in Chapter 14, along with the previously discussed status quo bias, have been attributed to loss aversion. Probability transformations are a little more involved. Expected utility is said to be "linear in probabilities," a 1% increase in probability has associated with it a constant change in value, regardless of the initial starting point. That is, for every 1% increase in the probability of an event, the expected utility increases by a constant amount. Behavioral research has shown that people tend not to evaluate risky decisions in this way. Instead, we tend to *transform* the probabilities with a "probability weighting function." This is a subjective distortion of the probabilities that naturally occurs when we are faced with risky decisions. In general, small probabilities tend to be over-weighted, and large probabilities tend to be under-weighted.

As mentioned in Chapter 14, the TO method is insensitive to loss aversion and probability transformations; the CE method is insensitive to loss aversion, but biased by probability transformations; and the PE method is biased by both (Bleichrodt, Pinto, and Wakker, 2001)! Because the TO method requires more questions to accurately elicit the utility function, there is no clear "best" method, and the decision analyst must select a procedure depending on the particular circumstances, such as time available or the familiarity of the decision maker with the assessment procedures.

Managerial and Policy Implications

The idea that people actually make decisions that are sometimes inconsistent with decision-analysis principles is not new. In fact, the premise of a book such as this one is that it is possible to improve one's decision-making skills. But now we have seen that individuals behave in certain specific and predictable ways. What implications does this have for managers and policy makers?

The most fundamental issue has to do with the reference point or status quo. What is the decision maker's reference point or status quo in a particular decision situation? How do people establish a reference point for decision-making purposes? Can the perception of the status quo be manipulated, and, if so, how? Complete answers to these questions are certainly beyond the scope of our discussion here, but we can discuss important examples in which the status quo plays an important role.

First is the problem of "sunk costs." As briefly mentioned earlier, managers frequently remain committed to a project that obviously has gone bad. In decision-analysis terms, the money that already has been spent on the project no longer should influence current and future decisions. Any decisions, particularly whether to continue or abandon a project, must be forward-looking—that is, consider only future cash flows. To account for the sunk costs, they would have to be accounted for on every branch and hence could not affect the relative ordering of the alternatives.

What do we say to an individual who seems unable to ignore sunk costs? One piece of advice is to help the decision maker reframe the decision with a more appropriate reference point. If the individual wants to "throw good money after bad," then he or she may be operating on the basis of an earlier reference point; abandoning the project may look like accepting a sure loss of the money already invested. From this perspective, it might seem quite reasonable instead to seek a risky gain by remaining committed to the project. An alternative reference point views the choice as a chance of either winning or losing the amount about to be invested in a project that is unlikely to yield the anticipated benefits. From the perspective of this new reference point, abandoning the project amounts to the avoidance of a losing venture; funds would be better invested elsewhere.

In other cases, a problem's frame may be specified with equal validity in several ways. Consider the case of seat belts. If people view seat belts as inconvenient and uncomfortable, then they may refuse to wear them; the status quo is the level of comfort when unbuckled. Suppose, however, the status quo were framed as how well off people are in general. Who would want to risk the loss of a healthy family, a productive life, and possibly much of one's savings? The use of a seat belt is a form of inexpensive insurance to avoid a possible dramatic loss relative to this new status quo.

A similar argument can be made in the area of environmental protection. People may view environmental programs as anything from inconveniences (being forced to separate recyclable materials from trash) to major economic impediments (adhering to EPA's complex regulations). The implied status quo is the current level of direct costs, relative to which the programs represent a sure loss. If, however, emphasis is given to the current overall condition of the community, nation, or world, then the increased cost induced by the programs can be viewed as a small amount of insurance necessary to avoid a large loss relative to our current overall welfare.

In the discussion so far, we have focused our attention on issues concerning the status quo or reference points. We turn now to the certainty effect, or the fact that we tend to overvalue sure outcomes relative to uncertain ones. This psychological phenomenon can have interesting effects on our decision making, especially under conditions of uncertainty.

In our Western culture, we abhor uncertainty. Indeed, it is appropriate to expend resources for information in order to reduce uncertainty. This is true only up to a point, however, as we discussed in Chapter 12. But where may the certainty effect lead? We may try too hard to eliminate uncertainty altogether. For example, in organizations, there may be a tendency to spend far too much effort and resources on tracking down elusive information in an effort to know the "truth." More insidious is a tendency to ignore uncertainty altogether. We often tend to view forecasts, for example, as perfect indicators of the future, ignoring their inherent uncertainty. The use of carefully assessed probabilistic forecasts is an important way to avoid this problem.

As a society, the certainty effect may be a factor in our preoccupation with certain kinds of health and environmental risks. Many individuals—activists in various causes—would prefer to eliminate risk altogether, and thus they call for stringent regulations on projects that appear to pose risks to the population or environment. Certainly these individuals play a valuable role in drawing our attention to important issues, but achieving zero risk in our society is not only impractical, but also impossible. A sound approach to the management of risk in our society requires a consideration of both the benefits and costs of reducing risk to various levels.

In this brief section, we have considered various implications of the behavioral paradoxes for the application of decision analysis (especially utility assessment), as well as for organizational decisions and policy making. But we have only scratched the surface here. As research progresses in this fertile area, many other behavioral paradoxes and their implications will be studied. The examples we have considered illustrate the pervasiveness of the effects as well as their importance.

A FINAL PERSPECTIVE

We have discussed a variety of inconsistencies in human behavior. Do these inconsistencies invalidate expected utility theory? The argument all along has been that people do not always make coherent decisions without some guidance. If a decision maker does wish to make coherent decisions, then a careful decision-analysis approach, including a careful assessment of personal preferences, can help.

It is easy to get the impression that utility and probability numbers reside in a decision maker's mind and that the assessment procedure simply elicits those numbers. But there is more to the process than that. Just as the process of structuring a decision problem helps the decision maker understand the problem better and possibly leads to the recognition of new alternatives for action, so may the assessment process provide a medium in which the decision maker actually can develop his or her preferences or beliefs about uncertainty. The assessment process helps to mold the decision maker's subjective preferences and beliefs. How many of us, for example, have given much thought to assessing a utility function for a cup of coffee (Problem 15.15) or considered the probability distribution for a grade in a decision-analysis course (Problem 8.11)? Certainly the assessed numbers do not already exist inside our heads; they come into being through the assessment procedure. This is exactly why assessment often requires hard thinking and why decisions are hard to make. Thus, perhaps the best way to think about the assessment process is in constructive terms. Reflecting on the decision problem faced and considering our preferences and beliefs about uncertainty provides a basis not only for building a model of the problem and necessary beliefs, but also for constructing those beliefs in the first place. This view may explain some of the behavioral paradoxes that we have discussed; individuals who have not thought long and hard in thoroughly developing their preferences and beliefs might have a tendency to make inconsistent judgments.

This constructive view of the assessment process is a fundamental matter. You may recall that we introduced these ideas back in Chapter 1 when we suggested that the decision-analysis process actually helps a decision maker develop his or her thoughts about the structure of the problem, beliefs about uncertainty, and preferences. Again, the idea of a requisite model is appropriate. A decision model is requisite in terms of preferences if it captures the essential preference issues that matter to the decision maker for the problem at hand. Thus, this constructive view suggests that decision analysis should provide an environment in which the decision maker can systematically develop his or her understanding of the problem, including preferences and beliefs about uncertainty. But how can we be sure that decision analysis does provide such an environment? More research is required to answer this question completely. The decision-analysis approach, however, does encourage decision makers to think about the issues in a systematic way. Working through the decision-analysis cycle (modeling, analyzing, performing sensitivity analysis, and then modeling again) should help the decision maker to identify and think clearly about the appropriate issues. Thus, the argument is that good initial decision-analysis structuring of a problem will lead to appropriate assessments and careful thought about important issues.

SUMMARY

We have covered a lot of ground in this chapter. We started with the axioms that underlie utility theory and showed how those axioms imply that an individual should make decisions that are consistent with the maximization of expected utility. Then we examined some of the behavioral paradoxes that have been documented. These are situations in which intelligent people make decisions that violate one or more of the axioms, and thus make decisions that are inconsistent with expected utility. These paradoxes do not invalidate the idea that we should still make decisions according to expected utility; recall that the basic goal of decision analysis is to help people improve their decision-making skills. But the paradoxes do have certain implications. We explored some of these implications, including issues involving utility elicitation. We ended with a constructive perspective of assessment, whereby it provides a medium within which the decision maker can explore and develop preferences and beliefs.

EXERCISES

15.1. In your own words, explain why the axioms that underlie expected utility are important to decision analysis.

15.2. From a decision-analysis perspective, why is it worthwhile to spend time studying the kinds of paradoxes described in this chapter?

15.3. Most people are learning constantly about themselves and their environment. Our tastes develop and change as our environment changes. As new technologies arise, new risks are discovered. What are the implications of this dynamic environment for decision analysis?

15.4. a. Find the value for p that makes you indifferent between

| **Lottery 1** | Win $1,000 with probability p |
| | Win $0 with probability $1 - p$ |

and

| **Lottery 2** | Win $400 for sure |

b. Now find the q that makes you indifferent between

> Lottery 3   Win $400 with probability 0.50
>
>   Win $0 with probability 0.50

and

> Lottery 4   Win $1,000 with probability q
>
>   Win $0 with probability $1 - q$

c. According to your assessment in part a, U($400) = p. In part b, U($400) = $2q$. Explain why this is the case.

d. To be consistent, your assessments should be such that $p = 2q$. Were your assessments consistent? Would you change them? Which assessment do you feel most confident about? Why?

QUESTIONS AND PROBLEMS

15.5.   We used the phrase "rules for clear thinking" to refer to the axioms described in this chapter. However, these "rules" do not cover every aspect of decision making as we have discussed it in this book. In particular, the axioms do not tell us in detail how to structure a problem, how to generate creative alternatives, or how to perform a sensitivity analysis. Can you give some "rules for clear thinking" that would help a decision maker in these aspects of decision making? (See Frisch and Clemen 1994.)

15.6.   Imagine that you collect bottles of wine as a hobby. How would you react to these situations?

a. You have just learned that one of the bottles (Wine A) that you purchased five years ago has appreciated considerably. A friend has offered to buy the bottle from you for $100. His offer is a fair price. Would you sell the bottle of wine?

b. A second bottle of wine (Wine B) is viewed by experts as being equivalent in value to Wine A. You never purchased a bottle of Wine B, but a casual acquaintance did. In conversation at a party, he offers to sell you his bottle of Wine B for $100. Would you buy it?

Many people would neither sell Wine A nor buy Wine B. Explain why this pattern of choices is inconsistent with expected utility. What other considerations might be taken into account?

15.7.   Consider the following two scenarios:

a. You have decided to see a show for which tickets cost $20. You bought your ticket in advance, but as you enter the theater, you find that you have lost the ticket. You did not make a note of your seat number, and the ticket is not recoverable or refundable in any way. Would you pay another $20 for a second ticket?

b. You have decided to see a show whose tickets cost $20. As you open your wallet to pay for the ticket, you discover that you have lost a $20 bill. Would you still buy a ticket to see the show?

Many individuals would not purchase a second ticket under the first scenario, but they would under the second. Explain why this is inconsistent with expected utility. How would you explain this kind of behavior?

15.8. Imagine yourself in the following two situations:

a. You are about to go shopping to purchase a stereo system at a local store. Upon reading the newspaper, you find that another stereo store across town has the system you are interested in for $1,089.99. You had been planning to spend $1,099.95, the best price you had found after considerable shopping. Would you drive across town to purchase the stereo system at the other store?

b. You are about to go shopping to purchase a popcorn popper at a local hardware store for $19.95, the best price you have seen yet. Upon reading the paper, you discover that a department store across town has the same popper for $9.99. Would you drive across town to purchase the popper at the department store?

Many people would drive across town to save money on the popcorn popper, but not on the stereo system. Why is this inconsistent with expected utility? What explanation can you give for this behavior?

15.9. A classified advertisement, placed by a car dealer, reads as follows:

NEW

2012 **BMW** 525i

Retail $48,838.50

WAS $37,998

NOW

$37,498

a. What is your reaction to this advertisement?

b. In the same paper, a computer dealer advertised a $500 discount on a computer system, marked down from $3,495 to $2,995. Which do you think is a better deal, the special offer on the car or the computer? Why?

15.10. Consider these two scenarios:

a. You have made a reservation to spend the weekend at the coast. To get the reservation, you had to make a nonrefundable $50 deposit. As the weekend approaches, you feel a bit out of sorts. On balance, you decide that you would be happier at home than at the coast. Of course, if you stay home, you forfeit the deposit. Would you stay home or go to the coast? What arguments would you use to support your position?

b. You have decided to spend the weekend at the coast and have made a reservation at your favorite resort. While driving over, you discover a new resort. After looking it over, you realize that you would rather spend your weekend there. Your reservation at the coast can be canceled easily at no charge. Staying at the new resort, however, would cost $50 more. Would you stay at the new resort or continue to the coast?

Are your decisions consistent in parts a and b? Explain why or why not.

15.11. Even without a formal assessment process, it often is possible to learn something about an individual's utility function just through the preferences revealed by choice behavior. Two persons, A and B, make the following bet: A wins $40 if it rains tomorrow and B wins $10 if it does not rain tomorrow.

a. If they both agree that the probability of rain tomorrow is 0.10, what can you say about their utility functions?

b. If they both agree that the probability of rain tomorrow is 0.30, what can you say about their utility functions?

c. Given no information about their probabilities, is it possible that their utility functions could be identical?

d. If they both agree that the probability of rain tomorrow is 0.20, could both individuals be risk-averse? Is it possible that their utility functions could be identical? Explain.

Source: R. L. Winkler (1972) *Introduction to Bayesian Inference and Decision*. New York: Holt.

15.12. Assume that you are interested in purchasing a new model of a personal computer whose reliability has not yet been perfectly established. Measure reliability in terms of the number of days in the shop over the first three years that you own the machine. (Does this definition of reliability pass the clarity test?) Now assess your utility function for computer reliability over the range from 0 days (best) to 50 days (worst). Use the assessment technique with which you feel most comfortable, and use computer assessment aids if they are available.

15.13. You are in the market for a new car. An important characteristic is the life span of the car. (Define lifespan as the number of miles driven until the car breaks down, requiring such extensive repairs that it would be cheaper to buy an equivalent depreciated machine.) Assess your utility function for automobile life span over the range from 40,000 to 200,000 miles.

15.14. Being a student, you probably have well-developed feelings about homework. Given the same amount of material learned, the less the better, right? (I thought so!) Define homework as the number of hours spent outside of class on various assignments that enter into your final grade. Now, assuming that the amount of material learned is the same in all instances, assess your utility function for homework over the range from 0 hours per week (best) to 20 hours per week (worst). (*Hint:* You may have to narrow the definition of homework. For example, does it make a difference what kind of course the homework is for? Does it matter whether the homework is term papers, case studies, short written assignments, oral presentations, or something else?)

15.15. We usually think of utility functions as always sloping upward (more is better) or downward (less is better—fewer nuclear power plant disasters, for example). But this is not always the case. In this problem, you must think about your utility function for coffee versus milk.

Imagine that you are about to buy a cup of coffee. Let c ($0 \leq c \leq 1$) represent the proportion of the contents of the cup accounted for by coffee, and $1 - c$ the proportion accounted for by milk.

a. Assess your utility function for c for $0 \leq c \leq 1$. Note that if you like a little milk in your coffee, the high point on your utility function may be at a value of c strictly between 0 and 1.

b. Compare (A) the mixture consisting of proportions c of coffee and $1 - c$ of milk in a cup and (B) the lottery yielding a cup of coffee with probability c and a cup of milk with probability $1 - c$. (The decision tree is shown in Figure 15.12.) Are the expected amounts of milk and coffee the same in A and B? [That is, if you calculate $E(c)$, is it the same in A and B?] Is there any value of c for which you are indifferent between A and B? (How about when c is 0 or 1?) Are you indifferent between A and B for the value of c at the high point of your utility function?

c. How would you describe your risk attitude with respect to c? Are you risk-averse or risk-prone, or would some other term be more appropriate?

15.16. In a court case, a plaintiff claimed that the defendant should pay her $3 million for damages. She did not expect the judge to award her this amount; her expected value actually was $1 million. The defendant also did not believe that the court would award the full $3 million, and shared the plaintiff's expected value of $1 million.

a. Assuming that the plaintiff is thinking about the award in terms of gains, explain why you might expect her to be risk-averse in this situation. If she is risk-averse, what kind of settlement offer might she accept from the defendant?

b. Assuming that the defendant is thinking about the situation in terms of losses, explain why you might expect him or her to be

FIGURE **15.12**
Decision tree for Problem 15.15.

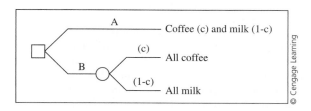

risk-seeking. What would this imply about settlement offers to which the defendant might agree? (*Hint:* Draw an example of a risk-seeking utility curve over the possible negative payoffs for the defendant. Now find the CE.)

c. Discuss your answers to parts a and b. What are the implications for settlements in real-world court cases? What would happen if the defendant's expected value were less than the plaintiff's?

CASE STUDIES

THE LIFE INSURANCE GAME

Peggy Ewen sat back in her chair and listened as Tom Pitman tried to explain. "I don't know what's going on," Tom said. "I have no trouble making the phone calls, and I seem to be able to set up in-home visits. I am making at least as many visits as anyone else in the office. For some reason, though, I cannot talk them into buying the product. I seem to be unlucky enough to have run into a lot of people who just are not interested in life insurance."

Peggy thought about this. Tom had been with the company for five months now. He was bright and energetic. He had gone through the training program easily, and had appeared to hit the ground running. His paperwork was always perfect. For some reason, though, his career selling life insurance was virtually stalled. His sales rate was only one-third that of the next best salesperson. Why?

Peggy asked, "How do you feel about going to the in-home visits?"

"Fine," Tom replied. "Well, I'm starting to feel a little apprehensive about it just because I'm becoming less sure of myself."

"Well, that's something we'll have to work on. But how do the visits go? What do you talk about? Tell me what a typical visit would be like."

"Let's see. Usually I'll come in, sit down, and we'll chat briefly. They'll offer me a cup of coffee. After a short visit, we get right down to business. I go through the presentation material provided by the company. Eventually we get around to talking about the reasons for purchasing life insurance. I really stress the importance of being able to make up for the loss of income. The presentation material stresses the idea of building up savings for sending kids to school or for retirement. You know, the idea of being sure that the extra money will be there down the road. But I really don't think that's why most people buy life insurance. I think they buy it to be sure that their family will be able to make up for a loss. For just a small premium, they can be sure that the loss won't happen, or at least they can minimize the loss."

Peggy seemed interested in Tom's account. "So you really stress the idea that for a little bit of money they can insure against the loss of income."

"Yes," Tom answered. "I'd rather have them look at life insurance as protection against a potential loss, rather than as a savings mechanism that would provide some sure amount in the future. Most of them know that there are better ways to save, anyway."

"And how would you classify your typical client? What kind of income bracket?"

"Mostly young couples just starting out," said Tom. "Maybe they've just had their first child. Not much income yet. Not much savings, either. We usually discuss this early on in the conversation. In general they seem to be quite aware of their financial situation. Occasionally they are even quite sensitive about it."

Peggy looked at Tom and grinned. "Tom, I do believe that there's something you can do right now to improve your sales rate."

Questions

1. About what issue is Peggy thinking?
2. What are the implications for people interested in selling financial securities such as insurance, annuities, and so on?
3. What are the implications for their customers?

NUCLEAR POWER PARANOIA

Ray Kaplan was disgusted. The rally against the power plant had gone poorly. The idea had been to get a lot of people out to show the utility company that the community did not support the idea of nuclear power. It was just too dangerous! Too much chance of an accident. Sure, the officials always pointed out that there had never been a serious nuclear power plant accident in the United States. They always pointed to the safeguards in the plants, and to the safety features required by federal regulations. "You're safer in our plant than on the freeway," they claimed. Well, the same officials met with the protesters again today and said the same old things. Ray was getting tired of it. He hopped on his motorcycle and rode home. Fast.

He was still ruminating about the rally while he broiled his steak over the charcoal that evening. As he snacked on a bowl of ice cream after dinner, he asked himself, "Can't they see the potential for disaster?"

The next day, Ray decided to mow his lawn and then ride out to the beach. About a mile from his house, he realized that he wasn't wearing his motorcycle helmet. Well, he thought, the beach was only about 20 miles away. Besides, it would be nice to feel the wind in his hair. The ride was nice, even though the traffic was heavier than he had expected. The fumes from one of the trucks really got to him briefly, but fortunately the exit for the beach was right there. As he lay down on his towel to soak up the sunshine, his mind went back to the rally. "Darn," he thought. "I'll probably develop an ulcer just worrying about that silly power plant."

Question

1. What do you think about Ray Kaplan's behavior?

THE MANAGER'S PERSPECTIVE

Ed Freeman just couldn't understand it. Why were the activists so blind? For years the information had been available showing just how safe nuclear power plants were. Study after study had concluded that the risk of fatalities from a nuclear power plant accident was far less than driving a car, flying in a commercial airliner, and many other commonplace activities in which people freely chose to engage. Sure, there had been some close calls, such as Three Mile Island, and there had been the terrible accidents at Chernobyl in the Soviet Union and Fukushima Daiichi in Japan. Still, the overall record of the nuclear power industry in the United States was excellent. No one could deny it if they would only compare the industry to others.

His risk assessors had gone through their own paces, documenting the safety features of his plant for the Nuclear Regulatory Commission; it was up to date and, in fact, one of the safest plants in the country. The experts had estimated the probability of an accident at

the plant as nearly zero. Furthermore, even if an accident were to occur, the safety systems that had been built in would minimize the public's exposure.

Given all this, he just could not understand the public opposition to the plant. He knew that these were bright people. They were articulate, well read, and able to marshal their supporters with great skill. But they seemed to ignore all of the data as well as the experts' reports and conclusions.

"I guess it takes all kinds," he sighed as he prepared to go back to work.

Questions

1. This case and "Nuclear Power Paranoia" go together. People often are willing to engage voluntarily in activities that are far more risky (in the sense of the probability of a serious injury or death) than living near a nuclear power plant. Why do you think this is the case?
2. What makes new technologies seem risky to you?

REFERENCES

The axioms of expected utility, along with the notion of subjective probability, were first discussed by Ramsey (1931), but the world appears to have ignored him.

Most economists refer to "von Neumann-Morgenstern utility functions" because in 1947 von Neumann and Morgenstern published their celebrated

Theory of Games and Economic Behavior in which they also set forth a set of axioms for choice behavior that leads to maximization of expected utility. The axioms subsequently appeared in a wide variety of forms and in many textbooks. Some examples are Luce and Raiffa (1957), Savage (1954), DeGroot (1970), and, more recently, French (1986). French's text is excellent for those interested in the axiomatic mathematics that underlie decision theory.

The various axioms have been debated widely. Our discussion of the transitivity axiom, for example, was suggested by Dr. Peter Fishburn as part of his acceptance speech for the Ramsey Medal, an award for distinguished contributions to decision analysis. If Peter Fishburn, one of the foremost scholars of decision theory, is willing to concede that intransitive preferences might not be unreasonable, perhaps we should pay attention! Fishburn (1989) summarizes many of the recent developments in the axioms and theory.

The text by von Winterfeldt and Edwards (1986) also contains much intriguing discussion of the axioms from the point of view of behavioral researchers and a discussion of the many paradoxes found in behavioral decision theory. Hogarth (1987) also covers this topic. Tversky and Kahneman (1981) provide an excellent and readable treatment of framing effects, and Kahneman and Tversky (1979) present a theory of behavioral decision making that accounts for many anomalies in individual decision behavior.

The fact that people do not normally follow the axioms perfectly has been the source of much debate about expected utility theory. Many theorists have attempted to relax the axioms in ways that are consistent with the observed patterns of choices that people make (e.g., Fishburn 1988). For the purpose of decision analysis, though, the question is whether we should model what people actually do or whether we should help them to adhere to axioms that are compelling but in some instances difficult to follow because of our own frailties.

This debate is taken up by Rex Brown (1992) and Ron Howard (1992) and is a central theme of a collection of articles in Edwards (1992). Luce and von Winterfeldt (1994) make an argument for decision analysis in which the status quo is explicitly used as an essential element in decision models, and subjective assessments are made relative to the status quo.

The debate about axioms is fine as far as it goes, but it is important to realize that many aspects of decision making are not covered by the axioms. In particular, the axioms tell you what to do once you have your problem structured and probabilities and utilities assessed. The axioms do indicate that decisions problems can be decomposed into issues of value (utility) and uncertainty (probability), but no guidance is provided regarding how to determine the important dimensions of value or the important uncertainties in a decision situation. The axioms provide little help in terms of creativity, sensitivity analysis, or even how to recognize a decision situation. Frisch and Clemen (1994) discuss this issue from the point of view of psychological research on decision making and the prescriptive goals of decision analysis.

The constructionist view of decision analysis that is presented in the last section of this chapter does not appear to be widely discussed among decision analysts, although such a view has substantial and fundamental implications for research in decision theory as well as in decision-analysis practice. For more discussion of this topic with regard to utility assessment, see von Winterfeldt and Edwards (1986, p. 356), Fischer (1979), and Payne, Bettman, and Johnson (1993). On the probability side, Shafer and Tversky (1986) view probability and structuring of inference problems in an interesting "constructive" way. Phillips's notion of the development of a requisite model (1982, 1984) and Watson and Buede's (1987) approach to decision analysis contain many of the elements of the constructionist view.

Our discussion of ways in which decision makers' perceptions might be manipulated has interesting implications for public policy. Is it appropriate for a governing body or regulator to establish policies that lead people to view a choice in a certain way? For example, should companies be required to have new employees explicitly opt out of a retirement plan rather than opt in? Standard practice in the past has been to have new employees opt in, but it has been shown that the percentage of employees participating in the retirement plan increases dramatically if the default is participation unless they explicitly opt out. In a very readable and provocative book, Thaler and Sunstein (2008) explore this and similar themes.

For many people, risk refers primarily to dangerous circumstances that may cause bodily injury, disease, or even death. The two cases, "Nuclear Power Paranoia" and "The Manager's Perspective," introduce the idea of risk to life and limb instead of risk in monetary gambles. Although one might think that measuring such risks would be a straightforward matter of assessing probability distributions for injuries or deaths—for example, with respect to options associated with building or siting a power plant—it turns out that people are very sensitive to certain kinds of risk. How individuals perceive risk has an important impact on how risks should be managed and how to communicate risk information to the public. For good introductory material, see Slovic (1987) and Morgan (1993).

Allais, M. (1953) "Le Comportement de l'Homme Rationnel Devant le Risque: Critique des Postulats et Axiomes de l'École Americaine." *Econometrica*, 21, 503–546.

Allais, M., and J. Hagen (eds.) (1979) *Expected Utility Hypotheses and the Allais Paradox*. Dordrecht, The Netherlands: Reidel.

Bazerman, M., and D. Moore (2008) *Judgment in Managerial Decision Making, 7th Ed*. New York: Wiley.

Brown, R. (1992) "The State of the Art of Decision Analysis: A Personal Perspective." *Interfaces*, 22, 5–14.

DeGroot, M. (1970) *Optimal Statistical Decisions*. New York: McGraw-Hill.

Edwards, W. (ed.) (1992) *Utility Theories: Measurements and Applications*. Boston, MA: Kluwer.

Fischer, G. (1979) "Utility Models for Multiple Objective Decisions: Do They Accurately Represent Human Preferences?" *Decision Sciences*, 10, 451–479.

Fishburn, P. C. (1988) *Nonlinear Preference and Utility Theory*. Baltimore: Johns Hopkins.

Fishburn, P. C. (1989) "Foundations of Decision Analysis: Along the Way." *Management Science*, 35, 387–405.

French, S. (1986) *Decision Theory: An Introduction to the Mathematics of Rationality*. London: Wiley.

Frisch, D., and R. Clemen (1994) "Beyond Expected Utility: Rethinking Behavioral Decision Research." *Psychological Bulletin*, 116, 46–54.

Hastie, R., and R. Dawes (2010) *Rational Choice in an Uncertain World: The Psychology of Judgment and Decision Making, 2nd Ed*. Thousand Oaks, CA: Sage.

Hershey, J. C., H. C. Kunreuther, and P. J. H. Shoemaker (1982) "Sources of Bias in Assessment Procedures for Utility Functions." *Management Science*, 28, 936–954.

Hogarth, R. (1987) *Judgment and Choice*, 2nd ed. New York: Wiley.

Howard, R. (1992) "Heathens, Heretics, and Cults: The Religious Spectrum of Decision Aiding." *Interfaces*, 22, 15–27.

Kahneman, D., and A. Tversky (1979) "Prospect Theory: An Analysis of Decision under Risk." *Econometrica*, 47, 263–291.

Luce, R. D., and H. Raiffa (1957) *Games and Decisions: Introduction and Critical Survey*. New York: Wiley.

Luce, R. D., and D. von Winterfeldt (1994) "What Common Ground Exists for Descriptive, Prescriptive, and Normative Utility Theories?" *Management Science*, 40, 263–279.

McCord, M., and R. De Neufville (1986) "'Lottery Equivalents': Reduction of the Certainty Effect Problem in Utility Assessment." *Management Science*, 32, 56–60.

Morgan, G. (1993) "Risk Analysis and Management." *Scientific American*, July, 32–41.

Payne, J., J. Bettman, and E. Johnson (1993) *The Adaptive Decision Maker*. Cambridge: Cambridge University Press.

Phillips, L. D. (1982) "Requisite Decision Modelling." *Journal of the Operational Research Society*, 33, 303–312.

Phillips, L. D. (1984) "A Theory of Requisite Decision Models." *Acta Psychologica*, 56, 29–48.

Plous, S. (1993) *The Psychology of Judgment and Decision Making*. New York: McGraw-Hill.

Ramsey, F. P. (1931) "Truth and Probability." In R. B. Braithwaite (ed.) *The Foundations of Mathematics and Other Logical Essays*. New York: Harcourt, Brace.

Samuelson, W. & R. Zeckhauser (1988) "Status quo bias in decision making," *Journal of Risk and Uncertainty*, 1, 7–59.

Savage, L. J. (1954) *The Foundations of Statistics*. New York: Wiley.

Shafer, G., and A. Tversky (1986) "Languages and Designs for Probability Judgment." *Cognitive Science*, 9, 309–339.

Slovic, P. (1987) "Perception of Risk." *Science*, 236, 280–285.

Swalm, R. (1966) "Utility Theory—Insights into Risk Taking." *Harvard Business Review*, 123–136.

Thaler, R. (1980) "Toward a positive theory of consumer choice," *Journal of Economic Behavior and Organization*, 1, 39–60.

Thaler, R., and C. Sunstein (2008) *Nudge: Improving Decisions about Health, Wealth, and Happiness*. New Haven, CT: Yale University Press.

Tversky, A., and D. Kahneman (1981) "The Framing of Decisions and the Psychology of Choice." *Science*, 211, 453–458.

von Neumann, J., and O. Morgenstern (1947) *Theory of Games and Economic Behavior*. Princeton, NJ: Princeton University Press.

von Winterfeldt, D., and W. Edwards (1986) *Decision Analysis and Behavioral Research*. Cambridge: Cambridge University Press.

Watson, S. R., and D. M. Buede (1987) *Decision Synthesis: The Principles and Practice of Decision Analysis*. Cambridge: Cambridge University Press.

EPILOGUE

We began the chapter with the Asian influenza example. This kind of study has been done repeatedly by many different experimenters, and the results are always the same; many of the subjects make inconsistent choices that depend on the framing of the problem. Of course, many of these experiments have been done using college students and other individuals who are not used to making this kind of decision. It would be nice to think that individuals who make difficult decisions often would not be susceptible to such inconsistencies. Unfortunately, such is not the case. Tversky and Kahneman (1981) report the same kinds of inconsistencies among decisions made by university faculty and physicians.

CHAPTER **16**

Conflicting Objectives I: Fundamental Objectives and the Additive Utility Function

WITH CONTRIBUTIONS BY JEFFERY GUYSE

The utility functions for money that we have considered have embodied an important fundamental trade-off: monetary return versus riskiness. We have argued all along that the basic reason for using a utility function as a preference model in decision making is to capture our attitudes about risk and return. Accomplishing high returns and minimizing exposure to risk are two conflicting objectives, and we already have learned how to model our preference trade-offs between these objectives using utility functions. Thus, we already have addressed two of the fundamental conflicting objectives that decision makers face.

We make many other trade-offs in our decisions, however. Some of the examples from Chapters 3 and 4 involved cost versus safety or fun versus salary. The FAA bomb-detection example balanced detection effectiveness, passenger acceptance, time to implement, and cost. Other examples are famil-iar: When purchasing cars or computers, we consider not only reliability and life span but also price, ease of use, maintenance costs, operating expenses, and so on. When deciding among school courses, you might be interested in

Jeffery Guyse, Professor of Technology and Operations Management at California State Polytechnic University, Pomona contributed to the behavioral and psychological aspects of this chapter.

FIGURE **16.1**
Four examples of decisions involving complicated preference trade-offs.

1. A mayor must decide whether to approve a major new electric power generating station. The city needs more power capacity, but the new plant would worsen the city's air quality. The mayor might consider the following issues:
- The health of residents
- The economic conditions of the residents
- The psychological state of the residents
- The economy of the city and the state
- Businesses
- Local politics

2. Imagine the issues involved in the treatment of heroin addicts. A policy maker might like to:
- Reduce the size of the addict pool
- Reduce costs to the city and its residents
- Reduce crimes against property and persons
- Improve the "quality of life" of addicts
- Improve the "quality of life" of non-addicts
- Curb organized crime
- Live up to the high ideals of civil rights and civil liberties
- Decrease the alienation of youth
- Get elected to higher political office

3. In choosing a site for a new airport near Mexico City, the head of the Ministry of Public Works had to balance such objectives as:
- Minimize the costs to the federal government
- Raise the capacity of airport facilities
- Improve the safety of the system
- Reduce noise levels
- Reduce access time to users
- Minimize displacement of people for expansion
- Improve regional development (roads, for instance)
- Achieve political aims

4. A doctor prescribing medical treatment must consider a variety of issues:
- Potential health complications for the patient (perhaps death)
- Money cost to the patient
- Patient's time spent being treated
- Cost to insurance companies
- Payments to the doctor
- Utilization of resources (nurses, hospital space, equipment)
- Information gained in treating this patient (may be helpful in treating others)

Source: Keeney, R., and Raiffa, H. (1976) *Decisions with Multiple Objectives: Preference and Value Tradeoffs*. Reprinted with the permission of Cambridge University Press.

factors such as the complementarity of material covered, importance in relation to your major and career goals, time schedule, and quality of the instructor. Still other examples and possible objectives appear in Figure 16.1 (abstracted from Keeney and Raiffa 1976).

As individuals, we usually can do a fair job of assimilating enough information so that we feel comfortable with a decision. In many cases, we end up saying things like, "Well, I can save some money now and buy a new car sooner," "You get what you pay for," and "You can't have everything." These intuitive statements reflect the informal trade-offs that we make. Understanding trade-offs in detail, however, may be critical for a company executive who is interested in acquiring hundreds of personal computers or a large fleet of automobiles for the firm.

In this chapter we will present a relatively straightforward way of dealing with conflicting objectives. Essentially, we will create an additive preference model; that is, we will calculate a utility score for each objective and then add the scores, weighting them appropriately according to the relative importance of the various objectives. The procedure is easy to use and intuitive. Computer programs are available that make the required assessment process fairly simple. But with the simple additive form comes limitations. Some of those limitations will be exposed in the problems at the end of the chapter. In Chapter 17, we will see how to construct more complicated preference models that are less limiting.

Where are we going? The first part of the chapter reviews some of the issues regarding identifying objectives, constructing objective hierarchies, and creating useful attribute scales. With objectives and attribute scales specified, we move on to the matter of understanding trade-offs. In the section titled "Trading Off Conflicting Objectives: The Basics," we will look at an example that offers a relatively simple choice involving three automobiles and two objectives. In this initial discussion, we will develop intuitive ways to trade off two conflicting objectives. The purpose of this discussion is to introduce ideas, help you focus on the primary issues involved, and provide a framework for thinking clearly.

The next section formally introduces the additive utility function and explores some of its properties. In particular, we introduce indifference curves and the marginal rate of substitution between objectives. We also show that the simple multiobjective approach described in Chapters 3 and 4 is consistent with the additive utility function.

The additive utility function is composed of two different kinds of elements, scores on individual attribute scales and weights for the corresponding objectives. Many different methods exist for assessing the scores and the weights, and these are the topics of the following sections.

In the last section of the chapter, we consider an actual example in which the city of Eugene, Oregon, evaluated four candidate sites for a new public library. The example shows the process of defining objectives and attribute scales, rating the alternatives on each attribute scale, assessing weights, and then putting all of the assessments together to obtain an overall comparison of the four sites.

OBJECTIVES AND ATTRIBUTES

In Chapter 3 we discussed at length the notion of conflicting objectives in decision making. Understanding objectives is an important part of the structuring process. We stressed the importance of identifying fundamental objectives, the essential reasons that matter in any given decision context. Fundamental objectives are organized into a hierarchy in which the lower levels of the hierarchy explain what is meant by the higher (more general) levels. Figure 16.2 shows a fundamental-objectives hierarchy for evaluating alternative-energy technologies. We also discussed the notion of means objectives, which are not important in and of themselves but help, directly or indirectly, to accomplish the fundamental objectives. Distinguishing means and fundamental objectives is important because we would like to measure the available alternatives relative to the fundamental objectives, the things we really care about.

The discussion in Chapter 3 also introduced attribute scales. Attribute scales provide the means to measure accomplishment of the fundamental objectives. Some attribute scales are easily defined; if minimizing cost is an objective, then measuring cost in dollars is an appropriate attribute scale. Others are more difficult. In Figure 16.2, for example, there is no obvious way to measure risks related to aesthetic aspects of the environment. In cases like these, we discussed the use of constructed scales and related measurements as proxies.

FIGURE **16.2**
Objectives hierarchy for evaluating alternative-energy technologies.

Source: von Winterfeldt and Edwards (1986).

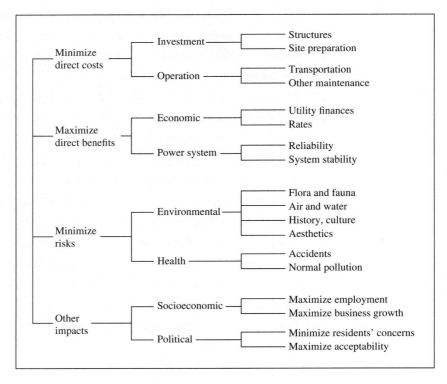

For convenience, we use the term attribute to refer to the quantity measured on an attribute scale. For example, if an objective is to minimize cost, then the attribute scale might be defined in terms of dollars, and we would refer to dollar cost as the attribute for this objective. Use of the term *attribute* is common in the decision analysis literature, and many authors use *multiattribute utility theory (MAUT)* to refer to topics covered in Chapters 16 and 17.

There are a number of essential criteria for fundamental objectives and their attributes. Many of these we discussed in Chapters 3 and 4, and you are encouraged to review those sections. Here is an encapsulation:

1. The set of objectives, as represented by the fundamental-objectives hierarchy, should be complete; it should include all relevant aspects of the decision. The fact that important objectives are missing can be indicated by reluctance to accept the results of an analysis or simply the gnawing feeling that something is missing. If the results "just don't feel right," ask yourself what is wrong with the alternatives that the analysis suggests should be preferred. Careful thought and an honest answer should reveal the missing objectives.

2. At the same time, the set of objectives should be as small as possible. Too many objectives can be cumbersome and hard to grasp. Keep in mind that the objectives hierarchy is meant to be a useful representation of objectives that are important to the decision maker. Furthermore, each objective should differentiate the available alternatives. If all of the alternatives are equivalent with regard to a particular objective (as measured by its corresponding attribute), then that objective will not be of any help in making the decision.

3. The set of fundamental objectives should not be redundant. That is, the same objectives should not be repeated in the hierarchy, and the objectives should not be closely related. This avoids double counting.

4. As far as possible, the set of objectives should be *decomposable*. That is, the decision maker should be able to think about each objective easily without having to consider others. For example, in evaluating construction bids, the cost of the project and the amount of time required may be important attributes. In most cases, we can think about these attributes separately; regardless of the cost, it is always preferable to complete the project sooner, and regardless of time to completion, it is always preferable to have a lower cost. Thus, the objectives would be decomposable into these two attributes, which can be considered independently. On the other hand, if you are deciding which course to take, you may want to choose the most interesting topic and at the same time minimize the amount of effort required. These attributes, however, are related in a way that does not permit decomposition; whether you want to put in a lot of effort may depend on how interested you are in the material. Hence, you may have to alter your set of objectives. For example, you might construct a scale that measures something like the extent to which the course inspires you to work harder and learn more.

5. Means and fundamental objectives should be distinguished. Even if fundamental objectives are difficult to measure and means objectives are used as proxies, it is important to remain clear on why the decision matters in the first place. Doing so can help avoid choosing an inappropriate alternative for the wrong reason.

6. Attribute scales must be operational. They should provide an easy way to measure performance of the alternatives or the outcomes on the fundamental objectives. Another way to put it is that the attribute scales should make it straightforward (if not easy) to fill in the cells in the consequence matrix.

TRADING OFF CONFLICTING OBJECTIVES: THE BASICS

The essential problem in multiobjective decision making is deciding how best to trade off increased value on one objective against lower value on another. Making these trade-offs is a subjective matter and requires the decision maker's judgment. In this section, we will look at a simple approach that captures the essence of trade-offs. We will begin with an example that involves only two objectives.

Choosing an Automobile: An Example

Suppose you are buying a car, and you are interested in both price and life span. You would like a long expected life span—that is, the length of time until you must replace the car—and a low price. (These assumptions are made for the purpose of this example; some people might enjoy purchasing a new car every 3 years, and for them a long life span may be meaningless.) Let us further suppose that you have narrowed your choices to three alternatives: the Portalo (a relatively expensive sedan with a reputation for longevity), the Norushi (renowned for its reliability), and the Standard Motors car (a relatively inexpensive domestic automobile). You have researched and evaluated all three cars on both attributes as shown in Table 16.1. Plotting these three alternatives on a graph with expected life span on the horizontal axis and price on the vertical axis yields Figure 16.3. The Portalo, Norushi, and Standard show up on the graph as three points arranged on an upward sloping curve. That the three points are ordered in this way reflects the notion, "You get what you pay for." If you want a longer expected life span, you have to pay more money.

Occasionally alternatives may be ruled out immediately by means of a dominance argument. For example, consider a hypothetical car that costs $15,000 and has an expected life span of 7 years (Point A in Figure 16.3).

TABLE **16.1**
Automobile purchase alternatives.

	Portalo	Norushi	Standard Motors
Price ($1,000s)	17	10	8
Life Span (Years)	12	9	6

FIGURE **16.3**
Graph of three cars, comparing price and expected life span.

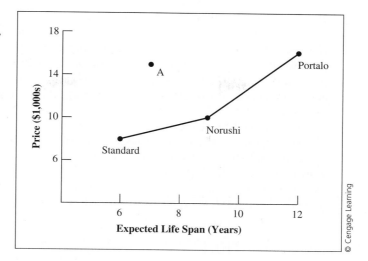

Such a car would be a poor choice relative to the Norushi, which gives a longer expected life for less money. Thus, A would be dominated by the Norushi.

Figure 16.3 shows that none of the three cars lies above and to the left of another car, and thus none of the cars under consideration is dominated. With this being the case, how can you choose? The question clearly is, "How much are you willing to pay to increase the life span of your car?" To answer this question, we will start with the Standard and assume that you will purchase it if the others are not better. Is it worthwhile to switch from the Standard to the Norushi? Note that the slope of the line connecting the Norushi and the Standard is $666.67 per year. The switch would be worthwhile if you were willing to pay at least $666.67 for each additional year of life span, or $2,000 to increase the expected life span by 3 years. Would you be willing to pay more than $2,000 to increase the expected life of your car by 3 years? This is a subjective assessment! If you would, then it is worthwhile to switch to the Norushi from the Standard. If not, do not switch.

For the sake of continuing the example, assume that you make the switch, and that you have decided that the Norushi is better for you than the Standard; you would pay at least $2,000 for the additional 3 years of life span. Now, should you switch to the Portalo? Notice that the slope of the line connecting the Norushi and the Portalo is $2,333.33 per year, or $7,000 for an additional 3 years. You were willing to pay at least $666.67 for an extra year. Now, what about an extra $7,000 for another 3 years? Are the extra years of expected life span worth this much to you? If so, make the switch to the Portalo. If not, stick with the Norushi.

This simple procedure permits you to move systematically through the alternatives. The idea is to start at one corner of the graph (for example, the Standard) and then consider switching with each of the other alternatives, always moving in the same direction. Once a switch is made, there is never a need to reconsider the previous alternative. (After all, the one to which you changed must be better.) If there were many cars to choose from, the procedure would be to plot them all on a graph, eliminate the dominated alternatives, and then systematically move through the nondominated set, beginning at the lower-left of the graph and considering the alternatives that are to the upper-right.

This procedure works well in the context of two conflicting objectives, and you can see how we are trading off the two. At each step we ask whether the additional benefit from switching (the increase in expected life span) is worth the cost (the increase in price). The same kind of procedure can be used with three or more attributes. The trade-offs become more complicated, however, and graphical interpretation is difficult.

THE ADDITIVE UTILITY FUNCTION

The preceding automobile example is intended to give you an intuitive idea of how tradeoffs work. This particular example is easy because it seems natural to many of us to think in terms of dollars, and we often can reduce nonmonetary attributes to dollars. But what if we wanted to trade off life span and reliability? We would like to have a systematic procedure that we can apply in any situation fairly easily. To do this, we must find satisfactory ways to answer two questions. The first question has to do with comparing the attribute levels of the available alternatives. We are comparing three different automobiles. How do they compare on the two attributes? Is the Portalo "twice as good" on life span as the Norushi? How does the Standard compare (quantitatively) to the Portalo on price? In the energy example in Figure 16.2, alternative technologies must be ranked on each of their attributes. For example, substantial differences may exist among these technologies on all of the detail attributes. To get anywhere with the construction of a quantitative model of preferences, we must assess numerical scores for each alternative that reflect the comparisons.

The second question asks how the attributes compare in terms of importance. In the automobile example, is life span twice as important as price, and exactly what does "twice as important" mean? In the alternative-energy example, how do the environmental and health risks compare in terms of importance within the "Minimize Risks" fundamental objective? As with the scores, numerical weights must be assessed for each attribute.

The model that we will adopt in this chapter is called the *additive utility function*. We assume that we have individual utility functions $U_1(x_1)$, ..., $U_m(x_m)$ for each of the m different attributes x_1 through x_m. These are utility functions just like those that we discussed in Chapters 14 and 15. In particular, we assume that each utility function assigns values of 0 and 1 to the worst and best levels respectively on that particular objective. The additive utility function is simply a weighted average of these different utility functions. For an outcome that has levels x_1, ..., x_m on the m objectives, we would calculate the utility of this outcome as

$$U(x_1, \ldots, x_m) = k_1 U_1(x_1) + \cdots + k_m U_m(x_m)$$

$$= \sum_{i=1}^{m} k_i U_i(x_i) \qquad (16.1)$$

where the weights are $k_1, \ldots, k_m$. All of the weights are positive, and they add up to 1.

First, you can see that this additive utility function also assigns values of 0 and 1 to the worst and best conceivable outcomes, respectively. To see this, look at what happens when we plug in the worst level x_i^- for each objective. The individual utility functions then assign 0 to the worst value on each objective $[U_i(x_i^-) = 0]$, and so the overall utility is also 0. If we plug in the best possible value for each objective x_i^+, the individual utility functions are each equal to 1 $[U_i(x_i^+) = 1]$, and so the overall utility becomes

$$U(x_1^+, \ldots, x_m^+) = k_1 U_1(x_1^+) + \cdots + k_m U_m(x_m^+)$$

$$= k_1 + \cdots + k_m$$

$$= 1$$

You can see that the additive utility function is consistent with what we developed in Chapters 3 and 4. In Chapter 3 we discussed how to assess "scores" by using attribute scales; you can see that the individual utility functions $U_i(x)$ in Equation (16.1) define the attribute scales. In Chapters 3 and 4 we had the attribute scales ranging from 0 to 100, whereas here we have defined the utility functions to range from 0 to 1. The transformation is simple enough; think of the 0 and 100 in Chapters 3 and 4 as 0% and 100%. In the case of quantitative natural scales we showed in Chapter 4 how to standardize those to a scale from 0 to 100, and in the case of constructed scales we had to make a subjective assessment of the value of the intermediate levels on the scale from 0 to 100. As we proceed through this chapter, we will examine some alternative ways of coming up with the individual utility functions.

In Chapter 4 we turned to the assessment of weights. We used a simple technique of comparing the importance of the range of one attribute with another. Later in this chapter we will discuss this and several other approaches for assessing weights.

Choosing an Automobile: Proportional Scores

To understand the additive utility function better, let us work through a simple example with the automobile choice. We will begin with the determination of the individual utility values, following the same proportional-scoring technique discussed in Chapter 4 (except that we will have the utility functions range from 0 to 1 rather than 0 to 100).

The first step is easy. The Standard is best on price and worst on life span, so assign it a 1 for price and a 0 for life span: $U_P(\text{Standard}) = 1$ and $U_L(\text{Standard}) = 0$, where the subscripts P and L represent price and life span, respectively. Do the opposite for the Portalo, which is worst on price and best on life span: $U_P(\text{Portalo}) = 0$ and $U_L(\text{Portalo}) = 1$. Now, how do we derive the corresponding scores for the Norushi? Because we have natural numerical measures for the objectives (dollars and years), we can simply scale the Norushi's price and life span. The general proportional utility formula is

$$U_i(x) = \frac{x - \text{Worst Value}}{\text{Best Value} - \text{Worst Value}}$$

$$= \frac{x - x_i^-}{x_i^+ - x_i^-} \qquad (16.2)$$

For the Norushi's price, we calculate the utility value of

$$U_P(\$10{,}000) = \frac{10{,}000 - 17{,}000}{8{,}000 - 17{,}000}$$

$$= 0.78$$

Likewise, the utility for the Norushi's life span is

$$U_L(9 \text{ years}) = \frac{9 - 6}{12 - 6}$$

$$= 0.50$$

The intuition behind these calculations is that 9 years is exactly halfway between 6 and 12 years [thus $U_L(\text{Norushi}) = 0.50$], whereas \$10,000 is 78% of the way from \$17,000 to \$8,000. Moreover, you can see that the values of 0 and 1, which we assigned to the Standard and the Portalo, are consistent with the general formula; plugging in the worst value for x yields $U_i(\text{Worst}) = 0$, and plugging in the best value gives $U_i(\text{Best}) = 1$. The utilities for the three cars are summarized in Table 16.2. As long as the objectives have natural numerical attributes, it is a straightforward matter to scale those attributes so that the utility of the best is 1, the utility of the worst is 0, and the intermediate alternatives have scores that reflect the relative distance between the best and worst.

Assessing Weights: Pricing Out the Objectives

Now we must assess the weights for price and life span. But before we decide on the weights once and for all, let us look at the implications of various weights. For the automobile example, we must assess k_P and k_L, which represent the weights for price and life span, respectively.

Suppose you were to decide that price and expected life span should be weighted equally, or $k_P = k_L = 0.5$. In general, we are going to calculate

$$U(\text{Price, Life Span}) = k_P U_P(\text{Price}) + k_L U_L(\text{Life Span})$$

TABLE **16.2**
Utilities for three cars on two attributes.

	Portalo	Norushi	Standard Motors
Price (U_P)	0.00	0.78	1.00
Life Span (U_L)	1.00	0.50	0.00

Thus, the weighted utilities would be

$$U(\text{Portalo}) = 0.5(0.00) + 0.5(1.00) = 0.50$$
$$U(\text{Norushi}) = 0.5(0.78) + 0.5(0.50) = 0.64$$
$$U(\text{Standard}) = 0.5(1.00) + 0.5(0.00) = 0.50$$

The Standard and the Portalo come out with exactly the same overall utility because of the way that price and life span are traded off against each other. Because the difference between 1 and 0 amounts to $9,000 in price versus 6 years in life span, the equal weight in this case says that one additional year of life span is worth $1,500. The Norushi comes out on top because you pay less than $1,500 per year for the 3 additional years in expected life span as compared to the Standard.

Suppose that you have little money to spend on a car. Then you might think that price should be twice as important as life span. To model this, let $k_P = 0.67$ and $k_L = 0.33$. Now the overall utilities for the cars are Portalo, 0.33; Norushi, 0.69; and Standard, 0.67. In this case the weights imply that an increase in life span of 1 year is only worth an increase in price of $750. (You can verify this by calculating the utility for a car that costs $8,750 and is expected to last 7 years; such a car will have the same weighted score as the Standard.) Again the Norushi comes out as being preferred to the Standard, because its 3-year increase in life span (relative to the Standard) is accompanied by only a $2,000 increase in price, whereas the weights indicate that the additional 3 years would be worth $2,250.

You may not be happy with either scheme. Perhaps you have thought carefully about the relative importance of expected life span and price, and you have decided that you would be willing to pay up to $600 for an extra year of expected life span. You have thus *priced out* the value of an additional year of expected life span. How can you translate this price into the appropriate weights? Take the Standard as your base case (although any of the three automobiles could be used for this). Essentially, you are saying that you would be indifferent between paying $8,000 for 6 years of expected life span and $8,600 for 7 years of expected life span. Using Equation (16.2), we can find that such a hypothetical car (Car B) would score $\frac{1}{6} = 0.167$ on expected life span (which is one-sixth of the way from the worst to the best case) and 0.933 on price ($8,600 is 0.933 of the way from the worst to the best case). Because you would be indifferent between the Standard and the hypothetical Car B, the weights must satisfy

$$U(\text{Standard}) = U(\text{Car B})$$
$$k_P \times 1.00 + k_L \times 0 = k_P \times 0.933 + k_L \times 0.167$$

Simplify this equation to find that or that

$$k_P \times (1.00 - 0.933) = k_L \times 0.167$$
$$k_P = k_L \frac{0.167}{0.067} = 2.50 k_L$$

Including the condition that the weights must sum to 1, we have

$$k_P = 2.50(1 - k_P)$$

or

$$k_P = 0.714 \quad \text{and} \quad k_L = 0.286$$

Note that these weights are consistent with what we did previously. The weight $k_P = 0.667$ implied a price of $750 per additional year of expected life span. With a still lower price per additional year ($600), we obtained a higher weight for k_P.

The final objective, of course, is to compare the cars in terms of their overall utilities:

$$U(\text{Portalo}) = 0.714 \times 0.00 + 0.286 \times 1.00 = 0.286$$
$$U(\text{Norushi}) = 0.714 \times 0.78 + 0.286 \times 0.50 = 0.700$$
$$U(\text{Standard}) = 0.714 \times 1.00 + 0.286 \times 0.00 = 0.714$$

The Standard comes out only slightly better than the Norushi. This is consistent with the switching approach described earlier. The weights here came from the assessment that 1 year of life span was worth only $600, not the $666.67 or more required to switch from the Standard to the Norushi.

Indifference Curves

The assessment that you would trade $600 for an additional year of life span can be used to construct *indifference curves*, which can be thought of as a set of alternatives (most being hypothetical) among which the decision maker is indifferent. For example, we already have established that you would be indifferent between the Standard and hypothetical Car B, which costs $8,600 and lasts 7 years. Thus, in Figure 16.4 we have a line that passes through the points for the Standard and the hypothetical Car B. All of the points along this particular line represent cars that would be equivalent to the Standard; all would have the same utility, 0.714.

FIGURE **16.4**
Indifference curves for the automobile decision.

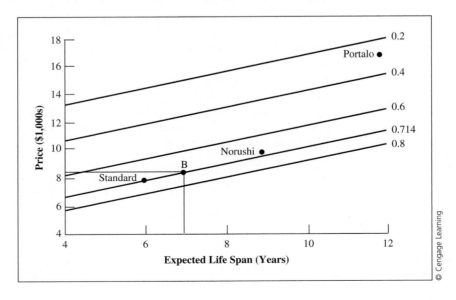

© Cengage Learning

Other indifference curves also are shown with their corresponding utilities. Note that the indifference curves have higher utilities as one moves down and to the right, because you would rather pay less money and have a longer life span. You can see that the Norushi and the Portalo are not preferred to the Standard because they lie above the 0.714 indifference curve.

The slope of the indifference curves in Figure 16.4 is related to the trade-off rate that was assessed. Specifically, the slope is $600 per year, the price that was assessed for each year of expected life span. This also is sometimes called the *marginal rate of substitution,* or the rate at which one attribute can be used to replace another.

When using the additive utility function, it is straightforward to calculate how much a utility point in objective i is worth in terms of objective j. Let us say that you want to know how much one utility unit of attribute i is worth in terms of utility units of attribute j. Then the marginal rate of substitution between i and j is simply k_i/k_j. Thus, in the automobile case, the marginal rate of substitution in terms of the utility scales is $0.286/0.714 = 0.40$. In other words, the increase of one utility point on the life-span scale is worth 40% of the increase of one point on the price scale.

Unfortunately, knowing the marginal rate of substitution in utility terms is not so useful. More useful would be knowing the substitution rate relative to the attributes because attributes are what we naturally care about. If you are using the additive utility function and proportional scores as we have done here, then the marginal rate of substitution in terms of the original attributes is easily calculated. Let M_{ij} denote the marginal rate of substitution between attributes i and j. Then, using $|x|$ to denote the absolute value of x,

$$M_{ij} = \frac{k_i/|x_i^+ - x_i^-|}{k_j/|x_j^+ - x_j^-|} \tag{16.3}$$

Thus, for the automobiles M_{LP} can be calculated as

$$M_{LP} = \frac{0.286/|12\,yr - 6\,yr|}{0.714/|\$8,000 - \$17,000|}$$

$$= \$600 \text{ per year}$$

In general, without proportional scores or with a nonadditive overall utility function, the marginal rate of substitution can vary depending on the values of the attributes x_i and x_j, and the reason is that the indifference curves may be just that—curves instead of straight lines. Moreover, calculating M_{ij} can be difficult, requiring calculus to determine the slope of an indifference curve at a particular point. It is often possible to graph approximate indifference curves, however, and doing so can provide insight into one's assessed trade-offs. We will return to indifference curves in Chapter 17.

ASSESSING INDIVIDUAL UTILITY FUNCTIONS

As you can see, the essence of using the additive utility function is to be able to assess the individual utility functions and the weights. In this section we look at some issues regarding the assessment of the individual utility functions.

FIGURE **16.5**
Proportional scores
for the prices of the
three cars.

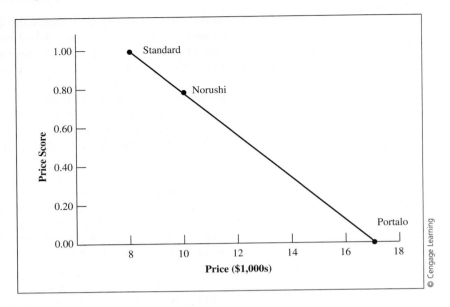

© Cengage Learning

Proportional Scores

In the example here and in Chapter 4, we have used the proportional scoring approach. In fact, we have just taken the original values and scaled them so that they now range from 0 (worst) to 1 (best). For the automobile example, Figure 16.5 graphs the price relative to a car's score on price. The graph shows a straight line, and we know about straight lines in this context: They imply risk neutrality and all of the unusual behavior associated with risk neutrality.

Let us think about what risk neutrality implies here with another simple example. Imagine that you face two career choices. You could decide to invest your life savings in an entrepreneurial venture, or you could take a job as a government bureaucrat. After considering the situation carefully, you conclude that your objectives are purely monetary, and you can think in terms of income and savings. (Actually, more than just monetary outcomes should influence your career choice!) The bureaucratic job has a well-defined career path and considerable security. After 10 years, you know with virtual certainty that you will make $60,000 per year and have $120,000 in the bank toward retirement. In contrast, becoming an entrepreneur is a risky proposition. The income and savings outcomes could range anywhere from zero dollars in the case of failure to some large amount in the event of success. Because of the uncertainty in income and savings, you decide to assess a continuous distribution for each and fit discrete approximations. The decision tree in Figure 16.6 shows your probability assessments and alternatives. You can see that for the entrepreneurial alternative, the expected values are $60,000 in income and $120,000 in savings, the same as the certain values associated with the bureaucratic job.

Now we assign scores to the outcomes. For income, the best is $120,000, the worst is 0, and $60,000 is halfway between. These outcomes receive

FIGURE **16.6**
A career decision.

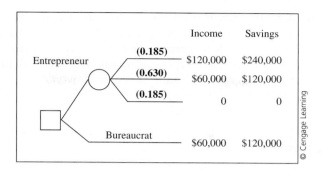

FIGURE **16.7**
A career decision
with proportional
scores.

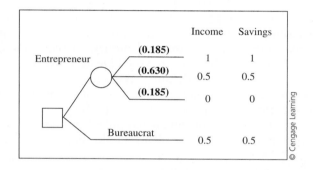

scores of 1, 0, and ½, respectively. Performing the same analysis for the savings dimension results in similar scores, and the decision tree with these scores appears in Figure 16.7.

We now calculate expected scores for the two alternatives; this requires calculating scores for each of the three possible outcomes. Let k_I and k_S represent the weights that we would assign to income and savings. The scores (U) for the possible outcomes are

$$U(\$60{,}000, \$120{,}000) = k_I \times 1.00 + k_S \times 1.00 = k_I + k_S$$
$$U(\$30{,}000, \$60{,}000) = k_I \times 0.50 + k_S \times 0.50 = (k_I + k_S) \times 0.50$$
$$U(\$0, \$0) = k_I \times 0.00 + k_S \times 0.00 = 0$$

Now we can calculate the expected utility (EU) for the entrepreneurial venture. That expected score is obtained by averaging the scores over the three branches:

$$EU(\text{Entrepreneur}) = 0.185(k_I + k_S) + 0.63[0.50(k_I + k_S)] + 0.185(0)$$
$$= 0.50(k_I + k_S)$$
$$= 0.50$$

because $k_I + k_S = 1$. Of course, the expected score for the bureaucratic option also is 0.50, and so, on the basis of expected scores, the two alternatives are equivalent. (In fact, it is interesting to note that the two alternatives have the same score regardless of the specific values of k_I and k_S.) It is obvious, however, that being an entrepreneur is riskier, but our assumption of risk neutrality ignores the risk and reports the same score. If each job really has the same expected scores in all relevant dimensions, would you be indifferent? (Probably not, but we will not guess about whether you would choose the riskier job or the more secure one!)

Ratios

Another way to assess utilities—and a particularly appropriate one for attributes that are not naturally quantitative—is to assess them on the basis of some ratio comparison. For example, let us return to the automobile example. Suppose that color is an important attribute in your automobile purchase decision. Clearly, this is not something that is readily measurable on a meaningful numerical scale. Using a ratio approach, you might conclude that to you blue is twice as good as red and that yellow is two and a half times as good as red. We could accomplish the same by assigning some number of points between 0 and 100 to each possible alternative on the basis of performance on the attribute. In this way, for example, you might assign 30 points to red, 60 points to blue, and 75 points to yellow. This could be represented graphically as in Figure 16.8.

To construct the utility curve for color, we must scale these assessments so that they range from 0 to 1. We need to find constants a and b so that

$$0 = a + 30b$$
$$1 = a + 75b$$

Solving these two equations simultaneously gives

$$a = -\frac{2}{3}$$
$$b = \frac{1}{45}$$

© Cengage Learning

FIGURE **16.8**
Graphically scoring alternatives based on assigned points.

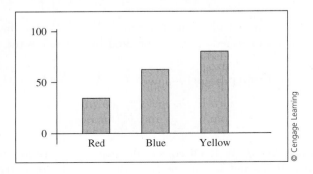

FIGURE **16.9**
Scaled scores for
colors using the
ratio method.

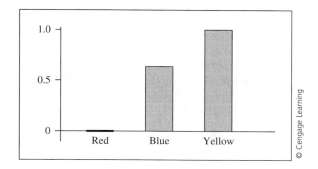

Applying these scaling constants, we can calculate U_C, the utilities for the three colors:

$$U_C(\text{Red}) = -\frac{2}{3} + \frac{30}{45} = 0$$

$$U_C(\text{Blue}) = -\frac{2}{3} + \frac{60}{45} = \frac{2}{3}$$

$$U_C(\text{Yellow}) = -\frac{2}{3} + \frac{75}{45} = 1$$

Figure 16.9 shows the scaled scores, which now represent your relative preference for the different colors. They may be used to calculate weighted scores for different cars in a decision problem in which color is one attribute to consider. For example, with appropriate trade-off weights for price, color, and life span, the weighted score for a blue Portalo would be

$$U(\$17{,}000,\ 12\ \text{Years},\ \text{Blue}) = k_P \times 0 + k_L \times 1 + k_C \times 0.667.$$

You can see how the ratio approach can be used to compare virtually any set of alternatives whether or not they are quantitatively measured.

Standard Utility-Function Assessment

In principle, assessing the individual utility functions need be no more complicated than the assessment procedures described in Chapters 14 and 15. For the automobile example, we would need to assess utility functions for price, life span, and color. If you face a decision that is complicated by both uncertainty and trade-offs, this is the best solution. The utility functions, having been assessed in terms of your preferences over uncertain situations, are models of your preferences in which your risk attitude is built in.

To see the effect of building in a risk attitude, let us return to the previous example about the two jobs. Suppose we assess utility functions for income and savings and find that

$$U_I(\$60{,}000) = 1$$
$$U_I(\$30{,}000) = 0.75$$
$$U_I(0) = 0$$

and

$$U_S(\$120{,}000) = 1$$
$$U_S(\$60{,}000) = 0.68$$
$$U_S(\$0) = 0$$

With these utilities, the expected score for becoming an entrepreneur is

$$EU(\text{Entrepreneur}) = 0.185(1k_I + 1k_S) + 0.63(0.75k_I + 0.68k_S)$$
$$+ 0.185(0k_I + 0k_S)$$
$$= 0.658k_I + 0.613k_S$$

Now compare EU(Entrepreneur) with EU(Bureaucrat):

$$EU(\text{Bureaucrat}) = 0.750k_I + 0.680k_S$$

Regardless of the specific values for the weights k_I and k_S, the expected score for being a bureaucrat always will be greater than the expected score for being an entrepreneur because the coefficients for k_I and k_S are larger for the bureaucrat than for the entrepreneur. This makes sense; the expected values (EMVs) for the two alternatives are equal for each attribute, but being an entrepreneur clearly is riskier. When we use a utility function that incorporates risk aversion, the utility of the riskier alternative is reduced.

ASSESSING WEIGHTS

In the examples here and in Chapter 4, we have seen two different methods of assessing weights for the additive utility function. The approach in the automobile example is called *pricing out* because it involves determining the value of one objective in terms of another (usually dollars). The summer-job example in Chapter 4, though, used an approach that we will call *swing weighting*. We will discuss both of these methods here along with a third method based on a comparison of lotteries.

Pricing Out

The pricing-out method for assessing weights is no more complicated than what was previously described in the automobile example. The essence of the procedure is to determine the marginal rate of substitution between one particular attribute (usually monetary) and any other attribute. Thus, we might say that a year of life span is worth $600. Or, in a decision regarding whether to accept a settlement offer or pursue a lawsuit, one might assess that it would be worth $350 in time and frustration to avoid an hour consulting with lawyers, giving depositions, or sitting in a courtroom. (And that would be on top of the cost of the lawyers' time!)

Assessing the marginal rate of substitution is straightforward in concept. The idea is to find your indifference point: the most you would pay for an incremental unit of benefit, or the least you would accept for an incremental unit of something undesirable. A common approach is to display your attributes in terms of their good and bad consequences. Then ask yourself "how much should I be willing to pay in order to change the bad consequence to the good one?" From this you can easily solve for (assuming proportional scoring) the marginal contributions of each attribute. This procedure uses money as the common metric for all attributes. Although this idea seems straightforward, it can be a difficult assessment to make, especially for attributes with which we have little buying or selling experience.

As you can see, pricing out is especially appropriate for direct determination of the marginal rate of substitution from one attribute scale to another. Because the additive utility function implies a constant marginal rate of substitution, pricing out is consistent with the notion of proportional scores. However, when the individual utility functions are nonlinear or not readily interpretable in terms of an interval scale (as they might not be with a constructed scale), then pricing out makes less sense. One would have to ask, "How much utility on Attribute Scale 1 would I be willing to give up for a unit increase on Attribute Scale 2?" This is a more difficult assessment, and in situations like this, one of the following weight-assessment procedures might be easier.

Swing Weighting

The swing-weighting approach can be used in virtually any weight-assessment situation. It requires a thought experiment in which the decision maker compares individual attributes directly by imagining (typically) hypothetical alternatives. We demonstrate the procedure in this section with the automobile example.

To assess swing weights, the first step is to create a table like that in Table 16.3 for the automobiles. The first row indicates the worst possible alternative, or the alternative that is at the worst level on each of the attributes. In the case of the automobiles, this would be a red car that lasts only 6 years and costs $17,000. This "worst case" provides a benchmark. Each of the succeeding rows "swings" one and only one of the attributes from worst to best. For example, the second row in Table 16.3 swings life span from 6 to 12 years and results in a red car that lasts 12 years and costs $17,000. The last row is for a car that is worst on price and life span ($17,000 and 6 years, respectively) but is your favorite color, yellow.

TABLE **16.3**
Swing-weight assessment table for automobile example.

Attribute Swung from Worst to Best	Consequence to Compare	Rank	Rate	Weight
Benchmark	6 years, $17,000, Red	4		
Life Span	12 years, $17,000, Red			
Price	6 years, $8,000, Red			
Color	6 years, $17,000, Yellow			

© Cengage Learning

TABLE **16.4**
Swing-weight assessment table with ranks assessed.

Attribute Swung from Worst to Best	Consequence to Compare	Rank	Rate	Weight
Benchmark	6 years, $17,000, Red	4	0	
Life Span	12 years, $17,000, Red	2		
Price	6 years, $8,000, Red	1	100	
Color	6 years, $17,000, Yellow	3		

© Cengage Learning

With the table constructed, the assessment can begin. The first step is to rank order the outcomes. You can see in Table 16.3, a "4" has been placed in the "Rank" column for the first row. There are four hypothetical cars to compare, and it is safe to assume that the benchmark car—the one that is worst on all the objectives—will rank fourth (worst) overall. The others must be compared to determine which ranks first (best), second, and third. Suppose that after some thought you conclude that the low-price car is the best, then the long life-span car, and finally the yellow car. Table 16.4 shows the partially completed table.

The next step is to fill in the "Rate" column in the table. You can see in Table 16.4 that two of the ratings are predetermined; the rating for the benchmark car is 0 and the rating for the top-ranked car is 100. The ratings for the other two cars must fall between 0 and 100. The comparison is relatively straightforward to make; how much less satisfaction do you get by swinging life span from 6 to 12 years as compared to swinging price from $17,000 to $8,000? What about swinging color from red to yellow as compared to swinging price? You can even think about it in percentage terms; considering the increase in satisfaction that results from swinging price from worst to best, what percentage of that increase do you get by swinging life span from worst to best?

Suppose that after careful thought, your conclusion is to assign 75 points to life span and 10 points to color. Essentially, this means that you think improving life span from worst to best is worth 75% of the value you get by improving the price from $17,000 to $8,000. Likewise, changing the color from yellow to red is worth only 10% of the improvement in price. With these assessments, the table can be completed and weights calculated. Table 16.5

TABLE **16.5**
Completed swing weight assessment table.

Attribute Swung from Worst to Best	Consequence to Compare	Rank	Rate	Weight	
Benchmark	6 years, $17,000, Red	4	0		
Life Span	12 years, $17,000, Red	2	75	.405	= 75/185
Price	6 years, $8,000, Red	1	100	.541	= 100/185
Color	6 years, $17,000, Yellow	3	10	.054	= 10/185
		Total	185	1.000	

© Cengage Learning

shows the completed table. The weights are the normalized ratings; recall that by convention we have the weights add up to 1. For example, k_P is calculated as $100/(100 + 75 + 10) = 0.541$. Likewise, we have $k_L = 75/(100 + 75 + 10) = 0.405$, and $k_C = 10/(100 + 75 + 10) = 0.054$.

With the weights determined, we can calculate the overall utility for different alternatives or outcomes. For example, we now can finish calculating the utility for a blue Portalo:

$$
\begin{aligned}
U(\$17{,}000, 12 \text{ Years, Blue}) &= k_P(0) + k_L(1) + k_C(0.667) \\
&= 0.541(0) + 0.405(1) + 0.054(0.667) \\
&= 0.441
\end{aligned}
$$

Why do swing weights work? The argument is straightforward. Here are the utilities for the hypothetical cars that you have considered:

$$
\begin{aligned}
U(\text{Worst Conceivable Outcome}) &= U(\$17{,}000, 6 \text{ Years, Red}) \\
&= k_P(0) + k_L(0) + k_C(0) \\
&= 0
\end{aligned}
$$

$$
U(\$8{,}000, 6 \text{ Years, Red}) = k_P(1) + k_L(0) + k_C(0) = k_P
$$

$$
U(\$17{,}000, 12 \text{ Years, Red}) = k_P(0) + k_L(1) + k_C(0) = k_L
$$

$$
U(\$17{,}000, 6 \text{ Years, Yellow}) = k_P(0) + k_L(0) + k_C(1) = k_C
$$

From the first two equations, you can see that the increase in satisfaction from swinging price from worst to best is just k_P. Likewise, the improvement from swinging any attribute from worst to best is simply the value of the corresponding weight. When you compare the relative improvements in utility by swinging the attributes one at a time, you are assessing the ratios k_L/k_P and k_C/k_P. These assessments, along with the constraint that the weights add to 1, allow us to calculate the weights. Figure 16.10 graphically shows how swing weights work.

Swing weights have a built-in advantage in that they are sensitive to the range of values that an attribute takes on. For example, suppose you are comparing two personal computers, and price is an attribute. One computer costs $1,900 and the other $2,000. When you work through the swing-weight assessment procedure, you probably will conclude that the increase in utility from swinging the price is pretty small. This would result, appropriately, in a small weight for price. But if the price difference is $1,000 rather than $100, the increase in utility experienced by swinging from worst to best would be much larger, resulting in a larger weight for price.

If you have a hard time thinking about the "Worst Conceivable Outcome," you might try reversing this procedure. That is, use as a benchmark the "Best Conceivable Outcome," best on all attributes, and consider decreases in satisfaction from swinging attributes from high to low. Assess relative decreases in satisfaction, and use those assessments in exactly the same way that we used the relative utility increases.

FIGURE **16.10**
Graphic
representation of
swing-weighting
procedure.

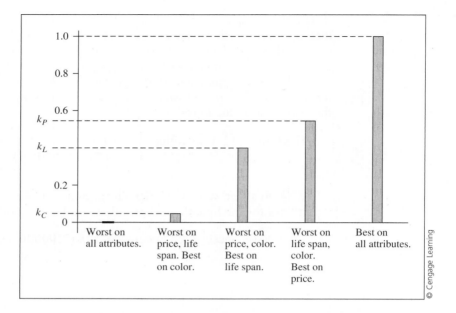

© Cengage Learning

Lottery Weights

It should come as no surprise that we also can use lottery-comparison techniques to assess weights. In fact, the technique we will use is a version of the probability equivalent assessment technique introduced in Chapter 14. The general assessment setup is shown in Figure 16.11.

The assessment of the probability p that makes you indifferent between the lottery and the sure thing turns out to be the weight for the one attribute that is best in the sure thing. We will see how this works in the case of the automobiles. Figure 16.12 shows the assessment decision for determining the weight associated with price.

Suppose that the indifference probability in Figure 16.12 turns out to be 0.55.

FIGURE **16.11**
Assessing weights
using a lottery
technique.

The task is to assess
the probability p
that makes you indif-
ferent between the
lottery (A) and the sure
thing (B).

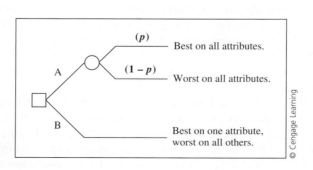

© Cengage Learning

FIGURE **16.12**
Assessing the
weight for price.

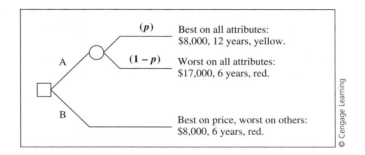

Write down the equation that is implied by the indifference U(B) = EU(A):

$$k_P U_P(\$8,000) + k_L U_L(6 \text{ Years}) + k_C U_C(\text{Red})$$
$$= 0.55[k_P U_P(\$8,000) + k_L U_L(12 \text{ Years}) + k_C U_C(\text{Yellow})]$$
$$+ 0.45[k_P U_P(\$17,000) + k_L U_L(6 \text{ Years}) + k_C U_C(\text{Red})]$$

As before, the individual utilities range from 0 to 1. This means that

$$U_P(\$8,000) = 1.00 \qquad U_P(\$17,000) = 0.00$$
$$U_L(12 \text{ Years}) = 1.00 \qquad U_L(6 \text{ Years}) = 0.00$$
$$U_C(\text{Yellow}) = 1.00 \qquad U_C(\text{Red}) = 0.00$$

Substitute these values into the equation to obtain

$$k_P \times 1 + k_L \times 0 + k_C \times 0 = 0.55[k_P \times 1 + k_L \times 1 + k_C \times 1]$$
$$+ 0.45[k_P \times 0 + k_L \times 0 + k_C \times 0]$$
$$k_P = 0.55[k_P + k_L + k_C]$$

Because $k_P + k_L + k_C = 1$, we have $k_P = 0.55$, which is simply the indifference probability that was assessed. Thus, we have a direct way to find the trade-off weight for the price attribute. Repeating this procedure one more time for the life-span attribute gives k_L, and then k_C follows because the weights must add to 1. Of course, a simple way to check for consistency is to repeat the procedure a third time for the color attribute. If assessed weights do not add to 1 and are not even close, then the additive model that we are using in this chapter is not appropriate. Chapter 17 discusses more complicated multiattribute utility models that may be able to accommodate such preferences.

Finally, you may have wondered why we always scale the individual utility functions from 0 to 1. The answer is contained in the preceding equations that underlie the weight-assessment techniques. In each case, we needed the values of 0 and 1 for best and worst cases in order to solve for the weights; the idea that scores are scaled from 0 to 1 is built into these assessment techniques. The result is that weights have very specific meanings. In particular, the swing-weight approach implies that we can interpret the weights in terms of improvements in utility that result from changing one attribute from low to high, and those low and high values may be specific to the alternatives being considered. The lottery-assessment method suggests that the weights can be interpreted as an indifference probability in a comparison of lotteries. The specific low and high values among the alternatives are important anchors for interpreting these indifference probabilities.

BIASES AND INCONSISTENCIES IN WEIGHT ASSESSMENT

In Chapter 14, we introduced the notion of *procedure invariance*. The weight-assessment methods that we just described are just different ways to measure one's preferences. Indeed, weights assessed with different methods can differ to some extent. Thus, strictly speaking, the different methods can lead to inconsistent weights. However, research has shown that when the different weights are used in a multiattribute utility function, the difference generally is not enough to have a large impact on choices.

Perhaps the most important behavioral issue with weight assessment is that assessment methods must be sensitive to the relevant range of each attribute. For example, if you are considering purchasing a new digital camera and have narrowed the choice to three cameras that all cost about the same, you wouldn't expect cost to play much of a role in the decision; you would assign relatively little weight to the cost attribute. For this reason we have avoided assessment methods that ask for direct "importance" ratings of the attributes; such methods have been shown to lead to weights that ignore the range of the attributes and hence can lead to considerable bias and inconsistency (Fischer, 1995). In the digital camera example, direct importance ratings might assign the same weight to cost whether the cameras are about the same or differ by several hundred dollars. All of the weight-assessment methods we have considered require the decision maker to consider the relevant range in one way or another.

The other bias we want to mention is more subtle. Called the *splitting bias*, it basically states that the weights assigned depend on the way the attributes are structured in a hierarchy (sometimes called a "value tree"). For example, in the automobile choice, one way to think about cost, life span, and color, is that they are three separate attributes. In this case, a default would be to assign a weight of 1/3 to each. Suppose though, that you separated them into monetary and non-monetary attributes. Then a default would be to assign a weight of 1/2 to the monetary attribute (cost) and share the other 1/2 between life span and color, each one receiving 1/4. In fact, research by Weber, Eisenführ, & von Winterfeldt, (1988) showed that people have precisely this tendency when assessing weights. There does not appear to be a good way to counter this bias aside from careful thought in the first place about how to structure and assess the weights and making the decision maker aware of the bias and the effects it might have on his or her judgments. Jacobi and Hobbs (2007) suggest a way to adjust the assessed weights in order to correct for the bias.

KEEPING CONCEPTS STRAIGHT: CERTAINTY VERSUS UNCERTAINTY

Up to this point we have been doing something that is, strictly speaking, not correct. We have been mixing up decision making under conditions of certainty with decision making under conditions of uncertainty. For example, the decision regarding which automobile to buy, as we have framed it, is one that is made under certainty regarding the outcomes; the Norushi, Portalo, and Standard Motors cars have particular characteristics (price, color, and advertised life span) that you know for sure when you buy them. On the other hand, we could reframe the problem and consider life span to be uncertain. In this case, we would assess a probability distribution over possible life spans for each car. The decision model we would create would require us to assess a utility function that covers all of the possible life-span outcomes so that we could appropriately value the probability distributions or lotteries for life span that come with each car. As we also saw, the entrepreneur-bureaucrat example involves uncertainty, and we needed an appropriate utility function in order to evaluate those two options in a way that made sense.

Why does it matter whether we are talking about certainty or uncertainty? Some of the utility-assessment methods we have talked about are appropriate for decisions under uncertainty, and some are not. When making decisions under certainty, we can use what are called *value functions* (also known as *ordinal utility functions*). Value functions are only required to rank-order sure outcomes in a way that is consistent with the decision maker's preferences for those outcomes. There is no concern with lotteries or uncertain outcomes. In fact, different value functions that rank sure outcomes in the same way may rank a set of lotteries in different ways.

If you face a decision under uncertainty, you should use what is called a *cardinal utility function*. A cardinal utility function appropriately incorporates your risk attitude so that lotteries are rank-ordered in a way that is consistent with your risk attitude. All of the discussion in Chapters 14 and 15 concerned cardinal utility; we constructed preference models to incorporate risk attitudes.

The good news is that most of the assessment techniques we have examined are appropriate for conditions of both certainty and uncertainty. Of the methods for assessing individual utility functions, only the ratio approach is, strictly speaking, limited only to decisions under certainty; nothing about this assessment method encodes the decision maker's attitude about risk. The proportional-scores technique is a special case; it may be used under conditions of uncertainty by a decision maker who is risk-neutral for the specified attributes. Of course, all of the lottery-based utility assessment methods from Chapters 14 and 15 are appropriate for decisions under uncertainty. And all of the weight-assessment methods described in this chapter can be used regardless of the presence or absence of uncertainty; once a specific multiattribute preference model is established, the weight-assessment methods amount to various ways of establishing indifference among specific lotteries or consequences. The weights can then be derived on the basis of these indifference judgments.

How much does the distinction between ordinal and cardinal utility models really matter? Although the distinction can be important in theoretical models of economic behavior, practical decision-analysis applications rarely distinguish between the two. Human decision makers need help understanding objectives and trade-offs, and all of the assessment techniques described in this chapter are useful in this regard. As always, we adopt a modeling view. The objective of assessing a multiattribute utility function is to gain insight and understanding of the decision maker's trade-offs among multiple objectives. Any assessment method or modeling technique that helps to do this—which includes all that are mentioned in this chapter—should result in a reasonable preference model that can lead the decision maker to a clear choice among available alternatives.

In a way, the situation is similar to the discussion on decreasing and constant risk aversion in Chapter 14, where we argued that it is difficult enough to determine the extent of a given individual's risk aversion, let alone whether it is decreasing or not. When facing multiple objectives, any approach that will help us to understand tradeoffs among objectives is welcome. Attention to preference ordering of lotteries rather than sure outcomes can be important in some situations but would come after obtaining a good basic understanding of the objectives and approximate trade-off weights.

A similar argument can be made for the additive utility function itself. Although strictly speaking it has some limitations and special requirements that will be explained in Chapter 17, it is an exceptionally useful and easy way to model preferences in many situations. Even if used only as an approximation, the additive utility function takes us a long way toward understanding our preferences and resolving a difficult decision.

AN EXAMPLE: LIBRARY CHOICES

With the discussion of assessing utility functions and weights behind us, we now turn to a realistic problem. This example will demonstrate the development of an additive utility function when there are many objectives. The issue is site selection for a new public library.

The Eugene Public Library

In 1986 a solution was sought for the overcrowded and inadequate conditions at the public library in Eugene, Oregon. The current building, with approximately 38,000 square feet of space, had been built in 1959 with the anticipation that it would serve satisfactorily for some 30 years. In the intervening years, Eugene's population had grown to the point that, on a per capita basis, the Eugene Public Library was one of the most heavily used public libraries in the western United States. All available space had been used. Even the basement, which had not been designed originally for patron use, had been converted to a periodicals reading room. Low-circulation materials had to be removed from the stacks and placed in storage to make room for patrons and books. Expansion was imperative; consultants estimated that 115,000 square feet of space were needed.

The current building could be expanded, but because of the original design it could not be operated as efficiently as a brand new building. Other potential sites were available, but all had their own benefits and drawbacks. After much thought, the possibilities were reduced to four sites in or near downtown Eugene, one of which was the current site. Some were less expensive for one reason or another; others had better opportunities for future expansion, and so on. How could the city choose from among them?

In evaluating the four proposed library sites, the first task was to create a fundamental-objectives hierarchy. What aspects of site location were important? The committee in charge of the study created the hierarchy shown in Figure 16.13 with seven root-level fundamental objectives and a second level of detail objectives. Parking, for example, was broken down into patron parking, off-site parking, night staff parking, and bookmobile space. (Without knowledge of Eugene's financial system, certain attributes in the "Related Cost" category may not make sense.) An important objective that is conspicuous by its absence is minimizing the cost of building a library. The committee's strategy was to compare the sites on the seven fundamental criteria first, and then consider the price tags for each. We will see later how this comparison can be made.

Comparing the four candidate sites (alternatives) required these four steps:

1. Evaluate the alternatives on each attribute.
2. Weight the attributes. This can be done with any of the three weight-assessment methods (although pricing out may be difficult because the overall cost is not included in this part of the analysis).
3. Calculate overall utility with the additive utility function.
4. Choose the alternative with the greatest overall utility.

Application of this procedure in the analysis of the four library sites produced the matrix shown in Table 16.6. The relative weights and the individual utilities are all shown in this table. (Actually, the committee's scores did not range from 0 to 1. Therefore, their scores have been rescaled here, and the weights have been adjusted to be consistent with the new numbers. Six attributes have been eliminated because they scored the same for all four sites.)

The overall utility is calculated and shown on a scale from 0 to 100, rather than from 0 to 1; this makes the table easier to read. Under each fundamental objective is a subtotal for each site. For example, the subtotal for Site 1 under "Parking" is

$$\text{Subtotal (Parking}_1) = [(0.053 \times 0.20 \times 1.00) + (0.053 \times 0.60 \times 0.00) \\ + (0.053 \times 0.20 \times 1.00)] \times 100 \\ = 2.12$$

(The factor of 100 at the end simply changes the scale so that it ranges from 0 to 100.) Once all individual utilities have been calculated for each

FIGURE **16.13**
Fundamental
objectives for
the Eugene Public
Library site
evaluation study.

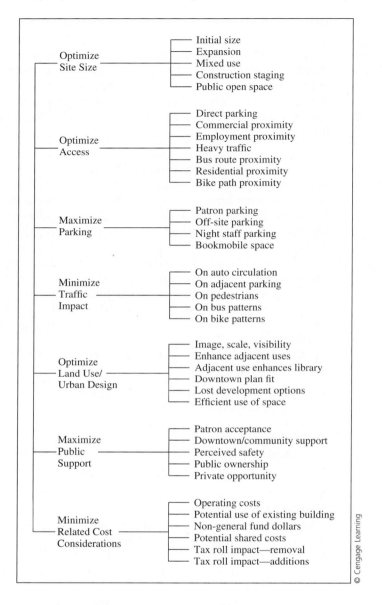

fundamental objective, they are simply added to find the overall utility for each site. For example,

$$U(\text{Site 1}) = 13.08 + 6.40 + 2.12 + 1.08 + 3.02 + 15.77 + 4.22$$
$$= 45.70$$

You can see that the overall weight given to a specific attribute is the product of the specific weight at the lower level and the overall weight for the fundamental objective. For example, Site 1 has U(Construction Staging) = 1.00.

TABLE **16.6**
Matrix of weights and utilities for four library sites.

Attributes	Percentage	Utilities			
		Site 1	Site 2	Site 3	Site 4
Site Size (21.1%)					
Initial	38	1.00	0.00	1.00	1.00
Expansion (Horizontal)	13	0.00	0.00	0.00	1.00
Mixed Use	25	0.00	1.00	1.00	1.00
Construction Staging	12	1.00	0.00	0.00	1.00
Public Open Space	12	1.00	0.00	0.00	0.00
Subtotals	*100*	*13.08*	*5.28*	*13.29*	*18.57*
Access (20.6%)					
Direct Parking	8	0.00	1.00	0.00	0.00
Commercial Proximity	23	0.00	1.00	0.67	1.00
Employment Proximity	15	0.50	1.00	0.00	1.00
Heavy Traffic	23	0.33	0.33	1.00	0.00
Bus Route Proximity	15	0.00	0.50	0.50	1.00
Residential Proximity	16	1.00	0.00	1.00	0.50
Subtotals	*100*	*6.40*	*12.58*	*12.75*	*12.57*
Parking (5.3%)					
Patron Parking	20	1.00	0.00	1.00	1.00
Off-Site Parking	60	0.00	1.00	0.33	0.33
Bookmobile Parking	20	1.00	0.00	1.00	1.00
Subtotals	*100*	*2.12*	*3.18*	*3.17*	*3.17*
Traffic Impacts (4.5%)					
Auto Circulation	47	0.00	0.75	1.00	0.00
Adjacent Parking	29	0.00	0.00	1.00	0.00
Bus Patterns	24	1.00	1.00	1.00	0.00
Subtotals	*100*	*1.08*	*2.67*	*4.50*	*0.00*
Land Use/Design (8.4%)					
Image/Scale/Visibility	13	0.00	1.00	0.00	0.00
Enhance Adjacent Uses	13	0.00	1.00	1.00	1.00
Adjacent Uses Enhance Library	38	0.00	1.00	1.00	0.00
Downtown Plan Fit	13	1.00	0.00	1.00	1.00
Lost Development Options	23	1.00	0.00	0.00	0.00
Subtotals	*100*	*3.02*	*5.38*	*5.38*	*2.18*

TABLE **16.6**
(Continued)

Attributes	Percentage	Utilities			
		Site 1	Site 2	Site 3	Site 4
Public Support (19.0%)					
Patron Acceptance	25	1.00	0.33	0.67	0.00
DT/Community Support	25	1.00	0.67	0.33	0.00
Perceived Safety	25	1.00	0.33	1.00	0.00
Public Ownership	17	0.00	1.00	1.00	0.00
Private Opportunity	8	1.00	0.00	1.00	1.00
Subtotals	*100*	*15.77*	*9.55*	*14.25*	*1.52*
Related Costs (21.1%)					
Operating Costs	20	0.00	1.00	1.00	1.00
Use of Existing Building	20	1.00	0.00	0.00	0.00
No General Fund Dollars	30	0.00	1.00	1.00	1.00
Tax Roll Impact, Removal	10	0.00	1.00	1.00	0.00
Tax Toll Impact, Added	20	0.00	1.00	1.00	1.00
Subtotals	*100*	*4.22*	*16.88*	*16.88*	*14.77*
Weighted Score		*45.70*	*55.51*	*70.22*	*52.78*

This utility then is multiplied by 0.12, the weight for construction staging, and then multiplied by 0.211, the weight for the fundamental attribute of "Site Size." Thus, in this grand scheme, the utilities are weighted by a product of the weights at the two levels in the hierarchy. To express this more formally, let k_i represent the weight of the ith fundamental objective, and k_{ij} and U_{ij} the weight and utility, respectively, for the jth attribute under fundamental objective i. If there are m fundamental objectives and n_i detail attributes under fundamental objective i, then the overall utility for a site is

$$U(\text{Site}) = k_1(k_{11}U_{11} + k_{12}U_{12} + k_{13}U_{13} + \cdots + k_{1n_1}U_{1n_1})$$
$$+ k_2(k_{21}U_{21} + k_{22}U_{22} + k_{23}U_{23} + \cdots + k_{2n}U_{2n_2})$$
$$+ \cdots + k_m(k_{m1}U_{m1} + k_{m2}U_{m2} + k_{m3}U_{m3} + \cdots + k_{mn_m}U_{mn_m})$$
$$= \sum_{i=1}^{m} k_i \left[\sum_{j=1}^{n_i} k_{ij}U_{ij} \right]$$

From these expressions, we can see that the utilities on the individual attributes are being weighted by the product of the appropriate weights and then added. Thus, we still have an additive score that is a weighted combination of the individual utilities, just as we did in the simpler two- and three-attribute preceding examples. Moreover, it also should be clear that as the hierarchy increases in the number of levels, the formula also grows, multiplying the individual utilities by all of the appropriate weights in the hierarchy.

The result of all of the calculations for the library example? Site 3 ranked the best with 70.22 points, Site 2 was second with 55.51 points, and Sites 4 and 1 (the current location) were ranked third and fourth overall with 52.78 and 45.70 points, respectively.

There is another interesting and intuitive way to interpret this kind of analysis. Imagine that 100 points are available to be awarded for each alternative, depending on how a given alternative ranks on each attribute. In the library case, 21.1 of the 100 points are awarded on the basis of "Site Size," 20.6 on the basis of "Access," 5.3 for "Parking," and so on. Within the "Site Size" category, the weights on the detail objectives determine how the 21.1 points for "Site Size" will be allocated; 38% of the 21.1 points (or 8.02 points) will be awarded on the basis of "Initial Size," 13% of the 21.1 points (2.74 points) will be awarded on the basis of "Expansion," and so on. We can see how this subdivision could continue through many layers in a hierarchy. Finally, when the ends of the branches are reached, we must determine utilities for the alternatives. If the utilities range from 0 to 1, then the utility indicates what proportion of the available points are awarded to the alternative for the particular detail attribute being considered. For example, Site 3 has a utility of 0.67 on "Commercial Proximity," so it receives 67% of the points available for this detail attribute. How many points are available? The weight of 23% tells us that 23% of the total points for "Access" are allocated to "Commercial Proximity," and the 20.6% weight for "Access" says that 20.6 points total are available for "Access." Thus, Site 3 earns $0.67 \times 0.23 \times 20.6 = 3.17$ points for "Commercial Proximity." For each detail attribute, calculate the points awarded to Site 3. Now add those points; the total is Site 3's overall utility (70.22) on a scale from 0 to 100.

Recall that cost was an important attribute that was not included in the analysis of the library sites. The committee studying the problem decided to ignore construction costs until the sites were well understood in terms of their other attributes. But now that we have ranked the sites on the basis of the attributes, we must consider money. Table 16.7 shows the costs associated with each site, along with the overall utilities from Table 16.6, and Figure 16.14 shows the same information, graphically plotting cost against overall utility.

TABLE 16.7
Cost and overall utility for four library sites.

Site	Cost ($ Million)	Overall Utility
1	21.74	45.70
2	18.76	55.51
3	24.48	70.22
4	24.80	52.78

© Cengage Learning

FIGURE **16.14**
Library site costs plotted against overall utility.

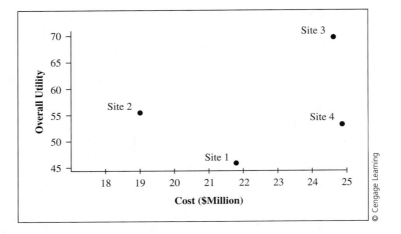

Table 16.7 and Figure 16.14 show clearly that Sites 1 and 4 are dominated. That is, if you like Site 4, then you should like Sites 2 or 3 even better, because each has a greater utility for less money. Likewise, Site 2 clearly dominates Site 1. Thus, Sites 1 and 4 can be eliminated from the analysis altogether on the basis of dominance. This leaves Sites 2 and 3. Is it worthwhile to pay the additional \$2.72 million to gain 14.71 additional points in terms of overall utility? Alternatively, is an increase of one point in the utility worth \$184,908?

Obviously, we are trying to price out the value of a single point on our 1-to-100 scale, just as we previously priced out the value of changes in attributes. But answering this question now is difficult because one point in the overall utility may have many components. One possible approach is to return to the detail attributes, look for specific attributes on which Site 3 is ranked higher than Site 2, and consider how much we would be willing to pay (in dollars) to bring Site 2 up to Site 3's level on this attribute. For example, Site 3 scored much higher than Site 2 for access during heavy traffic periods. The difference is that Site 2 is in a relatively congested area of downtown and on one of the city's main thoroughfares. In contrast, Site 3 is located at the edge of downtown, and access would be through relatively low-volume streets. How much would altering the traffic patterns be worth so that Site 2 would be just as good as Site 3 for this attribute? One million dollars? More?

Let us suppose that we have assessed that the difference between the sites in terms of access during heavy traffic is indeed worth \$1 million. It turns out that Site 3's advantage increases its weighted score by 3.17 points. (This is the difference between the sites in points awarded for this attribute.) Thus, the assessment would indicate that 3.17 points of overall utility are worth \$1 million, or \$315,457 per point of utility. This is greater than the \$184,908 per point required to switch from Site 2 to Site 3.

A pricing-out approach such as this can be used to assess the dollar value of one point of overall utility. Rather than making only one assessment, however, we should make several on different attributes where the two alternatives differ. For some of these assessments it may be possible to make estimates of true costs in terms of the market price of adjacent land, redesigning traffic patterns, constructing parking lots, and so on, and these cost estimates then might be helpful in assessing the dollar value of specific differences between sites. If the assessments in terms of prices per point of overall utility come out fairly close, then the average of these assessments can be used as a reasonable measure of the value of one point of overall utility. In the case of the library sites, if the final price per point is less than $184,908, then Site 2 is preferred; otherwise Site 3 is preferred. If the price per point turns out to be very close to $184,908, then the two sites are approximately equivalent.

The analysis probably would have been more complete had the committee elected to include minimizing cost as one of its fundamental objectives. In fact, all of the other attributes could have been priced out in terms of dollars, thus making the comparisons and trade-offs more intuitive. But it is not unusual for groups to ignore costs in an initial stage. The motivation often is political; it may be easier to gain constituent support by initially playing up the benefits of a project such as a new library before talking about the "bottom line."

USING SOFTWARE FOR MULTIPLE-OBJECTIVE DECISIONS

As you can imagine, multiple-objective decisions can become very complex. The library example involved only four alternatives and a relatively simple objectives hierarchy. Still, there were many assessments to make, and the calculations involved, though straightforward, are tedious. In Chapter 4 we demonstrated two methods that relieve you of the tedious calculations when modeling multiple-objective decisions. Both methods take advantage of the fact that PrecisionTree runs within a spreadsheet environment, providing easy access to side calculations. In the first method, you enter the attribute scores and weights into the spreadsheet with the corresponding utility functions. Then Excel® will calculate the overall utility of each alternative and PrecisionTree will calculate the expected utility. In the second method, you build a linked decision tree that takes its input values directly from the tree and outputs the expected utility value.

SUMMARY

This chapter has introduced the basics of making decisions that involve trade-offs. The basic problem is to create a model of the decision maker's preferences in terms of the various objectives. The first step in doing so, as discussed in detail in Chapter 3, is to understand which objectives are most important in making your decision; this requires introspection as to the fundamental objectives. The goal of this step is to create a fundamental-objectives hierarchy and a set of operational attribute scales to measure the performance of each alternative or outcome on each of the fundamental objectives.

To evaluate the alternatives, we introduced the additive utility function, which calculates an overall utility for an alternative or outcome as a weighted sum of individual utility functions for each fundamental objective. Assessing the individual utility functions is best done through a consistent method of comparison that results in utilities ranging from 0 to 1. We discussed three methods: calculation of proportional scores, assessment of ratios, and the conventional lottery-based assessment. Once these utility functions are established, weights must also be assessed. Several assessment procedures are possible here, all providing mechanisms for determining the rate at which the attributes can be traded off against one another. Sometimes trade-off rates can be assessed in terms of dollars by pricing out the other attributes. The swing-weighting and lottery-based assessment techniques can be used even if it is difficult to think of the attributes in dollar terms, and these techniques lead to clear interpretations of the assessed weights. With weights and individual utility functions determined, overall utilities are calculated by applying the additive utility formula. We demonstrated the procedure with an example in which potential sites for a public library were evaluated.

EXERCISES

16.1. Why is it important to think carefully about decision situations that involve multiple conflicting objectives?

16.2. Explain the general decision-analysis approach to dealing with multiple objectives.

16.3. Explain what is meant by the term *indifference curve*.

16.4. Explain the idea of dominance in the context of multiobjective decision making.

16.5. Imagine that you are working on a committee to develop an employment-conditions policy for your firm. During the discussion of safety, one committee member states that employee safety is twice as important as benefits such as flexible worktime, employer sponsored day care, and so on.
  a. How might you respond to such a statement?
  b. Suppose the statement was that employee safety was twice as important as insurance benefits. How might you translate this statement into a form (perhaps based on dollar values) so that it would be possible to evaluate various policy alternatives in terms of safety and insurance in a way that would be consistent with the statement?

16.6. Explain why proportional scores represent a risk attitude that is risk-neutral.

16.7. An MBA student evaluating weather outcomes for an upcoming party has concluded that a sunny day would be twice as good as a cloudy day, and a cloudy day would be three times as good as a rainy day. Use these assessments to calculate utilities that range from 0 to 1 for sunny, rainy, and cloudy days.

16.8. Explain in your own words why swing weights produce meaningful weights for evaluating alternatives.

16.9. A decision maker is assessing weights for two attributes using the swing-weight method. When he imagines swinging the attributes individually from worst to best, he concludes that his improvement in satisfaction from Attribute A is 70% of the improvement from swinging Attribute B. Calculate k_A and k_B.

16.10. Explain in your own words why the lottery method works to produce meaningful weights for evaluating alternatives.

16.11. A decision maker is assessing weights for three attributes using the lottery-assessment method. In considering the lotteries, she concludes that she is indifferent between:

    A. Win the best possible combination with probability 0.34
          Win the worst possible combination with probability 0.66

and

    B. Win a combination that is worst on Attributes 1 and 3 and best on 2

She also has concluded that she is indifferent between

    C. Win the best possible combination with probability 0.25
          Win the worst possible combination with probability 0.75

and

    D. Win a combination that is worst on Attributes 2 and 3 and best on 1

Find weights k_1, k_2, and k_3.

QUESTIONS AND PROBLEMS

16.12. Suppose that you are searching for an apartment in which to live while you go to school. Apartments near campus generally cost more than equivalent apartments farther away. Five apartments are available. One is right next to campus, and another is one mile away. The remaining apartments are two, three, and four miles away.

    a. Suppose you have a tentative agreement to rent the apartment that is one mile from campus. How much more would you be willing to pay in monthly rent to obtain the one next to campus? (Answer this question on the basis of your own personal experience. Other than rent and distance from campus, the two apartments are equivalent.)

    b. Now suppose you have a tentative agreement to rent the apartment that is four miles away. How much more would you be willing to pay in monthly rent to move to the apartment that is only three miles from campus?

    c. What are the implications of your answers to parts a and b? Would it be appropriate to rank the apartments in terms of distance using the proportional-scoring technique?

    d. Sketch an indifference curve that reflects the way you would trade off rent versus proximity to campus. Is your indifference curve a straight line?

16.13. A friend of yours is in the market for a new computer. Four different machines are under consideration. The four computers are essentially the same, but they vary in price and reliability. The least expensive model is also the least reliable, the most expensive is the most reliable, and the other two are in between.

a. Describe to your friend how you would approach the decision.

b. Define reliability in a way that would be appropriate for the decision. Do you need to consider risk?

c. How might your friend go about establishing a marginal rate of substitution between reliability and price?

16.14. Continuing Problem 16.13, the computers are described as follows:

    A. Price: $998.95 Expected number of days in the shop per year: 4

    B. Price: $1,300.00 Expected number of days in the shop per year: 2

    C. Price: $1,350.00 Expected number of days in the shop per year: 2.5

    D. Price: $1,750.00 Expected number of days in the shop per year: 0.5

The computer will be an important part of your friend's livelihood for the next 2 years. (After 2 years, the computer will have a negligible salvage value.) In fact, your friend can foresee that there will be specific losses if the computer is in the shop for repairs. The magnitude of the losses are uncertain but are estimated to be approximately $180 per day that the computer is down.

a. Can you give your friend any advice without doing any calculations?

b. Use the information given to determine weights k_P and k_R, where R stands for reliability. What assumptions are you making?

c. Calculate overall utilities for the computers. What do you conclude?

d. Sketch three indifference curves that reflect your friend's trade-off rate between reliability and price.

e. What considerations other than losses might be important in determining the tradeoff rate between cost and reliability?

16.15. Throughout the chapter we have assessed individual utility functions that range from 0 to 1. What is the advantage of doing this?

16.16. You are an up-and-coming developer in downtown Seattle and are interested in constructing a building on a site that you own. You have collected four bids from prospective contractors. The bids include both a cost (millions of dollars) and a time to completion (months):

Contractor	Cost ($ Million)	Time (months)
A	100	20
B	80	25
C	79	28
D	82	26

The problem now is to decide which contractor to choose. B has indicated that for another $20 million he could do the job in 18 months, and you have said that you would be indifferent between that and the original proposal. In talking with C, you have indicated that you would just as soon pay her an extra $4 million if she could get the job done in 26 months. Who gets the job? Explain your reasoning. (It may be convenient to plot the four alternatives on a graph.)

16.17. Once you decide that you are in the market for a personal computer, you have many different considerations. You should think about how you will use the computer, and so you need to know whether appropriate software is available and at what price. The "feel" of the computer, which is in some sense determined by the operating system and the user interface, can be critical. Are you an experienced user? Do you want to be able to program the machine, or will you (like most of us) rely on existing or over-the-counter software? If you intend to use the machine for number crunching, videos, or gaming, then processor speed may be important. Reliability and service are other matters. For many students, an important question is whether the computer will be compatible with other systems in any job they might eventually have. Finally, of course, price is important.

Create a fundamental-objectives hierarchy to compare your options. Take care in doing this; be sure that you establish the fundamental objectives and operational attributes that will allow you to make the necessary comparisons. (Note that the previously suggested attributes are *not* exhaustive, and some may not apply to you!)

Use your model to evaluate at least three different computers (preferably from different manufacturers). You will have to specify precisely the packages that you compare. It also might be worthwhile to include appropriate software. (Exactly what you compare is up to you, but make the packages meaningful.) Be sure that your utilities are such that the best alternative gets a 1 and the worst a 0 for each attribute. Assess weights using pricing out, swing weighting, or lottery weights. Calculate overall utilities for your alternatives.

Try using the utility functions for money and computer reliability that you assessed in Problems 14.12 and 15.12. You may have to rescale the utility functions to obtain scores so that the best alternative in this problem scores 1 and the worst scores 0.

16.18. When you choose a place to live, what objectives are you trying to accomplish? What makes some apartments better than others? Would you rather live close to campus or farther away and spend less money? What about the quality of the neighborhood? How about amenities such as a swimming pool?

Create a fundamental-objectives hierarchy that allows you to compare apartment options. Take care in doing this; be sure to establish the fundamental objectives and operational attributes that will allow you to make the necessary comparisons.

Once you are satisfied with your hierarchy, use it to compare available housing alternatives. Try ranking different apartments that are available. Be sure that your individual utilities follow the rules: Best takes a 1 and worst takes 0. (Try using the utility function for money that you assessed in Problem 14.12. You may have to rescale it so that your best alternative gets a 1 and worst gets a 0.) Assess weights using pricing out, swing weighting, or lottery weights. Evaluate your alternatives with the additive utility function.

16.19. What is important to you in choosing a job? Certainly salary is important, and for many people location matters a lot. Other considerations might involve promotion potential, the nature of the work, the organization itself, benefits, and so on.

Create a fundamental-objectives hierarchy that allows you to compare job offers. Be sure to establish the fundamental objectives and operational attributes that will allow you to make the necessary comparisons.

Once you are satisfied with your hierarchy, use it to compare your job offers. You also may want to think about your "ideal" job in order to compare your current offers with your ideal. You also might consider your imaginary worst possible job in all respects. (For the salary attribute, try using the utility function for money that you assessed in Problem 14.12, or some variation of it. You may have to rescale it so that your best alternative is 1 and worst 0.) Assess weights for the attributes using pricing out, swing weighting, or lottery weights, being careful to anchor your judgments in terms of both ideal and worst imaginable jobs. Evaluate your various job offers with the additive utility function. If possible, use a computer-based multiattribute decision program to do this problem.

16.20. How can you compare your courses? When you consider those that you have taken, it should be clear that some were better than others and that the good ones were, perhaps, good for different reasons. What are the important dimensions that affect the quality of a course? Some are obvious, such as the enthusiasm of an instructor, topic, and amount and type of work involved. Other aspects may not be quite so obvious; for example, how you perceive one course may depend on other courses you have had.

In this problem, the objective is to create a "template" that will permit consistent evaluation of your courses. The procedure is essentially the same as it is for any multiattribute decision, except that you will be able to use the template to evaluate future courses. Thus, we do not have a set of alternatives available to use for the determination of scores and weights. (You want to think, however, about current and recent courses in making your assessments.)

First, create a fundamental-objectives hierarchy that allows you to compare courses. Be sure to establish the fundamental objectives and operational attributes that will allow for the necessary comparisons. Constructing a set of objectives for comparing courses is considerably more difficult than comparing computers, apartments, or jobs. You may find that many of the attributes you consider initially will overlap with others, leading to a confusing array of attributes that are interdependent. It may take considerable thought to reduce the degree of redundancy in your hierarchy and to arrive at one that is complete, decomposable, small enough to be manageable, and involves attributes that are easy to think about.

Once you are satisfied with your objectives and attributes, imagine the best and worst courses for each attribute. Create attribute scales (constructed scales where appropriate) for each objective. The idea is to be able to return to these scales with any new course and determine utilities for each objective with relative ease. (Try using the homework utility function that you developed in Problem 15.14. You may have to rescale it so that your best alternative gets a 1 and the worst a 0.)

Once you have created the attribute scales, you are ready to assess the weights. Try the swing-weighting or lottery approach for assessing the weights. (Pricing out may be difficult to do in this particular example. Can you place a dollar value on your attributes?)

Finally, with scales and weights established, you are ready to evaluate courses. Try comparing three or four of your most recent courses. (Try evaluating one that you took more than a year ago. Can you remember enough about the course to assess the individual utilities with some degree of confidence?)

16.21. Refer to the discussion of the automobiles in the section on "Trading Off Conflicting Objectives: The Basics." We discussed switching first from the Standard to the Norushi, and then from the Norushi to the Portalo. Would it make sense to consider a direct switch from the Standard to the Portalo? Why or why not?

16.22. In Chapter 2 we discussed net present value (NPV) as a procedure for evaluating consequences that yield cash flows at different points in time. If x_i is the cash flow at year i and r is the discount rate, then the NPV is given by

$$\text{NPV} = \sum_{i=0}^{n} \frac{x_i}{(1+r)^i}$$

where the summation is over all future cash flows including the current x_0.

a. Explain how the NPV criterion is similar to the additive utility function that was discussed in this chapter. What are the attributes? What are the weights? Describe the way cash at time period i is traded off against cash at time period $i + 1$. (*Hint:* Review Chapter 2!)

b. Suppose that you can invest in one of two different projects. Each costs $20,000. The first project is riskless and will pay you $10,000 each year for the next 3 years. The second one is risky. There is a 50% chance that it will pay $15,000 each year for the next 3 years and a 50% chance that it will pay only $5,000 per year for the next 3 years. Your discount rate is 9%. Calculate the NPV for both the riskless and risky projects. Compare them. What can you conclude about the use of NPV for deciding among risky projects?

    c.   How might your NPV analysis in part b be modified to take risk into account? Could you use a utility function? How does the idea of a risk-adjusted discount rate fit into the picture? How could the interest rate be adjusted to account for risk? Would this be the same as using a utility function for money?

16.23. Following up Problem 16.22, even though we take riskiness into account, there still is difficulty with NPV as a decision criterion. Suppose that you are facing the two risky projects shown in Figure 16.15.

        Project A pays either $10,000 for each of 2 years or $100 for those 2 years. Project B pays $10,000 either in the first year or the second year and $100 in the other year. Assume that the cash flows are annual profits.

    a.   Which of these two risky investments would you prefer? Why?

    b.   Calculate the expected NPV for both projects, using the same 9% interest rate from Problem 16.22. Based on expected NPV, in which project would you invest?

    c.   After careful assessment, you have concluded that you are risk-averse and that your utility function can be adequately represented by $U(X_i) = \ln(X_i)$, where X_i represents cash flow during year i. Calculate the expected net present utility for each project. Net present utility is given by

$$\text{NPU} = \sum \frac{U(X_i)}{(1+r)^i}$$

    d.   NPU in part c should incorporate your attitude toward risk. Are your NPU calculations in part c consistent with your preferences in part a? What is there about these two projects that is not captured by your utility function? Can you think of any other way to model your preferences?

16.24. Instead of calculating a "discounted" utility as we did in Problem 16.23, let us consider calculating U(NPV). That is, calculate NPV first, using an appropriate interest rate, and then calculate a utility value for the NPV. For your utility function, use the exponential utility function $U(NPV) = 1 - e^{-NPV/5000}$. Use this approach to calculate the expected utility of Projects A and B in Figure 16.15. Which would

FIGURE 16.15
Decision tree for Problem 16.23.

Which of these two risky investments would you prefer?

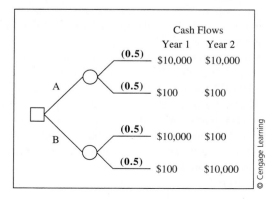

FIGURE **16.16**
Deciding between
alternative
chemicals in
Problem 16.25.

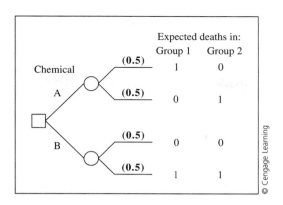

you choose? Are there any problems with using this procedure for
evaluating projects?

16.25. A policy maker in the Occupational Safety and Health Administration is
under pressure from industry to permit the use of certain chemicals in a
newly developed industrial process. Two different versions of the
process use two different chemicals, A and B. The risks associated with
these chemicals are not known with certainty, but the available
information indicates that they may affect two groups of people in the
following ways:

- *Chemical A* There is a 50% chance that Group 1 will be adversely
  affected, while Group 2 is unaffected; and a 50% chance that
  Group 2 is adversely affected, while Group 1 is unaffected.
- *Chemical B* There is a 50% chance that both groups will be adversely
  affected, and a 50% chance that neither group will be affected.

Assume that "adversely affected" means the same in every case—an
expected increase of one death in the affected group over the next 2 years.
The decision maker's problem looks like the decision tree in Figure 16.16.

a. Calculate the expected number of deaths for each chemical.

b. A decision maker who values consequences using an overall utility
    might calculate the utility for each consequence as

$$U(\text{Chemical}) = k_1 U_1(\text{Group 1 Deaths}) + k_2 U_2(\text{Group 2 Deaths})$$

For both U_1 and U_2, the best and worst possible outcomes are 0
deaths and 1 death, respectively. Thus,

$U_1(1 \text{ Death}) = 0$	$U_1(0 \text{ Deaths}) = 1$
$U_2(1 \text{ Death}) = 0$	$U_2(0 \text{ Deaths}) = 1$

Explain why k_1 and $k_2 = 1 - k_1$ may not be equal.

c. Assume that $k_1 = 0.4$. Show that the decision maker who evalu-
    ates the two chemicals in terms of their expected overall utilities

(as defined previously) would be indifferent between them. Does the value of k_1 matter?

d. Why might the decision maker *not* be indifferent between the two programs? (Most people think about the decision maker's risk attitude toward the number of deaths or lives saved. Besides this, think about the following: Suppose you are a member of Group 1, and the decision maker has chosen Chemical A. It turned out that Group 1 was affected. How would you feel? What would you do? What does this imply for the decision maker?)

16.26. Refer to the discussion of the three automobiles in the section "Trading Off Conflicting Objectives: The Basics." Suppose we had the following individual utility functions for price and life span:

Life Span	Price
$U_L(6 \text{ Years}) = 0.00$	$U_P(\$17,000) = 0.00$
$U_L(9 \text{ Years}) = 0.75$	$U_P(\$10,000) = 0.50$
$U_L(12 \text{ Years}) = 1.00$	$U_P(\$8,000) = 1.00$

The additive utility model discussed in this chapter would give us the following:

$$U(\text{Life Span, Price}) = k_L U_L(\text{Life Span}) + (1 - k)_L U_P(\text{Price})$$

a. With $k_L = 0.45$, calculate the utility for the three cars. Which would be chosen?

b. Suppose that you are not completely comfortable with the assessment of $k_L = 0.45$. How large could k_L be before the decision changes, and what would be the new choice? How small could k_L be before the decision changes, and what would be the new choice? Would you say that the choice among these three cars is very sensitive to the assessment of k_L?

16.27. Refer to Table 16.6. Your boss is a member of the library-site selection committee. She is not perfectly satisfied with the assessments shown in the table. Specifically, she wonders to what extent the assessed weights and individual utilities on the detail attributes could change without affecting the overall ranking of the four sites. Use an electronic spreadsheet to answer this question, and write a memo that discusses your findings. (*Hint:* There is no specific way to attack a sensitivity analysis like this. One possibility is to establish reasonable ranges for the weights and then create a tornado diagram. Be sure that your weights add to 1 in each category!)

16.28. Refer to Problem 16.11. Suppose that the decision maker has made a third assessment, concluding that she is indifferent between

E   Win the best possible combination with probability 0.18. Win the worst possible combination with probability 0.82

and

F   Win a combination that is worst on Attributes 1 and 2, and best on 3

What does this assessment imply for the analysis? Is it consistent with your answer for k_3 in Problem 16.11? What should you do now?

THE SATANIC VERSES

In early 1989, the Ayatollah Khomeini of Iran decreed that Salman Rushdie, the British author of *The Satanic Verses,* should be put to death. In many ways, Rushdie's novel satirized Islam and the Prophet Muhammed. Khomeini declared that Rushdie should die and that whoever killed him would go to Heaven.

Many bookstores in both Europe and the United States that carried *The Satanic Verses* found themselves in a bind. Some Muslims threatened violence unless the bookstores stopped selling the book. Some booksellers removed the book from their shelves and sold it only to customers who specifically asked for it. Others refused to sell it altogether on the grounds that it was too risky. Still others defied the threats. One bookseller in Berkeley, California, continued selling the book on the grounds that he would not allow anyone to interfere with the principle of freedom of the press. His store was bombed, and damage was substantial. His reaction? He increased security.

Questions

1. Imagine that you are the owner of a bookstore faced with the decision of what to do about *The Satanic Verses.* In deciding on a course of action, there are several conflicting objectives. Develop an objectives hierarchy and operational attribute scales.
2. What alternatives do you have?
3. What risks do you face? Do the risks differ depending on the alternative you choose? Sketch a simple influence diagram or decision tree for your problem.

DILEMMAS IN MEDICINE

In *Alpha and Omega: Ethics at the Frontiers of Life and Death,* author Ernlé Young specifies four fundamental principles that must be considered in making medical decisions: beneficence, nonmaleficence, justice, and autonomy. The following descriptions of these principles have been abstracted from the book (pp. 21–23):

*   *Beneficence* implies that the physician's most important duty is to provide services that are beneficial to the patient. In many cases, this can mean taking measures that are intended to preserve the patient's life.

*   *Nonmaleficence* is the duty not to cause harm to the patient. A medical aphorism of uncertain origin proclaims *primum non nocere*—above all, do no harm. Harm can mean different things in different situations and for different patients, and can include death, disability, separation from loved ones, or deprivation of pleasure or freedom. The difficulty is that many medical procedures entail at least some harm or the potential for harm. This always must be weighed against the potential benefits.

*   *Justice* in this context refers to the fair use of resources. It is, after all, impossible to do absolutely

everything that would be medically justifiable for all patients. Thus, decisions must be made regarding the allocation of scarce resources. The issue is how to make these decisions fairly or equitably. For example, how should we decide what patients have priority for receiving donated organs? Is it appropriate to admit a terminally ill patient to an intensive care unit?

- *Autonomy* requires allowing a patient to make his or her own decisions regarding medical treatment as far as is possible. The patient, operating as an independent, self-determining agent, should be able to obtain appropriate information and participate fully in the decisions regarding the course of treatment and, ultimately, the patient's life.

In most medical situations, these principles do not conflict. That is, the physician can provide beneficial care for the patient without causing harm, the treatment can be provided equitably, and the patient can easily make his or her own decisions. In a few cases, however, the principles are in conflict and it is impossible to accomplish all of them at once. For example, consider the case of a terminally ill patient who insists that everything possible be done to extend his or her life. Doing so may violate both nonmaleficence and justice while at the same time providing limited benefit. But not providing the requested services violates autonomy. Thus, the physician would be in a very difficult dilemma.

Questions

1. Discuss the relationship between the medical ethics here and decision making in the face of conflicting objectives. Sketch an objectives hierarchy for a physician who must cope with difficult problems such as those previously described. Can you explain or expand on the four fundamental objectives by developing lower-level objectives?

2. Neonatology is the study and treatment of newborn infants. Of particular concern is the treatment of low-birth-weight infants who are born prematurely. Often these babies are the victims of poor prenatal care and may be burdened with severe deformities. Millions of dollars are spent annually to save the lives of such infants. Discuss the ways in which the four principles conflict in this situation. Could you give any guidelines to a panel of doctors and hospital administrators grappling with such problems?

3. Terminally ill patients face the prospect of death within a relatively short period of time. In the case of cancer victims, their last months can be extremely painful. Increasing numbers of such patients consider taking their own lives, and much controversy has developed concerning euthanasia, or mercy killing. Imagine that a patient is terminally ill and mentions that he or she is considering suicide. If everything reasonable has been done to arrest the disease without success, this may be a reasonable option. Furthermore, the principle of autonomy should be respected here, provided that the patient is mentally stable and sound and understands fully the implications. But how deeply should the physician or loved one be involved? There are varying degrees of involvement. First, the physician might simply provide counseling and emotional support. The next step would be encouraging the patient by removing obstacles. Third, the physician might provide information about how to end one's life effectively and without trauma. The next step would be to assist in the procurement of the means to commit suicide. Helping the patient to end his or her life represents still another step, and actually killing the patient—by lethal injection or removal of a life support system, for example—would represent full involvement.

   Suppose that one of your loved ones were terminally ill and considering suicide. What issues would you want him or her to consider carefully? Draw an objectives hierarchy for the patient's decision.

   Now suppose that the patient has asked you to assist in his or her suicide. What issues would you want to consider when deciding on your level of involvement? Sketch an objectives hierarchy for your own decision. Compare this hierarchy with the patient's.

Source: E. Young (1989) *Alpha and Omega: Ethics at the Frontiers of Life and Death*, Palo Alto, CA: Stanford Alumni Association.

A MATTER OF ETHICS

Paul Lambert was in a difficult situation. When he started his current job 5 years ago, he understood clearly that he would be working on sensitive defense contracts for the government. In fact, his firm was a subcontractor for some major defense contractors. What he did not realize at the time—indeed, he only discovered this gradually over the past 2 years—was that the firm was overcharging. And it was not just a matter of a few dollars. In some cases, the government was overcharged by as much as a factor of 10.

Three weeks ago, he inadvertently came across an internal accounting memo that documented one particularly flagrant violation. He quietly made a copy and locked it in his desk. At the time, he was amazed, then righteously indignant. He resolved to take the evidence immediately to the appropriate authorities. But the more he thought about it, the more confused he became. Finally, he called his brother-in-law, Jim Grillich. Jim worked for another defense-related firm and agreed to have lunch with Paul. After exchanging stories about their families and comments on recent sporting events, Paul laid his cards on the table.

"Looks as though you could really make some waves," Jim commented, after listening to Paul's story.

"I guess I could. But I just don't know. If I blow the whistle, I'd feel like I'd have to resign. And then it would be tough to find another job. Nancy and I don't have a lot of savings, you know." The thought of dipping into their savings made Paul shake his head. "I just don't know."

The two men were silent for a long time. Then Paul continued, "To make matters worse, I really believe that the work that the company is doing, especially in the research labs, is important. It may have a substantial impact on our society over the next 20 years. The CEO is behind the research 100 percent, and I gather from the few comments I've overheard that he's essentially funding the research by overcharging on the subcontracts. So if I call foul, the research program goes down the drain."

"I know what you mean." Jim went on to recount a similar dilemma that he faced a few years before.

"So what did you do?"

"The papers are still in my desk. I always wanted to talk to someone about it. I even thought about calling you up, but I never did. After a while, it seemed like it was pretty easy just to leave the papers in there, locked up, safe and sound."

Questions

1. What trade-offs is Paul trying to make? What appear to be his fundamental objectives?
2. Suppose that Paul's take-home pay is currently $5,000 per month. In talking to an employment company, he is told that it will probably take two months to find a similar job if he leaves his current one, and he had better expect 3 months if he wants a better job. In looking at his savings account of $25,000, he decides that he cannot justify leaving his job, even though this means keeping quiet about the overcharging incident. Can you say anything about an implicit trade-off rate between the fundamental objectives that you identified previously?
3. Have you ever been in a situation in which it was difficult for you to decide whether to take an ethically appropriate action? Describe the situation. What made the decision difficult? What trade-offs did you have to make? What did you finally do?

FDA AND THE TESTING OF EXPERIMENTAL DRUGS

The Food and Drug Administration (FDA) of the federal government is one of the largest consumer-protection agencies in the world. One of the FDA's charges is to ensure that drugs sold to consumers do not pose health threats. As a result, the testing procedure that leads to a new drug's approval is rigorous and demanding. So much so, in fact, that some policy makers are calling for less stringent standards.

Here are some of the dilemmas that FDA faces:

- If an experimental drug shows promise in the treatment of a dangerous disease such as AIDS, should the testing procedure be abbreviated in order to get the drug to market more quickly?
- The FDA already is a large and costly bureaucracy. By easing testing standards, substantial dollars could be saved. But would it be more likely that a dangerous drug would be approved? What are the costs of such a mistake?

A fundamental trade-off is involved here. What are we gaining in the way of assurance of safe drugs, and what are we giving up by keeping the drugs away from the general public for an additional year or two?

Questions

1. What are the consequences (both good and bad) of keeping a drug from consumers for some required period of rigorous testing?
2. What are the consequences (both good and bad) of allowing drugs to reach consumers with less stringent testing?
3. Imagine that you are the FDA's commissioner. A pharmaceutical company requests special permission to rush a new AIDS drug to market. On the basis of a first round of tests, the company estimates that the new drug will save the lives of 200 AIDS victims in the first year. Your favorite pharmacologist expresses reservations, however, claiming that without running the complete series of tests, he fears that the drug may have as-yet-undetermined but serious side effects. What decision would you make? Why?
4. Suppose that the drug in Question 3 was for arthritis. It could be used by any individual who suffers from arthritis and, according to the preliminary tests, would be able to cure up to 80% of rheumatoid arthritis cases. But your pharmacologist expresses the same reservations as for the AIDS drug. Now what decision would you make? Why?

REFERENCES

The additive utility function has been described by many authors. The most comprehensive discussion, and the only one that covers swing weights, is that by von Winterfeldt and Edwards (1986). Keeney and Raiffa (1976) and Keeney (1980) also devote a lot of material to this preference model. Edwards and Barron (1994) discuss some heuristic approaches to assessing weights, including the use of only rank-order information about the objectives.

The basic idea of creating an additive utility function is fairly common and has been applied in a variety of settings. Moreover, this basic approach also has earned several different names. For example, a cost-benefit analysis typically prices out nonmonetary costs and benefits and then aggregates them. For an interesting critique of a cost-benefit analysis, see Bunn (1984, Chapter 5).

Other decision-aiding techniques also use the additive utility function implicitly or explicitly, including the Analytic Hierarchy Process (Saaty 1980) and goal programming with nonpreemptive weights (see Winston 1987). Conjoint analysis, a statistical technique used in market research to determine preference patterns of consumers on the basis of survey data, often is used to create additive utility functions. In all of these, some kind of subjective judgment forms the basis for the weights, and yet the interpretation of the weights is not always clear. For all of these alternative models, extreme care must be exercised in making the judgments on which the additive utility function is based. There is no substitute for thinking hard about trade-off issues. This text's view is that the decision-analysis approach discussed in this chapter provides the best systematic framework for making those judgments.

Finally, although there has been considerable research on biases in assessing multiattribute preference functions, our coverage has been necessarily brief. We encourage interested readers to follow up with references on behavioral decision theory given under *Further Reading* in Chapter 18.

Bunn, D. (1984) *Applied Decision Analysis*. New York: McGraw-Hill.

Edwards, W., and F. H. Barron (1994) "SMARTS and SMARTER: Improved Simple Methods for Multiattribute Utility Measurement." Organizational Behavior and Human Decision Processes, 60, 306–325.

Fischer, G. (1995). "Range sensitivity of attribute weights in multiattribute value models," *Organizational Behavior and Human Decision Processes*, 62, No. 3, 252–266.

Jacobi, S. K., and B.F. Hobbs (2007). Quantifying and mitigating the splitting bias and other value tree-induced weighting biases. *Decision Analysis*, 4, 194–210.

Keeney, R. (1980) *Siting Energy Facilities*. New York: Academic Press.

Keeney, R., and H. Raiffa (1976) *Decisions with Multiple Objectives*. New York: Wiley.

Saaty, T. (1980) *The Analytic Hierarchy Process*. New York: McGraw-Hill.

von Winterfeldt, D., and W. Edwards (1986) *Decision Analysis and Behavioral Research*. Cambridge: Cambridge University Press.

Winston, W. (1987) *Operations Research: Applications and Algorithms*. Boston: PWSKENT.

Weber, M., Eisenführ, and F. & D. von Winterfeldt (1988), "The effects of splitting attributes on weights in multiattribute utility measurement," *Management Science*, 34, No. 4, 431–445.

EPILOGUE

What happened with the Eugene Public Library? After much public discussion, an alternative emerged that had not been anticipated. An out-of-state developer expressed a desire to build a multistory office building in downtown Eugene (at Site 2, in fact) and proposed that the library could occupy the lower two floors of the building. By entering into a partnership with the developer, the city could save a lot in construction costs. Many citizens voiced concerns about the prospect of the city's alliance with a private developer, others were concerned about the complicated financing arrangement, and still others disapproved of the proposed location for a variety of reasons. However, the supporters pointed out that this might be the only way that Eugene would ever get a new library.

In March 1989, the proposal to accept the developer's offer was submitted to the voters. The result? They turned down the offer.

Eugene had still more chances to get a new library. In 1991, a study commissioned by the city concluded that a building vacated by Sears in downtown Eugene—only a few blocks from the current library—would be a suitable site for the new facility. In a March election of that year, nearly three-quarters of those who voted agreed with this assessment. Subsequent votes in May and November of 1994 to authorize issuance of bonds to pay for refurbishing the building and moving the library, however, were both narrowly defeated. Then in 1998, the Eugene City Council decided to dedicate downtown urban renewal funding to construct a new library, and in November the same year, voters approved additional funding. The new library was finally opened in 2002.

CHAPTER 17

Conflicting Objectives II: Multiattribute Utility Models with Interactions

The additive utility function described in Chapter 16 is an easy-to-use technique. It is lacking in certain instances, however, because it ignores certain fundamental characteristics of choices among multiattribute alternatives. We discussed one problem with proportional scores—they assume risk neutrality. Problem 16.22 demonstrated this in the important context of the common NPV choice criterion. More subtle are situations in which attributes interact. For example, two attributes may be substitutes for one another to some extent. Imagine a CEO who oversees several divisions. The simultaneous success of every division may not be terribly important; as long as some divisions perform well, cash flows, and profits will be adequate. In contrast, attributes can be complementary. An example might be the success of various phases of a research-and-development project. The success of each individual project is valuable in its own right. But the success of all phases might make possible an altogether new technology or process, thus leading to substantial synergistic gains. In this case, high achievement on all attributes (success in the various R&D phases) is worth more than the sum of the value obtained from the individual successes.

Such interactions cannot be captured by the additive utility function. That model is essentially an additive combination of preferences for individual attributes. To capture the kinds of interactions that we are talking about here, as well as risk attitudes,

FIGURE **17.1**
A utility surface
for two attributes
where the height of
the surface is the
utility U(x, y).

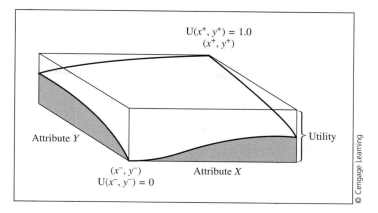

$U(x^+, y^+) = 1.0$
(x^+, y^+)

Attribute Y

Utility

(x^-, y^-)
$U(x^-, y^-) = 0$

Attribute X

© Cengage Learning

we must think more generally. Let us think in terms of a utility surface, such as the one depicted in Figure 17.1 for two attributes. Although it is possible to think about many attributes at once, we will develop multiattribute utility theory concepts using only two attributes. The ideas are readily extended to more attributes, and at the end of the chapter we will say a bit about multiattribute utility functions for three or more attributes.

Much of this chapter is fairly abstract and technical. The mathematics are necessary to do a good job with the material. After theoretical development, which is sprinkled with illustrative examples, we will work through a complete example that involves the assessment of a two-attribute utility function for managing a blood bank. We also discuss briefly how to deal with three or more attributes and demonstrate such a model in a large-scale electric-utility example.

MULTIATTRIBUTE UTILITY FUNCTIONS: DIRECT ASSESSMENT

To assess a utility function like the one in Figure 17.1, we can use the same basic approach that we already have used. For example, consider the reference-gamble method. The appropriate reference gamble has the worst pair (x^-, y^-) and the best pair (x^+, y^+) as the two possible outcomes:

Win (x^+, y^+) with probability p

Win (x^-, y^-) with probability $1 - p$

Now for any pair (x, y), where $x^- \leq x \leq x^+$ and $y^- \leq y \leq y^+$ find the probability p to use in the reference gamble that will make you indifferent between (x, y) and the reference gamble. As before, you can use p as your

FIGURE **17.2**
Directly assessing a
multiattribute utility.

The probability that
makes you indifferent
between the lottery and
the sure thing is your
utility value for (x, y).

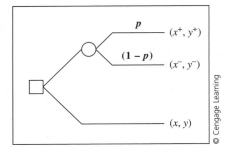

utility U(x, y) because U(x⁻, y⁻) = 0, and U(x⁺, y⁺) = 1. Figure 17.2 shows
the decision tree that represents the assessment situation. This is simply
the standard probability-equivalent utility assessment technique that we have
seen before.

You can see that we will wind up with many utility numbers after
making this assessment for a reasonable number of (x, y) pairs. There may
be several pairs with the same utility, and you should be indifferent among
such pairs. Thus, (x, y) pairs with the same utilities must fall on an indifference curve. One approach to understanding your multiattribute preferences is
simply to plot the assessed points on a graph, as in Figure 17.3, and sketch
rough indifference curves.

To find a good representation of preferences through direct assessment,
however, there is a drawback: You must assess utilities for a substantial
number of points. And even though it is straightforward to see how this
approach might be extended to three or more attributes, we run into the
problem that the more attributes being considered, the more points you must
assess, and the more complicated graphical representations become. It would
be convenient to use an easier method.

FIGURE **17.3**
Sketching
indifference
curves.

The point values are
the assessed utility
values for the
corresponding
(x, y) pair.

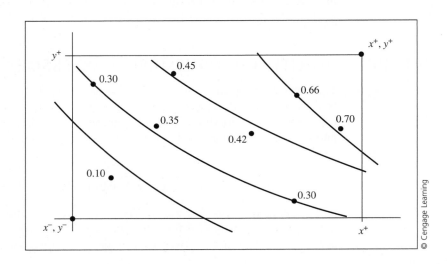

Another approach that would ease the assessment burden would be to think about a multiattribute utility function that is made up of the individual utility functions. Mathematically, we might represent the most general case as

$$U(x, y) = f[U_X(x), U_Y(y)]$$

The $f[\cdot, \cdot]$ notation means that $U(x,y)$ is a function of the individual utility functions $U_X(x)$ and $U_Y(y)$. In Chapter 16, the form we used was

$$U(x, y) = k_X U_X(x) + k_Y U_Y(y)$$

In this chapter we will consider

$$U(x, y) = c_1 + c_2 U_X(x) + c_2 U_Y(y) + c_4 U_X(x) U_Y(y)$$

The importance of any such formulation is that it greatly eases the assessment burden; as in Chapter 16, we require only the individual utility functions and enough information to put them together. Being able to break down the multiattribute utility function this way sometimes is called *separability*; the overall utility function can be "separated" into chunks that represent different attributes.

Is such an arrangement possible? Yes, but it requires some interesting conditions for the combined utility function. These conditions concern how the preferences interact among the attributes, a point suggested in the beginning of this chapter. We will digress briefly to discuss these conditions.

INDEPENDENCE CONDITIONS

Preferential Independence

One thing we need in order to have the kind of separability previously mentioned is *mutual preferential independence*. An attribute Y is said to be preferentially independent of X if preferences for specific outcomes of Y do not depend on the level of attribute X. As an example, let Y be the time to completion of a project and X its cost. If we prefer a project time of 5 days to one of 10 days, assuming that the cost is $10,000 in each case, and if we also prefer a project time of 5 days to one of 10 days assuming that the cost is $20,000 in each case, then Y is preferentially independent of X; it does not matter what the cost is—we still prefer the shorter completion time.

We need mutual preferential independence, so we also need the cost to be preferentially independent of the completion time. If we prefer lower cost no matter what the completion time, then X is preferentially independent of Y. Then we can say that the two attributes are mutually preferentially independent.

Preferential independence seems to be a pretty reasonable condition to assume, especially in cases like the one involving costs and time to completion. But it is easy to imagine situations in which preferential independence might not hold. For example, in Chapter 16 it was suggested that your preference for the amount of homework effort might depend on course topic. Bunn (1984) relates a nice hypothetical example in which preferential independence might not hold. Consider a decision with outcomes that affect both the place where you live and the automobile that you drive. Let X be an outcome variable that could denote either Los Angeles or an African farm, and Y an outcome variable denoting either a Cadillac or a Land Rover. The value of X (whether you live in Los Angeles or on an African farm) may well affect your preference for a Cadillac or a Land Rover. Therefore, Y would not be preferentially independent of X. Consider the reverse: You may prefer Los Angeles to an African farm (or vice versa) regardless of the car you own. Thus, one attribute would be preferentially independent of the other, but the two are not mutually preferentially independent.

It probably is fair to say that mutual preferential independence holds for many people and many situations, or that at least it is a reasonable approximation. Mutual preferential independence is like the decomposability property for an objectives hierarchy. If a decision maker has done a good job of building a decomposable hierarchy, mutual preferential independence probably is a reasonable assumption. But it should never be taken for granted.

If you recall the discussion about value functions and utility functions from Chapter 16, you will realize that mutual preferential independence, being about sure outcomes, is a condition that applies to value functions. In fact, mutual preferential independence is exactly the condition that is needed for the additive (ordinal) utility function to be appropriate when making a decision with no uncertainty. That is, when a decision maker's preferences display mutual preferential independence, then the additive utility function, assessed using any of the techniques described in Chapter 16, is appropriate for decisions under certainty. Once we move to decision under uncertainty, however, mutual preferential independence is not quite strong enough. Although it is a necessary condition for obtaining separability of a (cardinal) multiattribute utility function, it is not sufficient. Thus, we must look at stronger conditions.

Utility Independence

Utility independence is slightly stronger than preferential independence. An attribute Y is considered utility independent of attribute X if preferences for *uncertain choices* involving different levels of Y are independent of the value of X. Imagine assessing a certainty equivalent for a lottery involving only outcomes in Y. If the certainty equivalent for the Y lottery is the same no matter what the level of X, then Y is utility independent of X. If X also is utility independent of Y, then the two attributes are mutually utility independent.

Utility independence clearly is analogous to preferential independence, except that the assessments are made under conditions of uncertainty. For the preceding project evaluation example, suppose we assess that the certainty equivalent for an option giving, say, a 50% chance of $Y = 5$ days and a 50% chance of $Y = 10$ days does not depend on the level at which the cost X is fixed. As long as preferences for lotteries in the completion-time attribute are the same (as, say, measured by their certainty equivalents) regardless of the fixed level of cost, then completion time is utility independent of cost.

Keeney and Raiffa (1976) discuss an example in which utility independence might not hold. Suppose that X and Y are the rates of serious crime in two precincts of a metropolitan police division. In determining the joint utility function for this region's police chief, the issue of utility independence for X and Y would be faced. With Y fixed at 5, a relatively low rate of crime, he may be quite risk-averse to rates of crime in region X. He may not want to appear as though he is neglecting a particular precinct. Thus, his certainty equivalent for an option giving a 50% chance of $X = 0$ and a 50% chance of $X = 30$ may be 22 when Y is fixed at 5. If Y were fixed at the higher rate of 15, however, his certainty equivalent may be less risk-aversely assessed at 17. Thus, one must not assume that utility independence will hold in all cases. Even so, almost all reported multiattribute applications assume utility independence and thus are able to use a decomposable utility function.

DETERMINING WHETHER INDEPENDENCE EXISTS

How can you determine whether your preferences are preferentially independent? The simplest approach is to imagine a series of paired comparisons that involve one of the attributes. With the other attribute fixed at its lowest level, decide which outcome in each pair is preferred. Once this is done, imagine changing the level of the fixed attribute. Would your comparisons be the same? Would the comparisons be the same regardless of the fixed level of the other attribute? If so, then preferential independence holds.

Determining whether independence holds is a rather delicate matter. The following sample dialogue is taken from Keeney and Raiffa (1976). The notation has been changed to correspond to our notation here.

ANALYST: I would now like to investigate how you feel about various Y values when we hold fixed a particular value of X. For example, on the first page of this questionnaire [this is shown to the assessor] there is a list of 25 paired comparisons between Y evaluations; each element of the pair describes levels on the Y attributes alone. On this first page it is assumed that, throughout, the X evaluations are all the same, that is, x_1 [the fixed value for X is shown to the assessor]. Is this clear?

ASSESSOR: Crystal clear, but you are asking me for a lot of work.

ANALYST: Well, I have a devious purpose in mind, and it will not take as much time as you think to find out what I want. Now on the second page of the questionnaire [this is shown to the assessor] the identical set of 25 paired comparisons are repeated, but now the fixed, common level on the X attribute is changed from x_1 to x_2 [value is shown to the assessor]. Are you with me?

ASSESSOR: All the way.

ANALYST: On page 3, we have the same 25 paired comparisons but now the common value of the X value is x_3 [shown to the assessor].

ASSESSOR: You said this would not take long.

ANALYST: Well now, here comes the punch line. Suppose that you painstakingly respond to all of the paired comparisons on page 1 where x_1 is fixed. Now when you go to the next page would your responses change to these same 25 paired comparisons?

ASSESSOR: Let's see. In the second page all paired comparisons are the same except x_1 is replaced with x_2. What difference should that make?

ANALYST: Well, you tell me. If we consider this first comparison [pointed to on the questionnaire] does it make any difference if the X values are fixed at x_1 or x_2? There could be some interaction concerning how you view the paired comparison depending on the common value of X.

ASSESSOR: I suppose that might be the case in some other situation, but in the first comparison I prefer the left alternative to the right no matter what the X value is … as long as they are the same.

ANALYST: Okay. Would you now feel the same if you consider the second paired comparison?

ASSESSOR: Yes. And the third and so on. Am I being naive? Is there some trick here?

ANALYST: No, not at all. I am just checking to see if the X values have any influence on your responses to the paired comparisons. So I gather that you are telling me that your responses on page 1 carry over to page 2.

ASSESSOR: That's right.

ANALYST: And to page 3, where the X value is held fixed at x_3 [shown to assessor]?

ASSESSOR: Yes.

ANALYST: Well, on the basis of this information I now pronounce that for you attribute Y is preferentially independent of attribute X.

ASSESSOR: That's nice to know.

ANALYST: That's all I wanted to find out.

ASSESSOR: Aren't you going to ask me to fill out page 1?

ANALYST: No. That's too much work. There are less painful ways of getting that information.

Source: Keeney, R., and H. Raiffa (1976) *Decisions with Multiple Objectives: Preferences and Value Tradeoffs.* Reprinted with the permission of Cambridge University Press.

The dialogue describes how to check for preferential independence. Checking for utility independence would be much the same, except that the paired comparisons would be comparisons between lotteries involving attribute Y rather than sure outcomes. As long as the comparisons remain the same regardless of the fixed value for X, then Y can be considered utility independent of X. Of course, to establish mutual preferential or utility independence, the roles of X and Y would have to be reversed to determine whether paired comparisons of outcomes or lotteries in X depended on fixed values for Y. If each attribute turns out to be independent of the other, then mutual utility or preferential (whichever is appropriate) independence holds.

Using Independence

If a decision maker's preferences show mutual utility independence, then a two-attribute utility function can be written as a composition of the individual utility functions. As usual, the least preferred outcome (x^-, y^-) is assigned the utility value 0, and the most preferred pair (x^+, y^+) is assigned the utility value 1.

Under mutual utility independent preferences, the two-attribute utility function can be written as

---

$$U(x, y) = k_X U_X(x) + k_Y U_Y(y) + (1 - k_X - k_Y)U_X(x)U_Y(y),$$

where

$U_X(x)$ is a utility function on X scaled so that $U_X(x^-) = 0$ and $U_X(x^+) = 1$

$U_Y(y)$ is a utility function on Y scaled so that $U_Y(y^-) = 0$ and $U_Y(y^+) = 1$

Two important consequences for this utility function are:

$$k_X = U(x^+, y^-)$$
$$k_Y = U(x^-, y^+)$$

The product term $U_X(x)U_Y(y)$ in this utility function is what permits the modeling of interactions among attributes. The utility functions U_X and U_Y are *conditional utility functions,* and each must be assessed with the other attribute fixed at a particular level. For example, in assessing U_Y, imagine that X is fixed at a specific level.

To understand the two stated consequences regarding all we must do is plug the individual utilities into the equation. For example,

$$U(x^+, y^-) = k_X U_X(x^+) + k_Y U_Y(y^-) + (1 - k_X - k_Y)U_X(x^+)U_Y(y^-)$$
$$= k_X(1) + k_Y(0) + (1 - k_X - k_Y)(1)(0)$$
$$= k_X$$

This multiattribute utility function, called a *multilinear* expression, is not as bad as it looks! Look at it from the point of view of the X attribute. Think about fixing Y at a value (say, y_a); you get a conditional utility function for X, given that Y is fixed at y_a:

$$U(x, y_a) = k_X U_X(x) + k_Y U_Y(y_a) + (1 - k_X - k_Y)U_X(x)U_Y(y_a)$$
$$= k_Y U_Y(y_a) + [k_X + (1 - k_X - k_Y)U_Y(y_a)]U_X(x)$$

Because Y is fixed at y_a, the terms $k_Y U_Y(y_a)$ and $[k_X + (1 - k_X - k_Y)U_Y(y_a)]$ are just constants. Thus, $U(x, y_a)$ is simply a scaled version of $U_X(x)$. Now change to another y value, specifically y_b. What happens to the utility function for X? The expression now looks like

$$U(x, y_b) = k_Y U_Y(y_b) + [k_X + (1 - k_X - k_Y)U_Y(y_b)]U_X(x)$$

This is just another linear transformation of $U_X(x)$, and so $U(x, y_b)$ and $U(x, y_a)$ must be identical in terms of the way that lotteries involving the

X attribute would be ranked. We have scaled the utility function $U_X(x)$ in two different ways, but the scaling does not change the rank ordering of preferences. Now, notice that we can do exactly the same thing with the Y attribute; for different fixed values of X (x_a and x_b), the conditional utility functions are simply linear transformations of each other:

$$U(x_a, y) = k_X U_X(x_a) + [k_Y + (1 - k_X - k_Y)U_X(x_a)]U_Y(y)$$

$$U(x_b, y) = k_X U_X(x_b) + [k_Y + (1 - k_X - k_Y)U_X(x_b)]U_Y(y)$$

No matter what the level of one attribute, preferences over lotteries in the second attribute (Y) stay the same. This was the definition of utility independence in the last section. We have mutual utility independence because the conditional utility function for one attribute stays essentially the same no matter which attribute is held fixed.

ADDITIVE INDEPENDENCE

Look again at the multiattribute utility function

$$U(x, y) = k_X U_X(x) + k_Y U_Y(y) + (1 - k_X - k_Y)U_X(x)U_Y(y)$$

If $k_X + k_Y = 1$, then the utility function turns out to be simply additive:

$$U(x, y) = k_X U_X(x) + (1 - k_X)U_Y(y)$$

If this is the case, we have to assess only the two individual utility functions $U_X(x)$ and $U_Y(y)$ and the weighting constant k_X. This would be convenient: It would save having to assess k_Y. Of course, this is just the additive utility function from Chapter 16. How is this kind of multiattribute utility function related to the independence conditions? To be able to model preferences accurately with this additive utility function, we need *additive independence,* an even stronger condition than utility independence.

The statement of additive independence is the following: Suppose X and Y are mutually utility independent, and you are indifferent between Lotteries A and B:

A	(x^-, y^-)	with probability 0.5
	(x^+, y^+)	with probability 0.5
B	(x^-, y^+)	with probability 0.5
	(x^+, y^-)	with probability 0.5

If this is the case, then the utility function can be written as the weighted combination of the two utility functions, $U(x, y) = k_X U_X(x) + (1 - k_X)U_Y(y)$. You can see by writing out the expected utilities of the lotteries that they are equivalent:

$$EU(A) = 0.5[k_X U_X(x^-) + (1 - k_X)U_Y(y^-)] + 0.5[k_X U_X(x^+) + (1 - k_X)U_Y(y^+)]$$

$$= 0.5[k_X U_X(x^-) + (1 - k_X)U_Y(y^-) + k_X U_X(x^+) + (1 - k_X)U_Y(y^+)]$$

$$EU(B) = 0.5[k_XU_X(x^-) + (1-k_X)U_Y(y^+)] + 0.5[k_XU_X(x^+) + (1-k_X)U_Y(y^-)]$$
$$= 0.5[k_XU_X(x^-) + (1-k_X)U_Y(y^+) + k_XU_X(x^+) + (1-k_X)U_Y(y^-)]$$
$$= EU(A)$$

The intuition behind additive independence is that, in assessing uncertain outcomes over both attributes, we have to look at only one attribute at a time, and it does not matter what the other attribute's values are in the uncertain outcomes. This sounds a lot like utility independence. The difference is that, in the case of additive independence, changes in *lotteries* in one attribute do not affect preferences for lotteries in the other attribute; for utility independence, on the other hand, changes in *sure levels* of one attribute do not affect preferences for lotteries in the other attribute. Here is another way to say it: When we are considering a choice among risky prospects involving multiple attributes, if additive independence holds, then we can compare the alternatives one attribute at a time. In comparing Lotteries A and B above, we are indifferent because (1) for attribute X, each lottery gives us a 50% chance at x^- and a 50% chance at x^+; and (2) for Y, each lottery gives us a 50% chance at y^- and a 50% chance at y^+. Looking at the attributes one at a time, the two lotteries are the same.

The additive utility function from Chapter 16 requires additive independence of preferences across attributes in order to be an accurate model of a decision maker's preferences in decisions under uncertainty. Think back to some of the examples or problems. Do you think this idea of additive independence makes sense in purchasing a car? Think about reliability and quality of service, two attributes that might be important in this decision. When you purchase a new car, you do not know whether the reliability will be high or low, and you may not know the quality of the service. To some extent, however, the two attributes are substitutes for each other. Suppose you faced the hypothetical decision shown in Figure 17.4. Would you prefer Lottery A or B? Most of us probably would take A. If you have a clear preference for one or the other, then additive independence cannot hold.

Von Winterfeldt and Edwards (1986) discuss reports from behavioral decision theory that indicate additive independence usually does not hold. If this is the case, what is the justification for the use of the additive utility

FIGURE 17.4

An assessment lottery for a car purchase.

If you have a clear preference for A or B, then additive independence cannot hold.

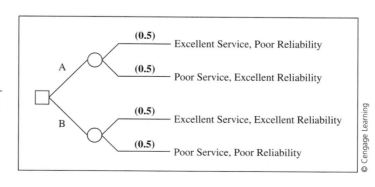

© Cengage Learning

function? Many multiattribute decisions that we make involve little or no uncertainty, and evidence has shown that the additive model is reasonable for most situations under conditions of certainty. And in extremely complicated situations with many attributes, the additive model may be a useful rough-cut approximation. It may turn out that considering the interactions among attributes is not critical to the decision at hand.

Finally, it is possible to use simple approximation techniques to include interactions within the additive utility framework. For example, suppose that we have a decision problem with many attributes that are, for the most part, additively independent of one another. The additive representation of the utility function does not allow for any interaction among the attributes. If this is appropriate for almost all of the possible outcomes, then we may use the additive representation while including a specific "bonus" or "penalty" (depending on which is appropriate) for those outcomes with noticeable interaction effects.

Raiffa (1982) has an interesting example. Suppose a city is negotiating a new contract with its police force. Two attributes are (1) increase in vacation for officers who have less than 5 years of service and (2) increase in vacation for officers who have more than 5 years of service. The city loses points in an additive value function for increases in vacation for either group. If either group is held to no increase, then the city loses no points for that particular group. But the city would be happy if all its officers could be held to no increase in vacation time; thus, no precedent is set for the other group. To capture this interaction, the city gets a "bonus" of some points in its overall utility if there is no increase in vacation for either group.

SUBSTITUTES AND COMPLEMENTS

In the multiattribute utility function, the interaction between the attributes is captured by the term $(1 - k_X - k_Y)U_X(x)U_Y(y)$. How can we interpret this? Keeney and Raiffa (1976) give an interesting interpretation of the coefficient $(1 - k_X - k_Y)$. The sign of $(1 - k_X - k_Y)$ can be interpreted in terms of whether x and y are complements or substitutes for each other. Suppose $(1 - k_X - k_Y)$ is positive. Now examine the multiattribute utility function:

$$U(x, y) = k_X U_X(x) + k_Y U_Y(y) + (1 - k_X - k_Y)U_X(x)U_Y(y)$$

Preferred values of X and Y will give high values to the conditional utility functions, and the positive coefficient $(1 - k_X - k_Y)$ will drive up the overall utility for the pair even higher. Thus, if $(1 - k_X - k_Y)$ is positive, the two attributes complement each other. On the other hand, if $(1 - k_X - k_Y)$ is negative, high values on each scale will result in a high product term, which must be subtracted in the multiattribute preference value. In this sense, preferred values of each attribute work against each other. But if one attribute is high and the other low, the subtraction effect is not as strong. Thus, if $(1 - k_X - k_Y)$ is negative, the two attributes are substitutes.

Keeney and Raiffa (1976) offer two examples. In one, imagine a corporation with two divisions that operate in different markets altogether, and let profits in each division represent two attributes of concern to the president. To a great extent, success by the two divisions could be viewed as substitutes. That is, if profit from one division was down while the other was up, the firm would get along fine. Financial success by one division would most likely ensure the overall success of the firm.

For an example of the complementary case, Keeney and Raiffa consider the problem a general would face in a battle being fought on two fronts. If we let the consequences on the two fronts represent two distinct attributes, then these two attributes may be complementary. That is, defeat on one front may be almost as bad as defeat on both fronts, and a completely successful outcome may be guaranteed only by victory on both.

ASSESSING A TWO-ATTRIBUTE UTILITY FUNCTION

Now that we have seen the basics of two-attribute utility functions, we are ready to assess one. The procedure is relatively straightforward. First, we determine whether mutual utility independence holds. Provided that it does, we then assess the individual utility functions. Finally, the scaling constants are determined in order to put the individual utility functions together.

The Blood Bank

In a hospital blood bank it is important to have a policy for deciding how much of each type of blood should be kept on hand. For any particular year, there is a "shortage rate," the percentage of units of blood demanded but not filled from stock because of shortages. Whenever there is a shortage, a special order must be placed to locate the required blood elsewhere or to locate donors. An operation may be postponed, but only rarely will a blood shortage result in a death. Naturally, keeping a lot of blood stocked means that a shortage is less likely. But there is also a rate at which blood is "outdated," or kept on the shelf the maximum amount of time, after which it must be discarded. Although having a lot of blood on hand means a low shortage rate, it probably also would mean a high outdating rate. Of course, the eventual outcome is unknown because it is impossible to predict exactly how much blood will be demanded. Should the hospital try to keep as much blood on hand as possible so as to avoid shortages? Or should the hospital try to keep a fairly low inventory in order to minimize the amount of outdated blood discarded? How should the hospital blood bank balance these two objectives?

Source: Keeney and Raiffa (1976).

The outcome at the blood bank depends on uncertain demand over the year as well as the specific inventory policy (stock level) chosen.

Thus, we can think of each possible inventory policy as a lottery over uncertain outcomes having two attributes, shortage and outdating. Shortage is measured as the annual percentage of units demanded but not in stock, while outdating is the percentage of units that are discarded due to aging. A high stock level probably will lead to less shortage but more outdating, and a low stock level will lead to more shortage and less outdating. To choose an appropriate stock level, we need to assess both the probability distribution over shortage and outdating outcomes for each possible stock level and the decision maker's utility function over these outcomes. Because each outcome has two attributes, we need a two-attribute utility function. Here we focus on the assessment of the utility function through the following steps:

1. The first step was to explain the problem to the nurse in charge of ordering blood. Maintaining an appropriate stock level was her responsibility, so it made sense to base an analysis of the problem on her personal preferences. She understood the importance of the problem and was motivated to think hard about her assessments. Without such understanding and motivation on her part, the entire project probably would have failed.

2. It was established that the annual outdating and shortage rates might range from 10% (worst case) to 0% (best case).

3. Did mutual utility independence hold? The nurse assessed a certainty equivalent for uncertain shortage rates (Attribute X), given a fixed outdating rate (Attribute Y). The certainty equivalent did not change for different outdating rates. Thus, shortage was found to be utility independent of outdating. Similar procedures showed the reverse to be true as well. Thus, shortage and outdating were mutually utility independent, implying the multilinear form for the utility function.

4. The next step was to assess the conditional utility functions $U_X(x)$ and $U_Y(y)$. In each case, the utility function was assessed conditional on the other attribute being held constant at 0. To assess $U_X(x)$, it was first established that preferences decreased as x increased. Using the lotteries that had been assessed earlier in the utility independence step, an exponential utility function was determined. Setting $U_X(0) = 1$ (best case) and $U_X(10) = 0$ (worst case), the utility function was

$$U_X(x) = 1 + 0.375(1 - e^{x/7.692})$$

Likewise, the second utility function was determined using the previously assessed certainty equivalents, and again an exponential form was used. The utility function was

$$U_Y(y) = 1 + 2.033(1 - e^{y/25})$$

This utility function also has $U_Y(0) = 1$ and $U_Y(10) = 0$.

5. Assessing the weights k_X and k_Y is the key to finding the two-attribute utility function. The trick is to use as much information as possible to set

up equations based on indifferent outcomes and lotteries, and then to solve the equations for the weights. Because we have two unknowns, k_X and k_Y, we will be solving two equations in two unknowns. To set up two equations, we will need two utility assessments.

Recall that the multilinear form can be written as

$$U(x, y) = k_X U_X(x) + k_Y U_Y(y) + (1 - k_X - k_Y)U_X(x)U_Y(y)$$

We also know that

$$U(10, 0) = k_X$$

$$U(0, 10) = k_X$$

These follow from steps 3 and 4 above, substituting $x^- = 10$, $x^+ = 0$, $y^- = 10$, and $y^+ = 0$.

The nurse determined that she was indifferent between the two outcomes $(x = 4.75, y = 0)$ and $(x = 0, y = 10)$. This first assessment indicates that, for her, avoiding shortages is more important than avoiding outdating. We can substitute each one of these points into the expression for the utility function, establishing the first equation relating k_X and k_Y:

$$U(4.75, 0) = k_X U_X(4.75) + k_Y U_Y(0) + (1 - k_X - k_Y)U_X(4.75)U_Y(0)$$
$$= k_X U_X(4.75) + k_Y(1) + (1 - k_X - k_Y)U_X(4.75)(1)$$

Because she was indifferent between (4.75, 0) and (0, 10), we have

$$U(4.75, 0) = U(0, 10) \qquad \text{(Because she is indifferent)}$$
$$= k_X \qquad \text{[from } U(0, 10) = k_X, \text{ above]}$$

Substituting, we obtain

$$k_X = k_X U_X(4.75) + k_Y + (1 - k_X - k_Y)U_X(4.75)$$
$$= k_Y + (1 - k_Y)U_X(4.75)$$
$$= k_Y + (1 - k_Y)[1 + 0.375(1 - e^{4.75/7.692})]$$
$$= k_Y + (1 - k_Y)(0.68)$$
$$= 0.68 + 0.32k_Y \qquad (17.1)$$

In the second assessment, the decision maker concluded that she was indifferent between the outcome (6, 6) and a 50–50 lottery between the outcomes (0, 0) and (10, 10). Using this assessment, we can find U(6, 6):

$$U(6, 6) = 0.5U(0, 0) + 0.5U(10, 10)$$
$$= 0.5(1) + 0.5(0)$$
$$= 0.5$$

This is just a standard assessment of a certainty equivalent for a 50–50 gamble between the best and worst outcomes. Now substitute U(6, 6) = 0.5

into the two attribute utility function to find a second equation in terms of k_X and k_Y:

$$0.5 = U(6, 6)$$
$$= k_X U_X(6) + k_Y U_Y(6) + (1 - k_X - k_Y) U_X(6) U_Y(6)$$

Substituting the values $X = 6$ and $Y = 6$ into the formulas for the individual utility functions gives

$$U_X(6) = 0.56$$
$$U_Y(6) = 0.45$$

Now plug these into the equation for $U(6, 6)$ to get

$$0.5 = k_X(0.56) + k_Y(0.45) + (1 - k_X - k_Y)(0.56)(0.45)$$

which simplifies to

$$0.248 = 0.308k_X + 0.198k_Y \qquad (17.2)$$

Now we have two linear equations in k_X and k_Y—Equations (17.1) and (17.2):

$$k_X = 0.680 + 0.320k_Y$$
$$0.248 = 0.308k_X + 0.198k_Y$$

Solving these two equations simultaneously for k_X and k_Y, we find that $k_X = 0.72$ and $k_Y = 0.13$. Thus, the two-attribute utility function can be written as

$$U(x, y) = 0.72U_X(x) + 0.13U_Y(y) + 0.15U_X(x)U_Y(y)$$

where $U_X(x)$ and $U_Y(y)$ are given by the exponential utility functions previously defined. Now we can find the utility for any (x, y) pair (as long as the x's and y's are each between 0 and 10, the range of the assessments). Any policy for ordering blood can be evaluated in terms of its expected utility. Table 17.1 shows utilities for different possible outcomes, and Figure 17.5 shows the indifference curves associated with the utility

TABLE **17.1**
Utility values for shortage and outdating in the blood bank.

x Values (Shortage)	y Values (Outdating)					
	0	2	4	6	8	10
0	1.00	0.95	0.90	0.85	0.79	0.72
2	0.90	0.86	0.81	0.76	0.70	0.64
4	0.78	0.74	0.69	0.64	0.59	0.54
6	0.62	0.58	0.54	0.50	0.45	0.40
8	0.40	0.37	0.34	0.31	0.27	0.23
10	0.13	0.11	0.08	0.06	0.03	0.00

FIGURE **17.5**

Indifference curves for nurse's utility function for shortage and outdating.

The numbers are U(x, y) for the corresponding indifference curve.

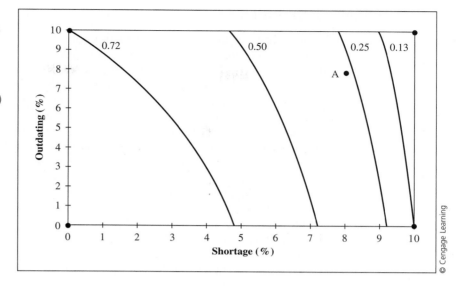

function. From Figure 17.5, we can verify the conditions and assessments that were used:

$$U(0, 0) = 1 \qquad U(10, 10) = 0$$
$$U(10, 0) = 0.13 = k_Y \qquad U(0, 10) = U(4.75, 0) = 0.72 = k_X$$
$$U(6, 6) = 0.50$$

The final assessed utility function is readily interpreted. The large value for k_X relative to k_Y means that the nurse is much more concerned about the percentage of shortage than she is about the percentage of outdating. This makes sense; most of us would agree that the objective of the blood bank is primarily to save lives, and we probably would rather throw out old blood than not have enough on hand when it is needed. The fact that $k_X + k_Y < 1$ means that the two attributes are complements rather than substitutes. We can see this in Figure 17.5. For example, imagine an outcome of (8, 8), for which the utility is 0.27 (Point A). Now imagine improving the shortage percentage to zero. This would increase the utility value to U(0, 8) = 0.79, for an approximate net increase of 0.52. On the other hand, improving the outdating percentage the same amount results in U(8, 0) = 0.40, for a net increase of 0.13. If we increased both at the same time, we would have U(0, 0) = 1.00, an increase of 0.73. The increase in utility from increasing both at once is greater than the sum of the individual increases (0.73 > 0.52 + 0.13 = 0.65). This is the sense in which there is an interaction. This kind of phenomenon is impossible in the additive utility function.

WHEN INDEPENDENCE FAILS

We have just dealt in depth with situations in which the assumption of mutual utility independence results in a reasonable model of preferences. This is not always true. Suppose we are interested in assessing a two-attribute utility function over attributes X and Y but have found that neither X nor Y is utility independent of the other. Then neither the multilinear nor additive forms for the utility function are appropriate. How can we obtain a reasonable $U(x, y)$ for decision-making purposes? Several possibilities exist. One is simply to perform a direct assessment as described at the beginning of this chapter. Pick the best and worst (x, y) pairs, assign them utility values of 1 and 0, and then use reference gambles to assess the utility values for other points.

A second approach is to transform the attributes into new attributes that are mutually independent and proceed to analyze the problem with the new set. Of course, the new set of attributes still must capture the critical aspects of the problem, and they must be measurable. Take the example previously discussed in which X and Y designate measures of the crime rates in two sections of a city. There may be a complicated preference structure for (x, y) pairs. For political reasons, the relative ordering of hypothetical lotteries for criminal activity in one section may be highly dependent on the level of crime in the other section. But suppose we define $s = (x + y)/2$ and $t = |x - y|$. Then s may be interpreted as an average crime index for the city and t as an indicator of the balance of criminal activity between the two sections. Any (x, y) outcome implies a unique (s, t) outcome, so it is easy to transform from one set of attributes to the other. Furthermore, even though x and y may not be utility independent, it may be reasonable to model s and t as being utility independent, thus simplifying the assessment procedure.

One of the most difficult and subtlest concepts in multiattribute utility theory is the notion of interaction among attributes. To use the additive utility function from Chapter 16, we must have no interaction at all. To use the multilinear utility function discussed in this chapter, we can have some interaction, but it must be of a limited form. (Any interactions must conform to the notion of utility independence.) The blood bank example demonstrated the nature of the interaction between two attributes that is possible with the multilinear utility function. In this section, we are concerned with situations in which the interactions are even more complicated than those that are possible in the multilinear case. Fortunately, evidence from behavioral research suggests that it is rarely, if ever, necessary to model extremely complex preference interactions.

Chapters 16 and 17 have presented many of the principles and decision-analysis techniques that are useful in making decisions in the face of conflicting objectives. Given the complexity of the techniques, it is important to keep in mind the modeling perspective that we have held all along. The objective of using the multiattribute decision-analysis techniques is to construct a model that is a reasonable representation of a decision maker's value structure. If minimal interactions exist among the attributes, then the additive utility function is appropriate. When attributes interact, it may be necessary to consider multiattribute utility theory, just as we have in this chapter.

MULTIATTRIBUTE UTILITY IN ACTION: BC HYDRO

Can multiattribute utility modeling be of use? Consider the situation of the British Columbia Hydro and Power Authority (BC Hydro):

Strategic Decisions at BC Hydro	In the late 1980s, BC Hydro found itself at an important juncture. Knowing that it would face many strategic decisions in the future, its directors wanted to prepare to make those decisions in the best possible way. It would have to make decisions regarding power-generation plants, placement of transmission lines, employee relations, how to communicate with public and special-interest groups, environmental impact of its activities and facilities, and policies for addressing large-scale problems such as global warming. To ensure that many different decisions would be coordinated and would all serve the organization's interests, Mr. Ken Peterson was appointed as Director of Strategic Planning. In short, Peterson's job was to make BC Hydro the leader in strategic planning among North American utility companies. To help Peterson get started, BC Hydro had a general mission statement. Like most such statements, however, BC Hydro's was broad and lacked details. It was certainly not up to the task of coordinating the myriad of diverse decisions that BC Hydro would face.

Realizing that he would need a way to think systematically about BC Hydro's strategic alternatives, Peterson enlisted Ralph Keeney and Tim McDaniels to help identify the organization's objectives and construct a multiattribute utility function. The project is described in Keeney (1992) and Keeney and McDaniels (1992). The process began with interviews of key decision makers in the organization to identify fundamental objectives. Once a satisfactory set of fundamental objectives was established, the process continued through all of the steps necessary to define and assess individual utility functions for the attributes and scaling constants for the multiattribute utility function. The final utility function involved 18 different attributes in six major groups (economics, environment, health and safety, equity, service quality, and public-service recognition). The hierarchy of objectives with corresponding attributes and ranges is shown in Table 17.2.

Keeney reports that the component utility functions were linear (i.e., proportional scores were used) for all but two of the attributes. The two that were not linear were annual government dividend and large customer outage duration. The individual utility functions for these two attributes are shown in Figure 17.6. Note that the dividend utility function shows risk aversion, but the outage utility function is risk-seeking.

The assessment proceeded by creating multiattribute utility functions for each of the groups and subgroups in Table 17.2. For example, two-attribute utility functions were created for service quality to small customers and large customers, each one covering the number of outages and outage duration for the corresponding customer type. These two utility functions were then combined with individual utility functions for new service and inquiries to create a four-attribute utility function for service. Finally, the service

TABLE **17.2**
Attributes and ranges for BC Hydro's strategic utility function.

	Worst Level	Best Level
Economics		
Levelized cost of energy from new sources (1989 $0.001/kWh)	55	35
Annualized dividend payable (1989 $ million)	0	200
Economic cost or resource losses (1989 $ million)	20	0
Environment		
Local Impacts Flora (hectares of mature forest lost)	10,000	0
Fauna (hectares of wildlife habitat lost)	10,000	0
Wilderness ecosystem (hectares of wilderness lost)	10,000	0
Recreation (hectares of recreational land lost)	10,000	0
Aesthetic (annual person-years of viewing high-voltage transmission lines in scenic terrain)	500,000	0
Global impact (megawatts generated from fossil fuels)	1,000	0
Health and Safety		
Public		
Mortality (annual person-years of life lost)	100	0
Morbidity (annual person-years of "severe" disability)	1,000	0
Employees		
Mortality (annual person-years of life lost)	100	0
Morbidity (annual person-years of lost work time)	1,000	0
Equity		
Equitable pricing (constructed scale: see Keeney 1992, section 12.3)	0.5	0
Equitable compensation (annual average number of individuals who feel they are inequitably treated)	500	0
Service Quality		
Small Customers		
Outages (annual number per customer)	2	0
Outage duration (hours per outage)	24	0
Large Customers		
Outages (annual number per customer)	2	0
Outage duration (hours per outage)	24	0
New service (installation time in workdays)	20	1
Inquiries (minutes until personal response)	1	0
Public-service recognition (constructed scale: see Keeney 1992, section 12.3)	0	4

Source: Keeney (1992, pp. 358–359).

FIGURE **17.6**
Two nonlinear
utility functions for
BC Hydro.
(a) A risk-averse
utility function for
government
dividend.
(b) A risk-prone
utility function for
duration of outages
to large customers.

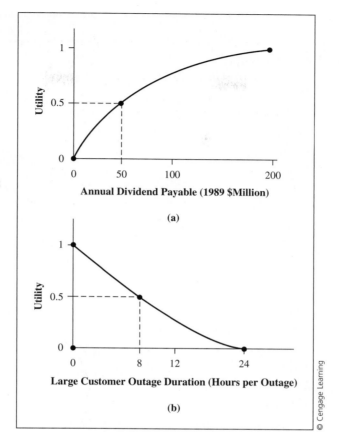

© Cengage Learning

utility function was combined with five similar utility functions for each of the other major groups.

All of the multiattribute utility functions (including the overall function for the six major groups) were additive except for the economic utility function. The reason for the nonadditive economic utility function is that the economic attributes were thought to be substitutes for each other to some extent. For the additive part of the model, it is possible to collapse the hierarchy and calculate the weight that any one attribute has in the overall utility function. This is done simply by multiplying the weight for the attribute times the weight for the group (or subgroup) in which it resides, and so on, until the top level of the objectives hierarchy is reached. (You will recall that we did this in the library example in Chapter 16.) The resulting scaling weights are shown in Table 17.3 for the additive attributes. (This table is taken from Keeney's (1992) Table 12.5. Scaling constants are given for public and worker health-and-safety aggregates rather than for the individual mortality and morbidity attributes. The same is true for small and large customer service attributes.)

Table 17.3 also shows in parentheses the scaling constants for the six major attribute groups, thus indicating the relative importance of these top-

TABLE **17.3**
Scaling constants
for BC Hydro's
strategic utility
function.

	Scaling Constant
Economics (0.395)	
Constants for multiplicative function:	
Levelized cost of energy	0.84
Annualized dividend	0.18
Resource cost	0.30
Scaling constant k	−0.76
Constants for additive function:	
Environment (0.250)	
Flora	0.023
Fauna	0.046
Wilderness ecosystem	0.093
Recreation	0.046
Aesthetic	0.023
Global impact	0.019
Health and Safety (0.089)	
Public	0.045
Worker	0.045
Equity (0.012)	
Equitable pricing	0.004
Equitable compensation	0.008
Service quality (0.250)	
Small customers	0.111
Large customers	0.125
New service	0.010
Inquiries	0.005
Public-service recognition (0.004)	0.004

level objectives. The most important of the six is the economic objective, accounting for almost 40% of the total weight. The table also shows the scaling constants for the three components in the economic utility function and the constant k that defines the interactions in this submodel. The economic utility function is given by

$$1 - 0.76U(x_1, x_2, x_3) = [1 - 0.76(0.84)U_1(x_1)]$$
$$[1 - 0.76(0.18)U_2(x_2)][1 - 0.76(0.30)U_3(x_3)] \qquad (17.3)$$

where x_1, x_2, and x_2 represent levelized energy costs, annual dividend, and resource losses, respectively. (This is a *multiplicative* utility function and is a special form of the general multilinear utility function. See the online supplement for more information.)

From Table 17.3, the overall utility of any given consequence can be calculated. First, find the individual utility for each attribute. Then, for the additive components, multiply each utility value times its weight and add up the resulting products. For the economic attributes, calculate the utility from Equation (17.3) and multiply the result times 0.395, the weight given to the economic component. Finally, add this product to the sum of the weighted utilities from the previous step. Of course, no one would do this in such a painstaking way by hand. Fortunately, it is very straightforward to program such utility calculations either into a specialized utility program or even in a spreadsheet.

Keeney (1992) shows how this utility function for BC Hydro can be used to generate important insights. For example, he shows the resource value in dollars of various attributes: Each hectare of wilderness lost is valued at $2,500, but a hectare of flora lost is worth $625. Each person-year of aesthetic deterioration is worth $13. One statistical fatality, for either an employee or a member of the general public, is worth $3 million. Many other economic trade-offs are listed in Keeney's Table 12.6 (1992). These are the amounts (but no more) that BC Hydro should be willing to sacrifice in order to save a hectare, a life, or a person-year of aesthetic damage. In addition to these trade-offs, Keeney lists a number of decision opportunities that arose from the analysis, including studying the implications of resource losses on economic activity, developing a database for fatalities, studying public environmental values, and understanding the process of responding to telephone inquiries.

Did the definition of strategic objectives and a strategic utility function have an impact on BC Hydro? Ken Peterson is quoted as saying:

> The structured set of objectives has influenced BC Hydro planning in many contexts. Two examples include our work to develop a decision framework for supply planning, and a case study of an investment to upgrade reliability, both of which have adopted a multiple objective structure. Less obvious has been an evolution in how key senior planners view planning issues. The notion of a utility function over a range of objectives (rather than a single objective, like costs) is evident in many planning contexts. The specific trade-offs in the elicitation process are less important than the understanding that trade-offs are unavoidable in electricity utility decisions and that explicit, well-structured, informed trade-offs can be highly useful. (*Interfaces*, November–December 1992, p. 109)

The use of multiattribute utility models has been a source of insight for many decision makers in diverse decision situations. For example, Keeney and Raiffa (1976) report applications involving fire department operations, strategic decision making by a technical consulting firm, evaluation of computer systems, siting of nuclear power facilities, the analysis of sites for the Mexico City airport, and many others. Other applications are described in von Winterfeldt and Edwards (1986).

SUMMARY

We have continued the discussion of making decisions in the face of conflicting objectives. Much of the chapter has been a rather technical discussion and treatment of independence conditions: preferential independence, utility independence, and additive independence. The differences among these have to do with the presence or absence of uncertainty. Preferential independence means that preferences for sure outcomes in one attribute do not depend on the level of other attributes. Utility independence requires that preferences for gambles or lotteries in an attribute do not depend on the level of other attributes. Additive independence is still stronger: Preferences over lotteries in one attribute must not depend on lotteries in the other attributes. The blood bank example showed how to apply mutual utility independence to assess a two-dimensional utility function that includes an interaction term. We saw that the attributes of shortage and outdating were complementary; they work together to increase the decision maker's utility. We briefly saw what to do when there are three or more attributes, and what to do if no independence properties hold. Finally, the BC Hydro application demonstrated multiattribute utility in a large-scale organizational setting.

EXERCISES

17.1. Explain what is meant when we speak of interaction between attributes. Why would the additive utility function from Chapter 16 be inappropriate if two attributes interact?

17.2. What are the advantages and disadvantages of directly assessing a multiattribute utility function?

17.3. Explain preferential independence in your own words. Can you cite an example from your own experience in which preferential independence holds? Can you cite an example in which it does not hold?

17.4. Explain in your own words the difference between preferential independence and utility independence.

17.5. Explain in your own words the difference between utility independence and additive independence. Why is it important to understand the concept of additive independence?

17.6. Suppose that a company would like to purchase a fairly complicated machine to use in its manufacturing operation. Several different machines are available, and their prices are more or less equivalent. But the machines vary considerably in their available technical support (Attribute X) and reliability (Attribute Y). Some machines have a high degree of reliability and relatively low support, while others are less reliable but have excellent field support. The decision maker determined what the best and worst scenarios were for both attributes, and an assessment then was made regarding the independence of the decision maker's preferences for these attributes. It was determined that utility independence held. Individual utility functions $U_X(x)$ and $U_Y(y)$ were assessed. Finally, the decision maker was found to be indifferent in comparing Lottery A with its alternative B:

A   Best on both reliability and support with probability 0.67

Worst on both reliability and support with probability 0.33

B   Best on reliability and worst on support

The decision maker also was indifferent between

C   Best on both reliability and support with probability 0.48

Worst on both reliability and support with probability 0.52

D   Worst on reliability and best on support

a.   What are the values for k_X and k_Y? Write out the decision maker's full two-attribute utility function for reliability and support.

b.   Are the two attributes substitutes or complements? Explain, both intuitively and on the basis of k_X and k_Y.

QUESTIONS AND PROBLEMS

17.7.   A hospital administrator is making a decision regarding the hospital's policy of treating individuals who have no insurance coverage. The policy involves examination of a prospective patient's financial resources. The issue is what level of net worth should be required in order for the patient to be provided treatment. Clearly, there are two competing objectives in this decision. One is to maximize the hospital's revenue, and the other is to provide as much care as possible to the uninsured poor. Attributes to measure achievement toward these two objectives are (1) prospective revenue (R), and (2) percentage of uninsured poor who are treated (P).

The two attributes were examined for independence, and the administrator concluded that they were mutually utility independent. Utility functions $U_R(r)$ and $U_P(p)$ for the two attributes were assessed. Then two more assessments were made. Lottery A and its certain alternative B were judged to be equivalent by the administrator:

A   Best on revenue, worst on treating poor with probability 0.65

Worst on revenue, best on treating poor with probability 0.35

B   Levels of revenue and treatment of poor that give $U_R(r) = 0.5$ and $U_P(p) = 0.5$

In the second assessment, Lottery C and its certain alternative D were judged to be equivalent:

C   Best on both revenue and treating poor with probability 0.46

Worst on both revenue and treating poor with probability 0.54

D   Worst on revenue and best on treating the poor

a.   Find values for k_R and k_P. Should the administrator consider these two attributes to be substitutes or complements? Why or why not?

b. Comment on using an additive utility model in this situation. Would such a model seriously compromise the analysis of the decision?

17.8. Suppose you face an investment decision in which you must think about cash flows in two different years. Regard these two cash flows as two different attributes, and let X represent the cash flow in Year 1, and Y the cash flow in Year 2. The maximum cash flow you could receive in any year is $20,000, and the minimum is $5,000. You have assessed your individual utility functions for X and Y, and have fitted exponential utility functions to them:

$$U_X(x) = 1.05 - 2.86e^{-x/5000}$$

$$U_Y(y) = 1.29 - 2.12e^{-y/10000}$$

Furthermore, you have decided that utility independence holds, and so these individual utility functions for each cash flow are appropriate regardless of the amount of the other cash flow. You also have made the following assessments:

- You would be indifferent between a sure outcome of $7,500 each year for 2 years and a risky investment with a 50% chance at $20,000 each year, and a 50% chance at $5,000 each year.
- You would be indifferent between getting (1) $18,000 the first year and $5,000 the second, and (2) getting $5,000 the first year and $20,000 the second.

a. Use these assessments to find the scaling constants k_X and k_Y. What does the value of $(1 - k_X - k_Y)$ imply about the cash flows of the different periods?

b. Use this utility function to choose between Alternatives A and B in Problem 16.23 (Figure 16.15).

c. Draw indifference curves for $U(x, y) = 0.25, 0.50$, and 0.75.

17.9. Refer to Problem 16.25. A decision maker who prefers Chemical B might be said to be sensitive to equity between the two groups. The eventual outcome with Chemical A is not equitable; one group is better off than the other. On the other hand, with Chemical B, both groups are treated the same. Let X and Y denote the expected increase in the number of deaths in Groups 1 and 2, respectively, and denote a decision maker's utility function as

$$U(x, y) = k_X U_X(x) + k_Y U_Y(y) + (1 - k_X - k_Y)U_X(x)U_Y(y)$$

What can you say about the value of $(1 - k_X - k_Y)$? Are X and Y complements or substitutes?

17.10. In Problem 14.12 and 15.12, you assessed individual utility functions for money (X) and computer reliability (Y). In this problem, we will use these assessed utility functions to put together a two-attribute utility function for use in a computer-purchase decision. (If you have not already worked Problems 14.12 and 15.12, do so before continuing. Even if you already have assessed these utility functions, review them and confirm that they are good models of your preferences. When you assessed them, did you consciously think about keeping all other important attributes at the same level?)

a. Are your preferences mutually utility independent? Your utility for money probably does not depend on your computer's level of reliability. But would you be less nervous about computer reliability if you had more money in the bank? Imagine that you have $5,000 in the bank. Now assess a certainty equivalent (in terms of computer downtime) for a 50–50 gamble between your computer being down for 20 days next year or not breaking down at all. Now imagine that you have $30,000 in the bank, and reassess your certainty equivalent. Is it the same? Are your preferences for money and computer reliability mutually utility independent?

b. Regardless of your answer to part a, let us assume that your preferences for money and computer reliability are mutually utility independent. Now make the following assessments:

   i. Assess a certainty equivalent (in terms of both attributes: computer downtime and money) for a 50–50 gamble between the worst outcome ($1,000 in the bank and 50 days of computer downtime) and the best outcome ($20,000 in the bank and no downtime).

   ii. Imagine the outcome that is $1,000 and no downtime (worst level in money, and best level in computer reliability). Assess a dollar amount x so that the outcome x dollars and 50 days of downtime is equivalent to $1,000 and no downtime.

c. Using your individual assessed utility functions from Problems 14.12 and 15.12, and assessments i and ii from part b, calculate k_X and k_Y. Write out your two-attribute utility function.

(*Note:* This problem can be done without having to fit a mathematical expression to your individual utility function. It can be done with a utility function expressed as a table or as a graph.)

17.11. Someday you probably will face a choice among job offers. Aside from the nature of the job itself, two attributes that are important for many people are salary and location. Some people prefer large cities, others prefer small towns. Some people do not have strong preferences about the size of the town in which they live; this would show up as a low weight for the population-size attribute in a multiattribute utility function. Assess a two-attribute utility function for salary (X) and population size (Y):

a. Determine whether your preferences for salary and town size are mutually utility independent.

b. If your preferences display mutual utility independence, assess the two individual utility functions and the weights k_X and k_Y. Draw indifference curves for your assessed utility function. If your preferences do not display mutual utility independence, then you need to think about alternative approaches. The simplest is to assess several utility points as described at the beginning of this chapter and "eyeball" the indifference curves.

c. What other attributes are important in a job decision? Would the two-attribute utility function you just assessed be useful as a first approximation if many of the other attributes were close in comparing two jobs?

17.12. Refer to Problem 16.17. For some of the attributes in your computer decision, you face uncertainty. The additive utility function assessed in Problem 16.17 essentially assumes that additive independence among attributes is reasonable.

a. Check some of your attributes with formal assessments for additive independence. Follow the example in the text in setting up the two lotteries. (One lottery is a 50–50 gamble between best and worst on both attributes. The other is a 50–50 gamble between (i) best on X, worst on Y; and (ii) worst on X, best on Y.)

b. How could you extend this kind of assessment for additive independence to more than two attributes?

17.13. In many cases a group of people must make a decision that involves multiple objectives. In fact, difficult decisions usually are dealt with by committees composed of individuals who represent different interests. For example, imagine a lumber mill owner and an environmentalist on a committee trying to decide on national forest management policy. It might make sense for the committee to try to assess a multiattribute "group utility function." But assessment of the weights would be a problem because different individuals probably would want to weight the attributes differently. Can you give any advice to a committee working on a problem that might help it to arrive at a decision? How should the discussions be structured? Can sensitivity analysis help in such a situation; if so, how?

CASE STUDY

A MINING INVESTMENT DECISION

A major U.S. mining firm faced a difficult capital-investment decision. The firm had the opportunity to bid on two separate parcels of land that had valuable ore deposits. The project involved planning, exploration, and eventually extraction of minerals. The firm had to decide how much to bid, whether to bid alone or with a partner, and how to develop the site if the bid were successful. Overall, the company would have to commit approximately $500 million to the project if it obtained the land.

Figure 17.7 shows a schematic version of the decision-tree model for this decision. Note that one of the immediate alternatives is not to bid at all, but to stay with and develop the firm's own property. Some of the key uncertainties are whether the bid is successful, the success of a competing venture, capital-investment requirements, operating costs, and product price.

Figure 17.8 shows cumulative distribution functions for net present value (NPV) from four

possible strategies. Strategy 25—develop own property with partner—stochastically dominates all of the other strategies considered, and hence appears to be a serious candidate for the chosen alternative. The decision makers realized, however, that while they did want most to maximize the project's NPV, they also had another objective, the maximization of product output (PO). Because of this, a two-attribute utility function for NPV and PO was constructed. The individual utility functions were assessed as exponential utility functions:

$$U_{PO}(po) = 1 - e^{-po/33.33}$$

$$U_{NPV}(npv) = 1 - e^{-(npv+100)/200}$$

The scaling constants also were assessed, yielding $k_{NPV} = 0.79$ and $k_{PO} = 0.16$. Using this two-attribute model, expected utilities and certainty equivalents—a

FIGURE **17.7**
Schematic decision tree for mining-investment decision.

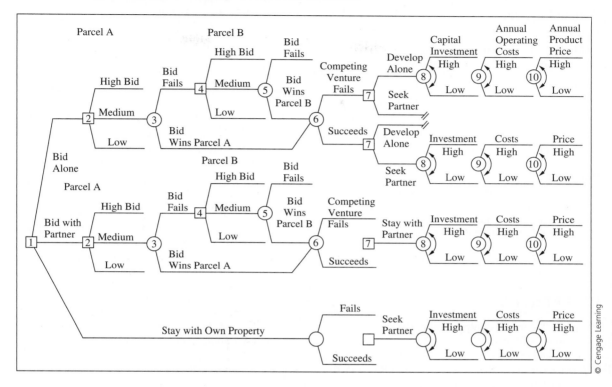

FIGURE **17.8**
Cumulative risk profiles for four strategies in mining-investment decision.

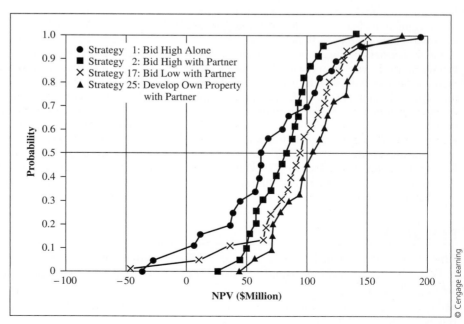

© Cengage Learning

TABLE **17.4**
Expected utilities (EU) and certainty equivalents (CE) for strategies in mining investment decision.

	Bid High Alone	Bid High with Partner	Bid Low with Partner	Develop Own Property with Partner	Do Nothing
EU	0.574	0.577	0.564	0.567	0.308
CE (NPV, in $ Million, PO = 50)	51	52	45	47	

© Cengage Learning

certain (NPV, PO) pair, with PO set to a specific level—were calculated. Table 17.4 shows the results for some of the strategies.

Questions

1. Which of the alternatives should be chosen? Why? Discuss the apparent conflict between the stochastic dominance results (Figure 17.8) and the results from the utility model.

2. The values of the scaling constants suggest that NPV and PO are viewed by the firm as complements. Can you explain intuitively why these two attributes would be complements rather than substitutes?

Source: A. C. Hax and K. M. Wiig (1977) "The Use of Decision Analysis in a Capital Investment Problem." In D. Bell, R. L. Keeney, and H. Raiffa (eds.) *Conflicting Objectives in Decisions*, pp. 277–297. New York: Wiley. Figures 16.8 and 16.9 reprinted by permission of the International Institute for Applied System Analysis (IIASA).

REFERENCES

Chapter 17 represents only the tip of the iceberg when it comes to general multiattribute utility modeling. If you are interested in reading more, the standard reference for multiattribute utility theory is Keeney and Raiffa (1976). Keeney (1980) covers most of the same material and is a little easier to read. Kirkwood (1997) provides a nice introduction to multiattribute value and utility models in a textbook format, and von Winterfeldt and Edwards (1986) have extensive discussion with an emphasis on behavioral issues. Keeney and von Winterfeldt (2007) focus on enhancing the usefulness of value models in practical applications. Further references and examples of applications can be obtained from all of these texts.

Keeney, R. (1980) *Siting Energy Facilities*. New York: Academic Press.

Keeney, R. (1992) *Value-Focused Thinking: A Path to Creative Decisionmaking*. Cambridge, MA: Harvard University Press.

Keeney, R., and T. McDaniels (1992) "Value-Focused Thinking about Strategic Decisions at BC Hydro." *Interfaces*, 22, 94–109.

Keeney, R., and H. Raiffa (1976) *Decisions with Multiple Objectives*. New York: Wiley.

Keeney, R., and D. von Winterfeldt (2007) "Practical Value Models" in: W. Edwards, R. F. Miles, and D. von Winterfeldt (2007) *Advances in Decision Analysis: From Foundations to Applications*. New York: Cambridge University Press, 232–252.

Kirkwood, C. (1997) *Strategic Decision Making: Multiobjective Decision Analysis with Spreadsheets*. Florence, KY: Cengage Learning.

Raiffa, H. (1982) *The Art and Science of Negotiation*. Cambridge, MA: Harvard University Press.

von Winterfeldt, D., and W. Edwards (1986) *Decision Analysis and Behavioral Research*. Cambridge: Cambridge University Press.

EPILOGUE

The Mining-Investment Decision. Hax and Wiig (1977) reported that the decision was to adopt Strategy 2—bid high with a partner. Just looking at NPV left the decision maker feeling uneasy. But with the product volume included in the two-attribute analysis, the decision maker was satisfied that the important objectives had been considered, so it was easy to adopt the strategy with the highest expected utility.

JOHN CARTER: HEDGING

John Carter was a farmer in Northern Massachusetts. John, like all of the farmers around him, grew apples and shipped his harvest to Boston for sale at the prevailing market price. The farm had been in John's family for three generations; from his inheritance and prudent management, John had built his net worth to $300,000. Like many of his neighbors, John was being pressed by increasing costs and by the failure of revenues to keep up with this increase. John worried that a really bad year could wipe him out and he might lose the farm.

John tried to project the amount of harvest and the price that it would bring at market. This year he believed the farm would earn revenues in the vicinity of $310,000. John's analysis of past costs indicated that the farm would incur $220,000 this year in fixed costs and that variable costs would be $0.03 per pound of apples produced. The tax schedule for farmers meant that John did not pay any taxes unless he earned over $25,000 in a year. Between $25,000 and $50,000, he would have to pay a marginal rate of 24 percent, so that his actual taxes on $50,000 would be 12 percent. Over $50,000, the marginal tax rate increased to 45.6 percent on earnings.

During the past few years, John had hedged his revenues using forward contracts. When he entered a forward contract, John had to guarantee the delivery of the contracted amount of apples at harvest. If John's own crop fell below the amount of apples that he had sold forward, he would have to buy enough apples on the open market to make up the difference. Any apples that John's farm produced above the amount specified in the contract would be sold at the prevailing market price. All transactions, including any payment received by John from the forward contract and any selling or buying of apples on the spot market at harvest would be settled at the same time in the fall.

John believed the price at harvest would best be approximated by a normal distribution with a mean of $0.2079 per pound and a standard deviation of $0.0247 per pound.[1] Forward contracts were only available in increments of 100 tons, and the current forward rate was $0.2079 per pound. In the past, John had assumed that he could predict with certainty what his land would produce, and he had usually hedged roughly half that amount. John sometimes wondered if that was the best policy for how much to hedge, given his forecast of what his farm would produce.

John Junior, home from college for spring vacation, had decided to help his father. He had produced a worksheet that modeled the future price of apples in an @RISK simulation. John Junior initially set up the model so that the harvest was exactly his father's forecast—743 tons of apples—and he agreed to help his father figure out what the ideal amount was to sell forward, given the assumption that apple production was known with certainty.

However, John Junior was concerned that his father's assumptions about the harvest did not capture all of the risks that the farm faced. After some prodding, John Junior was able to get his father to admit that his forecasts were not always right, and John Senior provided John Junior with data about actual market prices and harvest yields in the past (Exhibit 1). John Junior noted with some concern that his father's forecast for the upcoming harvest was simply the mean of the past ten years' harvests. In addition to the simple analysis his dad had asked him to do, John Junior decided to model the farm's profitability, factoring in uncertainty about how many tons of apples would actually be produced. He decided that production quantity was best approximated by a normal distribution with a mean of 743 tons (his father's forecast) and standard deviation of 87 tons.

After completing his basic model for his father and his "improved" model with the uncertainty about the size of the harvest, John Junior knew he could help decide how many tons of apples to sell forward. But something was nagging him. He suspected there was typically a relationship between the quantity of apples harvested and the price at market. After all, if his father had a bad year, other farmers might also have bad years, and this could affect price. As a result, he decided to add a correlation variable to his model to better capture the interaction between the harvest and

---

[1] The distributions in this example were based on data from *The CRB Commodity Yearbook*, 2001.

EXHIBIT **1**
John Carter:
Hedging.

	Carter's Production of Apples (tons)	Apple Price per Pound
1990	624.93	$0.2090
1991	627.06	$0.2510
1992	784.40	$0.1950
1993	792.41	$0.1840
1994	852.90	$0.1860
1995	784.89	$0.2400
1996	669.83	$0.2080
1997	665.43	$0.2210
1998	844.40	$0.1730
1999	783.26	$0.2120
Mean	742.95	$0.2079
Standard deviation	87	$0.0247

market price. To explore what correlation did for the decision of how much to sell forward, he decided to analyze how many tons his father should sell forward assuming 0 correlation between price and quantity, +0.99 correlation, and −0.99 correlation. He wondered whether the variables would be that highly correlated.

John Junior concluded, from talking over dinner with his father about risk preference, that his father was decreasingly risk averse and a logarithmic utility function would be an appropriate model of his risk preference. John Junior thus modeled the utility of the profit after tax of each hedging scenario. Based on the

results of the different simulations, John Junior hoped to explain to his father what the risks and implications were for the decision about forward contracts.

Source: This case was written by Lee Fiedler, MBA '02, under the supervision of Samuel Bodily, John Tyler Professor of Business Administration, Darden Graduate School of Business Administration, University of Virginia. Copyright © 2003 by the University of Virginia Darden School Foundation, Charlottesville, VA. All rights reserved. *To order copies, send an e-mail to* sales@ dardenbusinesspublishing.com *No part of this publication may be reproduced, stored in a retrieval system, used in a spreadsheet, or transmitted in any form or by any means—electronic, mechanical, photocopying, recording, or otherwise—without the permission of the Darden School Foundation.*

SLEEPMORE MATTRESS MANUFACTURING: PLANT CONSOLIDATION

W. Carl Lerhos, special assistant to the president of Sleepmore Mattress Manufacturing, had been asked to study the proposed consolidation of plants in three different locations. The company had just added several new facilities as a result of the acquisition of a competitor; some were in markets currently served by existing facilities. The president knew the dollar savings would be fairly easy to calculate for each location, but the qualitative factors and the tradeoffs

among them were more difficult to judge. This was the area in which he wanted Carl to spend most of his time.

The major objectives in evaluating a consolidation plan for the sites were to maximize manufacturing benefits, maximize sales benefits, and maximize direct financial benefits. These objectives would be composed of exploiting 13 attributes (see Exhibit 1). After spending some time looking at each attribute individually, Carl and the other officers of Sleepmore ranked them in order of most important to least important. They also added the best and worst possible outcomes for each attribute (see Exhibit 2).

EXHIBIT **1**
Hierarchy of
objectives.

I. **Maximize Manufacturing Benefits**
    a. Labor
    b. Management effectiveness
       1. Talent availability
       2. Plant size
    c. Operability
       1. Product-line complexity
       2. Training
       3. Production stability
    d. Facilities
       1. Layout
       2. Location
       3. Space availability
II. **Maximize Sales Benefits**
    a. Maximize service
    b. Maximize quality
III. **Maximize Direct Financial Benefits**
    a. Minimize initial cost
    b. Maximize ongoing benefit

EXHIBIT **2**
Thirteen attributes
selected for
evaluation of
consolidation.

Rank	Attribute	Worst Outcome	Best Outcome
1	Labor	Create hostile union	Eliminate hostile union
2	Quality	Drastically worsen quality	Strongly improve quality
3	Service	Lose business	Increase business
4	Annual savings	Lose $1 million/yr.	Save $1 million/yr.
5	Initial cost	Cost $5 million	Save $5 million
6	Management talent	Severely worsen management	Strongly improve management
7	Plant size (sales)	Create $35 million plant	Create $15 million plant
8	Plant location	Move from rural area to city	Move from city to rural area
9	Product-line complexity	Increased to full product line	Reduce product line
10	Space availability	Need a new facility (100,000 sq. ft.)	Save an expansion of 100,000 sq. ft.
11	Production stability	Increase demand variability	Decrease variability
12	Training	Train all new labor	Small layoff-no new training
13	Plant layout	Create poor layout	Eliminate poor layout

Measurements

In each case, the attributes were assigned a number from zero to ten, with ten being the best possible outcome mentioned in Exhibit 2. Each location was in a different region, and each of the three locations involved a decision between two alternatives—consolidate the plants there or keep them separate. The plants produced different product lines. Exhibits 3 to 5 give brief descriptions and scores of the three potential consolidation opportunities. Only the "consolidate" alternatives are scored; in other words, each "keep separate" alternative has a default score of five for each attribute (except for the attribute Plant size, which was undefined for the pair of plants prior to consolidation). Therefore, the attributes are really scored *relative to the current situation*, in which the plants are separate. The scores Carl assigned were based on subjective assessments after talking with the managers, and visiting the sites.

Weights

After Carl had scored each attribute on his scale of 0–10, he faced the more difficult task of deciding how important one attribute was compared with another. The quantitative attributes would be fairly easy to weigh. He knew that the company's discount rate (15%), along with its planning horizon (10 years), might help in this regard, but he was not quite sure how.

He had heard the president say, "The smaller a plant, the easier it is to manage. If we could improve from a $35 million plant size to a $15 million plant, the gain would be equivalent to a savings from the status quo of $1 million a year in operating costs." Carl made a quick mental calculation which suggested the weight for plant size would be one-half the weight for annual savings—he'd check it later.

The mattress-manufacturing industry required a lot of space. If a consolidation required a new plant or a significant addition, the hassle of moving, as well as

EXHIBIT **3**
Consolidation evaluated at Site 1: Merge Plant 1A into Plant 1B.

Attribute	Plant 1A	Plant 1B	Score for Combining
Labor	Poor	Excellent	9; large improvement
Quality	Poor	Good	9
Service	Poor	Good	8
Annual savings	High overhead	Efficient; merger saves $1 MM/yr.	_____
Initial cost	Save $1MM if plant merged	N/A	_____
Management talent	Poor	Excellent	9
Plant size (sales)	$3 million	$27 million	_____
Plant location	Large city	Rural area	10
Product-line complexity	2 major product lines	2 separate lines	0; very complex
Space availability	N/A	Has extra space; needs 0 new sq. ft.	_____
Production stability	Small demand/ high uncertainty	Large demand/ low uncertainty	7; reduce variation
Training	N/A	Extra labor available	7.5
Plant layout	Congested plant	Well laid out	7.5

EXHIBIT **4**
Consolidation
evaluated at Site 2:
Put Plant 2B into
Plant 2A.

Attribute	Plant 2A	Plant 2B	Score for Combining
Labor	Average	Poor	6
Quality	Average	Average	5
Service	Average	Good	7
Annual savings	Under capacity; merger saves $500K	Under capacity	_____
Initial cost	N/A	Save $1MM if merge plant	_____
Management talent	Average	Good	6
Plant size (sales)	$5 million	$10 million	_____
Plant location	Industrial park	Large city	6
Product-line complexity	2 major product lines	2 different lines	0; very complex
Space availability	Need to add 50K sq. ft. if merge	No room	_____
Production stability	Small demand/ high uncertainty	Counter cyclical demand	9; reduce variation
Training	Underutilized labor	Underutilized labor	9; small layoff
Plant layout	Excellent	Poor	9

hidden expenses, would be additional negative factors. The cost would be $25/sq. ft. for each additional square foot of space.

To help him in assigning weights to the other, more qualitative attributes, Carl pulled out his notes from a meeting attended by the president, the vice-president of operations, and the vice-president of human resources. At this meeting, held at the time of the acquisition, the list shown in Exhibit 2 had been generated and the relative importance of each attribute had been discussed.

The vice-president of human resources had said, "Labor is the most important, because the quality of labor determines the major aspects of plant performance (like quality, profitability, etc.). Experience has shown that a good labor force can overcome many obstacles, but a poor labor force leads to trouble. In fact, I think labor is twice as important as the average of all 13 attributes." Carl wondered about the context for this statement. He verified that the vice-president had the ranges of

Exhibit 2 in mind: improving labor relations from "create hostile union" to "eliminate hostile union" was twice as valuable as improving the average attribute from worst to best.

The vice-president of operations agreed with the comment about labor and said, "I think quality and service, although slightly less important than labor, are two other attributes that deserve more weight than average."

There seemed to be a consensus that management was the next most important qualitative attribute because, like labor, management would determine the fate of the plant. Unlike labor, however, management could be rather easily changed. Overall, this attribute was considered "average" in terms of importance.

The president then argued for consideration of plant location: "Plant location is as important as plant size. Our data show that plants in more congested areas (cities) tend to be less profitable than plants in rural areas."

EXHIBIT **5**
Consolidation evaluated at Site 3: Put Plant 3B into Plant 3A.

Attribute	Plant 3A	Plant 3B	Score for Combining
Labor	Below average	Good	3; may lose Plant 3A labor
Quality	Average	Average	5
Service	Average	Good	6
Annual savings	Under capacity; merger saves $200K/year	Efficient	_____
Initial cost	N/A	Save $2MM if merge	_____
Management talent	Average	Below average	6
Plant size (sales)	$9 million	$18 million	_____
Plant location	Large city	Suburb	4
Product-line complexity	2 major product lines	2 different lines	0; very complex
Space availability	Need 30K sq. ft. if merge	No room	_____
Production stability	Small demand/high uncertainty	Uncertain demand	6; demand not counter-cyclical
Training	Underutilized labor	N/A	3; some labor quits
Plant layout	Good	Cramped	7

The vice-president of operations said, "Because Sleepmore produces a different product line in different plants, consolidations could drastically increase complexity and reduce long-term efficiency. I move that product-line complexity be considered the next most important qualitative attribute, albeit its importance is about two-thirds the importance of management talent, in my opinion."

The remaining three attributes—stability, training, and layout—were agreed to have individual effects that were relatively small, but their combined effect was considered about twice that of product-line complexity.

The hardest task was to evaluate the tradeoffs that management would be willing to make between quantitative and qualitative factors. In this regard, the president had expressed difficulty to Carl in choosing between a situation with initial cost savings of $7 million and a situation where a hostile union was eliminated.

Decision

Carl had to figure out an effective way to combine all this information about both quantitative and qualitative factors to make decisions whether to consolidate at *each of the three sites*. He wondered how sensitive his decisions would be to the weights he assigned each attribute.

Source: This case was prepared by Samuel E. Bodily, John Tyler Professor of Business Administration, as a basis for class discussion rather than to illustrate effective or ineffective handling of an administrative situation. Copyright © by the University of Virginia Darden School Foundation, Charlottesville, VA, Rev. 10/95. All rights reserved. *To order copies, send an e-mail to* sales@dardenbusinesspublishing.com *No part of this publication may be reproduced, stored in a retrieval system, used in a spreadsheet, or transmitted in any form or by any means—electronic, mechanical, photocopying, recording, or otherwise—without the permission of the Darden School Foundation.*

SUSAN JONES (A)

DARDEN 🏛
BUSINESS PUBLISHING
UNIVERSITY *of* **VIRGINIA**

Susan sighed as she got up from the dinner table and looked out the window at the dogwood tree flowering in their front yard. "Thanks for cooking again tonight," she said to her husband, Rick. "I just haven't been able to get my mind off this job decision, and I'm afraid I would have burned the whole meal if it had been up to me."

Rick smiled at her knowingly, "You've got to let them know by the end of this week, don't you?" he asked. "Why don't you relax for a few minutes while I clean up; then we can hash it out once and for all."

With a grateful nod, Susan grabbed her diet soda from the table and headed into the living room, picking up a folder that held the three offer letters she needed to evaluate. As Rick loaded the dishwasher, Susan opened the folder and started reading the letters for the third time that day.

Susan and Rick

Born and raised in Dallas, Texas, Susan Jones received a Bachelor of Science degree from Harvard University in 1993, with a dual major in economics and international business. After graduation, she stayed in Boston to work for a multinational snack foods producer, analyzing international expansion opportunities in their foreign markets division. With four years of work experience under her belt, Susan applied to and was accepted at The Darden School, University of Virginia, to start in the fall of 1997.

Susan met her husband, Rick Jones, at Harvard, where he was a pre-med student a year behind her. They were married in 1995, while Rick was studying at Harvard Medical School to become an OB/GYN. Rick secured an internship at the University of Virginia Hospital and was able to join Susan in Charlottesville for her second year at Darden, but he was slated to return to Boston in July for his residency at the Brigham-Women's Hospital.

The Offers

Susan spent the summer between her first and second years of business school interning for a global consulting firm. She had a wonderful summer experience, traveling frequently to client sites around the country, and at the end of the summer she received an offer for permanent employment in the firm's Dallas office.

In the fall of her second year at Darden, Susan interviewed for management consulting and internal consulting positions. She received offers from four companies and quickly narrowed the decision down to two offers in addition to the offer she received from her internship: one as a management consultant for a start-up consulting firm that handled mostly local clients in Chicago and one as an internal consultant at a global beverage company in Boston.

The Decision

Rick finished loading the dishwasher and walked into the living room. "How's it going?" he asked his wife. "Oh, I don't know," she said. "Each of these offers has different good points, and it's like trying to compare apples to oranges. It would be so much easier if they were all on the same plane and all I had to decide on was the salary. But they're each in different cities, with different salaries; the only thing that is the same among them is relocation reimbursement!"

"Let's make a chart," Rick suggested, "and write out all the things that are different. Maybe if you look at everything all lined up it'll be easier to compare them." He picked up a pad of paper and a pencil and sat down, ready to write.

"The easiest place to start is with the hard facts," Susan began. "The offer in Texas pays $70,000 a year, which isn't bad when you consider that the cost of living there is about 70 percent of what it is in Boston. They'll also throw in a $15,000 sign-on bonus and pay for half of my second year tuition, which is worth another $10,000. The Boston offer is for $95,000, with a sign-on bonus of $12,000, and the Chicago offer is for $85,000, with a $15,000 sign-on bonus, but neither Boston nor Chicago is offering tuition reimbursement. The up-front money would sure come in handy to buy some new furniture, a few new suits, and all the luggage I'll need to get if I'm traveling a lot."

"What's the cost of living in Chicago, compared to Boston?" Rick asked.

"Chicago is a lot less expensive, too, about 75 percent of what Boston is, according to the web site I looked at," Susan replied. "In addition, Texas says

I can expect to get an annual bonus of 10 percent; Chicago is talking about an annual bonus of 12 percent; and Boston offers a 15 percent annual bonus.

"Since you'll be living in Boston, we'd only have to pay rent on one apartment if I live there, but it would have to be bigger, so let's assume the rent for me will be around $300 per month if I take that job. Housing's more affordable in Chicago than Boston, so I think I could find a small apartment there for around $1,000 per month. If I go back to Texas, I could move back home with Mom and not pay any rent at all."

"Now we're getting somewhere," Rick said, holding up the chart forming on his notepad. "Let's try to tackle some of the intangibles next. What about vacation and job travel?"

"Dallas and Chicago are offering three weeks of vacation, but Boston is only two. As for job travel, the Texas position would have me at client sites four days every week. That's a lot of time in hotels! If I go to Boston, there won't be any travel, except for occasional visits to district offices. Let's say I'll have about three days per month of travel out of Boston. In Chicago, I'd spend about five days a month on the road, but it would all be in the region, so just short flights or long car rides."

"How do you feel about all that travel?" Rick asked. "It could get pretty lonely in hotels every night of the week. How much would it be worth to you to not be travelling all the time?"

"If I'm not in Boston, I'll be lonely without you, anyway," his wife quipped, winking at him. "Seriously, I'm not crazy about being in hotels a lot, but if I'm in a different city from you, the travel isn't as big a deal. If we had to quantify it, I'd take about a $5,000 pay cut in Dallas to cut down that travel to five days a month, the same as in Boston. The difference in job travel between Chicago and Boston is almost negligible, though, so if they asked me to be on the road two more days a month in Chicago, I'd only ask for another thousand dollars in salary to make up the difference."

"You said you'd miss me," Rick said with a fake pout. "How often do you think you could work a visit to Boston into your schedule if you accept the Texas or Chicago job?"

"I'd want to be there every weekend, but that's not practical," Susan answered, ignoring his antics.

"Let's plan on twice a month to travel to Boston." She hopped up from the couch and went over to their computer, logging into an internet travel site. "The cheapest fare quoted for Dallas to Boston is around $260, and the cheapest out of Chicago is $275, but that's from O'Hare, which is a pain to get in and out of. Flying time is seven hours round trip from Chicago, then I'll add an extra two hours on to account for travel to and from the airport. Wow! Nine hours each trip in travel time alone!

"If I'm in Dallas, on the other hand, the firm will fly me directly from the client to Boston, unless there's a reason to be in the office on Friday. We'd have to make up the cost difference on any more expensive tickets, but it should be safe to assume that would be the equivalent of just paying for a trip to Boston ten times a year. The travel time round-trip is about six-and-one-half hours, plus two hours for getting to and from the airport from my mother's house. No significant difference from Chicago in travel time, and I'd say the chances are even that I'd be coming from closer to or farther from Boston, so we'll leave it at eight-and-one-half hours. How do we quantify the travel time?"

"We haven't dealt with vacation time, yet, either," Rick reminded her. "How close are those two?"

"That's easy," Susan said. "I'd gladly give up a week's vacation not to have to travel eight or nine hours every time I come to Boston!"

"Well, it looks like we've got just about everything, then," Rick said, putting down the pencil. "We've quantified the intangibles by either swapping them out or adjusting your salary, so all we have to do is 'run the numbers,' as you MBAs like to say. Fire up that Excel program, and let's find out where you'll be working next fall."

Source: This case was prepared by Noelle McCormick under the supervision of Dana Clyman, Associate Professor of Business Administration, to provide a basis for class discussion. This case was written as a basis for class discussion rather than to illustrate effective or ineffective handling of an administrative situation. Copyright © 1999 by the University of Virginia Darden School Foundation, Charlottesville, VA. All rights reserved. *To order copies, send an e-mail to* sales@dardenbusinesspublishing.com *No part of this publication may be reproduced, stored in a retrieval system, used in a spreadsheet, or transmitted in any form or by any means—electronic, mechanical, photocopying, recording, or otherwise—without the permission of the Darden School Foundation.*

SUSAN JONES (B)

DARDEN 🏛
BUSINESS PUBLISHING
UNIVERSITY *of* VIRGINIA

Susan walked into the kitchen carrying the pages she and her husband had worked on the night before to decide which job offer she would accept. "I know it says Dallas is the right job offer," she said, pouring a cup of coffee, "but I think we're not seeing everything. For instance, even though Dallas and Chicago are a wash as far as travel time to see you, it would be better for both of us if we could be in the same city to start with. Plus, it sounds like I might have more flexibility to move when you're finished with your residency if I take the Dallas offer, but if I take the Boston offer, I'd already be with you if you stay at Brigham-Women's. This model doesn't take factors like that into account."

"Maybe we're looking at this the wrong way," Rick said. "Instead of just looking at the pros and cons of each job offer, let's look at what we want, then figure out which job gets us closest to our ideal situation. I have to be at the hospital in fifteen minutes, so why don't you think more about this today, and we'll talk more when I get home tonight."

When Rick arrived home from work, the living room was awash in paper. "Wow!" he exclaimed, "You really did a lot of work on this job decision today! How are we going to wade through all this?"

"Well," Susan answered, "I tried to get all the factors down first, and then fit them together. But I found that when I started thinking about what's really important to me, the list kept getting bigger. There are a lot of aspects we didn't consider the first time around."

"Like what?" Rick asked. "I thought we were pretty thorough last night."

"Sure, we looked at all of the things in the offer letters, and even went beyond that to take into consideration travel back and forth to Boston and differences in cost of living. But those are all limited to what the companies are offering me. There are also other things that I want—things that are outside the terms of the letters but affect my decision nonetheless.

"Take my volunteer work," Susan started. "I've been volunteering at the women's shelter for the last year and a half, and it's very important to me. I'd like to volunteer at a women's shelter wherever I end up, but that takes dedicated time. And being near you is a big thing, obviously. I mean, I know we'll both be busy, but what if I take the Dallas offer and end up on an assignment that requires working weekends? We'd never see each other then. Plus, I have to think about where this will lead in a few years. Will I be able to transfer to whatever city you end up in after your residency? Will I have the skills to change jobs if I can't transfer? I don't even know if I'll want to be in consulting in three years."

"Whoa, there!" Rick laughed. "You certainly have been thinking a lot about this. Where do we stand right now?"

Susan replied, "There seem to be some tradeoffs among what I want for right now and what will be best for us in the future; we need to take both a long-term and short-term perspective. After a number of false starts, I finally have a list I'm satisfied with of what I want in the ideal job. Now we just need to tie it all together. Here's the list of what I want, in no particular order." Susan's list of objectives is in Exhibit 1.

Susan continued, "We learned about objective hierarchies in QA last year, and that seemed like a good framework to make some sense of all this. The idea is to establish which objectives are the *fundamental* objectives, by that I mean things that are an end in and of themselves; and which are *means* objectives, those that allow us to attain the fundamental objectives. Creating the hierarchy forces us to think about what's truly important in our lives, and not just the "hard numbers" of each offer.

"It can be kind of tricky to sort out, but we should be able to group the things on my wish list and create a map of how they're connected. Then we figure out attributes for measuring each objective and compare the job offers based on those attributes."

"That doesn't sound like anything we can't handle if we work together," Rick said, smiling. "Hand me a pencil; we can knock this out before dinner."

Source: This case was prepared by Noelle McCormick under the supervision of Dana Clyman, Associate Professor of Business Administration, to provide a basis for class discussion. This case was written as a basis for class discussion rather than to illustrate effective or ineffective handling of an administrative situation. Copyright © 1999 by the University of Virginia Darden School Foundation, Charlottesville, VA. All rights reserved. *To order copies, send an e-mail to sales@dardenbusinesspublishing.com. No part of this publication may be reproduced, stored in a retrieval system, used in a spreadsheet, or transmitted in any form or by any means—electronic, mechanical, photocopying, recording, or otherwise—without the permission of the Darden School Foundation.*

EXHIBIT **1**
Susan Jones (B).

Susan's Wish List:

1. High salary
2. See Rick as much as possible
3. Spend time with my parents
4. Volunteer at women's shelter
5. Minimize overall travel
6. Location with low cost of living
7. Enjoy work (people and projects)
8. Learn new skills
9. Challenging work environment
10. See friends
11. Pay off school loans
12. Location flexibility when Rick finishes residency
13. Good retirement plan
14. Good promotion prospects
15. High job responsibility
16. Career advancement opportunities
17. Be in a fun city
18. Good bonuses
19. Vacation time

CHAPTER **18**

Conclusion and Further Reading

We all have to face hard decisions from time to time. Sometimes we must make difficult personal decisions such as how to care for an elderly loved one or which one of several job offers to accept. Many policy decisions for corporations or governmental agencies are hard to make. In fact, as time goes by, it becomes increasingly clear that as a society we must grapple with some particularly thorny problems, such as competitiveness in the world marketplace, the risks associated with new technologies, social and economic inequities, and trade-offs between short-term economic benefits and long-term environmental stability.

The argument all along has been that decision analysis can help with such hard decisions. The cycle of structuring the decision, modeling uncertainty and preferences, analyzing the model, and then performing sensitivity analysis can lead a decision maker systematically through the issues that make the decision complicated and toward a requisite decision model—one that captures all of the essential elements of the problem. The objective is to arrive at a decision model that explicates the complex parts in a way that enables the decision maker to choose from the alternatives with insight and understanding. One common bonus is that the modeling-and-analysis process uncovers new alternatives that may dominate the original set.

At the same time that decision analysis provides a framework for tackling difficult decisions, it also furnishes the decision maker with a complete tool kit for constructing the necessary models of uncertainty and preferences. We have spent much time in considering probability and how to use it to model the uncertainty that a decision maker faces. Subjective assessment, theoretical models, and the use of data and simulation are all tools in the decision analyst's kit. We also discussed the tools available for modeling preferences. We considered in some depth the fundamental trade-off between risk and return. Finally, the last two chapters focused on the modeling of preferences when the decision maker must try to satisfy conflicting objectives.

Throughout the book the view of decision making has been optimistic. We all are subject to human foibles, but a person interested in making better decisions can use the principles and tools that we have discussed in order to do a better job. In day-to-day decisions, it may be simply a matter of thinking in terms of an informally decomposed problem: What is the nature of the problem? What are the objectives? What trade-offs must be made? What uncertainties are there? Is it a risky situation? More complicated situations may warrant considerable effort and careful use of the modeling tools.

Finally, in the process of reading the text and working through the problems, you may have learned something about yourself. You may have identified specific objectives that are important for you, or learned how you personally feel about uncertainty in your life and how you tend to deal with risky situations. If you have learned something about the tools of decision analysis, gained an understanding of what it means to build and analyze a model of a decision problem, and learned a little about your own decision-making personality, then your work has been worthwhile. If you feel that you are more prepared to face some of the complicated decisions that we all must face in the 21st century, then the goal of this text has been achieved.

A DECISION-ANALYSIS READING LIST

Where should you go from here? The references at the end of each chapter can lead you to more information on specific topics. You undoubtedly noticed that many of the references reappeared several times. In the sections that follow, we have listed a collection of books that provide everything from introductions to in-depth coverage of decision analysis and behavioral decision theory. And although we have not included them, many popular books are now available that cover topics like behavioral economics, behavioral finance, and the cognitive neuroscience of decision making.

Here are our favorites on decision analysis and behavioral decision theory:

Decision Analysis

- Ward Edwards, Ralph F. Miles, and Detlof von Winterfeldt (2007) *Advances in Decision Analysis: From Foundations to Applications.* New York: Cambridge University Press. A collection of chapters by leaders in decision analysis covering all aspects of the field. This book is a must-read for anyone claiming to be an expert in the field.

- John S. Hammond, Ralph L. Keeney, and Howard Raiffa. (1999) *Smart Choices.* Cambridge, MA: Harvard University Press. With an objective of bringing careful decision-analysis thinking to laypeople, the authors have produced the most readable explication of the decision analysis process.

- Ronald A. Howard and James Matheson (eds.) (1983) *The Principles and Applications of Decision Analysis* (2 volumes). Palo Alto, CA: Strategic Decisions Group. Since the early 1960s, Ron Howard has been practicing decision analysis and teaching the principles at Stanford University. This two-volume set contains many early papers presenting the principles and techniques that the authors and their colleagues have contributed to decision analysis.

- Ralph Keeney (1992) *Value-Focused Thinking: A Path to Creative Decision Making.* Cambridge, MA: Harvard University Press. As you know by now, this book provides all the details on understanding one's objectives and using them as a basis for decision-analysis models and improved decision making.

- Ralph Keeney and Howard Raiffa (1976) *Decisions with Multiple Objectives: Preferences and Value Tradeoffs.* New York: Wiley. Reprinted in 1993 by Cambridge University Press. This is *the* standard reference for multiattribute utility theory, although it also is good for decision analysis in general. Many applications are described. Much of the material is highly technical, although the mathematics are not difficult. Gems of insight and explanation are scattered through the technical material. Unfortunately, no problems are included.

- Craig W. Kirkwood, C. (1997), *Strategic Decision Making: Multiobjective Decision Analysis with Spreadsheets.* Florence, KY: Cengage Learning. Taking a practical, modeling-oriented approach, in many ways this book picks up where *Making Hard Decisions* leaves off. As the title indicates, the focus is largely on multiobjective decision making.

- M. Granger Morgan and Max Henrion (1990) *Uncertainty: A Guide to Dealing with Uncertainty in Quantitative Risk and Policy Analysis.* Cambridge: Cambridge University Press. The authors provide an in-depth treatment of the use of uncertainty for risk analysis. Especially good on the elicitation and use of expert judgment.

- Howard Raiffa (1968) *Decision Analysis.* Reading, MA: Addison-Wesley. Professor Raiffa is a founder of decision analysis, and he explains the

material well. The problems tend to be abstract. The text covers the
basics (and then some) and still is worthwhile after 45 years.

- Howard Raiffa (1982) *The Art and Science of Negotiation*. Cambridge,
  MA: Belknap Press. Raiffa discusses negotiations from a decision-
  theoretic point of view. A well-written (and easy-to-read!) book that
  provides deep insights and top-flight analytical tools.

- Howard Raiffa, John Richardson, and David Metcalfe (2007)
  *Negotiation Analysis: the Science and Art of Collaborative Decision
  Making*. Cambridge, MA: Belknap. Expanding on Raiffa's original *Art
  and Science of Negotiation*, this book adds material on individual
  decision analysis, behavioral decision theory, and game theory.

- David C. Skinner (1999) *Introduction to Decision Analysis, 3rd Ed*.
  Gainesville, FL: Probabilistic Publishing. The author covers all of the
  basics of decision analysis, including many useful tools and techniques
  that practitioners and consultants use in day-to-day practice.

- Detlof von Winterfeldt and Ward Edwards (1986) *Decision Analysis
  and Behavioral Research*. Cambridge: Cambridge University Press. An
  up-to-date and in-depth treatment of decision analysis from a behavioral
  perspective. Professor Edwards was involved in behavioral decision theory and decision analysis from their beginnings until his death in 2005,
  and the history the authors provide in Chapter 14 is an eye-opener.
  The authors have a strong slant toward applications and behavioral
  research that provides evidence on the applicability of decision-analysis
  tools. As with the Keeney and Raiffa book, there are no problems.

- Robert L. Winkler (2003) *An Introduction to Bayesian Inference and
  Decision, 2nd Ed*. Sugar Land, TX: Probabilisitic Publishing. An excellent
  introduction to decision theory. Professor Winkler is especially interested
  in Bayesian models of information, and the book is slanted more toward
  inference and statistics than toward applied decision analysis.

Behavioral Decision Making

- Max H. Bazerman and Don A. Moore (2009) *Judgment in Managerial
  Decision Making, 7th Ed*. New York: Wiley. Covers behavioral issues in
  judgment and decision making, including biases in negotiations. The
  authors offer insights to help the reader improve his or her decision
  making.

- Thomas Gilovich, Dale Griffin, and Daniel Kahneman (2002) *Heuristics
  and Biases: The Psychology of Intuitive Judgment*. Cambridge University
  Press, Cambridge, UK. A follow-up to the Kahneman, Slovic, and
  Tversky book (below), this is a compendium of some of the most important academic articles on the psychology of judgment and belief that
  appeared after 1982.

- Reid K. Hastie and Robyn M. Dawes (2010), *Rational Choice in and
  Uncertain World: The Psychology of Judgment and Decision Making,
  2nd Ed*. Thousand Oaks, CA: Sage. An easy-to-read introduction to the
  behavioral issues in decision analysis, with an emphasis on how to
  improve your decision-making skills.

- Robin M. Hogarth (1987) *Judgment and Choice, 2nd Ed.* New York: Wiley. An excellent introduction to behavioral decision theory, this is decision analysis from a psychological perspective. This book covers a broad range of topics and is very easy to read.
- Daniel Kahneman, Paul Slovic, and Amos Tversky (1982) *Judgment under Uncertainty: Heuristics and Biases.* Cambridge: Cambridge University Press. A reader filled with classic articles on behavioral decision theory.
- Daniel Kahneman and Amos Tversky (2000) *Choices, Values, and Frames.* Cambridge: Cambridge University Press. This collection of academic articles explores the behavioral issues associated with the assessment of preferences and use of those preferences in decision making.
- Scott Plous (1993) *The Psychology of Judgment and Decision Making.* New York: McGraw-Hill. A very readable introduction to behavioral decision theory, although the field has made great strides since.

AUTHOR INDEX

A

Abramson, B., 344
Adams, J. L., 238, 239
Allais, M., 693
Allen, M. S., 237
Amabile, T., 239
Amram, M., 569
Antikarov, V., 568
Arnott, D., 332

B

Baron, J., 242
Bazerman, M., 691, 802
Bell, D., 781
Beyth-Marom, R., 318
Black, F., 565
Bleichrodt, H., 657, 700
Bodily, S. E., 237, 250, 328, 561
Bostic, R., 659
Brown, R. B., 59
Bunn, D., 7, 753

C

Campbell, D. T., 241
Capen, E. C., 337
Celona, J., 656
Chelst, K., 250
Clemen, R., 704
Clemen, R. T., 5, 337
Copeland, T., 568

Copeland, T. E., 569
Corner, J., 12
Corner, J. L., 12
Craig, W., 801

D

Darling, S., 510
Dawes, R., 691, 802
de Bono, E., 243
Deneffe, D., 653
Dixit, A. K., 568

E

Edwards, W., 110, 181, 670, 691, 716, 753, 781, 801, 802
Eisenfuhr, F., 736

F

Finizza, A. J., 344
Fischer, G., 736
Fox, C., 337
Frisch, D., 704

G

Gilovich, T., 802
Glickman, S., 510
Grether, D., 659
Griffin, D., 802
Guyse, J., 637, 683, 713

H

Hagen, J., 693
Hamilton, C., 510
Hammond, J. S., 801
Harriman, E. H., 638, 640, 668
Hastie, R., 691, 802
Henrion, M., 346, 801
Herrnstein, R., 659
Hershey, J., 657, 699
Hobbs, B. F., 736
Hogarth, R., 336, 691, 803
Holloway, C. A., 299
Howard, R. A., 81, 546, 547, 657, 801
Hull, J. C., 564

J

Jacobi, S. K., 736

K

Kahneman, D., 330, 335, 692, 694, 712, 802, 803
Kautalika, N., 569
Keefer, D., 12, 328
Keelin, T., 255
Keenan, P. T., 569
Keeney, R. L., 6, 8, 48, 55, 243, 244, 245, 714, 753, 765, 771, 777, 781, 801
Kirkwood, C., 12, 801

SUBJECT INDEX

extreme
brownies

Mega Mallo Coconut
Brownie

Moby PB Cup
Blondie

Connie's *Today* Show
Peanut Butter Cup Brownie

extreme
brownies

50 recipes for the most over-the-top treats ever

connie weis

photography by renée comet

Andrews McMeel Publishing®

Kansas City · Sydney · London

extreme brownies

Andrews McMeel Publishing, LLC
an Andrews McMeel Universal company
1130 Walnut Street, Kansas City, Missouri 64106

www.andrewsmcmeel.com

14 15 16 17 18 WKT 10 9 8 7 6 5 4 3 2 1

ISBN: 978-1-4494-5032-8

Library of Congress Control Number: 2014930777

Design: Holly Ogden
Photography: Renée Comet
Digital/Photo Assistant: Steven Redfearn
Prop Stylist: Audrey Weppler

attention: schools and businesses
Andrews McMeel books are available at quantity discounts with bulk purchase for educational, business, or sales promotional use. For information, please e-mail the Andrews McMeel Special Sales Department: specialsales@amuniversal.com

On the cover, from top to bottom:
Holy Heavenly Hash Brownie
Cuppa-Cappuccino Brownie
Chocolate Amaretto Cheesecake Brownie

This book is lovingly dedicated to my husband, don,
who has always encouraged me to pursue my dreams,
even when I wanted to be the chick singer in a rock band.

Also, to the late peter coe,
founder of the Taste Unlimited specialty food stores,
who brought me into the foodie world,
where I always wanted to be.

contents

brownies 1

acknowledg ments

I didn't fit into the mold of a cookbook author that publishers pursue in today's world of high-profile "celebrity" chefs: those that have (or competed on) a TV show, own a string of successful restaurants, or maintain a food blog with thousands of followers.

Still, there are some wonderful people who recognized my passion for baking and believed in me enough to encourage me in my pursuit to have my cookbook published. Those include Michael L. Sand at Little, Brown and Company, who was kind enough to respond to my terrible proposal and gently encourage me to enlist the guidance of a literary agent. My slightly improved proposal landed in the hands of literary agent Sharon Bowers, whose personal knowledge of food and baking made her able to see that the recipes were the real deal and took me on as a client.

I also want to thank my editor, Jean Lucas, who again took a chance on a "no-name" and has guided me every step of the way in this journey, even though I am a computer idiot and have driven her crazy.

Huge thanks to the folks (all unpaid volunteers) that run the Old Beach Farmers Market in Virginia Beach, Virginia, specifically Laura Habr and Duff Kliewer. Without becoming a "brownie vendor," the recipes in this book would not have evolved into being. I also am so grateful to all of my customers at the market, many of whom have become dear friends. You have supported me week after week, even when I didn't bring your favorite brownie and promised you the week before that I would.

Finally, thank you to Hoda Kotb and all of the folks at the *Today* show, who enjoyed my brownies and invited me on to do a cooking segment. Hoda, your favorite brownie recipe is here but I know you won't bake it, so just let me know when you have a craving and I'll hook you up.

Whopping Malted
Milk Ball Brownies

why
i created great brownies . . .

How did I become so obsessed with brownies (and blondies) that I literally made them my life's work?

For starters, being an addicted chocoholic, I needed to get my fix, and I found that the brownies I purchased were lacking in true chocolate flavor and chewy texture. Even those from high-end bakeries and specialty food stores didn't deliver the goods, so I set about experimenting to create my own calorie-worthy over-the top treats.

Once I started rolling, I just couldn't stop. Here you will find fifty of my favorite creations, including my best-selling Caramel-Stuffed Sea Salt Brownies, Espresso Cacao Nib Coffee Marshmallow Brownies, Luscious Lemon Coconut White Chocolate Blondies, Holy Heavenly Hash Brownies, Raspberry Ripple Cheesecake Brownies, Triple Blueberry White Chocolate Blondies, Harlequin Truffle Brownies, and many others. Also included is *Today* show host Hoda Kotb's favorite, Connie's *Today* Show Peanut Butter Cup Brownies.

I call my concoctions "extreme" because they are. These are *not* the plain old chocolate and blond squares you have come to expect. My brownies look like none you've ever seen, and taste even better than they look. They're irresistibly fat with gorgeous glazes, frostings, nuts, fresh fruit sauces, candies, and layers of cheesecake and handmade marshmallows.

Fortunately, "extreme" doesn't equal difficult. Yes, many of my brownies and blondies have several steps, but if you look closely at the detailed instructions, they are all quite easy, and most steps (e.g., for glazes, frostings, and candied nuts) are accomplished in a matter of minutes. The end result will garner rave reviews from family and friends. I can attest to that, because after years of working on the recipes, I decided it wouldn't be a bad idea to jump on the farmers' market bandwagon and sell my creations. For four years, I have owned and operated a very successful brownie business at the Old Beach Farmers Market here in Virginia Beach, Virginia.

This cookbook is my passion, a culmination of my life's work, and it's finally time to share my recipes with others. Until now, my recipes were closely guarded, but I'm finally unlocking the vault to not only reveal my recipes but to provide the complete knowledge needed to make them *exactly as I do*.

With that in mind, the next time you're in the baking aisle of your local supermarket, bypass those boxes upon boxes of un-calorie-worthy brownie mixes and proceed directly to the baking ingredients.

I promise you, it will be well worth it!

ingredients
for making
extreme brownies and blondies

baking chocolates

bittersweet
Look at the cocoa mass percentages on the label. I tested all of the recipes in this book using Ghirardelli 60% Cacao Bittersweet Chips, and now it's my bittersweet chocolate of choice. If using other brands, do not exceed 63 percent cocoa mass.

milk
Preferred: Ghirardelli Milk Chocolate Baking Chips.

semisweet
Preferred: Hershey's Special Dark Chips. They are packaged as mildly sweet (not semisweet), but I love the flavor and size, and they melt beautifully for my chocolate drizzle. Acceptable substitute: Nestle Real Semi-Sweet Morsels.

unsweetened
Preferred: Guittard Classic "Oban" Cocoa Liquor (Unsweetened Chocolate) Wafers. Available from www.worldwidechocolate.com. Acceptable substitute: Baker's Unsweetened Baking Chocolate Squares.

white
Preferred: Baker's Premium White Chocolate Baking Bar or Ghirardelli White Chocolate Premium Baking Bar. Avoid white chocolate chips for your white chocolate blondie batter; they have a stabilizer that turns them into a gloopy mess when melted with butter.

baking powder
Preferred: Rumford brand. Make sure that whatever baking powder you use has "aluminum free" on the label to avoid a tinny flavor.

butter
Preferred: Plugrá Unsalted European-Style Butter. Acceptable substitute: Land O'Lakes Unsalted Butter. Avoid bargain or generic brands of butter; they often contain water that will strip your brownies of that coveted shiny sheen on top.

cocoa powder
Preferred: Dutch-processed cocoa: Valrhona Unsweetened Cocoa Powder. Acceptable substitute: Hershey's Special Dark Cocoa. For natural cocoa, Ghirardelli 100% Unsweetened Cocoa Powder.

eggs
Preferred: Large, cage-free. It's the humane thing to do for the hens that provide our eggs.

flour
Preferred: Pillsbury or Gold Medal all-purpose bleached flour.

nuts

peanuts
Preferred: Large Virginia salted peanuts, preferably from Plantation Peanuts, www.plantationpeanuts.com. For coarsely chopped peanuts, I use a nut grinder on the coarse setting. Recommended: Progressive International GFNC-2 Nut Chopper with Non-Skid Base, which is available through www.amazon.com.

pecans and walnuts
Preferred: Diamond brand. I do not like the mess or nut dust produced from chopping nuts, so I buy them in assorted sizes and store them in the refrigerator. If the recipe says "shelled walnuts" or "chopped walnuts," check the name on the Diamond package for the correct size nut: Shelled walnuts are large walnut pieces, almost but not quite walnut halves; chopped walnuts are about ¼-inch pieces.

salt
Use table salt, but never use iodized salt—it imparts a tinny flavor.

sugar
Preferred: Domino brand for all of my sugars (C&H on the West Coast). Acceptable substitute: Dixie Crystals. For granulated sugar, make sure the package indicates pure cane sugar.

vanilla extract
Preferred: Nielsen-Massey Madagascar Bourbon Pure Vanilla. Acceptable substitute: McCormick Pure Vanilla Extract. Always use pure, not imitation.

the right equipment

baking pan
The same size pan is used for every item in this book, so buy a good-quality heavy-weight shiny (not coated) pan. Recommended: 9 by 13-inch Chicago Metallic Commercial II Rectangular Cake Pan. Available through www.surlatable.com.

bowls

mixing bowls
I use melamine (hard plastic) mixing bowls that have a small spout for easy pouring. Recommended: Rosti Margrethe 1.5 Litre Mixing Bowl for the small mixing bowl to weigh dry ingredients, and the Rosti Margrethe 3 Litre Mixing Bowl to mix the batter. Available through www.amazon.com.

stainless-steel bowl
A 2-quart (8½-inch-diameter) stainless-steel mixing bowl can be used as the top for a double boiler. Available through restaurant supply stores.

cutting board
Use a dishwasher-safe, nonporous polypropylene cutting board dedicated to baking purposes only. Cutting boards that have been used for chopping garlic and onions retain their odor and taste no matter how well you wash them.

electric mixer
None of the brownie and blondie batters are made with a mixer; it adds too much volume and cools and thickens the chocolate too quickly, but most of the frostings are made using a handheld electric mixer. Handmade marshmallow is made in a heavy-duty stand mixer using the paddle attachment, not the whisk attachment, which can break the tines apart as the marshmallow thickens. The paddle attachment will produce almost the same volume as the whisk attachment without the risk of breaking.

knives
A high-carbon stainless-steel 10-inch chef's knife is good for cutting the slab, and a 4-inch paring knife can be slipped between the foil and the pan to loosen and remove the slab. Recommended: J. A. Henkels Twin Four Star Knives. Available through www.amazon.com.

measuring cups
You'll need both 1- and 2-cup Pyrex glass measuring cups for melting chocolate in a microwave oven.

measuring spoons
Have two sets—one for dry ingredients and one for wet. Take the spoons designated for dry ingredients off the ring and leave the spoons designated for wet

ingredients on the ring. Recommended: CIA Masters Collection 6-Piece Measuring Spoon Set. Available through www.amazon.com.

saucepan

The best pan for melting butter and chocolate together and to use as the bottom of a double boiler is a heavy-gauge stainless-steel 2-quart saucepan. Lightweight pans will burn the chocolate. Recommended: Cuisinart MCP19-18N MultiClad Pro Stainless Steel 2-Quart Saucepan with Cover. Available through www.amazon.com.

scale

You can use measuring cups and spoons for the recipes with good results, but a digital kitchen scale is far more consistent and efficient for baking. Look for one that weighs to within a tenth of an ounce. Recommended: Escali Arti 15-Pound/7-Kilogram Digital Scale. Available through www.amazon.com.

spatulas

silicone

I use light-colored silicone spatulas for my baking tasks and dark-colored silicone spatulas for pungent ingredients. Recommended: Le Creuset medium and small silicone spatulas. Available through www.surlatable.com.

small offset spatula

A small offset spatula is a must for smoothing brownie and blondie batter in the pan and spreading glazes, frostings, and handmade marshmallow. Recommended: Ateco 4½-inch offset spatula with wooden handle. Available through www.amazon.com.

strainer

You'll need a coarse, medium-mesh strainer that fits inside and can rest on the rim of the small (1.5 L) plastic mixing bowl, so it must be no wider than 6 inches across. Recommended: Norpro Stainless Steel 6-inch Strainer. Available through www.wayfair.com.

thermometers

candy

A candy thermometer is a must-have for making handmade marshmallow. Recommended: Taylor 5983n Candy/jelly Deep Fry Thermometer. Available through www.amazon.com.

oven

An oven that is off by as little as 25°F results in a big difference in baking times and texture. An oven thermometer will help you determine how accurate your oven is so you can correct settings as needed. Recommended: Taylor Oven Guide Thermometer. Available through www.amazon.com.

whisks

You'll need three sizes of stainless-steel whisks for these tasks: a small whisk to blend melting chocolate and butter, a medium whisk to blend the dry ingredients in the small mixing bowl, and a large whisk to blend the batter in the large mixing bowl. Recommended: Norpro 3 Piece Stainless Steel Balloon Whisk Set. Available through www.amazon.com.

pan
preparation

Materials needed to prepare a 9 by 13-inch pan include 12-inch-wide heavy-duty aluminum foil and solid vegetable (not butter-flavored) shortening, such as Crisco. Avoid pan sprays, as they tend to "pool" in places and have an unpleasant taste.

1   To prepare a 9 by 13-inch pan, using one finger, dab *very small portions* of Crisco on the interior bottom and sides of the pan. Then use your finger to spread the dabs around to entirely coat the interior with a very thin layer of shortening, which acts as a glue to hold the aluminum foil in place in the pan.

2   Turn the pan over on the counter, bottom side up. Tear off about a 16-inch length of aluminum foil. Position the foil (shiny side down) evenly over the bottom of the pan, and gently crease the foil over the edges, producing a foil template of the pan. Flip the pan over and place the foil in it, using the creased edges as a guide. Press the foil onto the greased interior, smoothing out any wrinkles. The foil should extend about 1½ inches up each side of the pan. Very lightly grease the foil in the same manner used to prepare the pan for the foil.

techniques
(and cool tips)
for extreme baking perfection

1 Use the designated ingredients and equipment as noted on pages xii–xv.

2 Read the entire recipe before you start to bake. There's nothing more frustrating than starting a recipe and finding you don't have a necessary ingredient, utensil, or piece of equipment. Plus, you want to make sure that ingredients marked "at room temperature" are indeed at room temperature and that you have allowed resting and chilling time for the slab as noted.

3 For best results, use a scale to weigh your ingredients. If you use measuring cups, spoon the flour into the measuring cup, then level off the top using a straight edge, such as the back of a steak knife or the side of a small offset spatula. Do not dip the measuring cup into the flour and level it off—that results in packing the flour, causing greater volume. Weights of cocoa powder vary greatly, but no matter what brand you choose, if you are measuring with a scale, use the weight as given in the recipe.

4 Have your eggs at room temperature. Cold eggs will do two undesirable things: They make the sugar (and salt) harder to dissolve, and they quickly cool down the melted butter/chocolate mixture, causing a thicker batter that is hard to spread. The more you spread a brownie batter around in the pan (which is necessary to do somewhat as brownie batter is thicker than cake batter and must be leveled out), the less likely you are to have that coveted shiny brownie top. It takes 3 to 4 hours for eggs to come to room temperature, especially if they're sitting on cold granite. To speed up the process, turn on the light (not the oven itself) in your oven and place the eggs on a kitchen towel on the middle rack. The oven will soon be much warmer than the kitchen, and your eggs should be ready in an hour or less. A ready egg does not have sweat on it, and the egg should feel as if it's at room temperature when you hold it in the palm of your hand.

5 Strain your granulated sugar. When weighing it out, place a coarse strainer in the small mixing bowl and weigh the sugar through the strainer. After you strain out (and discard) any large, coarse granules, you may need to add more sugar. After the strained, granulated sugar is in the small mixing bowl, remove the strainer, and if the recipe calls for it, add the brown sugar to the bowl. Then use one impeccably clean hand to squeeze the brown sugar, looking for (and discarding)

any large, hard lumps. Always add the salt to the *center top* of the weighed sugar(s). If you get distracted and can't remember whether you added the salt, simply wet the tip of one finger and touch the center of the sugar and taste it. If it tastes like salt, you know you added it.

6   After whisking a melted butter/chocolate mixture into an egg mixture, take the whisk out of the bowl. Use a silicone spatula, not the whisk, to fold in the dry ingredients. And here's my "whisk trick": After the butter/chocolate mixture and vanilla have been whisked into the egg mixture, I rest the handle of the whisk on the granite backsplash of my counter with the tines of the whisk hanging over the spout of the large mixing bowl. Gravity is at work dropping the chocolate mixture on the whisk back into the bowl, while I am at work gathering the dry ingredients needed for the next step.

7   Different add-ins (or subtractions) will change the baking times. If you were more generous with chocolate chips or nuts than the recipe calls for, or you chose to leave out the add-ins altogether, your baking time will vary. Start checking the center of the batter with a toothpick 2 minutes before the designated recipe time and continue to check it every 2 minutes. Your slab is baked if the toothpick comes out clean or has a few crumbs on it. I use round natural toothpicks on brownies and round colored toothpicks on blondies to better see the batter.

8   Always save the waxed wrapping that your butter sticks or pound butter bricks are packaged in— keep them in the refrigerator. They make dandy disposable spoon rests for chocolate-covered whisks and spatulas.

how to

remove the slab, and cut, store, freeze, and ship extreme brownies and blondies

1 Before removing the slab from the pan, always chill your brownie/blondie slab *very* well (at least 7 to 8 hours) in advance. This makes the slab quite firm and easier to handle while removing it from the pan, and the foil can be peeled off of the slab cleanly without sticking. To remove the brownie/ blondie slab from the pan, run a thin knife between the foil and the sides of the pan, then turn the pan over on a sharp angle and push on the center back of the pan, catching the top edge of the slab with your hand. Peel off and discard the foil and place the slab on a cutting board.

2   To get those desirable sharp, clean edges when cutting your brownies, you must first begin with a very well-chilled slab on a cutting board. Using a 10-inch chef's knife, place it directly over the middle of the slab (I use a ruler to find and lightly score the slab on each side) and press the knife directly down through the slab. Never drag a knife through the slab. You now have two equal-size halves. For absolutely perfect edges, the knife should be cleaned in hot water and dried completely before each and every cut. It is your choice whether to cut off the edges. I cut off (and eat) about ¼ inch of the sides that contained the corners of the baked slab, which tend to be a bit dryer. Cut each half in half in the same manner, then cut the four quarters into three equal pieces. You now have twelve 2¾-inch-square generous brownies. For bite-size squares, cut each well-chilled brownie into quarters.

3   Store your cut brownies/blondies in the refrigerator. Brownies or blondies with a firm top surface may be stored in the refrigerator in an airtight container with wax paper between each layer. Those with a delicate frosting, cheesecake, or sticky top, should first be placed individually on patty papers and stored (without stacking) in airtight containers. As for a great cheese, the taste and texture of brownies and blondies are best appreciated at room temperature. Store them chilled, but let them come to room temperature for at least 30 minutes before serving. (Patty papers are individually cut sheets of waxed paper that are widely used in restaurants to separate

and store hamburger patties. I use Heavy-Weight 4¾ by 5-inch Hamburger Patty Papers, which come in a box of 1,000 sheets. Available through www.amazon.com.)

4   Every item in this book (including those with cheesecake layers or handmade marshmallow) may be frozen without compromising the flavor or texture if done properly. For those items with a firm top surface, I generally freeze them in packages of six: I place six well-chilled brownies (two side-by-side strips of three) on an 18-inch-wide large sheet of plastic wrap. Bring the wrap tightly up over the brownies to completely cover and tuck in the sides. Place the wrapped 6-pack in a freezer-safe plastic bag, seal tightly, and freeze. For frosted, fragile, or sticky-topped items, place each brownie on a patty paper, then place them side by side in a container that allows them to be stored without the top surface of the brownie touching the lid, such as a plastic food storage container or pristine pizza box. If using a pizza box, after filling it with your brownies, place the box on a large sheet of plastic wrap and completely wrap the pizza box. Use freezer tape and a Sharpie to label and date the contents of your freezer bags, containers, or boxes. Freeze for up to 3 months. Thaw at room temperature (unwrapped) for 1 hour, or thaw (wrapped) in the refrigerator overnight. (I use Reynolds 2,000 feet by 18-inch wide PVC Foodservice Wrap Film with Slide Cutter, and 10 by 10 by 1¾-inch Corrugated Plain White Pizza/Bakery Box 50/Case both of which are available through www.amazon.com.)

5 I started shipping tins of brownies to family members and friends at Christmas many years ago. I try to ship only in colder weather, but if you are shipping in warmer climates, shipping stores are prepared with Styrofoam-lined boxes and freezer packs. I only ship brownies that I can wrap individually in plastic wrap, which includes plain (yet still extreme) brownies and those topped with firm chocolate glazes. Never ship items with a shorter shelf life; for example, those that contain more perishable elements, such as fresh fruit sauces or cheesecake layers. For the best presentation, tear off about a 10-inch length of 12-inch-wide plastic wrap and place it on a flat surface. Place the brownie, *top surface down*, on the plastic and tightly wrap the brownie, with the excess wrap on the back/bottom of the brownie. Place the individually wrapped brownies in a decorative tin (or box) and completely wrap the outside of the tin in plastic wrap. Place the wrapped tin in a Styrofoam peanut–lined box for protection while shipping. The wrapped brownies are fine at room temperature for 5 to 7 days, so I never ship overnight. I always ship my brownies on a Monday to make sure that they are not languishing in a hot warehouse over the weekend. My friend at the shipping store told me that the box will be handled with more care if marked FRAGILE rather than PERISHABLE, so that's what I write on the outside of the box.

Holy Heavenly Hash
Brownie

brownies

connie's "pms" brownies

makes 12 large squares or 24 smaller bars

This is my signature brownie, and I tell my customers it has taken me from "pre to post." Besides perfect texture, this dark, rich brownie has true chocolate flavor and is the treat I reach for when I'm really craving chocolate. Surprisingly, the cocoa powder brings more to the flavor party than the bittersweet chocolate, so use a very high-quality, high-fat (at least 20 percent) Dutch-processed dark cocoa powder.

Vegetable shortening for pan
3 sticks (12 ounces) unsalted butter
2 cups (12 ounces) 60% cacao bittersweet chocolate chips
6 large eggs, at room temperature
3 cups (1 pound 5 ounces) sugar
1 teaspoon salt
1 tablespoon pure vanilla extract
1¼ cups (5 ounces) cake flour
1 cup and 2 tablespoons (4.2 ounces) Dutch-processed unsweetened cocoa powder

1 To make the brownies, adjust an oven rack to the middle level of the oven and preheat to 350°F. Prepare a 9 by 13-inch baking pan with heavy-duty aluminum foil as shown on page xvi. Lightly grease the foil in the pan.

2 Cut the butter sticks into 1-inch slices. In a small, heavy saucepan, melt the butter pieces over the lowest setting; add the bittersweet chocolate chips. Stir with a small whisk until combined and the chocolate is melted and smooth. Turn off the heat but leave the saucepan on the burner while proceeding with the recipe.

3 Using a large whisk, lightly beat the eggs in a large mixing bowl. Place the sugar and salt in a separate small mixing bowl, then whisk into the eggs just until incorporated. Briefly whisk the melted chocolate mixture, then gradually whisk into the egg mixture until just combined. Briefly whisk in the vanilla.

4 Place the flour and cocoa powder in the small mixing bowl; whisk together to combine. Sift through a medium strainer directly onto the batter; stir in with a silicone spatula until just combined. Pour the batter into the prepared pan and spread evenly with a small offset spatula. Bake for 34 minutes, until a toothpick inserted in the center comes out clean. Transfer the pan to a cooling rack and let cool at room temperature for at least 15 minutes, then refrigerate the pan for 7 to 8 hours, or overnight. See page xix for instructions on removing and cutting the slab, and for refrigerated storage (up to 3 weeks) and freezing guidelines.

virginia peanut sea salt brownies

makes 12 large squares or 24 smaller bars

Virginia peanuts are like none other, and all modesty aside, I'm a Virginia peanut expert. I used to be the buyer for a group of specialty food stores, and every year I would go to the Virginia Food and Beverage Expo in Richmond, Virginia, which showcases the specialty foods made in the state. I sampled all of the Virginia peanut growers' products, and year after year, I thought the peanuts made by Plantation Peanuts (in Wakefield, Virginia) were the best. I love peanuts, and I love the combination of chocolate and sea salt, so the evolution of this brownie was a no-brainer.

brownie batter

Vegetable shortening for pan
2 sticks (8 ounces) unsalted butter
1⅓ cups (8 ounces) 60% cacao bittersweet chocolate chips
4 large eggs, at room temperature
2 cups (14 ounces) sugar
¾ teaspoon salt
1½ teaspoons pure vanilla extract
¾ cup and 1 tablespoon (3.3 ounces) cake flour
¾ cup and 2 tablespoons (2.8 ounces) Dutch-processed unsweetened cocoa powder
1½ cups (6 ounces) salted large Virginia peanuts
⅔ cup (4 ounces) semisweet chocolate chips

chocolate glaze

3½ teaspoons (0.06 ounce) canola oil
¾ cup and 1 tablespoon (5 ounces) semisweet or bittersweet chocolate chips

garnish

1 to 2 teaspoons Maldon flaked sea salt

1 To make the brownies, adjust an oven rack to the middle level of the oven and preheat to 350°F. Prepare a 9 by 13-inch baking pan with heavy-duty aluminum foil as shown on page xvi. Lightly grease the foil in the pan.

2 Cut the butter sticks into 1-inch slices. In a small, heavy saucepan, melt the butter pieces over the lowest setting; add the bittersweet chocolate chips. Stir with a small whisk until combined and the chocolate is melted and smooth. Turn off the heat, but leave the saucepan on the burner while proceeding with the recipe.

3 Using a large whisk, lightly beat the eggs in a large mixing bowl. Place the sugar and salt in a separate small mixing bowl, then whisk into the eggs just until incorporated. Briefly whisk the melted chocolate mixture, then gradually whisk into the egg mixture until just combined. Briefly whisk in the vanilla.

4 Place the flour and cocoa powder in the small mixing bowl; whisk together to combine. Sift through a medium strainer directly onto the batter; stir in with a silicone spatula until just combined. Sprinkle the peanuts and semisweet chocolate chips over the batter; fold in until just combined. Pour the batter into the prepared pan and spread evenly with a small offset spatula. Bake for 28 minutes, until a toothpick inserted in the center comes out clean. Transfer the pan to a cooling rack.

5 To make the chocolate glaze, bring a medium saucepan of water just to a boil. Place the canola oil and semisweet chocolate chips in a metal mixing bowl that will fit over the saucepan to form a double boiler. When the water comes to a boil, take the saucepan off the heat and place the mixing bowl over the hot water. Melt the chocolate chips until perfectly smooth, stirring occasionally with a silicone spatula. Pour the glaze over the brownie slab. Using a small offset spatula, spread the glaze evenly, then sprinkle the sea salt over the glaze. Let the glazed slab sit at room temperature for at least 30 minutes, then refrigerate the pan for 7 to 8 hours, or overnight. See page xix for instructions on removing and cutting the slab, and for refrigerated storage (up to 2 weeks) and freezing guidelines.

chookie brownies

makes 12 large squares

Can't decide between a chocolate chip cookie or a brownie? Well, now you don't have to. My Chookie Brownies are a delightful concoction of a baked chocolate chip cookie layer topped with a layer of dark, rich brownie. To send it over the top, there is a thick semisweet chocolate glaze, which helps secure an individual chocolate chip cookie for each brownie. The garnish cookies are made from the same dough as the base layer, and there will be a few extras. If you've ever worked in a restaurant kitchen, you know these will be designated as chef's treats, or "scooby" snacks.

chocolate chip cookie layer
1½ sticks (6 ounces) unsalted butter, at room temperature
½ cup (3.5 ounces) granulated sugar
1 packed cup (8 ounces) dark brown sugar
¾ teaspoon salt
2 large eggs, at room temperature
2 teaspoons pure vanilla extract
1 tablespoon (0.08 ounce) dark corn syrup
2 cups (9 ounces) bleached all-purpose flour
½ cup (2 ounces) cake flour
1 teaspoon baking soda
1 (12-ounce) package Hershey's Special Dark Chocolate Chips
Vegetable shortening for pan

brownie batter
1½ sticks (6 ounces) unsalted butter
1 cup (6 ounces) 60% cacao bittersweet chocolate chips
3 large eggs, at room temperature
1½ cups (10.5 ounces) sugar
½ teaspoon salt
1 teaspoon pure vanilla extract
½ cup and 1½ tablespoons (2.5 ounces) cake flour
½ cup and 1 tablespoon (2.1 ounces) Dutch-processed unsweetened cocoa powder

semisweet chocolate glaze
2½ tablespoons (0.09 ounce) canola oil
1 (10-ounce) package semisweet chocolate chips

1 To make the chocolate chip cookie layer, use a stand mixer fitted with the paddle attachment and beat the butter briefly on medium speed to soften. Place the sugars and salt in a small mixing bowl; gradually add to the butter, and beat on medium speed until lighter in color and creamy, 3 to 4 minutes. Increase the mixer speed to medium-high and add the eggs, one at a time, beating well after each addition. Scrape down the sides of the bowl with a silicone spatula and beat again briefly. Reduce the mixer speed to low; add the vanilla and corn syrup. Increase the speed to medium and beat for 30 seconds. Scrape down the sides of the bowl and beat again briefly.

2 Place the flours and baking soda in the small mixing bowl; whisk together to combine. Sift through a medium strainer onto a sheet of wax paper, then return the sifted mixture to the bowl. On low speed, add the dry ingredients to the wet mixture and beat until just combined. Sprinkle the chocolate chips into the batter

and beat on low speed until just combined. Remove the bowl and paddle from the mixer stand and thoroughly fold the dough with a silicone spatula to combine well. Cover the bowl tightly with plastic wrap and refrigerate for at least 30 minutes.

3   Prepare a 9 by 13-inch baking pan with heavy-duty aluminum foil as shown on page xvi. Lightly grease the foil in the pan.

4   Remove 1 cup (9 ounces) of the cookie dough and set it aside. Spread the remaining cookie dough evenly on the foil-lined bottom of the baking pan, then smooth it out as much as possible with a small offset spatula. Place the pan in the refrigerator to chill the dough for at least 1 hour before baking. Adjust an oven rack to the middle level of the oven and preheat to 350°F. Bake for 25 minutes, until the top is nicely browned and firm. Transfer the pan to a wire cooling rack. Maintain the oven temperature at 350°F.

5   While the cookie base is baking, line a half-sheet pan with parchment paper. Using a 1¼-inch scoop, form the remaining cookie dough into about twenty-two balls. Stagger them on the sheet pan and bake for 7 minutes, turn the pan, and bake an additional 4 to 5 minutes, until the cookies are lightly browned. Transfer the cookies to a cooling rack.

6   To make the brownies, cut the butter sticks into 1-inch slices. In a small, heavy saucepan, melt the butter pieces over the lowest setting; add the bittersweet chocolate chips. Stir with a small whisk until combined and the chocolate is melted and smooth. Turn off the heat but leave the saucepan on the burner while proceeding with the recipe.

7   Using a large whisk, lightly beat the eggs in a large mixing bowl. Place the sugar and salt in a separate small mixing bowl, then whisk into the eggs just until incorporated. Briefly whisk the melted chocolate mixture, then gradually whisk into the egg mixture until just combined. Briefly whisk in the vanilla.

8   Place the flour and cocoa powder in the small mixing bowl; whisk together to combine. Sift through a medium strainer directly onto the batter; stir in with a silicone spatula until just combined. Pour the batter over the cooled cookie dough layer and spread evenly with a small offset spatula. Bake for 25 minutes, until a toothpick inserted in the center comes out clean. Transfer the pan to a cooling rack and let cool at room temperature for at least 15 minutes.

9   To make the semisweet chocolate glaze, bring a medium saucepan of water just to a boil. Place the canola oil and the semisweet chocolate chips in a metal mixing bowl that will fit over the saucepan to form a double boiler. When the water comes to a boil, take the saucepan off the heat and place the mixing bowl over the hot water. Melt the chocolate chips until perfectly smooth, stirring occasionally with a silicone spatula. Pour the glaze over the brownie slab, then use a small offset spatula to spread it evenly. Let the glazed slab sit at room temperature for at least 1 hour, then refrigerate the pan for 7 to 8 hours, or overnight. See page xix for instructions on removing the slab from the pan and cutting it into 12 large squares. Garnish each brownie square with a chocolate chip cookie. See page xxi for refrigerated storage (up to 2 weeks) and freezing guidelines.

connie's caramel-stuffed sea salt brownies

makes 12 large squares or 24 smaller bars

Like everyone who is dedicated to baking and cooking, I am a cookbook junkie. My prerequisite for buying a cookbook is that as I peruse it, there has to be at least one intriguing recipe that I know I will want to make within a week. Otherwise, the book will sit collecting dust on a bookshelf with so many other virginal cookbooks—ones I've browsed through but never actually used. I have always said that if I take away one good recipe, inspiration, or tip from a cookbook (or magazine), the cost was well worth it. That said, I'm telling you now that this recipe is worth the price of this book. It is by far my most requested and sold brownie, and I can't believe I'm giving up my recipe with the techniques I developed to make it just so perfect. Oy!

caramel layer
⅓ cup and 1 teaspoon (3 ounces) heavy whipping cream
2 tablespoons (1 ounce) unsalted butter
12 ounces (about 43) Kraft Traditional Caramels
2 tablespoons and 1 teaspoon bleached all-purpose flour
1 teaspoon pure vanilla extract

brownie batter
Vegetable shortening for pan
2 sticks (8 ounces) unsalted butter
3 ounces unsweetened baking chocolate
1 cup (6 ounces) 60% cacao bittersweet chocolate chips
4 large eggs, at room temperature
1 cup (7 ounces) granulated sugar
1 packed cup (8 ounces) light brown sugar
¾ teaspoon salt
1½ teaspoons pure vanilla extract
1 cup (4.5 ounces) bleached all-purpose flour
½ teaspoon baking powder

milk chocolate glaze
3½ teaspoons (0.06 ounce) canola oil
¾ cup and 1 tablespoon (5 ounces) milk chocolate chips

garnish
1 to 2 teaspoons Maldon flaked sea salt

1   To make the caramel layer, place the cream and butter in a 2-quart saucier or saucepan. Begin to melt the mixture over medium-low heat. Unwrap the caramels, and as each is unwrapped, add it to the mixture. Cook over medium-low heat, stirring occasionally with a silicone spatula, until the caramels are melted and completely smooth. While the caramels are slowly melting, proceed with the brownie batter. Finish preparing the caramel once the brownie base is in the oven.

2   To make the brownies, adjust an oven rack to the middle level of the oven and preheat to 350°F. Prepare a 9 by 13-inch baking pan with heavy-duty aluminum foil as shown on page xvi. Lightly grease the foil in the pan.

3   Cut the butter sticks into 1-inch slices. In a small, heavy saucepan, melt the butter pieces over the lowest setting. While the butter is melting, chop the unsweetened chocolate into ¼-inch pieces and add to the melted butter along with the bittersweet chocolate chips. Use a small whisk to speed the melting process. When the chocolate is melted and completely smooth, turn off the heat but leave the saucepan on the burner while proceeding with the recipe.

4   Using a large whisk, lightly beat the eggs in a large mixing bowl. Place the sugars and salt in a separate small mixing bowl, then whisk into the eggs just until incorporated. Briefly whisk the melted chocolate mixture, then gradually whisk into the egg mixture until just combined. Briefly whisk in the vanilla.

5   Place the flour and baking powder in the small mixing bowl; whisk together to combine. Sift through a medium strainer directly onto the batter; stir in with a silicone spatula until just combined. Pour half (1 pound 4 ounces) of the brownie batter into the prepared pan. The best way to do this is by weight. Place the prepared pan on a scale, tare off (subtract) the weight of the pan, and scrape the correct weight of batter directly into the pan. Spread evenly with a small offset spatula; bake for 15 minutes, until a toothpick inserted in the center comes out clean. Transfer the pan to a cooling rack. Finish the caramel while the brownie base is baking. The caramel should be poured onto the very hot brownie base as soon as it is removed from the oven.

6   To finish the caramel layer, once the caramels are completely melted and smooth, sift (or strain) the flour directly onto the mixture, and stir in well. Remove the pan from the heat and stir in the vanilla. Pour the cooked caramel over the hot brownie base and spread evenly with a small offset spatula. Dollop the remaining brownie batter evenly over the caramel layer and carefully spread to the edges with the offset spatula, covering the caramel layer. Return the pan to the oven and bake for an additional 20 minutes. You should see some bubbling caramel around the edges of the brownie slab. Transfer the pan to a cooling rack and let cool at room temperature for at least 15 minutes.

9

10

7 To make the milk chocolate glaze, bring a medium saucepan of water just to a boil. Place the canola oil and milk chocolate chips in a metal mixing bowl that will fit over the saucepan to form a double boiler, When the water comes to a boil, take the saucepan off the heat and place the mixing bowl over the hot water. Stir with a small silicone spatula until the chocolate is melted and perfectly smooth. Pour the glaze evenly over the top of the warm brownie slab. Using a small offset spatula, spread the glaze evenly, then sprinkle the sea salt over the glaze. Let the glazed slab sit at room temperature for at least 30 minutes, then refrigerate the pan for 7 to 8 hours, or overnight. See page xix for instructions on removing and cutting the slab, and for refrigerated storage (up to 2 weeks) and freezing guidelines. The caramel next to the pan gets too hard and is unpleasant to eat; cut off and discard all of the edges around the brownie slab.

triple chocolate brownies

makes 12 large squares or 24 smaller bars

For those who want a more traditional (but still extreme) brownie that is not quite as intense as my "PMS" Brownie, this is for you. The triple chocolate barrage comes from unsweetened and bittersweet chocolate in the batter and semisweet chocolate in the drizzle. If you want to add chocolate chips to the batter, be my guest, but I like biting into this chewy brownie just the way it is, and it really doesn't need any more chocolate.

brownie batter
Vegetable shortening for pan
3 sticks (12 ounces) unsalted butter
4½ ounces unsweetened baking chocolate
1½ cups (9 ounces) 60% cacao bittersweet chocolate chips
6 large eggs, at room temperature
1½ cups (10.5 ounces) granulated sugar
1½ packed cups (12 ounces) light brown sugar
1 teaspoon salt
1 tablespoon pure vanilla extract
1½ cups (6.8 ounces) bleached all-purpose flour
¾ teaspoon baking powder

chocolate drizzle
1 tablespoon (0.05 ounce) unsalted butter
1 teaspoon (0.02 ounce) light corn syrup
¼ cup (1.5 ounces) semisweet chocolate chips
1 teaspoon very hot water

1 To make the brownies, adjust an oven rack to the middle level of the oven and preheat to 350°F. Prepare a 9 by 13-inch baking pan with heavy-duty aluminum foil as shown on page xvi. Lightly grease the foil in the pan.

2 Cut the butter sticks into 1-inch slices. In a small, heavy saucepan, melt the butter pieces over the lowest setting. While the butter is melting, chop the unsweetened chocolate into ¼-inch pieces and add to the melted butter along with the bittersweet chocolate chips. Use a small whisk to speed the melting process. When the chocolate is melted and completely smooth, turn off the heat but leave the saucepan on the burner while proceeding with the recipe.

3 Using a large whisk, lightly beat the eggs in a large mixing bowl. Place the sugars and salt in a separate small mixing bowl, then whisk into the eggs just until incorporated. Briefly whisk the melted chocolate mixture, then gradually whisk into the egg mixture until just combined. Briefly whisk in the vanilla. You can set aside the saucepan—no need to wash it—to use for the chocolate drizzle.

4 Place the flour and baking powder in the small mixing bowl; whisk together to combine. Sift through a medium strainer directly onto the batter; stir in with a silicone spatula until just combined. Pour the batter into the prepared pan and spread evenly with a small offset spatula. Bake for 34 minutes, until a toothpick inserted in the center comes out clean. Transfer the pan to a cooling rack and let cool at room temperature for at least 15 minutes.

5 To make the chocolate drizzle, melt the butter and corn syrup over low heat in a small, heavy saucepan. Remove the pan from the heat and add the chocolate chips; stir with a small silicone spatula until the chocolate is melted and smooth. Stir in the hot water to thin it out. Using the spatula, drizzle thin, random stripes over the top of the cooled brownie slab. Let the drizzle cool at room temperature for 30 minutes, then refrigerate the pan for 7 to 8 hours, or overnight. See page xix for instructions on removing and cutting the slab, and for refrigerated storage (up to 3 weeks) and freezing guidelines.

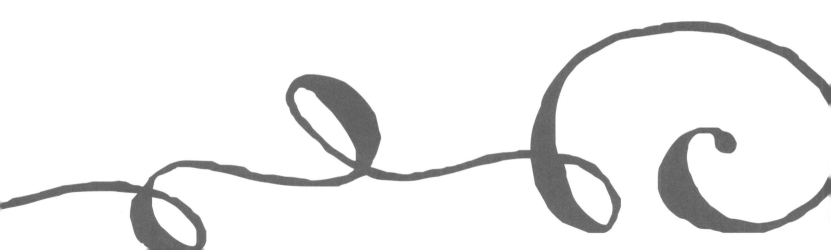

kitty kat krunch brownies

makes 12 large squares or 24 smaller bars

Inspiration for a new recipe can come from anywhere, but for me, it usually starts with a new ingredient I can incorporate into a brownie or blondie. The other day at the grocery store, I spied bags of Kit Kat Minis (unwrapped mini candy bars) cunningly displayed right by the registers, where we are at our most vulnerable. Well, they were too convenient (already unwrapped and cut) and too delicious to not use in a brownie. To emphasize the crunch of the mini candy bars, I caramelized chocolate puffed rice cereal for a topping on a luscious chocolate buttercream frosting. You may be wondering if the Kit Kats stay crunchy in the baked brownie. Yes. Yes, they do.

brownie batter
Vegetable shortening for pan
2 sticks (8 ounces) unsalted butter
3 ounces unsweetened baking chocolate
1 cup (6 ounces) 60% cacao bittersweet chocolate chips
4 large eggs, at room temperature
1 cup (7 ounces) granulated sugar
1 packed cup (8 ounces) light brown sugar
¾ teaspoon salt
1½ teaspoons pure vanilla extract
1 cup (4.5 ounces) bleached all-purpose flour
½ teaspoon baking powder
1 (8-ounce) bag Kit Kat Minis

candied chocolate rice cereal topping
Vegetable shortening for pan
1½ cups (1.3 ounces) chocolate puffed rice cereal, such as Cocoa Krispies
½ cup (3.5 ounces) granulated sugar
1 tablespoon water
1 teaspoon (0.02 ounce) light corn syrup
½ teaspoon kosher salt

chocolate buttercream frosting
½ cup and 1 tablespoon (5 ounces) heavy whipping cream
1¼ cups (7.5 ounces) 60% cacao bittersweet chocolate chips
10 tablespoons (5 ounces) unsalted butter, at room temperature
⅛ teaspoon salt
2 tablespoons unsweetened Dutch-processed cocoa powder
1 teaspoon vanilla extract

1   To make the brownies, adjust an oven rack to the middle level of the oven and preheat to 350°F. Prepare a 9 by 13-inch baking pan with heavy-duty aluminum foil as shown on page xvi. Lightly grease the foil in the pan.

2   Cut the butter sticks into 1-inch slices. In a small, heavy saucepan, melt the butter pieces over the lowest setting. While the butter is melting, chop the unsweetened chocolate into ¼-inch pieces and add to the melted butter along with the bittersweet chocolate chips. Use a small whisk to speed the melting process. When the chocolate is melted and completely smooth, turn off the heat but leave the saucepan on the burner while proceeding with the recipe.

3   Using a large whisk, lightly beat the eggs in a large mixing bowl. Place the sugars and salt in a separate small mixing bowl, then whisk into the eggs just until incorporated. Briefly whisk the melted chocolate mixture, then gradually whisk into the egg mixture until just combined. Briefly whisk in the vanilla.

4   Place the flour and baking powder in the small mixing bowl; whisk together to combine. Sift through a medium strainer directly onto the batter; stir in with a silicone spatula until just combined. Pour the batter into the prepared pan and spread evenly with a small offset spatula. Push the Kit Kat Minis into the batter; do not place any within ½ inch of the pan sides. Use the offset spatula to cover the candy with the batter. Bake for 28 minutes, until a toothpick inserted in the center comes out clean. Transfer the pan to a cooling rack.

5   To make the candied chocolate rice cereal topping, lightly grease a quarter-sheet pan with vegetable shortening, then line with parchment paper. Measure out the cereal; set aside. Place the sugar, water, corn syrup, and salt in a small, heavy saucepan; stir with a small silicone spatula just to combine. Bring to a boil over moderately high heat. Once the mixture comes to a boil, lower the heat to moderate and boil undisturbed until a medium amber-colored caramel forms, about 5 minutes. Remove the pan from the heat and stir in the cereal. Scrape the caramelized cereal onto the prepared pan and spread it out with a small offset spatula. Let cool at room temperature. Note: This makes more than you will need for the recipe, but the candied cereal topping can be stored in an airtight container at room temperature for up to 2 weeks. It's delicious to munch on for a snack and just wonderful on ice cream.

6   To make the frosting, bring a medium saucepan of water just to a simmer. Place the cream and chocolate chips in a metal mixing bowl that will fit over the saucepan to form a double boiler, making sure the bottom of the mixing bowl does not touch the simmering water. Stir the mixture with a silicone spatula until the chocolate is melted and completely smooth. Remove the mixing bowl from the double boiler and refrigerate the bowl until the mixture has cooled to the consistency of pudding, about 15 minutes. While the frosting mixture is chilling, cut up the candied chocolate rice cereal topping into ¼-inch pieces, using a sharp chef's knife.

7   Cut the butter into 1-inch pieces. Using a handheld electric mixer on medium speed, beat the butter pieces into the chilled cream mixture. Beat in the salt. Strain (or sift) the cocoa powder directly onto the mixture and beat in. Add the vanilla and beat in, starting on low and increasing to high speed, until the frosting is light and fluffy, about 1 minute. Dollop the frosting over the brownie slab. Using a small offset spatula, spread the frosting evenly. Garnish the frosting with some of the chopped candied chocolate rice cereal topping, then use the back of a metal spatula to lightly tap on the topping pieces to slightly embed them into the frosting. Refrigerate the pan for 7 to 8 hours, or overnight. See page xix for instructions on removing and cutting the slab, and for refrigerated storage (up to 2 weeks) and freezing guidelines.

big fat walnut chocolate chip brownies

makes 12 large squares or 24 smaller bars

When asked about my favorite brownie (and that happens all the time), I can never narrow it down to just one. Since I'm always developing new brownies and blondies, my favorite is usually whichever one I've just created, but this brownie is always among the first I rattle off and is the one most likely to be found in my refrigerator on any given day. Notice that shelled as well as chopped walnuts are listed in the ingredients. Look for those identifying names on the walnut packages: Shelled walnuts are large walnut pieces, almost but not quite walnut halves; chopped walnuts are about ¼-inch pieces. I buy different packages to suit my baking needs, but if you prefer, simply chop the shelled walnuts to add to the top of the batter.

Vegetable shortening for pan
1½ cups (6 ounces) shelled walnuts
3 sticks (12 ounces) unsalted butter
4½ ounces unsweetened baking chocolate
1½ cups (9 ounces) 60% cacao bittersweet chocolate chips
6 large eggs, at room temperature
1½ cups (10.5 ounces) granulated sugar
1½ packed cups (12 ounces) light brown sugar
1 teaspoon salt
1 tablespoon pure vanilla extract
1½ cups (6.8 ounces) bleached all-purpose flour
¾ teaspoon baking powder
⅔ cup (4 ounces) semisweet chocolate chips
¼ cup (1 ounce) chopped walnuts

1 To make the brownies, adjust an oven rack to the middle level of the oven and preheat to 350°F. Prepare a 9 by 13-inch baking pan with heavy-duty aluminum foil as shown on page xvi. Lightly grease the foil in the pan.

2 Sprinkle the 1½ cups of shelled walnuts out onto a quarter-sheet pan. Toast in the oven just until fragrant, about 7 minutes, then transfer the pan to a cooling rack. Maintain the oven temperature at 350°F.

3 Cut the butter sticks into 1-inch slices. In a small, heavy saucepan, melt the butter pieces over the lowest setting. While the butter is melting, chop the unsweetened chocolate into ¼-inch pieces and add to the melted butter along with the bittersweet chocolate chips. Use a small whisk to speed the melting process. When the chocolate is melted and completely smooth, turn off the heat but leave the saucepan on the burner while proceeding with the recipe.

4 Using a large whisk, lightly beat the eggs in a large mixing bowl. Place the sugars and salt in a separate small mixing bowl, then whisk into the eggs just until incorporated. Briefly whisk the melted chocolate mixture, then gradually whisk into the egg mixture until just combined. Briefly whisk in the vanilla.

5 Place the flour and baking powder in the small mixing bowl; whisk together to combine. Sift through a medium strainer directly onto the batter; stir in with a silicone spatula until just combined. Sprinkle the toasted walnuts and ½ cup of the semisweet chocolate chips over the batter; fold in until just combined. Pour the batter into the prepared pan and spread evenly with a small offset spatula. Place the remaining chocolate chips as well as the chopped walnuts evenly over the top of the batter. Bake for 35 minutes, until a toothpick inserted in the center comes out clean. Transfer the pan to a cooling rack and let cool at room temperature for at least 15 minutes, then refrigerate the pan for 7 to 8 hours, or overnight. See page xix for instructions on removing and cutting the slab, and for refrigerated storage (up to 3 weeks) and freezing guidelines.

crunchy candied pecan brownies

makes 12 large squares or 24 smaller bars

Although I live in Virginia, I'm not a native Southerner, which might explain why I much prefer walnuts to pecans. So, if pecans are the star of a particular brownie recipe, I'm going to enhance them. Large candied pecans grace the top of these brownies, and more are ground up and folded into the brownie batter itself, providing a textural and flavor experience not to be missed. Grinding candied nuts in a food processor bowl may scratch the interior of the bowl, so if you want to keep your processor bowl pristine, chop them up with a chef's knife.

candied pecans

4 tablespoons (2 ounces) granulated sugar
2 packed tablespoons (1 ounce) light brown sugar
½ teaspoon ground cinnamon
¼ teaspoon salt
1 egg white, at room temperature
2 cups (8 ounces) pecan halves

brownie batter

Vegetable shortening for pan
3 sticks (12 ounces) unsalted butter
4½ ounces unsweetened baking chocolate
1½ cups (9 ounces) 60% cacao bittersweet chocolate chips
6 large eggs, at room temperature
1½ cups (10.5 ounces) granulated sugar
1½ packed cups (12 ounces) light brown sugar
1 teaspoon salt
2 teaspoons pure vanilla extract
1½ cups (6.8 ounces) bleached all-purpose flour
¾ teaspoon baking powder

1   To make the candied pecans, adjust an oven rack to the middle level of the oven and preheat to 350°F. Line a half-sheet pan with a silicone baking mat. Place the sugars, cinnamon, and salt in a small bowl; whisk to combine. Place the egg white in a small mixing bowl; whisk until frothy. Add the pecans and stir with a silicone spatula. Sprinkle the sugar mixture over the pecans and fold in well. Turn the nuts out onto the prepared sheet pan and spread into a thin layer with the spatula. Bake for 13 minutes, then turn the nuts over with a metal spatula and spread out again. Continue baking until the nuts are fragrant and the sugar coating is caramelized, about another 6 minutes. Transfer the pan to a cooling rack.

2   To make the brownies, maintain the oven temperature at 350°F. Prepare a 9 by 13-inch baking pan with heavy-duty aluminum foil as shown on page xvi. Lightly grease the foil in the pan.

20

3 Cut the butter sticks into 1-inch slices. In a small, heavy saucepan, melt the butter pieces over the lowest setting. While the butter is melting, chop the unsweetened chocolate into ¼-inch pieces and add to the melted butter along with the bittersweet chocolate chips. Use a small whisk to speed the melting process. When the chocolate is melted and completely smooth, turn off the heat but leave the saucepan on the burner while proceeding with the recipe.

4 Using a large whisk, lightly beat the eggs in a large mixing bowl. Place the sugars and salt in a separate small mixing bowl, then whisk into the eggs just until incorporated. Briefly whisk the melted chocolate mixture, then gradually whisk into the egg mixture until just combined. Briefly whisk in the vanilla.

5 Place the flour and baking powder in the small mixing bowl; whisk together to combine. Sift through a medium strainer directly onto the batter; stir in with a silicone spatula until just combined.

6 Place 1½ cups of the candied pecans in the bowl of a food processor. Pulse until finely chopped, but not ground into a paste. Sprinkle the ground pecans over the batter; fold in until just combined. Pour the batter into the prepared pan and spread evenly with a small offset spatula. Place the remaining pecans evenly over the batter. Bake for 38 minutes, until a toothpick inserted in the center comes out clean. Transfer the pan to a cooling rack and let cool at room temperature for at least 15 minutes, then refrigerate the pan for 7 to 8 hours, or overnight. See page xix for instructions on removing and cutting the slab, and for refrigerated storage (up to 3 weeks) and freezing guidelines.

black walnut fudge frosted brownies

makes 12 large squares or 24 smaller bars

Black walnuts have a distinct flavor all their own, and they are very special to me. My mother, who died when I was twelve, used to make black walnut fudge and bring the saucepan into the living room, where we would sit and take turns stirring it vigorously with a wooden spoon until the fudge was thick and shiny. The nuts in the fudge were supplied by her best friend, Mollie, who let me tag along and help pick up the large green black walnut balls off the ground, making our hands black in the process. Then Mollie would do the arduous task of hulling and extracting the nuts. The black walnut fudge frosting is easy to make, and it really does have the consistency and taste of fudge, which for me must always contain black walnuts.

brownie batter
Vegetable shortening for pan
2 sticks (8 ounces) unsalted butter
3 ounces unsweetened baking chocolate
1 cup (6 ounces) 60% cacao bittersweet chocolate chips
4 large eggs, at room temperature
1 cup (7 ounces) granulated sugar
1 packed cup (8 ounces) light brown sugar
¾ teaspoon salt
1½ teaspoons pure vanilla extract
1 cup (4.5 ounces) bleached all-purpose flour
½ teaspoon baking powder

black walnut fudge frosting
1 stick (4 ounces) unsalted butter
6 tablespoons (3.4 ounces) whole milk
2 ounces unsweetened baking chocolate
1 pound confectioners' sugar
1 teaspoon pure vanilla extract
1 cup (4.5 ounces) chopped black walnuts

1 To make the brownies, adjust an oven rack to the middle level of the oven and preheat to 350°F. Prepare a 9 by 13-inch baking pan with heavy-duty aluminum foil as shown on page xvi. Lightly grease the foil in the pan.

2 Cut the butter sticks into 1-inch slices. In a small, heavy saucepan, melt the butter pieces over the lowest setting. While the butter is melting, chop the unsweetened chocolate into ¼-inch pieces and add to the melted butter along with the bittersweet chocolate chips. Use a small whisk to speed the melting process. When the chocolate is melted and completely smooth, turn off the heat but leave the saucepan on the burner while proceeding with the recipe.

3 Using a large whisk, lightly beat the eggs in a large mixing bowl. Place the sugars and salt in a separate small mixing bowl, then whisk into the eggs just until incorporated. Briefly whisk the melted chocolate mixture, then gradually whisk into the egg mixture until just combined. Briefly whisk in the vanilla. You can set aside the saucepan and whisk—no need to wash them—to use for the black walnut fudge frosting.

4 Place the flour and baking powder in the small mixing bowl; whisk together to combine. Sift through a medium strainer directly onto the batter; stir in with a silicone spatula until just combined. Pour the batter into the prepared pan and spread evenly with a small offset spatula. Bake for 28 minutes, until a toothpick inserted in the center comes out clean. Transfer the pan to a cooling rack.

5 To make the black walnut fudge frosting, cut the butter into ½-inch-thick slices. Place the butter and milk in the reserved saucepan and begin to cook over medium-low heat. Finely chop the unsweetened chocolate and add it to the melting butter mixture. Increase the heat to medium-high and cook, whisking constantly, until the butter and chocolate are melted and the mixture is slightly thickened; the mixture should not come to a boil. Remove the pan from the heat.

6 Strain (or sift) the confectioners' sugar into a medium bowl. Add the melted chocolate mixture; whisk well to combine. Whisk in the vanilla. Sprinkle the black walnuts over the frosting; stir in with a spatula. Pour the warm frosting over the still-warm brownie slab and spread evenly with a small offset spatula. Let the frosted slab sit at room temperature for at least 30 minutes, then refrigerate the pan for 7 to 8 hours, or overnight. See page xix for instructions on removing and cutting the slab, and for refrigerated storage (up to 2 weeks) and freezing guidelines.

la dolce vita hazelnut brownies

makes 12 large squares or 24 smaller bars

Europeans have long embraced the marriage of chocolate and hazelnuts with good reason; it's a marriage made in flavor heaven. This brownie is loaded with toasted whole hazelnuts, then topped with a chocolate hazelnut frosting and chopped milk chocolate hazelnut candy. After toasting the whole raw hazelnuts, it is a must to remove the skins as they are quite bitter. I have a kitchen towel designated just for this task, because rubbing off the skins causes stains that no laundry detergent (that I've tried) will remove.

brownie batter

1¼ cups (7 ounces) whole raw hazelnuts

Vegetable shortening for pan

2 sticks (8 ounces) unsalted butter

1⅓ cups (8 ounces) 60% cacao bittersweet chocolate chips

4 large eggs, at room temperature

2 cups (14 ounces) sugar

¾ teaspoon salt

1½ teaspoons vanilla extract

¾ cup and 1 tablespoon (3.3 ounces) cake flour

¾ cup and 2 tablespoons (2.8 ounces) Dutch-processed unsweetened cocoa powder

chocolate hazelnut buttercream frosting

½ cup and 1 tablespoon (5 ounces) heavy whipping cream

1¼ cups (7.5 ounces) 60% cacao bittersweet chocolate chips

10 tablespoons (5 ounces) unsalted butter, at room temperature

⅛ teaspoon salt

2 tablespoons unsweetened Dutch-processed cocoa powder

1 teaspoon hazelnut flavor

milk chocolate hazelnut candy garnish

1 (4.4-ounce) Milk Chocolate Hazelnut Candy Bar (Lindt)

1 To toast and skin the hazelnuts, adjust an oven rack to the middle level of the oven and preheat to 350°F. Spread the hazelnuts in a single layer onto a quarter-sheet pan. Toast the hazelnuts for 15 minutes, until the skins are uniformly cracked. Immediately pour the hot nuts into the center of a thick cotton kitchen towel. Pull the towel up around the nuts and twist tightly, making a sack. Place the towel sack in a plastic bag and let stand at room temperature for at least 10 minutes, allowing the nuts to steam. Discard the plastic bag but leave the nuts in the towel. Using your hands, rub the nuts vigorously in the towel against the kitchen counter, so the friction created by the nuts rubbing together removes most of the skins. Pick out the cleaned hazelnuts and place in a bowl; repeat the process until all of the nuts are skinned. Use your fingers to pick off any remaining skin. Maintain the oven temperature at 350°F.

2 To make the brownies, prepare a 9 by 13-inch baking pan with heavy-duty aluminum foil as shown on page xvi. Lightly grease the foil in the pan. Cut the butter sticks into 1-inch slices. In a small, heavy saucepan, melt the butter pieces over the lowest setting; add the bittersweet chocolate chips. Stir with a small whisk until combined and the chocolate is melted and smooth. Turn off the heat but leave the saucepan on the burner while proceeding with the recipe.

3 Using a large whisk, lightly beat the eggs in a large mixing bowl. Place the sugar and salt in a separate small mixing bowl, then whisk into the eggs just until incorporated. Briefly whisk the melted chocolate mixture, then gradually whisk into the egg mixture until just combined. Briefly whisk in the vanilla.

4 Place the flour and cocoa powder in the small mixing bowl; whisk together to combine. Sift through a medium strainer directly onto the batter; stir in with a silicone spatula until just combined. Sprinkle the hazelnuts over the batter and fold in until just combined. Pour the batter into the prepared pan and spread evenly with a small offset spatula. Bake for 26 minutes, until a toothpick inserted in the center comes out clean. Transfer the pan to a cooling rack.

5 To make the frosting, bring a medium saucepan of water just to a simmer. Place the cream and chocolate chips in a metal mixing bowl that will fit over the saucepan to form a double boiler. Make sure the bottom of the mixing bowl does not touch the simmering water. Stir the mixture with a silicone spatula until the chocolate is melted and completely smooth. Remove the mixing bowl from the double boiler and refrigerate the bowl until the mixture has cooled to the consistency of pudding, about 15 minutes. While the frosting mixture is chilling, cut up the hazelnut candy bar into ¼-inch pieces, using a sharp chef's knife.

6 Cut the butter into 1-inch pieces. Using a handheld electric mixer on medium speed, beat the butter pieces into the chilled cream mixture. Beat in the salt. Strain (or sift) the cocoa powder directly onto the mixture and beat in. Add the hazelnut flavor and beat in, starting on low and increasing to high speed, until the frosting is light and fluffy, about 1 minute. Dollop the frosting over the brownie slab. Using a small offset spatula, spread the frosting evenly. Garnish the frosting with the chopped candy bar, then use the back of a metal spatula to lightly tap on the candy pieces to slightly embed them into the frosting. Refrigerate the pan for 7 to 8 hours, or overnight. See page xix for instructions on removing and cutting the slab, and for refrigerated storage (up to 2 weeks) and freezing guidelines.

harlequin truffle brownies

makes 12 large squares or 24 smaller bars

The original French truffle was simply a roughly rolled hunk of chocolate ganache dusted in cocoa powder to emulate the coveted Black Périgord truffle mushroom. Today, almost every chocolatier gloms onto the name *truffle* to describe any chocolate candy in his or her collection. Consequently, I feel quite free to use the word in the title of this brownie, which is decadently dark and topped with a layer of chocolate ganache dusted with cocoa powder. The harlequin pattern on the cocoa powder is quite easy to make with a thin, sharp knife, and elevates this brownie to one I hope a French bistro would be proud to serve.

brownie batter

Vegetable shortening for pan

3 sticks (12 ounces) unsalted butter

2 cups (12 ounces) 60% cacao bittersweet chocolate chips

6 large eggs, at room temperature

3 cups (1 pound 5 ounces) sugar

1 teaspoon salt

1 tablespoon pure vanilla extract

1¼ cups (5 ounces) cake flour

1 cup and 2 tablespoons (4.2 ounces) Dutch-processed unsweetened cocoa powder

special dark chocolate ganache

¾ cup (6 ounces) heavy whipping cream

1¼ cups (7.5 ounces) Hershey's Special Dark Chocolate Chips

½ teaspoon pure vanilla extract

garnish

2 to 3 tablespoons Dutch-processed unsweetened cocoa powder

1 To make the brownies, adjust an oven rack to the middle level of the oven and preheat to 350°F. Prepare a 9 by 13-inch baking pan with heavy-duty aluminum foil as shown on page xvi. Lightly grease the foil in the pan.

2 Cut the butter sticks into 1-inch slices. In a small, heavy saucepan, melt the butter pieces over the lowest setting; add the bittersweet chocolate chips. Stir with a small whisk until combined and the chocolate is melted and smooth. Turn off the heat but leave the saucepan on the burner while proceeding with the recipe.

3 Using a large whisk, lightly beat the eggs in a large mixing bowl. Place the sugar and salt in a separate small mixing bowl, then whisk into the eggs just until incorporated. Briefly whisk the melted chocolate mixture, then gradually whisk into the egg mixture until just combined. Briefly whisk in the vanilla. You can set aside the saucepan and small whisk—no need to wash them—to use for the chocolate ganache.

4 Place the flour and cocoa powder in the small mixing bowl; whisk together to combine. Sift through a medium strainer directly onto the batter; stir in with a silicone spatula until just combined. Pour the batter into the prepared pan and spread evenly with a small offset spatula. Bake for 34 minutes, until a toothpick inserted in the center comes out clean. Transfer the pan to a cooling rack and let cool at room temperature while preparing the ganache.

5 To make the ganache, bring the cream just to a boil in the reserved small saucepan. Remove the pan from the heat and add the chocolate chips; shake the pan to cover the chips with the hot cream. Cover the pan tightly and let sit for 2 minutes, then gently blend together with a small whisk until the chocolate is incorporated and smooth. Add the vanilla and whisk briefly. Pour the ganache over the warm slab and spread evenly with a small offset spatula. Let sit at room temperature for at least 15 minutes, then refrigerate the pan for 7 to 8 hours, or overnight. See page xix for instructions on removing the slab from the pan and cutting it into 12 large squares.

6 Place four cut brownies close together in a square shape on a sheet of parchment paper. This placement will ensure that most of the cocoa powder spreads onto the brownies, not the parchment. Using a medium strainer, sift the cocoa powder to evenly cover the top of each brownie. Working with one brownie at a time, pick it up and tap it sideways on the parchment paper to knock off the excess cocoa powder; you just want a fine coating. Use a thin chef's (or paring) knife to lightly score diagonal lines about ¼ inch apart in one direction, and then repeat in the opposite direction, forming a diamond harlequin pattern. Repeat with the remaining brownies. Excess cocoa powder left on the parchment paper should be returned to the cocoa container for another use. See page xix for refrigerated storage (up to 2 weeks) and freezing guidelines.

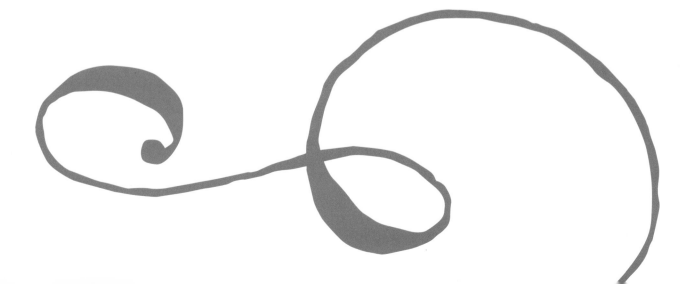

sea salt turtle pecan brownies

makes 12 large brownies

My husband loves those ubiquitous turtle candies, oozing with caramel, pecans, and chocolate, and every now and then (more than I should) I find myself buying "him" a box to enjoy. I decided to morph the flavors of one of my (oops, his) favorite candies into a brownie, since he finds my stash of turtle candies way too often. To correctly position the turtles on each brownie, you must decorate them after the brownies are cut, so allow plenty of time for them to bake and chill.

brownie batter
Vegetable shortening for pan
1¾ cups (6 ounces) pecan halves
2 sticks (8 ounces) unsalted butter
3 ounces unsweetened baking chocolate
1 cup (6 ounces) 60% cacao bittersweet chocolate chips
4 large eggs, at room temperature
1 cup (7 ounces) granulated sugar
1 packed cup (8 ounces) light brown sugar
¾ teaspoon salt
1½ teaspoons pure vanilla extract
1 cup (4.5 ounces) bleached all-purpose flour
½ teaspoon baking powder

caramel layer
⅓ cup and 1 teaspoon (3 ounces) heavy whipping cream
2 tablespoons (1 ounce) unsalted butter
12 ounces (about 43) Kraft Traditional Caramels
2 tablespoons and 1 teaspoon bleached all-purpose flour
1 teaspoon pure vanilla extract

turtle bodies
2 teaspoons (0.03 ounce) canola oil
½ cup (3 ounces) 60% cacao bittersweet chocolate chips

garnish
1 to 2 teaspoons Maldon flaked sea salt

1   To make the brownies, adjust an oven rack to the middle level of the oven and preheat to 350°F. Prepare a 9 by 13-inch baking pan with heavy-duty aluminum foil as shown on page xvi. Lightly grease the foil in the pan.

2   Sprinkle the pecans out onto a quarter-sheet pan. Toast in the oven just until fragrant, about 5 minutes, then transfer the pan to a cooling rack. Maintain the oven temperature at 350°F.

3   Cut the butter sticks into 1-inch slices. In a small, heavy saucepan, melt the butter pieces over the lowest setting. While the butter is melting, chop the unsweetened chocolate into ¼-inch pieces and add to the melted butter along with the bittersweet chocolate chips. Use a small whisk to speed the melting process. When the chocolate is melted and completely smooth, turn off the heat but leave the saucepan on the burner while proceeding with the recipe.

4 Using a large whisk, lightly beat the eggs in a large mixing bowl. Place the sugars and salt in a separate small mixing bowl, then whisk into the eggs just until incorporated. Briefly whisk the melted chocolate mixture, then gradually whisk into the egg mixture until just combined. Briefly whisk in the vanilla.

5 Place the flour and baking powder in the small mixing bowl; whisk together to combine. Sift through a medium strainer directly onto the batter; stir in with a silicone spatula until just combined.

6 Set aside 36 whole pecan halves to use later for the turtle heads, tails, and legs. Sprinkle the remaining pecans over the batter and fold in until just combined. Pour the batter into the prepared pan and spread evenly with a small offset spatula. Bake for 28 minutes, until a toothpick inserted in the center comes out clean. Transfer the pan to a cooling rack. Prepare the caramel layer while the brownie base is baking.

7 To make the caramel layer, place the cream and butter in a 2-quart saucier or saucepan. Begin to melt the mixture over medium-low heat. Unwrap the caramels, and as each is unwrapped, add it to the mixture. Cook over medium-low heat, stirring occasionally with a silicone spatula, until the caramels are melted and completely smooth. Sift (or strain) the flour directly onto the mixture; stir in well. Increase the heat to medium-high and bring the mixture to a full boil, stirring constantly; boil for 30

seconds. Remove the pan from the heat and stir in the vanilla. Pour the caramel over the hot brownie slab and spread evenly with a small offset spatula. Let the slab sit at room temperature for at least 30 minutes, then refrigerate the pan for 7 to 8 hours, or overnight. See page xix for information on removing and cutting the slab into 12 large squares. Leave the cut brownies on the cutting board.

8 To make the turtle bodies, place the oil and chocolate chips in a 1-cup Pyrex measuring cup. Microwave in 30-second intervals, stirring with a small, silicone spatula, until the chocolate is melted and smooth. Because the chocolate will set up quickly on the cool caramel, it's best to work with four brownies at a time when creating the turtles. To create the bodies, pour the chocolate into 3-inch ovals on the diagonal over four of the cut brownies. Immediately sprinkle sea salt only on the chocolate turtle bodies. Using the reserved toasted pecans, cut four pecan halves widthwise and place on each still warm chocolate turtle body to form the turtle heads and tails, slightly pushing the pecans into the chocolate. Cut eight pecan halves lengthwise to form four legs for each turtle and place in position. Repeat with the remaining brownies, forming twelve turtles. Refrigerate the brownies (still on the cutting board) for at least 30 minutes to set up the chocolate. See page xix for refrigerated storage (up to 2 weeks) and freezing guidelines.

crème de la crème de menthe brownies

makes 12 large squares or 24 smaller bars

I served these at a dinner party plated with a scoop of mint chocolate chip ice cream (garnished with a fresh mint leaf, of course) to rave reviews. Using the packaged Andes Crème de Menthe baking chips makes them a breeze to make, but if you can't find those, unwrap and chop up the individual candies. At Christmas I use a combination of the Andes Crème de Menthe and Peppermint Crunch baking chips inside the brownies as well as on top for a red and green holiday look.

brownie batter
Vegetable shortening for pan
2 sticks (8 ounces) unsalted butter
3 ounces unsweetened baking chocolate
1 cup (6 ounces) 60% cacao bittersweet chocolate chips
4 large eggs, at room temperature
1 cup (7 ounces) granulated sugar
1 packed cup (8 ounces) light brown sugar
¾ teaspoon salt
1½ teaspoons pure vanilla extract
1 cup (4.5 ounces) bleached all-purpose flour
½ teaspoon baking powder
1¼ cups (6 ounces) Andes Crème de Menthe baking chips

chocolate glaze
6 tablespoons (3 ounces) unsalted butter
1 tablespoon (0.08 ounce) light corn syrup
1 cup (6 ounces) 60% cacao bittersweet chocolate chips

garnish
¼ cup (1.5 ounces) Andes Crème de Menthe baking chips

1 To make the brownies, adjust an oven rack to the middle level of the oven and preheat to 350°F. Prepare a 9 by 13-inch baking pan with heavy-duty aluminum foil as shown on page xvi. Lightly grease the foil in the pan.

2 Cut the butter sticks into 1-inch slices. In a small, heavy saucepan, melt the butter pieces over the lowest setting. While the butter is melting, chop the unsweetened chocolate into ¼-inch pieces and add to the melted butter along with the bittersweet chocolate chips. Use a small whisk to speed the melting process. When the chocolate is melted and completely smooth, turn off the heat but leave the saucepan on the burner while proceeding with the recipe.

3 Using a large whisk, lightly beat the eggs in a large mixing bowl. Place the sugars and salt in a separate small mixing bowl, then whisk into the eggs just until incorporated. Briefly whisk the melted chocolate mixture, then gradually whisk into the egg mixture until just combined. Briefly whisk in the vanilla. You can set aside the saucepan and small whisk—no need to wash them—to use for the chocolate glaze.

4 Place the flour and baking powder in the small mixing bowl; whisk together to combine. Sift through a medium strainer directly onto the batter; stir in with a silicone spatula until just combined. Sprinkle the crème de menthe chips over the batter; fold in until just combined. Pour the batter into the prepared pan and spread evenly with a small offset spatula. Bake for 26 minutes, until a toothpick inserted in the center comes out clean. Transfer the pan to a cooling rack and let cool at room temperature for at least 15 minutes.

5 To make the chocolate glaze, slice the butter into ½-inch slices. Place the butter slices and corn syrup in the reserved small saucepan and melt over the lowest setting. Meanwhile, place the chocolate chips in a 2-cup Pyrex measuring cup. Microwave the chips on high power for 90 seconds, whisk with the reserved small whisk, then microwave for an additional 15 seconds. Whisk again. Pour the melted butter mixture into the melted chocolate and whisk gently until combined and completely smooth. Pour the glaze over the warm brownie slab and spread evenly with a small offset spatula. Sprinkle the crème de menthe baking chips evenly over the glaze while it is still warm and soft. Let the slab sit at room temperature for at least 30 minutes, then refrigerate the pan for 7 to 8 hours, or overnight. See page xix for instructions on removing and cutting the slab, and for refrigerated storage (3 weeks) and freezing guidelines.

barking toffee crunch brownies

makes 12 large squares or 24 smaller bars

My husband, Don, is crazy about English toffee, which I attribute to the fact that his maternal grandparents were from a little town in Cornwall, England, called Mousehole. Learning how to make really good English toffee is on my to-do list, but for the time being, Heath Bits 'O Brickle Toffee Bits (found in the baking section) does quite nicely. The easy and delicious crunchy chocolate bark garnishing this brownie is one I make at Christmas to give as little thank you gifts to my customers at the Market. I break it into larger shards and package it in clear polypropylene bags. My customers come back year after year, so they either love me, the brownies, or the free Christmas bark. I'm thinking it's the brownies . . .

crispy bark
1½ teaspoons (0.02 ounce) canola oil
2 ounces premium white baking chocolate
1⅓ cups (8 ounces) 60% cacao bittersweet chocolate chips
¾ cup (0.06 ounce) puffed rice cereal, such as Rice Krispies

brownie batter
Vegetable shortening for pan
2 sticks (8 ounces) unsalted butter
3 ounces unsweetened baking chocolate
1 cup (6 ounces) 60% cacao bittersweet chocolate chips
4 large eggs, at room temperature
1 cup (7 ounces) granulated sugar
1 packed cup (8 ounces) light brown sugar
¾ teaspoon salt
1½ teaspoons pure vanilla extract
1 cup (4.5 ounces) bleached all-purpose flour
½ teaspoon baking powder
1 (8-ounce) package English toffee baking bits, Heath Bits 'O Brickle Toffee Bits preferred

milk chocolate glaze
2½ tablespoons (0.09 ounce) canola oil
1 (10-ounce) package milk chocolate chips

1 To make the bark, line a half-sheet pan with parchment paper. Pour the oil into a 1-cup Pyrex measuring cup. Very finely chop the white chocolate; add it to the oil. Microwave on 50 percent power for 2 minutes. Stir with a small silicone spatula until the white chocolate is melted and completely smooth. Scrape the white chocolate into a resealable plastic sandwich bag and seal. Snip a very small (⅛-inch) corner off one side of the bag. Squeeze fine lines randomly over the parchment paper. Refrigerate the sheet pan until the chocolate is set, about 10 minutes.

2 Bring a medium saucepan of water just to a boil. Place the bittersweet chocolate chips in a metal mixing bowl that will fit over the saucepan to form a double boiler. When the water comes to a boil, take the saucepan off the heat and place the mixing bowl over the hot water. Melt the chocolate chips until perfectly smooth, stirring occasionally with a silicone spatula. Stir in the rice cereal. Pour the mixture over the white chocolate and spread thinly with a small offset spatula. Refrigerate the pan while proceeding with the recipe.

3 To make the brownies, adjust an oven rack to the middle level of the oven and preheat to 350°F. Prepare a 9 by 13-inch baking pan with heavy-duty aluminum foil as shown on page xvi. Lightly grease the foil in the pan.

4 Cut the butter sticks into 1-inch slices. In a small, heavy saucepan, melt the butter pieces over the lowest setting. While the butter is melting, chop the unsweetened chocolate into ¼-inch pieces and add to the melted butter along with the bittersweet chocolate chips. Use a small whisk to speed the melting process. When the chocolate is melted and completely smooth, turn off the heat but leave the saucepan on the burner while proceeding with the recipe.

5 Using a large whisk, lightly beat the eggs in a large mixing bowl. Place the sugars and salt in a separate small mixing bowl, then whisk into the eggs just until incorporated. Briefly whisk the melted chocolate mixture, then gradually whisk into the egg mixture until just combined. Briefly whisk in the vanilla.

6 Place the flour and baking powder in the small mixing bowl; whisk together to combine. Sift through a medium strainer directly onto the batter; stir in with a silicone spatula until just combined. Sprinkle the toffee bits over the batter; fold in until just combined. Pour the batter into the prepared pan and spread evenly with a small offset spatula. Bake for 28 minutes, until a toothpick inserted in the center comes out clean. Transfer the pan to a cooling rack and let cool at room temperature for 15 minutes.

7 To make the milk chocolate glaze, bring a medium saucepan of water just to a boil. Place the canola oil and chocolate chips in a metal mixing bowl that will fit over the saucepan to form a double boiler. When the water comes to a boil, take the saucepan off the heat and place the mixing bowl over the hot water. Melt the chocolate chips until perfectly smooth, stirring occasionally with a silicone spatula. Pour the glaze over the warm brownie slab, then use a small offset spatula to spread the glaze evenly. Let the glazed slab cool at room temperature for at least 15 minutes.

8 Using the parchment paper, transfer the chilled bark to a cutting board and cut into triangles, ¾ to 1 inch to a side, or into random shards. Slightly embed the triangles (with the smooth white chocolate-streaked bottom side up) randomly into the warm glaze. After placement, the triangles will melt slightly into the milk chocolate glaze. Refrigerate the pan for 7 to 8 hours, or overnight. See page xix for instructions on removing and cutting the slab, and for refrigerated storage (up to 3 weeks) and freezing guidelines.

holy heavenly hash brownies

makes 12 large squares or 24 smaller bars

I tried to duplicate the flavors of my favorite ice cream by topping this brownie with a layer of easy-to-make chocolate nougat garnished with mini-marshmallows, chopped almonds, and chocolate chips with a chocolate drizzle. I think the combination is, well, heavenly! There seems to be some debate over what nuts are used in a heavenly hash recipe (be it ice cream, fudge, or cake), but no recipe is written in stone, so if you have a preference for a different nut, by all means use it.

brownie batter

Vegetable shortening for pan

⅔ cup (3 ounces) roasted salted whole almonds

½ cup (3 ounces) semisweet chocolate chips

2 sticks (8 ounces) unsalted butter

3 ounces unsweetened baking chocolate

1 cup (6 ounces) 60% cacao bittersweet chocolate chips

4 large eggs, at room temperature

1 cup (7 ounces) granulated sugar

1 packed cup (8 ounces) light brown sugar

¾ teaspoon salt

1½ teaspoons pure vanilla extract

1 cup (4.5 ounces) bleached all-purpose flour

½ teaspoon baking powder

chocolate nougat

4 tablespoons (2 ounces) unsalted butter

1 cup (7 ounces) sugar

¼ cup (2.2 ounces) evaporated milk

7.2 ounces (1½ cups) marshmallow creme, such as Fluff

½ cup (3 ounces) 60% cacao bittersweet chocolate chips

¼ teaspoon salt

1 teaspoon pure vanilla extract

½ teaspoon pure chocolate extract

topping

1½ cups (2 ounces) miniature marshmallows

¼ cup (1 ounce) roasted salted whole almonds

2 tablespoons (1 ounce) semisweet chocolate chips

chocolate drizzle

1 tablespoon (0.05 ounce) unsalted butter

1 teaspoon (0.02 ounce) light corn syrup

¼ cup (1.5 ounces) semisweet chocolate chips

1 teaspoon very hot water

38

1 To make the brownies, adjust an oven rack to the middle level of the oven and preheat to 350°F. Prepare a 9 by 13-inch baking pan with heavy-duty aluminum foil as shown on page xvi. Lightly grease the foil in the pan.

2 Cut the almonds in half widthwise and place in a small bowl with the semisweet chocolate chips. Set aside.

3 Cut the butter sticks into 1-inch slices. In a small, heavy saucepan, melt the butter pieces over the lowest setting. While the butter is melting, chop the unsweetened chocolate into ¼-inch pieces and add to the melted butter along with the bittersweet chocolate chips. Use a small whisk to speed the melting process. When the chocolate is melted and completely smooth, turn off the heat but leave the saucepan on the burner while proceeding with the recipe.

4 Using a large whisk, lightly beat the eggs in a large mixing bowl. Place the sugars and salt in a separate small mixing bowl, then whisk into the eggs just until incorporated. Briefly whisk the melted chocolate mixture, then gradually whisk into the egg mixture until just combined. Briefly whisk in the vanilla. You can set aside the saucepan—no need to wash it—to use for the chocolate drizzle.

5 Place the flour and baking powder in the small mixing bowl; whisk together to combine. Sift through a medium strainer directly onto the batter; stir in with a silicone spatula until just combined. Sprinkle the almonds and semisweet chocolate chips over the batter; fold in until just combined. Pour the batter into the prepared pan and spread evenly with a small offset spatula. Bake for 28 minutes, until a toothpick inserted in the center comes out clean. Transfer the pan to a cooling rack and let cool at room temperature for at least 15 minutes, then transfer the pan to the freezer to chill the slab while preparing the chocolate nougat.

6 To make the chocolate nougat, cut the butter into ½-inch-thick slices. Place the butter, sugar, and evaporated milk in a medium (1½ to 2-quart) saucepan. Cook over medium-low heat, stirring occasionally with a silicone spatula, until the butter is melted and the sugar is completely dissolved. Increase the heat to medium-high and bring the mixture to a boil, then lower the heat to the lowest setting and boil gently for 5 minutes, without stirring. Remove the pan from the heat and stir in the marshmallow creme until very well incorporated, then add in the chocolate chips, salt, and extracts, stirring vigorously until the mixture is well blended. Dollop the nougat over the chilled brownie slab and spread evenly with a small offset spatula.

7 To position the toppings, evenly place the marshmallows over the nougat, gently pressing to slightly embed them. Cut the almonds in half, then embed them in the nougat; repeat with the chocolate chips.

8 To make the chocolate drizzle, melt the butter and corn syrup over low heat in the reserved saucepan. Remove the pan from the heat and add the chocolate chips; stir with a small silicone spatula until the chocolate is melted and smooth. Stir in the hot water to thin it out. Use the spatula to drizzle thin, random stripes over the top of the brownie slab. Let the slab sit at room temperature for 15 minutes, then refrigerate the pan for 7 to 8 hours, or overnight. See page xix for instructions on removing and cutting the slab, and for refrigerated storage (up to 2 weeks) and freezing guidelines.

mega mallo coconut brownies

makes 12 large squares or 24 smaller bars

When I was a child, my favorite candy treat was Boyer Mallo Cups, which have a yummy whipped marshmallow creme filling surrounded by milk chocolate and a hint of coconut. I hoarded the coin cards that were enclosed with each candy, and when the cards totaled five dollars, I sent them off to the Boyer company to get a free box of ten Mallo Cups. When my box of Mallo Cups arrived, I'm sure I was as excited as Ralphie in *A Christmas Story* when he received his Little Orphan Annie Decoder. I've used the snack-size Mallo Cups here, but they only seem to be available at Halloween. At other times of the year, I use fifteen full-size Mallo Cups. To enhance the Mallo Cup experience, I've tucked a little toasted coconut in the brownie batter and covered the top with a marbling of miniature marshmallows and a chocolate marshmallow glaze.

brownie batter

1 cup (2.8 ounces) unsweetened organic shredded coconut

1 (10-ounce) package snack-size Mallo Cups, or 15 regular-size Mallo Cups

Vegetable shortening for pan

2 sticks (8 ounces) unsalted butter

1⅓ cups (8 ounces) 60% cacao bittersweet chocolate chips

4 large eggs, at room temperature

2 cups (14 ounces) sugar

¾ teaspoon salt

1½ teaspoons pure vanilla extract

¾ cup and 1 tablespoon (3.3 ounces) cake flour

¾ cup and 2 tablespoons (2.8 ounces) Dutch-processed unsweetened cocoa powder

1 (10-ounce) bag miniature marshmallows

chocolate marshmallow glaze

1¼ cups (7.5 ounces) semisweet chocolate chips

1 cup and 1 tablespoon (5 ounces) marshmallow creme, such as Fluff

2 tablespoons heavy whipping cream

optional garnish

2 to 3 tablespoons Kraft vanilla mallow bits

2 to 3 tablespoons miniature chocolate chips

1 To toast the coconut, adjust an oven rack to the middle level of the oven and preheat to 350°F. Spread the coconut out evenly on a quarter-sheet pan. Bake for 4 minutes, or until the coconut is a light golden brown color and fragrant. Unwrap the Mallo Cups while the coconut is toasting; place them in a bowl and set aside. Transfer the coconut pan to a cooling rack. Maintain the oven temperature at 350°F.

2 To make the brownies, prepare a 9 by 13-inch baking pan with heavy-duty aluminum foil as shown on page xvi. Lightly grease the foil in the pan.

3 Cut the butter sticks into 1-inch slices. In a small, heavy saucepan, melt the butter pieces over the lowest setting; add the bittersweet chocolate chips. Stir with a small whisk until combined and the chocolate is melted and smooth. Turn off the heat but leave the saucepan on the burner while proceeding with the recipe.

4 Using a large whisk, lightly beat the eggs in a large mixing bowl. Place the sugar and salt in a separate small mixing bowl, then whisk into the eggs just until incorporated. Briefly whisk the melted chocolate mixture, then gradually whisk into the egg mixture until just combined. Briefly whisk in the vanilla. You can set aside the saucepan and small whisk—no need to wash them—to use later for the chocolate marshmallow glaze.

5 Place the flour and cocoa powder in the small mixing bowl; whisk together to combine. Sift through a medium strainer directly onto the batter; stir in with a silicone spatula until just combined. Sprinkle the toasted coconut over the batter; fold in until just combined. Pour the batter into the prepared pan and spread evenly with a small offset spatula. Push the Mallo Cups into the batter; do not place any within ½ inch of the pan sides. Use the offset spatula to cover the candy with the batter. Bake for 24 minutes, then remove the pan from the oven and sprinkle the marshmallows evenly over the brownie slab. Return the pan to the oven and bake an additional 5 minutes, or until the marshmallows are puffed. In the last 15 minutes of the brownie baking, prepare the chocolate marshmallow glaze; it must be ready but still warm after the brownie slab is removed from the oven with the puffed marshmallows.

6 To make the chocolate marshmallow glaze, place the chocolate chips, marshmallow creme, and cream in the reserved saucepan. Place over medium-low heat and cook, stirring constantly with a silicone spatula, until the chips are melted and the mixture is smooth. Turn the heat off but leave the pan on the burner. As soon as the brownie pan is transferred to a cooling rack, immediately dollop the chocolate marshmallow glaze over the puffed marshmallows. Even out the glaze with a small offset spatula, and use it to swirl lightly through the marshmallows and chocolate to create a marbled effect. Immediately sprinkle on the mini mallow bits, and then sprinkle on the mini chocolate chips. Let the brownie slab sit at room temperature for 30 minutes, then refrigerate for 7 to 8 hours, or overnight. See page xix for instructions on removing and cutting the slab, and for refrigerated storage (up to 2 weeks) and freezing guidelines.

rocky "road kill" brownies

makes 12 large squares or 24 smaller bars

Rocky Road is one of my favorite ice cream flavors. Whenever I open the carton, I grab a spoon and try to plunge it into the largest marshmallow ripple I can find. Sadly, marshmallows don't bake well in brownies; they just sort of melt and disappear. The good news is that they are fabulous baked lightly on top of brownies, so there's no more searching for elusive marshmallow ripples.

brownie batter

Vegetable shortening for pan

1 cup (4 ounces) chopped walnuts

2 sticks (8 ounces) unsalted butter

1⅓ cups (8 ounces) 60% cacao bittersweet chocolate chips

4 large eggs, at room temperature

2 cups (14 ounces) sugar

¾ teaspoon salt

1½ teaspoons pure vanilla extract

¾ cup and 1 tablespoon (3.3 ounces) cake flour

¾ cup and 2 tablespoons (2.8 ounces) Dutch-processed unsweetened cocoa powder

⅔ cup (4 ounces) semisweet chocolate chips

1 (10-ounce) bag miniature marshmallows

chocolate drizzle

1 tablespoon (0.05 ounce) unsalted butter

1 teaspoon (0.02 ounce) light corn syrup

¼ cup (1.5 ounces) semisweet chocolate chips

1 teaspoon very hot water

1 To make the brownies, adjust an oven rack to the middle level of the oven and preheat to 350°F. Prepare a 9 by 13-inch baking pan with heavy-duty aluminum foil as shown on page xvi. Lightly grease the foil in the pan.

2 Sprinkle the chopped walnuts onto a quarter-sheet pan. Toast in the oven just until fragrant, about 7 minutes, then transfer the pan to a cooling rack. Maintain the oven temperature at 350°F.

3 Cut the butter sticks into 1-inch slices. In a small, heavy saucepan, melt the butter pieces over the lowest setting; add the bittersweet chocolate chips. Stir with a small whisk until combined and the chocolate is melted and smooth. Turn off the heat but leave the saucepan on the burner while proceeding with the recipe.

4 Using a large whisk, lightly beat the eggs in a large mixing bowl. Place the sugar and salt in a separate small mixing bowl, then whisk into the eggs just until incorporated. Briefly whisk the melted chocolate mixture, then gradually whisk into the egg mixture until just combined. Briefly whisk in the vanilla. You can set aside the saucepan and whisk—no need to wash them—to use for the chocolate drizzle.

5 Place the flour and cocoa powder in the small mixing bowl; whisk together to combine. Sift through a medium strainer directly onto the batter; stir in with a silicone spatula until just combined. Sprinkle ¾ cup of the walnuts and ½ cup of the semisweet chocolate chips over the batter; fold in until just combined. Pour the batter into the prepared pan and spread evenly with a small offset spatula. Bake for 24 minutes, then remove the pan from the oven and sprinkle the marshmallows evenly over the brownie slab. Return the pan to the oven and bake an additional 6 minutes, until the marshmallows are puffed. Transfer the pan to a cooling rack and immediately sprinkle the remaining chopped walnuts evenly on the marshmallows, then sprinkle on the remaining chocolate chips. Return the pan to the oven for 1 minute. Transfer the pan to a cooling rack.

6 To make the chocolate drizzle, melt the butter and corn syrup over low heat in the reserved saucepan. Remove the pan from the heat and add the chocolate chips; stir with a small silicone spatula until the chocolate is melted and smooth. Stir in the hot water to thin it out. Use the spatula to drizzle thin, random stripes over the top of the brownie slab. Let the slab sit at room temperature for 15 minutes, then refrigerate the pan for 7 to 8 hours, or overnight. See page xix for instructions on removing and cutting the slab, and for refrigerated storage (up to 2 weeks) and freezing guidelines.

spotted cow brownies

makes 12 large squares or 24 smaller bars

This beautiful brownie is as fun to make as it is delicious, loaded with bittersweet chocolate chips and white chocolate chunks and a chocolate glaze with white "spots." It's always a big hit with kids, and often when parents ask their toddler what they would like, they point to this brownie. Do not substitute white chocolate baking chips for the baking squares; you will not get the desired taste or cowlike appearance in the brownies.

brownie batter
Vegetable shortening for pan
2 sticks (8 ounces) unsalted butter
3 ounces unsweetened baking chocolate
1½ cups (9 ounces) 60% cacao bittersweet chocolate chips
4.5 ounces premium white baking chocolate
4 large eggs, at room temperature
1 cup (7 ounces) granulated sugar
1 packed cup (8 ounces) light brown sugar
¾ teaspoon salt
1½ teaspoons pure vanilla extract
1 cup (4.5 ounces) bleached all-purpose flour
½ teaspoon baking powder

chocolate glaze
6 tablespoons (3 ounces) unsalted butter
1 tablespoon (0.08 ounce) light corn syrup
1 cup (6 ounces) 60% cacao bittersweet chocolate chips

white chocolate spots
1½ teaspoons canola oil
1.5 ounces premium white baking chocolate

1 To make the brownies, adjust an oven rack to the middle level of the oven and preheat to 350°F. Prepare a 9 by 13-inch baking pan with heavy-duty aluminum foil as shown on page xvi. Lightly grease the foil in the pan.

2 Cut the butter sticks into 1-inch slices. In a small, heavy saucepan, melt the butter pieces over the lowest setting. While the butter is melting, chop the unsweetened chocolate into ¼-inch pieces and add to the melted butter along with 1 cup (6 ounces) of the bittersweet chocolate chips. Use a small whisk to speed the melting process. When the chocolate is melted and completely smooth, turn off the heat but leave the saucepan on the burner while proceeding with the recipe.

3 Place the remaining ½ cup of bittersweet chocolate chips in a small bowl. Chop the white chocolate into ½-inch chunks; add to the bowl. Set aside.

4   Using a large whisk, lightly beat the eggs in a large mixing bowl. Place the sugars and salt in a separate small mixing bowl, then whisk into the eggs just until incorporated. Briefly whisk the melted chocolate mixture, then gradually whisk into the egg mixture until just combined. Briefly whisk in the vanilla. You can set aside the saucepan and small whisk—no need to wash them—to use for the chocolate glaze.

5   Place the flour and baking powder in the small mixing bowl; whisk together to combine. Sift through a medium strainer directly onto the batter; stir in with a silicone spatula until just combined. Sprinkle the white chocolate chunks and bittersweet chips over the batter; fold in until just combined. Pour the batter into the prepared pan and spread evenly with a small offset spatula. Bake for 26 minutes, until a toothpick inserted in the center comes out clean. Transfer the pan to a cooling rack and let cool at room temperature for at least 15 minutes.

6   To make the chocolate glaze, slice the butter into ½-inch slices. Place the butter slices and corn syrup in the reserved small saucepan and melt over the lowest setting. Meanwhile, place the chocolate chips in a 2-cup Pyrex measuring cup. Microwave the chips on high power for 90 seconds, whisk with the reserved small whisk, then microwave for an additional 15 seconds. Whisk again. Pour the melted butter mixture into the melted chocolate and whisk gently until combined and completely smooth. Pour the glaze over the warm brownie slab and spread evenly with a small offset spatula. Immediately prepare the white chocolate spots.

7   To make the spots, pour the oil into a 1-cup Pyrex measuring cup. Very finely chop the white chocolate; add it to the oil. Microwave on 50 percent power for 2 minutes. Stir with a small silicone spatula until the white chocolate is melted and completely smooth. Pour the white chocolate randomly into spots over the still warm glaze. Let the glazed slab sit at room temperature for at least 30 minutes, then refrigerate the pan for 7 to 8 hours, or overnight. See page xix for instructions on removing and cutting the slab, and for refrigerated storage (up to 3 weeks) and freezing guidelines.

tuxedo brownies

makes 12 large squares, 24 smaller bars, or sixty 1¹/₈-inch pieces

Like the name implies, this is one of my more elegant brownies. Although it is time consuming to cut the finished slab into 1¹/₈-inch squares, cleaning the knife carefully between each cut, I add this brownie to almost every bite-size brownie platter I make. Slowly biting through the glaze into that fluffy marshmallow frosting and then into the decadent brownie is a gastronomic experience not to be missed, and now you don't have to.

brownie batter

Vegetable shortening for pan

2 sticks (8 ounces) unsalted butter

1⅓ cups (8 ounces) 60% cacao bittersweet chocolate chips

4 large eggs, at room temperature

2 cups (14 ounces) sugar

¾ teaspoon salt

1½ teaspoons pure vanilla extract

¾ cup and 1 tablespoon (3.3 ounces) cake flour

¾ cup and 2 tablespoons (2.8 ounces) Dutch-processed unsweetened cocoa powder

fluffy white frosting

8 tablespoons (3.2 ounces) white all-vegetable shortening

1 stick (4 ounces) unsalted butter, at room temperature

1 cup (4.8 ounces) marshmallow creme, such as Fluff

1 teaspoon pure vanilla bean paste or 2 teaspoons pure vanilla extract

1 teaspoon clear imitation vanilla extract

1¼ cups (5 ounces) confectioners' sugar

chocolate glaze

6 tablespoons (3 ounces) unsalted butter

1 tablespoon (0.08 ounce) light corn syrup

1 cup (6 ounces) 60% cacao bittersweet chocolate chips

garnish

1 tablespoon white chocolate Callebaut Crispearls

1 tablespoon Valhrona Dark Chocolate Crunchy Pearls

1 To make the brownies, adjust an oven rack to the middle level of the oven and preheat to 350°F. Prepare a 9 by 13-inch baking pan with heavy-duty aluminum foil as shown on page xvi. Lightly grease the foil in the pan.

2 Cut the butter sticks into 1-inch slices. In a small, heavy saucepan, melt the butter pieces over the lowest setting; add the bittersweet chocolate chips. Stir with a small whisk until combined and the chocolate is melted and smooth. Turn off the heat but leave the saucepan on the burner while proceeding with the recipe.

3 Using a large whisk, lightly beat the eggs in a large mixing bowl. Place the sugar and salt in a separate small mixing bowl, then whisk into the eggs just until incorporated. Briefly whisk the melted chocolate mixture, then gradually whisk into the egg mixture until just combined. Briefly whisk in the vanilla.

4 Place the flour and cocoa powder in the small mixing bowl; whisk together to combine. Sift through a medium strainer directly onto the batter; stir in with a silicone spatula until just combined. Pour the batter into the prepared pan and spread evenly with a small offset spatula. Bake for 26 minutes, until a toothpick inserted in the center comes out clean. Transfer the pan to a cooling rack and let cool at room temperature for at least 15 minutes, then refrigerate the pan for 7 to 8 hours, or overnight. See page xix for instructions on removing the slab from the pan.

5 To make the fluffy white frosting, use a stand mixer fitted with the paddle attachment and beat together the shortening and butter on medium speed until well combined and completely smooth. Add the marshmallow creme and vanilla extracts to the mixing bowl and beat on medium-low speed until well combined. Add the confectioners' sugar (no need to sift) to the mixer bowl. Starting on low speed and gradually increasing to medium-high, beat until the mixture is fluffy, about 1 minute. Scrape down the sides of the bowl and beat again briefly. Dollop the frosting over the brownie slab and spread evenly with a small offset spatula. Place the slab (still on the cutting board) in the refrigerator while preparing the glaze.

6 To make the chocolate glaze, slice the butter into ½-inch slices. Place the butter slices and corn syrup in a small saucepan and melt over the lowest setting. Meanwhile, place the chocolate chips in a 2-cup Pyrex measuring cup. Microwave the chips on high power for 90 seconds, whisk with a small whisk, then microwave for an additional 15 seconds. Whisk again. Pour the melted butter mixture into the melted chocolate and whisk gently until combined and completely smooth. Pour the glaze over the fluffy white frosting and spread evenly with a small offset spatula to completely cover the frosting. Garnish the warm glaze with the white and dark chocolate crisp candies. Refrigerate the slab (still on the cutting board) until the frosting is firm, at least 2 hours. See page xix for instructions on cutting the slab, and for refrigerated storage (up to 3 weeks) and freezing guidelines.

peanut buttercream brownies

makes 12 large squares or 24 smaller bars

I have more peanut butter brownies and blondies in my repertoire than any other flavor simply because people love the combination of chocolate and peanut butter. However I marry the two, it sells. Feel free to leave out the unwrapped mini peanut butter cups inside the brownie if you like; the peanut butter in the frosting and the drizzle is more than enough to provide a powerful peanut butter fix.

brownie batter

Vegetable shortening for pan

2 sticks (8 ounces) unsalted butter

1⅓ cups (8 ounces) 60% cacao bittersweet chocolate chips

4 large eggs, at room temperature

2 cups (14 ounces) sugar

¾ teaspoon salt

1½ teaspoons pure vanilla extract

¾ cup and 1 tablespoon (3.3 ounces) cake flour

¾ cup and 2 tablespoons (2.8 ounces) Dutch-processed unsweetened cocoa powder

1 (8-ounce) bag unwrapped Reese's Minis peanut butter cups

peanut buttercream frosting

½ cup (4.5 ounces) creamy peanut butter

4 tablespoons (2 ounces) unsalted butter, at room temperature

⅛ teaspoon salt

2 cups (8 ounces) confectioners' sugar

3 tablespoons whole milk

1½ teaspoons vanilla extract

chocolate glaze

6 tablespoons (3 ounces) unsalted butter

1 tablespoon (0.08 ounce) light corn syrup

1 cup (6 ounces) 60% cacao bittersweet chocolate chips

peanut butter drizzle

2 teaspoons (0.03 ounce) canola oil

⅓ cup (2 ounces) peanut butter–flavored baking chips, such as Reese's

1 To make the brownies, adjust an oven rack to the middle level of the oven and preheat to 350°F. Prepare a 9 by 13-inch baking pan with heavy-duty aluminum foil as shown on page xvi. Lightly grease the foil in the pan.

2 Cut the butter sticks into 1-inch slices. In a small, heavy saucepan, melt the butter pieces over the lowest setting; add the bittersweet chocolate chips. Stir with a small whisk until combined and the chocolate is melted and smooth. Turn off the heat but leave the saucepan on the burner while proceeding with the recipe.

3 Using a large whisk, lightly beat the eggs in a large mixing bowl. Place the sugar and salt in a separate small mixing bowl, then whisk into the eggs just until incorporated. Briefly whisk the melted chocolate mixture, then gradually whisk into the egg mixture until just combined. Briefly whisk in the vanilla.

4 Place the flour and cocoa powder in the small mixing bowl; whisk together to combine. Sift through a medium strainer directly onto the batter; stir in with a silicone spatula until just combined. Sprinkle the mini peanut butter cups over the batter and fold in until just combined. Pour the batter into the prepared pan and spread evenly with a small offset spatula. Bake for 26 minutes, until a toothpick inserted in the center comes out clean. Transfer the pan to a cooling rack and let cool at room temperature for at least 15 minutes, then refrigerate the pan for 7 to 8 hours, or overnight. See page xix for instructions on removing the slab from the pan.

5 To make the peanut buttercream frosting, place the peanut butter, butter, and salt in a small mixing bowl. Using a hand mixer, beat together until the mixture is perfectly smooth. Add the confectioners' sugar (no need to sift) to the bowl along with the milk and vanilla; beat until well blended and fluffy. Dollop the frosting over the brownie slab, then spread evenly with a small offset spatula. Refrigerate the brownie slab (still on the cutting board) while preparing the chocolate glaze.

6 To make the chocolate glaze, slice the butter into ½-inch slices. Place the butter slices and corn syrup in the reserved small saucepan and melt over the lowest setting. Meanwhile, place the chocolate chips in a 2-cup Pyrex measuring cup. Microwave the chips on high power for 90 seconds, whisk with the reserved small whisk, then microwave for an additional 15 seconds. Whisk again. Pour the melted butter mixture into the melted chocolate and whisk gently until combined and completely smooth. Pour the glaze over the peanut buttercream frosting; spread evenly with a small offset spatula.

7 To make the peanut butter drizzle, place the oil and peanut butter chips in a 1-cup glass (Pyrex) measuring cup. Microwave on 50 percent power for 2 minutes, then stir with a small silicone spatula until the chips are melted and completely smooth. Pour the mixture in a thin stream randomly over the warm chocolate glaze. Refrigerate the slab (still on the cutting board) until the peanut buttercream frosting and glaze are quite firm, at least 2 hours. See page xix for instructions on cutting the slab, and for refrigerated (up to 3 weeks) and freezing guidelines.

raspberry rapture brownies

makes 12 large squares or 24 smaller bars

The flavor combination of tart raspberries and decadent chocolate is one of my favorites, and anytime I spy the two paired on a dessert menu I'm on it. You will only need two tablespoons of the fresh raspberry sauce for the raspberry fluff frosting, but it's quick and easy to make, and the leftover sauce is perfect for garnishing the plates when serving the brownies. It can also be frozen for later use in a trifle or on ice cream, pancakes, angel food cake or, well, the list goes on and on.

brownie batter
Vegetable shortening for pan
2 sticks (8 ounces) unsalted butter
1⅓ cups (8 ounces) 60% cacao bittersweet chocolate chips
4 large eggs, at room temperature
2 cups (14 ounces) sugar
¾ teaspoon salt
1½ teaspoons pure vanilla extract
¾ cup and 1 tablespoon (3.3 ounces) cake flour
¾ cup and 2 tablespoons (2.8 ounces) Dutch-processed unsweetened cocoa powder

raspberry sauce
6 ounces frozen (unthawed) or fresh raspberries
⅓ cup (2.3 ounces) sugar
2 teaspoons cornstarch

raspberry fluff frosting
¼ cup (1.6 ounces) white all-vegetable shortening
4 tablespoons (2 ounces) unsalted butter, at room temperature
2 tablespoons Raspberry Sauce
½ teaspoon pure red raspberry extract (optional)
1¼ cups (6 ounces) marshmallow creme, such as Fluff
¼ cup (1 ounce) confectioners' sugar

chocolate glaze
6 tablespoons (3 ounces) unsalted butter
1 tablespoon (0.08 ounce) light corn syrup
1 cup (6 ounces) 60% cacao bittersweet chocolate chips

garnish
2 tablespoons freeze-dried raspberries

1 To make the brownies, adjust an oven rack to the middle level of the oven and preheat to 350°F. Prepare a 9 by 13-inch baking pan with heavy-duty aluminum foil as shown on page xvi. Lightly grease the foil in the pan.

2 Cut the butter sticks into 1-inch slices. In a small, heavy saucepan, melt the butter pieces over the lowest setting; add the bittersweet chocolate chips. Stir with a small whisk until combined and the chocolate is melted and smooth. Turn off the heat but leave the saucepan on the burner while proceeding with the recipe.

3 Using a large whisk, lightly beat the eggs in a large mixing bowl. Place the sugar and salt in a separate small mixing bowl, then whisk into the eggs just until incorporated. Briefly whisk the melted chocolate mixture, then gradually whisk into the egg mixture until just combined. Briefly whisk in the vanilla. You can set aside the saucepan and whisk—no need to wash them—to use for the glaze.

4 Place the flour and cocoa powder in the small mixing bowl; whisk together to combine. Sift through a medium strainer directly onto the batter; stir in with a silicone spatula until just combined. Pour the batter into the prepared pan and spread evenly with a small offset spatula. Bake for 26 minutes, until a toothpick inserted in the center comes out clean. Transfer the pan to a cooling rack and let cool at room temperature for at least 15 minutes, then refrigerate the pan for 7 to 8 hours, or overnight. See page xix for instructions on removing the slab from the pan.

5 To make the raspberry sauce, combine the raspberries, sugar, and cornstarch in a 1-quart saucier or saucepan. Cover the pan tightly and cook over medium heat, stirring occasionally with a silicone spatula until the sugar dissolves, 8 to 10 minutes. Increase the heat to high and boil uncovered until the juices are thick and clear, stirring constantly with the spatula, about 2 minutes. Push the sauce through a medium-mesh strainer into a bowl, pressing on the berries with the spatula; discard the seeds. Transfer the strained sauce to a bowl and refrigerate, uncovered, for at least 15 minutes.

6 To make the frosting, place the shortening and butter in a small mixing bowl. Using a handheld electric mixer on medium speed, beat together until well combined and completely smooth. Add the raspberry sauce and raspberry extract, if using; beat on medium speed until combined. Add the marshmallow creme and beat on high speed until well incorporated. Add the confectioners' sugar (no need to sift) to the mixture. Beat (starting on low and increasing to high speed) until fluffy and smooth, about 2 minutes. Dollop the frosting over the brownie slab, then spread evenly with a small offset spatula. Refrigerate the brownie slab (still on the cutting board) while preparing the chocolate glaze.

7 To make the chocolate glaze, slice the butter into ½-inch slices. Place the butter slices and corn syrup in the reserved small saucepan and melt over the lowest setting. Meanwhile, place the chocolate chips in a 2-cup Pyrex measuring cup. Microwave the chips on high power for 90 seconds, whisk with the reserved small whisk, then microwave for an additional 15 seconds. Whisk again. Pour the melted butter mixture into the melted chocolate and whisk gently until combined and completely smooth. Pour the glaze over the raspberry fluff frosting. To make the garnish, pulse the raspberries briefly in a mini food processor, then sprinkle them evenly over the warm chocolate glaze. Refrigerate the slab (still on the cutting board) until the raspberry fluff frosting and glaze are quite firm, at least 2 hours. See page xix for instructions on cutting the slab, and for refrigerated (up to 2 weeks) and freezing guidelines.

espresso cacao nib coffee marshmallow brownies

makes 12 large squares or 24 smaller bars

When cacao nibs burst onto the baking scene (in the United States, almost exclusively from the Scharffen Berger Chocolate Maker), everyone wanted to include them in their desserts, and I was no exception. Cacao nibs are small pieces of cacao beans that have been roasted and hulled but not yet ground into the thick paste that is the basis for chocolate making. The first time I tried roasted cacao nibs I thought they tasted quite similar to roasted coffee beans, so I tended to use them in coffee-flavored brownies. I loved the little crunch they gave, but it bothered me that they were so bitter. Reluctantly, I abandoned the oh-so-cool nibs because I have a strict rule that every add-in (or add-on) ingredient must be one that I would enjoy on its own. Now that they have come out with sweetened cacao nibs, and even better, chocolate-covered cacao nibs, they are happily incorporated back into my baking repertoire.

brownie batter

Vegetable shortening for pan

2 teaspoons boiling water

2 tablespoons instant espresso powder

1½ sticks (6 ounces) unsalted butter

1 cup (6 ounces) 60% cacao bittersweet chocolate chips

3 large eggs, at room temperature

1½ cups (10.5 ounces) sugar

½ teaspoon salt

1 teaspoon pure vanilla extract

½ cup and 1½ tablespoons (2.5 ounces) cake flour

½ cup and 1 tablespoon (2.1 ounces) Dutch-processed unsweetened cocoa powder

coffee marshmallow layer

1 cup cold bottled spring water

3 tablespoons unflavored gelatin

2 cups (14 ounces) sugar

½ teaspoon salt

¾ cup (9 ounces) light corn syrup

2 teaspoons pure vanilla extract

2 teaspoons pure coffee extract

garnish

2 to 3 tablespoons organic chocolate-covered cacao nibs

1   To make the brownies, adjust an oven rack to the middle level of the oven and preheat to 350°F. Prepare a 9 by 13-inch baking pan with heavy-duty aluminum foil as shown on page xvi. Lightly grease the foil in the pan.

2   Add the 2 teaspoons of boiling water to the espresso powder; stir to dissolve. Set aside.

3   Cut the butter sticks into 1-inch slices. In a small, heavy saucepan, melt the butter pieces over the lowest setting; add the bittersweet chocolate chips. Stir with a small whisk until combined and the chocolate is melted and smooth. Turn off the heat but leave the saucepan on the burner while proceeding with the recipe.

4   Using a large whisk, lightly beat the eggs in a large mixing bowl. Place the sugar and salt in a separate small mixing bowl, then whisk into the eggs just until incorporated. Briefly whisk the melted chocolate mixture, then gradually whisk into the egg mixture until just combined. Briefly whisk in the vanilla.

5   Place the flour and cocoa powder in the small mixing bowl; whisk together to combine. Sift through a medium strainer directly onto the batter; stir in with a silicone spatula until just combined. Pour the batter into the prepared pan and spread evenly with a small offset spatula. Bake for 20 minutes, until a toothpick inserted in the center comes out clean. Transfer the pan to a cooling rack and cool at room temperature for at least 15 minutes, then place the pan in the freezer to chill the slab while preparing the coffee marshmallow layer.

6   To make the coffee marshmallow layer, place ½ cup of the water in the bowl of a stand mixer fitted with the paddle attachment. Sprinkle the gelatin over the surface of the water; set aside. Sift (or strain) the sugar into a 1½- to 2-quart heavy saucepan. Add the salt, corn syrup, and the remaining ½ cup of water. Place over moderately low heat and stir occasionally until the sugar is dissolved, about 7 minutes. Increase the heat to medium-high and bring the mixture to a boil. Lower the heat slightly, cover the pan, and boil for 2 minutes to allow any sugar crystals on the sides of the saucepan to dissolve. Remove the pan lid and increase the heat to medium-high. Insert a candy thermometer into the mixture, and let the syrup boil without stirring until the temperature reaches 240°F.

7   With the mixer on low speed, pour the syrup into the gelatin mixture. After all of the syrup has been added, gradually increase the speed to high and beat for 12 minutes. The sugar mixture is very hot—increase the mixer speed gradually so the syrup does not splash up out of the bowl. Reduce the speed to low and add the extracts. Increase the speed to high and beat an additional 4 minutes, until the mixture is lukewarm and the consistency of whipped marshmallow. Use a pastry scraper to dollop the slightly warm and thick marshmallow over the top of the brownie slab; quickly smooth the top with a small offset spatula. Sprinkle the top of the marshmallow with the chocolate-covered cacao nibs. Refrigerate the pan for 7 to 8 hours, or overnight. See page xix for instructions on removing and cutting the slab, and for refrigerated storage (up to 2 weeks) and freezing guidelines.

cuppa-cappuccino brownies

makes 12 large squares or 24 smaller bars

I am not a coffee drinker, but I'm a regular at a local coffee shop just for the mocha crumb cake. For some reason I really like coffee-flavored desserts, and I tend to order them when I spy them on a menu. Maybe there's a coffee drinker in me just waiting to emerge. When I was developing this recipe, I experimented with both pure coffee extract and instant espresso powder to bring out the coffee flavor in the brownie. The instant espresso powder made the coffee flavor come through beautifully, but the tablespoon of water necessary to dissolve the espresso powder stripped the top of the brownie of that desirable shiny surface. No problem—you'll never see the brownie surface in the dazzling finished product.

brownie batter

Vegetable shortening for pan
1 tablespoon boiling water
3 tablespoons (0.03 ounce) instant espresso powder
2 sticks (8 ounces) unsalted butter
3 ounces unsweetened baking chocolate
1 cup (6 ounces) 60% cacao bittersweet chocolate chips
4 large eggs, at room temperature
1 cup (7 ounces) granulated sugar
1 packed cup (8 ounces) light brown sugar
¾ teaspoon salt
1 teaspoon pure vanilla extract
1 cup (4.5 ounces) bleached all-purpose flour
½ teaspoon baking powder

cinnamon cream cheese frosting

1 (8-ounce) package cream cheese, at room temperature
6 tablespoons (3 ounces) unsalted butter, at room temperature
⅛ teaspoon salt
1½ cups (6 ounces) confectioners' sugar
1 teaspoon ground cinnamon
1 teaspoon pure vanilla extract

chocolate glaze

6 tablespoons (3 ounces) unsalted butter
1 tablespoon (0.08 ounce) light corn syrup
1 cup (6 ounces) 60% cacao bittersweet chocolate chips
½ teaspoon pure coffee extract

white chocolate cinnamon drizzle

2 teaspoons (0.03 ounce) canola oil
1½ ounces premium white baking chocolate
⅛ teaspoon ground cinnamon

1   To make the brownies, adjust an oven rack to the middle level of the oven and preheat to 350°F. Prepare a 9 by 13-inch baking pan with heavy-duty aluminum foil as shown on page xvi. Lightly grease the foil in the pan.

2   Add the tablespoon of boiling water to the espresso powder; stir to dissolve. Set aside.

58

3 Cut the butter sticks into 1-inch slices. In a small, heavy saucepan, melt the butter pieces over the lowest setting. While the butter is melting, chop the unsweetened chocolate into ¼-inch pieces and add to the melted butter along with the bittersweet chocolate chips. Use a small whisk to speed the melting process. When the chocolate is melted and completely smooth, turn off the heat but leave the saucepan on the burner while proceeding with the recipe.

4 Using a large whisk, lightly beat the eggs in a large mixing bowl. Place the sugars and salt in a separate small mixing bowl, then whisk into the eggs just until incorporated. Briefly whisk the melted chocolate mixture, then gradually whisk into the egg mixture until just combined. Briefly whisk in the vanilla and the dissolved espresso powder. You can set aside the saucepan—no need to wash it—to use for the chocolate glaze.

5 Place the flour and baking powder in the small mixing bowl; whisk together to combine. Sift through a medium strainer directly onto the batter; stir in with a silicone spatula until just combined. Pour the batter into the prepared pan and spread evenly with a small offset spatula. Bake for 26 minutes, until a toothpick inserted in the center comes out clean. Transfer the pan to a cooling rack and let cool at room temperature for at least 15 minutes, then refrigerate the pan for 7 to 8 hours, or overnight. See page xix for instructions on removing the slab from the pan.

6 To make the cinnamon cream cheese frosting, place the cream cheese, butter, and salt in a small mixing bowl. Using a hand mixer on high speed, beat the mixture until it is light and fluffy. Add the confectioners' sugar to the bowl (no need to sift) and beat until creamy and smooth. Add the cinnamon and vanilla and beat in until well combined. Dollop the frosting over the brownie slab and spread evenly with a small offset spatula. Refrigerate the slab (still on the cutting board) while preparing the chocolate glaze.

7 To make the chocolate glaze, slice the butter into ½-inch slices. Place the butter slices and corn syrup in the reserved small saucepan and melt over the lowest setting. Meanwhile, place the chocolate chips in a 2-cup Pyrex measuring cup. Microwave the chips on high power for 90 seconds, whisk with the reserved small whisk, then microwave for an additional 15 seconds. Whisk again. Pour the melted butter mixture into the melted chocolate and whisk gently until combined and completely smooth. Whisk in the coffee extract. Pour the glaze over the cinnamon cream cheese frosting and spread evenly with a small offset spatula.

8 To make the drizzle, pour the oil into a 1-cup Pyrex measuring cup. Very finely chop the white chocolate; add it to the oil. Microwave on 50 percent power for 2 minutes, then stir with a small silicone spatula until the white chocolate is melted and completely smooth. Stir in the ground cinnamon. Pour the white chocolate in a thin stream over the warm chocolate glaze in 1-inch parallel lines. Use a wire cake tester (or the tip of a sharp knife) to pull the white chocolate in the opposite direction back and forth through the glaze to create a pattern. Refrigerate the slab (still on the cutting board) until the cream cheese frosting and glaze are quite firm, at least 2 hours. See page xix for instructions on cutting the slab, and for refrigerated storage (up to 2 weeks) and freezing guidelines.

coo coo for coconut marshmallow brownies

makes 12 large squares or 24 smaller bars

I usually (make that always) have brownies in my refrigerator. When I was going through my handmade marshmallow phase, I found myself placing a slab of marshmallow on top of a brownie and thoroughly enjoying the combination; hence, the evolution of layering scratch brownies and marshmallow. Being a coconut freak, this is my favorite pairing, and truth be told, this is one of my all-time favorite brownies.

brownie batter

½ cup (1.4 ounces) unsweetened organic shredded coconut

Vegetable shortening for pan

1½ sticks (6 ounces) unsalted butter

1 cup (6 ounces) 60% cacao bittersweet chocolate chips

3 large eggs, at room temperature

1½ cups (10.5 ounces) sugar

½ teaspoon salt

1 teaspoon pure vanilla extract

½ cup and 1½ tablespoons (2.5 ounces) cake flour

½ cup and 1 tablespoon (2.1 ounces) Dutch-processed unsweetened cocoa powder

coconut marshmallow layer

1 cup cold bottled spring water

3 tablespoons unflavored gelatin

2 cups (14 ounces) sugar

½ teaspoon salt

¾ cup (9 ounces) light corn syrup

2 teaspoons pure vanilla extract

1 teaspoon clear vanilla extract

1 teaspoon coconut extract

garnish

½ cup (2 ounces) shredded sweetened coconut

1 To toast the unsweetened shredded coconut for the brownie batter, adjust an oven rack to the middle level of the oven and preheat to 350°F. Spread out the coconut evenly on a quarter-sheet pan. Bake for 4 minutes, until the coconut is very lightly browned and fragrant. Transfer the pan to a cooling rack. Maintain the oven temperature at 350°F. Reserve the pan—no need to wash it—to use later for toasting the sweetened coconut.

2 To make the brownies, prepare a 9 by 13-inch baking pan with heavy-duty aluminum foil as shown on page xvi. Lightly grease the foil in the pan.

3 Cut the butter sticks into 1-inch slices. In a small, heavy saucepan, melt the butter pieces over the lowest setting; add the bittersweet chocolate chips. Stir with a small whisk until combined and the chocolate is melted and smooth. Turn off the heat but leave the saucepan on the burner while proceeding with the recipe.

4 Using a large whisk, lightly beat the eggs in a large mixing bowl. Place the sugar and salt in a separate small mixing bowl, then whisk into the eggs just until incorporated. Briefly whisk the melted chocolate mixture, then gradually whisk into the egg mixture until just combined. Briefly whisk in the vanilla.

5 Place the flour and cocoa powder in the small mixing bowl; whisk together to combine. Sift through a medium strainer directly onto the batter; stir in with a silicone spatula until just combined. Sprinkle the toasted coconut over the batter; fold in until just combined. Pour the batter into the prepared pan and spread evenly with a small offset spatula. Bake for 20 minutes, until a toothpick inserted in the center comes out clean. Transfer the pan to a cooling rack and cool at room temperature for at least 15 minutes, then place the pan in the freezer to chill the slab while preparing the coconut marshmallow. While the oven is still at 350°F, toast the sweetened coconut as follows. Spread the coconut out evenly on the reserved sheet pan. Toast for 5 minutes, then turn the coconut with a metal spatula. Toast in additional 2-minute intervals, until the coconut is nicely browned. Transfer the pan to a cooling rack.

6 To make the coconut marshmallow layer, place ½ cup of the water in the bowl of a stand mixer fitted with the paddle attachment. Sprinkle the gelatin over the surface of the water; set aside. Sift (or strain) the sugar into a 1½- to 2-quart heavy saucepan. Add the salt, corn syrup, and the remaining ½ cup of water. Place over moderately low heat and stir occasionally until the sugar is dissolved, about 7 minutes. Increase the heat to medium-high and bring the mixture to a boil. Lower the heat slightly, cover the pan, and boil for 2 minutes to allow any sugar crystals on the sides of the saucepan to dissolve. Remove the pan lid and increase the heat to medium-high. Insert a candy thermometer into the mixture, and let the syrup boil without stirring until the temperature reaches 240°F.

7 With the mixer on low speed, pour the syrup into the gelatin mixture. After all of the syrup has been added, gradually increase the speed to high and beat for 12 minutes. The sugar mixture is very hot—increase the mixer speed gradually so the syrup does not splash up out of the bowl. Reduce the speed to low and add the extracts. Increase the speed to high and beat an additional 4 minutes, until the mixture is lukewarm and the consistency of whipped marshmallow. Use a pastry scraper to dollop the slightly warm and thick marshmallow over the top of the brownie slab; quickly smooth the top with a small offset spatula. Sprinkle the top of the marshmallow with the toasted sweetened coconut. Refrigerate the pan for 7 to 8 hours, or overnight. See page xix for instructions on removing and cutting the slab, and for refrigerated storage (up to 2 weeks) and freezing guidelines.

milk chocolate macadamia nut brownies

makes 12 large squares or 24 smaller bars

I used to buy raw, whole macadamia nuts and roast them to use in my brownies. One day I stumbled upon a bag of Mauna Loa Milk Chocolate Macadamias (found in the candy section of most stores), and I never looked back. It seemed only fitting to put them in a milk chocolate–based brownie topped with a milk chocolate glaze with a sprinkling of chopped dry-roasted macadamia nut pieces. Store any extra macadamia pieces in the refrigerator in an airtight container for the next use, unless you feel like munching.

brownie batter

Vegetable shortening for pan

2 sticks (8 ounces) unsalted butter

2⅔ cups (1 pound) milk chocolate chips

4 large eggs, at room temperature

½ cup (3.5 ounces) granulated sugar

1 packed cup (8 ounces) light brown sugar

¾ teaspoon salt

1 teaspoon pure vanilla extract

1½ cups (6.8 ounces) bleached all-purpose flour

½ teaspoon baking powder

2 tablespoons Dutch-processed cocoa powder

1 (6-ounce) package milk chocolate–covered macadamia nuts, such as Mauna Loa Milk Chocolate Macadamias

milk chocolate glaze

2 tablespoons canola oil

1⅓ cups (8 ounces) milk chocolate chips

garnish

3 tablespoons dry-roasted macadamia nut pieces

1 To make the brownies, adjust an oven rack to the middle level of the oven and preheat to 350°F. Prepare a 9 by 13-inch baking pan with heavy-duty aluminum foil as shown on page xvi. Lightly grease the foil in the pan.

2 Cut the butter sticks into 1-inch slices. In a small, heavy saucepan, melt the butter pieces over the lowest setting. Add the milk chocolate chips to the melted butter, stirring constantly with a small whisk until melted. When the chocolate is melted and completely smooth, turn off the heat but leave the saucepan on the burner while proceeding with the recipe.

3 Using a large whisk, lightly beat the eggs in a large mixing bowl. Place the sugars and salt in a separate small mixing bowl, then whisk into the eggs just until incorporated. Briefly whisk the melted chocolate mixture, then gradually whisk into the egg mixture until just combined. Briefly whisk in the vanilla.

4   Place the flour, baking powder, and cocoa powder in the small mixing bowl; whisk together to combine. Sift through a medium strainer directly onto the batter; stir in with a silicone spatula until just combined. Sprinkle the chocolate-covered macadamia nuts over the batter; fold in until just combined. Dollop the batter into the prepared pan and spread evenly with a small offset spatula. Bake for 30 minutes, until a toothpick inserted in the center comes out clean. Transfer the pan to a cooling rack and let cool at room temperature for at least 15 minutes before preparing the milk chocolate glaze.

5   To make the milk chocolate glaze, bring a medium saucepan of water just to a boil. Place the canola oil and milk chocolate chips in a metal mixing bowl that will fit over the saucepan to form a double boiler. When the water comes to a boil, take the saucepan off of the heat and place the mixing bowl over the hot water. Stir with a small silicone spatula until the chocolate is melted and perfectly smooth. Pour the glaze evenly over the top of the warm brownie slab. Using a small offset spatula, spread the glaze evenly, then sprinkle with the chopped dry-roasted macadamia nuts. Let the glazed slab sit at room temperature for at least 30 minutes, then refrigerate the pan for 7 to 8 hours, or overnight. See page xix for instructions on removing and cutting the slab, and for refrigerated storage (up to 3 weeks) and freezing guidelines.

spicy cinnamon baja brownies

makes 12 large squares or 24 smaller bars

I especially enjoy cooking Mexican food in the summer—probably because my garden produces great tomatoes, jalapeños, and cilantro, or more likely, as an excuse to continue my pursuit of the perfect margarita. Regardless, I needed a Mexican cuisine-influenced brownie for a dessert, as my friends fully expect to have some sort of brownie when they come for dinner. When I was creating this one, I kept increasing the cayenne pepper with each try, and it took me four attempts to get the heat just right. My apologies in advance to the entire Hispanic community; I know brownies will never appear on your dessert menu alongside your fabulous flan, churros, and dulce de leche cake. I just borrowed a few of your traditional ingredients to make (in my mind) this brownie more fiesta-like.

pine nut crunch
¾ cup (3.5 ounces) pine nuts
1 tablespoon (0.06) ounce egg white, at room temperature
2 tablespoons (1 ounce) granulated sugar
1 tablespoon (0.05 ounce) light brown sugar
¼ teaspoon ground cinnamon
⅛ teaspoon salt

brownie batter
Vegetable shortening for pan
3 sticks (12 ounces) unsalted butter
4.5 ounces unsweetened baking chocolate
1½ cups (9 ounces) 60% cacao bittersweet chocolate chips
6 large eggs, at room temperature
1½ cups (10.5 ounces) granulated sugar
1½ packed cups (12 ounces) light brown sugar
1 teaspoon salt
2 teaspoons pure vanilla extract
1½ cups (6.8 ounces) bleached all-purpose flour
¾ teaspoon baking powder
1½ teaspoons ground cinnamon
¾ and ⅛ teaspoon ground cayenne pepper
1 (10-ounce) bag Hershey's cinnamon baking chips

1 To make the pine nut crunch, adjust an oven rack to the middle level of the oven and preheat to 350°F. Place the pine nuts in a small, heavy saucepan. Toast the nuts over medium-low heat, tossing them often, until fragrant and very lightly toasted. Pour into a bowl and place in the freezer for 10 minutes to cool down the nuts. Line a half-sheet pan with a silicone baking mat. Place the tablespoon of egg white in a small mixing bowl; whisk until frothy. Add the toasted pine nuts and stir with a silicone spatula. Place the sugars, cinnamon, and salt in a small bowl; whisk to combine. Sprinkle the mixture over the nuts and stir in well. Turn the nuts out onto the sheet pan and spread into a thin layer with a small offset spatula. Bake for 13 minutes, then turn the nuts over with a metal spatula and spread out again. Continue baking until the nuts are fragrant and the sugar coating is caramelized, about another 5 minutes. Transfer the pan to a cooling rack. Let the nuts cool on the pan, separating them with your fingers as they cool. Set aside.

2 To make the brownies, maintain the oven temperature at 350°F. Prepare a 9 by 13-inch baking pan with heavy-duty aluminum foil as shown on page xvi. Lightly grease the foil in the pan.

3 Cut the butter sticks into 1-inch slices. In a small, heavy saucepan, melt the butter pieces over the lowest setting. While the butter is melting, chop the unsweetened chocolate into ¼-inch pieces and add to the melted butter along with the bittersweet chocolate chips. Use a small whisk to speed the melting process. When the chocolate is melted and completely smooth, turn off the heat but leave the saucepan on the burner while proceeding with the recipe.

4 Using a large whisk, lightly beat the eggs in a large mixing bowl. Place the sugars and salt in a separate small mixing bowl, then whisk into the eggs just until incorporated. Briefly whisk the melted chocolate mixture, then gradually whisk into the egg mixture until just combined. Briefly whisk in the vanilla.

5 Place the flour, baking powder, cinnamon, and cayenne in the small mixing bowl; whisk together to combine. Sift through a medium strainer directly onto the batter; stir in with a silicone spatula until just combined. Pour the cinnamon chips over the batter and stir in until just combined. Pour the batter into the prepared pan and spread evenly with a small offset spatula. Sprinkle the pine nut crunch evenly over the batter. Bake for 38 minutes, until a toothpick inserted in the center comes out clean. Transfer the pan to a cooling rack and let cool at room temperature for at least 15 minutes, then refrigerate the pan for 7 to 8 hours, or overnight. See page xix for instructions on removing and cutting the slab, and for refrigerated storage (up to 3 weeks) and freezing guidelines.

s'more galore brownies

makes 12 large squares

There are two kinds of people in the world—those who love s'mores and those who don't. Of course I love them, but oddly, I married a man who would never consider eating one. We've enjoyed a long, happy marriage in spite of this disparity. This galore-ious brownie is made with a handmade graham cracker crust that requires a pan with a removable bottom to roll out the dough, but I've included a traditional ground graham cracker crust recipe for those who don't have the pan. The crust is topped with layers of rich brownie and handmade marshmallow. For the "true s'more" experience, take a blowtorch and toast the marshmallow, preferably "à la minute," at the time of serving and not before. Then top with a chocolate candy, which by tradition (or strategic marketing) should be made by Hershey's.

handmade graham cracker crust dough

1½ sticks (6 ounces) unsalted butter, at room temperature

3 packed tablespoons (1.5 ounces) dark brown sugar

3 tablespoons (1.5 ounces) granulated sugar

½ teaspoon salt

3 tablespoons (2.3 ounces) dark corn syrup

1½ cups (6.8 ounces) all-purpose unbleached flour

⅓ cup and 2 tablespoons (2 ounces) whole wheat flour

¼ and ⅛ teaspoons baking soda

½ teaspoon ground cinnamon

brownie batter

Vegetable shortening for pan

1½ sticks (6 ounces) unsalted butter

1 cup (6 ounces) 60% cacao bittersweet chocolate chips

3 large eggs, at room temperature

1½ cups (10.5 ounces) sugar

½ teaspoon salt

1 teaspoon pure vanilla extract

½ cup and 1½ tablespoons (2.5 ounces) cake flour

½ cup and 1 tablespoon (2.1 ounces) Dutch-processed unsweetened cocoa powder

vanilla marshmallow layer

⅔ cup cold bottled spring water

2 tablespoons unflavored gelatin

1⅓ cups (9.3 ounces) sugar

¼ teaspoon salt

½ cup (6 ounces) light corn syrup

2 teaspoons pure vanilla extract

1 teaspoon clear vanilla extract

garnish

12 chocolate candies, such as Hershey or Ghirardelli Squares

1 To make the crust, using a stand mixer fitted with the paddle attachment, beat the butter, sugars, salt, and corn syrup on medium speed until light and fluffy, about 2 minutes. Place the flours, baking soda, and cinnamon in a small mixing bowl; whisk together to combine. On low speed, add the flour mixture to the mixer bowl and beat until just combined. Remove the bowl and paddle from the mixer stand and thoroughly fold the dough with a silicone spatula to combine well. Turn the dough out onto a large piece of plastic wrap. Using the plastic wrap, push the dough together to combine and incorporate any loose crumbs, then form into a large rectangle, about 5½ by 7 inches. Wrap the dough tightly in the plastic wrap and refrigerate for at least 1 hour.

2 Using a 9 by 13-inch baking pan with a removable bottom, draw a rectangle on a sheet of parchment paper by removing the bottom piece and tracing around it; cut out the parchment rectangle. Grease the bottom of the pan only with vegetable shortening. Place the pan bottom on a large sheet of newspaper; cover the greased bottom with the parchment square. Place the chilled dough on the parchment paper, then cover the dough with a large sheet of wax paper. Using a rolling pin, roll the dough out to the size of the pan bottom. Trim off the excess dough and place the pan bottom back into the sides of the pan. Use the dough trimmings to fill in any empty or thin areas in the dough crust, and use a small offset metal spatula to smooth the dough scraps into place. Place the pan in the refrigerator to chill the dough for at least 1 hour before baking. Adjust an oven rack to the middle level of the oven and preheat to 350°F. Bake for 22 minutes, until the top is browned and just firm. Transfer the pan to a wire cooling rack. Maintain the oven temperature at 350°F.

3 To make the brownies, cut the butter sticks into 1-inch slices. In a small, heavy saucepan, melt the butter pieces over the lowest setting; add the bittersweet chocolate chips. Stir with a small whisk until combined and the chocolate is melted and smooth. Turn off the heat but leave the saucepan on the burner while proceeding with the recipe.

4 Using a large whisk, lightly beat the eggs in a large mixing bowl. Place the sugar and salt in a separate small mixing bowl, then whisk into the eggs just until incorporated. Briefly whisk the melted chocolate mixture, then gradually whisk into the egg mixture until just combined. Briefly whisk in the vanilla.

5 Place the flour and cocoa powder in the small mixing bowl; whisk together to combine. Sift through a medium strainer directly onto the batter; stir in with a silicone spatula until just combined. Pour the batter over the Graham cracker crust and spread evenly with a small offset spatula. Bake for 26 minutes, until a toothpick inserted in the center comes out clean. Transfer the pan to a cooling rack and cool at room temperature for at least 15 minutes, then place the pan in the refrigerator to chill the slab while preparing the handmade marshmallow.

6 To make the vanilla marshmallow layer, place ⅓ cup of the water in the bowl of a stand mixer fitted with the paddle attachment. Sprinkle the gelatin over the surface of the water; set aside. Sift (or strain) the sugar into a 1½- to 2-quart heavy saucepan. Add the salt, corn syrup, and the remaining ⅓ cup of water. Place over moderately low heat and stir occasionally until the sugar is dissolved, about 7 minutes. Increase the heat to medium-high and bring the mixture to a boil. Lower the heat slightly, cover the pan, and boil for 2 minutes to allow any sugar crystals on the sides of the saucepan to dissolve. Remove the pan lid and increase the heat to medium-high. Insert a candy thermometer into the mixture, and let the syrup boil without stirring until the temperature reaches 240°F.

7   With the mixer on low speed, pour the syrup into the gelatin mixture. After all of the syrup has been added, gradually increase the speed to high and beat for 12 minutes. The sugar mixture is very hot—increase the mixer speed gradually so the syrup does not splash up out of the bowl. Reduce the speed to low and add the vanilla extracts. Increase the speed to high and beat an additional 4 minutes, until the mixture is lukewarm and the consistency of whipped marshmallow. Use a pastry scraper to dollop the slightly warm and thick marshmallow over the top of the brownie slab; quickly smooth the top with a small offset spatula. Let the slab cool at room temperature for 30 minutes, then refrigerate the pan for 7 to 8 hours, or overnight. See page xix for instructions on removing the slab from the pan and cutting it into 12 large squares. If desired, toast the top of each brownie by quickly moving a blowtorch back and forth over the marshmallow until lightly browned. After the marshmallow cools, garnish the top of each brownie with a chocolate candy. See page xix for instructions on refrigerated storage (up to 2 weeks) and freezing guidelines.

alternative graham cracker crust recipe

Vegetable shortening for pan
9 tablespoons (4.5 ounces) unsalted butter
3 cups fine crumbs (7.5 ounces) original graham crackers (about 13½ crackers)
3 tablespoons sugar
⅛ teaspoon salt
1 teaspoon ground cinnamon

1   To make the crust, adjust an oven rack to the middle level of the oven and preheat to 350°F. Prepare a 9 by 13-inch baking pan with heavy-duty aluminum foil as shown on page xvi. Lightly grease the foil in the pan.

2   Cut the butter into 1-inch chunks. In a small, heavy saucepan, melt the butter pieces over the lowest setting. Remove the pan from the heat and set aside.

3   Break up the graham crackers into 1-inch pieces directly into the bowl of a food processor, then add the sugar, salt, and cinnamon; pulse to process into fine crumbs. Pour the melted butter over the crumb mixture and pulse just to combine. Pour the crumb mixture into the prepared pan and shake to even out; then use a metal spatula to firmly press and flatten the mixture. Bake for 12 minutes, until the crust is firm.

snickering brownies

makes 12 large squares or 24 smaller bars

How can you possibly make a winning combination of peanut butter–flavored nougat, caramel, peanuts, and chocolate (a.k.a., the Snickers bar) even better? Stack it on top of a dark, rich brownie, and that's what I've done here. There are several steps to this brownie, but each is quite easy and the end result is so worth it! I am always emphasizing the importance of using quality ingredients, so try to use gourmet salted Virginia peanuts. I'm not suggesting this simply because I live in Virginia; you'll find that many non-Virginia chefs recommend them as well.

brownie batter

Vegetable shortening for pan

1½ sticks (6 ounces) unsalted butter

1 cup (6 ounces) 60% cacao bittersweet chocolate chips

3 large eggs, at room temperature

1½ cups (10.5 ounces) sugar

½ teaspoon salt

1 teaspoon pure vanilla extract

½ cup and 1½ tablespoons (2.5 ounces) cake flour

½ cup and 1 tablespoon (2.1 ounces) Dutch-processed unsweetened cocoa powder

peanut butter nougat

4 tablespoons (2 ounces) unsalted butter

1 cup (7 ounces) granulated sugar

¼ cup (2.2 ounces) evaporated milk

1½ cups (7.2 ounces) marshmallow creme, such as Fluff

¼ cup (2.2 ounces) creamy peanut butter

¼ teaspoon salt

1 teaspoon pure vanilla extract

caramel-peanut layer

⅓ cup and 1 teaspoon (3 ounces) heavy whipping cream

2 tablespoons (1 ounce) unsalted butter

12 ounces (about 43) Kraft Traditional Caramels

2 tablespoons and 1 teaspoon bleached all-purpose flour

1 teaspoon pure vanilla extract

1 cup and 2 tablespoons (4.5 ounces) large salted gourmet peanuts (preferably Virginia)

mixed chocolate glaze

2 tablespoons canola oil

⅔ cup (4 ounces) 60% cacao bittersweet chocolate chips

⅔ cup (4 ounces) milk chocolate chips

1   To make the brownies, adjust an oven rack to the middle level of the oven and preheat to 350°F. Prepare a 9 by 13-inch baking pan with heavy-duty aluminum foil as shown on page xvi. Lightly grease the foil in the pan.

2   Cut the butter sticks into 1-inch slices. In a small, heavy saucepan, melt the butter pieces over the lowest setting; add the bittersweet chocolate chips. Stir with a small whisk until combined and the chocolate is melted and smooth. Turn off the heat but leave the saucepan on the burner while proceeding with the recipe.

3   Using a large whisk, lightly beat the eggs in a large mixing bowl. Place the sugar and salt in a separate small mixing bowl, then whisk into the eggs just until incorporated. Briefly whisk the melted chocolate mixture, then gradually whisk into the egg mixture until just combined. Briefly whisk in the vanilla.

4   Place the flour and cocoa powder in the small mixing bowl; whisk together to combine. Sift through a medium strainer directly onto the batter; stir in with a silicone spatula until just combined. Pour the batter into the prepared pan and spread evenly with a small offset spatula. Bake for 21 minutes, until a toothpick inserted in the center comes out clean. Transfer the pan to a cooling rack and cool at room temperature for at least 15 minutes, then place the pan in the freezer to chill the slab while preparing the peanut butter nougat.

5   To make the peanut butter nougat, cut the butter into ½-inch-thick slices. Place the butter, sugar, and evaporated milk in a medium (1½- to 2-quart) saucepan. Cook over medium-low heat, stirring occasionally with a silicone spatula, until the butter is melted and the sugar is completely dissolved. Increase the heat to medium-high and bring the mixture to a boil, then lower the heat to low and boil gently for 5 minutes, without stirring. Remove the pan from the heat and stir in the fluff until very well incorporated, then stir in the peanut butter, salt, and vanilla, stirring vigorously until the mixture is well blended. Dollop the nougat over the chilled brownie slab and spread evenly with a small offset spatula. Place the pan in the refrigerator while preparing the caramel-peanut layer.

6   To make the caramel-peanut layer, place the cream and butter in a 2-quart saucier or saucepan. Begin to melt the mixture over medium-low heat. Unwrap the caramels, and as each is unwrapped, add it to the mixture. Cook over medium-low heat, stirring occasionally with a silicone spatula, until the caramels are melted and completely smooth. Sift (or strain) the flour directly onto the mixture; stir in well. Increase the heat to medium-high and bring the mixture to a full boil, stirring constantly; boil for 30 seconds. Remove the pan from the heat and stir in the vanilla. Sprinkle the peanuts evenly over the nougat layer, then pour the caramel over the nuts and spread evenly with a small offset spatula.

7   To make the mixed chocolate glaze, bring a medium saucepan of water just to a boil. Place the canola oil, bittersweet chocolate chips, and milk chocolate chips in a metal mixing bowl that will fit over the saucepan to form a double boiler. When the water comes to a boil, take the saucepan off the heat and place the mixing bowl over the hot water. Melt the chocolate chips, stirring occasionally with a silicone spatula, until all of the chips are melted and smooth. Pour the glaze over the caramel layer. Using a small offset spatula, spread the glaze evenly. Let the glazed slab sit at room temperature for at least 30 minutes, then refrigerate the pan for 7 to 8 hours, or overnight. See page xix for instructions on removing and cutting the slab, and for refrigerated storage (up to 2 weeks) and freezing guidelines.

whopping malted milk ball brownies

makes 12 large squares or 24 smaller bars

When I was a child I just didn't like malted milk balls—it had something to do with the texture when you bit into them. I ignored them until one year at the Fancy Food Show in New York I tasted a malted milk ball gelato that was up for an award. The crunch and flavor from the malted milk balls in the gelato was just terrific, and as soon as I came home I developed my own ice cream version. The malted milk balls retain their crunch in this milk chocolate–based brownie topped with a malted milk glaze, more malted milk balls, and a milk chocolate drizzle. Since my conversion, don't be surprised if you see me at a movie theater munching on a box of Whoppers, and no, I'm not sharing.

brownie batter

Vegetable shortening for pan

1 (5-ounce) box malted milk ball candies, such as Whoppers

2 sticks (8 ounces) unsalted butter

3⅓ cups (1 pound 4 ounces) milk chocolate chips

4 large eggs, at room temperature

½ cup (3.5 ounces) granulated sugar

1 packed cup (8 ounces) light brown sugar

¾ teaspoon salt

1 teaspoon pure vanilla extract

1½ cups (6.8 ounces) bleached all-purpose flour

½ teaspoon baking powder

2 tablespoons natural unsweetened cocoa powder

malted milk glaze

4 tablespoons (2 ounces) unsalted butter, at room temperature

⅓ cup (1.4 ounces) plain malted milk powder, such as Carnation

2 cups (8 ounces) 10x confectioners' sugar

1½ teaspoons vanilla extract

⅛ teaspoon salt

2 tablespoons (1.2 ounces) whole milk

garnish

⅔ cup (2.5 ounces) malted milk ball candies, such as Whoppers

milk chocolate drizzle

1½ teaspoons (0.02 ounce) canola oil

¼ cup (2 ounces) milk chocolate chips

1 To make the brownies, adjust an oven rack to the middle level of the oven and preheat to 350°F. Prepare a 9 by 13-inch baking pan with heavy-duty aluminum foil as shown on page xvi. Lightly grease the foil in the pan.

2 Use a sharp chef's knife to cut ¾ cup of the malted milk balls in half. Set aside.

3 Cut the butter sticks into 1-inch slices. In a small, heavy saucepan, melt the butter pieces over the lowest setting. Add 2⅔ cups (1 pound) of the milk chocolate chips to the melted butter, stirring constantly with a small whisk until melted. When the chocolate is melted and completely smooth, turn off the heat but leave the saucepan on the burner while proceeding with the recipe.

4 Using a large whisk, lightly beat the eggs in a large mixing bowl. Place the sugars and salt in a separate small mixing bowl, then whisk into the eggs just until incorporated. Briefly whisk the melted chocolate mixture, then gradually whisk into the egg mixture until just combined. Briefly whisk in the vanilla.

5 Place the flour, baking powder, and cocoa powder in the small mixing bowl; whisk together to combine. Sift through a medium strainer directly onto the batter; stir in with a silicone spatula until just combined. Sprinkle the cut malted milk balls and the remaining ⅔ cup of milk chocolate chips over the batter; fold in until just combined. Pour the batter into the prepared pan and spread evenly with a small offset spatula. Bake for 33 minutes, until a toothpick inserted in the center comes out clean. Transfer the pan to a cooling rack and let cool at room temperature for at least 15 minutes. Refrigerate the pan for 7 to 8 hours, or overnight. See page xix for instructions on removing the slab from the pan.

6 To make the malted milk glaze, place the butter and malted milk powder in a small mixing bowl. Using a handheld electric mixer on medium speed, beat together until well combined. Add the confectioners' sugar (no need to sift), vanilla, salt, and milk to the bowl and beat, starting on low and increasing to high, until well combined and smooth. Dollop the glaze over the chilled brownie slab and spread evenly with a small offset spatula. Chop the remaining malted milk balls in half and place them evenly (some cut side up, some cut side down) over the glaze, then use your fingertips to slightly embed them into the glaze.

7 To make the milk chocolate drizzle, pour the oil into a 1-cup Pyrex measuring cup; add the milk chocolate chips. Microwave on 50 percent power for 2 minutes. Stir with a small silicone spatula until the milk chocolate is melted and completely smooth. Using the spatula, drizzle thin, random stripes over the top of the brownie slab. Let the drizzle cool at room temperature for 15 minutes, then refrigerate the slab (still on the cutting board) until the glaze is firm, at least 2 hours. See page xix for instructions on removing and cutting the slab, and for refrigerated storage (up to 2 weeks) and freezing guidelines.

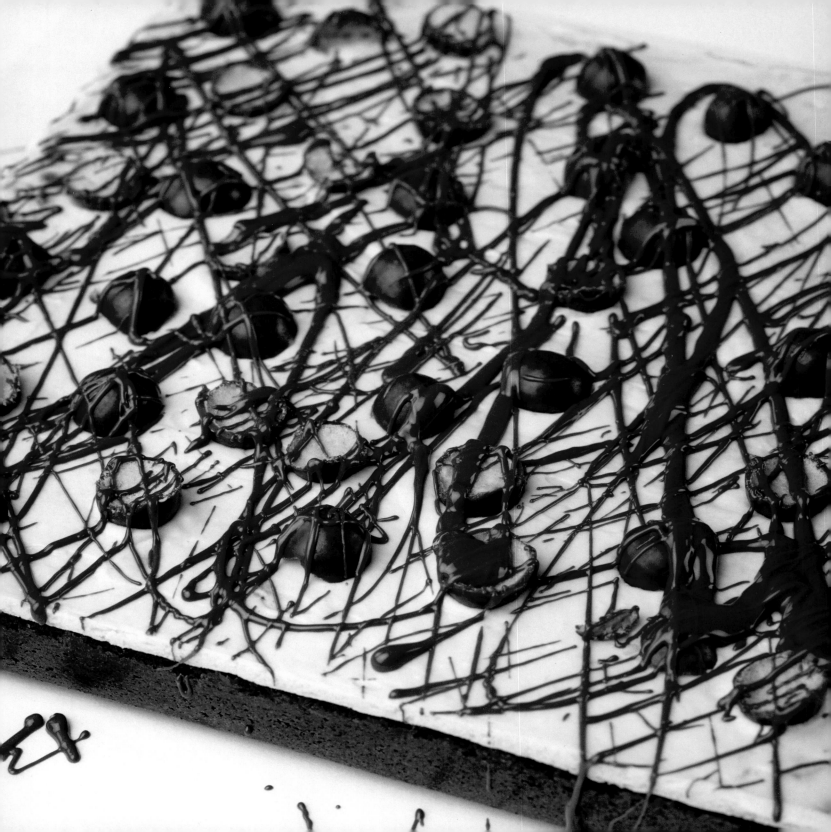

faux-germanic chocolate brownies

makes 12 large squares or 24 smaller bars

In spite of the name, German's Sweet Chocolate (or "German" Chocolate Cake) did not originate in Germany. Samuel German, an employee of the Walter Baker & Company, developed the dark baking chocolate in 1852, and the chocolate bar was given his name. The first published recipe for German's Chocolate Cake was printed in a Dallas newspaper in 1957, and the cake quickly gained popularity. As it was printed in other newspapers, the possessive form (German's) was dropped. I once worked with a charming chef named Melvin, and one day I asked him what was his favorite dessert. Without hesitation he answered German Chocolate Cake. I like to think that Melvin would especially enjoy these brownies.

brownie batter

Vegetable shortening for pan
2 sticks (8 ounces) unsalted butter
2 ounces unsweetened baking chocolate
1½ bars (6 ounces) German's Sweet Chocolate
4 large eggs, at room temperature
1 cup (7 ounces) granulated sugar
½ cup, packed (4 ounces) light brown sugar
½ teaspoon salt
1½ teaspoons pure vanilla extract
1 cup (4.5 ounces) bleached all-purpose flour
½ teaspoon baking powder

german chocolate frosting

1 cup (4 ounces) chopped pecans
1 cup (4 ounces) shredded sweetened coconut
1 stick (4 ounces) unsalted butter
1 cup (11 ounces) sweetened condensed milk
4 large egg yolks
¼ teaspoon salt
1 teaspoon pure vanilla extract

1 To make the brownies, adjust an oven rack to the middle level of the oven and preheat to 350°F. Prepare a 9 by 13-inch baking pan with heavy-duty aluminum foil as shown on page xvi. Lightly grease the foil in the pan.

2 Cut the butter sticks into 1-inch slices. In a small, heavy saucepan, melt the butter pieces over the lowest setting. While the butter is melting, chop the unsweetened and the sweet chocolate into ¼-inch pieces and add to the melted butter. Use a small whisk to speed the melting process. When the chocolate is melted and completely smooth, turn off the heat but leave the saucepan on the burner while proceeding with the recipe.

3 Using a large whisk, lightly beat the eggs in a large mixing bowl. Place the sugars and salt in a separate small mixing bowl, then whisk into the eggs just until incorporated. Briefly whisk the melted chocolate mixture, then gradually whisk into the egg mixture until just combined. Briefly whisk in the vanilla.

4 Place the flour and baking powder in the small mixing bowl; whisk together to combine. Sift through a medium strainer directly onto the batter; stir in with a silicone spatula until just combined. Pour the batter into the prepared pan and spread evenly with a small offset spatula. Bake for 24 minutes, until a toothpick inserted in the center comes out clean. Transfer the pan to a cooling rack.

5 To make the German chocolate frosting, toast the pecans and coconut while the oven is still hot. Sprinkle the chopped pecans and coconut onto a half-sheet pan. Bake for 7 minutes, until the pecans are fragrant and very lightly toasted. Transfer the pan to a cooling rack.

6 Cut the butter into ¼-inch slices. Place the butter slices in a 2-quart saucier or saucepan. Add the condensed milk and egg yolks. Cook over medium-low heat, stirring with a silicone spatula, until the butter is melted. Increase the heat to medium-high and bring the mixture to a low boil, stirring vigorously, and cook for 2 minutes until the mixture has thickened to the consistency of pudding. Remove the pan from the heat and stir in the salt, vanilla, pecans, and coconut. Dollop the frosting over the top of the brownie slab and spread evenly with a small offset spatula. Refrigerate the pan for 7 to 8 hours, or overnight. See page xix for instructions on removing and cutting the slab, and for refrigerated storage (up to 2 weeks) and freezing guidelines.

cookies 'n' cream extreme brownies

makes 12 large squares or 24 smaller bars

Who wouldn't love a decadent chewy brownie topped with fluffy vanilla frosting and topped with crunchy chocolate cookies? No one in my immediate circle of friends would object to that at all. I don't like crumbs on my frosting, so mini chocolate sandwich cookies work beautifully for the garnish and add a delightful crunchy bite. If you're at all like me, don't buy your mini cookies too far in advance of making this brownie. Once I crack open that pouch, they just seem to disappear . . .

brownie batter

Vegetable shortening for pan

2 sticks (8 ounces) unsalted butter

1⅓ cups (8 ounces) 60% cacao bittersweet chocolate chips

4 large eggs, at room temperature

2 cups (14 ounces) sugar

¾ teaspoon salt

1½ teaspoons pure vanilla extract

¾ cup and 1 tablespoon (3.3 ounces) cake flour

¾ cup and 2 tablespoons (2.8 ounces) Dutch-processed unsweetened cocoa powder

15 (from 2 [8.5-ounce] packages) White Fudge Covered Oreos (see Note)

fluffy white frosting

8 tablespoons (3.2 ounces) white all-vegetable shortening

1 stick (4 ounces) unsalted butter, at room temperature

1 cup (4.8 ounces) marshmallow creme, such as Fluff

1 teaspoon pure vanilla bean paste or 2 teaspoons pure vanilla extract

1 teaspoon clear imitation vanilla extract

1¼ cups (5 ounces) confectioners' sugar

cookie garnish

1¼ cups (or more) Oreo Mini Chocolate Sandwich Cookies

chocolate drizzle

2 tablespoons (1 ounce) unsalted butter

2 teaspoons (0.04 ounce) light corn syrup

½ cup (3 ounces) semisweet chocolate chips

2 teaspoons very hot water

1 To make the brownies, adjust an oven rack to the middle level of the oven and preheat to 350°F. Prepare a 9 by 13-inch baking pan with heavy-duty aluminum foil as shown on page xvi. Lightly grease the foil in the pan.

2 Cut the butter sticks into 1-inch slices. In a small, heavy saucepan, melt the butter pieces over the lowest setting; add the bittersweet chocolate chips. Stir with a small whisk until combined and the chocolate is melted and smooth. Turn off the heat but leave the saucepan on the burner while proceeding with the recipe.

80

3   Using a large whisk, lightly beat the eggs in a large mixing bowl. Place the sugar and salt in a separate small mixing bowl, then whisk into the eggs just until incorporated. Briefly whisk the melted chocolate mixture, then gradually whisk into the egg mixture until just combined. Briefly whisk in the vanilla.

4   Place the flour and cocoa powder in the small mixing bowl; whisk together to combine. Sift through a medium strainer directly onto the batter; stir in with a silicone spatula until just combined. Pour the batter into the prepared pan and spread evenly with a small offset spatula. Push the White Fudge Covered Oreos into the batter; do not place any within ½ inch of the pan sides. Use the offset spatula to cover the cookies with the batter. Bake for 28 minutes, until a toothpick inserted in the center comes out clean. Transfer the pan to a cooling rack and let cool at room temperature for at least 15 minutes, then refrigerate the pan for 7 to 8 hours, or overnight. See page xix for instructions on removing the slab from the pan.

5   To make the fluffy white frosting, use a stand mixer fitted with the paddle attachment, and beat together the shortening and butter on medium speed until well combined and completely smooth. Add the marshmallow creme and the vanilla extracts to the mixing bowl and beat on medium-low speed until well combined. Add the confectioners' sugar (no need to sift) to the mixer bowl. Starting on low speed and gradually increasing to medium-high, beat until the mixture is fluffy, about 1 minute. Scrape down the sides of the bowl and beat again briefly. Dollop the frosting over the brownie slab and spread evenly with a small offset spatula, then immediately garnish with the mini Oreos, slightly embedding them into the frosting with your fingertips.

6   To make the chocolate drizzle, melt the butter and corn syrup over low heat in a small, heavy saucepan. Remove the pan from the heat and add the chocolate chips; stir with a small silicone spatula until the chocolate is melted and smooth. Stir in the hot water to thin out. Using the spatula, drizzle random stripes liberally over the top of the brownie slab. Refrigerate the slab (still on the cutting board) until the frosting is quite firm, at least 2 hours. See page xix for instructions on cutting the slab, and for refrigerated storage (up to 2 weeks) and freezing guidelines.

note:

This is a limited edition cookie, available from mid November through the early winter months. Substitute regular Oreos when mini Oreos are not available.

connie's *today* show peanut butter cup brownies

makes 12 large squares or 24 smaller bars

When I'm in the kitchen, I like to listen to either the TV or radio (preferably NPR) for background fodder as I'm cooking. One day on the *Today* show, Hoda Kotb held up a package of brownies she'd bought at a grocery store as one of her favorite things that she likes to share with viewers. I made a mental note that my brownies looked a lot better, and one day I would send her some. About six months later I did, and I hoped I would get a reply from Hoda, maybe with an autographed picture. Instead, I had an email from the producer asking me if I would like to come on the show to do a cooking segment. I was thrilled, and in July 2012, some friends and I went to New York and had a blast with my 15 minutes of fame. One of the results of that appearance, however, is that I always have people at my booth asking for the *Today* show brownie, so as much as I like to change up my selection, this is one I always have to bring.

Vegetable shortening for pan
1 (12-ounce) package miniature peanut butter cups
3 sticks (12 ounces) unsalted butter
4½ ounces unsweetened baking chocolate
1½ cups (9 ounces) 60% cacao bittersweet chocolate chips
6 large eggs, at room temperature
1½ cups (10.5 ounces) granulated sugar
1½ packed cups (12 ounces) light brown sugar
1 teaspoon salt
1 tablespoon pure vanilla extract
1½ cups (6.8 ounces) bleached all-purpose flour
¾ teaspoon baking powder
2 tablespoons (0.07 ounce) coarsely chopped salted peanuts
¼ cup (1 ounce) milk chocolate chips

1 To make the brownies, adjust an oven rack to the middle level of the oven and preheat to 350°F. Prepare a 9 by 13-inch baking pan with heavy-duty aluminum foil as shown on page xvi. Lightly grease the foil in the pan.

2 Unwrap the peanut butter cups; set aside.

3 Cut the butter sticks into 1-inch slices. In a small, heavy saucepan, melt the butter pieces over the lowest setting. While the butter is melting, chop the unsweetened chocolate into ¼-inch pieces and add to the melted butter along with the bittersweet chocolate chips. Use a small whisk to speed the melting process. When the chocolate is melted and completely smooth, turn off the heat but leave the saucepan on the burner while proceeding with the recipe.

82

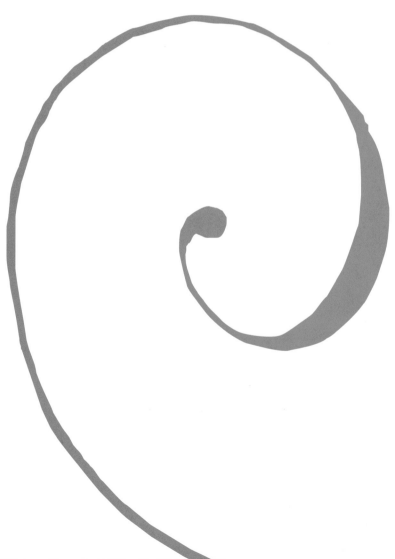

4 Using a large whisk, lightly beat the eggs in a large mixing bowl. Place the sugars and salt in a separate small mixing bowl, then whisk into the eggs just until incorporated. Briefly whisk the melted chocolate mixture, then gradually whisk into the egg mixture until just combined. Briefly whisk in the vanilla.

5 Place the flour and baking powder in the small mixing bowl; whisk together to combine. Sift through a medium strainer directly onto the batter; stir in with a silicone spatula until just combined. Pour the batter into the prepared pan and spread evenly with a small offset spatula. Push the peanut butter cups into the batter; do not place any within ½ inch of the pan sides. Use the offset spatula to cover the candy with the batter. Sprinkle the chopped peanuts over the batter, then place the milk chocolate chips evenly on the batter. Bake for 35 minutes, until a toothpick inserted in the center comes out clean. Transfer the pan to a cooling rack and let cool at room temperature for at least 15 minutes, then refrigerate the pan for 7 to 8 hours, or overnight. See page xix for instructions on removing and cutting the slab, and for refrigerated storage (up to 3 weeks) and freezing guidelines.

chocolate amaretto cheesecake brownies

makes 12 large squares or 24 smaller bars

Here's another holdover from my days of working in a restaurant. I used to serve this brownie with a large dollop of Amaretto-spiked whipped cream and a dusting of finely ground candied almonds. Here I've used amaretti cookies, which are available in most Italian grocery stores. Yes I know, you're only using a tiny amount of the cookies for the garnish, but the leftovers are great to nibble on or grind up to use in a cheesecake crust. You may be tempted to add almonds to the brownie itself (as I tried once), but I would advise against it. The textural pleasure of biting into a ganache-covered cheesecake brownie shouldn't be disrupted by a large crunchy nut. I've included my recipe for Amaretto Whipped Cream for those who want to gild the lily.

brownie batter
Vegetable shortening for pan
2 sticks (8 ounces) unsalted butter
1⅓ cups (8 ounces) 60% cacao bittersweet chocolate chips
4 large eggs, at room temperature
2 cups (14 ounces) sugar
¾ teaspoon salt
1½ teaspoons pure vanilla extract
¾ cup and 1 tablespoon (3.3 ounces) cake flour
¾ cup and 2 tablespoons (2.8 ounces) Dutch-processed unsweetened cocoa powder

chocolate amaretto cheesecake batter
1 cup (6 ounces) 60% cacao bittersweet chocolate chips
2 (8-ounce) packages cream cheese, at room temperature
1 cup (7 ounces) sugar
½ teaspoon salt
2 large eggs, at room temperature
¼ cup (1 ounce) Dutch-processed unsweetened cocoa powder
2 tablespoons bleached all-purpose flour
½ teaspoon pure vanilla extract
⅛ teaspoon pure almond extract
2 tablespoons Amaretto liqueur

chocolate almond ganache
¾ cup (6 ounces) heavy whipping cream
1¼ cups (7.5 ounces) bittersweet or semisweet chocolate chips
⅛ teaspoon pure almond extract

garnish
¼ cup (0.04 ounce) coarsely ground amaretti cookies, such as Lazzaroni Amaretti Cookie Snaps

1 To make the brownies, adjust an oven rack to the middle level of the oven and preheat to 350°F. Prepare a 9 by 13-inch baking pan with heavy-duty aluminum foil as shown on page xvi. Lightly grease the foil in the pan.

2 Cut the butter sticks into 1-inch slices. In a small, heavy saucepan, melt the butter pieces over the lowest setting; add the bittersweet chocolate chips. Stir with a small whisk until combined and the chocolate is melted and smooth. Turn off the heat but leave the saucepan on the burner while proceeding with the recipe.

3 Using a large whisk, lightly beat the eggs in a large mixing bowl. Place the sugar and salt in a separate small mixing bowl, then whisk into the eggs just until incorporated. Briefly whisk the melted chocolate mixture, then gradually whisk into the egg mixture until just combined. Briefly whisk in the vanilla. You can set aside the saucepan and small whisk—no need to wash them— to use for the chocolate ganache.

4 Place the flour and cocoa powder in the small mixing bowl; whisk together to combine. Sift through a medium strainer directly onto the batter; stir in with a silicone spatula until just combined. Pour the batter into the prepared pan and spread evenly with a small offset spatula. Bake for 25 minutes. While the brownie base is baking, prepare the chocolate Amaretto cheesecake batter.

5 To make the chocolate Amaretto cheesecake batter, place the chocolate chips in a 2-cup Pyrex measuring cup. Microwave the chips on high power for 90 seconds, stir with a small silicone spatula, then microwave for an additional 15 seconds. Stir until the chocolate is melted and smooth. Set aside to cool at room temperature.

6 Cut the cream cheese into 1-inch slices and place in the bowl of a stand mixer fitted with the paddle attachment. Beat on medium speed for 2 to 3 minutes, until perfectly smooth. Slowly add the sugar and salt; beat for an additional 2 to 3 minutes. On medium-low speed, add the eggs, one at a time, beating until just combined. Scrape down the sides of the bowl and beat again briefly. Remove the bowl and paddle from the mixer stand.

7 Place the cocoa powder and flour in the small mixing bowl; whisk to combine. Sift (or strain) the cocoa powder and flour directly onto the cheesecake batter. Return the bowl and paddle to the stand and beat on the lowest speed until just combined; scrape down the sides of the bowl. On medium-low speed add the melted chocolate, and then the extracts and Amaretto; beat on low speed until just combined. Remove the bowl and paddle from the mixer stand and fold the batter thoroughly with a silicone spatula to ensure that the batter on the bottom of the bowl is well incorporated and smooth.

8 After the brownie base has baked for 25 minutes, transfer the pan to a cooling rack. Pour the cheesecake batter evenly over the hot brownie base and spread evenly with a small offset spatula. Bake an additional 20 minutes, until the cheesecake layer is firm and set. The cheesecake layer will look baked around the edges and have tiny cracks; the rest will appear shiny. Transfer the pan to a cooling rack and let cool at room temperature for 15 minutes.

9 To make the chocolate almond ganache, bring the cream just to a boil in the reserved small saucepan. Remove the pan from the heat and add the chocolate chips; shake the pan to cover the chips with the hot cream. Cover the pan tightly and let sit for 2 minutes, then gently blend together with the small whisk until the chocolate is incorporated and smooth. Add the almond extract and whisk briefly. Pour the ganache over the warm brownie slab and spread evenly with a small offset spatula. Finely grind the Amaretti cookies in a mini food processor and sprinkle over the warm ganache. Let sit at room temperature for at least 15 minutes, then refrigerate the pan for 7 to 8 hours, or overnight. See page xix for instructions on removing and cutting the slab, and for refrigerated storage (up to 2 weeks) and freezing guidelines. If desired, serve with a dollop of Amaretto-flavored whipped cream, which should be made right before serving.

amaretto whipped cream

2 cups heavy whipping cream
8 tablespoons (2 ounces) confectioners' sugar
3 tablespoons (1.5 ounces) Amaretto liqueur

1 To make the Amaretto whipped cream, place all of the ingredients in the (preferably well-chilled) bowl of a stand mixer fitted with the whisk attachment. Starting on low speed and gradually increasing to high, beat until the cream holds soft peaks.

raspberry ripple cheesecake brownies

makes 12 large squares or 24 smaller bars

I think cheesecake and brownies rank high on most people's list of favorite desserts, so why not combine the two? Just to send this brownie over the top, I added ripples of fresh raspberry sauce to the cheesecake layer. When I worked as a pastry chef in fine dining, I served this brownie cut in half on the diagonal, plated with a dollop of freshly whipped mascarpone chantilly and a sprinkling of fresh raspberries. It always sold out, or "86'd" as we say in the biz.

raspberry sauce
1 (6 ounce) container raspberries
⅓ cup (2.3 ounces) sugar
2 teaspoons cornstarch

brownie batter
Vegetable shortening for pan
2 sticks (8 ounces) unsalted butter
1⅓ cups (8 ounces) 60% cacao bittersweet chocolate chips
4 large eggs, at room temperature
2 cups (14 ounces) sugar
¾ teaspoon salt
1½ teaspoons pure vanilla extract
¾ cup and 1 tablespoon (3.3 ounces) cake flour
¾ cup and 2 tablespoons (2.8 ounces) Dutch-processed
   unsweetened cocoa powder

cheesecake layer
8 ounces cream cheese, at room temperature
⅔ cup (4.8 ounces) sugar
¼ teaspoon salt
2 tablespoons (1 ounce) sour cream
1 teaspoon pure vanilla extract
1 large egg, at room temperature
2 tablespoons bleached all-purpose flour

1 To make the raspberry sauce, combine the raspberries, sugar, and cornstarch in a 1-quart saucier or saucepan. Cover the pan tightly and cook over medium heat, stirring occasionally with a silicone spatula until the sugar dissolves, 8 to 10 minutes. Increase the heat to high and boil (uncovered) until the juices are thick and clear, stirring constantly with the spatula, about 2 minutes. Push the sauce through a medium-mesh strainer into a bowl, pressing on the berries with the spatula; discard the seeds. Let sit at room temperature while making the brownie slab.

2 To make the brownies, adjust an oven rack to the middle level of the oven and preheat to 350°F. Prepare a 9 by 13-inch baking pan with heavy-duty aluminum foil as shown on page xvi. Lightly grease the foil in the pan.

3 Cut the butter sticks into 1-inch slices. In a small, heavy saucepan, melt the butter pieces over the lowest setting; add the bittersweet chocolate chips. Stir with a small whisk until combined and the chocolate is melted and smooth. Turn off the heat but leave the saucepan on the burner while proceeding with the recipe.

4 Using a large whisk, lightly beat the eggs in a large mixing bowl. Place the sugar and salt in a separate small mixing bowl, then whisk into the eggs just until incorporated. Briefly whisk the melted chocolate mixture, then gradually whisk into the egg mixture until just combined. Briefly whisk in the vanilla.

5 Place the flour and cocoa powder in the small mixing bowl; whisk together to combine. Sift through a medium strainer directly onto the batter; stir in with a silicone spatula until just combined. Pour the batter into the prepared pan and spread evenly with a small offset spatula. Bake for 22 minutes; while the brownie slab is in the oven, prepare the cheesecake layer.

6 To make the cheesecake layer, place the cream cheese, sugar, and salt in a small mixing bowl. Using a handheld electric mixer on medium speed, beat together until well combined. Add the sour cream, vanilla, and egg. Beat on medium speed just until combined, then beat in the flour. Set aside.

7 After the brownie slab has baked for 22 minutes, remove the pan from the oven and pour the cheesecake layer over the brownie layer. Use a small offset spatula to spread the batter evenly to the edges.

8 Place a resealable plastic sandwich bag inside a 1-cup Pyrex measuring cup, with the edges of the bag hanging over the sides of the cup. Pour the raspberry sauce into the plastic bag and seal. Snip a very small corner (about ⅛ inch) off of one side of the bottom of the bag. Slowly pipe parallel horizontal stripes of the raspberry sauce evenly over the cheesecake batter. Using the tip of a sharp knife, lightly pull the sauce back and forth through the cheesecake batter to create a rippled pattern. Return the pan to the oven and bake an additional 10 minutes, until the top is slightly puffed and the cheesecake layer is set when the pan is gently jiggled. Transfer the pan to a cooling rack and let cool at room temperature for 1 hour, then refrigerate the pan for 7 to 8 hours, or overnight. See page xix for instructions on removing and cutting the slab, and for refrigerated storage (up to 5 days) and freezing guidelines.

chunkie "pms" cheesecake brownies

makes 12 large squares or 24 smaller bars

I always have extra "PMS" Brownies on hand to use in the cheesecake for this recipe, and I save (and freeze) my cut "PMS" Brownie trimmings to use in the ganache. However, you may have to make a pan of "PMS" Brownies (page 3) prior to starting this recipe. The dazzling end result will more than make up for the additional prep—this is a showstopper dessert fit to end any fine dining experience.

brownie batter

Vegetable shortening for pan

1½ sticks (6 ounces) unsalted butter

1 cup (6 ounces) 60% cacao bittersweet chocolate chips

3 large eggs, at room temperature

1½ cups (10.5 ounces) sugar

½ teaspoon salt

1 teaspoon pure vanilla extract

½ cup and 1½ tablespoons (2.5 ounces) cake flour

½ cup and 1 tablespoon (2.1 ounces) Dutch-processed unsweetened cocoa powder

"pms" brownie cheesecake batter

2 pounds (four 8-ounce packages) cream cheese, at room temperature

1⅓ cups (9.3 ounces) sugar

½ teaspoon salt

4 large eggs, at room temperature

1 large egg yolk, at room temperature

2 tablespoons bleached all-purpose flour

1 tablespoon pure vanilla extract (preferably Tahitian vanilla)

2 tablespoons heavy whipping cream

2 cups (2 large brownies, 9.5 to 10 ounces) Connie's "PMS" Brownies (page 3)

brownie crumble chocolate ganache

½ cup (½ large brownie) Connie's "PMS" Brownie (page 3) or brownie trimmings

¾ cup (6 ounces) heavy whipping cream

1¼ cups (7.5 ounces) bittersweet chocolate chips

½ teaspoon pure vanilla extract

1   To make the brownies, adjust an oven rack to the middle level of the oven and preheat to 350°F. Prepare a 9 by 13-inch baking pan with heavy-duty aluminum foil as shown on page xvi. Lightly grease the foil in the pan.

2   Cut the butter sticks into 1-inch slices. In a small, heavy saucepan, melt the butter pieces over the lowest setting; add the bittersweet chocolate chips. Stir with a small whisk until combined and the chocolate is melted and smooth. Turn off the heat but leave the saucepan on the burner while proceeding with the recipe.

3 Using a large whisk, lightly beat the eggs in a large mixing bowl. Place the sugar and salt in a separate small mixing bowl, then whisk into the eggs just until incorporated. Briefly whisk the melted chocolate mixture, then gradually whisk into the egg mixture until just combined. Briefly whisk in the vanilla. You can set aside the saucepan and small whisk—no need to wash them—to use for the chocolate ganache.

4 Place the flour and cocoa powder in the small mixing bowl; whisk together to combine. Sift through a medium strainer directly onto the batter; stir in with a silicone spatula until just combined. Pour the batter into the prepared pan and spread evenly with a small offset spatula. Bake for 21 minutes, until a toothpick inserted in the center comes out clean. Transfer the pan to a cooling rack and cool. Lower the oven temperature to 325°F. While the brownie base is baking, prepare the cheesecake batter.

5 To make the cheesecake batter, cut the cream cheese into one-inch slices and place in the bowl of a stand mixer fitted with the paddle attachment. Beat on medium speed for 2 to 3 minutes, until creamy. Slowly add the sugar and salt; beat for an additional 2 to 3 minutes, until perfectly smooth. On medium-low speed, add the eggs and the egg yolk, one at a time, beating until just combined. On low speed, add the flour, vanilla, and cream until just combined. Scrape down the sides of the bowl and beat again briefly. Remove the bowl and paddle from the mixer stand and fold the batter thoroughly with a silicone spatula to ensure that the batter on the bottom of the bowl is well incorporated and smooth.

6 Cut the whole brownies into ¼-inch dice. Sprinkle the brownie pieces over the cheesecake batter, separating them with your fingertips as you drop them on the batter; fold in until just combined.

7 After the brownie base has baked for 21 minutes, transfer the pan to a cooling rack. Pour the cheesecake batter evenly over the hot brownie base and spread evenly with a small offset spatula. Bake at 325°F an additional 37 minutes, until the cheesecake layer is puffy and tiny cracks appear around the outer edges. Transfer the pan to a cooling rack and let cool at room temperature for 15 minutes.

8 To make the brownie crumble chocolate ganache, cut the brownie trimmings (or half-brownie) into ¼-inch dice; set aside. Bring the cream just to a boil in the reserved small saucepan. Remove the pan from the heat and add the chocolate chips; shake the pan to cover the chips with the hot cream. Cover the pan tightly and let sit for 2 minutes, then gently blend together with the small whisk until the chocolate is incorporated and smooth. Add the vanilla and whisk briefly. Pour about a third of the ganache evenly over the top of the cheesecake layer, then use a small offset spatula to smooth it out. Immediately sprinkle the brownie bits evenly over the ganache. Use a small silicone spatula to dollop the remaining ganache over the slab, specifically on top of the brownie bits. Refrigerate the pan for 7 to 8 hours, or overnight. See page xix for instructions on removing and cutting the slab, and for refrigerated storage (up to 2 weeks) and freezing guidelines.

91

red velvet brownies

makes 12 large squares or 24 smaller bars

As in red velvet cake, the chocolate should be prominent but not overly so, and this lovely red-hued, milk chocolate-based brownie nails its namesake. I like to serve these on Valentine's Day. Cut out brownie hearts by using a heart-shaped cookie cutter on the well-chilled brownie slab and frost them individually afterward. A heart-shaped chocolate candy in the center of each frosted brownie is the perfect garnish.

brownie batter

Vegetable shortening for pan

2¼ sticks (10 ounces) unsalted butter

3⅓ cups (1 pound 4 ounces) milk chocolate chips

5 large eggs, at room temperature

½ cup and 2 tablespoons (4.4 ounces) granulated sugar

1¼ packed cups (10 ounces) light brown sugar

1 teaspoon salt

1¼ teaspoons pure vanilla extract

2 tablespoons (1 ounce) red food color

2 cups (9 ounces) bleached all-purpose flour

1 teaspoon baking powder

3 tablespoons natural unsweetened cocoa powder

cream cheese frosting

3 ounces cream cheese, at room temperature (see Note)

5 tablespoons (2.5 ounces) unsalted butter, at room temperature

⅛ teaspoon salt

1 teaspoon pure vanilla extract

1¾ cups (7 ounces) confectioners' sugar

1 To make the brownies, adjust an oven rack to the middle level of the oven and preheat to 350°F. Prepare a 9 by 13-inch baking pan with heavy-duty aluminum foil as shown on page xvi. Lightly grease the foil in the pan.

2 Cut the butter sticks into 1-inch slices. In a small, heavy saucepan, melt the butter pieces over the lowest setting. Add the milk chocolate chips to the melted butter, stirring constantly with a small whisk until melted. When the chocolate is melted and completely smooth, turn off the heat but leave the saucepan on the burner while proceeding with the recipe.

3 Using a large whisk, lightly beat the eggs in a large mixing bowl. Place the sugars and salt in a separate small mixing bowl, then whisk into the eggs just until incorporated. Briefly whisk the melted chocolate mixture, then gradually whisk into the egg mixture until just combined. Briefly whisk in the vanilla and the red food color.

4 Place the flour, baking powder, and cocoa powder in the small mixing bowl; whisk together to combine. Sift through a medium strainer directly onto the batter; stir in with a silicone spatula until just combined. Pour the batter into the prepared pan and spread evenly with a small offset spatula. Bake for 40 minutes, until a toothpick inserted in the center comes out clean. Transfer the pan to a cooling rack and let cool at room temperature for at least 15 minutes. The top of the brownie slab will be puffed when it first comes out of the oven; it will settle as it cools. Refrigerate the pan for 7 to 8 hours, or overnight. See page xix for instructions on removing the slab from the pan.

5 To make the cream cheese frosting, place the cream cheese, butter, and salt in a small mixing bowl. Using a handheld electric mixer on medium speed, beat together until well combined. Add the vanilla and beat on medium speed just until combined. Add the confectioners' sugar (no need to sift) and beat, starting on low and increasing to high, until well combined and smooth. Dollop the frosting over the chilled brownie slab and spread evenly with a small offset spatula. Chill the slab (still on the cutting board) until the frosting is firm, about 1 hour. See page xix for instructions on cutting the slab, and for refrigerated storage (up to 2 weeks) and freezing guidelines.

93

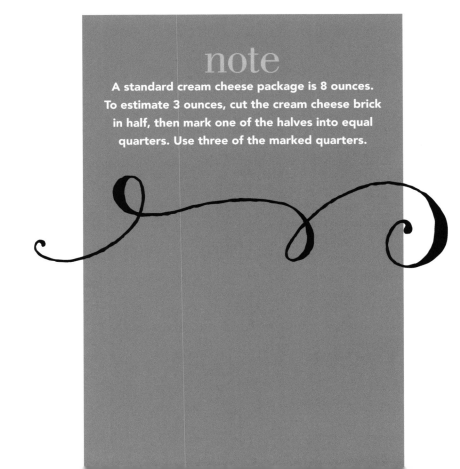

note

A standard cream cheese package is 8 ounces. To estimate 3 ounces, cut the cream cheese brick in half, then mark one of the halves into equal quarters. Use three of the marked quarters.

montmorency tart cherry black forest brownies

makes 12 large squares

I grew up with a lovely little orchard in our backyard. We had the usual apples, peaches, and pears, but my Dad also grew less conventional fruits like gooseberries, mulberries, and quince. By far my favorite fruit came from our sour cherry trees, and let me tell you, you have never tasted a real cherry pie until you've had one made with fresh, firm, tart cherries. Alas, these brownies aren't made with that precious fresh fruit, but they do contain dried tart Montmorency cherries. Don't even think about substituting dried cherry-flavored raisins. Horrors! For those who aren't familiar, a Black Forest cake is traditionally a chocolate cake topped with whipped cream, cherries, and chocolate curls. This is my very liberal brownie riff on that tantalizing German dessert.

chocolate shards

Vegetable shortening for pan

½ cup (3 ounces) semisweet chocolate chips

brownie batter

Vegetable shortening for pan

2 sticks (8 ounces) unsalted butter

3 ounces unsweetened baking chocolate

1 cup (6 ounces) 60% cacao bittersweet chocolate chips

4 large eggs, at room temperature

1 cup (7 ounces) granulated sugar

1 packed cup (8 ounces) light brown sugar

¾ teaspoon salt

1½ teaspoons pure vanilla extract

1 cup (4.5 ounces) bleached all-purpose flour

½ teaspoon baking powder

1 (5-ounce) package dried tart Montmorency cherries

fluffy white frosting

10 tablespoons (4 ounces) white all-vegetable shortening

1¼ sticks (5 ounces) unsalted butter, at room temperature

1¼ cups (6 ounces) marshmallow creme, such as Fluff

2½ teaspoons pure vanilla bean paste or pure vanilla extract

1¼ teaspoons clear imitation vanilla extract

1½ cups and 1 tablespoon (6.3 ounces) confectioners' sugar

garnish

12 jarred Maraschino or Morello cherries

1 To make the chocolate shards, lightly grease a half-sheet pan. Place a sheet of parchment paper securely on the greased pan. Bring a medium saucepan of water just to a boil. Place the chocolate chips in a metal mixing bowl that will fit over the saucepan to form a double boiler. When the water comes to a boil, take the saucepan off the heat and place the mixing bowl over the hot water. Stir with a small silicone spatula until the chocolate is melted and perfectly smooth. Pour the chocolate evenly over the parchment paper, then use a small offset spatula to spread the chocolate out into a rectangle, about 7 by 9-inches. Cover the chocolate with a second sheet of waxed paper. Roll the parchment paper–wrapped chocolate tightly into a ¾-inch wide cylinder. Refrigerate the roll on the sheet pan while proceeding with the recipe.

2 To make the brownies, adjust an oven rack to the middle level of the oven and preheat to 350°F. Prepare a 9 by 13-inch baking pan with heavy-duty aluminum foil as shown on page xvi. Lightly grease the foil in the pan.

3 Cut the butter sticks into 1-inch slices. In a small, heavy saucepan, melt the butter pieces over the lowest setting. While the butter is melting, chop the unsweetened chocolate into ¼-inch pieces and add to the melted butter along with the bittersweet chocolate chips. Use a small whisk to speed the melting process. When the chocolate is melted and completely smooth, turn off the heat but leave the saucepan on the burner while proceeding with the recipe.

4 Using a large whisk, lightly beat the eggs in a large mixing bowl. Place the sugars and salt in a separate small mixing bowl, then whisk into the eggs just until incorporated. Briefly whisk the melted chocolate mixture, then gradually whisk into the egg mixture until just combined. Briefly whisk in the vanilla.

5 Place the flour and baking powder in the small mixing bowl; whisk together to combine. Sift through a medium strainer directly onto the batter; stir in with a silicone spatula until just combined. Sprinkle the dried tart cherries over the batter; fold in until just combined. Dollop the batter into the prepared pan and spread evenly with a small offset spatula. Bake for 26 minutes, until a toothpick inserted in the center comes out clean and the top is browned. Transfer the pan to a cooling rack and let cool at room temperature for at least 15 minutes, then refrigerate the pan for 7 to 8 hours, or overnight. See page xix for instructions on removing the slab from the pan.

6 To make the fluffy white frosting, use a stand mixer fitted with the paddle attachment and beat together the shortening and butter on medium speed until well combined and completely smooth. Add the marshmallow creme and the vanilla extracts to the mixing bowl and beat on medium-low speed until well combined. Add the confectioners' sugar (no need to sift) to the mixer bowl. Starting on low speed and gradually increasing to medium-high, beat until the mixture is fluffy, about 1 minute. Scrape down the sides of the bowl and beat again briefly. Transfer ¼ cup of the frosting to a pastry bag fitted with a large star tip and set aside at room temperature. Dollop the remaining frosting over the chilled brownie slab and spread evenly with a small offset spatula. Unroll the chilled chocolate roll, discard the wax paper, and coarsely chop the chocolate shards; sprinkle evenly over the frosting. Use the back of a metal spatula to lightly tap on the shards and slightly embed them into the frosting. Refrigerate the slab (still on the cutting board) until the frosting is firm, at least 2 hours. See page xix for instructions on cutting the slab into squares. Pipe a decorative frosting star in the center of each brownie. Just before serving, place a well-drained cherry on top of the piped frosting. See page xix for refrigerated storage (up to 2 weeks) and freezing guidelines.

blondies

bombin' blondies

makes 12 large squares or 24 smaller bars

For years I struggled with blondies, and I suspect I had the same problem everyone else did; the batter rose up on the sides of the pan and down in the center. When baking is your business, every blondie must look perfect, and these do. My blondies are like a wonderful chewy, chocolate chip cookie morphed into a thick bar. The walnuts and coconut add additional crunch and flavor, and they really make these something special.

blondie batter
Vegetable shortening for pan
1 cup (4 ounces) shelled walnuts
3 sticks (12 ounces) unsalted butter
2½ cups and 2 tablespoons, firmly packed (1 pound 5 ounces) light brown sugar
3 large eggs, at room temperature
1 tablespoon pure vanilla extract
⅛ teaspoon pure almond extract
3⅓ cups and 2 tablespoons (15.5 ounces) bleached all-purpose flour
1 teaspoon salt
1¾ teaspoons baking powder
¾ cup (3 ounces) shredded sweetened coconut
1¾ cups (10 ounces) large semisweet chocolate baking chips (Hershey's Baking Melts), or 10 ounces semisweet chocolate chunks

chocolate drizzle
1½ teaspoons (0.03 ounce) unsalted butter
½ teaspoon (0.01 ounce) light corn syrup
1½ tablespoons (0.08 ounce) semisweet chocolate chips
½ teaspoon very hot water

1 To make the blondies, adjust an oven rack to the middle level of the oven and preheat to 350°F. Prepare a 9 by 13-inch baking pan with heavy-duty aluminum foil as shown on page xvi. Lightly grease the foil in the pan.

2 Sprinkle the walnuts out onto a quarter-sheet pan. Toast in the oven just until fragrant, about 7 minutes, then transfer the pan to a cooling rack. Maintain the oven temperature at 350°F.

3 Cut the butter sticks into 1-inch slices. Place the butter slices and brown sugar in a heavy 2-quart saucepan. Cook over the lowest setting until the sugar and butter dissolve, stirring frequently with a silicone spatula. Pour the sugar mixture into a large mixing bowl. Using the spatula, stir the eggs into the butter mixture one at a time, stirring vigorously after each addition. Stir in the extracts; scrape down the sides of the bowl.

4 Place the flour, salt, and baking powder in a small mixing bowl; whisk together to combine. Sift through a medium strainer directly onto the batter; stir in with the spatula until just combined.

5 Sprinkle the coconut, chocolate chips, and toasted walnuts over the batter; fold in until just combined. Scrape the batter into the prepared pan and spread evenly with a small offset spatula. Bake at 350°F for 20 minutes, then lower the oven temperature to 325°F and bake an additional 18 minutes, until a toothpick inserted in the center comes out clean. Transfer the pan to a cooling rack and let cool at room temperature for at least 15 minutes.

6 To make the chocolate drizzle, melt the butter and corn syrup over low heat in a small, heavy saucepan. Remove the pan from the heat and add the chocolate chips; stir with a small silicone spatula until the chocolate is melted and smooth. Stir in the hot water to thin it out. Using the spatula, drizzle thin, random stripes over the top of the blondie slab. Let the drizzle cool at room temperature for 30 minutes, then refrigerate the pan for 7 to 8 hours, or overnight. See page xix for instructions on removing and cutting the slab, and for refrigerated storage (up to 3 weeks) and freezing guidelines.

caramel crispie blondies

makes 12 large squares or 24 smaller bars

I like all of my brownies and blondies, but I don't necessarily love them all. Being a hopelessly addicted chocoholic, I naturally tend to favor those items that give me my chocolate fix. Still, I love it when one of my customers gravitates toward an item that I don't and buys it week after week. Marian, this is for you and Tom. Now that you'll be able to make them, I hope you will still come visit me at the market!

crispie rice cereal topping
Vegetable shortening for pan
1½ cups (1.3 ounces) puffed rice cereal (Rice Krispies)
½ cup (3.5 ounces) granulated sugar
1 tablespoon water
1 teaspoon (0.02 ounce) light corn syrup
½ teaspoon kosher salt

blondie batter
Vegetable shortening for pan
3 sticks (12 ounces) unsalted butter
2½ cups and 2 tablespoons, firmly packed (1 pound 5 ounces) light brown sugar
3 large eggs, at room temperature
1 tablespoon pure vanilla extract
3⅓ cups and 2 tablespoons (15.5 ounces) bleached all-purpose flour
1 teaspoon salt
1¾ teaspoons baking powder

caramel glaze
6 tablespoons (3 ounces) unsalted butter
¾ cup (6 ounces) heavy whipping cream
1 cup, firmly packed (8 ounces) dark brown sugar
1½ teaspoons pure vanilla extract
½ teaspoon salt
1 cup (4 ounces) confectioners' sugar

1 To make the crispy rice cereal topping, lightly grease a quarter-sheet pan and line with parchment paper. Measure out the cereal; set aside. Place the sugar, water, corn syrup, and salt in a small heavy saucepan; stir with a small silicone spatula just to combine. Bring to a boil over moderately high heat. Once the mixture comes to a boil, lower the heat to moderate and boil undisturbed until a medium-amber colored caramel forms, about 5 minutes. Remove the pan from the heat and stir in the rice cereal. Scrape the caramelized cereal onto the prepared pan and spread it out with a small offset spatula. Let cool at room temperature. Note: This makes more than you will need for the recipe, but leftovers can be stored in an airtight container at room temperature for up to 2 weeks. It's delicious as a snack to munch on and just wonderful on ice cream.

2 To make the blondies, adjust an oven rack to the middle level of the oven and preheat to 350°F. Prepare a 9 by 13-inch baking pan with heavy-duty aluminum foil as shown on page xvi. Lightly grease the foil in the pan.

3   Cut the butter sticks into 1-inch slices. Place the butter slices and brown sugar in a heavy 2-quart saucepan. Cook over the lowest setting until the sugar and butter dissolve, stirring frequently with a silicone spatula. Pour the sugar mixture into a large mixing bowl. Using the spatula, stir the eggs into the butter mixture one at a time, stirring vigorously after each addition. Stir in the vanilla.

4   Place the flour, salt, and baking powder in a small mixing bowl; whisk together to combine. Sift through a medium strainer directly onto the batter; stir in with the spatula until just combined. Scrape the batter into the prepared pan and spread evenly with a small offset spatula. Bake at 350°F for 20 minutes, then lower the oven temperature to 325°F and bake an additional 16 minutes, until a toothpick inserted in the center comes out clean. Transfer the pan to a cooling rack and let cool at room temperature for at least 15 minutes. Prepare the caramel glaze while the blondie is baking.

5   To make the caramel glaze, cut the butter into ½-inch slices. Place the butter slices, cream, and brown sugar in a small, heavy saucepan. Cook over medium heat, stirring occasionally with a silicone spatula, until the butter is melted and the mixture is smooth. Increase the heat to medium-high and bring to a full bubbling boil; boil for 2 minutes without stirring. Remove the pan from the heat and stir in the vanilla and salt. Let the mixture cool to room temperature, about 30 minutes, then sift (or strain) the confectioners' sugar directly onto the cooled brown sugar mixture; whisk in to make a smooth glaze. Pour the glaze over the warm blondie slab, then tilt the pan to spread evenly.

6   Using a sharp chef's knife, cut up the crispie rice cereal topping into ¼-inch pieces. Immediately sprinkle the pieces over the top of the warm caramel glaze. Let the slab cool at room temperature until the glaze is almost set, about 30 minutes, then refrigerate the pan for 7 to 8 hours, or overnight. See page xix for instructions on removing and cutting the slab, and for refrigerated (up to 2 weeks) and freezing guidelines.

roasted apple walnut blondies

makes 12 large squares or 24 smaller bars

For me, this is a seasonal blondie that I sell primarily in the fall, but good Granny Smith apples are available year round, and you can make it whenever you wish. Roasting the apples in advance serves two purposes. It removes most of the moisture that would otherwise make the blondies soggy, and it pre-cooks the apples in a lovely butter/sugar mixture that gives them great taste and texture. For those who aren't particularly fond of pumpkin pie (like me) this is a great blondie to serve at Thanksgiving.

roasted apples
2 teaspoons unsalted butter, at room temperature
2 large Granny Smith apples
2 tablespoons sugar

blondie batter
Vegetable shortening for pan
3 sticks (12 ounces) unsalted butter
2½ cups and 2 tablespoons, firmly packed (1 pound 5 ounces) light brown sugar
3 large eggs, at room temperature
1 tablespoon pure vanilla extract
3⅓ cups and 2 tablespoons (15.5 ounces) bleached all-purpose flour
1 teaspoon salt
1¾ teaspoons baking powder
1 teaspoon ground cinnamon
½ teaspoon ground ginger
1 cup (4 ounces) shelled walnuts

cinnamon cream cheese frosting
3 ounces cream cheese, at room temperature (see Note)
5 tablespoons (2.5 ounces) unsalted butter, at room temperature
⅛ teaspoon salt
¼ teaspoon ground cinnamon
1 teaspoon pure vanilla extract
1¾ cups (7 ounces) confectioners' sugar

garnish
2 tablespoons freeze-dried apple slices (preferably Granny Smith)

1   To make the roasted apples, adjust an oven rack to the middle level of the oven and preheat to 375°F. Smear the surface of a half-sheet pan with the butter.

2   Peel the apples, then cut them in half lengthwise. Cut out the core and seeds of each half, then cut each half in half widthwise. Slice the apple quarters into ¼-inch-thick slices. Cut the slices into ¼-inch dice; place in a small mixing bowl. Sprinkle the sugar over the diced apple; toss to coat. Turn the diced apple out onto the buttered pan and spread evenly. Roast in the oven for 14 minutes, until just tender and fragrant. Transfer the pan to a cooling rack and cool at room temperature. Lower the oven temperature to 350°F.

3   To make the blondies, prepare a 9 by 13-inch baking pan with heavy-duty aluminum foil as shown on page xvi. Lightly grease the foil in the pan.

4   Cut the butter sticks into 1-inch slices. Place the butter slices and brown sugar in a heavy 2-quart saucepan. Cook over the lowest setting until the sugar and butter dissolve, stirring frequently with a silicone spatula. Pour the sugar mixture into a large mixing bowl. Using the spatula, stir the eggs into the butter mixture one at a time, stirring vigorously after each addition. Stir in the vanilla; scrape down the sides of the bowl.

5   Place the flour, salt, baking powder, cinnamon, and ginger in a small mixing bowl; whisk together to combine. Sift through a medium strainer directly onto the batter; stir in with the spatula until just combined.

6   Sprinkle the walnuts and cooled apple bits over the batter; fold in until just combined. Scrape the batter into the prepared pan and spread evenly with a small offset spatula. Bake at 350°F for 20 minutes, then lower the oven

temperature to 325°F and bake an additional 18 minutes, until a toothpick inserted in the center comes out clean. Transfer the pan to a cooling rack and let cool at room temperature for at least 15 minutes, then refrigerate the pan for 7 to 8 hours, or overnight. See page xix for instructions on removing the slab from the pan.

7   To prepare the frosting, in a small mixing bowl using a handheld electric mixer, beat together the cream cheese, butter, and salt on high speed until well combined and smooth. Add the cinnamon and vanilla and beat on low speed until combined. Add the confectioners' sugar (no need to sift) to the cream cheese mixture. Beat (starting on low and increasing to high) until well combined and smooth. Dollop the frosting over the chilled blondie slab and spread evenly with a small offset spatula.

8   To make the garnish, break up the freeze-dried apple slices with your fingers into ½-inch pieces. Pulse the apple pieces in a mini food processor until coarsely crushed, then sprinkle them evenly over the frosting. Chill the slab (still on the cutting board) until the frosting is firm, at least 2 hours. See page xix for instructions on cutting the slab, and for refrigerated storage (up to 5 days) and freezing guidelines.

note

A standard cream cheese package is 8 ounces. To estimate 3 ounces, cut the cream cheese brick in half, then mark one of the halves into equal quarters. Use 3 of the marked quarters.

Spotted Cow Brownies

Dalmation Dog Blondies

dalmatian dog blondies

makes 12 large squares or 24 smaller bars

My Spotted Cow Brownie was such a hit that I wanted to turn it inside out with a white version—hence, my Dalmatian Dog Blondie. At the market, I always position them side by side, and customers who buy one usually buy the other as well. The ganache glaze accentuates the white chocolate in the blondie for those folks who just can't get enough white chocolate, and surprisingly (to me, a confirmed bittersweet chocoholic), they're very popular with customers.

blondie batter
Vegetable shortening for pan
1½ sticks (6 ounces) unsalted butter
6 ounces premium white baking chocolate
4 large eggs, at room temperature
2 cups (14 ounces) sugar
1 teaspoon salt
2 teaspoons pure vanilla extract
2½ cups (11.5 ounces) bleached all-purpose flour
½ teaspoon baking powder
1 cup (6 ounces) 60% cacao bittersweet chocolate chips

vanilla ganache glaze
⅓ cup and 1 tablespoon (3 ounces) heavy whipping cream
1½ cups (9 ounces) vanilla milk chips
   (Guittard Choc-Au-Lait)

chocolate spots
2 teaspoons (0.03 ounce) canola oil
¼ cup (1.5 ounces) 60% cacao bittersweet chocolate chips

1 To make the blondies, adjust an oven rack to the middle level of the oven and preheat to 350°F. Prepare a 9 by 13-inch baking pan with heavy-duty aluminum foil as shown on page xvi. Lightly grease the foil in the pan.

2 Cut the butter sticks into 1-inch slices. In a small, heavy saucepan, melt the butter pieces over the lowest setting. While the butter is melting, chop the white chocolate very finely and then add to the melted butter. Stir with a small whisk until combined and the white chocolate is melted and smooth. Remove the pan from the heat and set aside.

3 Using a large whisk, lightly beat the eggs in a large mixing bowl. Place the sugar and salt in a separate small mixing bowl, then whisk into the eggs just until incorporated. Briefly whisk the melted chocolate mixture, then gradually whisk into the egg mixture until just combined. Briefly whisk in the vanilla. You can set aside the saucepan and small whisk—no need to wash them— to use for the vanilla ganache glaze.

4 Place the flour and baking powder in the small mixing bowl; whisk together to combine. Sift through a medium strainer directly onto the batter; stir in with a silicone spatula until just combined.

5 Sprinkle the bittersweet chocolate chips over the batter; fold in until just combined. Dollop the batter into the prepared pan and spread evenly with a small offset spatula. Bake for 30 minutes, until a toothpick inserted in the center comes out clean and the top is browned. Transfer the pan to a cooling rack.

6 To make the vanilla ganache glaze, bring the cream just to a boil in the reserved small saucepan. Remove the pan from the heat and add the vanilla chips; shake the pan to cover the chips with the hot cream. Cover the pan tightly and let sit for 2 minutes, then gently blend together with the small whisk until the chips are incorporated and smooth. Pour the glaze over the hot blondie slab and spread evenly with a small offset spatula.

7 To make the spots, pour the oil into a 1-cup glass (Pyrex) measuring cup; add the chocolate chips. Microwave on 50 percent power for 2 minutes. Stir with a small silicone spatula until the chocolate is melted and completely smooth. Pour the chocolate randomly into spots over the still warm glaze. Let the glazed slab sit at room temperature for at least 30 minutes, then refrigerate the pan for 7 to 8 hours, or overnight. See page xix for instructions on removing and cutting the slab, and for refrigerated (up to 3 weeks) and freezing guidelines.

white chocolate raspberry blondies

makes 12 large squares or 24 smaller bars

Since I grow my own raspberries, I make IQF (Individually Quick Frozen) raspberries to use all year round by spreading them out onto a quarter-sheet pan right after picking (never rinse raspberries). I then freeze them in 6-ounce portions, which is the standard weight for the raspberry packages found in grocery stores. Because the frozen raspberries chill the batter (unfrozen raspberries are too fragile) this blondie will take longer to bake and the top will be uneven. No matter—it's topped with a delicious white chocolate cream cheese frosting. Biting into this blondie is like biting into a luscious piece of cake—only better.

blondie batter

Vegetable shortening for pan

1½ sticks (6 ounces) unsalted butter

6 ounces premium white baking chocolate

4 large eggs, at room temperature

2 cups (14 ounces) sugar

1 teaspoon salt

2 teaspoons pure vanilla extract

2½ cups (11.5 ounces) bleached all-purpose flour

½ teaspoon baking powder

6 ounces raspberries, frozen

white chocolate cream cheese frosting

2 ounces (2 squares) premium white baking chocolate

6 ounces (¾ brick) cream cheese, at room temperature

6 tablespoons (3 ounces) unsalted butter, at room temperature

1 teaspoon pure vanilla extract

1½ cups (6 ounces) confectioners' sugar

garnish

2 tablespoons freeze-dried raspberries

1 To make the blondies, adjust an oven rack to the middle level of the oven and preheat to 350°F. Prepare a 9 by 13-inch baking pan with heavy-duty aluminum foil as shown on page xvi. Lightly grease the foil in the pan.

2 Cut the butter sticks into 1-inch slices. In a small, heavy saucepan, melt the butter pieces over the lowest setting. While the butter is melting, chop the white chocolate very finely and then add to the melted butter. Stir with a small whisk until combined and the white chocolate is melted and smooth. Remove the pan from the heat and set aside.

3 Using a large whisk, lightly beat the eggs in a large mixing bowl. Place the sugar and salt in a separate small mixing bowl, then whisk into the eggs just until incorporated. Briefly whisk the melted chocolate mixture, then gradually whisk into the egg mixture until just combined. Briefly whisk in the vanilla.

4   Place the flour and baking powder in the small mixing bowl; whisk together to combine. Sift through a medium strainer directly onto the batter; stir in with a silicone spatula until just combined.

5   Sprinkle the frozen raspberries over the batter; fold in until just combined. Dollop the batter into the prepared pan and spread evenly with a small offset spatula. Bake for 40 minutes, until a toothpick inserted in the center comes out clean and the top is browned. Transfer the pan to a cooling rack and let cool at room temperature for at least 15 minutes, then refrigerate the pan for 7 to 8 hours, or overnight. See page xix for instructions on removing the slab from the pan.

6   To prepare the frosting, finely chop the white chocolate. Place in a small heat-proof bowl and microwave on 50 percent power for 2 minutes; stir until melted and smooth. Set aside. In a small mixing bowl using a handheld electric mixer, beat together the cream cheese and butter on high speed until well combined and smooth. Add the vanilla and the melted white chocolate and beat on low speed until combined. Add the confectioners' sugar (no need to sift) to the cream cheese mixture. Beat (starting on low and increasing to high) until well combined and smooth. Dollop the frosting over the chilled blondie slab and spread evenly with a small offset spatula. If desired, use a pastry comb over the surface of the frosting.

7   To make the garnish, pulse the raspberries briefly in a mini food processor until coarsely crushed, then sprinkle them evenly over the frosting. Chill the slab (still on the cutting board) until the frosting is firm, at least 2 hours. See page xix for instructions on cutting the slab, and for refrigerated storage (up to 5 days) and freezing guidelines.

moby pb cup blondies

makes 12 large squares or 24 smaller bars

It always surprises me that I have many customers who are die-hard white chocolate freaks—er, fans. Since peanut butter items do so well for me, I had to turn my attention to something peanut butter–laden for them. I came across these white peanut butter cups; chocolate was not in their title, so I correctly assumed that they contain no cocoa butter. I thought I'd try to work them into a blondie. I don't use or sell anything that I personally don't like, so of course, I had to try one. They were blissikins! I actually preferred them to my previously adored dark chocolate peanut butter cups. However, being a confirmed dark chocoholic, if we should meet and you bring this up, I will deny it.

blondie batter

Vegetable shortening for pan

1 (12-ounce) package White Peanut Butter Cups Miniatures (Reeses's)

1½ sticks (6 ounces) unsalted butter

6 ounces premium white baking chocolate

4 large eggs, at room temperature

2 cups (14 ounces) sugar

1 teaspoon salt

2 teaspoons pure vanilla extract

2½ cups (11.5 ounces) bleached all-purpose flour

½ teaspoon baking powder

vanilla ganache glaze

⅓ cup and 1 tablespoon (3 ounces) heavy whipping cream

1½ cups (9 ounces) vanilla milk chips (Guittard Choc-Au-Lait)

peanut butter drizzle

2 teaspoons (0.03 ounce) canola oil

⅓ cup (2 ounces) peanut butter flavored baking chips (Reese's)

garnish

2 tablespoons (0.07 ounce) coarsely chopped salted peanuts

1 To make the blondies, adjust an oven rack to the middle level of the oven and preheat to 350°F. Prepare a 9 by 13-inch baking pan with heavy-duty aluminum foil as shown on page xvi. Lightly grease the foil in the pan.

2 Unwrap the peanut butter cups; set aside.

3 Cut the butter sticks into 1-inch slices. In a small, heavy saucepan, melt the butter pieces over the lowest setting. While the butter is melting, chop the white chocolate very finely and then add to the melted butter. Stir with a small whisk until combined and the white chocolate is melted and smooth. Remove the pan from the heat and set aside.

4 Using a large whisk, lightly beat the eggs in a large mixing bowl. Place the sugar and salt in a separate small mixing bowl, then whisk into the eggs just until incorporated. Briefly whisk the melted chocolate mixture, then gradually whisk into the egg mixture until just combined. Briefly whisk in the vanilla. You can set aside the saucepan and small whisk—no need to wash them—to use for the vanilla ganache glaze.

5 Place the flour and baking powder in the small mixing bowl; whisk together to combine. Sift through a medium strainer directly onto the batter; stir in with a silicone spatula until just combined. Pour the batter into the prepared pan and spread evenly with a small offset spatula. Push the peanut butter cups into the batter; do not place any within ½ inch of the pan sides. Use the offset spatula to cover the candy with the batter. Bake for 30 minutes, until a toothpick inserted in the center comes out clean and the top is lightly browned. Transfer the pan to a cooling rack.

6 To make the vanilla ganache glaze, bring the cream just to a boil in the reserved small saucepan. Remove the pan from the heat and add the vanilla chips; shake the pan to cover the chips with the hot cream. Cover the pan tightly and let sit for 2 minutes, then gently blend together with the small whisk until the chips are incorporated and smooth. Pour the glaze over the hot blondie slab and spread evenly with a small offset spatula.

7 To make the peanut butter drizzle, place the oil and peanut butter chips in a 1-cup glass (Pyrex) measuring cup. Microwave on 50 percent power for 2 minutes, then stir with a small silicone spatula until the chips are melted and completely smooth. Pour the mixture in a thin stream randomly over the vanilla ganache glaze. Sprinkle the chopped peanuts over the glazed slab. Refrigerate the pan for 7 to 8 hours, or overnight. See page xix for instructions on removing and cutting the slab, and for refrigerated storage (up to 2 weeks) and freezing guidelines.

bunches of crunches
white chocolate blondies

makes 12 large squares or 24 smaller bars

Let's talk about texture. Sometimes I like a brownie that's silky and fudgy as my teeth sink into it; my signature "pms" Brownie comes immediately to mind. At other times, I want a bit of textural interplay in a brownie, and this one falls into that category. The Nestle Buncha Crunch candy works beautifully in this brownie for two reasons. First, the candy is coated, and when it is folded into the warm batter, there isn't any melting or what I call, bleeding. Second, it gives a delightful little crunch as you bite through the chocolate glaze into the brownie. The white chocolate candy on top further enhances both the textural and white chocolate profiles. Double the crunch—double the goodness!

blondie batter

Vegetable shortening for pan
1½ sticks (6 ounces) unsalted butter
6 ounces premium white baking chocolate
4 large eggs, at room temperature
2 cups (14 ounces) sugar
1 teaspoon salt
2 teaspoons pure vanilla extract
2½ cups (11.5 ounces) bleached all-purpose flour
½ teaspoon baking powder
1 (9-ounce) package Buncha Crunch candy (Nestle)

chocolate glaze

6 tablespoons (3 ounces) unsalted butter
1 tablespoon (0.08 ounce) light corn syrup
1 cup (6 ounces) 60% cacao bittersweet chocolate chips

garnish

2 to 3 tablespoons white chocolate crisp candies
   (Callebaut Crispearls)

1 To make the blondies, adjust an oven rack to the middle level of the oven and preheat to 350°F. Prepare a 9 by 13-inch baking pan with heavy-duty aluminum foil as shown on page xvi. Lightly grease the foil in the pan.

2 Cut the butter sticks into 1-inch slices. In a small, heavy saucepan, melt the butter pieces over the lowest setting. While the butter is melting, chop the white chocolate very finely and then add to the melted butter. Stir with a small whisk until combined and the white chocolate is melted and smooth. Remove the pan from the heat and set aside.

3 Using a large whisk, lightly beat the eggs in a large mixing bowl. Place the sugar and salt in a separate small mixing bowl, then whisk into the eggs just until incorporated. Briefly whisk the melted chocolate mixture, then gradually whisk into the egg mixture until just combined. Briefly whisk in the vanilla. You can set aside the saucepan and whisk—no need to wash them—to use for the chocolate glaze.

4 Place the flour and baking powder in the small mixing bowl; whisk together to combine. Sift through a medium strainer directly onto the batter; stir in with a silicone spatula until just combined.

5 Sprinkle the Buncha Crunch over the batter; fold in until just combined. Dollop the batter into the prepared pan and spread evenly with a small offset spatula. Bake for 30 minutes, until a toothpick inserted in the center comes out clean and the top is browned. Transfer the pan to a cooling rack and let cool at room temperature for at least 15 minutes.

6 To make the chocolate glaze, slice the butter into ½-inch slices. Place the butter slices and corn syrup in the reserved small saucepan and melt over the lowest setting. Meanwhile, place the chocolate chips in a 2-cup glass (Pyrex) measuring cup. Microwave the chips on high power for 90 seconds, whisk with the reserved small whisk, then microwave for an additional 15 seconds. Whisk again. Pour the melted butter mixture into the melted chocolate and whisk gently until combined and completely smooth. Pour the chocolate glaze over the warm blondie slab and spread evenly with a small offset spatula. Let the glaze cool at room temperature for 10 minutes before garnishing it with the white chocolate candies, then refrigerate the pan for 7 to 8 hours, or overnight. See page xix for instructions on removing and cutting the slab, and for refrigerated storage (up to 2 weeks) and freezing guidelines.

pretty in pink
cherry marshmallow blondies

makes 12 large squares

Your friend or your daughter is having a baby girl, and you offer to bring dessert to the baby shower. Have some fun! Tell them you are bringing vanilla cupcakes with pink frosting (insert yawn here) and instead, wow them with these fabulous blondies. The guests will forgive and forget when they sink their teeth into these beauties. My favorite taste testers who live next door, Anna and Sadie, served these at a sleepover and all of the girls loved them. I like to stock up on small heart-shaped chocolates that are sold around Valentine's Day for treats just like this. Store extra packages in a dark cupboard at room temperature.

blondie batter
Vegetable shortening for pan
1 (5-ounce) package dried tart Montmorency cherries
1½ sticks (6 ounces) unsalted butter
6 ounces premium white baking chocolate
4 large eggs, at room temperature
2 cups (14 ounces) sugar
1 teaspoon salt
2 teaspoons pure vanilla extract
2½ cups (11.5 ounces) bleached all-purpose flour
½ teaspoon baking powder

cherry marshmallow layer
1 cup (8 ounces) Just Tart Cherry Juice (Knudsen)
3 tablespoons unflavored gelatin (Knox)
2 cups (14 ounces) sugar
½ teaspoon salt
¾ cup (9 ounces) light corn syrup
½ teaspoon pure vanilla extract
1 teaspoon pure cherry extract
⅛ teaspoon red food color (optional)

optional garnish
12 white chocolate candy squares (such as Dove)

1 To make the blondies, adjust an oven rack to the middle level of the oven and preheat to 350°F. Prepare a 9 by 13-inch baking pan with heavy-duty aluminum foil as shown on page xvi. Lightly grease the foil in the pan.

2 Cut each large dried cherry in half with a chef's knife. Set aside.

3 Cut the butter sticks into 1-inch slices. In a small, heavy saucepan, melt the butter pieces over the lowest setting. While the butter is melting, chop the white chocolate very finely and then add to the melted butter. Stir with a small whisk until combined and the white chocolate is melted and smooth. Remove the pan from the heat and set aside.

4 Using a large whisk, lightly beat the eggs in a large mixing bowl. Place the sugar and salt in a separate small mixing bowl, then whisk into the eggs just until incorporated. Briefly whisk the melted chocolate mixture, then gradually whisk into the egg mixture until just combined. Briefly whisk in the vanilla.

5 Place the flour and baking powder in the small mixing bowl; whisk together to combine. Sift through a medium strainer directly onto the batter; stir in with a silicone spatula until just combined. Sprinkle the dried cherries over the batter; fold in until just combined. Dollop the batter into the prepared pan and spread evenly with a small offset spatula. Bake for 30 minutes, until a toothpick inserted in the center comes out clean and the top is very lightly browned. Transfer the pan to a cooling rack.

6 To make the cherry marshmallow layer, place ½ cup of the cherry juice in the bowl of a stand mixer fitted with the paddle attachment. Sprinkle the gelatin over the surface of the water; set aside. Sift (or strain) the sugar into a 1½ to 2-quart heavy saucepan. Add the salt, corn syrup, and the remaining ½ cup cherry juice. Place over moderately low heat and stir occasionally until the sugar is dissolved, about 7 minutes. Increase the heat to medium-high and bring the mixture to a boil. Lower the heat slightly, cover the pan, and boil for 2 minutes to allow any sugar crystals on the sides of the saucepan to dissolve. Remove the pan lid and increase the heat to medium-high. Insert a candy thermometer into the mixture, and let the syrup boil without stirring until the temperature reaches 240°F.

7 With the mixer on low speed, pour the syrup into the gelatin mixture. After all of the syrup has been added, gradually increase the speed to high and beat for 12 minutes. The sugar mixture is very hot—increase the mixer speed gradually so the syrup does not splash up out of the bowl. Reduce the speed to low and add the extracts and the red food color, if using. Increase the speed to high and beat an additional 4 minutes, until the mixture is lukewarm and the consistency of whipped marshmallow. Use a pastry scraper to dollop the slightly warm and thick marshmallow over the top of the brownie slab; quickly smooth the top with a small offset spatula. Refrigerate the pan for 7 to 8 hours, or overnight. See page xix for instructions on removing and cutting the slab, and for refrigerated storage (up to 2 weeks) and freezing guidelines. If using the candy garnish, press one into the center of each blondie after cutting. If freezing them, wait to add the candy garnish until right before serving.

red, white & blueberry white chocolate blondies

makes 12 large squares or 24 smaller bars

Did I create these to sell around the Fourth of July? Uh, yes I did. I have tried fresh blueberries in the batter, but found that dried wild blueberries work much better. Drying a fruit intensifies the flavor and the dried blueberries won't explode during baking, plus they add some nice chewy texture. You may be tempted to use red and blue sprinkles on the frosting in lieu of crushed freeze-dried raspberries and blueberries. Here's where I stand on sprinkles—they are only for children's cupcakes and ice cream treats, and even then only as a last resort. All garnishes should bring something more than decoration to the party. When serving, consider sprinkling each blondie with several fresh raspberries and blueberries.

raspberry sauce
1 (6-ounce) container raspberries, frozen (unthawed) or fresh
⅓ cup (2.3 ounces) sugar
2 teaspoons cornstarch

blondie batter
Vegetable shortening for pan
1½ sticks (6 ounces) unsalted butter
6 ounces premium white baking chocolate
4 large eggs, at room temperature
2 cups (14 ounces) sugar
1 teaspoon salt
2 teaspoons pure vanilla extract
2½ cups (11.5 ounces) bleached all-purpose flour
½ teaspoon baking powder
1 cup (6 ounces) dried blueberries, preferably wild

white chocolate cream cheese frosting
2 ounces (2 squares) premium white baking chocolate
6 ounces (¾ of a brick) cream cheese, at room temperature
6 tablespoons (3 ounces) unsalted butter, at room temperature
1 teaspoon pure vanilla extract
1½ cups (6 ounces) confectioners' sugar

garnish
1 tablespoon freeze-dried raspberries
1 tablespoon freeze-dried blueberries

1 To make the raspberry sauce, combine the raspberries, sugar, and cornstarch in a 1-quart saucier (or saucepan). Cover the pan tightly and cook over medium heat, stirring occasionally with a silicone spatula until the sugar dissolves, about 8 to10 minutes. Increase the heat to high and boil (uncovered) until the juices are thick and clear, stirring constantly with the spatula, about 2 minutes. Push the sauce through a medium-mesh strainer into a bowl, pressing on the berries with the spatula; discard the seeds. Transfer the strained sauce to a 1-cup glass (Pyrex) measuring cup. Refrigerate the sauce while proceeding with the recipe.

2 To make the blondies, adjust an oven rack to the middle level of the oven and preheat to 350°F. Prepare a 9 by 13-inch baking pan with heavy-duty aluminum foil as shown on page xvi. Lightly grease the foil in the pan.

3 Cut the butter sticks into 1-inch slices. In a small, heavy saucepan, melt the butter pieces over the lowest setting. While the butter is melting, chop the white chocolate very finely and then add to the melted butter. Stir with a small whisk until combined and the white chocolate is melted and smooth. Remove the pan from the heat and set aside.

4 Using a large whisk, lightly beat the eggs in a large mixing bowl. Place the sugar and salt in a separate small mixing bowl, then whisk into the eggs just until incorporated. Briefly whisk the melted chocolate mixture, then gradually whisk into the egg mixture until just combined. Briefly whisk in the vanilla.

5 Place the flour and baking powder in the small mixing bowl; whisk together to combine. Sift through a medium strainer directly onto the batter; stir in with a silicone spatula until just combined. Sprinkle the dried blueberries over the batter; fold in until just combined.

6 Dollop half of the batter (1 pound 6 ounces, see page 9) into the prepared pan and spread evenly with a small offset spatula. Slowly pour the raspberry sauce evenly over the blondie batter to within 1 inch of the pan sides; the sauce will not cover all of the batter. Dollop the remaining blondie batter on top of the raspberry sauce and smooth out with a small offset spatula. Bake for 30 minutes, until a toothpick inserted in the center comes out clean and the top is very lightly browned. Transfer the pan to a cooling rack and let cool at room temperature for at least 15 minutes, then refrigerate the pan for 7 to 8 hours, or overnight. See page xix for instructions on removing the slab from the pan.

7 To prepare the frosting, finely chop the white chocolate. Place in a small heat-proof bowl and microwave on 50 percent power for 2 minutes; stir until melted and smooth. Set aside. In a small mixing bowl using a handheld electric mixer, beat together the cream cheese and butter on high speed until well combined and smooth. Add the vanilla and the melted white chocolate and beat on low speed until combined. Add the confectioners' sugar (no need to sift) to the cream cheese mixture. Beat (starting on low and increasing to high) until well combined and smooth. Dollop the frosting over the chilled blondie slab and spread evenly with a small offset spatula.

8 To make the garnish, pulse the freeze-dried raspberries briefly in a mini food processor until coarsely crushed, then sprinkle them evenly over the frosting. Repeat with the freeze-dried blueberries. Don't be tempted to do them together—it just looks purple. Chill the slab (still on the cutting board) until the frosting is firm, at least 2 hours. See page xix for instructions on cutting the slab, and for refrigerated storage (up to 5 days) and freezing guidelines.

triple blueberry white chocolate blondies

makes 12 large squares or 24 smaller bars

This blondie incorporates blueberries three ways: fresh (or frozen) used in the blueberry sauce, dried (I prefer wild dried blueberries) used in the batter, and freeze-dried, used for the garnish. We grow several varieties of blueberries, but none are as good as the ones at Pungo Blueberries Etc., a charming pick-your-own blueberry and blackberry farm here in Virginia Beach. Normally I would never use any vanilla baking chips, but I want this ganache glaze to be somewhat stiff, and high-quality white baking chocolate produces a softer ganache. The vanilla ganache glaze, made with Guittard Choc-Au-Lait baking chips, is absolutely delicious and the texture is perfect.

blueberry sauce
1½ cups (7.5 ounces) frozen (unthawed) or fresh blueberries
⅓ cup (2.3 ounces) sugar
1 tablespoon cornstarch

blondie batter
Vegetable shortening for pan
1½ sticks (6 ounces) unsalted butter
6 ounces premium white baking chocolate
4 large eggs, at room temperature
2 cups (14 ounces) sugar
1 teaspoon salt
2 teaspoons pure vanilla extract
2½ cups (11.5 ounces) bleached all-purpose flour
½ teaspoon baking powder
1 cup (6 ounces) dried blueberries, preferably wild

vanilla ganache glaze
⅓ cup and 1 tablespoon (3 ounces) heavy whipping cream
1½ cups (9 ounces) vanilla milk chips (Guittard Choc-Au-Lait)

garnish
2 tablespoons freeze-dried blueberries

1   To make the blueberry sauce, combine the blueberries, sugar, and cornstarch in a 1-quart saucier (or saucepan). Cover the pan tightly and cook over medium-low heat, stirring occasionally with a silicone spatula until the sugar dissolves, 8 to 10 minutes. Increase the heat to high and bring to a boil stirring constantly with the spatula until the mixture is quite thick, about 1 minute. Push the sauce through a medium-mesh strainer into a bowl, pressing on the berries with the spatula; discard the solids. Transfer the strained sauce to a 1-cup glass (Pyrex) measuring cup. Refrigerate the sauce while proceeding with the recipe.

2   To make the blondies, adjust an oven rack to the middle level of the oven and preheat to 350°F. Prepare a 9 by 13-inch baking pan with heavy-duty aluminum foil as shown on page xvi. Lightly grease the foil in the pan.

3   Cut the butter sticks into 1-inch slices. In a small, heavy saucepan, melt the butter pieces over the lowest setting. While the butter is melting, chop the white chocolate very finely and then add to the melted butter. Stir with a small whisk until combined and the white chocolate is melted and smooth. Remove the pan from the heat and set aside.

4   Using a large whisk, lightly beat the eggs in a large mixing bowl. Place the sugar and salt in a separate small mixing bowl, then whisk into the eggs just until incorporated. Briefly whisk the melted chocolate mixture, then gradually whisk into the egg mixture until just combined. Briefly whisk in the vanilla. You can set aside the saucepan and small whisk—no need to wash them— to use for the vanilla ganache glaze.

5   Place the flour and baking powder in the small mixing bowl; whisk together to combine. Sift through a medium strainer directly onto the batter; stir in with a silicone spatula until just combined. Sprinkle the dried blueberries over the batter; fold in until just combined.

6   Dollop half of the batter (1 pound 6 ounces, see page 9) into the prepared pan and spread evenly with a small offset spatula. Slowly pour the blueberry sauce evenly over the blondie batter to within 1 inch of the pan sides; the sauce will not cover all of the batter. Dollop the remaining blondie batter on top of the blueberry sauce and smooth out with a small offset spatula. Bake for 30 minutes, until a toothpick inserted in the center comes out clean and the top is very lightly browned. Transfer the pan to a cooling rack.

7   To make the vanilla ganache glaze, bring the cream just to a boil in the reserved small saucepan. Remove the pan from the heat and add the vanilla chips; shake the pan to cover the chips with the hot cream. Cover the pan tightly and let sit for 2 minutes, then gently blend together with the small whisk until the chips are incorporated and smooth. Pour the glaze over the hot blondie slab and spread evenly with a small offset spatula.

8   To make the garnish, pulse the freeze-dried blueberries briefly in a mini food processor until coarsely crushed, then sprinkle them evenly over the warm glaze. Refrigerate the pan for 7 to 8 hours, or overnight. See page xix for instructions on removing and cutting the slab, and for refrigerated storage (up to 5 days) and freezing guidelines.

luscious lemon coconut white chocolate blondies

makes 12 large squares or 24 smaller bars

My second favorite cake (after Devil's Food) is Coconut Cake with Lemon Filling, so it is no surprise that I've come up with a blondie to mimic those flavors. One of my specials as a pastry chef was this blondie, cut into "fingers" and served with a scoop of toasted coconut ice cream resting on a pool of warm lemon curd with a sprinkling of fresh blackberries. At the restaurant, I was able to use pasteurized liquid egg yolk in the frosting, but at home I use a regular egg yolk, which is against health guidelines as it may contain salmonella. I have never made a batter (every single one has raw egg in it) that I haven't tasted, but it is your decision whether to use this frosting or substitute another. The line cooks that I worked with loved this dessert as much as I did; sorry Chef Todd Jurich, that may explain why we never had as many portions as we needed for service!

blondie batter

1 (7-ounce) bag shredded sweetened coconut

Vegetable shortening for pan

1½ sticks (6 ounces) unsalted butter

6 ounces premium white baking chocolate

4 large eggs, at room temperature

2 cups (14 ounces) sugar

1 teaspoon salt

2 teaspoons pure vanilla extract

2½ cups (11.5 ounces) bleached all-purpose flour

½ teaspoon baking powder

½ cup (3 ounces) premium white chocolate chips

lemon frosting

10 tablespoons (5 ounces) unsalted butter, at room temperature

1 large egg yolk, at room temperature

2⅔ cups (10.7 ounces) confectioners' sugar

¼ cup (2 ounces) heavy whipping cream

1 teaspoon pure lemon extract

⅛ teaspoon salt

Zest of 1 large lemon

2 tablespoons fresh lemon juice

garnish

2 to 3 tablespoons white chocolate crisp candies (Callebaut Crispearls)

1 To toast the coconut, adjust an oven rack to the middle level of the oven and preheat to 350°F. Spread the coconut out evenly onto a half-sheet pan. Bake for 5 minutes, then turn the coconut with a thin metal spatula, bringing it from the outer edges of the pan into the center. Bake for 4 additional minutes; repeat turning the coconut, then continue to bake in 2-minute intervals, turning the coconut until it is uniformly golden brown with just a bit of darker coconut color. Transfer the pan to a cooling rack and let cool at room temperature. Maintain the oven temperature at 350°F.

2 To make the blondies, prepare a 9 by 13-inch baking pan with heavy-duty aluminum foil as shown on page xvi. Lightly grease the foil in the pan.

3 Cut the butter sticks into 1-inch slices. In a small, heavy saucepan, melt the butter pieces over the lowest setting. While the butter is melting, chop the white chocolate very finely and then add to the melted butter. Stir with a small whisk until combined and the white chocolate is melted and smooth. Remove the pan from the heat and set aside.

4 Using a large whisk, lightly beat the eggs in a large mixing bowl. Place the sugar and salt in a separate small mixing bowl, then whisk into the eggs just until incorporated. Briefly whisk the melted chocolate mixture, then gradually whisk into the egg mixture until just combined. Briefly whisk in the vanilla.

5 Place the flour and baking powder in the small mixing bowl; whisk together to combine. Sift through a medium strainer directly onto the batter; stir in with a silicone spatula until just combined. Sprinkle the toasted coconut and white chocolate chips over the batter; fold in until just combined. Dollop the batter into the prepared pan and spread evenly with a small offset spatula. Bake for 30 minutes, until a toothpick inserted in the center comes out clean and the top is browned. Transfer the pan to a cooling rack and let cool at room temperature for at least 15 minutes, then refrigerate the pan for 7 to 8 hours, or overnight. See page xix for instructions on removing the slab from the pan.

6 To make the lemon frosting, place the butter and egg yolk in a small mixing bowl. Using a handheld electric mixer on medium speed, beat together until well combined. Add the confectioners' sugar (no need to sift) and beat in starting on low and increasing to high until the sugar is combined. Add the cream, lemon extract, and salt to the bowl. Starting on low speed and gradually increasing to high, beat the mixture until well combined. Using a Microplane zester, grate the yellow zest off the lemon directly onto the mixture, then cut the lemon in half and extract the juice; add 2 tablespoons of the juice to the mixture. Starting on low and increasing to high, beat in until well combined and fluffy. Dollop the frosting over the chilled blondie slab and spread evenly with a small offset spatula. Garnish the frosting with the white chocolate candies, then use the back of a metal spatula and lightly tap on the candies to slightly embed them into the frosting. Refrigerate the slab (still on the cutting board) until the frosting is firm, at least 2 hours. See page xix for instructions on cutting the slab, and for refrigerated storage (up to 2 weeks) and freezing guidelines.

cranberry pistachio "fruitcake" blondies

makes 12 large squares or 24 smaller bars

If I have friends and family over at Thanksgiving or Christmas, they can expect this delicious blondie to show up as one of the offered desserts; it's my version of fruitcake. If I'm even luckier and get to be a holiday guest, I show up with a tray of assorted bite-size brownies and blondies, and these will always be in the lineup. This whole brownie gig actually started one Christmas when I began sending brownie gift tins to friends and relatives in other states. Now, if I don't send the brownies off by mid-December, I start getting phone calls asking when they are coming. It's a lovely feeling knowing you are giving something that people actually look forward to, but now that this book is published, maybe I can go back to just sending cards.

blondie batter
Vegetable shortening for pan
1½ sticks (6 ounces) unsalted butter
6 ounces premium white baking chocolate
4 large eggs, at room temperature
2 cups (14 ounces) sugar
1 teaspoon salt
2 teaspoons pure vanilla extract
2½ cups (11.5 ounces) bleached all-purpose flour
½ teaspoon baking powder
1 (5-ounce) package sweetened dried cranberries
1 (6-ounce) package roasted and salted shelled pistachios

vanilla ganache glaze
⅓ cup and 1 tablespoon (3 ounces) heavy whipping cream
1½ cups (9 ounces) vanilla milk chips
  (Guittard Choc-Au-Lait)

1 To make the blondies, adjust an oven rack to the middle level of the oven and preheat to 350°F. Prepare a 9 by 13-inch baking pan with heavy-duty aluminum foil as shown on page xvi. Lightly grease the foil in the pan.

2 Cut the butter sticks into 1-inch slices. In a small, heavy saucepan, melt the butter pieces over the lowest setting. While the butter is melting, chop the white chocolate very finely and then add to the melted butter. Stir with a small whisk until combined and the white chocolate is melted and smooth. Remove the pan from the heat and set aside.

3   Using a large whisk, lightly beat the eggs in a large mixing bowl. Place the sugar and salt in a separate small mixing bowl, then whisk into the eggs just until incorporated. Briefly whisk the melted chocolate mixture, then gradually whisk into the egg mixture until just combined. Briefly whisk in the vanilla. You can set aside the saucepan and small whisk—no need to wash them—to use for the vanilla ganache glaze.

4   Place the flour and baking powder in the small mixing bowl; whisk together to combine. Sift through a medium strainer directly onto the batter; stir in with a silicone spatula until just combined. Sprinkle 1 cup of the dried cranberries and 1 cup of the pistachios over the batter; fold in until just combined. Dollop the batter into the prepared pan and spread evenly with a small offset spatula. Bake for 30 minutes, until a toothpick inserted in the center comes out clean and the top is very lightly browned. Transfer the pan to a cooling rack.

5   To make the vanilla ganache glaze, bring the cream just to a boil in the reserved small saucepan. Remove the pan from the heat and add the vanilla chips; shake the pan to cover the chips with the hot cream. Cover the pan tightly and let sit for 2 minutes, then gently blend together with a small whisk until the chips are incorporated and smooth. Pour the glaze over the hot blondie slab and spread evenly with a small offset spatula. Finely chop the remaining cranberries and sprinkle over the warm glaze, then place 3 tablespoons of the remaining pistachios on the glaze, slightly pushing them into it. Refrigerate the pan for 7 to 8 hours, or overnight. See page xix for instructions on removing and cutting the slab, and for refrigerated storage (up to 2 weeks) and freezing guidelines.

lemon mascarpone blondies

makes 12 large squares or 24 smaller bars

Here's my favorite summertime blondie—it's absolutely refreshing. This tart, slightly chewy, lemon blondie has an equally tart glaze to enhance it, and once you've tried it, you'll never make traditional lemon bars again. Mascarpone (pronounced mahs-car-POH-nay) cheese is basically an Italian triple-cream cream cheese, but now there are many fine American versions available. I like to serve these with fresh blackberries as well as a squiggle of blackberry coulis.

blondie batter
Vegetable shortening and 2 teaspoons flour for pan
2 sticks (8 ounces) unsalted butter
16 ounces mascarpone cheese
2 cups (14 ounces) sugar
4 large lemons, at room temperature
2 large eggs, at room temperature
1 teaspoon pure lemon extract
¼ cup (2 ounces) fresh lemon juice
2 cups (9 ounces) bleached all-purpose flour
1 teaspoon salt
1 teaspoon baking powder
¼ teaspoon baking soda

tart lemon glaze
2¼ cups (10 ounces) confectioners' sugar
2 large lemons, at room temperature
3 tablespoons (1.5 ounces) fresh lemon juice
½ teaspoon pure lemon extract
1 tablespoon (0.08 ounce) light corn syrup

1 To make the blondies, adjust an oven rack to the middle level of the oven and preheat to 350°F. Prepare a 9 by 13-inch baking pan with heavy-duty aluminum foil as shown on page xvi. Lightly grease the foil in the pan, then dust the interior bottom and sides of the pan with 2 teaspoons of flour. Knock out excess flour onto a sheet of newspaper for easy clean up.

2 Cut the butter sticks into 1-inch slices. Place the butter slices and mascarpone cheese in a heavy 2-quart saucepan. Cook over the lowest setting, gently whisking occasionally with a small whisk, until the butter and mascarpone are completely melted and smooth. Turn the heat off, but leave the saucepan on the burner while proceeding with the recipe.

3 Pour the sugar into the bowl of a food processor. Using a Microplane zester, grate the yellow zest from 4 lemons directly onto the sugar. Process until the sugar is fragrant and yellow, and the zest is broken down, about 10 seconds.

4 Using a large whisk, lightly beat the eggs in a large mixing bowl. Whisk the lemon sugar into the eggs just until incorporated. Gradually whisk the melted butter mixture into the egg/sugar mixture until just combined. Whisk in the lemon extract.

5 Extract enough juice from the lemons to equal ¼ cup. Whisk the ¼ cup lemon juice into the egg mixture until well incorporated.

6 Place the flour, salt, baking powder, and baking soda in a small mixing bowl; whisk together to combine. Sift through a medium strainer directly onto the batter; whisk in until just combined; the batter will be slightly lumpy. Pour the batter into the prepared pan and spread evenly with a small offset spatula. Bake for 32 minutes, until a toothpick inserted in the center comes out clean and the top is lightly browned. Transfer the pan to a cooling rack. Prepare the tart lemon glaze while the blondie is baking.

7 To make the tart lemon glaze, sift (or strain) the confectioners' sugar into the small mixing bowl. Using a Microplane zester, grate the yellow zest from the lemons directly onto the sugar. Extract enough lemon juice to equal 3 tablespoons. Add the lemon juice, lemon extract, and corn syrup to the confectioners' sugar; stir with a small silicone spatula until smooth. The glaze will be thick. Dollop it over the hot blondie slab, then spread evenly with a small offset spatula. Let the glazed slab sit at room temperature for at least 30 minutes, then refrigerate the pan for 7 to 8 hours, or overnight. See page xix for instructions on removing and cutting the slab, and for refrigerated storage (up to 2 weeks) and freezing guidelines.

127

metric
conversions
and equivalents

metric conversion formulas

to convert	multiply
Ounces to grams	Ounces by 28.35
Pounds to kilograms	Pounds by 0.454
Teaspoons to milliliters	Teaspoons by 4.93
Tablespoons to milliliters	Tablespoons by 14.79
Fluid ounces to milliliters	Fluid ounces by 29.57
Cups to milliliters	Cups by 236.59
Cups to liters	Cups by 0.236
Pints to liters	Pints by 0.473
Quarts to liters	Quarts by 0.946
Gallons to liters	Gallons by 3.785
Inches to centimeters	Inches by 2.54

approximate metric equivalents

volume

¼ teaspoon	1 milliliter
½ teaspoon	2.5 milliliters
¾ teaspoon	4 milliliters
1 teaspoon	5 milliliters
1¼ teaspoons	6 milliliters
1½ teaspoons	7.5 milliliters
1¾ teaspoons	8.5 milliliters
2 teaspoons	10 milliliters
1 tablespoon (0.5 fluid ounce)	15 milliliters
2 tablespoons (1 fluid ounce)	30 milliliters
¼ cup	60 milliliters
⅓ cup	80 milliliters
½ cup (4 fluid ounces)	120 milliliters
⅔ cup	160 milliliters
¾ cup	180 milliliters
1 cup (8 fluid ounces)	240 milliliters
1¼ cups	300 milliliters
1½ cups (12 fluid ounces)	360 milliliters
1⅔ cups	400 milliliters
2 cups (1 pint)	460 milliliters
3 cups	700 milliliters
4 cups (1 quart)	0.95 liter
1 quart plus ¼ cup	1 liter
4 quarts (1 gallon)	3.8 liters

weight

0.25 ounce	7 grams
0.5 ounce	14 grams
0.75 ounce	21 grams
1 ounce	28 grams
1.25 ounces	35 grams
1.5 ounces	42.5 grams
1.666 ounces	45 grams
2 ounces	57 grams
3 ounces	85 grams
4 ounces (¼ pound)	113 grams
5 ounces	142 grams
6 ounces	170 grams
7 ounces	198 grams
8 ounces (½ pound)	227 grams
16 ounces (1 pound)	454 grams
35.25 ounces (2.2 pounds)	1 kilogram

length

⅛ inch	3 millimeters
¼ inch	6 millimeters
½ inch	1.25 centimeters
1 inch	2.5 centimeters
2 inches	5 centimeters
2½ inches	6 centimeters
4 inches	10 centimeters
5 inches	13 centimeters
6 inches	15.25 centimeters
12 inches (1 foot)	30 centimeters

oven temperatures

To convert Fahrenheit to Celsius, subtract 32 from Fahrenheit, multiply the result by 5, then divide by 9.

description	fahrenheit	celsius	british gas mark
Very cool	200°	95°	0
Very cool	225°	110°	¼
Very cool	250°	120°	½
Cool	275°	135°	1
Cool	300°	150°	2
Warm	325°	165°	3
Moderate	350°	175°	4
Moderately hot	375°	190°	5
Fairly hot	400°	200°	6
Hot	425°	220°	7
Very hot	450°	230°	8
Very hot	475°	245°	9

common ingredients and their approximate equivalents

1 cup all-purpose flour = 140 grams
1 stick butter (4 ounces • ½ cup • 8 tablespoons) = 110 grams
1 cup butter (8 ounces • 2 sticks • 16 tablespoons) = 220 grams
1 cup brown sugar, firmly packed = 225 grams
1 cup granulated sugar = 200 grams

Information compiled from a variety of sources, including *Recipes into Type* by Joan Whitman and Dolores Simon (Newton, MA: Biscuit Books, 2000); *The New Food Lover's Companion* by Sharon Tyler Herbst (Hauppauge, NY: Barron's, 1995); and *Rosemary Brown's Big Kitchen Instruction Book* (Kansas City, MO: Andrews McMeel, 1998).

Cuppa-Cappuccino
Brownie

Raspberry Ripple
Cheesecake Brownie

index